LITERATURE
for Composition

■ LITERATURE

for Composition

ESSAYS, FICTION, POETRY, AND DRAMA

Third Edition

EDITED BY

Sylvan Barnet TUFTS UNIVERSITY

Morton Berman BOSTON UNIVERSITY

William Burto UNIVERSITY OF LOWELL

Marcia Stubbs WELLESLEY COLLEGE

■ HarperCollins*Publishers*

Sponsoring Editor: Lisa Moore
Development Editor: Judith Leet
Project Coordination, Text and Cover Design: PC&F, Inc.
Cover Artwork by David Hockney, "A Bigger Splash." Acrylic on canvas, 96" × 96".
    Copyright © David Hockney.
Production Manager: Michael Weinstein
Compositor: PC&F, Inc.
Printer and Binder: R.R. Donnelley & Sons Company
Cover Printer: The Lehigh Press, Inc.

Literature for Composition, Third Edition
Copyright © 1992 by Sylvan Barnet

Library of Congress Cataloging-in-Publication Data

```
Literature for composition : essays, fiction, poetry, and drama /
    edited by Sylvan Barnet ... [et al.]. -- 3rd ed.
        p.   cm.
    Includes index.
    ISBN 0-673-52129-X (student ed.). -- ISBN 0-673-52180-X
(teacher ed.)
    1. College readers.  2. English language--Rhetoric.  I. Barnet,
Sylvan
PE1417.L663  1991
808'.0427--dc20                                      91-16457
                                                        CIP
```

93 94 9 8 7 6 5

Photo Credits

Photograph of a scene from the opening production of *The Glass Menagerie* at the Playhouse in New York on March 31, 1945, starring Lorette Taylor, Julie Hayden, Eddie Dowling, and Anthony Ross. Reproduced by courtesy of the New York Public Library, The Billy Rose Collection.

Photograph of Claire Bloom as Nora in the 1971 production of *A Doll's House.* Photograph © by Martha Swope. Used by permission.

Photograph of the Greek Theater of Epidaurus on the Peloponnesus east of Nauplia. (Photograph: Frederick Ayer, Photo Researchers, Inc.)

Text Credits

Edward Albee, *The Sandbox,* copyright © 1960 by Edward Albee. Reprinted by permission of The Putnam Publishing Group.

A. R. Ammons, "Mountain Talk" is reprinted from *Collected Poems,* 1951–1971, by A. R. Ammons, by permission of W. W. Norton & Company, Inc. Copyright © 1972 by A. R. Ammons.

Sherwood Anderson, "The Egg" from *The Triumph of the Egg* by Sherwood Anderson. Copyright 1921 by B. W. Huebsch, Inc. Copyright renewed 1948 by Eleanor C. Anderson. Reprinted by permission of Harold Ober Associates Incorporated.

Maya Angelou, "Graduation" from *I Know Why the Caged Bird Sings* by Maya Angelou. Copyright © 1969 by Maya Angelou. Reprinted by permission of Random House, Inc.

José Armas, "El Tonto del Barrio" originally published in Pajarito Publications, 1979, from *Cuentos Chicanos,* revised edition, 1984, edited by Rudolfo A. Anaya and Antonio Mar-

(continued on page 1085)

■ CONTENTS

■ CHAPTER 6

Reading (and Writing about) Drama   153

■ CHAPTER 11

American Dreams and Nightmares   649

■ CHAPTER 12

The Individual and Society   771

▪ CHAPTER 13

Men, Women, God, and Gods 908

■ ALTERNATE
CONTENTS

Arranged by Literary Genre

ESSAYS

FICTION

POETRY

DRAMA

■ PREFACE

This book is based on the assumption that students in a composition course should encounter—if not at the start, then certainly by the midpoint—first-rate writing. By this we mean not simply competent prose but the powerful reports of experience that have been recorded by highly skilled writers past and present. We assume that the study of such writing yields pleasure and insight into life, and that it also yields a sense of what the best words in the best places can do.

Literature for Composition, Third Edition, is in large part an anthology of literature, but it is more: It also offers instruction in writing. Part One, "Getting Started," consists of seven chapters. Although each chapter includes works of literature, all of the introductory chapters aim primarily at helping students to read and to respond—in writing—to literature. The first two chapters discuss such procedures as annotating, free writing, listing, and keeping a journal; the third chapter discusses analysis and evaluation. All of these chapters include, as well, topics for discussion and writing.

The four remaining chapters of Part One discuss the four chief literary genres—the essay, fiction, drama, and poetry. These chapters include not only advice about reading and writing, but they also include works of literature; and again each work of literature is accompanied by suggested topics for discussion and writing. Chapters 4, 5, 6, and 7 thus offer a small anthology of literature, organized by genre, as well as an introduction to some ways of writing about literature.

Part Two is a thematic anthology of literature (including essays). Although Part One contains a fair amount of literature (for instance, five stories in the chapter on fiction, and two short plays in the chapter on drama), most of the literature appears in Part Two, where it is arranged into six themes: Strange Worlds; Innocence and Experience; Love and Hate; American Dreams and Nightmares; The Individual and Society; and Men, Women, and Gods. Here, as earlier, all of the essays, stories, poems, and plays are followed by questions and suggestions for writing. The aim of such questions and suggestions is to assist students to respond, to reflect on their responses, and perhaps to modify or expand them, aided by the act of writing.

The book concludes with three appendices, one on the research paper, one on manuscript form, and one containing a glossary of terms. The material on manuscript form may seem to be yet another discussion of writing, and some readers may wonder why it is put toward the back of the book. But manuscript form is chiefly a matter of editing rather than of drafting and revising. It is, so to speak, the final packaging of a product that develops during a complicated process, a process that begins with reading, responding, finding a topic, a thesis, and a voice, not with worrying about the width of margins or the form of citations. The last thing that one does in writing an essay, and therefore the last thing in our book, is to set it forth in a physical form fit for human consumption.

And now a few additional words about the literature in this book. Writers write about something. Of course they write essays or stories or poems or plays, but these are *about* something, for instance about love, which comes in many varieties. We arranged the works thematically so that we can give, if not responses to the whole of life, at least a spectrum of responses to large parts of it. By grouping the works according to themes, and by beginning each group with essays that help to set the reader to thinking about the theme, we hope to call attention not only to resemblances but to important differences, even between superficially similar works such as, say, two sonnets by Shakespeare. Obviously one work is not "right" and another "wrong." There is, after all, no one correct view of, say, love or happiness.

We trust that these multiple views are welcome, though we uneasily recall the Ballyhough railway station, which has two clocks that differ by six minutes. When an irritated traveler asked an attendant what was the use of having two clocks that didn't tell the same time, the attendant replied, "And what would we be wanting with two clocks if they told the same time?"

But works of literature are not clocks; we hope that each work will be valued for itself and will also be valued for the light it throws on other works of literature, and on life. Behind this hope, of course, is the assumption that good writing—the accurate report of powerful thinking and feeling—is a response to and an interpretation of life, and that it is therefore nourishing. We cannot do better than to quote Coleridge on this point:

> The heart should have fed upon truth, as insects on a leaf, till it be tinged with the color and shows its food in every minutest fiber.

A NOTE ON THE THIRD EDITION

Instructors familiar with earlier editions will notice major changes in this edition. The first three chapters of this book, on reading and responding, are entirely new. The next four chapters, on literary genres, are greatly expanded revisions of material that in earlier editions was at the rear of the book. These chapters, primarily concerned with helping students to write, now include many examples of annotations, lists, free writing, and journal entries by students, and they also now include many literary works. They constitute, in effect, a mini-anthology of literature arranged by genre. Part Two, the thematic anthology, has also been extensively revised in the light of our own experience and the experience of many other instructors who have taught the book. Almost half of the literary works in the book are new to this edition.

Note: An Instructor's Manual, with suggestions for teaching each selection, is available from the publisher. In addition, an impressive selection of videotapes and Harper audiotapes is also available to enrich students' experience of literature. Instructors are invited to learn more about the Harper-Collins video and audiotape library and request a complimentary copy of the Instructor's Manual from their HarperCollins representative or the publisher.

ACKNOWLEDGMENTS

In preparing the first two editions of *Literature for Composition* we were indebted to Judith Stanford, Donald A. Daiker, Clayton Hudnall, Michael Johnson, Charles Moran, Linda Robertson, Robert Schwegler, and Beverly Swan. In preparing the second edition we have profited greatly from suggestions made by Jim Streeter, Kathleen Shine Cain, Bertha Norman Booker, Margaret Blayney, Dorothy Trusock, Billie Varnum, Mickey Wadia, L. D. Galford, William Shelley, Leonard W. Engel, Bruce A. Reid, Raymond L. Thomas, Gary Zacharias, James R. Payne, Bill Kelly, Susan D. Tilka, JoAnna S. Mink, John P. Boots, Robin W. Bryant, Janice Slaughter, John O'Connor, Don K. Pierstorff, Bill Elliott, Patricia G. Morgan, Jim Schwartz, William Epperson, Diana Cardenas, Walter B. Connolly, Kathleen McWilliams, Kay Fortson, Joyce A. Ingram, Linda Cravens, Louis H. Pratt, Leesther Thomas, William McAndrew, Nancy Morris, Marie Foster, Donna Friedman, Sandra H. Harris, and Kathy J. Wright.

In preparing this latest edition, we have been greatly aided by the suggestions of the following reviewers:

Chris Grieco, Seton Hall University
Gerald Pike, University of California, Davis
Sally Harrold, Southwestern Oregon Community College
Judith Stanford, Rivier College
Christina Murphy, Texas Christian University
Elinor C. Flewellen, Santa Barbara City College
Loris Galford, McNeese State University
Pam Bourgeois, California State University, Northridge
Maureen Hoag, Wichita State University
Nancy Walker, Southwest Missouri State
Terry Santos, California State University, Los Angeles

At HarperCollins, Judith Leet and Lisa Moore carefully watched over this project. We wish also to thank Virginia Creeden, who secured copyright permission.

Sylvan Barnet
Morton Berman
William Burto
Marcia Stubbs

■ PART ONE

Getting Started

CHAPTER 1

The Writer

as Reader:

Reading and

Responding

Learning to write is in large measure learning to read. The text you must read most carefully is the one you produce, an essay you will ask someone else to read. It may start as a jotting in the margin of a book you are reading, or as a brief note in a journal, and it will go through several drafts before it becomes an essay. To produce something that another person will find worth reading, you must yourself read each draft with care, trying to imagine the effect that your words are likely to have on your reader. And if you write about literature, you will apply some of the same critical skills to your reading. That is, you will examine your responses to what you are reading and will try to account for them.

Let's begin by looking at a very short story by Kate Chopin (1851–1904). (The name is pronounced in the French way, something like "show pan.") Kate O'Flaherty, born into a prosperous family in St. Louis, in 1870 married Oscar Chopin, a French-Creole businessman from Louisiana. They lived in New Orleans, where they had six children. Oscar died of malaria in 1882, and in 1884 Kate returned to St. Louis, where, living with her mother and children, she began to write fiction.

■ KATE CHOPIN

Ripe Figs

Maman-Nainaine said that when the figs were ripe Babette might go to visit her cousins down on the Bayou-Lafourche where the sugar cane grows. Not that the ripening of figs had the least thing to do with it, but that is the way Maman-Nainaine was.

It seemed to Babette a very long time to wait; for the leaves upon the trees were tender yet, and the figs were like little hard, green marbles.

But warm rains came along and plenty of strong sunshine, and though Maman-Nainaine was as patient as the statue of la Madone, and Babette as restless as a humming-bird, the first thing they both knew it was hot summer-time. Every day Babette danced out to where the fig-trees were in a long line against the fence. She walked slowly beneath them, carefully peering be-tween the gnarled, spreading branches. But each time she came disconsolate away again. What she saw there finally was something that made her sing and dance the whole long day.

When Maman-Nainaine sat down in her stately way to breakfast, the fol-lowing morning, her muslin cap standing like an aureole about her white, placid face, Babette approached. She bore a dainty porcelain platter, which she set down before her godmother. It contained a dozen purple figs, fringed around with their rich, green leaves.

"Ah," said Maman-Nainaine arching her eyebrows, "how early the figs have ripened this year!"

"Oh," said Babette. "I think they have ripened very late."

"Babette," continued Maman-Nainaine, as she peeled the very plumpest figs with her pointed silver fruit-knife, "you will carry my love to them all down on Bayou-Lafourche. And tell your Tante Frosine I shall look for her at Toussaint—when the chrysanthemums are in bloom."

[1893]

Reading as Re-Creation

If we had been Chopin's contemporaries, we might have read this sketch in *Vogue* in 1893 or in an early collection of her works, *A Night in Acadie* (1897). But we are not Chopin's original readers, and, since we live in the late twentieth century, we inevitably read "Ripe Figs" in a somewhat different way. And this gets us to an important truth about writing and reading. A writer writes, sets forth his or her meaning, and attempts to guide the read-er's responses, as we all do when we write a letter home saying that we're thinking of dropping a course or asking for news or money or whatever. To this extent, the writer creates the written work and puts a meaning in it.

But the reader, whether reading that written work as a requirement or for recreation, *re-creates* it according to his or her experience and understand-ing. For instance, if the letter-writer's appeal for money is too indirect, the reader may miss it entirely or may sense it but feel that the need is not ur-gent. If, on the other hand, the appeal is direct or demanding, the reader may feel imposed upon, even assaulted. "Oh, but I didn't mean it that way," the writer later protests. Nevertheless, that's the way the reader took it. The let-ter is "out there," a physical reality standing between the writer and the read-er, but its *meaning* is something the reader as well as the writer makes.

Since all readers bring themselves to a written work, they each bring something individual. For instance, although many of Chopin's original readers knew that she wrote chiefly about the people of Louisiana, especially Creoles (descendants of the early French and Spanish settlers), Cajuns (descendants of the French whom the British had expelled from Canada in the eighteenth century), blacks, and mulattoes, those readers must have varied in their attitudes about such people. And many of today's readers do *not* (before they read a work by Chopin) know anything about her subject. Some readers may know where Bayou-Lafourche is, and they may have notions about what it looks like but most readers will not; indeed, many readers will not know that a bayou is a sluggish, marshy inlet or outlet of a river or lake. Moreover, even if a present-day reader in Chicago, Seattle, or Juneau knows what a bayou is, he or she may assume that "Ripe Figs" depicts a way of life still current, whereas a reader from Louisiana may see in the work a depiction of a lost way of life, a depiction of the good old days (or perhaps of the bad old days, depending on the reader's point of view). Much depends, we can say, on the reader's storehouse of experience.

To repeat: Reading is a *re*-creation; the author has tried to guide our reponses, but inevitably our own experiences, including, for instance, our ethnic background and our education, contribute to our responses.

Making Reasonable Inferences

Does this mean, then, that there is no use talking (or writing) about literature, since all of us perceive it in our relatively private ways, rather like the seven blind men in the fable? One man, you will recall, touched the elephant's tail (or was it his trunk?) and said that the elephant is like a snake; another touched the elephant's side and said the elephant is like a wall; a third touched the elephant's leg and said the elephant is like a tree, and so on. This familiar story is usually told in order to illustrate human limitations, but notice, too, that each of the blind men *did* perceive an aspect of the elephant—an elephant is massive, like a wall or a tree, and an elephant is (in its way) remarkably supple, as you know if you have given peanuts to one.

As readers we can and should make an effort to understand what an author seems to be getting at. For instance, we should make an effort to understand unfamiliar words. Perhaps we shouldn't look up every word that we don't know, at least on the first reading, but if certain unfamiliar words are repeated and thus seem especially important, we will probably want to look them up. It happens that in "Ripe Figs" a French word appears: "*Tante* Frosine" means "*Aunt* Frosine." Fortunately, the meaning of the word is not crucial, and the context probably makes it clear that Frosine is an adult, which is all that we really need to know about her. But a reader who does not know, for instance, that chrysanthemums bloom in late summer or early autumn will miss part of Chopin's meaning. The point is this: the writer is pitching, and she expects the reader to catch.

On the other hand, although writers tell us a good deal, they cannot tell us everything. We know that Maman-Nainaine is Babette's godmother, but we don't know exactly how old Maman-Nainaine and Babette are. Further,

Chopin tells us nothing of Babette's parents. It rather *sounds* as though Babette and her godmother live alone, but readers' opinions may differ. One reader may argue that Babette's parents must be dead or ill, whereas another may say that the status of her parents is irrelevant and that what counts is that Babette is supervised by only one person, a mature woman. In short, a text includes **indeterminacies** (passages that careful readers agree are open to various interpretations) and **gaps** (things left unsaid in the story, such as why a godmother rather than a mother takes care of Babette). As we work our way through a text, we keep reevaluating what we have read, pulling the details together to make sense of them, in a process called **consistency building**.

Whatever the gaps, careful readers are able to draw many reasonable inferences about Maman-Nainaine. What are some of these? We can list them:

She is older than Babette.
She has a "stately way," and she is "patient as the statue of la Madone."
She has an odd way (is it exasperating, or engaging, or a little of each?) of
     connecting actions with the seasons.
Given this last point, she seems to act slowly, to be very patient.
She apparently is used to being obeyed.

You may at this point want to go back and reread "Ripe Figs," to see what else you can say about Maman-Nainaine.

And now what of Babette?

She is young.
She is active and impatient ("restless as a hummingbird").
She is obedient.

And at this point, too, you may want to add to the list.

If you do add to the list, you might compare your additions with those of a classmate. The two of you may find that you disagree about what may reasonably be inferred from Chopin's words. Suppose, for instance, that your classmate said that although Babette is outwardly obedient, inwardly she probably hates Maman-Nainaine. Would you agree that this assertion is an acceptable inference? If you don't agree, how might you go about trying to convince your classmate that such a response is not justified?

Reading with Pen in Hand

It's probably best to read a work of literature straight through, enjoying it and letting yourself be carried along to the end. But then, when you have an overall view, you'll want to read it again, noticing (for example) how certain innocent-seeming details given early in the work prove to be especially important later.

Perhaps the best way to read attentively is, after a first reading, to mark the text, underlining or highlighting passages that seem especially interesting, and to jot notes or queries in the margins. (*Caution:* Annotate and highlight, but don't get so carried away that you highlight whole pages.) Here is

"Ripe Figs" once more, this time with the marks that a student added to it during and after a second reading.

KATE CHOPIN

Ripe Figs

Maman-Nainaine said that when the figs were ripe Babette might go to visit her cousins down on the Bayou-Lafourche where the sugar cane grows. Not that the ripening of figs had the least thing to do with it, but that is the way Maman-Nainaine was.

?

strange

It seemed to Babette a very long time to wait; for the leaves upon the trees were tender yet, and the figs were like little hard, green marbles.

But warm rains came along and plenty of strong sunshine, and though Maman-Nainaine was as patient as the statue of la Madone, and Babette as restless as a humming-bird, the first thing they both knew it was hot summer-time. Every day Babette danced out to where the fig-trees were in a long line against the fence. She walked slowly beneath them, carefully peering between the gnarled, spreading branches. But each time she came disconsolate away again. What she saw there finally was something that made her sing and dance the whole long day.

contrast between M-N and B

When Maman-Nainaine sat down in her stately way to breakfast, the following morning, her muslin cap standing like an aureole about her white, placid face, Babette approached. She bore a dainty porcelain platter, which she set down before her godmother. It contained a dozen purple figs, fringed around with their rich, green leaves.

another contrast

check this ?

ceremonious

"Ah," said Maman-Nainaine arching her eyebrows, "how early the figs have ripened this year!"

"Oh," said Babette. "I think they have ripened very late."

nice echo contrast like a song

time passes fast for M-N, slowly for B

"Babette," continued Maman-Nainaine, as she peeled the very plumpest figs with her pointed silver fruit-knife, "you will carry my love to them all down on Bayou-Lafourche. And tell your Tante Frosine I shall look for her at Toussaint—when the chrysanthemums are in bloom."

is M-N herself like a plump fig?

B entrusted with a message of love

opens with figs; ends with chrys. (autumn)

fulfillment? Equivalent to figs ripening?

Recording Your First Responses

Another useful way of getting at the meaning of a work of literature is to jot down your initial responses to it, recording your impressions as they come to you in any order—almost as though you're talking to yourself. Since no one else is going to read your notes, you can be entirely free and at ease. You can write in sentences or not; it's up to you. You can jot down these responses either before or after you annotate the text. Some readers find that annotating the text helps to produce ideas for further jottings, but others prefer to jot down a few thoughts immediately after a first reading, and then, stimulated by these thoughts, they reread and annotate the text.

Write whatever comes into your mind, whatever the literary work triggers in your own imagination, whatever you think are the important ideas or values of your own experience.

Here is a student's first response to "Ripe Figs."

> This is a very short story. I didn't know stories were this short, but I like it because you can get it all quickly and it's no trouble to reread it carefully. The shortness, though, leaves a lot of gaps for the reader to fill in. So much is <u>not</u> said. Your imagination is put to work.
>
> But I can see Maman-N sitting at her table—pleasantly powerful—no one you would want to argue with. She's formal and distant—and definitely has quirks. She wants to postpone Babette's trip, but we don't know why. And you can sense B's frustration. But maybe she's <u>teaching</u> her that something really good is worth waiting for and that anticipation is as much fun as the trip. Maybe I can develop this idea.
>
> Another thing. I can tell they are not poor—from two things. The pointed silver fruit knife and the porcelain platter, and the fact that Maman sits down to breakfast in a "stately" way. They are the leisure class. But I don't know enough about life on the bayous to go into this. Their life is different from mine; no one I know has that kind of peaceful rural life.

Audience and Purpose

Now, suppose that you are beginning the process of writing about "Ripe Figs" for someone else, not for yourself. The first question to ask yourself is: "For whom am I writing?" That is, Who is my *audience*? (Of course you probably are writing because an instructor has asked you to do so, but you must still imagine an audience. Your instructor may tell you, for instance, to write for your classmates, or to write for the readers of the college newspaper.) If you are writing for people who already are familiar with some of Chopin's work, you won't have to say much about the author, but if you are writing for an audience who perhaps has never heard of Chopin you may want to include a brief biographical note of the sort we gave. If you are writing for an audience who, you have reason to believe, has read several works by Chopin, you may want to make some comparisons, explaining how "Ripe Figs" resembles or differs from Chopin's other work.

In a sense, the audience is your collaborator; it helps you to decide what you will say. You are also helped by your sense of *purpose*. If your aim is to introduce readers to Chopin, you will make certain points. If your aim is to tell people what you think "Ripe Figs" means to say about human relationships, or about time, you will say some different things; if your aim is to have a little fun and to entertain an audience that is already familiar with "Ripe Figs," you may decide to write a parody (a humorous imitation) of the story.

A Writing Assignment on "Ripe Figs"

THE ASSIGNMENT

Let's assume that you want to describe "Ripe Figs" to someone who has not read it. You probably will briefly summarize the action, such as it is, and will mention where it takes place, who the characters are, including what their relationship is, and what, if anything, happens to them. Beyond that, you will probably try to explain as honestly as you can what makes "Ripe Figs" appealing or interesting—or trifling, or boring, or whatever.

Here is an essay that a student, Marilyn Brown, wrote for this assignment.

SAMPLE ESSAY

Ripening

Kate Chopin's "Ripe Figs" describes a growing season in a young girl's life. Maman-Nainaine agrees to allow young Babette to visit relatives away from home, but Babette must delay her trip until the figs ripen. Babette watches the signs of the natural world, impatiently observing, straining to have time pass at her own speed. At last, Babette finds that the figs have ripened, and she presents them to her godmother, Maman-Nainaine, who gives Babette her leave to go on the journey to Bayou-Lafourche.

Chopin sets the action within the context of the natural world. Babette, young and tender as the fig leaves, can't wait to "ripen." Her visit to Bayou-Lafourche is no mere pleasure trip but represents Babette's coming into her own season of maturity. Babette's desire to rush this process is tempered by a condition that Maman-Nainaine sets: Babette must wait until the figs ripen, since everything comes in its own season. Maman recognizes in the patterns of the natural world the rhythms of life. By asking Babette to await the ripening, the young girl is made to pay attention to these patterns as well.

In this work, Chopin asks her readers to see the relationship of human time to nature's seasons. Try as we may to push the process of maturity, growth or ripening happens in its own time. If we pay attention and wait with patience, the fruits of our own growth will be sweet, plump, and bountiful. Chopin uses natural imagery effectively, interweaving the young girl's growth with the rhythms of the seasons. In this way, the reader is connected with both processes in a very intimate and inviting way.

■ OTHER POSSIBILITIES FOR WRITING

But of course one might write a paper of a very different sort. Consider the following possibilities:

1. Write a sequel, moving from fall to spring.
2. Write a letter from Babette, now at Bayou-Lafourche, to Maman-Nainaine.
3. Imagine that Babette is now an old woman, writing her memoirs. What does she say about Maman-Nainaine?
4. Write a story based on your own experience of learning a lesson in patience.

■ CHAPTER 2

The Reader as Writer: Drafting and Writing

Pre-Writing: Getting Ideas

"All there is to writing," Robert Frost said, "is having ideas. To learn to write is to learn to have ideas." But how does one "learn to have ideas"? Among the methods are these: reading with a pen or pencil in hand, so that (as we have already seen) you can annotate the text; keeping a journal, in which you jot down reflections about your reading; talking with others (including your instructor) about the reading. Let's take another look at the first of these, annotating.

ANNOTATING A TEXT

In reading, if you own the book don't hesitate to mark it up, indicating (by highlighting or underlining or by making marginal notes) what puzzles you, what pleases or interests you, and what displeases or bores you. Later, of course, you'll want to think further about these responses, asking yourself, on rereading, if you still feel that way, and if not, why not, but these first responses will get you started.

Annotations of the sort given on page 7, which chiefly call attention to contrasts, indicate that the student is thinking about writing some sort of analysis of the story. That is, she is thinking of writing an essay in which she will examine the parts of a literary work either in an effort to see how they relate to each other or in an effort to see how one part relates to the whole.

MORE ABOUT GETTING IDEAS: A SECOND STORY BY KATE CHOPIN

Let's look at a story that is a little longer than "Ripe Figs," and then we'll discuss how in addition to annotating one might get ideas for writing about it.

The Story of an Hour

Knowing that Mrs. Mallard was afflicted with a heart trouble, great care was taken to break to her as gently as possible the news of her husband's death.

It was her sister Josephine who told her, in broken sentences, veiled hints that revealed in half concealing. Her husband's friend Richards was there, too, near her. It was he who had been in the newspaper office when intelligence of the railroad disaster was received, with Brently Mallard's name leading the list of "killed." He had only taken the time to assure himself of its truth by a second telegram, and had hastened to forestall any less careful, less tender friend in bearing the sad message.

She did not hear the story as many women have heard the same, with a paralyzed inability to accept its significance. She wept at once, with sudden, wild abandonment, in her sister's arms. When the storm of grief had spent itself she went away to her room alone. She would have no one follow her.

There stood, facing the open window, a comfortable, roomy armchair. Into this she sank, pressed down by a physical exhaustion that haunted her body and seemed to reach into her soul.

She could see in the open square before her house the tops of trees that were all aquiver with the new spring life. The delicious breath of rain was in the air. In the street below a peddler was crying his wares. The notes of a distant song which some one was singing reached her faintly, and countless sparrows were twittering in the eaves.

There were patches of blue sky showing here and there through the clouds that had met and piled above the other in the west facing her window. She sat with her head thrown back upon the cushion of the chair quite motionless, except when a sob came up into her throat and shook her, as a child who has cried itself to sleep continues to sob in its dreams.

She was young, with a fair, calm face, whose lines bespoke repression and even a certain strength. But now there was a dull stare in her eyes, whose gaze was fixed away off yonder on one of those patches of blue sky. It was not a glance of reflection, but rather indicated a suspension of intelligent thought.

There was something coming to her and she was waiting for it, fearfully. What was it? She did not know; it was too subtle and elusive to name. But she felt it, creeping out of the sky, reaching toward her through the sounds, the scents, the color that filled the air.

Now her bosom rose and fell tumultuously. She was beginning to recognize this thing that was approaching to possess her, and she was striving to beat it back with her will—as powerless as her two white slender hands would have been.

When she abandoned herself a little whispered word escaped her slightly parted lips. She said it over and over under her breath: "Free, free, free!" The vacant stare and the look of terror that had followed it went from her eyes. They stayed keen and bright. Her pulses beat fast, and the coursing blood warmed and relaxed every inch of her body.

She did not stop to ask if it were not a monstrous joy that held her. A clear and exalted perception enabled her to dismiss the suggestion as trivial.

She knew that she would weep again when she saw the kind, tender hands folded in death; the face that had never looked save with love upon her, fixed and gray and dead. But she saw beyond that bitter moment a long procession of years to come that would belong to her absolutely. And she opened and spread her arms out to them in welcome.

There would be no one to live for her during those coming years; she would live for herself. There would be no powerful will bending her in that blind persistence with which men and women believe they have a right to impose a private will upon a fellow creature. A kind intention or a cruel intention made the act seem no less a crime as she looked upon it in that brief moment of illumination.

And yet she had loved him—sometimes. Often she had not. What did it matter! What could love, the unsolved mystery, count for in face of this possession of self-assertion which she suddenly recognized as the strongest impulse of her being.

"Free! Body and soul free!" she kept whispering.

Josephine was kneeling before the closed door with her lips to the keyhole, imploring for admission. "Louise, open the door! I beg; open the door— you will make youself ill. What are you doing, Louise? For heaven's sake open the door."

"Go away. I am not making myself ill." No; she was drinking in a very elixir of life through that open window.

Her fancy was running riot along those days ahead of her. Spring days, and summer days, and all sorts of days that would be her own. She breathed a quick prayer that life might be long. It was only yesterday she had thought with a shudder that life might be long.

She arose at length and opened the door to her sister's importunities. There was a feverish triumph in her eyes, and she carried herself unwittingly like a goddess of Victory. She clasped her sister's waist, and together they descended the stairs. Richards stood waiting for them at the bottom.

Some one was opening the front door with a latchkey. It was Brently Mallard who entered, a little travel-stained, composedly carrying his gripsack and umbrella. He had been far from the scene of accident, and did not even know there had been one. He stood amazed at Josephine's piercing cry; at Richards' quick motion to screen him from the view of his wife.

But Richards was too late.

When the doctors came they said she had died of heart disease—of joy that kills.

[1894]

BRAINSTORMING FOR IDEAS FOR WRITING

Unlike annotating, which consists of making brief notes and small marks on the printed page, "brainstorming"—the free jotting down of ideas—asks that you jot down whatever comes to mind, without inhibition. Don't worry about spelling, about writing complete sentences, or about unifying your thoughts; just let one thought lead to another. Later you can review your jottings, deleting some, connecting with arrows others that are related, expanding still others, but for now you want to get going, and so there is no reason to look back. Thus you might jot down something about the title:

> Title speaks of an hour, and story covers an hour, but
> maybe takes five minutes to read

And then, perhaps prompted by "an hour," you might happen to add something to this effect:

> Doubt that a woman who got news of the death of her
> husband could move from grief to joy within an hour

Your next jotting might have little or nothing to do with this issue; it might simply say

> Enjoyed "Hour" more than "Ripe Figs" partly because
> "Hour" is so shocking

And then you might ask yourself

> By shocking, do I mean "improbable," or what? Come to
> think of it, maybe it's not so improbable. A lot
> depends on what the marriage was like.

FOCUSED FREE WRITING

Focused, or directed, free writing is a method related to brainstorming that some writers use to uncover ideas they may want to write about. Concentrating on one issue—for instance, a question that strikes them as worth puzzling over (What kind of person is Mrs. Mallard?)—they write at length, nonstop, for perhaps five or ten minutes.

Writers who find free writing helpful put down everything they can think of that has bearing on the one issue or question they are examining. They do not stop at this stage to evaluate the results, and they do not worry about niceties of sentence structure or of spelling. They just pour out their ideas in a steady stream of writing, drawing on whatever associations come to mind. If they pause in their writing, it is only to refer to the text, to search for more detail—perhaps a quotation—that will help them answer their question.

After the free-writing session, these writers usually go back and reread what they have written, highlighting or underlining what seems to be of value. Of course they find much that is of little or no use, but they also usually find that some strong ideas have surfaced and have received some development. At this point the writers are often able to make a scratch outline and then begin a draft.

Here is an example of one student's focused free writing:

What do I know about Mrs. Mallard? Let me put everything down here I know about her or can figure out from what Kate Chopin tells me. When she finds herself alone after the death of her husband, she says, "Free. Body and soul free" and before that she said, "Free, free, free." Three times. So she has suddenly perceived that she has not been free; she has been under the influence of a "powerful will." In this case it has been her husband, but she says no one, man nor woman, should impose their will on anyone else. So it's not a feminist issue--it's a power issue. No one should push anyone else around is what I guess Chopin means, force someone to do what the other person wants. I used to have a friend that did that to me all the time; he had to run everything. They say that fathers--before the women's movement--used to run things, with the father in charge of all the decisions, so maybe this is an honest reaction to having been pushed around by a husband. I think Mrs. Mallard is a believable character, even if the plot is not all that believable--all those things happening in such quick succession.

LISTING

In your preliminary thinking you may find it useful to make lists. In the previous chapter we saw that listing the traits of the two characters was helpful in thinking about Chopin's "Ripe Figs":

Maman-Nainaine
    older than Babette
    "stately way"
    "patient as the statue of la Madone"
    expects to be obeyed
    connects actions with seasons

Babette
> young
> active
> obedient

For "The Story of an Hour" you might list Mrs. Mallard's traits; or you might list the stages in her development. (Such a list is not the same as a summary of the plot. The list helps the writer to see the sequence of psychological changes.)

weeps (when she gets the news)
goes to room, alone
"pressed down by a physical exhaustion"
"dull stare"
"something coming to her"
strives to beat back "this thing"
"Free, free, free!" The "vacant stare went from her eyes"
"A clear and exalted perception"
rejects Josephine
"she was drinking in the very elixir of life"
gets up, opens door, "a feverish triumph in her eyes"
sees B, and dies

Of course, unlike brainstorming and annotating, which let you go in all directions, listing requires that you first make a decision about what you will be listing—traits of character, images, puns, or whatever. Once you make the decision, you can then construct the list, and, with a list in front of you, you will probably see patterns that you were not earlier fully conscious of.

ASKING QUESTIONS

If you feel stuck, ask yourself questions. (You'll recall that the assignment on "Ripe Figs" in effect asked the students to ask themselves questions about the work—for instance, question about the relationship between the characters—and about their responses to it: "You'll probably try to explain as honestly as you can what makes 'Ripe Figs' appealing or interesting—or trifling, or boring, or whatever.")

If you are thinking about a work of fiction, ask yourself questions about the plot and the characters—are they believable, are they interesting, and what does it all add up to? What does the story mean *to you?* One student found it helpful to jot down the following questions:

Plot
> Ending false? Unconvincing? Or prepared for?

Character?

> Mrs. M. unfeeling? Immoral?
> Mrs. M. unbelievable character?

What might her marriage have been like? Many gaps.
    (Can we tell what her husband was like?)
"And yet she loved him--sometimes." Fickle?
    Realistic?
What is "this thing that was approaching to possess
    her"?

Symbolism
    Set on spring day = symbolic of new life?

But, again, you don't have to be as tidy as this student was. You can begin by jotting down notes and queries about what you like or dislike and about what puzzles or amuses you. Here are the jottings of another student. They are, obviously, in no particular order—the student is "brainstorming," putting down whatever occurs to her—though it is equally obvious that one note sometimes led to the next:

Title nothing special. What might be a better
    title?
Could a woman who loved her husband be so heartless?
Is she heartless? Did she love him?
What are (were) Louise's feelings about her
    husband?
Did she want too much? What did she want?
Could this story happen today? Feminist
    interpretation?
Sister (Josephine)--a busybody?
Tricky ending--but maybe it could be true
"And yet she had loved him--sometimes. Often she had
    not."
Why does one love someone "sometimes"?
Irony: plot has reversal. Are characters ironic too?

These jottings will help the reader-writer to think about the story, to find a special point of interest and to develop a thoughtful argument about it.

KEEPING A JOURNAL

A journal is not a diary, a record of what the writer did each day ("today I read Chopin's 'Hour' "); rather, a journal is a place to store some of the thoughts that you may have inscribed on a scrap of paper or in the margin of the text—for instance, your initial response to the title of a work or to the ending. It's also a place to jot down some further reflections. These reflections may include thoughts about what the work means to you or what was said in the classroom about writing in general or about specific works. You may, for instance, want to reflect on why your opinion is so different from that of another student, or you may want to apply a concept such as "character" or "irony" or "plausibility" to a story that later you may write an essay about.

You might even make an entry in the form of a letter to the author or in the form of a letter from one character to another. Similarly, you might write a dialogue between characters in two works or between two authors, or you might record an experience of your own that is comparable to something in the work.

A student who wrote about "The Story of an Hour" began with the following entry in his journal. In reading this entry, notice that one idea stimulates another. The student was, quite rightly, concerned with getting and exploring ideas, not with writing a unified paragraph.

> Apparently a "well-made" story, but seems clever rather than moving or real. Doesn't seem plausible. Mrs. M's change comes out of the blue—maybe some women might respond like this, but probably not most.
>
> Does literature deal with unusual people, or with usual (typical?) people? Shouldn't it deal with typical? Maybe not. (Anyway, how can I know?) Is "typical" same as "plausible"? Come to think of it, prob. not.
>
> Anyway, whether Mrs. M is typical or not, is her change plausible, believable?
>
> Why did she change? Her husband dominated her life and controlled her action; he did "impose a private will upon a fellow creature." She calls this a crime? Why? Why not?

ARRIVING AT A THESIS

Having raised some questions, a reader goes back to the story, hoping to read it now with increased awareness. Some of the jottings will be dead ends, but some will lead to further ideas which can be arranged in lists. What the **thesis** of the essay will be—the idea that will be asserted and supported—is still in doubt, but there is no doubt about one thing: A good essay will have a thesis, a point, an argument. You ought to be able to state your point in a **thesis sentence**.

Consider these candidates as possible thesis sentences:

1. Mrs. Mallard dies soon after hearing that her husband has died.

    True, but scarcely a point that can be argued, or even developed. About the most the essayist can do with this sentence is to amplify it by summarizing the plot of the story, a task not worth doing. An analysis may include a sentence or two of summary, to give readers their bearings, but a summary is not an essay.

2.   The story is a libel on women.

In contrast to the first statement, this one can be developed into an argument. Probably the writer will try to demonstrate that Mrs. Mallard's behavior is despicable. Whether this point can be convincingly argued as another matter; the thesis may be untenable, but it is a thesis. A second problem, however, is this: Even if the writer demonstrates that Mrs. Mallard's behavior is despicable, he or she will have to go on to demonstrate that the presentation of one despicable woman constitutes a libel on women in general. That's a pretty big order.

3.   The story is clever but superficial because it is based on an unreal character.

Here, too, is a thesis, a point of view that can be argued. Whether or not this thesis is true is another matter. The writer's job will be to support it by presenting evidence. Probably the writer will have no difficulty in finding evidence that the story is "clever"; the difficulty probably will be in establishing a case that the characterization of Mrs. Mallard is "unreal." The writer will have to set forth some ideas about what makes a character real and then will have to show that Mrs. Mallard is an "unreal" (unbelievable) figure.

4.   The irony of the ending is believable partly because it is consistent with earlier ironies in the story.

It happens that the student who wrote the essay printed on page 24 began by drafting an essay based on the third of these thesis topics, but as she worked on a draft she found that she couldn't support her assertion that the character was unconvincing. In fact, she came to believe that although Mrs. Mallard's joy was the reverse of what a reader might expect, several early reversals in the story helped to make Mrs. Mallard's shift from grief to joy acceptable.

Writing a Draft

After jotting down notes and then adding more notes stimulated by rereading and further thinking, you'll probably be able to formulate a tentative thesis. At this point most writers find it useful to clear the air by glancing over their preliminary notes and by jotting down the thesis and a few especially promising notes—brief statements of what they think their key points may be. These notes may include some brief key quotations that the writer thinks will help to support the thesis.

Here are the notes (not the original brainstorming notes, but a later selection from them, with additions) and a draft (page 20) that makes use of them. The final version of the essay—the product produced by the process—is given on page 24.

```
title? Ironies in an Hour (?) An Hour of Irony (?) Kate
Chopin's Irony (?)

thesis: irony at end is prepared for by earlier ironies
```

chief irony: Mrs. M. dies just as she is beginning to
enjoy life

smaller ironies: 1. "sad message" brings her joy
                 2. Richards is "too late" at end;
                 3. Richards is too early at start

SAMPLE DRAFT

Now for the student's draft—not the first version, but a revised draft with
some of the irrelevancies of the first draft omitted and some evidence added.

The digits within the parentheses refer to the page numbers from which
the quotations are drawn, though with so short a work as "The Story of an
Hour," page references are hardly necessary. Check with your instructor to
find out if you must always give citations. (Detailed information about how to
document a paper is given on pages 1056-1067.)

Ironies in an Hour

    After we know how the story turns out, if we reread
it we find irony at the very start, as is true of many
other stories. Mrs. Mallard's friends assume,
mistakenly, that Mrs. Mallard was deeply in love with
her husband, Brently Mallard. They take great care to
tell her gently of his death. The friends mean well,
and in fact they do well. They bring her an hour of
life, an hour of freedom. They think their news is sad.
Mrs. Mallard at first expresses grief when she hears
the news, but soon she finds joy in it. So Richards's
"sad message" (12), though sad in Richards's eyes, is
in fact a happy message.

    Among the ironic details is the statement that when
Mallard entered the house, Richards tried to conceal
him from Mrs. Mallard, but "Richards was too late"
(14). This is ironic because earlier Richards
"hastened" (12) to bring his sad message; if he had at
the start been "too late" (14), Brently Mallard would
have arrived at home first, and Mrs. Mallard's life

would not have ended an hour later but would simply have gone on as it had before. Yet another irony at the end of the story is the diagnosis of the doctors. The doctors say she died of "heart disease--of joy that kills" (14). In one sense the doctors are right: Mrs. Mallard has experienced a great joy. But of course the doctors totally misunderstand the joy that kills her.

The central irony resides not in the well-intentioned but ironic actions of Richards, or in the unconsciously ironic words of the doctors, but in her own life. In a way she has been dead. She "sometimes" (13) loved her husband, but in a way she has been dead. Now, his apparent death brings her new life. This new life comes to her at the season of the year when "the tops of trees...were all aquiver with the new spring life" (12). But, ironically, her new life will last only an hour. She looks forward to "summer days" (13) but she will not see even the end of this spring day. Her years of marriage were ironic. They brought her a sort of living death instead of joy. Her new life is ironic too. It grows out of her moment of grief for her supposedly dead husband, and her vision of a new life is cut short.

Work Cited

Chopin, Kate. "The Story of an Hour." Literature
   for Composition. 3rd ed. Ed. Sylvan Barnet et al.
   New York: Harper, 1992. 12-14.

REVISING A DRAFT

The draft, although thoughtful and clear, is not yet a finished essay. The student went on to improve it in many small but important ways.

First, the draft needs a good introductory paragraph, a paragraph that will let readers know where the writer will be taking them. (In Chapter 4 we discuss introductory paragraphs.) Doubtless you know from your own experience as a reader that readers can follow an argument more easily—and with more pleasure—if early in the discussion the writer alerts them to the gist of the argument. (The title, too, can strongly suggest the thesis.) Second, some of the paragraphs could be clearer.

In revising paragraphs—or, for that matter, in revising an entire draft—writers unify, organize, clarify, and polish.

1. **Unity** is achieved partly by eliminating irrelevancies. Notice that in the final version, printed on page 24, the writer has deleted "as is true of many other stories."

2. **Organization** is largely a matter of arranging material into a sequence that will assist the reader to grasp the point.

3. **Clarity** is achieved largely by providing concrete details and quotations to support generalizations and by providing helpful transitions ("for instance," "furthermore," "on the other hand," "however").

4. **Polish** is small-scale revision. For instance, one deletes unnecessary repetitions. In the second paragraph of the draft, the phrase "the doctors" appears three times, but it appears only once in the final version of the paragraph. Similarly, in polishing, a writer combines choppy sentences into longer sentences and breaks overly long sentences into shorter sentences.

Later, after producing a draft that seems close to a finished essay, writers engage in yet another activity. They

5. **edit,** checking the accuracy of quotations by comparing them with the original, checking a dictionary for the spelling of doubtful words, checking a handbook for doubtful punctuation—for instance, whether a comma or a semicolon is needed in a particular sentence.

PEER REVIEW

Your instructor may encourage (or even require) you to discuss your draft with another student or with a small group of students. That is, you may be asked to get a review from your peers. Such a procedure is helpful in several ways. First, it gives the writer a real audience, readers who can point to what pleases or puzzles them, who make suggestions, who may often disagree (with the writer or with each other), and who frequently, though not intentionally, *misread*. Though writers don't necessarily like everything they hear (they seldom hear "This is perfect. Don't change a word!"), reading and discussing their work with others almost always gives them a fresh perspective on their work, and a fresh perspective may stimulate thoughtful revision. (Having your intensions *misread* because your writing isn't clear enough can be particularly stimulating.)

The writer whose work is being reviewed is not the sole beneficiary. When students regularly serve as readers for each other, they become better readers of their own work and consequently better revisers. As we said in Chapter 1, learning to write is in large measure learning to read.

If peer review is a part of the writing process in your course, the instructor may distribute a sheet with some suggestions and questions. Here is an example of such a sheet.

QUESTIONS FOR PEER REVIEW   ENGLISH 125a

Read each draft once, quickly. Then read it again,
with the following questions in mind.

1. What is the essay's topic? Is it one of the
   assigned topics, or a variation from it? Does
   the draft show promise of fulfilling the
   assignment?

2. Looking at the essay as a whole, what thesis
   (main idea) is stated or implied? If implied,
   try to state it in your own words.

3. Is the thesis plausible? How might it be
   strengthened?

4. Looking at each paragraph separately:
   a. What is the basic point? (If it isn't clear
      to you, ask for clarification.)
   b. How does the paragraph relate to the essay's
      main idea or to the previous paragraph?
   c. Should some paragraphs be deleted? Be
      divided into two or more paragraphs? Be
      combined? Be put elsewhere? (If you outline
      the essay by jotting down the gist of each
      paragraph, you will get help in answering
      these questions.)
   d. Is each sentence clearly related to the
      sentence that precedes and to the sentence
      that follows?
   e. Is each paragraph adequately developed?
   f. Are there sufficient details, perhaps brief
      supporting quotations from the text?

5. What are the paper's chief strengths?

6. Make at least two specific suggestions that you
   think will assist the author to improve the
   paper.

The Final Version

Here is the final version of the student's essay. The essay that was submitted to the instructor had been retyped, but here, so that you can easily
see how the draft has been revised, we print the draft with the final changes
written in by hand.

Ironies of Life in Kate Chopin's "The Story of an Hour"

~~Ironies in an Hour~~

Despite its title, Kate Chopin's "The Story of an Hour" ironically takes only a few minutes to read. In addition, the story turns out to have an ironic ending, but on rereading it one sees that the irony is not concentrated only in the outcome of the plot — Mrs. Mallard dies just when she is beginning to live — but is also present in many details.

After we know how the story turns out, if we reread it we find irony at the very start / ~~as is true of many other stories.~~ *Because* Mrs. Mallard's friends ∧ *and her sister* assume, mistakenly, that ~~Mrs. Mallard~~ *she* was deeply in love with her husband, Brently Mallard. ∧They take great care to tell her gently of his death. ~~The friends~~ *They* mean well, and in fact they <u>do</u> well, ~~They~~ bring∧*ing* her an hour of life, an hour of ∧*joyous* freedom. ∧ *but it is ironic that* They think their news is sad. *True,* ∧Mrs. Mallard at first expresses grief when she hears *(unknown to her friends)* the news, but soon ∧she finds joy in it. So Richards's "sad message" (12), though sad in Richards's eyes, is in fact a happy message.

small but significant Among the ∧ironic details is the statement ∧*near the end of the story* that when Mallard entered the house, Richards tried to conceal him from Mrs. Mallard, but "Richards was too late" (14). This is ironic because ~~earlier~~ *almost at the start of the story* Richards ∧ *in the second paragraph* "hastened" (12) to bring his sad message; if he had at the start been "too late" (14), Brently Mallard would have arrived at home first, and Mrs. Mallard's life would not have ended an hour later but would simply have gone on as it had before. Yet another irony at the end of the story is the diagnosis of the doctors. The doctors say she died of "heart disease--of joy that kills" (14). In one sense ~~the doctors~~ *they* are right: Mrs.

Mallard has *for the last hour* experienced a great joy. But of course the

doctors totally misunderstand the joy that kills her. *It is not joy at seeing her husband alive, but her realization that the great joy she experienced during the last hour is over.* ~~The central irony resides not in the well-~~ *all of these ironic details add richness to the story, but*

intentioned but ironic actions of Richards, or in the

unconsciously ironic words of the doctors, but in ~~her~~ *Mrs. Mallard's*

own life. ~~In a way she has been dead.~~ She "sometimes"

(13) loved her husband, but in a way she has been dead, *a body subjected to her husband's will*

Now, his apparent death brings her new life. *Appropriately,* This new

life comes to her at the season of the year when "the

tops of trees...were all aquiver with the new spring

life" (12). But, ironically, her new life will last

only an hour. *She is "Free, free, free"—but only until her husband walks through the doorway.* She looks forward to "summer days" (13)

but she will not see even the end of this spring day.

If Her years of marriage were ironic, ~~They brought~~ *bringing* her a

sort of living death instead of joy, Her new life is

ironic too, *not only because* It grows out of her moment of grief for her

supposedly dead husband, ~~and her vision of a new life~~ *but also because her vision of a long progression of years"*

is cut short, *within an hour on a spring day.*

Work Cited

Chopin, Kate. "The Story of an Hour." <u>Literature</u>
   <u>for Composition</u>. 3rd ed. Ed. Sylvan Barnet et al.
   New York: Harper, 1992. 12-14.

A BRIEF OVERVIEW OF
THE FINAL VERSION

Finally, as a quick review, let's look at several principles illustrated by this essay.

1. The **title of the essay** is not merely the title of the work discussed; rather, it gives the reader a clue, a small idea of the essayist's topic.

2. The **opening or introductory paragraph** does not begin by saying "In this story . . ." Rather, by naming the author and the title, it lets

the reader know exactly what story is being discussed. It also develops the writer's thesis so readers know where they will be going.

3. The **organization** is effective. The smaller ironies are discussed in the second and third paragraphs, the central (chief) irony in the last paragraph. That is, the essay does not dwindle or become anticlimactic; rather, it builds up from the least important to the most important point.

4. Some **brief quotations** are used, both to provide evidence and to let the reader hear—even if only fleetingly—Kate Chopin's writing.

5. The essay is chiefly devoted to **analysis** (how the parts relate to each other), not to summary (a brief restatement of the happenings). The writer, properly assuming that the reader has read the work, does not tell the plot in great detail. But, aware that the reader has not memorized the story, the writer gives helpful reminders.

6. The **present tense** is used in narrating the action: "Mrs. Mallard dies"; "Mrs. Mallard's friends and relatives all assume."

7. Although a **concluding paragraph** is often useful—if it does more than merely summarize what has already been clearly said—it is not essential in a short analysis. In this essay, the last sentence explains the chief irony and therefore makes an acceptable ending.

A Third Story by Kate Chopin

Here is one more of Chopin's stories. It is followed by some suggestions for writing.

The Storm

I

The leaves were so still that even Bibi thought it was going to rain. Bobinôt, who was accustomed to converse on terms of perfect equality with his little son, called the child's attention to certain sombre clouds that were rolling with sinister intention from the west, accompanied by a sullen, threatening roar. They were at Friedheimer's store and decided to remain there till the storm had passed. They sat within the door on two empty kegs. Bibi was four years old and looked very wise.

"Mama'll be 'fraid, yes," he suggested with blinking eyes.

"She'll shut the house. Maybe she got Sylvie helpin' her this evenin'," Bobinôt responded reassuringly.

"No; she ent got Sylvie. Sylvie was helpin' her yistiday," piped Bibi.

Bobinôt arose and going across to the counter purchased a can of shrimps, of which Calixta was very fond. Then he returned to his perch on the keg and sat stolidly holding the can of shrimps while the storm burst. It shook the wooden store and seemed to be ripping great furrows in the distant field. Bibi laid his little hand on his father's knee and was not afraid.

II

Calixta, at home, felt no uneasiness for their safety. She sat at a side window sewing furiously on a sewing machine. She was greatly occupied and did not notice the approaching storm. But she felt very warm and often stopped to mop her face on which the perspiration gathered in beads. She unfastened her white sacque at the throat. It began to grow dark, and suddenly realizing the situation she got up hurriedly and went about closing windows and doors.

Out on the small front gallery she had hung Bobinôt's Sunday clothes to air and she hastened out to gather them before the rain fell. As she stepped outside, Alcée Laballière rode in at the gate. She had not seen him very often since her marriage, and never alone. She stood there with Bobinôt's coat in her hands, and the big rain drops began to fall. Alcée rode his horse under the shelter of a side projection where the chickens had huddled and there were plows and a harrow piled up in the corner.

"May I come and wait on your gallery till the storm is over, Calixta?" he asked.

"Come 'long in, M'sieur Alcée."

His voice and her own startled her as if from a trance, and she seized Bobinôt's vest. Alcée, mounting to the porch, grabbed the trousers and snatched Bibi's braided jacket that was about to be carried away by a sudden gust of wind. He expressed an intention to remain outside, but it was soon apparent that he might as well have been out in the open: the water beat in upon the boards in driving sheets, and he went inside, closing the door after him. It was even necessary to put something beneath the door to keep the water out.

"My! what a rain! It's good two years since it rain' like that," exclaimed Calixta as she rolled up a piece of bagging and Alcée helped her to thrust it beneath the crack.

She was a little fuller of figure than five years before when she married; but she had lost nothing of her vivacity. Her blue eyes still retained their melting quality; and her yellow hair, dishevelled by the wind and rain, kinked more stubbornly than ever about her ears and temples.

The rain beat upon the low, shingled roof with a force and clatter that threatened to break an entrance and deluge them there. They were in the dining room—the sitting room—the general utility room. Adjoining was her bed room, with Bibi's couch along side her own. The door stood open, and the room with its white, monumental bed, its closed shutters, looked dim and mysterious.

Alcée flung himself into a rocker and Calixta nervously began to gather up from the floor the lengths of a cotton sheet which she had been sewing.

"If this keeps up, *Dieu sait*[2] if the levees goin' to stan' it!" she exclaimed.

---

[1] **gallery** porch, or passageway along a wall, open to the air but protected by a roof supported by columns

[2] *Dieu sait* God only knows

"What have you got to do with the levees?"

"I got enough to do! An' there's Bobinôt with Bibi out in that storm—if he only didn' left Friedheimer's!"

"Let us hope, Calixta, that Bobinôt's got sense enough to come in out of a cyclone."

She went and stood at the window with a greatly disturbed look on her face. She wiped the frame that was clouded with moisture. It was stiflingly hot. Alcée got up and joined her at the window, looking over her shoulder. The rain was coming down in sheets obscuring the view of far-off cabins and enveloping the distant wood in a gray mist. The playing of the lightning was incessant. A bolt struck a tall chinaberry tree at the edge of the field. It filled all visible space with a blinding glare and the crash seemed to invade the very boards they stood upon.

Calixta put her hands to her eyes, and with a cry, staggered backward. Alcée's arm encircled her, and for an instant he drew her close and spasmodically to him.

"*Bonté!*"[3] she cried, releasing herself from his encircling arm and retreating from the window, "the house'll go next! If I only knew w'ere Bibi was!" She would not compose herself; she would not be seated. Alcée clasped her shoulders and looked into her face. The contact of her warm, palpitating body when he had unthinkingly drawn her into his arms, had aroused all the old-time infatuation and desire for her flesh.

"Calixta," he said, "don't be frightened. Nothing can happen. The house is too low to be struck, with so many tall trees standing about. There! aren't you going to be quiet? say, aren't you?" He pushed her hair back from her face that was warm and steaming. Her lips were as red and moist as pomegranate seed. Her white neck and a glimpse of her full, firm bosom disturbed him powerfully. As she glanced up at him the fear in her liquid blue eyes had given place to a drowsy gleam that unconsciously betrayed a sensuous desire. He looked down into her eyes and there was nothing for him to do but to gather her lips in a kiss. It reminded him of Assumption.[4]

"Do you remember—in Assumption, Calixta?" he asked in a low voice broken by passion. Oh! she remembered; for in Assumption he had kissed her and kissed and kissed her; until his senses would well nigh fail, and to save her he would resort to a desperate flight. If she was not an immaculate dove in those days, she was still inviolate; a passionate creature whose very defenselessness had made her defense, against which his honor forbade him to prevail. Now—well, now—her lips seemed in a manner free to be tasted, as well as her round, white throat and her whiter breasts.

They did not heed the crashing torrents, and the roar of the elements made her laugh as she lay in his arms. She was a revelation in that dim, mysterious chamber; as white as the couch she lay upon. Her firm, elastic flesh that was knowing for the first time its birthright, was like a creamy lily that the sun invites to contribute its breath and perfume to the undying life of the world.

---

[3] *Bonté!* Heavens!

[4] **Assumption** a church feast on 15 August celebrating Mary's bodily ascent to Heaven

The generous abundance of her passion, without guile or trickery, was like a white flame which penetrated and found response in depths of his own sensuous nature that had never yet been reached.

When he touched her breasts they gave themselves up in quivering ecstasy, inviting his lips. Her mouth was a fountain of delight. And when he possessed her, they seemed to swoon together at the very borderland of life's mystery.

He stayed cushioned upon her, breathless, dazed, enervated, with his heart beating like a hammer upon her. With one hand she clasped his head, her lips lightly touching his forehead. The other hand stroked with a soothing rhythm his muscular shoulders.

The growl of the thunder was distant and passing away. The rain beat softly upon the shingles, inviting them to drowsiness and sleep. But they dared not yield.

The rain was over; and the sun was turning the glistening green world into a palace of gems. Calixta, on the gallery, watched Alcée ride away. He turned and smiled at her with a beaming face; and she lifted her pretty chin in the air and laughed aloud.

III

Bobinôt and Bibi, trudging home, stopped without at the cistern to make themselves presentable.

"My! Bibi, w'at will yo' mama say! You ought to be ashame'. You oughtn' put on those good pants. Look at 'em! An' that mud on yo' collar! How you got that mud on yo' collar, Bibi? I never saw such a boy!" Bibi was the picture of pathetic resignation. Bobinôt was the embodiment of serious solicitude as he strove to remove from his own person and his son's the signs of their tramp over heavy roads and through wet fields. He scraped the mud off Bibi's bare legs and feet with a stick and carefully removed all traces from his heavy brogans. Then, prepared for the worst—the meeting with an over-scrupulous housewife, they entered cautiously at the back door.

Calixta was preparing supper. She had set the table and was dripping coffee at the hearth. She sprang up as they came in.

"Oh, Bobinôt! You back! My! but I was uneasy. W'ere you been during the rain? An' Bibi? he ain't wet? he ain't hurt?" She had clasped Bibi and was kissing him effusively. Bobinôt's explanations and apologies which he had been composing all along the way, died on his lips as Calixta felt him to see if he were dry, and seemed to express nothing but satisfaction at their safe return.

"I brought you some shrimps, Calixta," offered Bobinôt, hauling the can from his ample side pocket and laying it on the table.

"Shrimps! Oh, Bobinôt! you too good fo' anything!" and she gave him a smacking kiss on the cheek that resounded. "*J'vous reponds,*[5] we'll have a feas' to night! umph-umph!"

Bobinôt and Bibi began to relax and enjoy themselves, and when the

[5] *J'vous reponds* Take my word; let me tell you

three seated themselves at table they laughed much and so loud that anyone might have heard them as far away as Laballière's.

IV

Alcée Laballière wrote to his wife, Clarisse, that night. It was a loving letter, full of tender solicitude. He told her not to hurry back, but if she and the babies liked it at Biloxi, to stay a month longer. He was getting on nicely; and though he missed them, he was willing to bear the separation a while longer—realizing that their health and pleasure were the first things to be considered.

V

As for Clarisse, she was charmed upon receiving her husband's letter. She and the babies were doing well. The society was agreeable; many of her old friends and acquaintances were at the bay. And the first free breath since her marriage seemed to restore the pleasant liberty of her maiden days. Devoted as she was to her husband, their intimate conjugal life was something which she was more than willing to forego for a while.

So the storm passed and everyone was happy.

[1898]

■ WRITING ABOUT "THE STORM"

As we said earlier, what you write will depend partly on your audience and on your purpose, as well as on your responses (for instance, pleasure or irritation). Consider the *differences* among these assignments:

1. Assume that you are trying to describe "The Storm" to someone who has not read it. Briefly summarize the action, and then try to explain why you think "The Storm" is (or is not) worth reading.
2. Assume that your readers are familiar with "The Story of an Hour" and "The Storm." Compare the implied attitudes, as you see them, toward marriage.
3. Write an essay arguing that "The Storm" is (or is not) immoral, or (a different thing) amoral. (By the way, because one of her slightly earlier works, a short novel called *The Awakening*, was widely condemned as sordid, Chopin was unable to find a publisher for "The Storm.")
4. In Part IV we are told that Alcée wrote a letter to Clarisse. Write his letter (500 words). Or write Clarisse's response (500 words).
5. You are writing to a high school teacher, urging that one of the three stories be taught in high school. Which one do you recommend, and why?

A Note about Literary Evaluations

One other point—and it is a big one. Until a decade or two ago, Chopin was regarded as a minor writer who worked in a minor field. She was called a "local colorist," that is, a writer who emphasizes the unique speech, mannerisms, and ways of thinking of the charming and somewhat eccentric characters associated with a particular locale. Other late nineteenth-century writers who are widely regarded as local colorists were Bret Harte (California), Sarah Orne Jewett and Mary E. Wilkins Freeman (New England), and Joel Chandler Harris (the old South). Because of the writers' alleged emphasis on the uniqueness and charm of a region, the reader's response is likely to be "How quaint" rather than "This is life as I feel it, or at least as I can imagine it."

Probably part of the reason for the relatively low value attributed to Chopin's work was that she was a woman, and it was widely believed that "serious and important literature" was (with a very few exceptions) written by men. In short, judgments, including literary evaluations, depend partly on cultural traditions.

A question: On the basis of the three stories by Chopin, do you think Chopin's interest went beyond presenting quaint folk for our entertainment? You might set forth your response in an essay of 500 words—after you have done some brainstorming, some thinking in a journal, and some drafting, revising, and editing.

■ CHAPTER 3

Analytic Writing:

An Overview

Why Write? Purpose and Audience

In Chapter 1 we briefly talked about audience and purpose, but a few further words may be useful. People write not only to communicate with others but also to clarify and to account for their responses to material that interests or excites or frustrates them. In putting words on paper you will have to take a second and a third look at what is in front of you and at what is within you. And so the process of writing is a way of learning. The last word is never said about complex thoughts and feelings, but when we write we hope to make at least a little progress in the difficult but rewarding job of talking about our responses. We learn, and then we hope to interest our reader because we are communicating our responses to material that for one reason or another is worth talking about.

When you write, you transform your responses into words that will let your reader share your perceptions, your enthusiasms, and even your doubts. This sharing is, in effect, teaching. Students often think that they are writing for the teacher, but this is a misconception. When you write, *you* are the teacher. An essay on literature is an attempt to help someone to see something as you see it.

If you are not writing for the teacher, for whom are you writing? For yourself, of course, but also for others. Occasionally, in an effort to help you develop an awareness that what you write depends partly on your audience, your instructor may specify an audience, suggesting that you write for high school students or for the readers of *The Atlantic* or *Ms*. But if an audience is not specified, write for your classmates. If you keep your classmates in mind as your audience, you will not write, "William Shakespeare, England's most famous playwright," because such a remark seems to imply that your reader does not know Shakespeare's nationality or trade. On the other hand,

you *will* write, "Sei Shōnagon, a lady of the court in medieval Japan," because
you can reasonably assume that your classmates do not know who she is.

Analysis

Most of the writing that you will do in college—not only in your English
courses but in courses in history, sociology, economics, fine arts, and
philosophy—will be analytic. **Analysis,** literally a separating of a whole into
parts, is a method we commonly use in thinking about complex matters and
in attempting to account for our responses. Watching Martina Navratilova play
tennis, we may admire her serve, or her backhand, or the execution of several brilliant plays, and then think more generally about the concentration and
flexibility that allow her to capitalize on her opponent's momentary weakness.
And of course when we want to improve our own game, we try to analyze
our performance. When writing is our game, we analyze our responses to a
work, trying to name them and account for them. We analyze our notes, looking for ideas that connect, searching for significant patterns, and later we analyze our drafts, looking for strengths and weaknesses. Similarly, in peer
review, discussed in Chapter 2, we analyze the draft of a fellow student, seeing how the parts (individual words, sentences, whole paragraphs, the tentative title, and everything else) relate to one another and fit together as a
whole.

To develop an analysis of a literary work, we tend, whether consciously
or not, to formulate questions and then to answer them. We ask such questions as:

What is the function of the setting in this story or play?
Why has this character been introduced?
What is the author trying to tell us?
How exactly can I describe the tone?
What is the difference in the assumptions between this essay and that one?

This book contains an anthology of literary works for you to respond to
and then write about, and after most of the works we pose some questions.
We also pose general questions on essays (page 87), fiction (page 120), drama
(174), and poetry (230). These questions may stimulate your thinking and
thus help you write. Our concern as teachers of writing is not so much with
the answers to these questions; we believe and we ask you to believe that
there are in fact no "right answers," only more or less persuasive ones, to
most questions about literature—as about life. Our aim, rather, is to help you
to pose questions that will stimulate your thinking.

Thinking Analytically: An Example

The following short poem is by Langston Hughes (1902-1967), an
African-American writer who was born in Joplin, Mississippi, lived part of his
youth in Mexico, spent a year at Columbia University, served as a merchant
seaman, and worked in a Paris nightclub, where he showed some of his poems

to Dr. Alain Locke, a strong advocate of African-American literature. Encouraged by Locke, when Hughes returned to the United States he continued to write, publishing fiction, plays, essays, and biographies; he also founded theaters, gave public readings, and was, in short, a highly visible presence. The poem that we reprint, "Harlem" (1951), provided Lorraine Hansberry with the title of her well-known play, *A Raisin in the Sun* (1958).

■ LANGSTON HUGHES

Harlem

What happens to a dream deferred?

> Does it dry up
> like a raisin in the sun?
> Or fester like a sore—
> And then run?   5
> Does it stink like rotten meat?
> Or crust and sugar over—
> like a syrupy sweet?

> Maybe it just sags
> like a heavy load.   10

> *Or does it explode?*
>   [1951]

Read the poem at least twice, and then think about its effect on you. Do you find the poem interesting? Do some things in it interest you more than others? Does anything in it puzzle you? Does the poem get you thinking about your own deferred dreams? Before reading any further, you might jot down your responses to some of these questions. And, whatever your responses, how can you account for them?

In Chapter 1 we emphasized the point that different readers will respond at least somewhat differently to any work. On the other hand, since writers want to communicate, they try to control their readers' responses, and they count on their readers to understand the denotations of words as they understand them. Thus, Hughes assumed that his readers knew that Harlem was the site of a large African-American community in New York City. A reader who confuses the title of the poem with Haarlem in the Netherlands will wonder what this poem is saying about the tulip-growing center in northern Holland.

Let's assume that the reader understands Hughes is talking about Harlem, New York, and, further, that the reader understands the "dream deferred" to refer to the unfulfilled hopes of African-Americans who live in a dominant white society. But Hughes does not say "hopes," he says "dream," and he does not say "unfulfilled," he says "deferred." You might ask yourself exactly what differences there are between these words. Next, when you have read the poem several times, you might think about which expression is better in the context, "Unfulfilled Hopes" or "Dream Deferred," and why?

WORKING TOWARD AN ANALYSIS OF "HARLEM"

Let's turn to an analysis of the poem, an examination of how the parts fit. As you look at the poem, think about the parts, and jot down whatever notes come to mind. After you have written your own notes, consider the annotations of one student:

These annotations chiefly get at the structure of the poem, the relationship of the parts. The student notices that the poem begins with a line set off by itself and ends with a line set off by itself, and he also notices that each of these lines is a question. Further, he indicates that each of these two lines is emphasized in other ways: The first begins further to the left than any of the other lines—as though the other lines are subheadings or are in some way subordinate—and the last is italicized. In short, he comments on the *structure* of the poem.

SOME JOURNAL ENTRIES

The student who made these annotations later wrote an entry in his journal:

Feb. 18. Since the title is "Harlem," it's obvious that the dream" is by African-American people. Also,

obvious that Hughes thinks that if the "dream" doesn't
become real there may be riots ("explode"). I like
"raisin in the sun" (maybe because I like the play),
and I like the business about "a syrupy sweet"--much
more pleasant than the festering sore and the rotten
meat. But if the dream becomes "sweet," what's wrong
with that? Why should something "sweet" explode?

Feb. 21. Prof. McCabe said to think of structure or
form of a poem as a sort of architecture, a building
with a foundation, floors, etc. topped by a roof--but
since we read a poem from top to bottom, it's like a
building upside down. Title is foundation (even though
it's at top); last line is roof, capping the whole. As
you read, you add layers. Foundation of "Harlem" is a
question (first line). Then, set back a bit from
foundation, or built on it by white space, a tall room
(7 lines high, with 4 questions); then, on top of this
room, another room (two lines, one statement, not a
question.) Funny; I thought that in poems all stanzas
are the same number of lines. Then--more white space,
so another unit--the roof. Man, this roof is going to
fall in--"explode." Not just the roof, maybe the whole
house.

Feb. 21, pm. I get it; one line at start, one line at
end; both are questions, but the last sort of says
(because it is in italics) that it is the most likely
answer to the question of the first line. The last line
is also a question, but it's still an answer. The big
stanza (7 lines) has 4 questions: 2 lines, 2 lines, 1
line, 2 lines. Maybe the switch to 1 line is to give
some variety, so as not to be dull? It's exactly in the
middle of the poem. I get the progress from raisin in
the sun (dried, but not so terrible), to festering sore
and to stinking meat, but I still don't see what's so
bad about "a syrupy sweet." Is Hughes saying that
after things are very bad they will get better? But
why, then, the explosion at the end?

Feb. 23. "Heavy load" and "sags" in next-to-last
stanza seems to me to suggest slaves with bales of
cotton, or maybe poor cotton pickers dragging big sacks
of cotton. Or maybe people doing heavy labor in Harlem.
Anyway, very tired. Different from running sore and
stinking meat earlier; not disgusting, but pressing
down, deadening. Maybe worse than a sore or rotten
meat--a hard, hopeless life. And then the last line.
Just one line, no fancy (and disgusting) simile. Boom!

Not just pressed down and tired, like maybe some racist
whites think (hope?) blacks will be? Bang! Will there
be survivors?

Drawing chiefly on these notes, the student jotted down some key ideas
to guide him through a draft of an analysis of the poem. (The organization of
the draft posed no problem; the student simply followed the organization of
the poem.)

> 11 lines; short, but powerful; explosive
> Question (first line)
> Answers (set off by space, & also indented)
> "raisin in the sun": shrinking ⎫
> "sore"   ⎬ disgusting
> "rotten meat"   ⎭
> "syrupy sweet": relief from disgusting comparisons
> Final question (last line): explosion?
>   explosive (powerful) because:
>   short, condensed, packed
>   in italics
>   stands by self — like first line
>   no fancy comparison; very direct

FINAL DRAFT

Here is the final analysis:

Langston Hughes's "Harlem"

"Harlem" is a poem that is only eleven lines long,
but it is charged with power. It explodes. Hughes sets
the stage, so to speak, by telling us in the title that
he is talking about Harlem, and then he begins by
asking "What happens to a dream deferred?" The rest of
the poem is set off by being indented, as though it is
the answer to his question. This answer is in three
parts (three stanzas, of different lengths).

In a way, it's wrong to speak of the answer, since
the rest of the poem consists of questions, but I think
Hughes means that each question (for instance, does a
"deferred" hope "dry up / like a raisin in the sun?")
really is an answer, something that really has happened
and that will happen again. The first question, "Does
it dry up / like a raisin in the sun?" is a famous line.
To compare hope to a raisin dried in the sun is to
suggest a terrible shrinking. The next two comparisons
are to a "sore" and to "rotten meat." These
comparisons are less clever, but they are very
effective because they are disgusting. Then, maybe
because of the disgusting comparisons, he gives a
comparison that is not at all disgusting. In this
comparison he says that maybe the "dream deferred"
will "crust over-- / like a syrupy sweet."

The seven lines with four comparisons are followed
by a stanza of two lines with just one comparison:

Maybe it just sags

like a heavy load.

So if we thought that this postponed dream might
finally turn into something "sweet," we were kidding
ourselves. Hughes comes down to earth, in a short
stanza, with an image of a heavy load, which probably
also calls to mind images of people bent under heavy
loads, maybe of cotton, or maybe just any sort of heavy
load carried by African-Americans in Harlem and
elsewhere.

The opening question ("What happens to a dream
deferred?") was followed by four questions in seven
lines, but now, with "Maybe it just sags / like a heavy
load" we get a statement, as though the poet at last
has found an answer. But at the end we get one more
question, set off by itself and in italics: "Or does it

explode?" This line itself is explosive for three
reasons: it is short, it is italicized, and it is a
stanza in itself. It's also interesting that this line,
unlike the earlier lines, does not use a simile. It's
almost as though Hughes is saying, "O.K., we've had
enough fancy ways of talking about this terrible
situation; here it is, straight."

■ QUESTION FOR DISCUSSION

The student's analysis suggests that the comparison with "a syrupy sweet" is a deliberately misleading happy ending that serves to make the real ending even more powerful. In class another student suggested that Hughes may be referring to African-Americans who play the Uncle Tom, people who adopt a smiling manner in order to cope with an oppressive society. Which explanation do you prefer, and why? What do you think of combining the two? Or can you offer a different explanation?

Analysis and Evaluation

When we evaluate, we say how good, how successful, how worthwhile, something is. If you reread the student's essay on "Harlem," you'll notice that he implies that the poem is worth reading. He doesn't say "In this excellent poem," but a reader of the essay probably comes away with the impression that the student thinks the poem is excellent. The writer might, of course, have included a more explicit evaluation, along these lines:

In "Harlem," every word counts, and every word is
effective. The image of the "heavy load" that "sags"
is not as unusual as the image of the raisin in the sun,
but it nevertheless is just right, adding a simple,
powerful touch just before the explosive ending.

In any case, if an analysis argues that the parts fit together effectively, it almost surely is implying a favorable evaluation. But only *"almost* surely." One might argue, for instance, that the parts fit, and so on, but that the work is immoral, or trivial, or unpleasant, or untrue to life. Even though one might grant that the work is carefully constructed, one's final evaluation of the work might be low. Evaluations are based on standards. If you offer an evaluation, make certain that your standards are clear to the reader.

Notice in the following three examples of evaluations of J. D. Salinger's *The Catcher in the Rye* that the writers let their readers know what their standards are. Each excerpt is from a review that was published when the book first appeared. In the first, Anne L. Goodman, writing in *The New Republic*

(16 July, 1951), began by praising Salinger's earlier short stories and then said of the novel:

> But the book as a whole is disappointing, and not merely because it is a re-working of a theme that one begins to suspect must obsess the author. Holden Caulfield, the main character who tells his own story, is an extraordinary portrait, but there is too much of him. He describes himself early on and, with the sureness of a wire recording, he remains strictly in character throughout.

Goodman then quotes a longish passage from *The Catcher*, and says,

> In the course of 277 pages the reader wearies of this kind of explicitness, repetition, and adolescence, exactly as one would weary of Holden himself.

Goodman lets us know that, in her opinion, 1) a book ought not simply to repeat a writer's earlier books, and also that, again in her opinion, 2) it's not enough to give a highly realistic portrait of a character; if the character is not a sufficiently interesting person, in the long run the book will be dull.

Another reviewer, Virgilia Peterson, writing in *New York Herald Tribune Book Review* (15 July 1951), found the book realistic in some ways, but unrealistic and therefore defective because its abundant profanity becomes unconvincing:

> There is probably not one phrase in the whole book that Holden Caulfield would not have used upon occasion, but when they are piled upon each other in cumulative monotony, the ear refuses to believe.

Ms. Peterson concluded her review, however, by confessing that she did not think she was in a position to evaluate a book about an adolescent, or at least *this* adolescent.

> . . . it would be interesting and highly enlightening to know what Holden Caulfield's contemporaries, male and female, think of him. Their opinion would constitute the real test of Mr. Salinger's validity. The question of authenticity is one to which no parent can really guess the reply.

Notice that here again the standard is clear—authenticity—but the writer confesses that she isn't sure about authenticity in this matter, and she defers to her juniors. Peterson's review is a rare example of an analysis offered by a writer who confesses an inability to evaluate.

Finally, here is a brief extract from a more favorable review, written by Paul Engle and published in the *Chicago Sunday Tribune Magazine of Books* (15 July 1951):

> The book ends with Holden in a mental institution for which the earlier events have hardly prepared the reader. But the story is an engaging and believable one for the most part, full of right observations and sharp insight, and a wonderful sort of grasp of how a boy can create his own world of fantasy and live form.

The first sentence implies that a good book prepares the reader for the end, and that in this respect *The Catcher* is deficient. The rest of the paragraph sets forth other standards that *The Catcher* meets (it is "engaging and believable," "full of right observations and sharp insight"), though one of the standards in Engle's last sentence ("live form") strikes us as obscure.

Choosing a Topic and Developing a Thesis

Because Hughes's "Harlem" is very short, the analysis may discuss the entire poem. But a short essay, or even a long one, can hardly discuss all aspects of a play or a novel or even of a long story. If you are writing about a long work, you'll have to single out an appropriate topic.

What is an appropriate topic? First, it must be a topic that you can work up some interest in or your writing will be mechanical and dull. (We say "work up some interest" because interest is commonly the result of some effort.) Second, an appropriate topic is compassable—that is, it is something you can cover with reasonable attention to detail in the few pages (and few days) you have to devote to it. If a work is fairly long, almost surely you will write an analysis of some part.

Unless you have an enormous amount of time for reflection and revision, you cannot write a meaningful essay of five hundred words or even a thousand words on "Shakespeare's *Hamlet*" or "The Fiction of Alice Walker." You cannot even write on "Character in *Hamlet*" or "Symbolism in Walker's *The Color Purple*." And probably you won't really want to write on such topics anyway. Probably *one* character or *one* symbol has caught your interest. Think of something in your annotations or "response" notes (described in Chapter 1) that has caught your attention. Trust your feelings; you are likely onto something interesting.

In Chapter 1 we talked about the value of asking yourself questions. To find an appropriate topic, ask yourself such questions as the following:

1. *What purpose does this serve?* For instance, why is this scene in the novel or play? Why is there a comic gravedigger in *Hamlet*? Why are these lines unrhymed? Why did the author call the work by this title?
2. *Why do I have this response?* Why do I feel that this work is more profound (or amusing, or puzzling) than that work? How did the author make this character funny or dignified or pathetic? How did the author communicate the idea that this character is a bore without boring me?

The first of these questions, "What purpose does this serve?" requires that you identify yourself with the author, wondering, for example, whether this opening scene is the best possible for this story. The second question, "Why do I have this response?" requires that you trust your feelings. If you are amused or puzzled or annoyed, assume that these responses are appropriate and follow them up, at least until a rereading of the work provides other responses. If you jot down notes reporting your responses and later think about them, you will probably find that you can select a topic.

Given an appropriate topic, you will find your essay easier to write and the finished version of it clearer and more persuasive if, at some point in your preparation, in note taking or in writing a first draft, you have converted your topic into a *thesis* (a proposition, a point, an argument) and constructed a *thesis statement* (a sentence stating your overall point).

Let's dwell a moment on the distinction between a topic and a thesis. It may be useful to think of it this way: A topic is a subject (for example, "The Role of Providence in *Hamlet*"); to arrive at a thesis, you have to make an arguable assertion (for example, "The role of Providence in *Hamlet* is not obvious, but it is crucial").

Of course some theses are more promising than others. Consider this thesis:

> The role of Providence in *Hamlet* is interesting.

This sentence indeed asserts a thesis, but it is vague and provides little direction, little help in generating ideas and in shaping your essay. Let's try again. It's almost always necessary to try again and again, for the process of writing is in large part a process of trial and error, of generating better and better ideas by evaluating—selecting or rejecting—ideas and options.

> The role of Providence is evident in the Ghost.

This is much better, and it could stimulate ideas for an interesting essay. Let's assume the writer rereads the play, looking for further evidence, and comes to believe that the Ghost is only one of several manifestations of Providence. The writer may stay with the Ghost or may (especially if the paper is long enough to allow for such a thesis to be developed) alter the thesis thus:

> The role of Providence is not confined to the Ghost but is found also in the killing of Polonius, in the surprising appearance of the pirate ship, and in the presence of the poisoned chalice.

Strictly speaking, the thesis here is given in the first part of the sentence ("The role of Providence is not confined to the Ghost"); the rest of the sentence provides an indication of how the argument will be supported.

Every literary work suggests its own topics for analysis to an active reader, and all essayists must set forth their own theses, but if you begin by seeking to examine one of your responses, you probably will soon be able to stake out a topic and to formulate a thesis.

A suggestion: With two or three other students, formulate a thesis about Kate Chopin's "The Storm" (in Chapter 2). By practicing with a group you will develop a skill that you will use when you have to formulate a thesis on your own.

An Analysis of a Story

If a story is short enough, you may be able to examine everything in it that you think is worth commenting on, but even if it is short you may nevertheless decide to focus on one element, such as the setting, or the construction of the plot, or the connection between two characters, or the degree of plausibility. Here is a story by James Thurber (1894–1961), the American humorist. It was first published in 1939.

■ JAMES THURBER
_____

The Secret Life of Walter Mitty

"We're going through!" The Commander's voice was like thin ice breaking. He wore his full-dress uniform, with the heavily braided white cap pulled down rakishly over one cold gray eye. "We can't make it, sir. It's spoiling for a hurricane, if you ask me." "I'm not asking you, Lieutenant Berg," said the Commander. "Throw on the power lights! Rev her up to 8,500! We're going through!" The pounding of the cylinders increased: ta-pocketa-pocketa-pocketa-*pocketa-pocketa*. The Commander stared at the ice forming on the pilot window. He walked over and twisted a row of complicated dials. "Switch on No. 8 auxiliary!" he shouted. "Switch on No. 8 auxiliary!" repeated Lieutenant Berg. "Full strength in No. 3 turret!" shouted the Commander. "Full strength in No. 3 turret!" The crew, bending to their various tasks in the huge, hurtling eight-engined Navy hydroplane, looked at each other and grinned. "The Old Man'll get us through," they said to one another. "The Old Man ain't afraid of Hell!" . . .

"Not so fast! You're driving too fast!" said Mrs. Mitty. "What are you driving so fast for?"

"Hmm?" said Walter Mitty. He looked at his wife, in the seat beside him, with shocked astonishment. She seemed grossly unfamiliar, like a strange woman who had yelled at him in a crowd. "You were up to fifty-five," she said. "You know I don't like to go more than forty. You were up to fifty-five." Walter Mitty drove on toward Waterbury in silence, the roaring of the SN202 through the worst storm in twenty years of Navy flying fading in the remote, intimate airways of his mind. "You're tensed up again," said Mrs. Mitty. "It's one of your days. I wish you'd let Dr. Renshaw look you over."

Walter Mitty stopped the car in front of the building where his wife went to have her hair done. "Remember to get those overshoes while I'm having my hair done," she said. "I don't need overshoes," said Mitty. She put her mirror back into her bag. "We've been all through that," she said, getting out of the car. "You're not a young man any longer." He raced the engine a little. "Why don't you wear your gloves? Have you lost your gloves?" Walter Mitty reached in a pocket and brought out the gloves. He put them on, but after she had turned and gone into the building and he had driven on to a red light, he took them off again. "Pick it up, brother!" snapped a cop as the light changed, and Mitty hastily pulled on his gloves and lurched ahead. He drove around the streets aimlessly for a time, and then he drove past the hospital on his way to the parking lot.

. . . "It's the millionaire banker, Wellington McMillan," said the pretty nurse. "Yes?" said Walter Mitty, removing his gloves slowly. "Who has the case?" "Dr. Renshaw and Dr. Benbow, but there are two specialists here, Dr.

Remington from New York and Dr. Pritchard-Mitford from London. He flew over." A door opened down a long, cool corridor and Dr. Renshaw came out. He looked distraught and haggard. "Hello, Mitty," he said. "We're having the devil's own time with McMillan, the millionaire banker and close personal friend of Roosevelt. Obstreosis of the ductal tract. Tertiary. Wish you'd take a look at him." "Glad to," said Mitty.

In the operating room there were whispered introductions: "Dr. Remington, Dr. Mitty, Mr. Pritchard-Mitford, Dr. Mitty." "I've read your book on streptothricosis," said Pritchard-Mitford, shaking hands. "A brilliant performance, sir." "Thank you," said Walter Mitty. "Didn't know you were in the States, Mitty," grumbled Remington. "Coals to Newcastle, bringing Mitford and me up here for a tertiary." "You are very kind," said Mitty. A huge, complicated machine, connected to the operating table, with many tubes and wires, began at this moment to go pocketa-pocketa-pocketa. "The new anesthetizer is giving way!" shouted an interne. "There is no one in the East who knows how to fix it!" "Quiet, man!" said Mitty, in a low, cool voice. He sprang to the machine, which was now going pocketa-pocketa-queep-pocketa-queep. He began fingering delicately a row of glistening dials. "Give me a fountain pen!" he snapped. Someone handed him a fountain pen. He pulled a faulty piston out of the machine and inserted the pen in its place. "That will hold for ten minutes," he said. "Get on with the operation." A nurse hurried over and whispered to Renshaw, and Mitty saw the man turn pale. "Coreopsis has set in," said Renshaw nervously. "If you would take over, Mitty?" Mitty looked at him and at the craven figure of Benbow, who drank, and at the grave, uncertain faces of the two great specialists. "If you wish," he said. They slipped a white gown on him; he adjusted a mask and drew on thin gloves; nurses handed him shining. . . .

"Back it up, Mac! Look out for that Buick!" Walter Mitty jammed on the brakes. "Wrong lane, Mac," said the parking-lot attendant, looking at Mitty closely. "Gee. Yeh," muttered Mitty. He began cautiously to back out of the lane marked "Exit Only." "Leave her sit there," said the attendant. "I'll put her away." Mitty got out of the car. "Hey, better leave the key." "Oh," said Mitty, handing the man the ignition key. The attendant vaulted into the car, backed it up with insolent skill, and put it where it belonged.

They're so damn cocky, thought Walter Mitty, walking along Main Street; they think they know everything. Once he had tried to take his chains off, outside New Milford, and he had got them wound around the axles. A man had had to come out in a wrecking car and unwind them, a young, grinning garageman. Since then Mrs. Mitty always made him drive to the garage to have the chains taken off. The next time, he thought, I'll wear my right arm in a sling; they won't grin at me then. I'll have my right arm in a sling and they'll see I couldn't possibly take the chains off myself. He kicked at the slush on the sidewalk. "Overshoes," he said to himself, and he began looking for a shoe store.

When he came out into the street again, with the overshoes in a box under his arm, Walter Mitty began to wonder what the other thing was his wife had told him to get. She had told him, twice, before they set out from their house for Waterbury. In a way he hated these weekly trips to town—he was always getting something wrong. Kleenex, he thought, Squibb's, razor blades? No. Toothpaste, toothbrush, bicarbonate, carborundum, initiative and referendum? He gave it up. But she would remember it. "Where's the what's-its-name?" she would ask. "Don't tell me you forgot the what's-its-name." A newsboy went by shouting something about the Waterbury trial.

. . . "Perhaps this will refresh your memory." The District Attorney suddenly thrust a heavy automatic at the quiet figure on the witness stand. "Have you ever seen this before?" Walter Mitty took the gun and examined it expertly. "This is my Webley-Vickers 50.80," he said calmly. An excited buzz ran around the courtroom. The Judge rapped for order. "You are a crack shot with any sort of firearms, I believe?" said the District Attorney, insinuatingly. "Objection!" shouted Mitty's attorney. "We have shown that the defendant could not have fired the shot. We have shown that he wore his right arm in a sling on the night of the fourteenth of July." Walter Mitty raised his hand briefly and the bickering attorneys were stilled. "With any known make of gun," he said evenly, "I could have killed Gregory Fitzhurst at three hundred feet *with my left hand.*" Pandemonium broke loose in the courtroom. A woman's scream rose above the bedlam and suddenly a lovely, dark-haired girl was in Walter Mitty's arms. The District Attorney struck at her savagely. Without rising from his chair, Mitty let the man have it on the point of the chin. "You miserable cur!" . . .

"Puppy biscuit," said Walter Mitty. He stopped walking and the buildings of Waterbury rose up out of the misty courtroom and surrounded him again. A woman who was passing laughed. "He said 'Puppy biscuit,' " she said to her companion. "That man said 'Puppy biscuit' to himself." Walter Mitty hurried on. He went into an A. & P., not the first one he came to but a smaller one farther up the street. "I want some biscuit for small, young dogs," he said to the clerk. "Any special brand, sir?" The greatest pistol shot in the world thought a moment. "It says 'Puppies Bark for It' on the box," said Walter Mitty.

His wife would be through at the hairdresser's in fifteen minutes, Mitty saw in looking at his watch, unless they had trouble drying it; sometimes they had trouble drying it. She didn't like to get to the hotel first; she would want him to be there waiting for her as usual. He found a big leather chair in the lobby, facing a window, and he put the overshoes and the puppy biscuit on the floor beside it. He picked up an old copy of *Liberty* and sank down into the chair. "Can Germany Conquer the World through the Air?" Walter Mitty looked at the pictures of bombing planes and of ruined streets.

. . . "The cannonading has got the wind up in young Raleigh, sir," said the sergeant. Captain Mitty looked up at him through tousled hair. "Get him to bed," he said wearily. "With the others. I'll fly alone." "But you can't, sir," said the sergeant anxiously. "It takes two men to handle that bomber and the Archies are pounding hell out of the air. Von Richtman's circus is between here and Saulier." "Somebody's got to get that ammunition dump," said Mitty. "I'm going over. Spot of brandy?" He poured a drink for the sergeant and one for himself. War thundered and whined around the dugout and battered at the door. There was a rending of wood and splinters flew through the room. "A bit of a near thing," said Captain Mitty carelessly. "The box barrage is closing in," said the sergeant. "We only live once, Sergeant," said Mitty, with his faint, fleeting smile. "Or do we?" He poured another brandy and tossed it off. "I never see a man could hold his brandy like you, sir," said the sergeant. "Begging your pardon, sir." Captain Mitty stood up and strapped on his huge Webley-Vickers automatic. "It's forty kilometers through hell, sir," said the sergeant. Mitty finished one last brandy. "After all," he said softly, "what isn't?" The pounding of the cannon increased; there was the rat-tat-tatting of machine guns, and from somewhere came the menacing pocket-pocketa-pocketa of the new flame-throwers. Walter Mitty walked to the door of the dugout humming "Auprès de Ma Blonde." He turned and waved to the sergeant. "Cheerio!" he said. . . .

Something struck his shoulder. "I've been looking all over this hotel for you," said Mrs. Mitty. "Why do you have to hide in this old chair? How did you expect me to find you?" "Things close in," said Walter Mitty vaguely. "What?" Mrs. Mitty said. "Did you get the what's-its-name? The puppy biscuit? What's in that box?" "Overshoes," said Mitty. "Couldn't you have put them on in the store?" "I was thinking," said Walter Mitty. "Does it ever occur to you that I am sometimes thinking?" She looked at him. "I'm going to take your temperature when I get you home," she said.

They went out through the revolving doors that made a faintly derisive whistling sound when you pushed them. It was two blocks to the parking lot. At the drugstore on the corner she said, "Wait here for me. I forgot something. I won't be a minute." She was more than a minute. Walter Mitty lighted a cigarette. It began to rain, rain with sleet in it. He stood up against the wall of the drugstore, smoking. . . . He put his shoulders back and his heels together. "To hell with the handkerchief," said Walter Mitty scornfully. He took one last drag on his cigarette and snapped it away. Then, with that faint, fleeting smile playing about his lips, he faced the firing squad; erect and motionless, proud and disdainful, Walter Mitty the Undefeated, inscrutable to the last.

[1942]

SOME JOURNAL ENTRIES

Before reading the following entries about "The Secret Life of Walter Mitty," write some of your own. You may want to think about what (if anything) you found amusing in the story, or about whether the story is dated, or about some aspect of Mitty's character or of his wife's. But the choice is yours.

A student wrote the following entry in her journal after the story was discussed in class.

<u>March 21</u>. Funny, I guess, especially the business about
him as a doctor performing an operation. and that
"pocketa-pocketa," but I don't think that it's as
hysterical as everyone else seems to think it is. And

how could anyone stand being married to a man like that? In fact, it's a good thing he has her to look after him. He ought to be locked up, driving into the "Exit Only" lane, talking to himself in the street, and having those crazy daydreams. No wonder the woman in the street laughs at him.

March 24. He's certainly a case, and she's not nearly as bad as everyone was saying. So she tells him to put his overshoes on; well, he ought to put them on, since Thurber says there is slush in the street, and he's no kid anymore. About the worst I can say of her is that she seems a little unreasonable in always wanting him to wait for her, rather than sometimes the other way around, but probably she's really telling him not to wander off, because if he ever drifts away there'll be no finding him. The joke, I guess, is that he's supposed to have these daydreams because he's henpecked, and henpecked men are supposed to be funny. Would people find the story just as funny if she had the daydreams, and he bullied her?

LIST NOTES

In preparation for writing a draft, the student reread the story, and jotted down some tentative notes based on her journal and on material that she had highlighted in the text. (At this point you may want to make your own list, based on your notes.)

Mitty helpless: he needs her
chains on tires
enters Exit Only
Waterbury
cop tells him to get going
fantasies
wife a nag? → causes his daydreams? Evidence?
makes him get to hotel first
overshoes
backseat driver?
"Does it ever occur to you that I am sometimes thinking?" Is he thinking, or just having dreams?
M. confuses Richthoven with someone called Richtman.
Funny—or anti-woman? Would it be funny if he nagged her, and she had daydreams?

Next, the student wrote a draft; then she revised the draft and submitted the revision (printed here) to some classmates for peer review. (The number enclosed within parentheses cites the source of a quotation.) Before reading the student's draft, you may want to write a draft based on your own notes and lists.

Sample Draft: Walter Mitty Is No Joke

James Thurber's "The Secret Life of Walter Mitty" seems to be highly regarded as a comic story about a man who is so dominated by his wife that he has to escape through fantasies. In my high school course in English, everyone found Mitty's dreams and his wife's bullying funny, and everyone seems to find them funny in college, too. Everyone except me.

If we look closely at the story, we see that Mitty is a pitiful man who <u>needs</u> to be told what to do. The slightest glimpse of reality sets him off on a daydream, as when he passes a hospital and immediately begins to imagine that he is a famous surgeon, or when he hears a newsboy shouting a headline about a crime and he imagines himself in a courtroom. The point seems to be that his wife nags him, so he escapes into daydreams. But the fact is that she <u>needs</u> to keep after him, because he <u>needs</u> someone to tell him what to do. It depends on what one considers nagging. She tells him he is driving too fast, and (given the date of the story, 1939) he probably is, since he is going 55 on a slushy or snowy road. She tells him to wear overshoes, and he probably ought to, since the weather is bad. He resents all of these orders, but he clearly is incompetent, since he delays when the traffic light turns from red to green, and he enters an "Exit Only" lane in a parking lot. We are also told that he can't put chains on tires.

In fact, he can't do anything right. All he can do is daydream, and the dreams, though they <u>are</u> funny, are proof of his inability to live in the real world. When his wife asks him why he didn't put the overshoes on in the store, instead of carrying them in a box, he says, "Does it ever occur to you that I am sometimes thinking?" (46). But he <u>doesn't</u> "think," he just daydreams. Furthermore, he can't even get things straight in his daydreams, since he gets everything mixed up, confusing Richthoven with Richtman, for example.

Is "The Secret Life of Walter Mitty" really a funny story about a man who daydreams because he is henpecked? Probably it is supposed to be so, but it's also a story about a man who is lucky to have a wife who can put up with him and keep him from getting killed on the road or lost in town.

Work Cited

Thurber, James. "The Secret Life of Walter Mitty." <u>Literature for Composition</u>. 3rd ed. Ed. Sylvan Barnet et al. New York: Harper, 1991. 43–46.

Introductions, Middles, Endings

INTRODUCTORY PARAGRAPHS

As the poet Byron said, at the beginning of a long part of a long poem, "Nothing so difficult as a beginning." Woody Allen thinks so, too. In an interview he said that the toughest part of writing is "to go from nothing to the first draft."

We can give two pieces of advice. Unfortunately, they are apparently contradictory.

1. *The opening paragraph is unimportant.* It's great if you can write a paragraph that will engage your readers and let them know where the essay will be taking them, but if you can't come up with such a paragraph, just put down anything in order to prime the pump.

2. *The opening paragraph is extremely important.* It must engage your read-
    ers, and probably by means of a thesis sentence it should let the readers
    know where the essay will be taking them.

The contradiction is, as we said, only apparent, not real. The first point is
relevant to the opening paragraph of a *draft*; the second point is relevant to
the opening paragraph of the *final version*. Almost all writers—professionals
as well as amateurs—find that the first paragraphs in their drafts are false
starts. Don't worry too much about the opening paragraphs of your draft;
you'll almost surely want to revise your opening later anyway. (Surprisingly
often your first paragraph may simply be deleted; your second, you may find,
is where your essay truly begins.)

When writing a first draft you merely need something—almost anything
may do—to break the ice. But in your finished paper the opening cannot be
mere throat-clearing. The opening should be interesting.

Among the commonest **uninteresting openings** are these:

1. A dictionary definition ("Webster says . . . ")
2. A restatement of your title. The title is (let's assume) "Romeo's Mat-
    uration," and the first sentence says, "This essay will study Romeo's
    maturation." True, there is an attempt at a thesis statement here, but no
    information beyond what has already been given in the title. There is no
    information about you, either, that is, no sense of your response to the
    topic, such as is present in, say, *"Romeo and Juliet* covers less than one
    week, but within this short period Romeo is impressively transformed
    from a somewhat comic infatuated boy to a thoughtful tragic hero."
3. A platitude, such as "Ever since the beginning of time men and women
    have fallen in love." Again, such a sentence may be fine if it helps you to
    start drafting, but because it sounds canned and because it is insufficient-
    ly interesting, it should not remain in your final version.

What is left? What *is* a good way for a final version to begin? Your introductory paragraph will be at least moderately interesting if it gives information, and it will be pleasing if the information provides a focus: that is, if it
goes beyond the title in letting the reader know exactly what your topic is and
where you are headed.

Let's assume that you agree: An opening paragraph should be *interesting*
and *focused*. Doubtless you will find your own ways of fulfilling these goals,
but you might consider using one of the following time-tested methods.

1. *Establish a connection between life and literature.* We have already sug-
    gested that a platitude (for instance, "Ever since the beginning of time
    men and women have fallen in love") usually makes a poor beginning be-
    cause it is dull, but you may find some other way of relating the work
    to daily experience. For instance:

```
Doubtless the popularity of Romeo and Juliet (the play

has been with us for almost four hundred years) is

partly due to the fact that it deals with a universal
```

experience. Still, no other play about love is so much
a part of our culture that the mere mention of the names
of the lovers immediately calls up an image. But when
we say that So-and-so is "a regular Romeo," exactly what
do we mean? And exactly what sort of lover is Romeo?

2. *Give an overview.* Here is an example:
    Langston Hughes's "Harlem" is about the destruction of
    the hopes of African-Americans. More precisely, Hughes
    begins by asking "What happens to a dream deferred?"
    and then offers several possibilities, the last of
    which is that it may "explode."

3. *Include a quotation.* The previous example illustrates this approach,
    also. Here is another example:
    One line from Langston Hughes's poem "Harlem" has
    become famous, "A raisin in the sun," but its fame is,
    in a sense, accidental; Lorraine Hansberry happened to
    use it for the title of a play. Doubtless she used it
    because it is impressive, but in fact the entire poem
    is worthy of its most famous line.

4. *Use a definition.* We have already suggested that a definition such as
    "Webster says . . ." is boring and therefore unusable, but consider
    the following:
    When we say that a character is the hero of a story, we
    usually mean that he is the central figure, and we
    probably imply that he is manly. But in Kafka's "The
    Metamorphosis" the hero is most <u>un</u>manly.

5. *Introduce a critical stance.* If your approach is feminist, or psychoana-
    lytic, or Marxist, or whatever, you may want to say so at the start.
    Example:
    Feminists have called our attention to the unfunny
    sexism of mother-in-law jokes, comments about women
    hooking men into marriage, and so forth. We can now see
    that the stories of James Thurber, long thought to be
    wholesome fun, are unpleasantly sexist.

Caution: We are not saying that these are the only ways to begin, and we certainly are not suggesting that you pack all five into the opening paragraph. We are saying only that after you have done some brainstorming and written some drafts, you may want to think about using one of these methods for your opening paragraph.

An Exercise: Write (either by yourself or in collaboration with one or two other students) an opening paragraph for an essay on one of Kate Chopin's stories and another for an essay on Hughes's "Harlem." (To write a useful opening paragraph you will, of course, first have to settle on the essay's thesis.)

MIDDLE PARAGRAPHS

The middle, or body, of your essay will develop your thesis by offering supporting evidence. Ideas for the body should emerge from the sketchy outline that emerged from your review of your brainstorming notes or your journal. Be sure that

1. *each paragraph makes a specific point* and that the point is sufficiently developed with evidence (a brief quotation is often the best evidence).
2. *each paragraph is coherent.* Read each sentence, starting with the second sentence, to see how it relates to the preceding sentence. Does it clarify, extend, reinforce, add an example? If you can't find the relationship, the sentence probably does not belong where it is. Rewrite it, move it, or strike it out.
3. *the connections between the paragraphs are clear.* Transitional words, such as "Furthermore," "On the other hand," "In the next stanza" will often give readers all the help they need in seeing how your points are connected.
4. *the paragraphs are in the best possible order.* A good way to test the organization is to jot down the topic sentence or topic idea of each paragraph, and then to see if your jottings are in a reasonable sequence.

CONCLUDING PARAGRAPHS

Concluding paragraphs, like opening paragraphs, are especially difficult, if only because they are so conspicuous. Readers often skim first paragraphs and last paragraphs to see if an essay is worth reading. With conclusions, as with openings, try to say something interesting. It is not in the least interesting to say, "Thus we see that Mrs. Mitty . . . " (and here you go on to echo your title or your first sentence).

What to do? When you are revising a draft, you might keep in mind the following widely practiced principles. They are not inflexible rules, but they often work.

1. *Hint that the end is near.* Expressions such as "Finally," "One other point must be discussed," and "In short," which alert the reader that the end is nigh, help to prevent the reader from feeling that the essay ends abruptly.

2. *Perhaps reassert the thesis, but put it in a slightly new light.* Not, "I have shown that Romeo and Hamlet are similar in some ways," but:

These similarities suggest that in some respects Romeo is an early study for Hamlet. Both are young men in love, both seek by the force of their passion to shape the world according to their own desires, and both die in the attempt. But compared with Hamlet, who at the end of the play understands everything that has happened, Romeo dies in happy ignorance; Romeo is spared the pain of knowing that his own actions will destroy Juliet, whereas Hamlet dies with the painful knowledge that his kingdom has been conquered by Norwegian invaders.

3. *Perhaps offer an evaluation.* You may find it appropriate to conclude your analysis with an evaluation, such as this:

Romeo is as convincing as he needs to be in a play about young lovers, but from first to last he is a relatively uncomplicated figure, the ardent lover. Hamlet is a lover, but he is also a good deal more, a figure whose complexity reveals a more sophisticated or a more mature author. Only five or six years separate Romeo and Juliet from Hamlet, but one feels that in those few years Shakespeare made a quantum leap in his grasp of human nature.

4. *Perhaps include a brief significant quotation from the work.* Example:

Romeo has won the hearts of audiences for almost four centuries, but, for all his charm, he is in the last analysis concerned only with fulfilling his own passion. Hamlet, on the other hand, at last fulfills not only his own wish but that of the Ghost, his father. "Remember me," the Ghost says, when he first appears to Hamlet and asks for revenge. Throughout the play Hamlet does remember the Ghost, and finally, at the

cost of his own life, Hamlet succeeds in avenging his
dead father.

A CHECKLIST FOR
REVISING PARAGRAPHS

1. Does the paragraph *say* anything? Does it have substance?
2. Does the paragraph have a topic sentence? If so, is it in the best place? If the paragraph doesn't have a topic sentence, might one improve the paragraph? Or does it have a clear topic idea?
3. If the paragraph is an opening paragraph, is it interesting enough to attract and to hold a reader's attention? If it is a later paragraph, does it easily evolve out of the previous paragraph, and lead into the next paragraph?
4. Does the paragraph contain some principle of development, for instance from general to particular?
5. Does each sentence clearly follow from the preceding sentence? Have you provided transitional words or cues to guide your reader? Would it be useful to repeat certain key words, for clarity?
6. What is the purpose of the paragraph? Do you want to summarize, or tell a story, or give an illustration, or concede a point, or what? Is your purpose clear to you, and does the paragraph fulfill your purpose?
7. Is the closing paragraph effective, and not an unnecessary restatement of the obvious?

Review: Writing an Analysis

Each writing assignment will require its own kind of thinking, but here are a few principles that usually are relevant:

1. Assume that your reader has already read the work you are discussing but is not thoroughly familiar with it—and of course does not know what you think and how you feel about the work. Early in your essay name the author, the work, and your thesis.
2. Do not tell the plot (or, at most, summarize it very briefly); instead, tell your reader what the work is about (not what happens, but what the happenings add up to).
3. Whether you are writing about character or plot or meter or anything else, you will probably be telling your reader something about how the work works, that is, how it develops. The stages by which a work advances may sometimes be marked fairly clearly. For instance (to oversimplify), a poem of two stanzas may ask a question in the first, and give an answer in the second, or it may express a hope in the first, and reveal a doubt in the second. Novels, of course, are customarily divided into chapters,

and even a short story may be printed with numbered parts. Virtually all works are built up out of parts, whether or not the parts are labeled.

4. In telling the reader how each part leads to the next, or how each part arises out of what has come before, you will probably be commenting on such things as (in a story) changes in a character's state of mind—marked perhaps by a change in the setting—or (in a poem) changes in the speaker's tone of voice—for instance from eager to resigned, or from cautious to enthusiastic. Probably you will in fact be describing not only the development of character or of tone or of plot, but also (and more important) you will be advancing your own thesis.

Revising Checklist: Eleven Questions to Ask Yourself

In this chapter, as in the earlier ones, we have tried to offer a concise course in writing essays. We will now condense our material even further. We think that if in the light of the following checklist you examine what you hope is your final draft, and if you then revise the draft where appropriate, you will turn in an effective essay.

1. Is the title of my essay at least moderately informative?
2. Do I identify the subject of my essay (author and title) and do I state my thesis early and clearly?
3. Is the organization reasonable? Does each point lead into the next, without irrelevancies?
4. Does the organization keep the reader interested? (An essay that moves from major points to minor points will make the later pages seem anticlimactic, and the reader will lose interest.)
5. Is each paragraph unified by a topic sentence or a topic idea? Are there adequate transitions from one paragraph to the next?
6. Are generalizations supported by appropriate specific details, especially by brief quotations from the text?
7. Is the opening paragraph interesting and, by its end, focused on the topic? Is the concluding paragraph conclusive without being repetitive?
8. Are the sentences clear and emphatic? Are needless words and inflated language eliminated? Is the tone reasonably consistent?
9. Is there only as much summary as is needed to let the reader follow the essay?
10. Are quotations accurate? Are they adequately introduced with a lead-in? That is, does the reader know who is speaking or where in the action the quotation is located? Are they only as long as they need to be? Is documentation provided when necessary?
11. Are the spelling and punctuation correct? Are other mechanical matters (such as margins, spacing, the form of the title, and citations) in correct form? Have I proofread carefully?

Two Short Stories

■ ALICE WALKER

Alice Walker was born in 1944 in Eatonton, Georgia, where her parents eked out a living as sharecroppers and dairy farmers; her mother also worked as a domestic. Walker attended Spelman College in Atlanta, and in 1965 finished her undergraduate work at Sarah Lawrence College near New York City. She then became active in the welfare rights movement in New York and in the voter registration movement in Georgia. Later she taught writing and literature in Mississippi, at Jackson State College and Tougaloo College, and at Wellesley College, the University of Massachusetts, and Yale University.

Walker has written essays, poetry, and fiction. Her best known novel, *The Color Purple* (1982), won a Pulitzer Prize and the National Book Award. She has said that her chief concern is "exploring the oppressions, the insanities, the loyalties, and the triumphs of black women."

Everyday Use

For your grandmama

I will wait for her in the yard that Maggie and I made so clean and wavy yesterday afternoon. A yard like this is more comfortable than most people know. It is not just a yard. It is like an extended living room. When the hard clay is swept clean as a floor and the fine sand around the edges lined with tiny, irregular grooves, anyone can come and sit and look up into the elm tree and wait for the breezes that never come inside the house.

Maggie will be nervous until after her sister goes: she will stand hopelessly in corners homely and ashamed of the burn scars down her arms and legs, eyeing her sister with a mixture of envy and awe. She thinks her sister had held life always in the palm of one hand, that "no" is a word the world never learned to say to her.

You've no doubt seen those TV shows where the child who has "made it" is confronted, as a surprise, by her own mother and father, tottering in weakly from backstage. (A pleasant surprise, of course: What would they do if parent and child came on the show only to curse out and insult each other?) On TV mother and child embrace and smile into each other's faces. Sometimes the mother and father weep, the child wraps them in her arms and leans across the table to tell how she would not have made it without their help. I have seen these programs.

Sometimes I dream a dream in which Dee and I are suddenly brought together on a TV program of this sort. Out of a dark and soft-seated limousine I am ushered into a bright room filled with many people. There I meet a smiling, gray, sporty man like Johnny Carson who shakes my hand and tells me what a fine girl I have. Then we are on the stage and Dee is embracing me with tears in her eyes. She pins on my dress a large orchid, even though she has told me once that she thinks orchids are tacky flowers.

In real life I am a large, big-boned woman with rough, man-working hands. In the winter I wear flannel nightgowns to bed and overalls during the day. I can kill and clean a hog as mercilessly as a man. My fat keeps me hot in zero weather. I can work outside all day, breaking ice to get water for washing. I can eat pork liver cooked over the open fire minutes after it comes steaming from the hog. One winter I knocked a bull calf straight in the brain between the eyes with a sledge hammer and had the meat hung up to chill before nightfall. But of course all this does not show on television. I am the way my daughter would want me to be: a hundred pounds lighter, my skin like an uncooked barley pancake. My hair glistens in the hot bright lights. Johnny Carson has much to do to keep up with my quick and witty tongue.

But that is a mistake. I know even before I wake up. Who ever knew a Johnson with a quick tongue? Who can even imagine me looking a strange white man in the eye? It seems to me I have talked to them always with one foot raised in flight, with my head turned in whichever way is farthest from them. Dee, though. She would always look anyone in the eye. Hesitation was no part of her nature.

"How do I look, Mama?" Maggie says, showing just enough of her thin body enveloped in pink skirt and red blouse for me to know she's there, almost hidden by the door.

"Come out into the yard," I say.

Have you ever seen a lame animal, perhaps a dog run over by some careless person rich enough to own a car, sidle up to someone who is ignorant enough to be kind to him? That is the way my Maggie walks. She has been like this, chin on chest, eyes on ground, feet in shuffle, ever since the fire that burned the other house to the ground.

Dee is lighter than Maggie, with nicer hair and a fuller figure. She's a woman now, though sometimes I forget. How long ago was it that the other house burned? Ten, twelve years? Sometimes I can still hear the flames and feel Maggie's arms sticking to me, her hair smoking and her dress falling off her in little black papery flakes. Her eyes seemed stretched open, blazed open by the flames reflected in them. And Dee. I see her standing off under the sweet gum tree she used to dig gum out of; a look of concentration on her face as she watched the last dingy gray board of the house fall in toward the red-hot brick chimney. Why don't you do a dance around the ashes? I'd wanted to ask her. She had hated the house that much.

I used to think she hated Maggie, too. But that was before we raised the money, the church and me, to send her to Augusta to school. She used to read to us without pity; forcing words, lies, other folks' habits, whole lives upon us two, sitting trapped and ignorant underneath her voice. She washed us in a river of make-believe, burned us with a lot of knowledge we didn't necessarily need to know. Pressed us to her with the serious way she read, to shove us away at just the moment, like dimwits, we seemed about to understand.

Dee wanted nice things. A yellow organdy dress to wear to her graduation from high school; black pumps to match a green suit she'd made from an old suit somebody gave me. She was determined to stare down any disaster in her efforts. Her eyelids would not flicker for minutes at a time. Often I fought off the temptation to shake her. At sixteen she had a style of her own: and knew what style was.

I never had an education myself. After second grade the school was closed down. Don't ask me why: in 1927 colored asked fewer questions than they do now. Sometimes Maggie reads to me. She stumbles along good-naturedly but can't see well. She knows she is not bright. Like good looks and money, quickness passed her by. She will marry John Thomas (who has mossy teeth in an earnest face) and then I'll be free to sit here and I guess just sing church songs to myself. Although I never was a good singer. Never could carry a tune. I was always better at a man's job. I used to love to milk till I was hoofed in the side in '49. Cows are soothing and slow and don't bother you, unless you try to milk them the wrong way.

I have deliberately turned my back on the house. It is three rooms, just like the one that burned, except the roof is tin; they don't make shingle roofs any more. There are no real windows, just some holes cut in the sides, like the portholes in a ship, but not round and not square, with rawhide holding the shutters up on the outside. This house is in a pasture, too, like the other one. No doubt when Dee sees it she will want to tear it down. She wrote me once that no matter where we "choose" to live, she will manage to come see us. But she will never bring her friends. Maggie and I thought about this and Maggie asked me, "Mama, when did Dee ever *have* any friends?"

She had a few. Furtive boys in pink shirts hanging about on washday after school. Nervous girls who never laughed. Impressed with her they worshiped the well-turned phrase, the cute shape, the scalding humor that erupted like bubbles in lye. She read to them.

When she was courting Jimmy T she didn't have much time to pay to us, but turned all her faultfinding power on him. He *flew* to marry a cheap gal from a family of ignorant flashy people. She hardly had time to recompose herself.

When she comes I will meet—but there they are!

Maggie attempts to make a dash for the house, in her shuffling way, but I stay her with my hand. "Come back here," I say. And she stops and tries to dig a well in the sand with her toe.

It is hard to see them clearly through the strong sun. But even the first glimpse of leg out of the car tells me it is Dee. Her feet were always neat-looking, as if God himself had shaped them with a certain style. From the other side of the car comes a short, stocky man. Hair is all over his head a foot long and hanging from his chin like a kinky mule tail. I hear Maggie suck in her breath. "Uhnnnh," is what it sounds like. Like when you see the wriggling end of a snake just in front of your foot on the road. "Uhnnnh."

Dee next. A dress down to the ground, in this hot weather. A dress so loud it hurts my eyes. There are yellows and oranges enough to throw back the light of the sun. I feel my whole face warming from the heat waves it throws out. Earrings, too, gold and hanging down to her shoulders. Bracelets dangling and making noises when she moves her arm up to shake the folds of the dress out of her armpits. The dress is loose and flows, and as she walks closer, I like it. I hear Maggie go "Uhnnnh" again. It is her sister's hair. It stands straight up like the wool on a sheep. It is black as night and around the edges are two long pigtails that rope about like small lizards disappearing behind her ears.

"Wa-su-zo-Tean-o!" she says, coming on in that gliding way the dress makes her move. The short stocky fellow with the hair to his navel is all grinning and he follows up with "Asalamalakim, my mother and sister!" He moves to hug Maggie but she falls back, right up against the back of my chair. I feel her trembling there and when I look up I see the perspiration falling off her chin.

"Don't get up," says Dee. Since I am stout it takes something of a push. You can see me trying to move a second or two before I make it. She turns, showing white heels through her sandals, and goes back to the car. Out she peeks next with a Polaroid. She stoops down quickly and lines up picture after picture of me sitting there in front of the house with Maggie cowering behind me. She never takes a shot without making sure the house is included. When a cow comes nibbling around the edge of the yard she snaps it and me and Maggie *and* the house. Then she puts the Polaroid in the back seat of the car, and comes up and kisses me on the forehead.

Meanwhile Asalamalakim is going through the motions with Maggie's hand. Maggie's hand is as limp as a fish, and probably as cold, despite the sweat, and she keeps trying to pull it back. It looks like Asalamalakim wants to shake hands but wants to do it fancy. Or maybe he don't know how people shake hands. Anyhow, he soon gives up on Maggie.

"Well," I say. "Dee."

"No, Mama," she says. "Not 'Dee,' Wangero Leewanika Kemanjo!"

"What happened to 'Dee'?" I wanted to know.

"She's dead," Wangero said. "I couldn't bear it any longer being named after the people who oppress me."

"You know as well as me you was named after your aunt Dicie," I said. Dicie is my sister. She named Dee. We called her "Big Dee" after Dee was born.

"But who was *she* named after?" asked Wangero.

"I guess after Grandma Dee," I said.

"And who was she named after?" asked Wangero.

"Her mother," I said, and saw Wangero was getting tired. "That's about as far back as I can trace it," I said. Though, in fact, I probably could have carried it back beyond the Civil War through the branches.

"Well," said Asalamalakim, "there you are."

"Uhnnnh," I heard Maggie say.

"There I was not," I said, "before 'Dicie' cropped up in our family, so why should I try to trace it that far back?"

He just stood there grinning, looking down on me like somebody inspecting a Model A car. Every once in a while he and Wangero sent eye signals over my head.

"How do you pronounce this name?" I asked.

"You don't have to call me by it if you don't want to," said Wangero.

"Why shouldn't I?" I asked. "If that's what you want us to call you, we'll call you."

"I know it might sound awkward at first," said Wangero.

"I'll get used to it," I said. "Ream it out again."

Well, soon we got the name out of the way. Asalamalakim had a name twice as long and three times as hard. After I tripped over it two or three times he told me to just call him Hakim-a-barber. I wanted to ask him was he a barber, but I didn't really think he was, so I didn't ask.

"You must belong to those beef-cattle peoples down the road," I said. They said "Asalamalakim" when they met you, too, but they didn't shake hands. Always too busy: feeding the cattle, fixing the fences, putting up salt-lick shelters, throwing down hay. When the white folks poisoned some of the herd the men stayed up all night with rifles in their hands. I walked a mile and a half just to see the sight.

Hakim-a-barber said, "I accept some of their doctrines, but farming and raising cattle is not my style." (They didn't tell me, and I didn't ask, whether Wangero [Dee] had really gone and married him.)

We sat down to eat and right away he said he didn't eat collards and pork was unclean. Wangero, though, went on through the chitlins and corn bread, the greens and everything else. She talked a blue streak over the sweet potatoes. Everything delighted her. Even the fact that we still used the benches her daddy made for the table when we couldn't afford to buy chairs.

"Oh, Mama!" she cried. Then turned to Hakim-a-barber. "I never knew how lovely these benches are. You can feel the rump prints," she said, running her hands underneath her and along the bench. Then she gave a sigh and her hand closed over Grandma Dee's butter dish. "That's it!" she said. "I knew there was something I wanted to ask you if I could have." She jumped up from the table and went over in the corner where the churn stood, the milk in it clabber by now. She looked at the churn and looked at it.

"This churn top is what I need," she said. "Didn't Uncle Buddy whittle it out of a tree you all used to have?"

"Yes," I said.

"Uh huh," she said happily. "And I want the dasher, too."

"Uncle Buddy whittle that, too?" asked the barber.

Dee (Wangero) looked up at me.

"Aunt Dee's first husband whittled the dash," said Maggie so low you almost couldn't hear her. "His name was Henry, but they called him Stash."

"Maggie's brain is like an elephant's," Wangero said, laughing. "I can use the churn top as a centerpiece for the alcove table," she said, sliding a plate over the churn, "and I'll think of something artistic to do with the dasher."

When she finished wrapping the dasher the handle stuck out. I took it for a moment in my hands. You didn't even have to look close to see where hands pushing the dasher up and down to make butter had left a kind of sink in the wood. In fact, there were a lot of small sinks; you could see where thumbs and fingers had sunk into the wood. It was beautiful light yellow wood, from a tree that grew in the yard where Big Dee and Stash had lived.

After dinner Dee (Wangero) went to the trunk at the foot of my bed and started rifling through it. Maggie hung back in the kitchen over the dishpan. Out came Wangero with two quilts. They had been pieced by Grandma Dee and then Big Dee and me had hung them on the quilt frames on the front porch and quilted them. One was in the Lone Star pattern. The other was Walk Around the Mountain. In both of them were scraps of dresses Grandma Dee had worn fifty and more years ago. Bits and pieces of Grandpa Jarrell's paisley shirts. And one teeny faded blue piece, about the piece of a penny matchbox, that was from Great Grandpa Ezra's uniform that he wore in the Civil War.

"Mama," Wangero said sweet as a bird. "Can I have these old quilts?"

I heard something fall in the kitchen, and a minute later the kitchen door slammed.

"Why don't you take one or two of the others?" I asked. "These old things was just done by me and Big Dee from some tops your grandma pieced before she died."

"No," said Wangero. "I don't want those. They are stitched around the borders by machine."

"That's make them last better," I said.

"That's not the point," said Wangero. "These are all pieces of dresses Grandma used to wear. She did all this stitching by hand. Imagine!" She held the quilts securely in her arms, stroking them.

"Some of the pieces, like those lavender ones, come from old clothes her mother handed down to her," I said, moving up to touch the quilts. Dee (Wangero) moved back just enough so that I couldn't reach the quilts. They already belonged to her.

"Imagine!" she breathed again, clutching them closely to her bosom.

"The truth is," I said, "I promised to give them quilts to Maggie, for when she marries John Thomas."

She gasped like a bee had stung her.

"Maggie can't appreciate these quilts!" she said. "She'd probably be backward enough to put them to everyday use."

"I reckon she would," I said. "God knows I been saving 'em for long enough with nobody using 'em. I hope she will!" I didn't want to bring up how I had offered Dee (Wangero) a quilt when she went away to college. Then she had told me they were old-fashioned, out of style.

"But they're *priceless!*" she was saying now, furiously; for she has a temper. "Maggie would put them on the bed and in five years they'd be in rags. Less than that!"

"She can always make some more," I said. "Maggie knows how to quilt."

Dee (Wangero) looked at me with hatred. "You just will not understand. The point is these quilts, *these* quilts!"

"Well," I said, stumped. "What would *you* do with them?"

"Hang them," she said. As if that was the only thing you *could* do with quilts.

Maggie by now was standing in the door. I could almost hear the sound her feet made as they scraped over each other.

"She can have them, Mama," she said, like somebody used to never winning anything, or having anything reserved for her. "I can 'member Grandma Dee without the quilts."

I looked at her hard. She had filled her bottom lip with checkerberry snuff and it gave her face a kind of dopey, hangdog look. It was Grandma Dee and Big Dee who taught her how to quilt herself. She stood there with her scarred hands hidden in the folds of her skirt. She looked at her sister with something like fear but she wasn't mad at her. This was Maggie's portion. This was the way she knew God to work.

When I looked at her like that something hit me in the top of my head and ran down to the soles of my feet. Just like when I'm in church and the spirit of God touches me and I get happy and shout. I did something I never had done before: hugged Maggie to me, then dragged her on into the room, snatched the quilts out of Miss Wangero's hands and dumped them into Maggie's lap. Maggie just sat there on my bed with her mouth open.

"Take one or two of the others," I said to Dee.

But she turned without a word and went out to Hakim-a-barber.

"You just don't understand," she said, as Maggie and I came out to the car.

"What don't I understand?" I wanted to know.

"Your heritage," she said. And then she turned to Maggie, kissed her, and said, "You ought to try to make something of yourself, too, Maggie. It's really a new day for us. But from the way you and Mama still live you'd never know it."

She put on some sunglasses that hid everything above the tip of her nose and her chin.

Maggie smiled; maybe at the sunglasses. But a real smile, not scared. After we watched the car dust settle I asked Maggie to bring me a dip of snuff. And then the two of us sat there just enjoying, until it was time to go in the house and go to bed.

[1973]

■ TOPICS FOR DISCUSSION AND WRITING

1. Alice Walker wrote the story, but the story is narrated by one of the characters, Mama. How would you characterize Mama?

2. At the end of the story, Dee tells Maggie, "It's really a new day for us. But from the way you and Mama still live you'd never know it." What does Dee mean? And how do Maggie and Mama respond?

3. On page 62 the narrator says, speaking of Maggie, "When I looked at her like that something hit me in the top of my head and ran down to the soles of my feet." What "hit" Mama? That is, what does she understand at this moment that she had not understood before?

4. In "Everyday Use" why does the family conflict focus on who will possess the quilts? Why are the quilts important? What do they symbolize?

■ JOSÉ ARMAS
_____

Born in 1944, José Armas has been a teacher (at the University of New Mexico and at the University of Albuquerque), publisher, critic, and community organizer. His interest in community affairs won him a fellowship, which in 1974–1975 brought him into association with the Urban Planning Department at the Massachusetts Institute of Technology. In 1980 he was awarded a writing fellowship by the National Endowment for the Arts, and he now writes a column on Hispanic affairs for *The Albuquerque Journal*.

El Tonto del Barrio[1]

Romero Estrado was called "El Cotoro"[2] because he was always whistling and singing. He made nice music even though his songs were spontaneous compositions made up of words with sounds that he liked but which seldom made any sense. But that didn't seem to bother either Romero or anyone else in the Golden Heights Centro where he lived. Not even the kids made fun of him. It just was not permitted.

Romero had a ritual that he followed almost every day. After breakfast he would get his broom and go up and down the main street of the Golden Heights Centro whistling and singing and sweeping the sidewalks for all the businesses. He would sweep in front of the Tortillería America,[3] the XXX Liquor Store, the Tres Milpas[4] Bar run by Tino Gabaldon, Barelas' Barber Shop, the used furniture store owned by Goldstein, El Centro Market of the Avila family, the Model Cities Office, and Lourdes Printing Store. Then, in the afternoons, he would come back and sit in Barelas' Barber Shop and spend the day looking at magazines and watching and waving to the passing people as he sang and composed his songs without a care in the world.

When business was slow, Barelas would let him sit in the barber's chair. Romero loved it. It was a routine that Romero kept every day except Sundays and Mondays when Barelas' Barber Shop was closed. After a period of years, people in the barrio got used to seeing Romero do his little task of sweeping the sidewalks and sitting in Barelas' Barber Shop. If he didn't show up one day someone assumed the responsibility to go to his house to see if he was ill. People would stop to say hello to Romero on the street and although he never initiated a conversation while he was sober, he always smiled and responded cheerfully to everyone. People passing the barber shop in the afternoons made it a point to wave even though they couldn't see him; they knew he was in there and was expecting some salutation.

When he was feeling real good, Romero would sweep in front of the houses on both sides of the block also. He took his job seriously and took great care to sweep cleanly, between the cracks and even between the sides

_____

[1] **El Tonto del Barrio**, the barrio dummy (in the United States, a barrio is a Spanish-speaking community).

[2] **El Cotoro**, The Parrot

[3] **Tortillería America**, America Tortilla Factory

[4] **Tres Milpas**, Three Cornfields

of buildings. The dirt and small scraps went into the gutter. The bottles and bigger pieces of litter were put carefully in cardboard boxes, ready for the garbage man.

If he did it the way he wanted, the work took him the whole morning. And always cheerful—always with some song.

Only once did someone call attention to his work. Frank Avila told him in jest that Romero had forgotten to pick up an empty bottle of wine from his door. Romero was so offended and made such a commotion that it got around very quickly that no one should criticize his work. There was, in fact, no reason to.

Although it had been long acknowledged that Romero was a little "touched," he fit very well into the community. He was a respected citizen.

He could be found at the Tres Milpas Bar drinking his occasional beer in the evenings. Romero had a rivalry going with the Ranchera songs on the jukebox. He would try to outsing the songs using the same melody but inserting his own selection of random words. Sometimes, like all people, he would "bust out" and get drunk.

One could always tell when Romero was getting drunk because he would begin telling everyone that he loved them.

"I looov youuu," he would sing to someone and offer to compose them a song.

"Ta bueno, Romero. Ta bueno, ya bete,"[5] they would tell him.

Sometimes when he got too drunk he would crap in his pants and then Tino would make him go home.

Romero received some money from Social Security but it wasn't much. None of the merchants gave him any credit because he would always forget to pay his bills. He didn't do it on purpose, he just forgot and spent his money on something else. So instead, the businessmen preferred to do little things for him occasionally. Barelas would trim his hair when things were slow. The Tortillería America would give him menudo[6] and fresh-made tortillas at noon when he was finished with his sweeping. El Centro Market would give him the overripe fruit and broken boxes of food that no one else would buy. Although it was unspoken and unwritten, there was an agreement that existed between Romero and the Golden Heights Centro. Romero kept the sidewalks clean and the barrio looked after him. It was a contract that worked well for a long time.

Then, when Seferino, Barelas' oldest son, graduated from high school he went to work in the barber shop for the summer. Seferino was a conscientious and sensitve young man and it wasn't long before he took notice of Romero and came to feel sorry for him.

One day when Romero was in the shop Seferino decided to act.

"Mira, Romero. Yo te doy 50 centavos por cada dia que me barres la banqueta. Fifty cents for every day you sweep the sidewalk for us. Qué te parece?"[7]

[5] **Ta bueno, ya bete** OK, now go away
[6] **menudo** tripe soup
[7] **Qué te parece?** How does that strike you?

Romero thought about it carefully.

"Hecho! Done!" he exclaimed. He started for home right away to get his broom.

"Why did you do that for, m'ijo?"[8] asked Barelas.

"It don't seem right, Dad. The man works and no one pays him for his work. Everyone should get paid for what they do."

"He don't need no pay. Romero has everything he needs."

"It's not the same, Dad. How would you like to do what he does and be treated the same way? It's degrading the way he has to go around getting scraps and handouts."

"I'm not Romero. Besides you don't know about these things, m'ijo. Romero would be unhappy if his schedule was upset. Right now everyone likes him and takes care of him. He sweeps the sidewalks because he wants something to do, not because he wants money."

"I'll pay him out of my money, don't worry about it then."

"The money is not the point. The point is that money will not help Romero. Don't you understand that?"

"Look, Dad. Just put yourself in his place. Would you do it? Would you cut hair for nothing?"

Barelas just knew his son was putting something over on him but he didn't know how to answer. It seemed to make sense the way Seferino explained it. But it still went against his "instinct." On the other hand, Seferino had gone and finished high school. He must know something. There were few kids who had finished high school in the barrio, and fewer who had gone to college. Barelas knew them all. He noted (with some pride) that Seferino was going to be enrolled at Harvard University this year. That must count for something, he thought. Barelas himself had never gone to school. So maybe his son had something there. On the other hand . . . it upset Barelas that he wasn't able to get Seferino to see the issue. How can we be so far apart on something so simple, he thought. But he decided not to say anything else about it.

Romero came back right away and swept the front of Barelas' shop again and put what little dirt he found into the curb. He swept up the gutter, put the trash in a shoe box and threw it in a garbage can.

Seferino watched with pride as Romero went about his job and when he was finished he went outside and shook Romero's hand. Seferino told him he had done a good job. Romero beamed.

Manolo was coming into the shop to get his hair cut as Seferino was giving Romero his wages. He noticed Romero with his broom.

"What's going on?" He asked. Barelas shrugged his shoulders. "Qué tiene Romero?[9] Is he sick or something?"

"No, he's not sick," explained Seferino, who had now come inside. He told Manolo the story.

"We're going to make Romero a businessman" said Seferino. "Do you realize how much money Romero would make if everyone paid him just fifty

---

[8] **m'ijo** (mi hijo), my son

[9] **Qué tiene Romero?** What's with Romero?

cents a day? Like my dad says, 'Everyone should be able to keep his dignity, no matter how poor.' And he does a job, you know."

"Well, it makes sense," said Manolo.

"Hey. Maybe I'll ask people to do that," said Seferino. "That way the poor old man could make a decent wage. Do you want to help, Manolo? You can go with me to ask people to pay him."

"Well," said Manolo as he glanced at Barelas, "I'm not too good at asking people for money."

This did not discourage Seferino. He went out and contacted all the businesses on his own, but no one else wanted to contribute. This didn't discourage Seferino either. He went on giving Romero fifty cents a day.

After a while, Seferino heard that Romero had asked for credit at the grocery store. "See, Dad. What did I tell you? Things are getting better for him already. He's becoming his own man. And look. It's only been a couple of weeks." Barelas did not reply.

But then the next week Romero did not show up to sweep any sidewalks. He was around but he didn't do any work for anybody the entire week. He walked around Golden Heights Centro in his best gray work pants and his slouch hat, looking important and making it a point to walk right past the barber shop every little while.

Of course, the people in the Golden Heights Centro noticed the change immediately, and since they saw Romero in the street, they knew he wasn't ill. But the change was clearly disturbing the community. They discussed him in the Tortillería America where people got together for coffee, and at the Tres Milpas Bar. Everywhere the topic of conversation was the great change that had come over Romero. Only Barelas did not talk about it.

The following week Romero came into the barber shop and asked to talk with Seferino in private. Barelas knew immediately something was wrong. Romero never initiated a conversation unless he was drunk.

They went into the back room where Barelas could not hear and then Romero informed Seferino, "I want a raise."

"What? What do you mean, a raise? You haven't been around for a week. You only worked a few weeks and now you want a raise?" Seferino was clearly angry but Romero was calm and insistent.

Romero correctly pointed out that he had been sweeping the sidewalks for a long time. Even before Seferino finished high school.

"I deserve a raise," he repeated after an eloquent presentation.

Seferino looked coldly at Romero. It was clearly a stand-off.

Then Seferino said, "Look, maybe we should forget the whole thing. I was just trying to help you out and look at what you do."

Romero held his ground. "I helped you out too. No one told me to do it and I did it anyway. I helped you many years."

"Well, let's forget about the whole thing then," said Seferino.

"I quit then," said Romero.

"Quit?" exclaimed Seferino as he laughed at Romero.

"Quit! I quit!" said Romero as he walked out the front of the shop past Barelas who was cutting a customer's hair.

Seferino came out shaking his head and laughing.

"Can you imagine that old guy?"

Barelas did not seem too amused. He felt he could have predicted that something bad like this would happen.

Romero began sweeping the sidewalks again the next day with the exception that when he came to the barber shop he would go around it and continue sweeping the rest of the sidewalks. He did this for the rest of the week. And the following Tuesday he began sweeping the sidewalk all the way up to the shop and then pushing the trash to the sidewalk in front of the barber shop. Romero then stopped coming to the barber shop in the afternoon.

The barrio buzzed with fact and rumor about Romero. Tino commented that Romero was not singing anymore. Even if someone offered to buy him a beer he wouldn't sing. Frank Avila said the neighbors were complaining because he was leaving his TV on loud the whole day and night. He still greeted people but seldom smiled. He had run up a big bill at the liquor store and when the manager stopped his credit, he caught Romero stealing bottles of whiskey. He was also getting careless about his dress. He didn't shave and clean like he used to. Women complained that he walked around in soiled pants, that he smelled bad. Even one of the little kids complained that Romero had kicked his puppy, but that seemed hard to believe.

Barelas felt terrible. He felt responsible. But he couldn't convince Seferino that what he had done was wrong. Barelas himself stopped going to the Tres Milpas Bar after work to avoid hearing about Romero. Once he came across Romero on the street and Barelas said hello but with a sense of guilt. Romero responded, avoiding Barelas' eyes and moving past him awkwardly and quickly. Romero's behavior continued to get erratic and some people started talking about having Romero committed.

"You can't do that," said Barelas when he was presented with a petition.

"He's flipped," said Tino, who made up part of the delegation circulating the petition. "No one likes Romero more than I do, you know that Barelas."

"But he's really crazy," said Frank Avila.

"He was crazy before. No one noticed," pleaded Barelas.

"But it was a crazy we could depend on. Now he just wants to sit on the curb and pull up the women's skirts. It's terrible. The women are going crazy. He's also running into the street stopping the traffic. You see how he is. What choice do we have?"

"It's for his own good," put in one of the workers from the Model Cities Office. Barelas dismissed them as outsiders. Seferino was there and wanted to say something but a look from Barelas stopped him.

"We just can't do that," insisted Barelas. "Let's wait. Maybe he's just going through a cycle. Look. We've had a full moon recently, qué no?[10] That must be it. You know how the moon affects people in his condition."

"I don't know," said Tino. "What if he hurts . . . ."

"He's not going to hurt anyone," cut in Barelas.

"No, Barelas. I was going to say, what if he hurts himself. He has no one

[10] **qué no?** right?

at home. I'd say, let him come home with me for a while but you know how stubborn he is. You can't even talk to him any more."

"He gives everyone the finger when they try to pull him out of the traffic," said Frank Avila. "The cops have missed him, but it won't be long before they see him doing some of his antics and arrest him. Then what? Then the poor guy is in real trouble."

"Well, look," said Barelas. "How many names you got on the list?"

Tino responded slowly, "Well, we sort of wanted you to start off the list."

"Let's wait a while longer," said Barelas. "I just know that Romero will come around. Let's wait just a while, okay?"

No one had the heart to fight the issue and so they postponed the petition.

There was no dramatic change in Romero even though the full moon had completed its cycle. Still, no one initiated the petition again and then in the middle of August Seferino left for Cambridge to look for housing and to register early for school. Suddenly everything began to change again. One day Romero began sweeping the entire sidewalk again. His spirits began to pick up and his strange antics began to disappear.

At the Tortillería America the original committee met for coffee and the talk turned to Romero.

"He's going to be all right now," said a jubilant Barelas. "I guarantee it."

"Well, don't hold your breath yet," said Tino. "The full moon is coming up again."

"Yeah," said Frank Avila dejectedly.

When the next full moon was in force the group was together again drinking coffee and Tino asked, "Well, how's Romero doing?"

Barelas smiled and said, "Well. Singing songs like crazy."

[1982]

■ TOPICS FOR DISCUSSION AND WRITING

1. What sort of man do you think Barelas is? In your response take account of the fact that the townspeople "sort of want" Barelas "to start off the list" of petitioners seeking to commit Romero.
2. The narrator, introducing the reader to Seferino, tells us that "Seferino was a conscientious and sensitive young man." Do you agree? Why, or why not?
3. What do you make of the last line of the story?
4. Do you think this story could take place in almost any community? If you did not grow up in a barrio, could it take place in your community?

■ CHAPTER 4

Reading

(and Writing about)

Essays

The word *essay* entered the English language in 1597, when Francis Bacon called a small book of ten short prose pieces *Essays*. Bacon borrowed the word from Michel de Montaigne, a French writer who in 1580 had published some short prose pieces under the title *Essais*—that is, "testings," or "attempts," from the French verb *essayer*, "to try." Montaigne's title indicated that his graceful and personal jottings—the fruit of pleasant study and meditation—were not fully thought-out treatises but rather sketches that could be amplified and amended.

If you keep a journal, you are working in Montaigne's tradition. You jot down your tentative thoughts, perhaps your responses to a work of literature, partly to find out what you think and how you feel. Montaigne said, in the preface to his book, "I am myself the subject of my book," and in all probability you are the real subject of your journal. Your entries—your responses to other writers and your reflections on those responses—require you to examine yourself.

The Essayist's Persona

Many of the essays that give readers the most pleasure are, like entries in a journal, chiefly reflective. An essay of this kind sets forth the writer's attitudes or states of mind, and the reader's interest in the essay is almost entirely in the way the writer sees things. It's not so much *what* the writers see and say as *how* they say what they see. Even in essays that are narrative—that is, in essays that recount events, such as a bit of biography—our interest is more in the essayists' *responses* to the events than in the events themselves.

When we read an essay, we almost say, "So that's how it feels to be you," and "Tell me more about the way you see things." The bit of history is less important than the memorable presence of the writer.

When you read an essay in this chapter or in a later chapter, try to imagine the kind of person who wrote it, the kind of person who seems to be speaking it. Then slowly reread the essay, noticing *how* the writer conveyed this personality or persona or "voice" (even while he or she was writing about a topic "out there"). The writer's persona may be revealed by common or uncommon words, for example, by short or long sentences, by literal or figurative language, or by familiar or erudite examples.

Let's take a simple, familiar example of words that establish a persona. Lincoln begins the Gettysburg Address with "Four score and seven years ago." He might have said "Eighty-seven years ago" —but the language would have lacked the biblical echo, and the persona would thus have been that of an ordinary person rather than that of a man who has about him something of the tone of an Old Testament prophet. This religious tone is entirely fitting, since President Lincoln was speaking at the dedication of a cemetery for "these hallowed dead" and was urging the members of his audience to give all of their energies to ensure that the dead men had not died in vain. By such devices as the choice of words, the length of sentences, and the sorts of evidence offered, an author sounds to the reader solemn or agitated or witty or genial or severe. If you read Martin Luther King's "I Have a Dream" (page 660), you will notice that he begins his essay (originally it was a speech, delivered at the Lincoln Memorial on the one-hundredth anniversary of Lincoln's Emancipation Proclamation) with these words: "Five score years ago . . . ." King is deliberately echoing Lincoln's words, partly in tribute to Lincoln, but also to help establish himself as the spiritual descendent of Lincoln and, further back, of the founders of the Judaeo-Christian traditition.

TONE

Only by reading closely can we hear in the mind's ear the writer's tone— friendly, or bitter, or indignant, or ironic (characterized by wry understatement or overstatement). Perhaps you have heard the line from Owen Wister's novel, *The Virginian:* "When you call me that, smile." Words spoken with a smile mean something different from the same words forced through clenched teeth. But while speakers can communicate, or, we might say, can guide the responses of their audience, by body language and by gestures, by facial expressions and by changes in tone of voice, writers have only words in ink on paper. As a writer, you are learning control of tone as you learn to take pains in your choice of words, in the way you arrange sentences, and even in the punctuation marks you may find yourself changing in your final draft. These skills will pay off doubly if you apply them to your reading, by putting yourself in the place of the writer whose work you are reading. As a reader, you must make some effort to "hear" the writer's tone as part of the meaning the words communicate. Skimming is not adequate to that task. Thinking carefully about the works in this book means, first of all, reading them carefully, listening for the sound of the speaking voice, so that you can respond to the persona—the personality or character the author presents in the essay.

Consider the following paragraph from the middle of "Black Men and Public Space," a short essay by Brent Staples. Staples is talking about growing up in a tough neighborhood. Of course the paragraph is only a small example; the tone depends, finally, on the entire essay, which we will print in a moment.

> As a boy I saw countless tough guys locked away; I have since buried several, too. They were babies, really—a teenage cousin, a brother of twenty-two, a childhood friend in his mid-twenties—all gone down in episodes of bravado played out on the streets. I came to doubt the virtues of intimidation early on. I chose, perhaps unconsciously, to remain a shadow—timid, but a survivor.

Judging only from these few lines, what sense of Staples do we get? Perhaps you will agree that we can probably say something along these lines:

1. He is relatively quiet and gentle. We sense this not simply because he tells us that he was "timid" but because (at least in this passage) he does not raise his voice either in a denunciation of white society for creating a system that produces black violence or in a denunciation of those blacks of his youth who engaged in violence.
2. He is perceptive; he sees that the "tough guys," despite the fact that some were in their twenties, were babies; their bravado was infantile and destructive.
3. He speaks with authority; he is giving a first-hand report.
4. He doesn't claim to be especially shrewd; he modestly says that he may have "unconsciously" adopted the behavior that enabled him to survive.
5. In saying that he is a "survivor" he displays a bit of wry humor. The usual image of a "survivor" is a guy in a Banana Republic outfit, gripping a knife, someone who survived a dog-eat-dog world by being tougher than the others. But Staples almost comically says he is a "survivor" who is "timid."

If your responses to the paragraph are somewhat different, jot them down and in a few sentences try to explain them.

Pre-Writing

IDENTIFYING THE TOPIC AND THESIS

Although we have emphasized the importance of the essayist's personality, essayists also make a point. They have a thesis or argument, and an argument implies taking a specific viewpoint toward a topic. In reading an essay, then, try to identify the topic. The topic of "Do-It-Yourself Brain Surgery" can't really be brain surgery; it must be do-it-yourself books, and the attitude probably will be amused contempt for such books. Even an essay that is largely narrative, like Brent Staples's, recounting a personal experience or a bit of history, probably will include an attitude toward the event that is being narrated, and it is that attitude—the interpretation of the event rather than the event itself—that may be the real topic of the essay.

It's time to look at Staples's essay. (Following the essay you will find a student's outline of it and another student's version of its thesis.) Staples, born in 1951, received a bachelor's degree from Widener University in Chester, Pennsylvania, and a Ph.D. from the University of Chicago. After working as a journalist in Chicago, he joined *The New York Times* in 1985, and he is now on the newspaper's editorial board, where he writes on politics and culture. His essay was first published in *Ms.* magazine in 1986 and reprinted in a slightly revised form—the form we give here—in *Harper's* in 1987.

■ BRENT STAPLES

Black Men and Public Space

My first victim was a woman—white, well dressed, probably in her late 1 twenties. I came upon her late one evening on a deserted street in Hyde Park, a relatively affluent neighborhood in an otherwise mean, impoverished section of Chicago. As I swung onto the avenue behind her, there seemed to be a discreet, uninflammatory distance between us. Not so. She cast back a worried glance. To her, the youngish black man—a broad six feet two inches with a beard and billowing hair, both hands shoved into the pockets of a bulky military jacket—seemed menacingly close. After a few more quick glimpses, she picked up her pace and was soon running in earnest. Within seconds, she disappeared into a cross street.

That was more than a decade ago. I was twenty-two years old, a graduate 2 student newly arrived at the University of Chicago. It was in the echo of that terrified woman's footfalls that I first began to know the unwieldy inheritance I'd come into—the ability to alter public space in ugly ways. It was clear that she thought herself the quarry of a mugger, a rapist, or worse. Suffering a bout of insomnia, however, I was stalking sleep, not defenseless wayfarers. As a softy who is scarcely able to take a knife to a raw chicken—let alone hold one to a person's throat—I was surprised, embarrassed, and dismayed all at once. Her flight made me feel like an accomplice in tyranny. It also made it clear that I was indistinguishable from the muggers who occasionally seeped into the area from the surrounding ghetto. That first encounter, and those that followed, signified that a vast, unnerving gulf lay between nighttime pedestrians—particularly women—and me. And I soon gathered that being perceived as dangerous is a hazard in itself. I only needed to turn a corner into a dicey situation, or crowd some frightened, armed person in a foyer somewhere, or make an errant move after being pulled over by a policeman. Where fear and weapons meet—and they often do in urban America—there is always the possibility of death.

In that first year, my first away from my hometown, I was to become 3 thoroughly familiar with the language of fear. At dark, shadowy intersections, I could cross in front of a car stopped at a traffic light and elicit the *thunk,*

thunk, thunk, thunk of the driver—black, white, male, or female—hammering down the door locks. On less traveled streets after dark, I grew accustomed to but never comfortable with people crossing to the other side of the street rather than pass me. Then there were the standard unpleasantries with policemen, doormen, bouncers, cabdrivers, and others whose business it is to screen out troublesome individuals *before* there is any nastiness.

I moved to New York nearly two years ago and I have remained an avid 4 night walker. In central Manhattan, the near-constant crowd cover minimizes tense one-on-one street encounters. Elsewhere—in SoHo, for example, where sidewalks are narrow and tightly spaced buildings shut out the sky— things can get very taut indeed.

After dark, on the warrenlike streets of Brooklyn where I live, I often 5 see women who fear the worst from me. They seem to have set their faces on neutral, and with their purse straps strung across their chests bandolier- style, they forge ahead as though bracing themselves against being tackled. I understand, of course, that the danger they perceive is not a hallucination. Women are particularly vulnerable to street violence, and young black males are drastically overrepresented among the perpetrators of that violence. Yet these truths are no solace against the kind of alienation that comes of being ever the suspect, a fearsome entity with whom pedestrians avoid making eye contact.

It is not altogether clear to me how I reached the ripe old age of twenty- 6 two without being conscious of the lethality nighttime pedestrians attributed to me. Perhaps it was because in Chester, Pennsylvania, the small, angry in- dustrial town where I came of age in the 1960s, I was scarcely noticeable against a backdrop of gang warfare, street knifings, and murders. I grew up one of the good boys, had perhaps a half-dozen fistfights. In retrospect, my shyness of combat has clear sources.

As a boy, I saw countless tough guys locked away; I have since buried 7 several, too. They were babies, really—a teenage cousin, a brother of twenty- two, a childhood friend in his mid-twenties—all gone down in episodes of bravado played out in the streets. I came to doubt the virtues of intimidation early on. I chose, perhaps unconsciously, to remain a shadow—timid, but a survivor.

The fearsomeness mistakenly attributed to me in public places often has 8 a perilous flavor. The most frightening of these confusions occurred in the late 1970s and early 1980s, when I worked as a journalist in Chicago. One day, rushing into the office of a magazine I was writing for with a deadline story in hand, I was mistaken for a burglar. The office manager called security and, with an ad hoc posse, pursued me through the labyrinthine halls, nearly to my editor's door. I had no way of proving who I was. I could only move briskly toward the company of someone who knew me.

Another time I was on assignment for a local paper and killing time be- 9 fore an interview. I entered a jewelry store on the city's affluent Near North Side. The proprietor excused herself and returned with an enormous red Doberman pinscher straining at the end of a leash. She stood, the dog ex- tended toward me, silent to my questions, her eyes bulging nearly out of her head. I took a cursory look around, nodded, and bade her good night.

Relatively speaking, however, I never fared as badly as another black 10
male journalist. He went to nearby Waukegan, Illinois, a couple of summers
ago to work on a story about a murderer who was born there. Mistaking the
reporter for the killer, police officers hauled him from his car at gunpoint and
but for his press credentials would probably have tried to book him. Such episodes are not uncommon. Black men trade tales like this all the time.

Over the years, I learned to smother the rage I felt at so often being 11
taken for a criminal. Not to do so would surely have led to madness. I now
take precautions to make myself less threatening. I move about with care,
particularly late in the evening. I give a wide berth to nervous people on subway platforms during the wee hours, particularly when I have exchanged business clothes for jeans. If I happen to be entering a building behind some people who appear skittish, I may walk by, letting them clear the lobby before
I return, so as not to seem to be following them. I have been calm and extremely congenial on those rare occasions when I've been pulled over by the
police.

And on late-evening constitutionals I employ what has proved to be an 12
excellent tension-reducing measure: I whistle melodies from Beethoven and
Vivaldi and the more popular classical composers. Even steely New Yorkers
hunching toward nighttime destinations seem to relax, and occasionally they
even join in the tune. Virtually everybody seems to sense that a mugger
wouldn't be warbling bright, sunny selections from Vivaldi's *Four Seasons*. It
is my equivalent of the cowbell that hikers wear when they know they are in
bear country.

[1986]

Summarizing

Summary should be clearly distinguished from analysis. The word "summary" is related to "sum," the total something adds up to. (We say "adds *up*
to" because the Greeks and Romans counted upward, and wrote the total at
the top.)

A summary is a condensation or abridgement; it briefly gives the reader
the gist of a longer work. It boils down the longer work, resembling the
longer work as a bouillion cube resembles a bowl of soup. A summary of Staples's "Black Men and Public Space" will reduce the essay, perhaps to a paragraph or two or even to a sentence. It will not call attention to Staples's various strategies, and it will not evaluate his views or his skill as a writer; it will
merely present the gist of what he says.

SUMMARY AND ANALYSIS

If, then, you are asked to write an analysis of something you have read,
you should not hand in a summary. On the other hand, a very brief summary
may appropriately appear within an analytic essay. Usually, in fact, the reader
needs some information, and the writer of the essay will briefly summarize

this information. For example, a student who wrote about Staples's essay is *summarizing* when she writes,

> Staples says that he is aware that his presence
> frightens many whites, especially women.

She is summarizing because she is reporting, without personal comment, what Staples said.

On the other hand, she is *analyzing* when she writes:

> By saying at the outset, "My first victim was a
> woman—white, well dressed, probably in her late
> twenties," Staples immediately catches the reader's
> attention and sets up expectations that will be
> undermined in the next paragraph.

In this sentence the writer is not reporting *what* Staples said but is explaining *how* he achieved an effect.

Here are a few principles that govern summaries:

1. A summary is much briefer than the original. It is not a paraphrase—a word-by-word translation of someone's words into your own. A paraphrase is usually at least as long as the original, whereas a summary is rarely longer than one-fourth the original, and usually is much briefer. An entire essay may be summarized in a sentence or two.
2. A summary usually achieves its brevity by omitting almost all the concrete details of the original, presenting only the sum that the details add up to.
3. A summary is accurate; it has no value if it misrepresents the point of the original.
4. The writer of a summary need not make the points in the same order as that of the original. If the writer of an essay has delayed revealing the main point until the end of the essay, the summary may rearrange the order, stating the main point first. Occasionally, when the original author has presented an argument in a disorderly or confusing sequence, one writes a summary in order to disengage the author's argument from its confusing structure.
5. A summary normally is written in the present tense because although the author wrote the piece last year or a hundred years ago, we assume in writing a summary that the piece speaks to us today.
6. Because a summary is openly based on someone else's views, it is usually not necessary to use quotation marks around key words or phrases from the original. Nor is it necessary to repeat "he says" or "she goes on to prove." From the opening sentence of a summary it should be clear that what follows is what the original author says.

Here is a summary of our comments on "summary":

> A summary is a condensation or abridgment. Its chief characteristics are: 1) it is rarely more than one-fourth as long as the original; 2) its brevity

is usually achieved by leaving out most of the concrete details of the original; 3) it is accurate; 4) it may rearrange the organization of the original, especially if a rearrangement will make things clearer; 5) it normally is in the present tense; 6) quoted words need not be enclosed in quotation marks.

PREPARING A SUMMARY

If you are summarizing an essay, you may find that the essay includes its own summary, perhaps at the start or more likely near the end. If it does, you're in luck.

If it doesn't, we suggest that on rereading you jot down, after reading each paragraph, a sentence summarizing the gist of the paragraph. (A very long or a poorly unified paragraph may require two sentences, but make every effort to boil the paragraph down to a dozen or so words.) Of course if a paragraph consists merely of a transitional sentence or two ("We will now turn to another example") you will lump it with the next paragraph. Similarly, if for some reason you encounter a series of very short paragraphs—for instance, three examples, each briefly stated, and all illustrating the same point—you probably will find that you can cover them with a single sentence. But if a paragraph runs to half a page or more of print, it's probably worth its own sentence of summary. In fact, your author may summarize the paragraph in the paragraph's opening sentence or in its final sentence.

Here is a student's paragraph-by-paragraph summary of Staples's "Black Men and Public Space." The numbers refer to Staples's paragraphs.

1. "First victim" was a white woman in Chicago, who hurried away.
2. Age 22, he realized--to his surprise and embarrassment--that he (a "youngish black man") could be perceived by strangers as a mugger. And, since his presence created fear, he was in a dangerous situation.
3, 4, 5. At intersections he heard drivers of cars lock their doors, and elsewhere he sensed hostility of bouncers and others.
   In NY, lots of tension on narrow sidewalks. Women are esp. afraid of him; he knows why, but that's "no solace."
6. He's not sure why it took him 22 years to see that others fear him, but prob. because in his hometown of Chester, Pa., there was lots of adolescent violence, though he stayed clear of it.
7. As a boy, he saw young toughs killed, and he kept clear, "timid, but a survivor."
8, 9, 10. Though he is gentle, he looks fearsome. Once, working as a journalist, he was mistaken for a burglar.

> Another time, in a jewelry store, the clerk brought out a
> guard dog. Another black journalist was covering a crime,
> but the police thought the journalist was the killer.
> Many blacks have had such experiences.
> 11. He has learned to smother his rage—and he keeps away
> from nervous people.
> 12. Walking late at night, he whistles familiar classical
> music, trying to reassure others that he is not a
> mugger.

When you have written your sentence summarizing the last paragraph, you may have done enough if the summary was intended simply for your own private use, for example, to help you review material for an examination. But if you are going to use it as the basis of a summary within an essay you are writing, you probably won't want to include a summary longer than three or four sentences; so your job will be to reduce and combine the sentences you have jotted down. Indeed, you may even want to reduce the summary to a single sentence.

A Suggested Exercise: Assuming that you find the sentences summarizing "Black Men and Public Space," reduce them to a summary no longer than four readable sentences. Then compare your version with the versions of two other students and, working as a group, produce a summary.

STATING THE THESIS OF AN ESSAY

Summarizing each stage of the essay forces a reader to be attentive and can assist the reader to formulate a **thesis sentence,** a sentence that (in the reader's opinion) sets forth the writer's central point. If an essay is essentially an argument—for example, a defense of (or an argument against) capital punishment—it will probably include one or more sentences that directly assert the thesis. "Black Men and Public Space," chiefly a narrative essay, is much less evidently an argument, but it does have a point, and some of its sentences come pretty close to summarizing the point. Here are three of those sentences:

> And I soon gathered that being perceived as dangerous is a hazard in itself. (2)
>
> The fearsomeness mistakenly attributed to me in public places often has a perilous flavor. (8)
>
> I now take precautions to make myself less threatening. (11)

We asked our students to formulate their own thesis sentence for Staples's essay. One student came up with the following sentence after first drafting a couple of tentative versions and then rereading the essay in order to modify them:

> In "Black Men and Public Space" Staples recognizes
> that because many whites fear a young black man and
> therefore may do violence to him, he may do well to try
> to cool the situation by making himself unthreatening.

Notice, again, that a thesis sentence states the *point* of the work. Don't confuse a thesis sentence with a summary of a narrative, such as "Staples at the age of twenty-two came to realize that his presence was threatening to whites, and he has since taken measures to make himself less threatening." This sentence, though true, doesn't clearly get at the point of the essay, the generalization that can be drawn from Staples's example.

Look again at the student's formulation of a thesis sentence (*not* the narrative summary sentence that we have just given). If you don't think that it fairly represents Staples's point, you may (if you are writing an essay about Staples's essay) want to come up with a sentence that seems more precise to you. Whether you use the sentence we have quoted or a sentence that you formulate for yourself, you can in any case of course disagree very strongly with what you take to be Staples's point. Your version of Staples's thesis should accurately reflect your understanding of Staples's point, but you need not agree with the point. You may think, for instance, that Staples is hypersensitive or (to mention only one other possibility) that he is playing the Uncle Tom.

A thesis sentence, then, whether the words are your own or the author's, is a very brief summary of the argument (not of the narrative) of the work. If you are writing an essay about an essay, you'll probably want to offer a sentence that reminds your reader of the point of the work you are discussing or gives the reader the gist of an unfamiliar work:

> Black males, however harmless, are in a perilous situation because whites, especially white women, perceive them as threatening.

Or:

> In "Black Men and Public Space" Staples recognizes that because many whites fear a young black man and therefore may do violence to him, a black man may do well to try to cool the situation by making himself non-threatening.

DRAFTING A SUMMARY

Sometimes, however, a fuller statement may be useful. For instance, if you are writing about a complex essay that makes six points, you may help your reader if you briefly restate all six. The length of your summary will depend on your purpose and the needs of your audience.

The following principles may help you to write your summary:

1. First, after having written sentences that summarize each paragraph or group of paragraphs, formulate the essay's thesis sentence. Formulating the sentence in writing will help you to stay with what you take to be the writer's main point.

2. Next, write a first draft by turning your summaries of the paragraphs into fewer and better sentences. For example, the student who wrote the paragraph-by-paragraph summary (page 76) of Staples's essay turned her first five sentences (on Staples's first paragraphs) into this:

> Staples's "first victim" was a white woman in
> Chicago. When she hurried away from him, he realized—
> to his surprise and embarrassment—that because he was
> large and black and young he seemed to her to be a
> mugger. And since his presence created fear, <u>he</u> was in
> a situation. Other experiences, such as hearing
> drivers lock their cars when they were waiting at an
> intersection, have made him aware of the hostility of
> others. Women are especially afraid of him, and
> although he knows why, this knowledge is "no solace."

The student turned the remaining sentences of the outline into the following summary:

> Oddly, it took him twenty-two years to see that
> others fear him. Perhaps it took this long because he
> grew up in a violent neighborhood, though he kept
> clear, "timid, but a survivor." Because he is black
> and large, whites regard him as fearsome and treat him
> accordingly (once a clerk in a jewelry store brought
> out a guard dog), but other blacks have been treated
> worse. He has learned to smother his rage, and in order
> to cool things he tries to reassure nervous people by
> keeping away from them and (when he is walking late at
> night) by whistling classical music.

3. Write a lead-in sentence, probably incorporating the gist of the thesis sentence. Here is an example:

> Brent Staples, in "Black Men and Public Space,"
> tells how his awareness that many white people
> regarded him as dangerous caused him to realize that
> <u>he</u> was in danger. His implicitly recommended
> solution is to try to cool the anxiety by adopting
> nonthreatening behavior.

After writing a lead-in, revise the draft of your summary, eliminating needless repetition, providing transitions, and adding whatever you think may be needed to clarify the work for someone who is unfamiliar with it. You may rearrange the points if you think the rearrangement will clarify matters.

4. Edit your draft for errors in grammar, punctuation, and spelling. Read it aloud to test it once more for readability. Sometimes only by reading aloud do we detect needless repetition or confusing phrases.

SOME WRITING ASSIGNMENTS

1. In a paragraph or two set forth what you take to be Staples's *purpose*. Do you think he was writing chiefly to clarify some ideas for himself—for instance, to explore how he came to discover the "alienation that comes of being ever the suspect"? Or writing to assist blacks? Or to assist whites? Or what? (You may of course conclude that none of these suggestions, or all, are relevant.)

2. If you think the essay is effective, in a paragraph or two addressed to your classmates try to account for its effectiveness. Do certain examples strike you as particularly forceful? If so, why? Do certain sentences seem especially memorable? Again, why? For example, if the opening and concluding paragraphs strike you as effective, explain why. On the other hand, if you are unimpressed by part or all of the essay, explain why.

3. The success of a narrative as a piece of writing often depends on the reader's willingness to identify with the narrator. From an examination of "Black Men and Public Space," what explanations can you give for your willingness (or unwillingness) to identify yourself with Staples? (Probably you will want to say something about his persona as you sense it from the essay.) In the course of a 500-word essay explaining your position, very briefly summarize Staples's essay and state his thesis.

4. Have *you* ever unintentionally altered public space? For instance, you might recall an experience in which, as a child, your mere presence caused adults to alter their behavior—for instance, to stop quarreling.

   After a session of brainstorming, in which you produce some possible topics, you'll want to try to settle on one. After you have chosen a topic and produced a first draft, if you are not satisfied with your first paragraph—for instance, if you feel that it is not likely to get and hold the reader's attention—you may want to imitate the strategy that Staples adopted for his first paragraph.

5. If you have ever been in the position of one of Staples's "victims," that is, if you have ever shown fear or suspicion of someone who, it turned out, meant you no harm (or if you can imagine being in that position), write an essay from the "victim's" point of view. Explain what happened, what you did and thought. Did you think at the time about the feelings of the person you avoided or fled from? Has reading Staples's essay prompted further reflections on your experience? (Suggested length: 750 words.)

Writing about an Essayist's Style

Since much of the pleasure we receive from an essay is derived from the essayist's style—the *how* with which an essayist conveys an attitude toward some aspect of reality—your instructor may ask you to analyze the writer's style.

Read the following essay by Joan Didion. While reading it, annotate it wherever you are inclined (you may want to express responses in the margin, underline puzzling words, or mark passages that strike you as especially effective or, for that matter, especially clumsy). Then reread the essay; since you will now be familiar with the essay as a whole, you may want to make further annotations, such as brief comments on Didion's use of repetition, or of short and long sentences.

Joan Didion, a fifth-generation Californian, was born in Sacramento in 1934. In 1956 she was graduated from the University of California, Berkeley, and in the same year she published her first story and won a contest sponsored by *Vogue* magazine. Since then she has written essays, stories, screenplays, and novels. All of her writing, she says, is an "act of saying *I*, of imposing oneself upon other people, of saying *listen to me, see it my way, change your mind*."

■ JOAN DIDION

Los Angeles Notebook

There is something uneasy in the Los Angeles air this afternoon, some 1 unnatural stillness, some tension. What it means is that tonight a Santa Ana will begin to blow, a hot wind from the northeast whining down through the Cajon and San Gorgonio Passes, blowing up sandstorms out along Route 66, drying the hills and the nerves to the flash point. For a few days now we will see smoke back in the canyons, and hear sirens in the night. I have neither heard nor read that a Santa Ana is due, but I know it, and almost everyone I have seen today knows it too. We know it because we feel it. The baby frets. The maid sulks. I rekindle a waning argument with the telephone company, then cut my losses and lie down, given over to whatever it is in the air. To live with the Santa Ana is to accept, consciously or unconsciously, a deeply mechanistic view of human behavior.

I recall being told, when I first moved to Los Angeles and was living on 2 an isolated beach, that the Indians would throw themselves into the sea when the bad wind blew. I could see why. The Pacific turned ominously glossy during a Santa Ana period, and one woke in the night troubled not only by the peacocks screaming in the olive trees but by the eerie absence of surf. The heat was surreal. The sky had a yellow cast, the kind of light sometimes called "earthquake weather." My only neighbor would not come out of her house for days, and there were no lights at night, and her husband roamed the place with a machete. One day he would tell me that he had heard a trespasser, the next a rattlesnake.

"On nights like that," Raymond Chandler once wrote about the Santa 3 Ana, "every booze party ends in a fight. Meek little wives feel the edge of the carving knife and study their husbands' necks. Anything can happen." That was the kind of wind it was. I did not know then that there was any basis for the effect it had on all of us, but it turns out to be another of these cases in which science bears out folk wisdom. The Santa Ana, which is named for one of the canyons it rushes through, is a *foehn* wind, like the *foehn* of Austria and Switzerland and the *hamsin* of Israel. There are a number of persistent malevolent winds, perhaps the best known of which are the mistral of France and the Mediterranean sirocco, but a *foehn* wind has distinct characteristics: it occurs on the leeward slope of a mountain range and, although the air begins as a cold mass, it is warmed as it comes down the mountain and appears finally as a hot dry wind. Whenever and wherever a *foehn* blows, doctors hear about headaches and nausea and allergies, about "nervousness," about "depression." In Los Angeles some teachers do not attempt to conduct formal classes during a Santa Ana, because the children become unmanageable. In Switzerland the suicide rate goes up during the *foehn*, and in the courts of some Swiss cantons the wind is considered a mitigating circumstance for crime. Surgeons are said to watch the wind, because blood does not clot normally during a *foehn*. A few years ago an Israeli physicist discovered that not only during such winds, but for the ten or twelve hours which precede them, the air carries an unusually high ratio of positive to negative ions. No one seems to know exactly why that should be; some talk about friction and others suggest solar disturbances. In any case the positive ions are there, and what an excess of positive ions does, in the simplest terms, is make people unhappy. One cannot get much more mechanistic than that.

Easterners commonly complain that there is no "weather" at all in 4 Southern California, that the days and the seasons slip by relentlessly, numbingly bland. That is quite misleading. In fact the climate is characterized by infrequent but violent extremes: two periods of torrential subtropical rains which continue for weeks and wash out the hills and send subdivisions sliding toward the sea; about twenty scattered days a year of the Santa Ana, which, with its incendiary dryness, invariably means fire. At the first prediction of a Santa Ana, the Forest Service flies men and equipment from northern California into the southern forests, and the Los Angeles Fire Department cancels its ordinary non-firefighting routines. The Santa Ana caused Malibu to burn the way it did in 1956, and Bel Air in 1961, and Santa Barbara in 1964. In the winter of 1966–67 eleven men were killed fighting a Santa Ana fire that spread through the San Gabriel Mountains.

Just to watch the front-page news out of Los Angeles during a Santa Ana 5 is to get very close to what it is about the place. The longest single Santa Ana period in recent years was in 1957, and it lasted not the usual three or four days but fourteen days, from November 21 until December 4. On the first day 25,000 acres of the San Gabriel Mountains were burning, with gusts reaching 100 miles an hour. In town, the wind reached Force 12, or hurricane force, on the Beaufort Scale; oil derricks were toppled and people ordered off the downtown streets to avoid injury from flying objects. On November 22 the fire in the San Gabriels was out of control. On November 24 six people were killed in automobile accidents, and by the end of the week the Los Angeles *Times* was keeping a box score of traffic deaths. On November 26 a prominent Pasadena attorney, depressed about money, shot and killed his wife, their two sons, and himself. On November 27 a South Gate divorcée, twenty-two, was murdered and thrown from a moving car. On November 30 the San Gabriel fire was still out of control, and the wind in town was blowing eighty miles an hour. On the first day of December four people died violently, and on the third the wind began to break.

It is hard for people who have not lived in Los Angeles to realize how 6 radically the Santa Ana figures in the local imagination. The city burning is Los Angeles's deepest image of itself: Nathanael West perceived that, in *The Day of the Locust;* and at the time of the 1965 Watts riots what struck the imagination most indelibly were the fires. For days one could drive the Harbor Freeway and see the city on fire, just as we had always known it would be in the end. Los Angeles weather is the weather of catastrophe, of apocalypse, and, just as the reliably long and bitter winters of New England determine the way life is lived there, so the violence and the unpredictability of the Santa Ana affect the entire quality of life in Los Angeles, accentuate its impermanence, its unreliability. The wind shows us how close to the edge we are.

[1968]

PRE-WRITING: ANNOTATIONS AND JOURNAL ENTRIES

While reading the essay a second time, one student, planning to write on Didion's style here, marked the first paragraph thus:

long sentence

short sentences

thesis?

There is some thing uneasy in the Los Angeles air this afternoon, some unnatural stillness, some tension. What it means is that tonight a Santa Ana will begin to blow, a hot wind from the northeast whining down through the Cajon and San Gorgonio Passes, blowing up sandstorms out along Route 66, drying the hills and the nerves to the flash point. For a few days now we will see smoke back in the canyons, and hear sirens in the night. I have neither heard nor read that a Santa Ana is due, but I know it, and almost everyone I have seen today knows it too. We know it because we feel it. The baby frets. The maid sulks. I rekindle a waning argument with the telephone company, then cut my losses and lie down, given over to whatever it is in the air. To live with the Santa Ana is to accept, consciously or unconsciously, a deeply mechanistic view of human behavior.

He marked other paragraphs in more or less the same way, and later in the day wrote the following entry in his journal:

Tuesday. She really seems to get the effect of this terrible, oppressive wind. Didion repeats a lot

("something...some...some," all in the first
sentence). I think she is trying to give us the feel of
a wind that won't let up, that keeps hammering at us and
driving us crazy. But what persona do I find in this
essay? I'm not sure. Sometimes she seems
schoolteacherish, with the lecture on foehn winds. And
in paragraph 4 when she says "This is quite
misleading," that's a little sharp. Maybe the wind is
getting her down!!

Tuesday night. I'm still not all that wild about the
tone in "That is quite misleading," but I guess
"schoolteacherish" isn't quite the way to describe
Didion on the whole. How many schoolteachers read
Raymond Chandler? She does sound a bit teachery in the
first sentence of the last paragraph ("It is hard for
people who have not lived in Los Angeles to realize
that...."), but I guess that a writer sometimes has to
give a little lecture. Maybe when she says "It is hard,
etc." she is really trying to be helpful, reassuring us
that if we don't realize whatever her point is, we
aren't therefore idiots. She knows that lots of her
readers don't know much about L.A., so she is being
helpful.

Later, drawing largely on his annotations in the text and on his entries
in his journal, this student jotted down the following notes in preparation for
drafting an essay on Didion's style in "Los Angeles Notebook":

persona (as revealed by style?)
    rather personal ("I recall being told," in para. 1)
    sometimes a bit of the school teacher
        (for instance on foehn wind, in 3
        "This is quite misleading" in 4)

but : very interesting; very informative; a good teacher
    she seems to know what she is talking about; details
    about foehn wind in para. 4; facts about
    what the Santa Ana did to Malibu in 1956, Bel Air in
    1961, Santa Barbara in 1964. Also facts about
    longest Santa Ana (14 days, in 1957) in para. 5.

style (chief characteristics that I see)
    some long sentences and some short sentences
        long sentences : Second: 45 words; prob. longest
            in essay; no, longest is next-to-last: 53
            words!!! The point? Long, blowing,

continuing wind? Certainly seems so in 3d
    sentence, with wind "whin<u>ing</u>, blow<u>ing</u>,
        dry<u>ing</u>"; it just keeps going on and on.
short sentences: "We know it because we feel it.
    The baby frets. The maid sulks."
    The point? Impatience? Inability to think, to
    accomplish anything that takes a little
    time? General nervousness?
repetition of words: "something," "some," "some"
    in first para. In 3, "about" appears three times
    in one sentence—and also three "ands" here. So,
    length plus repetition = suggestion of the
    driving, continuing wind

A SAMPLE ESSAY ON
DIDION'S "LOS ANGELES NOTEBOOK"

Ultimately the student wrote the following short essay. You'll notice that
it draws heavily on the notes on style, and hardly at all on the notes on persona. Notes written during pre-writing are a source to draw on. Resist the
temptation to work in, at all costs, everything you've produced.

Joan Didion's Style: Not Hot Air

In "Los Angeles Notebook" Joan Didion has a point
to make. A sentence at the end of her first paragraph
states the point concisely: "To live with the Santa Ana
is to accept, consciously or unconsciously, a deeply
mechanistic view of human behavior." But she doesn't
simply make the point; her essay tries to make the
point effectively, to make us <u>feel</u> the truth of what
she says. I think she succeeds, partly because she
knows what she is talking about (she gives lots of
details about the destructive effects of the wind) and
partly because she uses certain stylistic devices,
especially very short and very long sentences, and
repetition.

Her first sentence is probably of average length,
but it repeats "some" (once in the form of
"something") three times:

> There is something uneasy in the Los Angeles air
> this afternoon, some unnatural stillness, some
> tension.

The sentence is not monotonous, but the repetition
perhaps makes it seem a bit longer than it really is,
and the repetition suggests a lack of change, a lack of
progress. As the reader soon finds, it helps to suggest
the driving and unchanging wind. The second sentence,
forty-five words long, makes the point clear:

> What it means is that tonight a Santa Ana will begin
> to blow, a hot wind from the northeast whining down
> through the Cajon and San Gorgonio Passes, blowing
> up sandstorms out along Route 66, drying the hills
> and the nerves to the flash point.

The length of the sentence, and the use of whining,
blowing, and drying--continuous actions--makes the
sentence go on and on, giving an effect of the constant
wind.

The length of even this unusually long sentence is
exceeded by the next-to-last sentence in the essay,
fifty-three words about the catastrophic weather of
Los Angeles. But this next-to-last sentence, which
again suggests the relentless wind, is followed by a
sentence of only eleven words, and in fact Didion
earlier in the essay writes a number of fairly short or
even very short sentences. These short sentences, like
the long ones, contribute to the reader's response. If
the long sentences suggest the wind, the short
sentences suggest the nervousness, crankiness, or
fidgetiness of the person who experiences the wind, or
who even only senses the coming of the wind: "We know it
because we feel it. The baby frets. The maid sulks."
These choppy sentences seem to fret and sulk.

In "Los Angeles Notebook" Didion gives us many

facts about the destructive effect of the Santa Ana,
which, she explains, is a <u>foehn</u> wind. Her essay is
informative, and she is a good teacher, but her most
effective method of teaching is not the use of facts
but the use of a style that helps the reader to feel the
impact of this <u>foehn</u>.

SOME WRITING ASSIGNMENTS

1. Beginning with the third paragraph, Didion defines the Santa Ana. Would the essay have been clearer or more effective if the definition had introduced the essay? Explain. (Suggested length: one paragraph.)
2. In a paragraph explain Didion's last sentence. (How does it relate to the thesis sentence? How well does it summarize the essay?)
3. Write a paragraph in which you convey something of the feel of an experience. Possible topics: waiting in a long line, sitting through a boring lecture, waiting for a telephone call, walking a dog, running or swimming, thinking about getting out of bed.
4. In 500 to 750 words, let a reader sense the effect of some kind of weather on a community. Possible topics: Indian summer; the second day of continuous rain; the third day of a blizzard; a scorching Fourth of July.
5. "It had started to rain." Write a paragraph in which you communicate this fact without saying it. Instead, show a person performing an action that takes no more than five minutes.
6. With the aid of *New York Times Index* or *Newspaper Index* (an index to the *Chicago Tribune, Los Angeles Times, New Orleans Times-Picayune,* and *Washington Post*) write an update of "Los Angeles Notebook." What instances of the Santa Ana have occurred since Didion's essay was published in 1968? Or, do some research on unusual weather conditions (hurricanes, tornadoes, drought) in an area you are familiar with, and then write an essay reporting both the facts of the weather and the psychological experience of the inhabitants of the area. (Research may include conducting interviews.)

Summing Up: Getting Ideas for Writing about Essays

1. What kind of essay is it? Is it chiefly a presentation of facts (for example, an exposition, a report, or a history), or is it an argument, or is it a meditation?
2. What does it seem to add up to? If the essay is chiefly meditative or speculative, how much emphasis is placed on the persona? That is, if the essay is a sort of thinking-out-loud, is your interest chiefly in the ostensible topic or in the writer's mood and personality? If the essay is chiefly

a presentation of facts, does it also have a larger implication? For instance, if it narrates a happening (history), does the reader draw an inference—find a meaning—in the happening? If the essay is chiefly an argument, what is the thesis? How is the thesis supported? (Is it supported, for example, by induction, deduction, analogy, or emotional appeal?) Do you accept the assumptions (explicit and implicit)?

3. What is the tone of the essay? Is it, for example, solemn or playful? Is the tone consistent? If not, how do the shifts affect your understanding of the writer's point or your identification of the writer's persona?

4. What sort of *persona* does the writer create, and how does the writer create it? (For example, does the writer use colloquial, technical, or formal language? Short sentences or long ones? Personal anecdotes? Quotations from authorities?)

5. What is especially good (or bad) about the essay? Is it logically persuasive? Or entertaining? Or does it introduce an engaging persona? Or (if it is a narrative) does it tell a story effectively, using (where appropriate) description, dialogue, and commentary, and somehow make you feel that this story is worth reporting?

Five Essays

■ VIRGINIA WOOLF

Virginia Woolf (1882–1941) is known chiefly as a novelist, but she was also the author of short stories and essays, and in recent years the range of her power has been increasingly recognized.

Woolf was self-educated in the library of her father, Leslie Stephen, a distinguished man of letters. After her father's death she moved to Bloomsbury, an unfashionable part of London where she was part of a brilliant circle of friends—the Bloomsbury group—that included Clive Bell and Roger Fry (art critics), J. M. Keynes (an economist), Lytton Strachey (a biographer), and E. M. Forster (novelist and essayist). In 1907 she married Leonard Woolf, with whom ten years later she established the Hogarth Press, which published some of the most interesting literature of the period, including her own novels. Woolf experienced several mental breakdowns, and in 1941, fearing yet another, she drowned herself.

Professions for Women

When your secretary invited me to come here, she told me that your Society is concerned with the employment of women and she suggested that I might tell you something about my own professional experiences. It is true I am a woman; it is true I am employed, but what professional experiences have I had? It is difficult to say. My profession is literature; and in that profession there are fewer experiences for women than in any other, with the ex- 1 ception of the stage—fewer, I mean, that are peculiar to women. For the road was cut many years ago—by Fanny Burney, by Aphra Behn, by Harriet Martineau, by Jane Austen, by George Eliot—many famous women, and many more unknown and forgotten, have been before me, making the path smooth, and regulating my steps. Thus, when I came to write, there were very few material obstacles in my way. Writing was a reputable and harmless occupation. The family peace was not broken by the scratching of a pen. No demand was made upon the family purse. For ten and sixpence one can buy paper enough to write all the plays of Shakespeare—if one has a mind that way. Pianos and models, Paris, Vienna and Berlin, masters and mistresses, are not needed by a writer. The cheapness of writing paper is, of course, the reason why women have succeeded as writers before they have succeeded in the other professions.

But to tell you my story—it is a simple one. You have only got to figure 2 to yourselves a girl in a bedroom with a pen in her hand. She had only to move that pen from left to right—from ten o'clock to one. Then it occurred to her to do what is simple and cheap enough after all—to slip a few of those pages into an envelope, fix a penny stamp in the corner, and drop the envelope in the red box at the corner. It was thus that I became a journalist; and my effort was rewarded on the first day of the following month—a very glorious day it was for me—by a letter from an editor containing a check for one pound ten shillings and sixpence. But to show you how little I deserve to be called a professional woman, how little I know of the struggles and difficulties of such lives, I have to admit that instead of spending that sum upon bread and butter, rent, shoes and stockings, or butcher's bills, I went out and bought a cat—a beautiful cat, a Persian cat, which very soon involved me in bitter disputes with my neighbors.

What could be easier than to write articles and to buy Persian cats with 3 the profits? But wait a moment. Articles have to be about something. Mine, I seem to remember, was about a novel by a famous man. And while I was writing this review, I discovered that if I were going to review books I should need to do battle with a certain phantom. And the phantom was a woman, and when I came to know her better I called her after the heroine of a famous poem, The Angel in the House. It was she who used to come between me and my paper when I was writing reviews. It was she who bothered me and wasted my time and so tormented me that at last I killed her. You who come of a younger and happier generation may not have heard of her—you may not know what I mean by the Angel in the House. I will describe her as shortly as I can. She was intensely sympathetic. She was immensely charming. She was utterly unselfish. She excelled in the difficult arts of family life. She sacrificed herself daily. If there was chicken, she took the leg; if there was a draught she sat in it—in short she was so constituted that she never had a mind or a wish of her own but preferred to sympathize always with the minds and wishes of others. Above all—I need not say it—she was pure. Her purity was supposed to be her chief beauty—her blushes, her great grace. In those days—the last of Queen Victoria—every house had its Angel. And when I came to write I encountered her with the very first words. The shadow of her wings fell on my page; I heard the rustling of her skirts in the room. Directly, that is to say, I took my pen in hand to review that novel by a famous man, she slipped behind me and whispered: "My dear, you are a young woman. You are writing about a book that has been written by a man. Be sympathetic; be tender; flatter; deceive; use all the arts and wiles of our sex. Never let anybody guess that you have a mind of your own. Above all, be pure." And she made as if to guide my pen. I now record the one act for which I take some credit to myself, though the credit rightly belongs to some excellent ancestors of mine who left me a certain sum of money—shall we say five hundred pounds a year?—so that it was not necessary for me to depend solely on charm for my living. I turned upon her and caught her by the throat. I did my best to kill her. My excuse, if I were to be had up in a court of law, would be that I acted in self-defense. Had I not killed her she would have killed me. She would have plucked the heart out of my writing. For, as I found, directly I put pen to paper, you cannot review even a novel without having a mind of your own, without expressing what you think to be the truth about human relations, morality, sex. And all these questions, according to the Angel in the House, cannot be dealt with freely and openly by women; they must charm, they must conciliate, they must—to put it bluntly—tell lies if they are to succeed. Thus, whenever I felt the shadow of her wing or the radiance of her halo upon my page, I took up the inkpot and flung it at her. She died hard. Her fictitious nature was of great assistance to her. It is far harder to kill a phantom than a reality. She was always creeping back when I thought I had despatched her. Though I flatter myself that I killed her in the end, the struggle was severe; it took much time that had better have been spent upon learning Greek grammar; or in roaming the world in search of adventures. But it was a real experience; it was an experience that was bound to befall all women writers at that time. Killing the Angel in the House was part of the occupation of a woman writer.

But to continue my story. The Angel was dead; what then remained? You 4 may say that what remained was a simple and common object—a young woman in a bedroom with an inkpot. In other words, now that she had rid herself of falsehood, that young woman had only to be herself. Ah, but what is "herself"? I mean, what is a woman? I assure you, I do not know. I do not believe that you know. I do not believe that anybody can know until she has expressed herself in all the arts and professions open to human skill. That indeed is one of the reasons why I have come here—out of respect for you, who are in process of showing us by your experiments what a woman is, who are in process of providing us, by your failures and successes, with that extremely important piece of information.

But to continue the story of my professional experiences. I made one 5 pound ten and six by my first review; and I bought a Persian cat with the proceeds. Then I grew ambitious. A Persian cat is all very well, I said; but a Persian cat is not enough. I must have a motor car. And it was thus that I became a novelist—for it is a very strange thing that people will give you a motor car if you will tell them a story. It is a still stranger thing that there is nothing so delightful in the world as telling stories. It is far pleasanter than writing reviews of famous novels. And yet, if I am to obey your secretary and tell you my professional experiences as a novelist, I must tell you about a very strange experience that befell me as a novelist. And to understand it you must try first to imagine a novelist's state of mind. I hope I am not giving away professional secrets if I say that a novelist's chief desire is to be as unconscious as possible. He has to induce in himself a state of perpetual lethargy. He wants life to proceed with the utmost quiet and regularity. He wants to see the same faces, to read the same books, to do the same things day after day, month after month, while he is writing, so that nothing may break the illusion in which he is living—so that nothing may disturb or disquiet the mysterious nosings about, feelings round, darts, dashes and sudden discoveries of that very shy and illusive spirit, the imagination. I suspect that this state is the same both for men and women. Be that as it may, I want you to imagine me writing a novel in a state of trance. I want you to figure to yourselves a girl sitting with a pen in her hand, which for minutes, and indeed for hours, she never dips into the inkpot. The image that comes to my mind when I think of this girl is the image of a fisherman lying sunk in dreams on the verge of a deep lake with a rod held out over the water. She was letting her imagination sweep unchecked round every rock and cranny of the world that lies submerged in the depths of our unconscious being. Now came the experience, the experience that I believe to be far commoner with women writers than with men. The line raced through the girl's fingers. Her imagination had rushed away. It had sought the pools, the depths, the dark places where the largest fish slumber. And then there was a smash. There was an explosion. There was foam and confusion. The imagination had dashed itself against something hard. The girl was roused from her dream. She was indeed in a state of the most acute and difficult distress. To speak without figure she had thought of something, something about the body, about the passions which it was unfitting for her as a woman to say. Men, her reason told her, would be shocked. The consciousness of what men will say of a woman who speaks the truth about her passions had roused her from her artist's state of unconsciousness. She could write no more. The trance was over. Her imagination could work no longer. This I believe to be a very common experience with women writers—they are impeded by the extreme conventionality of the other sex. For though men sensibly allow themselves great freedom in these respects, I doubt that they realize or can control the extreme severity with which they condemn such freedom in women.

These then were two very genuine experiences of my own. These were 6 two of the adventures of my professional life. The first—killing the Angel in the House—I think I solved. She died. But the second, telling the truth about my own experiences as a body, I do not think I solved. I doubt that any woman has solved it yet. The obstacles against her are still immensely powerful—and yet they are very difficult to define. Outwardly, what is simpler than to write books? Outwardly, what obstacles are there for a woman rather than for a man? Inwardly, I think the case is very different; she has still many ghosts to fight, many prejudices to overcome. Indeed it will be a long time still, I think, before a woman can sit down to write a book without finding a phantom to be slain, a rock to be dashed against. And if this is so in literature, the freest of all professions for women, how is it in the new professions which you are now for the first time entering?

Those are the questions that I should like, had I time, to ask you. And 7 indeed, if I have laid stress upon these professional experiences of mine, it is because I believe that they are, though in different forms, yours also. Even when the path is nominally open—when there is nothing to prevent a woman from being a doctor, a lawyer, a civil servant—there are many phantoms and obstacles, as I believe, looming in her way. To discuss and define them is I think of great value and importance; for thus only can the labor be shared, the difficulties be solved. But besides this, it is necessary also to discuss the ends and the aims for which we are fighting, for which we are doing battle with these formidable obstacles. Those aims cannot be taken for granted; they must be perpetually questioned and examined. The whole position, as I see it—here is this hall surrounded by women practising for the first time in history I know not how many different professions—is one of extraordinary interest and importance. You have won rooms of your own in the house hither- to exclusively owned by men. You are able, though not without great labor and effort, to pay the rent. You are earning your five hundred pounds a year. But this freedom is only a beginning; the room is your own, but it is still bare. It has to be furnished; it has to be decorated; it has to be shared. How are you going to furnish it, how are you going to decorate it? With whom are you going to share it, and upon what terms? These, I think, are questions of the utmost importance and interest. For the first time in history you are able to ask them; for the first time you are able to decide for yourselves what the answers should be. Willingly would I stay and discuss those questions and answers—but not tonight. My time is up; and I must cease.

                                                                                      [1931]

■ TOPICS FOR DISCUSSION AND WRITING

1. How would you characterize Woolf's tone, especially her attitude toward her subject and herself, in the first paragraph?

2. What do you think Woolf means when she says (paragraph 3): "It is far harder to kill a phantom than a reality"?

3. Woolf conjectures (paragraph 6) that she has not solved the problem of "telling the truth about my own experiences as a body." Is there any rea- son to believe that today a woman has more difficulty than a man in tell- ing the truth about the experiences of the body?

4. In paragraph 7 Woolf suggests that phantoms as well as obstacles impede women from becoming doctors and lawyers. What might some of these phantoms be?

5. This essay is highly metaphoric. Speaking roughly (or, rather, as precisely as possible), what is the meaning of the metaphor of "rooms" in the final paragraph? What does Woolf mean when she says: "The room is your own, but it is still bare. . . . With whom are you going to share it, and upon what terms?"

6. Evaluate the last two sentences. Are they too abrupt and mechanical? Or do they provide a fitting conclusion to the speech? Explain.

The Death of the Moth

Moths that fly by day are not properly to be called moths; they do not 1
excite that pleasant sense of dark autumn nights and ivy-blossom which the
commonest yellow-underwing asleep in the shadow of the curtain never fails
to rouse in us. They are hybrid creatures, neither gay like butterflies nor
somber like their own species. Nevertheless the present specimen, with his
narrow hay-colored wings, fringed with a tassel of the same color, seemed to
be content with life. It was a pleasant morning, mid-September, mild, benig-
nant, yet with a keener breath than that of the summer months. The plow
was already scoring the field opposite the window, and where the share had
been, the earth was pressed flat and gleamed with moisture. Such vigor came
rolling in from the fields and the down beyond that it was difficult to keep the
eyes strictly turned upon the book. The rooks too were keeping one of their
annual festivities; soaring round the tree tops until it looked as if a vast net
with thousands of black knots in it had been cast up into the air; which, after
a few moments, sank slowly down upon the trees until every twig seemed
to have a knot at the end of it. Then, suddenly, the net would be thrown into
the air again in a wider circle this time, with the utmost clamor and vocifera-
tion, as though to be thrown into the air and settle slowly down upon the tree
tops were a tremendously, exciting experience.

The same energy which inspired the rooks, the ploughmen, the horses, 2
and even, it seemed, the lean bare-backed downs, sent the moth fluttering
from side to side of his square of the windowpane. One could not help watching him. One was, indeed, conscious of a queer feeling of pity for him. The
possibilities of pleasure seemed that morning so enormous and so various
that to have only a moth's part in life, and a day moth's at that, appeared a
hard fate, and his zest in enjoying his meager opportunities to the full, pathetic. He flew vigorously to one corner of his compartment, and, after waiting
there a second, flew across to the other. What remained for him but to fly
to a third corner and then to a fourth? That was all he could do, in spite of
the size of the downs, the width of the sky, the far-off smoke of houses, and
the romantic voice, now and then, of a steamer out at sea. What he could do
he did. Watching him, it seemed as if a fiber, very thin but pure, of the enormous energy of the world had been thrust into his frail and diminutive body.
As often as he crossed the pane, I could fancy that a thread of vital light became visible. He was little or nothing but life.

Yet, because he was so small, and so simple a form of the energy that 3
was rolling in at the open window and driving its way through so many narrow
and intricate corridors in my own brain and in those of other human beings,
there was something marvelous as well as pathetic about him. It was as if
someone had taken a tiny bead of pure life and decking it as lightly as possible
with down and feathers, had set it dancing and zigzagging to show us the true
nature of life. Thus displayed one could not get over the strangeness of it.
One is apt to forget all about life, seeing it humped and bossed and garnished
and cumbered so that it has to move with the greatest circumspection and
dignity. Again, the thought of all that life might have been had he been born
in any other shape caused one to view his simple activities with a kind of pity.

After a time, tired by his dancing apparently, he settled on the window 4
ledge in the sun, and, the queer spectacle being at an end, I forgot about him.
Then, looking up, my eye was caught by him.. He was trying to resume his
dancing, but seemed either so stiff or so awkward that he could only flutter
to the bottom of the window-pane; and when he tried to fly across it he failed.
Being intent on other matters I watched these futile attempts for a time
without thinking, unconsciously waiting for him to resume his flight, as one
waits for a machine, that has stopped momentarily, to start again without considering the reason of its failure. After perhaps a seventh attempt he slipped
from the wooden ledge and fell, fluttering his wings, on to his back on the
window sill. The helplessness of his attitude roused me. It flashed upon me
that he was in difficulties; he could no longer raise himself; his legs struggled
vainly. But, as I stretched out a pencil, meaning to help him to right himself,
it came over me that the failure and awkwardness were the approach of death.
I laid the pencil down again.

The legs agitated themselves once more. I looked as if for the enemy 5
against which he struggled. I looked out of doors. What had happened there?
Presumably it was midday, and work in the fields had stopped. Stillness and
quiet had replaced the previous animation. The birds had taken themselves
off to feed in the brooks. The horses stood still. Yet the power was there all
the same, massed outside, indifferent, impersonal, not attending to anything
in particular. Somehow it was opposed to the little hay-colored moth. It was
useless to try to do anything. One could only watch the extraordinary efforts
made by those tiny legs against an oncoming doom which could, had it chos-
en, have submerged an entire city, not merely a city, but masses of human
beings; nothing, I knew, had any chance against death. Nevertheless after a
pause of exhaustion the legs fluttered again. It was superb, this last protest,
and so frantic that he succeeded at last in righting himself. One's sympathies,
of course, were all on the side of life. Also, when there was nobody to care
or to know, this gigantic effort on the part of an insignificant little moth,
against a power of such magnitude, to retain what no one else valued or
desired to keep, moved one strangely. Again, somehow, one saw life, a pure
bead. I lifted the pencil again, useless though I knew it to be. But even as
I did so, the unmistakable tokens of death showed themselves. The body
relaxed, and instantly grew stiff. The struggle was over. The insignificant little
creature now knew death. As I looked at the dead moth, this minute wayside triumph of so great a force over so mean an antagonist filled me with
wonder. Just as life had been strange a few minutes before, so death was now
as strange. The moth having righted himself now lay most decently and un-
complainingly composed. O yes, he seemed to say, death is stronger than I
am.

[1941]

■ TOPICS FOR DISCUSSION AND WRITING

1. On the basis of the first paragraph, how would you describe Woolf's
    voice, or persona, in this essay? By what means does she try to engage
    our attention and interest?

2. Does the essay have a thesis sentence? If not, in a sentence or two of your own, try to state the essay's main point.
3. What is the season and the time span covered? How are these relevant to the thesis of the essay?
4. Reread the second paragraph, taking note as you do of the variety in sentence lengths. What sentences strike you as particularly effective? What makes them effective?
5. In paragraph three Woolf says, "One is apt to forget all about life, seeing it humped and bossed and garnished and cumbered so that it has to move with the greatest circumspection and dignity." What does she mean? Try to restate the idea in your own words.
6. Write an essay on an encounter with death or birth.

■ E. M. FORSTER
───────────────────────────────

E[dward] M[organ] Forster (1879–1970), born in London and educated at King's College, Cambridge, inherited enough money from an aunt so that he could write short stories, novels, and essays without worrying about making a living. Like Virginia Woolf, Forster belonged to the Bloomsbury Group, an informal society whose members included writers, artists, and the economist John Maynard Keynes.

My Wood

A few years ago I wrote a book which dealt in part with the difficulties 1 of the English in India. Feeling that they would have had no difficulties in India themselves, the Americans read the book freely. The more they read it the better it made them feel, and a check to the author was the result. I bought a wood with the check. It is not a large wood—it contains scarcely any trees, and it is intersected, blast it, by a public footpath. Still, it is the first property that I have owned, so it is right that other people should participate in my shame, and should ask themselves, in accents that will vary in horror, this very important question: What is the effect of property upon the character? Don't let's touch economics; the effect of private ownership upon the community as a whole is another question—a more important question, perhaps, but another one. Let's keep on psychology. If you own things, what's their effect on you? What's the effect on me of my wood?

In the first place, it makes me feel heavy. Property does have this effect. 2 Property produces men of weight, and it was a man of weight who failed to get into the Kingdom of Heaven. He was not wicked, that unfortunate millionaire in the parable, he was only stout; he stuck out in front, not to mention behind, and as he wedged himself this way and that in the crystalline entrance and bruised his well-fed flanks, he saw beneath him a comparatively slim camel passing through the eye of a needle and being woven into the robe of God. The Gospels all through couple stoutness and slowness. They point out what is perfectly obvious, yet seldom realized: that if you have a lot of things you cannot move about a lot, that furniture requires dusting, dusters require servants, servants require insurance stamps, and the whole tangle of them makes you think twice before you accept an invitation to dinner or go for a bathe in the Jordan. Sometimes the Gospels proceed further and say with Tolstoy that property is sinful; they approach the difficult ground of asceticism here, where I cannot follow them. But as to the immediate effects of property on people, they just show straightforward logic. It produces men of weight. Men of weight cannot, by definition, move like the lightning from the East unto the West, and the ascent of a fourteen-stone[1] bishop into a pulpit is thus the exact antithesis of the coming of the Son of Man. My wood makes me feel heavy.

In the second place, it makes me feel it ought to be larger.   3

The other day I heard a twig snap in it. I was annoyed at first, for I   4
thought that someone was blackberrying, and depreciating the value of the undergrowth. On coming nearer, I saw it was not a man who had trodden on the twig and snapped it, but a bird, and I felt pleased. My bird. The bird was not equally pleased. Ignoring the relation between us, it took fright as soon as it saw the shape of my face, and flew straight over the boundary hedge into a field, the property of Mrs. Henessy, where it sat down with a loud squawk. It had become Mrs. Henessy's bird. Something seemed grossly amiss here, something that would not have occurred had the wood been larger. I could not afford to buy Mrs. Henessy out, I dared not murder her, and limitations of this sort beset me on every side. Ahab did not want that vineyard—he only needed it to round off his property, preparatory to plotting a new curve—and all the land around my wood has become necessary to me in order to round off the wood. A boundary protects. But—poor little thing—the boundary ought in its turn to be protected. Noises on the edge of it. Children throw stones. A little more, and then a little more, until we reach the sea. Happy Canute! Happier Alexander! And after all, why should even the world be the limit of possession? A rocket containing a Union Jack, will, it is hoped, be shortly fired at the moon. Mars. Sirius. Beyond which . . . But these immensities ended by saddening me. I could not suppose that my wood was the destined nucleus of universal dominion—it is so very small and contains no mineral wealth beyond the blackberries. Nor was I comforted when Mrs. Henessy's bird took alarm for the second time and flew clean away from us all, under the belief that it belonged to itself.

In the third place, property makes its owner feel that he ought to do   5
something to it. Yet he isn't sure what. A restlessness comes over him, a vague sense that he has a personality to express—the same sense which, without any vagueness, leads the artist to an act of creation. Sometimes I think I will cut down such trees as remain in the wood, at other times I want to fill up the gaps between them with new trees. Both impulses are pretentious and empty. They are not honest movements towards money-making or beauty. They spring from a foolish desire to express myself and from an ina-

---

[1] A stone, an English unit of weight, is fourteen pounds; therefore, a fourteen-stone bishop would weigh 196 pounds.

bility to enjoy what I have got. Creation, property, enjoyment form a sinister trinity in the human mind. Creation and enjoyment are both very very good, yet they are often unattainable without a material basis, and at such moments property pushes itself in as a substitute, saying, "Accept me instead—I'm good enough for all three." It is not enough. It is, as Shakespeare said of lust, "The expense of spirit in a waste of shame": it is "Before, a joy proposed; behind, a dream." Yet we don't know how to shun it. It is forced on us by our economic system as the alternative to starvation. It is also forced on us by an internal defect in the soul, by the feeling that in property may lie the germs of self-development and of exquisite or heroic deeds. Our life on earth is, and ought to be, material and carnal. But we have not yet learned to manage our materialism and carnality properly; they are still entangled with the desire for ownership, where (in the words of Dante) "Possession is one with loss."

And this brings us to our fourth and final point: the blackberries.   6

Blackberries are not plentiful in this meager grove, but they are easily   7
seen from the public footpath which traverses it, and all too easily gathered. Foxgloves, too—people will pull up the foxgloves, and ladies of an educational tendency even grub for toadstools to show them on the Monday in class. Other ladies, less educated, roll down the bracken in the arms of their gentlemen friends. There is paper, there are tins. Pray, does my wood belong to me or doesn't it? And, if it does, should I not own it best by allowing no one else to walk there? There is a wood near Lyme Regis, also cursed by a public footpath, where the owner has not hesitated on this point. He has built high stone walls each side of the path, and has spanned it by bridges, so that the public circulate like termites while he gorges on the blackberries unseen. He really does own his wood, this able chap. Dives in Hell did pretty well, but the gulf dividing him from Lazarus could be traversed by vision, and nothing traverses it here.[2] And perhaps I shall come to this in time. I shall wall in and fence out until I really taste the sweets of property. Enormously stout, endlessly avaricious, pseudo-creative, intensely selfish, I shall weave upon my forehead the quadruple crown of possession until those nasty Bolshies come and take it off again and thrust me aside into the outer darkness.

[1936]

■ TOPICS FOR DISCUSSION AND WRITING

1. Much of the strength of the essay lies in its concrete presentation of generalities. Note, for example, that the essay is called "My Wood," but we might say that the general idea of the essay is "The Effect of Property on Its Owners." Forster gives four effects, chiefly through concrete statements. Put these four effects into four general statements.

2. How would you characterize Forster's persona in this essay? Point to some sentences to support your characterization.

3. Write an essay of 500 to 750 words on the effect a new possession

---

[2] According to Christ's parable in Luke 16:19–26, the rich man (unnamed, but traditionally known as *Dives*, the Latin word for "rich man") at whose gate the poor man Lazarus had begged was sent to hell, from where he could see Lazarus in heaven.

(perhaps a pet, a car, or a stereo set) had on you. In revising your essay, try to read it objectively to see if you maintain a consistent voice. Your readers should have a sense not only of your opinions but also of the sort of person who is expressing them.

4.   Write an essay of 500 to 750 words on the effect of some change in your life—say, graduating from school, or enduring a prolonged illness, or living for a while with a new member in your household (a grandparent, for example, or a stepparent). You may wish to imitate Forster's tone.

■ LANGSTON HUGHES

Langston Hughes (1902–1967) was born in Joplin, Mississippi. He lived part of his youth in Mexico, spent a year at Columbia University, served as a merchant seaman, and worked in a Paris nightclub, where he showed some of his poems to Dr. Alain Locke, a strong advocate of African-American literature. After returning to the United States, Hughes went on to publish poetry, fiction, plays, essays, and biographies.

Salvation

I was saved from sin when I was going on thirteen. But not really saved. 1 It happened like this. There was a big revival at my Auntie Reed's church. Every night for weeks there had been much preaching, singing, praying, and shouting, and some very hardened sinners had been brought to Christ, and the membership of the church had grown by leaps and bounds. Then just before the revival ended, they held a special meeting for children, "to bring the young lambs to the fold." My aunt spoke of it for days ahead. That night I was escorted to the front row and placed on the mourners' bench with all the other young sinners, who had not yet been brought to Jesus.

My aunt told me that when you were saved you saw a light, and something happened to you inside! And Jesus came into your life! And God was with you from then on! She said you could see and hear and feel Jesus in your soul. I believed her. I had heard a great many old people say the same thing and it seemed to me they ought to know. So I sat there calmly in the hot, crowded church, waiting for Jesus to come to me.

The preacher preached a wonderful rhythmical sermon, all moans and shouts and lonely cries and dire pictures of hell, and then he sang a song about the ninety and nine safe in the fold, but one little lamb was left out in the cold. Then he said: "Won't you come? Won't you come to Jesus? Young lambs, won't you come?" And he held out his arms to all us young sinners there on the mourners' bench. And the little girls cried. And some of them jumped up and went to Jesus right away. But most of us just sat there.

A great many old people came and knelt around us and prayed, old women with jet-black faces and braided hair, old men with work-gnarled hands. And the church sang a song about the lower lights are burning, some poor sinners to be saved. And the whole building rocked with prayer and song.

Still I kept waiting to *see* Jesus.   5

Finally all the young people had gone to the altar and were saved, but one boy and me. He was a rounder's son named Westley. Westley and I were surrounded by sisters and deacons praying. It was very hot in the church, and getting late now. Finally Westley said to me in a whisper: "God damn! I'm tired o' sitting here. Let's get up and be saved." So he got up and was saved.

Then I was left all alone on the mourners' bench. My aunt came and knelt at my knees and cried, while prayers and songs swirled all around me in the little church. The whole congregation prayed for me alone, in a mighty wail of moans and voices. And I kept waiting serenely for Jesus, waiting, waiting—but he didn't come. I wanted to see him, but nothing happened to me. Nothing! I wanted something to happen to me, but nothing happened.

I heard the songs and the minister saying: "Why don't you come? My dear child, why don't you come to Jesus? Jesus is waiting for you. He wants you. Why don't you come? Sister Reed, what is this child's name?"

"Langston," my aunt sobbed.

"Langston, why don't you come? Why don't you come and be saved? Oh, 10 Lamb of God! Why don't you come?"

Now it was really getting late. I began to be ashamed of myself, holding everything up so long. I began to wonder what God thought about Westley, who certainly hadn't seen Jesus either, but who was now sitting proudly on the platform, swinging his knickerbockered legs and grinning down at me, surrounded by deacons and old women on their knees praying. God had not struck Westley dead for taking his name in vain or for lying in the temple. So I decided that maybe to save further trouble, I'd better lie, too, and say that Jesus had come, and get up and be saved.

So I got up.

Suddenly the whole room broke into a sea of shouting, as they saw me rise. Waves of rejoicing swept the place. Women leaped in the air. My aunt threw her arms around me. The minister took me by the hand and led me to the platform.

When things quieted down, in a hushed silence, punctuated by a few ec-static "Amens," all the new young lambs were blessed in the name of God. Then joyous singing filled the room.

That night, for the last time in my life but one—for I was a big boy twelve 15 years old—I cried. I cried, in bed alone, and couldn't stop. I buried my head under the quilts, but my aunt heard me. She woke up and told my uncle I was crying because the Holy Ghost had come into my life, and because I had seen Jesus. But I was really crying because I couldn't bear to tell her that I had lied, that I had deceived everybody in the church, and I hadn't seen Jesus, and that now I didn't believe there was a Jesus any more, since he didn't come to help me.

[1940]

■ TOPICS FOR DISCUSSION AND WRITING

1. Do you find the piece amusing, or serious, or both? Explain.
2. How would you characterize the style or voice of the first three

sentences? Childlike, or sophisticated, or what? How would you characterize the final sentence? How can you explain the change in style or tone?

3. Why does Hughes bother to tell us, in paragraph 11, that Westley was
"swinging his knickerbockered legs and grinning"? Do you think that
Westley too may have cried that night? Give your reasons.

4. Is the episode told from the point of view of someone "going on thirteen," or from the point of view of a mature man? Cite evidence to support your position.

5. One of the Golden Rules of narrative writing is "Show, don't tell." In
about 500 words, report an experience—for instance, a death in the family, or a severe (perhaps unjust) punishment, or the first day in a new
school—that produced strong feelings. Like Hughes, you may want to
draw on an experience in which you were subjected to group pressure.
Do not explicitly state what the feelings were; rather, let the reader understand the feelings chiefly through concretely detailed actions. But, like
Hughes, you might state your thesis or basic position in your first paragraph and then indicate when and where the experience took place.

■ ALICE WALKER

Alice Walker was born in 1944 in Eatonton, Georgia, where her parents eked out a living as sharecroppers and dairy farmers; her mother
also worked as a domestic. Walker attended Spelman College in Atlanta,
and in 1965 finished her undergraduate work at Sarah Lawrence College
near New York City. She then became active in the welfare rights movement in New York and in the voter registration movement in Georgia.
Later she taught writing and literature in Mississippi, at Jackson State
College and Tougaloo College, and at Wellesley College, the University of
Massachusetts, and Yale University.

Walker has written essays, poetry, and fiction. Her best-known novel, *The Color Purple* (1982), won a Pulitzer Prize and the National Book
Award.

The essay reprinted here was originally published in 1967 in *The
American Scholar*, a quarterly journal whose audience is primarily
academic.

The Civil Rights Movement: What Good Was It?

Someone said recently to an old black lady from Mississippi, whose legs 1
had been badly mangled by local police who arrested her for "disturbing the
peace," that the Civil Rights Movement was dead, and asked, since it was
dead, what she thought about it. The old lady replied, hobbling out of his
presence on her cane, that the Civil Rights Movement was like herself, "if
it's dead, it shore ain't ready to lay down!"

This old lady is a legendary freedom fighter in her small town in the 2
Delta. She has been severely mistreated for insisting on her rights as an
American citizen. She has been beaten for singing Movement songs, placed
in solitary confinement in prisons for talking about freedom, and placed on
bread and water for praying aloud to God for her jailers' deliverance. For such
a woman the Civil Rights Movement will never be over as long as her skin
is black. It also will never be over for twenty million others with the same
"affliction," for whom the Movement can never "lay down," no matter how
it is killed by the press and made dead and buried by the white American public. As long as one black American survives, the struggle for equality with
other Americans must also survive. This is a debt we owe to those blameless
hostages we leave to the future, our children.

Still, white liberals and deserting Civil Rights sponsors are quick to justi- 3
fy their disaffection from the Movement by claiming that it is all over. "And
since it is over," they will ask, "would someone kindly tell me what has been
gained by it?" They then list statistics supposedly showing how much more
advanced segregation is now than ten years ago—in schools, housing, jobs.
They point to a gain in conservative politicians during the last few years. They
speak of ghetto riots and of the survey that shows that most policemen are
admittedly too anti-Negro to do their jobs in ghetto areas fairly and effectively. They speak of every area that has been touched by the Civil Rights Movement as somehow or other going to pieces.

They rarely talk, however, about human attitudes among Negroes that 4
have undergone terrific changes just during the past seven to ten years (not
to mention all those years when there was a Movement and only the Negroes
knew about it). They seldom speak of changes in personal lives because of
the influence of people in the Movement. They see general failure and few,
if any, individual gains.

They do not understand what it is that keeps the Movement from "laying 5
down" and Negroes from reverting to their former *silent* second-class status.
They have apparently never stopped to wonder why it is always the white
man—on his radio and in his newspaper and on his television—who says that
the Movement is dead. If a Negro were audacious enough to make such a
claim, his fellows might hanker to see him shot. The Movement is dead to
the white man because it no longer interests him. And it no longer interests
him because he can afford to be uninterested: he does not have to live by it,
with it, or for it, as Negroes must. He can take a rest from the news of beatings, killings, and arrests that reach him from North and South—if his skin is
white. Negroes cannot now and will never be able to take a rest from the in-
justices that plague them, for they—not the white man—are the target.

Perhaps it is naïve to be thankful that the Movement "saved" a large 6
number of individuals and gave them something to live for, even if it did
not provide them with everything they wanted. (Materially, it provided them
with precious little that they wanted.) When a movement awakens people to
the possibilities of life, it seems unfair to frustrate them by then denying what
they had thought was offered. But what was offered? What was promised?
What was it all about? What good did it do? Would it have been better, as some

have suggested, to leave the Negro people as they were, unawakened, unallied with one another, unhopeful about what to expect for their children in some future world?

I do not think so. If knowledge of my condition is all the freedom I get 7 from a "freedom movement," it is better than unawareness, forgottenness, and hopelessness, the existence that is like the existence of a beast. Man only truly lives by knowing; otherwise he simply performs, copying the daily habits of others, but conceiving nothing of his creative possibilities as a man, and accepting someone else's superiority and his own misery.

When we are children, growing up in our parents' care, we await the 8 spark from the outside world. Sometimes our parents provide it—if we are lucky—sometimes it comes from another source far from home. We sit, paralyzed, surrounded by our anxiety and dread, hoping we will not have to grow up into the narrow world and ways we see about us. We are hungry for a life that turns us on; we yearn for a knowledge of living that will save us from our innocuous lives that resemble death. We look for signs in every strange event; we search for heroes in every unknown face.

It was just six years ago that I began to be alive. I had, of course, been 9 living before—for I am now twenty-three—but I did not really know it. And I did not know it because nobody told me that I—a pensive, yearning, typical high-school senior, but Negro—existed in the minds of others as I existed in my own. Until that time my mind was locked apart from the outer contours and complexion of my body as if it and the body were strangers. The mind possessed both thought and spirit—I wanted to be an author or a scientist—which the color of the body denied. I had never seen myself and existed as a statistic exists, or as a phantom. In the white world I walked, less real to them than a shadow; and being young and well hidden among the slums, among people who also did not exist—either in books or in films or in the government of their own lives—I waited to be called to life. And, by a miracle, I was called.

There was a commotion in our house that night in 1960. We had managed 10 to buy our first television set. It was battered and overpriced, but my mother had gotten used to watching the afternoon soap operas at the house where she worked as maid, and nothing could satisfy her on days when she did not work but a continuation of her "stories." So she pinched pennies and bought a set.

I remained listless throughout her "stories," tales of pregnancy, abor- 11 tion, hypocrisy, infidelity, and alcoholism. All these men and women were white and lived in houses with servants, long staircases that they floated down, patios where liquor was served four times a day to "relax" them. But my mother, with her swollen feet eased out of her shoes, her heavy body relaxed in our only comfortable chair, watched each movement of the smartly coiffed women, heard each word, pounced upon each innuendo and inflection, and for the duration of these "stories" she saw herself as one of them. She placed herself in every scene she saw, with her braided hair turned blond, her two hundred pounds compressed into a sleek size-seven dress, her rough dark skin smooth and *white*. Her husband became "dark and handsome," talented, witty, urbane, charming. And when she turned to look at my father sitting near her in his sweat shirt with his smelly feet raised on the bed to "air," there was always a tragic look of surprise on her face. Then she would sigh and go out to the kitchen looking lost and unsure of herself. My mother, a truly great woman who raised eight children of her own and half a dozen of the neighbors' without a single complaint, was convinced that she did not exist compared to "them." She subordinated her soul to theirs and became a faithful and timid supporter of the "Beautiful White People." Once she asked me, in a moment of vicarious pride and despair, if I didn't think that "they" were "jest naturally smarter, prettier, better." My mother asked this: a woman who never got rid of any of her children, never cheated on my father, was never a hypocrite if she could help it, and never even tasted liquor. She could not even bring herself to blame "them" for making her believe what they wanted her to believe: that if she did not look like them, think like them, be sophisticated and corrupt-for-comfort's-sake like them, she was a nobody. Black was not a color on my mother; it was a shield that made her invisible.

Of course, the people who wrote the soap-opera scripts always made the 12 Negro maids in them steadfast, trusty, and wise in a home-remedial sort of way; but my mother, a maid for nearly forty years, never once identified herself with the scarcely glimpsed black servant's face beneath the ruffled cap. Like everyone else, in her daydreams at least, she thought she was free.

Six years ago, after half-heartedly watching my mother's soap operas and 13 wondering whether there wasn't something more to be asked of life, the Civil Rights Movement came into my life. Like a good omen for the future, the face of Dr. Martin Luther King, Jr., was the first black face I saw on our new television screen. And, as in a fairy tale, my soul was stirred by the meaning for me of his mission—at the time he was being rather ignominiously dumped into a police van for having led a protest march in Alabama—and I fell in love with the sober and determined face of the Movement. The singing of "We Shall Overcome"—that song betrayed by nonbelievers in it—rang for the first time in my ears. The influence that my mother's soap operas might have had on me became impossible. The life of Dr. King, seeming bigger and more miraculous than the man himself, because of all he had done and suffered, offered a pattern of strength and sincerity I felt I could trust. He had suffered much because of his simple belief in nonviolence, love, and brotherhood. Perhaps the majority of men could not be reached through these beliefs, but because Dr. King kept trying to reach them in spite of danger to himself and his family, I saw in him the hero for whom I had waited so long.

What Dr. King promised was not a ranch-style house and an acre of mani- 14 cured lawn for every black man, but jail and finally freedom. He did not promise two cars for every family, but the courage one day for all families everywhere to walk without shame and unafraid on their own feet. He did not say that one day it will be us chasing prospective buyers out of our prosperous well-kept neighborhoods, or in other ways exhibiting our snobbery and ignorance as all other ethnic groups before us have done; what he said was that we had a right to live anywhere in this country we chose, and a right to a meaningful well-paying job to provide us with the upkeep of our homes. He did not say we had to become carbon copies of the white American middle class; but he did say we had the right to become whatever we wanted to become.

Because of the Movement, because of an awakened faith in the newness 15 and imagination of the human spirit, because of "black and white together"— for the first time in our history in some human relationship on and off TV— because of the beatings, the arrests, the hell of battle during the past years, I have fought harder for my life and for a chance to be myself, to be something more than a shadow or a number, than I had ever done before in my life. Before, there had seemed to be no real reason for struggling beyond the effort for daily bread. Now there was a chance at that other that Jesus meant when He said we could not live by bread alone.

I have fought and kicked and fasted and prayed and cursed and cried my- 16 self to the point of existing. It has been like being born again, literally. Just "knowing" has meant everything to me. Knowing has pushed me out into the world, into college, into places, into people.

Part of what existence means to me is knowing the difference between 17 what I am now and what I was then. It is being capable of looking after myself intellectually as well as financially. It is being able to tell when I am being wronged and by whom. It means being awake to protect myself and the ones I love. It means being a part of the world community, and being *alert* to which part it is that I have joined, and knowing how to change to another part if that part does not suit me. To know is to exist: to exist is to be involved, to move about, to see the world with my own eyes. This, at least, the Movement has given me.

The hippies and other nihilists would have me believe that it is all the 18 same whether the people in Mississippi have a movement behind them or not. Once they have their rights, they say, they will run all over themselves trying to be just like everybody else. They will be well fed, complacent about things of the spirit, emotionless, and without that marvelous humanity and "soul" that the Movement has seen them practice time and time again. "What has the Movement done," they ask, "with the few people it has supposedly helped?" "Got them white-collar jobs, moved them into standardized ranch houses in white neighborhoods, given them nondescript gray flannel suits?" "What are these people now?" they ask. And then they answer themselves, "Nothings!"

I would find this reasoning—which I have heard many, many times from 19 hippies and nonhippies alike—amusing if I did not also consider it serious. For I think it is a delusion, a cop-out, an excuse to disassociate themselves from a world in which they feel too little has been changed or gained. The real question, however, it appears to me, is not whether poor people will adopt the middle-class mentality once they are well fed; rather, it is whether they will ever be well fed enough to be able to choose whatever mentality they think will suit them. The lack of a movement did not keep my mother from *wishing* herself bourgeois in her daydreams.

There is widespread starvation in Mississippi. In my own state of Georgia 20
there are more hungry families than Lester Maddox[1] would like to admit—or
even see fed. I went to school with children who ate red dirt. The Movement
has prodded and pushed some liberal senators into pressuring the government for food so that the hungry may eat. Food stamps that were two dollars
and out of the reach of many families not long ago have been reduced to fifty
cents. The price is still out of the reach of some families, and the government,
it seems to a lot of people, could spare enough free food to feed its own people. It angers people in the Movement that it does not; they point to the bil-
lions in wheat we send free each year to countries abroad. Their government's slowness while people are hungry, its unwillingness to believe that
there are Americans starving, its stingy cutting of the price of food stamps,
make many Civil Rights workers throw up their hands in disgust. But they
do not give up. They do not withdraw into the world of psychedelia. They apply what pressure they can to make the government give away food to hungry
people. They do not plan so far ahead in their disillusionment with society
that they can see these starving families buying identical ranch-style houses
and sending their snobbish children to Bryn Mawr and Yale. They take first
things first and try to get them fed.

They do not consider it their business, in any case, to say what kind of 21
life the people they help must lead. How one lives is, after all, one of the
rights left to the individual—when and if he has opportunity to choose. It is
not the prerogative of the middle class to determine what is worthy of aspira-
tion. There is also every possibility that the middle-class people of tomorrow
will turn out ever so much better than those of today. I even know some
middle-class people of today who are not *all* bad.

I think there are so few Negro hippies because middle-class Negroes, 22
although well fed, are not careless. They are required by the treacherous
world they live in to be clearly aware of whoever or whatever might be trying
to do them in. They are middle class in money and position, but they cannot
afford to be middle class in complacency. They distrust the hippie movement
because they know that it can do nothing for Negroes as a group but "love"
them, which is what all paternalists claim to do. And since the only way
Negroes can survive (which they cannot do, unfortunately, on love alone) is
with the support of the group, they are wisely wary and stay away.

A white writer tried recently to explain that the reason for the relatively 23
few Negro hippies is that Negroes have built up a "super-cool" that cracks
under LSD and makes them have a "bad trip." What this writer doesn't guess
at is that Negroes are needing drugs less than ever these days for any kind
of trip. While the hippies are "tripping," Negroes are going after power, which
is so much more important to their survival and their children's survival than
LSD and pot.

Everyone would be surprised if the Israelis ignored the Arabs and took 24
up "tripping" and pot smoking. In this country we are the Israelis. Everybody

[1] **Lester Maddox** Maddox (b. 1915) achieved national attention in 1964, when he
closed his restaurant rather than allow blacks to be served. In 1966 he was elected governor
of Georgia, running on a segregationist platform.

who can do so would like to forget this, of course. But for us to forget it for a minute would be fatal. "We Shall Overcome" is just a song to most Americans, *but we must do it*. Or die.

What good was the Civil Rights Movement? If it had just given this coun- 25 try Dr. King, a leader of conscience, for once in our lifetime, it would have been enough. If it had just taken black eyes off white television stories, it would have been enough. If it had fed one starving child, it would have been enough.

If the Civil Rights Movement is "dead," and if it gave us nothing else, it 26 gave us each other forever. It gave some of us bread, some of us shelter, some of us knowledge and pride, all of us comfort. It gave us our children, our husbands, our brothers, our fathers, as men reborn and with a purpose for living. It broke the pattern of black servitude in this country. It shattered the phony "promise" of white soap operas that sucked away so many pitiful lives. It gave us history and men far greater than Presidents. It gave us heroes, selfless men of courage and strength, for our little boys and girls to follow. It gave us hope for tomorrow. It called us to life.

Because we live, it can never die.   27

[1967]

■ TOPICS FOR DISCUSSION AND WRITING

1. Walker several times refers to "the Movement," assuming that her readers (a largely academic audience, in 1967) will know what she means. Reading the essay in the 1990s, are you clear about her meaning? On the basis of Walker's essay, try to define "the Movement" for a reader uncertain of its meaning.

2. Walker says (paragraph 5) that "it is always the white man—on his radio and in his newspaper and on his television—who says that the movement is dead." She was writing in 1967. Does her statement still apply? And if anyone today—black or white—says that the movement is dead, does that person probably mean that the movement has failed, or, on the contrary, that it has succeeded and therefore is no longer needed?

3. Explain what Walker means when she says in paragraph 24, "In this country we are the Israelis." How useful do you find the analogy?

4. In paragraph 18 Walker speaks of "hippies and other nihilists." Who or what are nihilists? And, for that matter, how would you describe hippies? Does Walker's equation of hippies and nihilists strike you as fair?

5. In this essay, Walker uses language which, were the essay to appear today, would be viewed as sexist. (One aspect of sexist language is the use of masculine nouns and pronouns to refer to persons of either sex.) How might you revise the third sentence of paragraph 7 to avoid the problem?

6. In paragraph 8, generalizing from her own childhood, Walker writes: ". . . growing up in our parents' care, we await the spark from the outside world." And the paragraph concludes: "We look for signs in every strange event." Reread the paragraph and think about how much of what Walker says in this paragraph characterized your own childhood. Who

were your heroes and heroines? How did they enter your life? And how did they influence it?

7. In this essay find two or three sentences or groups of sentences that strike you as especially interesting or moving and try to account for their affect on you.

CHAPTER 5

Reading

(and Writing about)

Fiction

Stories True and False

The word "story" comes from "history"; the stories that historians, biographers, and journalists narrate are supposed to be true accounts of what happened. The stories of novelists and short-story writers, however, are admittedly untrue; they are "fiction," things made up, imagined, manufactured. As readers, we come to a supposedly true story with expectations different from those we bring to fiction.

Consider the difference between reading a narrative in a newspaper and one in a book of short stories. If, while reading a newspaper, we come across a story of, say, a subway accident, we assume that the account is true, and we read it for the information about a relatively unusual event. Anyone hurt? What sort of people? In our neighborhood? Whose fault? When we read a book of fiction, however, we do not expect to encounter literal truths; we read novels and short stories not for facts but for pleasure and for some insight or for a sense of what an aspect of life means to the writer. Consider the following short story by Grace Paley.

■ GRACE PALEY

Born in New York City, Grace Paley attended Hunter College and New York University, but left without a degree. (She now teaches at Sarah Lawrence College.) While raising two children she wrote poetry and then, in the 1950s, turned to writing fiction.

Paley's chief subject is the life of little people struggling in the Big City. Of life she has said, "How daily life is lived is a mystery to me. You write about what's mysterious to you. What is it like? Why do people do this?" Of the short story she has said, "It can be just telling a little tale, or writing a complicated philosophical story. It can be a song, almost."

Samuel

Some boys are very tough. They're afraid of nothing. They are the ones 1 who climb a wall and take a bow at the top. Not only are they brave on the roof, but they make a lot of noise in the darkest part of the cellar where even the super hates to go. They also jiggle and hop on the platform between the locked doors of the subway cars.

Four boys are jiggling on the swaying platform. Their names are Alfred, Calvin, Samuel, and Tom. The men and the women in the cars on either side watch them. They don't like them to jiggle or jump but don't want to interfere. Of course some of the men in the cars were once brave boys like these. One of them had ridden the tail of a speeding truck from New York to Rockaway Beach without getting off, without his sore fingers losing hold. Nothing happened to him then or later. He had made a compact with other boys who preferred to watch: Starting at Eighth Avenue and Fifteenth Street, he would get to some specified place, maybe Twenty-third and the river, by hopping the tops of the moving trucks. This was hard to do when one truck turned a corner in the wrong direction and the nearest truck was a couple of feet too high. He made three or four starts before succeeding. He had gotten his idea from a film at school called *The Romance of Logging*. He had finished high school, married a good friend, was in a responsible job and going to night school.

These two men and others looked at the four boys jumping and jiggling on the platform and thought, It must be fun to ride that way, especially now the weather is nice and we're out of the tunnel and way high over the Bronx. Then they thought, These kids do seem to be acting sort of stupid. They *are* little. Then they thought of some of the brave things they had done when they were boys and jiggling didn't seem so risky.

The ladies in the car became very angry when they looked at the four boys. Most of them brought their brows together and hoped the boys could see their extreme disapproval. One of the ladies wanted to get up and say, Be careful you dumb kids, get off that platform or I'll call a cop. But three of the boys were Negroes and the fourth was something else she couldn't tell for sure. She was afraid they'd be fresh and laugh at her and embarrass her. She wasn't afraid they'd hit her, but she was afraid of embarrassment. Another lady thought, Their mothers never know where they are. It wasn't true in this particular case. Their mothers all knew that they had gone to see the missile exhibit on Fourteenth Street.

Out on the platform, whenever the train accelerated, the boys would 5 raise their hands and point them up to the sky to act like rockets going off, then they rat-tat-tatted the shatterproof glass pane like machine guns, although no machine guns had been exhibited.

For some reason known only to the motorman, the train began a sudden slowdown. The lady who was afraid of embarrassment saw the boys jerk forward and backward and grab the swinging guard chains. She had her own boy at home. She stood up with determination and went to the door. She slid it open and said, "You boys will be hurt. You'll be killed. I'm going to call the conductor if you don't just go into the next car and sit down and be quiet."

Two of the boys said, "Yes'm," and acted as though they were about to go. Two of them blinked their eyes a couple of times and pressed their lips together. The train resumed its speed. The door slid shut, parting the lady and the boys. She leaned against the side door because she had to get off at the next stop.

The boys opened their eyes wide at each other and laughed. The lady blushed. The boys looked at her and laughed harder. They began to pound each other's back. Samuel laughed the hardest and pounded Alfred's back until Alfred coughed and the tears came. Alfred held tight to the chain hook. Samuel pounded him even harder when he saw the tears. He said, "Why you bawling? You a baby, huh?" and laughed. One of the men whose boyhood had been more watchful than brave became angry. He stood up straight and looked at the boys for a couple of seconds. Then he walked in a citizenly way to the end of the car, where he pulled the emergency cord. Almost at once, with a terrible hiss, the pressure of air abandoned the brakes and the wheels were caught and held.

People standing in the most secure places fell forward, then backward. Samuel had let go of his hold on the chain so he could pound Tom as well as Alfred. All the passengers in the cars whipped back and forth, but he pitched only forward and fell head first to be crushed and killed between the cars.

The train had stopped hard, halfway into the station, and the conductor 10 called at once for the trainmen who knew about this kind of death and how to take the body from the wheels and brakes. There was silence except for passengers from other cars who asked, What happened! What happened! The ladies waited around wondering if he might be an only child. The men recalled other afternoons with very bad endings. The little boys stayed close to each other, leaning and touching shoulders and arms and legs.

When the policeman knocked at the door and told her about it, Samuel's mother began to scream. She screamed all day and moaned all night, though the doctors tried to quiet her with pills.

Oh, oh, she hopelessly cried. She did not know how she could ever find another boy like that one. However, she was a young woman and she became pregnant. Then for a few months she was hopeful. The child born to her was a boy. They brought him to be seen and nursed. She smiled. But immediately she saw that this baby wasn't Samuel. She and her husband together have had other children, but never again will a boy exactly like Samuel be known.

[1968]

You might think about the ways in which "Samuel" differs from a newspaper story of an accident in a subway. (You might even want to write a newspaper version of the happening.) In some ways, of course, Paley's story faintly resembles an account that might appear in a newspaper. Journalists are taught to give information about Who, What, When, Where, and Why, and Paley does provide this. Thus, the *characters* (Samuel and others) are the journalist's Who; the *plot* (the boys were jiggling on the platform, and when a man pulled the emergency cord one of them was killed) is the What; the *setting* (the subway, presumably in modern times) is the When and the Where; the *motivation* (the irritation of the man who pulls the emergency cord) is the Why.

To write about fiction you would think about these elements of fiction, asking yourself questions about each, both separately and how they work together. Much of the rest of this chapter will be devoted to examining such words as "character" and "plot," but before you read those pages notice the following questions we've posed about "Samuel" and try responding to them. Your responses will teach you a good deal about what fiction is, and some of the ways in which it works.

■ TOPICS FOR DISCUSSION AND WRITING

1. Paley wrote the story, but an unspecified person *tells* it. Describe the voice of this narrator in the first paragraph. Is the voice neutral and objective, or do you hear some sort of attitude, a point of view? If you do hear an attitude, what words or phrases in the story indicate it?

2. What do you know about the setting of "Samuel"? What can you infer about the neighborhood?

3. In the fourth paragraph we are told that "three of the boys were Negroes and the fourth was something else." Is race important in this story? Is Samuel "Negro" or "something else"? Does it matter?

4. Exactly *why* did a man walk "in a citizenly way to the end of the car, where he pulled the emergency cord"? Do you think the author blames him? What evidence can you offer to support your view? Do *you* blame him? Or do you blame the boys? Or anyone? Explain.

5. The story is called "Samuel," and it is, surely, about him. But what happens after Samuel dies? (You might want to list the events.) What else is the story about? (You might want to comment on why you believe the items in your list are important.)

6. Can you generalize about what the men think of the jigglers and about what the women think? Is Paley saying something about the sexes? About the attitudes of onlookers in a big city?

PLOT AND CHARACTER

In some stories, such as adventure stories, the emphasis is on physical action—wanderings and strange encounters. In Paley's "Samuel," however, although there is a violent death in the subway, the emphasis is less on an unusual happening than on other things: for instance, the contrast between some of the adults, the contrast between uptight adults and energetic children, and the impact of the death on Samuel's mother.

The novelist E. M. Forster, in a short critical study entitled *Aspects of the Novel* (1927), introduced a distinction between **flat characters** and **round**

characters. A *flat character* is relatively simple and usually has only one trait: loving wife (or jealous wife), tyrannical husband (or meek husband), braggart, pedant, hypocrite, or whatever. Thus, in "Samuel" we are told about a man "whose boyhood had been more watchful than brave." This man walks "in a citizenly way" to the end of the subway car, where he pulls the emergency cord. He is, so to speak, the conventional solid citizen. He is flat, or uncomplicated, but that is probably part of what the author is getting at. A *round character,* on the other hand, embodies several or even many traits that cohere to form a complex personality. Of course in a story as short as "Samuel" we can hardly expect to find fully rounded characters, but we can say that, at least by comparison with the "citizenly" man, the man who had once been a wild kid, had gone to night school, and now holds a "responsible job" is relatively round. Paley's story asserts rather than shows the development of the character, but much fiction does show such a development. Whereas a flat character is usually *static* (at the end of the story the character is pretty much what he or she was at the start), a round character is likely to be *dynamic,* changing considerably as the story progresses.

A frequent assignment in writing courses is to set forth a character sketch, describing some person in the story or novel. In preparing such a sketch, take these points into consideration:

1. What the character says (but consider that what he or she says need not be taken at face value; the character may be hypocritical, or self-deceived, or biased—you will have to detect this from the context).
2. What the character does.
3. What other characters say about the character.
4. What others *do*. (A character who serves as a contrast to another character is called a *foil*.)

A character sketch can be complex and demanding, but usually you will want to do more than write a character sketch. You will probably discuss the character's function, or trace the development of his or her personality, or contrast the character with another. (One of the most difficult topics, the narrator's personality, will be discussed later in this chapter under the heading "Narrative Point of View.") In writing on one of these topics you will probably still want to keep in mind the four suggestions for getting at a character, but you will also want to go further, relating your findings to additional matters that we discuss later.

Most discussions of fiction are concerned with happenings and with *why* they happen. Why does Samuel die? Because (to put it too simply) his youthful high spirits clash with the values of a "citizenly" adult. Paley never explicitly says anything like this, but a reader of the story tries to make sense out of the details, filling in the gaps.

Things happen, in most good fiction, at least partly because the people have certain personalities or character traits (moral, intellectual, and emotional qualities) and, given their natures, because they respond plausibly to other personalities. What their names are and what they look like may help you to understand them, but probably the best guide to characters is what they do and what they say. As we get to know more about their drives and goals—and especially about the choices they make—we enjoy seeing the writer complete the portraits, finally presenting us with a coherent and credible picture of people in action. In this view, plot and character are inseparable. Plot is not simply a series of happenings, but happenings that come out of character, that reveal character, and that influence character. Henry James puts it thus: "What is character but the determination of incident? What is incident but the illustration of character?" James goes on: "It is an incident for a woman to stand up with her hand resting on a table and look out at you in a certain way."

FORESHADOWING

Although some stories depend heavily on a plot with a surprise ending, other stories prepare the reader for the outcome, at least to some degree. The **foreshadowing** that would eliminate surprise, or greatly reduce it, and thus destroy a story that has nothing else to offer, is a powerful tool in the hands of a writer of serious fiction. In "Samuel," the reader perhaps senses even in the first paragraph that these "tough" boys who "jiggle and hop on the platform" may be vulnerable, may come to an unfortunate end. When a woman says, "You'll be killed," the reader doesn't yet know if she is right, but a seed has been planted.

Even in such a story as Faulkner's "A Rose for Emily" (p. 540), where we are surprised to learn near the end that Miss Emily has slept beside the decaying corpse of her dead lover, from the outset we expect something strange; that is, we are not surprised by the surprise, only by its precise nature. The first sentence of the story tell us that after Miss Emily's funeral (the narrator begins at the end) the townspeople cross her threshold "out of curiosity to see the inside of her house, which no one save an old manservant . . . had seen in at least ten years." As the story progresses, we see Miss Emily prohibiting people from entering the house, we hear that after a certain point no one ever sees Homer Barron again, that "the front door remained closed," and (a few paragraphs before the end of the story) that the townspeople "knew that there was one room in that region above the stairs which no one had seen in forty years." The paragraph preceding the revelation that "the man himself lay in the bed" is devoted to a description of Homer's dust-covered clothing and toilet articles. In short, however much we are unprepared for the precise revelation, we are prepared for some strange thing in the house; and, given Miss Emily's purchase of poison and Homer's disappearance, we have some idea of what will be revealed.

James Joyce's "Araby" (p. 350) is another example of a story in which the beginning is a preparation for all that follows. Consider the first two paragraphs. (A "blind" street is a dead-end street.)

> North Richmond Street, being blind, was a quiet street except at the hour when the Christian Brothers' school set the boys free. An uninhabited house of two storeys stood at the blind end, detached from its neighbours in a square ground. The other houses of the street, conscious of decent lives within them, gazed at one another with brown imperturbable faces.

The former tenant of our house, a priest, had died in the back drawing-room. Air, musty from having been long enclosed, hung in all the rooms, and the waste room behind the kitchen was littered with old useless papers. Among these I found a few paper-covered books, the pages of which were curled and damp: *The Abbot*, by Walter Scott, *The Devout Communicant* and *The Memoirs of Vidocq*. I liked the last best because its leaves were yellow. The wild garden behind the house contained a central apple-tree and a few straggling bushes under one of which I found the late tenant's rusty bicycle pump. He had been a very charitable priest; in his will he had left all his money to institutions and the furniture of his house to his sister.

Of course the full meaning of the passage will not become apparent until you have read the entire story. In a sense, a story has at least three lives:

when we read the story sentence by sentence, trying to turn the sequence of sentences into a consistent whole;

when we have finished reading the story and we think back on it as a whole, even if we think no more than "That was a waste of time," and

when we reread a story, knowing already even as we read the first line how it will turn out at the end.

Let's assume that you have not at some earlier time read the whole of "Araby." On the basis only of a reading of the first two paragraphs, what might you highlight or underline? Here are the words that one student marked:

blind	musty
quiet	kitchen was littered
set the boys free	leaves were yellow
brown imperturbable faces	wild garden . . . apple-tree
priest	charitable priest

No two readers will come up with exactly the same list (if you live on North Richmond Street, you will probably underline it and put an exclamation mark in the margin; and if you attended a parochial school, you'll probably underline "Christian Brothers' school"), but perhaps most readers—despite their varied experience—would agree that Joyce is giving us a picture of what he elsewhere called the "paralysis" of Ireland. How the story will turn out is, of course, unknown to a first-time reader. Perhaps the paralysis will increase, or perhaps it will be broken. Joyce goes on adding sentence to sentence, trying to shape the reader's response, and the reader goes on reading, making meaning out of the sentences.

SETTING AND ATMOSPHERE

Foreshadowing normally makes use of **setting.** The setting or environment in the first two paragraphs of Joyce's "Araby" is not mere geography, not mere locale: it provides an **atmosphere,** an air that the characters breathe, a world in which they move. Narrowly speaking, the setting is the physical surroundings—the furniture, the architecture, the landscape, the climate—and these often are highly appropriate to the characters who are associated with them. Thus, in Emily Brontë's *Wuthering Heights* the passionate Earnshaw family is associated with Wuthering Heights, the storm-exposed moorland, whereas the mild Linton family is associated with Thrushcross Grange in the sheltered valley below.

Broadly speaking, setting includes not only the physical surroundings but also a point (or several points) in time. The background against which we see the characters and the happenings may be specified as morning or evening, spring or fall. In a good story, this temporal setting will probably be highly relevant; it will probably be part of the story's meaning, perhaps providing an ironic contrast to or exerting an influence on the characters.

SYMBOLISM

Writers draw on experience, but an experience is not a happening through which the author necessarily passed; rather, it may be a thought, an emotion, or a vision that is meaningful and is embodied in the piece of fiction for all to read. Inevitably the writer uses **symbols.** Symbols are neither puzzles nor colorful details but are among the concrete embodiments that give the story whatever accuracy and meaning it has. Joyce's dead-end street, dead priest, apple tree, and rusty bicycle pump all help to define very precisely the condition of a thoroughly believable Dublin. In Hemingway's *A Farewell to Arms* the river in which Frederic Henry swims when he deserts the army is a river, as material as the guns he flees from.

On the other hand, Joyce's dead-end street, dead priest, and "central apple-tree," along with many other details, may suggest Eden after the Fall, a decaying world, and (for some readers) a failed religion. Frederic Henry's swim in the river may suggest that Henry is cleansing himself from the war. The "tender" leaves mentioned at the outset of Chopin's "Ripe Figs" (p. 3) may suggest Babette's immaturity; the ripening figs may suggest a stage in her maturity, and the chrysanthemums, mentioned at the end of the story, may suggest the two older women, Maman and Frosine, enjoying an autumnal blossoming, a "second bloom," so to speak. If so, we can say that these things are symbolic; they are themselves, but they also stand for something more than themselves.

NARRATIVE POINT OF VIEW

An author must choose a **point of view** (or sometimes, several points of view) from which he or she will narrate the story. The choice will contribute to the total effect that the story will have.

Narrative points of view can be divided into two sorts: **participant** (or **first-person**) and **nonparticipant** (or **third-person**). That is, the narrator may or may not be a character who participates in the story. Each of these two divisions can be subdivided:

I.　Participant (first-person)

　　A.　Narrator as a major character
　　B.　Narrator as a minor character

II.　Nonparticipant (third-person)

　　A.　Omniscient
　　B.　Selective omniscient
　　C.　Objective

Participant Points of View

In Frank O'Connor's "Guests of the Nation" (p. 355), the narrator is a major character. He, and not O'Connor, tells the story, and the story is chiefly about him; hence one can say that O'Connor uses a first-person (or participant) point of view. O'Connor has invented an Irishman who has fought against the English, and this narrator tells of the impact a happening had on him: "And anything that happened to me afterwards, I never felt the same about again."

But sometimes a first-person narrator tells a story that focuses on someone other than the narrator; he or she is a minor character, a peripheral witness, for example, to a story about Sally Jones, and we get the story of Sally filtered through, say, the eyes of her friend or brother or cat.

Nonparticipant Points of View

In a nonparticipant (third-person) point of view, the teller of the tale does not introduce himself or herself as a character. If the point of view is **omniscient,** the narrator relates what he or she wants to relate about the thoughts as well as the deeds of all the characters. The omniscient teller can enter the mind of any character; whereas the first-person narrator can only say "I was angry" or "Jack seemed angry," the omniscient teller can say, "Jack was inwardly angry but gave no sign; Jill continued chatting, but she sensed his anger." Thus, in Paley's "Samuel," the narrator tells us that Samuel's mother was "hopeful," but when the new baby was born "immediately she saw that this baby wasn't Samuel."

Furthermore, a distinction can be made between **neutral omniscience** (the narrator recounts deeds and thoughts but does not judge) and **editorial omniscience** (the narrator not only recounts but also judges). An editorially omniscient narrator knows what goes on in the minds of all the characters and might comment approvingly or disapprovingly: "He closed the book, having finished the story, but, poor fellow, he had missed the meaning."

Because a short story can scarcely hope to develop a picture of several minds effectively, authors may prefer to limit their omniscience to the minds of a few of their characters, or even to that of only one of the characters; that is, they may use **selective omniscience** as the point of view. Selective omniscience provides a focus, especially if it is limited to a single character. When thus limited, the author sees one character from outside and from inside, but sees the other characters only from the outside and from the impact they have on the mind of this selected receptor. When selective omniscience attempts to record mental activity ranging from consciousness to the unconscious, from clear perceptions to confused longings, it is sometimes labeled the **stream-of-consciousness** point of view. The following example is from Katherine Anne Porter's "The Jilting of Granny Weatherall" (p. 930):

> Her eyelids wavered and let in streamers of blue-gray light like tissue paper over her eyes. She must get up and pull the shades down or she'd never sleep. She was in bed again and the shades were not down. How could that happen? Better turn over, hide from the light, sleeping in the light gave you nightmares. "Mother, how do you feel now?" and a stinging wetness on her forehead. But I don't like having my face washed in cold water!

Finally, sometimes a third-person narrator does not enter even a single mind but records only what crosses an apparently dispassionate eye and ear. Such a point of view is **objective** (sometimes called the **camera** or **fly-on-the-wall** point of view). The absence of editorializing and of dissection of the mind often produces the effect of a play; we see and hear the characters in action. Much of Hemingway's "A Clean, Well-Lighted Place" (p. 937) is objective, consisting of bits of dialogue that make the story look like a play:

> "Last week he tried to commit suicide," one waiter said.
> "Why?"
> "He was in despair."
> "What about?"
> "Nothing."
> "How do you know it was nothing?"
> "He has plenty of money."
> They sat together at a table that was close against the wall near the door of the café and looked at the terrace where the tables were all empty except where the old man sat in the shadow of the leaves of the tree that moved slightly in the wind. A girl and a soldier went by in the street. The street light shone on the brass number on his collar. The girl wore no head covering and hurried beside him.
> "The guard will pick him up," one waiter said.
> "What does it matter if he gets what he's after?"

Style and Point of View

If you reread the preceding quotation from Hemingway's "A Clean, Well-Lighted Place," you will notice that except for one long sentence (immediately after the dialogue), it consists chiefly of short (and for the most part simple) sentences. The dialogue is almost abrupt, but even the other material strikes a reader as—well, not so much as "objective" as something else, though we may find it hard to give a name to what we hear. Let's begin by looking at the long sentence:

> They sat together at a table that was close against the wall near the door of the café and looked at the terrace where the tables were all empty except where the old man sat in the shadow of the leaves of the tree that moved slightly in the wind.

A sentence of fifty words is unusual, but what besides its length gives this sentence its distinctive sound? Suppose we rewrite it, keeping the essential information and even keeping it as one sentence:

> Sitting together at a table close against the wall near the door of the café, they looked at the terrace, whose tables were empty except one where the old man sat in the shadow of the leaves of a tree moved slightly by the wind.

The chief changes are these: Instead of Hemingway's "they sat . . . and looked," we have used subordination ("Sitting . . . , they looked"), and we have eliminated the flatness or bleakness of Hemingway's "that . . . where . . . where . . . that." Our sentence is almost as long as Hemingway's, but the impression it makes on a reader is different. (How might you describe the difference?) It contains the same information, but—on the highest level, so to speak—it says something different because its *style* is different, just as in daily life "Hi" says something a little different from "How do you do?" And a difference in style is a difference in meaning.

Just as we rewrote Hemingway's long sentence, we can rewrite his short sentences, this time combining three sentences into one. First, here is Hemingway's version:

> A girl and a soldier went by in the street. The street light shone on the brass number on his collar. The girl wore no head covering and hurried beside him.

Now our revision, into one sentence:

> A bare-headed girl and a soldier passed by, the girl hurrying to keep up with the man, whose brass number on his collar glittered under the street light.

The information again is roughly the same, but again the effect is different. Because the choppiness is gone, the bleakness is gone, or at least it is much less evident. We are, so to speak, in a subtly different world. Why? Because the *style* is different. Hemingway's short, almost disconnected sentences, then, do not really give an objective view of something "out there"; rather, Hemingway's choice of certain words and certain grammatical constructions *creates* what is allegedly "out there."

Obviously a story told by a first-person narrator will have a distinctive style—let's say the voice of an adolescent boy, or an elderly widow, or a madman. The voice of a third-person narrator—especially the voice of a supposedly objective narrator—will be much less distinctive, but if, especially on rereading, you listen carefully, you will probably hear a distinctive tone. (Look, for instance, at the first paragraph of Grace Paley's "Samuel.") Put it this way: Even a supposedly objective point of view is not purely objective, since it represents the writer's choice of a style, a way of reporting material with an apparently dispassionate voice.

After reading a story, you may want to think at least briefly about what the story might be like if told from a different point of view. You may find it instructive, for instance, to rewrite "Samuel" from the "citizenly" man's point of view, or "Ripe Figs" from Babette's.

DETERMINING AND DISCUSSING THE THEME

First, we can distinguish between story and theme in fiction. *Story* is concerned with "How does it turn out? What happens?" But **theme** is concerned with "What is it about? What does it add up to? What motif holds the happenings together? What does it make of life, and, perhaps, what wisdom does it offer?" In a good work of fiction, the details add up, or, to use Flannery O'Connor's words, they are "controlled by some overall purpose." In F. Scott Fitzgerald's *The Great Gatsby*, for example, there are many references to popular music, especially to jazz. These references contribute to our sense of the reality of Fitzgerald's depiction of America in the 1920s, but they do more: They help to comment on the shallowness of the white middle-class characters and they sometimes (very gently) remind us of an alternative culture. One might study Fitzgerald's references to music with an eye toward getting a deeper understanding of what the novel is about.

Suppose we think for a moment about the theme of Paley's "Samuel." Do we sense an "overall purpose" that holds the story together? Different readers inevitably will come up with different readings, that is, with different views of what the story is about. Here is one student's version:

    Whites cannot understand the feelings of blacks.

This statement gets an important element in the story—the conflict between the sober-minded adults and the jiggling boys, but it apparently assumes that all of the adults are white, an inference that cannot be supported by pointing to evidence in the story. Further, we cannot be certain that Samuel is black. And, finally, even if Samuel and his mother are black, surely white readers *do understand his youthful enthusiasm and his mother's inconsolable grief.*

    Here is a second statement:

    One should not interfere with the actions of others.

Does the story really offer such specific advice? This version of the theme seems to us to reduce the story to a too-simple code of action, a heartless rule of behavior, a rule that seems at odds with the writer's awareness of the mother's enduring grief.

A third version:

> Middle-class adults, acting from what seem to them
> to be the best of motives, may cause irreparable harm
> and grief.

This last statement seems to us to be one that can be fully supported by checking it against the story, but other equally valid statements can probably be made. How would you put it?

Summing Up: Getting Ideas for Writing about Fiction

Here are some questions that may help to stimulate ideas about stories. Not every question is, of course, relevant to every story, but if after reading a story and thinking about it, you then run your eye over these questions, you will probably find some questions that will help you to think further about the story—in short, that will help you to get ideas.

As we have said in earlier chapters, it's best to do your thinking with a pen or pencil in hand. If some of the following questions seem to you to be especially relevant to the story you will be writing about, jot down—freely, without worrying about spelling—your initial responses, interrupting your writing only to glance again at the story when you feel the need to check the evidence.

PLOT

1. Does the plot grow out of the characters, or does it depend on chance or coincidence? Did something at first strike you as irrelevant that later you perceived as relevant? Do some parts continue to strike you as irrelevant?

2. Does surprise play an important role, or does foreshadowing? If surprise is very important, can the story be read a second time with any interest? If so, what gives it this further interest?

3. What conflicts does the story include? Conflicts of one character against another? Of one character against the setting, or against society? Conflicts within a single character?

4. Are certain episodes narrated out of chronological order? If so, were you puzzled? Annoyed? On reflection, does the arrangement of episodes seem effective? Why, or why not? Are certain situations repeated? If so, what do you make out of the repetitions?

CHARACTER

1. Which character chiefly engages your interest? Why?
2. What purposes do minor characters serve? Do you find some who by their similarities and differences help to define each other or help to define the major character? How else is a particular character defined—by his or her words, actions (including thoughts and emotions), dress, setting, narrative point of view? Do certain characters act differently in the same, or in a similar, situation?
3. How does the author reveal character? By explicit authorial (editorial) comment, for instance, or, on the other hand, by revelation through dialogue? Through depicted action? Through the actions of other characters? How are the author's methods especially suited to the whole of the story?
4. Is the behavior plausible—that is, are the characters well motivated?
5. If a character changes, why and how does he or she change? (You may want to jot down each event that influences a change.) Or did you change your attitude toward a character not because the character changes but because you came to know the character better?
6. Are the characters round or flat? Are they complex, or, on the other hand, highly typical (for instance, one-dimensional representatives of a social class or age)? Are you chiefly interested in a character's psychology, or does the character strike you as standing for something, such as honesty or the arrogance of power?
7. How has the author caused you to sympathize with certain characters? How does your response—your sympathy or lack of sympathy—contribute to your judgment of the conflict?

POINT OF VIEW

1. Who tells the story? How much does the narrator know? Does the narrator strike you as reliable? What effect is gained by using this narrator?
2. How does the point of view help shape the theme? After all, the basic story of "Little Red Riding Hood"—what happens—remains unchanged whether told from the wolf's point of view or the girl's, but (to simplify grossly) if we hear the story from the wolf's point of view, we may feel that the story is about terrifying yet pathetic compulsive behavior; if from the girl's point of view, about terrified innocence.
3. It is sometimes said that the best writers are subversive, forcing readers to see something they do not want to see—something that is true but that violates their comfortable conventional ideas. Does this story oppose comfortable conventional views?
4. Does the narrator's language help you to construct a picture of the narrator's character, class, attitude, strengths, and limitations? (Jot down

some evidence, such as colloquial or—on the other hand—formal expressions, ironic comments, figures of speech.) How far can you trust the narrator? Why?

SETTING

1. Do you have a strong sense of the time and place? Is the story very much about, say, New England Puritanism, or race relations in the South in the late nineteenth century, or midwestern urban versus small-town life? If time and place are important, how and at what points in the story has the author conveyed this sense? If you do not strongly feel the setting, do you think the author should have made it more evident?
2. What is the relation of the setting to the plot and the characters? (For instance, do houses or rooms or their furnishings say something about their residents?) Would anything be lost if the descriptions of the setting were deleted from the story or the setting were changed?

SYMBOLISM

1. Do certain characters seem to you to stand for something in addition to themselves? Does the setting—whether a house, a farm, a landscape, a town, a period—have an extra dimension?)
2. If you do believe that the story has symbolic elements, do you think they are adequately integrated within the story, or do they strike you as being too obviously stuck in?

STYLE

1. How has the point of view shaped or determined the style?
2. How would you characterize the style? Simple? Understated? Figurative? Or what, and why?
3. Do you think that the style is consistent? If it isn't—for instance, if there are shifts from simple sentences to highly complex ones—what do you make of the shifts?

THEME

1. Is the title informative? What does it mean or suggest? Did the meaning seem to change after you read the story? Does the title help you to formulate a theme? If you had written the story, what title would you use?
2. Do certain passages—dialogue or description—seem to you to point especially toward the theme? Do you find certain repetitions of words or pairs of incidents highly suggestive and helpful in directing your thoughts

toward stating a theme? Flannery O'Connor, in *Mystery and Manners*, says, "In good fiction, certain of the details will tend to accumulate meaning from the action of the story itself, and when that happens, they become symbolic in the way they work." Does this story work that way?

3. Is the meaning of the story embodied in the whole story, or does it seem stuck in, for example in certain passages of editorializing?

4. Suppose someone asked you to state the point—the theme—of the story. Could you? And if you could, would you say that the theme of a particular story reinforces values you hold, or does it to some degree challenge them? Or is the concept of a theme irrelevant to this story?

Writing Fiction about Fiction

Your instructor may ask you to write a short story, perhaps even a story in the style of one of the authors you have studied, or a story that is in some way a variation of—perhaps a modernization of, or a response to—one of the stories you have studied. If you have read Poe's "The Cask of Amontillado," for instance, you might rewrite the story, setting it in the present and telling it from the point of view of the victim instead of the point of view of the murderer. And you might vary the plot, so that the would-be murderer is outwitted by the man who (he thinks) is so stupid.

Such an exercise, which requires you to read and reread a model, will teach you a good deal about the ways in which your author uses language and about the ways in which he or she uses the conventions of fiction. In short, you will learn much about the art of the short story. One thing you will surely learn is that writing a story is difficult; another is that it can be fun.

Here is an example, written by Lola Lee Loveall for a course taught by Diana Muir at Solano Community College. Ms. Loveall's story is a response to Kate Chopin's "The Story of an Hour" (p. 12). Notice that Loveall's first sentence is close to her source—a good way to get started, but by no means the only way; notice, too, that elsewhere in her story she occasionally echoes Chopin—for instance, in the references to the treetops, the sparrows, and the latchkey. A reader enjoys detecting these echoes.

What is especially interesting, however, is that before she conceived her story Loveall presumably said to herself something like, "Well, Chopin's story is superb, but suppose we shift the focus a bit. Suppose we think about what it would be like, *from the husband's point of view,* to live with a woman who suffered from 'heart trouble,' a person whom one had to treat with 'great care' " (Chopin's words, in the first sentence of "The Story of an Hour"). "And what about Mrs. Mallard's sister, Josephine—so considerate of Mrs. Mallard? What, exactly, would *Mr.* Mallard think of her? Wouldn't he see her as a pain in the neck? And what might he be prompted to do? That is, how might this character in this situation respond?" And so Loveall's characters and her plot began to take shape. As part of the game, she committed herself to writing a plot that, in its broad outline, resembled Chopin's by being highly ironic. But read it yourself.

Lola Lee Loveall
English 6

The Ticket
(A Different View of "The Story of an Hour")

Knowing full well his wife was afflicted with heart
trouble, Brently Mallard wondered how he was going to
break the news about the jacket. As he strode along his
boots broke through the shallow crust from the recent
rain, and dust kicked up from the well-worn wagon road
came up to flavor his breathing. At least, the gentle
spring rain had settled the dusty powder even as it had
sprinkled his stiffly starched shirt which was already
dampened from the exertion of stamping along. The
strenuous pace he set himself to cover the intervening
miles home helped him regain his composure. Mr. Brently
Mallard was always calm, cool, and confident.

However, he hadn't been this morning when he
stepped aboard the train, took off his jacket and
folded it neatly beside him, and settled in his seat on
the westbound train. He had been wildly excited.
Freedom was his. He was Free! He was off for
California, devil take the consequences! He would be
his old self again, let the chips fall where they may.
And he would have been well on his way, too, if that
accursed ticket agent hadn't come bawling out, "Mr.
Mallard, you left your ticket on the counter!" just
when Mallard himself had spied that nosy Jan Ardan
bidding her sister goodbye several car lengths down the
depot. How could he be so unfortunate to run into them
both twice this morning? Earlier, they had come into
the bank just as the banker had extended the thick
envelope.

"You understand, this is just an advance against
the estate for a while?"

Only Mallard's persuasiveness could have extracted that amount from the cagey old moneybags.

Mallard had carefully tucked it into his inside pocket.

This was the kind of spring day to fall in love—or lure an adventurer to the top of the next hill. Sparrows hovered about making happy sounds. Something about their movements reminded Mallard of his wife—quick, fluttering, then darting away.

He had loved her at first for her delicate ways. They had made a dashing pair—he so dark and worldly, she so fragile and fair—but her delicacy was a trap, for it disguised the heart trouble, bane of his life. Oh, he still took her a sip of brandy in bed in the morning as the doctor had suggested, although, of course, it wasn't his bed anymore. He had moved farther down the hall not long after her sister, Josephine, came to help, quick to come when Mrs. Mallard called, even in the middle of the night. After one such sudden appearance one night—"I thought I heard you call"—he had given up even sharing the same bed with his wife, although there had been little real sharing there for some time.

"No children!" the doctor had cautioned.

Mallard concentrated harder on the problem of the missing jacket. What to say? She would notice. Maybe not right away, but she would be aware. Oh, he knew Louise's reaction. She would apparently take the news calmly, then make a sudden stab toward her side with her delicate hands, then straighten and walk away—but not before he observed. A new jacket would cost money. Discussing money made the little drama happen more often, so now Mr. Mallard handled all the financial affairs, protecting her the best he could. After all, it was her inheritance, and he took great care with it, but there were the added costs: doctors, Josephine living with them, the medications, even his wife's brandy. Why, he checked it daily to be sure it was the proper strength. Of course, a man had to have a few pleasures, even if the cards did seem to fall against him more often than not. He manfully kept trying.

Everyone has a limit, though, and Mr. Mallard had reached his several days ago when the doctor had cautioned him again.

"She may go on like she is for years, or she may just keel over any time. However, the chances are she will gradually go downhill and need continual care. It is impossible to tell."

Mallard could not face "gradually go downhill." His manhood revolted against it. He was young, full of life. Let Josephine carry the chamber pot! After Louise's demise (whenever that occurred!) the simple estate which she had inherited reverted to Josephine. Let her earn it. Also, good old friend Richards was always about with a suggestion here or a word of comfort there for Louise. They'd really not care too much if Mallard were a long time absent.

As he drew nearer his home, Mallard continued to try to calm his composure, which was difficult for he kept hearing the sound of the train wheels as it pulled away, jacket, envelope, and all, right before his panic-stricken eyes: CALIFORNIA; California; california; california.

DUTY! It was his duty not to excite Louise. As he thought of duty he unconsciously squared his drooping shoulders, and the image of Sir Galahad flitted across his mind.

The treetops were aglow in the strange afterlight of the storm. A shaft of sunlight shot through the leaves and fell upon his face. He had come home.

He opened the front door with the latchkey.
Fortunately, it had been in his pants pocket.

Later, the doctors did not think Mr. Mallard's
reaction unusual, even when a slight smile appeared on
the bereaved husband's face. Grief causes strange
reactions.

"He took it like a man," they said.

Only later, when the full significance of his loss
reached him, did he weep.

Four Short Stories

■ EDGAR ALLAN POE

Edgar Allan Poe (1809–1849) was the son of traveling actors. His
father abandoned the family almost immediately, and his mother died
when Poe was two. The child was adopted—though never legally—by a
prosperous merchant and his wife in Richmond. The tensions were great,
aggravated by Poe's drinking and heavy gambling, and in 1827 Poe left
Richmond for Boston. He wrote, served briefly in the army, attended
West Point but left within a year, and became an editor for the remaining
eighteen years of his life. It was during these years, too, that he wrote
the poems, essays, and fiction—especially detective stories and horror
stories—that have made him famous.

The Cask of Amontillado

The thousand injuries of Fortunato I had borne as I best could, but when
he ventured upon insult, I vowed revenge. You, who so well know the nature
of my soul, will not suppose, however, that I gave utterance to a threat. At
length I would be avenged; this was a point definitely settled—but the very
definitiveness with which it was resolved precluded the idea of risk. I must
not only punish with impunity. A wrong is unredressed when retribution overtakes its redresser. It is equally unredressed when the avenger fails to make
himself felt as such to him who has done the wrong.

It must be understood that neither by word nor deed had I given Fortunato cause to doubt my good will. I continued, as was my wont, to smile in his
face, and he did not perceive that my smile *now* was at the thought of his
immolation.

He had a weak point—this Fortunato—although in other regards he was
a man to be respected and even feared. He prided himself on his connoisseur-
ship in wine. Few Italians have the true virtuoso spirit. For the most part
their enthusiasm is adopted to suit the time and opportunity to practice im-
posture upon the British and Austrian *millionaires*. In painting and gemmary

Fortunato, like his countrymen, was a quack, but in the matter of old wines he was sincere. In this respect I did not differ from him materially;—I was skillful in the Italian vintages myself, and bought largely whenever I could.

It was about dusk, one evening during the supreme madness of the carnival season, that I encountered my friend. He accosted me with excessive warmth, for he had been drinking much. The man wore motley. He had on a tight-fitting parti-striped dress, and his head was surmounted by the conical cap and bells. I was so pleased to see him, that I thought I should never have done wringing his hand.

I said to him— "My dear Fortunato, you are luckily met. How remarkably well you are looking to-day! But I have received a pipe[1] of what passes for Amontillado, and I have my doubts."

"How?" said he, "Amontillado? A pipe? Impossible! And in the middle of the carnival?"

"I have my doubts," I replied; "and I was silly enough to pay the full Amontillado price without consulting you in the matter. You were not to be found, and I was fearful of losing a bargain."

"Amontillado!"

"I have my doubts."

"Amontillado!"

"And I must satisfy them."

"Amontillado!"

"As you are engaged, I am on my way to Luchesi. If any one has a critical turn, it is he. He will tell me— "

"Luchesi cannot tell Amontillado from Sherry."

"And yet some fools will have it that his taste is a match for your own."

"Come, let us go."

"Whither?"

"To your vaults."

"My friend, no; I will not impose upon your good nature. I perceive you have an engagement. Luchesi—"

"I have no engagement; come."

"My friend, no. It is not the engagement, but the severe cold with which I perceive you are afflicted. The vaults are insufferably damp. They are encrusted with nitre."

"Let us go, nevertheless. The cold is merely nothing. Amontillado! You have been imposed upon; and as for Luchesi, he cannot distinguish Sherry from Amontillado."

Thus speaking, Fortunato possessed himself of my arm. Putting on a mask of black silk, and drawing a *roquelaure*[2] closely about my person, I suffered him to hurry me to my palazzo.

There were no attendants at home; they had absconded to make merry in honor of the time. I had told them that I should not return until the morning, and had given them explicit orders not to stir from the house. These

[1]**pipe** wine cask
[2]*roquelaure* short cloak

orders were sufficient, I well knew, to insure their immediate disappearance, one and all, as soon as my back was turned.

I took from their sconces two flambeaux, and giving one to Fortunato, bowed him through several suites of rooms to the archway that led into the vaults. I passed down a long and winding staircase, requesting him to be cautious as he followed. We came at length to the foot of the descent, and stood together on the damp ground of the catacombs of the Montresors.

The gait of my friend was unsteady, and the bells upon his cap jingled as he strode.

"The pipe," said he.

"It is farther on," said I; "but observe the white web-work which gleams from these cavern walls."

He turned towards me, and looked into my eyes with two filmy orbs that distilled the rheum of intoxication.

"Nitre?" he asked, at length.

"Nitre," I replied. "How long have you had that cough?"

"Ugh! ugh! ugh!—ugh! ugh! ugh!—ugh! ugh! ugh!—ugh! ugh! ugh!—ugh! ugh! ugh!"

My poor friend found it impossible to reply for many minutes.

"It is nothing," he said, at last.

"Come," I said, with decision, "we will go back; your health is precious. You are rich, respected, admired, beloved; you are happy, as once I was. You are a man to be missed. For me it is no matter. We will go back; you will be ill, and I cannot be responsible. Besides, there is Luchesi— "

"Enough," he said; "the cough is a mere nothing: it will not kill me. I shall not die of a cough."

"True—true," I replied; "and, indeed, I had no intention of alarming you unnecessarily—but you should use all proper caution. A draught of this Medoc will defend us from the damps."

Here I knocked off the neck of a bottle which I drew from a long row of its fellows that lay upon the mould.

"Drink," I said, presenting him the wine.

He raised it to his lips with a leer. He paused and nodded to me familiarly, while his bells jingled.

"I drink," he said, "to the buried that repose around us."

"And I to your long life."

He again took my arm, and we proceeded.

"These vaults," he said, "are extensive."

"The Montresors," I replied, "were a great and numerous family."

"I forget your arms."

"A huge human foot d'or, in a field azure; the foot crushes a serpent rampant whose fangs are imbedded in the heel."

"And the motto?"

"Nemo me impune lacessit." [3]

[3] *Nemo me impune lacessit* No one dare attack me with impunity (the motto of Scotland)

"Good!" he said.

The wine sparkled in his eyes and the bells jingled. My own fancy grew warm with the Medoc. We had passed through walls of piled bones, with casks and puncheons intermingling, into the inmost recesses of the catacombs. I paused again, and this time I made bold to seize Fortunato by an arm above the elbow.

"The nitre!" I said; "see, it increases. It hangs like moss upon the vaults. We are below the river's bed. The drops of moisture tickle among the bones. Come, we will go back ere it is too late. Your cough— "

"It is nothing," he said; "let us go on. But first, another draught of the Medoc."

I broke and reached him a flagon of De Grâve. He emptied it at a breath. His eyes flashed with a fierce light. He laughed and threw the bottle upwards with a gesticulation I did not understand.

I looked at him in surprise. He repeated the movement—a grotesque one.

"You do not comprehend?" he said.

"Not I," I replied.

"Then you are not of the brotherhood."

"How?"

"You are not of the masons." [4]

"Yes, yes," I said, "yes, yes."

"You? Impossible! A mason?"

"A mason," I replied.

"A sign," he said.

"It is this," I answered, producing a trowel from beneath the folds of my *roquelaure*.

"You jest," he exclaimed, recoiling a few paces. "But let us proceed to the Amontillado."

"Be it so," I said, replacing the tool beneath the cloak, and again offering him my arm. He leaned upon it heavily. We continued our route in search of the Amontillado. We passed through a range of low arches, descended, passed on, and descending again, arrived at a deep crypt, in which the foulness of the air caused our flambeaux rather to glow than flame.

At the most remote end of the crypt there appeared another less spacious. Its walls had been lined with human remains piled to the vault overhead, in the fashion of the great catacombs of Paris. Three sides of this interior crypt were still ornamented in this manner. From the fourth the bones had been thrown down, and lay promiscuously upon the earth, forming at one point a mound of some size. Within the wall thus exposed by the displacing of the bones, we perceived a still interior recess, in depth about four feet, in width three, in height six or seven. It seemed to have been constructed for no especial use within itself, but formed merely the interval between two of the colossal supports of the roof of the catacombs, and was backed by one of their circumscribing walls of solid granite.

[4] **of the masons** i.e., a member of the Freemasons, an international secret fraternity

It was in vain that Fortunato, uplifting his dull torch, endeavored to pry into the depths of the recess. Its termination the feeble light did not enable us to see.

"Proceed," I said; "herein is the Amontillado. As for Luchesi— "

"He is an ignoramus," interrupted my friend, as he stepped unsteadily forward, while I followed immediately at his heels. In an instant he had reached the extremity of the niche, and finding his progress arrested by the rock, stood stupidly bewildered. A moment more and I had fettered him to the granite. In its surface were two iron staples, distant from each other about two feet, horizontally. From one of these depended a short chain, from the other a padlock. Throwing the links about his waist, it was but the work of a few seconds to secure it. He was too much astounded to resist. Withdrawing the key I stepped back from the recess.

"Pass your hand," I said, "over the wall; you cannot help feeling the nitre. Indeed it is *very* damp. Once more let me *implore* you to return. No? Then I must positively leave you. But I must first render you all the little attentions in my power."

"The Amontillado!" ejaculated my friend, not yet recovered from his astonishment.

"True," I replied; "the Amontillado."

As I said these words I busied myself among the pile of bones of which I have before spoken. Throwing them aside, I soon uncovered a quantity of building-stone and mortar. With these materials and with the aid of my trowel, I began vigorously to wall up the entrance of the niche.

I had scarcely laid the first tier of masonry when I discovered that the intoxication of Fortunato had in a great measure worn off. The earliest indication I had of this was a low moaning cry from the depth of the recess. It was *not* the cry of a drunken man. There was then a long and obstinate silence. I laid the second tier, and the third, and the fourth; and then I heard the furious vibrations of the chain. The noise lasted for several minutes, during which, that I might hearken to it with the more satisfaction, I ceased my labors and sat down upon the bones. When at last the clanking subsided, I resumed the trowel, and finished without interruption the fifth, the sixth, and the seventh tier. The wall was now nearly upon a level with my breast. I again paused, and holding the flambeaux over the masonwork, threw a few feeble rays upon the figure within.

A succession of loud and shrill screams, bursting suddenly from the throat of the chained form, seemed to thrust me violently back. For a brief moment I hesitated—I trembled. Unsheathing my rapier, I began to grope with it about the recess; but the thought of an instant reassured me. I placed my hand upon the solid fabric of the catacombs, and felt satisfied. I reapproached the wall. I replied to the yells of him who clamored. I re-echoed—I aided—I surpassed them in volume and in strength. I did this, and the clamorer grew still.

It was now midnight, and my task was drawing to a close. I had completed the eighth, the ninth, and the tenth tier. I had finished a portion of the last and the eleventh; there remained but a single stone to be fitted and plastered in. I struggled with its weight; I placed it partially in its destined position. But now there came from out the niche a low laugh that erected the hairs upon my head. It was succeeded by a sad voice, which I had difficulty in recognizing as that of the noble Fortunato. The voice said—

"Ha! ha! ha!—he! he! he!—a very good joke indeed—an excellent jest. We will have many a rich laugh about it at the palazzo—he! he! he!—over our wine—he! he! he!"

"The Amontillado!" I said.

"He! he! he!—he! he! he!—yes, the Amontillado. But is it not getting late? Will not they be awaiting us at the palazzo, the Lady Fortunato and the rest? Let us be gone."

"Yes," I said, "let us be gone."

"For the love of God, Montresor!"

"Yes," I said, "for the love of God!"

But to these words I hearkened in vain for a reply. I grew impatient. I called aloud;

"Fortunato!"

No answer. I called again;

"Fortunato!"

No answer still. I thrust a torch through the remaining aperture and let it fall within. There came forth in return only a jingling of the bells. My heart grew sick—on account of the dampness of the catacombs. I hastened to make an end of my labor. I forced the last stone into its position; I plastered it up. Against the new masonry I reerected the old rampart of bones. For the half of a century no mortal has disturbed them. *In pace requiescat!*[5]

[1846]

■ TOPICS FOR DISCUSSION AND WRITING

1. To whom does Montresor tell his story? The story he tells happened fifty years earlier. Do we have any clues as to why he tells it now?

2. At the end of the story we learn that the murder occurred fifty years ago. Would the story be equally effective if Poe had had Montresor reveal that fact at the outset? Why, or why not?

3. Poe sets Montresor's story at dusk, "during the supreme madness of the carnival season." What is the "carnival season"? (If you are uncertain as to the meaning of "carnival," consult a dictionary.) What details of the story derive from the setting?

4. In the justifiably famous first line Montresor declares, "The thousand injuries of Fortunato I had borne as I best could, but when he ventured upon insult, I vowed revenge." Do we ever learn what those injuries and that insult were? What do we learn about Montresor from this declaration?

5. How does Montresor characterize Fortunato? What details of his portrait unwittingly enlist our sympathy for Fortunato? Does Montresor betray any sympathy for his victim?

6. "The Cask of Amontillado" is sometimes referred to as a "horror tale."

[5] *In pace requiescat!* May he rest in peace!

Do you think it has anything in common with horror movies? If so, what? (You might begin by making a list of the characteristics of horror movies.) Why do people take pleasure in horror movies? Does this story offer any of the same sorts of pleasure? In any case, why might a reader take pleasure in this story?

7. Construct a definition of madness (you may want to do a little research, but if you make use of your findings, be sure to give credit to your sources) and write an essay of 500–750 words arguing whether or not Montresor is mad. (*Note:* You may want to distinguish between Montresor at the time of the killing and Montresor at the present.)

8. If you have read Shiga's "Han's Crime" (page 133), do you think the judge would have found Montresor guilty? And if he found Montresor guilty, guilty of what? Explain, in an essay of 500 words.

■ SHIGA NAOYA (1883–1971)

Shiga (in Japanese, the family name is written first) was born into a rich family in Japan, in the harbor town of Ishinomaki. His mother died when he was twelve; his father, an official in a bank, took a second wife, and although the boy got along with his stepmother, he quarreled with his father, whom he regarded as grossly materialistic. Shiga published one novel, translated as *A Dark Night's Passing*, but he is chiefly known for his short stories, especially those dealing with family relationships.

Han's Crime

Translated by Lane Dunlop

In an unusual incident, a young Chinese juggler called Han severed his wife's carotid artery during a performance with a knife the size of a carver. The young wife died on the spot. Han was immediately arrested.

The act was witnessed by the owner-manager of the troupe, a Chinese stagehand, the introducer, and an audience of over three hundred. A policeman, sitting on a chair set up slightly above and at the edge of the audience, also saw it. But it was not at all known whether this incident, which had occurred before so many eyes, was a deliberate act or an accident.

For this performance, Han made his wife stand in front of a thick board the size of a rain shutter. From a distance of twelve feet, he hurled several of the carver-sized knives, each with a shout, to form an outline of her body not two inches removed from it.

The judge commenced by interrogating the owner-manager.

"Is that performance a particularly difficult one?"

"No. For an experienced performer, it is not that difficult. All that's required is an alert, healthy state of mind."

"If that's so, an incident like this should not have happened even as a mistake."

"Of course, unless one is sure of the performer—extremely sure—one cannot allow the performance."

"Well, then. Do you think it was a deliberate act?"

"No. I don't. The performance requires experience, instinctive skill and nothing else. But one cannot say that it will always come off with a machine-like precision. It's a fact that we never thought something like this would happen. But I do not think it is fair, now that is *has* happened, to say that we had considered the possibility and hold it against us."

"Well, what do you think it was?"

"I don't know."

The judge was perplexed. There was, here, the fact of homicide. But there was absolutely no proof as to whether it was premeditated murder or manslaughter (if the former, the judge thought, there was never such a cunning murder as this). Next calling in the Chinese stagehand, who had served with the troupe longer than Han, the judge questioned him.

"What is Han's ordinary behavior like?"

"He's a good person. He doesn't gamble, fool around with other women, or drink. About a year ago, he converted to Christianity. His English is good, and when he has the time he often reads collections of sermons."

"And his wife?"

"She was a good person too. As you know, people of our sort aren't always known for their strict morals. One often hears of somebody running off with somebody else's wife. Han's wife was a beautiful woman, although on the small side, and she now and then got solicitations of that sort. But she never took up with such people."

"What were their dispositions like?"

"Toward others, they were both extremely kind and gentle. They never thought of themselves and never got angry. And yet" (here the stagehand paused. Thinking a moment, he went on) "I'm afraid this may be to Han's detriment, but to tell the truth, strangely enough, those two, who were so kind, gentle, and self-effacing with others, when it came to their own relationship, were surprisingly cruel to each other."

"Why was that?"

"I don't know why."

"Had they always been that way?"

"No. About two years ago, the wife gave birth. The baby was premature, and died in three days or so. But after that, it was clear even to us that their relationship was slowly going to the bad. They would often have arguments over the most trivial things. At such times, Han would suddenly turn dead pale. But in the end, no matter what, he always fell silent. He never mistreated his wife. Of course, that's most likely because his religion forbade him to. But sometimes, when you looked at his face, there was a terrible, uncontrollable anger in it. Once, I suggested that if things were so bad between them it might be good to get a divorce. But Han said that even if his wife had reasons for seeking a divorce, he himself had none. Han followed his own will in the matter. He even said that there was no way he could love his wife. It was only natural, he said, if a woman he did not love gradually came not to love him. It was why he took to reading the Bible and collections of sermons. He seemed to think that by somehow calming his heart he could correct his fairly unruly feelings of hatred. After all, he had no reason to hate his wife. She, too, deserved sympathy. After their marriage, they had travelled about as road-players for nearly three years. Owing to an older brother's profligacy, the family back home was already broken up and gone. Even if she had left Han and gone back, nobody would have trusted a woman who'd been on the road four years enough to marry her. Bad as things were, she had no choice but to stay with Han."

"What is *your* opinion of the incident?"

"You mean whether it was deliberate or an accident?"

"Yes."

"Actually, I've thought a lot about that. But the more I've thought, the more I've come, by degrees, not to understand anything."

"Why is that?"

"I don't know why. I really do not. I think anyone would have the same problem. I asked the introducer what he thought, but he said he didn't know either."

"Well, at the instant it happened, what did you think?"

"I thought: He's murdered her. I did think that."

"Is that so?"

"But the introducer told me that he thought: He's bungled it."

"Is that so? But isn't that what he would think, not knowing too much about their relationship?"

"Maybe so. But later, I thought that my thinking he'd murdered her might also, in the same way, simply have been because I knew a good deal about their relationship."

"What was Han's demeanor just then?"

"He gave a short cry: 'Aa!' That was what drew my attention to what had happened. The blood suddenly gushed out of the wife's neck. Even so, she remained upright for a moment. Her body was held in place by the knife's sticking in the board behind her. Then, all of a sudden, her knees buckled, the knife came out and collapsing all together she fell forward. There was nothing anyone could do. We all of us just went stiff and watched. But I can't be sure of anything. I didn't have the leisure to observe Han's demeanor just then. But it seems to me that for those few seconds he was just like us. It was only afterward that I thought: He's murdered her at last. Han went dead pale and stood there with his eyes closed. We drew the curtain down and tried to revive the woman, but she was already dead. Han, his face bluish with excitement, blurted out: 'How could I make such a blunder?' Then he knelt, in a long silent prayer."

"Was his demeanor agitated then?"

"It was somewhat agitated."

"Good. If I have any further questions, I'll call you."

Dismissing the Chinese stagehand, the judge finally had Han himself brought in. Han, his face drawn and pale, was an intelligent-looking man. It was clear at a glance to the judge that he was suffering from nervous exhaustion. As soon as Han had seated himself, the judge said: "I've been questioning the owner-manager and the stagehand. I will now ask you some questions." Han nodded.

"Have you never loved your wife at all?"

"From the day I married her until the day she had the baby, I loved my wife with all my heart."

"Why did the birth become a source of discord?"

"Because I knew it wasn't my child."

"Do you know who the father was?"

"I have an idea it was my wife's cousin."

"Did you know the man?"

"He was a close friend of mine. It was he who suggested that we get married. He introduced me to her."

"Was there a relationship before she married you?"

"Of course there was. The baby was born the eighth month after the marriage."

"The stagehand said it was a premature birth."

"That's because I told him it was."

"The baby died shortly afterwards?"

"Yes."

"What was the cause of death?"

"It choked at the breast."

"Was that a deliberate act of your wife's?"

"She said it was an accident."

The judge, falling silent, looked intently at Han. Han, eyes lowered in his raised face, waited for the next question.

"Did your wife tell you about the relationship?"

"No, she didn't. Nor did I ask her about it. I felt that the baby's death was a judgement on her for what she'd done. I thought that I myself should be as forgiving as possible."

"But, in the end, you couldn't forgive her?"

"That's right. My feeling remained that the baby's death wasn't enough of a judgement. At times, when I thought about it by myself, I could be rather forgiving. But then, my wife would come in. She would go about her business. As I looked at her, at her body, I could not keep down my displeasure."

"You didn't think of divorcing her?"

"I often thought I'd like a divorce. But I never said anything."

"Why was that?"

"I was weak. And my wife had said that if I divorced her she would not survive."

"Did your wife love you?"

"She did not love me."

"If that was so, why did she say such a thing?"

"I think it was from the necessity of going on living. Her brother had broken up the household back home, and she knew that no respectable man would marry a woman who'd been the wife of a road-player. And her feet were too small for ordinary work."

"What were your sexual relations?"

"I believe they were probably not much different from those of an average couple."

"Did your wife feel any sympathy for you?"

"I can't think she felt any sympathy. I believe that for my wife living with me was an extraordinary hardship. But the patience with which she endured that hardship was beyond what one would have thought possible even for a man. My wife simply observed, with cruel eyes, the gradual destruction of my life. My writhing, desperate attempts to save myself, to enter upon my true life, she coolly, from the side and without the slightest wish to help, as if surrounding me, looked on at."

"Why were you unable to take a more assertive, resolute attitude?"

"Because I was thinking about various things."

"Various things? What sort of things?"

"I thought I would act in such a way as to leave no room for error. But, in the end, those thoughts never offered any solution."

"Did you ever think of killing your wife?"

Han did not answer. The judge repeated his question. Even then, Han did not answer immediately. Then, he said:

"I'd often thought, before then, that it would be good if she were dead."

"Then, if the law had allowed it, you might have killed her?"

"I was afraid of the law, and I had never had such thoughts before. It was merely because I was weak. But even though I was weak, my desire to live my own life was strong."

"So, after that, you thought about killing your wife?"

"I didn't make my mind up to it. But I did think about it."

"How long before the incident was this?"

"The night before. Toward daybreak."

"Had you quarrelled that evening?"

"Yes."

"What about?"

"Something so trivial it isn't worth mentioning."

"Tell me anyway."

"It was about food. When I'm hungry, I get irritable. The way she dawdled over the preparations for supper made me angry."

"Did you quarrel more violently than usual?"

"No. But I remained excited longer than usual. It was because lately I'd felt intolerably frustrated by the fact that I did not have a life of my own. I went to bed, but I couldn't sleep at all. I thought about all sorts of things. I felt as if my present existence in which, like a grub suspended in midair, I looked to one side and the other, always hesitating, without the courage to want what I wanted, without the courage to get rid of what was unbearable, was all due to my relationship with my wife. I could see no light in my future. A desire to seek the light was burning inside me. Or, if it was not, it was trying to catch fire. But my relationship with my wife would not let it. The flame was not out. It was smouldering, in a fitful, ugly way. What with the pain and unhappiness of it all, I was being poisoned. When the poisoning was complete, I would die. Although alive, I would be a dead man. And though this was what I had come to, I was still trying to put up with it. It would be good if she died—one part of me kept having that dirty, hateful thought. If this was how things were, why didn't I kill her? The consequences of such an act did not trouble me now. I might be put in jail. Who could tell how much better life in jail might be than this life? I would cross that bridge when I came to it. It would be enough if, in any way I could, I broke through whatever came up at the time it came up. Even if I broke through, and broke through, I might not break through all the way. But if I went on breaking through until the day I died, that would be my true life. I almost forgot that my wife was lying beside me. At last, I grew tired. But even though I was tired, it was not the sort of fatigue that leads to sleep. My thoughts began to blur. As my tensed up feelings relaxed, my dark thoughts of murder faded away. A feeling of loneliness came over me, as after a nightmare. I even felt pity for my own weak spirit, that the ability to think hard had, in a single night, become so feeble and forlorn. And then, at last, the night was over. It seemed to me that my wife hadn't slept either."

"When you got up, was everything as usual between you?"

"Neither of us said a word to each other."

"Why didn't you think of leaving your wife?"

"Do you mean that as a desired result, it would have come to the same thing?"

"Yes."

"For me, there was a great difference."

Saying this, Han looked at the judge and was silent. The judge, his face softening, nodded.

"But, between my thinking about such a thing and actually deciding to kill her, there was still a wide gap. That day, from early morning on, I felt insanely keyed up. Because of my bodily fatigue, my nerves were edgy, without elasticity. Unable to remain still, I stayed outside all morning. I walked about restlessly, away from the others. I kept thinking that no matter what I would have to do something. But I no longer thought of killing her, as I had the night before. And I was not at all worried about that day's performance. If I had been, I would not have chosen that particular act. We had many other acts. Finally, that evening, our turn came. Then also, I was not thinking of such a thing. As usual, I demonstrated to the audience that the knives were sharp by slicing through a slice of paper and sticking a knife into the stage. My wife, heavily made up and wearing a gaudy Chinese costume, came on. Her stage manner was no different from always. Greeting the audience with a winsome smile, she stepped up to the thick board and stood bolt upright with her back to it. A knife in my hand, I stood at a set distance straight across from her. For the first time since the night before, we exchanged looks. Only then did I realize the danger of having chosen this act for tonight. Unless I practiced the utmost care, I thought, there would be trouble. I must alleviate, as best I could, the day's restless agitation and my strained, edgy nerves. But no matter how I tried, a weariness that had eaten into my heart would not let me. I began to feel that I would not trust my own arm. Closing my eyes, I attempted to calm myself. My body started to sway. The moment came. I drove in the first knife above her head. It went in slightly higher than usual. Then I drove in one knife each under the pits of her arms which were raised to shoulder level. As each knife left my fingertips, something clung to it an instant, as if to hold it back. I felt as if I no longer knew where the knives would go in. Each time one hit, I thought: Thank God. Calm down, calm down, I thought. But I could feel in my arm the constraint that comes from a thing's having become conscious. I drove in a knife to the left of her throat. I was about to drive in the next one to the right, when suddenly a strange look came over her face. She must have felt an impulse of violent fear. Did she have a premonition that the knife about to fly at her would go through her neck? I don't know. I only felt that face of violent fear, thrown back at my heart with the same force as the knife. Dizziness struck me. But even so, with all my strength, almost without a target, as though aiming in the dark, I threw the knife . . . "

The judge was silent.

"I've killed her at last, I thought."

"How do you mean? That you'd done it on purpose?"

"Yes. I suddenly felt as if I had."

"Afterwards, you knelt by the body in silent prayer . . . ?"

"That was a trick that occurred to me at the moment. I knew everyone thought I seriously believed in Christianity. While pretending to pray, I was thinking about what attitude I should take."

"You felt sure that what you'd done was intentional?"

"Yes. And I thought right away I could make out it was an accident."

"But why did you think it was deliberate murder?"

"Because of my feelings, which were unhinged."

"So you thought you'd skillfully deceived the others?"

"Thinking about it later, I was shocked at myself. I acted surprised in a natural manner, was considerably agitated, and also displayed grief. But any perceptive person, I believe, could have seen that I was playacting. Recalling my behavior, I sweated cold sweat. That night, I decided that I would have to be found innocent. First of all, I was extremely encouraged by the fact that there was not a scrap of objective proof of my crime. Everyone knew we'd been on bad terms, of course, so there was bound to be a suspicion of murder. I couldn't do anything about that. But if I insisted, throughout, that it was an accident, that would be the end of it. That we'd gotten along badly might make people conjecture, but it was no proof. In the end, I thought, I would be acquitted for lack of evidence. Thinking back over the incident, I made up a rough version of my plea, as plausible as possible, so that it would seem like an accident. Soon, though, for some reason, a doubt rose up in me as to whether I myself believed it was murder. The night before, I had thought about killing her, but was that alone a reason for deciding, myself, that it was murder? Gradually, despite myself, I became unsure. A sudden excitement swept over me. I felt so excited I couldn't sit still. I was so happy, I was beside myself. I wanted to shout for joy."

"Was it because you yourself could now believe that it was an accident?"

"No. I'm still unsure of that. It was because it was completely unclear, even to myself, which it had been. It was because I could now tell the truth and be found innocent. Being found innocent meant everything to me now. For that purpose, rather than trying to deceive myself and insisting that it was an accident, it was far better to be able to be honest, even if it meant saying I didn't know which it was. I could no longer assert that it was an accident, nor, on the other hand, could I say that it was a deliberate act. I was so happy because come what may it was no longer a question of a confession of guilt."

Han felt silent. The judge, also, was silent for a moment. Then, as if to himself, he said: "On the whole, it seems to be the truth." And then: "By the way, do you not feel the slightest sorrow about your wife's death?"

"None whatsoever. And up to now, no matter what my feelings of hatred for her, I never imagined that I'd be able to talk so cheerfully about her death."

"That will be all. You may step down," the judge said. Han, after a slight wordless bow, left the room.

The judge felt an excitement, he could not put a name to it, surge up in him.

Quickly, he took up his pen. And, then and there, he wrote: "Innocent."

[1913]

■ TOPICS FOR DISCUSSION AND WRITING

1. What is the narrative point of view?
2. The first three paragraphs sound like a newspaper account. Why do you suppose Shiga adopts this tone?
3. The judge writes "Innocent." But of what is Han innocent? How does the last word of the story reflect on the title? Should Shiga have retitled the story? Does the meaning of the title change after you've read the story? What other title do you suggest? Why?
4. If you had been the judge, what other questions might you have asked the witnesses and the accused man?
5. Do you agree with the judge's verdict? Why or why not?
6. On what do you suppose the judge based his verdict?
7. How important is "intention" in the verdict? How important do you think intention is in justifying any crime? Is remorse important to the judge? Is it important to *your* judgment of criminality? Should it be important in assigning punishment?
8. On the basis of this story, what do you know (and what can you conjecture) about the society in which it takes place? What, for example, is the position of women? Of children? What are the expectations of justice?
9. The story was written by a Japanese author for a Japanese public. But the protagonist is Chinese. What effect do you think is gained by making Han a foreigner?
10. What do you think the verdict would probably be in an American court today? Why?

■ EUDORA WELTY

Eudora Welty was born in 1909 in Jackson, Mississippi. Although she earned a bachelor's degree at the University of Wisconsin, and she spent a year studying advertising in New York City at the Columbia University Graduate School of Business, she has lived almost all of her life in Jackson.

In the preface to her *Collected Stories* she says:

I have been told, both in approval and in accusation, that I seem to love all my characters. What I do in writing of any character is to try to enter into the mind, heart and skin of a human being who is not myself. Whether this happens to be a man or a woman, old or young, with skin black or white, the primary challenge lies in making the jump itself. It is the act of a writer's imagination that I set most high.

In addition to writing stories and novels, Welty has written a book about fiction, *The Eye of the Story* (1977), and a memoir, *One Writer's Beginnings* (1984).

A Worn Path

It was December—a bright frozen day in the early morning. Far out in the country there was an old Negro woman with her head tied in a red rag, coming along a path through the pinewoods. Her name was Phoenix Jackson. She was very old and small and she walked slowly in the dark pine shadows, moving a little from side to side in her steps, with the balanced heaviness and lightness of a pendulum in a grandfather clock. She carried a thin, small cane made from an umbrella, and with this she kept tapping the frozen earth in front of her. This made a grave and persistent noise in the still air, that seemed meditative like the chirping of a solitary little bird.

She wore a dark striped dress reaching down to her shoe tops, and an equally long apron of bleached sugar sacks, with a full pocket: all neat and tidy, but every time she took a step she might have fallen over her shoe-laces, which dragged from her unlaced shoes. She looked straight ahead. Her eyes were blue with age. Her skin had a pattern all its own of numberless branching wrinkles and as though a whole little tree stood in the middle of her forehead, but a golden color ran underneath, and the two knobs of her cheeks were illuminated by a yellow burning under the dark. Under the red rag her hair came down on her neck in the frailest of ringlets, still black, and with an odor like copper.

Now and then there was a quivering in the thicket. Old Phoenix said, "Out of my way, all you foxes, owls, beetles, jack rabbits, coons, and wild animals! . . . Keep out from under these feet, little bob-whites. . . . Keep the big wild hogs out of my path. Don't let none of those come running my direction. I got a long way." Under her small black-freckled hand her cane, limber as a buggy whip, would switch at the brush as if to rouse up any hiding things.

On she went. The woods were deep and still. The sun made the pine needles almost too bright to look at, up where the wind rocked. The cones dropped as light as feathers. Down in the hollow was the mourning dove—it was not too late for him.

The path ran up a hill. "Seem like there is chains about my feet, time I get this far," she said, in the voice of argument old people keep to use with themselves. "Something always take a hold of me on this hill—pleads I should stay."

After she got to the top she turned and gave a full, severe look behind her where she had come. "Up through pines," she said at length. "Now down through oaks."

Her eyes opened their widest, and she started down gently. But before she got to the bottom of the hill a bush caught her dress.

Her fingers were busy and intent, but her skirts were full and long, so that before she could pull them free in one place they were caught in another. It was not possible to allow the dress to tear. "I in the thorny bush," she said. "Thorns, you doing your appointed work. Never want to let folks pass—no sir. Old eyes thought you was a pretty little *green* bush."

Finally, trembling all over, she stood free, and after a moment dared to stoop for her cane.

"Sun so high!" she cried, leaning back and looking, while the thick tears went over her eyes. "The time getting all gone here."

At the foot of this hill was a place where a log was laid across the creek.

"Now comes the trial," said Phoenix.

Putting her right foot out, she mounted the log and shut her eyes. Lifting her skirt, levelling her cane fiercely before her, like a festival figure in some parade, she began to march across. Then she opened her eyes and she was safe on the other side.

"I wasn't as old as I thought," she said.

But she sat down to rest. She spread her skirts on the bank around her and folded her hands over her knees. Up above her was a tree in a pearly cloud of mistletoe. She did not dare to close her eyes, and when a little boy brought her a little plate with a slice of marble-cake on it she spoke to him. "That would be acceptable," she said. But when she went to take it there was just her own hand in the air.

So she left that tree, and had to go through a barbed-wire fence. There she had to creep and crawl, spreading her knees and stretching her fingers like a baby trying to climb the steps. But she talked loudly to herself: she could not let her dress be torn now, so late in the day, and she could not pay for having her arm or leg sawed off if she got caught fast where she was.

At last she was safe through the fence and risen up out in the clearing. Big dead trees, like black men with one arm, were standing in the purple stalks of the withered cotton field. There sat a buzzard.

"Who you watching?"

In the furrow she made her way along.

"Glad this not the season for bulls," she said, looking sideways, "and the good Lord made his snakes to curl up and sleep in the winter. A pleasure I don't see no two-headed snake coming around that tree, where it come once. It took a while to get by him, back in the summer."

She passed through the old cotton and went into a field of dead corn. It whispered and shook and was taller than her head. "Through the maze now," she said, for there was no path.

Then there was something tall, black, and skinny there, moving before her.

At first she took it for a man. It could have been a man dancing in the field. But she stood still and listened, and it did not make a sound. It was as silent as a ghost.

"Ghost," she said sharply, "who be you the ghost of? For I have heard of nary death close by."

But there was no answer—only the ragged dancing in the wind.

She shut her eyes, reached out her hand, and touched a sleeve. She found a coat and inside that an emptiness, cold as ice.

"You scarecrow," she said. Her face lighted. "I ought to be shut up for good," she said with laughter. "My senses is gone, I too old. I the oldest people I ever know. Dance, old scarecrow," she said, "while I dancing with you."

She kicked her foot over the furrow, and with mouth drawn down, shook her head once or twice in a little strutting way. Some husks blew down and whirled in streamers about her skirts.

Then she went on, parting her way from side to side with the cane, through the whispering field. At last she came to the end, to a wagon track where the silver grass blew between the red ruts. The quail were walking around like pullets, seeming all dainty and unseen.

"Walk pretty," she said. "This the easy place. This the easy going."

She followed the track, swaying through the quiet bare fields, through the little strings of trees silver in their dead leaves, past cabins silver from weather, with the doors and windows boarded shut, all like old women under a spell sitting there. "I walking in their sleep," she said, nodding her head vigorously.

In a ravine she went where a spring was silently flowing through a hollow log. Old Phoenix bent and drank. "Sweet-gum makes the water sweet," she said, and drank more. "Nobody know who made this well, for it was here when I was born."

The track crossed a swampy part where the moss hung as white as lace from every limb. "Sleep on, alligators, and blow your bubbles." Then the track went into the road.

Deep, deep the road went down between the high green-colored banks. Overhead the live-oaks met, and it was as dark as a cave.

A black dog with a lolling tongue came up out of the weeds by the ditch. She was meditating, and not ready, and when he came at her she only hit him a little with her cane. Over she went in the ditch, like a little puff of milk-weed.

Down there, her senses drifted away. A dream visited her, and she reached her hand up, but nothing reached down and gave her a pull. So she lay there and presently went to talking. "Old woman," she said to herself, "that black dog come up out of the weeds to stall you off, and now there he sitting on his fine tail, smiling at you."

A white man finally came along and found her—a hunter, a young man, with his dog on a chain.

"Well, Granny!" he laughed. "what are you doing there?"

"Lying on my back like a June-bug waiting to be turned over, mister," she said, reaching up her hand.

He lifted her up, gave her a swing in the air, and set her down. "Anything broken, Granny?"

"No sir, them old dead weeds is springy enough," said Phoenix, when she had got her breath. "I thank you for your trouble."

"Where do you live, Granny?" he asked, while the two dogs were growling at each other.

"Away back yonder, sir, behind the ridge. You can't even see it from here."

"On your way home?"

"No, sir, I going to town."

"Why, that's too far! That's as far as I walk when I come out myself, and I get something for my trouble." He patted the stuffed bag he carried, and there hung down a little closed claw. It was one of the bob-whites, with its beak hooked bitterly to show it was dead. "Now you go on home, Granny!"

"I bound to go to town, mister," said Phoenix. "The time come around."

He gave another laugh, filling the whole landscape. "I know you old colored people! Wouldn't miss going to town to see Santa Claus!"

But something held Old Phoenix very still. The deep lines in her face went into a fierce and different radiation. Without warning, she had seen with her own eyes a flashing nickel fall out of the man's pocket onto the ground.

"How old are you, Granny?" he was saying.

"There is no telling, mister," she said, "no telling."

Then she gave a little cry and clapped her hands and said, "Git on away from here, dog! Look! Look at that dog!" She laughed as if in admiration. "He ain't scared of nobody. He a big black dog." She whispered, "Sic him!"

"Watch me get rid of that cur," said the man. "Sic him, Pete! Sic him!"

Phoenix heard the dogs fighting, and heard the man running and throwing sticks. She even heard a gunshot. But she was slowly bending forward by that time, further and further forward, the lids stretched down over her eyes, as if she were doing this in her sleep. Her chin was lowered almost to her knees. The yellow palm of her hand came out from the fold of her apron. Her fingers slid down and along the ground under the piece of money with the grace and care they would have in lifting an egg from under a sitting hen. Then she slowly straightened up, she stood erect, and the nickel was in her apron pocket. A bird flew by. Her lips moved. "God watching me the whole time. I come to stealing."

The man came back, and his own dog panted about them. "Well, I scared him off that time," he said, and then he laughed and lifted his gun and pointed it at Phoenix.

She stood straight and faced him.

"Doesn't the gun scare you?" he said, still pointing it.

"No, sir, I seen plenty go off closer by, in my day, and for less than what I done," she said, holding utterly still.

He smiled, and shouldered the gun. "Well, Granny," he said, "you must be a hundred years old, and scared of nothing. I'd give you a dime if I had any money with me. But you take my advice and stay home, and nothing will happen to you."

"I bound to go on my way, mister," said Phoenix. She inclined her head in the red rag. Then they went in different directions, but she could hear the gun shooting again and again over the hill.

She walked on. The shadows hung from the oak trees to the road like curtains. Then she smelled wood-smoke, and smelled the river, and she saw a steeple and the cabins on their steep steps. Dozens of little black children whirled around her. There ahead was Natchez shining. Bells were ringing. She walked on.

In the paved city it was Christmas time. There were red and green electric lights strung and crisscrossed everywhere, and all turned on in the daytime. Old Phoenix would have been lost if she had not distrusted her eyesight and depended on her feet to know where to take her.

She paused quietly on the sidewalk where people were passing by. A lady came along in the crowd, carrying an armful of red-, green-, and silver-wrapped presents; she gave off perfume like the red roses in hot summer, and Phoenix stopped her.

"Please, missy, will you lace up my shoe?" She held up her foot.

"What do you want, Grandma?"

"See my shoe," said Phoenix. "Do all right for out in the country, but wouldn't look right to go in a big building."

"Stand still then, Grandma," said the lady. She put her packages down on the sidewalk beside her and laced and tied both shoes tightly.

"Can't lace 'em with a cane," said Phoenix. "Thank you, missy. I doesn't mind asking a nice lady to tie up my shoe, when I gets out on the street."

Moving slowly and from side to side, she went into the big building and into a tower of steps, where she walked up and around and around until her feet knew to stop.

She entered a door, and there she saw nailed up on the wall the document that had been stamped with the gold seal and framed in the gold frame, which matched the dream that was hung up in her head.

"Here I be," she said. There was a fixed and ceremonial stiffness over her body.

"A charity case, I suppose," said an attendant who sat at the desk before her.

But Phoenix only looked above her head. There was sweat on her face, the wrinkles in her skin shone like a bright net.

"Speak up, Grandma," the woman said. "What's your name? We must have your history, you know. Have you been here before? What seems to be the trouble with you?"

Old Phoenix only gave a twitch to her face as if a fly were bothering her.

"Are you deaf?" cried the attendant.

But then the nurse came in.

"Oh, that's just old Aunt Phoenix," she said. "She doesn't come for herself—she has a little grandson. She makes these trips just as regular as clockwork. She lives away back off the old Natchez Trace." She bent down. "Well, Aunt Phoenix, why don't you just take a seat? We won't keep you standing after your long trip." She pointed.

The old woman sat down, bolt upright in the chair.

"Now, how is the boy?" asked the nurse.

Old Phoenix did not speak.

"I said, how is the boy?"

But Phoenix only waited and stared straight ahead, her face very solemn and withdrawn into rigidity.

"Is his throat any better?" asked the nurse. "Aunt Phoenix, don't you hear me? Is your grandson's throat any better since the last time you came for the medicine?"

With her hands on her knees, the old woman waited, silent, erect and motionless, just as if she were in armor.

"You mustn't take up our time this way, Aunt Phoenix," the nurse said. "Tell us quickly about your grandson, and get it over. He isn't dead, is he?"

At last there came a flicker and then a flame of comprehension across her face, and she spoke.

"My grandson. It was my memory had left me. There I sat and forgot why I made my long trip."

"Forgot?" The nurse frowned. "After you came so far?"

Then Phoenix was like an old woman begging a dignified forgiveness for waking up frightened in the night. "I never did go to school, I was too old at the Surrender," she said in a soft voice. "I'm an old woman without an education. It was my memory fail me. My little grandson, he is just the same, and I forgot it in the coming."

"Throat never heals, does it?" said the nurse, speaking in a loud, sure voice to Old Phoenix. By now she had a card with something written on it, a little list. "Yes. Swallowed lye. When was it—January—two-three years ago— "

Phoenix spoke unasked now. "No, missy, he not dead, he just the same. Every little while his throat begin to close up again, and he not able to swallow. He not get his breath. He not able to help himself. So the time come around, and I go on another trip for the soothing medicine."

"All right. The doctor said as long as you came to get it, you could have it," said the nurse. "But it's an obstinate case."

"My little grandson, he sit up there in the house all wrapped up, waiting by himself," Phoenix went on. "We is the only two left in the world. He suffer and it don't seem to put him back at all. He got a sweet look. He going to last. He wear a little patch quilt and peep out holding his mouth open like a little bird. I remembers so plain now. I not going to forget him again, no, the whole enduring time. I could tell him from all the others in creation."

"All right." The nurse was trying to hush her now. She brought her a bottle of medicine. "Charity," she said, making a check mark in a book.

Old Phoenix held the bottle close to her eyes and then carefully put it into her pocket.

"I thank you," she said.

"It's Christmas time, Grandma," said the attendant. "Could I give you a few pennies out of my purse?"

"Five pennies is a nickel," said Phoenix stiffly.

"Here's a nickel," said the attendant.

Phoenix rose carefully and held out her hand. She received the nickel and then fished the other nickel out of her pocket and laid it beside the new one. She stared at her palm closely, with her head on one side.

Then she gave a tap with her cane on the floor.

"This is what come to me to do," she said. "I going to the store and buy my child a little windmill they sells, made out of paper. He going to find it hard to believe there such a thing in the world. I'll march myself back where he waiting, holding it straight up in his hand."

She lifted her free hand, gave a little nod, turned round, and walked out of the doctor's office. Then her slow step began on the stairs, going down.

[1941]

■ TOPICS FOR DISCUSSION AND WRITING

1. If you do not know the legend of the Phoenix, look it up in a dictionary or, better, in an encyclopedia. Then carefully reread the story, to learn whether the story in any way connects with the legend.
2. What do you think of the hunter?
3. What would be lost if the episode (with all of its dialogue) of Phoenix falling into the ditch and being helped out of it by the hunter were omitted?
4. Is Christmas a particularly appropriate time in which to set the story? Why or why not?
5. What do you make of the title?

■ JOHN UPDIKE

John Updike (b. 1932) grew up in Shillington, Pennsylvania, where his father was a teacher and his mother was a writer. After receiving a B.A. degree from Harvard he studied drawing at Oxford for a year, but an offer from *The New Yorker* magazine brought him back to the United States. He at first served as a reporter for the magazine, but soon began contributing poetry, essays, and fiction. Today he is one of America's most prolific and well-known writers.

A & P

In walks these three girls in nothing but bathing suits. I'm in the third checkout slot, with my back to the door, so I don't see them until they're over by the bread. The one that caught my eye first was the one in the plaid green two-piece. She was a chunky kid, with a good tan and a sweet broad soft-looking can with those two crescents of white just under it, where the sun never seems to hit, at the top of the backs of her legs. I stood there with my hand on a box of HiHo crackers trying to remember if I rang it up or not. I ring it up again and the customer starts giving me hell. She's one of these cash-register-watchers, a witch about fifty with rouge on her cheekbones and no eyebrows, and I know it made her day to trip me up. She'd been watching cash registers for fifty years and probably never seen a mistake before.

By the time I got her feathers smoothed and her goodies into a bag—she gives me a little snort in passing, if she'd been born at the right time they would have burned her over in Salem—by the time I get her on her way the girls had circled around the bread and were coming back, without a pushcart, back my way along the counters, in the aisle between the checkouts and the Special bins. They didn't even have shoes on. There was this chunky one, with the two-piece—it was bright green and the seams on the bra were still sharp and her belly was still pretty pale so I guessed she just got it (the suit)—there was this one, with one of those chubby berry-faces, the lips all bunched together under her nose, this one, and a tall one, with black hair that hadn't quite frizzed right, and one of these sunburns right across under the eyes, and a chin that was too long—you know, the kind of girl other girls think is very "striking" and "attractive" but never quite makes it, as they very well know, which is why they like her so much—and then the third one, that wasn't quite so tall. She was the queen. She kind of led them, the other two peeking around and making their shoulders round. She didn't look around, not this queen, she just walked straight on slowly, on these long white prima-donna legs. She came down a little hard on her heels, as if she didn't walk in her bare feet that much, putting down her heels and then letting the weight move along to her toes as if she was testing the floor with every step, putting a little deliberate extra action into it. You never know for sure how girls' minds work (do they really think it's a mind in there or just a little buzz like a bee in a glass jar?) but you got the idea she had talked the other two into coming in here with her, and now she was showing them how to do it, walk slow and hold yourself straight.

She had on a kind of dirty pink—beige maybe, I don't know—bathing suit with a little nubble all over it and, what got me, the straps were down. They were off her shoulders looped loose around the cool tops of her arms, and I guess as a result the suit had slipped on her, so all around the top of the cloth there was this shining rim. If it hadn't been there you wouldn't have known there could have been anything whiter than those shoulders. With the straps pushed off, there was nothing between the top of the suit and the top of her head except just *her,* this clean bare plane of the top of her chest down from the shoulder bones like a dented sheet of metal tilted in the light. I mean, it was more than pretty.

She had sort of oaky hair that the sun and salt had bleached, done up in a bun that was unravelling, and a kind of prim face. Walking into the A & P with your straps down, I suppose it's the only kind of face you *can* have. She held her head so high her neck, coming up out of those white shoulders, looked kind of stretched, but I didn't mind. The longer her neck was, the more of her there was.

She must have felt in the corner of her eye me and over my shoulder Stokesie in the second slot watching, but she didn't tip. Not this queen. She kept her eyes moving across the racks, and stopped, and turned so slow it made my stomach rub the inside of my apron, and buzzed to the other two, who kind of huddled against her for relief, and then they all three of them went up the cat and dog food-breakfast cereal-macaroni-rice-raisins-seasonings-spreads-spaghetti-soft drinks-crackers-and-cookies aisle. From the third slot I look straight up this aisle to the meat counter, and I watched them all the way. The fat one with the tan sort of fumbled with the cookies, but on second thought she put the package back. The sheep pushing their carts down the aisle—the girls were walking against the usual traffic (not that we have one-way signs or anything)—were pretty hilarious. You could see them, when Queenie's white shoulders dawned on them, kind of jerk, or hop, or hiccup, but their eyes snapped back to their own baskets and on they pushed. I bet you could set off dynamite in the A & P and the people would by and large keep reaching and checking oatmeal off their lists and muttering "Let me see, there was a third thing, began with A, asparagus, no, ah, yes, applesauce!" or whatever it is they do mutter. But there was no doubt, this jiggled them. A few house slaves in pin curlers even look around after pushing their carts past to make sure what they had seen was correct.

You know, it's one thing to have a girl in a bathing suit down on the beach, where what with the glare nobody can look at each other much anyway, and another thing in the cool of the A & P, under the fluorescent lights, against all those stacked packages, with her feet paddling along naked over our checker-board green-and-cream rubber-tile floor.

"Oh, Daddy," Stokesie said beside me. "I feel so faint."

"Darling," I said. "Hold me tight." Stokesie's married, with two babies chalked up on his fuselage already, but as far as I can tell that's the only difference. He's twenty-two, and I was nineteen this April.

"Is it done?" he asks, the responsible married man finding his voice. I forgot to say he thinks he's going to be a manager some sunny day, maybe in 1990 when it's called the Great Alexandrov and Petrooshki Tea Company or something.

What he meant was, our town is five miles from a beach, with a big summer colony out on the Point, but we're right in the middle of town, and the women generally put on a shirt or shorts or something before they get out of the car into the street. And anyway these are usually women with six children and varicose veins mapping their legs and nobody, including them, could care less. As I say, we're right in the middle of town, and if you stand at our front doors you can see two banks and the Congregational church and the newspaper store and three real estate offices and about twenty-seven old freeloaders tearing up Central Street because the sewer broke again. It's not as if we're on the Cape; we're north of Boston and there's people in this town haven't seen the ocean for twenty years.

The girls had reached the meat counter and were asking McMahon something. He pointed, they pointed, and they shuffled out of sight behind a pyramid of Diet Delight peaches. All that was left for us to see was old McMahon patting his mouth and looking after them sizing up their joints. Poor kids, I began to feel sorry for them, they couldn't help it.

Now here comes the sad part of the story, at least my family says it's sad, but I don't think it's so sad myself. The store's pretty empty, it being Thursday afternoon, so there was nothing much to do except lean on the register and wait for the girls to show up again. The whole store was like a pinball machine and I didn't know which tunnel they'd come out of. After a while they come around out of the far aisle, around the light bulbs, records at discount of the Caribbean Six or Tony Martin Sings or some such gunk you wonder they waste the wax on, sixpacks of candy bars, and plastic toys done up in cellophane that fall apart when a kid looks at them anyway. Around they come, Queenie still leading the way, and holding a little gray jar in her hand. Slots Three through Seven are unmanned and I could see her wondering between Stokes and me, but Stokesie with his usual luck draws an old party in baggy gray pants who stumbles up with four giant cans of pineapple juice (what do these bums *do* with all that pineapple juice? I've often asked myself) so the girls come to me. Queenie puts down the jar and I take it into my fingers icy cold. Kingfish Fancy Herring Snacks in Pure Sour Cream: 49¢. Now her hands are empty, not a ring or a bracelet, bare as God made them, and I wonder where the money's coming from. Still with the prim look she lifts a folded dollar bill out of the hollow at the center of her nubbled pink top. The jar went heavy in my hand. Really, I thought that was so cute.

Then everybody's luck begins to run out. Lengel comes in from haggling with a truck full of cabbages on the lot and is about to scuttle into the door marked MANAGER behind which he hides all day when the girls touch his eye. Lengel's pretty dreary, teaches Sunday school and the rest, but he doesn't miss that much. He comes over and says, "Girls, this isn't the beach."

Queenie blushes, though maybe it's just a brush of sunburn I was noticing for the first time, now that she was so close. "My mother asked me to pick up a jar of herring snacks." Her voice kind of startled me, the way voices do when you see the people first, coming out so flat and dumb yet kind of tony, too, the way it ticked over "pick up" and "snacks." All of a sudden I slid right down her voice into her living room. Her father and the other men were standing around in ice-cream coats and bow ties and the women were in sandals picking up herring snacks on toothpicks off a big glass plate and they were all holding drinks the color of water with olives and sprigs of mint in them. When my parents have somebody over they get lemonade and if it's a real racy affair Schlitz in tall glasses with "They'll Do It Every Time" cartoons stencilled on.

"That's all right," Lengel said. "But this isn't the beach." His repeating this struck me as funny, as if it had just occurred to him, and he had been thinking all these years the A & P was a great big dune and he was the head lifeguard. He didn't like my smiling—as I say he doesn't miss much—but he concentrates on giving the girls that sad Sunday-school-superintendent stare.

Queenie's blush was no sunburn now, and the plump one in plaid, that I liked better from the back—a really sweet can—pipes up, "We weren't doing any shopping. We just came in for the one thing."

"That makes no difference," Lengel tells her, and I could see from the way his eyes went that he hadn't noticed she was wearing a two-piece before. "We want you decently dressed when you come in here."

"We *are* decent," Queenie says suddenly, her lower lip pushing, getting sore now that she remembers her place, a place from which the crowd that runs the A & P must look pretty crummy. Fancy Herring Snacks flashed in her very blue eyes.

"Girls, I don't want to argue with you. After this come in here with your shoulders covered. It's our policy." He turns his back. That's policy for you. Policy is what the kingpins want. What the others want is juvenile delinquency.

All this while, the customers had been showing up with their carts but, you know, sheep, seeing a scene, they had all bunched up on Stokesie, who shook open a paper bag as gently as peeling a peach, not wanting to miss a word. I could feel in the silence everybody getting nervous, most of all Lengel, who asks me, "Sammy, have you rung up this purchase?"

I thought and said "No" but it wasn't about that I was thinking. I go through the punches, 4, 9, GROC, TOT—it's more complicated than you think and after you do it often enough, it begins to make a little song, that you hear words to, in my case "Hello (*bing*) there, you (*gung*) hap-py *pee*pul (*splat*)!"— the *splat* being the drawer flying out. I uncrease the bill, tenderly as you may imagine, it just having come from between the two smoothest scoops of vanilla I had ever known were there, and pass a half and a penny into her narrow pink palm and nestle the herrings in a bag and twist its neck and hand it over, all the time thinking.

The girls, and who'd blame them, are in a hurry to get out, so I say "I quit" to Lengel quick enough for them to hear, hoping they'll stop and watch me, their unsuspected hero. They keep right on going, into the electric eye; the door flies open and they flicker across the lot to their car, Queenie and Plaid and Big Tall Goony-Goony (not that as raw material she was so bad), leaving me with Lengel and a kink in his eyebrow.

"Did you way something, Sammy?"

"I said I quit."

"I thought you did."

"You didn't have to embarrass them."

"It was they who were embarrassing us."

I started to say something that came out "Fiddle-de-doo." It's a saying of my grandmother's, and I know she would have been pleased.

"I don't think you know what you're saying," Lengel said.

"I know you don't," I said. "But I do." I pull the bow at the back of my apron and start shrugging it off my shoulders. A couple customers that had been heading for my slot begin to knock against each other, like scared pigs in a chute.

Lengel sighs and begins to look very patient and old and gray. He's been a friend of my parents for years. "Sammy, you don't want to do this to your Mom and Dad," he tells me. It's true, I don't. But it seems to me that once you begin a gesture it's fatal not to go through with it. I fold the apron, "Sammy" stitched in red on the pocket, and put it on the counter, and drop the bow tie on top of it. The bow tie is theirs, if you've ever wondered. "You'll feel this for the rest of your life," Lengel says, and I know that's true, too, but remembering how he made that pretty girl blush makes me so scrunchy inside I punch the No Sale tab and the machine whirs "pee-pul" and the drawer splats out. One advantage to this scene taking place in summer, I can follow this up with a clean exit, there's no fumbling around getting your coat and galoshes, I just saunter into the electric eye in my white shirt that my mother ironed the night before, and the door heaves itself open, and outside the sunshine is skating round on the asphalt.

I look around for my girls, but they're gone, of course. There wasn't anybody but some young married screaming with her children about some candy they didn't get by the door of a powder-blue Falcon station wagon. Looking back in the big windows, over the bags of peat moss and aluminum lawn furniture stacked on the pavement, I could see Lengel in my place in the slot, checking the sheep through. His face was dark gray and his back stiff, as if he'd just had an injection of iron, and my stomach kind of fell as I felt how hard the world was going to be to me hereafter.

[1962]

■ TOPICS FOR DISCUSSION AND WRITING

1. In what sort of community is this A & P located? To what extent does this community resemble yours?

2. Do you think Sammy is a male chauvinist pig? Why, or why not? And if you think he is, do you find the story offensive? Again, why or why not?

3. In the last line of the story Sammy says, "I felt how hard the world was going to be to me hereafter." Do you think the world is going to be hard to Sammy? Why, or why not? And if it is hard to him, is this because of a virtue or a weakness in Sammy?

4. Write Lengel's version of the story (500–1000 words) as he might narrate it to his wife during dinner.

5. Speaking of contemporary fiction Updike said:

    I want stories to startle and engage me within the first few sentences, and in their middle to widen or deepen or sharpen my knowledge of human activity, and to end by giving me a sensation of completed statement.

    Let's assume that you share Updike's view of what a story should do. To what extent do you think "A & P" fulfills these demands? (You may want to put your response in the form of a letter to Updike.)

■ CHAPTER 6

Reading

(and Writing about)

Drama

The college essays you write about plays will be similar in many respects to analytic essays about fiction. Unless you are writing a review of a performance, you probably won't try to write about all aspects of a play. Rather, you'll choose one significant aspect as your topic. For instance, if you are writing about Tennessee Williams's *The Glass Menagerie*, you might compare the aspirations of Jim Connor and Tom Wingfield, or you might compare Tom's illusions with those of his sister, Laura, and his mother, Amanda. Or you might examine the symbolism, perhaps limiting your essay topic to the glass animals but perhaps extending it to include other symbols, such as the fire escape, the lighting, and the Victrola. Similarly, if you are writing an analysis, you might decide to study the construction of one scene of a play or (if the play does not have a great many scenes) even the construction of the entire play.

A list of questions on page 174 may help you to find a topic for the particular play you choose to write about.

A Sample Essay

The following essay discusses the structure of *The Glass Menagerie*. It mentions various characters, but since its concern is with the arrangement of scenes, it does not (for instance) examine any of the characters in detail. Of course an essay might well be devoted to examining (for example) Williams's assertion that "There is much to admire in Amanda, and as much to love and pity as there is to laugh at," but an essay on the structure of the play is probably not the place to talk about Williams's characterization of Amanda.

PRELIMINARY NOTES

After deciding to write on the structure of the play, with an eye toward seeing the overall pattern that the parts form, the student reread *The Glass Menagerie*, jotted down some notes briefly summarizing each of the seven scenes, with an occasional comment, and then typed them. On rereading the typed notes, he added a few observations in handwriting.

nagging

1. begins with Tom talking to audience;
   ~~says he is a magician~~
   America, in 1930s
      "shouting and confusion"
   Father deserted
   Amanda nagging; ~~is she a bit cracked?~~
   Tom: bored, angry
   Laura: embarrassed, depressed

2. Laura: quit business school; sad, but
      Jim's name is mentioned, so,
      lighter tone introduced

out-and-out battle ——

3. Tom and Amanda argue
      Tom almost destroys glass menagerie
   Rage: Can things get any worse?

reconcil-iation, and false hopes— then final collapse

4. T and A reconciled
      T to try to get a "gentleman caller"

5. T tells A that Jim will visit
      things are looking up

6. Jim arrives; L terrified
      still, Aman thinks things can work out

7. Lights go out (foreshadowing dark ending?)
      Jim a jerk, clumsy; breaks unicorn, but
      L doesn't seem to mind. Maybe he <u>is</u> the
      right guy to draw her into normal world.
      Jim reveals he is engaged:
         "Desolation."
   Tom escapes into merchant marine, but
      can't escape memories. Speaks to
      audience. L. blows out candles (does
      this mean he forgets her? No, because
      he is remembering her right now. I don't
      get it, if the candles are supposed
      to be symbolic.)

These notes enabled the student to prepare a rough draft, which he then submitted to some classmates for peer review. (On peer review, see page 23.)

Notice that the final version of the essay, printed below, is *not* merely a summary (a brief retelling of the plot). Although it does indeed include summary, it chiefly is devoted to showing *how* the scenes are related.

Title is focused; it announces topic and thesis	**The Solid Structure of The Glass Menagerie**
Opening paragraph closes in on thesis	In the "Production Notes" Tennessee Williams calls The Glass Menagerie a "memory play," a term that the narrator in the play also uses. Memories often consist of fragments of episodes that are so loosely connected that they seem chaotic, and therefore we might think that The Glass Menagerie will consist of very loosely related episodes. However, the play covers only one episode, and though it gives the illusion of random talk, it really has a firm structure and moves steadily toward a foregone conclusion.
Reasonable organization; the paragraph touches on the beginning and the end	Tennessee Williams divides the play into seven scenes. The first scene begins with a sort of prologue, and the last scene concludes with a sort of epilogue that is related to the prologue. In the prologue Tom addresses the audience and comments on the 1930s as a time when America was "blind" and was a place of
Brief but effective quotations	"shouting and confusion." Tom also mentions that our lives consist of expectations, and though he does not say that our expectations are unfulfilled, near the end of the prologue he quotes a postcard that his father wrote to the family he deserted: "Hello––Goodbye." In the epilogue Tom tells us that he followed his "father's footsteps," deserting the family. And just before the epilogue, near the end of Scene VII, we see what can be considered

another desertion: Jim explains to Tom's sister
Laura that he is engaged and therefore

cannot visit Laura again. Thus the end is
closely related to the beginning, and the play
is the steady development of the initial
implications.

The first three scenes show things going
from bad to worse. Amanda is a nagging mother
who finds her only relief in talking about the
past to her crippled daughter Laura and her
frustrated son Tom. When she was young she was
beautiful and was eagerly courted by rich young
men, but now the family is poor and this
harping on the past can only bore or infuriate
Tom and embarrass or depress Laura, who have no
happy past to look back to, who see no happy
future, and who can only be upset by Amanda's
insistence that they should behave as she
behaved long ago. The second scene deepens the

despair: Amanda learns that the timorous Laura
has not been attending a business school but
has retreated in terror from this
confrontation with the contemporary world.
Laura's helplessness is made clear to the
audience, and so is Amanda's lack of
understanding. Near the end of the second
scene, however, Jim's name is introduced; he is
a boy Laura had a crush on in high school, and
so the audience gets a glimpse of a happier
Laura and a sense that possibly Laura's world
is wider than the stifling tenement in which
she and her mother and brother live. But in the
third scene things get worse, when Tom and
Amanda have so violent an argument that they
are no longer on speaking terms. Tom is so

angry with his mother that he almost by
accident destroys his sister's treasured
collection of glass animals, the fragile,
lifeless world that is her refuge. The
apartment is literally full of the "shouting
and confusion" that Tom spoke of in his
prologue.

Useful summary and
transition

   The first three scenes have revealed a
progressive worsening of relations; the next
three scenes reveal a progressive improvement
in relations. In Scene IV Tom and his mother
are reconciled, and Tom reluctantly—
apparently in an effort to make up with his
mother—agrees to try to get a friend to come
to dinner so that Laura will have "a gentleman
caller." In Scene V Tom tells his mother that
Jim will come to dinner on the next night, and
Amanda brightens, because she sees a
possibility of security for Laura at last. In
Scene VI Jim arrives, and despite Laura's
initial terror, there seems, at least in
Amanda's mind, to be the possiblity that things
will go well.

   The seventh scene, by far the longest, at
first seems to be fulfilling Amanda's hopes.
Despite the ominous fact that the lights go out
because Tom has not paid the electric bill, Jim
is at ease. He is an insensitive oaf, but that
doesn't seem to bother Amanda, and almost
miraculously he manages to draw Laura somewhat
out of her sheltered world. Even when Jim in
his clumsiness breaks the horn off Laura's
treasured glass unicorn, she is not upset. In
fact, she is almost relieved because the loss
of the horn makes the animal less "freakish"

and he "will feel more at home with the other horses." In a way, of course, the unicorn symbolizes the crippled Laura, who at least for the moment feels less freakish and isolated now that she is somewhat reunited with society through Jim. But this is a play about life in a blind and confused world, and though in a previous age the father escaped, there can be no escape now. Jim reveals that he is engaged, Laura relapses into "desolation," Amanda relapses into rage and bitterness, and Tom relapses into dreams of escape. In a limited sense Tom does escape. He leaves the family and joins the merchant marine, but his last speech or epilogue tells us that he cannot escape the memory of his sister: "Oh, Laura, Laura, I tried to leave you behind me, but I am more faithful than I intended to be!" And so the

The essayist is thinking and commenting, not merely summarizing the plot

end of the last scene brings us back again to the beginning of the first scene: we are still in a world of "the blind" and of "confusion." But now at the end of the play the darkness is deeper, the characters are lost forever in their unhappiness as Laura "blows the candles out," the darkness being literal but also symbolic of their extinguished hopes.

Numerous devices, such as repeated references to the absent father, to Amanda's youth, to Laura's Victrola, and of course to Laura's glass menagerie help to tie the scenes together

Useful, thoughtful summary of thesis

into a unified play. But beneath these threads of imagery and recurring motifs is a fundamental pattern that involves the movement from nagging (Scenes I and II) to open hostilities (Scene III) to temporary

reconciliation (Scene IV) to false hopes
(Scenes V and VI) to an impossible heightening
of false hopes and then, in a swift descent, to
an inevitable collapse (Scene VII). Tennessee
Williams has constructed his play carefully.
G. B. Tennyson says that a "playwright must
'build' his speeches, as the theatrical

Effective quotation from
an outside source

expression has it" (13). But a playwright must
do more, he must also build his play out of
scenes. Like Ibsen, if Williams had been
introduced to an architect he might have said,
"Architecture is my business too."

Works Cited

Documentation

Tennyson, G. B. <u>An Introduction to Drama</u>.
        New York: Holt, 1967.
Williams, Tennessee. <u>The Glass Menagerie</u>.
        <u>Literature for Composition</u>. Ed. Sylvan
        Barnet et al. 3rd ed. New York:
        HarperCollins, 1991. 721-767.

Types of Plays

Most of the world's great plays written before the twentieth century may
be regarded as one of two kinds: **tragedy** or **comedy**. Roughly speaking,
tragedy dramatizes the conflict between the vitality of the single life and the
laws or limits of life. The tragic hero reaches a height, going beyond the experience of others but at the cost of his or her life. Comedy, on the other
hand, dramatizes the vitality of the laws of social life. In comedy, the good
life is seen to reside in the shedding of an individualism that isolates, in favor
of a union with a genial and enlightened society. These points must be amplified a bit before we go on to the further point that, of course, any important
play does much more than can be put into such crude formulas.

TRAGEDY

Tragic heroes usually go beyond the standards to which reasonable people adhere; they do some fearful deed which ultimately destroys them. This
deed is often said to be an act of *hubris*, a Greek word meaning something

like "overweening pride." It may involve, for instance, violating a taboo, such as that against taking life. But if the hubristic act ultimately destroys the man or woman who performs it, it also shows that person (paradoxically) to be in some way more fully a living being—a person who has experienced life more fully, whether by heroic action or by capacity for enduring suffering—than the other characters in the play. (If the tragic hero does not die, he or she is usually left in some deathlike state, as is the blind Oedipus in *Oedipus Rex*.) In tragedy we see humanity pushed to an extreme; the hero enters a world unknown to most and reveals magnificence. After the hero's departure from the stage, we are left in a world of littler people.

What has just been said may (or may not) be true of most tragedies, but it certainly is not true of all. If you are writing about a tragedy, you might consider whether the points just made are illustrated in your play. Is the hero guilty of *hubris?* Does the hero seem a greater person than the others in the play? An essay examining such questions probably requires not only a character sketch but also some comparison with other characters.

Tragedy commonly involves **irony** of two sorts: unconsciously ironic deeds and unconsciously ironic speeches. **Ironic deeds** have some consequence more or less the reverse of what the doer intends. Macbeth thinks that by killing Duncan he will gain happiness, but he finds that his deed brings him sleepless nights. Brutus thinks that by killing Caesar he will bring liberty to Rome, but he brings tyranny. In an **unconsciously ironic speech**, the speaker's words mean one thing to him but something more significant to the audience, as when King Duncan, baffled by Cawdor's treason, says:

> There's no art
> To find the mind's construction in the face:
> He was a gentleman on whom I build
> An absolute trust.

At this moment Macbeth, whom we have already heard meditating the murder of Duncan, enters. Duncan's words are true, but he does not apply them to Macbeth, as the audience does. A few moments later Duncan praises Macbeth as "a peerless kinsman." Soon Macbeth will indeed become peerless, when he kills Duncan and ascends to the throne.[1] Sophocles' use of ironic deeds and speeches is so pervasive, especially in *Oedipus Rex*, that **Sophoclean irony** has become a critical term.

When the deed backfires or has a reverse effect, such as Macbeth's effort to gain happiness has, we have what Aristotle (the first—and still the

---

[1] **Dramatic irony** (ironic deeds, or happenings, and unconsciously ironic speeches) must be distinguished from **verbal irony,** which is produced when the speaker is *conscious* that his words mean something different from what they say. In *Macbeth* Lennox says: "The gracious Duncan / Was pitied of Macbeth. Marry, he was dead! / And the right valiant Banquo walked too late. / . . . / Men must not walk too late." He *says* nothing about Macbeth having killed Duncan and Banquo, but he *means* that Macbeth has killed them.

greatest—drama critic) called a **peripeteia,** or a **reversal.** When a character comes to perceive what has happened (Macbeth's "I have lived long
enough: my way of life / Is fall'n into the sere, the yellow leaf"), he experiences (in Aristotle's language) an **anagnorisis,** or **recognition.** Strictly speaking, for Aristotle the recognition was a matter of literal
identification—for example, the recognition that Oedipus was the son of a
man he killed. In *Macbeth,* the recognition in this sense is that Macduff,
"from his mother's womb / Untimely ripped," is the man who fits the
prophecy that Macbeth can be conquered only by someone not "of woman
born."

In his analysis of drama, Aristotle says that the tragic hero comes to
grief through his **hamartia,** a term sometimes translated as **tragic flaw** but
perhaps better translated as **tragic error,** since *flaw* implies a moral fault.
Thus it is a great error for Oedipus (however apparently justifiable his action)
to kill a man old enough to be his father, and to marry a woman old enough
to be his mother. If we hold to the translation *flaw,* we begin to hunt for a
fault in the tragic hero's character; and we say, for instance, that Oedipus
is rash, or some such thing. In doing this, we may diminish or even overlook
the hero's grandeur.

COMEDY

Although in tragedy the hero usually seems to embody certain values
that are superior to those of the surrounding society, in comedy the fullest
life is seen to reside *within* enlightened social norms: At the beginning of a
comedy we find banished dukes, unhappy lovers, crabby parents, jealous
husbands, and harsh laws; but at the end we usually have a unified and genial
society, often symbolized by a marriage feast to which everyone, or almost
everyone, is invited. Early in *A Midsummer Night's Dream,* for instance, we
meet quarreling young lovers and a father who demands that his daughter
either marry a man she does not love or enter a convent. Such is the Atheni-
an law. At the end of the play the lovers are properly matched, to everyone's
satisfaction.

Speaking broadly, most comedies fall into one of two classes: **satiric
comedy** or **romantic comedy.** In satiric comedy, the emphasis is on the
obstructionists—the irate fathers, hardheaded businessmen, and other
members of the Establishment who at the beginning of the play seem to hold
all of the cards, preventing joy from reigning. They are held up to ridicule
because they are repressive monomaniacs enslaved to themselves, acting
mechanistically (always irate, always hardheaded) instead of responding
genially to the ups and downs of life. The outwitting of these obstructionists,
usually by the younger generation, often provides the resolution of the plot.
Ben Jonson, Molière, and George Bernard Shaw are in this tradition; their
comedy, according to an ancient Roman formula, "chastens morals with
ridicule"—that is, it reforms folly or vice by laughing at it. On the other
hand, in romantic comedy (one thinks of Shakespeare's *A Midsummer*

Night's Dream, As You Like It, and *Twelfth Night*) the emphasis is on a pair or pairs of delightful people who engage our sympathies as they run their obstacle race to the altar. There are obstructionists here too, but the emphasis is on festivity.

In writing about comedy you may, of course, be concerned with the function of one scene or character, but whatever your topic, you may find it helpful to begin by trying to decide whether the play is primarily romantic or primarily satiric (or something else). One way of getting at this is to ask yourself to what degree you sympathize with the characters. Do you laugh *with* them, sympathetically, or on the other hand do you laugh *at* them, regarding them as at least somewhat contemptible?

Aspects of Drama

THEME

If we have read or seen a drama thoughtfully, we ought to be able to formulate its **theme,** its underlying idea, and perhaps we can even go so far as to say its moral attitudes, its view of life, its wisdom. Some critics, it is true, have argued that the concept of theme is meaningless. They hold that *Macbeth,* for example, gives us only an extremely detailed history of one imaginary man. In this view, *Macbeth* says nothing to you or me; it only says what happened to some imaginary man. Even *Julius Caesar* says nothing about the historical Julius Caesar or about the nature of Roman politics. Here we can agree; no one would offer Shakespeare's play as evidence of what the historical Caesar said or did. But surely the view that the concept of theme is meaningless, and that a work tells us only about imaginary creatures, is a desperate one. We *can* say that we see in *Julius Caesar* the fall of power, or (if we are thinking of Brutus) the vulnerability of idealism, or some such thing.

To the reply that these are mere truisms, we can counter: Yes, but the truisms are presented in such a way that they take on life and become a part of us rather than remaining things of which we say, "I've heard it said, and I guess it's so." The play offers instruction, in a pleasant and persuasive way. And surely we are in no danger of equating the play with the theme that we sense underlies it. We recognize that the play presents the theme with such detail that our statement is only a wedge to help us enter into the play, so we can appropriate it more fully.

Some critics (influenced by Aristotle's statement that a drama is an imitation of an action) use **action** in a sense equivalent to theme. In this sense, the action is the underlying happening—the inner happening—for example, "the enlightenment of a character," or "the coming of unhappiness to a character," or "the finding of the self by self-surrender." One might say that the theme of *Macbeth,* for example, is embodied in some words that Macbeth himself utters: "Blood will have blood." Of course this is not to say that these words and no other words embody the theme or the action; it is only to say that these words seem to the writer (and, if the essay is effective, to the reader) to bring us close to the center of the play.

PLOT

Plot is variously defined, sometimes as equivalent to *story* (in this sense a synopsis of *Julius Caesar* has the same plot as *Julius Caesar*), but more often, and more usefully, as the dramatist's particular *arrangement of the story*. Thus, because Shakespeare's *Julius Caesar* begins with a scene dramatizing an encounter between plebeians and tribunes, its plot is different from that of a play on Julius Caesar in which such a scene (not necessary to the story) is omitted.

Handbooks on drama often suggest that a plot (arrangement of happenings) should have a **rising action,** a **climax,** and a **falling action.** This sort of plot can be diagramed as a pyramid: The tension rises through complications or **crises** to a climax, at which point the climax is the apex, and the tension allegedly slackens as we witness the **dénouement** (literally, *unknotting*). Shakespeare sometimes used a pyramidal structure, placing his climax neatly in the middle of what seems to us to be the third of five acts. In *Hamlet*, the protagonist proves to his own satisfaction Claudius's guilt in 3.2, with the play within the play; but almost immediately he begins to worsen his position, by failing to kill Claudius when he is an easy target (3.3) and by contaminating himself with the murder of Polonius (3.4). In *Romeo and Juliet*, the first half shows Romeo winning Juliet, but when in 3.1 he kills her cousin Tybalt, Romeo sets in motion the second half of the play, the losing of Juliet and of his own life.

Of course, no law demands such a structure, and a hunt for the pyramid usually causes the hunter to overlook all the crises but the middle one. William Butler Yeats once suggestively diagramed a good plot not as a pyramid but as a line moving diagonally upward, punctuated by several crises. Perhaps it is sufficient to say that a good plot has its moments of tension, but the location of these will vary with the play. They are the product of **conflict,** but it should be noted that not all conflict produces tension; there is conflict but little tension in a ball game when the home team is ahead 10–0 and the visiting pitcher comes to bat in the ninth inning with two out and none on base.

Regardless of how a plot is diagramed, the **exposition** is that part that tells the audience what it has to know about the past, the **antecedent action.** Two gossiping servants who tell each other that after a year away in Paris the young master is coming home tomorrow with a new wife are giving the audience the exposition. But the exposition may also extend far into the play, being given in small, explosive revelations.

Exposition has been discussed as though it consists simply of informing the audience about events, but exposition can do much more. It can give us an understanding of the characters who themselves are talking about other characters, it can evoke a mood, and it can generate tension. When we summarize the opening act, and treat it as "mere exposition," we are probably losing what is in fact dramatic in it.

In fact, exposition usually includes *foreshadowing*. Details given in the exposition, which we may at first take as mere background, often turn out to be highly relevant to later developments. For instance, in the very short first scene of *Macbeth* the Witches introduce the name of Macbeth, but in such words as "Fair is foul" and "when the battle's lost and won" they also give glimpses of what will happen: Macbeth will become foul, and though he will seem to win (he becomes king) he will lose the most important battle. Similarly, during the exposition in the second scene we learn that Macbeth has loyally defeated Cawdor, who betrayed King Duncan, and Macbeth has been given Cawdor's title. Later we will find that, like Cawdor, Macbeth betrays Duncan. That is, in giving us the background about Cawdor, the exposition is also telling us (though we don't know it, when we first see or read the play) something about what will happen to Macbeth.

In writing about an aspect of plot, you may want to consider one of the following topics:

1. Is the plot improbable? If so, is the play therefore weak?
2. Does a scene that might at first glance seem unimportant or even irrelevant serve an important function?
3. If certain actions that could be shown onstage take place offstage, is there a reason? In *Macbeth*, for instance, why do you suppose the murder of Duncan takes place offstage, whereas Banquo and Macduff's family are murdered onstage? Why, then, might Shakespeare have preferred not to show us the murder of Duncan? What has he gained? (A good way to approach this sort of question is to think of what your own reaction would be if the action were shown on the stage.)
4. If there are several conflicts—for example, between pairs of lovers or between parents and their children and also between the parents themselves—how are these conflicts related? Are they parallel? Or contrasting?
5. Does the arrangement of scenes have a structure? For instance, do the scenes depict a rise and then a fall?
6. Does the plot seem satisfactorily concluded? Are there loose threads? If so, is the apparent lack of a complete resolution a weakness in the play? Or does it serve a function?

GESTURES

The language of a play, broadly conceived, includes the **gestures** that the characters make and the settings in which they make them. As Ezra Pound says, "The medium of drama is not words, but persons moving about on a stage using words." Because plays are meant to be seen, make every effort to visualize the action when you read a play. Ibsen is getting at something important when he tells us in a stage direction that Nora "walks cautiously over to the door to the study and listens." Her silent actions tell us as much about her as many of her speeches do.

Gesture can be interpreted even more broadly: The mere fact that a character enters, leaves, or does not enter may be highly significant. John

Russell Brown comments on the actions and the absence of certain words that in *Hamlet* convey the growing separation between King Claudius and his wife, Gertrude:

> Their first appearance together with a public celebration of marriage is a large and simple visual effect, and Gertrude's close concern for her son suggests a simple, and perhaps unremarkable modification. . . . But Claudius enters without Gertrude for his "Prayer Scene" (3.2) and, for the first time, Gertrude enters without him for the Closet Scene (3.4) and is left alone, again for the first time, when Polonius hides behind the arras. Thereafter earlier accord is revalued by an increasing separation, often poignantly silent and unexpected. When Claudius calls Gertrude to leave with him after Hamlet has dragged off Polonius' body, she makes no reply; twice more he urges her and she is still silent. But he does not remonstrate or question; rather he speaks of his own immediate concerns and, far from supporting her with assurances, becomes more aware of his own fears:
>
> O, come away!
My soul is full of discord and dismay. (4.1.44–45)
>
> Emotion has been so heightened that it is remarkable that they leave together without further words. The audience has been aware of a new distance between Gertrude and Claudius, of her immobility and silence, and of his self-concern, haste, and insistence.*

SETTING

Drama of the nineteenth and early twentieth centuries (for example, the plays of Henrik Ibsen, Anton Chekhov, and George Bernard Shaw) is often thought to be "realistic," but even a realistic playwright or stage designer selects from among many available materials. A **realistic setting** (indication of the **locale**), then, can say a great deal, and can even serve as a symbol. Over and over again in Ibsen we find the realistic setting of a nineteenth-century drawing room, with its heavy draperies and its bulky furniture, helping to convey his vision of a bourgeois world that oppresses the individual who struggles to affirm other values.

Twentieth-century dramatists are often explicit about the symbolic qualities of the setting. Here is an example from Eugene O'Neill's *Desire under the Elms:* Only a part of the initial stage direction is given.

> The house is in good condition but in need of paint. Its walls are a sickly grayish, the green of the shutters faded. Two enormous elms are on each side of the house. They bend their trailing branches down over the roof. They appear to protect and at the same time subdue. There is a sinister maternity in their aspect, a crushing, jealous absorption. . . . They are like exhausted women resting their sagging breasts and hands and hair on its roof. . . .

Not surprisingly, the action in the play includes deeds of "sinister maternity" (a mother kills her infant) and "jealous absorption."

Shakespeare's Plays in Performance (New York: St. Martin's, 1967), p. 139.

In *The Glass Menagerie* Tennessee Williams tells us that

> the apartment faces an alley and is entered by a fire escape, a structure whose name is a touch of accidental poetic truth, for all of these huge buildings are always burning with the slow and implacable fires of human desperation.

CHARACTERIZATION AND MOTIVATION

Characterization, or personality, is defined, as in fiction (see page 111), by what the characters do (a stage direction tells us that "Nora dances more and more wildly"), by what they say (she asks her husband to play the piano), by what others say about them, and by the setting in which they move. The characters are also defined in part by other characters whom they in some degree resemble or from whom they in some degree differ. Hamlet, Laertes, and Fortinbras have each lost their fathers, but Hamlet spares the praying King Claudius, whereas Laertes, seeking vengeance on Hamlet for murdering Laertes's father, says he would cut Hamlet's throat in church; Hamlet meditates about the nature of action, but Fortinbras leads the Norwegians in a military campaign and ultimately acquires Denmark.

Other plays, of course, also provide examples of such **foils,** or characters who set one another off. Macbeth and Banquo both hear prophecies, but they act and react differently; Brutus is one kind of assassin, Cassius another, and Casca still another. Any analysis of a character, then, will probably have to take into account, in some degree, the other characters who help to show what he or she is, and who thus help to set forth his or her **motivation** (grounds for action, inner drives, goals).

Organizing an Analysis of a Character

As you read and reread, you'll annotate the text and will jot down (in whatever order they come to you) your thoughts about the character you are studying. Reading, with a view toward writing, you'll want to

1. jot down traits as they come to mind ("kind," "forgetful," "enthusiastic");
2. look back at the text, searching for supporting evidence (characteristic actions, brief supporting quotations); and of course you will also look for counterevidence so that you may modify your earlier impressions.

Brainstorming leads to an evaluation of your ideas and to a shaping of them. Evaluating and shaping lead to a tentative outline, and a tentative outline leads to the search for supporting evidence—the material that will constitute the body of your essay.

When you set out to write a first draft, review your annotations and notes and see if you can summarize your view of the character in one or two sentences:

X is. . . ,

or

Although X is . . . , she is also . . . .

That is, try to formulate a thesis sentence or a thesis paragraph, a proposition that you will go on to support.

You want to let your reader know early, probably in your first sentence—and almost certainly by the end of your first paragraph—which character you are writing about and what your overall thesis is.

FIRST DRAFT

Here is the first draft of an opening paragraph that identifies the character and sets forth a thesis.

Romeo is a very interesting character, I think. In the beginning of the play Romeo is very adolescent. Romeo is smitten with puppy love for a woman named Rosaline. He desires to show all of his friends that he knows how a lover is supposed to act. When he sees Juliet he experiences true love. From the point when he sees Juliet he experiences true love, and from this point he steadily matures in Romeo and Juliet. He moves from a self-centered man to a man who lives not for himself but only for Juliet.

Later the student edited the draft. We reprint the original, with the additional editing in handwriting.

Romeo ~~is a very interesting character, I think. In~~ the ~~beginning of the play Romeo is very~~ begins as an adolescent, ~~Romeo is~~ smitten with puppy love for ~~a woman named~~ Rosaline, and a desire ~~He desires~~ to show all of his friends that he knows how a lover is supposed to act. When he sees Juliet, however, he experiences true love, and this ~~From~~ ~~the~~ point ~~when he sees Juliet he experiences true love, and from this point~~ he steadily matures, ~~in Romeo and Juliet. He moves~~ moving *adolescent*

from a self-centered ~~man~~ to a man who lives ~~not for himself but~~ only for Juliet.

Here is a revised version of another effective opening paragraph, effective partly because it identifies the character and offers a thesis.

> In the last speech of <u>Macbeth</u>, Malcolm character-
> izes Lady Macbeth as "fiend-like," and indeed she
> invokes evil spirits and prompts her husband to commit
> murder. But despite her bold pose, her role in the
> murder, and her belief that she will be untroubled by
> guilt, she has a conscience that torments her and that
> finally drives her to suicide. She is not a mere
> heartless villain; she is a human being who is less
> strong--and more moral--than she thinks she is.

Notice that the paragraph quotes a word ("fiend-like") from the text. It happens that the writer goes on to argue that this word is *not* a totally accurate description, but the quotation nevertheless helps to bring the reader into close contact with the subject of the essay.

Notice also that in writing about literature we do not ordinarily introduce the thesis formally. We do not, that is, say "In this paper it is my intention to prove that . . . ." Such a sentence may be perfectly appropriate in a paper in Political Science, but in a paper on literature it is out of place.

The body of your essay will be devoted, of course, to supporting your thesis. If you have asserted that although Lady Macbeth is cruel and domineering she nevertheless is endowed with a conscience, you will go on in your essay to support those assertions with references to passages that demonstrate them. This does *not* mean that you tell the plot of the whole work; an essay on a character is by no means the same as a summary of the plot. But since you must support your generalizations, you will have to make brief references to specific episodes that reveal her personality, and almost surely you will quote an occasional word or passage.

There are many possible ways to organize an essay on a character. Much will depend, of course, on your purpose and thesis. For instance, you may want to show how the character develops—gains knowledge, or matures, or disintegrates. Or, again, you may want to show what the character contributes to the story or play as a whole. Or, to give yet another example, you may want to show that the character is unbelievable. Still, although no single organization is always right, two methods are common and effective. One is to let the organization of your essay follow closely the sequence of the literary work;

that is, you might devote a paragraph to Lady Macbeth as we perceive her in the first act, and then in subsequent paragraphs go on to show that her character is later seen to be more complex than it at first appears. Such an essay may trace your changing responses. This does not mean that you need to write five paragraphs, one on her character in each of the five acts. But it does mean that you might begin with Lady Macbeth as you perceive her in, say, the first act, and then go on to the additional revelations of the rest of the play.

A second effective way of organizing an essay on a character is to set forth, early in the essay, the character's chief traits—let's say the chief strengths and two or three weaknesses—and then go on to study each trait you have listed. Here the organization would (in order to maintain the reader's interest) probably begin with the most obvious points and then move on to the less obvious, subtler points. The body of your essay, in any case, is devoted to offering evidence that supports your generalizations about the character.

What about a concluding paragraph? the concluding paragraph ought *not* to begin with the obviousness of "Thus we see," or "In conclusion," or "I recommend this play because . . . ." In fact, after you have given what you consider a sound sketch of the character, it may be appropriate simply to quit. Especially if your essay has moved from the obvious traits to the more subtle and more important traits, and if your essay is fairly short (say, fewer than 500 words), a reader may not need a conclusion. Further, there probably is no reason to blunt what you have just said by adding an unnecessary and merely repetitive summary. But if you do feel that a conclusion is necessary, you may find it effective to write a summary of the character, somewhat as you did in your opening. For the conclusion, relate the character's character to the entire drama—that is, try to give the reader a sense of the role that the character plays.

Writing a Review

Your instructor may ask you to write a review of a local production. A review requires analytic skill but it is not identical with an analysis. First of all, a reviewer normally assumes that the reader is unfamiliar with the production being reviewed, and unfamiliar with the play if the play is not a classic. Thus, the first paragraph usually provides a helpful introduction, along these lines:

> Marsha Norman's new play, *'night, Mother,* a tragedy with only two actors and one set, shows us a woman's preparation for suicide. Jesse has concluded that she no longer wishes to live, and so she tries to put her affairs into order, which chiefly means preparing her rather uncomprehending mother to get along without her.

Inevitably some retelling of the plot is necessary if the play is new, and a summary of a sentence or two is acceptable even for a familiar play, but the review will chiefly be concerned with

1. describing,
2. analyzing, and, especially,
3. evaluating.

(By the way, don't confuse description with analysis. Description tells what something—for instance, the set or the costumes—looks like; analysis tells us how it works, what it adds up to, what it contributes to the total effect.) If the play is new, much of the evaluation may center on the play itself, but if the play is a classic, the evaluation probably will be devoted chiefly to the acting, the set, and the direction.

Other points:

1. **Save the playbill;** it will give you the names of the actors, and perhaps a brief biography of the author, a synopsis of the plot, and a photograph of the set, all of which may be helpful.
2. **Draft your review as soon as possible,** while the performance is still fresh in your mind. If you can't draft it immediately after seeing the play, at least jot down some notes about the setting and the staging, the acting, and the audience's responses.
3. If possible, **read the play**—ideally, before the performance and again after it.
4. **In your first draft, don't worry about limitations of space;** write as long a review as you can, putting down everything that comes to mind. Later you can cut it to the required length, retaining only the chief points and the necessary supporting details. But in your first draft try to produce a fairly full record of the performance and your response to it, so that a day or two later, when you revise, you won't have to trust a fading memory for details.

A Sample Review

If you read reviews of plays in *Time, Newsweek,* or a newspaper, you will soon develop a sense of what reviews do. The following example, an undergraduate's review of a college production of *Macbeth,* is typical except in one respect: Reviews of new plays, as we have already suggested, customarily include a few sentences summarizing the plot and classifying the play (a tragedy, a farce, a rock musical, or whatever), perhaps briefly putting it in the context of the author's other works. Because *Macbeth* is so widely known, however, the writer of this review chose not to risk offending her readers by telling them that *Macbeth* is a tragedy by Shakespeare.

PRELIMINARY JOTTINGS

During the two intermissions and immediately after the end of the performance, the reviewer made a few jottings, which the next day she rewrote thus:

Compare with last year's <u>Midsummer Night's Dream</u>
Set: barren;
    pipe framework at rear. Duncan exits on it. Useful?
witches: powerful, not funny
stage: battlefield? barren land?
    costume: earth-colored rags
    they seduce--even caress--Mac.
Macbeth
    ~~witches caress him e~~
    strong; also gentle (with Lady M)
Lady Macb.
    sexy in speech about unsexing her
    too attractive? Prob. ok
Banquo's ghost: naturalistic; covered with blood
Duncan: terrible; worst actor except for Lady
    Macduff's boy
costumes: leather, metal; only Duncan in robes
pipe framework used for D, and murder of Lady Macduff
forest; branches unrealistic; stylized? or cheesy?

THE FINISHED VERSION

The published review appears below, accompanied by some marginal notes in which we comment on its strengths.

Title implies thesis

An Effective <u>Macbeth</u>

Opening paragraph is informative, letting the reader know the reviewer's overall attitude

    <u>Macbeth</u> at the University Theater is a thoughtful and occasionally exciting production, partly because the director, Mark Urice, has trusted Shakespeare and has not imposed a gimmick on the play. The characters do not wear cowboy costumes as they did in last year's production of <u>A Midsummer Night's Dream.</u>

Reviewer promptly turns to a major issue

    Probably the chief problem confronting a director of <u>Macbeth</u> is how to present the witches so that they are powerful supernatural forces and not silly things that look as though they came from a Halloween party. Urice gives us ugly but not absurdly grotesque witches, and he introduces them most effectively. The stage seems to be a bombed-out battlefield littered with rocks and great chunks of earth, but some of these begin to stir--the earth seems to come alive--and the clods move, unfold, and become the witches, dressed in brown and dark gray rags. The suggestion is that the witches are a part of nature, elemental forces that can hardly be escaped. This effect is increased by the moans and creaking noises that they make, all of which could be comic but which in this production are impressive.

First sentence of this paragraph provides an effective transition

The witches' power over Macbeth is further emphasized by their actions. When the witches first meet Macbeth, they encircle him, touch him, caress him, even embrace him, and he seems helpless, almost their plaything. Moreover, in the scene in which he imagines that he sees a dagger, the director has arranged for one of the witches to appear, stand near Macbeth, and guide his hand toward the invisible dagger. This is, of course, not in the text, but the interpretation is reasonable rather than intrusive. Finally, near the end of the play, just before Macduff kills Macbeth, a witch appears and laughs at Macbeth as Macduff explains that he was not "born of woman." There is no doubt that throughout the tragedy Macbeth has been a puppet of the witches.

Paragraph begins with a broad assertion and then offers supporting details

Stephen Beers (Macbeth) and Tina Peters (Lady Macbeth) are excellent. Beers is sufficiently brawny to be convincing as a battlefield hero, but he also speaks the lines sensitively, so the audience feels that in addition to being a hero, he is a man of gentleness. One can believe Lady Macbeth when she says that she fears he is "too full o' the

Reference to a particular scene

milk of human kindness" to murder Duncan. Lady Macbeth is especially effective in the scene in which she asks the spirits to "unsex her." During this speech she is reclining on a bed and as she delivers the lines she becomes increasingly sexual in her bodily motions, deriving excitement from her own stimulating words. Her attachment to Macbeth is strongly sexual, and so is his attraction to her. The scene when she persuades him to kill Duncan ends with their passionately embracing. The strong attraction of each for the other, so evident in the early part of the play, disappears after the murder, when Macbeth keeps his distance from Lady Macbeth and does not allow her to touch him. The acting of the other performers is effective, except for John Berens (Duncan), who recites the lines mechanically and seems not to take much account of their meaning.

Description, but also analysis

The set consists of a barren plot, at the rear of which stands a spidery framework of piping of the sort used by construction companies, supporting a catwalk. This framework fits with the costumes (lots of armor, leather, heavy boots), suggesting a sort of elemental, primitive, and somewhat sadistic world. The catwalk, though effectively used when Macbeth goes off to murder Duncan (whose room is presumably upstairs and offstage) is not much used in later scenes. For the most part it is an

*Concrete details to
support evaluation*

interesting piece of scenery but not otherwise helpful. For instance, there is no reason
why the scene with Macduff's wife and children
is staged on it. The costumes are not in any
way Scottish—no plaids—but in several scenes
the sound of a bagpipe is heard, adding another
weird or primitive tone to the production.

Summary

This Macbeth appeals to the eye, the ear,
and the mind. The director has given us a
unified production that makes sense and that is
faithful to the spirit of Shakespeare's play.

Much of what we want to say about this review we have already said in
our marginal notes, but three additional points should be made:

1. The reviewer's feelings and evaluations are clearly expressed, not in
   such expressions as "furthermore I feel," and "it is also my opinion," but
   in such expressions as "a thoughtful and occasionally exciting production," "excellent," and "appeals to the eye, the ear, and the mind."
2. The evaluations are supported by details. For instance, the evaluation
   that the witches are effectively presented is supported by a brief description of their appearance.
3. The reviewer is courteous, even when (as in the discussion of the catwalk, in the next-to-last paragraph) she is talking about aspects of the
   production she doesn't care for.

Summing Up: Getting Ideas for Writing about Drama

The following questions may help you to formulate ideas for an essay on
a play.

PLOT AND CONFLICT

1. Does the exposition introduce elements that will be ironically fulfilled?
   During the exposition do you perceive things differently from the way the
   characters perceive them?
2. Are certain happenings or situations recurrent? If so, what significance
   do you attach to them?
3. If there is more than one plot, do the plots seem to you to be related?

Is one plot clearly the main plot and another plot a sort of subplot, a minor variation on the theme?

4. Do any scenes strike you as irrelevant?

5. Are certain scenes so strongly foreshadowed that you anticipated them? If so, did the happenings in these scenes merely fulfill your expectations, or did they also surprise you?

6. What kinds of conflict are there? One character against another, one group against another, one part of a personality against another part in the same person?

7. How is the conflict resolved? By an unambiguous triumph of one side or by a triumph that is also in some degree a loss for the triumphant side? Do you find the resolution satisfying, or unsettling, or what? Why?

CHARACTER

1. A dramatic character is not likely to be thoroughly realistic, a copy of someone we might know. Still, we can ask if the character is consistent and coherent. We can also ask if the character is complex or is, on the other hand, a rather simple representative of some human type.

2. How is the character defined? Consider what the character says and does and what others say about him or her and do to him or her. Also consider other characters who more or less resemble the character in question, because the similarities—and the differences—may be significant.

3. How trustworthy are the characters when they characterize themselves? When they characterize others?

4. Do characters change as the play goes on, or do we simply know them better at the end?

5. What do you make of the minor characters? Are they merely necessary to the plot, or are they foils to other characters? Or do they serve some other functions?

6. If a character is tragic, does the tragedy seem to you to proceed from a moral flaw, from an intellectual error, from the malice of others, from sheer chance, or from some combination of these?

7. What are the character's goals? To what degree do you sympathize with them? If a character is comic, do you laugh *with* or *at* the character?

8. Do you think the characters are adequately motivated?

9. Is a given character so meditative that you feel he or she is engaged less in a dialogue with others than in a dialogue with the self? If so, do you feel that this character is in large degree a spokesperson for the author, commenting not only on the world of the play but also on the outside world?

NONVERBAL LANGUAGE

1. If the playwright does not provide full stage directions, try to imagine for at least one scene what gestures and tones might accompany each speech. (The first scene is usually a good one to try your hand at.)

2. What do you make of the setting? Does it help to reveal character? Do changes of scene strike you as symbolic? If so, symbolic of what?

THE PLAY ON FILM

1. If the play has been turned into a film, what has been added? What has been omitted? Why?
2. Has the film medium been used to advantage—for example, in focusing attention through close-ups or reaction shots (shots showing not the speaker but a person reacting to the speaker). Or do some of the inventions, such as outdoor scenes that were not possible in the play, seem mere busywork, distracting from the urgency or the conflict or the unity of the play?

Two Short Plays

■ SUSAN GLASPELL

Susan Glaspell (1882–1948) was born in Davenport, Iowa, and educated at Drake University in Des Moines. In 1903 she married George Cram Cook and, with Cook and other writers, actors, and artists, in 1915 founded the Provincetown Players, a group that remained vital until 1929. Glaspell wrote *Trifles* (1916) for the Provincetown Players, but she also wrote stories, novels, and a biography of her husband. In 1931 she won the Pulitzer Prize for *Alison's House*, a play about the family of a deceased poet who in some ways resembles Emily Dickinson.

Trifles

SCENE: *The kitchen in the now abandoned farmhouse of* JOHN WRIGHT, *a gloomy kitchen, and left without having been put in order—unwashed pans under the sink, a loaf of bread outside the breadbox, a dish towel on the table—other signs of incompleted work. At the rear the outer door opens, and the* SHERIFF *comes in, followed by the* COUNTY ATTORNEY *and* HALE. *The* SHERIFF *and* HALE *are men in middle life, the* COUNTY ATTORNEY *is a young man; all are much bundled up and go at once to the stove. They are followed by the two women—the* SHERIFF'S WIFE *first; she is a slight wiry woman, a thin nervous face.* MRS. HALE *is larger and would ordinarily be called more comfortable looking, but she is disturbed now and looks fearfully about as she enters. The women have come in slowly and stand close together near the door.*

COUNTY ATTORNEY [*rubbing his hands*]. This feels good. Come up to the fire, ladies.

MRS. PETERS [*after taking a step forward*]. I'm not—cold.

SHERIFF [*unbuttoning his overcoat and stepping away from the stove as if to the beginning of official business*]. Now, Mr. Hale, before we move things about, you explain to Mr. Henderson just what you saw when you came here yesterday morning.

COUNTY ATTORNEY. By the way, has anything been moved? Are things just as you left them yesterday?

SHERIFF [*looking about*]. It's just the same. When it dropped below zero last night, I thought I'd better send Frank out this morning to make a fire for us—no use getting pneumonia with a big case on; but I told him not to touch anything except the stove—and you know Frank.

COUNTY ATTORNEY. Somebody should have been left here yesterday.

SHERIFF. Oh—yesterday. When I had to send Frank to Morris Center for that man who went crazy—I want you to know I had my hands full yesterday. I knew you could get back from Omaha by today, and as long as I went over everything here myself—

COUNTY ATTORNEY. Well, Mr. Hale, tell just what happened when you came here yesterday morning.

HALE. Harry and I had started to town with a load of potatoes. We came along the road from my place; and as I got here, I said, "I'm going to see if I can't get John Wright to go in with me on a party telephone." I spoke to Wright about it once before, and he put me off, saying folks talked too much anyway, and all he asked was peace and quiet—I guess you know about how much he talked himself; but I thought maybe if I went to the house and talked about it before his wife, though I said to Harry that I didn't know as what his wife wanted made much difference to John—

COUNTY ATTORNEY. Let's talk about that later, Mr. Hale. I do want to talk about that, but tell now just what happened when you got to the house.

HALE. I didn't hear or see anything; I knocked at the door, and still it was all quiet inside. I knew they must be up, it was past eight o'clock. So I knocked again, and I thought I heard somebody say, "Come in." I wasn't sure, I'm not sure yet, but I opened the door—this door [*indicating the door by which the two women are still standing*], and there in that rocker—[*pointing to it*] sat Mrs. Wright. [*They all look at the rocker.*]

COUNTY ATTORNEY. What—was she doing?

HALE. She was rockin' back and forth. She had her apron in her hand and was kind of—pleating it.

COUNTY ATTORNEY. And how did she—look?

HALE. Well, she looked queer.

COUNTY ATTORNEY. How do you mean—queer?

HALE. Well, as if she didn't know what she was going to do next. And kind of done up.

COUNTY ATTORNEY. How did she seem to feel about your coming?

HALE. Why, I don't think she minded—one way or other. She didn't pay much attention. I said, "How do, Mrs. Wright, it's cold, ain't it?" And she said, "Is it?"—and went on kind of pleating at her apron. Well, I was surprised; she didn't ask me to come up to the stove, or to set down, but just sat there, not even looking at me, so I said, "I want to see John." And then she—laughed. I guess you would call it a laugh. I thought of Harry and the team outside, so I said a little sharp: "Can't I see John?" "No," she says, kind o' dull like. "Ain't he home?" says I. "Yes," says she, "he's home." "Then why can't I see him?" I asked her, out of patience. " 'Cause he's dead," says she. *"Dead?"* says I. She just nodded her head, not getting a bit excited, but rockin' back and forth. "Why—where is he?" says I, not knowing what to say. She just pointed upstairs—like that [*himself pointing to the room above*]. I got up, with the idea of going up there. I walked from there to here—then I says, "Why, what did he die of?" "He died of a rope around his neck," says she, and just went on pleatin' at her apron. Well, I went out and called Harry. I thought I might—need help. We went upstairs, and there he was lyin'—

COUNTY ATTORNEY. I think I'd rather have you go into that upstairs, where you can point it all out. Just go on now with the rest of the story.

HALE. Well, my first thought was to get that rope off. I looked . . . [*Stops, his face twitches.*] . . . but Harry, he went up to him, and he said, "No, he's dead all right, and we'd better not touch anything." So we went back downstairs. She was still sitting that same way. "Has anybody been notified?" I asked. "No," says she, unconcerned. "Who did this, Mrs. Wright?" said Harry. He said it businesslike—and she stopped pleatin' of her apron. "I don't know," she says. "You don't *know?*" says Harry. "No," says she, "Weren't you sleepin' in the bed with him?" says Harry. "Yes," says she, "but I was on the inside." "Somebody slipped a rope round his neck and strangled him, and you didn't wake up?" says Harry. "I didn't wake up," she said after him. We must 'a looked as if we didn't see how that could be, for after a minute she said, "I sleep sound." Harry was going to ask her more questions, but I said maybe we ought to let her tell her story first to the coroner, or the sheriff, so Harry went fast as he could to Rivers' place, where there's a telephone.

COUNTY ATTORNEY. And what did Mrs. Wright do when she knew that you had gone for the coroner?

HALE. She moved from that chair to this over here . . . [*Pointing to a small chair in the corner.*] . . . and just sat there with her hands held together and looking down. I got a feeling that I ought to make some conversation, so I said I had come in to see if John wanted to put in a telephone, and at that she started to laugh, and then she stopped and looked at me—scared. [*The* COUNTY ATTORNEY, *who has had his notebook out, makes a note.*] I dunno, maybe it wasn't scared. I wouldn't like to say it was. Soon Harry got back, and then Dr. Lloyd came, and you, Mr. Peters, and so I guess that's all I know that you don't.

COUNTY ATTORNEY [*looking around*]. I guess we'll go upstairs first—and then out to the barn and around there. [*To the* SHERIFF.] You're convinced that there was nothing important here—nothing that would point to any motive?

SHERIFF. Nothing here but kitchen things.

[*The* COUNTY ATTORNEY, *after again looking around the kitchen, opens the door of a cupboard closet. He gets up on a chair and looks on a shelf. Pulls his hand away, sticky.*]

COUNTY ATTORNEY. Here's a nice mess.

[*The women draw nearer.*]

MRS. PETERS [*to the other woman*]. Oh, her fruit; it did freeze. [*To the* LAWYER.] She worried about that when it turned so cold. She said the fir'd go out and her jars would break.

SHERIFF. Well, can you beat the women! Held for murder and worryin' about her preserves.

COUNTY ATTORNEY. I guess before we're through she may have something more serious than preserves to worry about.

HALE. Well, women are used to worrying over trifles.

[*The two women move a little closer together.*]

COUNTY ATTORNEY [*with the gallantry of a young politician*]. And yet, for all their worries, what would wc do without the ladies? [*The women do not unbend. He goes to the sink, takes a dipperful of water from the pail and, pouring it into a basin, washes his hands. Starts to wipe them on the roller towel, turns it for a cleaner place.*] Dirty towels! [*Kicks his foot against the pans under the sink.*] Not much of a housekeeper, would you say, ladies?

MRS. HALE [*stiffly*]. There's a great deal of work to be done on a farm.

COUNTY ATTORNEY. To be sure. And yet . . . [*With a little bow to her.*] . . . I know there are some Dickson county farmhouses which do not have such roller towels. [*He gives it a pull to expose its full length again.*]

MRS. HALE. Those towels get dirty awful quick. Men's hands aren't always as clean as they might be.

COUNTY ATTORNEY. Ah, loyal to your sex, I see. But you and Mrs. Wright were neighbors. I suppose you were friends, too.

MRS. HALE [*shaking her head*]. I've not seen much of her of late years. I've not been in this house—it's more than a year.

COUNTY ATTORNEY. And why was that? You didn't like her?

MRS. HALE. I liked her all well enough. Farmers' wives have their hands full, Mr. Henderson. And then—

COUNTY ATTORNEY. Yes—?

MRS. HALE [*looking about*]. It never seemed a very cheerful place.

COUNTY ATTORNEY. No—it's not cheerful. I shouldn't say she had the homemaking instinct.

MRS. HALE. Well, I don't know as Wright had, either.

COUNTY ATTORNEY. You mean that they didn't get on very well?

MRS. HALE. No, I don't mean anything. But I don't think a place'd be any cheerfuler for John Wright's being in it.

COUNTY ATTORNEY. I'd like to talk more of that a little later. I want to get the lay of things upstairs now. [*He goes to the left, where three steps lead to a stair door.*]

SHERIFF. I suppose anything Mrs. Peters does'll be all right. She was to take in some clothes for her, you know, and a few little things. We left in such a hurry yesterday.

COUNTY ATTORNEY. Yes, but I would like to see what you take, Mrs. Peters, and keep an eye out for anything that might be of use to us.

MRS. PETERS. Yes, Mr. Henderson.

[*The women listen to the men's steps on the stairs, then look about the kitchen.*]

MRS. HALE. I'd hate to have men coming into my kitchen, snooping around and criticizing. [*She arranges the pans under sink which the LAWYER had shoved out of place.*]

MRS. PETERS. Of course it's no more than their duty.

MRS. HALE. Duty's all right, but I guess that deputy sheriff that came out to make the fire might have got a little of this on. [*Gives the roller towel a pull.*] Wish I'd thought of that sooner. Seems mean to talk about her for not having things slicked up when she had to come away in such a hurry.

MRS. PETERS [*who has gone to a small table in the left rear corner of the room, and lifted one end of a towel that covers a pan*]. She had bread set. [*Stands still.*]

MRS. HALE [*eyes fixed on a loaf of bread beside the breadbox, which is on a low shelf at the other side of the room. Moves slowly toward it*]. She was going to put this in there. [*Picks up loaf, then abruptly drops it. In a manner of returning to familiar things.*] It's a shame about her fruit. I wonder if it's all gone. [*Gets up on the chair and looks.*] I think there's some here that's all right, Mrs. Peters. Yes—here; [*Holding it toward the window.*] this is cherries, too. [*Looking again.*] I declare I believe that's the only one. [*Gets down, bottle in her hand. Goes to the sink and wipes it off on the outside.*] She'll feel awful bad after all her hard work in the hot weather. I remember the afternoon I put up my cherries last summer. [*She puts the bottle on the big kitchen table, center of the room, front table. With a sigh, is about to sit down in the rocking chair. Before she is seated realizes what chair it is; with a slow look at it, steps back. The chair, which she has touched, rocks back and forth.*]

MRS. PETERS. Well, I must get those things from the front room closet. [*She goes to the door at the right, but after looking into the other room steps back.*] You coming with me, Mrs. Hale? You could help me carry them. [*They go into the other room; reappear,* MRS. PETERS *carrying a dress and skirt,* MRS. HALE *following with a pair of shoes.*]

MRS. PETERS. My, it's cold in there. [*She puts the cloth on the big table, and hurries to the stove.*]

MRS. HALE [*examining the skirt*]. Wright was close. I think maybe that's why she kept so much to herself. She didn't even belong to the Ladies' Aid. I suppose she felt she couldn't do her part, and then you don't enjoy things when you feel shabby. She used to wear pretty clothes and be lively, when she was Minnie Foster, one of the town girls singing in the choir. But that— oh, that was thirty years ago. This all you was to take in?

MRS. PETERS. She said she wanted an apron. Funny thing to want, for there isn't much to get you dirty in jail, goodness knows. But I suppose just to make her feel more natural. She said they was in the top drawer in this cupboard. Yes, here. And then her little shawl that always hung behind the door. [*Opens stair door and looks.*] Yes, here it is. [*Quickly shuts door leading upstairs.*]

MRS. HALE [*abruptly moving toward her*]. Mrs. Peters?

MRS. PETERS. Yes, Mrs. Hale?

MRS. HALE. Do you think she did it?

MRS. PETERS [*in a frightened voice*]. Oh, I don't know.

MRS. HALE. Well, I don't think she did. Asking for an apron and her little shawl. Worrying about her fruit.

MRS. PETERS [*starts to speak, glances up, where footsteps are heard in the room above. In a low voice*]. Mr. Peters says it looks bad for her. Mr. Henderson is awful sarcastic in speech, and he'll make fun of her sayin' she didn't wake up.

MRS. HALE. Well, I guess John Wright didn't wake when they was slipping that rope under his neck.

MRS. PETERS. No, it's strange. It must have been done awful crafty and still. They say it was such a—funny way to kill a man, rigging it all up like that.

MRS. HALE. That's just what Mr. Hale said. There was a gun in the house. He says that's what he can't understand.

MRS. PETERS. Mr. Henderson said coming out that what was needed for the case was a motive; something to show anger, or—sudden feeling.

MRS. HALE [*who is standing by the table*]. Well, I don't see any signs of anger around here. [*She puts her hand on the dish towel which lies on the table, stands looking down at the table, one half of which is clean, the other half messy.*] It's wiped here. [*Makes a move as if to finish work, then turns and looks at loaf of bread outside the breadbox. Drops towel. In that voice of coming back to familiar things.*] Wonder how they are finding things upstairs? I hope she had it a little more red-up there. You know, it seems kind of *sneaking.* Locking her up in town and then coming out here and trying to get her own house to turn against her!

MRS. PETERS. But, Mrs. Hale, the law is the law.

MRS. HALE. I s'pose 'tis. [*Unbuttoning her coat.*] Better loosen up your things, Mrs. Peters. You won't feel them when you go out.

[MRS. PETERS *takes off her fur tippet, goes to hang it on hook at the back of room, stands looking at the under part of the small corner table.*]

MRS. PETERS. She was piecing a quilt. [*She brings the large sewing basket, and they look at the bright pieces.*]

MRS. HALE. It's log cabin pattern. Pretty, isn't it? I wonder if she was goin' to quilt or just knot it?

[*Footsteps have been heard coming down the stairs. The* SHERIFF *enters, followed by* HALE *and the* COUNTY ATTORNEY.]

SHERIFF. They wonder if she was going to quilt it or just knot it. [*The men laugh, the women look abashed.*]

COUNTY ATTORNEY [*rubbing his hands over the stove*]. Frank's fire didn't do much up there, did it? Well, let's go out to the barn and get that cleared up. [*The men go outside.*]

MRS. HALE [*resentfully*]. I don't know as there's anything so strange, our takin' up our time with little things while we're waiting for them to get the evidence. [*She sits down at the big table, smoothing out a block with decision.*] I don't see as it's anything to laugh about.

MRS. PETERS [*apologetically*]. Of course they've got awful important things on their minds. [*Pulls up a chair and joins* MRS. HALE *at the table.*]

MRS. HALE [*examining another block*]. Mrs. Peters, look at this one. Here, this is the one she was working on, and look at the sewing! All the rest of it has been so nice and even. And look at this! It's all over the place! Why, it looks as if she didn't know what she was about! [*After she has said this, they look at each other, then started to glance back at the door. After an instant* MRS. HALE *has pulled at a knot and ripped the sewing.*]

MRS. PETERS. Oh, what are you doing, Mrs. Hale?

MRS. HALE [*mildly*]. Just pulling out a stitch or two that's not sewed very good. [*Threading a needle.*] Bad sewing always made me fidgety.

MRS. PETERS [*nervously*]. I don't think we ought to touch things.

MRS. HALE. I'll just finish up this end. [*Suddenly stopping and leaning forward.*] Mrs. Peters?

MRS. PETERS. Yes, Mrs. Hale?

MRS. HALE. What do you suppose she was so nervous about?

MRS. PETERS. Oh—I don't know. I don't know as she was nervous. I sometimes sew awful queer when I'm just tired. [MRS. HALE *starts to say something, looks at* MRS. PETERS, *then goes on sewing.*] Well, I must get these things wrapped up. They may be through sooner than we think. [*Putting apron and other things together.*] I wonder where I can find a piece of paper, and string.

MRS. HALE. In that cupboard, maybe.

MRS. PETERS [*looking in cupboard*]. Why, here's a birdcage. [*Holds it up.*] Did she have a bird, Mrs. Hale?

MRS. HALE. Why, I don't know whether she did or not—I've not been here for so long. There was a man around last year selling canaries cheap, but I don't know as she took one; maybe she did. She used to sing real pretty herself.

MRS. PETERS [*glancing around*]. Seems funny to think of a bird here. But she must have had one, or why should she have a cage? I wonder what happened to it?

MRS. HALE. I s'pose maybe the cat got it.

MRS. PETERS. No, she didn't have a cat. She's got that feeling some people have about cats—being afraid of them. My cat got in her room, and she was real upset and asked me to take it out.

MRS. HALE. My sister Bessie was like that. Queer, ain't it?

MRS. PETERS [*examining the cage*]. Why, look at this door. It's broke. One hinge is pulled apart.

MRS. HALE [*looking, too*]. Looks as if someone must have been rough with it.

MRS. PETERS. Why, yes. [*She brings the cage forward and puts it on the table.*]

MRS. HALE. I wish if they're going to find any evidence they'd be about it. I don't like this place.

MRS. PETERS. But I'm awful glad you came with me, Mrs. Hale. It would be lonesome for me sitting here alone.

MRS. HALE. It would, wouldn't it? [*Dropping her sewing.*] But I tell you what I do wish, Mrs. Peters. I wish I had come over sometimes when *she* was here. I—[*Looking around the room.*]—wish I had.

MRS. PETERS. But of course you were awful busy, Mrs. Hale—your house and your children.

MRS. HALE. I could've come. I stayed away because it weren't cheerful—and that's why I ought to have come. I—I've never liked this place. Maybe because it's down in a hollow, and you don't see the road. I dunno what it is, but it's a lonesome place and always was. I wish I had come over to see Minnie Foster sometimes. I can see now—[*Shakes her head.*]

MRS. PETERS. Well, you mustn't reproach yourself, Mrs. Hale. Somehow we just don't see how it is with other folks until—something comes up.

MRS. HALE. Not having children makes less work—but it makes a quiet house, and Wright out to work all day, and no company when he did come in. Did you know John Wright, Mrs. Peters?

MRS. PETERS. Not to know him; I've seen him in town. They say he was a good man.

MRS. HALE. Yes—good; he didn't drink, and kept his word as well as most, I guess, and paid his debts. But he was a hard man, Mrs. Peters. Just to pass the time of day with him. [*Shivers.*] Like a raw wind that gets to the bone. [*Pauses, her eye falling on the cage.*] I should think she would 'a wanted a bird. But what do you suppose went with it?

MRS. PETERS. I don't know, unless it got sick and died. [*She reaches over and swings the broken door, swings it again; both women watch it.*]

MRS. HALE. You weren't raised round here, were you? [MRS. PETERS *shakes her head.*] You didn't know—her?

MRS. PETERS. Not till they brought her yesterday.

MRS. HALE. She—come to think of it, she was kind of like a bird herself—real sweet and pretty, but kind of timid and—fluttery. How—she—did—change. [*Silence; then as if struck by a happy thought and relieved to get back to everyday things.*] Tell you what, Mrs. Peters, why don't you take the quilt in with you? It might take up her mind.

MRS. PETERS. Why, I think that's a real nice idea, Mrs. Hale. There couldn't possible be any objection to it, could there? Now, just what would I take? I wonder if her patches are in here—and her things. [*They look in the sewing basket.*]

MRS. HALE. Here's some red. I expect this has got sewing things in it [*Brings out a fancy box.*] What a pretty box. Looks like something somebody would give you. Maybe her scissors are in here. [*Opens box. Suddenly puts her hand to her nose.*] Why—[MRS. PETERS *bends nearer, then turns her face away.*] There's something wrapped up in this piece of silk.

MRS. PETERS. Why, this isn't her scissors.

MRS. HALE [*lifting the silk*]. Oh, Mrs. Peters—it's—[MRS. PETERS *bends closer.*]

MRS. PETERS. It's the bird.

MRS. HALE [*jumping up*]. But, Mrs. Peters—look at it. Its neck! Look at its neck! It's all—other side *to.*

MRS. PETERS. Somebody—wrung—its neck.

[*Their eyes meet. A look of growing comprehension of horror. Steps are heard outside.* MRS. HALE *slips box under quilt pieces, and sinks into her chair. Enter* SHERIFF *and* COUNTY ATTORNEY. MRS. PETERS *rises.*]

COUNTY ATTORNEY [*as one turning from serious things to little pleasantries*]. Well, ladies, have you decided whether she was going to quilt it or knot it?

MRS. PETERS. We think she was going to—knot it.

COUNTY ATTORNEY. Well, that's interesting, I'm sure. [*Seeing the birdcage.*] Has the bird flown?

MRS. HALE [*putting more quilt pieces over the box*]. We think the—cat got it.

COUNTY ATTORNEY [*preoccupied*]. Is there a cat?

[MRS. HALE *glances in a quick covert way at* MRS. PETERS.]

MRS. PETERS. Well, not now. They're superstitious, you know. They leave.

COUNTY ATTORNEY [*to* SHERIFF PETERS, *continuing an interrupted conversation*]. No sign at all of anyone having come from the outside. Their own rope. Now let's go up again and go over it piece by piece. [*They start upstairs.*] It would have to have been someone who knew just the—

[MRS. PETERS *sits down. The two women sit there not looking at one another,*

*but as if peering into something and at the same time holding back. When they
talk now, it is the manner of feeling their way over strange ground, as if afraid
of what they are saying, but as if they cannot help saying it.*]

MRS. HALE. She liked the bird. She was going to bury it in that pretty
box.

MRS. PETERS [*in a whisper*]. When I was a girl—my kitten—there was a
boy took a hatchet, and before my eyes—and before I could get there—
[*Covers her face an instant.*] If they hadn't held me back, I would have—
[*Catches herself, looks upstairs where steps are heard, falters weakly.*]—hurt
him.

MRS. HALE [*with a slow look around her*]. I wonder how it would seem
never to have had any children around. [*Pause.*] No, Wright wouldn't like the
bird—a thing that sang. She used to sing. He killed that, too.

MRS. PETERS [*moving uneasily*]. We don't know who killed the bird.

MRS. HALE. I knew John Wright.

MRS. PETERS. It was an awful thing was done in this house that night,
Mrs. Hale. Killing a man while he slept, slipping a rope around his neck that
choked the life out of him.

MRS. HALE. His neck. Choked the life out of him.

[*Her hand goes out and rests on the birdcage.*]

MRS. PETERS [*with a rising voice*]. We don't know who killed him. We
don't *know*.

MRS. HALE [*her own feeling not interrupted*]. If there'd been years and
years of nothing, then a bird to sing to you, it would be awful—still, after the
bird was still.

MRS. PETERS [*something within her speaking*]. I know what stillness is.
When we homesteaded in Dakota, and my first baby died—after he was two
years old, and me with no other then—

MRS. HALE [*moving*]. How soon do you suppose they'll be through, looking for evidence?

MRS. PETERS. I know what stillness is. [*Pulling herself back.*] The law has
got to punish crime, Mrs. Hale.

MRS. HALE [*not as if answering that*]. I wish you'd seen Minnie Foster
when she wore a white dress with blue ribbons and stood up there in the
choir and sang. [*A look around the room.*] Oh, I *wish* I'd come over here once
in a while! That was a crime! That was a crime! Who's going to punish that?

MRS. PETERS [*looking upstairs*]. We mustn't—take on.

MRS. HALE. I might have known she needed help! I know how things can
be—for women. I tell you, it's queer, Mrs. Peters. We live close together and
we live far apart. We all go through the same things—it's all just a different
kind of the same thing. [*Brushes her eyes, noticing the bottle of fruit, reaches
out for it.*] If I was you, I wouldn't tell her her fruit was gone. Tell her it *ain't*.
Tell her it's all right. Take this in to prove it to her. She—she may never know
whether it was broke or not.

MRS. PETERS [*takes the bottle, looks about for something to wrap it in; takes
petticoat from the clothes brought from the other room, very nervously begins
winding this around the bottle. In a false voice*]. My, it's a good thing the men
couldn't hear us. Wouldn't they just laugh! Getting all stirred up over a little

thing like a—dead canary. As if that could have anything to do with—with—wouldn't they *laugh!*

[*The men are heard coming downstairs.*]

MRS. HALE [*under her breath*]. Maybe they would—maybe they wouldn't.

COUNTY ATTORNEY. No, Peters, it's all perfectly clear except a reason for doing it. But you know juries when it comes to women. If there was some definite thing. Something to show—something to make a story about—a thing that would connect up with this strange way of doing it.

[*The women's eyes meet for an instant. Enter* HALE *from outer door.*]

MRS. HALE. Well, I've got the team around. Pretty cold out there.

COUNTY ATTORNEY. I'm going to stay here awhile by myself. [*To the* SHERIFF.] You can send Frank out for me, can't you? I want to go over everything. I'm not satisfied that we can't do better.

SHERIFF. Do you want to see what Mrs. Peters is going to take in?

[*The* LAWYER *goes to the table, picks up the apron, laughs.*]

COUNTY ATTORNEY. Oh I guess they're not very dangerous things the ladies have picked up. [*Moves a few things about, disturbing the quilt pieces which cover the box. Steps back.*] No, Mrs. Peters doesn't need supervising. For that matter, a sheriff's wife is married to the law. Ever think of it that way, Mrs. Peters?

MRS. PETERS. Not—just that way.

SHERIFF [*chuckling*]. Married to the law. [*Moves toward the other room.*] I just want you to come in here a minute, George. We ought to take a look at these windows.

COUNTY ATTORNEY [*scoffingly*]. Oh, windows!

SHERIFF. We'll be right out, Mr. Hale.

[HALE *goes outside. The* SHERIFF *follows the* COUNTY ATTORNEY *into the other room. Then* MRS. HALE *rises, hands tight together, looking intensely at* MRS. PETERS, *whose eyes take a slow turn, finally meeting* MRS. HALE'S. *A moment* MRS. HALE *holds her, then her own eyes point the way to where the box is concealed. Suddenly* MRS. PETERS *throws back quilt pieces and tries to put the box in the bag she is wearing. It is too big. She opens box, starts to take the bird out, cannot touch it, goes to pieces, stands there helpless. Sound of a knob turning in the other room.* MRS. HALE *snatches the box and puts it in the pocket of her big coat. Enter* COUNTY ATTORNEY *and* SHERIFF.]

COUNTY ATTORNEY [*facetiously*]. Well, Henry, at least we found out that she was not going to quilt it. She was going to—what is it you call it, ladies?

MRS. HALE [*her hand against her pocket*]. We call it—knot it, Mr. Henderson.

CURTAIN

[1916]

■ TOPICS FOR DISCUSSION AND WRITING

1. Briefly describe the setting, indicating what it "says" and what atmosphere it evokes.

2. Even before the first word of dialogue is spoken, what do you think

the play tells us (in the entrance of the characters) about the distinction between the men and the women?

3. How would you characterize Mr. Henderson, the county attorney?

4. In what way or ways are Mrs. Peters and Mrs. Hale different from each other?

5. Several times the men "laugh" or "chuckle." In their contexts, what do these expressions of amusement convey?

6. On page 185, *"the women's eyes meet for an instant."* What do you think this bit of action "says"? What do you understand by the exchange of glances?

7. On page 184, when Mrs. Peters tells of the boy who killed her cat, she says, "If they hadn't held me back, I would have—(*catches herself, looks upstairs where steps are heard, falters weakly*)—hurt him."
What do you think she was about to say before she faltered? Why do you suppose Glaspell included this speech about Mrs. Peters's girlhood?

8. On page 181, Mrs. Hale, looking at a quilt, wonders whether Mrs. Wright "was going to quilt it or just knot it." The men are amused by the women's concern with this topic, and the last line of the play returns to the issue. What do you make of this emphasis on the matter?

9. We never see Mrs. Wright on stage. Nevertheless, by the end of *Trifles* we know a great deal about her. In an essay of 500–750 words explain both what we know about her—physical characteristics, habits, interests, personality, life before her marriage and after—and *how* we know these things.

10. The title of the play is ironic—the "trifles" are important. What other ironies do you find in the play? (On irony, see Glossary.)

11. Do you think the play is immoral? Explain.

12. Assume that the canary has been found, thereby revealing a possible motive, and that Minnie is indicted for murder. You are the defense attorney. In 500 words set forth your defense. (Take any position you wish. For instance, you may want to argue that she committed justifiable homicide or that—on the basis of her behavior as reported by Mr. Hale—she is innocent by reason of insanity.)

13. Assume that the canary had been found and Minnie Wright convicted. Compose the speech you think she might have delivered before the sentence was given.

■ HARVEY FIERSTEIN

Harvey Fierstein was born in Brooklyn, New York, the son of parents who had emigrated from Eastern Europe. While studying painting at Pratt Institute he acted in plays and revues, and one of his plays was produced in 1973, but he did not achieve fame until his *Torch Song Trilogy* (1976–1979) moved from Off Broadway to Broadway in 1982. *Torch Song*

Trilogy won the Theatre World Award, the Tony Award, and the Drama Desk Award. In addition, Fierstein won the Best Actor Tony Award and the Best Actor Drama Desk Award. He later received a third Tony Award for the book for the musical version of *La Cage aux Folles* (1983).

On Tidy Endings

The curtain rises on a deserted, modern Upper West Side apartment. In the bright daylight that pours in through the windows we can see the living room of the apartment. Far Stage Right is the galley kitchen, next to it the multilocked front door with intercom. Stage Left reveals a hallway that leads to the two bedrooms and baths.

Though the room is still fully furnished (couch, coffee table, etc.), there are boxes stacked against the wall and several photographs and paintings are on the floor leaving shadows on the wall where they once hung. Obviously someone is moving out. From the way the boxes are neatly labeled and stacked, we know that this is an organized person.

From the hallway just outside the door we hear the rattling of keys and two arguing voices:

JIM [*Offstage*]. I've got to be home by four. I've got practice.

MARION [*Offstage*]. I'll get you to practice, don't worry.

JIM [*Offstage*]. I don't want to go in there.

MARION [*Offstage*]. Jimmy, don't make Mommy crazy, alright? We'll go inside, I'll call Aunt Helen and see if you can go down and play with Robbie. [*The door opens.* MARION *is a handsome woman of forty. Dressed in a business suit, her hair conservatively combed,* SHE *appears to be going to a business meeting.* JIM *is a boy of eleven. His playclothes are typical, but someone has obviously just combed his hair.* MARION *recovers the key from the lock.*]

JIM. Why can't I just go down and ring the bell?

MARION. Because I said so.

[*As* MARION *steps into the room* SHE *is struck by some unexpected emotion.* SHE *freezes in her path and stares at the empty apartment.* JIM *lingers by the door.*]

JIM. I'm going downstairs.

MARION. Jimmy, please.

JIM. This place gives me the creeps.

MARION. This was your father's apartment. There's nothing creepy about it.

JIM. Says you.

MARION. You want to close the door, please?

[JIM *reluctantly obeys*]

MARION. Now, why don't you go check your room and make sure you didn't leave anything.

JIM. It's empty.

MARION. Go look.

JIM. I looked last time.

MARION [*Trying to be patient*]. Honey, we sold the apartment. You're never going to be here again. Go make sure you have everything you want.

JIM. But Uncle Arthur packed everything.

MARION [*Less patiently*]. Go make sure.

JIM. There's nothing in there.

MARION [*Exploding*]. I said make sure!

[JIM *jumps, then realizing that* SHE*'s not kidding, obeys*]

MARION. Everything's an argument with that one. [SHE *looks around the room and breathes deeply. There is sadness here. Under her breath:*] I can still smell you. [*Suddenly not wanting to be alone*] Jimmy? Are you okay?

JIM [*Returning*]. Nothing. Told you so.

MARION. Uncle Arthur must have worked very hard. Make sure you thank him.

JIM. What for? Robbie says, [*Fey mannerisms*] "They love to clean up things!"

MARION. Sometimes you can be a real joy.

JIM. Did you call Aunt Helen?

MARION. Do I get a break here? [*Approaching the* BOY *understandingly*] Wouldn't you like to say good-bye?

JIM. To who?

MARION. To the apartment. You and your daddy spent a lot of time here together. Don't you want to take one last look around?

JIM. Ma, get a real life.

MARION. "Get a real life." [*Going for the phone*] Nice. Very nice.

JIM. Could you call already?

MARION [*Dialing*]. Jimmy, what does this look like I'm doing?

[JIM *kicks at the floor impatiently. Someone answers the phone at the other end*]

MARION [*Into the phone*]. Helen? Hi, we're upstairs. . . . No, we just walked in the door. Jimmy wants to know if he can come down. . . . Oh, thanks.

[*Hearing that,* JIM *breaks for the door*]

MARION [*Yelling after him*]. Don't run in the halls! And don't play with the elevator buttons!

[*The door slams shut behind him*]

MARION [*Back to the phone*]. Hi. . . . No, I'm okay. It's a little weird being here. . . . No. Not since the funeral, and then there were so many people. Jimmy told me to get "a real life." I don't think I could handle anything realer. . . . No, please. Stay where you are. I'm fine. The doorman said Arthur would be right back and my lawyer should have been here already. . . . Well, we've got the papers to sign and a few other odds and ends to clean up. Shouldn't take long.

[*The intercom buzzer rings*]

MARION. Hang on, that must be her. [MARION *goes to the intercom and speaks*] Yes? . . . Thank you. [*Back to the phone*] Helen? Yeah, it's the lawyer. I'd better go. . . . Well, I could use a stiff drink, but I drove down. Listen, I'll stop by on my way out. Okay? Okay. 'Bye.

[SHE *hangs up the phone, looks around the room. That uncomfortable feeling returns to her quickly.* SHE *gets up and goes to the front door, opens it and looks out. No one there yet.* SHE *closes the door, shakes her head knowing that* SHE's *being silly and starts back into the room.* SHE *looks around, can't make it and retreats to the door.* SHE *opens it, looks out, closes it, but stays right there, her hand on the doorknob. The bell rings.* SHE *throws open the door*]

MARION. That was quick.

[JUNE LOWELL *still has her finger on the bell. Her arms are loaded with contracts.* MARION's *contemporary,* JUNE *is less formal in appearance and more hyper in her manner*]

JUNE. *That* was quicker. What, were you waiting by the door?

MARION [*Embarrassed*]. No. I was just passing it. Come on in.

JUNE. Have you got your notary seal?

MARION. I think so.

JUNE. Great. Then you can witness. I left mine at the office and thanks to gentrification I'm double-parked downstairs. [*Looking for a place to dump her load*] Where?

MARION [*Definitely pointing to the coffee table*]. Anywhere. You mean you're not staying?

JUNE. If you really think you need me I can go down and find a parking lot. I think there's one over on Columbus. So, I can go down, park the car in the lot and take a cab back if you really think you need me.

MARION. Well . . . ?

JUNE. But you shouldn't have any problems. The papers are about as straightforward as papers get. Arthur is giving you power of attorney to sell the apartment and you're giving him a check for half the purchase price. Everything else is just signing papers that state that you know that you signed the other papers. Anyway, he knows the deal, his lawyers have been over it all with him, it's just a matter of signatures.

MARION [*Not fine*]. Oh, fine.

JUNE. Unless you just don't want to be alone with him . . . ?

MARION. With Arthur? Don't be silly.

JUNE [*Laying out the papers*]. Then you'll handle it solo? Great. My car thanks you, the parking lot thanks you, and the cab driver that wouldn't have gotten a tip thanks you. Come have a quick look-see.

MARION [*Joining her on the couch*]. There are a lot of papers here.

JUNE. Copies. Not to worry. Start here.

[MARION *starts to read*]

JUNE. I ran into Jimmy playing Elevator Operator.

[MARION *jumps*]

JUNE. I got him off at the sixth floor. Read on.

MARION. This is definitely not my day for dealing with him.

[JUNE *gets up and has a look around*]

JUNE. I don't believe what's happening to this neighborhood. You made quite an investment when you bought this place.

MARION. Collin was always very good at figuring out those things.

JUNE. Well, he sure figured this place right. What, have you tripled your money in ten years?

MARION. More.

JUNE. It's a shame to let it go.

MARION. We're not ready to be a two-dwelling family.

JUNE. So, sublet it again.

MARION. Arthur needs the money from the sale.

JUNE. Arthur got plenty already. I'm not crying for Arthur.

MARION. I don't hear you starting in again, do I?

JUNE. Your interests and your wishes are my only concern.

MARION. Fine.

JUNE. I still say we should contest Collin's will.

MARION. June . . . !

JUNE. You've got a child to support.

MARION. And a great job, and a husband with a great job. Tell me what Arthur's got.

JUNE. To my thinking, half of everything that should have gone to you. And more. All of Collin's personal effects, his record collection . . .

MARION. And I suppose their three years together meant nothing.

JUNE. When you compare them to your sixteen-year marriage? Not nothing, but not half of everything.

MARION [*Trying to change the subject*]. June, who gets which copies?

JUNE. Two of each to Arthur. One you keep. The originals and anything else come back to me. [*Looking around*] I still say you should've sublet the apartment for a year and then sold it. You would've gotten an even better price. Who wants to buy an apartment when they know someone died in it. No one. And certainly no one wants to buy an apartment when they know the person died of AIDS.

MARION [*Snapping*]. June. Enough!

JUNE [*Catching herself*]. Sorry. That was out of line. Sometimes my mouth does that to me. Hey, that's why I'm a lawyer. If my brain worked as fast as my mouth I would have gotten a real job.

MARION [*Holding out a stray paper*]. What's this?

JUNE. I forgot. Arthur's lawyer sent that over yesterday. He found it in Collin's safety-deposit box. It's an insurance policy that came along with some consulting job he did in Japan. He either forgot about it when he made out his will or else he wanted you to get the full payment. Either way, it's yours.

MARION. Are you sure we don't split this?

JUNE. Positive.

MARION. But everything else . . . ?

JUNE. Hey, Arthur found it, his lawyer sent it to me. Relax, it's all yours. Minus my commission, of course. Go out and buy yourself something. Anything else before I have to use my cut to pay the towing bill?

MARION. I guess not.

JUNE [*Starting to leave*]. Great. Call me when you get home. [*Stopping at the door and looking back*] Look, I know that I'm attacking this a little coldly. I am aware that someone you loved has just died. But there's a time and place for everything. This is about tidying up loose ends, not holding hands. I hope you'll remember that when Arthur gets here. Call me.

[And SHE's gone]

[MARION *looks ill at ease to be alone again.* SHE *nervously straightens the papers into neat little piles, looks at them and then remembers:*]

MARION. Pens. We're going to need pens.

[*At last a chore to be done.* SHE *looks in her purse and finds only one.* SHE *goes to the kitchen and opens a drawer where* SHE *finds two more.* SHE *starts back to the table with them but suddenly remembers something else.* SHE *returns to the kitchen and begins going through the cabinets until* SHE *finds what* SHE*'s looking for: a blue Art Deco teapot. Excited to find it,* SHE *takes it back to the couch. Guilt strikes.* SHE *stops, considers putting it back, wavers, then:*]

MARION [*To herself*]. Oh, he won't care. One less thing to pack.

[SHE *takes the teapot and places it on the couch next to her purse.* SHE *is happier. Now* SHE *searches the room with her eyes for any other treasures* SHE *may have overlooked. Nothing here.* SHE *wanders off into the bedroom.*
We hear keys outside the front door. ARTHUR *lets himself into the apartment carrying a load of empty cartons and a large shopping bag.*
ARTHUR *is in his mid-thirties, pleasant looking though sloppily dressed in work clothes and slightly overweight.*
ARTHUR *enters the apartment just as* MARION *comes out of the bedroom carrying a framed watercolor painting.* THEY *jump at the sight of each other.*]

MARION. Oh, hi, Arthur. I didn't hear the door.

ARTHUR [*Staring at the painting*]. Well hello, Marion.

MARION [*Guiltily*]. I was going to ask you if you were thinking of taking this painting because if you're not going to then I'll take it. Unless, of course, you want it.

ARTHUR. No. You can have it.

MARION. I never really liked it, actually. I hate cats. I didn't even like the show. I needed something for my college dorm room. I was never the rock star poster type. I kept it in the back of a closet for years until Collin moved in here and took it. He said he liked it.

ARTHUR. I do too.

MARION. Well, then you keep it.

ARTHUR. No. Take it.

MARION. We've really got no room for it. You keep it.

ARTHUR. I don't want it.

MARION. Well, if you're sure.

ARTHUR [*Seeing the teapot*] You want the teapot?

MARION. If you don't mind.

ARTHUR. One less thing to pack.

MARION. Funny, but that's exactly what I thought. One less thing to pack. You know, my mother gave it to Collin and me when we moved in to our first apartment. Silly sentimental piece of junk, but you know.

ARTHUR. That's not the one.

MARION. Sure it is. Hall used to make them for Westinghouse back in the thirties. I see them all the time at antiques shows and I always wanted to buy another, but they ask such a fortune for them.

ARTHUR. We broke the one your mother gave you a couple of years ago. That's a reproduction. You can get them almost anywhere in the Village for eighteen bucks.

MARION. Really? I'll have to pick one up.

ARTHUR. Take this one. I'll get another.

MARION. No, it's yours. You bought it.

ARTHUR. One less thing to pack.

MARION. Don't be silly. I didn't come here to raid the place.

ARTHUR. Well, was there anything else of Collin's that you thought you might like to have?

MARION. Now I feel so stupid, but actually I made a list. Not for me. But I started thinking about different people; friends, relatives, you know, that might want to have something of Collin's to remember him by. I wasn't sure just what you were taking and what you were throwing out. Anyway, I brought the list. [*Gets it from her purse*] Of course these are only suggestions. You probably thought of a few of these people yourself. But I figured it couldn't hurt to write it all down. Like I said, I don't know what you are planning on keeping.

ARTHUR [*Taking the list*]. I was planning on keeping it all.

MARION. Oh, I know. But most of these things are silly. Like his high school yearbooks. What would you want with them?

ARTHUR. Sure. I'm only interested in his Gay period.

MARION. I didn't mean it that way. Anyway, you look it over. They're only suggestions. Whatever you decide to do is fine with me.

ARTHUR [*Folding the list*]. It would have to be, wouldn't it. I mean, it's all mine now. He did leave this all to me.

[MARION *is becoming increasingly nervous, but tries to keep a light approach as* SHE *takes a small bundle of papers from her bag*]

MARION. While we're on the subject of what's yours. I brought a batch of condolence cards that were sent to you care of me. Relatives mostly.

ARTHUR [*Taking them*]. More cards? I'm going to have to have another printing of thank-you notes done.

MARION. I answered these last week, so you don't have to bother. Unless you want to.

ARTHUR. Forge my signature?

MARION. Of course not. They were addressed to both of us and they're mostly distant relatives or friends we haven't seen in years. No one important.

ARTHUR. If they've got my name on them, then I'll answer them myself.

MARION. I wasn't telling you not to, I was only saying that you don't have to.

ARTHUR. I understand.

[MARION *picks up the teapot and brings it to the kitchen*]

MARION. Let me put this back.

ARTHUR. I ran into Jimmy in the lobby.

MARION. Tell me you're joking.

ARTHUR. I got him to Helen's.

MARION. He's really racking up the points today.

ARTHUR. You know, he still can't look me in the face.

MARION. He's reacting to all of this in strange ways. Give him time. He'll come around. He's really very fond of you.

ARTHUR. I know. But he's at that awkward age: under thirty. I'm sure in twenty years we'll be the best of friends.

MARION. It's not what you think.

ARTHUR. What do you mean?

MARION. Well, you know.

ARTHUR. No I don't know. Tell me.

MARION. I thought that you were intimating something about his blaming you for Collin's illness and I was just letting you know that it's not true. [*Foot in mouth,* SHE *braves on*] We discussed it a lot and . . . uh . . . he understands that his father was sick before you two ever met.

ARTHUR. I don't believe this.

MARION. I'm just trying to say that he doesn't blame you.

ARTHUR. First of all, who asked you? Second of all, that's between him and me. And third and most importantly, of course he blames me. Marion, he's eleven years old. You can discuss all you want, but the fact is that his father died of a "fag" disease and I'm the only fag around to finger.

MARION. My son doesn't use that kind of language.

ARTHUR. Forget the language. I'm talking about what he's been through. Can you imagine the kind of crap he's taken from his friends? That poor kid's been chased and chastised from one end of town to the other. He's got to have someone to blame just to survive. He can't blame you, you're all he's got. He can't blame his father; he's dead. So, Uncle Arthur gets the shaft. Fine, I can handle it.

MARION. You are so wrong, Arthur. I know my son and that is not the way his mind works.

ARTHUR. I don't know what you know. I only know what I know. And all I know is what I hear and see. The snide remarks, the little smirks . . . And it's not just the illness. He's been looking for a scapegoat since the day you and Collin first split up. Finally he has one.

MARION [*Getting very angry now*]. Wait. Are you saying that if he's going to blame someone it should be me?

ARTHUR. I think you should try to see things from his point of view.

MARION. Where do you get off thinking you're privy to my son's point of view?

ARTHUR. It's not that hard to imagine. Life's rolling right along, he's having a happy little childhood, when suddenly one day his father's moving out. No explanations, no reasons, none of the fights that usually accompany such things. Divorce is hard enough for a kid to understand when he's listened to years of battles, but yours?

MARION. So what should we have done? Faked a few months' worth of fights before Collin moved out?

ARTHUR. You could have told him the truth, plain and simple.

MARION. He was seven years old at the time. How the hell do you tell a seven-year-old that his father is leaving his mother to go sleep with other men?

ARTHUR. Well, not like that.

MARION. You know, Arthur, I'm going to say this as nicely as I can: Butt out. You're not his mother and you're not his father.

ARTHUR. Thank you. I wasn't acutely aware of that fact. I will certainly keep that in mind from now on.

MARION. There's only so much information a child that age can handle.

ARTHUR. So it's best that he reach his capacity on the street.

MARION. He knew about the two of you. We talked about it.

ARTHUR. Believe me, he knew before you talked about it. He's young, not stupid.

MARION. It's very easy for you to stand here and criticize, but there are aspects that you will just never be able to understand. You weren't there. You have no idea what it was like for me. You're talking to someone who thought that a girl went to college to meet a husband. I went to protest rallies because I liked the music. I bought a guitar because I thought it looked good on the bed! This lifestyle, this knowledge that you take for granted, was all a little out of left field for me.

ARTHUR. I can imagine.

MARION. No, I don't think you can. I met Collin in college, married him right after graduation and settled down for a nice quiet life of Kids and Careers. You think I had any idea about this? Talk about life's little surprises. You live with someone for sixteen years, you share your life, your bed, you have a child together, and then you wake up one day and he tells you that to him it's all been a lie. A lie. Try that on for size. Here you are the happiest couple you know, fulfilling your every life fantasy and he tells you he's living a lie.

ARTHUR. I'm sure he never said that.

MARION. Don't be so sure. There was a lot of new ground being broken back then and plenty of it was muddy.

ARTHUR. You know that he loved you.

MARION. What's that supposed to do, make things easier? It doesn't. I was brought up to believe, among other things, that if you had love that was enough. So what if I wasn't everything he wanted. Maybe he wasn't exactly everything I wanted either. So, you know what? You count your blessings and you settle.

ARTHUR. No one has to settle. Not him. Not you.

MARION. Of course not. You can say, "Up yours!" to everything and everyone who depends and needs you, and go off to make yourself happy.

ARTHUR. It's not that simple.

MARION. No. This is simpler. Death is simpler. [*Yelling out*] Happy now? [THEY *stare at each other.* MARION *calms the rage and catches her breath.* ARTHUR *holds his emotions in check*]

ARTHUR. How about a nice hot cup of coffee? Tea with lemon? Hot cocoa with a marshmallow floating in it?

MARION [*Laughs*]. I was wrong. You *are* a mother.

[ARTHUR *goes into the kitchen and starts preparing things.* MARION *loafs by the doorway.*]

MARION. I lied before. He *was* everything I ever wanted.

[ARTHUR *stops, looks at her, and then changes the subject as* HE *goes on with his work.*]

ARTHUR. When I came into the building and saw Jimmy in the lobby I absolutely freaked for a second. It's amazing how much they look alike. It was like seeing a little miniature Collin standing there.

MARION. I know. He's like Collin's clone. There's nothing of me in him.

ARTHUR. I always kinda hoped that when he grew up he'd take after me. Not much chance, I guess.

MARION. Don't do anything fancy in there.

ARTHUR. Please. Anything we can consume is one less thing to pack.

MARION. So you've said.

ARTHUR. So *we've* said.

MARION. I want to keep seeing you and I want you to see Jim. You're still part of this family. No one's looking to cut you out.

ARTHUR. Ah, who'd want a kid to grow up looking like me anyway. I had enough trouble looking like this. Why pass on the misery?

MARION. You're adorable.

ARTHUR. Is that like saying I have a good personality?

MARION. I think you are one of the most naturally handsome men I know.

ARTHUR. Natural is right, and the bloom is fading.

MARION. All you need is a few good nights' sleep to kill those rings under your eyes.

ARTHUR. Forget the rings under my eyes, [*Grabbing his middle*]. . . how about the rings around my moon?

MARION. I like you like this.

ARTHUR. From the time that Collin started using the wheelchair until he died, about six months, I lost twenty-three pounds. No gym, no diet. In the last seven weeks I've gained close to fifty.

MARION. You're exaggerating.

ARTHUR. I'd prove it on the bathroom scale, but I sold it in working order.

MARION. You'd never know.

ARTHUR. Marion, *you'd* never know, but ask my belt. Ask my pants. Ask my underwear. Even my stretch socks have stretch marks. I called the ambulance at five A.M., he was gone at nine and by nine-thirty, I was on a first-name basis with Sara Lee. I can quote the business hours of every ice-cream parlor, pizzeria and bakery on the island of Manhattan. I know the location of every twenty-four-hour grocery in the greater New York area, and I have memorized the phone numbers of every Mandarin, Szechuan and Hunan restaurant with free delivery.

MARION. At least you haven't wasted your time on useless hobbies.

ARTHUR. Are you kidding? I'm opening my own Overeater's Hotline. We'll have to start small, but expansion is guaranteed.

MARION. You're the best, you know that? If I couldn't be everything that Collin wanted then I'm grateful that he found someone like you.

ARTHUR [*Turning on her without missing a beat*]. Keep your goddamned gratitude to yourself. I didn't go through any of this for you. So your thanks are out of line. And he didn't find "someone like" me. It was me.

MARION [*Frightened*]. I didn't mean . . .

ARTHUR. And I wish you'd remember one thing more: He died in my arms, not yours.

[MARION *is totally caught off guard.* SHE *stares disbelieving, openmouthed.* ARTHUR *walks past her as* HE *leaves the kitchen with place mats.* HE *puts them on the coffee table. As* HE *arranges the papers, and place mats* HE *speaks, never looking at her.*]

ARTHUR. Look, I know you were trying to say something supportive. Don't waste your breath. There's nothing you can say that will make any of this easier for me. There's no way for you to help me get through this. And that's your fault. After three years you still have no idea or understanding of who I am. Or maybe you do know but refuse to accept it. I don't know and I don't care. But at least understand, from my point of view, who you are: You are my husband's *ex*-wife. If you like, the mother of *my* stepson. Don't flatter yourself into thinking you're any more than that. And whatever you are, you're certainly not my friend.

[HE *stops, looks up at her, then passes her again as* HE *goes back to the kitchen.* MARION *is shaken, working hard to control herself.* SHE *moves toward the couch.*]

    MARION. Why don't we just sign these papers and I'll be out of your way.

    ARTHUR. Shouldn't you say *I'll* be out of *your* way? After all, I'm not just signing papers. I'm signing away my home.

    MARION [*Resolved not to fight,* SHE *gets her purse*]. I'll leave the papers here. Please have them notarized and returned to my lawyer.

    ARTHUR. Don't forget my painting.

    MARION [*Exploding*]. What do you want from me, Arthur?

    ARTHUR [*Yelling back*]. I want you the hell out of my apartment! I want you out of my life! And I want you to leave Collin alone!

    MARION. The man's dead. I don't know how much more alone I can leave him.

[ARTHUR *laughs at the irony, but behind the laughter is something much more desperate*].

    ARTHUR. Lots more, Marion. You've got to let him go.

    MARION. For the life of me, I don't know what I did or what you think I did, for you to treat me like this. But you're not going to get away with it. You will not take your anger out on me. I will not stand here and be badgered and insulted by you. I know you've been hurt and I know you're hurting but you're not the only one who lost someone here.

    ARTHUR [*Topping her*]. Yes I am! You didn't just lose him. I did! You lost him five years ago when he divorced you. This is not your moment of grief and loss, it's mine! [*Picking up the bundle of cards and throwing it toward her*] These condolences do not belong to you, they're mine. [*Tossing her list back to her*] His things are not yours to give away, they're mine! This death does not belong to you, it's mine! Bought and paid for outright. I suffered for it, I bled for it.

    I was the one who cooked his meals. I was the one who spoon-fed them. I pushed his wheelchair. I carried and bathed him. I wiped his backside and changed his diapers. I breathed life into and wrestled fear out of his heart. I kept him alive for two years longer than any doctor thought possible and when it was time I was the one who prepared him for death.

    I paid in full for my place in his life and I will *not* share it with you. We are not the two widows of Collin Redding. Your life was not here. Your husband didn't just die. You've got a son and a life somewhere else. Your husband's sitting, waiting for you at home, wondering, as I am, what the hell you're doing here and why you can't let go.

[MARION *leans back against the couch.* SHE*'s blown away.* ARTHUR *stands staring at her*]

ARTHUR [*Quietly*]. Let him go, Marion. He's mine. Dead or alive; mine. [*The teakettle whistles.* ARTHUR *leaves the room, goes to the kitchen and pours the water as* MARION *pulls herself together.* ARTHUR *carries the loaded tray back into the living room and sets it down on the coffee table.* HE *sits and pours a cup*]

ARTHUR. One marshmallow or two?

[MARION *stares, unsure as to whether the attack is really over or not*]

ARTHUR [*Placing them in her cup*]. Take three, they're small.

[MARION *smiles and takes the offered cup*]

ARTHUR [*Campily*]. Now let me tell you how I *really* feel.

[MARION *jumps slightly, then* THEY *share a small laugh. Silence as* THEY *each gather themselves and sip their refreshments*]

MARION [*Calmly*]. Do you think that I sold the apartment just to throw you out?

ARTHUR. I don't care about the apartment . . .

MARION. . . . Because I really didn't. Believe me.

ARTHUR. I know.

MARION. I knew the expenses here were too much for you, and I knew you couldn't afford to buy out my half . . . I figured if we sold it, that you'd at least have a nice chunk of money to start over with.

ARTHUR. You could've given me a little more time.

MARION. Maybe. But I thought the sooner you were out of here, the sooner you could go on with your life.

ARTHUR. Or the sooner you could go on with yours.

MARION. Maybe. [*Pause to gather her thoughts*] Anyway, I'm not going to tell you that I have no idea what you're talking about. I'd have to be worse than deaf and blind not to have seen the way you've been treated. Or mistreated. When I read Collin's obituary in the newspaper and saw my name and Jimmy's name and no mention of you . . . [*Shakes her head, not knowing what to say*] You know that his secretary was the one who wrote that up and sent it in. Not me. But I should have done something about it and I didn't. I know.

ARTHUR. Wouldn't have made a difference. I wrote my own obituary for him and sent it to the smaller papers. They edited me out.

MARION. I'm sorry. I remember, at the funeral, I was surrounded by all of Collin's family and business associates while you were left with your friends. I knew it was wrong. I knew I should have said something but it felt good to have them around me and you looked like you were holding up . . . Wrong. But saying that it's all my fault for not letting go . . . ? There were other people involved.

ARTHUR. Who took their cue from you.

MARION. Arthur, you don't understand. Most people that we knew as a couple had no idea that Collin was Gay right up to his death. And even those that did know only found out when he got sick and the word leaked out that it was AIDS. I don't think I have to tell you how stupid and ill-informed most people are about homosexuality. And AIDS . . . ? The kinds of insane behavior that word inspires . . . ?

Those people at the funeral, how many times did they call to see how he was doing over these years? How many of them ever went to see him in the hospital? Did any of them even come here? So, why would you expect them to act any differently after his death?

So, maybe that helps to explain their behavior, but what about mine, right? Well, maybe there is no explanation. Only excuses. And excuse number one is that you're right, I have never really let go of him. And I am jealous of you. Hell, I was jealous of anyone that Collin ever talked to, let alone slept with . . . let alone loved.

The first year, after he moved out, we talked all the time about the different men he was seeing. And I always listened and advised. It was kind of fun. It kept us close. It kept me a part of his intimate life. And the bottom line was always that he wasn't happy with the men he was meeting. So, I was always allowed to hang on to the hope that one day he'd give it all up and come home. Then he got sick.

He called me, told me he was in the hospital and asked if I'd come see him. I ran. When I got to his door there was a sign, INSTRUCTIONS FOR VISITORS OF AN AIDS PATIENT. I nearly died.

ARTHUR. He hadn't told you?

MARION. No. And believe me, a sign is not the way to find these things out. I was so angry . . . And he was so sick . . . I was sure that he'd die right then. If not from the illness then from the hospital staff's neglect. No one wanted to go near him and I didn't bother fighting with them because I understood that they were scared. I was scared. That whole month in the hospital I didn't let Jimmy visit him once.

You learn.

Well, as you know, he didn't die. And he asked if he could come stay with me until he was well. And I said yes. Of course, yes. Now, here's something I never thought I'd ever admit to anyone: had he asked to stay with me for a few weeks I would have said no. But he asked to stay with me until he was well and knowing there was no cure I said yes. In my craziness I said yes because to me that meant forever. That he was coming back to me forever. Not that I wanted him to die, but I assumed from everything I'd read . . . And we'd be back together for whatever time he had left. Can you understand that?

[ARTHUR *nods*.]

MARION [*Gathers her thoughts again*]. Two weeks later he left. He moved in here. Into this apartment that we had bought as an investment. Never to live in. Certainly never to live apart in. Next thing I knew, the name Arthur starts appearing in every phone call, every dinner conversation.

"Did you see the doctor?"

"Yes. Arthur made sure I kept the appointment."

"Are you going to your folks for Thanksgiving?"

"No. Arthur and I are having some friends over."

I don't know which one of us was more of a coward, he for not telling or me for not asking about you. But eventually you became a given. Then, of course, we met and became what I had always thought of as friends.

[ARTHUR *winces in guilt*]

MARION. I don't care what you say, how could we not be friends with someone so great in common: love for one of the most special human beings there ever was. And don't try and tell me there weren't times when you en-joyed me being around as an ally. I can think of a dozen occasions when we ganged up on him, teasing him with our intimate knowledge of his personal habits.

[ARTHUR *has to laugh*]

MARION. Blanket stealing? Snoring? Excess gas, no less? [*Takes a mo-ment to enjoy this truce*] I don't think that my loving him threatened your rela-tionship. Maybe I'm not being truthful with myself. But I don't. I never tried to step between you. Not that I ever had the opportunity. Talk about being joined at the hip! And that's not to say I wasn't jealous. I was. Terribly. Hate-fully. But always lovingly. I was happy for Collin because there was no way to deny that he was happy. With everything he was facing, he was happy. Love did that. You did that.

He lit up with you. He came to life. I envied that and all the time you spent together, but more, I watched you care for him (sometimes *overcare* for him), and I was in awe. I could never have done what you did. I never would have survived. I really don't know how you did.

ARTHUR. Who said I survived?

MARION. Don't tease. You did an absolutely incredible thing. It's not as if you met him before he got sick. You entered a relationship that you knew in all probability would end this way and you never wavered.

ARTHUR. Of course I did. Don't have me sainted, Marion. But sometimes you have no choice. Believe me, if I could've gotten away from him I would've. But I was a prisoner of love.

[HE *makes a campy gesture and pose*]

MARION. Stop.

ARTHUR. And there were lots of pluses. I got to quit a job I hated, stay home all day and watch game shows. I met a lot of doctors and learned a lot of big words. [ARTHUR *jumps up and goes to the pile of boxes where* HE *extracts one and brings it back to the couch.*]

And then there was all the exciting traveling I got to do. This box has a souvenir from each one of our trips. Wanna see? [MARION *nods.* HE *opens the box and pulls things out one by one. Holding up an old bottle*]

This is from the house we rented in Reno when we went to clear out his lungs. [*Holding handmade potholders*]

This is from the hospital in Reno. Collin made them. They had a great arts and crafts program. [*Copper bracelets*]

These are from a faith healer in Philly. They don't do much for a fever, but they look great with a green sweater. [*Glass ashtrays*]

These are from our first visit to the clinic in France. Such lovely people. [*A Bible*]

This is from our second visit to the clinic in France. [*A bead necklace*]

A Voodoo doctor in New Orleans. Next time we'll have to get there earli-er in the year. I think he sold all the pretty ones at Mardi Gras. [*A tiny piñata*]

Then there was Mexico. Black market drugs and empty wallets. [*Now pulling things out at random*]

L.A., San Francisco, Houston, Boston . . . We traveled everywhere they offered hope for sale and came home with souvenirs. [ARTHUR *quietly pulls a few more things out and then begins to put them all back into the box slowly. Softly as* HE *works:*] Marion, I would have done anything, traveled anywhere to avoid . . . or delay . . . Not just because I loved him so desperately, but when you've lived the way we did for three years . . . the battle becomes your life. [HE *looks at her and then away*] His last few hours were beyond any scenario I had imagined. He hadn't walked in nearly six months. He was totally incontinent. If he spoke two words in a week I was thankful. Days went by without his eyes ever focusing on me. He just stared out at I don't know what. Not the meals as I fed him. Not the TV I played constantly for company. Just out. Or maybe in.

It was the middle of the night when I heard his breathing become labored. His lungs were filling with fluid again. I knew the sound. I'd heard it a hundred times before. So, I called the ambulance and got him to the hospital.

They hooked him up to the machines, the oxygen, shot him with morphine and told me that they would do what they could to keep him alive.

But, Marion, it wasn't the machines that kept him breathing. He did it himself. It was that incredible will and strength inside him. Whether it came from his love of life or fear of death, who knows. But he'd been counted out a hundred times and a hundred times he fought his way back.

I got a magazine to read him, pulled a chair up to the side of his bed and holding his hand, I wondered whether I should call Helen to let the cleaning lady in or if he'd fall asleep and I could sneak home for an hour. I looked up from the page and he was looking at me. Really looking right into my eyes. I patted his cheek and said, "Don't worry, honey, you're going to be fine."

But there was something else in his eyes. He wasn't satisfied with that. And I don't know why, I have no idea where it came from, I just heard the words coming out of my mouth, "Collin, do you want to die?"

His eyes filled and closed, he nodded his head.

I can't tell you what I was thinking, I'm not sure I was. I slipped off my shoes, lifted his blanket and climbed into bed next to him. I helped him to put his arms around me, and mine around him, and whispered as gently as I could into his ear, "It's alright to let go now. It's time to go on." And he did.

Marion, you've got your life and your son. All I have is an intangible place in a man's history. Leave me that. Respect that.

MARION. I understand.

[ARTHUR *suddenly comes to life, running to get the shopping bag that* HE*'d left at the front door*]

ARTHUR. Jeez! With all the screamin' and sad storytelling I forgot something. [HE *extracts a bouquet of flowers from the bag*] I brung you flowers and everything.

MARION. You brought *me* flowers?

ARTHUR. Well, I knew you'd never think to bring me flowers and I felt that on an occasion such as this somebody oughta get flowers from somebody.

MARION. You know, Arthur, you're really making me feel like a worthless piece of garbage.

ARTHUR. So what else is new? [HE *presents the flowers*] Just promise me one thing: Don't press one in a book. Just stick them in a vase and when they fade just toss them out. No more memorabilia.

MARION. Arthur, I want to do something for you and I don't know what. Tell me what you want.

ARTHUR. I want little things. Not much. I want to be remembered. If you get a Christmas card from Collin's mother make sure she sent me one too. If his friends call to see how you are, ask if they've called me. Have me to dinner so I can see Jimmy. Let me take him out now and then. Invite me to his wedding. [THEY BOTH *laugh*]

MARION. You've got it.

ARTHUR [*Clearing the table*]. Let me get all this cold cocoa out of the way. We still have the deed to do.

MARION [*Checking her watch*]. And I've got to get Jimmy home in time for practice.

ARTHUR. Band practice?

MARION. Baseball. [*Picking her list off the floor*] About this list, you do what you want.

ARTHUR. Believe me, I will. But I promise to consider your suggestions. Just don't rush me. I'm not ready to give it all away. [ARTHUR *is off to the kitchen with his tray and the phone rings.* HE *answers in the kitchen*] "Hello? . . . Just a minute. [*Calling out*] It's your eager Little Leaguer.

[MARION *picks up the living room extension and* ARTHUR *hangs his up*]

MARION [*Into phone*]. Hello, honey. . . . I'll be down in five minutes. No. You know what? You come up here and get me. . . . No, I said you should come up here . . . . I said I want you to come up here. . . . Because I said so. . . . Thank you. [SHE *hangs the receiver*]

ARTHUR [*Rushing to the papers*]. Alright, where do we start on these?

MARION [*Getting out her seal*]. I guess you should just start signing everything and I'll stamp along with you. Keep one of everything on the side for yourself.

ARTHUR. Now I feel so rushed. What am I signing?

MARION. You want to do this another time?

ARTHUR. No. Let's get it over with. I wouldn't survive another session like this.

[HE *starts to sign and* SHE *starts her job*]

MARION. I keep meaning to ask you; how are you?

ARTHUR [*At first puzzled and then:*] Oh, you mean my health? Fine. No. I'm fine. I've been tested, and nothing. We were very careful. We took many precautions. Collin used to make jokes about how we should invest in rubber futures.

MARION. I'll bet.

ARTHUR [*Stops what* HE'*s doing*]. It never occurred to me until now. How about you?

MARION [*Not stopping*]. Well, we never had sex after he got sick.

ARTHUR. But before?

MARION [*Stopping but not looking up*]. I have the antibodies in my blood. No signs that it will ever develop into anything else. And it's been five years so my chances are pretty good that I'm just a carrier.

ARTHUR. I'm so sorry. Collin never told me.

MARION. He didn't know. In fact, other than my husband and the doctors, you're the only one I've told.

ARTHUR. You and your husband . . . ?

MARION. Have invested in rubber futures. There'd only be a problem if we wanted to have a child. Which we do. But we'll wait. Miracles happen every day.

ARTHUR. I don't know what to say.

MARION. Tell me you'll be be there if I ever need you.

[ARTHUR *gets up, goes to her and puts his arm around her.* THEY *hold each other.* HE *gently pushes her away to make a joke.*]

ARTHUR. Sure! Take something else that should have been mine.

MARION. Don't even joke about things like that.

[*The doorbell rings.* THEY *pull themselves together*]

ARTHUR. You know we'll never get these done today.

MARION. So, tomorrow.

[ARTHUR *goes to open the door as* MARION *gathers her things.* HE *opens the doors and* JIMMY *is standing in the hall*]

JIM. C'mon, Ma. I'm gonna be late.

ARTHUR. Would you like to come inside?

JIM. We've gotta go.

MARION. Jimmy, come on.

JIM. Ma!

[SHE *glares.* HE *comes in.* ARTHUR *closes the door*]

MARION [*Holding out the flowers*]. Take these for Mommy.

JIM [*Taking them*]. Can we go?

MARION [*Picking up the painting*]. Say good-bye to your Uncle Arthur.

JIM. 'Bye, Arthur. Come on.

MARION. Give him a kiss.

ARTHUR. Marion, don't.

MARION. Give your uncle a kiss good-bye.

JIM. He's not my uncle.

MARION. No. He's a hell of a lot more than your uncle.

ARTHUR [*Offering his hand*]. A handshake will do.

MARION. Tell Uncle Arthur what your daddy told you.

JIM. About what?

MARION. Stop playing dumb. You know.

ARTHUR. Don't embarrass him.

MARION. Jimmy, please.

JIM [HE *regards his* MOTHER*'s softer tone and then speaks*]. He said that after me and Mommy he loved you the most.

MARION [*Standing behind him*]. Go on.

JIM. And that I should love you too. And make sure that you're not lonely or very sad.

ARTHUR. Thank you.

[ARTHUR *reaches down to the* BOY *and* THEY *hug.* JIM *gives him a little peck on the cheek and then breaks away*]

MARION [*Going to open the door*]. Alright, kid, you done good. Now let's blow this joint before you muck it up.

[JIM *rushes out the door.* MARION *turns to* ARTHUR]

MARION. A child's kiss is magic. Why else would they be so stingy with them. I'll call you.

[ARTHUR *nods understanding.* MARION *pulls the door closed behind her.* ARTHUR *stands quietly as the lights fade to black*]

THE END

NOTE: *If being performed on film, the final image should be of* ARTHUR *leaning his back against the closed door on the inside of the apartment and* MARION *leaning on the outside of the door. A moment of thought and then* THEY BOTH *move on.*

[1987]

■ TOPICS FOR DISCUSSION AND WRITING

1. We first hear about AIDS on page 190. Were you completely surprised, or did you think the play might introduce the subject? That is, did the author in any way prepare you for the subject? If so, how?

2. So far as the basic story goes, June (the lawyer) is not necessary. Marion could have brought the papers with her. Why do you suppose Fierstein introduces June? What function(s) does she serve? How would you characterize her?

3. On page 191 Marion says of the teapot, "One less thing to pack." Arthur says the same words a moment later, and then he repeats them yet again. A little later, while drinking cocoa, he repeats the words, and Marion says, "So you've said," to which Arthur replies, "So we've said." Exactly what tone do you think should be used when Marion first says these words? When Arthur says them? And what significance, if any, do you attach to the fact that both characters speak these words?

4. A reviewer of the play said that Arthur is "bitchy" in many of his responses to Marion. What do you suppose the reviewer meant by this? Does the term imply that Fierstein presents a stereotype of the homosexual? If so, what is this stereotype? If you think that the term applies (even though you might not use such a word yourself), do you think that Fierstein's portrayal of Arthur is stereotypical? If it is stereotypical, is this a weakness in the play?

5. Arthur says that Jimmy blames him for Collin's death, but Marion denies it. Who do you think is right? Can a reader be sure? Why, or why not?

6. When Arthur tells Marion that she should have told Jimmy why Collin left her, Marion says, "How the hell do you tell a seven-year-old that his father is leaving his mother to go sleep with other men?" Arthur replies, "Well, not like that." What does Arthur mean? How *might* Marion have told Jimmy? Do you think she should have told Jimmy?

7. Do you agree with a reader who found Marion an unconvincing character because she is "so passive and unquestioningly loving in her regard for her ex-husband"? If you disagree, how would you argue your case?

8. During the course of the play, what (if anything) does Marion learn? What (if anything) does Arthur learn? What (if anything) does Jimmy learn? What (if anything) does the reader or viewer learn from the play?

9. One reader characterized the play as "propaganda." Do you agree? Why, or why not? And if you think "On Tidy Endings" is propaganda, are you implying that it is therefore deficient as a work of art?

CHAPTER 7

Reading
(and Writing about)
Poetry

The Speaker and the Poet

The **speaker,** or **voice,** or **mask,** or **persona** (Latin for "mask") that speaks a poem is not usually identical with the poet who writes it. The author assumes a role, or counterfeits the speech of a person in a particular situation. Robert Browning, for instance, in "My Last Duchess" invented a Renaissance duke who, in his palace, talks about his first wife and his art collection with an emissary from a count who is negotiating to offer his daughter in marriage to the duke.

In reading a poem, then, the first and most important question to ask yourself is this: Who is speaking? If an audience and a setting are suggested, keep them in mind too, although these are not always indicated in a poem. For instance, Emily Dickinson's "Wild Nights" (1861) is the utterance of an impassioned lover, but we need not assume that the beloved is actually in the presence of the lover. In fact, since the second line says, "Were I with thee," the reader must assume that the person addressed is *not* present. The poem apparently represents a state of mind—a sort of talking to oneself—rather than an address to another person.

■ EMILY DICKINSON (1830–1886)

Wild Nights—Wild Nights

Wild Nights—Wild Nights,
Were I with Thee
Wild Nights should be
Our luxury!   4

Futile—the Winds
To a Heart in port—

Done with the Compass—
Done with the Chart!   8

Rowing in Eden—
Ah, the Sea!
Might I but moor—Tonight—
In Thee.   12
                    [c. 1861]

Clearly the speaker is someone passionately in love. The following questions invite you to look more closely at how the speaker of "Wild Nights" is
characterized.

■ QUESTIONS FOR DISCUSSION

1. How does this poem communicate the speaker's state of mind? For ex-
    ample, in the first stanza (lines 1-4), what—beyond the meaning of the
    words—is communicated by the repetition of "Wild Nights"? In the last
    stanza (lines 9-12), what is the tone of "Ah, the Sea!"? ("Tone" means
    something like emotional coloring, as for instance when one speaks of
    a "businesslike tone," a "bitter tone," or an "eager tone.")
2. Paraphrase (that is, put into your own words) the second stanza. What
    does this stanza communicate about the speaker's love for the beloved?
    Compare your paraphrase and the original. What does the form of the
    original sentences (the *omission*, for instance, of the verbs of lines 5 and
    6 and of the subject in lines 7 and 8) communicate?
3. Paraphrase the last stanza. How does "Ah, the Sea!" fit into your
    paraphrase? If you had trouble fitting it in, do you think the poem would
    be better off without it? If not, why not?

    The voice speaking a poem may, of course, have the ring of the author's
own voice, and to make a distinction between speaker and author may at
times seem perverse. In fact, some poetry (especially contemporary American poetry) is highly autobiographical. Still, even in autobiographical poems
it may be convenient to distinguish between author and speaker. The speaker
of a given poem is, let's say, Sylvia Plath in her role as parent, or Sylvia Plath
in her role as daughter, not simply Sylvia Plath the poet.

The Language of Poetry: Diction and Tone

    How is a voice or mask or persona created? From the whole of language,
the author consciously or unconsciously selects certain words and grammatical constructions; this selection constitutes the persona's diction. It is, then,
partly by the diction that we come to know the speaker of a poem. Just as
in life there is a difference between people who speak of a "belly-button," a
"navel," or an "umbilicus," so in poetry there is a difference between speakers who use one word rather than another. Of course it is also possible that
all three of these words are part of a given speaker's vocabulary, and the

speaker's choice among the three would depend on the situation. That is, in addressing a child, the speaker would probably use the word "belly-button"; in addressing an adult other than a family member or close friend, the speaker might be more likely to use "navel"; and if the speaker is a physician addressing an audience of physicians, he or she might be most likely to use "umbilicus." But this is only to say, again, that the dramatic situation in which one finds oneself helps to define oneself, helps to establish the particular role that one is playing.

Of course some words are used in virtually all poems: *I, see, and,* and the like. Still, the grammatical constructions in which they appear may help to define the speaker. In Dickinson's "Wild Nights," for instance, expressions such as "Were I with Thee" and "Might I" indicate a speaker of an earlier century than ours, and probably an educated speaker.

Speakers have attitudes toward themselves, their subjects, and their audiences, and, consciously or unconsciously, they choose their words, pitch, and modulation accordingly; all these add up to their tone. In written literature, tone must be detected without the aid of the ear, although it's a good idea to read poetry aloud, trying to find the appropriate tone of voice. That is, the reader must understand by the selection and sequence of words the way the words are meant to sound—playful, angry, confidential, or ironic, for example. The reader must catch what Frost calls "the speaking tone of voice somehow entangled in the words and fastened to the page for the ear of the imagination."

WRITING ABOUT THE SPEAKER: ROBERT FROST'S "THE TELEPHONE"

Robert Frost once said that

everything written is as good as it is dramatic. . . . [A poem is] heard as sung or spoken by a person in a scene—in a character, in a setting. By whom, where and when is the question. By the dreamer of a better world out in a storm in autumn; by a lover under a window at night.

Suppose, in reading a poem Frost published in 1916, we try to establish "by whom, where and when" it is spoken. We may not be able to answer all three questions in great detail, but let's see what the poem suggests. As you read it, you'll notice—alerted by the quotation marks—that there are *two* speakers; the poem is a tiny drama. Thus, the closing quotation marks at the end of line 9 signal to us that the first speech is finished.

■ ROBERT FROST (1874–1963)

The Telephone

"When I was just as far as I could walk
From here today
There was an hour

All still
When leaning with my head against a flower   5
I heard you talk.
Don't say I didn't, for I heard you say—
You spoke from that flower on the window sill—
Do you remember what it was you said?"

"First tell me what it was you thought you heard."   10

"Having found the flower and driven a bee away,
I leaned my head,
And holding by the stalk,
I listened and I thought I caught the word—
What was it? Did you call me by my name?   15
Or did you say—
Someone said 'Come'—I heard it as I bowed."

"I may have thought as much, but not aloud."

"Well, so I came."

[1916]

Suppose we ask: Who are these two speakers? What is their relationship? What's going on between them? Where are they? We don't think that these questions can be answered with absolute certainty, but we do think some answers are more probable than others. For instance, line 8 ("You spoke from that flower on the window sill") tells us that the speakers are in a room, probably of a home—rather than, say, in a railroad station—but we can't say whether the home is a farmhouse, or a house in a village, town, or city, or an apartment.

Let's put the questions (even if they may turn out to be unanswerable) into a more specific form.

■ QUESTIONS

1. One speaker speaks lines 1-9, 11-17, and 19. The other speaks lines 10 and 18. Do you think you can tell the gender of each speaker? For sure, probably, or not at all? On what do you base your answer?

2. Try to visualize this miniature drama. In line 7 the first speaker says, "Don't say I didn't, . . ." What happens—what do you see in your mind's eye—after line 6 that causes the speaker to say this?

3. Why do you suppose the speaker of lines 10 and 18 says so little? How would your characterize the tone of these two lines? What sort of relationship do you think exists between the two speakers?

4. How would you characterize the tone of lines 11-17? Of the last line of the poem?

If you haven't jotted down your responses, we suggest that you do so before reading what follows.

JOURNAL ENTRIES

Given questions somewhat like the preceding ones, students were asked to try to identify the speakers by sex, to speculate on their relationship, and then to add whatever they wished to say. One student recorded the following thoughts:

> These two people care about each other—maybe husband and wife, or lovers—and a man is doing most of the talking, though I can't prove it. He has walked as far as possible—that is, as far as possible and still get back on the same day—and he seemed to hear the other person call him. He claims that she spoke to him "from that flower on the window sill," and that's why I think the second person is a woman. She's at home, near the window. Somehow I even imagine she was at the window near the kitchen sink, maybe working while he was out on this long walk.
>
> Then she speaks one line; she won't say if she did or didn't speak. She is very cautious, or suspicious: "First tell me what it was you thought you heard." Maybe she doesn't want to say something and then have her husband embarrass her by saying, "No, that's not what I thought." Or maybe she just doesn't feel like talking. Then he claims that he heard her speaking through a flower, as though the flower was a telephone, just as though it was hooked up to the flower on the window sill. But at first he won't say what he supposedly heard, or "thought" he heard. Instead, he says that maybe it was someone else: "<u>Someone</u> said 'Come.'" Is he teasing her? Pretending that she may have a rival?
>
> Then she speaks—again just one line, saying, "I may have thought as much, but not aloud." She won't admit that she <u>did</u> think this thought. And then the man says, "Well, so I came." Just like that; short and sweet. No more fancy talk about flowers as telephones. He somehow (through telepathy?) got the message, and so here he is. He seems like a sensitive guy, playful (the stuff about the flowers as telephones) but also he knows when to stop kidding around.

Another student also identified the couple as a man and woman and thought that this dialogue occurs after a quarrel:

As the poem goes on, we learn that the man wants to be with the woman, but it starts by telling us that he walked as far away from her as he could. He doesn't say why, but I think from the way the woman speaks later in the poem, they had a fight and he walked out. Then, when he stopped to rest, he thought he heard her voice. He really means that he was thinking of her and he was hoping she was thinking of him. So he returns, and he tells her he heard her calling him, but he pretends he heard her call him through a flower on their window sill. He can't admit that he was thinking about her. This seems very realistic to me; when someone feels a bit ashamed, it's sometimes hard to admit that you were wrong, and you want the other person to tell you that things are OK anyhow. And judging from line 7, when he says "Don't say I didn't," it seems that she is going to interrupt him by denying it. She is still angry, or maybe she doesn't want to make up too quickly. But he wants to pretend that she called him back. So when he says, "Do you remember what it was you said?" she won't admit that she was thinking of him, and she says, "First tell me what it was you thought you heard." She's testing him a little. So he goes on, with the business about flowers as telephones, and he says "someone" called him. He understands that she doesn't want to be pushed into forgiving him, so he backs off. Then she is willing to admit that she did think about him, but still she doesn't quite admit it. She is too proud to say openly that she wants him back but she does say, "I may have thought as much, . . ." And then, since they both have preserved their dignity, and also both have admitted that they care about the other, he can say, "Well, so I came."

■ TOPICS FOR WRITING

1. In a paragraph or two or three, *evaluate* one of these two entries recorded by students. Do you think the comments are weak, plausible, or convincing, and *why* do you think so? Can you offer additional supporting evidence or, on the other hand, counterevidence? You may want to set forth your own scenario.

2. Two small questions: In a sentence or two, offer a suggestion as to why in line 11 Frost wrote, "and driven a bee away." After all, the bee plays no role in the poem. Second, in line 17 Frost has the speaker say, "I

heard it as I bowed." Of course "bowed" rhymes with "aloud," but let's assume that the need for a rhyme did not dictate the choice of this word. Do you think "I heard it as I bowed" is better than, say, "I heard it as I waited," or "I heard it as I listened"? Why?

3. Write an essay of 500 words either about an uncanny experience of your own or about a quarrel or disagreement that was resolved in a way you had not expected.

PARAPHRASE

Our interest in the shifting tones of the voice that speaks the words should not, of course, cause us to neglect the words themselves, the gist of the idea expressed. Sometimes a line may be obscure, for instance because a word is no longer current, or is current only in a region. The Anglo-Irish poet William Butler Yeats (1865–1939) begins one poem with

The friends that have it I do wrong . . . .

Because the idiom "to have it" (meaning "to believe that," "to think that") is unfamiliar to many readers today, a discussion of the poem might include a paraphrase—a rewording, a translation into more familiar language, such as

The friends who think that I am doing the wrong thing . . . .

Another brief example: In a poem by Emily Dickinson (1830–86), the following line appears:

The sun engrossed the East. . . .

"Engrossed" here has (perhaps among other meanings) a special commercial meaning, "to acquire most or all of a commodity; to monopolize a market," and so a paraphrase of the line might go thus:

The sun took over all of the east.

The point of paraphrase is to help you, or your reader, understand at least the surface meaning, and the act of paraphrasing will usually help you to understand at least some of the implicit meaning. Furthermore, a paraphrase makes you see that the poet's words—if the poem is a good one—are exactly right, better than any words we might substitute. It becomes clear that the thing said in the poem—not only the rough "idea" expressed but the precise tone with which it is expressed—is a sharply defined experience.

Figurative Language

Robert Frost has said, "Poetry provides the one permissible way of saying one thing and meaning another." This, of course, is an exaggeration, but it shrewdly suggests the importance of figurative language—saying one thing in terms of something else. Words have their literal meanings, but they can also be used so that something other than the literal meaning is implied. "My love is a rose" is, literally, nonsense, for a person is not a five-petaled, many-stamened plant with a spiny stem. But the suggestions of rose (at least for Robert Burns, who compared his beloved to a rose in the line, "My love is like a red, red rose") include "delicate beauty," "soft," and "perfumed," and thus the word *rose* can be meaningfully applied—figuratively rather than literally—to "my love." The girl is fragrant; her skin is perhaps like a rose in texture and (in some measure) color; she will not keep her beauty long. The poet, that is, has communicated his perception very precisely.

People who write about poetry have found it convenient to name the various kinds of figurative language. Just as the student of geology employs such special terms as *kames* and *eskers*, the student of literature employs special terms to name things as accurately as possible. The following paragraphs discuss the most common terms.

In a **simile,** items from different classes are explicitly compared by a connective such as *like, as,* or *than,* or by a verb such as *appears* or *seems.* (If the objects compared are from the same class, for example, "Tokyo is like Los Angeles," no simile is present.)

> Float like a butterfly, sting like a bee.
> —Muhammad Ali

> It is a beauteous evening, calm and free.
> The holy time is quiet as a Nun,
> Breathless with adoration.
> —William Wordsworth

> All of our thoughts will be fairer than doves.
> —Elizabeth Bishop

> Seems he a dove? His feathers are but borrowed.
> —Shakespeare

A **metaphor** asserts the identity, without a connective such as *like* or a verb such as *appears*, of terms that are literally incompatible.

> Umbrellas clothe the beach in every hue.
> —Elizabeth Bishop

> The
> whirlwind fife-and-drum of the storm bends the salt
> marsh grass
> —Marianne Moore

Two common types of metaphor have Greek names. In **synecdoche** the whole is replaced by the part, or the part by the whole. For example, *bread* in "Give us this day our daily bread" replaces all sorts of food. In **metonymy** something is named that replaces something closely related to it. For example, James Shirley names certain objects, using them to replace social classes (royalty and the peasantry) to which they are related:

Scepter and crown must tumble down
And in the dust be equal made
With the poor crooked scythe and spade.

The attribution of human feelings or characteristics or abstractions or two inanimate objects is called **personification.**

Memory,
that exquisite blunderer.
—Amy Clampitt

There's Wrath who has learnt every trick of guerilla warfare,
The shamming dead, the night-raid, the feinted retreat.
—W. H. Auden

Hope, thou bold taster of delight.
—Richard Crashaw

Crashaw's personification, "Hope, thou bold taster of delight," is also an example of the figure called **apostrophe,** an address to a person or thing not literally listening. Wordsworth begins a sonnet by apostrophizing Milton:

Milton, thou shouldst be living at this hour.

What conclusions can we draw about figurative language? First, figurative language, with its literally incompatible terms, forces the reader to attend to the *connotations* (suggestions, associations) rather than to the *denotations* (dictionary definitions) of one of the terms. Second, although figurative language is said to differ from ordinary speech, it is found in ordinary speech as well as in poetry and other literary forms. "It rained cats and dogs," "War is hell," "Don't be a pig," "Mr. Know-it-all," and other tired figures are part of our daily utterances. But through repeated use, these, and most of the figures we use, have lost whatever impact they once had and are only a shade removed from expressions which, though once figurative, have become literal: the *eye* of a needle, a *branch* office, the *face* of a clock. Third, good figurative language is usually concrete, condensed, and interesting.

We should mention, too, that figurative language is not limited to literary writers; it is used by scientists and social scientists—by almost everyone who is concerned with effective expression. Take, for instance, R. H. Tawney's *Religion and the Rise of Capitalism* (1926), a classic of economics. Among the titles of Tawney's chapters are "The Economic Revolution," "The Puritan Movement," and "The New Medicine for Poverty," all of which include metaphors. (To take only the last: Poverty is seen as a sick person or a disease.) Or take this sentence from Tawney (almost any sentence will serve equally well to reveal his bent for metaphor): "By the end of the sixteenth century the divorce between religious theory and economic realities had long been evident." Figures are not a fancy way of speaking. Quite the opposite:

Writers use figures because they are forceful and exact. Literal language would not only be less interesting, it would also be less precise.

Imagery and Symbolism

WILLIAM BLAKE: "THE SICK ROSE"

When we read *rose* we may more or less call to mind a picture of a rose, or perhaps we are reminded of the odor or texture of a rose. Whatever in a poem appeals to any of our senses (including sensations of heat as well as of sight, smell, taste, touch, sound) is an image. In short, images are the sensory content of a work, whether literal or figurative. When a poet says "My rose" and is speaking about a rose, we have no figure of speech—though we still have an image. If, however, "My rose" is a shortened form of "My love is a rose," some would say that the poet is using a metaphor; but others would say that because the first term is omitted ("My love is"), the rose is a symbol. A poem about the transience of a rose might compel the reader to feel that the transience of female beauty is the larger theme even though it is never explicitly stated.

Some symbols are **conventional symbols**—people have agreed to accept them as standing for something other than their literal meanings: A poem about the cross would probably be about Christianity; similarly, the rose has long been a symbol for love. In Virginia Woolf's novel *Mrs. Dalloway,* the husband communicates his love by proffering this conventional symbol: "He was holding out flowers—roses, red and white roses. (But he could not bring himself to say he loved her; not in so many words.)" Objects that are not conventional symbols, however, may also give rise to rich, multiple, indefinable associations. The following poem uses the traditional symbol of the rose, but uses it in a nontraditional way:

> O rose, thou art sick!
> The invisible worm
> That flies in the night,
> In the howling storm,
>
> Has found out thy bed
> Of crimson joy,
> And his dark secret love
> Does thy life destroy.
>   [1794]
>   —William Blake, "The Sick Rose"

A reader might perhaps argue that the worm is invisible (line 2) merely because it is hidden within the rose, but an "invisible worm / That flies in the night" is more than a long, slender, soft-bodied, creeping animal; and a rose that has, or is, a "bed / Of crimson joy" is more than a gardener's rose. Blake's worm and rose suggest things beyond themselves—a stranger, more vibrant world than the world we are usually aware of. They are, in short, symbolic, though readers will doubtless differ in their interpretations. Perhaps we find ourselves half thinking, for example, that the worm is male, the rose female, and that the poem is about the violation of virginity. Or that the poem is about the destruction of beauty: Woman's beauty, rooted in joy, is destroyed by a power that feeds on her. But these interpretations are not fully satisfying: The poem presents a worm and a rose, and yet it is not merely about a worm and a rose. These objects resonate, stimulating our thoughts toward something else, but the something else is elusive. This is not to say, however, that symbols mean whatever any reader says they mean. A reader could scarcely support, we imagine, an interpretation arguing that the poem is about the need to love all aspects of nature. All interpretations are not equally valid; it's the writer's job to offer a reasonably persuasive interpretation.

A symbol, then, is an image so loaded with significance that it is not simply literal, and it does not simply stand for something else; it is both itself *and* something else that it richly suggests, a kind of manifestation of something too complex or too elusive to be otherwise revealed. Blake's poem is about a blighted rose and at the same time about much more. In a symbol, as Thomas Carlyle wrote, "the Infinite is made to blend with the Finite, to stand visible, and as it were, attainable there."

Verbal Irony and Paradox

Among the most common devices in poems is **verbal irony.** The speaker's words mean more or less the opposite of what they seem to say. Sometimes verbal irony takes the form of **overstatement,** or **hyperbole,** as when Lady Macbeth says, while sleep-walking, "All the perfumes of Arabia will not sweeten this little hand." Sometimes it takes the form of **understatement,** as when Andrew Marvell's speaker in "To His Coy Mistress" (page 564) remarks with cautious wryness, "The grave's a fine and private place, / But none, I think, do there embrace," or when Sylvia Plath sees an intended suicide as "the big strip tease." Speaking broadly, intensely emotional contemporary poems like those of Plath often use irony to undercut—and thus make acceptable—the emotion presented.

Another common device in poems is **paradox:** the assertion of an apparent contradiction, as in Marvell's "am'rous birds of prey" in "To His Coy Mistress." Normally we think of amorous birds as gentle—doves, for example—and not as birds of prey, such as hawks. Another example of an apparent contradiction: In "Auld Lang Syne" there is the paradox that the remembrance of joy evokes a kind of sadness.

Structure

The arrangement of the parts, the organization of the entire poem, is its **structure.** Sometimes the poem is divided into blocks of, say, four lines each, but even if the poem is printed as a solid block it probably has some principle of organization. It may move, for example, from sorrow in the first

two lines to joy in the next two or from a question in the first three lines to
an answer in the last line.

Consider this short poem by an English poet of the seventeenth century.

■ ROBERT HERRICK (1591–1674)

Upon Julia's Clothes

Whenas in silk my Julia goes,
Then, then (methinks) how sweetly flows
That liquefaction of her clothes.

Next, when I cast mine eyes, and see
That brave* vibration, each way free
O, how that glittering taketh me.

[1648]

One student began thinking about this poem by copying it, double-
spaced, and by making the following notes on his copy.

STUDENT ESSAY: "HERRICK'S JULIA, JULIA'S HERRICK"

Upon Julia's Clothes

3 { Whenas in silk *(my Julia)* goes, — *cool tone?*
   Then, then (methinks) how sweetly flows
   That liquefaction of her clothes.

"Then, then"—
more
excited?   3 { Next, when I cast mine eyes, and see
almost at   That brave vibration, each way free,
a loss   O, how that glittering taketh me. — *free to do what?*
for words? emotional?   *free from what?*

The student got some further ideas by thinking about several of the
questions that, at the end of this chapter, we suggest you ask yourself while
rereading a poem. Among the questions are these:

* *splendid*

Does the poem proceed in a straightforward way, or at some point or points
does the speaker reverse course, altering his or her tone or perception?
What is the effect on you of the form?

With such questions in mind, the student was stimulated to see if there
is some sort of reversal or change in Herrick's poem, and if there is, how it
is related to the structure. After rereading the poem several times, thinking
about it in the light of these questions and perhaps others that came to mind,
he produced the following notes:

> Two stanzas, each of three lines, with the same
> structure

> Basic structure of 1st stanza: When X (one line), then
> Y (two lines)

> Basic structure of second stanza: Next (one line), then
> Z (two lines)

When he marked the text, after reading the poem a few times, he noticed that the last line—an exclamation of delight ("O, how that glittering
taketh me")—is much more personal than the rest of the poem. A little further thought enabled him to refine this last perception:

> Although the pattern of stanzas is repeated, the
> somewhat analytic, detached tone of the beginning
> ("Whenas," "Then," "Next") changes to an open,
> enthusiastic confession of delight in what the poet
> sees.

Further thinking led to this:

> Although the title is "Upon Julia's Clothes," and the
> first five lines describe Julia's silken dress, the
> poem finally is not only about Julia's clothing but
> about the effect of Julia (moving in silk that
> liquefies or seems to become a liquid) on the poet.

This is a nice observation, but when the student looked again at the
poem the next day, and started to write about it, he found that he was able
to refine his observation.

> Even at the beginning, the speaker is not entirely
> detached, for he speaks of "my Julia."

In writing about Herrick's "Upon Julia's Clothes," the student tells us,
the thoughts did not come quickly or neatly. After two or three thoughts, he
started to write. Only after drafting a paragraph, and rereading the poem, did
he notice that the personal element appears not only in the last line ("taketh
me") but even in the first line ("*my* Julia"). In short, for almost all of us, the
only way to get to a good final essay is to read, to think, to jot down ideas,

to write a draft, and to revise and revise again. Having gone through such processes, the student came up with the following excellent essay.

By the way, the student did not hit on the final version of his title ("Herrick's Julia, Julia's Herrick") until shortly before he typed his final version. His preliminary title was

Structure and Personality in
Herrick's "Upon Julia's Clothing"

That's a bit heavy-handed but at least it is focused, as opposed to such an uninformative title as "On a Poem." He soon revised his tentative title to

Julia, Julia's Clothing, and Julia's Poet

That's quite a good title: It is neat, and it is appropriate, since it moves (as the poem and the essay do) from Julia and her clothing to the poet. Of course it doesn't tell the reader exactly what the essay will be about, but it does stimulate the reader's interest. The essayist's final title, however, is even better:

Herrick's Julia, Julia's Herrick

Again, it is neat (the balanced structure, and structure is part of the student's topic), and it moves (as the poem itself moves) from Julia to the poet.

Herrick's Julia, Julia's Herrick

Robert Herrick's "Upon Julia's Clothes" begins as a description of Julia's clothing and ends as an expression of the poet's response not just to Julia's clothing but to Julia herself. Despite the apparently objective or detached tone of the first stanza and the first two lines of the second stanza, the poem finally conveys a strong sense of the speaker's excitement.

The first stanza seems to say, "Whenas" X (one line), "Then" Y (two lines). The second stanza repeats this basic structure of one line of assertion and two lines describing the consequence: "Next" (one line), "then" (two lines). But the logic or coolness of "Whenas," "Then," and "Next," and of such rather scientific language as "liquefaction" (a more technical-sounding word than "melting") and "vibration," is undercut by the breathlessness or

excitement of "Then, then" (that is very different
from a simple "Then"). It is also worth mentioning
that although there is a personal rather than a fully
detached note even in the first line, in "my Julia,"
this expression scarcely reveals much feeling. In
fact, it reveals a touch of male chauvinism, a
suggestion that the woman is a possession of the
speaker's. Not until the last line does the speaker
reveal that, far from Julia being his possession, he is
possessed by Julia: "O, how that glittering taketh
me." If he begins coolly, objectively, and somewhat
complacently, and uses a structure that suggests a
somewhat detached mind, in the exclamatory "O" he
nevertheless at last confesses (to our delight) that he
is enraptured by Julia.

Other things, of course, might be said about this poem. For instance, the
writer says nothing about the changes in the meter, and their possible value
in the poem. Nor does he say anything about the sounds of any of the words
(he might have commented on the long vowels in "sweetly flows," and shown
how the effect would have been different if instead of "sweetly flows" Herrick
had written "swiftly flits"), but such topics might be material for another essay. Furthermore, another reader might have found the poem less
charming—even offensive in its exclusive concern with Julia's appearance.
Still, the essay we have given is, in itself, an interesting and perceptive discussion of the way in which the poet used a repeated structure to set forth a
miniature drama in which observation is, at the end, replaced by emotion.

You may want to think about the structure of the following poem by
Christina Rossetti, an English poet. One of her brothers, Dante Gabriel Rossetti, was a painter, and it was thought (at least by yet another brother) that
the poem refers to his model, Elizabeth Siddal, whom he afterwards married.

■ CHRISTINA ROSSETTI (1830–1894)

In an Artist's Studio

One face looks out from all his canvases,
   One selfsame figure sits or walks or leans:
   We found her hidden just behind those screens,
That mirror gave back all her loveliness.   4

A queen in opal or in ruby dress,
    A nameless girl in freshest summer-greens
    A saint, an angel—every canvas means
The same one meaning, neither more nor less   8
He feeds upon her face by day and night,
    And she with true kind eyes looks back on him,
Fair as the moon and joyful as the light:
    Not wan with waiting, not with sorrow dim;   12
Not as she is, but was when hope shone bright;
    Not as she is, but as she fills his dream.

                     [1856]

This poem is a sonnet. We discuss the form later, on page 229, but if you study the rhymes here you will notice that the first eight lines are united by rhymes, and the next six by different rhymes. A reader might, for a start at least, think about whether what is said has any relation to these units. The first eight lines are about the model, but are the next six equally about her or about someone else?

■ TOPICS FOR DISCUSSION

1.   What do we know about the model in the first eight lines? What do we know about her in the last two lines?
2.   How are the contrasts (between then and now, between model and painter) communicated by the repetition of "Not as she is," in lines 13 and 14?

Explication

A line-by-line commentary on what is going on in a text is an explication (literally, unfolding, or spreading out). Although your explication will for the most part move steadily from the beginning to the end of the selection, try to avoid writing along these lines (or, one might say, along this one line): "In line one . . . . In the second line . . . . In the third line . . . ." That is, don't hesitate to write such things as

> The poem begins . . . . In the next line . . . . The speaker
> immediately adds . . . . He then introduces . . . . The
> next stanza begins by saying . . . .

And of course you can discuss the second line before the first if that seems the best way of handling the passage.

An explication is not concerned with the writer's life or times, and it is not a paraphrase (a rewording)—though it may include paraphrase if a passage in the original seems unclear perhaps because of an unusual word or an unfamiliar expression. On the whole, however, an explication goes beyond paraphrase, seeking to make explicit what the reader perceives as implicit in the work. To this end it calls attention, as it proceeds, to the implications of words (for instance, to their tone), the function of rhymes (for instance, how they may connect ideas, as in *throne* and *alone*), the development of contrasts, and any other contributions to the meaning.

A SAMPLE EXPLICATION

Take this short poem (published in 1917) by the Irish poet William Butler Yeats (1865–1939). The "balloon" in the poem is a dirigible, a blimp.

■ WILLIAM BUTLER YEATS

The Balloon of the Mind

Hands, do what you're bid:
Bring the balloon of the mind
That bellies and drags in the wind
Into its narrow shed.

[1917]

A student began thinking about the poem by copying it, double-spaced. Then she jotted down her first thoughts.

sounds abrupt

Hands, do what you're bid:
Bring the balloon of the mind
That bellies and drags in the wind
Into its narrow shed.

— balloon imagined by the mind? Or a mind like a balloon?
no real rhymes?
line seems to drag — it's so long!

Later she wrote some notes in a journal.

> I'm still puzzled about the meaning of the words, "The balloon of the mind." Does "balloon of the mind" mean a balloon that belongs to the mind, sort of like "a disease of the heart"? If so, it means a balloon that the mind <u>has</u>, a balloon that the mind possesses, I guess by imagining it. Or does it mean that the mind is <u>like</u> a balloon, as when you say "he's a pig of a man," meaning he is like a pig, he is a pig? Can it mean both? What's a balloon that the mind imagines? Something like dreams of fame, wealth? Castles in Spain.

Is Yeats saying that the "hands" have to work hard
to make dreams a reality? Maybe. But maybe the idea
really is that the mind is <u>like</u> a balloon--hard to keep
under control, floating around. Very hard to keep the
mind on the job. If the mind is like a balloon, it's
hard to get it into the hangar (shed).

"Bellies." Is there such a verb? In this poem it
seems to mean something like "puffs out" or "flops
around in the wind." Just checked <u>The American Heritage</u>
<u>Dictionary</u>, and it says "belly" can be a verb, "to
swell out," "to bulge." Well, you learn something
every day.

A later entry:

OK; I think the poem is about a writer trying to
keep his balloon-like mind from floating around,
trying to keep the mind under control, trying to keep
it working at the job of writing something, maybe
writing something with the "clarity, unity, and
coherence" I keep hearing about in this course.

Here is the student's final version of the explication.

Yeats's "Balloon of the Mind" is about writing
poetry, specifically about the difficulty of getting
one's floating thoughts down in lines on the page. The
first line, a short, stern, heavily stressed command to
the speaker's hands, perhaps implies by its severe or
impatient tone that these hands will be disobedient or
inept or careless if not watched closely: the poor
bumbling body so often fails to achieve the goals of
the mind. The bluntness of the command in the first
line is emphasized by the fact that all the subsequent
lines have more syllables. Furthermore, the first line
is a grammatically complete sentence, whereas the
thought of line 2 spills over into the next lines,
implying the difficulty of fitting ideas into
confining spaces, that is, of getting one's thoughts
into order, especially into a coherent poem.

Lines 2 and 3 amplify the metaphor already stated in
the title (the product of the mind is an airy but
unwieldy balloon), and they also contain a second
command, "Bring." Alliteration ties this command,
"Bring," to the earlier "bid"; it also ties both of
these verbs to their object, "balloon," and to the
verb that most effectively describes the balloon,
"bellies." In comparison with the abrupt first line of
the poem, lines 2 and 3 themselves seem almost swollen,
bellying and dragging, an effect aided by using
adjacent unstressed syllables ("of the," "[bell]ies
and," "in the") and by using an eye rhyme ("mind" and
"wind") rather than an exact rhyme. And then comes the
short last line: almost before we could expect it, the
cumbersome balloon-- here, the idea that is to be
packed into the stanza--is successfully lodged in its
"narrow shed." Aside from the relatively colorless
"into," the only words of more than one syllable in the
poem are "balloon," "bellies," and "narrow," and all
three emphasize the difficulty of the task. But after
"narrow"-- the word itself almost looks long and
narrow, in this context like a hangar--we get the
simplicity of the monosyllable "shed." The difficult
job is done, the thought is safely packed away, the
poem is completed--but again with an off rhyme ("bid"
and "shed"), for neatness can go only so far when hands
and mind and a balloon are involved.

Note: The reader of an explication needs to see the text, and because the ex-
plicated text is usually short, it is advisable to quote it all. (Remember, your
imagined audience probably consists of your classmates; even if they have already read the work you are explicating, they have not memorized it, and so
you helpfully remind them of the work by quoting it.) You can quote the entire
text at the outset, or you can quote the first unit (for example, a stanza), then
explicate that unit, and then quote the next unit, and so on. And if the poem

or passage of prose is longer than, say, six lines, it is advisable to number each line at the right for easy reference.

Rhythm and Versification: A Glossary for Reference

Rhythm (most simply, in English poetry, stresses at regular intervals) has a power of its own. A highly pronounced rhythm is common in such forms of poetry as charms, college yells, and lullabies; all of them are aimed at inducing a special effect magically. It is not surprising that *carmen*, the Latin word for poem or song, is also the Latin word for *charm* and the word from which our word *charm* is derived.

In much poetry, rhythm is only half heard, but its presence is suggested by the way poetry is printed. Prose (from Latin *prorsus*, "forward," "straight on") keeps running across the paper until the right-hand margin is reached; then, merely because the paper has given out, the writer or printer starts again at the left, with a small letter. But verse (Latin *versus*, "a turning") often ends well short of the right-hand margin. The next line begins at the left—usually with a capital—not because paper has run out but because the rhythmic pattern begins again. Lines of poetry are continually reminding us that they have a pattern.

Note that a mechanical, unvarying rhythm may be good to put the baby to sleep, but it can be deadly to readers who want to stay awake. Poets vary their rhythm according to their purposes; they ought not to be so regular that they are (in W. H. Auden's words) "accentual pests." In competent hands, rhythm contributes to meaning; it says something. Ezra Pound has a relevant comment: "Rhythm *must* have meaning. It can't be merely a careless dash off, with no grip and no real hold to the words and sense, a tumty tum tumty tum tum ta."

Consider this description of Hell from *Paradise Lost* (stressed syllables are marked by ´; unstressed syllables by ˘):

Rocks, caves, lakes, fens, bogs, dens, and shades of death.

The normal line in *Paradise Lost* is written in iambic feet—alternate unstressed and stressed syllables—but in this line Milton immediately follows one heavy stress with another, helping to communicate the "meaning"—the oppressive monotony of Hell. As a second example, consider the function of the rhythm in two lines by Alexander Pope:

When Ajax strives some rock's vast weight to throw.
The line too labors, and the words move slow.

The stressed syllables do not merely alternate with the unstressed ones; rather the great weight of the rock is suggested by three consecutive stressed words, "rock's vast weight," and the great effort involved in moving it is suggested by another three consecutive stresses, "line too labors," and by yet another three, "words move slow." Note, also the abundant pauses within the lines. In the first line, for example, unless one's speech is slovenly, one must pause at least slightly after "Ajax," "strives," "rock's," "vast," "weight," and "throw." The grating sounds in "Ajax" and "rock's" do their work, too, and so do the explosive *t*'s.

When Pope wishes to suggest lightness, he reverses his procedure, and he groups *un*stressed syllables:

> Not so, when swift Camilla scours the plain.
> Flies o'er th' unbending corn, and skims along the main.

This last line has twelve syllables and is thus longer than the line about Ajax, but the addition of *along* helps to communicate lightness and swiftness because in this line (it can be argued) neither syllable of *along* is strongly stressed. If *along* is omitted, the line still makes grammatical sense and becomes more "regular," but it also becomes less imitative of lightness.

The very regularity of a line may be meaningful too. Shakespeare begins a sonnet thus:

> When I do count the clock that tells the time.

This line about a mechanism runs with appropriate regularity. (It is worth noting, too, that "*c*ount the *c*lock" and "*t*ells the *t*ime" emphasize the regularity by the repetition of sounds and syntax.) But notice what Shakespeare does in the middle of the next line:

> And see the brave day sunk in hideous night.

The technical vocabulary of **prosody** (the study of the principles of verse structure, including meter, rhyme and other sound effects, and stanzaic patterns) is large. An understanding of these terms will not turn anyone into a poet, but it will enable you to write about some aspects of poetry more efficiently. The following are the chief terms of prosody.

METER

Most poetry written in English has a pattern of stressed (accented) sounds, and this pattern is the **meter** (from the Greek word for "measure"). Strictly speaking, we really should not talk of "unstressed" or "unaccented" syllables, since to utter a syllable—however lightly—is to give it some stress. It is really a matter of *relative* stress, but the fact is that "unstressed" or "unaccented" are parts of the established terminology of versification.

In a line of poetry, the **foot** is the basic unit of measurement. It is on rare occasions a single stressed syllable; but generally a foot consists of two or three syllables, one of which is stressed. The repetition of feet, then, produces a pattern of stresses throughout the poem.

Two cautions:

1. A poem will seldom contain only one kind of foot throughout; significant variations usually occur, but one kind of foot is dominant.
2. In reading a poem, one chiefly pays attention to the sense, not to presupposed metrical pattern. By paying attention to the sense, one often finds

(reading aloud is a great help) that the stress falls on a word that according to the metrical pattern would be unstressed. Or a word that according to the pattern would be stressed may be seen to be unstressed. Furthermore, by reading for sense one finds that not all stresses are equally heavy; some are almost as light as unstressed syllables, and sometimes there is a **hovering stress**—that is, the stress is equally distributed over two adjacent syllables. To repeat: One reads for sense, allowing the syntax to help indicate the stresses.

Metrical Feet. The most common feet in English poetry are the six listed below.

Iamb (adjective: **iambic**): one unstressed syllable followed by one stressed syllable. The iamb, said to be the most common pattern in English speech, is surely the most common in English poetry. The following example has four iambic feet:

˘ ´ ˘ ´ ˘ ´ ˘ ´
My heart is like a sing - ing bird.
　　—Christina Rossetti

Trochee (trochaic): one stressed syllable followed by one unstressed.

´ ˘ ´ ˘ ´ ˘ ´ ˘ ´ ˘
We were very tired, we were very merry
　　—Edna St. Vincent Millay

Anapest (anapestic): two unstressed syllables followed by one stressed.

˘ ˘ ´ ˘ ˘ ´ ˘ ˘ ´ ˘ ˘ ´
There are man - y who say that a dog has his day.
　　—Dylan Thomas

Dactyl (dactylic): one stressed syllable followed by two unstressed. This trisyllabic foot, like the anapest, is common in light verse or verse suggesting joy, but its use is not limited to such material, as Longfellow's *Evangeline* shows. Thomas Hood's sentimental "The Bridge of Sighs" begins:

´ ˘ ˘ ´ ˘ ˘
Take her up tenderly.

Spondee (spondaic): two stressed syllables; most often used as a substitute for an iamb or trochee.

´ ´ ˘ ´ ˘ ´ ˘ ´
Smart lad, to slip betimes away.
　　—A. E. Housman

Pyrrhic: two unstressed syllables; it is often not considered a legitimate foot in English.

Metrical Lines. A metrical line consists of one or more feet and is named for the number of feet in it. The following names are used:

monometer: one foot	**pentameter:** five feet
dimeter: two feet	**hexameter:** six feet
trimeter: three feet	**heptameter:** seven feet
tetrameter: four feet	

A line is scanned for the kind and number of feet in it, and the **scansion** tells you if it is, say, anapestic trimeter (three anapests):

⏑ ⏑ ′ ⏑ ⏑ ⏑ ′ ⏑ ⏑ ′

As I came to the edge of the woods.

> —Robert Frost

Or, in another example, iambic pentameter:

⏑ ′ ⏑ ′ ⏑ ′ ⏑ ′ ⏑ ′

The sum - mer thun - der, like a wood - en bell

> —Louise Bogan

A line ending with a stress has a **masculine ending;** a line ending with an extra unstressed syllable has a **feminine ending.** The **caesura** (usually indicated by the symbol / /) is a slight pause within the line. It need not be indicated by punctuation (notice the fourth and fifth lines in the following quotation), and it does not affect the metrical count:

> Awake, my St. John! / / leave all meaner things
> To low ambition, / / and the pride of kings.
> Let us / / (since Life can little more supply
> Than just to look about us / / and to die)
> Expatiate free / / o'er all this scene of Man;
> A mighty maze! / / but not without a plan;
> A wild, / / where weeds and flowers promiscuous shoot;
> Or garden, / / tempting with forbidden fruit.
>> —Alexander Pope

The varying position of the caesura helps to give Pope's lines an informality that plays against the formality of the pairs of rhyming lines.

An **end-stopped line** concludes with a distinct syntactical pause, but a **run-on line** has its sense carried over into the next line without syntactical pause. (The running-on of a line is called **enjambment.**) In the following passage, only the first is a run-on line:

> Yet if we look more closely we shall find
> Most have the seeds of judgment in their mind:
> Nature affords at least a glimmering light;
> The lines, though touched but faintly, are drawn right.
>> —Alexander Pope

Meter produces **rhythm,** recurrences at equal intervals, but rhythm (from a Greek word meaning "flow") is usually applied to larger units than feet. Often it depends most obviously on pauses. Thus, a poem with run-on lines will have a different rhythm from a poem with end-stopped lines, even though both are in the same meter. And prose, though it is unmetrical, can have rhythm, too.

In addition to being affected by syntactical pause, rhythm is affected by pauses attributable to consonant clusters and to the length of words. Polysyllabic words establish a different rhythm from monosyllabic words, even in metrically identical lines. One can say, then, that rhythm is altered by shifts in meter, syntax, and the length and ease of pronunciation. But even with no such shift, even if a line is repeated verbatim, a reader may sense a change in rhythm. The rhythm of the final line of a poem, for example, may well differ from that of the line before, even though in all other respects the lines are identical, as in Frost's "Stopping by Woods on a Snowy Evening" (page 837) which concludes by repeating "And miles to go before I sleep." One may simply sense that this final line ought to be spoken, say, more slowly and with more stress on "miles."

PATTERNS OF SOUND

Though rhythm is basic to poetry, **rhyme**—the repetition of the identical or similar stressed sound or sounds—is not. Rhyme is, presumably, pleasant in itself; it suggests order; and it also may be related to meaning, for it brings two words sharply together, often implying a relationship, as in the now trite *dove* and *love*, or in the more imaginative *throne* and *alone*.

Perfect, or **exact, rhyme:** Differing consonant sounds are followed by identical stressed vowel sounds, and the following sounds, if any, are identical (*foe—toe; meet—fleet; buffer—rougher*). Notice that perfect rhyme involves identity of sound, not of spelling. *Fix* and *sticks*, like *buffer* and *rougher,* are perfect rhymes.

Half-rhyme (or **off-rhyme**): Only the final consonant sounds of the words are identical; the stressed vowel sounds as well as the initial consonant sounds, if any, differ (*soul—oil; mirth—forth; trolley—bully*).

Eye-rhyme: The sounds do not in fact rhyme, but the words look as though they would rhyme (*cough—bough*).

Masculine rhyme: The final syllables are stressed and, after their differing initial consonant sounds, are identical in sound (*stark—mark; support—retort*).

Feminine rhyme (or **double rhyme**): Stressed rhyming syllables are followed by identical unstressed syllables (*revival—arrival; flatter—batter*). **Triple rhyme** is a kind of feminine rhyme in which identical stressed vowel sounds are followed by two identical unstressed syllables (*machinery—scenery; tenderly—slenderly*).

End rhyme (or **terminal rhyme**): The rhyming words occur at the ends of the lines.

Internal rhyme: At least one of the rhyming words occurs within the line (Oscar Wilde's "Each narrow *cell* in which we *dwell*").

Alliteration: sometimes defined as the repetition of initial sounds ("All the *a*wful *a*uguries," or "*B*ring me my *b*ow of *b*urning gold"), and sometimes as the prominent repetition of a consonant ("a*f*ter li*f*e's *f*it*f*ul *f*ever").

Assonance: the repetition, in words of proximity, of identical vowel sounds preceded and followed by differing consonant sounds. Whereas *tide* and *hide* are rhymes, *tide* and *mine* are assonantal.

Consonance: the repetition of identical consonant sounds and differing vowel sounds in words in proximity (*fail—feel; rough—roof; pitter—patter*). Sometimes consonance is more loosely defined merely as the repetition of a consonant (*fail—peel*).

Onomatopoeia: the use of words that imitate sounds, such as *hiss* and *buzz.* There is a mistaken tendency to see onomatopoeia everywhere—for example, in *thunder* and *horror.* Many words sometimes thought to be onomatopoeic are not clearly imitative of the thing they refer to; they merely contain some sounds that, when we know what the word means, seem to have some resemblance to the thing they denote. Tennyson's lines from "Come down, O maid" are usually cited as an example of onomatopoeia:

> The moan of doves in immemorial elms
> And murmuring of innumerable bees.

STANZAIC PATTERNS

Lines of poetry are commonly arranged in a rhythmical unit called a stanza (from an Italian word meaning "room" or "stopping-place"). Usually all the stanzas in a poem have the same rhyme pattern. A stanza is sometimes called a **verse,** though *verse* may also mean a single line of poetry. (In discussing stanzas, rhymes are indicated by identical letters. Thus, *abab* indicates that the first and third lines rhyme with each other, while the second and fourth lines are linked by a different rhyme. An unrhymed line is denoted by *x*.) Common stanzaic forms in English poetry are the following:

Couplet: a stanza of two lines, usually, but not necessarily, with end-rhymes. *Couplet* is also used for a pair of rhyming lines. The **octosyllabic couplet** is iambic or trochaic tetrameter:

> Had we but world enough and time.
> This coyness, lady, were no crime.
>> —Andrew Marvell

Heroic couplet: a rhyming couplet of iambic pentameter, often "closed," that is, containing a complete thought, with a fairly heavy pause at the end of the first line and a still heavier one at the end of the second. Commonly, there is a parallel or an *antithesis* (contrast) within a line or between the two lines. It is called heroic because in England, especially in the eighteenth century, it was much used for heroic (epic) poems.

> Some foreign writers, some our own despise;
> The ancients only, or the moderns, prize.
>> —Alexander Pope

Triplet (or **tercet**): a three-line stanza, usually with one rhyme.

> Whenas in silks my Julia goes
> Then, then (methinks) how sweetly flows
> That liquefaction of her clothes.
>> —Robert Herrick

Quatrain: a four-line stanza, rhymed or unrhymed. The **heroic** (or **elegiac) quatrain** is iambic pentameter, rhyming *abab*. That is, the first and third lines rhyme (so they are designated *a*), and the second and fourth lines rhyme (so they are designated *b*).

Sonnet: a fourteen-line poem, predominantly in iambic pentameter. The rhyme is usually according to one of two schemes. The **Italian** (or

Petrarchan[1]) **sonnet** has two divisions: The first eight lines (rhyming *abba abba* are the **octave,** the last six (rhyming *cd cd cd,* or a variant) are the **sestet.** Gerard Manley Hopkins's "God's Grandeur" (page 978) is an Italian sonnet. The second kind of sonnet, the **English** (or **Shakespearean**) **sonnet,** is usually arranged into three quatrains and a couplet, rhyming *abab cdcd efef gg.* (For examples see pages 560-561.) In many sonnets there is a marked correspondence between the rhyme scheme and the development of the thought. Thus an Italian sonnet may state a generalization in the octave and a specific example in the sestet. Or an English sonnet may give three examples—one in each quatrain—and draw a conclusion in the couplet.

BLANK VERSE AND FREE VERSE

A good deal of English poetry is unrhymed, much of it in **blank verse,** that is, unrhymed iambic pentameter. Introduced into English poetry by Henry Howard, Earl of Surrey, in the middle of the sixteenth century, late in the century it became the standard medium (especially in the hands of Christopher Marlow and Shakespeare) of English drama. In the seventeenth century, Milton used it for *Paradise Lost,* and it has continued to be used in both dramatic and nondramatic literature. For example see the first scene of *Hamlet* (page 407), until the Ghost appears.

The second kind of unrhymed poetry fairly common in English, especially in the twentieth century, is **free verse** (or **vers libre**): rhythmical lines varying in length, adhering to no fixed metrical pattern and usually unrhymed. The pattern is often largely based on repetition and parallel grammatical structure. For an example, see T. S. Eliot's "The Love Song of J. Alfred Prufrock" (page 840).

Summing Up: Getting Ideas for Writing about Poetry

If you are going to write about a fairly short poem (say, under thirty lines), it's not a bad idea to copy out the poem, writing or typing it double-spaced. By writing it out you will be forced to notice details, down to the punctuation. After you have copied the poem, proofread it carefully against the original. Catching an error—even the addition or omission of a comma—may help you to notice a detail in the original that you might otherwise have overlooked. And of course, now that you have the poem with ample space between the lines, you have a worksheet with room for jottings.

A good essay is based on a genuine response to a poem; a response may

---

[1] So called after Francesco Petrarch (1304–1374), the Italian poet who perfected and popularized the form

be stimulated in part by first reading the poem aloud and then considering the following questions.

FIRST RESPONSE

1. What was your response to the poem on first reading? Did some parts especially please or displease you, or puzzle you? After some study—perhaps checking the meanings of some of the words in a dictionary and reading the poem several times—did you modify your initial response to the parts and to the whole?

SPEAKER AND TONE

1. Who is the speaker? (Consider age, sex, personality, frame of mind, and tone of voice.) Is the speaker defined fairly precisely (for instance, an older woman speaking to a child), or is the speaker simply a voice meditating? (Jot down your first impressions, then reread the poem and make further jottings, if necessary.)
2. Do you think the speaker is fully aware of what he or she is saying, or does the speaker unconsciously reveal his or her personality and values? What is your attitude toward this speaker?
3. Is the speaker narrating or reflecting on an earlier experience or attitude? If so, does he or she convey a sense of new awareness, such as of regret for innocence lost?

AUDIENCE

1. To whom is the speaker speaking? What is the situation (including time and place)? (In some poems, a listener is strongly implied, but in others, especially those in which the speaker is meditating, there may be no audience other than the reader, who "overhears" the speaker.)

STRUCTURE AND FORM

1. Does the poem proceed in a straightforward way, or at some point or points does the speaker reverse course, altering his or her tone or perception? If there is a shift, what do you make of it?
2. Is the poem organized into sections? If so, what are these sections—stanzas, for instance—and how does each section (characterized, perhaps, by a certain tone of voice, or a group of rhymes) grow out of what precedes it?
3. What is the effect on you of the form—say, quatrains (stanzas of four lines) or blank verse (unrhymed lines of ten syllables)? If the sense overflows the form, running without pause from (for example) one quatrain into the next, what effect is created?

CENTER OF INTEREST AND THEME

1. What is the poem about? Is the interest chiefly in a distinctive character, or in meditation? That is, is the poem chiefly psychological or chiefly philosophical?
2. Is the theme stated explicitly (directly) or implicitly? How might you state the theme in a sentence?

DICTION

1. Do certain words have rich and relevant associations that relate to other words and help to define the speaker or the theme or both?
2. What is the role of figurative language, if any? Does it help to define the speaker or the theme?
3. What do you think is to be taken figuratively or symbolically, and what literally?

SOUND EFFECTS

1. What is the role of sound effects, including repetitions of sound (for instance, alliteration) and of entire words, and shifts in versification?
2. If there are off-rhymes (for instance "dizzy" and "easy," or "home" and "come"), what effect do they have on you? Do they, for instance, add a note of tentativeness or uncertainty?
3. If there are unexpected stresses or pauses, what do they communicate about the speaker's experience? How do they affect you?

Ten Poems

■ EMILY DICKINSON
_____

Emily Dickinson (1830–1886) was born into a proper New England family in Amherst, Massachusetts. Although she spent her seventeenth year a few miles away, at Mount Holyoke Seminary (now Mount Holyoke College), in the next twenty years she left Amherst only five or six times, and in her last twenty years she may never have left her house. Her brother was probably right when he said that having seen something of the rest of the world—she had visited Washington with her father, when he was a member of Congress—"she could not resist the feeling that it was painfully hollow. It was to her so thin and unsatisfying in the face of the Great Realities of Life." Dickinson lived with her parents (a somewhat reclusive mother and an austere, remote father) and a younger sister; a married brother lived in the house next door. She did, however, form some passionate attachments, to women as well as men, but there is no evidence that they found physical expression.

By the age of twelve Dickinson was writing witty letters, but she apparently did not write more than an occasional poem before her late twenties. At her death—she died in the house where she was born—she left 1,775 poems, only seven of which had been published (anonymously) during her lifetime.

A Narrow Fellow in the Grass

A narrow Fellow in the Grass
Occasionally rides—
You may have met Him—did you not
His notice sudden is—   4

The Grass divides as with a Comb—
A spotted shaft is seen—
And then it closes at your feet
And opens further on—   8

He likes a Boggy Acre
A Floor too cool for Corn—
Yet when a Boy, and Barefoot—
I more than once at Noon   12
Have passed, I thought, a Whip lash
Unbraiding in the Sun
When stooping to secure it
It wrinkled, and was gone—   16

Several of Nature's People
I know, and they know me—
I feel for them a transport
Of cordiality—   20

But never met this Fellow
Attended, or alone
Without a tighter breathing
And Zero at the Bone—   24

[c. 1865]

■ TOPICS FOR DISCUSSION AND WRITING

1. Many of Dickinson's poems are rather like riddles. In this poem who or what is the "narrow Fellow in the Grass"?

2. How would you describe the speaker of this poem? What relationship does the speaker seem to establish with the reader?

3. In lines 17–20 Dickinson refers to "Several of Nature's People." Who or what might these be, in Amherst in the later nineteenth century? Check "transport" and "cordiality" in a dictionary, to see which meanings you think are especially relevant.

Apparently with no surprise

Apparently with no surprise
To any happy Flower
The Frost beheads it at its play—
In accidental power—
The blonde Assassin passes on—   5
The Sun proceeds unmoved
To measure off another Day
For an Approving God.

[c. 1884]

■ TOPICS FOR DISCUSSION AND WRITING

1. What is the implication of the action described in lines 1–3?
2. Why is the frost's power called "accidental"?
3. Why is the assassin called "blonde"? What does this word contribute to the poem?
4. Do you find the last line shocking? Why, or why not?

■ GERARD MANLEY HOPKINS

Gerard Manley Hopkins (1884–1889) was born near London and was educated at Oxford, where he studied Classics. A convert from Anglicanism to Roman Catholicism, he was ordained a Jesuit priest in 1877. After serving as a parish priest and teacher, he was appointed Professor of Greek at the Catholic University in Dublin

Hopkins published only a few poems during his lifetime, partly because he believed that the pursuit of literary fame was incompatible with his vocation as a priest, and partly because he was aware that his highly individual style might puzzle readers. (In the following poem notice, for example, an archaic word [*brinded,* for *brindled*], compound words [*rose-moles, Fresh-firecoal chestnut-falls*], and an original stanza form of six lines, four lines, and a half-line.)

Pied° Beauty

Glory be to God for dappled things—
    For skies of couple-colour as a brinded° cow;
        For rose-moles all in stipple° upon trout that swim;
Fresh-firecoal chestnut-falls°; finches' wings;   4
    Landscape plotted and pieced—fold, fallow, and plough;°
        And áll trádes, their gear and tackle and trim.°

Pied of two or more colors   2 **brinded** brindled, brownish-orange streaked with gray   3 **stipple** dots, colored specks   4 **chestnut-falls** freshly fallen chestnuts, which look like glowing coals   5 **fold, fallow, and plough** (i.e., fields 1) fenced to contain animals, 2) lying fallow, 3) cultivated   6 **tackle and trim** equipment

All things counter, original, spare,° strange;
> Whatever is fickle, freckled (who knows how?)   8
>> With swift, slow; sweet, sour; adazzle, dim;
He fathers-forth whose beauty is past change:
>> Praise him.

>> [1877]

■ TOPICS FOR DISCUSSION AND WRITING

1. The poem begins by praising God and then quickly introduces landscape elements and the animal and vegetable worlds. Why do you suppose Hopkins introduced these before human elements? By the way, exactly where in the poem do you find the first implication of the human world?
2. What might be some specific examples of the "gear and tackle and trim" (line 6) that Hopkins would have seen in the late nineteenth century? What "gear and tackle and trim" have you seen that appeals to you?
3. What is the connection between the first line and line 10? Do you find the relationship contradictory? Or *apparently* contradictory rather than truly contradictory?
4. Read the poem aloud, at least twice. Do certain phrases or even whole lines especially appeal to you? If so, try to explain why they give pleasure.
5. As the introductory biographical note says, Hopkins was a Roman Catholic priest. Do you think that a reader has to be a Roman Catholic—or any sort of Christian—to enjoy the poem? Explain.

■ THOMAS HARDY
_____

Thomas Hardy (1840–1928) was born near Dorchester, in southwest England, where at fifteen he was apprenticed to an architect. At the age of twenty-one he went to London to practice as an architect, but he soon turned to writing fiction and poetry. Between 1872 and 1896 he achieved fame as a novelist; among his novels are *The Return of the Native* (1878) and *Tess of the D'Urbervilles*. With the hostile reception of *Jude the Obscure* (1896) he abandoned writing fiction and concentrated on writing poetry.

Transformations

Portion of this yew
Is a man my grandsire knew,
Bosomed here at its foot:
This branch may be his wife,
A ruddy human life   5
Now turned to a green shoot.

7 **spare** rare

These grasses must be made
Of her who often prayed,
Last century, for repose;
And the fair girl long ago   10
Whom I often tried to know
May be entering the rose.

So, they are not underground,
But as nerves and veins abound
In the growths of upper air,   15
And they feel the sun and rain,
And the energy again
That made them what they were!
                    [1917]

■ TOPICS FOR DISCUSSION AND WRITING

1. What is your sense of the speaker's tone in the first stanza? In the last?
    In lines 7–8 the speaker conjectures that "These grasses must be
    made / Of her who often prayed." What sort of visual connection is sug-
    gested between the grasses and the woman?
2. How might the speaker know that someone "often prayed, / Last century,
    before"?
3. At what stage of life is the speaker? How do you know?
4. What do you think Hardy means by "the energy . . . / That made them
    what they were"?
5. Do you find the poem far-fetched, or do you feel that the poet has made
    his assertions plausible? Explain.

■ ROBERT FROST

Robert Frost (1874–1963) was born in California. After his father's
death in 1885 Frost's mother brought the family to New England, where
she taught in high schools in Massachusetts and New Hampshire. Frost
studied for part of one term at Dartmouth College in New Hampshire,
then did odd jobs (including teaching), and from 1897 to 1899 was enrolled as a special student at Harvard. He then farmed in New Hampshire, published a few poems in local newspapers, left the farm and
taught again, and in 1912 left for England, where he hoped to achieve
more popular success as a writer. By 1915 he had won a considerable
reputation, and he returned to the United States, settling on a farm in
New Hampshire and cultivating the image of the country-wise farmer-
poet. In fact he was well read in the classics, the Bible, and in English
and American literature.

Among Frost's many comments about literature, here are three:
"Writing is unboring to the extent that it is dramatic"; "Every poem
is . . . a figure of the will braving alien entanglements"; and, finally, a

poem "begins in delight and ends in wisdom. . . . It runs a course of lucky events, and ends in a clarification of life—not necessarily a great clarification, such as sects and cults are founded on, but in a momentary stay against confusion."

The Need of Being Versed in Country Things

The house had gone to bring again
To the midnight sky a sunset glow.
Now the chimney was all of the house that stood,
Like a pistil after the petals go.   4

The barn opposed across the way,
That would have joined the house in flame
Had it been the will of the wind, was left
To bear forsaken the place's name.   8

No more it opened with all one end
For teams that came by the stony road
To drum on the floor with scurrying hoofs
And brush the mow with the summer load.   12

The birds that came to it through the air
At broken windows flew out and in,
Their murmur more like the sigh we sigh
From too much dwelling on what has been.   16

Yet for them the lilac renewed its leaf,
And the aged elm, though touched with fire;
And the dry pump flung up an awkward arm;
And the fence post carried a strand of wire.   20

For them there was really nothing sad.
But though they rejoiced in the nest they kept,
One had to be versed in country things
Not to believe the phoebes wept.   24

[1923]

■ TOPICS FOR DISCUSSION AND WRITING

1. By the end of the second stanza the reader understands that the farm-house has been destroyed by a fire. Why do you suppose (putting aside the matter of rhyme) in line 2 Frost wrote "a sunset glow" instead of (say) "a burst of flame"? And what is the effect of the simile in line 4? That is, what do these comparisons contribute to the poem? (If you are unsure of the meaning of "pistil," check a dictionary.)

2. In the fifth stanza Frost uses personifications: "the lilac *renewed* its leaf," the "pump *flung up an awkward arm*," and "the fence post *carried* a strand of wire." What other personifications do you find in the

poem? What effect do these personifications have on you? And why do
you suppose there are no personifications in the last two lines of the
poem?

3. In a sentence or two or three, characterize the speaker. (Of course you
can probably characterize him or her by means of an adjective or two or
three; use the rest of the allotment to provide evidence, such as brief
quotations.)

4. Much of the poem describes a scene, but the speaker also interprets the
scene. How would you summarize the interpretation? How might you
paraphrase the title? Does the speaker convince you of the "need" to be
"versed in country things"?

5. Do you think the poem is sentimental? Or, on the other hand, cynical?
Explain.

6. Suppose you were to write a parody of "The Need of Being Versed in
Country Things." What scene might you use, or what objects might you
personify? (A parody is an amusing imitation of the style of another work,
often with an inappropriate subject. Thus, one might parody a sports
writer by imitating his or her style, but the subject would not be an ath-
letic event but, say, students engaged in peer review.) Suggestion: Consider the possibility of using your neighborhood or your workplace as a
subject.

Design

I found a dimpled spider, fat and white,
On a white heal-all,* holding up a moth
Like a white piece of rigid satin cloth—
Assorted characters of death and blight   4
Mixed ready to begin the morning right,
Like the ingredients of witches' broth—
A snow-drop spider, a flower like froth,
And dead wings carried like a paper kite.   8

What had that flower to do with being white,
The wayside blue and innocent heal-all?
What brought the kindred spider to that height,
Then steered the white moth thither in the night?   12
What but design of darkness to appall?—
If design govern in a thing so small.

[1936]

■ TOPICS FOR DISCUSSION AND WRITING

1. Do you find the spider, as described in line 1, cute or disgusting or
what? Why?

*heal-all a flower, usually blue

2. What alternatives are suggested by "If" in the last line? Which alternative do you believe, or prefer to believe?

3. The word "design" can mean "pattern" (as in "a pretty design"), or it can mean "intention," especially an evil intention (as in "He had designs on her"). Does Frost use the word in one sense or in both? Explain.

■ ELIZABETH BISHOP

Elizabeth Bishop (1911–1979) was born in Worcester, Massachusetts. Because her father died when she was eight months old and her mother was confined to a sanitarium four years later, Bishop was raised by relatives in New England and Nova Scotia. After graduating from Vassar College in 1934, where she was co-editor of the student literary magazine, she lived (on a small private income) for a while in Key West, France, and Mexico, and then for much of her adult life in Brazil, before returning to the United States to teach at Harvard. Her financial independence enabled her to write without worrying about the sales of her books and without having to devote energy to distracting jobs.

The Fish

I caught a tremendous fish
and held him beside the boat
half out of water, with my hook
fast in a corner of his mouth.
He didn't fight.   5
He hadn't fought at all.
He hung a grunting weight,
battered and venerable
and homely. Here and there
his brown skin hung in strips   10
like ancient wall-paper,
and its pattern of darker brown
was like wall-paper:
shapes like full-blown roses
stained and lost through age.   15
He was speckled with barnacles,
fine rosettes of lime,
and infested
with tiny white sea-lice,
and underneath two or three   20
rags of green weed hung down.
While his gills were breathing in
the terrible oxygen
—the frightening gills,
fresh and crisp with blood,   25

that can cut so badly—
I thought of the coarse white flesh
packed in like feathers,
the big bones and the little bones,
the dramatic reds and blacks   30
of his shiny entrails,
and the pink swim-bladder
like a big peony.
I looked into his eyes
which were far larger than mine   35
but shallower, and yellowed,
the irises backed and packed
with tarnished tinfoil
seen through the lenses
of old scratched isinglass.   40
They shifted a little, but not
to return my stare.
—It was more like the tipping
of an object toward the light.
I admired his sullen face,   45
the mechanism of his jaw,
and then I saw
that from his lower lip
—if you could call it a lip—
grim, wet, and weapon-like,   50
hung five old pieces of fish-line,
or four and a wire leader
with the swivel still attached,
with all their five big hooks
grown firmly in his mouth.   55
A green line, frayed at the end
where he broke it, two heavier lines,
and a fine black thread
still crimped from the strain and snap
when it broke and he got away.   60
Like medals with their ribbons
frayed and wavering,
a five-haired beard of wisdom
trailing from his aching jaw.
I stared and stared   65
and victory filled up
the little rented boat,
from the pool of bilge
where oil had spread a rainbow
around the rusted engine   70
to the bailer rusted orange,

the sun-cracked thwarts,
the oarlocks on their strings,
the gunnels—until everything
was rainbow, rainbow, rainbow!   75
And I let the fish go.

[1946]

■ TOPICS FOR DISCUSSION AND WRITING

1. In line 9 Bishop calls the fish "homely" and in succeeding lines compares
    him to a series of stained, scratched, and tarnished domestic objects.
    When (in line 44) she reports that she "admired his sullen face," did that
    take you by surprise, or had she prepared you for her admiration?
    Explain.
2. In lines 66–67 we're told that "victory filled up / the little rented boat."
    Whose victory was it? Or do you think the lines are deliberately
    ambiguous?
3. Why does the speaker pause in her story to describe the condition of the
    rented boat? Is a comparison between the boat and the fish implied?
4. What causes the "rainbow" in line 69? How do you understand "every-
    thing / was rainbow, rainbow, rainbow!" in lines 74–75?
5. Why does the speaker let the fish go? Is this ending a surprise, or has it
    been prepared for? Explain.

■ WILLIAM STAFFORD

William Stafford was born in Hutchinson, Kansas, in 1914 and was
educated at the University of Kansas and the State University of Iowa. A
conscientious objector during World War II, he worked for the Brethren
Service and the Church World Service. After the war he taught at several
universities and then settled at Lewis and Clark College in Portland, Oregon. In addition to writing several books of poems, Stafford is the author
of *Down in My Heart* (1947), an account of his experiences as a conscientious objector.

Traveling Through the Dark

Traveling through the dark I found a deer
dead on the edge of the Wilson River road.
It is usually best to roll them into the canyon:
the road is narrow; to swerve might make more dead.

By glow of the tail-light I stumbled back of the car   5
and stood by the heap, a doe, a recent killing;
she had stiffened already, almost cold.
I dragged her off; she was large in the belly.

My fingers touching her side brought me the reason—
her side was warm; her fawn lay there waiting,   10
alive, still, never to be born.
Beside that mountain road I hesitated.

The car aimed ahead its lowered parking lights;
under the hood purred the steady engine.
I stood in the glare of the warm exhaust turning red;   15
around our group I could hear the wilderness listen.

I thought hard for us all—my only swerving—
then pushed her over the edge into the river.

[1960]

■ TOPICS FOR DISCUSSION AND WRITING:

1. What do we know (or believe we know) about the speaker of these
   lines?
2. Rereading the second stanza, note the pauses in line 6. What do they
   seem to tell you about the speaker's frame of mind?
3. Line 11 also has three pauses. In reading the line what do you sense
   about the speaker's feelings?
4. Line twelve tells us that the speaker hesitated—and then the poem
   hesitates. Instead of moving forward to the conclusion of the story,
   the fourth stanza offers some description. What is described and how
   is it described? Try to imagine the poem without stanza 4. Do you
   find the stanza necessary? If so, why?
5. In the final stanza who does "us all" refer to? Does it include the
   same members as "our group" (in line 15) or not? Why does the
   speaker characterize his thinking (in line 17) as "swerving"?
6. In light of your reading of the poem, what meanings does the title
   have?
7. What choices does the speaker of "Traveling" have? Do you think he
   makes the right choice? Explain.

■ A. R. AMMONS

A[rchibald] R[andolph] Ammons was born in a farmhouse near
Whiteville, North Carolina, in 1926. After serving in the navy during
World War II he attended Wake Forest University, where he studied chiefly biology and chemistry. From 1951 to 1952, after briefly serving as a
high school principal, he did graduate work at the University of California,
Berkeley; but he left without a degree and for ten years worked as an
executive
in a glass manufacturing company in New Jersey. He published his first
book of poetry in 1955, when he was thirty, and his second in 1964, the
year in which he began teaching at Cornell, where he is a professor of
English. As the critic Helen Vendler says, although in his poetry Ammons

often sees "the natural world as emblematic of spiritual or intellectual meaning," he is also a poet of "humor and self-deprecation, visible in his colloquy
with the mountain [in 'Mountain Talk']."

Mountain Talk

I was going along a dusty highroad
when the mountain
across the way
turned me to its silence:
oh I said how come   5
I don't know your
massive symmetry and rest:
nevertheless, said the mountain,
would you want
to be   10
lodged here with
a changeless prospect, risen
to an unalterable view:
so I went on
counting my numberless fingers.   15
                           [1970]

■ TOPICS FOR DISCUSSION AND WRITING

1. In the first line do you imagine a traveler on foot, a recreational mountain
    climber, a worker, or what? Does the rest of the poem support more
    than one definition of the speaker?
2. Line 4 ("turned me to its silence:") employs unusual diction. Did you try
    to read it (as we at first did) as if it were "turned to me"—and then real-
    ized your mistake? Do you find other places in the poem where the lan-
    guage catches you off balance? For example, assuming that you're willing
    to go along with mountains that talk back to us (and with poets who ask
    them questions), what do you make of this mountain starting its speech
    with "nevertheless"?
3. Line 9 consists of two syllables. Suppose lines 9 and 10 were combined.
    How would the meaning change? Would anything else change? Next try
    putting the word "risen," now at the end of line 12, at the beginning of
    line 13. What difference, if any, does it make?
4. How does the speaker respond to the mountain? What does it mean to
    call fingers numberless? Has the speaker's original question been an-
    swered to his satisfaction, or yours?
5. Try writing in your journal: "I was going along a . . . ." Then see what
    inanimate objects along the way you can develop an interesting conversa-
    tion with.

■ N. SCOTT MOMADAY

N. Scott Momaday (b. 1934) was born in Lawton, Oklahoma, of Cherokee and Kiowa descent. After attending reservation, parochial, and private schools he attended the University of New Mexico, and University of Virginia, the Stanford University, where he received his M.A. and Ph.D. degrees. He has taught at the University of California at Santa Barbara and Berkeley, Stanford University, and the University of Arizona, Tucson. Momaday's most widely known work is *The Way to Rainy Mountain* (1969), a lyrical imaginative history of the Kiowa and a memoir of his developing awareness of his heritage. He has also written a novel, essays, and poems in a variety of forms. We print a poem from *The Gourd Dancer* (1976), a book that includes some poems indebted to Indian oral traditions.

The Eagle-Feather Fan

The eagle is my power,
And my fan is an eagle.
It is strong and beautiful
In my hand. And it is real.
My fingers hold upon it   5
As if the beaded handle
Were the twist of bristlecone.
The bones of my hand are fine
And hollow; the fan bears them.
My hand veers in the thin air   10
Of the summits. All morning
It scuds on the cold currents;
All afternoon it circles
To the singing, to the drums.
                    [1976]

■ TOPICS FOR DISCUSSION AND WRITING

1. In the first two lines the speaker seems to assert his possession of both the power of the eagle and the fan. At what point does he begin to relinquish possession and control?

2. What effect do the singing and drums have? As the eagle "scuds" and "circles" (in lines 12 and 13) what do we imagine the speaker to be doing?

3. Imagine or write a prose paragraph describing the scene depicted in "The Eagle-Feather Fan." What advantage does the poem have over a prose "translation"?

4. Compare "The Eagle-Feather Fan" to any one or two of the poems about nature in this section, focusing on the relationship between human consciousness and the natural environment.

■ PART TWO

A Thematic

Anthology

■ CHAPTER 8

Strange Worlds

ESSAY

■ JUANITA MIRANDA

Juanita Miranda was born in 1953 in Havana, but was brought up in Florida. She has written, under a pseudonym, two books of science fiction and, under another pseudonym, several essays on the Bible.

In Defense of Fantasy

We often hear that literature gives us an image of life. This idea is usually connected with the belief that literature teaches us. After all, if literature does not resemble life, how (one might wonder) can it teach us anything?

And since today the most popular form of literature is the novel—a form in which people who live in a recognizable society speak prose that sounds like everyday speech—it is roughly true that most of our books give us at least the illusion of life. Even today, decades after the publication of *The Catcher in the Rye,* probably millions of young people see themselves in Holden Caulfield and in Phoebe. And yet, surely we do not always want our literature to be about people like ourselves. Sometimes we want it to be about matters that apparently are remote. As Dr. Johnson said, some two hundred years ago,

> Babies do not want to hear about babies; they like to be told of giants and castles, and of somewhat which can stretch and stimulate their little minds.

But, it may be objected, we are not babies, we do not want fairy tales. Yet if we think for a moment, we will probably agree that most of the novels that please us also stretch our minds, for they strike a balance between two poles: On the one hand, they seem plausible, in one way or another lifelike, and on the other hand, they tell "a good story," that is, they stretch our minds by containing something of the unusual, the surprising, the attention-getting.

Suppose we begin by looking, very briefly, not at a novel but at the biblical story of David and Goliath, in 1 Samuel 17, a story whose chief purpose originally was to inform its audience that David was suited to become a king. The Bible tells us that the Philistine champion, Goliath, was "six cubits and a span" (nine feet, nine inches). Surely that's arresting. But, as we shall see, the story of David and Goliath also gives us plenty of convincing details, both in its descriptions and in its dialogue.

> And there went out a champion out of the camp of the Philistines, named Goliath, of Gath, whose height was six cubits and a span. And he had an helmet of brass upon his head, and he was armed with a coat of mail; and the weight of the coat was five thousand shekels of brass. And the staff of his spear was like a weaver's beam; and his spear's head weighed six hundred shekels of iron, and one bearing a shield went before him.
>
> And he stood and cried unto the armies of Israel, and said unto them, "Why are ye come out to set your battle in array? Am not I a Philistine, and ye servants to Saul? Choose you a man for you, and let him come down to me. If he be able to fight with me, and to kill me, then will we be your servants; but if I prevail against him, and kill him, then shall ye be our servants and serve us."
>
> And the Philistine said, "I defy the armies of Israel this day; give me a man, that we may fight together."
>
> When Saul and all Israel heard those words of the Philistine, they were dismayed, and greatly afraid.

David, the young shepherd, hears Goliath, and he determines to fight this giant who insults "the living God." By the way, since many people know the story not from actually reading it but only at second hand, it's worth mentioning that the story (short as it is) is far richer than my abridgment of it. For instance, it includes an apparently irrelevant but thoroughly convincing episode that in fact serves to emphasize the obstacles that David must overcome even before he slays Goliath. David's older brother finds David near the battlefield instead of far away with the sheep, and, such is the way of older brothers, he rebukes David:

> Why camest thou down hither? And with whom hast thou left those few sheep in the wilderness? I know thy pride, and the naughtiness of thine heart, for thou art come down that thou mightest see the battle.

Other nice touches—touches not strictly necessary to the narrative but enriching it—are King Saul's initial reluctance to believe that so young and inexperienced a man could fight so great a warrior as Goliath, and (after David assures Saul that he has killed a lion) Saul's arming of David with "an helmet of brass" and "a coat of mail." But David, having never used such materials, puts them off—we may also sense that he wishes the victory to be entirely his own and not something to be shared with Saul—and so David prepares in his own way:

He took his staff in his hand, and chose him five smooth stones out of the brook, and put them in a shepherd's bag which he had . . . and his sling was in his hand, and he drew near to the Philistine. . . .

And when the Philistine looked about and saw David, he disdained him, for he was but a youth, and ruddy, and of a fair countenance. And the Philistine said unto David, "Am I a dog, that thou comest to me with staves?" And the Philistine cursed David by his gods. And the Philistine said to David, "Come to me, and I will give thy flesh unto the fowls of the air, and to the beasts of the field."

Then said David to the Philistine, "Thou comest to me with a sword, and with a spear, and with a shield, but I come to thee in the name of the Lord of hosts, the God of the armies of Israel, whom thou hast defied. This day will the Lord deliver thee into mine hand, and I will smite thee, and take thine head from thee, and I will give the carcases of the host of the Philistines this day unto the fowls of the air, and to the wild beasts of the earth, that all the earth may know that there is a God in Israel. . . .

And it came to pass, when the Philistine arose, and came and drew nigh to meet David, that David hasted, and ran toward the army to meet the Philistine. And David put his hand in his bag, and took thence a stone, and slang it, and smote the Philistine in his forehead, that the stone sunk into his forehead, and he fell upon his face to the earth.

So David prevailed over the Philistine with a sling and with a stone, and smote the Philistine, and slew him; but there was no sword in the hand of David. Therefore David ran, and stood upon the Philistine, and took his sword, and drew it out of the sheath thereof, and slew him, and cut off his head therewith.

The Philistine's scorn when he sees David, David's reply (a mixture of scorn and piety, for David announces that he comes "in the name of the Lord"), the observation that David was eager to do battle (he "*ran* toward the army to meet the Philistine"), the explanation that David cut off Goliath's head with Goliath's own sword—all of these details help us to see the scene, to believe in the characters, and yet of course the whole story is, on the literal level, remote from our experience. We don't encounter people almost ten feet tall, we don't have kings arm us, we don't fight with slingshots, and many of us don't believe that God fights on our behalf. Moreover, our daily experience may not provide us with many instances in which the underdog triumphs, or even—not quite the same thing—instances in which virtue triumphs, and yet we get all of this in the story of David and Goliath. But the writer of the story gives us not only a plot that fulfills our wishes, as "Jack the Giant-Killer" does, but also convincing details, and despite the (to the rational mind) improbability of the whole story, the story delights and continues to delight on each rereading.

Nor can even the nonbeliever feel that this is only an idle tale; it is evident that the story-teller knows too much about human psychology (remember, again, such details as the scornful older brother, Saul's initial reluctance and then his offer of superfluous help, and David's rejection of the offer) to be easily dismissed as a spinner of fantastic empty tales.

Or we can approach the matter from another side, and argue that all literature is fantasy. After all, Hamlet and Macbeth, like Holden and Phoebe, 5 never existed, and even Julius Caesar, who of course did exist, did not say the things Shakespeare makes him say. All literature, then, can be thought of as "fantasy" in the sense of being something made up, imagined. Thus, Robert Frost begins a short poem, "Stopping by Woods on a Snowy Evening," with this stanza:

> Whose woods these are I think I know,
> His house is in the village though;
> He will not see me stopping here
> To watch his woods fill up with snow.

It is of course conceivable that Frost had a thought of this sort while stopping in the woods on a snowy evening, but readers understand that the entire poem was not written in a woods. Moreover, readers are to pretend, to imagine, to fantasize, that they are with the speaker of the poem, overhearing him as he meditates, though—another fantastic bit—he doesn't seem to know they are there. The whole is fantastic—and yet the poem seems very down to earth. As we read any work of literature, then, there is the pretense that we are not in our comfortable living room but are in an imagined world. Writers themselves often use the metaphor of a work of literature as a means of travel to a new world. Emily Dickinson, for example, begins one of her most famous poems by asserting that "There is no frigate like a book / To take us lands away," and John Keats compares reading to traveling in "realms of gold." The world of literature, we are told, is different from the world of the reader.

But how different? Think again of the idea that a good story probably cannot afford utterly to neglect either of two poles: it must have enough reality in it to convince us that it is not nonsense, and it must have enough strangeness in it—it must be enough of "a good story"—to hold our interest and make us want to keep on reading. Thus, if it happens to deal with a kid named Holden Caulfield it deals with someone who in many ways resembles all of us (we are, or have been, students, have been annoyed by phonies, hold ideals, and so on) and who in many ways (most notably in his gift for expression) is not at all like us.

Some writers, for some reasons, prefer to put their characters in relatively unrealistic circumstances, and prefer to draw characters who are not especially realistic. If they are writing a short work of prose fiction, they are writing a tale rather than a story; if they are writing a long work of prose fiction, they are writing a romance rather than a novel. Hawthorne, in his preface to *The House of the Seven Gables,* speaks for such writers:

> When a writer calls his work a romance, he wishes to claim a certain latti-
> tude, both as to its fashion and material, which he would not have felt himself
> entitled to assume had he professed to be writing a novel.

In the tale and the romance we are likely to feel, more than in the story and the novel, that we are in the world of myth and ritual, of symbolism. "Symbolism" is a big word with many possible meanings, but it may be enough to say that here it is used in Henry James's sense, as when he said that symbolism is the presentation "of objects casting . . . far behind them a shadow more curious . . . than the apparent figure." In the story of David and

Goliath we do not quite get symbolism in this sense, because the figures themselves (except for Goliath's height) are quite convincing, but surely they cast long shadows. David's "shadow" suggests youthful piety, enthusiasm, strength, and success; Goliath's suggests the inadequacy of boasting, brute strength, and false religion. That is, because the boy and the giant are sharply etched, the story of David and Goliath does not immediately force our minds to brood about the implications (and perhaps leave David and Goliath behind), but implications or shadows are surely present and important. Further, the story of David and Goliath is none the worse for being, from a common-sense viewpoint, highly improbable. This improbability is not a weakness. If it were more probable—if Goliath were not a giant, and if David were more experienced and more heavily armed—it would be more realistic but much less memorable, less touching.

Like Hawthorne, Herman Melville was chiefly a writer of romances. In *The Confidence Man* he expresses puzzlement that people expect to find in fiction a "severe fidelity to real life." He goes on to say that he hopes his readers will read the book as "tolerantly as they sit at a play, and with much the same expectations and feelings." Melville continues:

> And as, in real life, the properties will not allow people to act out themselves with that unreserve permitted to the stage; so, in books of fiction, they look not only for more entertainment, but, at bottom, even for more reality, than real life itself can show. Thus, though they want novelty, they want nature, too; but nature unfettered, exhilarated, in effect transformed. In this way of thinking, the people in a fiction, like the people in a play, must dress as nobody exactly dresses, talk as nobody exactly talks, act as nobody exactly acts. It is with fiction as with religion; it should present another world, and yet one to which we feel a tie.

Melville's last words, "one to which we feel a tie," are especially important. The writer's world may be set on Mars, or it may include ghosts, but it must (if the work is to be more than a moment's idle entertainment) convince readers that it deals with human affairs. What is improbable (and boring) about so much science fiction, and what makes most of it so trivial, is not that it is set in the future, or that people have ray guns, but that it is so remote from human psychology. Writers on science fiction usually define the genre by saying, more or less, that science fiction presents with verisimilitude some enormous change in the environment. It offers much that is new, and it often succeeds in making the technology of this imagined world believable. But a convincing physical environment is not enough to make us "feel a tie." Despite all of the apparent realism (for example, some scientific language) of a science fiction work, the work may seem utterly remote from life, not because people move about in rockets rather than in automobiles but because there is so much concern with technology and so little concern with feelings. On the other hand, a fable in which animals talk, or a ghost story in which the dead come back to seek revenge, may seem to a reader close to human life.

One might contrast the remote (psychological as well as temporal) worlds of most science fiction with the world of the fairy tale. What, one might ask, can be more remote from human experience than, say, the story of Sleeping Beauty? A prophecy is uttered that at the age of fifteen the princess will prick her finger on a spindle and will fall into a deathlike sleep for a hundred years. In order to prevent the prophecy from coming true, the king bans all spindles, but the girl nevertheless pricks her finger on a spindle as predicted, and falls asleep, to be awakened at last by the handsome young man. Now, one reads this story—or, rather, first hears it told by an elder, and then treasures it ever after—for the strangeness of the story itself, for the world of royalty, prophecy, a beautiful princess and a handsome prince. Most people (since they are neither literary critics nor psychologists) never bother to analyze the story— to give it a "meaning"—but surely part of the story's appeal is that despite its apparent remoteness it sets forth a world "to which we feel a tie." What is that tie? If we stand back form the story, we can say that it reveals the adolescent's fear of new experience (especially of sexual maturing), a paralyzing withdrawal or isolation from reality, and then (after a protective interval that ends with the loving kiss of the prince), the return to reality. It is scarcely going too far to say that "Sleeping Beauty," like many other fairy tales, alluringly sets forth our cultural values. These tales, in Dr. Johnson's words, "stretch and stimulate . . . little minds," and thus help children to grow (however unconsciously) into social adults. Allowing, of course, for great differences, something of the general pattern of "Sleeping Beauty" can be seen in Frost's "Stopping by Woods," where the movement is from a longing for extinction ("the woods are lovely, dark and deep") to the return to the larger world of life ("But I have promises to keep, / And miles to go before I sleep").

For Edgar Allan Poe, like his contemporaries Hawthorne and Melville, 10 a writer of romances, mere realism was "pitiable stuff," the accurate depiction of "decayed cheeses." A defense of romance or fantasy need not, however, with Poe dismiss realistic writing. For one thing, if writing is nothing but realistic, it dismisses itself; the realistic writing that endures is writing that manages to give not only a sense of the real—Poe's decayed cheeses— but also a sense of its meaning or importance to us, a sense, we might say, of the archetypal. To go back to our two poles: The realistic story that we willingly read a second and a third time has in it more than just realism, more than just convincing dialogue (a tape recorder can give us that) and descriptions of clothes and houses. It is, as one says, "a good story," which means that it has in it something of the unusual, but this unusual element is not the merely freakish; rather, it is something we feel a tie to.

[1987]

■ TOPICS FOR DISCUSSION AND WRITING

1. Take one of the relatively unrealistic works in this book—any selection in this chapter will do—and test it against Miranda's essay. Does the essay help you to enjoy the work? Or does the work refute the essay?

2. Do you find Miranda's discussion of the story of David and Goliath helpful? Why, or why not?

3. Briefly summarize a fairy tale that interests you, and then try to account for your interest in it. You may or may not want to draw on Miranda's essay.

FICTION

■ E D G A R   A L L A N   P O E

Edgar Allan Poe (1809–1849) was born in Boston, the son of traveling actors. Orphaned before he was three, he was brought up by the John Allan family in Richmond, Virginia, but his relations with John Allan were severely strained. Poe spent a year at the University of Virginia, where he incurred gambling debts; he then served a hitch in the army, published a book of poems at his own expense, and received an appointment to West Point, where he stayed only briefly. He then set out on a career as an editor and an author of essays, fiction, and poetry which often had a dream-like quality. By the age of twenty-six he had established something of a literary reputation, but his personal life was unstable and he had difficulty holding an editorial job. On his way from Richmond to a job in Philadelphia he got off the train at Baltimore, where he collapsed in the street. He was taken to a hospital but died shortly after.

The Fall of the House of Usher

Son coeur est un luth suspendu;
Sitôt qu'on le touche il résonne.
                    —*De Béranger*[1]

During the whole of a dull, dark, and soundless day in the autumn of the year, when the clouds hung oppressively low in the heavens, I had been passing alone, on horseback, through a singularly dreary tract of country, and at length found myself, as the shades of the evening drew on, within view of the melancholy House of Usher. I know not how it was—but, with the first glimpse of the building, a sense of insufferable gloom pervaded my spirit. I say insufferable; for the feeling was unrelieved by any of that half-pleasurable, because poetic, sentiment with which the mind usually receives even the sternest natural images of the desolate or terrible. I looked upon the scene before me—upon the mere house, and the simple landscape features of the domain—upon the bleak walls—upon the vacant eye-like windows—upon a few rank sedges—and upon a few white trunks of decayed trees—with an utter depression of soul which I can compare to no earthly sensation more properly than to the after-dream of the reveller upon opium—the bitter lapse into every-day life—the hideous dropping off of the veil. There was an iciness, a sinking, a sickening of the heart—an unredeemed dreariness of thought which no goading of the imagination could torture into aught of the sublime. What was it—I paused to think—what was it that so unnerved me in the contemplation of the House of Usher? It was a mystery all insoluble; nor could

[1]From "Le Refus," by Pierre-Jean de Béranger. The lines may be translated thus: "His heart is a lute, tightly strung; / The instant one touches it, it resounds."

I grapple with the shadowy fancies that crowded uupon me as I pondered. I was forced to fall back upon the unsatisfactory conclusion, that while, beyond doubt, there *are* combinations of very simple natural objects which have the power of thus affecting us, still the analysis of this power lies among considerations beyond our depth. It was possible, I reflected, that a mere different arrangement of the particulars of the scene, of the details of the picture, would be sufficient to modify, or perhaps to annihilate its capacity for sorrowful impression; and, acting upon this idea, I reined my horse to the precipitous brink of a black and lurid tarn[2] that lay in unruffled lustre by the dwelling, and gazed down—but with a shudder even more thrilling than before—upon the remodelled and inverted images of the gray sedge, and the ghastly tree-stems, and the vacant and eye-like windows.

Nevertheless, in this mansion of gloom I now proposed to myself a sojourn of some weeks. Its proprietor, Roderick Usher, had been one of my boon companions in boyhood; but many years had elapsed since our last meeting. A letter, however, had lately reached me in a distant part of the country—a letter from him—which, in its wildly importunate nature, had admitted of no other than a personal reply. The MS. gave evidence of nervous agitation. The writer spoke of acute bodily illness—of a mental disorder which oppressed him—and of an earnest desire to see me, as his best and indeed his only personal friend, with a view of attempting, by the cheerfulness of my society, some alleviation of his malady. It was the manner in which all this, and much more, was said—it was the apparent *heart* that went with his request—which allowed me no room for hesitation; and I accordingly obeyed forthwith what I still considered a very singular summons.

Although, as boys, we had been even intimate associates, yet I really knew little of my friend. His reserve had been always excessive and habitual. I was aware, however, that his very ancient family had been noted, time out of mind, for a peculiar sensibility of temperament, displaying itself, through long ages, in many works of exalted art, and manifested, of late, in repeated deeds of munificent yet unobtrusive charity, as well as in a passionate devotion to the intricacies, perhaps even more than to the orthodox and easily recognizable beauties, of musical science. I had learned, too, the very remarkable fact, that the stem of the Usher race, all time-honored as it was, had put forth, at no period, an enduring branch; in other words, that the entire family lay in the direct line of descent, and had always, with very trifling and very temporary variation, so lain. It was this deficiency, I considered, while running over in thought the perfect keeping of the character of the premises with the accredited character of the people, and while speculating upon the possible influence which the one, in the long lapse of centuries, might have exercised upon the other—it was this deficiency, perhaps, of collateral issue, and the consequent undeviating transmission, from sire to son, of the patrimony with the name, which had, at length, so identified the two as to merge the original title of the estate in the quaint and equivocal appellation of the "House of Usher"—an appellation which seemed to include, in the minds of the peasantry who used it, both the family and the family mansion.

[2] **tarn** small mountain lake

I have said that the sole effect of my somewhat childish experiment—that of looking down within the tarn—had been to deepen the first singular impression. There can be no doubt that the consciousness of the rapid increase of my superstition—for why should I not so term it?—served mainly to accelerate the increase itself. Such, I have long known, is the paradoxical law of all sentiments having terror as a basis. And it might have been for this reason only, that, when I again uplifted my eyes to the house itself, from its image in the pool, there grew in my mind a strange fancy—a fancy so ridiculous, indeed, that I but mention it to show the vivid force of the sensations which oppressed me. I had so worked upon my imagination as really to believe that about the whole mansion and domain there hung an atmosphere peculiar to themselves and their immediate vicinity—an atmosphere which had no affinity with the air of heaven, but which had reeked up from the decayed trees, and the gray wall, and the silent tarn—a pestilent and mystic vapor, dull, sluggish, faintly discernible, and leaden-hued.

Shaking off from my spirit what *must* have been a dream, I scanned more narrowly the real aspect of the building. Its principal feature seemd to be that of an excessive antiquity. The discoloration of ages had been great. Minute fingi overspread the whole exterior, hanging in a fine tangled web-work from the eaves. Yet all this was apart from any extraordinary dilapidation. No portion of the masonry had fallen; and there appeared to be a wild inconsistency between its still perfect adaptation of parts, and the crumbling condition of the individual stones. In this there was much that reminded me of the specious totality of old wood-work which has rotted for long years in some neglected vault, with no disturbance from the breath of the external air. Beyond this indication of extensive decay, however, the fabric gave little token of instability. Perhaps the eye of a scrutinizing observer might have discovered a barely perceptible fissure, which, extending from the roof of the building in front, made its way down the wall in a zigzag direction, until it became lost in the sullen waters of the tarn.

Noticing these things, I rode over a short causeway to the house. A servant in waiting took my horse, and I entered the Gothic archway of the hall. A valet, of stealthy step, thence conducted me, in silence, through many dark and intricate passages in my progress to the *studio* of his master. Much that I encountered on the way contributed, I know not how, to heighten the vague sentiments of which I have already spoken. While the objects around me— while the carvings of the ceilings, the sombre tapestries of the walls, the ebon blackness of the floors, and the phantasmagoric armorial trophies which rattled as I strode, were but matters to which, or to such as which, I had been accustomed from my infancy—while I hesitated not to acknowledge how familiar was all this—I still wondered to find how unfamiliar were the fancies which ordinary images were stirring up. On one of the staircases, I met the physician of the family. His countenance, I thought, wore a mingled expression of low cunning and perplexity. He accosted me with trepidation and passed on. The valet now threw open a door and ushered me into the presence of his master.

The room in which I found myself was very large and lofty. The windows were long, narrow, and pointed, and at so vast a distance from the black oaken floor as to be altogether inaccessible from within. Feeble gleams of encrimsoned light made their way through the trellissed panes, and served to render sufficiently distinct the more prominent objects around; the eye, however, struggled in vain to reach the remoter angles of the chamber, or the recesses of the vaulted and fretted ceiling. Dark draperies hung upon the walls. The general furniture was profuse, comfortless, antique, and tattered. Many books and musical instruments lay scattered about, but failed to give any vitality to the scene. I felt that I breathed an atmosphere of sorrow. An air of stern, deep, and irredeemable gloom hung over and pervaded all.

Upon my entrance, Usher arose from a sofa on which he had been lying at full length, and greeted me with a vivacious warmth which had much in it, I at first thought, of an overdone cordiality—of the constrained effort of the *ennuyé*[3] man of the world. A glance, however, at his countenance convinced me of his perfect sincerity. We sat down; and for some moments, while he spoke not, I gazed upon him with a feeling half of pity, half of awe. Surely, man had never before so terribly altered, in so brief a period, as had Roderick Usher! It was with difficulty that I could bring myself to admit the identity of the wan being before me with the companion of my early boyhood. Yet the character of his face had been at all times remarkable. A cadaverousness of complexion; an eye large, liquid, and luminous beyond comparison; lips somewhat thin and very pallid but of a surpassingly beautiful curve; a nose of a delicate Hebrew model, but with a breadth of nostril unusual in similar formations; a finely moulded chin, speaking, in its want of prominence, of a want of moral energy; hair of a more than web-like softness and tenuity;—these features, with an inordinate expansion above the regions of the temple, made up altogether a countenance not easily to be forgotten. And now in the mere exaggeration of the prevailing character of these features, and of the expression they were wont to convey, lay so much of change that I doubted to whom I spoke. The now ghastly pallor of the skin, and the now miraculous lustre of the eye, above all things startled and even awed me. The silken hair, too, had been suffered to grow all unheeded, and as, in its wild gossamer texture, it floated rather than fell about the face, I could not, even with effort, connect its Arabasque[4] expression with any idea of simple humanity.

In the manner of my friend I was at once struck with an incoherence—an inconsistency; and I soon found this to arise from a series of feeble and futile struggles to overcome an habitual trepidancy—an excessive nervous agitation. For something of this nature I had indeed been prepared, no less by his letter, than by reminiscences of certain boyish traits, and by conclusions deduced from his peculiar physical confirmation and temperament. His action was alternately vivacious and sullen. His voice varied rapidly from a tremulous indecision (which the animal spirits seemed utterly in abeyance) to that species of energetic concision—that abrupt, weighty, unhurried, and hollow-sounding enunciation—that leaden, self-balanced, and perfectly modulated guttural utterance, which may be observed in the lost drunkard, or the irreclaimable eater of opium, during the periods of his most intense excitement.

[3] **ennuyé** bored
[4] **Arabesque** intricate

It was thus that he spoke of the object of my visit, of his earnest desire to see me, and of the solace he expected me to afford him. He entered, at some length, into what he conceived to be the nature of his malady. It was, he said, a constitutional and a family evil, and one for which he despaired to find a remedy—a mere nervous affection, he immediately added, which would undoubtedly soon pass off. It displayed itself in a host of unnatural sensations. Some of these, as he detailed them, interested and bewildered me; although, perhaps, the terms and the general manner of their narration had their weight. He suffered much from a morbid acuteness of the senses; the most insipid food was alone endurable; he could wear only garments of certain texture; the odors of all flowers were oppressive; his eyes were tortured by even a faint light; and there were but peculiar sounds, and these from stringed instruments, which did not inspire him with horror.

To an anomalous species of terror I found him a bounden slave. "I shall perish," said he, "I *must* perish in this deplorable folly. Thus, thus, and not otherwise, shall I be lost. I dread the events of the future, not in themselves, but in their results. I shudder at the thought of any, even the most trivial, incident, which may operate upon this intolerable agitation of soul. I have, indeed, no abhorrence of danger, except in its absolute effect—in terror. In this unnerved, in this pitiable, condition I feel that the period will sooner or later arrive when I must abandon life and reason together, in some struggle with the grim phantasm, FEAR."

I learned, moreover, at intervals, and through broken and equivocal hints, another singular feature of his mental condition. He was enchained by certain superstitious impressions in regard to the dwelling which he tenanted, and whence, for many years, he had never ventured forth—in regard to an influence whose supposititious force was conveyed in terms too shadowy here to be re-stated—an influence which some peculiarities in the mere form and substance of his family mansion had, by dint of long sufferance, he said, obtained over his spirit—an effect which the *physique* of the gray walls and turrets, and of the dim tarn into which they all looked down, had, at length, brought about upon the *morale* of his existence.

He admitted, however, although with hesitation, that much of the peculiar gloom which thus afflicted him could be traced to a more natural and far more palpable origin—to the severe and long-continued illness—indeed to the evidently approaching dissolution—of a tenderly beloved sister, his sole companion for many long years, his last and only relative on earth. "Her decease," he said, with a bitterness which I can never foget, "would leave him (him, the hopeless and the frail) the last of the ancient race of the Ushers." While he spoke, the lady Madeline (for so was she called) passed through a remote portion of the apartment, and, without having noticed my presence, disappeared. I regarded her with an utter astonishment not unmingled with dread; and yet I found it impossible to account for such feelings. A sensation of stupor oppressed me as my eyes followed her retreating steps. When a door, at length, closed upon her, my glance sought instinctively and eagerly the countenance of the brother; but he had buried his face in his hands and I could only perceive that a far more than ordinary wanness had overspread the emaciated fingers through which trickled many passionate tears.

The disease of the lady Madeline had long baffled the skill of her physicians. A settled apathy, a gradual wasting away of the person, and frequent although transient affections of a partially cataleptical character were the unusual diagnosis. Hitherto she had steadily borne up against the pressure of her malady, and had not betaken herself finally to bed; but on the closing in of the evening of my arrival at the house, she succumbed (as her brother told me at night with inexpressible agitation) to the prostrating power of the destroyer; and I learned that the glimpse I had obtained of her person would thus probably be the last I should obtain—that the lady, at least while living, would be seen by me no more.

For several days ensuing, her name was unmentioned by either Usher or myself; and during this period I was busied in earnest endeavors to alleviate the melancholy of my friend. We painted and read together, or I listened, as if in a dream, to the wild improvisations of his speaking guitar. And thus, as a closer and still closer intimacy admitted me more unreservedly into the recesses of his spirit, the more bitterly did I perceive the futility of all attempt at cheering a mind from which darkness, as if an inherent positive quality, poured forth upon all objects of the moral and physical universe in one unceasing radiation of gloom.

I shall ever bear about me a memory of the many solemn hours I thus spent alone with the master of the House of Usher. Yet I should fail in any attempt to convey an idea of the exact character of the studies, or of the occupations, in which he involved me, or led me the way. An excited and highly distempered ideality threw a sulphureous lustre over all. His long improvised dirges will ring forever in my ears. Among other things, I hold painfully in mind a certain singular perversion and amplification of the wild air of the last waltz of Von Weber. From the paintings over which his elaborate fancy brooded, and which grew, touch by touch, into vaguenesses at which I shuddered and more thrillingly, because I shuddered knowing not why—from these paintings (vivid as their images now are before me) I would in vain endeavor to educe more than a small portion which should lie within the compass of merely written words. By the utter simplicity, by the nakedness of his designs, he arrested and overawed attention. If ever mortal painted an idea, that mortal was Roderick Usher. For me at least, in the circumstances then surrounding me, there arose out of the pure abstractions which the hypochondriac contrived to throw upon his canvas, an intensity of intolerable awe, no shadow of which felt I ever yet in the contemplation of the certainly glowing yet too concrete reveries of Fuseli.

One of the phantasmagoric conceptions of my friend, partaking not so rigidly of the spirit of abstraction, may be shadowed forth, although feebly, in words. A small picture presented the interior of an immensely long and rectangular vault or tunnel, with low walls, smooth, white, and without interruption or device. Certain accessory points of the design served well to convey the idea that this excavation lay at an exceeding depth below the surface of the earth. No outlet was observed in any portion of its vast extent, and no torch or other artificial source of light was discernible; yet a flood of intense rays rolled throughout, and bathed the whole in a ghastly and inappropriate splendor.

I have just spoken of that morbid condition of the auditory nerve which rendered all music intolerable to the sufferer, with the exception of certain effects of stringed instruments. It was, perhaps, the narrow limits to which he thus confined himself upon the guitar which gave birth, in great measure, to the fantastic character of his performances. But the fervid *facility* of his *impromptus* could not be so accounted for. They must have been, and were, in the notes, as well as in the words of his wild fantasias (for he not unfrequently accompanied himself with rhymed verbal improvisations), the result of that intense mental collectedness and concentration to which I have previously alluded as observable only in particular moments of the highest artificial excitement. The words of one of these rhapsodies I have easily remembered. I was, perhaps, the most forcibly impressed with it as he gave it, because, in the under or mystic current of its meaning, I fancied that I perceived, and for the first time, a full consciousness of the part of Usher of the tottering of his lofty reason upon her throne. The verses, which were entitled "The Haunted Palace," ran very nearly, if not accurately, thus:—

I.

In the greenest of our valleys,
    By good angels tenanted,
Once a fair and stately palace—
    Radiant palace—reared its head.
In the monarch Thought's dominion—
    It stood there!
Never seraph spread a pinion
    Over fabric half so fair.

II.

Banners yellow, glorious, golden,
    On its roof did float and flow
(This—all this—was in the olden
    Time long ago);
And every gentle air that dallied,
    In that sweet day,
Along the ramparts plumed and pallid,
    A winged odor went away.

III.

Wanderers in that happy valley
    Through two luminous windows saw
Spirits moving musically
    To a lute's well-tunèd law;
Round about a throne, where sitting
    (Porphyrogene!)[5]
In state his glory well befitting,
    The ruler of the realm was seen.

[5] **Porphyrogene** born to the purple, i.e., royal

IV.

And all with pearl and ruby glowing
    Was the fair palace door,
Through which came flowing, flowing, flowing
    And sparkling evermore,
A troop of Echoes whose sweet duty
    Was but to sing,
In voices of surpassing beauty,
    The wit and wisdom of their king.

V.

But evil things, in robes of sorrow,
    Assailed the monarch's high estate;
(Ah, let us mourn, for never morrow
    Shall dawn upon him, desolate!)
And, round about his home, the glory
    That blushed and bloomed
Is but a dim-remembered story
    Of the old time entombed.

VI.

And travellers now within that valley,
    Through the red-litten windows see
Vast forms that move fantastically
    To a discordant melody;
While, like a rapid ghastly river,
    Through the pale door;
A hideous throng rush out forever,
    And laugh—but smile no more.

I well remember that suggestions arising from this ballad led us into a train of thought wherein there became manifest an opinion of Usher's which I mention not so much on account of its novelty (for other men have thought thus), as on account of the pertinacity with which he maintained it. This opinion, in its general form, was that of the sentience of all vegetable things. But, in his disordered fancy, the idea had assumed a more daring character, and trespassed, under certain conditions, upon the kingdom of inorganization. I lack words to express the full extent, or the earnest *abandon* of his persuasion. The belief, however, was connected (as I have previously hinted) with the gray stones of the home of his forefathers. The conditions of the sentence had been here, he imagined, fulfilled in the method of collocation of these stones—in the order of their arrangement, as well as in that of the many *fungi* which overspread them, and of the decayed trees which stood around—above all, in the long undisturbed endurance of this arrangement, and in its reduplication in the still waters of the tarn. Its evidence—the evidence of the sentience—was to be seen, he said (and I here started as he spoke), in the gradual yet certain condensation of an atmosphere of their own about the waters and the walls. The result was discoverable, he added, in that silent yet importunate and terrible influence which for centuries had moulded the destinies of his family, and which made *him* what I now saw him—what he was. Such opinions need no comment, and I will make none.

Our books—books which, for years, had formed no small portion of the mental existence of the invalid—were, as might be supposed, in strict keeping with this character of phantasm. We pored together over such works as the "Ververt et Chartreuse" of Gresset; the "Belphegor" of Machiavelli; the "Heaven and Hell" of Swedenborg; the "Subterranean Voyage of Nicholas Klimm" of Holberg; the "Chiromancy" of Robert Flud, of Jean D'Indaginé, and of Dela Chambre; the "Journey into the Blue Distance of Tieck"; and the "City of the Sun of Campanella." One favorite volume was a small octavo edition of the "Directorium Inquisitorium," by the Dominican Eymeric de Gironne; and there were passages in Pomponius Mela, about the old African Satyrs and Œgipans, over which Usher would sit dreaming for hours. His chief delight, however, was found in the perusal of an exceedingly rare and curious book in quarto Gothic—the manual of a forgotten church—the *Vigiliæ Mortuorum secundum Chorum Ecclesiæ Maguntinæ.*

I could not help thinking of the wild ritual of this work, and of its probable influence upon the hypochondriac, when, one evening, having informed me abruptly that the lady Madeline was no more, he stated his intention of preserving her corpse for a fortnight (previously to its final interment), in one of the numerous vaults within the main walls of the building. The worldly reason, however, assigned for this singular proceeding, was one which I did not feel at liberty to dispute. The brother had been led to his resolution (so he told me) by consideration of the unusual character of the malady of the deceased, of certain obtrusive and eager inquiries on the part of her medical men, and of the remote and exposed situation of the burial-ground of the family. I will not deny that when I called to mind the sinister countenance of the person whom I met upon the staircase, on the day of my arrival at the house, I had no desire to oppose what I regarded as at best but a harmless, and by no means an unnatural, precaution.

At the request of Usher, I personally aided him in the arrangements for the temporary entombment. The body having been encoffined, we two alone bore it to its rest. The vault in which we placed it (and which had been so long unopened that our torches, half smothered in its oppressive atmosphere, gave us little opportunity for investigation) was small, damp, and entirely without means of admission for light; lying, at great depth, immediately beneath that portion of the building in which was my own sleeping apartment. It had been used, apparently, in remote feudal times, for the worst purposes of a donjonkeep, and, in later days, as a place of deposit for powder, or some other highly combustible substance, as a portion of its floor, and the whole interior of a long archway through which we reached it, were carefully sheathed with copper. The door, of massive iron, had been, also, similarly protected. Its immense weight caused an unusually sharp, grating sound, as it moved upon its hinges.

Having deposited our mournful burden upon tressels within this region of horror, we partially turned aside the yet unscrewed lid of the coffin, and looked upon the face of the tenant. A striking similitude between the brother and sister now first arrested my attention; and Usher, divining, perhaps, my thoughts, murmured out some few words from which I learned that the deceased and himself had been twins, and that sympathies of a scarcely intelligible nature had always existed between them. Our glances, however, rested not long upon the dead—for we could not regard her unawed. The disease which had thus entombed the lady in the maturity of youth, had left, as usual in all maladies of a strictly cataleptical character, the mockery of a faint blush upon the bosom and the face, and that suspiciously lingering smile upon the lip which is so terrible in death. We replaced and screwed down the lid, and, having secured the door of iron, made our way, with toil, into the scarcely less gloomy apartments of the upper portion of the house.

And now, some days of bitter grief having elapsed, an observable change came over the features of the mental disorder of my friend. His ordinary manner had vanished. His ordinary occupations were neglected or forgotten. He roamed from chamber to chamber with hurried, unequal, and objectless step. The pallor of his countenance had assumed, if possible, a more ghastly hue— but the luminousness of his eye had utterly gone out. The once occasional huskiness of his tone was heard no more; and a tremulous quaver, as if of extreme terror, habitually characterized his utterance. There were times, indeed, when I thought his unceasingly agitated mind was laboring with some oppressive secret to divulge which he struggled for the necessary courage. At times, again, I was obliged to resolve all into the mere inexplicable vagaries of madness, for I beheld him gazing upon vacancy for long hours, in an attitude of the profoundest attention, as if listening to some imaginary sound. It was no wonder that his condition terrified—that it infected me. I felt creeping upon me, by slow yet certain degrees, the wild influences of his own fantastic yet impressive superstitions.

It was, especially, upon retiring to bed late in the night of the seventh or eighth day after the placing of the lady Madeline within the donjon, that I experienced the full power of such feelings. Sleep came not near my couch—while the hours waned and waned away. I struggled to reason off the nervousness which had dominion over me. I endeavored to believe that much, if not all of what I felt, was due to the bewildering influence of the gloomy furniture of the room—of the dark and tattered draperies, which, tortured into motion by the breath of a rising tempest, swayed fitfully to and fro upon the walls, and rustled uneasily about the decorations of the bed. But my efforts were fruitless. An irrepressible tremor gradually pervaded my frame; and, at length, there sat upon my very heart an incubus of utterly causeless alarm. Shaking this off with a gasp and a struggle, I uplifted myself upon the pillows, and, peering earnestly within the intense darkness of the chamber, hearkened—I know not why, except that an instinctive spirit prompted me— to certain low and indefinite sounds which came, through the pauses of the storm, at long intervals, I knew not whence. Overpowered by an intense sentiment of horror, unaccountable yet unendurable, I threw on my clothes with haste (for I felt that I should sleep no more during the night), and endeavored to arouse myself from the pitiable condition into which I had fallen, by pacing rapidly to and fro through the apartment.

I had taken but few turns in this manner, when a light step on an adjoining staircase arrested my attention. I presently recognized it as that of Usher. In an instant afterward he rapped, with a gentle touch, at my door, and entered, bearing a lamp. His countenance was, as usual, cadaverously wan—but, moreover, there was a species of mad hilarity in his eyes—an evidently restrained *hysteria* in his whole demeanor. His air appalled me—but any thing was preferable to the solitude which I had so long endured, and I even welcomed his presence as a relief.

"And you have not seen it?" he said abruptly, after having stared about him for some moments in silence—"you have not then seen it?—but, stay! you shall." Thus speaking, and having carefully shaded his lamp, he hurried to one of the casements, and threw it freely open to the storm.

The impetuous fury of the entering gust nearly lifted us from our feet. It was, indeed, a tempestuous yet sternly beautiful night, and one wildly singular in its terror and its beauty. A whirlwind had apparently collected its force in our vicinity; for there were frequent and violent alterations in the direction of the wind; and the exceeding density of the clouds (which hung so low as to press upon the turrets of the house) did not prevent our perceiving the life-like velocity with which they flew careering from all points against each other, without passing away into the distance. I say that even their exceeding density did not prevent our perceiving this—yet we had no glimpse of the moon or stars, nor was there any flashing forth of the lightning. But the under surfaces of the huge masses of agitated vapor, as well as all terrestial objects immediately around us, were glowing in the unnatural light of a faintly luminous and distinctly visible gaseous exhalation which hung about and enshrouded the mansion.

"You must not—you shall not behold this!" said I, shuddering, to Usher, as I led him, with a gentle violence, from the window to a seat. "These appearances, which bewilder you, are merely electrical phenomena not uncommon—or it may be that they have their ghastly origin in the rank miasma of the tarn. Let us close this casement;—the air is chilling and dangerous to your frame. Here is one of your favorite romances. I will read, and you shall listen:—and so we will pass away this terrible night together."

The antique volume which I had taken up was the "Mad Trist"[6] of Sir Launcelot Canning; but I had called it a favorite of Usher's more in sad jest than in earnest; for, in truth, there is little in its uncouth and unimaginative prolixity which could have had interest for the lofty and spiritual ideality of my friend. It was, however, the only book immediately at hand; and I indulged a vague hope that the excitement which now agitated the hypochondriac, might find relief (for the history of mental disorder is full of similar anomalies) even in the extremeness of the folly which I should read. Could I have judged, indeed, by the wild overstrained air of vivacity with which he hearkened, or apparently hearkened, to the words of the tale, I might well have congratulated myself upon the success of my design.

I had arrived at that well-known portion of the story where Ethelred, the hero of the Trist, having sought in vain for peaceable admission into the dwelling of the hermit, proceeds to make good an entrance by force. Here, it will be remembered, the words of the narrative run thus:

"And Ethelred, who was by nature of a doughty heart, and who was now

[6] Poe has invented the story and the author. A "trist" (i.e., tryst) is an appointed meeting.

mighty withal, on account of the powerfulness of the wine which he had drunken, waited no longer to hold parley with the hermit, who, in sooth, was of an obstinate and maliceful turn, but, feeling the rain upon his shoulders, and fearing the risking of the tempest, uplifted his mace outright, and, with blows, made quickly room in the plankings of the door for his gauntleted hand; and now pulling therewith sturdily, he so cracked, and ripped, and tore all asunder, that the noise of the dry and hollow-sounding wood alarumed and reverberated throughout the forest."

And the termination of this sentence I started and, for a moment, paused; for it appeared to me (although I at once concluded that my excited fancy had deceived me)—it appeared to me that, from some very remote portion of the mansion, there came, indistinctly to my ears, what might have been, in its exact similarity of character, the echo (but a stifled and dull one certainly) of the very cracking and ripping sound which Sir Launcelot had so particularly described. It was, beyond doubt, the coincidence alone which had arrested my attention; for, amid the rattling of the sashes of the casements, and the ordinary commingled noises of the still increasing storm, the sound, in itself, had nothing, surely, which should have interested or disturbed me. I continued the story:

"But the good champion Ethelred, now entering within the door, was sore enraged and amazed to perceive no signal of the maliceful hermit; but, in the stead thereof, a dragon of a scaly and prodigious demeanor, and of a fiery tongue, which sate in guard before a palace of gold, with a floor of silver; and upon the wall there hung a shield of shining brass with this legend enwritten—

Who entereth herein, a conqueror hath bin;
Who slayeth the dragon, the shield he shall win.

And Ethelred uplifted his mace, and struck upon the head of the dragon, which fell before him, and gave up his pesty breath, with a shriek so horrid and harsh, and withal so piercing, that Ethelred had fain to close his ears with his hands against the dreadful noise of it, the like whereof was never before heard."

Here again I paused abruptly, and now with a feeling of wild amazement— for there could be no doubt whatever that, in this instance, I did actually hear (although from what direction it proceeded I found it impossible to say) a low and apparently distant, but harsh, protracted, and most unusual screaming or grating sound—the exact counterpart of what my fancy had already conjured up for the dragon's unnatural shriek as described by the romancer.

Oppressed, as I certainly was, upon the occurrence of this second and most extraordinary coincidence, by a thousand conflicting sensations, in which wonder and extreme terror were predominant, I still retained sufficient presence of mind to avoid exciting, by any observation, the sensitive nervousness of my companion. I was by no means certain that he had noticed the sounds in question; although, assuredly, a strange alteration had, during the last few minutes, taken place in his demeanor. From a position fronting my own, he had gradually brought round his chair, so as to sit with his face to the door of the chamber; and thus I could but partially perceive his features, although I saw that his lips trembled as if he were murmuring inaudibly. His head had dropped upon his breast—yet I knew that he was not asleep, from the wide and rigid opening of the eye as I caught a glance of it in profile. The motion of his body, too, was at variance with this idea—for he rocked from side to side with a gentle yet constant and uniform sway. Having rapidly taken notice of all this, I resumed the narrative of Sir Launcelot, which thus proceeded:

"And now, the champion, having escaped from the terrible fury of the dragon, bethinking himself of the brazen shield, and of the breaking up of the enchantment which was upon it, removed the carcass from out of the way before him, and approached valorously over the silver pavement of the castle to where the shield was upon the wall; which in sooth tarried not for his full coming, but fell down at his feet upon the silver floor, with a mighty great and terrible ringing sound."

No sooner had these syllables passed my lips, than—as if a shield of brass had indeed, at the moment, fallen heavily upon a floor of silver—I became aware of a distinct, hollow, metallic, and clangorous, yet apparently muffled, reverberation. Completely unnerved, I leaped to my feet; but the measured rocking movement of Usher was undisturbed. I rushed to the chair in which he sat. His eyes were bent fixedly before him, and throughout his whole countenance there reigned a stony rigidity. But, as I placed my hand upon his shoulder, there came a strong shudder over his whole person; a sickly smile quivered about his lips; and I saw that he spoke in a low, hurried, and gibbering murmur, as if unconscious of my presence. Bending closely over him, I at length drank in the hideous import of his words.

"Now hear it?—yes, I hear it, and *have* heard it. Long—long—long—many minutes, many hours, many days, have I heard it—yet I dared not—oh, pity me, miserable wretch that I am!—I dared not—I *dared* not speak! *We have put her living in the tomb!* Said I not that my senses were acute? I *now* tell you that I heard her first feeble movements in the hollow coffin, I heard them— many, many days ago—yet I dared not—*I dared not speak!* And now—to-night—Ethelred—ha! ha!—the breaking of the hermit's door, and the death-cry of the dragon, and the clangor of the shield—say, rather, the rending of her coffin, and the grating of the iron hinges of her prison, and her struggles within the coppered archway of the vault! Oh! whither shall I fly? Will she not be here anon? Is she not hurrying to upbraid me for my haste? Have I not heard her footstep on the stair? Do I not distinguish that heavy and horrible beating of her heart? Madman!"—here he sprang furiously to his feet, and shrieked out his syllables, as if in the effort he were giving up his soul—"*Madman! I tell you that she now stands without the door!*"

As if in the superhuman energy of his utterance there had been found the potency of a spell, the huge antique panels to which the speaker pointed threw slowly back, upon the instant, their ponderous and ebony jaws. It was the work of the rushing gust—but then without those doors there *did* stand the lofty and enshrouded figure of the lady Madeline of Usher. There was blood upon her white robes, and the evidence of some bitter struggle upon every portion of her emaciated frame. For a moment she remained trembling and reeling to and fro upon the threshold—then, with a low moaning cry, fell heavily inward upon the person of her brother, and in her violent and now final death-agonies, bore him to the floor a corpse, and a victim to the terrors he had anticipated.

From that chamber, and from that mansion, I fled aghast. The storm was still abroad in all its wrath as I found myself crossing the old causeway. Suddenly there shot along the path a wild light, and I turned to see whence a gleam so unusual could have issued; for the vast house and its shadows were alone behind me. The radiance was that of the full, setting, and blood-red moon, which now shone vividly through that once barely discernible fissure, of which I have before spoken as extending from the roof of the building, in a zigzag direction, to the base. While I gazed, this fissure rapidly widened— there came a fierce breath of the whirlwind—the entire orb of the satellite burst at once upon my sight—my brain reeled as I saw the mighty walls rushing asunder—there was a long tumultuous shouting sound like the voice of a thousand waters—and the deep and dank tarn at my feet closed sullenly and silently over the fragments of the *"House of Usher."*

[1839]

■ TOPICS FOR DISCUSSION AND WRITING

1. Is it reasonable to say that the decaying mansion is a metaphor for the mind of Roderick Usher? If so, what evidence supports this view?

2. What might have been Poe's reason(s) for introducing the romance of the knight and the dragon? In any case, what is the effect of this interpolated story?

3. There is very little drama, in the sense of scenes with dialogue. Rather, most of the story is devoted to the narrator's report of what happened. Why do you suppose Poe chose this method? What is the effect of Poe's decision to let the narrator tell so much of the story in his own words?

4. Do you take the narrator to be a reliable narrator? Is it possible that he is insane? After all, can we believe (to take a single example) that Madeline broke open a coffin whose lid had been tightly screwed down and pushed open a door of "massive iron"? Is the story, then, about a mad narrator?

5. We learn that Madeline is Roderick's twin. What other instances of doubling do you find in the story?

6. Imitating as closely as possible the style of Poe's narrator, describe a college building.

■ JEAN RHYS

"Jean Rhys" was the pseudonym used by Ella Gwendolen Rees Williams (1890?–1979). She was born in the West Indies, in Dominica (at that time a British colony), and was educated there and in England. After a term at the London Academy of Dramatic Arts, she joined a touring

musical company, married a man who was soon convicted of illegal financial dealings, divorced him, lived with the writer Ford Madox Ford, and
married twice again.

In addition to writing stories and five novels, she wrote an autobiography, *Smile Please: An Unfinished Autobiography* (1979).

I Used to Live Here Once

She was standing by the river looking at the stepping stones and remembering each one. There was the round unsteady stone, the pointed one, the
flat one in the middle—the safe stone where you could stand and look round.
The next wasn't so safe for when the river was full the water flowed over it
and even when it showed dry it was slippery. But after that it was easy and
soon she was standing on the other side.

The road was much wider than it used to be but the work had been done
carelessly. The felled trees had not been cleared away and the bushes looked
trampled. Yet it was the same road and she walked along feeling extraordinarily happy.

It was a fine day, a blue day. The only thing was that the sky had a glassy
look that she didn't remember. That was the only word she could think of.
Glassy. She turned the corner, saw that what had been the old pavé[1] had been
taken up, and there too the road was much wider, but it had the same unfinished look.

She came to the worn stone steps that led up to the house and her heart
began to beat. The screw pine was gone, so was the mock summer house
called the ajoupa, but the clove tree was still there and at the top of the steps
the rough lawn stretched away, just as she remembered it. She stopped and
looked towards the house that had been added to and painted white. It was
strange to see a car standing in front of it.

There were two children under the big mango tree, a boy and a little girl,
and she waved to them and called "Hello" but they didn't answer her or turn
their heads. Very fair children, as Europeans born in the West Indies so often
are: as if the white blood is asserting itself against all odds.

The grass was yellow in the hot sunlight as she walked towards them.
When she was quite close she called again, shyly: "Hello." Then, "I used to
live here once," she said.

Still they didn't answer. When she said for the third time "Hello" she was
quite near them. Her arms went out instinctively with the longing to touch
them.

It was the boy who turned. His gray eyes looked straight into hers. His
expression didn't change. He said: "Hasn't it gone cold all of a sudden. D'you
notice? Let's go in. "Yes let's," said the girl.

Her arms fell to her sides as she watched them running across the grass
to the house. That was the first time she knew.

[1976]

[1]**pavé** cobblestone pavement

■ TOPICS FOR DISCUSSION AND WRITING

1. One of our students, who had lived in the West Indies (where the story is set) argued that the story is about a woman who, after having deserted the islands, returns to them and is now deliberately snubbed (that is, treated as though she doesn't exist). Do you think this is what the story is about? Are you convinced by the student's description that this is the way West Indians treat those who leave and then return?

2. What do you make out of the following details: (1) that the sky has an unfamiliar "glassy" look; (2) that the children don't reply; (3) that the boy comments on a sudden chilliness?

■ ELIZABETH BOWEN

Elizabeth Bowen (1899–1973) was born in Dublin, Ireland, but she was of Anglo-Irish stock and received her schooling in England. During the First World War she served as a nurse in a military hospital. She married an Englishman in 1923 and published her first book—a collection of stories—in the same year. For twelve years she and her husband lived near Oxford, but then they moved to London. During the Second World War she worked for the Ministry of Information. After the war she returned to her family home in Ireland, though she spent her last years in England.

Bowen wrote stories and novels—often with a hallucinatory quality that struck readers as a counterpart to the absurdity of life—as well as some critical essays.

The Demon Lover

Towards the end of her day in London Mrs. Drover went round to her shut-up house to look for several things she wanted to take away. Some belonged to herself, some to her family, who were by now used to their country life. It was late August; it had been a steamy, showery day: at the moment the trees down the pavement glittered in an escape of humid yellow afternoon sun. Against the next batch of clouds, already piling up ink-dark, broken chimneys and parapets stood out. In her once familiar street, as in any unused channel, an unfamiliar queerness had silted up: a cat wove itself in and out of railings, but no human eye watched Mrs. Drover's return. Shifting some parcels under her arm, she slowly forced round her latchkey in an unwilling lock, then gave the door, which had warped, a push with her knee. Dead air came out to meet her as she went in.

The staircase window having been boarded up, no light came down into the hall. But one door, she could just see, stood ajar, so she went quickly through into the room and unshuttered the big window in there. Now the prosaic woman, looking about her, was more perplexed than she knew by everything that she saw, by traces of her long former habit of life—the yellow smoke-stain up the white marble mantelpiece, the ring left by a vase on the top of the escritoire; the bruise in the wallpaper where, on the door being thrown open widely, the china handle had always hit the wall. The piano, having gone away to be stored, had left what looked like claw-marks on its part of the parquet. Though not much dust had seeped in, each object wore a film of another kind; and, the only ventilation being the chimney, the whole drawing-room smelled of the cold hearth. Mrs. Drover put down her parcels on the escritoire and left the room to proceed upstairs; the things she wanted were in a bedroom closet.

She had been anxious to see how the house was—the part-time caretaker she shared with some neighbors was away this week on his holiday, known to be not yet back. At the best of times he did not look in often, and she was never sure that she trusted him. There were some cracks in the structure, left by the last bombing, on which she was anxious to keep an eye. Not that one could do anything—

A shaft of refracted daylight now lay across the hall. She stopped dead and stared at the hall table—on this lay a letter addressed to her.

She thought first—then the caretaker *must* be back. All the same, who,   5 seeing the house shuttered, would have dropped a letter in at the box? It was not a circular, it was not a bill. And the post office redirected, to the address in the country, everything for her that came through the post. The caretaker (even if he *were* back) did not know she was due in London today—her call here had been planned to be a surprise—so his negligence in the manner of this letter, leaving it to wait in the dusk and the dust, annoyed her. Annoyed, she picked up the letter, which bore no stamp. But it cannot be important, or they would know . . . She took the letter rapidly upstairs with her, without a stop to look at the writing till she reached what had been her bedroom, where she let in light. The room looked over the garden and other gardens: the sun had gone in; as the clouds sharpened and lowered, the trees and rank lawns seemed already to smoke with dark. Her reluctance to look again at the letter came from the fact that she felt intruded upon—and by someone contemptuous of her ways. However, in the tenseness preceding the fall of rain she read it: it was a few lines.

> Dear Kathleen: You will not have forgotten that today is our anniversary, and the day we said. The years have gone by at once slowly and fast. In view of the fact that nothing has changed, I shall rely upon you to keep your promise. I was sorry to see you leave London, but was satisfied that you would be back in time. You may expect me, therefore, at the hour arranged. Until then . . .
>
>   K.

Mrs. Drover looked for the date: it was today's. She dropped the letter on to the bed-springs, then picked it up to see the writing again—her lips, beneath the remains of lipstick, beginning to go white. She felt so much the change in her own face that she went to the mirror, polished a clear patch in it, and looked at once urgently and stealthily in. She was confronted by a woman of forty-four, with eyes starting out under a hat-brim that had been rather carelessly pulled down. She had not put on any more powder since she left the shop where she ate her solitary tea. The pearls her husband had given her on their marriage hung loose around her now rather thinner throat, slipping in the V of the pink wool jumper her sister knitted last autumn as they sat round the fire. Mrs. Drover's most normal expression was one of controlled worry, but of assent. Since the birth of the third of her little boys, attended by a quite serious illness, she had had an intermittent muscular flicker to the left of her mouth, but in spite of this she could always sustain a manner that was at once energetic and calm.

Turning from her own face as precipitately as she had gone to meet it, she went to the chest where the things were, unlocked it, threw up the lid, and knelt to search. But as rain began to come crashing down she could not keep from looking over her shoulder at the stripped bed on which the letter lay. Behind the blanket of rain the clock of the church that still stood struck six—with rapidly heightening apprehension she counted each of the slow strokes. "The hour arranged . . . My God," she said, "what hour? How should I . . . ? After twenty-five years . . ."

The young girl talking to the soldier in the garden had not ever completely seen his face. It was dark; they were saying goodbye under a tree. Now and then—for it felt, from not seeing him at this intense moment, as though she had never seen him at all—she verified his presence for these few moments longer by putting out a hand, which he each time pressed, without very much kindness, and painfully, on to one of the breast buttons of his uniform. That cut of the button on the palm of her hand was, principally, what she was to carry away. This was so near the end of a leave from France that she could only wish him already gone. It was August 1916. Being not kissed, being drawn away from and looked at intimidated Kathleen till she imagined spectral glitters in the place of his eyes. Turning away and looking back up the lawn she saw, through branches of trees, the drawing-room window light: she caught a breath for the moment when she could go running back there into the safe arms of her mother and sister, and cry: "What shall I do, what shall I do? He has gone."

Hearing her catch her breath, her fiancé said, without feeling: "Cold?"

"You're going away such a long way."

"Not so far as you think."   10

"I don't understand?"

"You don't have to," he said. "You will. You know what we said."

"But that was—suppose you—I mean, suppose."

"I shall be with you," he said, "sooner or later. You won't forget that. You need do nothing but wait."

Only a little more than a minute later she was free to run up the silent 15 lawn. Looking in through the window at her mother and sister, who did not for the moment perceive her, she already felt that unnatural promise drive down between her and the rest of all human kind. No other way of having given herself could have made her feel so apart, lost and foresworn. She could not have plighted a more sinister troth.

Kathleen behaved well when, some months later, her fiancé was reported missing, presumed killed. Her family not only supported her but were able to praise her courage without stint because they could not regret, as a husband for her, the man they knew almost nothing about. They hoped she would, in a year or two, console herself—and had it been only a question of consolation things might have gone much straighter ahead. But her trouble, behind just a little grief, was a complete dislocation from everything. She did not reject other lovers, for these failed to appear: for years she failed to attract men—and with the approach of her thirties she became natural enough to share her family's anxiousness on this score. She began to put herself out, to wonder; and at thirty-two she was very greatly relieved to find herself being courted by William Drover. She married him, and the two of them settled down in this quiet, arboreal part of Kensington: in this house the years piled up, her children were born, and they all lived till they were driven out by the bombs of the next war. Her movements as Mrs. Drover were circumscribed, and she dismissed any idea that they were still watched.

As things were—dead or living the letter-writer sent her only a threat. Unable, for some minutes, to go on kneeling with her back exposed to the empty room, Mrs. Drover rose from the chest to sit on an upright chair whose back was firmly against the wall. The desuetude of her former bedroom, her married London home's whole air of being a cracked cup from which memory, with its reassuring power, had either evaporated or leaked away, made a crisis—and at just this crisis the letter-writer had, knowledgeably, struck. The hollowness of the house this evening canceled years on years of voices, habits, and steps. Through the shut windows she only heard rain fall on the roofs around. To rally herself, she said she was in a mood—and for two or three seconds shutting her eyes, told herself that she had imagined the letter. But she opened them—there it lay on the bed.

On the supernatural side of the letter's entrance she was not permitting her mind to dwell. Who, in London, knew she meant to call at the house today? Evidently, however, this had been known. The caretaker, had he come back, had had no cause to expect her: he would have taken the letter in his pocket, to forward it, at his own time, through the post. There was no other sign that the caretaker had been in—but, if not? Letters dropped in at doors of deserted houses do not fly or walk to tables in halls. They do not sit on the dust of empty tables with the air of certainty that they will be found. There is needed some human hand—but nobody but the caretaker had a key. Under circumstances she did not care to consider, a house can be entered without a key. It was possible that she was not alone now. She might be being waited for, downstairs. Waited for—until when? Until "the hour arranged." At least that was not six o'clock: six has struck.

She rose from the chair and went over and locked the door.

The thing was, to get out. To fly? No, not that: she had to catch her train. As a woman whose utter dependability was the keystone of her family life she was not willing to return to the country, to her husband, her little boys, and her sister, without the objects she had come up to fetch. Resuming work at the chest she set about making up a number of parcels in a rapid, fumbling-decisive way. These, with her shopping parcels, would be too much to carry; these meant a taxi—at the thought of the taxi her heart went up and her normal breathing resumed. I will ring up the taxi now; the taxi cannot come too soon: I shall hear the taxi out there running its engine, till I walk calmly down to it through the hall. I'll ring up—But no: the telephone is cut off . . . She tugged at a knot she had tied wrong.

The idea of flight . . . He was never kind to me, not really. I don't remember him kind at all. Mother said he never considered me. He was set on me, that was what it was—not love. Not love, not meaning a person well. What did he do, to make me promise like that? I can't remember—But she found that she could.

She remembered with such dreadful acuteness that the twenty-five years since then dissolved like smoke and she instinctively looked for the weal left by the button on the palm of her hand. She remembered not only all that he said and did but the complete suspension of her existence during that August week. I was not myself—they all told me so at the time. She remembered—but with one white burning blank as where acid has dropped on a photograph: *under no conditions* could she remember his face.

So, wherever he may be waiting, I shall not know him. You have no time to run from a face you do not expect.

The thing was to get to the taxi before any clock struck what could be the hour. She would slip down the street and round the side of the square to where the square gave on the main road. She would return in the taxi, safe, to her own door, and bring the solid driver into the house with her to pick up the parcels from room to room. The idea of the taxi driver made her decisive, bold: she unlocked her door, went to the top of the staircase, and listened down.

She heard nothing—but while she was hearing nothing the *passé* air of the staircase was disturbed by a draught that traveled up to her face. It emanated from the basement: down there a door or window was being opened by someone who chose this moment to leave the house.

The rain had stopped; the pavements steamily shone as Mrs. Drover let herself out by inches from her own front door into the empty street. The unoccupied houses opposite continued to meet her look with their damaged stare. Making towards the thoroughfare and the taxi, she tried not to keep looking behind. Indeed, the silence was so intense—one of those creeks of London silence exaggerated this summer by the damage of war—that no tread could have gained on hers unheard. Where her street debouched on the square where people went on living, she grew conscious of, and checked, her unnatural pace. Across the open end of the square two buses impassively passed each other: women, a perambulator, cyclists, a man wheeling a barrow signalized, once again, the ordinary flow of life. At the square's most populous corner should be—and was—the short taxi rank. This evening, only one taxi—but this, although it presented its blank rump, appeared already to be alertly waiting for her. Indeed, without looking round the driver started his engine as she panted up from behind and put her hand on the door. As she did so, the clock struck seven. The taxi faced the main road: to make the trip back to her house it would have to turn—she had settled back on the seat and the taxi *had* turned before she, surprised by its knowing movement, recollected that she had not "said where." She leaned forward to scratch at the glass panel that divided the driver's head from her own.

The driver braked to what was almost a stop, turned round, and slid the glass panel back: the jolt of this flung Mrs. Drover forward till her face was almost into the glass. Through the aperture driver and passenger, not six inches between them, remained for an eternity eye to eye. Mrs. Drover's mouth hung open for some seconds before she could issue her first scream. After that she continued to scream freely and to beat with her gloved hands on the glass all round as the taxi, accelerating without mercy, made off with her into the hinterland of deserted streets.

[1941]

■ TOPICS FOR DISCUSSION AND WRITING

1. In a paragraph explain how Mrs. Drover's home helps to characterize her life. In a second paragraph, indicate to what degree she is a sympathetic figure. Be sure to support your view with evidence from the text.
2. Evaluate the view that the story is about a woman whose earlier frustration in love led to a nervous breakdown, and that the sight of the house now triggers hallucinations concerning a letter, a man leaving the basement, and a taxi driver.
3. In an essay of 500 words argue that the story is (1) a ghost story, or (2) a story about a woman with hallucinations; or (3) show that neither of these two views can be argued conclusively.
4. If you have read Joyce Carol Oates's "Where Are You Going" (page 294), in two paragraphs compare Bowen's demon lover and Arnold Friend.

■ JOHN CHEEVER
_____

John Cheever (1912–1982) was born in Quincy, Massachusetts. His father was a businessman who deserted his family after the crash of 1929; his mother was an Englishwoman who, after the father's desertion, operated a successful gift shop. When Cheever was expelled from school for being a troublesome youth (he smoked, and his grades were poor), he wrote a story about it, which he published in 1930 (he was not yet eighteen) in *The New Republic*. He was chiefly a writer of short stories—many were published in *The New Yorker*—but one of his novels, *The Wapshot Chronicle*, won the National Book Award for 1957. In 1978 his collected short stories won the Pulitzer Prize.

His characters are usually affluent suburbanites who, so to speak, are put on trial.

The Enormous Radio

Jim and Irene Westcott were the kind of people who seem to strike that satisfactory average of income, endeavor, and respectability that is reached by the statistical reports in college alumni bulletins. They were the parents of two young children, they had been married nine years, they lived on the twelfth floor of an apartment house near Sutton Place,[1] they went to the theatre on an average of 10.3 times a year, and they hoped someday to live

_____

[1] **Sutton Place** a fashionable address in New York City. Westchester, mentioned in the next sentence, is an affluent suburb.

in Westchester. Irene Westcott was a pleasant, rather plain girl with soft brown hair and a wide, fine forehead upon which nothing at all had been written, and in the cold weather she wore a coat of fitch skins died to resemble mink. You could not say that Jim Westcott looked younger than he was, but you could at least say of him that he seemed to feel younger. He wore his graying hair cut very short, he dressed in the kind of clothes his class had worn at Andover,[2] and his manner was earnest, vehement, and intentionally naïve. The Westcotts differed from their friends, their classmates, and their neighbors only in an interest they shared in serious music. They went to a great many concerts—although they seldom mentioned this to anyone—and they spent a good deal of time listening to music on the radio.

Their radio was an old instrument, sensitive, unpredictable, and beyond repair. Neither of them understood the mechanics of radio—or of any of the other appliances that surrounded them—and when the instrument faltered, Jim would strike the side of the cabinet with his hand. This sometimes helped. One Sunday afternoon, in the middle of a Schubert[3] quartet, the music faded away altogether. Jim struck the cabinet repeatedly, but there was no response; the Schubert was lost to them forever. He promised to buy Irene a new radio, and on Monday when he came home from work he told her that he had got one. He refused to describe it, and said it would be a surprise for her when it came.

The radio was delivered at the kitchen door the following afternoon, and with the assistance of her maid and the handyman Irene uncrated it and brought it into the living room. She was struck at once with the physical ugliness of the large gumwood cabinet. Irene was proud of her living room, she had chosen its furnishings and colors as carefully as she chose her clothes, and now it seemed to her that the new radio stood among her intimate possessions like an aggressive intruder. She was confounded by the number of dials and switches on the instrument panel, and she studied them thoroughly before she put the plug into a wall socket and turned the radio on. The dials flooded with a malevolent green light, and in the distance she heard the music of a piano quintet. The quintet was in the distance for only an instant; it bore down upon her with a speed greater than light and filled the apartment with the noise of music amplified so mightily that it knocked a china ornament from a table to the floor. She rushed to the instrument and reduced the volume. The violent forces that were snared in the ugly gumwood cabinet made her uneasy. Her children came home from school then, and she took them to the Park. It was not until later in the afternoon that she was able to return to the radio.

The maid had given the children their suppers and was supervising their baths when Irene turned on the radio, reduced the volume, and sat down to listen to a Mozart[4] quintet that she knew and enjoyed. The music came through clearly. The new instrument had a much purer tone, she thought, than the old one. She decided that tone was most important and that she

[2] **Andover** a distinguished boarding school in Massachusetts
[3] **Schubert** Franz Peter Schubert (1797–1828), Austrian composer
[4] **Mozart** Wolfgang Amadeus Mozart (1756–1791), Austrian Composer

could conceal the cabinet behind a sofa. But as soon as she had made her peace with the radio, the interference began. A crackling sound like the noise of a burning powder fuse began to accompany the singing of the strings. Beyond the music, there was a rustling that reminded Irene unpleasantly of the sea, and as the quintet progressed, these noises were joined by many others. She tried all the dials and switches but nothing dimmed the interference, and she sat down, disappointed and bewildered, and tried to trace the flight of the melody. The elevator shaft in her building ran beside the living-room wall, and it was the noise of the elevator that gave her a clue to the character of the static. The rattling of the elevator cables and the opening and closing of the elevator doors were reproduced in her loudspeaker, and, realizing that the radio was sensitive to electrical currents of all sorts, she began to discern through the Mozart the ringing of telephone bells, the dialing of phones, and the lamentation of a vacuum cleaner. By listening more carefully, she was able to distinguish doorbells, elevator bells, electric razors, and Waring mixers, whose sounds had been picked up from the apartments that surrounded hers and transmitted through her loudspeaker. The powerful and ugly instrument, with its mistaken sensitivity to discord, was more than she could hope to master, so she turned the thing off and went into the nursery to see her children.

When Jim Westcott came home that night, he went to the radio confidently and worked the controls. He had the same sort of experience Irene had had. A man was speaking on the station Jim had chosen, and his voice swung instantly from the distance into a force so powerful that it shook the apartment. Jim turned the volume control and reduced the voice. Then, a minute or two later, the interference began. The ringing of telephones and doorbells set in, joined by the rasp of the elevator doors and the whir of cooking appliances. The character of the noise had changed since Irene had tried the radio earlier; the last of the electric razors was being unplugged, the vacuum cleaners had all been returned to their closets, and the static reflected that change in pace that overtakes the city after the sun goes down. He fiddled with the knobs but couldn't get rid of the noises, so he turned the radio off and told Irene that in the morning he'd call the people who had sold it to him and give them hell.

The following afternoon, when Irene returned to the apartment from a luncheon date, the maid told her that a man had come and fixed the radio. Irene went into the living room before she took off her hat or her furs and tried the instrument. From the loudspeaker came a recording of the "Missouri Waltz." It reminded her of the thin, scratchy music from an old-fashioned phonograph that she sometimes heard across the lake where she spent her summers. She waited until the waltz had finished, expecting an explanation of the recording, but there was none. The music was followed by silence, and then the plaintive and scratchy record was repeated. She turned the dial and got a satisfactory burst of Caucasian music—the thump of bare feet in the dust and the rattle of coin jewelry—but in the background she could hear the ringing of bells and a confusion of voices. Her children came home from school then, and she turned off the radio and went to the nursery.

When Jim came home that night, he was tired, and he took a bath and changed his clothes. Then he joined Irene in the living room. He had just turned on the radio when the maid announced dinner, so he left it on, and he and Irene went to the table.

Jim was too tired to make even pretense of sociability, and there was nothing about the dinner to hold Irene's interest, so her attention wandered from the food to the deposits of silver polish on the candlesticks and from there to the music in the other room. She listened for a few minutes to a Chopin[5] prelude and then was surprised to hear a man's voice break in. "For Christ's sake, Kathy," he said, "do you always have to play the piano when I get home?" The music stopped abruptly. "It's the only chance I have," a woman said. "I'm at the office all day." "So am I," the man said. He added something obscene about an upright piano, and slammed a door. The passionate and melancholy music began again.

"Did you hear that?" Irene asked.

"What?" Jim was eating his dessert.

"The radio. A man said something while the music was still going on— something dirty."

"It's probably a play."

"I don't think it *is* a play," Irene said.

They left the table and took their coffee into the living room. Irene asked Jim to try another station. He turned the knob. "Have you seen my garters?" a man asked. "Button me up," a woman said. "Have you seen my garters?" the man said again. "Just button me up and I'll find your garters," the woman said. Jim shifted to another station. "I wish you wouldn't leave apple cores in the ashtrays," a man said. "I hate the smell."

"This is strange," Jim said.

"Isn't it?" Irene said.

Jim turned the knob again. " 'On the coast of Coromandel where the early pumpkins blow,' " a woman with a pronounced English accent said, " 'in the middle of the woods lived the Yonghy-Bonghy-Bò. Two old chairs, and half a candle, one old jug without a handle. . . . ' "[6]

"My God!" Irene cried. "That's the Sweeneys' nurse."

" 'These were all his worldly goods,' " the British voice continued.

"Turn that thing off," Irene said. "Maybe they can hear *us*." Jim switched the radio off. "That was Miss Armstrong, the Sweeneys' nurse," Irene said. "She must be reading to the little girl. They live in 17-B. I've talked with Miss Armstrong in the Park. I know her voice very well. We must be getting other people's apartments."

"That's impossible," Jim said.

"Well, that was the Sweeneys' nurse," Irene said hotly. "I know her voice. I know it very well. I'm wondering if they can hear us."

Jim turned the switch. First from a distance and then nearer, nearer, as if borne on the wind, came the pure accents of the Sweeneys' nurse again: " *'Lady Jingly! Lady Jingly!'* " she said, " *'sitting where the pumpkins blow, will you come and be my wife?* said the Yonghy-Bonghy-Bó. . . . ' "

[5] **Chopin** Frédéric François Chopin (1810–1849), Polish composer
[6] **"On the coast . . . a handle"** from "The Courtship of Yonghy-Bonghy-Bò," by Edward Lear (1812–1888)

Jim went over to the radio and said "Hello" loudly into the speaker.

" '*I am tired of living singly,*' " the nurse went on, " '*on this coast so wild and shingly, I'm a-weary of my life; if you'll come and be my wife, quite serene would be my life. . . .* ' "

"I guess she can't hear us," Irene said. "Try something else."

Jim turned to another station, and the living room was filled with the uproar of a cocktail party that had overshot its mark. Someone was playing the piano and singing the "Whiffenpoof Song," and the voices that surrounded the piano were vehement and happy. "Eat some more sandwiches," a woman shrieked. There were screams of laughter and a dish of some sort crashed to the floor.

"Those must be the Fullers, in 11-E," Irene said. "I knew they were giving a party this afternoon. I saw her in the liquor store. Isn't this too divine? Try something else. See if you can get those people in 18-C."

The Westcotts overheard that evening a monologue on salmon fishing in Canada, a bridge game, running comments on home movies of what had apparently been a fortnight at Sea Island, and a bitter family quarrel about an overdraft at the bank. They turned off their radio at midnight and went to bed, weak with laughter. Sometime in the night, their son began to call for a glass of water and Irene got one and took it to his room. It was very early. All the lights in the neighborhood were extinguished, and from the boy's window she could see the empty street. She went into the living room and tried the radio. There was some faint coughing, a moan, and then a man spoke. "Are you all right, darling?" he asked. "Yes," a woman said wearily. "Yes, I'm all right, I guess," and then she added with great feeling, "But, you know, Charlie, I don't feel like myself any more. Sometimes there are about fifteen or twenty minutes in the week when I feel like myself. I don't like to go to another doctor, because the doctor's bills are so awful already, but I just don't feel like myself, Charlie. I just never feel like myself." They were not young, Irene thought. She guessed from the timbre of their voices that they were middle-aged. The restrained melancholy of the dialogue and the draft from the bedroom window made her shiver, and she went back to bed.

The following morning, Irene cooked breakfast for the family—the maid didn't come up from her room in the basement until ten—braided her daughter's hair, and waited at the door until her children and her husband had been carried away in the elevator. Then she went into the living room and tried the radio. "I don't want to go to school," a child screamed. "I hate school. I won't go to school. I hate school." "You will go to school," an enraged woman said. "We paid eight hundred dollars to get you into that school and you'll go if it kills you." The next number on the dial produced the worn record of the "Missouri Waltz." Irene shifted the control and invaded the privacy of several breakfast tables. She overheard demonstrations of indigestion, carnal love, abysmal vanity, faith, and despair. Irene's life was nearly as simple and sheltered as it appeared to be, and the forthright and sometimes brutal language that came from the loudspeaker that morning astonished and troubled her. She continued to listen until her maid came in. Then she turned off the radio quickly, since this insight, she realized, was a furtive one.

Irene had a luncheon date with a friend that day, and she left her apartment at a little after twelve. There were a number of women in the elevator when it stopped at her floor. She stared at their handsome and impassive faces, their furs, and the cloth flowers in their hats. Which one of them had been to Sea Island? she wondered. Which one had overdrawn her bank account? The elevator stopped at the tenth floor and a woman with a pair of Skye terriers joined them. Her hair was rigged high on her head and she wore a mink cape. She was humming the "Missouri Waltz."

Irene had two Martinis at lunch, and she looked searchingly at her friend and wondered what her secrets were. They had intended to go shopping after lunch, but Irene excused herself and went home. She told the maid that she was not to be disturbed; then she went into the living room, closed the doors, and switched on the radio. She heard, in the course of the afternoon, the halting conversation of a woman entertaining her aunt, the hysterical conclusion of a luncheon party, and a hostess briefing her maid about some cocktail guests. "Don't give the best Scotch to anyone who hasn't white hair," the hostess said. "See if you can get rid of that liver paste before you pass those hot things, and could you lend me five dollars? I want to tip the elevator man."

As the afternoon waned, the conversations increased in intensity. From where Irene sat, she could see the open sky above the East River. There were hundreds of clouds in the sky, as though the south wind had broken the winter into pieces and were blowing it north, and on her radio she could hear the arrival of cocktail guests and the return of children and businessmen from their schools and offices. "I found a good-sized diamond on the bathroom floor this morning," a woman said. "It must have fallen out of that bracelet Mrs. Dunston was wearing last night." "We'll sell it," a man said. "Take it down to the jeweler on Madison Avenue and sell it. Mrs. Dunston won't know the difference, and we could use a couple of hundred bucks. . . . " " 'Oranges and lemons, say the bells of St. Clement's,' " the Sweeneys' nurse sang. " 'Halfpence and farthings, say the bells of St. Martin's. When will you pay me? say the bells at old Bailey. . . . ' " "It's not a hat," a woman cried, and at her back roared a cocktail party. "It's not a hat, it's a love affair. That's what Walter Florell said. He said it's not a hat, it's a love affair," and then, in a lower voice, the same woman added, "Talk to somebody, for Christ's sake, honey, talk to somebody. If she catches you standing here not talking to anybody, she'll take us off her invitation list, and I love these parties."

The Westcotts were going out for dinner that night, and when Jim came home, Irene was dressing. She seemed sad and vague, and he brought her a drink. They were dining with friends in the neighborhood, and they walked to where they were going. The sky was broad and filled with light. It was one of those splendid spring evenings that excite memory and desire, and the air that touched their hands and faces felt very soft. A Salvation Army band was on the corner playing "Jesus Is Sweeter." Irene drew on her husband's arm and held him there for a minute, to hear the music. "They're really such nice people, aren't they?" she said. "They have such nice faces. Actually, they're so much nicer than a lot of the people we know." She took a bill from her purse and walked over and dropped it into the tambourine. There was in her face, when she returned to her husband, a look of radiant melancholy that he was not familiar with. And her conduct at the dinner party that night seemed strange to him, too. She interrupted her hostess rudely and stared at the people across the table from her with an intensity for which she would have punished her children.

It was still mild when they walked home from the party, and Irene looked up at the spring stars. " 'How far that little candle throws its beams,' " she exclaimed. " 'So shines a good deed in a naughty world.' " [7] She waited that night until Jim had fallen asleep, and then went into the living room and turned on the radio.

Jim came home at about six the next night. Emma, the maid, let him in, and he had taken off his hat and was taking off his coat when Irene ran into the hall. Her face was shining with tears and her hair was disordered. "Go up to 16-C, Jim!" she screamed. "Don't take off your coat. Go up to 16-C. Mr. Osborn's beating his wife. They've been quarreling since four o'clock, and now he's hitting her. Go up there and stop him."

From the radio in the living room, Jim heard screams, obscenities, and thuds. "You know you don't have to listen to this sort of thing," he said. He strode into the living room and turned the switch. "It's indecent," he said. "It's like looking in windows. You know you don't have to listen to this sort of thing. You can turn it off."

"Oh, it's so horrible, it's so dreadful," Irene was sobbing. "I've been listening all day, and it's so depressing."

"Well, if it's so depressing, why do you listen to it? I bought this damned radio to give you pleasure," he said. "I paid a great deal of money for it. I thought it might make you happy. I wanted to make you happy."

"Don't, don't don't, don't quarrel with me," she moaned, and laid her head on his shoulder. "All the others have been quarreling all day. Everybody's been quarreling. They're all worried about money. Mrs. Hutchinson's mother is dying of cancer in Florida and they don't have enough money to send her to the Mayo Clinic. At least, Mr. Hutchinson says they don't have enough money. And some woman in this building is having an affair with the handyman—with that hideous handyman. It's too disgusting. And Mrs. Melville has heart trouble and Mr. Hendricks is going to lose his job in April and Mrs. Hendricks is horrid about the whole thing and that girl who plays the 'Missouri Waltz' is a whore, a common whore, and the elevator man has tuberculosis and Mr. Osborn has been beating Mrs. Osborn." She wailed, she trembled with grief and checked the stream of tears down her face with the heel of her palm.

"Well, why do you have to listen?" Jim asked again. "Why do you have to listen to this stuff if it makes you so miserable?"

"Oh, don't, don't, don't," she cried. "Life is too terrible, too sordid and awful. But we've never been like that, have we, darling? Have we? I mean, we've always been good and decent and loving to one another, haven't we? And we have two children, two beautiful children. Our lives aren't sordid, are they, darling? Are they?" She flung her arms around his neck and drew his face down to hers. "We're happy, aren't we, darling? We are happy, aren't we?"

[7] **How far . . . world** from Shakespeare's *The Merchant of Venice*, V. i. 101–102

"Of course we're happy," he said tiredly. He began to surrender his resentment. "Of course we're happy. I'll have that damned radio fixed or taken away tomorrow." He stroked her soft hair. "My poor girl," he said.

"You love me, don't you?" she asked. "And we're not hypercritical or worried about money or dishonest, are we?"

"No, darling," he said.

A man came in the morning and fixed the radio. Irene turned it on cautiously and was happy to hear a California-wine commercial and a recording of Beethoven's[8] Ninth Symphony, including Schiller's "Ode to Joy." She kept the radio on all day and nothing untoward came from the speaker.

A Spanish suite was being played when Jim came home. "Is everything all right?" he asked. His face was pale, she thought. They had some cocktails and went in to dinner to the "Anvil Chorus" from *Il Trovatore*. This was followed by Debussy's "La Mer."

"I paid the bill for the radio today," Jim said. It cost four hundred dollars. I hope you'll get some enjoyment out of it."

"Oh, I'm sure I will," Irene said.

"Four hundred dollars is a good deal more than I can afford," he went on. "I wanted to get something that you'd enjoy. It's the last extravagance we'll be able to indulge in this year. I see that you haven't paid your clothing bills yet. I saw them on your dressing table." He looked directly at her. "Why did you tell me you'd paid them? Why did you lie to me?"

"I just didn't want you to worry, Jim," she said. She drank some water. "I'll be able to pay my bills out of this month's allowance. There were the slipcovers last month, and that party."

"You've got to learn to handle the money I give you a little more intelligently, Irene," he said. "You've got to understand that we don't have as much money this year as we had last. I had a very sobering talk with Mitchell today. No one is buying anything. We're spending all our time promoting new issues, and you know how long that takes. I'm not getting any younger, you know. I'm thirty-seven. My hair will be gray next year. I haven't done as well as I'd hoped to do. And I don't suppose things will get any better."

"Yes, dear," she said.

"We've got to start cutting down," Jim said. "We've got to think of the children. To be perfectly frank with you, I worry about money a great deal. I'm not at all sure of the future. No one is. If anything should happen to me, there's the insurance, but that wouldn't go very far today. I've worked awfully hard to give you and the children a comfortable life," he said bitterly. "I don't like to see all my energies, all of my youth, wasted in fur coats and radios and slipcovers and—"

"Please, Jim," she said. "Please. They'll hear us."

"*Who'll hear us?* Emma can't hear us."

"The radio."

"Oh, I'm sick!" he shouted. "I'm sick to death of your apprehensiveness.

[8]**Beethoven** Ludwig van Beethoven (1770–1827), German composer. Other names mentioned in the next few lines are: Johann Christian Friedrich von Schiller (1759–1805), German poet; *Il Trovatore*, opera by Giuseppe Verdi (1813–1901); Claude Achille Debussy (1862–1918), French composer.

The radio can't hear us. Nobody can hear us. And what if they can hear us? Who cares?"

Irene got up from the table and went into the living room. Jim went to the door and shouted at her from there. "Why are you so Christly all of a sudden? What's turned you overnight into a convent girl? You stole your mother's jewelry before they probated her will. You never gave your sister a cent of that money that was intended for her—not even when she needed it. You made Grace Howland's life miserable, and where was all your piety and your virtue when you went to that abortionist? I'll never forget how cool you were. You packed your bag and went off to have that child murdered as if you were going to Nassau. If you'd had any reasons, if you'd had any good reasons—"

Irene stood for a minute before the hideous cabinet, disgraced and sickened, but she held her hand on the switch before she extinguished the music and the voices, hoping that the instrument might speak to her kindly, that she might hear the Sweeneys' nurse. Jim continued to shout at her from the door. The voice on the radio was suave and noncommittal. "An early-morning railroad disaster in Tokyo," the loudspeaker said, "killed twenty-nine people. A fire in a Catholic hospital near Buffalo for the care of blind children was extinguished early this morning by nuns. The temperature is forty-seven. The humidity is eighty-nine."

[1947]

■ TOPICS FOR DISCUSSION AND WRITING

1. How are the Westcotts characterized in the first two paragraphs? What details particularly prepare you for their ordeal?
2. How early did you become aware that the radio is—to say the least—peculiar?
3. Overall, what effect does the radio have on the lives of the Westcotts? At the story's end are they better off than they were before they acquired the radio?
4. Is Cheever saying that no one is decent? Explain.
5. The story ends with the "suave and noncommittal" voice of a radio announcer reciting, first, the facts of two disasters and then the weather. What do you think this passage contributes to the story?
6. "The Enormous Radio" was published in 1947. Do you think the story could be written today? If so, what would you substitute for the radio? How would the substitution change the story?

■ RAY BRADBURY

Ray Bradbury (b. 1920) was born in Waukegan, Illinois, and educated there and in Los Angeles. While a high school student he published his first science fiction in the school's magazine, and by 1941 he was publishing professionally.

The story printed here is from *The Martian Chronicles* (1950), a collection of linked short stories. Among his other works are *Fahrenheit 451* (1953), *Something Wicked This Way Comes* (1962), and *Death Is a Lonely Business* (1985).

October 2026:

THE MILLION-YEAR PICNIC

Somehow the idea was brought up by Mom that perhaps the whole family would enjoy a fishing trip. But they weren't Mom's words; Timothy knew that. They were Dad's words, and Mom used them for him somehow.

Dad shuffled his feet in a clutter of Martian pebbles and agreed. So immediately there was a tumult and a shouting, and very quickly the camp was tucked into capsules and containers, Mom slipped into traveling jumpers and blouse, Dad stuffed his pipe full with trembling hands, his eyes on the Martian sky, and the three boys piled yelling into the motorboat, none of them really keeping an eye on Mom and Dad, except Timothy.

Dad pushed a stud. The water boat sent a humming sound up into the sky. The water shook back and the boat nosed ahead, and the family cried, "Hurrah!"

Timothy sat in the back of the boat with Dad, his small fingers atop Dad's hairy ones, watching the canal twist, leaving the crumbled place behind where they had landed in their small family rocket all the way from Earth. He remembered the night before they left Earth, the hustling and hurrying, the rocket that Dad had found somewhere, somehow, and the talk of a vacation on Mars. A long way to go for a vacation, but Timothy said nothing because of his younger brothers. They came to Mars and now, first thing, or so they said, they were going fishing.

Dad had a funny look in his eyes as the boat went up-canal. A look that 5 Timothy couldn't figure. It was made of strong light and maybe a sort of relief. It made the deep wrinkles laugh instead of worry or cry.

So there went the cooling rocket, around a bend, gone.

"How far are we going?" Robert splashed his hand. It looked like a small crab jumping in the violet water.

Dad exhaled. "A million years."

"Gee," said Robert.

"Look, kids." Mother pointed one soft long arm. "There's a dead city." 10

They looked with fervent anticipation and the dead city lay dead for them alone, drowsing in a hot silence of summer made on Mars by a Martian weatherman.

And Dad looked as if he was pleased that it was dead.

It was a futile spread of pink rocks sleeping on a rise of sand, a few tumbled pillars, one lonely shrine, and then the sweep of sand again. Nothing else for miles. A white desert around the canal and a blue desert over it.

Just then a bird flew up. Like a stone thrown across a blue pond, hitting, falling deep, and vanishing.

Dad got a frightened look when he saw it. "I thought it was a rocket." 15

Timothy looked at the deep ocean sky, trying to see Earth and the war and the ruined cities and the men killing each other since the day he was born. But he saw nothing. The war was as removed and far off as two flies battling to the death in the arch of a great high and silent cathedral. And just as senseless.

William Thomas wiped his forehead and felt the touch of his son's hand
on his arm, like a young tarantula, thrilled. He beamed at his son. "How goes
it, Timmy?"

"Fine, Dad."

Timothy hadn't quite figured out what was ticking inside the vast adult
mechanism beside him. The man with the immense hawk nose, sunburnt,
peeling—and the hot blue eyes like agate marbles you play with after school
in summer back on Earth, and the long thick columnar legs in the loose riding
breeches.

"What are you looking at so hard, Dad?"   20

"I was looking for Earthian logic, common sense, good government,
peace, and responsibility."

"All that up there?"

"No. I didn't find it. It's not there any more. Maybe it'll never be there
again. Maybe we fooled ourselves that it was ever there."

"Huh?"

"See the fish," said Dad, pointing.   25

There rose a soprano clamor from all three boys as they rocked the boat
in arching their tender necks to see. They *oohed* and *ahed*. A silver ring fish
floated by them, undulating, and closing like an iris, instantly, around food particles, to assimilate them.

Dad looked at it. His voice was deep and quiet.

"Just like war. War swims along, sees food, contracts. A moment later—
Earth is gone.

"William," said Mom.

"Sorry," said Dad.   30

They sat still and felt the canal water rush cool, swift and glassy. The
only sound was the motor hum, the glide of water, the sun expanding the air.

"When do we see the Martians?" cried Michael.

"Quite soon, perhaps," said Father. "Maybe tonight."

"Oh, but the Martians are a dead race now," said Mom.

"No, they're not. I'll show you some Martians, all right," Dad said 35
presently.

Timothy scowled at that but said nothing. Everything was odd now. Vaca-
tions and fishing and looks between people.

The other boys were already engaged making shelves of their small
hands and peering under them toward the seven-foot stone banks of the
canal, watching for Martians.

"What do they look like?" demanded Michael.

"You'll know them when you see them." Dad sort of laughed, and Timothy saw a pulse beating time in his cheek.

Mother was slender and soft, with a woven plait of spun-gold hair over 40
her head in a tiara, and eyes the color of the deep cool canal water where
it ran in shadow, almost purple, with flecks of amber caught in it. You could
see her thoughts swimming around in her eyes, like fish—some bright, some
dark, some fast, quick, some slow and easy, and sometimes, like when she
looked up where Earth was, being nothing but color, and nothing else. She

at in the boat's prow, one hand resting on the side lip, the other on the lap of her dark blue breeches, and a line of sunburnt soft neck showing where her blouse opened like a white flower.

She kept looking ahead to see what was there, and, not being able to see it clearly enough, she looked backward toward her husband, and through his eyes, reflected then, she saw what was ahead; and since he added part of himself to this reflection, a determined firmness, her face relaxed and she accepted it and she turned back, knowing suddenly what to look for.

Timothy looked too. But all he saw was a straight pencil line of canal going violet through a wide shallow valley penned by low, eroded hills, and on until it fell over the sky's edge. And this canal went on and on through cities that would have rattled like beetles in a dry skull if you shook them. A hundred or two hundred cities dreaming hot summer-day dreams and cool summer-night dreams.

They had come millions of miles for this outing—fish. But there had been a gun on the rocket. This was a vacation. But why all the food, more than enough to last them years and years, left hidden back there near the rocket? Vacation. Just behind the veil of the vacation was not a soft face of laughter, but something hard and bony and perhaps terrifying. Timothy could not lift the veil, and the two other boys were busy being ten and eight years old, respectively.

"No Martians yet. Nuts." Robert put his V-shaped chin on his hands and glared at the canal.

Dad had brought an atomic radio along, strapped to his wrist. It func- 45 tioned on an old-fashioned principle: you held it against the bones near your ear and it vibrated singing or talking to you. Dad listened to it now. His face looked like one of those fallen Martian cities, caved in, sucked dry, almost dead.

Then he gave it to Mom to listen. Her lips dropped open.

"What—— " Timothy started to question, but never finished what he wished to say.

For at that moment there were two titanic, marrow-jolting explosions that grew upon themselves, followed by a half-dozen minor concussions.

Jerking his head up, Dad notched the boat speed higher immediately. The boat leaped and jounced and spanked. This shook Robert out of his funk and elicited yelps of frightened but ecstatic joy from Michael, who clung to Mom's legs and watched the water pour by his nose in a wet torrent.

Dad swerved the boat, cut speed, and ducked the craft into a little branch 50 canal and under an ancient, crumbling stone wharf that smelled of crab flesh. The boat rammed the wharf hard enough to throw them all forward, but no one was hurt and Dad was already twisted to see if the ripples on the canal were enough to map their route into hiding. Water lines went across, lapped the stones, and rippled back to meet each other, settling, to be dappled by the sun. It all went away.

Dad listened. So did everybody.

Dad's breathing echoed like fists beating against the cold wet wharf stones. In the shadow, Mom's cat eyes just watched Father for some clue to what next.

Dad relaxed and blew out a breath, laughing at himself.

"The rocket, of course. I'm getting jumpy. The rocket."

Michael said, "What happened, Dad, what happened?" 55

"Oh, we just blew up our rocket, is all," said Timothy, trying to sound matter-of-fact. "I've heard rockets blown up before. Ours just blew."

"Why did we blow up our rocket?" asked Michael. "Huh, Dad?"

"It's part of the game, silly!" said Timothy.

"A game!" Michael and Robert loved the word.

"Dad fixed it so it would blow up and no one'd know where we landed 60 or went! In case they ever came looking, see?"

"Oh boy, a secret!"

"Scared by my own rocket," admitted Dad to Mom. "I *am* nervous. It's silly to think there'll ever be any more rockets. Except *one*, perhaps, if Edwards and his wife get through with *their* ship."

He put his tiny radio to his ear again. After two minutes he dropped his hand as you would drop a rag.

"It's over at last," he said to Mom. "The radio just went off the atomic beam. Every other world station's gone. They dwindled down to a couple in the last few years. Now the air's completely silent. It'll probably remain silent."

"For how long?" asked Robert. 65

"Maybe—your great-grandchildren will hear it again," said Dad. He just sat there, and the children were caught in the center of his awe and defeat and resignation and acceptance.

Finally he put the boat out into the canal again, and they continued in the direction in which they had originally started.

It was getting late. Already the sun was down the sky, and a series of dead cities lay ahead of them.

Dad talked very quietly and gently to his sons. Many times in the past he had been brisk, distant, removed from them, but now he patted them on the head with just a word and they felt it.

"Mike, pick a city." 70

"What, Dad?"

"Pick a city, Son. Any one of these cities we pass."

"All right," said Michael. "How do I pick?"

"Pick the one you like the most. You, too, Robert and Tim. Pick the city you like best."

"I want a city with Martians in it," said Michael. 75

"You'll have that," said Dad. "I promise." His lips were for the children, but his eyes were for Mom.

They passed six cities in twenty minutes. Dad didn't say anything more about the explosions; he seemed much more interested in having fun with his sons, keeping them happy, than anything else.

Michael liked the first city they passed, but this was vetoed because everyone doubted quick first judgments. The second city nobody liked. It was an Earth Man's settlement, built of wood and already rotting into sawdust. Timothy liked the third city because it was large. The fourth and fifth were too small and the sixth brought acclaim from everyone, including Mother, who joined in the Gees, Goshes, and Look-at-thats!

There were fifty or sixty huge structures still standing, streets were dusty but paved, and you could see one or two old centrifugal fountains still pulsing wetly in the plazas. That was the only life—water leaping in the late sunlight.

"This is the city," said everybody.   80

Steering the boat to a wharf, Dad jumped out.

"Here we are. This is ours. This is where we live from now on!"

"From now on?" Michael was incredulous. He stood up, looking, and then turned to blink back at where the rocket used to be. "What about the rocket? What about Minnesota?"

"Here," said Dad.

He touched the small radio to Michael's blond head. "Listen."   85
Michael listened.

"Nothing," he said.

"That's right. Nothing. Nothing at all any more. No more Minneapolis, no more rockets, no more Earth."

Michael considered the lethal revelation and began to sob little dry sobs.

"Wait a moment," said Dad the next instant. "I'm giving you a lot more   90
in exchange, Mike!"

"What?" Michael held off the tears, curious, but quite ready to continue in case Dad's further revelation was as disconcerting as the original.

"I'm giving you this city, Mike. It's yours."

"Mine?"

"For you and Robert and Timothy, all three of you, to own for your-selves."

Timothy bounded from the boat. "Look, guys, all for *us!* All of *that!*" He   95
was playing the game with Dad, playing it large and playing it well. Later, after it was all over and things had settled, he could go off by himself and cry for ten minutes. But now it was still a game, still a family outing, and the other kids must be kept playing.

Mike jumped out with Robert. They helped Mom.

"Be careful of your sister," said Dad, and nobody knew what he meant until later.

They hurried into the great pink-stoned city whispering among them-selves, because dead cities have a way of making you want to whisper, to watch the sun go down.

"In about five days," said Dad quietly, "I'll go back down to where our rocket was and collect the food hidden in the ruins there and bring it here; and I'll hunt for Bert Edwards and his wife and daughters there."

"Daughters?" asked Timothy. "How many?"   100
"Four."

"I can see that'll cause trouble later." Mom nodded slowly.

"Girls." Michael made a face like an ancient Martian stone image. "Girls."

"Are they coming in a rocket too?"

"Yes. If they make it. Family rockets are made for travel to the Moon,   105
not Mars. We were lucky we got through."

"Where did you get the rocket?" whispered Timothy, for the other boys were running ahead.

"I saved it. I saved it for twenty years, Tim. I had it hidden away, hoping I'd never have to use it. I suppose I should have given it to the government for the war, but I kept thinking about Mars. . . ."

"And a picnic!"

"Right. This is between you and me. When I saw everything was finishing on Earth, after I'd waited until the last moment, I packed us up. Bert Edwards had a ship hidden, too, but we decided it would be safer to take off separately, in case anyone tried to shoot us down."

"Why'd you blow up the rocket, Dad?"   110

"So we can't go back ever. And so if any of those evil men ever come to Mars they won't know we're here."

"Is that why you look up all the time?"

"Yes, it's silly. They won't follow us, ever. They haven't anything to follow with. I'm being too careful, is all."

Michael came running back. "Is this really *our* city, Dad?"

"The whole darn planet belongs to us, kids. The whole darn planet."   115

They stood there, King of the Hill, Top of the Heap, Ruler of All They Surveyed, Unimpeachable Monarchs and Presidents, trying to understand what it meant to own a world and how big a world really was.

Night came quickly in the thin atmosphere, and Dad left them in the square by the pulsing fountain, went down to the boat and came walking back carrying a stack of paper in his big hands.

He laid the papers in a clutter in an old courtyard and set them afire. To keep warm, they crouched around the blaze and laughed, and Timothy saw the little letters leap like frightened animals when the flames touched and engulfed them. The papers crinkled like an old man's skin and the cremation surrounded innumerable words:

"GOVERNMENT BONDS; Business Graph, 1999; Religious Prejudice: An Essay; The Science of Logistics; Problems of the Pan-American Unity; Stock Report for July 3, 1998; the War Digest . . ."

Dad had insisted on bringing these papers for this purpose. He sat there   120
and fed them into the fire, one by one, with satisfaction, and told his children what it all meant.

"It's time I told you a few things. I don't suppose it was fair, keeping so much from you. I don't know if you'll understand, but I have to talk even if only part of it gets over to you."

He dropped a leaf in the fire.

"I'm burning a way of life, just like that way of life is being burned clean of Earth right now. Forgive me if I talk like a politician. I am, after all, a former state governor, and I was honest and they hated me for it. Life on Earth never settled down to doing anything very good. Science ran too far ahead of us too quickly, and the people got lost in a mechanical wilderness, like children making over pretty things, gadgets, helicopters, rockets; emphasizing the wrong items, emphasizing machines instead of how to run the machines. Wars got bigger and bigger and finally killed Earth. That's what the silent radio means. That's what we ran away from.

"We were lucky. There aren't any more rockets left. It's time you knew this isn't a fishing trip at all. I put off telling you. Earth is gone. Interplanetary travel won't be back for centuries, maybe never. But that way of life proved itself wrong and strangled itself with its own hands. You're young. I'll tell you this again every day until it sinks in."

He paused to feed more papers to the fire.   125

"Now we're alone. We and a handful of others who'll land in a few days. Enough to start over. Enough to turn away from all that back on Earth and strike out on a new line—— "

The fire leaped up to emphasize his talking. And then all the papers were gone except one. All the laws and beliefs of Earth were burnt into small hot ashes which soon would be carried off in a wind.

Timothy looked at the last thing that Dad tossed in the fire. It was a map of the World, and it wrinkled and distorted itself hotly and went—flimpf—and was gone like a warm, black butterfly. Timothy turned away.

"Now I'm going to show you the Martians," said Dad. "Come on, all of you. Here, Alice." He took her hand.

Michael was crying loudly, and Dad picked him up and carried him, and   130 they walked down through the ruins toward the canal.

The canal. Where tomorrow or the next day their future wives would come up in a boat, small laughing girls now, with their father and mother.

The night came down around them, and there were stars. But Timothy couldn't find Earth. It had already set. That was something to think about.

A night bird called among the ruins as they walked. Dad said, "Your mother and I will try to teach you. Perhaps we'll fail. I hope not. We've had a good lot to see and learn from. We planned this trip years ago, before you were born. Even if there hadn't been a war we would have come to Mars, I think, to live and form our own standard of living. It would have been another century before Mars would have been really poisoned by the Earth civilization. Now, of course—— "

They reached the canal. It was long and straight and cool and wet and reflective in the night.

"I've always wanted to see a Martian," said Michael. "Where are they,   135 Dad? You promised."

"There they are," said Dad, and he shifted Michael on his shoulder and pointed straight down.

The Martians were there. Timothy began to shiver.

The Martians were there—in the canal—reflected in the water. Timothy and Michael and Robert and Mom and Dad.

The Martians stared back up at them for a long, long silent time from the rippling water. . . .

[1951]

■ TOPICS FOR DISCUSSION AND WRITING

1. Reread the story, marking on the first two or three pages those passages that turn out—in the light of the rest of the story—to be hints of something special that is to come.

2. Would the story be equally effective—or more so or less so—if the last sentence were omitted?

■ GABRIEL GARCÍA MÁRQUEZ

Gabriel García Márquez (b. 1928) was born in Aracataca, a small village in Colombia. After being educated in Bogota, where he studied journalism and law, he worked as a journalist in Latin America, Europe, and the United States. He began writing fiction when he was in Paris, and at twenty-seven he published his first novel, *La hojarasca* (*Leaf Storm*, 1955). During most of the 1960s he lived in Mexico, where he wrote film scripts and the novel that made him famous: *Cien años de soledad* (1967), translated in 1970 as *A Hundred Years of Solitude*. In 1982 García Márquez was awarded the Nobel Prize in Literature. A socialist, he now lives in Mexico because his presence is not welcome in Colombia.

A Very Old Man with Enormous Wings:

A TALE FOR CHILDREN

Translated by Gregory Rabassa

On the third day of rain they had killed so many crabs inside the house that Pelayo had to cross his drenched courtyard and throw them into the sea, because the newborn child had a temperature all night and they thought it was due to the stench. The world had been sad since Tuesday. Sea and sky were a single ash-gray thing and the sands of the beach, which on March nights glimmered like powdered light, had become a stew of mud and rotten shellfish. The light was so weak at noon that when Pelayo was coming back to the house after throwing away the crabs, it was hard for him to see what it was that was moving and groaning in the rear of the courtyard. He had to go very close to see that it was an old man, a very old man, lying face down in the mud, who, in spite of his tremendous efforts, couldn't get up, impeded by his enormous wings.

Frightened by that nightmare, Pelayo ran to get Elisenda, his wife, who was putting compresses on the sick child, and he took her to the rear of the courtyard. They both looked at the fallen body with mute stupor. He was dressed like a ragpicker. There were only a few faded hairs left on his bald skull and very few teeth in his mouth, and his pitiful condition of a drenched great-grandfather had taken away any sense of grandeur he might have had. His huge buzzard wings, dirty and half-plucked, were forever entangled in the mud. They looked at him so long and so closely that Pelayo and Elisenda very soon overcame their surprise and in the end found him familiar. Then they dared speak to him, and he answered in an incomprehensible dialect with a strong sailor's voice. That was how they skipped over the inconvenience of the wings and quite intelligently concluded that he was a lonely castaway from some foreign ship wrecked by the storm. And yet, they called in a neighbor woman who knew everything about life and death to see him, and all she needed was one look to show them their mistake.

"He's an angel," she told them. "He must have been coming for the child, but the poor fellow is so old that the rain knocked him down."

On the following day everyone knew that a flesh-and-blood angel was held captive in Pelayo's house. Against the judgment of the wise neighbor woman, for whom angels in those times were the fugitive survivors of a celestial conspiracy, they did not have the heart to club him to death. Pelayo watched over him all afternoon from the kitchen, armed with his bailiff's club, and before going to bed he dragged him out of the mud and locked him up with the hens in the wire chicken coop. In the middle of the night, when the rain stopped, Pelayo and Elisenda were still killing crabs. A short time afterward the child woke up without a fever and with a desire to eat. Then they felt magnanimous and decided to put the angel on a raft with fresh water and provisions for three days and leave him to his fate on the high seas. But when they went out into the courtyard with the first light of dawn, they found the whole neighborhood in front of the chicken coop having fun with the angel, without the slightest reverence, tossing him things to eat through the openings in the wire as if he weren't a supernatural creature but a circus animal.

Father Gonzaga arrived before seven o'clock, alarmed at the strange 5 news. By that time onlookers less frivolous than those at dawn had already arrived and they were making all kinds of conjectures concerning the captive's future. The simplest among them thought that he should be named mayor of the world. Others of sterner mind felt that he should be promoted to the rank of five-star general in order to win all wars. Some visionaries hoped that he could be put to stud in order to implant on earth a race of winged wise men who could take charge of the universe. But Father Gonzaga, before becoming a priest, had been a robust woodcutter. Standing by the wire, he reviewed his catechism in an instant and asked them to open the door so that he could take a close look at that pitiful man who looked more like a huge decrepit hen among the fascinated chickens. He was lying in a corner drying his open wings in the sunlight among the fruit peels and breakfast leftovers that the early risers had thrown him. Alien to the impertinences of the world, he only lifted his antiquarian eyes and murmured something in his dialect when Father Gonzaga went into the chicken coop and said good morning to him in Latin. The parish priest had his first suspicion of an imposter when he saw that he did not understand the language of God or know how to greet His ministers. Then he noticed that seen close up he was much too human: he had an unbearable smell of the outdoors, the back side of his wings was strewn with parasites and his main feathers had been mistreated by terrestrial winds, and nothing about him measured up to the proud dignity of angels. Then he came out of the chicken coop and in a brief sermon warned the curious against the risks of being ingenuous. He reminded them that the devil had the bad habit of making use of carnival tricks in order to confuse the unwary. He argued that if wings were not the essential element in determining the difference between a hawk and an airplane, they were even less so in the recognition of angels. Nevertheless, he promised to write a letter to his bishop so that the latter would write to his primate so that the latter would write to the Supreme Pontiff in order to get the final verdict from the highest courts.

His prudence fell on sterile hearts. The news of the captive angel spread with such rapidity that after a few hours the courtyard had the bustle of a marketplace and they had to call in troops with fixed bayonets to disperse the mob that was about to knock the house down. Elisenda, her spine all twisted from sweeping up so much marketplace trash, then got the idea of fencing in the yard and charging five cents admission to see the angel.

The curious came from far away. A traveling carnival arrived with a flying acrobat who buzzed over the crowd several times, but no one paid attention to him because his wings were not those of an angel but, rather, those of a sidereal bat. The most unfortunate invalids on earth came in search of health: a poor woman who since childhood had been counting her heartbeats and had run out of numbers; a Portuguese man who couldn't sleep because the noise of the stars disturbed him; a sleepwalker who got up at night to undo the things he had done while awake; and many others with less serious ailments. In the midst of that shipwreck disorder that made the earth tremble, Pelayo and Elisenda were happy with fatigue, for in less than a week they had crammed their rooms with money and the line of pilgrims waiting their turn to enter still reached beyond the horizon.

The angel was the only one who took no part in his own act. He spent his time trying to get comfortable in his borrowed nest, befuddled by the hellish heat of the oil lamps and sacramental candles that had been placed along the wire. At first they tried to make him eat some mothballs, which, according to the wisdom of the wise neighbor woman, were the food prescribed for angels. But he turned them down, just as he turned down the papal lunches that the penitents brought him, and they never found out whether it was because he was an angel or because he was an old man that in the end he ate nothing but eggplant mush. His only supernatural virtue seemed to be patience. Especially during the first days, when the hens pecked at him, searching for the stellar parasites that proliferated in his wings, and the cripples pulled out feathers to touch their defective parts with, and even the most merciful threw stones at him, trying to get him to rise so they could see him standing. The only time they succeeded in arousing him was when they burned his side with an iron for branding steers, for he had been motionless for so many hours that they thought he was dead. He awoke with a start, ranting in his hermetic language and with tears in his eyes, and he flapped his wings a couple of times, which brought on a whirlwind of chicken dung and lunar dust and a gale of panic that did not seem to be of this world. Although many thought that his reaction had been one not of rage but of pain, from then on they were careful not to annoy him, because the majority understood that his passivity was not that of a hero taking his ease but that of a cataclysm in repose.

Father Gonzaga held back the crowd's frivolity with formulas of maidservant inspiration while awaiting the arrival of a final judgment on the nature of the captive. But the mail from Rome showed no sense of urgency. They spent their time finding out if the prisoner had a navel, if his dialect had any connection with Aramaic, how many times he could fit on the head of a pin, or whether he wasn't just a Norwegian with wings. Those meager letters might have come and gone until the end of time if a providential event had not put an end to the priest's tribulations.

It so happened that during those days, among so many other carnival at- 10 tractions, there arrived in town the traveling show of the woman who had been changed into a spider for having disobeyed her parents. The admission to see her was not only less than the admission to see the angel, but people were permitted to ask her all manner of questions about her absurd state and to examine her up and down so that no one would ever doubt the truth of her horror. She was a frightful tarantula the size of a ram and with the head of a sad maiden. What was most heart-rending, however, was not her outlandish shape but the sincere affliction with which she recounted the details of her misfortune. While still practically a child she had sneaked out of her parents' house to go to a dance, and while she was coming back through the woods after having danced all night without permission, a fearful thunderclap rent the sky in two and through the crack came the lightning bolt of brimstone that changed her into a spider. Her only nourishment came from the meatballs that charitable souls chose to toss into her mouth. A spectacle like that, full of so much human truth and with such a fearful lesson, was bound to defeat without even trying that of a haughty angel who scarcely deigned to look at mortals. Besides, the few miracles attributed to the angel showed a certain mental disorder, like the blind man who didn't recover his sight but grew three new teeth, or the paralytic who didn't get to walk but almost won the lottery, and the leper whose sores sprouted sunflowers. Those consolation miracles, which were more like mocking fun, had already ruined the angel's reputation when the woman who had been changed into a spider finally crushed him completely. That was how Father Gonzaga was cured forever of his insomnia and Pelayo's courtyard went back to being as empty as during the time it had rained for three days and crabs walked through the bedrooms.

The owners of the house had no reason to lament. With the money they saved they built a two-story mansion with balconies and gardens and high netting so that crabs wouldn't get in during the winter, and with iron bars on the windows so that angels wouldn't get in. Pelayo also set up a rabbit warren close to town and gave up his job as bailiff for good, and Elisenda bought some satin pumps with high heels and many dresses of iridescent silk, the kind worn on Sunday by the most desirable women in those times. The chicken coop was the only thing that didn't receive any attention. If they washed it down with creolin and burned tears of myrrh inside it every so often, it was not in homage to the angel but to drive away the dungheap stench that still hung everywhere like a ghost and was turning the new house into an old one. At first, when the child learned to walk, they were careful that he not get too close to the chicken coop. But then they began to lose their fears and got used to the smell, and before the child got his second teeth he'd gone inside the chicken coop to play, where the wires were falling apart. The angel was no less standoffish with him than with other mortals, but he tolerated the most ingenious infamies with the patience of a dog who had no illusions. They both came down with chicken pox at the same time. The doctor who took care of the child couldn't resist the temptation to listen to the angel's heart, and he found so much whistling in the heart and so many sounds in his kidneys that it seemed impossible for him to be alive. What surprised him most, however, was the logic of his wings. They seemed so natural on that completely human organism that he couldn't understand why other men didn't have them too.

When the child began school it had been some time since the sun and rain had caused the collapse of the chicken coop. The angel went dragging himself about here and there like a stray dying man. They would drive him out of the bedroom with a broom and a moment later find him in the kitchen. He seemed to be in so many places at the same time that they grew to think that he'd been duplicated, that he was reproducing himself all through the house, and the exasperated and unhinged Elisenda shouted that it was awful living in that hell full of angels. He could scarcely eat and his antiquarian eyes had also become so foggy that he went about bumping into posts. All he had left were the bare cannulae of his last feathers. Pelayo threw a blanket over him and extended him the charity of letting him sleep in the shed, and only then did they notice that he had a temperature at night, and was delirious with the tongue twisters of an old Norwegian. That was one of the few times they became alarmed, for they thought he was going to die and not even the wise neighbor woman had been able to tell them what to do with dead angels.

And yet he not only survived his worst winter, but seemed improved with the first sunny days. He remained motionless for several days in the farthest corner of the courtyard, where no one would see him, and at the beginning of December some large, stiff feathers began to grow on his wings, the feathers of a scarecrow, which looked more like another misfortune of decrepitude. But he must have known the reason for those changes, for he was quite careful that no one should notice them, that no one should hear the sea chanteys that he sometimes sang under the stars. One morning Elisenda was cutting some bunches of onions for lunch when a wind that seemed to come from the high seas blew into the kitchen. Then she went to the window and caught the angel in his first attempts at flight. They were so clumsy that his fingernails opened a furrow in the vegetable patch and he was on the point of knocking the shed down with the ungainly flapping that slipped on the light and couldn't get a grip on the air. But he did manage to gain altitude. Elisenda let out a sigh of relief, for herself and for him, when she saw him pass over the last houses, holding himself up in some way with the risky flapping of a senile vulture. She kept watching him even when she was through cutting the onions and she kept on watching until it was no longer possible for her to see him, because then he was no longer an annoyance in her life but an imaginary dot on the horizon of the sea.

[1968]

■ TOPICS FOR DISCUSSION AND WRITING

1.   The subtitle is "A Tale for Children." Do you think that the story is more suited to children than to adults? What in the story do you think children would especially like, or dislike?

2.   Is the story chiefly about our inability to perceive and respect the miraculous world? Explain.

3.   In a paragraph characterize the narrator of the story.

4.   Devoting a paragraph to each, characterize Pelayo, Elisenda, their son, and the man with wings.

■ JOYCE CAROL OATES

Joyce Carol Oates was born in 1938 in Millerport, New York. She won a scholarship to Syracuse University, from which she graduated (Phi Beta Kappa and valedictorian) in 1960. She then did graduate work in English, first at the University of Wisconsin and then at Rice University, but she withdrew from Rice in order to be able to devote more time to writing. Her first collection of stories, *By the North Gate*, was published in 1963; since then she has published steadily—stories, poems, essays, and (in twenty years) sixteen novels.

Where Are You Going, Where Have You Been?

To Bob Dylan

Her name was Connie. She was fifteen and she had a quick nervous giggling habit of craning her neck to glance into mirrors or checking other people's faces to make sure her own was all right. Her mother, who noticed everything and knew everything and who hadn't much reason any longer to look at her own face, always scolded Connie about it. "Stop gawking at yourself, who are you? You think you're so pretty?" she would say. Connie would raise her eyebrows at these familiar complaints and look right through her mother, into a shadowy vision of herself as she was right at that moment: she knew she was pretty and that was everything. Her mother had been pretty once too, if you could believe those old snapshots in the album, but now her looks were gone and that was why she was always after Connie.

"Why don't you keep your room clean like your sister? How've you got your hair fixed—what the hell stinks? Hair spray? You don't see your sister using that junk."

Her sister June was twenty-four and still lived at home. She was a secretary in the high school Connie attended, and if that wasn't bad enough—with her in the same building—she was so plain and chunky and steady that Connie had to hear her praised all the time by her mother and her mother's sisters. June did this, June did that, she saved money and helped clean the house and cooked and Connie couldn't do a thing, her mind was all filled with trashy daydreams. Their father was away at work most of the time and when he came home he wanted supper and he read the newspaper at supper and after supper he went to bed. He didn't bother talking much to them, but around his bent head Connie's mother kept picking at her until Connie wished her mother were dead and she herself were dead and it were all over. "She makes me want to throw up sometimes," she complained to her friends. She had a high, breathless, amused voice which made everything she said sound a little forced, whether it was sincere or not.

There was one good thing: June went places with girlfriends of hers, girls who were just as plain and steady as she, and so when Connie wanted to do that her mother had no objections. The father of Connie's best girlfriend drove the girls the three miles to town and left them off at a shopping plaza, so that they could walk through the stores or go to a movie, and when he came to pick them up again at eleven he never bothered to ask what they had done.

They must have been familiar sights, walking around that shopping plaza 5 in their shorts and flat ballerina slippers that always scuffed the sidewalk, with charm bracelets jingling on their thin wrists; they would lean together to whisper and laugh secretly if someone passed by who amused or interested them. Connie had long dark blond hair that drew anyone's eye to it, and she wore part of it pulled up on her head and puffed out and the rest of it she let fall down her back. She wore a pullover jersey blouse that looked one way when she was at home and another way when she was away from home. Everything about her had two sides to it, one for home and one for anywhere that was not home: her walk that could be childlike and bobbing, or languid enough to make someone think she was hearing music in her head, her mouth which was pale and smirking most of the time, but bright and pink on these evenings out, her laugh which was cynical and drawling at home— "Ha, ha, very funny" —but high-pitched and nervous anywhere else, like the jingling of the charms on her bracelet.

Sometimes they did go shopping or to a movie, but sometimes they went across the highway, ducking fast across the busy road, to a drive-in restaurant where older kids hung out. The restaurant was shaped like a big bottle, though squatter than a real bottle, and on its cap was a revolving figure of a grinning boy who held a hamburger aloft. One night in midsummer they ran across, breathless with daring, and right away someone leaned out a car window and invited them over, but it was just a boy from high school they didn't like. It made them feel good to be able to ignore him. They went up through the maze of parked and cruising cars to the bright-lit, fly-infested restaurant, their faces pleased and expectant as if they were entering a sacred building that loomed out of the night to give them what haven and what blessing they yearned for. They sat at the counter and crossed their legs at the ankles, their thin shoulders rigid with excitement, and listened to the music that made everything so good: the music was always in the background like music at a church service, it was something to depend upon.

A boy named Eddie came in to talk with them. He sat backward on his stool, turning himself jerkily around in semicircles and then stopping and turning again, and after a while he asked Connie if she would like something to eat. She said she did and so she tapped her friend's arm on her way out— her friend pulled her face up into a brave droll look—and Connie said she would meet her at eleven, across the way. "I just hate to leave her like that," Connie said earnestly, but the boy said that she wouldn't be alone for long. So they went out to his car and on the way Connie couldn't help but let her eyes wander over the windshields and faces all around her, her face gleaming with a joy that had nothing to do with Eddie or even this place; it might have been the music. She drew her shoulders up and sucked in her breath with the pure pleasure of being alive, and just at that moment she happened to glance at a face just a few feet from hers. It was a boy with shaggy black hair, in a convertible jalopy painted gold. He stared at her and then his lips widened into a grin. Connie slit her eyes at him and turned away, but she couldn't help glancing back and there he was still watching her. He wagged a finger and laughed and said, "Gonna get you, baby," and Connie turned away again without Eddie noticing anything.

She spent three hours with him, at the restaurant where they ate hamburgers and drank Cokes in wax cups that were always sweating, and then down an alley a mile or so away, and when he left her off at five to eleven only the movie house was still open at the plaza. Her girlfriend was there, talking with a boy. When Connie came up the two girls smiled at each other and Connie said, "How was the movie?" and the girl said, "*You* should know." They rode off with the girl's father, sleepy and pleased, and Connie couldn't help but look at the darkened shopping plaza with its big empty parking lot and its signs that were faded and ghostly now, and over at the drive-in restaurant where cars were still circling tirelessly. She couldn't hear the music at this distance.

Next morning June asked her how the movie was and Connie said, "So-so."

She and that girl and occasionally another girl went out several times a   10
week that way, and the rest of the time Connie spent around the house—it was summer vacation—getting in her mother's way and thinking, dreaming, about the boys she met. But all the boys fell back and dissolved into a single face that was not even a face, but an idea, a feeling, mixed up with the urgent insistent pounding of the music and the humid night air of July. Connie's mother kept dragging her back to the daylight by finding things for her to do or saying, suddenly, "What's this about the Pettinger girl?"

And Connie would say nervously, "Oh, her. That dope." She always drew thick clear lines between herself and such girls, and her mother was simple and kindly enough to believe her. Her mother was so simple, Connie thought, that it was maybe cruel to fool her so much. Her mother went scuffling around the house in old bedroom slippers and complained over the telephone to one sister about the other, then the other called up and the two of them complained about the third one. If June's name was mentioned her mother's tone was approving, and if Connie's name was mentioned it was disapproving. This did not really mean she disliked Connie and actually Connie thought that her mother preferred her to June because she was prettier, but the two of them kept up a pretense of exasperation, a sense that they were tugging and struggling over something of little value to either of them. Sometimes, over coffee, they were almost friends, but something would come up—some vexation that was like a fly buzzing suddenly around their heads—and their faces went hard with contempt.

One Sunday Connie got up at eleven—none of them bothered with church—and washed her hair so that it could dry all day long, in the sun. Her parents and sisters were going to a barbecue at an aunt's house and Connie said no, she wasn't interested, rolling her eyes to let her mother know just what she thought of it. "Stay home alone then," her mother said sharply. Connie sat out back in a lawn chair and watched them drive away, her father quiet and bald, hunched around so that he could back the car out, her mother with a look that was still angry and not at all softened through the windshield, and in the back seat poor old June all dressed up as if she didn't know what a barbecue was, with all the running yelling kids and the flies. Connie sat with her eyes closed in the sun, dreaming and dazed with the warmth about her as if this were a kind of love, the caresses of love, and her mind slipped over onto thoughts of the boy she had been with the night before and how nice he had been, how sweet it always was, not the way someone like June would suppose but sweet, gentle, the way it was in movies and promised in songs; and when she opened her eyes she hardly knew where she was, the back yard ran off into weeds and a fence line of trees and behind it the sky was perfectly blue and still. The asbestos "ranch house" that was now three years old startled her—it looked small. She shook her head as if to get awake.

It was too hot. She went inside the house and turned on the radio to drown out the quiet. She sat on the edge of her bed, barefoot, and listened for an hour and a half to a program called XYZ Sunday jamboree, record after record of hard, fast, shrieking songs she sang along with, interspersed by exclamations from "Bobby King": "An' look here you girls at Napoleon's— Son and Charley want you to pay real close attention to this song coming up!"

And Connie paid close attention herself, bathed in a glow of slow-pulsed joy that seemed to rise mysteriously out of the music itself and lay languidly about the airless little room, breathed in and breathed out with each gentle rise and fall of her chest.

After a while she heard a car coming up the drive. She sat up at once,   15
startled, because it couldn't be her father so soon. The gravel kept crunching all the way in from the road—the driveway was long—and Connie ran to the window. It was a car she didn't know. It was an open jalopy, painted a bright gold that caught the sunlight opaquely. Her heart began to pound and her fingers snatched at her hair, checking it, and she whispered "Christ, Christ," wondering how bad she looked. The car came to a stop at the side door and the horn sounded four short taps as if this were a signal Connie knew.

She went into the kitchen and approached the door slowly, then hung out the screen door, her bare toes curling down off the step. There were two boys in the car and now she recognized the driver: he had shaggy, shabby black hair that looked crazy as a wig and he was grinning at her.

"I ain't late, am I?" he said

"Who the hell do you think you are?" Connie said.

"Toldja I'd be out, didn't I?"

"I don't even know who you are."   20

She spoke sullenly, careful to show no interest or pleasure, and he spoke in a fast bright monotone. Connie looked past him to the other boy, taking her time. He had fair brown hair, with a lock that fell onto his forehead. His sideburns gave him a fierce, embarrassed look, but so far he hadn't even bothered to glance at her. Both boys wore sunglasses. The driver's glasses were metallic and mirrored everything in miniature.

"You wanta come for a ride?" he said.

Connie smirked and let her hair fall loose over one shoulder.

"Don'tcha like my car? New paint job," he said. "Hey."

"What?"   25

"You're cute."

She pretended to fidget, chasing flies away from the door.

"Don'tcha believe me, or what?" he said.

"Look, I don't even know who you are," Connie said in disgust.

"Hey, Ellie's got a radio, see. Mine's broke down." He lifted his friend's 30
arm and showed her the little transistor the boy was holding, and now Connie
began to hear the music. It was the same program that was playing inside the
house.

"Bobby King?" she said.

"I listen to him all the time. I think he's great."

"He's kind of great," Connie said reluctantly.

"Listen, that guy's *great*. He knows where the action is."

Connie blushed a little, because the glasses made it impossible for her 35
to see just what this boy was looking at. She couldn't decide if she liked him
or if he was just a jerk, and so she dawdled in the doorway and wouldn't come
down or go back inside. She said, "What's all that stuff painted on your car?"

"Can'tcha read it?" He opened the door very carefully, as if he was afraid
it might fall off. He slid out just as carefully, planting his feet firmly on the
ground, the tiny metallic world in his glasses slowing down like gelatine
hardening and in the midst of it Connie's bright green blouse. "This here is
my name, to begin with," he said. ARNOLD FRIEND was written in tarlike black
letters on the side, with a drawing of a round grinning face that reminded Connie of a pumpkin, except it wore sunglasses. "I wanta introduce myself, I'm
Arnold Friend and that's my real name and I'm gonna be your friend, honey,
and inside the car's Ellie Oscar, he's kinda shy." Ellie brought his transistor
radio up to his shoulder and balanced it there. "Now these numbers are a
secret code, honey," Arnold Friend explained. He read off the numbers 33,
19, 17 and raised his eyebrows at her to see what she thought of that, but she
didn't think much of it. The left rear fender had been smashed and around
it was written, on the gleaming gold background: DONE BY CRAZY WOMAN
DRIVER. Connie had to laugh at that. Arnold Friend was pleased at her laughter and looked up at her. "Around the other side's a lot more—you wanta come
and see them?"

"No."

"Why not?"

"Why should I?"

"Don'tcha wanta see what's on the car? Don'tcha wanta go for a ride?" 40

"I don't know."

"Why not?"

"I got things to do."

"Like what?"

He laughed as if she had said something funny. He slapped his thighs. 45
He was standing in a strange way, leaning back against the car as if he were
balancing himself. He wasn't tall, only an inch or so taller than she would be
if she came down to him. Connie liked the way he was dressed, which was
the way all of them dressed: tight faded jeans stuffed into black, scuffled
boots, a belt that pulled his waist in and showed how lean he was, and a white
pullover shirt that was a little soiled and showed the hard small muscles of
his arms and shoulders. He looked as if he probably did hard work, lifting and
carrying things. Even his neck looked muscular. And his face was a familiar
face, somehow: the jaw and chin and cheeks slightly darkened, because he

hadn't shaved for a day or two, and the nose long and hawklike, sniffing as if she were a treat he was going to gobble up and it was all a joke.

"Connie, you ain't telling the truth. This is your day set aside for a ride with me and you know it," he said, still laughing. The way he straightened and recovered from his fit of laughing showed that it had been all fake.

"How do you know what my name is?" she said suspiciously.

"It's Connie."

"Maybe and maybe not."

"I know my Connie," he said, wagging his finger. Now she remembered 50 him even better, back at the restaurant, and her cheeks warmed at the thought of how she sucked in her breath just at the moment she passed him—how she must have looked at him. And he had remembered her. "Ellie and I come out here especially for you," he said. "Ellie can sit in back. How about it?"

"Where?"

"Where what?"

"Where're we going?"

He looked at her. He took off the sunglasses and she saw how pale the skin around his eyes was, like holes that were not in shadow but instead in light. His eyes were like chips of broken glass that catch the light in an amiable way. He smiled. It was as if the idea of going for a ride somewhere, to some place, was a new idea to him.

"Just for a ride, Connie sweetheart."   55

"I never said my name was Connie," she said.

"But I know what it is. I know your name and all about you, lots of things," Arnold Friend said. He had not moved yet but stood still leaning back against the side of his jalopy. "I took a special interest in you, such a pretty girl, and found out all about you like I know your parents and sister are gone somewheres and I know where and how long they're going to be gone, and I know who you were with last night, and your best girlfriend's name is Betty. Right?"

He spoke in a simple lilting voice, exactly as if he were reciting the words to a song. His smile assured her that everything was fine. In the car Ellie turned up the volume on his radio and did not bother to look around at them.

"Ellie can sit in the back seat," Arnold Friend said. He indicated his friend with a casual jerk of his chin, as if Ellie did not count and she should not bother with him.

"How'd you find out all that stuff?" Connie said.   60

"Listen: Betty Schultz and Tony Fitch and Jimmy Pettinger and Nancy Pettinger," he said, in a chant. "Raymond Stanley and Bob Hutter—"

"Do you know all those kids?"

"I know everybody."

"Look, you're kidding. You're not from around here."

"Sure."   65

"But—how come we never saw you before?"

"Sure you saw me before," he said. He looked down at his boots, as if he were a little offended. "You just don't remember."

"I guess I'd remember you," Connie said.

"Yeah?" He looked up at this, beaming. He was pleased. He began to mark time with the music from Ellie's radio, tapping his fists lightly together. Connie looked away from his smile to the car, which was painted so bright it almost hurt her eyes to look at it. She looked at that name. ARNOLD FRIEND. And up at the front fender was an expression that was familiar—MAN THE FLY-ING SAUCERS. It was an expression kids had used the year before, but didn't use this year. She looked at it for a while as if the words meant something to her that she did not yet know.

"What're you thinking about? Huh?" Arnold Friend demanded. "Not 70 worried about your hair blowing around in the car, are you?"

"No."

"Think I maybe can't drive good?"

"How do I know?"

"You're a hard girl to handle. How come?" he said. "Don't you know I'm your friend? Didn't you see me put my sign in the air when you walked by?"

"What sign?"   75

"My sign." And he drew an X in the air, leaning out toward her. They were maybe ten feet apart. After his hand fell back to his side the X was still in the air, almost visible. Connie let the screen door close and stood perfectly still inside it, listening to the music from her radio and the boy's blend together. She stared at Arnold Friend. He stood there so stiffly relaxed, pretending to be relaxed, with one hand idly on the door handle as if he were keeping himself up that way and had no intention of ever moving again. She recognized most things about him, the tight jeans that showed his thighs and buttocks and the greasy leather boots and the tight shirt, and even that slippery friendly smile of his, that sleepy dreamy smile that all the boys used to get across ideas they didn't want to put into words. She recognized all this and also the singsong way he talked, slightly mocking, kidding, but serious and a little melancholy, and she recognized the way he tapped one fist against the other in homage of the perpetual music behind him. But all these things did not come together.

She said suddenly, "Hey, how old are you?"

His smile faded. She could see then that he wasn't a kid, he was much older—thirty, maybe more. At this knowledge her heart began to pound faster.

"That's a crazy thing to ask. Can'tcha see I'm your own age?"

"Like hell you are."   80

"Or maybe a coupla years older, I'm eighteen."

"Eighteen?" she said doubtfully.

He grinned to reassure her and lines appeared at the corners of his mouth. His teeth were big and white. He grinned so broadly his eyes became slits and she saw how thick the lashes were, thick and black as if painted with a black tarlike material. Then he seemed to become embarrassed, abruptly, and looked over his shoulder at Ellie. "*Him,* he's crazy," he said. "Ain't he a riot, he's a nut, a real character." Ellie was still listening to the music. His sunglasses told nothing about what he was thinking. He wore a bright orange shirt unbuttoned halfway to show his chest; which was a pale, bluish chest and not muscular like Arnold Friend's. His shirt collar was turned up all around and the very tips of the collar pointed out past his chin as if they were protecting him. He was pressing the transistor radio up against his ear and sat there in a kind of daze, right in the sun.

"He's kinda strange," Connie said.

"Hey, she says you're kinda strange! Kinda strange!" Arnold Friend 85 cried. He pounded on the car to get Ellie's attention. Ellie turned for the first time and Connie saw with shock that he wasn't a kid either—he had a fair, hairless face, cheeks reddened slightly as if the veins grew too close to the surface of his skin, the face of a forty-year-old baby. Connie felt a wave of dizziness rise in her at this sight and she stared at him as if waiting for something to change the shock of the moment, make it all right again. Ellie's lips kept shaping words, mumbling along with the words blasting in his ear.

"Maybe you two better go away," Connie said faintly.

"What? How come?" Arnold Friend cried. "We come out here to take you for a ride. It's Sunday." He had the voice of the man on the radio now. It was the same voice, Connie thought. "Don'tcha know it's Sunday all day and honey, no matter who you were with last night today you're with Arnold Friend and don't you forget it!—Maybe you better step out here," he said, and this last was in a different voice. It was a little flatter, as if the heat was finally getting to him.

"No. I got things to do."

"Hey."

"You two better leave."

"We ain't leaving until you come with us."

"Like hell I am—"

"Connie, don't fool around with me. I mean, I mean, don't fool *around*." he said, shaking his head. He laughed incredulously. He placed his sunglasses on top of his head, carefully, as if he were indeed wearing a wig, and brought the stems down behind his ears. Connie stared at him, another wave of dizziness and fear rising in her so that for a moment he wasn't even in focus but was just a blur, standing there against his gold car, and she had the idea that he had driven up the driveway all right but had come from nowhere before that and belonged nowhere and that everything about him and even about the music that was so familiar to her was only half real.

"If my father comes and sees you— "

"He ain't coming. He's at a barbecue."

"How do you know that?"

"Aunt Tillie's. Right now they're—uh—they're drinking. Sitting around," he said vaguely, squinting as if he were staring all the way to town and over to Aunt Tillie's back yard. Then the vision seemed to get clear and he nodded energetically. "Yeah. Sitting around. There's your sister in a blue dress, huh? And high heels, the poor sad bitch—nothing like you, sweetheart! And your mother's helping some fat woman with the corn, they're cleaning the corn— husking the corn— " "What fat woman?" Connie cried.

"How do I know what fat woman, I don't know every goddam fat woman in the world!" Arnold laughed.

"Oh, that's Mrs. Hornsby . . . Who invited her?" Connie said. She felt 100 a little light-headed. Her breath was coming quickly.

"She's too fat. I don't like them fat. I like them the way you are honey," he said, smiling sleepily at her. They stared at each other for a while, through the screen door. He said softly, "Now what you're going to do is this: you're going to come out that door. You're going to sit up front with me and Ellie's going to sit in the back, the hell with Ellie, right? This isn't Ellie's date. You're my date. I'm your lover, honey."

"What? You're crazy— "

"Yes, I'm your lover. You don't know what that is, but you will," he said. "I know that too. I know all about you. But look: it's real nice and you couldn't ask for nobody better than me, or more polite. I always keep my word. I'll tell you how it is, I'm always nice at first, the first time. I'll hold you so tight you won't think you have to try to get away or pretend anything because you'll know you can't. And I'll come inside you where it's all secret and you'll give in to me and you'll love me— "

"Shut up! You're crazy!" Connie said. She backed away from the door. She put her hands against her ears as if she'd heard something terrible, something not meant for her. "People don't talk like that, you're crazy," she muttered. He heart was almost too big now for her chest and its pumping made sweat break out all over her. She looked out to see Arnold Friend pause and then take a step toward the porch lurching. He almost fell. But, like a clever drunken man, he managed to catch his balance. He wobbled in his high boots and grabbed hold of one of the porch posts.

"Honey?" he said. "You still listening?"   105

"Get the hell out of here!"

"Be nice, honey. Listen."

"I'm going to call the police— "

He wobbled again and out of the side of his mouth came a fast spat curse, an aside not meant for her to hear. But even this "Christ!" sounded forced. Then he began to smile again. She watched this smile come, awkward as if he were smiling from inside a mask. His whole face was a mask, she thought wildly, tanned down onto his throat but then running out as if he had plastered makeup on his face but had forgotten about his throat.

"Honey—? Listen, here's how it is. I always tell the truth and I promise   110 you this: I ain't coming in that house after you."

"You better not! I'm going to call the police if you—if you don't— "

"Honey," he said, talking right through her voice, "honey, I'm not coming in there but you are coming out here. You know why?"

She was panting. The kitchen looked like a place she had never seen before, some room she had run inside but which wasn't good enough, wasn't going to help her. The kitchen window had never had a curtain, after three years, and there were dishes in the sink for her to do—probably—and if you ran your hand across the table you'd probably feel someting sticky there.

"You listening, honey? Hey?"

" —going to call the police— "   115

"Soon as you touch the phone I don't need to keep my promise and can come inside. You won't want that."

She rushed forward and tried to lock the door. Her fingers were shaking. "But why lock it," Arnold Friend said gently, talking right into her face. "It's just a screen door. It's just nothing." One of his boots was at a strange angle, and if his foot wasn't in it. It pointed out to the left, bent at the ankle. "I mean, anybody can break through a screen door and glass and wood and iron or anything else if he needs to, anybody at all and specially Arnold Friend. If the place got lit up with a fire honey you'd come runnin, out into my arms, right into my arms an' safe at home—like you knew I was your lover and'd stopped fooling around. I don't mind a nice shy girl but I don't like no fooling around." Part of those words were spoken with a slight rhythmic lilt, and Connie somehow recognized them—the echo of a song from last year, about a girl rushing into her boyfriend's arms and coming home again—

Connie stood barefoot on the linoleum floor, staring at him. "What do you want?" she whispered.

"I want you," he said.

"What?"   120

"Seen you that night and thought, that's the one, yes sir. I never needed to look any more."

"But my father's coming back. He's coming to get me. I had to wash my hair first—" She spoke in a dry, rapid voice, hardly raising it for him to hear.

"No, your Daddy is not coming and yes, you had to wash your hair and you washed it for me. It's nice and shining and all for me, I thank you, sweetheart," he said, with a mock bow, but again he almost lost his balance. He had to bend and adjust his boots. Evidently his feet did not go all the way down; the boots must have been stuffed with something so that he would seem taller. Connie stared out at him and behind him Ellie in the car, who seemed to be looking off toward Connie's right into nothing. This Ellie said, pulling the words out of the air one after another as if he were just discovering them, "You want me to pull out the phone?"

"Shut your mouth and keep it shut," Arnold Friend said, his face red from bending over or maybe from embarrassment because Connie had seen his boots. "This ain't none of your business."

"What—what are you doing? What do you want?" Connie said. "If I call   125 the police they'll get you, they'll arrest you—"

"Promise was not to come in unless you touch that phone, and I'll keep that promise," he said. He resumed his erect position and tried to force his shoulders back. He sounded like a hero in a movie, declaring something important. He spoke too loudly and it was as if he were speaking to someone behind Connie. "I ain't made plans for coming in that house where I don't belong but just for you to come out to me, the way you should. Don't you know who I am?"

"You're crazy," she whispered. She backed away from the door but did not want to go into another part of the house, as if this would give him permission to come through the door. "What you do. . . You're crazy, you. . . "

"Huh? What're you saying, honey?"

Her eyes darted everywhere in the kitchen. She could not remember what it was, this room.

"This is how it is, honey: you come out and we'll drive away, have a nice   130 ride. But if you don't come out we're gonna wait till your people come home and then they're all going to get it."

"You want that telephone pulled out?" Ellie said. He held the radio away from his ear and grimaced, as if without the radio the air was too much for him.

"I toldja shut up, Ellie," Arnold Friend said, "you're deaf, get a hearing aid, right? Fix yourself up. This little girl's no trouble and's gonna be nice to me, so Ellie keep to yourself, this ain't your date—right? Don't hem in on me. Don't hog. Don't crush. Don't bird dog. Don't trail me," he said in a rapid meaningless voice, as if he were running through all the expressions he'd learned but was no longer sure which one of them was in style, then rushing on to new ones, making them up with his eyes closed, "Don't crawl under my fence, don't squeeze in my chipmunk hole, don't sniff my glue, suck my popsicle, keep your own greasy fingers on yourself!" He shaded his eyes and peered in at Connie, who was backed against the kitchen table. "Don't mind him honey he's just a creep. He's a dope. Right? I'm the boy for you and like I said you come out here nice like a lady and give me your hand, and nobody else gets hurt, I mean, your nice old bald-headed daddy and your mummy and your sister in her high heels. Because listen: why bring them in this?"

"Leave me alone," Connie whispered.

"Hey, you know that old woman down the road, the one with the chickens and stuff—you know her?"

"She's dead!"   135

"Dead? What? You know her?" Arnold Friend said.

"She's dead—"

"Don't you like her?"

"She's dead—she's—she isn't here anymore—"

"But don't you like her, I mean, you got something against her? Some   140 grudge or something?" Then his voice dipped as if he were conscious of a rudeness. He touched the sunglasses perched on top of his head as if to make sure they were still there. "Now you be a good girl."

"What are you going to do?"

"Just two things, or maybe three," Arnold Friend said. "But I promise it won't last long and you'll like me the way you get to like people you're close to. You will. It's all over for you here, so come on out. You don't want your people in any trouble, do you?"

She turned and bumped against a chair or something, hurting her leg, but she ran into the back room and picked up the telephone. Something roared in her ear, a tiny roaring, and she was so sick with fear that she could do nothing but listen to it—the telephone was clammy and very heavy and her fingers groped down to the dial but were too weak to touch it. She began to scream into the phone, into the roaring. She cried out, she cried for her mother, she felt her breath start jerking back and forth in her lungs as if it were something Arnold Friend were stabbing her with again and again with no tenderness. A noisy sorrowful wailing rose all about her and she was locked inside it the way she was locked inside this house.

After a while she could hear again. She was sitting on the floor with her wet back against the wall.

Arnold Friend was saying from the door, "That's a good girl. Put the   145 phone back."

She kicked the phone away from her.

"No, honey. Pick it up. Put it back right."

She picked it up and put it back. The dial tone stopped.

"That's a good girl. Now you come outside."

She was hollow with what had been fear, but what was now just an empti- 150
ness. All that screaming had blasted it out of her. She sat, one leg cramped
under her, and deep inside her brain was something like a pinpoint of light
that kept going and would not let her relax. She thought I'm not going to see
my mother again. She thought, I'm not going to sleep in my bed again. Her
bright green blouse was all wet.

Arnold Friend said, in a gentle-loud voice that was like a stage voice,
"The place where you came from ain't there any more, and where you had
in mind to go is canceled out. This place you are now—inside your daddy's
house—is nothing but a cardboard box I can knock down any time. You know
that and always did know it. You hear me?"

She thought, I have got to think. I have to know what to do.

"We'll go out to a nice field, out in the country here where it smells so
nice and it's sunny," Arnold Friend said. "I'll have my arms tight around you
so you won't need to try to get away and I'll show you what love is like, what
it does. The hell with this house! It looks solid all right," he said. He ran a
fingernail down the screen and the noise did not make Connie shiver, as it
would have the day before. "Now put your hand on your heart, honey. Feel
that? That feels solid too, but we know better, be nice to me, be sweet like
you can because what else is there for a girl like you but to be sweet and pretty and give in?—and get away before her people come back?"

She felt her pounding heart. Her hand seemed to enclose it. She thought
for the first time in her life that it was nothing that was hers, that belonged
to her, but just a pounding, living thing inside this body that wasn't really hers
either.

"You don't want them to get hurt," Arnold Friend went on. "Now get up, 155
honey. Get up all by yourself."

She stood.

"Now turn this way. That's right. Come over here to me—Ellie, put that
away, didn't I tell you? You dope. You miserable creepy dope," Arnold Friend
said. His words were not angry but only part of an incantation. The incantation was kindly. "Now come out through the kitchen to me honey, and let's
see a smile, try it, you're a brave sweet little girl and now they're eating corn
and hot dogs cooked to bursting over an outdoor fire, and they don't know
one thing about you and never did and honey you're better than them because
not a one of them would have done this for you."

Connie felt the linoleum under her feet; it was cool. She brushed her hair
back out of her eyes. Arnold Friend let go of the post tentatively and opened
his arms for her, his elbows pointing in toward each other and his wrists limp,
to show that this was an embarrassed embrace and a little mocking, he didn't
want to make her self-conscious.

She put out her hand against the screen. She watched herself push the
door slowly open as if she were safe back somewhere in the other doorway,
watching this body and this head of long hair moving out into the sunlight
where Arnold Friend waited.

"My sweet little blue-eyed girl," he said, in a half-sung sigh that had noth- 160 ing to do with her brown eyes but was taken up just the same by the vast sunlit reaches of the land behind him on all sides of him, so much land that Connie had never seen before and did not recognize except to know that she was going to it.

[1966]

■ TOPICS FOR DISCUSSION AND WRITING

1. In a paragraph characterize Connie. Then in a second paragraph explain whether you think the early characterization of Connie prepares us for her later behavior.
2. Is Arnold Friend clairvoyant—definitely, definitely not, or maybe? Explain.
3. In an essay of 500 words evaluate the view that Arnold Friend is both Satan and the incarnation of Connie's erotic desires.
4. What do you make out of the fact that Oates dedicated the story to Bob Dylan? Is she perhaps contrasting Dylan's music with the escapist (or in some other way unwholesome) music of other popular singers?
5. In an essay of 500 words evaluate the view that Oates has given the old ballad, "The Demon Lover" (page 309), a moral interpretation.
6. If you have read Flannery O'Connor's "A Good Man Is Hard to Find" (page 941), compare and contrast Arnold Friend and the Misfit.
7. This story, like Elizabeth Bowen's "The Demon Lover" (page 268), is indebted to the ballad called "The Demon Lover" (page 309). If you have read Bowen's story, in an essay of 500 words explain why you prefer one story to the other.
8. Joyce Carol Oates has said: "I am concerned with only one thing, the moral and social conditions of my generation." What moral and social conditions do you find reflected in "Where Are You Going, Where Have You Been?" Does the story reflect "concern"? If so, how?
9. What music do you like? Why do you like it? How did you come to know it? Has your life been influenced by the popular music of your generation? How seriously do you take the lyrics of songs you like? (Give one or two examples of song lyrics you do or do not take seriously.)

POETRY

A NOTE ON POPULAR BALLADS

The first two poems are folk ballads, anonymous songs passed down orally from generation to generation. Such works are also called "popular ballads," narrative poems created for the populace rather than for a sophisticated audience. But of course sophisticated literary writers have sometimes imitated aspects of the popular ballad. For an example of a "literary ballad," see Keats's "La Belle Dame sans Merci" (page 311).

During the process of oral transmission, a folk ballad inevitably undergoes changes. Somewhat as a stone is smoothed by the force of a river, a folk ballad loses its rough spots. For example, the less memorable stanzas may simply be forgotten, and weak lines may be strengthened. So the work, whatever its origin, finally becomes a communal product. Among the chief characteristics of folk ballads are (1) abrupt transitions (probably caused by the loss of less memorable transitional stanzas), which create highly dramatic, sometimes unexplained scenes; (2) repetition of words, phrases, and even entire lines; (3) stock or conventional diction, often with alliteration, such as "red, red rose," "white, white steed," "wealthy wife," "stout and stalwart sons"; and (4) impersonality (the speaker does not offer an opinion on what happens).

■ ANONYMOUS
_____

The Wife of Usher's Well

There lived a wife at Usher's Well,
    And a wealthy wife was she;
She had three stout and stalwart sons,
    And sent them o'er the sea.   4

They hadna been a week from her,
    A week but barely ane,
Whan word came to the carlin° wife
    That her three sons were gane.   8

They hadna been a week from her,
    A week but barely three,
Whan word came to the carlin wife
    That her sons she'd never see.   12

"I wish the wind may never cease,
    Nor [fashes°] in the flood,
Till my three sons came hame to me,
    In earthly flesh and blood."   16

It fell about the Martinmass,°
    When nights are lang and mirk,
The carlin wife's three sons came hame,
    And their hats were o' the birk.°   20

7 **carlin** peasant 14 **fashes** troubles 17 **Martinmass** November 1 20 **birk** birch

It neither grew in syke° nor ditch,
    Nor yet in ony sheugh; °
But at the gates o Paradise,
    That birk grew fair eneugh,   24

"Blow up the fire, my maidens!
    Bring water from the well!
For a' my house shall feast this night,
    Since my three sons are well."   28

And she has made to them a bed,
    She's made it large and wide,
And she's ta'en her mantle her about,
    Sat down at the bed-side.   32

Up then crew the red, red cock,
    And up and crew the grey;
The eldest to the youngest said,
    " 'Tis time we were away."   36

The cock he hadna craw'd but once,
    And clapp'd his wings at a',
When the youngest to the eldest said,
    "Brother, we must awa'.   40

"The cock doth craw, the day doth daw,
    The channerin° worm doth chide;
Gin° we be mist out o' our place,
    A sair° pain we maun° bide.   44

"Fare ye weel, my mother dear!
    Fareweel to barn and byre!°
And fare ye weel, the bonny lass
    That kindles my mother's fire!"   48

■ TOPICS FOR DISCUSSION AND WRITING

1. In a sentence or two, summarize the narrative. That is, tell the story as briefly as possible.

2. Notice that the poem does not tell how the sons were lost. We are told in line 12 that the wife learns she will never see them again, and we are told in line 23 that the birch from which their hats are made grew at "the gates o Paradise." So we infer that they are dead, but the poet does not

---

21 **syke** rivulet 22 **sheugh** ditch 42 **channerin** scolding 43 **Gin** If 44 **sair** sore; **maun** must 46 **byre** shed

explicitly say so. Nor, for that matter, do we get any description of the appearance of any of the people, except for the lass in the last line, who is "bonny." Consider the mother. We are not told what she looked like, or what her thoughts or feelings are. Yet we know her thoughts and feelings, and we can characterize her.

In a sentence or two, characterize the mother. Then, in the first paragraph of an essay of 250 words, explain what your evidence is. Then try to explain the effect on the reader of the lack of explicit detail in the poem. In your final sentence or two, indicate whether you believe that the poem effectively sets the mother forth. (Most instructors in composition courses urge their students to give concrete details in their writing. Is it possible that additional details in this poem would not be useful?)

3. Medieval ghosts, for the most part, appear like ordinary mortals. They are not transparent, and they do not wear white sheets. Do you assume that the mother knows her sons are ghosts? At what point does she realize this?

4. In the last four stanzas, the sons talk about leaving, but there are no screams or tears. Do you assume they are glad to leave? Or, on the other hand, are they deeply regretful that they must leave? Exactly what, besides their mother, are they leaving? Indicate, without making excessive claims, what implications or associations may legitimately be found in the last stanza, especially in the last two lines.

■ ANONYMOUS

The Demon Lover

"O where have you been, my long, long love,
  This long seven years and mair?"
"O I'm come to seek my former vows
  Ye granted me before." 4

"O hold your tongue of your former vows,
  For they will breed sad strife;
O hold your tongue of your former vows,
  For I am become a wife." 8

He turned him right and round about,
  And the tear blinded his ee:
"I wad never hae trodden on Irish ground,
  If it had not been for thee. 12

"I might hae had a king's daughter,
  Far, far beyond the sea;
I might have had a king's daughter,
  Had it not been for love o thee." 16

"If ye might have had a king's daughter,
　　Yer sel ye had to blame;
Ye might have taken the king's daughter,
　　For ye kend° that I was nane.　　　　　　　　　20

"If I was to leave my husband dear,
　　And my two babes also,
O what have you to take me to,
　　If with you I should go?"　　　　　　　　　24

"I hae seven ships upon the sea—
　　The eighth brought me to land—
With four-and-twenty bold mariners,
　　And music on every hand."　　　　　　　　　28

She has taken up her two little babes,
　　Kissed them baith cheek and chin:
"O fair ye weel, my ain two babes,
　　For I'll never see you again."　　　　　　　　　32

She set her foot upon the ship,
　　No mariners could she behold;
But the sails were o the taffetie,
　　And the masts o the beaten gold.　　　　　　　　　36

They had not sailed a league, a league,
　　A league but barely three,
With dismal grew his countenance,
　　And drumlie° grew his ee.　　　　　　　　　40

They had not sailed a league, a league,
　　A league but barely three,
Until she espied his cloven foot,
　　And she wept right bitterlie.　　　　　　　　　44

"O hold your tongue of your weeping," says he,
　　"Of your weeping now let me be;
I will show you how the lilies grow
　　On the banks of Italy."　　　　　　　　　48

"O what hills are yon, yon pleasant hills,
　　That the sun shines sweetly on?"
"O yon are the hills of heaven," he said.
　　"Where you will never win."°　　　　　　　　　52

20 **kend** knew　40 **drumlie** gloomy　52 **win** gain, get to

"O whaten mountain is yon," she said,
    "All so dreary wi frost and snow?"
"O yon is the mountain of hell," he cried,
    "Where you and I will go."   56

He strack the tap-mast wi his hand,
    The fore-mast wi his knee,
And he brake that gallant ship in twain,
    And sank her in the sea.   60

■ TOPICS FOR DISCUSSION AND WRITING

1. What takes place between lines 28 and 29?
2. What is the first hint that supernatural forces are at work?
3. What does the "cloven foot" (line 43) signify? Is the spirit motivated by malice? By love? By both?
4. In a paragraph offer a character sketch of the Wife. You may include a brief moral judgment, but devote most of your paragraph to describing her actions in such a way that they reveal a personality. This personality may, of course, be rather complex.

■ JOHN KEATS

    John Keats (1795–1821), son of a London stable keeper, was taken out of school when he was fifteen and was apprenticed to a surgeon and apothecary. In 1816 he was licensed to practice as an apothecary-surgeon, but he almost immediately abandoned medicine and decided to make a career as a poet. His progress was amazing; he quickly moved from routine verse to major accomplishments, publishing books of poems—to mixed reviews—in 1817, 1818, and 1820, before dying of tuberculosis at the age of twenty-five. Today he is esteemed as one of England's greatest poets.

La Belle Dame sans Merci*

O what can ail thee, knight-at-arms,
    Alone and palely loitering?
The sedge has withered from the lake,
    And no birds sing.   4

O what can ail thee, knight-at-arms,
    So haggard and so woe-begone?
The squirrel's granary is full,
    And the harvest's done.   8

*The beautiful, pitiless lady

I see a lily on thy brow,
    With anguish moist and fever dew,
And on thy cheeks a fading rose
    Fast withereth too.   12

"I met a lady in the meads,
    Full beautiful—a faery's child,
Her hair was long, her foot was light,
    And her eyes were wild.   16

"I made a garland for her head,
    And bracelets too, and fragrant zone;°
She looked at me as she did love,
    And made sweet moan.   20

"I set her on my pacing steed,
    And nothing else saw all day long,
For sidelong would she bend and sing
    A faery's song.   24

"She found me roots of relish sweet,
    And honey wild, and manna dew,
And sure in language strange she said
    'I love thee true.'   28

"She took me to her elfin grot,
    And there she wept and sighed full sore,
And there I shut her wild wild eyes
    With kisses four.   32

"And there she lulléd me to sleep,
    And there I dreamed—Ah! woe betide!
The latest dream I ever dreamt
    On the cold hill side.   36

"I saw pale kings and princes too,
    Pale warriors, death-pale were they all;
They cried, 'La Belle Dame sans Merci
    Thee hath in thrall!'   40

"I saw their starved lips in the gloam
    With horrid warning gapéd wide,
And I awoke, and found me here,
    On the cold hill's side.   44

18 **zone** belt of flowers

"And this is why I sojourn here,
 Alone and palely loitering,
Though the sedge is withered from the lake,
 And no birds sing."   48

[1819]

■ TOPICS FOR DISCUSSION AND WRITING

1. In the first three stanzas the speaker describes the knight as pale, haggard, and so forth. In the rest of the poem the knight recounts his experience. In a few sentences summarize the knight's experience, and indicate why it has caused him to appear as he now does.

2. The *femme fatale*—the dangerously seductive woman—appears in much literature. If you are familiar with one such work, compare it with Keats's poem.

3. What characteristics of the popular ballad (see the introductory note on page 306) do you find in this poem? What characteristic does it *not* share with popular ballads? Set forth your response in an essay of 500 words.

■ EMILY DICKINSON

Emily Dickinson (1830–1886) was born into a proper New England family in Amherst, Massachusetts. Although she spent her seventeenth year a few miles away, at Mount Holyoke Seminary (now Mount Holyoke College), in her twenties and thirties she left Amherst only five or six times, and in her last twenty years she may never have left her house. Her brother was probably right when he said that having seen something of the rest of the world—she had visited Washington with her father, when he was a member of Congress—"she could not resist the feeling that it was painfully hollow. It was to her so thin and unsatisfying in the face of the Great Realities of Life." Dickinson lived with her parents (a somewhat reclusive mother and an austere, remote father) and a younger sister; a married brother lived in the house next door. She did, however, form some passionate attachments, to women as well as men, but there is no evidence that they found physical expression.

By the age of twelve Dickinson was writing witty letters, but she apparently did not write more than an occasional poem before her late twenties. At her death—she died in the house where she was born—she left 1,775 poems, only seven of which had been published (anonymously) during her lifetime.

Because I could not stop for Death

Because I could not stop for Death—
He kindly stopped for me—
The Carriage held but just Ourselves—
And Immortality.   4

We slowly drove—He knew no haste
And I had put away
My labor and my leisure too,
For His Civility—   8

We passed the School, where Children strove
At Recess—in the Ring—
We passed the Fields of Gazing Grain—
We passed the Setting Sun—   12

Or rather—He passed Us—
The Dews drew quivering and chill—
For only Gossamer, my Gown—
My Tippet—only Tulle—   16

We paused before a House that seemed
A Swelling of the Ground—
The Roof was scarcely visible—
The Cornice—in the Ground—   20

Since then—'tis Centuries—and yet
Feels shorter than the Day
I first surmised the Horses' Heads
Were toward Eternity—   24

[c. 1863]

■ TOPICS FOR DISCUSSION AND WRITING

1. Reread the poem noticing how often time is referred or alluded to and the various ways in which we are made aware of time passing. Does it pass slowly or swiftly for the speaker? Explain.
2. Characterize death as it appears in lines 1–8.
3. What is the significance of the details and their arrangement in the third stanza? Why "strove" rather than "played" (line 9)? What meanings does "Ring" (line 10) have? Is "Gazing Grain" better than "Golden Grain"?
4. The "House" in the fifth stanza is a sort of riddle. What is the answer? Does this stanza introduce an aspect of death not present—or present only very faintly—in the rest of the poem? Explain.
5. Write the words "Time Passes." Then in one (typed) page or less, show us a character engaged in an action that takes a specific period of time, from a few minutes to a few hours, but no more than one day. Without telling us directly, describe the action so that we can guess how much time has passed (approximately) and how the character feels, both about the activity in which he or she is engaged and about the passing of time.

■ JOHN HALL WHEELOCK

John Hall Wheelock (1908–1978) was born in Far Rockaway, Long Island, New York. In 1928, while an undergraduate at Harvard, he published a book of poems. After doing graduate work at the Universities of Berlin and Göttingen, he settled in New York, where he worked as an editor for Scribner's.

Earth

"A planet doesn't explode of itself," said drily
The Martian astronomer, gazing off into the air—
"That they were able to do it is proof that highly
Intelligent beings must have been living there."

[1961]

■ TOPICS FOR DISCUSSION AND WRITING

1. What is the "it" (line 3) that has been done?
2. How do you think the Martian astronomer would characterize himself or herself? How do you think the author would characterize the astronomer?

■ CRAIG RAINE

Born in England in 1945, Raine graduated from Oxford, where after his graduation he was appointed a lecturer. Since 1981 he has been poetry editor for the English publisher, Faber and Faber. He gives frequent readings of his poetry both in England and in America.

A Martian Sends a Postcard Home

Caxtons° are mechanical birds with many wings
and some are treasured for their markings—

they cause the eyes to melt
or the body to shriek without pain.

I have never seen one fly,   5
sometimes they perch on the hand.

Mist is when the sky is tired of flight
and rests its soft machine on ground:

1 **Caxtons** William Caxton (c. 1422–1491) was the first English printer of books.

then the world is dim and bookish
like engravings under tissue paper   5

Rain is when the earth is television.
It has the property of making colours darker.

Model T° is a room with the lock inside—
a key is turned to free the world

for movement, so quick there is a film   10
to watch for anything missed.

But time is tied to the wrist
or kept in a box, ticking with impatience.

In homes, a haunted apparatus sleeps,
that snores when you pick it up.   15

If the ghost cries, they carry it
to their lips and soothe it to sleep

with sounds. And yet, they wake it up
deliberately, by tickling with a finger.

Only the young are allowed to suffer   20
openly. Adults go to a punishment room

with water but nothing to eat.
They lock the door and suffer the noises

alone. No one is exempt
and everyone's pain has a different smell.   25

At night, when all the colours die,
they hide in pairs

and read about themselves—
in colour, with their eyelids shut.

[1979]

- TOPICS FOR DISCUSSION AND WRITING

1. When you first encountered the title, what was your response? Did it
   strike you as odd that a Martian would communicate with Mars by means
   of a postcard? How might we expect the Martian to communicate?

13 **Model T** A Ford automobile made between 1908 and 1928.

2. Write your own Martian report, describing some earthly activities or
    things, presenting them as they might be perceived (or misperceived) by
    a visitor from Mars. Your report may or may not imply a value judgment.

DRAMA

■ W. W. JACOBS and
   LOUIS N. PARKER

William Wymark Jacobs (1863–1943), born in England, wrote some
twenty volumes of short stories, chiefly whimsical pieces about British
barge crews, longshoremen, and other coastal workers. Some of his stories, however, including "The Monkey's Paw," are tales of horror.

Louis Napoleon Parker (1852–1944) was born in France but lived
most of his life in England, where he was active as a dramatist, composer, and director of civic pageants. He adapted several of Jacobs's stories into short plays.

The Monkey's Paw

Characters

MR. WHITE	SERGEANT-MAJOR MORRIS
MRS. WHITE	MR. SAMPSON
HERBERT	

*Scene: The living-room of an old-fashioned cottage on the outskirts of Fulham.
Set corner-wise in the left angle at the back a deep window; further front, L.,
three or four steps lead up to a door. Further forward a dresser, with plates,
glasses, etc. R. C. at back an alcove with the street door fully visible. On the
inside of the street door, a wire letter-box. On the right a cupboard, then a fireplace. In the center a round table. Against the wall, L. back, an old-fashioned
piano. A comfortable armchair each side of the fireplace. Other chairs. On the
mantelpiece a clock, old china figures, etc. An air of comfort pervades the room.*

I

At the rise of the curtain, MRS. WHITE, *a pleasant-looking old woman, is
seated in the armchair below the fire, attending to a kettle which is steaming
on the fire, and keeping a laughing eye on* MR. WHITE *and* HERBERT. *These two
are seated at the right angle of the table nearest the fire with a chessboard between them.* MR. WHITE *is evidently losing. His hair is ruffled; his spectacles are*

high up on his forehead. HERBERT, *a fine young fellow, is looking with satisfaction at the move he has just made.* MR. WHITE *makes several attempts to move, but thinks better of them. There is a shaded lamp on the table. The door is tightly shut. The curtains of the window are drawn; but every now and then the wind is heard whistling outside.*

MR. WHITE [*moving at last, and triumphant*]. There, Herbert, my boy! Got you, I think.

HERBERT. Oh, you're a deep 'un, Dad, aren't you?

MRS. WHITE. Mean to say he's beaten you at last?

HERBERT. Lor', no! Why, he's overlooked—

MR. WHITE [*very excited*]. I see it! Lemme have that back!

HERBERT. Not much. Rules of the game!

MR. WHITE [*disgusted*]. I don't hold with them scientific rules. You turn what ought to be an innocent relaxation—

MRS. WHITE. Don't talk so much, Father. You put him off—

HERBERT [*laughing*]. Not he!

MR. WHITE [*trying to distract his attention*]. Hark at the wind.

HERBERT [*drily*]. Ah! I'm listening. Check.

MR. WHITE [*still trying to distract him*]. I should hardly think Sergeant-major Morris'd come to-night.

HERBERT. Mate. [*Rises, goes up L.*]

MR. WHITE [*with an outbreak of disgust and sweeping the chessmen off the board*]. That's the worst of living so far out. Your friends can't come for a quiet chat, and you addle your brains over a confounded—

HERBERT. Now, Father! Morris'll turn up all right.

MR. WHITE [*still in a temper*]. Lovers' Lane, Fulham! Ho! of all the beastly, slushy, out-o'-the-way places to live in—! Pathway's a bog, and the road's a torrent. [*To* MRS. WHITE, *who has risen, and is at his side*] What's the County Council thinking of, that's what I want to know? Because this is the only house in the road it doesn't matter if nobody can get near it I s'pose.

MRS. WHITE. Never mind, dear. Perhaps you'll win tomorrow. [*She moves to back of table.*]

MR. WHITE. Perhaps I'll—perhaps I'll—What d'you mean? [*Bursts out laughing.*] There! You always know what's going on inside o' me, don't you, Mother?

MRS. WHITE. Ought to, after thirty years, John.

She goes to dresser, and busies herself wiping tumblers on tray there. He rises, goes to fireplace and lights pipe.

HERBERT [*down C.*]. And it's not such a bad place, Dad, after all. One of the few old-fashioned houses left near London. None o' your stucco villas. Homelike, I call it. And so do you, or you wouldn't ha' bought it. [*Rolls a cigarette.*]

MR. WHITE [*R., growling*]. Nice job I made o' that, too! With two hundred pounds owin' on it.

HERBERT [*on back of chair, C.*]. Why, I shall work that off in no time, Dad. Matter o' three years, with the rise promised me.

MR. WHITE. If you don't get married.

HERBERT. Not me. Not that sort.

MRS. WHITE. I wish you would, Herbert. A good, steady lad—

She brings the tray with a bottle of whiskey, glasses, a lemon, spoons, buns, and a knife to the table.

HERBERT. Lots o' time, Mother. Sufficient for the day—as the sayin' goes. Just now my dynamos don't leave me any time for love-making. Jealous, they are, I tell you!

MR. WHITE [*chuckling*]. I lay awake o' nights often, and think: If Herbert took a nap, and let his what-d' you-callums—dynamos, run down, all Fulham would be in darkness. Lord! what a joke! [*Gets R. C.*]

HERBERT. Joke! And me with the sack! Pretty idea of a joke you've got, I don't think.

Knock at outer door.

MRS. WHITE. Hark!

Knock repeated, louder.

MR. WHITE [*going toward door*]. That's him. That's the Sergeant-major. [*He unlocks door, back.*]

HERBERT [*removes chessboard*]. Wonder what yarn he's got for us to-night. [*Places chessboard on piano.*]

MRS. WHITE [*goes up right, busies herself putting the other armchair nearer fire, etc.*]. Don't let the door slam, John!

MR. WHITE *opens the door a little, struggling with it. Wind.* SERGEANT-MAJOR MORRIS, *a veteran with a distinct military appearance—left arm gone—dressed as a commissionaire, is seen to enter.* MR. WHITE *helps him off with his coat, which he hangs up in the outer hall.*

MR. WHITE [*at the door*]. Slip in quick! It's as much as I can do to hold it against the wind.

SERGEANT. Awful! Awful! [*Busy taking off his cloak, etc.*] And a mile up the road—by the cemetery—it's worse. Enough to blow the hair off your head.

MR. WHITE. Give me your stick.

SERGEANT. If 'twasn't I knew what a welcome I'd get—

MR. WHITE [*preceding him into the room*]. Sergeant-major Morris!

MRS. WHITE. Tut! tut! So cold you must be! Come to the fire; do'ee, now.

SERGEANT. How are you, marm? [*To* HERBERT] How's yourself, laddie? Not on duty yet, eh? Day-week, eh?

HERBERT [*C.*] No sir. Night-week. But there's half an hour yet.

SERGEANT [*sitting in the armchair above the fire, which* MRS. WHITE *is motioning him toward*].

MR. WHITE *mixes grog for* MORRIS.

Thank'ee kindly, marm. That's good—hah! That's a sight better than the trenches at Chitral. That's better than settin' in a puddle with the rain pourin' down in buckets, and the natives takin' pot-shots at you.

MRS. WHITE. Didn't you have no umbrellas? [*Corner below fire, kneels before it, stirs it, etc.*]

SERGEANT. Umbrell—? Ho! ho! That's good! Eh, White? That's good. Did ye hear what she said? Umbrellas—*And* goloshes! *and* hot-water bottles!—Ho, yes! No offence, marm, but it's easy to see you was never a soldier.

HERBERT [*rather hurt*]. Mother spoke out o' kindness, sir.

SERGEANT. And well I know it; and no offense intended. No, marm, 'ardship, 'ardship is the soldier's lot. Starvation, fever, and get yourself shot. That's a bit o' my own.

MRS. WHITE. You don't look to've taken much harm—except—[*Indicates his empty sleeve. She takes kettle to table, then returns to fire.*]

SERGEANT [*showing a medal hidden under his coat*]. And that I got this for. No, marm. Tough. Thomas Morris is tough.

MR. WHITE *is holding a glass of grog under the* SERGEANT'S *nose.*

And sober. What's this now?

MR. WHITE. Put your nose in it; you'll see.

SERGEANT. Whiskey? And hot? And sugar? And a slice o' lemon? No. I said I'd never—but seein' the sort o' night—Well! [*Waving the glass at them*] Here's another thousand a year.

MR. WHITE [*sits R. of table, also with a glass*]. Same to you and many of 'em.

SERGEANT [*to* HERBERT, *who has no glass*]. What? Not you?

HERBERT [*laughing and sitting across chair, C.*]. Oh! 'tisn't for want of being sociable. But my work don't go with it! Not if 'twas ever so little. I've got to keep a cool head, a steady eye, and a still hand. The fly-wheel might gobble me up.

MRS. WHITE. Don't, Herbert. [*Sits in armchair below fire.*]

HERBERT [*laughing*]. No fear, Mother.

SERGEANT. Ah! you electricians!—Sort o' magicians, you are. Light! says you—and light it is. And, power! says you—and the trams go whizzin'. And, knowledge! says you—and words go 'ummin' to the ends o' the world. It fair beats me—and I've *seen* a bit in my time, too.

HERBERT [*nudging his father*]. Your Indian magic? All a fake, governor. The fakir's fake.

SERGEANT. Fake, you call it? I tell you, I've *seen* it.

HERBERT [*nudges his father with his foot*]. Oh, come, now! such as what? Come, now!

SERGEANT. I've seen a cove with no more clothes on than a babby, [*to* MRS. WHITE] if you know what I mean—take an empty basket—empty, mind!—as empty as—as this here glass—

MR. WHITE. Hand it over, Morris. [*Hands it to* HERBERT, *who goes quickly behind table and fills it.*]

SERGEANT. Which was not my intentions, but used for illustration.

HERBERT [*while mixing*]. Oh I've seen the basket trick; and I've read how it was done. Why, I could do it myself, with a bit o' practice. Ladle out something stronger. [HERBERT *brings him the glass.*]

SERGEANT. Stronger?—what do you say to an old fakir chuckin' a rope up in the air—in the air, mind you!—and swarming up it, same as if it was 'ooked on—vanishing clean out o' sight?—I've seen that.

HERBERT *goes to table, plunges a knife into a bun, and offers it to the* SERGEANT *with exaggerated politeness.*

SERGEANT [*eyeing it with disgust*]. Bun—? What for?
HERBERT. That yarn takes it.

MR. and MRS. WHITE *delighted.*

SERGEANT. Mean to say you doubt my word?
MRS. WHITE. No, no! He's only taking you off.—You shouldn't, Herbert.
MR. WHITE. Herbert always was one for a bit o' fun!

HERBERT *puts bun back on table, comes round in front, and moving the chair out of the way, sits cross-legged on the floor at his father's side.*

SERGEANT. But it's true. Why, if I chose, I could tell you things—But there! you don't get no more yarns out o' *me*.
MR. WHITE. Nonsense, old friend. [*Puts down his glass.*] You're not going to get shirty about a bit o' fun. [*Moves his chair nearer* MORRIS*'s*]. What was that you started telling me the other day about a monkey's paw or something? [*Nudges* HERBERT, *and winks at* MRS. WHITE.]
SERGEANT [*gravely*]. Nothing. Leastways, nothing worth hearing.
MRS. WHITE [*with astonished curiosity*]. Monkey's *paw*—?
MR. WHITE. Ah—you was tellin' me—
SERGEANT. Nothing. Don't go on about it. [*Puts his empty glass to his lips—then stares at it.*] *What?* Empty again? There! When I begin thinkin' o' the paw, it makes me that absent-minded—
MR. WHITE [*rises and fills glass*]. You said you always carried it on you.
SERGEANT. So I do, for fear o' what might happen. [*Sunk in thought*] Ay—ay!
MR. WHITE [*handing him his glass refilled*]. There. [*Sits again in same chair.*]
MRS. WHITE. What's it for?
SERGEANT. You wouldn't believe me, if I was to tell you.
HERBERT. *I* will, every word.
SERGEANT. Magic, then!—Don't you laugh!
HERBERT. I'm not. Got it on you now?
SERGEANT. Of course.
HERBERT. Let's see it.

Seeing the SERGEANT *embarrassed with his glass,* MRS. WHITE *rises, takes it from him, places it on mantelpiece and remains standing.*

SERGEANT. Oh, it's nothing to look at. [*Hunting in his pocket*] Just an ordinary—little paw—dried to a mummy. [*Produces it and holds it towards* MRS. WHITE.] Here.
MRS. WHITE [*who has leant foward eagerly to see it, starts back with a little cry of disgust*]. Oh!
HERBERT. Give us a look. [MORRIS *passes the paw to* MR. WHITE, *from whom* HERBERT *takes it.*] Why, it's all dried up!

SERGEANT. I said so.

Wind.

MRS. WHITE [*with a slight shudder*]. Hark at the wind! [*Sits again in her old place.*]

MR. WHITE [*taking the paw from* HERBERT]. And what might there be special about it.

SERGEANT [*impressively*]. That there paw has had a spell put upon it!

MR. WHITE. No? [*In great alarm he thrusts the paw back into* MORRIS*'s hand.*]

SERGEANT [*pensively, holding the paw in the palm of his hand*]. Ah! By an old fakir. He was a very holy man. He'd sat all doubled up in one spot goin' on for fifteen year; thinkin' o' things. And he wanted to show that fate ruled people. That everything was cut and dried from the beginning, as you might say. That there warn't no gettin' away from it. And that, if you tried to, you caught it hot. [*Pauses solemnly.*] So he put a spell on this bit of a paw. It might ha' been anything else, but he took the first thing that came handy. Ah! He put a spell on it, and made it so that three people [*looking at them and with deep meaning*] could each have three wishes.

All but MRS. WHITE *laugh rather nervously.*

MRS. WHITE. Ssh! Don't!

SERGEANT [*more gravely*]. But—! But, mark you, though the wishes was granted, those three people would have cause to wish they *hadn't* been.

MR. WHITE. But how *could* the wishes be granted?

SERGEANT. He didn't say. It would all happen so natural, you might think it a coincidence if so disposed.

HERBERT. Why haven't you tried it, sir?

SERGEANT [*gravely, after a pause*]. I have.

HERBERT [*eagerly*]. You've had your three wishes?

HERBERT [*gravely*]. Yes.

MRS. WHITE. Were they granted?

SERGEANT [*staring at the fire*]. They were.

A pause.

MR. WHITE. Has anybody else wished?

SERGEANT. Yes. The first owner had his three wish—[*Lost in recollection*] Yes, oh yes, he had his three wishes all right. I don't know what his first two were, [*very impressively*] but the third was for death. [*All shudder.*] That's how I got the paw.

A pause.

HERBERT [*cheerfully*]. Well! Seems to me you've only got to wish for things that *can't* have any bad luck about 'em— [*Rises.*]

SERGEANT [*shaking his head*]. Ah!

MR. WHITE [*tentatively*]. Morris—if you've had your three wishes—it's no good to you, now—what do you keep it for?

SERGEANT [*still holding the paw; looking at it*]. Fancy, I s'pose. I did have some idea of selling it, but I don't think I will. It's done mischief enough already. Besides, people won't buy. Some of 'em think it's a fairy-tale. And some want to try it first, and pay after.

Nervous laugh from the others.

MRS. WHITE. If you could have another three wishes, would you?

SERGEANT [*slowly—weighing the paw in his hand, and looking at it*]. I don't know—I don't know—[*Suddenly, with violence, flinging it in the fire*] No! I'm damned if I would!

Movement from all.

MR. WHITE [*rises and quickly snatches it out of the fire*]. What are you doing? [WHITE *goes R. C.*]

SERGEANT [*rising and following him and trying to prevent him*]. Let it burn! Let the infernal thing burn!

MRS. WHITE [*rises*]. Let it burn, Father!

MR. WHITE [*wiping it on his coat-sleeve*]. No. If you don't want it, give it to me.

SERGEANT [*violently*]. I won't! I won't! My hands are clear of it. I threw it on the fire. If you keep it, don't blame me, whatever happens. Here! Pitch it back again.

MR. WHITE [*stubbornly*]. I'm going to keep it. What do you say, Herbert?

HERBERT [*L. C., laughing*]. I say, keep it if you want to. Stuff and nonsense, anyhow.

MR. WHITE [*looking at the paw thoughtfully*]. Stuff and nonsense. Yes. I wonder—[*casually*] I wish— [*He was going to say some ordinary thing, like "I wish I were certain."*]

SERGEANT [*misunderstanding him; violently*]. Stop! Mind what you're doing. That's not the way.

MR. WHITE. What *is* the way?

MRS. WHITE [*moving away, up R. C. to back of table, and beginning to put the tumblers straight, and the chairs in their places*)]. Oh, don't have anything to do with it, John.

Takes glasses on tray to dresser, L., busies herself there, rinsing them in a bowl of water on the dresser, and wiping them with a cloth.

SERGEANT. That's what I say, marm. But if I warn't to tell him, he might go wishing something he didn't mean to. You hold it in your right hand, and wish aloud. But I warn you! I warn you!

MRS. WHITE. Sounds like *The Arabian Nights*. Don't you think you might wish me four pair o' hands?

MR. WHITE [*laughing*]. Right you are, Mother!—I wish—

SERGEANT [*pulling his arm down*]. Stop it! If you must wish, wish for something sensible. Look here! I can't stand this. Gets on my nerves. Where's my coat? [*Goes into alcove.*]

MR. WHITE *crosses to fireplace and carefully puts the paw on mantelpiece. He is absorbed in it to the end of the tableau.*

HERBERT. I'm coming your way, to the works, in a minute. Won't you wait? [*Goes up C., helps* MORRIS *with his coat.*]

SERGEANT [*putting on his coat*]. No. I'm all shook up. I want fresh air. I don't want to be here when you wish. And wish you will as soon's my back's turned. I know. I know. But I've warned you, mind.

MR. WHITE [*helping him into his coat*]. All right, Morris. Don't you fret about us. [*Gives him money.*] Here.

SERGEANT [*refusing it*]. No. I won't—

MR. WHITE [*forcing it into his hand*]. Yes, you will.

Opens door.

SERGEANT [*turning to the room*]. Well, good night all. [*To* WHITE] Put it in the fire.

ALL. Good night   *Exit* SERGEANT.

MR. WHITE *closes door, comes towards fireplace, absorbed in the paw.*

HERBERT [*down L.*]. If there's no more in this than there is in his other stories, we shan't make much out of it.

MRS. WHITE [*comes down R. C. to* WHITE]. Did you give him anything for it, Father?

MR. WHITE. A trifle. He didn't want it, but I made him take it.

MRS. WHITE. There, now! You shouldn't. Throwing your money about.

MR. WHITE [*looking at the paw which he has picked up again*]. I wonder—

HERBERT. What?

MR. WHITE. I wonder, whether we hadn't better chuck it on the fire?

HERBERT [*laughing*]. Likely! Why, we're all going to be rich and famous and happy.

MRS. WHITE. Throw it on the fire, indeed, when you've given money for it! So like you, Father.

HERBERT. Wish to be an emperor, Father, to begin with. Then you can't be henpecked!

MRS. WHITE [*going for him front of table with a duster*]. You young—! [*Follows him to back of table.*]

HERBERT [*running away from her round behind table*]. Steady with that duster, Mother!

MR. WHITE. Be quiet, there! [HERBERT *catches* MRS. WHITE *in his arms and kisses her.*] I wonder— [*He has the paw in his hand.*] I don't know what to wish for and that's a fact. [*He looks about him with a happy smile.*] I seem to've got all I want.

HERBERT [*with his hands on the old man's shoulders*]. Old Dad! If you'd only cleared the debt on the house, you'd be quite happy, wouldn't you! [*Laughing.*] Well—go ahead!—wish for the two hundred pounds: that'll just do it.

MR. WHITE [*half laughing*]. Shall I? [*Crosses to R.C.*]

HERBERT. Go on! Here!—I'll play slow music. [*Crosses to piano.*]

MRS. WHITE. Don't 'ee, John. Don't have nothing to do with it!

HERBERT. Now, Dad! [*Plays.*]

MR. WHITE. I will! [*Holds up the paw, as if half ashamed.*] I wish for two hundred pounds.

Crash on the piano. At the same instant MR. WHITE *utters a cry and lets the paw drop.*

MRS. WHITE and HERBERT. What's the matter?

MR. WHITE [*gazing with horror at the paw*]. It moved! As I wished, it twisted in my hand like a snake.

HERBERT [*goes down R., and picks the paw up*]. Nonsense, Dad. Why, it's as stiff as a bone. [*Lays it on the mantelpiece.*]

MRS. WHITE. Must have been your fancy, Father.

HERBERT [*laughing*]. Well—? [*Looking round the room*] I don't see the money; and I bet I never shall.

MR. WHITE [*relieved*]. Thank God, there's no harm done! But it gave me a shock.

HERBERT. Half-past eleven. I must get along. I'm on at midnight. [*Goes up C., fetches his coat, etc.*] We've had quite a merry evening.

MRS. WHITE. I'm off to bed. Don't be late for breakfast, Herbert.

HERBERT. I shall walk home as usual. Does me good. I shall be with you about nine. Don't wait, though.

MRS. WHITE. You know your father never waits.

HERBERT. Good night, Mother. [*Kisses her. She lights candle on dresser, L., goes upstairs and exits.*]

HERBERT [*coming to his father, R., who is sunk in thought*]. Good night, Dad. You'll find the cash tied up in the middle of the bed.

MR. WHITE [*staring, seizes* HERBERT*'s hand*]. It moved, Herbert.

HERBERT. Ah! And a monkey hanging by his tail from the bed-post, watching you count the golden sovereigns.

MR. WHITE [*accompanying him to the door*]. I wish you wouldn't joke, my boy.

HERBERT. All right, Dad. [*Opens door.*] Lord! What weather! Good night. [*Exit.*]

The old man shakes his head, closes the door, locks it, puts the chain up, slips the lower bolt, has some difficulty with the upper bolt.

MR. WHITE. This bolt's stiff again! I must get Herbert to look to it in the morning.

Comes into the room, puts out the lamp, crosses towards steps; but is irresistibly attracted toward fireplace. Sits down and stares into the fire. His expression changes: he sees something horrible.

MR. WHITE [*with an involuntary cry*]. Mother! Mother!

MRS. WHITE [*appearing at the door at the top of the steps with candle*]. What's the matter? [*Comes down R. C.*]

MR. WHITE [*mastering himself. Rises*]. Nothing—I—haha!—I saw faces in the fire.

MRS. WHITE. Come along.

She takes his arm and draws him toward the steps. He looks back frightened toward fireplace as they reach the first step.

TABLEAU CURTAIN

II

Bright sunshine. The table, which has been moved nearer the window, is laid for breakfast. MRS. WHITE *busy about the table.* MR. WHITE *standing in the window looking off R. The inner door is open, showing the outer door.*

MR. WHITE. What a morning Herbert's got for walking home!

MRS. WHITE [*L. C.*]. What's o'clock? [*Looks at clock on mantelpiece.*] Quarter to nine, I declare. He's off at eight. [*Crosses to fire.*]

MR. WHITE. Takes him half an hour to change and wash. He's just by the cemetery now.

MRS. WHITE. He'll be here in ten minutes.

MR. WHITE [*coming to the table*]. What's for breakfast?

MRS. WHITE. Sausages. [*At the mantelpiece*] Why, if here isn't that dirty monkey's paw! [*Picks it up, looks at it with disgust, puts it back. Takes sausages in dish from before the fire and places them on table.*] Silly thing! The idea of us listening to such nonsense!

MR. WHITE [*goes up to window again*]. Ay—the Sergeant-major and his yarns! I suppose all old soldiers are alike—

MRS. WHITE. Come on, Father. Herbert hates us to wait.

They both sit and begin breakfast.

MRS. WHITE. How could wishes be granted, nowadays?

MR. WHITE. Ah! Been thinking about it all night, have you?

MRS. WHITE. You kept me awake, with your tossing and tumbling—

MR. WHITE. Ay, I had a bad night.

MRS. WHITE. It was the storm, I expect. How it blew!

MR. WHITE. I didn't hear it. I was asleep and not asleep, if you know what I mean.

MRS. WHITE. And all that rubbish about its making you unhappy if your wish *was* granted! How could two hundred pounds hurt you, eh, Father?

MR. WHITE. Might drop on my head in a lump. Don't see any other way. And I'd try to bear that. Though, mind you, Morris said it would happen so naturally that you might take it for a coincidence, if so disposed.

MRS. WHITE. Well—it hasn't happened. That's all I know. And it isn't going to. [*A letter is seen to drop in the letter-box.*] And how you can sit there and talk about it—[*Sharp postman's knock; she jumps to her feet.*] What's that?

MR. WHITE. Postman, o' course.

MRS. WHITE [*seeing the letter from a distance; in an awed whisper*]. He's brought a letter, John!

MR. WHITE [*laughing*]. What did you think he'd bring? Ton o' coals?

MRS. WHITE. John—! John—! Suppose—?

MR. WHITE. Suppose what?

MRS. WHITE. Suppose it was two hundred pounds!

MR. WHITE [*suppressing his excitement*]. Eh!—Here! Don't talk nonsense. Why don't you fetch it?

MRS. WHITE [*crosses and takes letter out of the box*]. It's thick, John—[*feels it*]—and—and it's got something crisp inside it. [*Takes letter to* WHITE *R. C.*]

MR. WHITE. Who—who's it for?

MRS. WHITE. You.

MR. WHITE. Hand it over, then. [*Feeling and examining it with ill-concealed excitement*] The idea! What a superstitious old woman you are! Where are my specs?

MRS. WHITE. Let me open it.

MR. WHITE. Don't you touch it. Where are my specs? [*Goes to R.*]

MRS. WHITE. Don't let sudden wealth sour your temper, John.

MR. WHITE. *Will* you find my specs?

MRS. WHITE [*taking them off mantelpiece*]. Here, John, here. [*As he opens the letter*] Take care! Don't tear it!

MR. WHITE. Tear what?

MRS. WHITE. If it was banknotes, John!

MR. WHITE [*taking a thick, formal document out of the envelope and a crisp-looking slip*]. You've gone dotty.—You've made me nervous. [*Reads.*] "Sir, Enclosed please find receipt for interest on the mortgages of £200 on your house, duly received."

They look at each other, MR. WHITE *sits down to finish his breakfast silently.* MRS. WHITE *goes to the window.*

MRS. WHITE. That comes of listening to tipsy old soldiers.

MR. WHITE [*pettish*]. What does?

MRS. WHITE. You thought there was banknotes in it.

MR. WHITE [*injured*]. I didn't. I said all along—

MRS. WHITE. How Herbert will laugh, when I tell him!

MR. WHITE [*with gruff good-humor*]. You're not going to tell him. You're going to keep your mouth shut. That's what you're going to do. Why, I should never hear the last of it.

MRS. WHITE. Serve you right. I shall tell him. You know you like his fun. See how he joked you last night when you said the paw moved. [*She is looking through the window towards R.*]

MR. WHITE. So it did. It did move. That I'll swear to.

MRS. WHITE [*abstractedly: she is watching something outside*]. You thought it did.

MR. WHITE. I say it did. There was no thinking about it. You saw how it upset me, didn't you?

She doesn't answer.

Didn't you?—Why don't you listen? [*Turns round.*] What is it?

MRS. WHITE. Nothing.

MR. WHITE [*turns back to his breakfast*]. Do you see Herbert coming?

MRS. WHITE. No.

MR. WHITE. He's about due. What *is* it?

MRS. WHITE. Nothing. Only a man. Looks like a gentleman. Leastways, he's in black, and he's got a top-hat on.

MR. WHITE. What about him? [*He is not interested; goes on eating.*]

MRS. WHITE. He stood at the garden-gate as if he wanted to come in. But he couldn't seem to make up his mind.

MR. WHITE. Oh, go on! You're full o' fancies.

MRS. WHITE. He's going—no; he's coming back.

MR. WHITE. Don't let him see you peeping.

MRS. WHITE [*with increasing excitement*]. He's looking at the house. He's got his hand on the latch. No. He turns away again. [*Eagerly*] John! He looks like a sort of lawyer.

MR. WHITE. What of it?

MRS. WHITE. Oh, you'll only laugh again. But suppose—suppose he's coming about the two hundred—

MR. WHITE. You're not to mention it again!—You're a foolish old woman.— Come and eat your breakfast. [*Eagerly*] Where is he now?

MRS. WHITE. Gone down the road. He has turned back. He seems to've made up his mind. Here he comes!—Oh, John, and me all untidy! [*Crosses to fire R.*]

Knock.

MR. WHITE [*to* MRS. WHITE, *who is hastily smoothing her hair, etc.*]. What's it matter? He's made a mistake. Come to the wrong house [*Crosses to fireplace.*]

MRS. WHITE *opens the door.* MR. SAMPSON, *dressed from head to foot in solemn black, with a top-hat, stands in the doorway.*

SAMPSON [*outside*]. Is this Mr. White's?

MRS. WHITE. Come in, sir. Please step in.

She shows him into the room; goes R.; he is awkward and nervous.

You must overlook our being so untidy; and the room all anyhow; and John in his garden-coat. [*To* MR. WHITE, *reproachfully*] Oh, John.

SAMPSON [*to* MR. WHITE]. Morning. My name is Sampson.

MRS. WHITE [*offering a chair*]. Won't you please be seated?

SAMPSON *stands quite still up C.*

SAMPSON. Ah—thank you—no, I think not—I think not. [*Pause.*]

MR. WHITE [*awkwardly, trying to help him*]. Fine weather for the time o' year.

SAMPSON. Ah—yes—yes— [*Pause; he makes a renewed effort.*] My name is Sampson—I've come—

MRS. WHITE. Perhaps you was wishful to see Herbert; he'll be home in a minute. [*Pointing*] Here's his breakfast waiting—

SAMPSON [*interrupting her hastily*]. No, no! [*Pause.*] I've come from the electrical works—

MRS. WHITE. Why, you might have come *with* him.

MR. WHITE *sees something is wrong, tenderly puts his hand on her arm.*

SAMPSON. No—no—I've come—*alone.*

MRS. WHITE [*with a little anxiety*]. Is anything the matter?

SAMPSON. I was asked to call—

MRS. WHITE [*abruptly*]. Herbert! Has anything happened? Is he hurt? Is he hurt?

MR. WHITE [*soothing her*]. There, there, Mother. Don't you jump to conclusions. Let the gentleman speak. You've not brought bad news, I'm sure, sir.

SAMPSON. I'm—sorry—

MRS. WHITE. Is he hurt?

SAMPSON *bows.*

MRS. WHITE. Badly?

SAMPSON. Very badly. [*Turns away.*]

MRS. WHITE [*with a cry*]. John—! [*She instinctively moves towards* MR. WHITE.]

MR. WHITE. Is he in pain?

SAMPSON. He is not in pain.

MRS. WHITE. Oh, thank God! Thank God for that! Thank—[*She looks in a startled fashion at* MR. WHITE—*realizes what* SAMPSON *means, catches his arm and tries to turn him towards her.*] Do you mean—?

SAMPSON *avoids her look; she gropes for her husband: he takes her two hands in his, and gently lets her sink into the armchair above the fireplace, then he stands on her right, between her and* SAMPSON.

MR. WHITE [*hoarsely*]. Go on, sir.

SAMPSON. He was telling his mates a story. Something that had happened here last night. He was laughing, and wasn't noticing and—and—[*hushed*] the machinery caught him—

A little cry from MRS. WHITE, *her face shows her horror and agony.*

MR. WHITE [*vague, holding* MRS. WHITE*'s hand*]. The machinery caught him—yes—and him the only child—it's hard, sir—very hard—

SAMPSON [*subdued*]. The Company wished me to convey their sincere sympathy with you in your great loss—

MR. WHITE [*staring blankly*]. Our—great—loss—!

SAMPSON. I was to say further—[*as if apologizing*] I am only their servant—I am only obeying orders—

MR. WHITE. Our—great—loss—

SAMPSON [*laying an envelope on the table and edging towards the door*]. I was to say, the Company disclaim all responsibility, but, in consideration of your son's services, they wish to present you with a certain sum as compensation. [*Gets to door.*]

MR. WHITE. Our—great—loss—[*Suddenly, with horror*] How—how much?

SAMPSON [*in the doorway*]. Two hundred pounds. [*Exit.*]

MRS. WHITE *gives a cry. The old man takes no heed of her, smiles faintly, puts out his hands like a sightless man, and drops, a senseless heap, to the floor.* MRS. WHITE *stares at him blankly and her hands go out helplessly towards him.*

TABLEAU CURTAIN

III

Night. On the table a candle is flickering at its last gasp. The room looks neglected. MR. WHITE *is dozing fitfully in the armchair.* MRS. WHITE *is in the window peering through the blinds towards L.*

MR. WHITE *starts, wakes, looks around him.*

MR. WHITE [*fretfully*]. Jenny—Jenny.

MRS. WHITE [*in the window*]. Yes.

MR. WHITE. Where are you?

MRS. WHITE. At the window.

MR. WHITE. What are you doing?

MRS. WHITE. Looking up the road.

MR. WHITE [*falling back*]. What the use, Jenny? What's the use?

MRS. WHITE. That's where the cemetery is; that's where we've laid him.

MR. WHITE. Ay—ay—a week to-day—what o'clock is it?

MRS. WHITE. I don't know.

MR. WHITE. We don't take much account of time now, Jenny, do we?

MRS. WHITE. Why should we? He don't come home. He'll never come home again. There's nothing to think about—

MR. WHITE. Or to talk about [*Pause.*] Come away from the window; you'll get cold.

MRS. WHITE. It's colder where *he* is.

MR. WHITE. Ay—gone for ever—

MRS. WHITE. And taken all our hopes with him—

MRS. WHITE. And all our *wishes*—

MRS. WHITE. Ay, and all our— [*With a sudden cry*] John!

She comes quickly to him; he rises.

MR. WHITE. Jenny! For God's sake! What's the matter?

MRS. WHITE [*with dreadful eagerness*]. The *paw*! The monkey's paw!

MR. WHITE [*bewildered*]. Where? Where is it? What's wrong with it?

MRS. WHITE. I want it! You haven't done away with it?

MR. WHITE. I haven't seen it—since—why?

MRS. WHITE. I want it! Find it! Find it!

MR. WHITE [*groping on the mantelpiece*]. Here! Here it is! What do you want of it? [*He leaves it there.*]

MRS. WHITE. Why didn't I think of it? Why didn't *you* think of it?

MR. WHITE. Think of what?

MRS. WHITE. The *other two* wishes!

MR. WHITE [*with horror*]. What?

MRS. WHITE. We've only had one.

MR. WHITE [*tragically*]. Wasn't that enough?

MRS. WHITE. No! We'll have one more. [WHITE *crosses to R. C.* MRS. WHITE *takes the paw and follows him.*] Take it. Take it quickly. And wish—

MR. WHITE [*avoiding the paw*]. Wish what?

MRS. WHITE. Oh, John! John! Wish our boy alive again!

MR. WHITE. Good God! Are you mad?

MRS. WHITE. Take it. Take it and wish. [*With a paroxysm of grief*] Oh, my boy! My boy!

MR. WHITE. Get to bed. Get to sleep. You don't know what you're saying.

MRS. WHITE. We had the first wish granted—why not the second?

MR. WHITE [*hushed*]. He's been dead ten days, and—Jenny! Jenny! I only knew him by his clothing—if you wasn't allowed to see him then—how could you bear to see him *now?*

MRS. WHITE. I don't care. Bring him back.

MR. WHITE [*shrinking from the paw*]. I daren't touch it!

MRS. WHITE [*thrusting it in his hand*]. Here! Here! Wish!

MR. WHITE [*trembling*]. Jenny!

MRS. WHITE [*fiercely*]. *Wish.* [*She goes on frantically whispering "Wish."*]

MR. WHITE [*shuddering, but overcome by her insistence*]. I-I—wish—my—son—alive again.

He drops it with a cry. The candle goes out. Utter darkness. He sinks into a chair. MRS. WHITE *hurries to the window and draws the blind back. She stands in the moonlight. Pause.*

MRS. WHITE [*drearily*]. Nothing.

MR. WHITE. Thank God! Thank God!

MRS. WHITE. Nothing at all. Along the whole length of the road not a living thing. [*Closes blind.*] And nothing, nothing, nothing left in our lives, John.

MR. WHITE. Except each other, Jenny—and memories.

MRS. WHITE [*coming back slowly to the fireplace*]. We're too old. We were only alive in him. We can't begin again. We can't feel anything now, John, but emptiness and darkness. [*She sinks into armchair.*]

MR. WHITE. 'Tisn't for long, Jenny. There's that to look forward to.

MRS. WHITE. Every minute's long, now.

MR. WHITE [*rising*]. I can't bear the darkness!

MRS. WHITE. It's dreary—dreary.

MR. WHITE [*crosses to dresser*]. Where's the candle? [*Finds it and brings it to table.*] And the matches? Where are the matches? We musn't sit in the dark. 'Tisn't wholesome. [*Lights match; the other candlestick is close to him.*] There. [*Turning with the lighted match toward* MRS. WHITE, *who is rocking and moaning*] Don't take on so, Mother.

MRS. WHITE. I'm a mother no longer.

MR. WHITE [*lights candle*]. There now; there now. Go on up to bed. Go on, now—I'm a-coming.

MRS. WHITE. Whether I'm here or in bed, or wherever I am, I'm with my boy, I'm with—

A low single knock at the street door.

MRS. WHITE [*starting*]. What's that!

MR. WHITE [*mastering his horror*]. A rat. The house is full of 'em.

A louder single knock; she starts up. He catches her by the arm.

Stop! What are you going to do?

MRS. WHITE [*wildly*]. It's my boy! It's Herbert! I forgot it was a mile away! What are you holding me for? I must open the door!

The knocking continues in single knocks at irregular intervals, constantly growing louder and more insistent.

MR. WHITE [*still holding her*]. For God's sake!

MRS. WHITE [*struggling*]. Let me go!

MR. WHITE. Don't open the door! [*He drags her towards left front.*]

MRS. WHITE. Let me go!

MR. WHITE. Think what you might see!

MRS. WHITE [*struggling fiercely*]. Do you think I fear the child I bore! Let me go! [*She wrenches herself loose and rushes to the door which she tears open.*] I'm coming, Herbert! I'm coming!

MR. WHITE [*cowering in the extreme corner, left front.*] Don't 'ee do it! Don't 'ee do it!

MRS. WHITE *is at work on the outer door, where the knocking still continues. She slips the chain, slips the lower bolt, unlocks the door.*

MR. WHITE [*suddenly*]. The paw! Where's the monkey's paw? [*He gets on his knees and feels along the floor for it.*]

MRS. WHITE [*tugging at the top bolt*]. John! The top bolt's stuck. I can't move it. Come and help. Quick!

MR. WHITE [*wildly groping*]. The paw! There's a wish left.

The knocking is now loud, and in groups of increasing length between the speeches.

MRS. WHITE. D'ye hear him? John! Your child's knocking!

MR. WHITE. Where is it? Where did it fall?

MRS. WHITE [*tugging desperately at the bolt*]. Help! Help! Will you keep your child from his home?

MR. WHITE. Where did it fall? I can't find it—I can't find—

The knocking is now tempestuous, and there are blows upon the door as of a body beating against it.

MRS. WHITE. Herbert! Herbert! My boy! Wait! Your mother's opening to you! Ah! It's moving! It's moving!

MR. WHITE. God forbid! [*Finds the paw.*] Ah!

MRS. WHITE [*slipping the bolt*]. Herbert!

MR. WHITE [*has raised himself to his knees; he holds the paw high*]. I wish him dead. [*The knocking stops abruptly*]. I wish him dead and at peace!

MRS. WHITE [*flinging the door open simultaneously*]. *Herb—*

A flood of moonlight. Emptiness. The old man sways in prayer on his knees. The old woman lies half swooning, wailing against the door-post.

CURTAIN

[1910]

■ TOPICS FOR DISCUSSION AND WRITING

1. In a paragraph, characterize Mr. White and Herbert, basing your remarks only on what they reveal of themselves during the game of chess at the start of the play.

2. Sergeant-major Morris tells the Whites that the fakir who put a spell on the paw had a purpose: "And he wanted to show that fate ruled people. That everything was cut and dried from the beginning, as you might say. That there warn't no gettin' away from it. And that, if you tried to, you caught it hot." In a paragraph explain how the plot of the play illustrates this point.

3. In the third scene, Mrs. White persuades Mr. White to wish that Herbert return alive. Imagine, for a moment, that the playwright handled the story differently. In this imagined version, Mr. White wants Herbert to return, but Mrs. White tries to dissuade him. Despite her pleas, he makes the wish—but then, when he hears the knocking at the door, he realizes that she is right not to want to bring Herbert back from the dead. In an essay of 250 words explain why you think one version—the printed one, or the one we have sketched—is superior to the other.

CHAPTER 9

Innocence and Experience

ESSAYS

■ PLATO

Plato (427–347 B.C.), born in Athens, the son of an aristocratic family, wrote thirty dialogues in which Socrates is the chief speaker. Socrates, about twenty-five years older than Plato, was a philosopher who called himself a gadfly to Athenians. For his efforts at stinging them into thought, the Athenians executed him in 399 B.C. "The Myth of the Cave" is the beginning of Book VII of Plato's dialogue entitled *The Republic*. Socrates is talking with Glaucon.

For Plato, true knowledge is philosophic insight or awareness of the Good, not mere opinion or the knack of getting along in this world by remembering how things have usually worked in the past. To illustrate his idea that awareness of the Good is different from the ability to recognize the things of this shabby world, Plato (through his spokesman Socrates) resorts to an allegory: men imprisoned in a cave see on a wall in front of them the shadows or images of objects that are really behind them, and they hear echoes, not real voices. (The shadows are caused by the light from a fire behind the objects, and the echoes by the cave's acoustical properties.) The prisoners, unable to perceive the real objects and the real voices, mistakenly think that the shadows and the echoes are real, and some of them grow highly adept at dealing with this illusory world. Were Plato writing today, he might have made the cave a movie theater: We see on the screen in front of us images caused by an object (film, passing in front of light) that is behind us. Moreover, the film itself is an illusory image, for it bears only the traces of a yet more real world—the world that was photographed—outside of the movie theater. And when we leave the theater to go into the real world, our eyes have become so

accustomed to the illusory world that we at first blink with discomfort—
just as Plato's freed prisoners do when they move out of the cave—at the
real world of bright day, and we long for the familiar darkness. So too,
Plato suggests, dwellers in ignorance may prefer the familiar shadows of
their unenlightened world ("the world of becoming") to the bright world
of the eternal Good ("the world of being") that education reveals.

We have just used the word "education." You will notice that the first
sentence in the translation (by Benjamin Jowett) says that the myth will
show "how far our nature is enlightened or unenlightened" In the original
Greek the words here translated "enlightened" and "unenlightened" are
paideia and *apaideusia*. No translation can fully catch the exact meanings
of these elusive words. Depending on the context, *paideia* may be translated as "enlightenment," education," "civilization," "culture," "knowledge
of the good."

The Myth of the Cave

And now, I said, let me show in a figure how far our nature is enlightened 1
or unenlightened—Behold! human beings living in an underground den, which
has a mouth open toward the light and reaching all along the den; here they
have been from their childhood, and have their legs and necks chained so that
they cannot move, and can only see before them, being prevented by the
chains from turning round their heads. Above and behind them a fire is blazing
at a distance, and between the fire and the prisoners there is a raised way;
and you will see, if you look, a low wall built along the way, like the screen
which marionette players have in front of them, over which they show the
puppets.

I see.

And do you see, I said, men passing along the wall carrying all sorts of
vessels, and statues and figures of animals made of wood and stone and various materials, which appear over the wall? Some of them are talking, others
silent.

You have shown me a strange image, and they are strange prisoners.

Like ourselves, I replied; and they see only their own shadows, or the 5
shadows of one another, which the fire throws on the opposite wall of the
cave?

True, he said; how could they see anything but the shadows if they were
never allowed to move their heads?

And of the objects which are being carried in like manner they would only
see the shadows?

Yes, he said.

And if they were able to converse with one another, would they not suppose that they were naming what was actually before them?

Very true.   10

And suppose further that the prison had an echo which came from the
other side, would they not be sure when one of the passersby spoke that the
voice which they heard came from the passing shadow?

No question, he replied.

To them, I said, the truth would be literally nothing but the shadows of the images.

That is certain.

And now look again, and see what will naturally follow if the prisoners 15 are released and disabused of their error. At first, when any of them is liberated and compelled suddenly to stand up and turn his neck round and walk and look toward the light, he will suffer sharp pains; the glare will distress him, and he will be unable to see the realities of which in his former state he had seen the shadows; and then conceive some one saying to him, that what he saw before was an illusion, but that now, when he is approaching nearer to being and his eye is turned toward more real existence, he has a clearer vision—what will be his reply? And you may further imagine that his instructor is pointing to the objects as they pass and requiring him to name them— will he not be perplexed? Will he not fancy that the shadows which he formerly saw are truer than the objects which are now shown to him?

Far truer.

And if he is compelled to look straight at the light, will he not have a pain in his eyes which will make him turn away to take refuge in the objects of vision which he can see, and which he will conceive to be in reality clearer than the things which are now being shown to him?

True, he said.

And suppose once more, that he is reluctantly dragged up a steep and rugged ascent, and held fast until he is forced into the presence of the sun himself, is he not likely to be pained and irritated? When he approaches the light his eyes will be dazzled, and he will not be able to see anything at all of what are now called realities.

Not all in a moment, he said.   20

He will require to grow accustomed to the sight of the upper world. And first he will see the shadows best, next the reflections of men and other objects in the water, and then the objects themselves; then he will gaze upon the light of the moon and the stars and the spangled heaven; and he will see the sky and the stars by night better than the sun or the light of the sun by day?

Certainly.

Last of all he will be able to see the sun, and not mere reflections of him in the water, but he will see him in his own proper place, and not in another; and he will contemplate him as he is.

Certainly.

He will then proceed to argue that this is he who gives the season and 25 the years, and is the guardian of all that is in the visible world, and in a certain way the cause of all things which he and his fellows have been accustomed to behold?

Clearly, he said, he would first see the sun and then reason about him.

And when he remembered his old habitation, and the wisdom of the den and his fellow-prisoners, do you not suppose that he would felicitate himself on the change, and pity them?

Certainly, he would.

And if they were in the habit of conferring honors among themselves on those who were quickest to observe the passing shadows and to remark which of them went before, and which followed after, and which were together; and who were therefore best able to draw conclusions as to the future, do you think that he would care for such honors and glories, or envy the possessors of them? Would he not say with Homer,

Better to be the poor servant of a poor master,

and to endure anything, rather than think as they do and live after their manner?

Yes, he said, I think that he would rather suffer anything than entertain 30 these false notions and live in this miserable manner.

Imagine once more, I said, such an one coming suddenly out of the sun to be replaced in his old situation; would he not be certain to have his eyes full of darkness?

To be sure, he said.

And if there were a contest, and he had to compete in measuring the shadows with the prisoners who had never moved out of the den, while his sight was still weak, and before his eyes had become steady (and the time which would be needed to acquire this new habit of sight might be very considerable), would he not be ridiculous? Men would say of him that up he went and down he came without his eyes; and that it was better not even to think of ascending; and if any one tried to loose another and lead him up to the light, let them only catch the offender, and they would put him to death.

No question, he said.

This entire allegory, I said, you may now append, dear Glaucon, to the 35 previous argument; the prison-house is the world of sight, the light of the fire is the sun, and you will not misapprehend me if you interpret the journey upwards to be the ascent of the soul into the intellectual world according to my poor belief, which, at your desire, I have expressed—whether rightly or wrongly God knows. But, whether true or false, my opinion is that in the world of knowledge the idea of good appears last of all, and is seen only with an effort; and, when seen, is also inferred to be the universal author of all things beautiful and right, parent of light and of the lord of light in this visible world, and the immediate source of reason and truth in the intellectual; and that this is the power upon which he who would act rationally either in public or private life must have his eye fixed.

I agree, he said, as far as I am able to understand you.

Moreover, I said, you must not wonder that those who attain to this beatific vision are unwilling to descend to human affairs; for their souls are ever hastening into the upper world where they desire to dwell; which desire of theirs is very natural, if our allegory may be trusted.

Yes, very natural.

And is there anything surprising in one who passes from divine contemplations to the evil state of man, misbehaving himself in a ridiculous manner; if, while his eyes are blinking and before he has become accustomed to the surrounding darkness, he is compelled to fight in courts of law, or in other places, about the images or the shadows of images of justice, and is endeavoring to meet the conceptions of those who have never yet seen absolute justice?

Anything but surprising, he replied.   40

Any one who has common sense will remember that the bewilderments of the eyes are of two kinds, and arise from two causes, either from coming out of the light or from going into the light, which is true of the mind's eye, quite as much as of the bodily eye; and he who remembers this when he sees any one whose vision is perplexed and weak, will not be too ready to laugh; he will first ask whether that soul of man has come out of the brighter life, and is unable to see because unaccustomed to the dark, or having turned from darkness to the day is dazzled by excess of light. And he will count the one happy in his condition and state of being, and he will pity the other; or, if he have a mind to laugh at the soul which comes from below into the light, there will be more reason in this than in the laugh which greets him who returns from above out of the light into the den.

That, he said, is very just distinction.

But then, if I am right, certain professors of education must be wrong when they say that they can put a knowledge into the soul which was not there before, like sight into blind eyes.

They undoubtedly say this, he replied.

Whereas, our argument shows that the power and capacity of learning 45 exists in the soul already; and that just as the eye was uanble to turn from darkness to light without the whole body, so too the instrument of knowledge can only by the movement of the whole soul be turned from the world of becoming into that of being, and learn by degrees to endure the sight of being, and of the brightest and best of being, or in other words, of the good.

Very true.

And must there not be some art which will effect conversion in the easiest and quickest manner; not implanting the faculty of sight, for that exists already, but has been turned in the wrong direction, and is looking away from the truth?

Yes, he said, such an art may be presumed.

And whereas the other so-called virtues of the soul seem to be akin to bodily qualities, for even when they are not originally innate they can be implanted later by habit and exercise, the virtue of wisdom more than anything else contains a divine element which always remains, and by this conversion is rendered useful and profitable; or, on the other hand, hurtful and useless. Did you never observe the narrow intelligence flashing from the keen eye of a clever rogue—how eager he is, how clearly his paltry soul sees the way to his end; he is the reverse of blind, but his keen eyesight is forced into the service of evil, and he is mischievous in proportion to his cleverness?

Very true, he said.   50

But what if there had been a circumcision of such natures in the days of their youth; and they had been severed from those sensual pleasures, such as eating and drinking, which, like leaden weights, were attached to them at their birth, and which drag them down and turn the vision of their souls upon the things that are below—if, I say, they had been released from these impediments and turned in the opposite direction, the very same faculty in them would have seen the truth as keenly as they see what their eyes are turned to now.

Very likely.

Yes, I said; and there is another thing which is likely, or rather a necessary inference from what has preceded, that neither the uneducated and uninformed of the truth, nor yet those who never make an end of their education, will be able ministers of State; not the former, because they have no single aim of duty which is the rule of all their actions, private as well as public; nor the latter, because they will not act at all except upon compulsion, fancying that they are already dwelling apart in the islands of the blest.

Very true, he replied.

Then, I said, the business of us who are the founders of the State will 55 be to compel the best minds to attain that knowledge which we have already shown to be the greatest of all—they must continue to ascend until they arrive at the good; but when they have ascended and seen enough we must not allow them to do as they do now.

What do you mean?

I mean that they remain in the upper world: but this must not be allowed; they must be made to descend again among the prisoners in the den, and partake of their labors and honors, whether they are worth having or not.

But is not this unjust? he said; ought we to give them a worse life, when they might have a better?

You have again forgotten, my friend, I said, the intention of the legislator, who did not aim at making any one class in the State happy above the rest; the happiness was to be in the whole State, and he held the citizens together by persuasion and necessity, making them benefactors of the State, and therefore benefactors of one another; to this end he created them, not to please themselves, but to be his instruments in binding up the State.

True, he said, I had forgotten.   60

Observe, Glaucon, that there will be no justice in compelling our philosophers to have a care and providence of others; we shall explain to them that in other States, men of their class are not obliged to share in the toils of politics: and this is reasonable, for they grow up at their own sweet will, and the government would rather not have them. Being self-taught, they cannot be expected to show any gratitude for a culture which they have never received. But we have brought you into the world to be rulers of the hive, kings of yourselves and of the other citizens, and have educated you far better and more perfectly than they have been educated, and you are better able to share in the double duty. Wherefore each of you, when his turn comes, must go down to the general underground abode, and get the habit of seeing in the dark. When you have acquired the habit, you will see ten thousand times better than the inhabitants of the den, and you will know what the several images are, and what they represent, because you have seen the beautiful and just and good in their truth. And thus our State which is also yours will be a reality, and not a dream only, and will be administered in a spirit unlike that of other States, in which men fight with one another about shadows only and are distracted in the struggle for power, which in their eyes is a great good. Whereas the truth is that the State in which the rulers are most reluctant to govern is always the best and most quietly governed, and the State in which they are most eager, the worst.

Quite true, he replied.

And will our pupils, when they hear this, refuse to take their turn at the toils of State, when they are allowed to spend the greater part of their time with one another in the heavenly light?

Impossible, he answered; for they are just men, and the commands which we impose upon them are just; there can be no doubt that every one of them will take office as a stern necessity, and not after the fashion of our present rulers of State.

Yes, my friend, I said; and there lies the point. You must contrive for your 65 future rulers another and a better life than that of a ruler, and then you may have a well-ordered State; for only in the State which offers this, will they rule who are truly rich, not in silver and gold, but in virtue and wisdom, which are the true blessings of life. Whereas if they go to the administration of public affairs, poor and hungering after their own private advantage, thinking that hence they are to snatch the chief good, order there can never be; for they will be fighting about office, and the civil and domestic broils which thus arise will be the ruin of the rulers themselves and of the whole State.

Most true, he replied.

And the only life which looks down upon the life of political ambition is that of true philosophy. Do you know of any other?

Indeed, I do not, he said.

And those who govern ought not to be lovers of the task? For, if they are, there will be rival lovers, and they will fight.

No question.   70

Who then are those whom we shall compel to be guardians? Surely they will be the men who are wisest about affairs of State, and by whom the State is best administered, and who at the same time have other honors and another and a better life than that of politics?

They are the men, and I will choose them, he replied.

And now shall we consider in what way such guardians will be produced, and how they are to be brought from darkness to light—as some are said to have ascended from the world below to the gods?

By all means, he replied.

The process, I said, is not the turning over of an oyster-shell,[1] but the turning round of a soul passing from a day which is little better than night to the true day of being, that is, the ascent from below which we affirm to be true philosophy?

Quite so.

■ TOPICS FOR DISCUSSION AND WRITING

1.   Plato is not merely reporting one of Socrates' conversations; he is teaching. What advantages does a dialogue have over a narrative or an essay as a way of teaching philosophy? How is the form of a dialogue especially suited to solving a problem?

[1] An allusion to a game in which two parties fled or pursued according as an oystershell which was thrown into the air fell with the dark or light side uppermost.

2. If you don't know the etymology of the word "conversion," look it up in a dictionary. How is the etymology appropriate to Plato's idea about education?

3. In paragraph 19, describing the prisoner as "reluctantly dragged" upward and "forced" to look at the sun, Socrates asks: "Is he not likely to be pained and irritated?" Can you recall experiencing pain and irritation while learning something you later were glad to have learned? Can you recall learning something new *without* experiencing pain and irritation?

4. "The State in which rulers are most reluctant to govern is always the best and most quietly governed, and the State in which they are most eager, the words" (paragraph 61). What does Socrates mean? Using examples from contemporary politics, defend this proposition, or argue against it.

5. Can you account for the power of this myth or fable? In our introductory comment (page 334) we tried to clarify the message by saying that a movie theater might serve as well as a cave, but in fact if the story were recast using a movie theater, would the emotional power be the same? Why or why not?

6. The metaphors of education as conversion and ascent are linked by the metaphor of light. Consider such expressions as "I see" (meaning "I understand") and "Let me give an illustration" (from the Latin *in* = in, *lustrare* = to make bright). What other expressions about light are used metaphorically to describe intellectual comprehension?

7. Write an allegory of your own, for instance using a sport, college, business activity, or a family in order to explain some aspect of reality.

■ MAYA ANGELOU
_____

Maya Angelou, born Marguerita Johnson in 1928 in St. Louis, spent her early years in California and Arkansas. She has worked as a cook, a streetcar conductor, a television screenwriter, and an actress, and she has written poems and five autobiographical books. The following selection comes from her first autobiography, *I Know Why the Caged Bird Sings* (1970).

Graduation

The children in Stamps trembled visibly with anticipation. Some adults were excited too, but to be certain the whole young population had come down with graduation epidemic. Large classes were graduating from both the grammar school and the high school. Even those who were years removed from their own day of glorious release were anxious to help with preparations as a kind of dry run. The junior students who were moving into the vacating classes' chairs were tradition-bound to show their talents for leadership and management. They strutted through the school and around the campus exerting pressure on the lower grades. Their authority was so new that occasionally if they pressed a little too hard it had to be overlooked. After all, next term was coming, and it never hurt a sixth grader to have a play sister in the eighth grade, or a tenth-year student to be able to call a twelfth grader Bubba. So all was endured in a spirit of shared understanding. But the graduating classes themselves were the nobility. Like travelers with exotic destinations on their minds, the graduates were remarkably forgetful. They came to school without their books, or tablets or even pencils. Volunteers fell over themselves to secure replacements for the missing equipment. When accepted, the willing workers might or might not be thanked, and it was of no importance to the pregraduation rites. Even teachers were respectful of the now quiet and aging seniors, and tended to speak to them, if not as equals, as beings only slightly lower than themselves. After tests were returned and grades given, the student body, which acted like an extended family, knew who did well, who excelled, and what piteous ones had failed.

Unlike the white high school, Lafayette County Training School distinguished itself by having neither lawn, nor hedges, nor tennis court, nor climbing ivy. Its two buildings (main classrooms, the grade school and home economics) were set on a dirt hill with no fence to limit either its boundaries or those of bordering farms. There was a large expanse to the left of the school which was used alternately as a baseball diamond or a basketball court. Rusty hoops on the swaying poles represented the permanent recreational equipment, although bats and balls could be borrowed from the P.E. teacher if the borrower was qualified and if the diamond wasn't occupied.

Over this rocky area relieved by a few shady tall persimmon trees the graduating class walked. The girls often held hands and no longer bothered to speak to the lower students. There was a sadness about them, as if this old world was not their home and they were bound for higher ground. The boys, on the other hand, had become more friendly, more outgoing. A decided change from the closed attitude they projected while studying for finals. Now they seemed not ready to give up the old school, the familiar paths and classrooms. Only a small percentage would be continuing on to college—one of the South's A & M (agricultural and mechanical) schools, which trained Negro youths to be carpenters, farmers, handymen, masons, maids, cooks and baby nurses. Their future rode heavily on their shoulders, and blinded them to the collective joy that had pervaded the lives of the boys and girls in the grammar school graduating class.

Parents who could afford it had ordered new shoes and ready-made clothes for themselves from Sears and Roebuck or Montgomery Ward. They also engaged the best seamstresses to make the floating graduating dresses and to cut down secondhand pants which would be pressed to a military slickness for the important event.

Oh, it was important, all right. Whitefolks would attend the ceremony, 5 and two or three would speak of God and home, and the Southern way of life, and Mrs. Parsons, the principal's wife, would play the graduation march while the lower-grade graduates paraded down the aisles and took their seats below the platform. The high school seniors would wait in empty classrooms to make their dramatic entrance.

In the Store I was the person of the moment. The birthday girl. The center. Bailey had graduated the year before, although to do so he had had to forfeit all pleasures to make up for his time lost in Baton Rouge.

My class was wearing butter-yellow piqué dresses, and Momma launched out on mine. She smocked the yoke into tiny crisscrossing puckers, then shirred the rest of the bodice. Her dark fingers ducked in and out of the lemony cloth as she embroidered raised daisies around the hem. Before she considered herself finished she had added a crocheted cuff on the puff sleeves, and a pointy crocheted collar.

I was going to be lovely. A walking model of all the various styles of fine hand sewing and it didn't worry me that I was only twelve years old and merely graduating from the eighth grade. Besides, many teachers in Arkansas Negro schools had only that diploma and were licensed to impart wisdom.

The days had become longer and more noticeable. The faded beige of former times had been replaced with strong and sure colors. I began to see my classmates' clothes, their skin tones, and the dust that waved off pussy willows. Clouds that lazed across the sky were objects of great concern to me. Their shiftier shapes might have held a message that in my new happiness and with a little bit of time I'd soon decipher. During that period I looked at the arch of heaven so religiously my neck kept a steady ache. I had taken to smiling more often, and my jaws hurt from the unaccustomed activity. Between the two physical sore spots, I suppose I could have been uncomfortable, but that was not the case. As a member of the winning team (the graduating class of 1940) I had outdistanced unpleasant sensations by miles. I was headed for the freedom of open fields.

Youth and social approval allied themselves with me and we trammeled 10 memories of slights and insults. The wind of our swift passage remodeled my features. Lost tears were pounded to mud and then to dust. Years of withdrawal were brushed aside and left behind, as hanging ropes of parasitic moss.

My work alone had awarded me a top place and I was going to be one of the first called in the graduating ceremonies. On the classroom blackboard, as well as on the bulletin board in the auditorium, there were blue stars and white stars and red stars. No absences, no tardinesses, and my academic work was among the best of the year. I could say the preamble to the Constitution even faster than Bailey. We timed ourselves often: "We the people of the United States in order to form a more perfect union . . ." I had memorized the Presidents of the United States from Washington to Roosevelt in chronological as well as alphabetical order.

My hair pleased me too. Gradually the black mass had lengthened and thickened, so that it kept at last to its braided pattern, and I didn't have to yank my scalp off when I tried to comb it.

Louise and I had rehearsed the exercises until we tired out ourselves. Henry Reed was class valedictorian. He was a small, very black boy with hooded eyes, a long, broad nose and an oddly shaped head. I had admired him for years because each term he and I vied for the best grades in our class. Most often he bested me, but instead of being disappointed I was pleased that we shared top places between us. Like many Southern Black children, he lived with his grandmother, who was as strict as Momma and as kind as she knew how to be. He was courteous, respectful and soft-spoken to elders, but on the playground he chose to play the roughest games. I admired him. Anyone, I reckoned, sufficiently afraid or sufficiently dull could be polite. But to be able to operate at a top level with both adults and children was admirable.

His valedictory speech was entitled "To Be or Not To Be." The rigid tenth-grade teacher had helped him to write it. He'd been working on the dramatic stresses for months.

The weeks until graduation were filled with heady activities. A group of small children were to be presented in a play about buttercups and daisies and bunny rabbits. They could be heard throughout the building practicing their hops and their little songs that sounded like silver bells. The older girls (nongraduates, of course) were assigned the task of making refreshments for the night's festivities. A tangy scent of ginger, cinnamon, nutmeg and chocolate wafted around the home economics building as the budding cooks made samples for themselves and their teachers.

In every corner of the workshop, axes and saws split fresh timber as the woodshop boys made sets and stage scenery. Only the graduates were left out of the general bustle. We were free to sit in the library at the back of the building or look in quite detachedly, naturally, on the measures being taken for our event.

Even the minister preached on graduation the Sunday before. His subject was, "Let your light so shine that men will see your good works and praise your Father, Who is in Heaven." Although the sermon was purported to be addressed to us, he used the occasion to speak to backsliders, gamblers, and general ne'er-do-wells. But since he had called our names at the beginning of the service we were mollified.

Among Negroes the tradition was to give presents to children going only from one grade to another. How much more important this was when the person was graduating at the top of the class. Uncle Willie and Momma had sent away for a Mickey Mouse watch like Bailey's. Louise gave me four embroidered handkerchiefs. (I gave her three crocheted doilies.) Mrs. Sneed, the minister's wife, made me an underskirt to wear for graduation, and nearly every customer gave me a nickel or maybe even a dime with the instruction "Keep on moving to high ground," or some such encouragement.

Amazingly the great day finally dawned and I was out of bed before I knew it. I threw open the back door to see it more clearly, but Momma said, "Sister, come away from that door and put your robe on."

I hoped the memory of that morning would never leave me. Sunlight was itself still young, and the day had none of the insistence maturity would bring it in a few hours. In my robe and barefoot in the backyard, under cover of going to see about my new beans, I gave myself up to the gentle warmth and thanked God that no matter what evil I had done in my life He had allowed me to live to see this day. Somewhere in my fatalism I had expected to die, accidentally, and never have the chance to walk up the stairs in the auditorium and gracefully receive my hard-earned diploma. Out of God's merciful bosom I had won reprieve.

Bailey came out in his robe and gave me a box wrapped in Christmas paper. He said he had saved his money for months to pay for it. It felt like a box of chocolates, but I knew Bailey wouldn't save money to buy candy when we had all we could want under our noses.

He was as proud of the gift as I. It was a soft-leather-bound copy of a

collection of poems by Edgar Allan Poe, or, as Bailey and I called him, "Eap."
I turned to "Annabel Lee" and we walked up and down the garden rows, the
cool dirt between our toes, reciting the beautifully sad lines.

Momma made a Sunday breakfast although it was only Friday. After we
finished the blessing, I opened my eyes to find the watch on my plate. It was
a dream of a day. Everything went smoothly and to my credit, I didn't have
to be reminded or scolded for anything. Near evening I was too jittery to attend to chores, so Bailey volunteered to do all before his bath.

Days before, we had made a sign for the Store and as we turned out the
lights Momma hung the cardboard over the doorknob. It read clearly:
CLOSED. GRADUATION.

My dress fitted perfectly and everyone said that I looked like a sunbeam 25
in it. On the hill, going toward the school, Bailey walked behind with Uncle
Willie, who muttered, "Go on, Ju." He wanted him to walk ahead with us because it embarrassed him to have to walk so slowly. Bailey said he'd let the
ladies walk together, and the men would bring up the rear. We all laughed,
nicely.

Little children dashed by out of the dark like fireflies. Their crepe-paper
dresses and butterfly wings were not made for running and we heard more
than one rip, dryly, and the regretful "uh uh" that followed.

The school blazed without gaiety. The windows seemed cold and unfriendly from the lower hill. A sense of ill-fated timing crept over me, and if
Momma hadn't reached for my hand I would have drifted back to Bailey and
Uncle Willie, and possibly beyond. She made a few slow jokes about my feet
getting cold, and tugged me along to the now-strange building.

Around the front steps, assurance came back. There were my fellow
"greats," the graduating class. Hair brushed back, legs oiled, new dresses
and pressed pleats, fresh pocket handkerchiefs and little handbags, all
homesewn. Oh, we were up to snuff, all right. I joined my comrades and
didn't even see my family go in to find seats in the crowded auditorium.

The school band struck up a march and all classes filed in as had been
rehearsed. We stood in front of our seats, as assigned, and on a signal from
the choir director, we sat. No sooner had this been accomplished than the
band started to play the national anthem. We rose again and sang the song,
after which we recited the pledge of allegiance. We remained standing for a
brief minute before the choir director and the principal signaled to us, rather
desperately I thought, to take our seats. The command was so unusual that
our carefully rehearsed and smooth-running machine was thrown off. For a
full minute we fumbled for our chairs and bumped into each other awkwardly.
Habits change or solidify under pressure, so in our state of nervous tension
we had been ready to follow our usual assembly pattern: the American National Anthem, then the pledge of allegiance, then the song every Black person I knew called the Negro National Anthem. All done in the same key, with
the same passion and most often standing on the same foot.

Finding my seat at last, I was overcome with a presentiment of worse 30
things to come. Something unrehearsed, unplanned, was going to happen,
and we were going to be made to look bad. I distinctly remember being explicit in the choice of pronoun. It was "we," the graduating class, the unit,
that concerned me then.

The principal welcomed "parents and friends" and asked the Baptist minister to lead us in prayer. His invocation was brief and punchy, and for a second I thought we were getting back on the high road to right action. When the principal came back to the dais, however, his voice had changed. Sounds always affected me profoundly and the principal's voice was one of my favorites. During assembly it melted and lowed weakly into the audience. It had not been in my plan to listen to him, but my curiosity was piqued and I straightened up to give him my attention.

He was talking about Booker T. Washington, our "late great leader," who said we can be as close as the fingers on the hand, etc. . . . Then he said a few vague things about friendship and the friendship of kindly people to those less fortunate than themselves. With that his voice nearly faded, thin, away. Like a river diminishing to a stream and then to a trickle. But he cleared his throat and said, "Our speaker tonight, who is also our friend, came from Texarkana to deliver the commencement address, but due to the irregularity of the train schedule, he's going to, as they say, 'speak and run.' " He said that we understood and wanted the man to know that we were most grateful for the time he was able to give us and then something about how we were willing always to adjust to another's program, and without more ado—"I give you Mr. Edward Donleavy."

Not one but two white men came through the door offstage. The shorter one walked to the speaker's platform, and the tall one moved over to the center seat and sat down. But that was our principal's seat, and already occupied. The dislodged gentleman bounced around for a long breath or two before the Baptist minister gave him his chair, then with more dignity than the situation deserved, the minister walked off the stage.

Donleavy looked at the audience once (on reflection, I'm sure that he wanted only to reassure himself that we were really there), adjusted his glasses and began to read from a sheaf of papers.

He was glad "to be here and to see the work going on just as it was in 35 the other schools."

At the first "Amen" from the audience I willed the offender to immediate death by choking on the word. But Amen's and Yes, sir's began to fall around the room like rain through a ragged umbrella.

He told us of the wonderful changes we children in Stamps had in store. The Central School (naturally, the white school was Central) had already been granted improvements that would be in use in the fall. A well-known artist was coming from Little Rock to teach art to them. They were going to have the newest microscopes and chemistry equipment for their laboratory. Mr. Donleavy didn't leave us long in the dark over who made these improvements available to Central High. Nor were we to be ignored in the general betterment scheme he had in mind.

He said that he had pointed out to people at a very high level that one of the first-line football tacklers at Arkansas Agricultural and Mechanical College had graduated from good old Lafayette County Training School. Here fewer Amen's were heard. Those few that did break through lay dully in the air with the heaviness of habit.

He went on to praise us. He went on to say how he had bragged that "one of the best basketball players at Fisk sank his first ball right here at Lafayette County Training School."

The white kids were going to have a chance to become Galileos and Madame Curies and Edisons and Gauguins, and our boys (the girls weren't even in on it) would try to be Jesse Owenses and Joe Louises. 40

Owens and the Brown Bomber were great heroes in our world, but what school official in the white-goddom of Little Rock had the right to decide that those two men must be our only heroes? Who decided that for Henry Reed to become a scientist he had to work like George Washington Carver, as a bootblack, to buy a lousy microscope? Bailey was obviously always going to be too small to be an athlete, so which concrete angel glued to what country seat had decided that if my brother wanted to become a lawyer he had to first pay penance for his skin by picking cotton and hoeing corn and studying correspondence books at night for twenty years?

The man's dead words fell like bricks around the auditorium and too many settled in my belly. Constrained by hard-learned manners I couldn't look behind me, but to my left and right the proud graduating class of 1940 had dropped their heads. Every girl in my row had found something new to do with her handkerchief. Some folded the tiny squares into love knots, some into triangles, but most were wadding them, then pressing them flat on their yellow laps.

On the dais, the ancient tragedy was being replayed. Professor Parsons sat, a sculptor's reject, rigid. His large, heavy body seemed devoid of will or willingness, and his eyes said he was no longer with us. The other teachers examined the flag (which was draped stage right) or their notes, or the windows which opened on our now-famous playing diamond.

Graduation, the hush-hush magic time of frills and gifts and congratulations and diplomas, was finished for me before my name was called. The accomplishment was nothing. The meticulous maps, drawn in three colors of ink, learning and spelling decasyllabic words, memorizing the whole of *The Rape of Lucrece*—it was nothing. Donleavy had exposed us.

We were maids and farmers, handymen and washerwomen, and anything higher that we aspired to was farcical and presumptuous. Then I wished that Gabriel Prosser and Nat Turner had killed all whitefolks in their beds and that Abraham Lincoln had been assassinated before the signing of the Emancipation Proclamation, and that Harriet Tubman had been killed by that blow on her head and Christopher Columbus had drowned in the *Santa Maria*. 45

It was awful to be Negro and have no control over my life. It was brutal to be young and already trained to sit quietly and listen to charges brought against my color and no chance of defense. We should all be dead. I thought I should like to see us all dead, one on top of the other. A pyramid of flesh with the whitefolks on the bottom, as the broad base, then the Indians with their silly tomahawks and teepees and wigwams and treaties, the Negroes with their mops and recipes and cotton sacks and spirituals sticking out of their mouths. The Dutch children should all stumble in their wooden shoes and break their necks. The French should choke to death on the Louisiana Purchase (1803) while silkworms ate all the Chinese with their stupid pigtails. As a species, we were an abomination. All of us.

Donleavy was running for election, and assured our parents that if he won we could count on having the only colored paved playing field in that part of Arkansas. Also—he never looked up to acknowledge the grunts of acceptance—also, we were bound to get some new equipment for the home economics building and the workshop.

He finished, and since there was no need to give any more than the most perfunctory thank-you's, he nodded to the men on the stage, and the tall white man who was never introduced joined him at the door. They left with the attitude that now they were off to something really important. (The graduation ceremonies at Lafayette County Training school had been a mere preliminary.)

The ugliness they left was palpable. An uninvited guest who wouldn't leave. The choir was summoned and sang a modern arrangement of "Onward, Christian Soldiers," with new words pertaining to graduates seeking their place in the world. But it didn't work. Elouise, the daughter of the Baptist minister, recited "Invictus," and I could have cried at the impertinence of "I am the master of my fate, I am the captain of my soul."

My name had lost its ring of familiarity and I had to be nudged to go and   50 receive my diploma. All my preparations had fled. I neither marched up to the stage like a conquering Amazon, nor did I look in the audience for Bailey's nod of approval. Marguerite Johnson, I heard the name again, my honors were read, there were noises in the audience of appreciation, and I took my place on the stage as rehearsed.

I thought about colors I hated: ecru, puce, lavender, beige and black.

There was shuffling and rustling around me, then Henry Reed was giving his valedictory address, "To Be or Not to Be." Hadn't he heard the white-folks? We couldn't *be*, so the question was a waste of time. Henry's voice came out clear and strong. I feared to look at him. Hadn't he got the message? There was no "nobler in the mind" for Negroes because the world didn't think we had minds, and they let us know it. "Outrageous fortune"? Now, that was a joke. When the ceremony was over I had to tell Henry Reed some things. That is, if I still cared. Not "rub," Henry, "erase." "Ah, there's the erase." Us.

Henry had been a good student in elocution. His voice rose on tides of promise and fell on waves of warnings. The English teacher had helped him to create a sermon winging through Hamlet's soliloquy. To be a man, a doer, a builder, a leader, or to be a tool, an unfunny joke, a crusher of funky toad-stools. I marveled that Henry could go through with the speech as if we had a choice.

I had been listening and silently rebutting each sentence with my eyes closed; then there was a hush, which in an audience warns that something unplanned is happening. I looked up and saw Henry Reed, the conservative, the proper, the A student, turn his back to the audience and turn to us (the proud graduating class of 1940) and sing, nearly speaking,

Lift ev'ry voice and sing
Till earth and heaven ring
Ring with the harmonies of Liberty . . .

It was the poem written by James Weldon Johnson. It was the music composed by J. Rosamond Johnson. It was the Negro National Anthem. Out of habit we were singing it.

Our mothers and fathers stood in the dark hall and joined the hymn of 55 encouragement. A kindergarten teacher led the small children onto the stage and the buttercups and daisies and bunny rabbits marked time and tried to follow:

Stony the road we trod
Bitter the chastening rod
Felt in the days when hope, unborn, had died.
Yet with a steady beat
Have not our weary feet
Come to the place for which our fathers sighed?

Every child I knew had learned that song with his ABC's and along with "Jesus Loves Me This I Know." But I personally had never heard it before. Never heard the words, despite the thousands of times I had sung them. Never thought they had anything to do with me.

On the other hand, the words of Patrick Henry had made such an impression on me that I had been able to stretch myself tall and trembling and say, "I know not what course others may take, but as for me, give me liberty or give me death."

And now I heard, really for the first time:

We have come over a way that with tears has been watered,
We have come, treading our path through the blood of the slaughtered.

While echoes of the song shivered in the air, Henry Reed bowed his head, said "Thank you," and returned to his place in the line. The tears that slipped down many faces were not wiped away in shame.

We were on top again. As always, again. We survived. The depths had 60 been icy and dark, but now a bright sun spoke to our souls. I was no longer simply a member of the proud graduating class of 1940; I was a proud member of the wonderful, beautiful Negro race.

Oh, Black known and unknown poets, how often have your auctioned pains sustained us? Who will compute the lonely nights made less lonely by your songs, or the empty pots made less tragic by your tales?

If we were a people much given to revealing secrets, we might raise monuments and sacrifice to the memories of our poets, but slavery cured us of that weakness. It may be enough, however, to have it said that we survive in exact relationship to the dedication of our poets (include preachers, musicians and blues singers).

[1969]

■ TOPICS FOR DISCUSSION AND WRITING

1. In the first paragraph notice such overstatements as "glorious release," "the graduating classes themselves were the nobility," and "exotic desti-

nations." Find further examples in the next few pages. What is the function of this diction?

2. How would you define "poets" as Angelou uses the word in the last sentence?

3. Characterize the writer as you perceive her up to the middle of paragraph 29. Support your characterizations with references to specific passages. Next, characterize her in the paragraph beginning "It was awful to be Negro" (paragraph 46). Next, characterize her on the basis of the entire essay. Finally, in a sentence, try to describe the change, telling the main attitudes or moods that she goes through.

FICTION

■ JAMES JOYCE

James Joyce (1882–1941) was born into a middle-class family in Dublin, Ireland. His father drank, became increasingly irresponsible and unemployable, and the family sank in the social order. Still, Joyce received a strong classical education at excellent Jesuit schools and at University College, Dublin, where he studied modern languages. In 1902, at the age of twenty, he left Ireland so that he might spend the rest of his life writing about life in Ireland. ("The shortest way to Tara," he said, "is via Holyhead," i.e., the shortest way to the heart of Ireland is to take ship away.) In Trieste, Zurich, and Paris he supported his family in a variety of ways, sometimes teaching English in a Berlitz school of language. His fifteen stories, collected under the title of *Dubliners*, were written between 1904 and 1907, but he could not get them published until 1914. Next came a highly autobiographical novel, *Portrait of the Artist as a Young Man* (1916). *Ulysses* (1922), a large novel covering eighteen hours in Dublin, was for some years banned by the United States Post Office, though few if any readers today find it offensive. He spent most of the rest of his life working on *Finnegans Wake* (1939).

Araby

North Richmond Street, being blind, was a quiet street except at the hour when the Christian Brothers' School set the boys free. An uninhabited house of two stories stood at the blind end, detached from its neighbors in a square ground. The other houses of the street, conscious of decent lives within them, gazed at one another with brown imperturbable faces.

The former tenant of our house, a priest, had died in the back drawing-room. Air, musty from having been long enclosed, hung in all the rooms, and the waste room behind the kitchen was littered with old useless papers. Among these I found a few paper-covered books, the pages of which were curled and damp: *The Abbot,* by Walter Scott, *The Devout Communicant* and *The Memoirs of Vidocq.* I liked the last best because its leaves were yellow. The wild garden behind the house contained a central apple-tree and a few straggling bushes under one of which I found the late tenant's rusty bicycle-pump. He had been a very charitable priest; in his will he had left all his money to institutions and the furniture of his house to his sister.

When the short days of winter came dusk fell before we had well eaten our dinners. When we met in the street the houses had grown somber. The space of sky above us was the color of ever-changing violet and towards it the lamps of the street lifted their feeble lanterns. The cold air stung us and we played till our bodies glowed. Our shouts echoed in the silent street. The career of our play brought us through the dark muddy lanes behind the houses where we ran the gantlet of the rough tribes from the cottages, to the back doors of the dark dripping gardens where odors arose from the ashpits, to the dark odorous stables where a coachman smoothed and combed the horse or shook music from the buckled harness. When we returned to the street light from the kitchen windows had filled the areas. If my uncle was seen turning the corner we hid in the shadow until we had seen him safely housed. Or if Mangan's sister came out on the doorstep to call her brother in to his tea we watched her from our shadow peer up and down the street. We waited to see whether she would remain or go in and, if she remained, we left our shadow and walked up to Mangan's steps resignedly. She was waiting for us, her figure defined by the light from the half-opened door. Her brother always teased her before he obeyed and I stood by the railings looking at her. Her dress swung as she moved her body and the soft rope of her hair tossed from side to side.

Every morning I lay on the floor in the front parlor watching her door. The blind was pulled down to within an inch of the sash so that I could not be seen. When she came out on the doorstep my heart leaped. I ran to the hall, seized my books and followed her. I kept her brown figure always in my eye and, when we came near the point at which our ways diverged, I quickened my pace and passed her. This happened morning after morning. I had never spoken to her, except for a few casual words, and yet her name was like a summons to all my foolish blood.

Her image accompanied me even in places the most hostile to romance.   5 On Saturday evenings when my aunt went marketing I had to go to carry some of the parcels. We walked through the flaring streets, jostled by drunken men and bargaining women, amid the curses of laborers, the shrill litanies of shop-boys who stood on guard by the barrels of pigs' cheeks, the nasal chanting of street-singers, who sang a *come-all-you* about O'Donovan Rossa, or a ballad about the troubles in our native land. These noises converged in a single sensation of life for me: I imagined that I bore my chalice safely through a throng of foes. Her name sprang to my lips at moments in strange prayers and praises which I myself did not understand. My eyes were often full of tears (I could not tell why) and at times a flood from my heart seemed to pour itself out into my bosom. I thought little of the future. I did not know whether I would ever speak to her or not or, if I spoke to her, how I could tell her of my confused adoration. But my body was like a harp and her words and gestures were like fingers running upon the wires.

One evening I went into the back drawing-room in which the priest had died. It was a dark rainy evening and there was no sound in the house. Through one of the broken panes I heard the rain impinge upon the earth, the fine incessant needles of water playing in the sodden beds. Some distant lamp or lighted window gleamed below me. I was thankful that I could see so little. All my senses seemed to desire to veil themselves and, feeling that I was about to slip from them, I pressed the palms of my hands together until they trembled, murmuring: *O love! O love!* many times.

At last she spoke to me. When she addressed the first words to me I was so confused that I did not know what to answer. She asked me was I going to *Araby*. I forget whether I answered yes or no. It would be a splendid bazaar, she said; she would love to go.

—And why can't you? I asked.

While she spoke she turned a silver bracelet round and round her wrist. She could not go, she said, because there would be a retreat that week in her convent. Her brother and two other boys were fighting for their caps and I was alone at the railings. She held one of the spikes, bowing her head towards me. The light from the lamp opposite our door caught the white curve of a neck, lit up her hair that rested there and, falling, lit up the hand upon the railing. It fell over one side of her dress and caught the white border of a petticoat, just visible as she stood at ease.

—It's well for you, she said. 10

—If I go, I said, I will bring you something.

What innumerable follies laid waste my waking and sleeping thoughts after that evening! I wished to annihilate the tedious intervening days. I chafed against the work of school. At night in my bedroom and by day in the classroom her image came between me and the page I strove to read. The syllables of the word *Araby* were called to me through the silence in which my soul luxuriated and cast an Eastern enchantment over me. I asked for leave to go to the bazaar on Saturday night. My aunt was surprised and hoped it was not some Freemason affair. I answered few questions in class, I watched my master's face pass from amiability to sternness; he hoped I was not beginning to idle. I could not call my wandering thoughts together. I had hardly any patience with the serious work of life which, now that it stood between me and my desire, seemed to me child's play, ugly monotonous child's play.

On Saturday morning I reminded my uncle that I wished to go to the bazaar in the evening. He was fussing at the hall-stand, looking for the hat-brush, and answered me curtly:

—Yes, boy, I know.

As he was in the hall I could not go into the front parlor and lie at the 15 window. I left the house in bad humor and walked slowly towards the school. The air was pitilessly raw and already my heart misgave me.

When I came home to dinner my uncle had not yet been home. Still it was early. I sat staring at the clock for some time and, when its ticking began to irritate me, I left the room. I mounted the staircase and gained the upper part of the house. The high cold empty gloomy rooms liberated me and I went from room to room singing. From the front window I saw my companions playing below in the street. Their cries reached me weakened and indistinct and, leaning my forehead against the cool glass, I looked over at the dark house where she lived. I may have stood there for an hour, seeing nothing but the brown-clad figure cast by my imagination, touched discreetly by the lamplight at the curved neck, at the hand upon the railings and at the border below the dress.

When I came downstairs again I found Mrs. Mercer sitting at the fire. She was an old garrulous woman, a pawnbroker's widow, who collected used stamps for some pious purpose. I had to endure the gossip of the tea-table. The meal was prolonged beyond an hour and still my uncle did not come. Mrs. Mercer stood up to go: she was sorry she couldn't wait any longer, but it was after eight o'clock and she did not like to be out late, as the night air was bad for her. When she had gone I began to walk up and down the room, clenching my fists. My aunt said:

—I'm afraid you may put off your bazaar for this night of Our Lord.

At nine o'clock I heard my uncle's latchkey in the halldoor. I heard him talking to himself and heard the hall-stand rocking when it had received the weight of his overcoat. I could interpret these signs. When he was midway through his dinner I asked him to give me the money to go to the bazaar. He had forgotten.

—The people are in bed and after their first sleep now, he said.   20

I did not smile. My aunt said to him energetically:

—Can't you give him the money and let him go? You've kept him late enough as it is.

My uncle said he was very sorry he had forgotten. He said he believed in the old saying: *All work and no play makes Jack a dull boy.* He asked me where I was going and, when I had told him a second time he asked me did I know *The Arab's Farewell to His Steed.* When I left the kitchen he was about to recite the opening lines of the piece to my aunt.

I held a florin tightly in my hand as I strode down Buckingham Street towards the station. The sight of the streets thronged with buyers and glaring with gas recalled to me the purpose of my journey. I took my seat in a third-class carriage of a deserted train. After an intolerable delay the train moved out of the station slowly. It crept onward among ruinous houses and over the twinkling river. At Westland Row Station a crowd of people pressed to the carriage doors; but the porters moved them back, saying that it was a special train for the bazaar. I remained alone in the bare carriage. In a few minutes the train drew up beside an improvised wooden platform. I passed out on to the road and saw by the lighted dial of a clock that it was ten minutes to ten. In front of me was a large building which displayed the magical name.

I could not find any sixpenny entrance and, fearing that the bazaar would   25
be closed, I passed in quickly through a turnstile, handing a shilling to a weary-looking man. I found myself in a big hall girdled at half its height by a gallery. Nearly all the stalls were closed and the greater part of the hall was

in darkness. I recognized a silence like that which pervades a church after a service. I walked into the center of the bazaar timidly. A few people were gathered about the stalls which were still open. Before a curtain, over which the words *Café Chantant* were written in colored lamps, two men were counting money on a salver. I listened to the fall of the coins.

Remembering with difficulty why I had come I went over to one of the stalls and examined porcelain vases and flowered tea-sets. At the door of the stall a young lady was talking and laughing with two young gentlemen. I remarked their English accents and listened vaguely to their conversation.

—O, I never said such a thing!

—O, but you did!

—O, but I didn't!

—Didn't she say that?   30

—Yes. I heard her.

—O, there's a . . . fib!

Observing me the young lady came over and asked me did I wish to buy anything. The tone of her voice was not encouraging; she seemed to have spoken to me out of a sense of duty. I looked humbly at the great jars that stood like eastern guards at either side of the dark entrance to the stall and murmured:

—No, thank you.

The young lady changed the position of one of the vases and went back 35 to the two young men. They began to talk of the same subject. Once or twice the young lady glanced at me over her shoulder.

I lingered before her stall, though I knew my stay was useless, to make my interest in her wares seem the more real. Then I turned away slowly and walked down the middle of the bazaar. I allowed the two pennies to fall against the sixpence in my pocket. I heard a voice call from one end of the gallery that the light was out. The upper part of the hall was now completely dark.

Gazing up into the darkness I saw myself as a creature driven and derided by vanity; and my eyes burned with anguish and anger.

[1905]

■   TOPICS FOR DISCUSSION AND WRITING

1. Joyce wrote a novel called *A Portrait of the Artist as a Young Man*. Write an essay of about 500 words on "Araby" as a portrait of the artist as a boy.

2. In an essay of about 500 words, consider the role of images of darkness and blindness and what they reveal to us about "Araby" as a story of the fall from innocence into painful awareness.

3. How old, approximately, is the narrator of "Araby" at the time of the experience he describes? How old is he at the time he tells his story? On what evidence do you base your estimates?

4. The boy, apparently an only child, lives with an uncle and aunt, rather than with parents. Why do you suppose Joyce put him in this family setting rather than some other?

5. The story is rich in images of religion. This in itself is not surprising, for the story is set in Roman Catholic Ireland, but the religious images are

not simply references to religious persons or objects. In an essay of 500 to 750 words, discuss how these images reveal the narrator's state of mind.

■ FRANK O'CONNOR
_____

"Frank O'Connor" was the pen name of Michael O'Donovan (1903–1966), who was born in Cork, Ireland. Poverty compelled his family to take him out of school after the fourth grade. He worked at odd jobs and then, during "the troubles"—the armed conflict of 1918–1921 that led to the establishment (1922) of the Irish Free State—he served in the Irish Republican Army, fighting the British until he was captured. After his release from prison he worked as a librarian and as a director (1935–1939) of the Abbey Theatre in Dublin. Still later, in the 1950s, he lived in the United States, teaching at Northwestern University and Harvard University.

Among his books—stories, novels, autobiographies, plays, translations of Gaelic poetry, and criticism—is *The Lonely Voice*, a study of the short story.

Guests of the Nation

I

At dusk the big Englishman, Belcher, would shift his long legs out of the ashes and say "Well, chums, what about it?" and Noble or me would say "All right, chum" (for we had picked up some of their curious expressions), and the little Englishman, Hawkins, would light the lamp and bring out the cards. Sometimes Jeremiah Donovan would come up and supervise the game and get excited over Hawkins's cards, which he always played badly, and shout at him as if he was one of our own "Ah, you divil, you, why didn't you play the tray?"

But ordinarily Jeremiah was a sober and contented poor devil like the big Englishman, Belcher, and was looked up to only because he was a fair hand at documents, though he was slow enough even with them. He wore a small cloth hat and big gaiters over his long pants, and you seldom saw him with his hands out of his pockets. He reddened when you talked to him, tilting from toe to heel and back, and looking down all the time at his big farmer's feet. Noble and me used to make fun of his broad accent, because we were from the town.

I couldn't at the time see the point of me and Noble guarding Belcher and Hawkins at all, for it was my belief that you could have planted that pair down anywhere from this to Claregalway and they'd have taken root there like a native weed. I never in my short experience seen two men to take to the country as they did.

They were handed on to us by the Second Battalion when the search for them became too hot, and Noble and myself, being young, took over with a natural feeling of responsibility, but Hawkins made us look like fools when he showed that he knew the country better than we did.

"You're the bloke they calls Bonaparte," he says to me. "Mary Brigid O'Connell told me to ask you what you done with the pair of her brother's socks you borrowed."

For it seemed, as they explained it, that the Second used to have little evenings, and some of the girls of the neighborhood turned in, and, seeing they were such decent chaps, our fellows couldn't leave the two Englishmen out of them. Hawkins learned to dance "The Walls of Limerick," "The Siege of Ennis," and "The Waves of Tory" as well as any of them, though, naturally, we couldn't return the compliment, because our lads at that time did not dance foreign dances on principle.

So whatever privileges Belcher and Hawkins had with the Second they just naturally took with us, and after the first day or two we gave up all pretense of keeping a close eye on them. Not that they could have got far, for they had accents you could cut with a knife and wore khaki tunics and overcoats with civilian pants and boots. But it's my belief that they never had any idea of escaping and were quite content to be where they were.

It was a treat to see how Belcher got off with the old woman of the house where we were staying. She was a great warrant to scold, and cranky even with us, but before ever she had a chance of giving our guests, as I may call them, a lick of her tongue, Belcher had made her his friend for life. She was breaking sticks, and Belcher, who hadn't been more than ten minutes in the house, jumped up from his seat and went over to her.

"Allow me, madam," he says, smiling his queer little smile, "please allow me"; and he takes the bloody hatchet. She was struck too paralytic to speak, and after that, Belcher would be at her heels, carrying a bucket, a basket, or a load of turf, as the case might be. As Noble said, he got into looking before she leapt, and hot water, or any little thing she wanted, Belcher would have it ready for her. For such a huge man (and though I am five foot ten myself I had to look up at him) he had an uncommon shortness—or should I say lack?—of speech. It took us some time to get used to him, walking in and out, like a ghost, without a word. Especially because Hawkins talked enough for a platoon, it was strange to hear big Belcher with his toes in the ashes come out with a solitary "Excuse me, chum," or "That's right, chum." His one and only passion was cards, and I will say for him that he was a good cardplayer. He could have fleeced myself and Noble, but whatever we lost to him Hawkins lost to us, and Hawkins played with the money Belcher gave him.

Hawkins lost to us because he had too much old gab, and we probably 10 lost to Belcher for the same reason. Hawkins and Noble would spit at one another about religion into the early hours of the morning, and Hawkins worried the soul out of Noble, whose brother was a priest, with a string of questions that would puzzle a cardinal. To make it worse, even in treating of holy subjects, Hawkins had a deplorable tongue. I never in all my career met a man who could mix such a variety of cursing and bad language into an argument. He was a terrible man, and a fright to argue. He never did a stroke of work, and when he had no one else to talk to, he got stuck in the old woman.

He met his match in her, for one day when he tried to get her to complain profanely of the drought, she gave him a great comedown by blaming it entirely on Jupiter Pluvius (a deity neither Hawkins nor I had ever heard of, though

Noble said that among the pagans it was believed that he had something to do with the rain). Another day he was swearing at the capitalists for starting the German war when the old lady laid down her iron, puckered up her little crab's mouth, and said: "Mr. Hawkins, you can say what you like about the war, and think you'll deceive me because I'm only a simple poor countrywoman, but I know what started the war. It was the Italian Count that stole the heathen divinity out of the temple in Japan. Believe me, Mr. Hawkins, nothing but sorrow and want can follow the people that disturb the hidden powers."

A queer old girl, all right.

II

We had our tea one evening, and Hawkins lit the lamp and we all sat into cards. Jeremiah Donovan came in too, and sat down and watched us for a while, and it suddenly struck me that he had no great love for the two Englishmen. It came as a great surprise to me, because I hadn't noticed anything about him before.

Late in the evening a really terrible argument blew up between Hawkins and Noble, about capitalists and priests and love of your country.

"The capitalists," says Hawkins with an angry gulp, "pays the priests to   15 tell you about the next world so as you won't notice what the bastards are up to in this."

"Nonsense, man!" says Noble, losing his temper. "Before ever a capitalist was thought of, people believed in the next world."

Hawkins stood up as though he was preaching a sermon.

"Oh, they did, did they?" he says with a sneer. "They believed all the things you believe, isn't that what you mean? And you believe that God created Adam, and Adam created Shem, and Shem created Jehoshaphat. You believe all that silly old fairytale about Eve and Eden and the apple. Well, listen to me, chum. If you're entitled to hold a silly belief like that, I'm entitled to hold my silly belief—which is that the first thing your God created was a bleeding capitalist, with morality and Rolls-Royce complete. Am I right, chum?" he says to Belcher.

"You're right, chum," says Belcher with his amused smile, and got up from the table to stretch his long legs into the fire and stroke his moustache. So, seeing that Jeremiah Donovan was going, and that there was no knowing when the argument about religion would be over, I went out with him. We strolled down to the village together, and then he stopped and started blushing and mumbling and saying I ought to be behind, keeping guard on the prisoners. I didn't like the tone he took with me, and anyway I was bored with life in the cottage, so I replied by asking him what the hell he wanted guarding them at all for. I told him I'd talked it over with Noble, and that we'd both rather be out with a fighting column.

"What use are those fellows to us?" says I.   20

He looked at me in surprise and said: "I thought you knew we were keeping them as hostages."

"Hostages?" I said.

"The enemy have prisoners belonging to us," he says, "and now they're talking of shooting them. If they shoot our prisoners, we'll shoot theirs."

"Shoot them?" I said.

"What else did you think we were keeping them for?" he says.   25

"Wasn't it very unforeseen of you not to warn Noble and myself of that in the beginning?" I said.

"How was it?" says he. "You might have known it."

"We couldn't know it, Jeremiah Donovan," says I. "How could we when they were on our hands so long?"

"The enemy have our prisoners as long and longer," says he.

"That's not the same thing at all," says I.   30

"What difference is there?" says he.

I couldn't tell him, because I knew he wouldn't understand. If it was only an old dog that was going to the vet's, you'd try and not get too fond of him, but Jeremiah Donovan wasn't a man that would ever be in danger of that.

"And when is this thing going to be decided?" says I.

"We might hear tonight," he says. "Or tomorrow or the next day at latest. So if it's only hanging round here that's a trouble to you, you'll be free soon enough."

It wasn't the hanging round that was a trouble to me at all by this time.   35
I had worse things to worry about. When I got back to the cottage the argument was still on. Hawkins was holding forth in his best style, maintaining that there was no next world, and Noble was maintaining that there was; but I could see that Hawkins had had the best of it.

"Do you know what, chum?" he was saying with a saucy smile. "I think you're just as big a bleeding unbeliever as I am. You say you believe in the next world, as you know just as much about the next world as I do, which is sweet damn-all. What's heaven? You don't know. Where's heaven? You don't know. You know sweet damn-all! I ask you again, do they wear wings?"

"Very well, then," says Noble, "they do. Is that enough for you? They do wear wings."

"Where do they get them, then? Who makes them? Have they a factory for wings? Have they a sort of store where you hands in your chit and takes your bleeding wings?"

"You're an impossible man to argue with," says Noble. "Now, listen to me—" And they were off again.

It was long after midnight when we locked up and went to bed. As I blew   40
out the candle I told Noble that Jeremiah Donovan was after telling me. Noble took it very quietly. When we'd been in bed about an hour he asked me did I think we ought to tell the Englishmen. I didn't think we should, because it was more than likely that the English wouldn't shoot our men, and even if they did, the brigade officers, who were always up and down with the Second Battalion and knew the Englishmen well, wouldn't be likely to want them plugged. "I think so too," says Noble. "It would be great cruelty to put the wind up them now."

"It was very unforeseen of Jeremiah Donovan anyhow," says I.

It was next morning that we found it so hard to face Belcher and Hawkins. We went about the house all day scarcely saying a word. Belcher didn't seem to notice; he was stretched into the ashes as usual, with his usual look of waiting in quietness for something unforeseen to happen, but Hawkins noticed and put it down to Noble's being beaten in the argument of the night before.

"Why can't you take a discussion in the proper spirit?" he says severely. "You and your Adam and Eve! I'm a Communist, that's what I am. Communist or anarchist, it all comes to much the same thing." And for hours he went round the house, muttering when the fit took him. "Adam and Eve! Adam and Eve! Nothing better to do with their time than picking bleeding apples!"

III

I don't know how we got through that day, but I was very glad when it was over, the tea things were cleared away, and Belcher said in his peaceable way: "Well, chums, what about it?" We sat round the table and Hawkins took out the cards, and just then I heard Jeremiah Donovan's footstep on the path and a dark presentiment crossed my mind. I rose from the table and caught him before he reached the door.

"What do you want?" I asked. 45

"I want those two soldier friends of yours," he says, getting red.

"Is that the way, Jeremiah Donovan?" I asked.

"That's the way. There were four of our lads shot this morning, one of them a boy of sixteen."

"That's bad," I said.

At that moment Noble followed me out, and the three of us walked down 50 the patch together, talking in whispers. Feeney, the local intelligence officer, was standing by the gate.

"What are you going to to about it?" I asked Jeremiah Donovan.

"I want you and Noble to get them out; tell them they're being shifted again; that'll be the quietest way."

"Leave me out of that," says Noble under his breath.

Jeremiah Donovan looks at him hard.

"All right," he says. "You and Feeney get a few tools from the shed and 55 dig a hole by the far end of the bog. Bonaparte and myself will be after you. Don't let anyone see you with the tools. I wouldn't like it to go beyond ourselves."

We saw Feeney and Noble go round to the shed and went in ourselves. I left Jeremiah Donovan to do the explanations. He told them that he had orders to send them back to the Second Battalion. Hawkins let out a mouthful of curses, and you could see that though Belcher didn't say anything, he was a bit upset too. The old woman was for having them stay in spite of us, and she didn't stop advising them until Jeremiah Donovan lost his temper and turned on her. He had a nasty temper, I noticed. It was pitch-dark in the cottage by this time, but no one thought of lighting the lamp, and in the darkness the two Englishmen fetched their topcoats and said good-bye to the old woman.

"Just as a man makes a home of a bleeding place, some bastard at headquarters thinks you're too cushy and shunts you off," says Hawkins, shaking her hand.

"A thousand thanks, madam," says Belcher. "A thousand thanks for everything"—as though he'd made it up.

We went round to the back of the house and down towards the bog, it was only then that Jeremiah Donovan told them. He was shaking with excitement.

"There were four of our fellows shot in Cork this morning and now you're   60
to be shot as a reprisal."

"What are you talking about?" snaps Hawkins. "It's bad enough being mucked about as we are without having to put up with your funny jokes."

"It isn't a joke," says Donovan. "I'm sorry, Hawkins, but it's true," and begins on the usual rigmarole about duty and how unpleasant it is.

I never noticed that people who talk a lot about duty find it much of a trouble to them.

"Oh, cut it out!" says Hawkins.

"Ask Bonaparte," says Donovan, seeing that Hawkins isn't taking him   65
seriously. "Isn't it true, Bonaparte?"

"It is," I say, and Hawkins stops.

"Ah, for Christ's sake, chum."

"I mean it, chum," I say.

"You don't sound as if you meant it."

"If he doesn't mean it, I do," says Donovan, working himself up.   70

"What have you against me, Jeremiah Donovan?"

"I never said I had anything against you. But why did your people take out four of our prisoners and shoot them in cold blood?"

He took Hawkins by the arm and dragged him on, but it was impossible to make him understand that we were in earnest. I had the Smith and Wesson in my pocket and I kept fingering it and wondering what I'd do if they put up a fight for it or ran, and wishing to God they'd do one or the other. I knew if they did run for it, that I'd never fire on them. Hawkins wanted to know was Noble in it, and when we said yes, he asked us why Noble wanted to plug him. Why did any of us want to plug him? What had he done to us? Weren't we all chums? Didn't we understand him and didn't he understand us? Did we imagine for an instant that he'd shoot us for all the so-and-so officers in the so-and-so British Army?

By this time we'd reached the bog, and I was so sick I couldn't even answer him. We walked along the edge of it in the darkness, and every now and then Hawkins would call a halt and begin all over again, as if he was wound up, about our being chums, and I knew that nothing but the sight of the grave would convince him that we had to do it. And all the time I was hoping that something would happen; that they'd run for it or that Noble would take over the responsibility from me. I had the feeling that it was worse on Noble than on me.

IV

At last we saw the lantern in the distance and made towards it. Noble was   75
carrying it, and Feeney was standing somewhere in the darkness behind him, and the picture of them so still and silent in the bogland brought it home to me that we were in earnest, and banished the last bit of hope I had.

Belcher, on recognizing Noble, said: "Hallo, chum," in his quiet way, but Hawkins flew at him at once, and the argument began all over again, only this

time Noble had nothing to say for himself and stood with his head down, holding the lantern between his legs.

It was Jeremiah Donovan who did the answering. For the twentieth time,
as though it was haunting his mind, Hawkins asked if anybody thought he'd
shoot Noble.

"Yes, you would," says Jeremiah Donovan.

"No, I wouldn't, damn you!"

"You would, because you'd know you'd be shot for not doing it."   80

"I wouldn't, not if I was to be shot twenty times over. I wouldn't shoot
a pal. And Belcher wouldn't—isn't that right, Belcher?"

"That's right chum," Belcher said, but more by way of answering the
question than of joining in the argument. Belcher sounded as though
whatever unforeseen thing he'd always been waiting for had come at last.

"Anyway, who says Noble would be shot if I wasn't? What do you think
I'd do if I was in his place, out in the middle of a blasted bog?"

"What would you do?" asks Donovan.

"I'd go with him wherever he was going, of course. Share my last bob   85
with him and stick by him through thick and thin. No one can ever say of me
that I let down a pal."

"We had enough of this," says Jeremiah Donovan, cocking his revolver.
"Is there any message you want to send?"

"No, there isn't."

"Do you want to say your prayers?"

Hawkins came out with a cold-blooded remark that even shocked me and
turned on Noble again.

"Listen to me, Noble," he says. "You and me are chums. You can't come   90
over to my side, so I'll come over to your side. That show you I mean what
I say? Give me a rifle and I'll go along with you and the other lads."

Nobody answered him. We knew that was no way out.

"Hear what I'm saying?" he says. "I'm through with it. I'm a deserter
or anything else you like. I don't believe in your stuff, but it's no worse than
mine. That satisfy you?"

Noble raised his head, but Donovan began to speak and he lowered it
again without replying.

"For the last time, have you any messages to send?" says Donovan in a
cold, excited sort of voice.

"Shut up, Donovan! You don't understand me, but these lads do. They're 95
not the sort to make a pal and kill a pal. They're not the tools of any
capitalist."

I alone of the crowd saw Donovan raise his Webley to the back of
Hawkins's neck, and as he did so I shut my eyes and tried to pray. Hawkins
had begun to say something else when Donovan fired, and as I opened my
eyes at the bang, I saw Hawkins stagger at the knees and lie out flat at Noble's
feet, slowly and as quiet as a kid falling asleep, with the lantern-light on his
lean legs and bright farmer's boots. We all stood very still, watching him settle
out in the last agony.

Then Belcher took out a handkerchief and began to tie it about his own
eyes (in our excitement we'd forgotten to do the same for Hawkins), and, see-

ing it wasn't big enough, turned and asked for the loan of mine. I gave it to him and he knotted the two together and pointed with his foot at Hawkins.

"He's not quite dead," he says. "Better give him another."

Sure enough, Hawkins's left knee is beginning to rise. I bend down and put my gun to his head; then, recollecting myself, I get up again. Belcher understands what's in my mind.

"Give him his first," he says. "I don't mind. Poor bastard, we don't know   100
what's happening to him now."

I knelt and fired. By this time I didn't seem to know what I was doing. Belcher, who was fumbling a bit awkwardly with the handkerchiefs, came out with a laugh as he heard the shot. It was the first time I heard him laugh and it sent a shudder down my back; it sounded so unnatural.

"Poor bugger!" he said quietly. "And last night he was so curious about it all. It's very queer, chums, I always think. Now he knows as much about it as they'll ever let him know, and last night he was all in the dark."

"Donovan helped him to tie the handkerchiefs about his eyes. "Thanks, chum," he said. Donovan asked if there were any messages he wanted sent.

"No, chum," he says. "Not for me. If any of you would like to write to Hawkins's mother, you'll find a letter from her in his pocket. He and his mother were great chums. But my missus left me eight years ago. Went away with another fellow and took the kid with her. I like the feeling of a home, as you may have noticed, but I couldn't start again after that."

It was an extraordinary thing, but in those few minutes Belcher said   105
more than in all the weeks before. It was just as if the sound of the shot had started a flood of talk in him and he could go on the whole night like that, quite happily, talking about himself. We stood round like fools now that he couldn't see us any longer. Donovan looked at Noble, and Noble shook his head. Then Donovan raised his Webley, and at that moment Belcher gives his queer laugh again. He may have thought we were talking about him, or perhaps he noticed the same thing I'd noticed and couldn't understand it.

"Excuse me, chums," he says. "I feel I'm talking the hell of a lot, and so silly, about my being so handy about a house and things like that. But this thing came on me suddenly. You'll forgive me, I'm sure."

"You don't want to say a prayer?" asked Donovan.

"No, chum," he says. "I don't think it would help. I'm ready, and you boys want to get it over."

"You understand that we're only doing our duty?" says Donovan.

Belcher's head was raised like a blind man's, so that you could only see   110
his chin and the tip of his nose in the lantern-light.

"I never could make out what duty was myself," he said. "I think you're all good lads, if that's what you mean. I'm not complaining."

Noble, just as if he couldn't bear any more of it, raised his fist at Donovan, and in a flash Donovan raised his gun and fired. The big man went over like a sack of meal, and this time there was no need of a second shot.

I don't remember much about the burying, but that it was worse than all the rest because we had to carry them to the grave. It was all mad lonely with nothing but a patch of lantern-light between ourselves and the dark, and birds hooting and screeching all round, disturbed by the guns. Noble went through

Hawkins's belongings to find the letter from his mother, and then joined his hands together. He did the same with Belcher. Then, when we'd filled in the grave, we separated from Jeremiah Donovan and Feeney and took our tools back to the shed. All the way we didn't speak a word. The kitchen was dark and cold as we'd left it, and the old woman was sitting over the hearth, saying her beads. We walked past her into the room, and Noble struck a match to light the lamp. She rose quietly and came to the doorway with all her cantankerousness gone.

"What did ye do with them?" she asked in a whisper, and Noble started so that the match went out in his hand.

"What's that?" he asked without turning round.   115

"I heard ye," she said.

"What did you hear?" asked Noble.

"I heard ye. Do ye think I didn't hear ye, putting the spade back in the houseen?"

Noble struck another match and this time the lamp lit for him.

"Was that what ye did to them?" she asked.   120

Then, by God, in the very doorway, she fell on her knees and began praying, and after looking at her for a minute or two Noble did the same by the fireplace. I pushed my way out past her and left them at it. I stood at the door, watching the stars and listening to the shrieking of the birds dying out over the bogs. It is so strange what you feel at times like that you can't describe it. Noble says he saw everything ten times the size, as though there were nothing in the whole world but that little patch of bog with the two Englishmen stiffening into it, but with me it was as if the patch of bog where the Englishmen were was a million miles away, and even Noble and the old woman, mumbling behind me, and the birds and the bloody stars were all far away, and I was somehow very small and very lost and lonely like a child astray in the snow. And anything that happened to me afterwards, I never felt the same about again.

[1931]

■ TOPICS FOR DISCUSSION AND WRITING

1. Although the narrator, Noble, and Donovan are all patriotic Irishmen, Donovan's attitude toward the English prisoners is quite different from that of the other two. How does that difference in attitude help point up the story's theme?

2. How does the constant bickering between Noble and Hawkins help to prepare us for the conclusion of the story? How does it contribute to the theme?

3. When he hears he is about to be shot, Hawkins, to save his life, volunteers to join the Irish cause. Is his turnabout simply evidence of his cowardice and hypocrisy? Explain.

4. Throughout most of the story Belcher is shy and speaks little; just before his execution, however, he suddenly becomes loquacious. Is he trying to stall for time? Would it have been more in character for Belcher to have remained stoically taciturn to the end, or do the narrator's remarks about Belcher's change make it plausible?

5. Does the old woman's presence in the story merely furnish local color or picturesqueness? If so, is it necessary or desirable? Or does her presence further contribute to the story's meaning? If so, how?
6. The following is the last paragraph of an earlier version. Which is the more effective conclusion? Why?

So then, by God, she fell on her two knees by the door, and began telling her beads, and after a minute or two Noble went on his knees by the fireplace, so I pushed my way past her, and stood at the door, watching the stars and listening to the damned shrieking of the birds. It is so strange what you feel at such moments, and not to be written afterwards. Noble says he felt he seen everything ten times as big, perceiving nothing around him but the little patch of black bog with the two Englishmen stiffening into it; but with me it was the other way, as though the patch of bog where the two Englishmen were was a thousand miles away from me, and even Noble mumbling just behind me and the old woman and the birds and the bloody stars were all far away, and I was somehow very small and very lonely. And nothing that ever happened me after I never felt the same about again.

7. How does the point of view (see page 121) help to emphasize the narrator's development from innocence to awareness? If the story had been told in the third person, how would it have affected the story's impact?

■ HISAYE YAMAMOTO

Hisaye Yamamoto was born in 1921 in Redondo Beach, California. Before the Second World War she contributed to the Japan-California *Daily News*, but when the United States entered the war she and her family were interned, along with more than a hundred thousand other persons of Japanese ancestry. She was sent to the Colorado River Relocation Center in Poston, Arizona, where she wrote for the camp's newspaper.

Yamamoto writes chiefly of rural Japanese-Americans, usually setting her stories in the depression or in the 1940s. "Yoneko's Earthquake" appeared in *Best American Short Stories of 1952*. Five of her stories have been collected in a volume called *Seventeen Syllables* (1985).

Yoneko's Earthquake

Yoneko Hosoume became a free-thinker on the night of March 10, 1933, only a few months after her first actual recognition of God. Ten years old at the time, of course she had heard rumors about God all along, long before Marpo came. Her cousins who lived in the city were all Christians, living as they did right next door to a Baptist church exclusively for Japanese people. These city cousins, of whom there were several, had been baptized en masse, and were very proud of their condition. Yoneko was impressed when she heard of this and thereafter was given to referring to them as "my cousins, the Christians." She, too, yearned at times after Christianity, but she realized the absurdity of her whim, seeing that there was no Baptist church for Japanese in the rural community she lived in. Such a church would have been impractical, moreover, since Yoneko, her father, her mother, and her little brother Seigo, were the only Japanese thereabouts. They were the only ones, too, whose agriculture was so diverse as to include blackberries, cabbages, rhubarb, potatoes, cucumbers, onions, and cantaloupes. The rest of the countryside there was like one vast orange grove.

Yoneko had entered her cousins' church once, but she could not recall the sacred occasion without mortification. It had been one day when the cousins had taken her and Seigo along with them to Sunday school. The church was a narrow, wooden building mysterious-looking because of its unusual bluish-gray paint and its steeple, but the basement schoolroom inside had been disappointingly ordinary, with desks, a blackboard, and erasers. They had all sung "Let Us Gather at the River" in Japanese. This goes:

Mamonaku kanata no
Nagare no soba de
Tanoshiku ai-masho
Mata tomodachi to

Mamonaku ai-masho
Kirei-na, kirei-na kawa de
Tanoshiku ai-masho
Mata tomodachi to.

Yoneko had not known the words at all, but always clever in such situations, she had opened her mouth and grimaced nonchalantly to the rhythm. What with everyone else singing at the top of his lungs, no one had noticed that she was not making a peep. Then everyone had sat down again and the man had suggested, "Let us pray." Her cousins and the rest had promptly curled their arms on the desks to make nests for their heads, and Yoneko had done the same. But not Seigo. Because when the room had become so still that one was aware of the breathing, the creaking, and the chittering in the trees outside, Seigo, sitting with her, had suddenly flung his arm around her neck and said with concern, "Sis, what are you crying for? Don't cry." Even the man had laughed and Yoneko had been terribly ashamed that Seigo should thus disclose them to be interlopers. She had pinched him fiercely and he had begun to cry, so she had had to drag him outside, which was a fortunate move, because he had immediately wet his pants. But he had been only three then, so it was not very fair to expect dignity of him.

So it remained for Marpo to bring the word of God to Yoneko, Marpo with the face like brown leather, the thin mustache like Edmund Lowe's, [1] and the rare, breathtaking smile like white gold. Marpo, who was twenty-seven years old, was a Filipino and his last name was lovely, something like Humming Wing, but no one ever ascertained the spelling of it. He ate principally rice, just as though he were Japanese, but he never sat down to the Hosoume table, because he lived in the bunkhouse out by the barn and cooked on his own kerosene stove. Once Yoneko read somewhere that Filipinos trapped

---

[1] **Edmund Lowe** a movie actor popular in the 1930s

wild dogs, starved them for a time, then, feeding them mountains of rice, killed them at the peak of their bloatedness, thus insuring themselves meat ready to roast, stuffing and all, without further ado. This, the book said, was considered a delicacy. Unable to hide her disgust and her fascination, Yoneko went straightway to Marpo and asked, "Marpo, is it true that you eat dogs?" and he, flashing that smile, answered "Don't be funny, honey!" This caused her no end of amusement, because it was a poem, and she completely forgot about the wild dogs.

Well, there seemed to be nothing Marpo could not do. Mr. Hosoume said Marpo was the best hired man he had ever had, and he said this often, because it was an irrefutable fact among Japanese in general that Filipinos in general were an indolent lot. Mr. Hosoume ascribed Marpo's industry to his having grown up in Hawaii, where there is known to be considerable Japanese influence. Marpo had gone to a missionary school there and he owned a Bible given him by one of his teachers. This had black leather covers that gave as easily as cloth, golden edges, and a slim purple ribbon for a marker. He always kept it on the little table by his bunk, which was not a bed with springs but a low, three-plank shelf with a mattress only. On the first page of the book, which was stiff and black, his teacher had written in large swirls of white ink, "As we draw near to God, He will draw near to us."

What, for instance, could Marpo do? Why, it would take an entire, leisurely evening to go into his accomplishments adequately, because there was not only Marpo the Christian and Marpo the best hired man, but Marpo the athlete, Marpo the musician (both instrumental and vocal), Marpo the artist, and Marpo the radio technician:

(1) As an athlete, Marpo owned a special pair of black shoes, equipped with sharp nails on the soles, which he kept in shape with the regular application of neatsfoot oil. Putting these on, he would dash down the dirt road to the highway, a distance of perhaps half a mile, and back again. When he first came to work for the Hosoumes, he undertook this sprint every evening before he went to get his supper but, as time went on, he referred to these shoes less and less and, in the end, when he left, he had not touched them for months. He also owned a muscle-builder sent him by Charles Atlas which, despite his unassuming size, he could stretch the length of his outspread arms; his teeth gritted then and his whole body became temporarily victim to a jerky vibration. (2) As an artist, Marpo painted larger-than-life water colors of his favorite movie stars, all of whom were women and all of whom were blonde, like Ann Harding and Jean Harlow, and tacked them up on his walls. He also made for Yoneko a folding contraption of wood holding two pencils, one with lead and one without, with which she, too, could obtain double-sized likenesses of any picture she wished. It was a fragile instrument, however, and Seigo splintered it to pieces one day when Yoneko was away at school. He claimed he was only trying to copy Boob McNutt from the funny paper when it failed. (3) As a musician, Marpo owned a violin for which he had paid over one hundred dollars. He kept this in a case whose lining was red velvet, first wrapping it gently in a brilliant red silk scarf. This scarf, which weighed nothing, he tucked under his chin when he played, gathering it up delicately by the center and flicking it once to unfurl it—a gesture Yoneko prized. In addition to this, Marpo was a singer, with a soft tenor which came

out in professional quavers and rolled r's when he applied a slight pressure
to his Adam's apple with thumb and forefinger. His violin and vocal repertoire
consisted of the same numbers, mostly hymns and Irish folk airs. He was especially addicted to "The Rose of Tralee" and the "Londonderry Air." (4) Finally, as a radio technician who had spent two previous winters at a
specialists' school in the city, Marpo had put together a bulky table-size radio
which brought in equal proportions of static and entertainment. He never got
around to building a cabinet to house it and its innards of metal and glass remained public throughout its lifetime. This was just as well, for not a week
passed without Marpo's deciding to solder one bit or another. Yoneko and Seigo became a part of the great listening audience with such fidelity that Mr.
Hosoume began remarking the fact that they dwelt more with Marpo than
with their own parents. He eventually took a serious view of the matter and
bought the naked radio from Marpo, who thereupon put away his radio manu-
als and his soldering iron in the bottom of his steamer trunk and divided more
time among his other interests.

However, Marpo's versatility was not revealed, as it is here, in a lump.
Yoneko uncovered it fragment by fragment every day, by dint of unabashed
questions, explorations among his possessions, and even silent observation,
although this last was rare. In fact, she and Seigo visited with Marpo at least
once a day and both of them regularly came away amazed with their findings.
The most surprising thing was that Marpo was, after all this, a rather shy
young man meek to the point of speechlessness in the presence of Mr. and
Mrs. Hosoume. With Yoneko and Seigo, he was somewhat more self-
confident and at ease.

It is not remembered now just how Yoneko and Marpo came to open
their protracted discussion on religion. It is sufficient here to note that Yoneko
was an ideal apostle, adoring Jesus, desiring Heaven, and fearing Hell. Once
Marpo had enlightened her on these basics, Yoneko never questioned their
truth. The questions she put up to him, therefore, sought neither proof of
her exegeses nor balm for her doubts, but simply additional color to round
out her mental images. For example, who did Marpo suppose was God's
favorite movie star? Or, what sound did Jesus' laughter have (it must be like
music, she added, nodding sagely, answering herself to her own satisfaction),
and did Marpo suppose that God's sense of humor would have appreciated
the delicious chant she had learned from friends at school today:

There ain't no bugs on us,
There ain't no bugs on us,
There may be bugs on the rest of you mugs,
But there ain't no bugs on us!

Or, did Marpo believe Jesus to have been exempt from stinging eyes when
he shampooed that long, naturally wavy hair of his?

To shake such faith, there would have been required a most monstrous
upheaval of some sort, and it might be said that this is just what happened.
For early on the evening of March 10, 1933, a little after five o'clock this was,
as Mrs. Hosoume was getting supper, as Marpo was finishing up in the fields
alone because Mr. Hosoume had gone to order some chicken fertilizer, and
as Yoneko and Seigo were listening to Skippy, a tremendous roar came out

of nowhere and the Hosoume house began shuddering violently as though some giant had seized it in his two hands and was giving it a good shaking. Mrs. Hosoume, who remembered similar, although milder experiences, from her childhood in Japan, screamed, *"Jishin, jishin!"* [2] before she ran and grabbed Yoneko and Seigo each by a hand and dragged them outside with her. She took them as far as the middle of the rhubarb patch near the house, and there they all crouched, pressed together, watching the world about them rock and sway. In a few minutes, Marpo, stumbling in from the fields, joined them, saying, "Earthquake, earthquake!" and he gathered them all in his arms, as much to protect them as to support himself.

Mr. Hosoume came home later that evening in a stranger's car, with another stranger driving the family Reo. Pallid, trembling, his eyes wildly staring, he could have been mistaken for a drunkard, except that he was famous as a teetotaler. It seemed that he had been on the way home when the first jolt came, that the old green Reo had been kissed by a broken live wire dangling from a suddenly leaning pole. Mr. Hosoume, knowing that the end had come by electrocution, had begun to writhe and kick and this had been his salvation. His hands had flown from the wheel, the car had swerved into a ditch, freeing itself from the sputtering wire. Later, it was found that he was left permanently inhibited about driving automobiles and permanently incapable of considering electricity with calmness. He spent the larger part of his later life weakly, wandering about the house or fields and lying down frequently to rest because of splitting headaches and sudden dizzy spells.

So it was Marpo who went back into the house as Yoneko screamed, "No, Marpo, no!" and brought out the Hosoumes' kerosene stove, the food, the blankets, while Mr. Hosoume huddled on the ground near his family.

The earth trembled for days afterwards. The Hosoumes and Marpo Humming Wing lived during that time on a natural patch of Bermuda grass between the house and the rhubarb patch remembering to take three meals a day and retire at night. Marpo ventured inside the house many times despite Yoneko's protests and reported the damage slight: a few dishes had been broken; a gallon jug of mayonnaise had fallen from the top pantry shelf and spattered the kitchen floor with yellow blobs and pieces of glass.

Yoneko was in constant terror during this experience. Immediately on learning what all the commotion was about, she began praying to God to end this violence. She entreated God, flattered Him, wheedled Him, commanded Him, but He did not listen to her at all—inexorably, the earth went on rumbling. After three solid hours of silent, desperate prayer, without any results whatsoever, Yoneko began to suspect that God was either powerless, callous, downright cruel, or nonexistent. In the murky night, under a strange moon wearing a pale ring of light, she decided upon the last as the most plausible theory. "Ha," was one of the things she said tremulously to Marpo, when she was not begging him to stay out of the house, "you and your God!"

The others soon oriented themselves to the catastrophe with philosophy, saying how fortunate they were to live in the country where the peril was less than in the city and going so far as to regard the period as a sort of vacation

---

[2] *jishin* earthquake (Japanese)

from work, with their enforced alfresco existence a sort of camping trip. They tried to bring Yoneko to partake of this pleasant outlook, but she, shivering with each new quiver, looked on them as dreamers who refused to see things as they really were. Indeed, Yoneko's reaction was so notable that the Hosoume household thereafter spoke of the event as "Yoneko's earthquake."

After the earth subsided and the mayonnaise was mopped off the kitchen floor, life returned to normal, except that Mr. Hosoume stayed at home most of the time. Sometimes, if he had a relatively painless day, he would have supper on the stove when Mrs. Hosoume came in from the fields. Mrs. Hosoume and Marpo did all the field labor now, except on certain overwhelming days when several Mexicans were hired to assist them. Marpo did most of the driving, too, and it was now he and Mrs. Hosoume who went into town on the weekly trip for groceries. In fact, Marpo became indispensable and both Mr. and Mrs. Hosoume often told each other how grateful they were for Marpo.

When summer vacation began and Yoneko stayed at home, too, she found the new arrangement rather inconvenient. Her father's presence cramped her style: for instance, once when her friends came over and it was decided to make fudge, he would not permit them, saying fudge used too much sugar and that sugar was not a plaything; once when they were playing paper dolls, he came along and stuck his finger up his nose and pretended he was going to rub some snot off onto the dolls. Things like that. So, on some days, she was very much annoyed with her father.

Therefore when her mother came home breathless from the fields one day and pushed a ring at her, a gold-colored ring with a tiny glasslike stone in it, saying, "Look, Yoneko, I'm going to give you this ring. If your father asks where you got it, say you found it on the street." Yoneko was perplexed but delighted both by the unexpected gift and the chance to have some secret revenge on her father, and she said, certainly, she was willing to comply with her mother's request. Her mother went back to the fields then and Yoneko put the pretty ring on her middle finger, taking up the loose space with a bit of newspaper. It was similar to the rings found occasionally in boxes of Crackerjack, except that it appeared a bit more substantial.

Mr. Hosoume never asked about the ring; in fact, he never noticed she was wearing one. Yoneko thought he was about to, once, but he only reproved her for the flamingo nail polish she was wearing, which she had applied from a vial brought over by Yvonne Fournier, the French girl two orange groves away. "You look like a Filipino," Mr. Hosoume said sternly, for it was another irrefutable fact among Japanese in general that Filipinos in general were a gaudy lot. Mrs. Hosoume immediately came to her defense, saying that in Japan, if she remembered correctly, young girls did the same thing. In fact, she remembered having gone to elaborate lengths to tint her fingernails: she used to gather, she said, the petals of the red *tsubobana* or the purple *kogane* (which grows on the underside of stones), grind them well, mix them with some alum powder, then cook the mixture and leave it to stand overnight in an envelope of either persimmon or sugar potato leaves (both very strong leaves). The second night, just before going to bed, she used to obtain threads by ripping a palm leaf (because real thread was dear) and tightly bind the paste to her fingernails under shields of persimmon or sugar potato leaves. She would be helpless for the night, the fingertips bound so well that they were alternately numb or aching, but she would grit her teeth and tell herself that the discomfort indicated the success of the operation. In the morning, finally releasing her fingers, she would find the nails shining with a translucent red-orange color.

Yoneko was fascinated, because she usually thought of her parents as having been adults all their lives. She thought that her mother must have been a beautiful child, with or without bright fingernails, because, though surely past thirty, she was even yet a beautiful person. When she herself was younger, she remembered, she had at times been so struck with her mother's appearance that she had dropped to her knees and mutely clasped her mother's legs in her arms. She had left off this habit as she learned to control her emotions, because at such times her mother had usually walked away, saying, "My, what a clinging child you are. You've got to learn to be a little more independent." She also remembered she had once heard someone comparing her mother to "a dewy, half-opened rosebud."

Mr. Hosoume, however, was irritated. "That's no excuse for Yoneko to begin using paint on her fingernails," he said. "She's only ten."

"Her Japanese age is eleven,[3] and we weren't much older," Mrs. Hosoume said.

"Look," Mr. Hosoume said, "if you're going to contradict every piece of advice I give the children, they'll end up disobeying us both and doing what they very well please. Just because I'm ill just now is no reason for them to start being disrespectful."

"When have I ever contradicted you before?" Mrs. Hosoume said.

"Countless times," Mr. Hosoume said.

"Name one instance," Mrs. Hosoume said.

Certainly there had been times, but Mr. Hosoume could not happen to mention the one requested instance on the spot and he became quite angry. "That's quite enough of your insolence," he said. Since he was speaking in Japanese, his exact accusation was that she was *nama-iki,* which is a shade more revolting than being merely insolent.

"*Nama-iki, nama-iki?*" said Mrs. Hosoume. "How dare you? I'll not have anyone calling me *nama-iki!*"

"At that, Mr. Hosoume went up to where his wife was ironing and slapped her smartly on the face. It was the first time he had ever laid hands on her. Mrs. Hosoume was immobile for an instant, but she resumed her ironing as though nothing had happened, although she glanced over at Marpo, who happened to be in the room reading a newspaper. Yoneko and Seigo forgot they were listening to the radio and stared at their parents, thunderstruck.

"Hit me again," said Mrs. Hosoume quietly, as she ironed. "Hit me all you wish."

---

[3] **Her Japanese age is eleven** By Japanese reckoning a child becomes one year old on the first New Year's Day following his or her birth.

Mr. Hosoume was apparently about to, but Marpo stepped up and put his hand on Mr. Hosoume's shoulder. "The children are here," said Marpo, "the children."

"Mind your own business," said Mr. Hosoume in broken English. "Get out of here!"

Marpo left, and that was about all. Mrs. Hosoume went on ironing, Yoneko and Seigo turned back to the radio, and Mr. Hosoume muttered that Marpo was beginning to forget his place. Now that he thought of it, he said, Marpo had been increasingly impudent towards him since his illness. He said just because he was temporarily an invalid was no reason for Marpo to start being disrespectful. He added that Marpo had better watch his step or that he might find himself jobless one of these fine days.

And something of the sort must have happened. Marpo was here one day and gone the next, without even saying good-bye to Yoneko and Seigo. That was also the day the Hosoume family went to the city on a weekday afternoon, which was most unusual. Mr. Hosoume, who now avoided driving as much as possible, handled the cumbersome Reo as though it were a nervous stallion, sitting on the edge of the seat and hugging the steering wheel. He drove very fast and about halfway to the city struck a beautiful collie which had dashed out barking from someone's yard. The car jerked with the impact, but Mr. Hosoume drove right on and Yoneko, wanting suddenly to vomit, looked back and saw the collie lying very still at the side of the road.

When they arrived at the Japanese hospital, which was their destination, Mr. Hosoume cautioned Yoneko and Seigo to be exemplary children and wait patiently in the car. It seemed hours before he and Mrs. Hosoume returned, she walking with very small, slow steps and he assisting her. When Mrs. Hosoume got in the car, she leaned back and closed her eyes. Yoneko inquired as to the source of her distress, for she was obviously in pain, but she only answered that she was feeling a little under the weather and that the doctor had administered some necessarily astringent treatment. At that, Mr. Hosoume turned around and advised Yoneko and Seigo that they must tell no one of coming to the city on a weekday afternoon, absolutely no one, and Yoneko and Seigo readily assented. On the way home, they passed the place of the encounter with the collie, and Yoneko looked up and down the stretch of road but the dog was nowhere to be seen.

Not long after that, the Hosoumes got a new hired hand, an old Japanese man who wore his gray hair in a military cut and who, unlike Marpo, had no particular interests outside working, eating, sleeping, and playing an occasional game of goh[4] with Mr. Hosoume. Before he came Yoneko and Seigo played sometimes in the empty bunkhouse and recalled Marpo's various charms together. Privately, Yoneko was wounded more than she would admit even to herself that Marpo should have subjected her to such an abrupt desertion. Whenever her indignation became too great to endure gracefully, she would console herself by telling Seigo that, after all, Marpo was a mere Filipino, an eater of wild dogs.

[4] **goh** a Japanese game for two, played with pebblelike counters on a board

Seigo never knew about the disappointing new hired man, because he suddenly died in the night. He and Yoneko had spent the hot morning in the nearest orange grove, she driving him to distraction by repeating certain words he could not bear to hear: she had called him Serge, a name she had read somewhere, instead of Seigo; and she had chanted off the name of the tires they were rolling around like hoops as Goodrich Silver-TO-town, Goodrich Silver-TO-town, instead of Goodrich Silvertown. This had enraged him, and he had chased her around the trees most of the morning. Finally she had taunted him from several trees away by singing "You're a Yellow-streaked Coward," which was one of several small songs she had composed. Seigo had suddenly grinned and shouted, "Sure!" and walked off, leaving her, as he intended, with a sense of emptiness. In the afternoon, they had per-spired and followed the potato-digging machine and the Mexican workers, both hired for the day, around the field, delighting in unearthing marble-sized, smooth-skinned potatoes that both the machine and the men had missed. Then, in the middle of the night, Seigo began crying, complaining of a stomach ache. Mrs. Hosoume felt his head and sent her husband for the doc-tor, who smiled and said Seigo would be fine in the morning. He said it was doubtless the combination of green oranges, raw potatoes, and the July heat. But as soon as the doctor left, Seigo fell into a coma and a drop of red blood stood out on his underlip, where he had evidently bit it. Mr. Hosoume again fetched the doctor, who was this time very grave and wagged his head, saying several times, "It looks very bad." So Seigo died at the age of five.

Mrs. Hosoume was inconsolable and had swollen eyes in the morning for weeks afterwards. She now insisted on visiting the city relatives each Sunday, so that she could attend church services with them. One Sunday, she stood up and accepted Christ. It was through accompanying her mother to many of these services that Yoneko finally learned the Japanese words to "Let Us Gather at the River." Mrs. Hosoume also did not seem interested in discuss-ing anything but God and Seigo. She was especially fond of reminding visitors how adorable Seigo had been as an infant, how she had been unable to refrain from dressing him as a little girl and fixing his hair in bangs until he was two. Mr. Hosoume was very gentle with her and when Yoneko accidently caused her to giggle once, he nodded and said, "Yes, that's right, Yoneko, we must make your mother laugh and forget about Seigo." Yoneko herself did not think about Seigo at all. Whenever the thought of Seigo crossed her mind, she in-stantly began composing a new song, and this worked very well.

One evening, when the new hired man had been with them a while, Yoneko was helping her mother with the dishes when she found herself being examined with such peculiarly intent eyes that, with a start of guilt, she began searching in her mind for a possible crime she had lately committed. But Mrs. Hosoume only said, "Never kill a person, Yoneko, because if you do, God will take from you someone you love."

"Oh, that," said Yoneko quickly, "I don't believe in that, I don't believe in God." And her words tumbling pell-mell over one another, she went on eagerly to explain a few of her reasons why. If she neglected to mention the test she had given God during the earthquake, it was probably because she was a little upset. She had believed for a moment that her mother was going to ask about the ring (which, alas, she had lost already, somewhere in the flumes[5] along the cantaloupe patch).

[1951]

■ TOPICS FOR DISCUSSION AND WRITING

1. Why does Mrs. Hosoume tell Yoneko not to tell Mr. Hosoume where the ring came from?
2. Why does Mr. Hosoume strike his wife?
3. Why does Marpo disappear on the same day that Mrs. Hosoume goes to the hospital?
4. Why does Mrs. Hosoume say—out of the blue, so far as Yoneko is concerned—"Never kill a person, Yoneko"?

■ ALICE MUNRO

Alice Munro was born in 1931 in Wingham, Ontario, Canada, a relatively rural community and the sort of place in which she sets much of her fiction. She began publishing stories when she was an undergraduate at the University of Western Ontario. She left Western after two years, worked in a library and in a bookstore. She then married and moved to Victoria, British Columbia, where she founded a bookstore. She continued to write while raising three children. She divorced and remarried; much of her fiction concerns marriage or divorce, which is to say it concerns shifting relationships in a baffling world.

How I Met My Husband

We heard the plane come over at noon, roaring through the radio news, and we were sure it was going to hit the house, so we all ran out into the yard. We saw it come in over the treetops, all red and silver, the first close-up plane I ever saw. Mrs. Peebles screamed.

"Crash landing," their little boy said. Joey was his name.

"It's okay," said Dr. Peebles. "He knows what he's doing." Dr. Peebles was only an animal doctor, but had a calming way of talking, like any doctor.

This was my first job—working for Dr. and Mrs. Peebles, who had bought an old house out on the Fifth Line, about five miles out of town. It was just when the trend was starting of town people buying up old farms, not to work them but to live on them.

We watched the plane land across the road, where the fairgrounds used to be. It did make a good landing field, nice and level for the old race track, and the barns and display sheds torn down now for scrap lumber so there was nothing in the way. Even the old grandstand bays had burned.

---

[5] **flumes** artificial channels made to conduct water

"All right," said Mrs. Peebles, snappy as she always was when she got over her nerves. "Let's go back in the house. Let's not stand here gawking like a set of farmers."

She didn't say that to hurt my feelings. It never occurred to her.

I was just setting the dessert down when Loretta Bird arrived, out of breath, at the screen door.

"I thought it was going to crash into the house and kill youse all!"

She lived on the next place and the Peebleses thought she was a country-woman, they didn't know the difference. She and her husband didn't farm, he worked on the roads and had a bad name for drinking. They had seven children and couldn't get credit at the HiWay Grocery. The Peebleses made her welcome, not knowing any better, as I say, and offered her dessert.

Dessert was never anything to write home about, at their place. A dish of Jello-O or sliced bananas or fruit out of a tin. "Have a house without a pie, be ashamed until you die," my mother used to say, but Mrs. Peebles operated differently.

Loretta Bird saw me getting the can of peaches.

"Oh, never mind," she said. "I haven't got the right kind of stomach to trust what comes out of those tins, I can only eat home canning."

I could have slapped her. I bet she never put down fruit in her life.

"I know what he's landed here for," she said. "He's got permission to use the fairgrounds and take people up for rides. It costs a dollar. It's the same fellow who was over at Palmerston[1] last week and was up the lakeshore before that. I wouldn't go up, if you paid me."

"I'd jump at the chance," Dr. Peebles said. "I'd like to see this neighborhood from the air."

Mrs. Peebles said she would just as soon see it from the ground. Joey said he wanted to go and Heather did, too. Joey was nine and Heather was seven.

"Would you, Edie?" Heather said.

I said I didn't know. I was scared, but I never admitted that, especially in front of children I was taking care of.

"People are going to be coming out here in their cars raising dust and trampling your property, if I was you I would complain," Loretta said. She hooked her legs around the chair rung and I knew we were in for a lengthy visit. After Dr. Peebles went back to his office or out on his next call and Mrs. Peebles went for her nap, she would hang around me while I was trying to do the dishes. She would pass remarks about the Peebleses in their own house.

"She wouldn't find time to lay down in the middle of the day, if she had seven kids like I got."

She asked me did they fight and did they keep things in the dresser drawer not to have babies with. She said it was a sin if they did. I pretended I didn't know what she was talking about.

[1] **Palmerston** a town in Ontario, Canada

I was fifteen and away from home for the first time. My parents had made the effort and sent me to high school for a year, but I didn't like it. I was shy of strangers and the work was hard, they didn't make it nice for you or explain the way they do now. At the end of the year the averages were published in the paper, and mine came out on the very bottom, 37 percent. My father said that's enough and I didn't blame him. The last thing I wanted, anyway, was to go on and end up teaching school. It happened the very day the paper came out with my disgrace in it, Dr. Peebles was staying at our place for dinner, having just helped one of our cows have twins, and he said I looked smart to him and his wife was looking for a girl to help. He said she felt tied down, with the two children, out in the country. I guess she would, my mother said, being polite, though I could tell from her face she was wondering what on earth it would be like to have only two children and no barn work, and then to be complaining.

When I went home I would describe to them the work I had to do, and it made everybody laugh. Mrs. Peebles had an automatic washer and dryer, the first I ever saw. I have had those in my own home for such a long time now it's hard to remember how much of a miracle it was to me, not having to struggle with the wringer and hang up and haul down. Let alone not having to heat water. Then there was practically no baking. Mrs. Peebles said she couldn't make pie crust, the most amazing thing I ever heard a woman admit. I could, of course, and I could make light biscuits and a white cake and dark cake, but they didn't want it, she said they watched their figures. The only thng I didn't like about working there, in fact, was feeling half hungry a lot of the time. I used to bring back a box of doughnuts made out at home, and hide them under my bed. The children found out, and I didn't mind sharing, but I thought I better bind them to secrecy.

The day after the plane landed Mrs. Peebles put both children in the car and drove over to Chesley, to get their hair cut. There was a good woman then at Chesley for doing hair. She got hers done at the same place, Mrs. Peebles did, and that meant they would be gone a good while. She had to pick a day Dr. Peebles wasn't going out into the country, she didn't have her own car. Cars were still in short supply then, after the war.

I loved being left in the house alone, to do my work at leisure. The kitchen was all white and bright yellow, with fluorescent lights. That was before they ever thought of making the appliances all different colors and doing the cupboards like dark old wood and hiding the lighting. I loved light. I loved the double sink. So would anybody new-come from washing dishes in a dishpan with a rag-plugged hole on an oilcloth-covered table by light of a coal-oil lamp. I kept everything shining.

The bathroom too. I had a bath in there once a week. They wouldn't have minded if I took one oftener, but to me it seemed like asking too much, or maybe risking making it less wonderful. The basin and the tub and the toilet were all pink, and there were glass doors with flamingoes painted on them, to shut off the tub. The light had a rosy cast and the mat sank under your feet like snow, except that it was warm. The mirror was three-way. With the mirror all steamed up and the air like a perfume cloud, from things I was allowed to use, I stood up on the side of the tub and admired myself naked, from three directions. Sometimes I thought about the way we lived out at home and the way we lived here and how one way was so hard to imagine when you were living the other way. But I thought it was still a lot easier, living the way we lived at home, to picture something like this, the painted flamingoes and the warmth and the soft mat, than it was anybody knowing only things like this to picture how it was the other way. And why was that?

I was through my jobs in no time, and had the vegetables peeled for supper and sitting in cold water besides. Then I went into Mrs. Peebles' bedroom. I had been in there plenty of times, cleaning, and I always took a good look in her closet, at the clothes she had hanging there. I wouldn't have looked in her drawers, but a closet is open to anybody. That's a lie. I would have looked in drawers, but I would have felt worse doing it and been more scared she could tell.

Some clothes in her closet she wore all the time, I was quite familiar with them. Others she never put on, they were pushed to the back. I was disappointed to see no wedding dress. But there was one long dress I could just see the skirt of, and I was hungering to see the rest. Now I took note of where it hung and lifted it out. It was satin, a lovely weight on my arm, light bluish-green in color, almost silvery. It had a fitted, pointed waist and a full skirt and an off-the-shoulder fold hiding the little sleeves.

Next thing was easy. I got out of my own things and slipped it on. I was slimmer at fifteen than anybody would believe who knows me now and the fit was beautiful. I didn't, of course, have a strapless bra on, which was what it needed, I just had to slide my straps down my arms under the material. Then I tried pinning up my hair, to get the effect. One thing led to another. I put on rouge and lipstick and eyebrow pencil from her dresser. The heat of the day and the weight of the satin and all the excitement made me thirsty, and I went out to the kitchen, got-up as I was, to get a glass of ginger ale with ice cubes from the refrigerator. The Peebleses drank ginger ale, or fruit drinks, all day, like water, and I was getting so I did too. Also there was no limit on ice cubes which I was so fond of I would even put them in a glass of milk.

I turned from putting the ice tray back and saw a man watching me through the screen. It was the luckiest thing in the world I didn't spill the ginger ale down the front of me then and there.

"I never meant to scare you. I knocked but you were getting the ice out, you didn't hear me."

I couldn't see what he looked like, he was dark the way somebody is pressed up against a screen door with the bright daylight behind them. I only knew he wasn't from around here.

"I'm from the plane over there. My name is Chris Watters and what I was wondering was if I could use that pump."

There was a pump in the yard. That was the way the people used to get their water. Now I noticed he was carrying a pail.

"You're welcome," I said. "I can get it from the tap and save you pumping." I guess I wanted him to know we had piped water, didn't pump ourselves.

"I don't mind the exercise." He didn't move, though, and finally he said "Were you going to a dance?"

Seeing a stranger there had made me entirely forget how I was dressed.

"Or is that the way ladies around here generally get dressed up in the afternoon?"

I didn't know how to joke back then. I was too embarrassed.

"You live here? Are you the lady of the house?"

"I'm the hired girl."

Some people change when they find that out, their whole way of looking at you and speaking to you changes, but his didn't.

"Well, I just wanted to tell you you look very nice. I was so surprised when I looked in the door and saw you. Just because you looked so nice and beautiful."

I wasn't even old enough then to realize how out of the common it is, for a man to say something like that to a woman, or somebody he is treating like a woman. For a man to say a word like *beautiful*. I wasn't old enough to realize or to say anything back, or in fact to do anything but wish he would go away. Not that I didn't like him, but just that it upset me so, having him look at me, and me trying to think of something to say.

He must have understood. He said good-bye, and thanked me, and went and sarted filling his pail from the pump. I stood behind the Venetian blinds in the dining room, watching him. When he had gone, I went into the bedroom and took the dress off and put it back in the same place. I dressed in my own clothes and took my hair down and washed my face, wiping it on Kleenex, which I threw in the wastebasket.

The Peebleses asked me what kind of man he was. Young, middle-aged, short, tall? I couldn't say.

"Good-looking?" Dr. Peebles teased me.

I couldn't think a thing but that he would be coming to get his water again, he would be talking to Dr. or Mrs. Peebles, making friends with them, and he would mention seeing me that first afternoon, dressed up. Why not mention it? He would think it was funny. And no idea of the trouble it would get me into.

After supper the Peebleses drove into town to go to a movie. She wanted to go somewhere with her hair fresh done. I sat in my bright kitchen wondering what to do, knowing I would never sleep. Mrs. Peebles might not fire me, when she found out, but it would give her a different feeling about me altogether. This was the first place I ever worked but I already had picked up things about the way people feel when you are working for them. They like to think you aren't curious. Not just that you aren't dishonest, that isn't enough. They like to feel you don't notice things, that you don't think or wonder about anything but what they liked to eat and how they liked things ironed, and so on. I don't mean they weren 't kind to me, because they were. They had me eat my meals with them (to tell the truth I expected to, I didn't know there were families who don't) and sometimes they took me along in the car. But all the same.

I went up and checked on the children being asleep and then I went out.

I had to do it. I crossed the road and went in the old fairgrounds gate. The plane looked unnatural sitting there, and shining with the moon. Off at the far side of the fairgrounds, where the bush was taking over, I saw his tent.

He was sitting outside it smoking a cigarette. He saw me coming.

"Hello, were you looking for a plane ride? I don't start taking people up till tomorrow." Then he looked again and said, "Oh, it's you. I didn't know you without your long dress on."

My heart was knocking away, my tongue was dried up. I had to say something. But I couldn't. My throat was closed and I was like a deaf-and-dumb.

"Did you want a ride? Sit down. Have a cigarette."

I couldn't even shake my head to say no, so he gave me one.

"Put it in your mouth or I can't light it. It's a good thing I'm used to shy ladies."

I did. It wasn't the first time I had smoked a cigarette, actually. My girl-friend out home, Muriel Lowe, used to steal them from her brother.

"Look at your hand shaking. Did you just want to have a chat, or what?"

In one burst I said, "I wisht you wouldn't say anything about that dress."

"What dress? Oh, the long dress."

"It's Mrs. Peebles'. "

"Whose? Oh, the lady you work for? Is that it? She wasn't home so you got dressed up in her dress, eh? You got dressed up and played queen. I don't blame you. You're not smoking the cigarette right. Don't just puff. Draw it in. Did anybody ever show you how to inhale? Are you scared I'll tell on you? Is that it?"

I was so ashamed at having to ask him to connive this way I couldn't nod. I just looked at him and he saw *yes*.

"Well I won't. I won't in the slightest way mention it or embarrass you. I give you my word of honor."

Then he changed the subject, to help me out, seeing I couldn't even thank him.

"What do you think of this sign?"

It was a board sign lying practically at my feet.

SEE THE WORLD FROM THE SKY. ADULTS $1.00, CHILDREN 50¢. QUALIFIED PILOT.

"My old sign was getting pretty beat up, I thought I'd make a new one. That's what I've been doing with my time today."

The lettering wasn't all that handsome, I thought. I could have done a better one in half an hour.

"I'm not an expert at sign making."

"It's very good," I said.

"I don't need it for publicity, word of mouth is usually enough. I turned away two carloads tonight. I felt like taking it easy. I didn't tell them ladies were dropping in to visit me."

Now I remembered the children and I was scared again, in case one of them had waked up and called me and I wasn't there.

"Do you have to go so soon?"

I remembered some manners. "Thank you for the cigarette."

"Don't forget. You have my word of honor."

I tore off across the fairgrounds, scared I'd see the car heading home from town. My sense of time was mixed up, I didn't know how long I'd been out of the house. But it was all right, it wasn't late, the children were asleep. I got in bed myself and lay thinking what a lucky end to the day, after all, and among things to be grateful for I could be grateful Loretta Bird hadn't been the one who caught me.

The yard and borders didn't get trampled, it wasn't as bad as that. All the same it seemed very public, around the house. The sign was on the fairgrounds gate. People came mostly after supper but a good many in the afternoon, too. The Bird children all came without fifty cents between them and hung on the gate. We got used to the excitement of the plane coming in and taking off, it wasn't excitement anymore. I never went over, after that one time, but would see him when he came to get his water. I would be out on the steps doing sitting-down work, like preparing vegetables, if I could.

"Why don't you come over? I'll take you up in my plane."

"I'm saving my money," I said, because I couldn't think of anything else.

"For what? For getting married?"

I shook my head.

"I'll take you up for free if you come sometime when it's slack. I thought you would come, and have another cigarette."

I made a face to hush him, because you never could tell when the children would be sneaking around the porch, or Mrs. Peebles herself listening in the house. Sometimes she came out and had a conversation with him. He told her things he hadn't bothered to tell me. But then I hadn't thought to ask. He told her he had been in the war, that was where he learned to fly a plane, and now he couldn't settle down to ordinary life, this was what he liked. She said she couldn't imagine anybody liking such a thing. Though sometimes, she said, she was almost bored enough to try anything herself, she wasn't brought up to living in the country. It's all my husband's idea, she said. This was news to me.

"Maybe you ought to give flying lessons," she said.

"Would you take them?"

She just laughed.

Sunday was a busy flying day in spite of it being preached against from two pulpits. We were all sitting out watching. Joey and Heather were over on the fence with the Bird kids. Their father had said they could go, after their mother saying all week they couldn't.

A car came down the road past the parked cars and pulled up right in the drive. It was Loretta Bird who got out, all importance, and on the driver's side another woman got out, more sedately. She was wearing sunglasses.

"This is a lady looking for the man that flies the plane," Loretta Bird said. "I heard her inquire in the hotel coffee shop where I was having a Coke and I brought her out."

"I'm sorry to bother you," the lady said. "I'm Alice Kelling, Mr. Waters' fiancée."

This Alice Kelling had on a pair of brown and white checked slacks and a yellow top. Her bust looked to me rather low and bumpy. She had a worried face. Her hair had had a permanent, but had grown out, and she wore a yellow band to keep it off her face. Nothing in the least pretty or even young-looking about her. But you could tell from how she talked she was from the city, or educated, or both.

Dr. Peebles stood up and introduced himself and his wife and me and asked her to be seated.

"He's up in the air right now, but you're welcome to sit and wait. He gets his water here and he hasn't been yet. He'll probably take his break about five."

"That is him, then?" said Alice Kelling, wrinkling and straining at the sky.

"He's not in the habit of running out on you, taking a different name?" Dr. Peebles laughed. He was the one, not his wife, to offer iced tea. Then she sent me into the kitchen to fix it. She smiled. She was wearing sunglasses too.

"He never mentioned his fiancée," she said.

I loved fixing iced tea with lots of ice and slices of lemon in tall glasses. I ought to have mentioned before, Dr. Peebles was an abstainer, at least around the house, or I wouldn't have been allowed to take the place. I had to fix a glass for Loretta Bird too, though it galled me, and when I went out she had settled in my lawn chair, leaving me the steps.

"I knew you was a nurse when I first heard you in that coffee shop."

"How would you know a thing like that?"

"I get my hunches about people. Was that how you met him, nursing?"

"Chris? Well yes. Yes, it was."

"Oh, were you overseas?" said Mrs. Peebles.

"No, it was before he went overseas. I nursed him when he was stationed at Centralia and had a ruptured appendix. We got engaged and then he went overseas. My, this is refreshing, after a long drive."

"He'll be glad to see you," Dr. Peebles said. "It's a rackety kind of life, isn't it, not staying one place long enough to really make friends."

"Youse've had a long engagement," Loretta Bird said.

Alice Kelling passed that over. "I was going to get a room at the hotel, but when I was offered directions I came on out. Do you think I could phone them?"

"No need," Dr. Peebles said. "You're five miles away from him if you stay at the hotel. Here, you're right across the road. Stay with us. We've got rooms on rooms, look at this big house."

Asking people to stay, just like that, is certainly a country thing, and maybe seemed natural to him now, but not to Mrs. Peebles, from the way she said, oh yes, we have plenty of room. Or to Alice Kelling, who kept protesting, but let herself be worn down. I got the feeling it was a temptation to her to be that close. I was trying for a look at her ring. Her nails were painted red, her fingers were freckled and wrinkled. It was a tiny stone. Muriel Lowe's cousin had one twice as big.

Chris came to get his water, late in the afternoon just as Dr. Peebles had predicted. He must have recognized the car from a way off. He came smiling.

"Here I am chasing after you to see what you're up to," called Alice Kelling. She got up and went to meet him and they kissed, just touched, in front of us.

"You're going to spend a lot on gas that way," Chris said.

Dr. Peebles invited Chris to stay for supper since he had already put up the sign that said: NO MORE RIDES TILL 7 P.M. Mrs. Peebles wanted it served in the yard, in spite of the bugs. One thing strange to anybody from the country is this eating outside. I had made a potato salad earlier and she had made a jellied salad, that was one thing she could do, so it was just a matter of getting those out, and some sliced meat and cucumbers and fresh leaf lettuce. Loretta Bird hung around for some time saying, "Oh, well, I guess I better get home to those yappers," and, "It's so nice just sitting here, I sure hate to get up," but nobody invited her, I was relieved to see, and finally she had to go.

That night after rides were finished Alice Kelling and Chris went off somewhere in her car. I lay awake till they got back. When I saw the car lights sweep my ceiling I got up to look down on them through the slats of my blind. I don't know what I thought I was going to see. Muriel Lowe and I used to sleep on her front veranda and watch her sister and her sister's boyfriend saying good night. Afterward we couldn't get to sleep, for longing for somebody to kiss us and rub up against us and we would talk about suppose you were out in a boat with a boy and he wouldn't bring you in to shore unless you did it, or what if somebody got you trapped in a barn, you would have to, wouldn't you, it wouldn't be your fault. Muriel said her two girl cousins used to try with a toilet paper roll that one of them was a boy. We wouldn't do anything like that; just lay and wondered.

All that happened was that Chris got out of the car on one side and she got out on the other and they walked off separately—him toward the fairgrounds and her toward the house. I got back in bed and imagined about me coming home with him, not like that.

Next morning Alice Kelling got up late and I fixed a grapefruit for her the way I had learned and Mrs. Peebles sat down with her to visit and have another cup of coffee. Mrs. Peebles seemed pleased enough now, having company. Alice Kelling said she guessed she better get used to putting in a day just watching Chris take off and come down, and Mrs. Peebles said she didn't know if she should suggest it because Alice Kelling was the one with the car, but the lake was only twenty-five miles away and what a good day for a picnic.

Alice Kelling took her up on the idea and by eleven o'clock they were in the car, with Joey and Heather and a sandwich lunch I had made. The only thing was that Chris hadn't come down, and she wanted to tell him where they were going.

"Edie'll go over and tell him," Mrs. Peebles said. "There's no problem."

Alice Kelling wrinkled her face and agreed.

"Be sure and tell him we'll be back by five!"

I didn't see that he would be concerned about knowing this right away, and I thought of him eating whatever he ate over there, alone, cooking on his camp stove, so I got to work and mixed up a crumb cake and baked it, in between the other work I had to do; then, when it was a bit cooled, wrapped it in a tea towel. I didn't do anything to myself but take off my apron and comb my hair. I would like to have put some makeup on, but I was too afraid it would remind him of the way he first saw me, and that would humiliate me all over again.

He had come and put another sign on the gate: NO RIDES THIS P.M. APOLO-GIES. I worried that he wasn't feeling well. No sign of him outside and the tent flap was down. I knocked on the pole.

"Come in," he said, in a voice that would just as soon have said *Stay out*. I lifted the flap.

"Oh, it's you. I'm sorry. I didn't know it was you."

He had been just sitting on the side of the bed, smoking. Why not at least sit and smoke in the fresh air?

"I brought a cake and hope you're not sick," I said.

"Why would I be sick? Oh—that sign. That's all right. I'm just tired of talking to people. I don't mean you. Have a seat." He pinned back the tent flap. "Get some fresh air in here."

I sat on the edge of the bed, there was no place else. It was one of those fold-up cots, really: I remembered and gave him his fiancée's message.

He ate some of the cake. "Good."

"Put the rest away for when you're hungry later."

"I'll tell you a secret. I won't be around here much longer."

"Are you getting married?"

"Ha ha. What time did you say they'd be back?"

"Five o'clock."

"Well, by that time this place will have seen the last of me. A plane can get further than a car." He unwrapped the cake and ate another piece of it, absent-mindedly.

"Now you'll be thirsty."

"There's some water in the pail."

"It won't be very cold. I could bring some fresh. I could bring some ice from the refrigerator."

"No," he said. "I don't want you to go. I want a nice long time of saying good-bye to you."

He put the cake away carefully and sat beside me and started those little kisses, so soft, I can't ever let myself think about them, such kindness in his face and lovely kisses, all over my eyelids and neck and ears, all over, then me kissing back as well as I could (I had only kissed a boy on a dare before, and kissed my own arms for practice) and we lay back on the cot and pressed together, just gently, and he did some other things, not bad things or not in a bad way. It was lovely in the tent, that smell of grass and hot tent cloth with the sun beating down on it, and he said, "I wouldn't do you any harm for the world." Once, when he had rolled on top of me and we were sort of rocking together on the cot, he said softly, "Oh, no," and freed himself and jumped up and got the water pail. He splashed some of it on his neck and face, and the little bit left, on me lying there.

"That's to cool us off, miss."

When we said good-bye I wasn't at all sad, because he held my face and said, "I'm going to write you a letter. I'll tell you where I am and maybe you can come and see me. Would you like that? Okay then. You wait." I was really glad I think to get away from him, it was like he was piling presents on me I couldn't get the pleasure of till I considered them alone.

No consternation at first about the plane being gone. They thought he had taken somebody up, and I didn't enlighten them. Dr. Peebles had phoned he had to go to the country, so there was just us having supper, and then Loretta Bird thrusting her head in the door and saying, "I see he's took off."

"What?" said Alice Kelling, and pushed back her chair.

"The kids come and told me this afternoon he was taking down his tent. Did he think he'd run through all the business there was around here? He didn't take off without letting you know, did he?"

"He'll send me word," Alice Kelling said. "He'll probably phone tonight. He's terribly restless, since the war."

"Edie, he didn't mention to you, did he?" Mrs. Peebles said. "When you took over the message?"

"Yes," I said. So far so true.

"Well why didn't you say?" All of them were looking at me. "Did he say where he was going?"

"He said he might try Bayfield," I said. What made me tell such a lie? I didn't intend it.

"Bayfield, how far is that?" said Alice Kelling.

Mrs. Peebles said, "Thirty, thirty-five miles."

"That's not far. Oh, well, that's really not far at all. It's on the lake, isn't it?"

You'd think I'd be ashamed of myself, setting her on the wrong track. I did it to give him more time, whatever time he needed. I lied for him, and also, I have to admit, for me. Women should stick together and not do things like that. I see that now, but didn't then. I never thought of myself as being in any way like her, or coming to the same troubles, ever.

She hadn't taken her eyes off me. I thought she suspected my lie.

"When did he mention this to you?"

"Earlier."

"When you were over at the plane?"

"Yes."

"You must've stayed and had a chat." She smiled at me, not a nice smile. "You must've stayed and had a little visit with him."

"I took a cake," I said, thinking that telling some truth would spare me telling the rest.

"We didn't have a cake," said Mrs. Peebles rather sharply.

"I baked one."

Alice Kelling said, "That was very friendly of you."

"Did you get permission," said Loretta Bird. "You never know what these girls'll do next," she said. "It's not they mean harm so much, as they're ignorant."

"The cake is neither here nor there," Mrs. Peebles broke in. "Edie, I wasn't aware you knew Chris that well."

I didn't know what to say.

"I'm not surprised," Alice Kelling said in a high voice. "I knew by the look of her as soon as I saw her. We get them at the hospital all the time." She looked hard at me with a stretched smile. "Having their babies. We have to put them in a special ward because of their diseases. Little country tramps. Fourteen and fifteen years old. You should see the babies they have, too."

"There was a bad woman here in town had a baby that pus was running out of its eyes," Loretta Bird put in.

"Wait a minute," said Mrs. Peebles. "What is this talk? Edie. What about you and Mr. Watters? Were you intimate with him?"

"Yes," I said. I was thinking of us lying on the cot and kissing, wasn't that intimate? And I would never deny it.

They were all one minute quiet, even Loretta Bird.

"Well," said Mrs. Peebles. "I am surprised. I think I need a cigarette. This is the first of any such tendencies I've seen in her," she said, speaking to Alice Kelling, but Alice Kelling was looking at me.

"Loose little bitch." Tears ran down her face. "Loose little bitch, aren't you? I knew as soon as I saw you. Men despise girls like you. He just made use of you and went off, you know that, don't you? Girls like you are just nothing, they're just public conveniences, just filthy little rags!"

"Oh now," said Mrs. Peebles.

"Filthy," Alice Kelling sobbed. "Filthy little rags!"

"Don't get yourself upset," Loretta Bird said. She was swollen up with pleasure at being in on this scene. "Men are all the same."

"Edie, I'm very surprised," Mrs. Peebles said. "I thought your parents were so strict. You don't want to have a baby, do you?"

I'm still ashamed of what happened next. I lost control, just like a six-year-old, I started howling. "You don't get a baby from just doing that!"

"You see. Some of them are that ignorant," Loretta Bird said.

But Mrs. Peebles jumped up and caught my arms and shook me.

"Calm down. Don't get hysterical. Calm down. Stop crying. Listen to me. Listen. I'm wondering, if you know what being intimate means. Now tell me. What did you think it meant?"

"Kissing," I howled.

She let go. "Oh, Edie. Stop it. Don't be silly. It's all right. It's all a misunderstanding. Being intimate means a lot more than that. Oh I *wondered*."

"She's trying to cover up, now," said Alice Kelling. "Yes. She's not so stupid. She sees she got herself in trouble."

"I believe her," Mrs. Peebles said. "This is an awful scene."

"Well there is one way to find out," said Alice Kelling, getting up. "After all, I am a nurse."

Mrs. Peebles drew a breath and said, "No. No. Go to your room, Edie. And stop that noise. This is too disgusting."

I heard the car start in a little while. I tried to stop crying, pulling back each wave as it started over me. Finally I succeeded, and lay heaving on the bed.

Mrs. Peebles came and stood in the doorway.

"She's gone," she said. "That Bird woman too. Of course, you know you should never have gone near that man and that is the cause of all this trouble.

I have a headache. As soon as you can, go and wash your face in cold water and get at the dishes and we will not say any more about this."

Nor we didn't. I didn't figure out till years later the extent of what I had been saved from. Mrs. Peebles was not very friendly to me afterward, but she was fair. Not very friendly is the wrong way of describing what she was. She had never been very friendly. It was just that now she had to see me all the time and it got on her nerves, a little.

As for me, I put it all out of my mind like a bad dream and concentrated on waiting for my letter. The mail came every day except Sunday, between one-thirty and two in the afternoon, a good time for me because Mrs. Peebles was always having her nap. I would get the kitchen all cleaned and then go up to the mailbox and sit in the grass, waiting. I was perfectly happy, waiting, I forgot all about Alice Kelling and her misery and awful talk and Mrs. Peebles and her chilliness and the embarrassment of whether she told Dr. Peebles and the face of Loretta Bird, getting her fill of other people's troubles. I was always smiling when the mailman got there, and continued smiling even after he gave me the mail and I saw today wasn't the day. The mailman was a Carmichael. I knew by his face because there are a lot of Carmichaels living out by us and so many of them have a sort of sticking-out top lip. So I asked his name (he was a young man, shy, but good-humored, anybody could ask him anything) and then I said, "I knew by your face!" He was pleased by that and always glad to see me and got a little less shy. "You've got the smile I've been waiting on all day!" he used to holler out the car window.

It never crossed my mind for a long time a letter might not come. I believed in it coming just like I believed the sun would rise in the morning. I just put off my hope from day to day, and there was the goldenrod out around the mailbox and the children gone back to school, and the leaves turning, and I was wearing a sweater when I went to wait. One day walking back with the hydro bill stuck in my hand, that was all, looking across at the fairgrounds with the full-blown milkweed and dark teasels, so much like fall, it just struck me: *No letter was ever going to come.* It was an impossible idea to get used to. No, not impossible. If I thought about Chris's face when he said he was going to write to me, it was impossible, but if I forgot that and thought about the actual tin mailbox, empty, it was plain and true. I kept on going to meet the mail, but my heart was heavy now like a lump of lead. I only smiled because I thought of the mailman counting on it, and he didn't have an easy life, with the winter driving ahead.

Till it came to me one day there were women doing this with their lives, all over. There were women just waiting and waiting by mailboxes for one letter or another. I imagined me making this journey day after day and year after year, and my hair starting to go gray, and I thought, I was never made to go on like that. So I stopped meeting the mail. If there were women all through life waiting, and women busy and not waiting, I knew which I had to be. Even though there might be things the second kind of women have to pass up and never know about, it still is better.

I was surprised when the mailman phoned the Peebleses' place in the evening and asked for me. He said he missed me. He asked if I would like to go to Goderich, where some well-known movie was on, I forget now what. So I said yes, and I went out with him for two years and he asked me to marry him, and we were engaged a year more while I got my things together, and then we did marry. He always tells the children the story of how I went after him by sitting by the mailbox every day, and naturally I laugh and let him, because I like for people to think what pleases them and makes them happy.

[1974]

■ TOPICS FOR DISCUSSION AND WRITING

1. Since Edie tells the story, we know about the other characters only as much as she tells us. Do you think her view of Mrs. Peebles and of Loretta Bird is accurate? On what do you base your answer?

2. Edie offers explicit comments about Mrs. Peebles and Loretta Bird, but not about Alice Kelling, or at least not to the same degree. Why?

3. Characterize Edie.

4. What do you think of the title? Why?

■ LILIANA HEKER

Liliana Heker, born in Argentina in 1943, achieved fame in 1966 with the publication of her first book. She has continued to write fiction, and she has also been influential in her role as the editor of a literary magazine. "The Stolen Party," first published in Spanish in 1982, was translated and printed in *Other Fires: Short Fiction by Latin American Women* (1985), edited and translated by Alberto Manguel.

The Stolen Party

As soon as she arrived she went straight to the kitchen to see if the monkey was there. It was: what a relief! She wouldn't have liked to admit that her mother had been right. *Monkeys at a birthday?* her mother had sneered. *Get away with you, believing any nonsense you're told!* She was cross, but not because of the monkey, the girl thought; it's just because of the party.

"I don't like you going," she told her. "It's a rich people's party."

"Rich people go to Heaven too," said the girl, who studied religion at school.

"Get away with Heaven," said the mother. "The problem with you, young lady, is that you like to fart higher than your ass."

The girl didn't approve of the way her mother spoke. She was barely nine, and one of the best in her class.

"I'm going because I've been invited," she said. "And I've been invited because Luciana is my friend. So there."

"Ah yes, your friend," her mother grumbled. She paused. "Listen, Rosaura," she said at last. "That one's not your friend. You know what you are to them? The maid's daughter, that's what."

Rosaura blinked hard: she wasn't going to cry. Then she yelled: "Shut up! You know nothing about being friends!"

Every afternoon she used to go to Luciana's house and they would both finish their homework while Rosaura's mother did the cleaning. They had their tea in the kitchen and they told each other secrets. Rosaura loved everything in the big house, and she also loved the people who lived there.

"I'm going because it will be the most lovely party in the whole world, Luciana told me it would. There will be a magician, and he will bring a monkey and everything."

The mother swung around to take a good look at her child, and pompously put her hands on her hips.

"Monkeys at a birthday?" she said. "Get away with you, believing any nonsense you're told!"

Rosaura was deeply offended. She thought it unfair of her mother to accuse other people of being liars simply because they were rich. Rosaura too wanted to be rich, of course. If one day she managed to live in a beautiful palace, would her mother stop loving her? She felt very sad. She wanted to go to that party more than anything else in the world.

"I'll die if I don't go," she whispered, almost without moving her lips.

And she wasn't sure whether she had been heard, but on the morning of the party she discovered that her mother had starched her Christmas dress. And in the afternoon, after washing her hair, her mother rinsed it in apple vinegar so that it would be all nice and shiny. Before going out, Rosaura admired herself in the mirror, with her white dress and glossy hair, and thought she looked terribly pretty.

Señora Ines also seemed to notice. As soon as she saw her, she said: "How lovely you look today, Rosaura."

Rosaura gave her starched skirt a slight toss with her hands and walked into the party with a firm step. She said hello to Luciana and asked about the monkey. Luciana put on a secretive look and whispered into Rosaura's ear: "He's in the kitchen. But don't tell anyone, because it's a surprise."

Rosaura wanted to make sure. Carefully she entered the kitchen and there she saw it: deep in thought, inside its cage. It looked so funny that the girl stood there for a while, watching it, and later, every so often, she would slip out of the party unseen and go and admire it. Rosaura was the only one allowed into the kitchen. Señora Ines had said: "You yes, but not the others, they're much too boisterous, they might break something." Rosaura had never broken anything. She even managed the jug of orange juice, carrying it from the kitchen into the dining room. She held it carefully and didn't spill a single drop. And Señora Ines had said: "Are you sure you can manage a jug as big as that?" Of course she could manage. She wasn't a butterfingers, like the others. Like that blonde girl with the bow in her hair. As soon as she saw Rosaura, the girl with the bow had said:

"And you? Who are you?"

"I'm a friend of Luciana," said Rosaura.

"No," said the girl with the bow, "you are not a friend of Luciana because I'm her cousin and I know all her friends. And I don't know you."

"So what," said Rosaura. "I come here every afternoon with my mother and we do our homework together."

"You and your mother do your homework together?" asked the girl, laughing.

"I and Luciana do our homework together," said Rosaura, very seriously. The girl with the bow shrugged her shoulders.

"That's not being friends," she said. "Do you go to school together?"

"No."

"So where do you know her from?" said the girl, getting impatient.

Rosaura remembered her mother's words perfectly. She took a deep breath.

"I'm the daughter of the employee," she said.

Her mother had said very clearly: "If someone asks, you say you're the daughter of the employee; that's all." She also told her to add: "And proud of it." But Rosaura thought that never in her life would she dare say something of the sort.

"What employee?" said the girl with the bow. "Employee in a shop?"

"No," said Rosaura angrily. "My mother doesn't sell anything in any shop, so there."

"So how come she's an employee?" said the girl with the bow.

Just then Señora Ines arrived saying *shh shh*, and asked Rosaura if she wouldn't mind helping serve out the hotdogs, as she knew the house so much better than the others.

"See?" said Rosaura to the girl with the bow, and when no one was looking she kicked her in the shin.

Apart from the girl with the bow, all the others were delightful. The one she liked best was Luciana, with her golden birthday crown; and then the boys. Rosaura won the sack race, and nobody managed to catch her when they played tag. When they split into two teams to play charades, all the boys wanted her for their side. Rosaura felt she had never been so happy in all her life.

But the best was still to come. The best came after Luciana blew out the candles. First the cake. Señora Ines had asked her to help pass the cake around, and Rosaura had enjoyed the task immensely, because everyone called out to her, shouting "Me, me!" Rosaura remembered a story in which there was a queen who had the power of life or death over her subjects. She had always loved that, having the power of life or death. To Luciana and the boys she gave the largest pieces, and to the girl with the bow she gave a slice so thin one could see through it.

After the cake came the magician, tall and bony, with a fine red cape. A true magician: he could untie handkerchiefs by blowing on them and make a chain with links that had no openings. He could guess what cards were pulled out from a pack, and the monkey was his assistant. He called the monkey "partner." "Let's see here, partner," he would say, "turn over a card." And, "Don't run away, partner: time to work now."

The final trick was wonderful. One of the children had to hold the monkey in his arms and the magician said he would make him disappear.

"What, the boy?" they all shouted.

"No, the monkey!" shouted back the magician.

Rosaura thought that this was truly the most amusing party in the whole world.

The magician asked a small fat boy to come and help, but the small fat boy got frightened almost at once and dropped the monkey on the floor. The magician picked him up carefully, whispered something in his ear, and the monkey nodded almost as if he understood.

"You mustn't be so unmanly, my friend," the magician said to the fat boy.

"What's unmanly?" said the fat boy.

The magician turned around as if to look for spies.

"A sissy," said the magician. "Go sit down."

Then he stared at all the faces, one by one. Rosaura felt her heart tremble.

"You, with the Spanish eyes," said the magician. And everyone saw that he was pointing at her.

She wasn't afraid. Neither holding the monkey, nor when the magician made him vanish; not even when, at the end, the magician flung his red cape over Rosaura's head and uttered a few magic words . . . and the monkey reappeared, chattering happily, in her arms. The children clapped furiously. And before Rosaura returned to her seat, the magician said:

"Thank you very much, my little countess."

She was so pleased with the compliment that a while later, when her mother came to fetch her, that was the first thing she told her.

"I helped the magician and he said to me, 'Thank you very much, my little countess.' "

It was strange because up to then Rosaura had thought that she was angry with her mother. All along Rosaura had imagined that she would say to her: "See that the monkey wasn't a lie?" But instead she was so thrilled that she told her mother all about the wonderful magician.

Her mother tapped her on the head and said: "So now we're a countess!"

But one could see that she was beaming.

And now they both stood in the entrance, because a moment ago Señora Ines, smiling, had said: "Please wait here a second."

Her mother suddenly seemed worried.

"What is it?" she asked Rosaura.

"What is what?" said Rosaura. "It's nothing; she just wants to get the presents for those who are leaving, see?"

She pointed at the fat boy and at a girl with pigtails who were also waiting there, next to their mothers. And she explained about the presents. She knew, because she had been watching those who left before her. When one of the girls was about to leave, Señora Ines would give her a bracelet. When a boy left, Señora Ines gave him a yo-yo. Rosaura preferred the yo-yo because it sparkled, but she didn't mention that to her mother. Her mother might have said: "So why don't you ask for one, you blockhead?" That's what her mother was like. Rosaura didn't feel like explaining that she'd be horribly ashamed to be the odd one out. Instead she said:

"I was the best-behaved at the party."

And she said no more because Señora Ines came out into the hall with two bags, one pink and one blue.

First she went up to the fat boy, gave him a yo-yo out of the blue bag, and the fat boy left with his mother. Then she went up to the girl and gave her a bracelet out of the pink bag, and the girl with the pigtails left as well.

Finally she came up to Rosaura and her mother. She had a big smile on her face and Rosaura liked that. Señora Ines looked down at her, then looked up at her mother, and then said something that made Rosaura proud:

"What a marvelous daughter you have, Herminia."

For an instant, Rosaura thught that she'd give her two presents: the bracelet and the yo-yo. Señora Ines bent down as if about to look for something. Rosaura also leaned forward, stretching out her arm. But she never completed the movement.

Señora Ines didn't look in the pink bag. Nor did she look in the blue bag. Instead she rummaged in her purse. In her hand appeared two bills.

"You really and truly earned this," she said handing them over. "Thank you for all your help, my pet."

Rosaura felt her arms stiffen, stick close to her body, and then she noticed her mother's hand on her shoulder. Instinctively she pressed herself against her mother's body. That was all. Except her eyes. Rosaura's eyes had a cold, clear look that fixed itself on Señora Ines's face.

Señora Ines, motionless, stood there with her hand outstretched. As if she didn't dare draw it back. As if the slightest change might shatter an infinitely delicate balance.

[1982]

■ TOPICS FOR DISCUSSION AND WRITING

1. The first paragraph tells us, correctly, that Rosaura's mother is wrong about the monkey. By the time the story is over, is the mother right about anything? If so, what?

2. Characterize Señora Ines. Why does she offer Rosaura money instead of a yo-yo or a bracelet? By the way, do you assume she is speaking deceptively when she tells Rosaura that she bars other children from the kitchen on the grounds that "they might break something"? On what do you base your view?

3. What do you make of the last paragraph? Why does Señora Ines stand with her hand outstretched, "as if she didn't dare draw it back"? What "infinitely delicate balance" might be shattered?

■ JAMAICA KINCAID

Jamaica Kincaid (b. 1949) was born in St. John's, Antigua, in the West Indies. She was educated at the Princess Margaret School in Antigua, and, briefly, at Westchester Community College and Franconia College. Since 1974 she has been a contributor to *The New Yorker.*

Kincaid is the author of four books, *At the Bottom of the River*

(1983, a collection of short pieces, including "Girl"), *Annie John* (1985,
a second book recording a girl's growth, including "Columbus in
Chains"), *A Small Place* (1988, a passionate essay about the destructive
effects of colonialism), and *Lucy* (1990, a short novel about a young
black woman who comes to the United States from the West Indies).

Girl

Wash the white clothes on Monday and put them on the stone heap;
wash the color clothes on Tuesday and put them on the clothesline to dry;
don't walk barehead in the hot sun; cook pumpkin fritters in very hot sweet
oil; soak your little clothes right after you take them off; when buying cotton
to make yourself a nice blouse, be sure that it doesn't have gum on it, because that way it won't hold up well after a wash; soak salt fish overnight
before you cook it; is it true that you sing benna in Sunday School?; always
eat your food in such a way that it won't turn someone else's stomach; on
Sundays try to walk like a lady and not like the slut you are so bent on becoming; don't sing benna[1] in Sunday School; you mustn't speak to wharf-rat
boys, not even to give directions; don't eat fruits on the street—flies will follow you; *but I don't sing benna on Sundays at all and never in Sunday school;*
this is how to sew on a button; this is how to make a buttonhole for the button you have just sewed on; this is how to hem a dress when you see the
hem coming down and so to prevent yourself from looking like the slut I
know you are so bent on becoming; this is how you iron your father's khaki
shirt so that it doesn't have a crease; this is how you iron your father's khaki
pants so that they don't have a crease; this is how you grow okra—far from
the house, because okra tree harbors red ants; when you are growing
dasheen, make sure it gets plenty of water or else it makes your throat itch
when you are eating it; this is how you sweep a corner; this is how you
sweep a whole house; this is how you sweep a yard; this is how you smile
to someone you don't like too much; this is how you set a table for dinner
with an important guest; this is how you smile to someone you don't like at
all; this is how you smile to someone you like completely; this is how you
set a table for tea; this is how you set a table for dinner; this is how you set
a table for lunch; this is how you set a table for breakfast; this is how to behave in the presence of men who don't know you very well, and this way
they won't recognize immediately the slut I have warned you against becoming; be sure to wash every day, even if it is with your own spit; don't squat
down to play marbles—you are not a boy, you know; don't pick people's
flowers—you might catch something; don't throw stones at blackbirds, because it might not be a blackbird at all; this is how to make a bread pudding;
this is how to make doukona[2]; this is how to make pepper pot; this is how
to make a good medicine for a cold; this is how to make a good medicine to
throw away a child before it even becomes a child; this is how to catch a fish;

[1]**benna** Calypso music
[2]**doukona** spicy pudding made of plantains

this is how to throw back a fish you don't like, and that way something bad won't fall on you; this is how to bully a man; this is how a man bullies you; this is how to love a man, and if this doesn't work there are other ways, and if they don't work don't feel too bad about giving up; this is how to spit up in the air if you feel like it, and this is how to move quick so that it doesn't fall on you; this is how to make ends meet; always squeeze bread to make sure it's fresh; *but what if the baker won't let me feel the bread?*; you mean to say that after all you are really going to be the kind of woman who the baker won't let near the bread?

[1978]

■ TOPICS FOR DISCUSSION AND WRITING

1. Identify the two characters whose voices we hear in this story. Explain what we know about them (their circumstances and their relationship). How old, approximately, is "girl"? Cite specific evidence from the text.
2. What do we learn about the relationship from frequent repetition of "this is how"? Are there other words or phrases frequently repeated? If so, what are they?
3. Imitating the structure of "Girl," compose a comparable piece, based on some repeated conversation in your family.

Columbus in Chains

Outside, as usual, the sun shone, the trade winds blew; on her way to put some starched clothes on the line, my mother shooed some hens out of her garden; Miss Dewberry baked the buns, some of which my mother would buy for my father and me to eat with our afternoon tea; Miss Henry brought the milk, a glass of which I would drink with my lunch, and another glass of which I would drink with the bun from Miss Dewberry; my mother prepared our lunch; my father noted some perfectly idiotic thing his partner in house-building, Mr. Oatie, had done, so that over lunch he and my mother could have a good laugh.

The Anglican church bell struck eleven o'clock—one hour to go before lunch. I was then sitting at my desk in my classroom, in Antigua. We were having a history lesson—the last lesson of the morning. For taking first place in the second form, over all the other girls, I had been given a prize, a copy of a book called "Roman Britain," and I was made prefect of my class. What a mistake the prefect part had been, for I was among the worst-behaved in my class. Now I had to sit in the prefect's seat—the first seat in the front row, the seat from which I could stand up and survey quite easily my classmates. From where I sat I could see out the window. Sometimes when I looked out, I could see the sexton going over to the minister's house. The sexton's daughter, Hilarene, a disgusting model of good behavior and keen attention to scholarship, sat next to me, since she took second place. The minister's daughter, Ruth, sat in the last row, the row reserved for all the dunce girls. Hilarene, of course, I could not stand. A girl that good would never do for me. I would probably not have cared so much for first place if I could be sure it would not go to her. Ruth I liked, because she was such a dunce and came from England and had yellow hair. When I first met her, I used to walk her home and sing bad songs to her just to see her turn pink, as if I had just spilled hot water all over her.

Our books, "A History of the West Indies," were open in front of us. Our day had begun with morning prayers, then a geometry lesson, then it was over to the science building for a lesson in "Introductory Physics" (not a subject we cared much for), taught by the most dingy-toothed Mr. Slacks, a teacher from Canada, then precious recess, and now this, our history lesson. Recess had the usual drama: this time, I coaxed Gwen out of her disappointment at not being allowed to join the junior choir. Her father—how many times had I wished he would become a leper and so be banished to a leper colony for the rest of my long and happy life with Gwen—had forbidden it, giving as his reason that she lived too far away from church, where choir rehearsals were conducted, and that it would be dangerous for her, a young girl, to walk home alone at night in the dark. Of course, all the streets had lamplight, but it was useless to point that out to him. Oh, how it would have pleased us to press and rub our knees together as we sat in our pew while pretending to pay close attention to Mr. Simmons, our choir-master, as he waved his baton up and down and across, and how it would have pleased us even more to walk home together, alone in the "early dusk" (the way Gwen had phrased it, a ready phrase always on her tongue), stopping, if there was a full moon, to lie down in a pasture and expose our bosoms in the moonlight. We had heard that full moonlight would make our breasts grow to a size we would like. Poor Gwen! When I first heard from her that she was one of the children, right on the spot I told her that I would love only her, since her mother already had so many other people to love.

Our teacher, Miss Edward, paced up and down in front of the class in her usual way. In front of her desk stood a small table, and on it stood the dunce cap. The dunce cap was in the shape of a coronet, with an adjustable opening in the back, so that it could fit any head. It was made of cardboard with a shiny gold paper covering and the word "DUNCE" in shiny red paper on the front. When the sun shone on it, the dunce cap was all aglitter, almost as if you were being tricked into thinking it a desirable thing to wear. As Miss Edward paced up and down, she would pass between us and the dunce cap like an eclipse. Each Friday morning, we were given a small test to see how well we had learned the things taught to us all week. The girl who scored lowest was made to wear the dunce cap all day the following Monday. On many Mondays, Ruth wore it—only, with her short yellow hair, when the dunce cap was sitting on her head she looked like a girl attending a birthday party in "The Schoolgirl's Own Annual."

It was Miss Edward's way to ask one of us a question the answer to which 125 she was sure the girl would not know and then put the same question to another girl who she was sure would know the answer. The girl who did not answer correctly would then have to repeat the correct answer in the exact words of the other girl. Many times, I had heard my exact words repeated over and over again, and I liked it especially when the girl doing the repeating was one I didn't care about very much. Pointing a finger at Ruth, Miss Edward asked a question the answer to which was "On the third of November, 1493, a Sunday morning, Christopher Columbus discovered Dominica." Ruth, of course, did not know the answer, as she did not know the answer to many questions about the West Indies. I could hardly blame her. Ruth had come all the way from England. Perhaps she did not want to be in the West Indies at all. Perhaps she wanted to be in England, where no one would remind her constantly of the terrible things her ancestors had done; perhaps she had felt even worse when her father was in charge of a mission in Africa. I could see how Ruth felt from looking at her face. Her ancestors had been the masters, while ours had been the slaves. She had such a lot to be ashamed of, and by being with us every day she was always being reminded. We could look everybody in the eye, for our ancestors had done nothing wrong except just sit somewhere, defenseless. Of course, sometimes, what with our teachers and our books, it was hard for us to tell on which side we really now belonged— with the masters or the slaves—for it was all history, it was all in the past, and everybody behaved differently now, and all of us celebrated Queen Victoria's birthday, even though she had been dead a long time. But we knew quite well what had happened, and I was sure that if the tables had been turned we would have acted differently; I was sure we would have taken a proper interest in the Europeans and said, "How nice," and then gone home to tell our friends about it.

I was sitting at my desk, having these thoughts to myself. I don't know how long it had been since I lost track of what was going on around me. I had not noticed that the girl who was asked the question after Ruth failed—a girl named Hyacinth—had only got a part of the answer correct. I had not noticed that after these two attempts Miss Edward had launched into a harangue about what a worthless bunch we were compared to girls of the past. In fact, I was no longer on the same chapter we were studying. I was way ahead, at the end of the chapter about Columbus's third voyage. In this chapter, there was a picture of Columbus that took up a whole page, and it was in color—one of only five color pictures in the book. In this picture, Columbus was seated in the bottom of a ship. He was wearing the usual three-quarter trousers and a shirt with enormous sleeves, both the trousers and shirt made of maroon-colored velvet. His hat, which was cocked up on one side of his head, had a gold feather in it, and his black shoes had huge gold buckles. His hands and feet were bound up in chains, and he was sitting there staring off into space, looking quite dejected and miserable. The picture had as a title "Columbus in Chains," printed at the bottom of the page. What had happened was that the usually quarrelsome Columbus had got into a disagreement with people who were even more quarrelsome, and a man named Bobadilla, representing King Ferdinand and Queen Isabella, had sent him back to Spain fettered in chains attached to the bottom of a ship. What just deserts, I thought, for I did not like Columbus. How I loved this picture! Shortly after I first discovered it in my history book, I heard my mother read out loud to my father a letter she had just received from her sister, who still lived with her mother and father in the very same Dominica, which is where my mother came from. Ma Chess was fine, wrote my aunt, but Pa Chess was not well. Pa Chess was having a bit of trouble with his limbs; he was no longer able to go about as he pleased; often he had to depend on someone else to do one thing or another for him. Since I had long ago managed to convince my parents that

I was the most innocent, most virtuous child who ever lived, they often felt free to speak frankly to each other in my presence. Whenever I found myself alone with them—and that was quite often—I would get a faraway look on my face, as if to say, I am not really here and you don't interest me with your big thoughts. If that wasn't too successful, I would start to hum a little childish song to myself, while playing with my collar or my shoelaces. My parents would soon start to speak quite openly to each other about many things. It was in just such an atmosphere that my mother read out loud to my father the letter she had just received from her sister. After she read the part about Pa Chess's stiff limbs, she turned to my father and laughed as she said, "So the great man can no longer just get up and go. How I would love to see his face now!" When I next saw the picture of Columbus sitting there all locked up in his chains, I wrote under it the words "The Great Man Can No Longer Just Get Up and Go." I had written this out with my fountain pen, and in Old English lettering—a script I had just recently mastered. As I sat there looking at the picture, I traced the words with my pen over and over, so that the letters grew big and you could read what I had written from not very far away. I don't know how long it was before I heard that my name, Annie John, was being said by this bellowing dragon in the form of Miss Edward bearing down on me.

I had never been a favorite of hers. Her favorite was Hilarene. It must have pained Miss Edward that I so often beat out Hilarene. Not that I liked Miss Edward and wanted her to like me back, but all my other teachers regarded me with much affection, would always tell my mother that I was the most charming student they had ever had, beamed at me when they saw me coming, and were very sorry when they had to write some version of this on my report card: "Annie is an unusually bright girl. She is well behaved in class, at least in the presence of her masters and mistresses, but behind their backs and outside the classroom quite the opposite is true." When my mother read this or something like it, she would burst into tears. She had hoped to display, with a great flourish, my report card to her friends, along with whatever prize I had won. Instead, the report card would have to take a place at the bottom of an old trunk in which she kept any important thing that had to do with me. I became not a favorite of Miss Edward's in the following way: Each Friday afternoon, the girls in the lower forms were given, instead of a last lesson period, an extra-long recess. We were to use this in lady-like recreation— walks, chats about the novels and poems we were reading, showing each other the new embroidery stitches we had learned to master in home class, or something just as seemly. Instead, some of the girls would play a game of cricket or rounders or stones, but most of us would go to the far end of the school grounds and play band. In this game, of which teachers and parents disapproved and which was sometimes absolutely forbidden, we would place our arms around each other's waist or shoulders, forming lines of ten or so girls, and then we would dance from one end of the school grounds to the other. As we danced, we would chant these words: "Tee la la la, come go. Tee la la la, come go." Sometimes one group of girls would sing, "Tee la la la," and the others would answer, "Come go." Up and down the schoolyard, away from our teachers, we would dance and sing. At the end of recess—

forty-five minutes—we were missing ribbons and and other ornaments from our hair, the pleats of our linen tunics were flattened out, the collars of our blouses were pulled out, and we were soaking wet all the way down to our bloomers. When the school bell rang, we would make a whooping sound, as if in a great panic, and then we would throw ourselves on top of each other as we laughed and shrieked. We would then run back to our classes, where we prepared to file into the auditorium for evening prayers. After that, it was home for the weekend. But how could we go straight home after all that excitement? No sooner were we on the street than we would form little groups, depending on the direction we were headed in. I was never keen on joining them on the way home, because I was sure I would run into my mother. Instead, my friends and I would go to a secluded part of the churchyard and sit on the tombstones of people who had been buried there way before slavery was abolished, in 1833. We would sit on these stones and sing bad songs, use forbidden words, and, of course, show each other various parts of our bodies. While some of us watched, the others would walk up and down on the large tombstones showing off their legs. It was immediately a popular idea; everybody soon wanted to do it. It wasn't long before many girls—the ones whose mothers didn't pay strict attention to what they were doing—started to come to school on Fridays wearing not bloomers under their uniforms but underpants trimmed with lace and satin frills. It also wasn't long before an end came to all that. One Friday afternoon, Miss Edward, on her way home from school, took a shortcut through the churchyard. She must have heard the commotion we were making because there she suddenly was, saying, "What is the meaning of this?"—just the very thing someone like her would say if she came unexpectedly on something like us. It was obvious that I was the ringleader. Oh, how I wished the ground would open up and take her in, but it did not. We all shamefacedly, slunk home, I with Miss Edward at my side. Tears came to my mother's eyes when she heard what I had done. It was apparently such a bad thing that my mother couldn't bring herself to repeat my misdeed to my father in my presence. I got the usual punishment of dinner alone, outside under the tree, but added on to that I was not allowed to go to the library on Saturday, and on Sunday, after Sunday school and dinner, I was not allowed to take a stroll in the botanical gardens, where Gwen was waiting for me in the bamboo grove.

That happened when I was in the first form. Now here Miss Edward stood. Her whole face was on fire. Her eyes were bulging out of her head. I was sure that any minute they would land at my feet and roll away. The small pimples on her face, already looking as if they were constantly irritated, now ballooned into huge, on-the-verge-of-exploding boils. Her head shook from side to side. Her strange bottom, which she carried high in the air, seemed to rise up so high in the air that it almost touched the ceiling. Why did I not pay attention, she said. My impertinence was beyond endurance. She then found a hundred words for the different forms my impertinence took. On she went. I was just getting used to this amazing bellowing when suddenly she was speechless. In fact, everything stopped. Her eyes stopped, her bottom stopped, her pimples stopped. Yes, she had got close enough so that her eyes caught a glimpse of what I had done to my textbook. The glimpse soon led to closer inspection. It was bad enough that I had defaced my schoolbook by writing in it. That I should write under the picture of Columbus "The Great Man . . " was just too much. I had gone too far this time, defaming one of the great men in history, Christopher Columbus, discoverer of the island that was my home. And now look at me. I was not even hanging my head in remorse. Had my peers ever seen anyone so arrogant, so blasphemous?

I was sent to the headmistress, Miss Blake. As punishment, I was removed from my position as prefect, and my place was taken by the odious Hilarene. As an added punishment, I was ordered to copy Books I and II of "Paradise Lost," by John Milton, and to have it done a week from that day. I then couldn't wait to get home to lunch and the comfort of my mother's kiss and arms. I had nothing to worry about there yet; it would be a while before my mother and father heard of my bad deeds. What a terrible morning! Seeing my mother would be such a tonic—something to pick me up.

When I got home, my mother kissed me absent-mindedly. My father had 5 got home ahead of me, and they were already deep in conversation, my father regaling her with some unusually outlandish thing the oaf Mr. Oatie had done. I washed my hands and took my place at table. My mother brought me my lunch. I took one smell of it, and I could tell that it was the hated breadfruit. My mother said not at all, it was a new kind of rice imported from Belgium, and not breadfruit, mashed and forced through a ricer, as I thought. She went back to talking to my father. My father could hardly get a few words out of his mouth before she was a jellyfish of laughter. I sat there, putting my food in my mouth. I could not believe that she couldn't see how miserable I was and so reach out a hand to comfort me and caress my cheek, the way she usually did when she sensed that something was amiss with me. I could not believe how she laughed at everything he said, how much she liked him. Until then, I had always thought that she liked him because he was my father; now I could see that she liked him just for himself. I remembered that, the other day, they were sitting outside and when I walked up to them I noticed her hand resting lightly on the nape of his neck. I was taken aback then. Now I ate my meal. The more I ate of it, the more I was sure that it was breadfruit. When I finished, my mother got up to remove my plate. As she started out the door, I said, "Tell me, really, the name of the thing I just ate."

My mother said, "You just ate some breadfruit, I made it look like rice so that you would eat it. It's very good for you, filled with lots of vitamins." As she said this, she laughed. She was standing half inside the door, half outside. Her body was in the shade of our house, but her head was in the sun. When she laughed, her mouth opened to show off big, shiny, sharp white teeth. It was as if my mother had suddenly turned into a crocodile.

[1983]

■ TOPICS FOR DISCUSSION AND WRITING

1. On reading the first paragraph only, what do we know about the narrator and her family? What is the mood of this paragraph?

2. On reading the second paragraph only, what do we know or what can we guess about the narrator's age, sex, and other characteristics?

3. Why does Annie John dislike Columbus? Explain the title of the story. To what (in the story) does it literally refer? Does it have any metaphorical meaning as well?

4. Who is Ruth? What is her function in "Columbus in Chains"?

5. In a paragraph of your own, contrast the mood of the first paragraph of the story with that of the last paragraph.

6. In an essay of approximately 500 words characterize the relationship between Annie John and her mother, tracing the changes that occur.

7. Read an historical account of the British rule of Antigua. In two or three paragraphs, summarize the parts of that history which are relevant to Annie John's understanding of it and compare the historical account with Annie John's version.

POETRY

■ WILLIAM BLAKE

William Blake (1757–1827) was born in London and at fourteen was apprenticed for seven years to an engraver. A Christian visionary poet, he made his living by giving drawing lessons and by illustrating books, including his own *Songs of Innocence* (1789) and *Songs of Experience* (1794). These two books represent, he said, "two contrary states of the human soul." ("The Lamb" comes from *Innocence*, "The Tyger" from *Experience*.) In 1809 Blake exhibited his art, but the show was a failure. Not until he was in his sixties, when he stopped writing poetry, did he achieve any public recognition—and then it was as a painter.

The Lamb

Little Lamb, who made thee?
  Dost thou know who made thee?
Gave thee life, and bid thee feed?
By the stream and o'er the mead;
Gave thee clothing of delight,   5
Softest clothing, wooly, bright;
Gave thee such a tender voice,

Making all the vales rejoice?
    Little Lamb, who made thee?
    Dost thou know who made thee?   10

    Little Lamb, I'll tell thee,
    Little Lamb I'll tell thee:
He is calléd by thy name,
For he calls himself a Lamb.
He is meek, and he is mild;   15
He became a little child.
I a child, and thou a lamb,
We are calléd by his name.
    Little Lamb, God bless thee!
    Little Lamb, God bless thee!   20
                [1789]

The Tyger

Tyger! Tyger! burning bright
In the forests of the night,
What immortal hand or eye
Could frame thy fearful symmetry?   4

In what distant deeps or skies
Burnt the fire of thine eyes?
On what wings dare he aspire?
What the hand dare seize the fire?   8

And what shoulder, and what art,
Could twist the sinews of thy heart?
And, when thy heart began to beat
What dread hand? and what dread feet?   12

What the hammer? what the chain?
In what furnace was thy brain?
What the anvil? what dread grasp
Dare its deadly terrors clasp?   16

When the stars threw down their spears,
And watered heaven with their tears,
Did he smile his work to see?
Did he who made the lamb make thee?   20

Tyger! Tyger! burning bright
In the forests of the night,
What immortal hand or eye,
Dared frame thy fearful symmetry?   24
                [1792]

■ TOPICS FOR DISCUSSION AND WRITING

1. Why does Blake answer his question in "The Lamb" but not in "The Tyger"? Do you think that the questions in "The Tyger" are answerable?

2. In his book entitled *Innocence and Experience*, the critic E. D. Hirsch, Jr., suggests that in the fifth stanza "the stars" are the rebellious angels who "threw down their spears" when God defeated them and hurled Lucifer and his followers out of heaven. Does this interpretation strike you as plausible? Interesting?

■ GERARD MANLEY HOPKINS

Gerard Manley Hopkins (1844–1889) was born near London and was educated at Oxford, where he studied the classics. A convert from Anglicanism to Roman Catholicism, he was ordained a Jesuit priest in 1877. After serving as a parish priest and teacher, he was appointed Professor of Greek at the Catholic University in Dublin.

Hopkins published only a few poems during his lifetime, partly because he believed that the pursuit of literary fame was incompatible with his vocation as a priest, and partly because he was aware that his highly individual style might puzzle readers.

Spring and Fall:

TO A YOUNG CHILD

Márgarét áre you griéving
Over Goldengrove unleaving?
Leáves, líke the things of mán, you
With your fresh thoughts care for, can you?
Ah! ás the héart grows older   5
It will come to such sights colder
By and by, nor spare a sigh
Though worlds of wanwood leafmeal lie;
And yet you will weep and know why.
Now no matter, child, the name: 10
Sórrow's springs áre the same.
Nor mouth had, no nor mind, expressed
What héart heárd of, ghost° guéssed:
It is the blight mán was bórn for,
It is Margaret you mourn for.   15

[1880]

13 **ghost** spirit

■ TOPICS FOR DISCUSSION AND WRITING

1.   What is the speaker's age? His tone? What is the relevance of the title to
     Margaret? What meanings are in "Fall"? Is there more than one meaning
     to "spring"? (Notice especially the title and line 11.)
2.   What is meant by Margaret's "fresh thoughts" (line 4)? Paraphrase lines
     3–4 and lines 12–13.
3.   "Wanwood" and "leafmeal" are words coined by Hopkins. What are their
     suggestions?
4.   What does "blight" mean in line 14?
5.   Why is it not contradictory for the speaker to say that Margaret weeps
     for herself (line 15) after saying that she weeps for "Goldengrove unleav-
     ing" (line 2)?

■ A. E. HOUSMAN
_____

          Alfred Edward Housman (1859–1936) was born in rural Shropshire,
     England, and educated in classics and philosophy at Oxford University.
     Although he was a brilliant student, his final examination was unexpected-
     ly weak—in fact, he failed—and he did not receive the academic appoint-
     ment that he had anticipated. He began working as a civil servant at the
     British Patent Office, but in his spare time he wrote scholarly articles on
     Latin literature, and these writings in 1892 won him an appointment as
     Professor of Latin at the University of London. In 1911 he was appointed
     to Cambridge. During his lifetime he published (in addition to his scholar-
     ly writings) only two thin books of poetry, *A Shropshire Lad* (1898) and
     Last Poems (1922), and a highly readable lecture called *The Name and
     Nature of Poetry* (1933). After his death a third book of poems, *More
     Poems* (1936) was published.

When I Was One-and-Twenty

When I was one-and-twenty
     I heard a wise man say,
"Give crowns and pounds and guineas
     But not your heart away;
Give pearls away and rubies   5
     But keep your fancy free."
But I was one-and-twenty,
     No use to talk to me.

When I was one-and-twenty
     I heard him say again,   10
"The heart out of the bosom
     Was never given in vain;

'Tis paid with sighs a plenty
    And sold for endless rue."
And I am two-and-twenty,   15
    And oh, 'tis true, 'tis true.
[1896]

■ TOPICS FOR DISCUSSION AND WRITING

1.   In line 6, what does "fancy" mean?
2.   In your own words, what is the advice of the "wise man"?
3.   In a paragraph, indicate what you think the speaker's attitude is toward himself. In a second paragraph, indicate what *our* attitude toward him is.

■ E. E. CUMMINGS

     Edwin Estlin Cummings (1894–1962) grew up in Cambridge, Massachusetts, and was graduated from Harvard, where he became interested in modern literature and art, especially in the movements called cubism and futurism. His father, a conservative clergyman and a professor at Harvard, seems to have been baffled by the youth's interests, but Cummings's mother encouraged his artistic activities, including his use of unconventional punctuation as a means of expression.

     Politically liberal in his youth, Cummings became more conservative after a visit to Russia in 1931, but early and late his work emphasizes individuality and freedom of expression.

anyone lived in a pretty how town

anyone lived in a pretty how town
(with up so floating many bells down)
spring summer autumn winter
he sang his didn't he danced his did.   4

Women and men(both little and small)
cared for anyone not at all
they sowed their isn't they reaped their same
sun moon stars rain   8

children guessed(but only a few
and down they forgot as up they grew
autumn winter spring summer)
that noone loved him more by more   12

when by now and tree by leaf
she laughed his joy she cried his grief

bird by snow and stir by still
anyone's any was all to her   16

someones married their everyones
laughed their cryings and did their dance
(sleep wake hope and then)they
said their nevers they slept their dream   20

stars rain sun moon
(and only the snow can begin to explain
how children are apt to forget to remember
with up so floating many bells down)   24

one day anyone died i guess
(and noone stopped to kiss his face)
busy folk buried them side by side
little by little and was by was   28

all by all and deep by deep
and more by more they dream their sleep
noone and anyone earth by april
wish by spirit and if by yes.   32

Women and men(both dong and ding)
summer autumn winter spring
reaped their sowing and went their came
sun moon stars rain   36

1940]

■ TOPICS FOR DISCUSSION AND WRITING

1.   Put into normal order (as far as possible) the words of the first two stan-
     zas and then compare your version with Cummings's. What does
     Cummings gain—or lose?
2.   Characterize the "anyone" who "sang his didn't" and "danced his did." In
     your opinion, how does he differ from the people who "sowed their isn't
     they reaped the same"?
3.   Some readers interpret "anyone died" (line 25) to mean that the child
     matured and became as dead as the other adults. How might you support
     or refute this interpretation?

■ ROBERT HAYDEN

    Robert Hayden (1913–1980) was born in Detroit, Michigan. His
parents divorced when he was a child, and he was brought up by a

neighboring family, whose name he adopted. In 1942, at the age of
twenty-nine he graduated from Detroit City College (now Wayne State
University), and he received a master's degree from the University of
Michigan. He taught at Fisk University from 1946 to 1969 and after that,
for the remainder of his life, at the University of Michigan. In 1979 he
was appointed Consultant in Poetry to the Library of Congress, the first
African-American to hold the post.

Those Winter Sundays

Sundays too my father got up early
and put his clothes on in the blueblack cold,
then with cracked hands that ached
from labor in the weekday weather made
banked fires blaze. No one ever thanked him.   5

I'd wake and hear the coal splintering, breaking.
When the rooms were warm, he'd call,
and slowly I would rise and dress,
fearing the chronic angers of that house,

Speaking indifferently to him,   10
who had driven out the cold
and polished my good shoes as well.
What did I know, what did I know
of love's austere and lonely offices?

[1962]

■ TOPICS FOR DISCUSSION AND WRITING

1. In line 1 what does the word "too" tell us about the father? What does it
   suggest about the speaker (and the implied hearer) of the poem?
2. What do you take to be the speaker's present attitude toward his father?
   What circumstances, do you imagine, prompted his memory of "Those
   Winter Sundays"? What line or lines suggest those circumstances to you?
3. What is the meaning of "offices" in the last line? What does this word
   suggest that other words Hayden might have chosen do not?

■ LOUISE GLÜCK

   Louise Glück (b. 1943) was born in New York City and attended
Sarah Lawrence College and Columbia University. She has taught at God-
dard College in Vermont and at Warren Wilson College in North Carolina.
Her volume of poems, *The Triumph of Achilles* (1985), won the National
Book Critics Circle Award for poetry.

Gretel in Darkness

This is the world we wanted. All who would have seen us dead
Are dead. I hear the witch's cry
Break in the moonlight through a sheet of sugar: God rewards.
Her tongue shrivels into gas. . . .

                                    Now, far from women's arms   5
And memory of women, in our father's hut
We sleep, are never hungry.
Why do I not forget?
My father bars the door, bars harm
From this house, and it is years.   10

No one remembers. Even you, my brother,
Summer afternoons you look at me as though you meant
To leave, as though it never happened. But I killed for you.
I see armed firs, the spires of that gleaming kiln come back, come back—

Nights I turn to you to hold me but you are not there.   15
Am I alone? Spies
Hiss in the stillness, Hansel we are there still, and it is real, real,
That black forest, and the fire in earnest.

                                                   [1975]

■ TOPICS FOR DISCUSSION AND WRITING

1. If you are not thoroughly familiar with the story of Hansel and Gretel,
   read the story in *Grimm's Fairy Tales*. Why, according to the poem, does
   the episode with the witch mean so much more to Gretel than to
   Hansel?
2. How, as the poem develops, is the first sentence of the poem modified?

DRAMA

A Note on the Elizabethan Theater

Shakespeare's theater was wooden, round or polygonal (the Chorus in
Henry V calls it a "wooden O"). About eight hundred spectators could stand
in the yard in front of—and perhaps along the two sides of—the stage that jutted from the rear wall, and another fifteen hundred or so spectators could sit

in the three roofed galleries that ringed the stage. That portion of the galleries that was above the rear of the stage was sometimes used by actors. Entry to the stage was normally gained by doors at the rear but some use was made of a curtained alcove—or perhaps a booth—between the doors, which allowed characters to be "discovered" (revealed) as in the modern proscenium theater, which normally employs a curtain. A performance was probably uninterrupted by intermissions or by long pauses for the changing of scenery; a group of characters leaves the stage, another enters, and if the locale was changed, the new characters somehow tell us. (Modern editors customarily add indications of locales to help a reader, but it should be understood that the action on the Elizabethan stage was continuous.)

A Note on the Text of Hamlet

Shakespeare's *Hamlet* comes to us in three versions. The first, known as the First Quarto (Q1), was published in 1603. It is an illegitimate garbled version, perhaps derived from the memory of the actor who played Marcellus (this part is conspicuously more accurate than the rest of the play) in a short version of the play. The second printed version (Q2), which appeared in 1604, is almost twice as long as Q1; all in all, it is the best text we have, doubtless published (as Q1 was not) with the permission of Shakespeare's theatrical company. The third printed version, in the First Folio (the collected edition of Shakespeare's plays, published in 1623), is also legitimate, but it seems to be an acting version, for it lacks some two hundred lines of Q2. On the other hand, the Folio text includes some ninety lines not found in Q2. Because Q2 is the longest version, giving us more than the play as Shakespeare conceived it than either of the other texts, it serves as the basic version for this text. Unfortunately, the printers of it often worked carelessly: Words and phrases are omitted, there are plain misreadings of what must have been in Shakespeare's manuscript, and speeches are sometimes wrongly assigned. It was therefore necessary to turn to the First Folio for many readings. It has been found useful, also, to divide the play into acts and scenes; these divisions, not found in Q2 (and only a few are found in the Folio), are purely editorial additions, and they are therefore enclosed in square brackets.

■ WILLIAM SHAKESPEARE

William Shakespeare (1564–1616) was born in Stratford, England, of middle-class parents. Nothing of interest is known about his early years, but by 1590 he was acting and writing plays in London. By the end of the following decade he had worked in all three Elizabethan dramatic genres—tragedy, comedy, and history. *Romeo and Juliet*, for example, was written about 1595, the year of *Richard II*, and in the following year he wrote *A Midsummer Night's Dream*. *Julius Caesar* (1599) probably preceded *As You Like It* by one year, and *Hamlet* probably followed *As You Like It* by less than a year. Among the plays that followed *King Lear* (1605–1606) were *Macbeth* (1605–1606) and several "romances"—plays that have happy endings but that seem more meditative and closer to tragedy than such comedies as *A Midsummer Night's Dream, As You Like It,* and *Twelfth Night.*

The Tragedy of Hamlet
Prince of Denmark

[Dramatis Personae

CLAUDIUS, *King of Denmark*
HAMLET, *son to the late and nephew to the present King*
POLONIUS, *Lord Chamberlain*
HORATIO, *friend to Hamlet*
LAERTES, *son to Polonius*
VOLTEMAND
CORNELIUS
ROSENCRANTZ
GUILDENSTERN } *courtiers*
OSRIC
A GENTLEMAN
A PRIEST
MARCELLUS } *officers*
BARNARDO
FRANCISCO, *a soldier*
REYNALDO, *servant to Polonius*
PLAYERS
TWO CLOWNS, *gravediggers*
FORTINBRAS, *Prince of Norway*
A NORWEGIAN CAPTAIN
ENGLISH AMBASSADORS
GERTRUDE, *Queen of Denmark, mother to Hamlet*
OPHELIA, *daughter to Polonius*
GHOST OF HAMLET'S FATHER
LORD, LADIES, OFFICERS, SOLDIERS, SAILORS, MESSENGERS, ATTENDANTS

Scene: Elsinore]

[ACT I

Scene I. *A guard platform of the castle.*]

Enter BARNARDO *and* FRANCISCO, *two sentinels.*

BARNARDO. Who's there?
FRANCISCO. Nay, answer me, stand and unfold°[1] yourself.

[1] The degree sign (°) indicates a footnote, which is keyed to the text by the line number. Text references are printed in **boldface** type; the annotation follows in lightface type.

I.i.2 **unfold** disclose

BARNARDO. Long live the King!°
FRANCISCO. Barnardo?
BARNARDO. He.   5
FRANCISCO. You come most carefully upon your hour.
BARNARDO. 'Tis now struck twelve. Get thee to bed, Francisco.
FRANCISCO. For this relief much thanks. 'Tis bitter cold,
     And I am sick at heart.
BARNARDO. Have you had quiet guard?
FRANCISCO.   Not a mouse stirring.   10
BARNARDO. Well, good night.
     If you do meet Horatio and Marcellus,
     The rivals° of my watch, bid them make haste.
                    Enter HORATIO *and* MARCELLUS.
FRANCISCO. I think I hear them. Stand, ho! Who is there?
HORATIO. Friends to this ground.
MARCELLUS.   And liegemen to the Dane.°   15
FRANCISCO. Give you° goodnight.
MARCELLUS.   O, farewell, honest soldier.
     Who hath relieved you?
FRANCISCO.   Barnardo hath my place.
     Give you good night.
                                        Exit FRANCISCO.

MARCELLUS.   Holla, Barnardo!
BARNARDO.   Say—
     What, is Horatio there
FRANCISCO.   A piece of him.
BARNARDO. Welcome, Horatio. Welcome, good Marcellus.   20
MARCELLUS. What, has this thing appeared again tonight?
BARNARDO. I have seen nothing.
MARCELLUS. Horatio says 'tis but our fantasy,
     And will not let belief take hold of him
     Touching this dreaded sight twice seen of us;   25
     Therefore I have entreated him along
     With us to watch the minutes of this night,
     That, if again this apparition come,
     He may approve° our eyes and speak to it.
HORATIO. Tush, tush, 'twill not appear.
BARNARDO.   Sit down awhile,   30
     And let us once again assail your ears,
     That are so fortified against our story,
     What we have two nights seen.

3 **Long live the King** (perhaps a password, perhaps a greeting) 13 **rivals** partners 15 **liegemen to the Dane** loyal subjects to the King of Denmark 16 **Give you**
God give you 29 **approve** confirm

HORATIO.   Well, sit we down,
   And let us hear Barnardo speak of this.
BARNARDO. Last night of all,   35
   When yond same star that's westward from the pole°
   Had made his course t'illume that part of heaven
   Where now it burns, Marcellus and myself,
   The bell then beating one—
                    Enter GHOST.
MARCELLUS. Peace, break thee off. Look where it comes again.   40
BARNARDO. In the same figure like the king that's dead.
MARCELLUS. Thou art a scholar; speak to it, Horatio.
BARNARDO. Looks 'a not like the king? Mark it, Horatio.
HORATIO. Most like: it harrows me with fear and wonder.
BARNARDO. It would be spoke to.
MARCELLUS.   Speak to it, Horatio.   45
HORATIO. What art thou that usurp'st this time of night,
   Together with that fair and warlike form
   In which the majesty of buried Denmark°
   Did sometimes march? By heaven I charge thee, speak.
MARCELLUS. It is offended.
BARNARDO.   See, it stalks away.   50
HORATIO. Stay! Speak, speak. I charge thee, speak.
                         Exit GHOST.

MARCELLUS. 'Tis gone and will not answer.
BARNARDO. How now, Horatio? You tremble and look pale.
   Is not this something more than fantasy?
   What think you on't?   55
HORATIO. Before my God, I might not this believe
   Without the sensible and true avouch°
   Of mine own eyes.
MARCELLUS.   Is it not like the King?
HORATIO. As thou art to thyself.
   Such was the very armor he had on   60
   When he the ambitious Norway° combated:
   So frowned he once, when, in an angry parle,°
   He smote the sledded Polacks° on the ice.
   'Tis strange.
MARCELLUS. Thus twice before, and jump° at this dead hour,   65
   With martial stalk hath he gone by our watch.
HORATIO. In what particular thought to work I know not;
   But, in the gross and scope° of my opinion,
   This bodes some strange eruption to our state.

36 **pole** polestar 48 **buried Denmark** the buried King of Denmark 57 **sensible
and true avouch** sensory and true proof 61 **Norway** King of Norway 62 **parle**
parley 63 **sledded Polacks** Poles in sledges 65 **jump** just 68 **gross and scope**
general drift

MARCELLUS. Good now, sit down, and tell me he that knows,   70
    Why this same strict and most observant watch
    So nightly toils the subject° of the land,
    And why such daily cast of brazen cannon
    And foreign mart° for implements of war,
    Why such impress° of shipwrights, whose sore task   75
    Does not divide the Sunday from the week,
    What might be toward° that this sweaty haste
    Doth make the night joint-laborer with the day?
    Who is't that can inform me?
HORATIO.   That can I.
    At least the whisper goes so: our last king,   80
    Whose image even but now appeared to us,
    Was, as you know, by Fortinbras of Norway,
    Thereto pricked on by a most emulate pride,
    Dared to the combat; in which our valiant Hamlet
    (For so this side of our known world esteemed him)   85
    Did slay this Fortinbras, who, by a sealed compact
    Well ratified by law and heraldry,°
    Did forfeit, with his life, all those his lands
    Which he stood seized° of, to the conqueror;
    Against the which a moiety competent°   90
    Was gagèd° by our King, which had returned
    To the inheritance of Fortinbras,
    Had he been vanquisher, as, by the same comart°
    And carriage of the article designed,°
    His fell to Hamlet. Now, sir, young Fortinbras,   95
    Of unimprovèd° mettle hot and full,
    Hath in the skirts° of Norway here and there
    Sharked up° a list of lawless resolutes,°
    For food and diet, to some enterprise
    That hath a stomach in't;° which is no other,   100
    As it doth well appear unto our state,
    But to recover of us by strong hand
    And terms compulsatory, those foresaid lands
    So by his father lost; and this, I take it,
    Is the main motive of our preparations,   105
    The source of this our watch, and the chief head°
    Of this posthaste and romage° in the land.

72 **toils the subject** makes the subjects toil 74 **mart** trading 75 **impress** forced
service 77 **toward** in preparation 87 **law and heraldry** heraldic law (governing the
combat) 89 **seized** possessed 90 **moiety competent** equal portion 91 **gagèd**
engaged, pledged 93 **comart** agreement 94 **carriage of the article designed**
import of the agreement drawn up 96 **unimprovèd** untried 97 **skirts** borders
98 **Sharked up** collected indiscriminately (as a shark gulps its prey) 98 **resolutes**
desperadoes 100 **hath a stomach in't** i.e., requires courage 106 **head** fountainhead,
origin 107 **romage** bustle

BARNARDO. I think it be no other but e'en so;
　　Well may it sort° that this portentous figure
　　Comes armèd through our watch so like the King　　110
　　that was and is the question of these wars.
HORATIO. A mote it is to trouble the mind's eye:
　　In the most high and palmy state of Rome,
　　A little ere the mightiest Julius fell,
　　The graves stood tenantless, and the sheeted dead　　115
　　Did squeak and gibber in the Roman streets;°
　　As stars with trains of fire and dews of blood,
　　Disasters° in the sun; and the moist star,°
　　Upon whose influence Neptune's empire stands,
　　Was sick almost to doomsday with eclipse.　　120
　　And even the like precurse° of feared events,
　　As harbingers° preceding still° the fates
　　And prologue to the omen° coming on,
　　Have heaven and earth together demonstrated
　　Unto our climatures° and countrymen.　　125
　　　　　　　Enter GHOST.
　　But soft, behold, lo where it comes again!
　　I'll cross it,° though it blast me.—Stay, illusion.
　　　　　　　　　It spreads his° arms.
　　If thou hast any sound or use of voice,
　　Speak to me.
　　If there be any good thing to be done　　130
　　That may to thee do ease and grace to me,
　　Speak to me.
　　If thou art privy to thy country's fate,
　　Which happily° foreknowing may avoid.
　　O, speak!　　135
　　Or if thou hast uphoarded in the life
　　Extorted° treasure in the womb of earth,
　　For which, they say, you spirits oft walk in death,
　　　　　　　　　The cock crows.
　　Speak of it. Stay and speak. Stop it, Marcellus.
MARCELLUS. Shall I strike at it with my partisan°?　　140
HORATIO. Do, if it will not stand.
BARNARDO.　　　　　　'Tis here.
HORATIO.　　　　　　　　'Tis here.

---

109 **sort** befit　116 **Did squeak. . . Roman streets** (the break in the sense which
follows this line suggests that a line has dropped out)　118 **Disasters** threatening
signs　118 **moist star** moon　121 **precurse** precursor, foreshadowing　122 **harbingers**
forerunners　122 **still** always　123 **omen** calamity　125 **climatures** regions　127 **cross
it** (1) cross its path, confront it, (2) make the sign of the cross in front of it　127 s.d.
his i.e., its, the ghost's (though possibly what is meant is that Horatio spreads his own
arms, making a cross of himself)　134 **happily** haply, perhaps　137 **Extorted** ill-won
140 **partisan** pike (a long-handled weapon)

MARCELLUS.   'Tis gone.
                                            Exit GHOST.

We do it wrong, being so majestical,
To offer it the show of violence,
For it is as the air, invulnerable,   145
And our vain blows malicious mockery.
BARNARDO. It was about to speak when the cock crew.
HORATIO. And then it started, like a guilty thing
Upon a fearful summons. I have heard,
The cock, that is the trumpet to the morn,   150
Doth with his lofty and shrill-sounding throat
Awake the god of day, and at his warning,
Whether in sea or fire, in earth or air,
Th' extravagant and erring° spirit hies
To his confine; and of the truth herein   155
This present object made probation.°
MARCELLUS. It faded on the crowing of the cock.
Some say that ever 'gainst° that season comes
Wherein our Savior's birth is celebrated,
This bird of dawning singeth all night long,   160
And then, they say, no spirit dare stir abroad,
The nights are wholesome, then no planets strike,°
No fairy takes,° nor witch hath power to charm:
So hallowed and so gracious is that time.
HORATIO. So have I heard and do in part believe it.   165
But look, the morn in russet mantle clad
Walks o'er the dew of yon high eastward hill.
Break we our watch up, and by my advice
Let us impart what we have seen tonight
Unto young Hamlet, for upon my life   170
This spirit, dumb to us, will speak to him.
Do you consent we shall acquaint him with it,
As needful in our loves, fitting our duty?
MARCELLUS. Let's do't, I pray, and I this morning know
Where we shall find him most convenient. *Exeunt.*   175

[Scene II. *The castle.*]

Flourish.° Enter CLAUDIUS, *King of Denmark,* GERTRUDE *the Queen, Coun-cilors,* POLONIUS *and his son* LAERTES, HAMLET, *Cum aliis°* [*including* VOLTE-MAND *and* CORNELIUS].

---

154 **extravagant and errring** out of bounds and wandering   156 **probation** proof
158 **'gainst** just before   162 **strike** exert an evil influence   163 **takes** be-
witches   I.ii.s.d.   **Flourish** fanfare of trumpets s.d. **cum aliis** with others (Latin)

KING. Though yet of Hamlet our dear brother's death
    The memory be green, and that it us befitted
    To bear our hearts in grief, and our whole kingdom
    To be contracted in one brow of woe,
    Yet so far hath discretion fought with nature   5
    That we with wisest sorrow think of him
    Together with remembrance of ourselves.
    Therefore our sometime sister,° now our Queen,
    Th' imperial jointress° to this warlike state,
    Have we, as 'twere, with a defeated joy,   10
    With an auspicious° and a dropping eye,
    With mirth in funeral, and with dirge in marriage,
    In equal scale weighing delight and dole,
    Taken to wife. Nor have we herein barred
    Your better wisdoms, which have freely gone   15
    With this affair along. For all, our thanks.
    Now follows that you know young Fortinbras,
    Holding a weak supposal of our worth,
    Or thinking by our late dear brother's death
    Our state to be disjoint and out of frame,°   20
    Colleaguèd with this dream of his advantage,°
    He hath not failed to pester us with message,
    Importing the surrender of those lands
    Lost by his father, with all bands of law,
    To our most valiant brother. So much for him.   25
    Now for ourself and for this time of meeting.
    Thus much the business is: we have here writ
    To Norway, uncle of young Fortinbras—
    Who, impotent and bedrid, scarcely hears
    Of this his nephew's purpose—to suppress   30
    His further gait° herein, in that the levies,
    The lists, and full proportions° are all made
    Out of his subject;° and we here dispatch
    You, good Cornelius, and you, Voltemand,
    For bearers of this greeting to old Norway,   35
    Giving to you no further personal power
    To business with the King, more than the scope
    Of these delated articles° allow.
    Farewell, and let your haste commend your duty.
CORNELIUS, VOLTEMAND. In that, and all things, will we show our duty.   40

---

8 our sometime sister my (the royal "we") former sister-in-law **9 jointress** joint
tenant, partner **11 auspicious** joyful **20 frame** order **21 advantage** superiority
31 gait proceeding **32 proportions** supplies for war **33 Out of his subject** i.e., out
of old Norway's subjects and realm **38 delated articles** detailed documents

KING. We doubt it nothing. Heartily farewell.

                      Exit VOLTEMAND *and* CORNELIUS.

  And now, Laertes, what's the news with you?
  You told us of some suit. What is't, Laertes?
  You cannot speak of reason to the Dane
  And lose your voice.° What wouldst thou beg, Laertes,   45
  That shall not be my offer, not thy asking?
  The head is not more native° to the heart,
  The hand more instrumental to the mouth,
  Than is the throne of Denmark to thy father.
  What wouldst thou have, Laertes?

LAERTES.   My dread lord,   50
  Your leave and favor to return to France,
  From whence, though willingly I came to Denmark
  To show my duty in your coronation,
  Yet now I must confess, that duty done,
  My thoughts and wishes bend again toward France   55
  And bow them to your gracious leave and pardon.

KING. Have you your father's leave? What says Polonius?

POLONIUS. He hath, my lord, wrung from me my slow leave
  By laborsome petition, and at last
  Upon his will I sealed my hard consent.°   60
  I do beseech you give him leave to go.

KING. Take thy fair hour, Laertes. Time be thine,
  And thy best graces spend it at thy will.
  But now, my cousin° Hamlet, and my son——

HAMLET. [*Aside*] A little more than kin, and less than kind!°   65

KING. How is it that the clouds still hang on you?

HAMLET. Not so, my lord. I am too much in the sun.°

QUEEN. Good Hamlet, cast thy nighted color off,
  And let thine eye look like a friend on Denmark.
  Do not forever with thy vailèd° lids   70
  Seek for thy noble father in the dust.
  Thou know'st 'tis common; all that lives must die,
  Passing through nature to eternity.

HAMLET. Ay, madam, it is common.°

QUEEN.   If it be,
  Why seems it so particular with thee?   75

HAMLET. Seems, madam? Nay, it is. I know not "seems."
  'Tis not alone my inky cloak, good mother,

---

45 **lose your voice** waste your breath 47 **native** related 60 **Upon his...hard**
consent to his desire I gave my reluctant consent 64 **cousin** kinsman 65 **kind** (pun
on the meanings "kindly" and "natural"; though doubly related—**more than kin**—
Hamlet asserts that he neither resembles Claudius in nature or feels kindly toward
him) 67 **sun** sunshine of royal favor (with a pun on "son") 70 **vailèd** lowered
74 **common** (1) universal (2) vulgar

Nor customary suits of solemn black,
Nor windy suspiration° of forced breath,
No, nor the fruitful river in the eye,   80
 Nor the dejected havior of the visage,
 Together with all forms, moods, shapes of grief,
 That can denote me truly. These indeed seem,
 For they are actions that a man might play,
 But I have that within which passes show;   85
 These but the trappings and the suits of woe.
KING. 'Tis sweet and commendable in your nature, Hamlet,
 To give these mourning duties to your father,
 But you must know your father lost a father,
 That father lost, lost his, and the survivor bound   90
 In filial obligation for some term
 To do obsequious° sorrow. But to persever
 In obstinate condolement° is a course
 Of impious stubbornness. 'Tis unmanly grief.
 It shows a will most incorrect to heaven,   95
 A heart unfortified, a mind impatient,
 An understanding simple and unschooled.
 For what we know must be and is as common
 As any the most vulgar° thing to sense,
 Why should we in our peevish opposition   100
 Take it to heart? Fie, 'tis a fault to heaven,
 A fault against the dead, a fault to nature,
 To reason most absurd, whose common theme
 Is death of fathers, and who still hath cried,
 From the first corse° till he that died today,   105
 "This must be so." We pray you throw to earth
 This unprevailing° woe, and think of us
 As of a father, for let the world take note
 You are the most immediate to our throne,
 And with no less nobility of love   110
 Than that which dearest father bears his son
 Do I impart toward you. For your intent
 In going back to school in Wittenberg,
 It is most retrograde° to our desire
 And we beseech you, bend you° to remain   115
 Here in the cheer and comfort of our eye,
 Our chiefest courtier, cousin, and our son.
QUEEN. Let not thy mother lose her prayers, Hamlet.
 I pray thee stay with us, go not to Wittenberg.

---

79 **windy suspiration** heavy sighing   92 **obsequious** suitable to obsequies (funerals)
93 **condolement** mourning   99 **vulgar** common   105 **corse** corpse   107 **unprevail-
ing** unavailing   114 **retrograde** contrary   115 **bend you** incline

HAMLET. I shall in all my best obey you, madam.   120
KING. Why, 'tis a loving and a fair reply.
    Be as ourself in Denmark. Madam, come.
    This gentle and unforced accord of Hamlet
    Sits smiling to my heart, in grace whereof
    No jocund health that Denmark drinks today,   125
    But the great cannon to the clouds shall tell,
    And the King's rouse° the heaven shall bruit° again,
    Respeaking earthly thunder. Come away.
                           Flourish. Exeunt all but HAMLET.
HAMLET. O that this too too sullied° flesh would melt,
    Thaw, and resolve itself into a dew,   130
    Or that the Everlasting had not fixed
    His canon° 'gainst self-slaughter. O God, God,
    How weary, stale, flat and unprofitable
    Seem to me all the uses of this world!
    Fie on't, ah, fie, 'tis an unweeded garden   135
    That grows to seed. Things rank and gross in nature
    Possess it merely.° That it should come to this:
    But two months dead, nay, not so much, not two,
    So excellent a king, that was to this
    Hyperion° to a satyr, so loving to my mother   140
    That he might not beteem° the winds of heaven
    Visit her face too roughly. Heaven and earth,
    Must I remember? Why, she would hang on him
    As if increase of appetite had grown
    By what it fed on; and yet within a month—   145
    Let me not think on't; frailty, thy name is woman—
    A little month, or ere those shoes were old
    With which she followed my poor father's body
    Like Niobe,° all tears, why she, even she—
    O God, a beast that wants discourse of reason°   150
    Would have mourned longer—married with my uncle,
    My father's brother, but no more like my father
    Than I to Hercules. Within a month,
    Ere yet the salt of most unrighteous tears
    Had left the flushing° in her gallèd eyes,   155
    She married. O, most wicked speed, to post°

---

127 **rouse** deep drink   127 **bruit** announce noisily   129 **sullied** (Q2 has **sallied,** here
modernized to **sullied,** which makes sense and is therefore given; but the Folio
reading, **solid,** which fits better with **melt,** is quite possibly correct)   132 **canon**
law   137 **merely** entirely   140 **Hyperion** the sun god, a model of beauty   141 **beteem**
allow   149 **Niobe** (a mother who wept profusely at the death of her children)
150 **wants discourse of reason** lacks reasoning power   155 **left the flushing**
stopped reddening   156 **post** hasten

With such dexterity to incestuous° sheets!
It is not, nor it cannot come to good.
But break my heart, for I must hold my tongue.
       Enter HORATIO, MARCELLUS, *and* BARNARDO.
HORATIO. Hail to your lordship!
HAMLET.   I am glad to see you well.   160
    Horatio—or I do forget myself.
HORATIO. The same, my lord, and your poor servant ever.
HAMLET. Sir, my good friend, I'll change° that name with you.
    And what make you from Wittenberg, Horatio?
    Marcellus.   165
MARCELLUS. My good lord!
HAMLET. I am very glad to see you. [*To* BARNARDO] Good even, sir.
    But what, in faith, make you from Wittenberg?
HORATIO. A truant disposition, good my lord.
HAMLET. I would not hear your enemy say so,   170
    Nor shall you do my ear that violence
    To make it truster° of your own report
    Against yourself. I know you are no truant.
    But what is your affair in Elsinore?
    We'll teach you to drink deep ere you depart.   175
HORATIO. My lord, I came to see your father's funeral.
HAMLET. I prithee do not mock me, fellow student.
    I think it was to see my mother's wedding.
HORATIO. Indeed, my lord, it followed hard upon.
HAMLET. Thrift, thrift, Horatio. The funeral baked meats   180
    Did coldly furnish forth the marriage tables.
    Would I had met my dearest° foe in heaven
    Or ever I had seen that day, Horatio!
    My father, methinks I see my father.
HORATIO. Where, my lord?
HAMLET.   In my mind's eye, Horatio.   185
HORATIO. I saw him once. 'A° was a goodly king.
HAMLET. 'A was a man, take him for all in all,
    I shall not look upon his like again.
HORATIO. My lord, I think I saw him yesternight.
HAMLET. Saw? Who?   190
HORATIO. My lord, the King your father.
HAMLET.   The King my father?
HORATIO. Season your admiration° for a while
    With an attent ear till I may deliver
    Upon the witness of these gentlemen
    This marvel to you.

---

157 **incestuous** (canon law considered marriage with a deceased brother's widow to be incestuous) 163 **change** exchange 172 **truster** believer 182 **dearest** most intensely felt 186 **'A** he 192 **Season your admiration** control your wonder

HAMLET.   For God's love let me hear!   195
HORATIO. Two nights together had these gentlemen,
    Marcellus and Barnardo, on their watch
    In the dead waste and middle of the night
    Been thus encountered. A figure like your father,
    Armèd at point exactly, cap-a-pe,°   200
    Appears before them, and with solemn march
    Goes slow and stately by them. Thrice he walked
    By their oppressed and fear-surprisèd eyes,
    Within his truncheon's length,° whilst they, distilled°
    Almost to jelly with the act° of fear,   205
    Stand dumb and speak not to him. This to me
    In dreadful° secrecy impart they did,
    And I with them the third night kept the watch,
    Where, as they had delivered, both in time,
    Form of the thing, each word made true and good,   210
    The apparition comes. I knew your father.
    These hands are not more like.
HAMLET.   But where was this?
MARCELLUS. My lord, upon the platform where we watched.
HAMLET. Did you not speak to it?
HORATIO.   My lord, I did;
    But answer made it none. Yet once methought   215
    It lifted up it° head and did address
    Itself to motion like as it would speak:
    But even then the morning cock crew loud,
    And at the sound it shrunk in haste away
    And vanished from our sight.
HAMLET.   'Tis very strange.   220
HORATIO. As I do live, my honored lord, 'tis true,
    And we did think it writ down in our duty
    To let you know of it.
HAMLET. Indeed, indeed, sirs, but this troubles me.
    Hold you the watch tonight?
ALL.   We do, my lord.   225
HAMLET. Armed, say you?
ALL. Armed, my lord.
HAMLET. From top to toe?
ALL.   My lord, from head to foot.
HAMLET. Then saw you not his face.
HORATIO. Oh, yes, my lord. He wore his beaver° up.   230
HAMLET. What, looked he frowningly?

200 **cap-a-pe** head to foot 204 **truncheon's length** space of a short staff
204 **distilled** reduced 205 **act** action 207 **dreadful** terrified 216 **it** its 230 **beaver**
visor, face guard

HORATIO. A countenance more in sorrow than in anger.
HAMLET. Pale or red?
HORATIO. Nay, very pale.
HAMLET.   And fixed his eyes upon you?
HORATIO. Most constantly.
HAMLET.   I would I had been there.   235
HORATIO. It would have much amazed you.
HAMLET. Very like, very like. Stayed it long?
HORATIO. While one with moderate haste might tell° a hundred.
BOTH. Longer, longer.
HORATIO. Not when I saw't.
HAMLET.   His beard was grizzled,° no?   240
HORATIO. It was as I have seen it in his life,
    A sable silvered.°
HAMLET.   I will watch tonight.
    Perchance 'twill walk again.
HORATIO.   I warr'nt it will.
HAMLET. If it assume my noble father's person,
    I'll speak to it though hell itself should gape   245
    And bid me hold my peace. I pray you all,
    If you have hitherto concealed this sight,
    Let it be tenable° in your silence still,
    And whatsomever else shall hap tonight,
    Give it an understanding but no tongue;   250
    I will requite your loves. So fare you well.
    Upon the platform 'twixt eleven and twelve
    I'll visit you.
ALL.   Our duty to your honor.
HAMLET. Your loves, as mine to you. Farewell.
                        Exeunt [all but HAMLET].
    My father's spirit—in arms? All is not well.   255
    I doubt° some foul play. Would the night were come!
    Till then sit still, my soul. Foul deeds will rise,
    Though all the earth o'erwhelm them, to men's eyes.
                                Exit.

[Scene III. *A room.*]

Enter LAERTES *and* OPHELIA, *his sister.*
LAERTES. My necessaries are embarked. Farewell.
    And, sister, as the winds give benefit
    And convoy° is assistant, do not sleep,
    But let me hear from you.
OPHELIA.   Do you doubt that?

---

238 **tell** count 240 **grizzled** gray 242 **sable silvered** black mingled with white
248 **tenable** held 256 **doubt** suspect I.ii.3 **convoy** conveyance

LAERTES. For Hamlet, and the trifling of his favor,   5
    Hold it a fashion and a toy° in blood,
    A violet in the youth of primy° nature,
    Forward,° not permanent, sweet, not lasting,
    The perfume and suppliance° of a minute,
    No more.
OPHELIA   No more but so?
LAERTES   Think it no more.   10
    For nature crescent° does not grow alone
    In thews° and bulk, but as this temple° waxes,
    The inward service of the mind and soul
    Grows wide withal. Perhaps he loves you now,
    And now no soil nor cautel° doth besmirch   15
    The virtue of his will; but you must fear,
    His greatness weighed,° his will is not his own.
    For he himself is subject to his birth.
    He may not, as unvalued° persons do,
    Carve for himself; for on his choice depends   20
    The safety and health of this whole state;
    And therefore must his choice be circumscribed
    Unto the voice and yielding of that body
    Whereof he is the head. Then if he says he loves you,
    It fits your wisdom so far to believe it   25
    As he in his particular act and place
    May give his saying deed, which is no further
    Than the main voice of Denmark goes withal.
    Then weigh what loss your honor may sustain
    If with too credent° ear you list his songs,   30
    Or lose your heart, or your chaste treasure open
    To his unmastered importunity.
    Fear it, Ophelia, fear it, my dear sister,
    And keep you in the rear of your affection,
    Out of the shot and danger of desire.   35
    The chariest maid is prodigal enough
    If she unmask her beauty to the moon.
    Virtue itself scapes not calumnious strokes.
    The canker° galls the infants of the spring
    Too oft before their buttons° be disclosed,   40
    And in the morn and liquid dew of youth
    Contagious blastments are most imminent.
    Be wary then; best safety lies in fear;
    Youth to itself rebels, though none else near.

6 **toy** idle fancy   7 **primy** springlike   8 **Forward** premature   9 **suppliance** diversion
11 **crescent** growing   12 **thews** muscles and sinews   12 **temple** i.e., the body
15 **cautel** deceit   17 **greatness weighed** high rank considered   19 **unvalued** of low
rank   30 **credent** credulous   39 **canker** cankerworm   40 **buttons** buds

OPHELIA. I shall the effect of this good lesson keep   45
    As watchman to my heart, but, good my brother,
    Do not, as some ungracious° pastors do,
    Show me the steep and thorny way to heaven,
    Whiles, like a puffed and reckless libertine,
    Himself the primrose path of dalliance treads   50
    And recks not his own rede.°
                Enter POLONIUS.
LAERTES.   O, fear me not.
    I stay too long. But here my father comes.
    A double blessing is a double grace;
    Occasion smiles upon a second leave.
POLONIUS Yet here, Laertes? Aboard, aboard, for shame!   55
    The wind sits in the shoulder of your sail,
    And you are stayed for. There—my blessing with thee,
    And these few precepts in thy memory
    Look thou character.° Give thy thoughts no tongue,
    Nor any unproportioned° thought his act.   60
    Be thou familiar, but by no means vulgar.
    Those friends thou hast, and their adoption tried,
    Grapple them unto thy soul with hoops of steel,
    But do not dull thy palm with entertainment
    Of each new-hatched, unfledged courage.° Beware   65
    Of entrance to a quarrel; but being in,
    Bear't that th' opposèd may beware of thee.
    Give every man thine ear, but few thy voice;
    Take each man's censure,° but reserve thy judgment.
    Costly thy habit as thy purse can buy,   70
    But not expressed in fancy; rich, not gaudy,
    For the apparel oft proclaims the man,
    And they in France of the best rank and station
    Are of a most select and generous, chief in that.°
    Neither a borrower nor a lender be,
    For loan oft loses both itself and friend,
    And borrowing dulleth edge of husbandry.°
    This above all, to thine own self be true,
    And it must follow, as the night the day,
    Thou canst not then be false to any man.   75
    Farewell. My blessing season this° in thee!
LAERTES. Most humbly do I take my leave, my lord.

47 **ungracious** lacking grace 51 **recks not his own rede** does not heed his own
advice 59 **character** inscribe 60 **unproportioned** unbalanced 65 **courage** gallant
youth 69 **censure** opinion 74 **Are of. . .in that** show their fine taste and their
gentlemanly instincts more in that than in any other point of manners (Kittredge)
77 **husbandry** thrift 81 **season this** make fruitful this (advice)

POLONIUS. The time invites you. Go, your servants tend.°
LAERTES. Farewell, Ophelia, and remember well
    What I have said to you.
OPHELIA.   'Tis in my memory locked,   80
    And you yourself shall keep the key of it.
LAERTES. Farewell   *Exit* LAERTES.
POLONIUS. What is't, Ophelia, he hath said to you?
OPHELIA. So please you, something touching the Lord Hamlet.
POLONIUS. Marry,° well bethought.   85
    'Tis told me he hath very oft of late
    Given private time to you, and you yourself
    Have of your audience been most free and bounteous.
    If it be so—as so 'tis put on me,
    And that in way of caution—I must tell you   90
    You do not understand yourself so clearly
    As it behooves my daughter and your honor.
    What is between you? Give me up the truth.
OPHELIA. He hath, my lord, of late made many tenders°
    Of his affection to me.   95
POLONIUS. Affection pooh! You speak like a green girl,
    Unsifted° in such perilous circumstance.
    Do you believe his tenders, as you call them?
OPHELIA. I do not know, my lord, what I should think.
POLONIUS. Marry, I will teach you. Think yourself a baby   100
    That you have ta'en these tenders for true pay
    Which are not sterling. Tender yourself more dearly,
    Or (not to crack the wind of the poor phrase)
    Tend'ring it thus you'll tender me a fool.°
OPHELIA. My lord, he hath importuned me with love   105
    In honorable fashion.
POLONIUS. Ay, fashion you may call it. Go to, go to.
OPHELIA. And hath given countenance to his speech, my lord,
    With almost all the holy vows of heaven.
POLONIUS. Ay, springes to catch woodcocks.° I do know,   110
    When the blood burns, how prodigal the soul
    Lends the tongue vows. These blazes, daughter,
    Giving more light than heat, extinct in both,
    Even in their promise, as it is a-making,
    You must not take for fire. From this time   115
    Be something scanter of your maiden presence.
    Set your entreatments° at a higher rate

---

83 **tend** attend 90 **Marry** (a light oath, from "By the Virgin Mary") 99 **tenders**
offers (in line 103 it has the same meaning, but in line 106 Polonius speaks of **tenders**
in the sense of counters or chips; in line 109 **Tend'ring** means "holding," and
tender means "give," "present") 102 **Unsifted** untried 109 **tender me a fool**
(1) present me with a fool (2) present me with a baby 115 **springes to catch woodcocks** snares to catch stupid birds 122 **entreatments** interviews

Than a command to parley. For Lord Hamlet,
Believe so much in him that he is young,
And with a larger tether may he walk   125
Than may be given you. In few, Ophelia,
Do not believe his vows, for they are brokers,°
Not of that dye° which their investments° show,
But mere implorators° of unholy suits,
Breathing like sanctified and pious bonds,°   130
The better to beguile. This is for all:
I would not, in plain terms, from this time forth
Have you so slander° any moment leisure
As to give words or talk with the Lord Hamlet.
Look to't, I charge you. Come your ways.   135

OPHELIA. I shall obey, my lord.   *Exeunt.*

[Scene IV. *A guard platform.*]

Enter HAMLET, HORATIO, *and* MARCELLUS.

HAMLET. The air bites shrewdly;° it is very cold.
HORATIO. It is a nipping and an eager° air.
HAMLET. What hour now?
HORATIO.   I think it lacks of twelve.
MARCELLUS. No, it is struck.
HORATIO. Indeed? I heard it not. It then draws near the season   5
Wherein the spirit held his wont to walk.

A flourish of trumpets, and two pieces go off.
What does this mean, my lord?
HAMLET. The King doth wake° tonight and takes his rouse,°
Keeps wassail, and the swagg'ring upspring° reels,
And as he drains his draughts of Rhenish° down   10
The kettledrum and trumpet thus bray out
The triumph of his pledge.°
HORATIO.   Is it a custom?
HAMLET. Ay, marry, is't,
But to my mind, though I am native here
And to the manner born, it is a custom   15
More honored in the breach than the observance.
This heavy-headed revel east and west
Makes us traduced and taxed of° other nations.
They clepe° us drunkards and with swinish phrase
Soil our addition,° and indeed it takes   20

---

127 **brokers** procurers 128 **dye** i.e., kind 128 **investments** garments 129 **implorators** solicitors 130 **bonds** pledges 133 **slander** disgrace I.iv.1 **shrewdly** bitterly
2 **eager** sharp 8 **wake** hold a revel by night 8 **takes his rouse** carouses
9 **upspring** (a dance) 10 **Rhenish** Rhine wine 12 **The triumph of his pledge** the achievement (of drinking a wine cup in one draught) of his toast 18 **taxed of** blamed by 19 **clepe** call 20 **addition** reputation (literally, "title of honor")

From our achievements, though performed at height,
The pith and marrow of our attribute.°
So oft it chances in particular men
That for some vicious mole° of nature in them,
As in their birth, wherein they are not guilty,   25
(Since nature cannot choose his origin)
By the o'ergrowth of some complexion,°
Oft breaking down the pales° and forts of reason,
Or by some habit that too much o'erleavens°
The form of plausive° manners, that (these men,   30
Carrying, I say, the stamp of one defect,
Being nature's livery, or fortune's star°)
Their virtues else, be they as pure as grace,
As infinite as man may undergo,
Shall in the general censure° take corruption   35
From that particular fault. The dram of evil
Doth all the noble substance of a doubt,
To his own scandal.°
                    Enter GHOST.
HORATIO.   Look, my lord, it comes.
HAMLET. Angels and ministers of grace defend us!
Be thou a spirit of health° or goblin damned,   40
Bring with thee airs from heaven or blasts from hell,
Be thy intents wicked or charitable,
Thou com'st in such a questionable° shape
That I will speak to thee. I'll call thee Hamlet,
King, father, royal Dane. O, answer me!   45
Let me not burst in ignorance, but tell
Why thy canonized° bones, hearsèd in death,
Have burst their cerements,° why the sepulcher
Wherein we saw thee quietly interred
Hath oped his ponderous and marble jaws   50
To cast thee up again. What may this mean
That thou, dead corse, again in complete steel,
Revisits thus the glimpses of the moon,
Making night hideous, and we fools of nature
So horridly to shake our disposition°   55

---

22 **attribute** reputation   24 **mole** blemish   27 **complexion** natural disposition
28 **pales** enclosures   29 **o'er-leavens** mixes with, corrupts   30 **plausive** pleasing
32 **nature's livery, or fortune's star** nature's equipment (i.e., "innate"), or a
person's destiny determined by the stars   35 **general censure** popular judgment
36–38 **The dram . . . own scandal** (though the drift is clear, there is no agreement as
to the exact meaning of these lines)   40 **spirits of health** good spirit
43 **questionable** (1) capable of discourse (2) dubious   47 **canonized** buried according
to the canon or ordinance of the church   48 **cerements** waxed linen shroud   55 **shake
our disposition** disturb us

With thoughts beyond the reaches of our souls?
Say, why is this? Wherefore? What should we do?

GHOST beckons HAMLET.

HORATIO. It beckons you to go away with it,
　　As if it some impartment° did desire
　　To you alone.
MARCELLUS.　　　　Look with what courteous action　　　　60
　　It waves you to a more removèd ground.
　　But do not go with it.
HORATIO.　　　　　　　No, by no means.
HAMLET. It will not speak. Then I will follow it.
HORATIO. Do not, my lord.
HAMLET.　　　　　　　Why, what should be the fear?
　　I do not set my life at a pin's fee,　　　　　　　65
　　And for my soul, what can it do to that,
　　Being a thing immortal as itself?
　　It waves me forth again. I'll follow it.
HORATIO. What if it tempt you toward the flood, my lord,
　　Or to the dreadful summit of the cliff　　　　　70
　　That beetles° o'er his base into the sea,
　　And there assume some other horrible form,
　　Which might deprive your sovereignty of reason°
　　And draw you into madness? Think of it.
　　The very place puts toys° of desperation,　　　　75
　　Without more motive, into every brain
　　That looks so many fathoms to the sea
　　And hears it roar beneath.
HAMLET　　　　　　　　It waves me still.
　　Go on; I'll follow thee.
MARCELLUS. You shall not go, my lord.
HAMLET.　　　　　　　　Hold off your hands.　　　80
HORATIO. Be ruled. You shall not go.
HAMLET.　　　　　　　My fate cries out
　　And makes each petty artere° in this body
　　As hardy as the Nemean lion's nerve.°
　　Still am I called! Unhand me, gentlemen.
　　By heaven, I'll make a ghost of him that lets° me!　　85
　　I say, away! Go on. I'll follow thee.

Exit GHOST, and HAMLET.

HORATIO. He waxes desperate with imagination.
MARCELLUS. Let's follow. 'Tis not fit thus to obey him.

---

59 **impartment** communication　71 **beetles** juts out　73 **deprive your sovereignty of reason** destroy the sovereignty of your reason　75 **toys** whims, fancies　82 **artere** artery　83 **Nemean lion's nerve** sinews of the mythical lion slain by Hercules 85 **lets** hinders

HORATIO. Have after! To what issue will this come?
MARCELLUS. Something is rotten in the state of Denmark.   90
HORATIO. Heaven will direct it.
MARCELLUS.   Nay, let's follow him.   *Exeunt.*

[Scene V. *The battlements.*]

Enter GHOST *and* HAMLET.

HAMLET. Whither wilt thou lead me? Speak; I'll go no further.
GHOST. Mark me.
HAMLET.   I will.
GHOST.   My hour is almost come,
    When I to sulf'rous and tormenting flames
    Must render up myself.
HAMLET.   Alas, poor ghost.
GHOST. Pity me not, but lend thy serious hearing   5
    To what I shall unfold.
HAMLET.   Speak. I am bound to hear.
GHOST. So art thou to revenge, when thou shalt hear.
HAMLET. What?
GHOST. I am thy father's spirit,
    Doomed for a certain term to walk the night,   10
    And for the day confined to fast in fires,
    Till the foul crimes° done in my days of nature
    Are burnt and purged away. But that I am forbid
    To tell the secrets of my prison house,
    I could a tale unfold whose lightest word   15
    Would harrow up thy soul, freeze thy young blood,
    Make thy two eyes like stars start from their spheres,°
    Thy knotted and combinèd locks to part,
    And each particular hair to stand an end
    Like quills upon the fearful porpentine.°   20
    But this eternal blazon° must not be
    To ears of flesh and blood. List, list, O, list!
    If thou didst ever thy dear father love——
HAMLET. O God!
GHOST. Revenge his foul and most unnatural murder.   25
HAMLET. Murder?
GHOST. Murder most foul, as in the best it is,
    But this most foul, strange, and unnatural.
HAMLET. Haste me to know't, that I, with wings as swift
    As meditation° or the thoughts of love,   30
    May sweep to my revenge.

I.v.12 **crimes** sins 17 **spheres** (in Ptolemaic astronomy, each planet was fixed in a hollow transparent shell concentric with the earth) 20 **fearful porpentine** timid porcupine 21 **eternal blazon** revelation of eternity 30 **meditation** thought

GHOST.   I find thee apt,
   And duller shouldst thou be than the fat weed
   That roots itself in ease on Lethe wharf,°
   Wouldst thou not stir in this. Now, Hamlet, hear.
   'Tis given out that, sleeping in my orchard,   35
   A serpent stung me. So the whole ear of Denmark
   Is by a forgèd process° of my death
   Rankly abused. But know, thou noble youth,
   The serpent that did sting thy father's life
   Now wears his crown.
HAMLET.   O my prophetic soul!   40
   My uncle?
GHOST. Ay, that incestuous, that adulterate° beast,
   With witchcraft of his wits, with traitorous gifts—
   O wicked wit and gifts, that have the power
   So to seduce!—won to his shameful lust   45
   The will of my most seeming-virtuous queen.
   O Hamlet, what a falling-off was there,
   From me, whose love was of that dignity
   That it went hand in hand even with the vow
   I made to her in marriage, and to decline   50
   Upon a wretch whose natural gifts were poor
   To those of mine.
   But virtue, as it never will be moved,
   Though lewdness° court it in a shape of heaven,
   So lust, though to a radiant angel linked,   55
   Will sate itself in a celestial bed
   And prey on garbage.
   But soft, methinks I scent the morning air;
   Brief let me be. Sleeping within my orchard,
   My custom always of the afternoon,   60
   Upon my secure° hour thy uncle stole
   With juice of cursed hebona° in a vial,
   And in the porches of my ears did pour
   The leperous distillment, whose effect
   Holds such an enmity with blood of man   65
   That swift as quicksilver it courses through
   The natural gates and alleys of the body,
   And with a sudden vigor it doth posset°
   And curd, like eager° droppings into milk,
   The thin and wholesome blood. So did it mine,   70
   And a most instant tetter° barked about

---

33 **Lethe wharf** bank of the river of forgetfulness in Hades   37 **forgèd process** false
account   42 **adulterate** adulterous   54 **lewdness** lust   61 **secure** unsuspecting
62 **hebona** a poisonous plant   68 **posset** curdle   69 **eager** acid   71 **tetter** scab

Most lazarlike° with vile and loathsome crust
All my smooth body.
Thus was I, sleeping, by a brother's hand
    Of life, of crown, of queen at once dispatched,   75
    Cut off even in the blossoms of my sin,
    Unhouseled, disappointed, unaneled,°
    No reck'ning made, but sent to my account
    With all my imperfections on my head.
    O, horrible! O, horrible! Most horrible!   80
    If thou hast nature in thee, bear it not.
    Let not the royal bed of Denmark be
    A couch for luxury° and damnèd incest.
    But howsomever thou pursues this act,
    Taint not thy mind, nor let thy soul contrive   85
    Against thy mother aught. Leave her to heaven
    And to those thorns that in her bosom lodge
    To prick and sting her. Fare thee well at once.
    The glowworm shows the matin° to be near
    And 'gins to pale his uneffectual fire.   90
    Adieu, adieu, adieu. Remember me.   *Exit.*
HAMLET. O all you host of heaven! O earth! What else?
    And shall I couple hell? O fie! Hold, hold, my heart,
    And you, my sinews, grow not instant old,
    But bear me stiffly up. Remember thee?   95
    Ay, thou poor ghost, whiles memory holds a seat
    In this distracted globe.° Remember thee?
    Yea, from the table° of my memory
    I'll wipe away all trivial fond° records,
    All saws° of books, all forms, all pressures° past   100
    That youth and observation copied there,
    And thy commandment all alone shall live
    Within the book and volume of my brain,
    Unmixed with baser matter. Yes, by heaven!
    O most pernicious woman!   105
    O villain, villain, smiling, damnèd villain!
    My tables—meet it is I set it down
    That one may smile, and smile, and be a villain.
    At least I am sure it may be so in Denmark. [*Writes.*]
    So, uncle, there you are. Now to my word: 110
    It is "Adieu, adieu, remember me."
    I have sworn't.
HORATIO *and* MARCELLUS. (*Within*) My lord, my lord!
                Enter HORATIO *and* MARCELLUS.

72 **lazarlike** leperlike   77 **Unhouseled, disappointed, unaneled** without the sacrament of communion, unabsolved, without extreme unction   83 **luxury** lust   89 **matin**
morning   97 **globe** i.e., his head   98 **table** tablet, notebook   99 **fond** foolish   100
saws maxims   100 **pressures**

MARCELLUS.   Lord Hamlet!
HORATIO.   Heavens secure him!
HAMLET. So be it!
MARCELLUS. Illo, ho, ho,° my lord!   115
HAMLET. Hillo, ho, ho, boy! Come, bird, come.
MARCELLUS. How is't, my noble lord?
HORATIO.   What news, my lord?
HAMLET. O, wonderful!
HORATIO. Good my lord, tell it.
HAMLET.   No, you will reveal it.
HORATIO. Not I, my lord, by heaven.
MARCELLUS.   Nor I, my lord.   120
HAMLET. How say you then? Would heart of man once think it?
     But you'll be secret?
BOTH.   Ay, by heaven, my lord.
HAMLET. There's never a villain dwelling in all Denmark
     But he's an arrant knave.
HORATIO. There needs no ghost, my lord, come from the grave   125
     To tell us this.
HAMLET.   Why, right, you are in the right;
     And so, without more circumstance° at all,
     I hold it fit that we shake hands and part:
     You, as your business and desire shall point you,
     For every man hath business and desire   130
     Such as it is, and for my own poor part,
     Look you, I'll go pray.
HORATIO. These are but wild and whirling words, my lord.
HAMLET. I am sorry they offend you, heartily;
     Yes, faith, heartily.
HORATIO.   There's no offense, my lord.   135
HAMLET. Yes, by Saint Patrick, but there is, Horatio,
     And much offense too. Touching this vision here,
     It is an honest ghost,° that let me tell you.
     For your desire to know what is between us,
     O'ermaster't as you may. And now, good friends,   140
     As you are friends, scholars, and soldiers,
     Give me one poor request.
HORATIO. What is't, my lord? We will.
HAMLET. Never make known what you have seen tonight.
BOTH. My lord, we will not.
HAMLET.   Nay, but swear't.
HORATIO.   In faith,   145
     My lord, not I.
MARCELLUS.   Nor I, my lord—in faith.

---

115 **Illo, ho, ho** (falconer's call to his hawk)   127 **circumstance** details   138 **honest ghost** i.e., not a demon in his father's shape

HAMLET. Upon my sword.
MARCELLUS.   We have sworn, my lord, already.
HAMLET. Indeed, upon my sword, indeed.

                                   GHOST *cries under the stage.*

GHOST. Swear.
HAMLET. Ha, ha, boy, say'st thou so? Art thou there, truepenny?°   150
    Come on. You hear this fellow in the cellarage.
    Consent to swear.
HORATIO.   Propose the oath, my lord.
HAMLET. Never to speak of this that you have seen.
    Swear by my sword.
GHOST. [*Beneath*] Swear.   155
HAMLET. *Hic et ubique?*° Then we'll shift our ground.
    Come hither, gentlemen,
    And lay your hands again upon my sword.
    Swear by my sword
    Never to speak of this that you have heard.   160
GHOST. [*Beneath*] Swear by his sword.
HAMLET. Well said, old mole! Canst work i' th' earth so fast?
    A worthy pioner!° Once more remove, good friends.
HORATIO. O day and night, but this is wondrous strange!
HAMLET. And therefore as a stranger give it welcome.   165
    There are more things in heaven and earth, Horatio,
    Than are dreamt of in your philosophy.
    But come:
    Here as before, never, so help you mercy,
    How strange or odd some'er I bear myself   170
    (As I perchance hereafter shall think meet
    To put an antic disposition° on),
    That you, at such times seeing me, never shall
    With arms encumb'red° thus, or this headshake,
    Or by pronouncing of some doubtful phrase,   175
    As "Well, well, we know," or "We could, an if we would,"
    Or "If we list to speak," or "there be, an if they might,"
    Or such ambiguous giving out, to note
    That you know aught of me—this do swear,
    So grace and mercy at your most need help you.   180
GHOST. [*Beneath*] Swear.   [*They swear.*]
HAMLET. Rest, rest, perturbèd spirit. So, gentlemen,
    With all my love I do commend me° to you,
    And what so poor a man as Hamlet is
    May do t' express his love and friending to you,   185

---

150 **truepenny** honest fellow   156 **Hic et ubique** here and everywhere (Latin)   163
pioner digger of mines   172 **antic disposition** fantastic behavior   174 **encumb'red**
folded   183 **commend me** entrust myself

God willing, shall not lack. Let us go in together,
And still your fingers on your lips, I pray.
The time is out of joint. O cursèd spite,
That ever I was born to set it right!
Nay, come, let's go together.   *Exeunt.*   190

[ACT II

Scene I. *A room.*]

Enter old POLONIUS, *with his man* REYNALDO.

POLONIUS. Give him this money and these notes, Reynaldo.
REYNALDO. I will, my lord.
POLONIUS. You shall do marvell's° wisely, good Reynaldo,
   Before you visit him, to make inquire
   Of his behavior.
REYNALDO.   My lord, I did intend it.   5
POLONIUS. Marry, well said, very well said. Look you sir,
   Inquire me first what Danskers° are in Paris,
   And how, and who, what means, and where they keep,°
   What company, at what expense; and finding
   By this encompassment° and drift of question   10
   That they do know my son, come you more nearer
   Than your particular demands° will touch it.
   Take you as 'twere some distant knowledge of him,
   As thus, "I know his father and his friends,
   And in part him." Do you mark this, Reynaldo?   15
REYNALDO. Ay, very well, my lord.
POLONIUS. "And in part him, but," you may say, "not well,
   But if't be he I mean, he's very wild,
   Addicted so and so." And there put on him
   What forgeries° you please; marry, none so rank   20
   As may dishonor him—take heed of that—
   But, sir, such wanton, wild, and usual slips
   As are companions noted and most known
   To youth and liberty.
REYNALDO.   As gaming, my lord.
POLONIUS. Ay, or drinking, fencing, swearing, quarreling,   25
   Drabbing.° You may go so far.
REYNALDO. My lord, that would dishonor him.
POLONIUS. Faith, no, as you may season it in the charge.
   You must not put another scandal on him,
   That he is open to incontinency.°   30

II.i.3 **marvell's** marvelous(ly) 7 **Danskers** Danes 8 **keep** dwell 10 **encompass-
ment** circling 12 **demands** questions 20 **forgeries** inventions 26 **Drabbing** wench-
ing 30 **incontincy** habitual licentiousness

That's not my meaning. But breathe his faults so quaintly°
That they may seem the taints of liberty,
The flash and outbreak of a fiery mind,
A savageness in unreclaimèd blood,
Of general assault.°
REYNALDO.   But, my good lord——   35
POLONIUS. Wherefore should you do this?
REYNALDO.   Ay, my lord,
I would know that.
POLONIUS.   Marry, sir, here's my drift,
And I believe it is a fetch of warrant.°
You laying these slight sullies on my son
As 'twere a thing a little soiled i' th' working,   40
Mark you,
Your party in converse, him you would sound,
Having ever seen in the prenominate crimes°
The youth you breathe of guilty, be assured
He closes with you in this consequence:°   45
"Good sir," or so, or "friend," or "gentleman" —
According to the phrase or the addition°
Of man and country—
REYNALDO.   Very good, my lord.
POLONIUS. And then, sir, does 'a° this—'a does—
What was I about to say? By the mass, I was about   50
to say something! Where did I leave?
REYNALDO. At "closes in the consequence," at "friend or so,"
and "gentleman."
POLONIUS. At "closes in the consequence"—Ay, marry!
He closes thus: "I know the gentleman;   55
I saw him yesterday, or t'other day,
Or then, or then, with such or such, and, as you say,
There was 'a gaming, there o'ertook in's rouse,
There falling out at tennis"; or perchance,
"I saw him enter such a house of sale,"   60
Videlicet,° a brothel, or so forth.
See you now—
Your bait of falsehood take this carp of truth,
And thus do we of wisdom and of reach,°
With windlasses° and with assays of bias,°   · 65
By indirections find directions out.

---

31 **quaintly** ingeniously, delicately   35 **Of general assault** common to all men
38 **fetch of warrant** justifiable device   43 **Having...crimes** if he has ever seen in
the aforementioned crimes   45 **He closes...this consequence** he falls in with you
in this conclusion   47 **addition** title   49 **'a** he   61 **Videlicet** namely   64 **reach** far-
reaching awareness(?)   65 **windlasses** circuitous courses   65 **assays of bias** indirect
attempts (metaphor from bowling; bias=curved course)

So, by my former lecture and advice,
Shall you my son. You have me, have you not?
REYNALDO. My lord, I have.
POLONIUS.   God bye ye, fare ye well.
REYNALDO. Good my lord.   70
POLONIUS. Observe his inclination in yourself.°
REYNALDO. I shall, my lord.
POLONIUS. And let him ply his music.
REYNALDO.   Well, my lord.
POLONIUS. Farewell.   *Exit* REYNALDO.

Enter OPHELIA.

                       How now, Ophelia, what's the matter?
OPHELIA. O my lord, my lord, I have been so affrighted!   75
POLONIUS. With what, i' th' name of God?
OPHELIA. My lord, as I was sewing in my closet,°
Lord Hamlet, with his doublet all unbraced,°
No hat upon his head, his stockings fouled,
Ungartered, and down-gyvèd° to his ankle,   80
Pale as his shirt, his knees knocking each other,
And with a look so piteous in purport,°
As if he had been loosèd out of hell
To speak of horrors—he comes before me.
POLONIUS. Mad for thy love?
OPHELIA.   My lord, I do not know,   85
But truly I do fear it.
POLONIUS.   What said he?
OPHELIA. He took me by the wrist and held me hard;
Then goes he to the length of all his arm,
And with his other hand thus o'er his brow
He falls to such perusal of my face   90
As 'a would draw it. Long stayed he so.
At last, a little shaking of mine arm,
And thrice his head thus waving up and down,
He raised a sigh so piteous and profound
As it did seem to shatter all his bunk   95
And end his being. That done, he lets me go,
And, with his head over his shoulder turned,
He seemed to find his way without his eyes,
For out o' doors he went without their helps,
And to the last bended their light on me.   100
POLONIUS. Come, go with me. I will go seek the King.
This is the very ecstasy° of love,
Whose violent property fordoes° itself

---

71 **in yourself** for yourself 77 **closet** private room 78 **doublet all unbraced** jacket
entirely unlaced 80 **down-gyvèd** hanging down like fetters 82 **purport** expression 102 **ecstasy** madness 103 **property fordoes** quality destroys

And leads the will to desperate undertakings
As oft as any passions under heaven   105
That does afflict our natures. I am sorry.
What, have you given him any hard words of late?
OPHELIA. No, my good lord; but as you did command,
  I did repel his letters and denied
  His access to me.
POLONIUS.   That hath made him mad.   110
  I am sorry that with better heed and judgment
  I had not quoted° him. I feared he did but trifle
  And meant to wrack thee; but beshrew my jealousy.°
  By heaven, it is as proper° to our age
  To cast beyond ourselves° in our opinions   115
  As it is common for the younger sort
  To lack discretion. Come, go we to the King.
  This must be known, which, being kept close, might move
  More grief to hide than hate to utter love.°
  Come.   *Exeunt.*   120

[Scene II. *The castle.*]

Flourish. Enter KING *and* QUEEN, ROSENCRANTZ, *and* GUILDENSTERN
                          [*with others*].

KING. Welcome, dear Rosencrantz and Guildenstern.
  Moreover that° we much did long to see you,
  The need we have to use you did provoke
  Our hasty sending. Something have you heard
  Of Hamlet's transformation: so call it,   5
  Sith° nor th' exterior nor the inward man
  Resembles that it was. What it should be,
  More than his father's death, that thus hath put him
  So much from th' understanding of himself,
  I cannot dream of. I entreat you both   10
  That, being of so° young days brought up with him,
  And sith so neighbored to his youth and havior,°
  That you vouchsafe your rest° here in our court
  Some little time, so by your companies
  To draw him on to pleasures, and to gather   15
  So much as from occasion you may glean,
  Whether aught to us unknown afflicts him thus,
  That opened° lies within our remedy.

---

112 **quoted** noted   113 **beshrew my jealousy** curse on my suspicions   114 **proper**
natural   115 **To cast beyond ourselves** to be overcalculating   117–19 **Come,
go. . .utter love** (the general meaning is that while telling the King of Hamlet's love
may anger the King, more grief would come from keeping it secret)   II.ii.2 **Moreover
that** beside the fact that   6 **Sith** since   11 **of so** from such   12 **youth and havior**
behavior in his youth   13 **vouchsafe your rest** consent to remain   18 **opened** revealed

QUEEN. Good gentlemen, he hath much talked of you,
    And sure I am, two men there is not living   20
    To whom he more adheres. If it will please you
    To show us so much gentry° and good will
    As to expend your time with us awhile
    For the supply and profit of our hope,
    Your visitation shall receive such thanks   25
    As fits a king's remembrance.
ROSENCRANTZ.   Both your Majesties
    Might, by the sovereign power you have of us,
    Put your dread pleasures more into command
    Than to entreaty.
GUILDENSTERN.   But we both obey,
    And here give up ourselves in the full bent°   30
    To lay our service freely at your feet,
    To be commanded.
KING. Thanks Rosencrantz and gentle Guildenstern.
QUEEN. Thanks, Guildenstern and gentle Rosencrantz.
    And I beseech you instantly to visit   35
    My too much changèd son. Go, some of you,
    And bring these gentlemen where Hamlet is.
GUILDENSTERN. Heavens make our presence and our practices
    Pleasant and helpful to him!
QUEEN.   Ay, amen!
    Exeunt ROSENCRANTZ *and* GUILDENSTERN [*with some Attendants*].
                  Enter POLONIUS.
POLONIUS. Th' ambassadors from Norway, my good lord,   40
    Are joyfully returned.
KING. Thou still° hast been the father of good news.
POLONIUS. Have I, my lord? Assure you, my good liege,
    I hold my duty, as I hold my soul,
    Both to my God and to my gracious king;   45
    And I do think, or else this brain of mine
    Hunts not the trail of policy so sure°
    As it hath used to do, that I have found
    The very cause of Hamlet's lunacy.
KING. O, speak of that! That do I long to hear.   50
POLONIUS. Give first admittance to th' ambassadors.
    My news shall be the fruit to that great feast.
KING. Thyself do grace to them and bring them in.
                        [*Exit* POLONIUS.]
    He tells me, my dear Gertrude, he hath found
    The head and source of all your son's distemper.   55

---

22 **gentry** courtesy 30 **in the full bent** entirely (the figure is of a bow bent to its
capacity) 42 **still** always 47 **Hunts not...so sure** does not follow clues of political
doings with such sureness

QUEEN. I doubt° it is no other but the main,°
    His father's death and our o'erhasty marriage.
KING. Well, we shall sift him.
                Enter POLONIUS, VOLTEMAND, *and* CORNELIUS.
                      Welcome, my good friends.
    Say, Voltemand, what from our brother Norway?
VOLTEMAND. Most fair return of greetings and desires.   60
    Upon our first,° he sent out to suppress
    His nephew's levies, which to him appeared
    To be a preparation 'gainst the Polack;
    But better looked into, he truly found
    It was against your Highness, whereat grieved,   65
    That so his sickness, age, and impotence
    Was falsely borne in hand,° sends out arrests
    On Fortinbras; which he, in brief, obeys,
    Receives rebuke from Norway, and in fine,°
    Makes vow before his uncle never more   70
    To give th' assay° of arms against your Majesty.
    Whereon old Norway, overcome with joy,
    Gives him threescore thousand crowns in annual fee
    And his commission to employ those soldiers,
    So levied as before, against the Polack,   75
    With an entreaty, herein further shown,
                            [Gives a paper.]
    That it might please you to give quiet pass
    Through your dominions for this enterprise,
    On such regards of safety and allowance°
    As therein are set down.
KING.   It likes us well;   80
    And at our more considered time° we'll read,
    Answer, and think upon this business.
    Meantime, we thank you for your well-took labor.
    Go to your rest; at night we'll feast together.
    Most welcome home!   *Exeunt* AMBASSADORS.
POLONIUS.   This business is well ended.   85
    My liege and madam, to expostulate°
    What majesty should be, what duty is,
    Why day is day, night night, and time is time,
    Were nothing but to waste night, day, and time.
    Therefore, since brevity is the soul of wit,°   90
    And tediousness the limbs and outward flourishes,
    I will be brief. Your noble son is mad.

---

56 **doubt** suspect 56 **main** principal point 61 **first** first audience 67 **borne in hand** deceived 69 **in fine** finally 71 **assay** trial 79 **regards of safety and allowance** i.e., conditions 81 **considered time** time proper for considering 86 **expostulate** discuss 90 **wit** wisdom, understanding

Mad call I it, for, to define true madness,
What is't but to be nothing else but mad?
But let that go.
QUEEN.   More matter, with less art.   95
POLONIUS. Madam, I swear I use no art at all.
That he's mad, 'tis true: 'tis true 'tis pity,
And pity 'tis 'tis true—a foolish figure.°
But farewell it, for I will use no art.
Mad let us grant him then; and now remains   100
That we find out the cause of this effect,
Or rather say, the cause of this defect,
For this effect defective comes by cause.
Thus it remains, and the remainder thus.
Perpend.°   105
I have a daughter: have, while she is mine,
Who in her duty and obedience, mark,
Hath given me this. Now gather, and surmise.
                                  [*Reads*] *the letter.*
"To the celestial, and my soul's idol, the most
    beautified Ophelia" —   110
That's an ill phrase, a vile phrase; "beautified" is a
    vile phrase. But you shall hear. Thus:
"In her excellent white bosom, these, &c."
QUEEN. Came this from Hamlet to her?
POLONIUS. Good madam, stay awhile. I will be faithful.   115
    "Doubt thou the stars are fire,
        Doubt that the sun doth move;
    Doubt° truth to be a liar,
        But never doubt I love.
O dear Ophelia, I am ill at these numbers.° I have   120
not art to reckon my groans; but that I love thee
best, O most best, believe it. Adieu.
    Thine evermore, most dear lady, whilst this
        machine° is to him, Hamlet."
This in obedience hath my daughter shown me,   125
And more above° hath his solicitings,
As they fell out by time, by means, and place,
All given to mine ear.
KING.   But how hath she
    Received his love?
POLONIUS.   What do you think of me?
KING. As of a man faithful and honorable.   130

98 **figure** figure of rhetoric 105 **Perpend** consider carefully 118 **Doubt** suspect
120 **ill at these numbers** unskilled in verses 124 **machine** complex device (here,
his body) 126 **more above** in addition

POLONIUS. I would fain prove so. But what might you think,
    When I had seen this hot love on the wing
    (As I perceived it, I must tell you that,
    Before my daughter told me), what might you,
    Or my dear Majesty your Queen here, think,   135
    If I had played the desk or table book,°
    Or given my heart a winking,° mute and dumb,
    Or looked upon this love with idle sight?
    What might you think? No, I went round to work
    And my young mistress thus I did bespeak: 140
    "Lord Hamlet is a prince, out of thy star.°
    This must not be." And then I prescripts gave her,
    That she should lock herself from his resort,
    Admit no messengers, receive no tokens.
    Which done, she took the fruits of my advice,   145
    And he, repellèd, a short tale to make,
    Fell into a sadness, then into a fast,
    Thence to a watch,° thence into a weakness,
    Thence to a lightness,° and, by this declension,
    Into the madness wherein now he raves,   150
    And all we mourn for.
KING.   Do you think 'tis this?
QUEEN. It may be, very like.
POLONIUS. Hath there been such a time, I would fain know that,
    That I have positively said " 'Tis so,"
    When it proved otherwise?
KING.   Not that I know.   155
POLONIUS. [*Pointing to his head and shoulder*]   Take this
       from this, if this be otherwise.
    If circumstances lead me, I will find
    Where truth is hid, though it were hid indeed
    Within the center.°
KING.   How may we try it further?
POLONIUS. You know sometimes he walks four hours together   160
    Here in the lobby.
QUEEN.   So he does indeed.
POLONIUS. At such a time I'll loose my daughter to him.
    Be you and I behind an arras° then.
    Mark the encounter. If he love her not,
    And be not from his reason fall'n thereon,   165
    Let me be no assistant for a state
    But keep a farm and carters.

---

136 **played the desk or table book** i.e., been a passive recipient of secrets
137 **winking** closing of the eyes 141 **star** sphere 148 **watch** wakefulness
149 **lightness** mental derangement 159 **center** center of the earth 163 **arras**
tapestry hanging in front of a wall

KING.   We will try it.
                    Enter HAMLET *reading on a book.*
QUEEN. But look where sadly the poor wretch comes reading.
POLONIUS. Away, I do beseech you both, away.
                                              Exit KING *and* QUEEN.
    I'll board him presently.° O, give me leave,   170
    How does my good Lord Hamlet?
HAMLET. Well, God-a-mercy.
POLONIUS. Do you know me, my lord?
HAMLET. Excellent well. You are a fishmonger.°
POLONIUS. Not I, my lord.   175
HAMLET. Then I would you were so honest a man.
POLONIUS. Honest, my lord?
HAMLET. Ay, sir. To be honest, as this world goes, is to be
    one man picked out of ten thousand.
POLONIUS. That's very true, my lord.   180
HAMLET. For if the sun breed maggots in a dead dog,
    being a good kissing carrion°——Have you a daugh-
    ter?
POLONIUS. I have, my lord.
HAMLET. Let her not walk i' th' sun. Conception° is a bless-   185
    ing, but as your daughter may conceive, friend, look
    to't.
POLONIUS. [*Aside*] How say you by that? Still harping on my
    daughter. Yet he knew me not at first. 'A said I was
    a fishmonger. 'A is far gone, far gone. And truly in   190
    my youth I suffered much extremity for love, very
    near this. I'll speak to him again.—What do you read,
    my lord?
HAMLET. Words, words, words.
POLONIUS. What is the matter, my lord?   195
HAMLET. Between who?
POLONIUS. I mean the matter° that you read, my lord.
HAMLET. Slanders, sir; for the satirical rogue says here that
    old men have gray beards, that their faces are wrinkled,
    their eyes purging thick amber and plumtree gum, and   200
    that they have a plentiful lack of wit, together with
    most weak hams. All which, sir, though I most power-
    fully and potently believe, yet I hold it not honesty°
    to have it thus set down; for you yourself, sir, should
    be old as I am if, like a crab, you could go back-   205
    ward.

---

170 **board him presently** accost him at once   174 **fishmonger** dealer in fish (slang
for a procurer)   182 **a good kissing carrion** (perhaps the meaning is "a good piece of
flesh to kiss," but many editors emend *good* to *god*, taking the word to refer to the
sun)   185 **Conception** (1) understanding (2) becoming pregnant   197 **matter** (Polonius
means "subject matter," but Hamlet pretends to take the word in the sense of
"quarrel")   203 **honesty** decency

POLONIUS. [*Aside*] Though this be madness, yet there is
method in't. Will you walk out of the air, my lord?

HAMLET. Into my grave.

POLONIUS. Indeed, that's out of the air. [*Aside*] How 210
pregnant° sometimes his replies are! A happiness° that
often madness hits on, which reason and sanity could
not so prosperously be delivered of. I will leave him and
suddenly contrive the means of meeting between him
and my daughter.—My lord, I will take my leave of 215
you.

HAMLET. You cannot take from me anything that I will more
willingly part withal—except my life, except my life, except my life.

        Enter GUILDENSTERN *and* ROSENCRANTZ.

POLONIUS. Fare you well, my lord. 220

HAMLET. These tedious old fools!

POLONIUS. You go to seek the Lord Hamlet? There he is.

ROSENCRANTZ. [*To* POLONIUS] God save you, sir!

                              [*Exit* POLONIUS.]

GUILDENSTERN. My honored lord! 225

ROSENCRANTZ. My most dear lord!

HAMLET. My excellent good friends! How dost thou, Guildenstern? Ah, Rosencrantz! Good lads, how do you
both?

ROSENCRANTZ. As the indifferent° children of the earth. 230

GUILDENSTERN. Happy in that we are not overhappy.
On Fortune's cap we are not the very button.

HAMLET. Nor the soles of her shoe?

ROSENCRANTZ. Neither, my lord.

HAMLET. Then you live about her waist, or in the middle of 235
her favors?

GUILDENSTERN. Faith, her privates° we.

HAMLET. In the secret parts of Fortune? O, most true!
She is a strumpet. What news?

ROSENCRANTZ. None, my lord, but that the world's grown honest. 240

HAMLET. Then is doomsday near. But your news is not true.
Let me question more in particular. What have you, my
good friends, deserved at the hands of Fortune that
she sends you to prison hither? 245

GUILDENSTERN. Prison, my lord?

HAMLET. Denmark's a prison.

ROSENCRANTZ. Then is the world one.

---

211 **pregnant** meaningful 211 **happiness** apt turn of phrase 230 **indifferent** ordinary 237 **privates** ordinary men (with a pun on "private parts")

HAMLET. A goodly one, in which there are many confines, wards,° and dungeons, Denmark being one o'   250
th' worst.

ROSENCRANTZ. We think not so, my lord.

HAMLET. Why, then 'tis none to you, for there is nothing either good or bad but thinking makes it so. To me it is   255
a prison.

ROSENCRANTZ. Why then your ambition makes it one. 'Tis too narrow for your mind.

HAMLET. O God, I could be bounded in a nutshell and count myself a king of infinite space, were it not that I have bad dreams.   260

GUILDENSTERN. Which dreams indeed are ambition, for the very substance of the ambitious is merely the shadow of a dream.

HAMLET. A dream itself is but a shadow.

ROSENCRANTZ. Truly, and I hold ambition of so airy and light   265
a quality that it is but a shadow's shadow.

HAMLET. Then are our beggars bodies, and our monarchs and outstretched heroes the beggars' shadows.° Shall we to th' court? For, by my fay,° I cannot
reason.   270

BOTH. We'll wait upon you.

HAMLET. No such matter. I will not sort you with the rest of my servants, for, to speak to you like an honest man, I am most dreadfully attended. But in the beaten way of friendship, what make you at   275
Elsinore?

ROSENCRANTZ. To visit you, my lord; no other occasion.

HAMLET. Beggar that I am, I am even poor in thanks, but I thank you; and sure, dear friends, my thanks are too dear a halfpenny.° Were you not sent for?   280
Is it your own inclining? Is it a free visitation?
Come, come, deal justly with me. Come, come;
nay, speak.

GUILDENSTERN. What should we say, my lord?

HAMLET. Why anything—but to th' purpose. You were sent   285
for, and there is a kind of confession in your looks, which your modesties have not craft enough to color.
I know the good King and Queen have sent for
you.

ROSENCRANTZ. To what end, my lord?   290

250 **wards** cells 267–69 **Then are. . .beggars' shadows** i.e., by your logic, beggars
(lacking ambition) are substantial, and great men are elongated shadows 269 **fay**
faith 280 **too dear a halfpenny** i.e., not worth a halfpenny

HAMLET. That you must teach me. But let me conjure you
by the rights of our fellowship, by the consonancy of our
youth, by the obligation of our ever-preserved love, and
by what more dear a better proposer can charge you
withal, be even and direct with me, whether you were   295
sent for or no.

ROSENCRANTZ. [*Aside to* GUILDENSTERN] What say you?

HAMLET. [*Aside*] Nay then, I have an eye of you.—If you love
me, hold not off.

GUILDENSTERN. My lord, we were sent for.   300

HAMLET. I will tell you why; so shall my anticipation prevent your discovery,° and your secrecy to the King
and Queen molt no feather. I have of late, but wherefore I know not, lost all my mirth, forgone all custom
of exercises; and indeed, it goes so heavily with   305
my disposition that this goodly frame, the earth,
seems to me a sterile promontory; this most excellent canopy, the air, look you, this brave o'er-
hanging firmament, this majestical roof fretted° with
golden fire: why, it appeareth nothing to me but a   310
foul and pestilent congregation of vapors. What a
piece of work is a man, how noble in reason, how
infinite in faculties, in form and moving how express°
and admirable, in action how like an angel, in apprehension how like a god: the beauty of the world,   315
the paragon of animals; and yet to me, what is this
quintessence of dust? Man delights not me; nor woman
neither, though by your smiling you seem to say
so.

ROSENCRANTZ. My lord, there was no such stuff in my   320
thoughts.

HAMLET. Why did ye laugh then, when I said "Man delights
not me"?

ROSENCRANTZ. To think, my lord, if you delight not in man,
what lenten° entertainment the players shall receive   325
from you. We coted° them on the way, and hither are
they coming to offer you service.

HAMLET. He that plays the king shall be welcome; his Majesty shall have tribute of me; the adventurous knight
shall use his foil and target;° the lover shall not sigh   330
gratis; the humorous man° shall end his part in peace;
the clown shall make those laugh whose lungs are

302 **prevent your discovery** forestall your disclosure   309 **fretted** adorned
313 **express** exact   325 **lenten** meager   326 **coted** overtook   330 **target** shield
331 **humorous man** i.e., eccentric man (among stock characters in dramas were men
dominated by a "humor" or odd trait)

tickle o' th' sere;° and the lady shall say her mind freely,
or° the blank verse shall halt° for't. What players are
they?   335

ROSENCRANTZ. Even those you were wont to take such delight in, the tragedians of the city.

HAMLET. How chances it they travel? Their residence, both
in reputation and profit, was better both ways.

ROSENCRANTZ. I think their inhibition° comes by the means   340
of the late innovation.°

HAMLET. Do they hold the same estimation they did when
I was in the city? Are they so followed?

ROSENCRANTZ. No indeed, are they not.

HAMLET. How comes it? Do they grow rusty?   345

ROSENCRANTZ. Nay, their endeavor keeps in the wonted
pace, but there is, sir, an eyrie° of children, little
eyases, that cry out on the top of question° and are
most tyrannically° clapped for't. These are now the
fashion, and so berattle the common stages° (so they   350
call them) that many wearing rapiers are afraid of
goosequills° and dare scarce come thither.

HAMLET. What, are they children? Who maintains 'em? How
are they escoted?° Will they pursue the quality° no
longer than they can sing? Will they not say after-   355
wards, if they should grow themselves to common
players (as it is most like, if their means are no
better), their writers do them wrong to make them
exclaim against their own succession?°

ROSENCRANTZ. Faith, there has been much to-do on both   360
sides, and the nation holds it no sin to tarre° them to
controversy. There was, for a while, no money bid for
argument° unless the poet and the player went to cuffs
in the question.

HAMLET. Is't possible?   365

GUILDENSTERN. O, there has been much throwing about of
brains.

HAMLET. Do the boys carry it away?

---

333 **tickle o' th' sere** on hair trigger (**sere**=part of the gunlock)   334 **or** else
334 **halt** limp   340 **inhibition** hindrance   341 **innovation** (probably an allusion to
the companies of child actors that had become popular and were offering serious
competition to the adult actors)   347 **eyrie** nest   348 **eyases, that . . . of question**
unfledged hawks that cry shrilly above others in matters of debate   349 **tyrannically**
violently   350 **berattle the common stages** cry down the public theaters (with
the adult acting companies)   352 **goosequills** pens (of satirists who ridicule the public
theaters and their audiences)   354 **escoted** financially supported   354 **quality**
profession of acting   359 **succession** future   361 **tarre** incite   363 **argument** plot
of a play

ROSENCRANTZ. Ay, that they do, my lord—Hercules and his
load° too.   370

HAMLET. It is not very strange, for my uncle is King of Denmark, and those that would make mouths at him while
my father lived give twenty, forty, fifty, a hundred
ducats apiece for his picture in little. 'Sblood,° there
is something in this more than natural, if philosophy   375
could find out.

                                        A flourish.

GUILDENSTERN. There are the players.

HAMLET. Gentlemen, you are welcome to Elsinore. Your
hands, come then. Th' appurtenance of welcome is
fashion and ceremony. Let me comply with you in   380
this garb,° lest my extent° to the players (which I
tell you must show fairly outwards) should more
appear like entertainment than yours. You are welcome. But my uncle-father and aunt-mother are de-
ceived.   385

GUILDENSTERN. In what, my dear lord?

HAMLET. I am but mad north-northwest:° when the wind
is southerly I know a hawk from a handsaw.°

                                        Enter POLONIUS.

POLONIUS. Well be with you, gentlemen.

HAMLET. Hark you, Guildenstern, and you too; at each ear   390
a hearer. That great baby you see there is not yet out
of his swaddling clouts.

ROSENCRANTZ. Happily° he is the second time come to
them, for they say an old man is twice a child.

HAMLET. I will prophesy he comes to tell me of the players.   395
Mark it.—You say right, sir; a Monday morning, 'twas
then indeed.

POLONIUS. My lord, I have news to tell you.

HAMLET. My lord, I have news to tell you. When Roscius°
was an actor in Rome——   400

POLONIUS. The actors are come hither, my lord.

HAMLET. Buzz, buzz.°

POLONIUS. Upon my honor——

HAMLET. Then came each actor on his ass——

POLONIUS. The best actors in the world, either for tragedy,   405

369–70 **Hercules and his load** i.e., the whole world (with a reference to the Globe
Theatre, which had a sign that represented Hercules bearing the globe)   374 **'Sblood**
by God's blood   380 **comply** be courteous   381 **garb** outward show   381 **extent** behavior   387 **north-northwest** i.e., on one point of the compass only   388 **hawk from
a handsaw** (**hawk** can refer not only to a bird but to a kind of pickax; **handsaw**—a
carpenter's tool—may involve a similar pun on "hernshaw," a heron)   393 **Happily**
perhaps   399 **Roscius** (a famous Roman comic actor)   402 **Buzz, buzz** (an interjec-
tion, perhaps indicating that the news is old)

comedy, history, pastoral, pastoral-comical, historical-
pastoral, tragical-historical, tragical-comical-historical-
pastoral; scene individable,° or poem unlimited.°
Seneca° cannot be too heavy, nor Plautus° too light.
For the law of writ and the liberty,° these are the   410
only men.

HAMLET. O Jeptha, judge of Israel,° what a treasure hadst
thou!

POLONIUS. What a treasure had he, my lord?

HAMLET. Why,   415

    "One fair daughter, and no more,
      The which he lovèd passing well."

POLONIUS. [*Aside*] Still on my daughter.

HAMLET. Am I not i' th' right, old Jeptha?

POLONIUS. If you call me Jeptha, my lord, I have a daugh-   420
ter that I love passing well.

HAMLET. Nay, that follows not.

POLONIUS. What follows then, my lord?

HAMLET. Why,

        "As by lot, God wot,"   425
and then, you know,
      "It came to pass, as most like it was."
The first row of the pious chanson° will show you more,
for look where my abridgment° comes.

Enter the PLAYERS.

You are welcome, masters, welcome, all. I am glad   430
to see thee well. Welcome, good friends. O, old
friend, why, thy face is valanced° since I saw thee
last. Com'st thou to beard me in Denmark? What,
my young lady° and mistress? By'r Lady, your lady-
ship is nearer to heaven than when I saw you   435
last by the altitude of a chopine.° Pray God your
voice, like a piece of uncurrent gold, be not cracked
within the ring.°—Masters, you are all welcome.

---

408 **scene individable** plays observing the unities of time, place, and action
408 **poem unlimited** plays not restricted by the tenets of criticism 409 **Seneca**
(Roman tragic dramatist) 410 **Plautus** (Roman comic dramatist) 410–11 **For the law
of writ and the liberty** (perhaps "for sticking to the text and for improvising";
perhaps "for classical plays and for modern loosely written plays") 412 **Jeptha, judge
of Israel** (the title of a ballad on the Hebrew judge who sacrificed his daughter; see
Judges 11) 428 **row of the pious chanson** stanza of the scriptural song
429 **abridgment** (1) i.e., entertainers, who abridge the time (2) interrupters
432 **valanced** fringed (with a beard) 434 **young lady** i.e., boy for female roles
436 **chopine** thick-soled shoe 437–38 **like a piece. . .the ring** (a coin was unfit for
legal tender if a crack extended from the edge through the ring enclosing the monarch's
head. Hamlet, punning on **ring,** refers to the change of voice that the boy actor will
undergo)

We'll e'en to't like French falconers, fly at any-
thing we see. We'll have a speech straight. Come,   440
give us a taste of your quality. Come, a passionate
speech.

PLAYER. What speech, my good lord?

HAMLET. I heard thee speak me a speech once, but it was
never acted, or if it was, not above once, for the   445
play, I remember, pleased not the million; 'twas
caviary to the general,° but it was (as I received it,
and others, whose judgments in such matters cried
in the top of° mine) an excellent play, well digested
in the scenes, set down with as much modesty as   450
cunning.° I remember one said there were no
sallets° in the lines to make the matter savory;
nor no matter in the phrase that might indict the
author of affectation, but called it an honest method, as
wholesome as sweet, and by very much more hand-   455
some than fine.° One speech in't I chiefly loved.
'Twas Aeneas' tale to Dido, and thereabout of it
especially when he speaks of Priam's slaughter. If
it live in your memory, begin at this line—let me
see, let me see: 460
    "The rugged Pyrrhus, like th' Hyrcanian beast°——"
'Tis not so; it begins with Pyrrhus:
    "The rugged Pyrrhus, he whose sable° arms,
    Black as his purpose, did the night resemble
    When he lay couchèd in th' ominous horse,°   465
    Hath now this dread and black complexion smeared
    With heraldry more dismal.° Head to foot
    Now is he total gules, horridly tricked°
    With blood of fathers, mothers, daughters, sons,
    Baked and impasted° with the parching streets,   470
    That lend a tyrannous and a damnèd light
    To their lord's murder. Roasted in wrath and fire,
    And thus o'ersizèd° with coagulate gore,
    With eyes like carbuncles, the hellish Pyrrhus
    Old grandsire Priam seeks."   475
So, proceed you.

POLONIUS. Fore God, my lord, well spoken, with good
accent and good discretion.

---

447 **caviary to the general** i.e., too choice for the multitude   449 **in the top of**
overtopping   450–51 **modesty as cunning** restraint as art   452 **sallets** salads, spicy
jests   455–56 **more handsome than fine** well-proportioned rather than ornamented
461 **Hyrcanian beast** i.e., tiger (Hyrcania was in Asia)   463 **sable** black
465 **ominous horse** i.e., wooden horse at the siege of Troy   467 **dismal** ill-omened
468 **total gules, horridly tricked** all red, horridly adorned   470 **impasted** encrusted
473 **o'ersizèd** smeared over

PLAYER.   "Anon he finds him,
    Striking too short at Greeks. His antique sword,   480
    Rebellious to his arm, lies where it falls,
    Repugnant to command.° Unequal matched,
    Pyrrhus at Priam drives, in rage strikes wide,
    But with the whiff and wind of his fell sword
    Th' unnervèd father falls. Then senseless Ilium,°   485
    Seeming to feel this blow, with flaming top
    Stoops to his base,° and with a hideous crash
    Takes prisoner Pyrrhus' ear. For lo, his sword,
    Which was declining on the milky head
    Of reverend Priam, seemed i' th' air to stick.   490
    So as a painted tyrant° Pyrrhus stood,
    And like a neutral to his will and matter°
    Did nothing.
    But as we often see, against° some storm,
    A silence in the heavens, the rack° stand still,   495
    The bold winds speechless, and the orb below
    As hush as death, anon the dreadful thunder
    Doth rend the region, so after Pyrrhus' pause,
    A rousèd vengeance sets him new awork,
    And never did the Cyclops' hammers fall   500
    On Mars's armor, forged for proof eterne,°
    With less remorse than Pyrrhus' bleeding sword
    Now falls on Priam.
    Out, out, thou strumpet Fortune! All you gods,
    In general synod° take away her power,   505
    Break all the spokes and fellies° from her wheel,
    And bowl the round nave° down the hill of heaven,
    As low as to the fiends."
POLONIUS. This is too long.
HAMLET. It shall to the barber's, with your beard.—   510
    Prithee say on. He's for a jig or a tale of bawdry, or
    he sleeps. Say on; come to Hecuba.
PLAYER. "But who (ah woe!) had seen the mobled° queen——"
HAMLET. "The mobled queen"?
POLONIUS. That's good. "Mobled queen" is good.   515
PLAYER. "Run barefoot up and down, threat'ning the flames
    With bisson rheum;° a clout° upon that head
    Where late the diadem stood, and for a robe,
    About her lank and all o'erteemèd° loins,

---

482 **Repugnant to command** disobedient 485 **senseless Ilium** insensate Troy
487 **Stoops to his base** collapses (**his**=its) 491 **painted tyrant** tyrant in a
picture 492 **matter** task 494 **against** just before 495 **rack** clouds 501 **proof
eterne** eternal endurance 505 **synod** council 506 **fellies** rims 507 **nave** hub
513 **mobled** muffled 517 **bisson rheum** blinding tears 517 **clout** rag
519 **o'erteemèd** exhausted with childbearing

A blanket in the alarm of fear caught up—   520
Who this had seen, with tongue in venom steeped
'Gainst Fortune's state would treason have pronounced.
But if the gods themselves did see her then,
When she saw Pyrrhus make malicious sport
In mincing with his sword her husband's limbs,   525
The instant burst of clamor that she made
(Unless things mortal move them not at all)
Would have made milch° the burning eyes of heaven
And passion in the gods."

POLONIUS. Look, whe'r° he has not turned his color, and   530
    has tears in's eyes. Prithee no more.

HAMLET. 'Tis well. I'll have thee speak out the rest of this
    soon. Good my lord, will you see the players well
    bestowed?° Do you hear? Let them be well used,
    for they are the abstract and brief chronicles of the   535
    time. After your death you were better have a bad
    epitaph than their ill report while you live.

POLONIUS. My lord, I will use them according to their
    desert.

HAMLET. God's bodkin,° man, much better! Use every man   540
    after his desert, and who shall scape whipping? Use
    them after your own honor and dignity. The less they
    deserve, the more merit is in your bounty. Take them
    in.

POLONIUS. Come, sirs.   545

HAMLET. Follow him, friends. We'll hear a play tomorrow.
    [*Aside to* PLAYER] Dost thou hear me, old friend? Can
    you play *The Murder of Gonzago?*

PLAYER. Ay, my lord.

HAMLET. We'll ha't tomorrow night. You could for a   550
    need study a speech of some dozen or sixteen lines
    which I would set down and insert in't, could you
    not?

PLAYER. Ay, my lord.

HAMLET. Very well. Follow that lord, and look you mock   555
    him not. My good friends, I'll leave you till night. You
    are welcome to Elsinore.
                  Exeunt POLONIUS *and* PLAYERS.

ROSENCRANTZ. Good my lord.
                 Exeunt [ROSENCRANTZ *and* GUILDENSTERN].

HAMLET. Ay, so, God bye to you.—Now I am alone.
    O, what a rogue and peasant slave am I!   560
    Is it not monstrous that this player here,
    But in a fiction, in a dream of passion,°

---

528 **milch** moist (literally, "milk-giving")   530 **whe'r** whether   534 **bestowed** housed
540 **God's bodkin** by God's little body   562 **dream of passion** imaginary emotion

Could force his soul so to his own conceit°
That from her working all his visage wanned,
Tears in his eyes, distraction in his aspect,   565
A broken voice, and his whole function° suiting
With forms° to his conceit? And all for nothing!
For Hecuba!
What's Hecuba to him, or he to Hecuba,
That he should weep for her? What would he do   570
Had he the motive and the cue for passion
That I have? He would drown the stage with tears
And cleave the general ear with horrid speech,
Make mad the guilty and appall the free,°
Confound the ignorant, and amaze indeed   575
The very faculties of eyes and ears.
Yet I,
A dull and muddy-mettled° rascal, peak
Like John-a-dreams,° unpregnant of° my cause,
And can say nothing. No, not for a king,   580
Upon whose property and most dear life
A damned defeat was made. Am I a coward?
Who calls me villain? Breaks my pate across?
Plucks off my beard and blows it in my face?
Tweaks me by the nose? Gives me the lie i' th' throat   585
As deep as to the lungs? Who does me this?
Ha, 'swounds,° I should take it, for it cannot be
But I am pigeon-livered° and lack gall
To make oppression bitter, or ere this
I should ha' fatted all the region kites°   590
With this slave's offal. Bloody, bawdy villain!
Remorseless, treacherous, lecherous, kindless° villain!
O, vengeance!
Why, what an ass am I! This is most brave,°
That I, the son of a dear father murdered,   595
Prompted to my revenge by heaven and hell,
Must, like a whore, unpack my heart with words
And fall a-cursing like a very drab,°
A stallion!° Fie upon't, foh! About,° my brains.
Hum—   600
I have heard that guilty creatures sitting at a play

---

563 **conceit** imagination   566 **function** action   567 **forms** bodily expressions
574 **appall the free** terrify (make pale?) the guiltless   578 **muddy-mettled** weak-
spirited   578–79 **peak / Like John-a-dreams** mope like a dreamer   579 **unpregnant
of** unquickened by   587 **'swounds** by God's wounds   588 **pigeon-livered** gentle as a
dove   590 **region kites** kites (scavenger birds) of the sky   592 **kindless** unnatural   594 **brave** fine   598 **drab** prostitute   599 **stallion** male prostitute (perhaps one
should adopt the Folio reading, **scullion**=kitchen wench)   599 **About** to work

Have by the very cunning of the scene
Been struck so to the soul that presently°
They have proclaimed their malefactions.
For murder, though it have no tongue, will speak   605
With most miraculous organ. I'll have these players
Play something like the murder of my father
Before mine uncle. I'll observe his looks,
I'll tent° him to the quick. If 'a do blench,°
I know my course. The spirit that I have seen   610
May be a devil, and the devil hath power
T' assume a pleasing shape, yea, and perhaps
Out of my weakness and my melancholy,
As he is very potent with such spirits,
Abuses me to damn me. I'll have grounds   615
More relative° than this. The play's the thing
Wherein I'll catch the conscience of the King.   *Exit*.

[ACT III

Scene I. *The castle*.]

Enter KING, QUEEN, POLONIUS, OPHELIA, ROSENCRANTZ, GUILDENSTERN, LORDS.

KING. And can you by no drift of conference°
    Get from him why he puts on his confusion,
    Grating so harshly all his days of quiet
    With turbulent and dangerous lunacy?
ROSENCRANTZ. He does confess he feels himself distracted,   5
    But from what cause 'a will by no means speak.
GUILDENSTERN. Nor do we find him forward to be sounded,°
    But with a crafty madness keeps aloof
    When we would bring him on to some confession
    Of his true state.
QUEEN.   Did he receive you well?   10
ROSENCRANTZ. Most like a gentleman.
GUILDENSTERN. But with much forcing of his disposition.°
ROSENCRANTZ. Niggard of question,° but of our demands
    Most free in his reply.
QUEEN.   Did you assay° him
    To any pastime?   15
ROSENCRANTZ. Madam, it so fell out that certain players
    We o'erraught° on the way; of these we told him,

603 **presently** immediately   609 **tent** probe   609 **blench** flinch   616 **relative**
(probably "pertinent," but possibly "able to be related plausibly")   III.i.1 **drift of**
conference management of conversation   7 **forward to be sounded** willing to be
questioned   12 **forcing of his disposition** effort   13 **Niggard of question** uninclined
to talk   14 **assay** tempt   17 **o'erraught** overtook

And there did seem in him a kind of joy
To hear of it. They are here about the court,
And, as I think, they have already order   20
This night to play before him.
POLONIUS.   'Tis most true,
And he beseeched me to entreat your Majesties
To hear and see the matter.
KING. With all my heart, and it doth much content me
To hear him so inclined.   25
Good gentlemen, give him a further edge
And drive his purpose into these delights.
ROSENCRANTZ. We shall, my lord.
                         Exeunt ROSENCRANTZ *and* GUILDENSTERN.
KING.   .   Sweet Gertrude, leave us too,
For we have closely° sent for Hamlet hither,
That he, as 'twere by accident, may here   30
Affront° Ophelia.
Her father and myself (lawful espials°)
Will so bestow ourselves that, seeing unseen,
We may of their encounter frankly judge
And gather by him, as he is behaved,   35
If't be th' affliction of his love or no
That thus he suffers for.
QUEEN.   I shall obey you.
And for your part, Ophelia, I do wish
That your good beauties be the happy cause
Of Hamlet's wildness. So shall I hope your virtues   40
Will bring him to his wonted way again,
To both your honors.
OPHELIA.   Madam, I wish it may.
                              [*Exit* QUEEN.]
POLONIUS. Ophelia, walk you here.—Gracious, so please you,
We will bestow ourselves. [*To* OPHELIA] Read on this book,
That show of such an exercise may color°   45
Your loneliness. We are oft to blame in this,
'Tis too much proved, that with devotion's visage
And pious action we do sugar o'er
The devil himself.
KING.   [*Aside*] O, 'tis too true.
How smart a lash that speech doth give my conscience!   50
The harlot's cheek, beautied with plast'ring art,
Is not more ugly to the thing that helps it
Than is my deed to my most painted word.
O heavy burden!

---

29 **closely** secretly 31 **Affront** meet face to face 32 **espials** spies 45 **exercise may color** act of devotion may give a plausible hue to (the book is one of devotion)

POLONIUS. I hear him coming. Let's withdraw, my lord.   55
[Exeunt KING and POLONIUS.]
Enter HAMLET.

HAMLET. To be or not to be: that is the question:
    Whether 'tis nobler in the mind to suffer
    The slings and arrows of outrageous fortune,
    Or to take arms against a sea of troubles,
    And by opposing end them. To die, to sleep—   60
    No more—and by a sleep to say we end
    The heartache, and the thousand natural shocks
    That flesh is heir to! 'Tis a consummation
    Devoutly to be wished. To die, to sleep—
    To sleep—perchance to dream: ay, there's the rub,°   65
    For in that sleep of death what dreams may come
    When we have shuffled off this mortal coil,°
    Must give us pause. There's the respect°
    That makes calamity of so long life:°
    For who would bear the whips and scorns of time,   70
    Th' oppressor's wrong, the proud man's contumely,
    The pangs of despised love, the law's delay,
    The insolence of office, and the spurns
    That patient merit of th' unworthy takes,
    When he himself might his quietus° make   75
    With a bare bodkin?° Who would fardels° bear,
    To grunt and sweat under a weary life,
    But that the dread of something after death,
    The undiscovered country, from whose bourn°
    No traveler returns, puzzles the will,   80
    And makes us rather bear those ills we have,
    Than fly to others that we know not of?
    Thus conscience° does make cowards of us all,
    And thus the native hue of resolution
    Is sicklied o'er with the pale cast° of thought,   85
    And enterprises of great pitch° and moment,
    With this regard° their currents turn awry,
    And lose the name of action.—Soft you now,
    The fair Ophelia!—Nymph, in thy orisons°
    Be all my sins remembered.
OPHELIA.   Good my lord,   90
    How does your honor for this many a day?

---

65 **rub** impediment (obstruction to a bowler's ball)   67 **coil** (1) turmoil (2) a ring of rope
(here the flesh encircling the soul)   68 **respect** consideration   69 **makes calamity
of so long life** (1) makes calamity so long-lived (2) makes living so long a calamity
75 **quietus** full discharge (a legal term)   76 **bodkin** dagger   76 **fardels** burdens
79 **bourn** region   83 **conscience** self-consciousness, introspection   85 **cast** color
86 **pitch** height (a term from falconry)   87 **regard** consideration   89 **orisons** prayers

HAMLET. I humbly thank you; well, well, well.

OPHELIA. My lord, I have remembrances of yours
　That I have longèd long to redeliver.
　I pray you now, receive them.

HAMLET.　　　　　　　　　　No, not I,   95
　I never gave you aught.

OPHELIA. My honored lord, you know right well you did,
　And with them words of so sweet breath composed
　As made these things more rich. Their perfume lost,
　Take these again, for to the noble mind   100
　Rich gifts wax poor when givers prove unkind.
　There, my lord.

HAMLET. Ha, ha! Are you honest?°

OPHELIA. My lord?

HAMLET. Are you fair?   105

OPHELIA. What means your lordship?

HAMLET. That if you be honest and fair, your honesty should
　admit no discourse to your beauty.°

OPHELIA. Could beauty, my lord, have better commerce than
　with honesty?   110

HAMLET. Ay, truly; for the power of beauty will sooner
　transform honesty from what it is to a bawd° than the
　force of honesty can translate beauty into his likeness.
　This was sometime a paradox, but now the time gives
　it proof. I did love you once.   115

OPHELIA. Indeed, my lord, you made me believe so.

HAMLET. You should not have believed me, for virtue can-
　not so inoculate° our old stock but we shall relish of it.°
　I loved you not.

OPHELIA. I was the more deceived.   120

HAMLET. Get thee to a nunnery. Why wouldst thou be
　a breeder of sinners? I am myself indifferent hon-
　est,° But yet I could accuse me of such things that
　it were better my mother had not borne me: I am
　very proud, revengeful, ambitious, with more of-   125
　fenses at my beck° than I have thoughts to put them
　in, imagination to give them shape, or time to act
　them in. What should such fellows as I do crawling
　between earth and heaven? We are arrant knaves
　all; believe none of us. Go thy ways to a nunnery.   130
　Where's your father?

---

103 **Are you honest** (1) are you modest (2) are you chaste (3) have you integrity
107-08 **your honesty. . . to your beauty** your modesty should permit no approach to
your beauty　112 **bawd** procurer　118 **inoculate** graft　118 **relish of it** smack of it
(our old sinful nature)　122-23 **indifferent honest** moderately virtuous　126 **beck** call

OPHELIA. At home, my lord.

HAMLET. Let the doors be shut upon him, that he may play
the fool nowhere but in's own house. Farewell.

OPHELIA. O help him, you sweet heavens!   135

HAMLET. If thou dost marry, I'll give thee this plague for
thy dowry: be thou as chaste as ice, as pure as snow,
thou shalt not escape calumny. Get thee to a nunnery.
Go, farewell. Or if thou wilt needs marry, marry a
fool, for wise men know well enough what monsters°   140
you make of them. To a nunnery, go, and quickly too.
Farewell.

OPHELIA. Heavenly powers, restore him!

HAMLET. I have heard of your paintings, well enough. God
hath given you one face, and you make yourselves   145
another. You jig and amble, and you lisp; you nickname God's creatures and make your wantonness
your ignorance.° Go to, I'll no more on't; it hath
made me mad. I say we will have no moe° marriage.
Those that are married already—all but one—shall   150
live. The rest shall keep as they are. To a nunnery,
go.   *Exit.*

OPHELIA. O what a noble mind is here o'erthrown!
The courtier's, soldier's, scholar's, eye, tongue, sword,
Th' expectancy and rose° of the fair state,   155
The glass of fashion, and the mold of form,°
Th' observed of all observers, quite, quite down!
And I, of ladies most deject and wretched,
That sucked the honey of his musicked vows,
Now see that noble and most sovereign reason   160
Like sweet bells jangled, out of time and harsh,
That unmatched form and feature of blown° youth
Blasted with ecstasy.° O, woe is me
T' have seen what I have seen, see what I see!
                    Enter KING *and* POLONIUS.

KING. Love? His affections° do not that way tend,   165
Nor what he spake, though it lacked form a little,
Was not like madness. There's something in his soul
O'er which his melancholy sits on brood,
And I do doubt° the hatch and the disclose
Will be some danger; which for to prevent,   170
I have in quick determination
Thus set it down: he shall with speed to England

---

140 **monsters** horned beasts, cuckolds   147–48 **make your wantonness your
ignorance** excuse your wanton speech by pretending ignorance   149 **moe** more
155 **expectancy and rose** i.e., fair hope   156 **The glass...of form** the mirror of
fashion, and the pattern of excellent behavior   162 **blown** blooming   163 **ecstasy** madness   165 **affections** inclinations   169 **doubt** fear

For the demand of our neglected tribute.
Haply the seas, and countries different,
With variable objects, shall expel   175
This something-settled° matter in his heart,
Whereon his brains still beating puts him thus
From fashion of himself. What think you on't?
POLONIUS. It shall do well. But yet do I believe
The origin and commencement of his grief   180
Sprung from neglected love. How now, Ophelia?
You need not tell us what Lord Hamlet said;
We heard it all. My lord, do as you please,
But if you hold it fit, after the play,
Let his queen mother all alone entreat him   185
To show his grief. Let her be round° with him,
And I'll be placed, so please you, in the ear
Of all their conference. If she find him not,°
To England send him, or confine him where
Your wisdom best shall think.
KING.   It shall be so.   190
Madness in great ones must not unwatched go.

                                                        Exeunt.

[Scene II. *The castle.*]

Enter HAMLET *and three of the* PLAYERS.

HAMLET. Speak the speech, I pray you, as I pronounced
it to you, trippingly on the tongue. But if you mouth it,
as many of our players do, I had as lief the town
crier spoke my lines. Nor do not saw the air too
much with your hand, thus, but use all gently, for in   5
the very torrent, tempest, and (as I may say) whirl-
wind of your passion, you must acquire and beget
a temperance that may give it smoothness. O, it offends
me to the soul to hear a robustious periwig-pated°
fellow tear a passion to tatters, to very rags, to split   10
the ears of the groundlings,° who for the most part
are capable of° nothing but inexplicable dumb shows°
and noise. I would have such a fellow whipped for
o'erdoing Termagant. It out herods Herod.° Pray you
avoid it.   15

---

176 **something-settled** somewhat settled   186 **round** blunt   188 **find him not** does
not find him out   III.ii.9 **robustious periwig-pated** boisterous wig-headed
11 **groundlings** those who stood in the pit of the theater (the poorest and presumably
most ignorant of the audience)   12 **are capable of** are able to understand
12 **dumb shows** (it had been the fashion for actors to preface plays or parts of plays
with silent mime)   14 **Termagant . . . Herod** (boisterous characters in the old
mystery plays)

PLAYER. I warrant your honor.

HAMLET. Be not too tame neither, but let your own discretion be your tutor. Suit the action to the word, the
word to the action, with this special observance, that
you o'erstep not the modesty of nature. For any-   20
thing so o'erdone is from° the purpose of playing,
whose end, both at the first and now, was and is, to
hold, as 'twere, the mirror up to nature; to show
virtue her own feature, scorn her own image, and the
very age and body of the time his form and pres-   25
sure.° Now, this overdone, or come tardy off, though
it makes the unskillful laugh, cannot but make the
judicious grieve, the censure of the which one must
in your allowance o'erweigh a whole theater of others.
O, there be players that I have seen play, and heard   30
others praise, and that highly (not to speak it profanely), that neither having th' accent of Christians,
nor the gait of Christian, pagan, nor man, have so
strutted and bellowed that I have thought some of
Nature's journeymen° had made men, and not made   35
them well, they imitated humanity so abomina-
bly.

PLAYER. I hope we have reformed that indifferently° with us,
sir.

HAMLET. O, reform it altogether! And let those that play   40
your clowns speak no more than is set down for them,
for there be of them that will themselves laugh, to
set on some quantity of barren spectators to laugh
too, though in the meantime some necessary question
of the play be then to be considered. That's villainous   45
and shows a most pitiful ambition in the fool that uses
it. Go make you ready.

                                        Exit PLAYERS.

          Enter POLONIUS, GUILDENSTERN, *and* ROSENCRANTZ.

How now, my lord? Will the King hear this piece of
work?

POLONIUS. And the Queen too, and that presently.   50

HAMLET. Bid the players make haste.   *Exit* POLONIUS.

Will you two help to hasten them?

ROSENCRANTZ. Ay, my lord.   *Exeunt they two.*

HAMLET. What, ho, Horatio!

          Enter HORATIO.

HORATIO. Here, sweet lord, at your service.   55

---

21 **from** contrary to   25–26 **pressure** image, impress   35 **journeymen** workers not
yet masters of their craft   38 **indifferently** tolerably

HAMLET. Horatio, thou art e'en as just a man
  As e'er my conversation coped withal.°
HORATIO. O, my dear lord——
HAMLET.   Nay, do not think I flatter.
  For what advancement° may I hope from thee,
  That no revenue hast but thy good spirits   60
  To feed and clothe thee? Why should the poor be flattered?
  No, let the candied° tongue lick absurd pomp,
  And crook the pregnant° hinges of the knee
  Where thrift° may follow fawning. Dost thou hear?
  Since my dear soul was mistress of her choice   65
  And could of men distinguish her election,
  S'hath sealed thee° for herself, for thou hast been
  As one, in suff'ring all, that suffers nothing,
  A man that Fortune's buffets and rewards
  Hast ta'en with equal thanks; and blest are those   70
  Whose blood° and judgment are so well commeddled°
  That they are not a pipe for Fortune's finger
  To sound what stop she please. Give me that man
  That is not passion's slave, and I will wear him
  In my heart's core, ay, in my heart of heart,   75
  As I do thee. Something too much of this—
  There is a play tonight before the King.
  One scene of it comes near the circumstance
  Which I have told thee, of my father's death.
  I prithee, when thou seest that act afoot,   80
  Even with the very comment° of thy soul
  Observe my uncle. If his occulted° guilt
  Do not itself unkennel in one speech,
  It is a damnèd ghost that we have seen,
  And my imaginations are as foul   85
  As Vulcan's stithy.° Give him heedful note,
  For I mine eyes will rivet to his face,
  And after we will both our judgments join
  In censure of his seeming.°
HORATIO.   Well, my lord.
  If 'a steal aught the whilst this play is playing,   90
  And scape detecting, I will pay the theft.
    Enter TRUMPETS *and* KETTLEDRUMS, KING, QUEEN, POLONIUS, OPHE-
    LIA, ROSENCRANTZ, GUILDENSTERN, *and other* LORDS *attendant with*
    his GUARD *carrying torches. Danish March. Sound a Flourish.*

57 **coped withal** met with   59 **advancement** promotion   62 **candied** sugared,
flattering   63 **pregnant** (1) pliant (2) full of promise of good fortune   64 **thrift**
profit   67 **S' hath sealed thee** she (the soul) has set a mark on you   71 **blood**
passion   71 **commeddled** blended   81 **very comment** deepest wisdom   82 **occulted**
hidden   86 **stithy** forge, smithy   89 **censure of his seeming** judgment on his looks

HAMLET. They are coming to the play: I must be idle;°
  Get you a place.

KING. How fares our cousin Hamlet?

HAMLET. Excellent, i' faith of the chameleon's dish;° I eat   95
  the air, promise-crammed; you cannot feed capons
  so.

KING. I have nothing with this answer, Hamlet; these words
  are not mine.

HAMLET. No, nor mine now. [*To* POLONIUS] My lord, you   100
  played once i' th' university, you say?

POLONIUS. That did I, my lord, and was accounted a good
  actor.

HAMLET. What did you enact?

POLONIUS. I did enact Julius Caesar. I was killed i' th' Capi-   105
  tol; Brutus killed me.

HAMLET. It was a brute part of him to kill so capital a calf
  there. Be the players ready?

ROSENCRANTZ. Ay, my lord. They stay upon your patience.   110

QUEEN. Come hither, my dear Hamlet, sit by me.

HAMLET. No, good mother. Here's metal more attractive.°

POLONIUS. [*to the* KING] O ho! Do you mark that?

HAMLET. Lady, shall I lie in your lap?   115

> [*He lies at* OPHELIA's *feet.*]

OPHELIA. No, my lord.

HAMLET. I mean, my head upon your lap?

OPHELIA. Ay, my lord.

HAMLET. Do you think I meant country matters?°

OPHELIA. I think nothing, my lord.   120

HAMLET. That's a fair thought to lie between maids'
  legs.

OPHELIA. What is, my lord?

HAMLET. Nothing.

OPHELIA. You are merry, my lord.   125

HAMLET. Who, I?

OPHELIA. Ay, my lord.

HAMLET. O God, your only jig-maker!° What should a
  man do but be merry? For look you how cheerfully
  my mother looks, and my father died within's two   130
  hours.

OPHELIA. Nay, 'tis twice two months, my lord.

HAMLET. So long? Nay then, let the devil wear black, for
  I'll have a suit of sables.° O heavens! Die two months

---

92 **be idle** play the fool 95 **the chameleon's dish** air (on which chameleons were
thought to live) 112–13 **attractive** magnetic 119 **country matters** rustic doings (with
a pun on the vulgar word for the pudendum) 128 **jig-maker** composer of songs and
dances (often a Fool, who performed them) 134 **sables** (pun on "black" and
"luxurious furs")

ago, and not forgotten yet? Then there's hope a   135
great man's memory may outlive his life half a year.
But by'r Lady, 'a must build churches then, or else
shall 'a suffer not thinking on, with the hobbyhorse,°
whose epitaph is "For O, for O, the hobbyhorse is
forgot!"   140

The trumpets sound. Dumb show follows:

Enter a KING *and a* QUEEN *very lovingly, the* QUEEN *embracing him,
and he her. She kneels; and makes show of protestation unto him.
He takes her up, and declines his head upon her neck. He lies him
down upon a bank of flowers. She, seeing him asleep, leaves him.
Anon come in another man: takes off his crown, kisses it, pours poison in the sleeper's ears, and leaves him. The* QUEEN *returns, finds
the* KING *dead, makes passionate action. The poisoner, with some
three or four, come in again, seem to condole with her. The dead body
is carried away. The poisoner woos the* QUEEN *with gifts; she seems
harsh awhile, but in the end accepts love.*

Exeunt.

OPHELIA. What means this, my lord?

HAMLET. Marry, this is miching mallecho;° it means mischief.

OPHELIA. Belike this show imports the argument° of the
play.   145

Enter PROLOGUE.

HAMLET. We shall know by this fellow. The players cannot
keep counsel; they'll tell all.

OPHELIA. Will 'a tell us what this show meant?

HAMLET. Ay, or any show that you will show him. Be not
you ashamed to show, he'll not shame to tell you   150
what it means.

OPHELIA. You are naught,° you are naught; I'll mark the
play.

PROLOGUE. For us, and for our tragedy,
   Here stooping to your clemency,   155
   We beg your hearing patiently.   *[Exit.]*

HAMLET. Is this a prologue, or the posy of a ring?°

OPHELIA. 'Tis brief, my lord.

HAMLET. As woman's love.

Enter [two PLAYERS *as]* KING *and* QUEEN.

PLAYER KING. Full thirty times hath Phoebus' cart° gone round   160
   Neptune's salt wash° and Tellus'° orbèd ground,
   And thirty dozen moons with borrowed sheen
   About the world have times twelve thirties been,

---

138 **hobbyhorse** mock horse worn by a performer in the morris dance   142 **miching
mallecho** sneaking mischief   144 **argument** plot   152 **naught** wicked, improper
157 **posy of a ring** motto inscribed in a ring   160 **Phoebus' cart** the sun's chariot
161 **Neptune's salt wash** the sea   161 **Tellus** Roman goddess of the earth

Since love our hearts, and Hymen did our hands,
Unite commutual in most sacred bands.   165
PLAYER QUEEN. So many journeys may the sun and moon
  Make us again count o'er ere love be done!
  But woe is me, you are so sick of late,
  So far from cheer and from your former state,
  That I distrust° you. Yet, though I distrust,   170
  Discomfort you, my lord, it nothing must.
  For women fear too much, even as they love,
  And women's fear and love hold quantity,
  In neither aught, or in extremity.°
  Now what my love is, proof° hath made you know,   175
  And as my love is sized, my fear is so.
  Where love is great, the littlest doubts are fear;
  Where little fears grow great, great love grows there.
PLAYER KING. Faith, I must leave thee, love, and shortly too;
  My operant° powers their functions leave to do: 180
  And thou shalt live in this fair world behind,
  Honored, beloved, and haply one as kind
  For husband shalt thou——
PLAYER QUEEN.   O, confound the rest!
  Such love must needs be treason in my breast.
  In second husband let me be accurst!   185
  None wed the second but who killed the first.
HAMLET. [*Aside*] That's wormwood.°
PLAYER QUEEN. The instances° that second marriage move°
  Are base respects of thrift,° but none of love.
  A second time I kill my husband dead   190
  When second husband kisses me in bed.
PLAYER KING. I do believe you think what now you speak,
  But what we do determine oft we break.
  Purpose is but the slave to memory,
  Of violent birth, but poor validity,°   195
  Which now like fruit unripe sticks on the tree,
  But fall unshaken when they mellow be.
  Most necessary 'tis that we forget
  To pay ourselves what to ourselves is debt.
  What to ourselves in passion we propose,   200
  The passion ending, doth the purpose lose.
  The violence of either grief or joy

---

170 **distrust** am anxious about 173-74 **And women's... in extremity** (perhaps the
idea is that women's anxiety is great or little in proportion to their love. The previous
line, unrhymed, may be a false start that Shakespeare neglected to delete) 175 **proof**
experience 180 **operant** active 187 **wormwood** a bitter herb 188 **instances**
motives 188 **move** induce 189 **respects of thrift** considerations of profit
195 **validity** strength

Their own enactures° with themselves destroy:
Where joy most revels, grief doth most lament;
Grief joys, joy grieves, on slender accident.   205
This world is not for aye, nor 'tis not strange
That even our loves should with our fortunes change,
For 'tis a question left us yet to prove,
Whether love lead fortune, or else fortune love.
The great man down, you mark his favorite flies;   210
The poor advanced makes friends of enemies;
And hitherto doth love on fortune tend,
For who not needs shall never lack a friend;
And who in want a hollow friend doth try,
Directly seasons him° his enemy.   215
But, orderly to end where I begun,
Our wills and fates do so contrary run
That our devices still are overthrown;
Our thoughts are ours, their ends none of our own.
So think thou wilt no second husband wed,   220
But die thy thoughts when thy first lord is dead.
PLAYER QUEEN. Nor earth to me give food, nor heaven light,
Sport and repose lock from me day and night,
To desperation turn my trust and hope,
An anchor's° cheer in prison be my scope,   225
Each opposite that blanks° the face of joy
Meet what I would have well, and it destroy:
Both here and hence pursue me lasting strife,
If, once a widow, ever I be wife!
HAMLET. If she should break it now!   230
PLAYER KING. 'Tis deeply sworn. Sweet, leave me here awhile;
My spirits grow dull, and fain I would beguile
The tedious day with sleep.
PLAYER QUEEN.   Sleep rock thy brain,

                                              [He] sleeps.
And never come mischance between us twain!   *Exit.*
HAMLET. Madam, how like you this play?   235
QUEEN. The lady doth protest too much, methinks.
HAMLET. O, but she'll keep her word.
KING. Have you heard the argument?° Is there no
    offense in't?
HAMLET. No, no, they do but jest, poison in jest; no   240
    offense i' th' world.
KING. What do you call the play?

---

203 **enactures** acts   215 **seasons him** ripens him into   225 **anchor's** anchorite's,
hermit's   226 **opposite that blanks** adverse thing that blanches   238 **argument** plot

HAMLET. *The Mousetrap.* Marry, how? Tropically.° This play
is the image of a murder done in Vienna: Gonzago
is the Duke's name; his wife, Baptista. You shall see   245
anon. 'Tis a knavish piece of work, but what of that?
Your Majesty, and we that have free° souls, it touches
us not. Let the galled jade winch;° our withers are
unwrung.

Enter LUCIANUS.

This is one Lucianus, nephew to the King.   250
OPHELIA. You are as good as a chorus, my lord.
HAMLET. I could interpret° between you and your love, if
I could see the puppets dallying.
OPHELIA. You are keen,° my lord, you are keen.
HAMLET. It would cost you a groaning to take off mine   255
edge.
OPHELIA. Still better, and worse.
HAMLET. So you mistake° your husbands.—Begin, murderer.
Leave thy damnable faces and begin. Come, the croak-
ing raven doth bellow for revenge.   260
LUCIANUS. Thoughts black, hands apt, drugs fit, and time agreeing,
Confederate season,° else no creature seeing,
Thou mixture rank, of midnight weeds collected,
With Hecate's ban° thrice blasted, thrice infected,
Thy natural magic and dire property°   265
On wholesome life usurps immediately.

Pours the poison in his ears.

HAMLET. 'A poisons him i' th' garden for his estate. His
name's Gonzago. The story is extant, and written in
very choice Italian. You shall see anon how the mur-
derer gets the love of Gonzago's wife.   270
OPHELIA. The King rises.
HAMLET. What, frighted with false fire?°
QUEEN. How fares my lord?
POLONIUS. Give o'er the play.
KING. Give me some light. Away!   275
POLONIUS. Lights, lights, lights!

Exeunt all but HAMLET *and* HORATIO.

HAMLET. Why, let the strucken deer go weep,
          The hart ungallèd play:
      For some must watch, while some must sleep;
          Thus runs the world away.   280

243 **Tropically** figuratively (with a pun on "trap") 247 **free** innocent 248 **galled jade
winch** chafed horse wince 252 **interpret** (like a showman explaining the action of
puppets) 254 **keen** (1) sharp (2) sexually aroused 258 **mistake** err in taking
262 **Confederate season** the opportunity allied with me 264 **Hecate's ban** the curse of
the goddess of sorcery 265 **property** nature 272 **false fire** blank discharge of firearms

Would not this, sir, and a forest of feathers°—if the rest
of my fortunes turn Turk° with me—with two Provincial
roses° on my razed° shoes, get me a fellowship in a
cry° of players?

HORATIO. Half a share.   285

HAMLET. A whole one, I.
    For thou dost know, O Damon dear,
        This realm dismantled was
    Of Jove himself; and now reigns here
        A very, very—pajock.°   290

HORATIO. You might have rhymed.°

HAMLET. O good Horatio, I'll take the ghost's word for a
thousand pound. Didst perceive?

HORATIO. Very well, my lord.

HAMLET. Upon the talk of poisoning?   295

HORATIO. I did very well note him.

HAMLET. Ah ha! Come, some music! Come, the recorders!°
    For if the King like not the comedy,
    Why then, belike he likes it not, perdy.°   300
Come, some music!

        Enter ROSENCRANTZ *and* GUILDENSTERN.

GUILDENSTERN. Good my lord, vouchsafe me a word with
you.

HAMLET. Sir, a whole history.

GUILDENSTERN. The King, sir——   305

HAMLET. Ay, sir, what of him?

GUILDENSTERN. Is in his retirement marvelous distem-
p'red.

HAMLET. With drink, sir?

GUILDENSTERN. No, my lord, with choler.°   310

HAMLET. Your wisdom should show itself more richer to
signify this to the doctor, for for me to put him to
his purgation would perhaps plunge him into more
choler.

GUILDENSTERN. Good my lord, put your discourse into some   315
frame,° and start not so wildly from my affair.

HAMLET. I am tame, sir; pronounce.

GUILDENSTERN. The Queen, your mother, in most great affliction of spirit hath sent me to you.

HAMLET. You are welcome.   320

---

281 **feathers** (plumes were sometimes part of a costume) 282 **turn Turk** i.e., go
bad, treat me badly 282–83 **Provincial roses** rosettes like the roses of Provence (?)
283 **razed** ornamented with slashes 284 **cry** pack, company 290 **pajock** peacock
291 **You might have rhymed** i.e., rhymed "was" with "ass" 297–98 **recorders** flute-
like instruments 300 **perdy** by God (French: *par dieu*) 310 **choler** anger (but Hamlet
pretends to take the word in its sense of "biliousness") 316 **frame** order, control

GUILDENSTERN. Nay, good my lord, this courtesy is not of
the right breed. If it shall please you to make me a
wholesome answer, I will do your mother's commandment: if not, your pardon and my return shall be the end
of my business.   325

HAMLET. Sir, I cannot.

ROSENCRANTZ. What, my lord?

HAMLET. Make you a wholesome° answer; my wit's diseased. But, sir, such answer as I can make, you shall
command, or rather, as you say, my mother. There-   330
fore no more, but to the matter. My mother, you
say——

ROSENCRANTZ. Then thus she says: your behavior hath
struck her into amazement and admiration.°

HAMLET. O wonderful son, that can so astonish a mother!   335
But is there no sequel at the heels of this mother's
admiration? Impart.

ROSENCRANTZ. She desires to speak with you in her closet
ere you go to bed.

HAMLET. We shall obey, were she ten times our mother.   340
Have you any further trade with us?

ROSENCRANTZ. My lord, you once did love me.

HAMLET. And do still, by these pickers and stealers.°

ROSENCRANTZ. Good my lord, what is your cause of distemper? You do surely bar the door upon your own liberty,   345
if you deny your griefs to your friend.

HAMLET. Sir, I lack advancement.°

ROSENCRANTZ. How can that be, when you have the
voice of the King himself for your succession in
Denmark?   350

Enter the PLAYERS *with recorders.*

HAMLET. Ay, sir, but "while the grass grows"—the proverb°
is something musty. O, the recorders. Let me see one.
To withdraw° with you—why do you go about to
recover the wind° of me as if you would drive me into
a toil?°   355

GUILDENSTERN. O my lord, if my duty be too bold, my love is
too unmannerly.°

HAMLET. I do not well understand that. Will you play upon
this pipe?

328 **wholesome** sane   334 **admiration** wonder   343 **pickers and stealers**
i.e., hands (with reference to the prayer; "Keep my hands from picking and stealing")
347 **advancement** promotion   351 **proverb** ("While the grass groweth, the horse star-
veth")   353 **withdraw** speak in private   354 **recover the wind** get on the windward
side (as in hunting)   355 **toil** snare   356–57 **if my duty. . .too unmannerly**
i.e., if these questions seem rude, it is because my love for you leads me beyond good
manners.

GUILDENSTERN. My lord, I cannot. 360

HAMLET. I pray you.

GUILDENSTERN. Believe me, I cannot.

HAMLET. I pray you.

GUILDENSTERN. Believe me, I cannot.

HAMLET. I do beseech you.

GUILDENSTERN. I know no touch of it, my lord.

HAMLET. It is as easy as lying. Govern these ventages° 365
with your fingers and thumb, give it breath with your
mouth, and it will discourse most eloquent music. Look
you, these are the stops.

GUILDENSTERN. But these cannot I command to any
utt'rance of harmony; I have not the skill. 370

HAMLET. Why, look you now, how unworthy a thing you
make of me! You would play upon me; you would seem
to know my stops; you would pluck out the heart of my
mystery; you would sound me from my lowest note to
the top of my compass;° and there is much music, 375
excellent voice, in this little organ,° yet cannot you
make it speak. 'Sblood, do you think I am easier to be
played on than a pipe? Call me what instrument you
will, though you can fret° me, you cannot play upon
me. 380

Enter POLONIUS.

God bless you, sir!

POLONIUS. My lord, the Queen would speak with you, and
presently.

HAMLET. Do you see yonder cloud that's almost in shape
of a camel? 385

POLONIUS. By th' mass and 'tis, like a camel indeed.

HAMLET. Methinks it is like a weasel.

POLONIUS. It is backed like a weasel.

HAMLET. Or like a whale.

POLONIUS. Very like a whale. 390

HAMLET. Then I will come to my mother by and by. [*Aside*]
They fool me to the top of my bent.° —I will come
by and by.°

POLONIUS. I will say so. *Exit.*

HAMLET. "By and by" is easily said. Leave me, friends. 395

[*Exeunt all but* HAMLET.]

'Tis now the very witching time of night,
When churchyards yawn, and hell itself breathes out

---

365 **ventages** vents, stops on a recorder　375 **compass** range of voice　376 **organ**
i.e., the recorder　379 **fret** vex (with a pun alluding to the frets, or ridges, that guide
the fingering on some instruments)　392 **They fool . . . my bent** they compel me to
play the fool to the limit of my capacity　393 **by and by** very soon

Contagion to this world. Now could I drink hot blood
And do such bitter business as the day
Would quake to look on. Soft, now to my mother.   400
O heart, lose not thy nature; let not ever
The soul of Nero° enter this firm bosom.
Let me be cruel, not unnatural;
I will speak daggers to her, but use none.
My tongue and soul in this be hypocrites: 405
How in my words somever she be shent,°
To give them seals° never, my soul, consent!   *Exit.*

[Scene III. *The castle.*]

Enter KING, ROSENCRANTZ, *and* GUILDENSTERN.

KING. I like him not, nor stands it safe with us
To let his madness range. Therefore prepare you.
I your commission will forthwith dispatch,
And he to England shall along with you.
The terms° of our estate may not endure   5
Hazard so near's° as doth hourly grow
Out of his brows.
GUILDENSTERN.   We will ourselves provide.
Most holy and religious fear it is
To keep those many many bodies safe
That live and feed upon your Majesty.   10
ROSENCRANTZ. The single and peculiar° life is bound
With all the strength and armor of the mind
To keep itself from noyance,° but much more
That spirit upon whose weal depends and rests
The lives of many. The cess of majesty°   15
Dies not alone, but like a gulf° doth draw
What's near it with it; or it is a massy wheel
Fixed on the summit of the highest mount,
To whose huge spokes ten thousand lesser things
Are mortised and adjoined, which when it falls,   20
Each small annexment, petty consequence,
Attends° the boist'rous ruin. Never alone
Did the King sigh, but with a general groan.
KING. Arm° you, I pray you, to this speedy voyage,
For we will fetters put about this fear,   25
Which now goes too free-footed.
ROSENCRANTZ.   We will haste us.
Exeunt GENTLEMEN.

---

402 **Nero** (Roman emperor who had his mother murdered)   406 **shent** rebuked
407 **give them seals** confirm them with deeds   III.iii.5 **terms** conditions   6 **near's**
near us   11 **peculiar** individual, private   13 **noyance** injury   15 **cess of majesty**
cessation (death) of a king   16 **gulf** whirlpool   22 **Attends** waits on, participates in
24 **Arm** prepare

Enter POLONIUS.

POLONIUS. My lord, he's going to his mother's closet.°
  Behind the arras I'll convey myself
  To hear the process.° I'll warrant she'll tax him home,°
  And, as you said, and wisely was it said,   30
  'Tis meet that some more audience than a mother,
  Since nature makes them partial, should o'erhear
  The speech of vantage.° Fare you well, my liege.
  I'll call upon you ere you go to bed
  And tell you what I know.

KING.   Thanks, dear my lord.   35

Exit [POLONIUS].

  O, my offense is rank, it smells to heaven;
  It hath the primal eldest curse° upon't,
  A brother's murder. Pray can I not,
  Though inclination be as sharp as will.
  My stronger guilt defeats my strong intent,   40
  And like a man to double business bound
  I stand in pause where I shall first begin,
  And both neglect. What if this cursèd hand
  Were thicker than itself with brother's blood,
  Is there not rain enough in the sweet heavens   45
  To wash it white as snow? Whereto serves mercy
  But to confront° the visage of offense?
  And what's in prayer but this twofold force,
  To be forestallèd ere we come to fall,
  Or pardoned being down? Then I'll look up.   50
  My fault is past. But, O, what form of prayer
  Can serve my turn? "Forgive me my foul murder"?
  That cannot be, since I am still possessed
  Of those effects° for which I did the murder,
  My crown, mine own ambition, and my queen.   55
  May one be pardoned and retain th' offense?
  In the corrupted currents of this world
  Offense's gilded hand may shove by justice,
  And oft 'tis seen the wicked prize itself
  Buys out the law. But 'tis not so above.   60
  There is no shuffling;° there the action lies
  In his true nature, and we ourselves compelled,
  Even to the teeth and forehead of our faults,
  To give in evidence. What then? What rests?°
  Try what repentance can. What can it not?   65
  Yet what can it when one cannot repent?

27 **closet** private room   29 **process** proceedings   29 **tax him home** censure him
sharply   33 **of vantage** from an advantageous place   37 **primal eldest curse** (curse
of Cain, who killed Abel)   47 **confront** oppose   54 **effects** things gained   61 **shuffling**
trickery   64 **rests** remains

O wretched state! O bosom black as death!
O limèd° soul, that struggling to be free
Art more engaged!° Help, angels! Make assay.°
Bow, stubborn knees, and, heart with strings of steel,   70
Be soft as sinews of the newborn babe.
All may be well.   [*He kneels.*]
                    Enter HAMLET.
HAMLET. Now might I do it pat, now 'a is a-praying,
    And now I'll do't. And so 'a goes to heaven,
    And so am I revenged. That would be scanned.°   75
    A villain kills my father, and for that
    I, his sole son, do this same villain send
    To heaven.
    Why, this is hire and salary, not revenge.
    'A took my father grossly, full of bread,°   80
    With all his crimes broad blown,° as flush° as May;
    And how his audit° stands, who knows save heaven?
    But in our circumstance and course of thought,
    'Tis heavy with him; and am I then revenged,
    To take him in the purging of his soul,   85
    When he is fit and seasoned for his passage?
    No.
    Up, sword, and know thou a more horrid hent.°
    When he is drunk asleep, or in his rage,
    Or in th' incestuous pleasure of his bed,   90
    At game a-swearing, or about some act
    That has no relish° of salvation in't—
    Then trip him, that his heels may kick at heaven,
    And that his soul may be as damned and black
    As hell, whereto it goes. My mother stays.   95
    This physic° but prolongs thy sickly days.   *Exit.*
KING. [*Rises*] My words fly up, my thoughts remain below.
    Words without thoughts never to heaven go.   *Exit.*

                [Scene IV. *The* QUEEN's *closet.*]
            Enter [QUEEN] GERTRUDE *and* POLONIUS.

POLONIUS. 'A will come straight. Look you lay home° to him.
    Tell him his pranks have been too broad° to bear with,
    And that your Grace hath screened and stood between

---

68 **limèd** caught (as with birdlime, a sticky substance spread on boughs to snare
birds)   69 **engaged** ensnared   69 **assay** an attempt   75 **would be scanned** ought to
be looked into   80 **bread** i.e., wordly gratification   81 **crimes broad blown** sins in full
bloom   81 **flush** vigorous   82 **audit** account   88 **hent** grasp (here, occasion for seizing)   92 **relish** flavor   96 **physic** (Claudius' purgation by prayer, as Hamlet thinks in
line 85)   III.iv.1 **lay home** thrust (rebuke) him sharply   2 **broad** unrestrained

Much heat and him. I'll silence me even here.
Pray you be round with him.　　　　　　　　　　　　　　　5
HAMLET. (*Within*) Mother, Mother, Mother!
QUEEN. I'll warrant you; fear me not. Withdraw; I hear him
　　coming.　　　　　　　　　　[POLONIUS *hides behind the arras.*]
　　　　　　　　　　　Enter HAMLET.
HAMLET. Now, Mother, what's the matter?
QUEEN. Hamlet, thou hast thy father much offended.　　　　　10
HAMLET. Mother, you have my father much offended.
QUEEN. Come, come, you answer with an idle° tongue.
HAMLET. Go, go, you question with a wicked tongue.
QUEEN. Why, how now, Hamlet?
HAMLET.　　　　　　　　　　　What's the matter now?
QUEEN. Have you forgot me?
HAMLET.　　　　　　　　　No, by the rood,° not so!　　　　15
　　You are the Queen, your husband's brother's wife,
　　And, would it were not so, you are my mother.
QUEEN. Nay, then I'll set those to you that can speak.
HAMLET. Come, come, and sit you down. You shall not budge.
　　You go not till I set you up a glass°　　　　　　　　　　20
　　Where you may see the inmost part of you!
QUEEN. What wilt thou do? Thou wilt not murder me?
　　Help, ho!
POLONIUS. [*Behind*] What, ho! Help!
HAMLET. [*Draws*] How now? A rat? Dead for a ducat, dead!　　25
　　　　　[*Makes a pass through the arras and*] *kills* POLONIUS.
POLONIUS. [*Behind*] O, I am slain!
QUEEN.　　　　　　　　　O, me, what hast thou done?
HAMLET. Nay, I know not. Is it the King?
QUEEN. O, what a rash and bloody deed is this!
HAMLET. A bloody deed—almost as bad, good Mother,
　　As kill a king, and marry with his brother.　　　　　　　30
QUEEN As kill a king?
HAMLET.　　　　　　　Ay, lady, it was my word.
　　　　　　　　　[*Lifts up the arras and sees* POLONIUS.]
　　Thou wretched, rash, intruding fool, farewell!
　　I took thee for thy better. Take thy fortune.
　　Thou find'st to be too busy is some danger.—
　　Leave wringing of your hands. Peace, sit you down　　　　35
　　And let me wring your heart, for so I shall
　　If it be made of penetrable stuff,
　　If damnèd custom have not brazed° it so
　　That it be proof° and bulwark against sense.°

---

12 **idle** foolish　15 **rood** cross　20 **glass** mirror　38 **brazed** hardened like brass
39 **proof** armor　39 **sense** feeling

QUEEN. What have I done that thou dar'st wag thy tongue   40
    In noise so rude against me?

HAMLET.   Such an act
    That blurs the grace and blush of modesty,
    Calls virtue hypocrite, takes off the rose
    From the fair forehead of an innocent love,
    And sets a blister° there, makes marriage vows   45
    As false as dicers' oaths. O, such a deed
    As from the body of contraction° plucks
    The very soul, and sweet religion makes
    A rhapsody° of words! Heaven's face does glow
    O'er this solidity and compound mass   50
    With heated visage, as against the doom
    Is thoughtsick at the act.°

QUEEN.   Ay me, what act,
    That roars so loud and thunders in the index?°

HAMLET. Look here upon this picture, and on this,
    The counterfeit presentment° of two brothers.   55
    See what a grace was seated on this brow:
    Hyperion's curls, the front° of Jove himself,
    An eye like Mars, to threaten and command,
    A station° like the herald Mercury
    New lighted on a heaven-kissing hill—   60
    A combination and a form indeed
    Where every god did seem to set his seal
    To give the world assurance of a man.
    This was your husband. Look you now what follows.
    Here is your husband, like a mildewed ear   65
    Blasting his wholesome brother. Have you eyes?
    Could you on this fair mountain leave to feed,
    And batten° on this moor? Ha! Have you eyes?
    You cannot call it love, for at your age
    The heyday° in the blood is tame, it's humble,   70
    And waits upon the judgment, and what judgment
    Would step from this to this? Sense° sure you have,
    Else could you not have motion, but sure that sense
    Is apoplexed,° for madness would not err,
    Nor sense to ecstasy° was ne'er so thralled   75
    But it reserved some quantity of choice

---

45 **sets a blister** brands (as a harlot)　47 **contraction** marriage contract
49 **rhapsody** senseless string　49–52 **Heaven's face. . .the act** i.e., the face of
heaven blushes over this earth (compounded of four elements), the face hot, as if
Judgment Day were near, and it is thoughtsick at the act　53 **index** prologue
55 **counterfeit presentment** represented image　57 **front** forehead　59 **station**
bearing　68 **batten** feed gluttonously　70 **heyday** excitement　72 **Sense** feeling
74 **apoplexed** paralyzed　75 **ecstasy** madness

To serve in such a difference. What devil was't
That thus hath cozened you at hoodman-blind?°
Eyes without feeling, feeling without sight,
Ears without hands or eyes, smelling sans° all,   80
Or but a sickly part of one true sense
Could not so mope.°
O shame, where is thy blush? Rebellious hell,
If thou canst mutine in a matron's bones,
To flaming youth let virtue be as wax   85
And melt in her own fire. Proclaim no shame
When the compulsive ardor° gives the charge,
Since frost itself as actively doth burn,
And reason panders will.°

QUEEN.   O Hamlet, speak no more.
Thou turn'st mine eyes into my very soul.   90
And there I see such black and grainèd° spots,
As will not leave their tinct.°

HAMLET.   Nay, but to live
In the rank sweat of an enseamèd° bed,
Stewed in corruption, honeying and making love
Over the nasty sty——

QUEEN.   O, speak to me no more.   95
These words like daggers enter in my ears.
No more, sweet Hamlet.

HAMLET.   A murderer and a villain,
A slave that is not twentieth part the tithe°
Of your precedent lord, a vice° of kings,
A cutpurse of the empire and the rule,   100
That from a shelf the precious diadem stole
And put it in his pocket——

QUEEN.   No more.

Enter GHOST.

HAMLET. A king of shreds and patches—
Save me and hover o'er me with your wings,
You heavenly guards! What would your gracious figure?   105

QUEEN. Alas, he's mad.

HAMLET. Do you not come your tardy son to chide,
That, lapsed in time and passion, lets go by
Th' important acting of your dread command?
O, say!   110

---

78 cozened you at hoodman-blind cheated you at blindman's bluff **80 sans**
without **82 mope** be stupid **87 compulsive ardor** compelling passion **89 reason
panders will** reason acts as a procurer for desire **91 grainèd** dyed in grain (fast
dyed) **92 tinct** color **93 enseamèd** (perhaps "soaked in grease," i.e., sweaty;
perhaps "much wrinkled") **98 tithe** tenth part **99 vice** (like the Vice, a fool and
mischief-maker in the old morality plays)

GHOST. Do not forget. This visitation
 Is but to whet thy almost blunted purpose.
 But look, amazement on thy mother sits.
 O, step between her and her fighting soul!
 Conceit° in weakest bodies strongest works.   115
 Speak to her, Hamlet.
HAMLET.   How is it with you, lady?
QUEEN. Alas, how is't with you,
 That you do bend your eye on vacancy,
 And with th' incorporal° air do hold discourse?
 Forth at your eyes your spirits wildly peep,   120
 And as the sleeping soldiers in th' alarm
 Your bedded hair° like life in excrements°
 Start up and stand an end.° O gentle son,
 Upon the heat and flame of thy distemper
 Sprinkle cool patience. Whereon do you look?   125
HAMLET. On him, on him! Look you, how pale he glares!
 His form and cause conjoined, preaching to stones,
 Would make them capable.°—Do not look upon me,
 Lest with this piteous action you convert
 My stern effects.° Then what I have to do   130
 Will want true color; tears perchance for blood.
QUEEN. To whom do you speak this?
HAMLET.   Do you see nothing there?
QUEEN. Nothing at all; yet all that is I see.
HAMLET. Nor did you nothing hear?
QUEEN.   No, nothing but ourselves.
HAMLET. Why, look you there! Look how it steals away!   135
 My father, in his habit° as he lived!
 Look where he goes even now out at the portal!

                                                        Exit GHOST.

QUEEN. This is the very coinage of your brain.
 This bodiless creation ecstasy
 Is very cunning in.
HAMLET.   Ecstasy?   140
 My pulse as yours doth temperately keep time
 And makes as healthful music. It is not madness
 That I have uttered. Bring me to the test,
 And I the matter will reword, which madness
 Would gambol° from. Mother, for love of grace,   145
 Lay not that flattering unction° to your soul,

---

115 **Conceit** imagination 119 **incorporal** bodiless 122 **bedded hair** hair laid flat
122 **excrements** outgrowths (here, the hair) 123 **an end** on end 128 **capable** recep-
tive 129-30 **convert / My stern effects** divert my stern deeds 136 **habit** garment
(Q1, though a "bad" quarto, is probably correct in saying that at line 102 the ghost
enters "in his nightgown," i.e., dressing gown) 145 **gambol** start away
146 **unction** ointment

That not your trespass but my madness speaks.
It will but skin and film the ulcerous place
Whiles rank corruption, mining° all within,
Infects unseen. Confess yourself to heaven, 150
Repent what's past, avoid what is to come,
And do not spread the compost° on the weeds
To make them ranker. Forgive me this my virtue.
For in the fatness of these pursy° times
Virtue itself of vice must pardon beg, 155
Yea, curb° and woo for leave to do him good.
QUEEN. O Hamlet, thou hast cleft my heart in twain.
HAMLET. O, throw away the worser part of it,
And live the purer with the other half.
Good night—but go not to my uncle's bed. 160
Assume a virtue, if you have it not.
That monster custom, who all sense doth eat,
Of habits devil, is angel yet in this,
That to the use° of actions fair and good
He likewise gives a frock or livery° 165
That aptly is put on. Refrain tonight,
And that shall lend a kind of easiness
To the next abstinence; the next more easy;
For use almost can change the stamp of nature,
And either° the devil, or throw him out 170
With wondrous potency. Once more, good night,
And when you are desirous to be blest,
I'll blessing beg of you.—For this same lord,
I do repent; but heaven hath pleased it so,
To punish me with this, and this with me, 175
That I must be their° scourge and minister.
I will bestow° him and will answer well
The death I gave him. So again, good night.
I must be cruel only to be kind.
Thus bad begins, and worse remains behind. 180
One word more, good lady.
QUEEN.   What shall I do?
HAMLET. Not this, by no means, that I bid you do:
Let the bloat King tempt you again to bed,
Pinch wanton on your cheek, call you his mouse,
And let him, for a pair of reechy° kisses, 185

---

149 **mining** undermining 152 **compost** fertilizing substance 154 **pursy** bloated
156 **curb** bow low 164 **use** practice 165 **livery** characteristic garment (punning on
"habits" in line 163) 170 **either** (probably a word is missing after **either;** among
suggestions are "master," "curb," and "house"; but possibly **either** is a verb meaning
"make easier") 176 **their** i.e., the heavens' 177 **bestow** stow, lodge 185 **reechy** foul
(literally "smoky")

Or paddling in your neck with his damned fingers,
Make you to ravel° all this matter out,
That I essentially am not in madness,
But mad in craft. 'Twere good you let him know,
For who that's but a queen, fair, sober, wise,   190
Would from a paddock,° from a bat, a gib,°
Such dear concernings hide? Who would do so?
No, in despite of sense and secrecy,
Unpeg the basket on the house's top,
Let the birds fly, and like the famous ape,   195
To try conclusions,° in the basket creep
And break your own neck down.
QUEEN. Be thou assured, if words be made of breath,
And breath of life, I have no life to breathe
What thou hast said to me.   200
HAMLET. I must to England; you know that?
QUEEN.   Alack,
I had forgot. 'Tis so concluded on.
HAMLET. There's letters sealed, and my two school-fellows,
Whom I will trust as I will adders fanged,
They bear the mandate;° they must sweep my way   205
And marshall me to knavery. Let it work;
For 'tis the sport to have the enginer
Hoist with his own petar,° and 't shall go hard
But I will delve one yard below their mines
And blow them at the moon. O, 'tis most sweet   210
When in one line two crafts° directly meet.
This man shall set me packing:
I'll lug the guts into the neighbor room.
Mother, good night. Indeed, this counselor
Is now most still, most secret, and most grave,   215
Who was in life a foolish prating knave.
Come, sir, to draw toward an end with you.
Good night, Mother
              [*Exit the* QUEEN. *Then*] *exit* HAMLET, *tugging in* POLONIUS.

[ACT IV

Scene I. *The castle.*]

Enter KING *and* QUEEN, *with* ROSENCRANTZ *and* GUILDENSTERN.

KING. There's matter in these sighs. These profound heaves
You must translate; 'tis fit we understand them.
Where is your son?

187 **ravel** unravel, reveal 191 **paddock** toad 191 **gib** tomcat 196 **To try
conclusions** to make experiments 205 **mandate** command 208 **petar** bomb
211 **crafts** (1) boats (2) acts of guile, crafty schemes

QUEEN. Bestow this place on us a little while
                   [*Exeunt* ROSENCRANTZ *and* GUILDENSTERN.]
    Ah, mine own lord, what have I seen tonight!   5
KING. What, Gertrude? How does Hamlet?
QUEEN. Mad as the sea and wind when both contend
    Which is the mightier. In his lawless fit,
    Behind the arras hearing something stir,
    Whips out his rapier, cries, "A rat, a rat!"   10
    And in this brainish apprehension° kills
    The unseen good old man.
KING.   O heavy deed!
    It had been so with us, had we been there.
    His liberty is full of threats to all,
    To you yourself, to us, to every one.   15
    Alas, how shall this bloody deed be answered?
    It will be laid to us, whose providence°
    Should have kept short, restrained, and out of haunt°
    This mad young man. But so much was our love
    We would not understand what was most fit,   20
    But, like the owner of a foul disease,
    To keep it from divulging, let it feed
    Even on the pith of life. Where is he gone?
QUEEN. To draw apart the body he hath killed;
    O'er whom his very madness, like some ore   25
    Among a mineral° of metals base,
    Shows itself pure. 'A weeps for what is done.
KING. O Gertrude, come away!
    The sun no sooner shall the mountains touch
    But we will ship him hence, and this vile deed   30
    We must with all our majesty and skill
    Both countenance and excuse. Ho, Guildenstern!
             Enter ROSENCRANTZ *and* GUILDENSTERN.
    Friends both, go join you with some further aid:
    Hamlet in madness hath Polonius slain,
    And from his mother's closet hath he dragged him.   35
    Go seek him out; speak fair, and bring the body
    Into the chapel. I pray you haste in this.
             [*Exeunt* ROSENCRANTZ *and* GUILDENSTERN.]
    Come, Gertrude, we'll call up our wisest friends
    And let them know both what we mean to do
    And what's untimely done . . .°   40

IV.i.11 **brainish apprehension** mad imagination 17 **providence** foresight 18 **out of haunt** away from association with others 25–26 **ore / Among a mineral** vein of gold in a mine 40 **done . . .** (evidently something has dropped out of the text. Capell's conjecture, "So, haply slander," is usually printed)

Whose whisper o'er the world's diameter,
As level as the cannon to his blank°
Transports his poisoned shot, may miss our name
And hit the woundless° air. O, come away!
My soul is full of discord and dismay.   *Exeunt.*   45

[Scene II. *The castle.*]

Enter HAMLET.

HAMLET. Safely stowed.

GENTLEMEN. (*Within*) Hamlet! Lord Hamlet!

HAMLET. But soft, what noise? Who calls on Hamlet?
   O, here they come.

Enter ROSENCRANTZ *and* GUILDENSTERN.

ROSENCRANTZ. What have you done, my lord, with the dead
   body?   5

HAMLET. Compounded it with dust, whereto 'tis kin.

ROSENCRANTZ. Tell us where 'tis, that we may take it thence
   And bear it to the chapel.

HAMLET. Do not believe it.

ROSENCRANTZ. Believe what?   10

HAMLET. That I can keep your counsel and not mine own.
   Besides, to be demanded of° a sponge, what replication°
   should be made by the son of a king?

ROSENCRANTZ. Take you me for a sponge, my lord?

HAMLET. Ay, sir, that soaks up the King's countenance,°   15
   his rewards, his authorities. But such officers do the
   King best service in the end. He keeps them, like an
   ape, in the corner of his jaw, first mouthed, to be last
   swallowed. When he needs what you have gleaned,
   it is but squeezing you and, sponge, you shall be dry   20
   again.

ROSENCRANTZ. I understand you not, my lord.

HAMLET. I am glad of it: a knavish speech sleeps in a foolish
   ear.

ROSENCRANTZ. My lord, you must tell us where the body is   25
   and go with us to the King.

HAMLET. The body is with the King, but the King is not
   with the body. The King is a thing——

GUILDENSTERN. A thing, my lord?

HAMLET. Of nothing. Bring me to him. Hide fox, and all   30
   after.°   *Exeunt.*

---

42 **blank** white center of a target 44 **woundless** invulnerable IV.ii.12 **demanded of**
questioned by 12 **replication** reply 15 **countenance** favor 30– **Hide fox, and all
after** (a cry in a game such as hide-and-seek; Hamlet runs from the stage)

[Scene III. *The castle.*]

Enter KING, *and two or three.*

KING. I have sent to seek him and to find the body:
How dangerous is it that this man goes loose!
Yet must not we put the strong law on him:
He's loved of the distracted° multitude,
Who like not in their judgment, but their eyes,   5
And where 'tis so, th' offender's scourge is weighed,
But never the offense. To bear° all smooth and even,
This sudden sending him away must seem
Deliberate pause.° Diseases desperate grown
By desperate appliance are relieved,   10
Or not at all.
            Enter ROSENCRANTZ, [GUILDENSTERN,] *and all the rest.*
            How now? What hath befall'n?
ROSENCRANTZ. Where the dead body is bestowed, my lord,
We cannot get from him.
KING.   But where is he?
ROSENCRANTZ. Without, my lord; guarded, to know your pleasure.
KING. Bring him before us.
ROSENCRANTZ.   Ho! Bring in the lord.   15
                    They enter.
KING. Now, Hamlet, where's Polonius?
HAMLET. At supper.
KING. At supper? Where?
HAMLET. Not where he eats, but where 'a is eaten. cer-
tain convocation of politic° worms are e'en at him. Your   20
worm is your only emperor for diet. We fat all crea-
tures else to fat us, and we fat ourselves for maggots.
Your fat king and your lean beggar is but variable
service°—two dishes, but to one table. That's the
end.   25
KING. Alas, alas!
HAMLET. A man may fish with the worm that hath eat of
a king, and eat of the fish that hath fed of that worm.
KING. What dost thou mean by this?
HAMLET. Nothing but to show you how a king may go a   30
progress° through the guts of a beggar.
KING. Where is Polonius?
HAMLET. In heaven. Send thither to see. If your messenger find him not there, seek him i' th' other place
yourself. But if indeed you find him not within this   35

IV.iii.4 **distracted** bewildered, senseless   7 **bear** carry out   9 **pause** planning
20 **politic** statesmanlike, shrewd   23–24 **variable service** different courses
31 **progress** royal journey

month, you shall nose him as you go up the stairs into
the lobby.

KING. [*To* ATTENDANTS] Go seek him there.

HAMLET. 'A will stay till you come.

[*Exeunt* ATTENDANTS.]

KING. Hamlet, this deed, for thine especial safety,　　　　　40
Which we do tender° as we dearly grieve
For that which thou hast done, must send thee hence
With fiery quickness. Therefore prepare thyself.
The bark is ready and the wind at help,
Th' associates tend,° and everything is bent　　　　　45
For England.

HAMLET.　　　　　For England?

KING.　　　　　　　　　Ay, Hamlet.

HAMLET.　　　　　　　　　　　　Good.

KING. So is it, if thou knew'st our purposes.

HAMLET. I see a cherub° that sees them. But come, for
England! Farewell, dear Mother.

KING. Thy loving father, Hamlet.　　　　　50

HAMLET. My mother—father and mother is man and wife,
man and wife is one flesh, and so, my mother. Come,
for England!　　　　　*Exit.*

KING. Follow him at foot;° tempt him with speed aboard.
Delay it not; I'll have him hence tonight.　　　　　55
Away! For everything is sealed and done
That else leans° on th' affair. Pray you make haste.

[*Exeunt all but the* KING.]

And, England, if my love thou hold'st at aught—
As my great power thereof may give thee sense,
Since yet thy cicatrice° looks raw and red　　　　　60
After the Danish sword, and thy free awe°
Pays homage to us—thou mayst not coldly set
Our sovereign process,° which imports at full
By letters congruing to that effect
The present° death of Hamlet. Do it, England,　　　　　65
For like the hectic° in my blood he rages,
And thou must cure me. Till I know 'tis done,
Howe'er my haps,° my joys were ne'er begun.

Exit.

---

41 **tender** hold dear　45 **tend** wait　48 **cherub** angel of knowledge　54 **at foot** closely　57 **leans** depends　60 **cicatrice** scar　61 **free awe** uncompelled submission　62–63 **coldly set / Our sovereign process** regard slightly our royal command　65 **present** instant　66 **hectic** fever　68 **haps** chances, fortunes

[Scene IV. *A plain in Denmark.*]

Enter FORTINBRAS *with his Army over the stage.*

FORTINBRAS. Go, Captain, from me greet the Danish king.
Tell him that by his license Fortinbras
Craves the conveyance of° a promised march
Over his kingdom. You know the rendezvous.
If that his Majesty would aught with us,   5
We shall express our duty in his eye;°
And let him know so.
CAPTAIN.   I will do't, my lord.
FORTINBRAS. Go softly° on.

                    [*Exeunt all but the* CAPTAIN.]
Enter HAMLET, ROSENCRANTZ, &c.

HAMLET. Good sir, whose powers° are these?
CAPTAIN. They are of Norway, sir.   10
HAMLET. How purposed, sir, I pray you?
CAPTAIN. Against some part of Poland.
HAMLET. Who commands them, sir?
CAPTAIN. The nephew to old Norway, Fortinbras.
HAMLET. Goes it against the main° of Poland, sir,   15
Or for some frontier?
CAPTAIN. Truly to speak, and with no addition,°
We go to gain a little patch of ground
That hath in it no profit but the name.
To pay five ducats, five, I would not farm it,   20
Nor will it yield to Norway or the Pole
A ranker° rate, should it be sold in fee.°
HAMLET. Why, then the Polack never will defend it.
CAPTAIN. Yes, it is already garrisoned.
HAMLET. Two thousand souls and twenty thousand ducats   25
Will not debate° the question of this straw.
This is th' imposthume° of much wealth and peace,
That inward breaks, and shows no cause without
Why the man dies. I humbly thank you, sir.
CAPTAIN. Good bye you, sir.   [*Exit*].
ROSENCRANTZ.   Will't please you go, my lord?   30
HAMLET. I'll be with you straight. Go a little before.
                    [*Exeunt all but* HAMLET.]
How all occasions do inform against me
And spur my dull revenge! What is a man,
If his chief good and market° of his time

IV.iv. 3 **conveyance of** escort for   6 **in his eye** before his eyes (i.e., in his
presence)   8 **softly** slowly   9 **powers** forces   15 **main** main part   17 **with no
addition** plainly   22 **ranker** higher   22 **in fee** outright   26 **debate** settle
27 **imposthume** abscess, ulcer   34 **market** profit

Be but to sleep and feed? A beast, no more.   35
Sure he that made us with such large discourse,°
Looking before and after, gave us not
That capability and godlike reason
To fust° in us unused. Now, whether it be
Bestial oblivion,° or some craven scruple   40
Of thinking too precisely on th' event°—
A thought which, quartered, hath but one part wisdom
And ever three parts coward—I do not know
Why yet I live to say, "This thing's to do,"
Sith I have cause, and will, and strength, and means   45
To do't. Examples gross° as earth exhort me.
Witness this army of such mass and charge,°
Led by a delicate and tender prince,
Whose spirit, with divine ambition puffed,
Makes mouths at the invisible event,°   50
Exposing what is mortal and unsure
To all that fortune, death, and danger dare,
Even for an eggshell. Rightly to be great
Is not° to stir without great argument,°
But greatly° to find quarrel in a straw   55
When honor's at the stake. How stand I then,
That have a father killed, a mother stained,
Excitements° of my reason and my blood,
And let all sleep, while to my shame I see
The imminent death of twenty thousand men   60
That for a fantasy and trick of fame°
Go to their graves like beds, fight for a plot
Whereon the numbers cannot try the cause,
Which is not tomb enough and continent°
To hide the slain? O, from this time forth,   65
My thoughts be bloody, or be nothing worth!   *Exit.*

[Scene V. *The castle.*]

Enter HORATIO, [QUEEN] GERTRUDE, *and a* GENTLEMAN.
QUEEN. I will not speak with her.
GENTLEMAN. She is importunate, indeed distract.
    Her mood will needs be pitied.
QUEEN.   What would she have?

36 **discourse** understanding 39 **fust** grow moldy 40 **oblivion** forgetfulness
41 **event** outcome 46 **gross** large, obvious 47 **charge** expense 50 **Makes mouths
at the invisible event** makes scornful faces at (is contemptuous of) the unseen
outcome 54 **not** (the sense seems to require "not not") 54 **argument** reason
55 **greatly** i.e., nobly 58 **Excitements** incentives 61 **fantasy and trick of fame**
illusion and trifle of reputation 64 **continent** receptacle, container

GENTLEMAN. She speaks much of her father, says she hears
   There's tricks i' th' world, and hems, and beats her heart,   5
   Spurns enviously at straws,° speaks things in doubt°
   That carry but half sense. Her speech is nothing,
   Yet the unshapèd use of it doth move
   The hearers to collection;° they yawn° at it,
   And botch the words up fit to their own thoughts,   10
   Which, as her winks and nods and gestures yield them,
   Indeed would make one think there might be thought,
   Though nothing sure, yet much unhappily.
HORATIO. 'Twere good she were spoken with, for she may strew
   Dangerous conjectures in ill-breeding minds.   15
QUEEN. Let her come in.   *[Exit* GENTLEMAN.]
   [*Aside*] To my sick soul (as sin's true nature is)
   Each toy seems prologue to some great amiss;°
   So full of artless jealousy° is guilt
   It spills° itself in fearing to be spilt.   20
             Enter OPHELIA [*distracted.*]
OPHELIA. Where is the beauteous majesty of Denmark?
QUEEN. How now, Ophelia?
OPHELIA. (*She sings.*) How should I your truelove know
          From another one?
          By his cockle hat° and staff   25
          And his sandal shoon.°
QUEEN. Alas, sweet lady, what imports this song?
OPHELIA. Say you? Nay, pray you mark.
          He is dead and gone, lady,   (*Song*)
             He is dead and gone;   30
          At his head a grass-green turf,
             At his heels a stone.
    O, ho!
QUEEN. Nay, but Ophelia——
OPHELIA. Pray you mark.   35
   [*Sings.*] White his shroud as the mountain snow——
                Enter KING.
QUEEN. Alas, look here, my lord.
OPHELIA.   Larded° all with sweet flowers   (*Song*)
          Which bewept to the grave did not go
          With truelove showers   40

IV.v.6 **Spurns enviously at straws** objects spitefully to insignificant matters 6 **in
doubt** uncertainly 8–9 **Yet the...to collection** i.e., yet the formless manner of it
moves her listeners to gather up some sort of meaning 9 **yawn** gape 18 **amiss** misfortune 19 **artless jealousy** crude suspicion 20 **spills** destroys 25 **cockle hat** (a
cockleshell on the hat was the sign of a pilgrim who had journeyed to shrines overseas.
The association of lovers and pilgrims was a common one) 26 **shoon** shoes
38 **Larded** decorated

KING. How do you, pretty lady?

OPHELIA. Well, God dild° you! They say the owl was a
   baker's daughter.° Lord, we know what we are, but
   know not what we may be. God be at your table!

KING. Conceit° upon her father.   45

OPHELIA. Pray let's have no words of this, but when they
   ask you what it means, say you this:

   Tomorrow is Saint Valentine's day.°   (*Song*)
      All in the morning betime,
   And I a maid at your window,   50
      To be your Valentine.

   Then up he rose and donned his clothes
      And dupped° the chamber door,
   Let in the maid, that out a maid
      Never departed more.   55

KING. Pretty Ophelia.

OPHELIA. Indeed, la, without an oath, I'll make an end on't:
   [*Sings.*] By Gis° and by Saint Charity,
      Alack, and fie for shame!
   Young men will do't if they come to't,   60
      By Cock,° they are to blame,
   Quoth she, "Before you tumbled me,
      You promised me to wed."
   He answers:
   "So would I 'a' done, by yonder sun,   65
      An thou hadst not come to my bed."

KING. How long hath she been thus?

OPHELIA. I hope all will be well. We must be patient, but I
   cannnot choose but weep to think they would lay him
   i' th' cold ground. My brother shall know of it; and   70
   so I thank you for your good counsel. Come, my coach!
   Good night, ladies, good night. Sweet ladies, good
   night, good night.   *Exit.*

KING. Follow her close; give her good watch, I pray you.

                                              [*Exit* HORATIO.]

   O, this is the poison of deep grief; it springs   75
   All from her father's death—and now behold!
   O Gertrude, Gertrude,
   When sorrows come, they come not single spies,
   But in battalions: first, her father slain;
   Next, your son gone, and he most violent author   80

---

42 **dild** yield, i.e., reward   43 **baker's daughter** (an allusion to a tale of a baker's
daughter who begrudged bread to Christ and was turned into an owl)   45 **Conceit**
brooding   48 **Saint Valentine's day** Feb. 14 (the notion was that a bachelor would
become the true love of the first girl he saw on this day)   53 **dupped** opened (did
up)   58 **Gis** (contraction of "Jesus")   61 **Cock** (1) God (2) phallus

Of his own just remove; the people muddied,°
Thick and unwholesome in their thoughts and whispers
For good Polonius' death, and we have done but greenly°
In huggermugger° to inter him; poor Ophelia
Divided from herself and her fair judgment,   85
Without the which we are pictures or mere beasts;
Last, and as much containing as all these,
Her brother is in secret come from France,
Feeds on his wonder,° keeps himself in clouds,
And wants not buzzers° to infect his ear   90
With pestilent speeches of his father's death,
Wherein necessity, of matter beggared,°
Will nothing stick° our person to arraign
In ear and ear. O my dear Gertrude, this,
Like a murd'ring piece,° in many places   95
Gives me superfluous death.

                                              A noise within.
                    Enter a MESSENGER.
QUEEN.   Alack, what noise is this?
KING. Attend, where are my Switzers?° Let them guard the door.
    What is the matter?
MESSENGER.   Save yourself, my lord.
    The ocean, overpeering of his list,°
    Eats not the flats with more impiteous haste   100
    Than young Laertes, in a riotous head,°
    O'erbears your officers. The rabble call him lord
    And, as the world were now but to begin,
    Antiquity forgot, custom not known,
    The ratifiers and props of every word,   105
    They cry "Choose we! Laertes shall be king!"
    Caps, hands, and tongues applaud it to the clouds,
    "Laertes shall be king! Laertes king!"
                                              A noise within.
QUEEN. How cheerfully on the false trail they cry!
    O, this is counter,° you false Danish dogs!   110
                    Enter LAERTES *with others.*
KING. The doors are broke.
LAERTES. Where is this king?—Sirs, stand you all without.
ALL. No let's come in.
LAERTES.   I pray you give me leave.
ALL. We will, we will.

---

81 **muddied** muddled 83 **greenly** foolishly 84 **huggermugger** secret haste
89 **wonder** suspicion 90 **wants not buzzers** does not lack talebearers 92 **of
matter beggared** unprovided with facts 93 **Will nothing stick** will not hesitate
95 **murd'ring piece** (a cannon that shot a kind of shrapnel) 97 **Switzers** Swiss
guards 99 **list** shore 101 **in a riotous head** with a rebellious force 110 **counter** (a
hound runs counter when he follows the scent backward from the prey)

LAERTES. I thank you. Keep the door.

> [*Exeunt his* FOLLOWERS.]

                   O thou vile King,   115

Give me my father.

QUEEN.   Calmly, good Laertes.

LAERTES. That drop of blood that's calm proclaims me bastard,
    Cries cuckold° to my father, brands the harlot
    Even here between the chaste unsmirchèd brow
    Of my true mother.

KING.   What is the cause, Laertes,   120
    That thy rebellion looks so giantlike?
    Let him go, Gertrude. Do not fear° our person.
    There's such divinity doth hedge a king
    That treason can but peep to° what it would,
    Acts little of his will. Tell me, Laertes,   125
    Why thou art thus incensed. Let him go, Gertrude.
    Speak, man.

LAERTES. Where is my father?

KING.   Dead.

QUEEN.   But not by him.

KING. Let him demand his fill.

LAERTES. How came he dead? I'll not be juggled with.   130
    To hell allegiance, vows to the blackest devil,
    Conscience and grace to the profoundest pit!
    I dare damnation. To this point I stand,
    That both the worlds I give to negligence,°
    Let come what comes, only I'll be revenged   135
    Most throughly for my father.

KING.   Who shall stay you?

LAERTES. My will, not all the world's.
    And for my means, I'll husband them° so well
    They shall go far with little.

KING.   Good Laertes,
    If you desire to know the certainty   140
    Of your dear father, is't writ in your revenge
    That swoopstake° you will draw both friend and foe,
    Winner and loser?

LAERTES. None but his enemies.

KING.   Will you know them then?

LAERTES. To his good friends thus wide I'll ope my arms   145
    And like the kind life-rend'ring pelican°
    Repast° them with my blood.

---

118 **cuckold** man whose wife is unfaithful 122 **fear** fear for 124 **peep to** i.e., look at from a distance 134 **That both...to negligence** i.e., I care not what may happen (to me) in this world or the next 138 **husband them** use them economically 142 **swoopstake** in a clean sweep 146 **pelican** (thought to feed its young with its own blood) 147 **Repast** feed

KING.   Why, now you speak
   Like a good child and a true gentleman.
   That I am guiltless of your father's death,
   And am most sensibly° in grief for it,   150
   It shall as level to your judgment 'pear
   As day does to your eye.
                          A noise within: "Let her come in."
LAERTES. How now? What noise is that?
                          Enter OPHELIA.
   O heat, dry up my brains; tears seven times salt
   Burn out the sense and virtue° of mine eye!   155
   By heaven, thy madness shall be paid with weight
   Till our scale turn the beam.° O rose of May,
   Dear maid, kind sister, sweet Ophelia!
   O heavens, is't possible a young maid's wits
   Should be as mortal as an old man's life?   160
   Nature is fine° in love, and where 'tis fine,
   It sends some precious instance° of itself
   After the thing it loves.
OPHELIA. They bore him barefaced on the bier   *(Song)*
            Hey non nony, nony, hey nony   165
         And in his grave rained many a tear——
            Fare you well, my dove!
LAERTES. Hadst thou thy wits, and didst persuade revenge,
   It could not move thus.
OPHELIA. You must sing "A-down a-down, and you call him   170
   a-down-a." O, how the wheel° becomes it! It is the
   false steward, that stole his master's daughter.
LAERTES. This nothing's more than matter.°
OPHELIA. There's rosemary, that's for remembrance. Pray
   you, love, remember. And there is pansies, that's for   175
   thoughts.
LAERTES. A document° in madness, thoughts and remembrance fitted.
OPHELIA. There's fennel° for you, and columbines. There's
   rue for you, and here's some for me. We may call it   180
   herb of grace o' Sundays. O, you must wear your rue
   with a difference. There's a daisy. I would give you
   some violets, but they withered all when my father

---

150 **sensibly** acutely 155 **virtue** power 157 **turn the beam** weigh down the bar (of
the balance) 161 **fine** refined, delicate 162 **instance** sample 171 **wheel** (of uncertain
meaning, but probably a turn or dance of Ophelia's, rather than Fortune's wheel)
173 **This nothing's more than matter** this nonsense has more meaning than matters
of consequence 177 **document** lesson 179 **fennel** (the distribution of flowers in the
ensuing lines has symbolic meaning, but the meaning is disputed. Perhaps **fennel**, flattery; **columbines**, cuckoldry; **rue**, sorrow for Ophelia and repentance for the Queen;
daisy, dissembling; **violets**, faithfulness. For other interpretations, see J. W. Lever in
Review of English Studies, New Series 3 [1952], pp. 123-29)

died. They say 'a made a good end.

[*Sings*]   For bonny sweet Robin is all my joy.   185

LAERTES. Thought and affliction, passion, hell itself,
    She turns to favor° and to prettiness.

OPHELIA. And will 'a not come again?   (*Song*)
    And will 'a not come again?
      No, no, he is dead,   190
      Go to thy deathbed,
    He never will come again.

    His beard was as white as snow,
    All flaxen was his poll.°
      He is gone, he is gone,   195
      And we cast away moan.
    God 'a' mercy on his soul!

And of all Christian souls, I pray God. God bye you.   [*Exit.*]

LAERTES. Do you see this, O God?

KING. Laertes, I must commune with your grief,   200
    Or you deny me right. Go but apart,
    Make choice of whom your wisest friends you will,
    And they shall hear and judge 'twixt you and me.
    If by direct or by collateral° hand
    They find us touched,° we will our kingdom give,   205
    Our crown, our life, and all that we call ours,
    To you in satisfaction; but if not,
    Be you content to lend your patience to us,
    And we shall jointly labor with your soul
    To give it due content.

LAERTES.   Let this be so.   210
    His means of death, his obscure funeral—
    No trophy, sword, nor hatchment° o'er his bones,
    No noble rite nor formal ostentation°—
    Cry to be heard, as 'twere from heaven to earth,
    That I must call't in question.

KING.   So you shall;   215
    And where th' offense is, let the great ax fall.
    I pray you go with me.   *Exeunt.*

[Scene VI. *The castle.*]

Enter HORATIO *and others.*

HORATIO. What are they that would speak with me?

GENTLEMAN. Seafaring men, sir. They say they have letters
    for you.

---

187 **favor** charm, beauty   194 **All flaxen was his poll** white as flax was his head
204 **collateral** indirect   205 **touched** implicated   212 **hatchment** tablet bearing the
coat of arms of the dead   213 **ostentation** ceremony

HORATIO. Let them come in.   [*Exit* ATTENDANT.]
    I do not know from what part of the world   5
    I should be greeted, if not from Lord Hamlet.
                Enter SAILORS.
SAILOR. God bless you, sir.
HORATIO. Let Him bless thee too.
SAILOR. 'A shall, sir, an't please Him. There's a letter for
    you, sir—it came from th' ambassador that was bound   10
    for England—if your name be Horatio, as I am let to
    know it is.
HORATIO. [*Reads the letter.*] "Horatio, when thou shalt
    have overlooked° this, give these fellows some means
    to the King. They have letters for him. Ere we were   15
    two days old at sea, a pirate of very warlike appoint-
    ment° gave us chase. Finding ourselves too slow of
    sail, we put on a compelled valor, and in the grapple
    I boarded them. On the instant they got clear of
    our ship; so I alone became their prisoner. They have   20
    dealt with me like thieves of mercy, but they knew
    what they did: I am to do a good turn for them. Let
    the King have the letters I have sent, and repair thou
    to me with as much speed as thou wouldest fly death.
    I have words to speak in thine ear will make thee   25
    dumb; yet are they much too light for the bore° of the
    matter. These good fellows will bring thee where I
    am. Rosencrantz and Guildenstern hold their course
    for England. Of them I have much to tell thee. Fare-
    well.   30
        He that thou knowest thine, HAMLET,"
    Come, I will give you way for these your letters,
    And do't the speedier that you may direct me
    To him from whom you brought them.   *Exeunt.*

             [Scene VII. *The castle*.]
           Enter KING *and* LAERTES.

KING. Now must your conscience my acquittance seal,
    And you must put me in your heart for friend,
    Sith you have heard, and with a knowing ear,
    That he which hath your noble father slain
    Pursued my life.
LAERTES.   It well appears. But tell me   5
    Why you proceeded not against these feats

IV.vi.14 **overlooked** surveyed   17 **appointment** equipment   26 **bore** caliber (here,
"importance")

So criminal and so capital° in nature,
As by your safety, greatness, wisdom, all things else,
You mainly° were stirred up.

KING.   O, for two special reasons,   10
Which may to you perhaps seem much unsinewed,°
But yet to me they're strong. The Queen his mother
Lives almost by his looks, and for myself—
My virtue or my plague, be it either which—
She is so conjunctive° to my life and soul,
That, as the star moves not but in his sphere,   15
I could not but by her. The other motive
Why to a public count° I might not go
Is the great love the general gender° bear him,
Who, dipping all his faults in their affection,
Would, like the spring that turneth wood to stone,°   20
Convert his gyves° to graces; so that my arrows,
Too slightly timbered° for so loud a wind,
Would have reverted to my bow again,
And not where I had aimed them.

LAERTES. And so have I a noble father lost,   25
A sister driven into desp'rate terms,°
Whose worth, if praises may go back again,°
Stood challenger on mount of all the age
For her perfections. But my revenge will come.

KING. Break not your sleeps for that. You must not think   30
That we are made of stuff so flat and dull
That we can let our beard be shook with danger,
And that it pastime. You shortly shall hear more.
I loved your father, and we love ourself,
And that, I hope, will teach you to imagine——   35

                    Enter a MESSENGER *with letters.*
How now? What news?

MESSENGER.   Letters, my lord, from Hamlet:
These to your Majesty; this to the Queen.

KING. From Hamlet? Who brought them?

MESSENGER. Sailors, my lord, they say; I saw them not.
They were given me by Claudio; he received them   40
Of him that brought them.

KING.   Laertes, you shall hear them.—
Leave us.   *Exit* MESSENGER.
[*Reads.*] "High and mighty, you shall know I am set

IV.vii.7 **capital** deserving death 9 **mainly** powerfully 10 **unsinewed** weak
14 **conjunctive** closely united 17 **count** reckoning 18 **general gender** common
people 20 **spring that turneth wood to stone** (a spring in Shakespeare's county
was so charged with lime that it would petrify wood placed in it) 21 **gyves** fetters
22 **timbered** shafted 26 **terms** conditions 27 **go back again** revert to what is past

naked° on your kingdom. Tomorrow shall I beg leave to
see your kingly eyes; when I shall (first asking your   45
pardon thereunto) recount the occasion of my sudden
and more strange return.

HAMLET."

What should this mean? Are all the rest come back?
Or is it some abuse,° and no such thing?   50
LAERTES. Know you the hand?
KING.   'Tis Hamlet's character.° "Naked"!
And in a postscript here, he says "alone."
Can you devise° me?
LAERTES. I am lost in it, my lord. But let him come.
It warms the very sickness in my heart   55
That I shall live and tell him to his teeth,
"Thus did'st thou."
KING.   If it be so, Laertes
(As how should it be so? How otherwise?),
Will you be ruled by me?
LAERTES.   Ay, my lord,
So you will not o'errule me to a peace.   60
KING. To thine own peace. If he be now returned,
As checking at° his voyage, and that he means
No more to undertake it, I will work him
To an exploit now ripe in my device,
Under the which he shall not choose but fall;   65
And for his death no wind of blame shall breathe,
But even his mother shall uncharge the practice°
And call it accident.
LAERTES.   My lord, I will be ruled;
The rather if you could devise it so
That I might be the organ.
KING.   It falls right.   70
You have been talked of since your travel much,
And that in Hamlet's hearing, for a quality
Wherein they say you shine. Your sum of parts
Did not together pluck such envy from him
As did that one, and that, in my regard,   75
Of the unworthiest siege.°
LAERTES.   What part is that, my lord?
KING. A very riband in the cap of youth,
Yet needful too, for youth no less becomes
The light and careless livery that it wears
Than settled age his sables and his weeds,°   80

---

44 **naked** destitute 50 **abuse** deception 51 **character** handwriting 53 **devise**
advise 62 **checking at** turning away from (a term in falconry) 67 **uncharge the**
practice not charge the device with treachery 76 **siege** rank 80 **sables and his**
weeds i.e., sober attire

Importing health and graveness. Two months since
Here was a gentleman of Normandy.
I have seen myself, and served against, the French,
And they can° well on horseback, but this gallant
Had witchcraft in't. He grew unto his seat,   85
And to such wondrous doing brought his horse
As had he been incorpsed and deminatured
With the brave beast. So far he topped my thought
That I, in forgery° of shapes and tricks,
Come short of what he did.

LAERTES.   A Norman was't?   90

KING. A Norman.

LAERTES. Upon my life, Lamord.

KING.   The very same.

LAERTES. I know him well. He is the brooch° indeed
And gem of all the nation.

KING. He made confession° of you,   95
And gave you such a masterly report,
For art and exercise in your defense,
And for your rapier most especial,
that he cried out 'twould be a sight indeed
If one could match you. The scrimers° of their nation   100
He swore had neither motion, guard, nor eye,
If you opposed them. Sir, this report of his
Did Hamlet so envenom with his envy
That he could nothing do but wish and beg
Your sudden coming o'er to play with you.   105
Now, out of this——

LAERTES.   What out of this, my lord?

KING. Laertes, was your father dear to you?
Or are you like the painting of a sorrow,
A face without a heart?

LAERTES.   Why ask you this?

KING. Not that I think you did not love your father,   110
But that I know love is begun by time,
And that I see, in passages of proof,°
Time qualifies° the spark and fire of it.
There lives within the very flame of love
A kind of wick or snuff° that will abate it,   115
And nothing is at a like goodness still,°
For goodness, growing to a plurisy,°
Dies in his own too-much. That we would do

---

84 **can** do   89 **forgery** invention   93 **brooch** ornament   95 **confession** report
100 **scrimers** fencers   112 **passages of proof** proved cases   113 **qualifies** diminishes
115 **snuff** residue of burnt wick (which dims the light)   116 **still** always   117 **plurisy**
fullness, excess

We should do when we would, for this "would" changes,
And hath abatements and delays as many   120
As there are tongues, are hands, are accidents,
And then this "should" is like a spendthrift sigh,°
That hurts by easing. But to the quick° of th' ulcer—
Hamlet comes back; what would you undertake
To show yourself in deed your father's son   125
More than in words?

LAERTES.   To cut his throat i' th' church!

KING. No place indeed should murder sanctuarize;°
Revenge should have no bounds. But, good Laertes,
Will you do this? Keep close within your chamber.
Hamlet returned shall know you are come home.   130
We'll put on those° shall praise your excellence
And set a double varnish on the fame
The Frenchman gave you, bring you in fine° together
And wager on your heads. He, being remiss,
Most generous, and free from all contriving,   135
Will not peruse the foils, so that with ease,
Or with a little shuffling, you may choose
A sword unbated,° and, in a pass of practice,°
Requite him for your father.

LAERTES.   I will do't,
And for that purpose I'll anoint my sword.   140
I bought an unction of a mountebank,°
So mortal that, but dip a knife in it,
Where it draws blood, no cataplasm° so rare,
Collected from all simples° that have virtue°
Under the moon, can save the thing from death   145
That is but scratched withal. I'll touch my point
With this contagion, that, if I gall him slightly,
It may be death.

KING.   Let's further think of this,
Weigh what convenience both of time and means
May fit us to our shape.° If this should fail,   150
And that our drift look through° our bad performance,
'Twere better not assayed. Therefore this project
Should have a back or second, that might hold
If this did blast in proof.° Soft, let me see.

122 **spendthrift sigh** (sighing provides ease, but because it was thought to thin the
blood and so shorten life it was spendthrift)   123 **quick** sensitive flesh   127 **sanctuarize** protect   131 **We'll put on those** we'll incite persons who   133 **in fine** finally
138 **unbated** not blunted   138 **pass of practice** treacherous thrust   141 **mountebank**
quack   143 **cataplasm** poultice   144 **simples** medicinal herbs   144 **virtue** power (to
heal)   150 **shape** role   151 **drift look through** purpose show through   154 **blast in
proof** burst (fail) in performance

We'll make a solemn wager on your cunnings—   155
I ha't!
When in your motion you are hot and dry—
As make your bouts more violent to that end—
And that he calls for drink, I'll have prepared him
A chalice for the nonce,° whereon but sipping,   160
If he by chance escape your venomed stuck,°
Our purpose may hold there.—But stay, what noise?

      Enter QUEEN.

QUEEN. One woe doth tread upon another's heel.
 So fast they follow. Your sister's drowned, Laertes.
LAERTES. Drowned! O, where?   165
QUEEN. There is a willow grows askant° the brook,
 That shows his hoar° leaves in the glassy stream:
 Therewith° fantastic garlands did she make
 Of crowflowers, nettles, daisies, and long purples,
 That liberal° shepherds give a grosser name,   170
 But our cold maids do dead men's fingers call them.
 There on the pendent boughs her crownet° weeds
 Clamb'ring to hang, an envious sliver° broke,
 When down her weedy trophies and herself
 Fell in the weeping brook. Her clothes spread wide,   175
 And mermaidlike awhile they bore her up,
 Which time she chanted snatches of old lauds,°
 As one incapable° of her own distress,
 Or like a creature native and indued°
 Unto that element. But long it could not be   180
 Till that her garments, heavy with their drink,
 Pulled the poor wretch from her melodious lay
 To muddy death
LAERTES.   Alas, then she is drowned?
QUEEN. Drowned, drowned.
LAERTES. Too much of water hast thou, poor Ophelia,   185
 And therefore I forbid my tears; but yet
 It is our trick;° nature her custom holds,
 Let shame say what it will: when these are gone,
 The woman° will be out. Adieu, my lord.
 I have a speech o' fire, that fain would blaze,   190
 But that this folly drowns it.   *Exit.*
KING.   Let's follow, Gertrude.
 How much I had to do to calm his rage!

---

160 **nonce** occasion 161 **stuck** thrust 166 **askant** aslant 167 **hoar** silver-gray
168 **Therewith** i.e., with willow twigs 170 **liberal** free-spoken, coarse-mouthed
172 **crownet** coronet 173 **envious sliver** malicious branch 177 **lauds** hymns
178 **incapable** unaware 179 **indued** in harmony with 187 **trick** trait, way
189 **woman** i.e., womanly part of me

Now fear I this will give it start again;
Therefore let's follow.   *Exeunt.*

[ACT V

Scene I. *A churchyard.*]

Enter two CLOWNS.°

CLOWN. Is she to be buried in Christian burial when she
willfully seeks her own salvation?

OTHER. I tell thee she is. Therefore make her grave
straight.° The crowner° hath sate on her, and finds it
Christian burial.   5

CLOWN. How can that be, unless she drowned herself in her
own defense?

OTHER. Why, 'tis found so.

CLOWN. It must be *se offendendo;*° it cannot be else. For
here lies the point: if I drown myself wittingly, it argues   10
an act, and an act hath three branches—it is to act,
to do, to perform. Argal,° she drowned herself wittingly.

OTHER. Nay, but hear you, Goodman Delver.

CLOWN. Give me leave. Here lies the water—good. Here   15
stands the man—good. If the man go to this water
and drown himself, it is, will he nill he,° he goes;
mark you that. But if the water come to him and
drown him, he drowns not himself. Argal, he that is
not guilty of his own death, shortens not his own   20
life.

OTHER. But is this law?

CLOWN. Ay marry, is't—crowner's quest° law.

OTHER. Will you ha' the truth on't? If this had not been a
gentlewoman, she should have been buried out o'   25
Christian burial.

CLOWN. Why, there thou say'st. And the more pity that
great folk should have count'nance° in this world to
drown or hang themselves more than their even-
Christen.° Come, my spade. There is no ancient   30
gentlemen but gard'ners, ditchers, and gravemakers.
They hold up° Adam's profession.

OTHER. Was he a gentleman?

V.i.s.d. **Clowns** rustics 4 **straight** straightway 4 **crowner** coroner 9 **se offendendo** (blunder for **se defendendo**, a legal term meaning "in self-defense") 12 **Argal**
(blunder for Latin **ergo**, "therefore") 17 **will he nill he** will he or will he not
(whether he will or will not) 23 **quest** inquest 28 **count'nance** privilege 29–30 **even-
Christen** fellow Christian 32 **hold up** keep up

CLOWN. 'A was the first that ever bore arms.°

OTHER. Why, he had none.   35

CLOWN. What, art a heathen? How dost thou understand
    the Scripture? The Scripture says Adam digged. Could
    he dig without arms? I'll put another question to thee.
    If thou answerest me not to the purpose, confess
    thyself——   40

OTHER. Go to.

CLOWN. What is he that builds stronger than either the
    mason, the shipwright, or the carpenter?

OTHER. The gallowsmaker, for that frame outlives a thou-
    sand tenants.   45

CLOWN. I like thy wit well, in good faith. The gallows does
    well. But how does it well? It does well to those that
    do ill. Now thou dost ill to say the gallows is built strong-
    er than the church. Argal, the gallows may do well to
    thee. To't again, come.   50

OTHER. Who builds stronger than a mason, a shipwright,
    or a carpenter?

CLOWN. Ay, tell me that, and unyoke.°

OTHER. Marry, now I can tell.

CLOWN. To't.   55

OTHER. Mass,° I cannot tell.

            Enter HAMLET *and* HORATIO *afar off.*

CLOWN. Cudgel thy brains no more about it, for your dull
    ass will not mend his pace with beating. And when
    you are asked this question next, say "a gravemaker."
    The houses he makes lasts till doomsday. Go, get   60
    get thee in, and fetch me a stoup° of liquor.

            [*Exit Other* CLOWN.]

In youth when I did love, did love,   (*Song*)
    Methought it was very sweet
To contract—O—the time for—a—my behove,°
    O, methought there—a—was nothing—a—meet.   65

HAMLET. Has this fellow no feeling of his business? 'A sings
    in gravemaking.

HORATIO. Custom hath made it in him a property of easi-
    ness.°

HAMLET. 'Tis e'en so. The hand of little employment hath   70
    the daintier sense.°

34 **bore arms** had a coat of arms (the sign of a gentleman)   53 **unyoke** i.e., stop
work for the day   56 **Mass** by the mass   61 **stoup** tankard   64 **behove** advantage
68–69 **in him a property of easiness** easy for him   71 **hath the daintier sense** is
more sensitive (because it is not calloused)

CLOWN. But age with his stealing steps   *(Song)*
      Hath clawed me in his clutch,
      And hath shipped me into the land,
      As if I had never been such.   75

                    [Throws up a skull.]

HAMLET. That skull had a tongue in it, and could sing
once. How the knave jowls° it to the ground, as if
'twere Cain's jawbone, that did the first murder! This
might be the pate of a politician, which this ass now   80
o'erreaches,° one that would circumvent God, might
it not?

HORATIO. It might, my lord.

HAMLET. Or of a courtier, which could say "Good morrow, sweet lord! How dost thou, sweet lord?" This   85
might be my Lord Such-a-one, that praised my Lord
Such-a-one's horse when 'a went to beg it, might it
not?

HORATIO. Ay, my lord.

HAMLET. Why, e'en so, and now my Lady Worm's, chapless,° and knocked about the mazzard° with a sexton's   90
spade. Here's fine revolution, an we had the trick
to see't. Did these bones cost no more the breeding
but to play at loggets° with them? Mine ache to think
on't.

CLOWN. A pickax and a spade, a spade,   *(Song)* 95
      For and a shrouding sheet;
      O, a pit of clay for to be made
      For such a guest is meet.

                [Throws up another skull.]

HAMLET. There's another. Why may not that be the skull
of a lawyer? Where be his quiddities° now, his quilli-   100
ties,° his cases, his tenures,° and his tricks? Why
does he suffer this mad knave now to knock him
about the sconce° with a dirty shovel, and will not
tell him of his action of battery? Hum! This fellow
might be in's time a great buyer of land, with his   105
statutes, his recognizances, his fines,° his double
vouchers, his recoveries. Is this the fine° of his fines,

---

77 **jowls** hurls 81 **o'erreaches** (1) reaches over (2) has the advantage over
89–90 **chapless** lacking the lower jaw 90 **mazzard** head 93 **loggets** (a game in
which small pieces of wood were thrown at an object) 100 **quiddities** subtle arguments (from Latin **quidditas**, "whatness") 100–101 **quillities** fine distinctions
101 **tenures** legal means of holding land 103 **sconce** head 106 **his statutes, his
recognizances, his fines** his documents giving a creditor control of a debtor's land,
his bonds of surety, his documents changing an entailed estate into fee simple
(unrestricted ownership) 107 **fine** end

and the recovery of his recoveries, to have his fine
pate full of fine dirt? Will his vouchers vouch him no
more of his purchases, and double ones too, than   110
the length and breadth of a pair of indentures?° The
very conveyances° of his lands will scarcely lie in
this box, and must th' inheritor himself have no more,
ha?

HORATIO. Not a jot more, my lord.   115

HAMLET. Is not parchment made of sheepskins?

HORATIO. Ay, my lord, and of calveskins too.

HAMLET. They are sheep and calves which seek out assur-
ance° in that. I will speak to this fellow. Whose grave's
this, sirrah?   120

CLOWN. Mine, sir.
    [*Sings.*]   O, a pit of clay for to be made
                For such a guest is meet.

HAMLET. I think it be thine indeed, for thou liest in't.

CLOWN. You lie out on't, sir, and therefore 'tis not yours.   125
For my part, I do not lie in't, yet it is mine.

HAMLET. Thou dost lie in't, to be in't and say it is thine.
'Tis for the dead, not for the quick;° therefore thou
liest.

CLOWN. 'Tis a quick lie, sir; 'twill away again from me to   130
you.

HAMLET. What man dost thou dig it for?

CLOWN. For no man, sir.

HAMLET. What woman then?

CLOWN. For none neither.   135

HAMLET. Who is to be buried in't?

CLOWN. One that was a woman, sir; but, rest her soul,
she's dead.

HAMLET. How absolute° the knave is! We must speak by
the card,° or equivocation° will undo us. By the   140
Lord, Horatio, this three years I have took note of
it, the age is grown so picked° that the toe of the
peasant comes so near the heel of the courtier he
galls his kibe.° How long hast thou been a grave-
maker?   145

CLOWN. Of all the days i' th' year, I came to't that day that
our last king Hamlet overcame Fortinbras.

HAMLET. How long is that since?

---

111 **indentures** contracts 112 **conveyances** legal documents for the transference of
land 118–119 **assurance** safety 128 **quick** living 139 **absolute** positive, decided
139–40 **by the card** by the compass card, i.e., exactly 140 **equivocation** ambiguity
142 **picked** refined 144 **kibe** sore on the back of the heel

CLOWN. Cannot you tell that? Every fool can tell that. It
    was that very day that young Hamlet was born—he   150
    that is mad, and sent into England.
HAMLET. Ay, marry, why was he sent into England?
CLOWN. Why, because 'a was mad. 'A shall recover his wits
    there; or, if 'a do not, 'tis no great matter there.
HAMLET. Why?   155
CLOWN. 'Twill not be seen in him there. There the men
    are as mad as he.
HAMLET. How came he mad?
CLOWN. Very strangely, they say.
HAMLET. How strangely?   160
CLOWN. Faith, e'en with losing his wits.
HAMLET. Upon what ground?
CLOWN. Why, here in Denmark. I have been sexton here,
    man and boy, thirty years.
HAMLET. How long will a man lie i' th' earth ere he rot?   165
CLOWN. Faith, if 'a be not rotten before 'a die (as we have
    many pocky corses° nowadays that will scarce hold
    the laying in), 'a will last you some eight year or nine
    year. A tanner will last you nine year.
HAMLET. Why he, more than another?   170
CLOWN. Why, sir, his hide is so tanned with his trade that
    'a will keep out water a great while, and your water
    is a sore decayer of your whoreson dead body. Here's
    a skull now hath lien you i' th' earth three and twenty
    years.   175
HAMLET. Whose was it?
CLOWN. A whoreson mad fellow's it was. Whose do you
    think it was?
HAMLET. Nay, I know not.
CLOWN. A pestilence on him for a mad rogue! 'A poured a   180
    flagon of Rhenish on my head once. This same skull, sir,
    was, sir, Yorick's skull, the King's jester.
HAMLET. This?
CLOWN. E'en that.
HAMLET. Let me see. [*Takes the skull.*] Alas, poor Yorick! 185
    I knew him, Horatio, a fellow of infinite jest, of most
    excellent fancy. He hath borne me on his back a thou-
    sand times. And now how abhorred in my imagination
    it it is! My gorge rises at it. Here hung those lips
    that I have kissed I know not how oft. Where be your   190
    gibes now? Your gambols, your songs, your flashes of
    merriment that were wont to set the table on a
    roar? Not one now to mock your own grinning? Quite

---

167 **pocky corses** bodies of persons who had been infected with the pox (syphilis)

chapfall'n°? Now get you to my lady's chamber, and tell
her, let her paint an inch thick, to this favor° she must   195
come. Make her laugh at that. Prithee, Horatio, tell me
one thing.

HORATIO. What's that, my lord?

HAMLET. Dost thou think Alexander looked o' this fashion
i' th' earth?   200

HORATIO. E'en so.

HAMLET. And smelt so? Pah!   [*Puts down the skull.*]

HORATIO. E'en so, my lord.

HAMLET. To what base uses we may return, Horatio! Why
may not imagination trace the noble dust of Alex-   205
ander till 'a find it stopping a bunghole?

HORATIO. 'Twere to consider too curiously,° to consider so.

HAMLET. No, faith, not a jot, but to follow him thither with
modesty enough,° and likelihood to lead it; as thus: 210
Alexander died, Alexander was buried, Alexander
returneth to dust; the dust is earth; of earth we make
loam; and why of that loam whereto he was converted
might they not stop a beer barrel?
Imperious Caesar, dead and turned to clay,   215
Might stop a hole to keep the wind away.
O, that that earth which kept the world in awe
Should patch a wall t' expel the winter's flaw!°
But soft, but soft awhile! Here comes the King.

   Enter KING, QUEEN, LAERTES, *and a coffin, with* LORDS
    attendant [*and a* DOCTOR OF DIVINITY].

The Queen, the courtiers. Who is this they follow?   220
And with such maimèd° rites? This doth betoken
The corse they follow did with desp'rate hand
Fordo it° own life. 'Twas of some estate.°
Couch° we awhile, and mark. [*Retires with* HORATIO.]

LAERTES. What ceremony else?

HAMLET.   That is Laertes,   225
A very noble youth. Mark.

LAERTES. What ceremony else?

DOCTOR. Her obsequies have been as far enlarged
As we have warranty. Her death was doubtful,°
And, but that great command o'ersways the order,   230
She should in ground unsanctified been lodged
Till the last trumpet. For charitable prayers,
Shards,° flints, and pebbles should be thrown on her.

---

194 **chapfall'n** (1) down in the mouth (2) jawless   195 **favor** facial appearance
207 **curiously** minutely   210 **with modesty enough** without exaggeration
218 **flaw** gust   221 **maimèd** incomplete   223 **Fordo it** destroy its   223 **estate** high rank
224 **Couch** hide   229 **doubtful** suspicious   233 **Shards** broken pieces of pottery

Yet here she is allowed her virgin crants,°
Her maiden strewments,° and the bringing home   235
Of bell and burial.
LAERTES. Must there no more be done?
DOCTOR.   No more be done.
We should profane the service of the dead
To sing a requiem and such rest to her
As to peace-parted souls.
LAERTES.   Lay her i' th' earth,   240
And from her fair and unpolluted flesh
May violets spring! I tell thee, churlish priest,
A minist'ring angel shall my sister be
When thou liest howling!
HAMLET.   What, the fair Ophelia?
QUEEN. Sweets to the sweet! Farewell.   245
                                        [*Scatters flowers.*]
I hoped thou shouldst have been my Hamlet's wife.
I thought thy bride bed to have decked, sweet maid,
And not have strewed thy grave.
LAERTES.   O, treble woe
Fall ten times treble on that cursèd head
Whose wicked deed thy most ingenious sense°   250
Deprived thee of! Hold off the earth awhile,
Till I have caught her once more in mine arms.
                                        Leaps in the grave.
Now pile your dust upon the quick and dead
Till of this flat a mountain you have made
T'o'ertop old Pelion° or the skyish head   255
Of blue Olympus.
HAMLET. [*Coming forward*] What is he whose grief
Bears such an emphasis, whose phrase of sorrow
Conjures the wand'ring stars,° and makes them stand
Like wonder-wounded hearers? This is I,
Hamlet the Dane.
LAERTES.   The devil take thy soul!   260
                                [Grapples with him.]°

---

234 **crants** garlands   235 **strewments** i.e., of flowers   250 **most ingenious sense**
finely endowed mind   255 **Pelion** (according to classical legend, giants in their fight
with the gods sought to reach heaven by piling Mount Pelion and Mount Ossa on Mount
Olympus)   258 **wand'ring stars** planets   260 s.d. **Grapples with him** (Q1, a bad
quarto, presumably reporting a version that toured, has a previous direction saying
"Hamlet leaps in after Laertes." Possibly he does so, somewhat hysterically. But such a
direction—absent from the two good texts, Q2 and F—makes Hamlet the aggressor,
somewhat contradicting his next speech. Perhaps Laertes leaps out of the grave to attack Hamlet)

HAMLET. Thou pray'st not well.
　　I prithee take thy fingers from my throat,
　　For, though I am not splenitive° and rash,
　　Yet have I in me something dangerous,
　　Which let thy wisdom fear. Hold off thy hand.　　　265
KING. Pluck them asunder.
QUEEN.　　　　　　　　　Hamlet, Hamlet!
ALL. Gentlemen!
HORATIO.　　　　　Good my lord, be quiet.

　　　　　　　　　　　　　　[ATTENDANTS *part them.*]

HAMLET. Why, I will fight with him upon this theme
　　Until my eyelids will no longer wag.
QUEEN. O my son, what theme?　　　　　　　　　　270
HAMLET. I loved Ophelia. Forty thousand brothers
　　Could not with all their quanity of love
　　Make up my sum. What wilt thou do for her?
KING. O, he is mad, Laertes.
QUEEN. For love of God forbear him.　　　　　　　275
HAMLET. 'Swounds, show me what thou't do.
　　Woo't weep? Woo't fight? Woo't fast? Woo't tear thyself?
　　Woo't drink up eisel?° Eat a crocodile?
　　I'll do't. Dost thou come here to whine?
　　To outface me with leaping in her grave?　　　　280
　　Be buried quick with her, and so will I.
　　And if thou prate of mountains, let them throw
　　Millions of acres on us, till our ground,
　　Singeing his pate against the burning zone,°
　　Make Ossa like a wart! Nay, an thou'lt mouth,　　285
　　I'll rant as well as thou.
QUEEN.　　　　　　　　This is mere madness;
　　And thus a while the fit will work on him.
　　Anon, as patient as the female dove
　　When that her golden couplets are disclosed,°
　　His silence will sit drooping.
HAMLET.　　　　　　　　Hear you, sir.　　　　290
　　What is the reason that you use me thus?
　　I loved you ever. But it is no matter.
　　Let Hercules himself do what he may,
　　The cat will mew, and dog will have his day.
KING. I pray thee, good Horatio, wait upon him.　　295

　　　　　　　　　　　Exit HAMLET *and* HORATIO.

　　[*To* LAERTES] Strengthen your patience in our last night's speech.
　　We'll put the matter to the present push.°

---

263 **splenitive** fiery (the spleen was thought to be the seat of anger)　278 **eisel** vinegar　284 **burning zone** sun's orbit　289 **golden couplets are disclosed** (the dove lays two eggs, and the newly hatched [**disclosed**] young are covered with golden down)　297 **present push** immediate test

Good Gertrude, set some watch over your son.
This grave shall having a living° monument.
An hour of quiet shortly shall we see;   300
Till then in patience our proceeding be.   *Exeunt.*

[Scene II. *The castle.*]

Enter HAMLET *and* HORATIO.

HAMLET. So much for this, sir; now shall you see the other.
     You do remember all the circumstance?
HORATIO. Remember it, my lord!
HAMLET. Sir, in my heart there was a kind of fighting
     That would not let me sleep. Methought I lay   5
     Worse than the mutines in the bilboes.° Rashly
     (And praised be rashness for it) let us know,
     Our indiscretion sometime serves us well
     When our deep plots do pall,° and that should learn us
     There's a divinity that shapes our ends,   10
     Rough-hew them how we will.
HORATIO.   That is most certain.
HAMLET. Up from my cabin,
     My sea gown scarfed about me, in the dark
     Groped I to find out them, had my desire,
     Fingered° their packet, and in fine° withdrew   15
     To mine own room again, making so bold,
     My fears forgetting manners, to unseal
     Their grand commission; where I found, Horatio—
     Ah, royal knavery!—an exact command,
     Larded° with many several sorts of reasons,   20
     Importing Denmark's health, and England's too,
     With, ho, such bugs and goblins in my life,°
     That on the supervise,° no leisure bated,°
     No, not to stay the grinding of the ax,
     My head should be struck off.
HORATIO.   Is't possible?   25
HAMLET. Here's the commission; read it at more leisure.
     But wilt thou hear now how I did proceed?
HORATIO. I beseech you.
HAMLET. Being thus benetted round with villains,
     Or° I could make a prologue to my brains,   30
     They had begun the play. I sat me down,
     Devised a new commission, wrote it fair.

299 **living** lasting (with perhaps also a reference to the plot against Hamlet's
life) V.ii.6 **mutines in the bilboes** mutineers in fetters 9 **pall** fail 15 **Fingered**
stole 15 **in fine** finally 20 **Larded** enriched 22 **such bugs and goblins in my life**
such bugbears and imagined terrors if I were allowed to live 23 **supervise** reading
23 **leisure bated** delay allowed 30 **Or** ere

I once did hold it, as our statists° do,
A baseness to write fair,° and labored much
How to forget that learning, but, sir, now   35
It did me yeoman's service. Wilt thou know
Th' effect° of what I wrote?
HORATIO.   Ay, good my lord.
HAMLET. An earnest conjuration from the King,
As England was his faithful tributary,
As love between them like the palm might flourish,   40
As peace should still her wheaten garland wear
And stand a comma° 'tween their amities,
And many suchlike as's of great charge,°
That on the view and knowing of these contents,
Without debatement further, more or less,   45
He should those bearers put to sudden death,
Not shriving° time allowed.
HORATIO.   How was this sealed?
HAMLET. Why, even in that was heaven ordinant.°
I had my father's signet in my purse,
Which was the model° of that Danish seal,   50
Folded the writ up in the form of th' other,
Subscribed it, gave't th' impression, placed it safely,
The changeling never known. Now, the next day
Was our sea fight, and what to this was sequent
Thou knowest already.   55
HORATIO. So Guildenstern and Rosencrantz go to't.
HAMLET. Why, man, they did make love to this employment.
They are not near my conscience; their defeat
Does by their own insinuation° grow.
'Tis dangerous when the baser nature comes   60
Between the pass° and fell° incensèd points
Of mighty opposites.
HORATIO.   Why, what a king is this!
HAMLET. Does it not, think thee, stand me now upon°—
He that hath killed my king, and whored my mother,
Popped in between th' election° and my hopes,   65
Thrown out his angle° for my proper life,°
And with such coz'nage°—is't not perfect conscience
To quit° him with this arm? And is't not to be damned

---

33 **statists** statesmen   34 **fair** clearly   37 **effect** purport   42 **comma** link   43 **great
charge** (1) serious exhortation (2) heavy burden (punning on **as's** and "asses")
47 **shriving** absolution   48 **ordinant** ruling   50 **model** counterpart   59 **insinuation**
meddling   61 **pass** thrust   61 **fell** cruel   63 **stand me now upon** become incumbent
upon me   65 **election** (the Danish monarchy was elective)   66 **angle** fishing line
66 **my proper life** my own life   67 **coz'nage** trickery   68 **quit** pay back

To let this canker of our nature come
In further evil?　　　　　　　　　　　　　　　　70
HORATIO. It must be shortly known to him from England
What is the issue of the business there.
HAMLET. It will be short; the interim's mine,
And a man's life's no more than to say "one."
But I am very sorry, good Horatio,　　　　　　　75
That to Laertes I forgot myself,
For by the image of my cause I see
The portraiture of his. I'll court his favors.
But sure the bravery° of his grief did put me
Into a tow'ring passion.
HORATIO.　　　　　　　Peace, who comes here?　　80
　　　　　　　Enter young OSRIC, *a courtier.*
OSRIC. Your lordship is right welcome back to Denmark.
HAMLET. I humbly thank you, sir. [*Aside to* HORATIO]
Dost know this waterfly?
HORATIO. [*Aside to* HAMLET] No, my good lord.
HAMLET. [*Aside to* HORATIO] Thy state is the more gra-　　85
cious, for 'tis a vice to know him. He hath much
land, and fertile. Let a beast be lord of beasts,
and his crib shall stand at the king's mess.° 'Tis a
chough,° but, as I say, spacious° in the possession of
dirt.　　　　　　　　　　　　　　　　　90
OSRIC. Sweet lord, if your lordship were at leisure, I should
impart a thing to you from his Majesty.
HAMLET. I will receive it, sir, with all diligence of spirit.
Put your bonnet to his right use. 'Tis for the head.
OSRIC. I thank your lordship, it is very hot.　　　95
HAMLET. No, believe me, 'tis very cold; the wind is north-
erly.
OSRIC. It is indifferent cold, my lord, indeed.
HAMLET. But yet methinks it is very sultry and hot for my
complexion.°　　　　　　　　　　　　　100
OSRIC. Exceedingly, my lord; it is very sultry, as 'twere—I
cannot tell how. But, my lord, his Majesty bade me
signify to you that 'a has laid a great wager on your
head. Sir, this is the matter——
HAMLET. I beseech you remember.　　　　　　105
　　　　　　　[HAMLET *moves him to put on his hat.*]
OSRIC. Nay, good my lord; for my ease, in good faith. Sir,
here is newly come to court Laertes—believe me,
an absolute gentleman, full of most excellent differ-

79 **bravery** bravado　88 **mess** table　89 **chough** jackdaw (here, chatterer)
89 **spacious** well off　100 **complexion** temperament

ences,° of very soft society and great showing. Indeed,
to speak feelingly° of him, he is the card° or calendar   110
of gentry; for you shall find in him the continent° of
what part a gentleman would see.

HAMLET. Sir, his definement° suffers no perdition° in you,
though, I know, to divide him inventorially would
dozy° th' arithmetic of memory, and yet but yaw   115
neither in respect of his quick sail.° But, in the verity
of extolment, I take him to be a soul of great article,°
and his infusion° of such dearth and rareness as, to
make true diction° of him, his semblable° is his mirror,
and who else would trace him, his umbrage,° nothing   120
more.

OSRIC. Your lordship speaks most infallibly of him.

HAMLET. The concernancy,° sir? Why do we wrap the gentleman in our more rawer breath?

OSRIC. Sir?   125

HORATIO. Is't not possible to understand in another tongue?
You will to't,° sir, really.

HAMLET. What imports the nomination of this gentleman?

OSRIC. Of Laertes?   130

HORATIO. [*Aside to* HAMLET] His purse is empty already.
All's golden words are spent.

HAMLET. Of him, sir.

OSRIC. I know you are not ignorant——

HAMLET. I would you did, sir; yet, in faith, if you did, it   135
would not much approve° me. Well, sir?

OSRIC. You are not ignorant of what excellence Laertes
is——

HAMLET. I dare not confess that, lest I should compare
with him in excellence; but to know a man well were   140
to know himself.

OSRIC. I mean, sir, for his weapon; but in the imputa-
tion° laid on him by them, in his meed° he's un-
fellowed.

HAMLET. What's his weapon?   145

OSRIC. Rapier and dagger.

HAMLET. That's two of his weapons—but well.

---

109 **differences** distinguishing characteristics   110 **feelingly** justly   110 **card** chart
111 **continent** summary   113 **definement** description   113 **perdition** loss
115 **dozy** dizzy   115-16 **and yet...quick sail** i.e., and yet only stagger despite all
(yaw neither) in trying to overtake his virtues   118 **article** (literally, "item," but here
perhaps "traits" or "importance")   118 **infusion** essential quality   119 **diction**
description   119 **semblable** likeness   120 **umbrage** shadow   123 **concernancy**
meaning   127 **will to't** will get there   136 **approve** commend   142–43 **imputation**
reputation   143 **meed** merit

OSRIC. The King, sir, hath wagered with him six Barbary
    horses, against the which he has impawned,° as I take
    it, six French rapiers and poniards, with their assigns,°   150
    as girdle, hangers,° and so. Three of the carriages,°
    in faith, are very dear to fancy, very responsive°
    to the hilts, most delicate carriages, and of very liberal
    conceit.°

HAMLET. What call you the carriages?   155

HORATIO. [*Aside to* HAMLET] I knew you must be edified by
    the margent° ere you had done.

OSRIC. The carriages, sir, are the hangers.

HAMLET. The phrase would be more germane to the matter
    if we could carry a cannon by our sides. I would   160
    it might be hangers till then. But on! Six Barbary
    horses against six French swords, their assigns, and
    three liberal-conceited carriages—that's the French
    bet against the Danish. Why is this all impawned, as
    you call it?   165

OSRIC. The King, sir, hath laid, sir, that in a dozen
    passes between yourself and him he shall not exceed
    you three hits; he hath laid on twelve for nine, and
    it would come to immediate trial if your lordship
    would vouchsafe the answer.   170

HAMLET. How if I answer no?

OSRIC. I mean, my lord, the opposition of your person in
    trial.

HAMLET. Sir, I will walk here in the hall. If it please
    his Majesty, it is the breathing time of day with me.°   175
    Let the foils be brought, the gentleman willing, and
    the King hold his purpose, I will win for him an I
    can; if not, I will gain nothing but my shame and
    the odd hits.

OSRIC. Shall I deliver you e'en so?   180

HAMLET. To this effect, sir, after what flourish your nature
    will.

OSRIC. I commend my duty to your lordship.

HAMLET. Yours, yours. [*Exit* OSRIC.] He does well to
    commend it himself; there are no tongues else for's   185
    turn.

HORATIO. This lapwing° runs away with the shell on his
    head.

---

149 **impawned** wagered 150 **assigns** accompaniments 151 **hangers** straps hanging
the sword to the belt 151 **carriages** (an affected word for hangers) 152 **responsive**
corresponding 154 **liberal conceit** elaborate design 157 **margent** i.e., marginal
(explanatory) comment 175 **breathing time of day with me** time when I take
exercise 187 **lapwing** (the new-hatched) lapwing was thought to run around with half
its shell on its head)

HAMLET. 'A did comply, sir, with his dug° before 'a sucked
it. Thus has he, and many more of the same breed
that I know the drossy age dotes on, only got the tune
of the time and, out of an habit of encounter,° a kind of
yeasty° collection, which carries them through and
through the most fanned and winnowed opinions; and
do but blow them to their trial, the bubbles are
out.° 195

Enter a LORD.

LORD. My lord, his Majesty commended him to you by
young Osric, who brings back to him that you attend
him in the hall. He sends to know if your pleasure
hold to play with Laertes, or that you will take longer
time. 200

HAMLET. I am constant to my purposes; they follow the
King's pleasure. If his fitness speaks, mine is ready;
now or whensoever, provided I be so able as now.

LORD. The King and Queen and all are coming down. 205

HAMLET. In happy time.

LORD. The Queen desires you to use some gentle enter-
tainment° to Laertes before you fall to play.

HAMLET. She well instructs me.   [*Exit* LORD.]

HORATIO. You will lose this wager, my lord. 210

HAMLET. I do not think so. Since he went into France
I have been in continual practice. I shall win at the
odds. But thou wouldst not think how ill all's here
about my heart. But it is no matter.

HORATIO. Nay, good my lord—— 215

HAMLET. It is but foolery, but it is such a kind of gain-
giving° as would perhaps trouble a woman.

HORATIO. If your mind dislike anything, obey it. I will forestall their repair hither and say you are not fit.

HAMLET. Not a whit, we defy augury. There is special providence in the fall of a sparrow.° If it be now, 'tis not 220
to come; if it be not to come, it will be now; if it be
not now, yet it will come. The readiness is all. Since no
man of aught he leaves knows, what is't to leave
betimes?° Let be. 225

---

189 **'A did comply, sir, with his dug** he was ceremoniously polite to his mother's
breast   192 **out of an habit of encounter** out of his own superficial way of meeting
and conversing with people   193 **yeasty** frothy   195-96 **the bubbles are out** i.e., they
are blown away (the reference is to the "yeasty collection")   207-08 **to use some gentle entertainment** to be courteous   216-17 **gain-giving** misgiving   221 **the fall of a
sparrow** (cf. Matthew 10:29 "Are not two sparrows sold for a farthing? and one of
them shall not fall on the ground without your Father")   225 **betimes** early

A table prepared. [*Enter*] TRUMPETS, DRUMS, *and* OFFICERS *with cushions;* KING, QUEEN, [OSRIC,] *and all the* STATE, [*with*] *foils, daggers,* [*and stoups of wine borne in*]; *and* LAERTES].

KING. Come, Hamlet, come, and take this hand from me.
                    [*The* KING *puts* LAERTES' *hand into* HAMLET'*s.*]
HAMLET. Give me your pardon, sir. I have done you wrong.
    But pardon't, as you are a gentleman.
    This presence° knows, and you must needs have heard,
    How I am punished with a sore distraction.   230
    What I have done
    That might your nature, honor, and exception°
    Roughly awake, I here proclaim was madness.
    Was't Hamlet wronged Laertes? Never Hamlet.
    If Hamlet from himself be ta'en away,   235
    And when he's not himself does wrong Laertes,
    Then Hamlet does it not, Hamlet denies it.
    Who does it then? His madness. If't be so,
    Hamlet is of the faction° that is wronged;
    His madness is poor Hamlet's enemy.   240
    Sir, in this audience,
    Let my disclaiming from a purposed evil
    Free me so far in your most generous thoughts
    That I have shot my arrow o'er the house
    And hurt my brother.
LAERTES.   I am satisfied in nature,   245
    Whose motive in this case should stir me most
    To my revenge. But in my terms of honor
    I stand aloof, and will no reconcilement
    Till by some elder masters of known honor
    I have a voice and precedent° of peace   250
    To keep my name ungored. But till that time
    I do receive your offered love like love,
    And will not wrong it.
HAMLET.   I embrace it freely,
    And will this brother's wager frankly play.
    Give us the foils. Come on.
LAERTES.   Come, one for me.   255
HAMLET. I'll be your foil°, Laertes. In mine ignorance
    Your skill shall, like a star i' th' darkest night,
    Stick fiery off° indeed.
LAERTES.   You mock me, sir.

---

229 **presence** royal assembly   232 **exception** disapproval   239 **faction** party, side
250 **voice and precedent** authoritative opinion justified by precedent   256 **foil**
(1) blunt sword (2) background (of metallic leaf) for a jewel   258 **Stick fiery off** stand
out brilliantly

HAMLET. No, by this hand.

KING. Give them the foils, young Osric. Cousin Hamlet,   260
     You know the wager?

HAMLET.   Very well, my lord.
     Your grace has laid the odds o' th' weaker side.

KING. I do not fear it, I have seen you both;
     But since he is bettered,° we have therefore odds.

LAERTES. This is too heavy; let me see another.   265

HAMLET. This likes me well. These foils have all a length?

                                   Prepare to play.

OSRIC. Ay, my good lord.

KING. Set me the stoups of wine upon that table.
     If Hamlet give the first or second hit,
     Or quit° in answer of the third exchange,   270
     Let all the battlements their ordnance fire.
     The King shall drink to Hamlet's better breath,
     And in the cup an union° shall he throw
     Richer than that which four successive kings
     In Denmark's crown have worn. Give me the cups,   275
     And let the kettle° to the trumpet speak,
     The trumpet to the cannoneer without,
     The cannons to the heavens, the heaven to earth,
     "Now the King drinks to Hamlet." Come, begin.

                                   Trumpets the while.

     And you, the judges, bear a wary eye.   280

HAMLET. Come on, sir.

LAERTES.   Come, my lord.   *They play.*

HAMLET.   One.

LAERTES.   No.

HAMLET.   Judgment?

OSRIC. A hit, a very palpable hit.

     Drum, trumpets, and shot. Flourish; a piece goes off.

LAERTES.   Well, again.

KING. Stay, give me drink. Hamlet, this pearl is thine.
     Here's to thy health. Give him the cup.

HAMLET. I'll play this bout first; set it by awhile.   285
     Come. [*They play.*] Another hit. What say you?

LAERTES. A touch, a touch; I do confess't.

KING. Our son shall win.

QUEEN.   He's fat,° and scant of breath.
     Here, Hamlet, take my napkin, rub thy brows.
     The Queen carouses to thy fortune, Hamlet.   290

HAMLET. Good madam!

KING.   Gertrude, do not drink.

---

264 **bettered** has improved (in France)   270 **quit** repay, hit back   273 **union** pearl
276 **kettle** kettledrum   288 **fat** (1) sweaty (2) out of training

QUEEN. I will, my lord; I pray you pardon me. [*Drinks.*]

KING. [*Aside*] It is the poisoned cup; it is too late.

HAMLET. I dare not drink yet, madam—by and by.

QUEEN. Come, let me wipe thy face. 295

LAERTES. My lord, I'll hit him now.

KING.   I do not think't.

LAERTES. [*Aside*] And yet it is almost against my conscience.

HAMLET. Come for the third, Laertes. You do but dally.

  I pray you pass with your best violence;

  I am sure you make a wanton° of me. 300

LAERTES. Say you so? Come on.   [*They*] *play.*

OSRIC. Nothing neither way.

LAERTES. Have at you now!

     In scuffling they change rapiers, [*and both are wounded*].

KING.   Part them. They are incensed.

HAMLET. Nay, come—again!   [*The* QUEEN *falls.*]

OSRIC.   Look to the Queen there, ho!

HORATIO. They bleed on both sides. How is it, my lord? 305

OSRIC. How is't, Laertes?

LAERTES. Why, as a woodcock to mine own springe,° Osric.

  I am justly killed with mine own treachery.

HAMLET. How does the Queen?

KING.   She sounds° to see them bleed.

QUEEN. No, no, the drink, the drink! O my dear Hamlet! 310

  The drink, the drink! I am poisoned.   [*Dies.*]

HAMLET. O villainy! Ho! Let the door be locked.

  Treachery! Seek it out.   [LAERTES *falls.*]

LAERTES. It is here, Hamlet. Hamlet, thou art slain;

  No med'cine in the world can do thee good. 315

  In thee there is not half an hour's life.

  The treacherous instrument is in thy hand,

  Unbated and envenomed. The foul practice°

  Hath turned itself on me. Lo, here I lie,

  Never to rise again. Thy mother's poisoned. 320

  I can no more. The King, the King's to blame.

HAMLET. The point envenomed too?

  Then, venom, to thy work.   *Hurts the* KING.

ALL. Treason! Treason!

KING. O, yet defend me, friends. I am but hurt. 325

HAMLET. Here, thou incestuous, murd'rous, damnèd Dane,

  Drink off this potion. Is thy union here?

  Follow my mother.   KING *dies.*

LAERTES.   He is justly served.

  It is a poison tempered° by himself.

---

300 **wanton** spoiled child   307 **springe** snare   309 **sounds** swoons   318 **practice** deception   329 **tempered** mixed

Exchange forgiveness with me, noble Hamlet.   330
Mine and my father's death come not upon thee,
Nor thine on me!   *Dies.*
HAMLET. Heaven make thee free of it! I follow thee.
I am dead, Horatio. Wretched Queen, adieu!
You that look pale and tremble at this chance,   335
That are but mutes° or audience to this act,
Had I but time (as this fell sergeant,° Death,
Is strict in his arrest) O, I could tell you—
But let it be. Horatio, I am dead;
Thou livest; report me and my cause aright   340
To the unsatisfied.°
HORATIO.   Never believe it.
I am more an antique Roman° than a Dane.
Here's yet some liquor left.
HAMLET.   As th' art a man,
Give me the cup. Let go. By heaven, I'll ha't!
O God, Horatio, what a wounded name,   345
Things standing thus unknown, shall live behind me!
If thou didst ever hold me in thy heart,
Absent thee from felicity° awhile,
And in this harsh world draw thy breath in pain,
To tell my story.   *A march afar off.* [*Exit* OSRIC.]
            What warlike noise is this?   350
                                    Enter OSRIC.
OSRIC. Young Fortinbras, with conquest come from Poland,
To th' ambassadors of England gives
This warlike volley.
HAMLET.   O, I die, Horatio!
The potent poison quite o'ercrows° my spirit.
I cannot live to hear the news from England,   355
But I do prophesy th' election lights
On Fortinbras. He has my dying voice.
So tell him, with th' occurrents,° more and less,
Which have solicited°—the rest is silence.   *Dies.*
HORATIO. Now cracks a noble heart. Good night, sweet Prince, 360
And flights of angels sing thee to thy rest.   [*March within.*]
Why does the drum come hither?
                Enter FORTINBRAS, *with the* AMBASSADORS *with*
                    Drum, Colors, and ATTENDANTS.
FORTINBRAS. Where is this sight?

---

336 **mutes** performers who have no words to speak   337 **fell sergeant** dread sheriff's
officer   341 **unsatisfied** uninformed   342 **antique Roman** (with reference to the old
Roman fashion of suicide)   348 **felicity** i.e., the felicity of death   354 **o'ercrows** overpowers (as a triumphant cock crows over its weak opponent)   358 **occurrents** occur-
rences   359 **solicited** incited

HORATIO.   What is it you would see?
If aught of woe or wonder, cease your search.
FORTINBRAS. This quarry° cries on havoc.° O proud Death, 365
What feast is toward° in thine eternal cell
That thou so many princes at a shot
So bloodily hast struck?
AMBASSADOR.   The sight is dismal;
And our affairs from England come too late.
The ears are senseless that should give us hearing 370
To tell him his commandment is fulfilled,
That Rosencrantz and Guildenstern are dead.
Where should we have our thanks?
HORATIO.   Not from his° mouth,
Had it th' ability of life to thank you.
He never gave commandment for their death. 375
But since, so jump° upon this bloody question,
You from the Polack wars, and you from England,
Are here arrived, give order that these bodies
High on a stage° be placèd to the view,
And let me speak to th' yet unknowing world 380
How these things came about. So shall you hear
Of carnal, bloody, and unnatural acts,
Of accidental judgments, casual° slaughters,
Of deaths put on by cunning and forced cause,
And, in this upshot, purposes mistook 385
Fall'n on th' inventors' heads. All this can I
Truly deliver.
FORTINBRAS.   Let us haste to hear it,
And call the noblest to the audience.
For me, with sorrow I embrace my fortune.
I have some rights of memory° in this kingdom, 390
Which now to claim my vantage doth invite me.
HORATIO. Of that I shall have also cause to speak,
And from his mouth whose voice will draw on° more.
But let this same be presently performed,
Even while men's minds are wild, lest more mischance 395
On° plots and errors happen.
FORTINBRAS.   Let four captains
Bear Hamlet like a soldier to the stage,
For he was likely, had he been put on,°
To have proved most royal; and for his passage°

365 **quarry** heap of slain bodies 365 **cries on havoc** proclaims general slaughter 366 **toward** in preparation 373 **his** (Claudius') 376 **jump** precisely 379 **stage** platform 383 **casual** not humanly planned, chance 390 **rights of memory** remembered claims 393 **voice will draw on** vote will influence 396 **On** on top of 398 **put on** advanced (to the throne) 399 **passage** death

The soldiers' music and the rite of war   400
Speak loudly for him.
Take up the bodies. Such a sight as this
Becomes the field,° but here shows much amiss.
Go, bid the soldiers shoot.
Exeunt marching; after the which a peal of ordnance are shot off.

FINIS

[1600–1601]

■ TOPICS FOR DISCUSSION AND WRITING

Act I

1. The first scene (like many other scenes in this play) is full of expressions of uncertainty. What are some are these uncertainties? The Ghost first appears at I.i.42. Does his appearance surprise us, or have we been prepared for it? Or is there both preparation and surprise? Do the last four speeches of I.i help to introduce a note of hope? If so, how?

2. Does the King's opening speech in I.ii reveal him to be an accomplished public speaker—or are lines 10–14 offensive? In his second speech (lines 41–49), what is the effect of naming Laertes four times? Claudius sometimes uses the royal pronouns ("we," "our"), sometimes the more intimate "I" and "my." Study his use of these in lines 1–4 and in 106–117. What do you think he is getting at?

3. Hamlet's first soliloquy (I.ii.129–159) reveals that more than just his father's death distresses him. Be as specific as possible about the causes of Hamlet's anguish here. What traits does Hamlet reveal in his conversation with Horatio (I.ii.160–254)?

4. What do you make of Polonius's advice to Laertes (I.iii.55–80)? Is it sound? Sound advice, but here uttered by a fool? Ignoble advice? How would one follow the advice of line 78: "to thine own self be true"? In his words to Ophelia in I.iii.101–135, what does he reveal about himself?

5. Can I.iv.17–38 reasonably be taken as a speech on the "tragic flaw"? (On this idea, see page 163.) Or is the passage a much more limited discussion, a comment simply on Danish drinking habits?

6. Hamlet is convinced in I.v.95–104 that the Ghost has told the truth, indeed, the only important truth. But do we detect in 105–112 a hint of a tone suggesting that Hamlet delights in hating villainy? If so, can it be said that later this delight grows, and that in some scenes (e.g., III.iii) we feel that Hamlet has almost become a diabolic revenger? Explain.

Act II

1. Characterize Polonius on the basis of II.i.1–74.

2. In light of what we have seen of Hamlet, is Ophelia's report of his strange behavior when he visits her understandable?

403 **field** battlefield

3. Why does II.ii.33–34 seem almost comic? How do these lines help us to form a view about Rosencrantz and Guildenstern?

4. Is "the hellish Pyrrhus" (II.ii.536) Hamlet's version of Claudius? Or is he Hamlet, who soon will be responsible for the deaths of Polonius, Rosencrantz and Guildenstern, Claudius, Gertrude, Ophelia, and Laertes? Explain.

5. Is the player's speech (II.ii.541ff) a huffing speech? If so, why? To distinguish it from the poetry of the play itself? To characterize the bloody deeds that Hamlet cannot descend to?

6. In II.ii.629–687 Hamlet rebukes himself for not acting. Why has he not acted? Because he is a coward (line 513)? Because he has a conscience? Because no action can restore his father and his mother's purity? Because he doubts the Ghost? What reason(s) can you offer?

Act III

1. What do you make out of Hamlet's assertion to Ophelia: "I loved you not" (III.i.122)? Of his characterization of himself as full of "offenses" (III.i.130–131)? Why is Hamlet so harsh to Ophelia?

2. In III.iii.36–72 Claudius's conscience afflicts him. But is he repentant? What makes you say so?

3. Is Hamlet other than abhorrent in III.iii.73–96? Do we want him to kill Claudius at this moment, when Claudius (presumably with his back to Hamlet) is praying? Why?

4. The Ghost speaks of Hamlet's "almost blunted purpose" (III.iv.112). Is the accusation fair? Explain.

5. How would your characterize the Hamlet who speaks in III.iv.203–218?

Act IV

1. Is Gertrude protecting Hamlet when she says he is mad (IV.i.7), or does she believe that he is mad? If she believes he is mad, does it follow that she no longer feels ashamed and guilty? Explain.

2. Why should Hamlet hide Polonius's body (in IV.ii)? Is he feigning madness? Is he on the edge of madness? Explain.

3. How can we explain Hamlet's willingness to go to England (IV.iii.52)?

4. Judging from IV.v., what has driven Ophelia mad? Is Laertes heroic, or somewhat foolish? Consider also the way Claudius treats him in IV.vii.

Act V

1. Would anything be lost if the Gravediggers in V.i were omitted?

2. To what extent do we judge Hamlet severely for sending Rosencrantz and Guildenstern to their deaths, as he reports in V.ii? On the whole, do we think of Hamlet as an intriguer? What other intrigues has he engendered? How successful were they?

3. Does V.ii.254–260 show a paralysis of the will, or a wise recognition that more is needed than mere human scheming? Explain.

4. Does V.ii.336 suggest that Laertes takes advantage of a momentary pause and unfairly stabs Hamlet? Is the exchange of weapons accidental,

or does Hamlet (as in Olivier's film version), realizing that he has been betrayed, deliberately get possession of Laertes's deadly weapon?

5. Fortinbras is often cut from the play. How much is lost by the cut? Explain.

6. Fortinbras gives Hamlet a soldier's funeral. Is this ridiculous? Can it fairly be said that, in a sense, Hamlet has been at war? Explain.

General Questions

1. Hamlet in V.ii.10–11 speaks of a "divinity that shapes our ends." To what extent does "divinity" (or Fate or mysterious Chance) play a role in the happenings?

2. How do Laertes, Fortinbras, and Horatio help to define Hamlet for us?

3. T. S. Eliot says (in "Shakespeare and the Stoicism of Seneca") that Hamlet, having made a mess, "dies fairly well pleased with himself." Evaluate.

■ CHAPTER 10

Love and Hate

ESSAYS

■ SEI SHŌNAGON

Sei Shōnagon was a Japanese woman who, in the tenth century, served for some ten years as a lady-in-waiting to the empress in Kyoto. Her *Pillow Book*—a marvellous collection of lists, eyewitness reports, and brief essays—established the Japanese tradition of *zuihitsu*, "spontaneous writing" (literally, "to follow the brush").

Not much is known about Sei Shōnagon. Her book tells us nothing of her early years, and the date and circumstances of her death are unknown. Scholars conjecture that she was born about 965 and that she became a lady-in-waiting during the early 990s. It is evident from her book that she was witty, snobbish, and well versed in the etiquette of love at court.

The passage that we here reprint appears in a list entitled "Hateful Things."

A Lover's Departure

A lover who is leaving at dawn announces that he has to find his fan and his paper. "I know I put them somewhere last night," he says. Since it is pitch dark, he gropes about the room, bumping into the furniture and muttering, "Strange! Where on earth can they be?" Finally he discovers the objects. He thrusts the paper into the breast of his robe with a great rustling sound; then he snaps open his fan and busily fans away with it. Only now is he ready to take his leave. What charmless behavior! "Hateful" is an understatement.

Equally disagreeable is the man who, when leaving in the middle of the night, takes care to fasten the cord of his headdress. This is quite unnecessary; he could perfectly well put it gently on his head without tying the cord. And why must he spend time adjusting his cloak or hunting costume? Does

515

he really think someone may see him at this time of night and criticize him for not being impeccably dressed?

A good lover will behave as elegantly at dawn as at any other time. He drags himself out of bed with a look of dismay on his face. The lady urges him on: "Come, my friend, it's getting light. You don't want anyone to find you here." He gives a deep sigh, as if to say that the night has not been nearly long enough and that it is agony to leave. Once up, he does not instantly pull on his trousers. Instead he comes close to the lady and whispers whatever was left unsaid during the night. Even when he is dressed, he still lingers, vaguely pretending to be fastening his sash.

Presently he raises the lattice, and the two lovers stand together by the side door while he tells her how he dreads the coming day, which will keep them apart; then he slips away. The lady watches him go, and this moment of parting will remain among her most charming memories.

Indeed, one's attachment to a man depends largely on the elegance of 5 his leave-taking. When he jumps out of bed, scurries about the room, tightly fastens his trouser-sash, rolls up the sleeves of his Court cloak, overrobe, or hunting costume, stuffs his belongings into the breast of his robe and then briskly secures the outer sash—one really begins to hate him.

■ TOPICS FOR DISCUSSION AND WRITING

1.   What are your first responses to this passage? Later—even if only thirty minutes later—reread the passage and think about whether your responses change.

2.   On the basis of this short extract, how would you characterize Sei Shōnagon? Can you imagine that you and she might become close friends or lovers?

3.   Write a journal entry or two on the topic "Hateful Things."

■ JILL TWEEDIE
_____

Jill Tweedie was born in 1936 of an English family in the Middle East. She grew up in England and then lived ten years in Canada before returning to England. The author of a novel and of books of essays (some of the essays have been collected under the title *It's Only Me*), she now lives in London and writes articles for the *Guardian*.

The Experience

'*Some day my prince will come...*'

I have no particular qualifications to write about love but then, who has? There are no courses of higher learning offered in the subject except at the University of Life, as they say, and there I have put in a fair amount of work. So I offer my own thoughts, experiences and researches into love in the only spirit possible to such an enterprise—a combination of absolute humility and utter arrogance that will cause the reader either to deride my wrong-headedness or, with luck, to recognise some of the same lessons.

I am a white, Anglo-Saxon, heterosexual, happily married, middle-income female whose experience of what is called love spans forty years of the mid-twentieth century in one of the most fortunate parts of the globe. I mention this because I am profoundly aware of the limits these facts give to my vision; also because, in spite of such advantages, my experience of love has hardly been uplifting and yet, because of them too, I have at least been vouchsafed a glimpse of what love might be, some day.

I took my first steps in what I was told was love when the idea of high romance and living happily ever after still held sway. They said that whatever poisoned apple I might bite would surely be dislodged by a Prince's kiss and I would then rise from all the murderous banalities of living and, enfolded in a strong man's arms, gallop away on a white charger to the better land called love. The way it turned out, this dream of love did not do much to irradiate my life. The ride was nice enough but 'twas better to travel than to arrive and—oh, shame—there was more than one Prince. Of two previous marriages and a variety of other lovings, very little remains and that mostly ugly. However sweet love's initial presence, when it goes it leaves horrid scars. Unlike friendship and other forms of love, the tide of male/female sex love does not ebb imperceptibly, leaving the stones it reveals gleaming and covetable. No. It only shows that what was taken to be precious is simply a bare, dull pebble like any other.

Loving, lovers fill each other's lives, Siamese twins joined at the heart, bees that suck honey from each other's blossoms. When love ebbs, nothing remains. Ex-lovers rarely meet again or write or offer each other even those small kindnesses and comforts that strangers would not withhold. Birthdays, high days and holidays pass unmarked where once they were entered in New Year diaries and planned for months ahead. Photographs of the beloved are discarded or curl up, yellowing, in some dusty drawer. What was once the world becomes a no-man's-land, fenced with barbed wire, where trespassers are prosecuted and even the civilities given a passing acquaintance are forbidden. What was most intimate—private thoughts, dreams, nightmares and childhood panics soothed in warm arms—are now merely coinage for a pub joke, a hostess flippancy, worth a line or two in the local paper or the old school magazine. Divorced. Separated. Split.

For the first man I thought I loved, and therefore married, I bear, at 5 most, a distant anger for injuries received. For the second I carefully suppress the good times, burying them with the bad. All those hours, weeks, months, years passed in the same bed have vanished, leaving only the traces of an old wound, an ache where a growth was removed.

Was either a part of love, ever? Of a kind. The best we could manage at the time, a deformed seedling planted in infertile ground. The three of us, each of them and me, carried loads on our backs when we met, all the clobber of past generations. This I must do, that you must be, this is good, that is bad, you must, I must, we must. By the time we met, we were already proficient puppeteers, hands stuck up our stage dolls, our real selves well concealed behind the striped canvas. You Punch, me Judy. Me Jane, you Tarzan.

I had a conventional 1940s and 1950s childhood, cut to the pattern of time. I adored and admired my father and my father did not adore or admire me. My mother was there like the curtains and the carpets were there, taken for loving granted in early childhood and then ruthlessly discarded, the living symbol of everything my world did not regard and that I, therefore, did not wish to become. Rejecting her caused a very slight wreckage inside, nothing you'd notice, though transfusions would later be necessary. Powerful unloving father, powerless loving mother. Cliché.

So I did what I could to make my way and married an older man. Love and marriage go together like a horse and carriage. This act imposed certain conditions. First of all, you cannot grow up if you marry a father figure because this is no part of the contract, and besides, growing up is a disagreeable occupation. Then, of course, a continuing virginity of mind, if not of body, is essential because Daddy's girl has never known other men and any evidence of sexual curiosity or, worse, a touch of ribaldry might cause him to withdraw his protection. Indeed, a daughter must not know much of anything at all because Daddy must teach and daughter learn, for ever. Competence, independence, self-sufficiency, talent in anything but the most girlish endeavours, toughness of any kind, is against the rules. Light-heartedness, giggling, little tantrums and a soupçon of mischief are permitted because Daddy is a Daddy, after all, and likes to be amused after a long day or even smack a naughty bum, in his wisdom. My first marriage was a romper room and each day I laid plans to negotiate the next, with my thumb stuck endearingly in my mouth.

To begin with, we both enjoyed the game we didn't know we were playing. He was a proper husband in the eyes of the outside world, protective and admonitory, and I was a proper wife, that is to say, a child; charming and irresponsible. But quite soon these playful rituals began to harden into concrete, so that we could no longer move, even if we wished, as long as we were together. For a few years I was satisfied enough, the drama of my life absorbed me, it was a stage and I was the star. First a house to play with and later, in case the audience began to cough and fidget, a pregnancy to hold them riveted. Later, like Alice in Wonderland, I came across the cake labelled 'eat me' and whenever my husband was away at work, I ate and I grew. My legs stuck out of the windows, my arms snaked round the doors, my head above an endless neck loomed through the chimney and my heartbeat rocked the room. Each day, just before 5 p.m., I nibbled the other side of Alice's cake and, in the nick of time, shrank to being a little woman again. Hullo, darling, how was your day? Me? Oh, nothing happened. Terrified, I knew that one day I wouldn't make it down again and my husband, returning from work, would fall back in horror at the monster who had taken over his home and push me out into the big wide world.

Writing this now perhaps suggests that I was aware of a pretence and set 10 up my false self knowingly, for reward. Not so. The boundaries given me in girlhood were strictly defined, allowing only minimum growth and that mainly physical. To sprout the titivating secondary sexual characteristics was expected, but woe betide the *enfant terrible* who tried to burst that tight cocoon and emerge as a full-grown adult in mind as well as body. The penalty was ill-defined but all-pervasive, like those sci-fi novels of a postnuclear generation bred to fear the radioactive world above their subterranean tunnels that threatens isolation, mutilation and death. The reward for my self-restraint (in the most literal sense) was a negative one—be good and tractable and you will be looked after—but it was none the less powerful for that. So my real self, or hints of it, was as frightening to me as I feared it would be to my husband, a dark shadow given to emerging at less and less acceptable times. I was Mr Rochester[1] secure in his mansion but I was also his mad wife in the attic. I had to conceal her existence to preserve my way of life but all the time she was setting matches to the bedding, starting a flame at the hem of the curtains, hoping to burn the mansion down.

Things became more and more schizoid. The demure façade of a prim girl hid a raucous fishwife who folded her massive arms against her chest and cursed. She horrified me, so much so—threatening, as she did, my exile from society—that in spite of increasing marital quarrels and even spurts of pure hatred, never once did I let that fishwife out to hurl the oaths she could have hurled or yelled the truths she knew. How could I, without revealing what I really was, to him and to myself?

The inner split opened wider. When my husband said he loved me, I knew he meant he loved the doll I had created and I accepted his love smugly enough, on her behalf. She was worth it. She wore the right clothes, she said the right things, the span of her waist would bring tears to your eyes and the tiny staccato of her heels across a floor would melt the sternest heart. She turned her head upon its graceful stem just so and her camellia hands, laced on her lap, could make a stone bleed. She smiled just enough to give a man the wildest expectations and frowned just enough to make him feel safe. This doll is a good doll. This doll is a marriageable doll. This doll is a real doll.

I knew, of course, that my doll self was only a front but it was the one I had deliberately created in response to popular demand. My real self knew all the things the doll did not wish to know. She was human and therefore hopelessly unfeminine, she had no pretty ways. Her voice was harsh, pumped from the guts instead of issuing sweetly from the throat, and every now and then she howled and the doll was forced to look at her face, bare as a picked bone. No wonder the poor dolly gathered up her ruffled skirts and ran shrieking down corridors to find reassurance in a man's eyes. See my soft red lips, my white skin, feel how smooth the shaven legs, smell the scented underarms, tell me you love me, dolly me.

There were, of course, other ways to accommodate the spectre within and other ways became more necessary as the spectre grew stronger and rattled the bars of the cage. My husband was a man of uncertain temper. I was quite aware of this before we married. He came from a country ravaged by war, his home had been destroyed, his brother killed, his family made refugees and he, corralled off the streets of his town, had spent two years starving in the polar wastes of a Russian prison camp. Understandably, he was outside the conventional pale. I was afraid of him.

The fear was seductive. The dolly shook with it at times, was martyred 15 by it. Hit, punched, she fell to the floor and lay, a poor pale victim, her lashes fanned against an appealingly white cheek stained, briefly, dull red. Later, kindly, she accepted the remorse of her attacker, grovelling before her. Yes, I forgive you, she said. And well she might forgive, because down in the dun-

[1] **Mr. Rochester** In Charlotte Brontë's *Jane Eyre* (1847), the hero Rochester keeps his lunatic wife secluded.

geon beneath, her other self was quiet for the time being, gorged to quies-
cence on the thick hot adrenalin provided by the man. A small price to pay.

I do not know how many people stand at the altar repeating the marriage
vows and knowing, however unclearly, that what they say is false and what
they do calamitous. My doll stood stiffly in her stiff dress, the groom beside
her, and there was not a hope for them. Upbringing had set us against each
other from the start and each was busily preparing to hammer the other into
an appropriate frame. After the service well-wishers launched our raft with
champagne; lashed together, not far out, we sank.

Next time, I chose more carefully. The doll, anyway, was aware that her
days were numbered. Winning ways must be adjusted if they are to go on being useful and a good actress acknowledges that she has aged out of *ingénue*
roles before the casting director says don't call us. Besides, I was no longer
enamoured of my puppet and did not want to extend her life much further.
She had become more obstacle than defence, the way a wall, originally built
to keep enemies out, can come to be a prison keeping you in.

So I let my real self out on probation, to be called in only now and then
for discipline. And now I needed a male with all the right worldly appurtenances, whom I could use as a hermit crab uses a shell, to reach full growth
without exposing vulnerable flesh. Using him, I could flex my own muscles
in safety until they were strong enough to risk exposure.

So I fell in love with my second husband. This time, the emotion was
much more powerful because I knew he had seen something of my real self
before he took me on. I thought him beautiful, a golden man, flamboyant and
seductively hollow, like a rocket into which I could squeeze myself and guide
the flight, using his engines. He was so large he filled a room, his laugh set
it shaking, his shining head topped everyone, he drew all eyes. In the turmoil
of his wake I found breathing space, I could advance or retreat as I chose.
He had another desirable asset and that was his lack of self-restraint. He
never talked if he could shout, he never saved if he could spend, he was full
of tall stories and the drinks were always on him. All of which combined to
make him a natural force and natural forces can be harnessed for other ends.
By his noisy, infuriating, unpredictable, ebullient and blustering existence he
made me look, in comparison, a good, calm, reasonable and deeply feminine
woman and thus I was able, over the years with him, to allow my real self out
for airings in the sure knowledge that though I might not be as adorable as
the doll, I was bound to appear more acceptable than I actually was.

There were drawbacks, of course. Originally, the space within our rela- 20
tionship was almost entirely taken up with the volume of his ego and I made
do in a little left-over corner. He breathed deeply, his lungs fully expanded,
and I breathed lightly, in short thin gasps, and there was air enough for both
of us. But then things changed. I learned a trade, began to work, worked hard
and earned money. Hey, he said, getting a little stuffy in here, isn't it? Sorry,
darling, I said. I breathed more deeply and new ideas rushed in. The voices
of American women reached me, ideas on women's rights that linked me to
the clamour of the outside world. For the first time I saw myself face to face,
recognised myself, realised that I was not my own creation, uniquely formed
in special circumstances, but much of a muchness with other women, a fairly

standard female product made by a conveyor-belt society. Inner battles, to be fought for myself alone, became outer battles, to be fought alongside the whole female sex. Release, euphoria. Look, said my husband, I haven't enough room. Neither have I, I said. I would not placate, I would not apologise, I would not give ground any more because I was connected now to a larger army that waged a bigger war, and rescue was at hand. The slaves had revolted and even the most abject gained strength for their individual skirmishes from the growing awareness that they were not personally slavish but merely enslaved. My poor man had his problems, too, but I felt no pity, then. The walls of our relationship were closing in, we fought each other as the oxygen gave out and finally I made it into the cold, invigorating fresh air. The dolly died of double pneumonia but I was still alive.

That is a brief sketch of two marriages, founded on something we all called love because we lived in the romantic West and what other reason is allowed for marriage, if not love? On the surface, of course, the upheavals were not so apparent, being thought of as private quarrels, and I have anyway condensed them greatly—they were actually spread over seven years each, the seven years they say it takes a human to replace every cell of body skin. In the lulls between there were good times, when we laughed together and shared quite a deal of tenderness and celebrated the birth of children, and just ordinary times when we went about the business of marriage, the paying of bills, the buying of goods, the cooking and the cleaning and the entertainment of friends, as every couple does. I make very little of them because the world made so much, crowding round the happy wife, the successful husband, and abruptly turning away, turning a blind and embarrassed eye to the sobbing wife and the angry, frustrated husband. Besides, the violence was endemic and perhaps because of that, ignored as much as possible. Each of us thought we were building new houses, especially designed for us, but we didn't know about the quicksand beneath or the death-watch beetles munching the timbers. An all-pervading dishonesty hung over our enterprise. I was not what I pretended and neither were they. I sold my soul for a mess of sacrificial femininity, sugar and spice and all things nice. They built a prison with their own masculinity, so constricting it made them red in the face, choleric. And the impulsion to act out our roles, the sheer effort it took, left little time or energy to investigate small sounds of protest within. What reward, anyway, would there be for such investigation? In fact, only penalties would be paid. Loss of social approval, isolation from friends and family, accusations of bizarre behaviour and, for the woman, selfishness, that sin forbidden to any female unless she be extraordinarily rich, beautiful or old. To let the human being show behind the mask of gender was to risk even madness. They might come and take us away to the funny farm, make arrangements for derangement.

Much safer to be what they wanted, what was considered respectable. Much better to lean heavily upon each other for support and set up a quarrel, some drama, whenever the inner voices grew querulous and needed to be drowned. *Men*, said my mother, wiping my tears away. *Women*, said my father, soothing a husband. They sounded calm and quite pleased. Well, it was all very natural, wasn't it?

Long before all this, in my very first close encounter with the opposite sex, the pattern was laid down. I was ten at the time and jaunted daily back and forth to school on a bus. Every morning a boy was also waiting at the stop, he with his mates and I with mine. I liked the way he looked, I laughed a little louder when he was about. One afternoon, on the way home, it happened. I was sitting right at the front of the bus and he was two rows behind. There came a rustle, sounds of suppressed mirth, a hand stuck itself over my shoulder and thrust a small piece of paper at me. I unfolded it. There upon the graph-lined page were fat letters in pencil. 'Dear Girl,' said the letters, 'I love you.'

I read the message and stared out of the window and watched the grass that lined the road grow as green as emeralds, as if a light had been lit under every leaf. An ache started at my chest and spread through every vein until I was heavy, drugged with glucose, banjaxed by that most potent of love-surrogates—thick undiluted narcissism. A boy, a stranger, a member of the male sex, encased in his own unknown life, lying on his unknown bed, had thought of me and, by doing so, given me surreality. Until that moment 'I' was who I thought I was. From then on for a very long time, 'I' was whoever a man thought I was. That pencilled note signalled the end of an autonomy I was not to experience again for many years. As I turned towards that boy, tilting my chin, narrowing my eyes, pulling down my underlip to show my pearly teeth, giving him my first consciously manufactured, all synthetic skin-deep smile, I entered into my flawed inheritance.

Looking back on all this and other episodes of lust and affection, encoun- 25 ters that lasted a week or a year, the picture seems at first glance chaotic and a gloomy sort of chaos at that. Love and failure. By the standards of my time, success in love is measured in bronze and gold and diamonds, anniversaries of the day when love was firstly publicly seen to be there, at the altar. Thus I am found wanting, like any other whose marriage and relationships have ended in separation, and to be found wanting is meant to induce a sense of failure because those who do not conform must be rendered impotent.

In fact, people of my generation, like all the generations before, have had little chance of success in love of any kind. Many of those who offer the longevity of their marriage as proof of enduring love are often only revealing their own endurance in the face of ravaging compromises and a resulting anaesthesia that has left them half-way dead. In the name of that love they have jettisoned every grace considered admirable in any other part or act of life: honesty, dignity, self-respect, courtesy, kindness, integrity, steadfastness of principle. They have said those things to each other that are unsayable and done those things that are undoable and there is no health in them. They have not been true to themselves and therefore they are false to everyone else, including their children. The man has become and been allowed to become an autocrat, a tin-pot dictator in love's police state. The woman has lowered herself upon the floor to lick his jackboots. Or, sometimes, vice versa. What would never have been permitted strangers is given a free licence under love—abuse, insults, petty denigration, physical attack, intrusions on personal privacy, destruction of personal beliefs, destruction of any other friendships, destruction of sex itself. In order to enter the kingdom of love they have shrunk themselves to the space of less than one and, atrophied in every part, they claim love's crown. Two individuals who could have reached some stature have settled for being pygmies whose life's work, now, is the similar distortion of their offspring.

If love takes any other form than this tight, monogamous, heterosexual, lifelong reproductive unit, blessed by the law, the State, the priests and sanctified by gods, it is dismissed as an aberration, hounded as a perversion, insulted as a failure and refused the label 'love'. The incredible shrinking couple is presented to the world as the central aim and reward of life, a holy grail for which it is never too early to begin searching. Worst of all, we are given to believe that these dwarfish twosomes form the rock upon which all the rest of life is built, from the mental health of children to whole political systems and to remain outside it is to opt out of a cosmic responsibility and threaten the very roots of the human community. Love is all, they say. Love makes the world go round, they say. And you know it's true love, they say, when two people remain together from youth to death.

But you don't and it doesn't and you can't. The truth is that we have not yet created upon this earth the conditions in which true love can exist. Most of us are quite aware that most of mankind's other developments, emotional or technological, have been dependent upon certain prerequisites. Fire had to be discovered before we could develop a taste for cooked food and a pot to cook it in. Mass literacy was only posssible after the invention of printing and printing itself depended on the much earlier Chinese discovery of paper-making. The geodesic dome was an absolute impossibility before the computer age. The emotions are based on something of the same rules. Men's lives were not overshadowed by the certainty of death (and this is still so in some primitive tribes) until life itself was safer and death could be seen inevitably to arrive without sudden injury or accident. Unlike his fellow Greeks, Xenophanes was a monotheist, largely because he guessed that the physical characteristics of the earth changed with time and belief in one universal god is dependent upon belief in universal rules. And man can only be said to have become truly self-conscious after Freud's delineation of the unconscious. Just so has love its necessary prerequisites, its birth-time in history, its most favourable climatic conditions.

So for all that we lay claim to an eternal heritage of love, man's bosom companion since the dawn of time, we have got it wrong. We have called other emotions love and they do not smell as sweet. Love itself has been very nearly impossible for most of us most of our history and is only just becoming possible today. I failed in love, like many others, because given the tools I had to hand the work could not be done. More hopelessly still, the very blueprint was flawed, rough sketch of the eventual edifice without a single practical instruction, without a brick or a nail, without a vital part or principle. Dreams are not enough.

[1979]

■ TOPICS FOR DISCUSSION AND WRITING

1. On the basis of the first three paragraphs, characterize Tweedie.
2. In paragraph 9 Tweedie alludes to a passage in which Alice eats a piece of cake and grows bigger. Whether or not you have read *Alice in Wonderland,* explain what Tweedie means when she says she ate this cake, and

then, just before 5 p.m., "in the nick of time" she ate from the other side of the cake and "shrank to being a little woman again."

3. Tweedie uses many metaphors, some extended (a doll, in paragraphs 12–14), some brief (a hermit crab, in paragraph 18). Choose two or three of her metaphors and discuss them, explaining why you think they are effective or ineffective.

4. In paragraph 26 Tweedie generalizes about people of her age. Judging from what you know of her generation (she was born in 1936), do you think her generalizations here are sound? Why, or why not?

5. In paragraph 28 Tweedie says that "we have not yet created upon this earth the conditions in which love can exist." In a paragraph explain to a reader why Tweedie comes to this conclusion, and then, in a paragraph or two, explain why you do or do not find her position convincing.

6. Imagine that you are one of Tweedie's two former husbands. In this persona write an essay of 500 words describing the marriage.

7. In an essay of 750–1000 words compare the ideas about love and marriage in Tweedie's "The Experience" with those in either Virginia Woolf's "Lappin and Lapinova" (p. 525) or Fay Weldon's "In the Great War" (p. 548).

8. Can you identify the popular song whose first line is the epigraph to this essay? (An epigraph, from the Greek *epigraphein*, "write on," is a quotation at the beginning of a work that in some way illuminates or comments on it.) Whether or not you can identify the epigraph to Tweedie's essay, explain what sort of comment it makes. (In the next essay you write, try to find an appropriate epigraph.)

FICTION

■ VIRGINIA WOOLF

Virginia Woolf (1882–1941) is known chiefly as a novelist, but she was also the author of short stories and essays, and in recent years the range of her power has been increasingly recognized.

Woolf was self-educated in the library of her father, Leslie Stephen, an important English scholar, literary critic, and biographer. In 1907 she married Leonard Woolf, with whom ten years later she established the Hogarth Press, which published some of the most interesting literature of the period, including her own novels. Woolf experienced several mental breakdowns, and in 1941, fearing yet another, she drowned herself.

Lappin and Lapinova[1]

They were married. The wedding march pealed out. The pigeons fluttered. Small boys in Eaton jackets threw rice: a fox terrier sauntered across the path; and Ernest Thorburn led his bride to the car through the small inquisitive crowd of complete strangers which always collects in London to enjoy others people's happiness or unhappiness. Certainly he looked handsome and she looked shy. More rice was thrown, and the car moved off.

That was on Tuesday. Now it was Saturday. Rosalind had still to get used to the fact that she was Mrs. Ernest Thorburn. Perhaps she never would get used to the fact that she was Mrs. Ernest Anybody, she thought, as she sat in the bow window of the hotel looking over the lake to the mountains, and waited for her husband to come down to breakfast. Ernest was a difficult name to get used to. It was not the name she would have chosen. She would have preferred Timothy, Antony, or Peter. He did not look like Ernest either. The name suggested the Albert Memorial,[2] mahogany sideboards, steel engravings of the Prince Consort with his family—her mother-in-law's dining-room in Porchester Terrace in short.

But here he was. Thank goodness he did not look like Ernest—no. But what did he look like? She glanced at him sideways. Well, when he was eating toast he looked like a rabbit. Not that anyone else would have seen a likeness to a creature so diminutive and timid in this spruce, muscular young man with the straight nose, the blue eyes, and the very firm mouth. But that made it all the more amusing. His nose twitched very slightly when he ate. So did her pet rabbit's. She kept watching his nose twitch; and then she had to explain, when he caught her looking at him, why she laughed.

"It's because you're like a rabbit, Ernest," she said. "Like a wild rabbit," she added, looking at him. "A hunting rabbit; a King Rabbit; a rabbit that makes laws for all the other rabbits."

Ernest had no objection to being that kind of rabbit, and since it amused her to see him twitch his nose—he had never known that his nose twitched—he twitched it on purpose. And she laughed and laughed; and he laughed too, so that the maiden ladies and the fishing man and the Swiss waiter in his greasy jacket all guessed right; they were very happy. But how long does such happiness last? they asked themselves; and each answered according to his own circumstances.

At lunch time, seated on a clump of heather beside the lake, "Lettuce, rabbit?" said Rosalind, holding out the lettuce that had been provided to eat with the hard-boiled eggs. "Come and take it out of my hand," she added, and he stretched out and nibbled the lettuce and twitched his nose.

---

[1] **Lappin and Lapinova** *lapin* is French for rabbit

[2] **Albert Memorial** a memorial, in Hyde Park, London, dedicated in 1872 to Prince Albert (1819–1861), consort of Queen Victoria. A bronze statue of the prince stands in a tabernacle which rests on a platform. The platform's corners are adorned with sculptural groups representing Industry, Commerce, Agriculture, and Science. The whole is a memorial to Victorian culture, which by Woolf's time was much ridiculed.

"Good rabbit, nice rabbit," she said, patting him, as she used to pat her tame rabbit at home. But that was absurd. He was not a tame rabbit, whatever he was. She turned it into French. "Lapin," she called him. But whatever he was, he was not a French rabbit. He was simply and solely English—born at Porchester Terrace, educated at Rugby; now a clerk in His Majesty's Civil Service. So she tried "Bunny" next; but that was worse. "Bunny" was someone plump and soft and comic; he was thin and hard and serious. Still, his nose twitched. "Lappin," she exclaimed suddenly; and gave a little cry as if she had found the very word she looked for.

"Lappin, Lappin, King Lappin," she repeated. It seemed to suit him exactly; he was not Ernest, he was King Lappin. Why? She did not know.

When there was nothing new to talk about on their long solitary walks— and it rained, as everyone had warned them that it would rain; or when they were sitting over the fire in the evening, for it was cold, and the maiden ladies had gone and the fishing man, and the waiter only came if you rang the bell for him, she let her fancy play with the story of the Lappin tribe. Under her hands—she was sewing; he was reading—they became very real, very vivid, very amusing. Ernest put down the paper and helped her. There were the black rabbits and the red; there were the enemy rabbits and the friendly. There were the wood in which they lived and the outlying prairies and the swamp. Above all there was King Lappin, who, far from having only the one trick—that he twitched his nose—became as the days passed an animal of the greatest character; Rosalind was always finding new qualities in him. But above all he was a great hunter.

"And what," said Rosalind, on the last day of the honeymoon, "did the King do to-day?"

In fact they had been climbing all day; and she had worn a blister on her heel; but she did not mean that.

"To-day," said Ernest, twitching his nose as he bit the end off his cigar, "he chased a hare." He paused; struck a match, and twitched again.

"A woman hare," he added.

"A white hare!" Rosalind exclaimed, as if she had been expecting this. "Rather a small hare; silver grey; with big bright eyes?"

"Yes," said Ernest, looking at her as she had looked at him, "a smallish animal; with eyes popping out of her head, and two little front paws dangling." It was exactly how she sat, with her sewing dangling in her hands; and her eyes, that were so big and bright, were certainly a little prominent.

"Ah, Lapinova," Rosalind murmured.

"Is that what she's called?" said Ernest—"the real Rosalind?" He looked at her. He felt very much in love with her.

"Yes; that's what she's called," said Rosalind. "Lapinova." And before they went to bed that night it was all settled. He was King Lappin; she was Queen Lapinova. They were the opposite of each other; he was bold and determined; she wary and undependable. He ruled over the busy world of rabbits; her world was a desolate, mysterious place, which she ranged mostly by moonlight. All the same, their territories touched; they were King and Queen.

Thus when they came back from their honeymoon they possessed a private world, inhabited, save for the one white hare, entirely by rabbits. No one guessed that there was such a place, and that of course made it all the more amusing. It made them feel, more even than most young married couples, in league together against the rest of the world. Often they looked slyly at each other when people talked about rabbits and woods and traps and shooting. Or they winked furtively across the table when Aunt Mary said that she could never bear to see a hare in a dish—it looked so like a baby; or when John, Ernest's sporting brother, told them what price rabbits were fetching that autumn in Wiltshire, skins and all. Sometimes when they wanted a gamekeeper, or a poacher or a Lord of the Manor, they amused themselves by distributing the parts among their friends. Ernest's mother, Mrs. Reginald Thorburn, for example, fitted the part of the Squire to perfection. But it was all secret—that was the point of it; nobody save themselves knew that such a world existed.

Without that world, how, Rosalind wondered, that winter could she have lived at all? For instance, there was the golden-wedding party, when all the Thorburns assembled at Porchester Terrace to celebrate the fiftieth anniversary of that union which had been so blessed—had it not produced Ernest Thorburn? and so fruitful—had it not produced nine other sons and daughters into the bargain, many themselves married and also fruitful? She dreaded that party. But it was inevitable. As she walked upstairs she felt bitterly that she was an only child and an orphan at that; a mere drop among all those Thorburns assembled in the great drawing-room with the shiny satin wallpaper and the lustrous family portraits. The living Thorburns much resembled the painted; save that instead of painted lips they had real lips; out of which came jokes; jokes about schoolrooms, and how they had pulled the chair from under the governess; jokes about frogs and how they had put them between the virgin sheets of maiden ladies. As for herself, she had never even made an apple-pie bed. Holding her present in her hand she advanced toward her mother-in-law sumptuous in yellow satin; and toward her father-in-law decorated with a rich yellow carnation. All round them on tables and chairs there were golden tributes, some nestling in cotton wool; others branching resplendent—candlesticks; cigar boxes; chains; each stamped with the goldsmith's proof that it was solid gold, hallmarked, authentic. But her present was only a little pinchbeck[3] box pierced with holes; an old sand caster, an eighteenth-century relic, once used to sprinkle sand over wet ink. Rather a senseless present she felt—in an age of blotting paper; and as she proffered it, she saw in front of her the stubby black handwriting in which her mother-in-law when they were engaged had expressed the hope that "My son will make you happy." No, she was not happy. Not at all happy. She looked at Ernest, straight as a ramrod with a nose like all the noses in the family portraits; a nose that never twitched at all.

Then they went down to dinner. She was half hidden by the great chrysanthemums that curled their red and gold petals into large tight balls. Everything was gold. A gold-edged card with gold initials intertwined recited the list of all the dishes that would be set one after another before them. She dipped her spoon in a plate of clear golden fluid. The raw white fog outside

---

[3] **pinchbeck** imitation gold

had been turned by the lamps into a golden mesh that blurred the edges of the plates and gave the pineapples a rough golden skin. Only she herself in her white wedding dress peering ahead of her with her prominent eyes seemed insoluble as an icicle.

As the dinner wore on, however, the room grew steamy with heat. Beads of perspiration stood out on the men's foreheads. She felt that her icicle was being turned to water. She was being melted; dispersed; dissolved into nothingness; and would soon faint. Then through the surge in her head and the din in her ears she heard a woman's voice exclaim, "But they breed so!"

The Thorburns—yes; they breed so, she echoed; looking at all the round red faces that seemed doubled in the giddiness that overcame her; and magnified in the gold mist that enhaloed them. "They breed so." Then John bawled:

"Little devils! . . . Shoot'em! Jump on'em with big boots! That's the only way to deal with 'em . . . rabbits!"

At that word, that magic word, she revived. Peeping between the chrysanthemums she saw Ernest's nose twitch. It rippled, it ran with successive twitches. And at that a mysterious catastrophe befell the Thorburns. The golden table became a moor with the gorse in full bloom; the din of voices turned to one peal of lark's laughter ringing down from the sky. It was a blue sky—clouds passed slowly. And they had all been changed—the Thorburns. She looked at her father-in-law, a furtive little man with dyed moustaches. His foible was collecting things—seals, enamel boxes, trifles from eighteenth-century dressing tables which he hid in the drawers of his study from his wife. Now she saw him as he was—a poacher, stealing off with his coat bulging with pheasants and partridges to drop them stealthily into a three-legged pot in his smoky little cottage. That was her real father-in-law—a poacher. And Celia, the unmarried daughter, who always nosed out other people's secrets, the little things they wished to hide—she was a white ferret[4] with pink eyes, and a nose clotted with earth from her horrid underground nosings and pokings. Slung round men's shoulders, in a net, and thrust down a hole—it was a pitiable life—Celia's; it was none of her fault. So she saw Celia. And then she looked at her mother-in-law—whom they dubbed The Squire. Flushed, coarse, a bully—she was all that, as she stood returning thanks, but now that Rosalind—that is Lapinova—saw her, she saw behind her the decayed family mansion, the plaster peeling off the walls, and heard her, with a sob in her voice, giving thanks to her children (who hated her) for a world that had ceased to exist. There was a sudden silence. They all stood with their glasses raised; they all drank; then it was over.

"Oh, King Lappin!" she cried as they went home together in the fog, "if your nose hadn't twitched just at that moment, I should have been trapped!"

"But you're safe," said King Lappin, pressing her paw.

"Quite safe," she answered.

And they drove back through the Park, King and Queen of the marsh, of the mist, and of the gorse-scented moor.

Thus time passed; one year; two years of time. And on a winter's night,

---

[4] **ferret** ferrets—albino polecats—were often used to hunt rats and rabbits

which happened by a coincidence to be the anniversary of the golden-wedding party—but Mrs. Reginald Thorburn was dead; the house was to let; and there was only a caretaker in residence—Ernest came home from the office. They had a nice little home; half a house above a saddler's shop in South Kensington, not far from the tube[5] station. It was cold, with fog in the air, and Rosalind was sitting over the fire, sewing.

"What d'you think happened to me to-day?" she began as soon as he had settled himself down with his legs stretched to the blaze. "I was crossing the stream when—"

"What stream?" Ernest interrupted her.

"The stream at the bottom, where our wood meets the black wood," she explained.

Ernest looked completely blank for a moment.

"What the deuce are you talking about?" he asked.

"My dear Ernest!" she cried in dismay, "King Lappin," she added, dangling her little front paws in the firelight. But his nose did not twitch. Her hands—they turned to hands—clutched the stuff she was holding; her eyes popped half out of her head. It took him five minutes at least to change from Ernest Thorburn to King Lappin; and while she waited she felt a load on the back of her neck, as if somebody were about to wring it. At last he changed to King Lappin; his nose twitched; and they spent the evening roaming the woods much as usual.

But she slept badly. In the middle of the night she woke, feeling as if something strange had happened to her. She was stiff and cold. At last she turned on the light and looked at Ernest lying beside her. He was sound asleep. He snored. But even though he snored, his nose remained perfectly still. It looked as if it had never twitched at all. Was it possible that he was really Ernest; and that she was really married to Ernest? A vision of her mother-in-law's dining-room came before her; and there they sat, she and Ernest, grown old, under the engravings, in front of the sideboard. . . . It was their golden-wedding day. She could not bear it.

"Lappin, King Lappin!" she whispered, and for a moment his nose seemed to twitch of its own accord. But he still slept. "Wake up, Lappin, wake up!" she cried.

Ernest woke; and seeing her sitting bolt upright beside him he asked: "What's the matter?"

"I thought my rabbit was dead!" she whimpered. Ernest was angry.

"Don't talk such rubbish, Rosalind," he said. "Lie down and go to sleep." He turned over. In another moment he was sound asleep and snoring.

But she could not sleep. She lay curled up on her side of the bed, like a hare in its form.[6] She had turned out the light, but the street lamp lit the ceiling faintly, and the trees outside made a lacy network over it as if there were a shadowy grove on the ceiling in which she wandered, turning, twisting, in and out, round and round, hunting, being hunted, hearing the bay of

[5] **tube** subway
[6] **form** the resting place of a hare

hounds and horns; flying, escaping . . . until the maid drew the blinds and brought their early tea.

Next day she could settle to nothing. She seemed to have lost something. She felt as if her body had shrunk; it had grown small, and black and hard. Her joints seemed stiff too, and when she looked in the glass, which she did several times as she wandered about the flat, her eyes seemed to burst out of her head, like currants in a bun. The rooms also seemed to have shrunk. Large pieces of furniture jutted out at odd angles and she found herself knocking against them. At last she put on her hat and went out. She walked along the Cromwell Road; and every room she passed and peered into seemed to be a dining-room where people sat eating under steel engravings, with thick yellow lace curtains, and mahogany sideboards. At last she reached the Natural History Museum; she used to like it when she was a child. But the first thing she saw when she went in was a stuffed hare standing on sham snow with pink glass eyes. Somehow it made her shiver all over. Perhaps it would be better when dusk fell. She went home and sat over the fire, without a light, and tried to imagine that she was out alone on a moor; and there was a stream rushing; and beyond the stream a dark wood. But she could get no further than the stream. At last she squatted down on the bank on the wet grass, and sat crouched in her chair, with her hands dangling empty, and her eyes glazed, like glass eyes, in the firelight. Then there was the crack of a gun. . . . She started as if she had been shot. It was only Ernest, turning his key in the door. She waited, trembling. He came in and switched on the light. There he stood, tall, handsome, rubbing his hands that were red with cold.

"Sitting in the dark?" he said.

"Oh, Ernest, Ernest!" she cried, starting up in her chair.

"Well, what's up now?" he asked briskly, warming his hands at the fire.

"It's Lapinova . . . " she faltered, glancing wildly at him out of her great started eyes. "She's gone, Ernest. I've lost her!"

Ernest frowned. He pressed his lips tight together.

"Oh, that's what's up, is it?" he said, smiling rather grimly at his wife. For ten seconds he stood there, silent; and she waited, feeling hands tightening at the back of her neck.

"Yes," he said at length. "Poor Lapinova . . . " He straightened his tie at the looking-glass over the mantelpiece.

"Caught in a trap," he said, "killed," and sat down and read the newspaper.

So that was the end of that marriage.

■ TOPICS FOR DISCUSSION AND WRITING

1. What is the point of view and the tone of the first paragraph? Of the second?

2. We are told that Rosalind and Ernest—King Lappin and Queen Lapinova—"were the opposite of each other; he was bold and determined; she wary and undependable." Are these brief characterizations adequate, or are the characters more complex?

3. Why, at the golden-wedding party, does Rosalind feel that she is being "dissolved into nothingness"?
4. The story ends with this sentence: "So that was the end of that marriage." Why did the marriage end? And what, if anything, does this rather flat sentence add to the story?
5. Write a story, a narrative essay, or a journal entry about the end of a relationship. The relationship need not be between husband and wife, or lovers, or friends. It might be between a teacher and a student, a coach and an athlete, or siblings, for example.

■ ZORA NEALE HURSTON
─────────────────────────────

Zora Neale Hurston (c. 1901–1960) was brought up in Eatonville, Florida, a town said to be the first all-black self-governing town in the United States. Her mother died in 1904, and when Hurston's father remarried, Hurston felt out of place. In 1914, then at about the age of fourteen, she joined a traveling theatrical group as a maid, hoping to save money for school. Later, by working at such jobs as manicurist and waitress, she put herself through college, entering Howard University in 1923. After receiving a scholarship, she transferred in 1926 to Barnard College in New York, where she was the first black student in the college. After graduating from Barnard in 1928 she taught drama, worked as an editor, and studied anthropology. But when grant money ran out in 1932 she returned to Eatonville to edit the folk material that she had collected during four years of fieldwork, and to do some further writing. She steadily published from 1932 to 1938—stories, folklore, and two novels— but she gained very little money. Further, although she played a large role in the Harlem Renaissance in the 1930s, she was criticized by Richard Wright and other influential black authors for portraying blacks as stereotypes and for being politically conservative. To many in the 1950s her writing seemed reactionary, almost embarrassing in an age of black protest, and she herself—working as a domestic, a librarian, and a substitute teacher—was almost forgotten. She died in a county welfare home in Florida and is buried in an unmarked grave.

Sweat

It was eleven o'clock of a Spring night in Florida. It was Sunday. Any other night, Delia Jones would have been in bed for two hours by this time. But she was a washwoman, and Monday morning meant a great deal to her. So she collected the soiled clothes on Saturday when she returned the clean things. Sunday night after church, she sorted them and put the white things to soak. It saved her almost a half day's start. A great hamper in the bedroom held the clothes that she brought home. It was so much neater than a number of bundles lying around.

She squatted in the kitchen floor beside the great pile of clothes, sorting them into small heaps according to color, and humming a song in a mournful key, but wondering through it all where Sykes, her husband, had gone with her horse and buckboard. [1]

Just then something long, round, limp and black fell upon her shoulders and slithered to the floor beside her. A great terror took hold of her. It softened her knees and dried her mouth so that it was a full minute before she could cry out or move. Then she saw that it was the big bull whip her husband liked to carry when he drove.

She lifted her eyes to the door and saw him standing there bent over with laughter at her fright. She screamed at him.

"Sykes, what you throw dat whip on me like dat? You know it would skeer me—looks just like a snake, an' you knows how skeered Ah is of snakes."

"Course Ah knowed it! That's how come Ah done it." He slapped his leg with his hand and almost rolled on the ground in his mirth. "If you such a big fool dat you got to have a fit over a earth worm or a string, Ah don't keer how bad Ah skeer you."

"You aint got no business doing it. Gawd knows it's a sin. Some day Ah'm gointuh drop dead from some of yo' foolishness. 'Nother thing, where you been wid mah rig? Ah feeds dat pony. He aint fuh you to be drivin' wid no bull whip."

"Yo sho is one aggravatin' nigger woman!" he declared and stepped into the room. She resumed her work and did not answer him at once. "Ah done tole you time and again to keep them white folks' clothes outa dis house."

He picked up the whip and glared down at her. Delia went on with her work. She went out into the yard and returned with a galvanized tub and set it on the washbench. She saw that Sykes had kicked all of the clothes together again, and now stood in her way truculently, his whole manner hoping, *praying*, for an argument. But she walked calmly around him and commenced to re-sort the things.

"Next time, Ah'm gointer to kick 'em outdoors," he threatened as he struck a match along the leg of his corduroy breeches.

Delia never looked up from her work, and her thin, stooped shoulders sagged further.

"Ah aint for no fuss t'night Sykes. Ah just come from taking sacrament at the church house."

He snorted scornfully. "Yeah, you just come from de church house on a Sunday night, but heah you is gone to work on them clothes. You aint nothing but a hypocrite. One of them amen-corner Christians—sing, whoop, shout, then come home and wash white folks clothes on the Sabbath."

He stepped roughly upon the whitest pile of things, kicking them helter-skelter as he crossed the room. His wife gave a little scream of dismay, and quickly gathered them together again.

"Sykes, you quit grindin' dirt into these clothes! How can Ah git through by Sat'day if Ah don't start on Sunday?"

"Ah don't keer if you never git through. Anyhow, Ah done promised Gawd

---

[1] **buckboard** an open wagon

and a couple of other men, Ah aint gointer have it in mah house. Don't gimme no lip neither, else Ah'll throw 'em out and put mah fist up side yo' head to boot."

Delia's habitual meekness seemed to slip from her shoulders like a blown scarf. She was on her feet; her poor little body, her bare knuckly hands bravely defying the strapping hulk before her.

"Looka heah, Sykes, you done gone too fur. Ah been married to you fur fifteen years, and Ah been takin' in washin' for fifteen years. Sweat, sweat, sweat! Work and sweat, cry and sweat, pray and sweat!"

"What's that go to do with me?" he asked brutally.

"What's it got to do with you, Sykes? Mah tub of suds is filled yo' belly with vittles more times than yo' hands is filled it. Mah sweat is done paid for this house and Ah reckon Ah kin keep on sweatin' in it."

She seized the iron skillet from the stove and struck a defensive pose, which act surprised him greatly, coming from her. It cowed him and he did not strike her as he usually did.

"Naw you won't," she panted, "that ole snaggle-toothed black woman you runnin' with aint comin' heah to pile up on *mah* sweat and blood. You aint paid for nothin' on this place, and Ah'm gointer stay right heah till Ah'm toted out foot foremost."

"Well, you better quit gittin' me riled up, else they'll be totin' you out sooner than you expect. Ah'm so tired of you Ah don't know whut to do. Gawd! how Ah hates skinny wimmen!"

A little awed by this new Delia, he sidled out of the door and slammed the back gate after him. He did not say where he had gone, but she knew too well. She knew very well that he would not return until nearly daybreak also. Her work over, she went on to bed but not to sleep at once. Things had come to a pretty pass!

She lay awake, gazing upon the debris that cluttered their matrimonial trail. Not an image left standing along the way. Anything like flowers had long ago been drowned in the salty stream that had been pressed from her heart. Her tears, her sweat, her blood. She had brought love to the union and he had brought a longing for the flesh. Two months after the wedding, he had given her the first brutal beating. She had the memory of numerous trips to Orlando with all of his wages when he had returned to her penniless, even before the first year had passed. She was young and soft then, but now she thought of her knotty, muscled limbs, her harsh knuckly hands, and drew herself up into an unhappy little ball in the middle of the big feather bed. Too late now to hope for love, even if it were not Bertha it would be someone else. This case differed from the others only in that she was bolder than the others. Too late for everything except her little home. She had built it for her old days, and planted one by one the trees and flowers there. It was lovely to her, lovely.

Somehow before sleep came, she found herself saying aloud: "Oh well, whatever goes over the Devil's back, is got to come under his belly. Sometime or ruther, Sykes, like everybody else, is gointer reap his sowing." After that she was able to build a spiritual earthworks against her husband. His shells could no longer reach her. *Amen*. She went to sleep and slept until he announced his presence in bed by kicking her feet and rudely snatching the cover away.

"Gimme some kivah heah, an' git yo' damn foots over on yo' own side! Ah oughter mash you in yo' mouf fuh drawing dat skillet on me."

Delia went clear to the rail without answering him. A triumphant indifference to all that he was or did.

The week was as full of work for Delia as all other weeks, and Saturday found her behind her little pony, collecting and delivering clothes.

It was a hot, hot day near the end of July. The village men on Joe Clarke's porch even chewed cane listlessly. They did not hurl the cane-knots as usual. They let them dribble over the edge of the porch. Even conversation had collapsed under the heat.

"Heah comes Delia Jones," Jim Merchant said, as the shaggy pony came 'round the bend of the road toward them. The rusty buckboard was heaped with baskets of crisp, clean laundry.

"Yep," Joe Lindsay agreed. "Hot or col', rain or shine, jes ez reg'lar ez de weeks roll roun' Delia carries 'em an' fetches 'em on Sat'day."

"She better if she wanter eat," said Moss. "Syke Jones aint wuth de shot an' powder hit would tek tuh kill 'em. Not to *bub* he aint."

"He sho' aint," Walter Thomas chimed in. "It's too bad, too, cause she wuz a right pritty lil trick when he got huh. Ah'd uh mah'ied huh mahseff if he hadnter beat me to it."

Delia nodded briefly at the men as she drove past.

"Too much knockin' will ruin *any* 'oman. He done beat huh 'nough tuh kill three women, let 'lone change they looks," said Elijah Mosely. "How Syke kin stommuck dat big black greasy Mogul[2] he's layin' roun' wid, gits me. Ah swear dat eight-rock couldn't kiss a sardine can Ah done thowed out de back do' 'way las' yeah."

"Aw, she's fat, thass how come. He's allus been crazy 'bout fat women," put in Merchant. "He'd a' been tied up wid one long time ago if he could a' found one tuh have him. Did Ah tell yuh 'bout him come sidlin' roun' *mah* wife—bringin' her a basket uh pee-cans outa his yard fuh a present? Yes-sir, mah wife! She tol' him tuh take 'em right straight back home, cause Delia works so hard ovah dat washtub she reckon everything en de place taste lak sweat an' soapsuds. Ah jus' wisht Ah'd a' caught 'im 'roun' dere! Ah'd a' made his hips ketch on fiah down dat shell road."

"Ah know he done it, too. Ah sees 'im grinnin' at every 'oman dat passes," Walter Thomas said. "But even so, he useter eat some mighty big hunks uh humble pie tuh git dat lil' 'oman he got. She wuz ez pritty ez a speckled pup! Dat wuz fifteen yeahs ago. He useter be so skeered uh losin' huh, she could make him do some parts of a husband's duty. Dey never wuz de same in de mind."

"There oughter be a law about him," said Lindsay. "He aint fit tuh carry guts tuh a bear."

[2] **Mogul** big person

Clarke spoke for the first time. "Taint no law on earth dat kin make a man be decent if it aint in 'im. There's plenty men dat takes a wife lak dey do a joint uh sugar-cane. It's round, juicy an' sweet when dey gits it. But dey squeeze an' grind, squeeze an' grind an' wring tell dey wring every drop uh pleasure dat's in 'em out. When dey's satisfied dat dey is wrung dry, dey treats 'em jes lak dey do a cane-chew. Dey thows 'em away. Dey knows whut dey is doin' while dey is at it, an' hates theirselves fuh it but they keeps on hangin' after huh tell she's empty. Den dey hates huh fuh bein' a cane-chew an' in de way."

"We oughter take Syke an' dat stray 'oman uh his'n down in Lake Howell swamp an' lay on de rawhide till they cain't say 'Lawd a' mussy.' He allus wuz uh ovahbearin' niggah, but since dat white 'oman from up north done teached 'im how to run a automobile, he done got too biggety to live— an' we oughter kill 'im," Old Man Anderson advised.

A grunt of approval went around the porch. But the heat was melting their civic virtue and Elijah Moseley began to bait Joe Clarke.

"Come on, Joe, git a melon outa dere an' slice it up for yo' customers. We'se all sufferin' wid de heat. De bear's done got *me!*"

"Thass right, Joe, a watermelon is jes' whut Ah needs tuh cure de ep-pizudicks,"[3] Walter Thomas joined forces with Moseley. "Come on dere, Joe. We all is steady customers an' you aint set us up in a long time. Ah chooses dat long, bowlegged Floridy favorite."

"A god, an' be dough. You all gimme twenty cents and slice away," Clarke retorted. "Ah needs a col' slice m'self. Heah, everybody chip in. Ah'll lend y'll mah meat knife."

The money was quickly subscribed and the huge melon brought forth. At that moment, Sykes and Bertha arrived. A determined silence fell on the porch and the melon was put away again.

Merchant snapped down the blade of his jackknife and moved toward the store door.

"Come on in, Joe, an' gimme a slab uh sow belly an' uh pound uh coffee—almost fuhgot 'twas Sat'day. Got to git on home." Most of the men left also.

Just then Delia drove past on her way home, as Sykes was ordering magnificently for Bertha. It pleased him for Delia to see.

"Git whutsoever yo' heart desires, Honey. Wait a minute, Joe. Give huh two bottles uh strawberry soda-water, uh quart uh parched groundpeas, an' a block uh chewin' gum."

With all this they left the store, with Sykes reminding Bertha that this was his town and she could have it if she wanted it.

The men returned soon after they left, and held their watermelon feast. "Where did Syke Jones git dat 'oman from nohow?" Lindsay asked.

"Ovah Apopka. Guess dey musta been cleanin' out de town when she lef'. She don't look lak a thing but a hunk uh liver wid hair on it."

"Well, she sho' kin squall," Dave Carter contributed. "When she gits

---

[3] **eppizudicks** i.e., epizootic, an epidemic among animals

ready tuh laff, she jes' opens huh mouf an' latches it back tuh de las' notch. No ole grandpa alligator down in Lake Bell aint got nothin' on huh."

Bertha had been in town three months now. Sykes was still paying her room rent at Della Lewis'—the only house in town that would have taken her in. Sykes took her frequently to Winter Park to "stomps."[4] He still assured her that he was the swellest man in the state.

"Sho' you kin have dat lil' ole house soon's Ah kin git dat 'oman outa dere. Everything b'longs tuh me an' you sho' kin have it. Ah sho' 'bominates uh skinny 'oman. Lawdy, you sho' is got one portly shape on you! You kin git *anything* you wants. Dis is *mah* town an' you sho' kin have it.

Delia's work-worn knees crawled over the earth in Gethsemane and on the rocks of Calvary[5] many, many times during these months. She avoided the villagers and meeting places in her efforts to be blind and deaf. But Bertha nullified this to a degree, by coming to Delia's house to call Sykes out to her at the gate.

Delia and Sykes fought all the time now with no peaceful interludes. They slept and ate in silence. Two or three times Delia had attempted a timid friendliness, but she was repulsed each time. It was plain that the breaches must remain agape.

The sun had burned July to August. The heat streamed down like a million hot arrows, smiting all things living upon the earth. Grass withered, leaves browned, snakes went blind in shedding and men and dogs went mad. Dog days!

Delia came home one day and found Sykes there before her. She wondered, but started to go on into the house without speaking, even though he was standing in the kitchen door and she must either stoop under his arm or ask him to move. He made no room for her. She noticed a soap box beside the steps, but paid no particular attention to it, knowing that he must have brought it there. As she was stooping to pass under his outstretched arm, he suddenly pushed her backward, laughingly.

"Look in de box dere Delia, Ah done brung yuh somethin'!"

She nearly fell upon the box in her stumbling, and when she saw what it held, she all but fainted outright.

"Syke! Syke, mah Gawd! You take dat rattlesnake 'way from heah! You *gottuh*. Oh, Jesus, have mussy!"

"Ah aint gut tuh do nuthin' uh de kin'—fact is Ah aint got tuh do nothin' but die. Taint no use uh you puttin' on airs makin' out lak you sceered uh dat snake—he's gointer stay right heah tell he die. He wouldn't bite me cause Ah knows how tuh handle 'im. Nohow he wouldn't risk breakin' out his fangs 'gin yo' skinny laigs."

"Naw, now Syke, don't keep dat thing 'roun' heah tuh skeer me tuh death. You knows Ah'm even feared uh earth worms. Thass de biggest snake Ah evah did see. Kill 'im Syke, please."

---

[4] **stomps** dances

[5] **Gethsemane . . . Calvary** Gethsemane was the garden where Jesus prayed just before he was betrayed (Matthew 26:36–47); Calvary was the hill where he was crucified

"Doan ast me tuh do nothin' fuh yuh. Goin' 'roun' tryin' to be so damn asterperious. Naw, Ah aint gonna kill it. Ah think uh damn sight mo' uh him dan you! Dat's a nice snake an' anybody doan lak 'im kin jes' hit de grit."

The village soon heard that Sykes had the snake, and came to see and ask questions.

"How de hen-fire did you ketch dat six-foot rattler, Syke?" Thomas asked.

"He's full uh frogs so he caint hardly move, thass how Ah eased up on 'm. But Ah'm a snake charmer an' knows how tuh handle 'em. Shux, dat aint nothin'. Ah could ketch one eve'y day if Ah so wanted tuh."

"Whut he needs is a heavy hick'ry club leaned real heavy on his head. Dat's de bes 'way tuh charm a rattlesnake."

"Naw, Walt, y'll jes' don't understand dese diamon' backs lak Ah do," said Sykes in a superior tone of voice.

The village agreed with Walter, but the snake stayed on. His box remained by the kitchen door with its screen wire covering. Two or three days later it had digested its meal of frogs and literally came to life. It rattled at every movement in the kitchen or the yard. One day as Delia came down the kitchen steps she saw his chalky-white fangs curved like scimitars hung in the wire meshes. This time she did not run away with averted eyes as usual. She stood for a long time in the doorway in a red fury that grew bloodier for every second that she regarded the creature that was her torment.

That night she broached the subject as soon as Sykes sat down to the table.

"Syke, Ah wants you tuh take dat snake 'way fum heah. You done starved me an' Ah put up widcher, you done beat me an Ah took dat, but you done kilt all mah insides bringin' dat varmint heah."

Sykes poured out a saucer full of coffee and drank it deliberately before he answered her.

"A whole lot Ah keer 'bout how you feels inside uh out. Dat snake aint goin' no damn wheah till Ah gits ready fuh 'im tuh go. So fur as beatin' is concerned, yuh aint took near all dat you gointer take ef yuh stay 'roun' *me*."

Delia pushed back her plate and got up from the table. "Ah hates you, Sykes," she said calmly. "Ah hates you tuh de same degree dat Ah useter love yuh. Ah done took an' took till mah belly is full up tuh mah neck. Dat's de reason Ah got mah letter fum de church an' moved mah membership tuh Woodbridge—so Ah don't haftuh take no sacrament wid yuh. Ah don't wantuh see yuh, 'roun' me atall. Lay 'roun' wid dat 'oman all yuh wants tuh, but gwan 'way fum me an' mah house. Ah hates yuh lak uh suck-egg dog."

Sykes almost let the huge wad of corn bread and collard greens he was chewing fall out of his mouth in amazement. He had a hard time whipping himself to the proper fury to try to answer Delia.

"Well, Ah'm glad you does hate me. Ah'm sho' tiahed uh you hangin' ontuh me. Ah don't want yuh. Look at yuh stringey ole neck! Yo' raw-bony laigs an' arms is enough tuh cut uh man tuh death. You looks jes' lak de devvul's doll-baby tuh *me*. You cain't hate me no worse dan Ah hates you. Ah been hatin' *you* fuh years."

"Yo' ole black hide don't look lak nothin' tuh me, but uh passle uh wrin-

kled up rubber, wid yo' big ole yeahs flappin' on each side lak up paih uh buzzard wings. Don't think Ah'm gointuh be run 'way fum mah house neither.
Ah'm goin' tuh de white folks about *you*, mah young man, de very nex' time
you lay yo' han's on me. Mah cup is done run ovah." Delia said this with no
signs of fear and Sykes departed from the house, threatening her, but made
not the slightest move to carry out any of them.

That night he did not return at all, and the next day being Sunday, Delia
was glad that she did not have to quarrel before she hitched up her pony and
drove the four miles to Woodbridge.

She stayed to the night service—"love feast"—which was very warm and
full of spirit. In the emotional winds her domestic trials were borne far and
wide so that she sang as she drove homeward,

> "Jurden water,[6] black an' col'
> Chills de body, not de soul
> An' Ah wantah cross Jurden in uh calm time."

She came from the barn to the kitchen door and stopped.

"Whut's de mattah, ol' satan, you aint kickin' up yo' racket?" She addressed the snake's box. Complete silence. She went on into the house with
a new hope in its birth struggles. Perhaps her threat to go to the white folks
had frightened Sykes! Perhaps he was sorry! Fifteen years of misery and suppression had brought Delia to the place where she would hope *anything* that
looked towards a way over or through her wall of inhibitions.

She felt in the match safe behind the stove at once for a match. There
was only one there.

"Dat niggah wouldn't fetch nothin heah tuh save his rotten neck, but he
kin run thew whut Ah brings quick enough. Now he done toted off nigh on
tuh haff uh box uh matches. He done had dat 'oman heah in mah house, too."

Nobody but a woman could tell how she knew this even before she struck
the match. But she did and it put her into a new fury.

Presently she brought in the tubs to put the white things to soak. This
time she decided she need not bring the hamper out of the bedroom; she
would go in there and do the sorting. She picked up the pot-bellied lamp and
went in. The room was small and the hamper stood hard by the foot of the
white iron bed. She could sit and reach through the bedposts—resting as she
worked.

"Ah wantah cross Jurden in uh calm time." She was singing again. The
mood of the "love feast" had returned. She threw back the lid of the basket
almost gaily. Then, moved by both horror and terror, she sprang back toward
the door. *There lay the snake in the basket!* He moved sluggishly at first, but
even as she turned round and round, jumped up and down in an insanity of
fear, he began to stir vigorously. She saw him pouring his awful beauty from
the basket upon the bed, then she seized the lamp and ran as fast as she
could to the kitchen. The wind from the open door blew out the light and the

---

[6] **Jurden water** the River Jordan, which the Jews had to cross in order to reach the
promised land

darkness added to her terror. She sped to the darkness of the yard, slamming the door after her before she thought to set down the lamp. She did not feel safe even on the ground, so she climbed up in the hay barn.

There for an hour or more she lay sprawled upon the hay a gibbering wreck.

Finally she grew quiet, and after that, coherent thought. With this, stalked through her a cold, bloody rage. Hours of this. A period of introspection, a space of retrospection, then a mixture of both. Out of this an awful calm.

"Well, Ah done de bes' Ah could. If things aint right, Gawd knows taint mah fault."

She went to sleep—a twitchy sleep—and woke up to a faint gray sky. There was a loud hollow sound below. She peered out. Sykes was at the wood-pile, demolishing a wire-covered box.

He hurried to the kitchen door, but hung outside there some minutes before he entered, and stood some minutes more inside before he closed it after him.

The gray in the sky was spreading. Delia descended without fear now, and crouched beneath the low bedroom window. The drawn shade shut out the dawn, shut in the night. But the thin walls held back no sound.

"Dat ol' scratch is woke up now!" She mused at the tremendous whirr inside, which every woodsman knows, is one of the sound illusions. The rattler is a ventriloquist. His whirr sounds to the right, to the left, straight ahead, behind, close under foot—everywhere but where it is. Woe to him who guesses wrong unless he is prepared to hold up his end of the argument! Sometimes he strikes without rattling at all.

Inside, Sykes heard nothing until he knocked a pot lid off the stove while trying to reach the match safe in the dark. He had emptied his pockets at Bertha's.

The snake seemed to wake up under the stove and Sykes made a quick leap into the bedroom. In spite of the gin he had had, his head was clearing now.

"Mah Gawd!" he chattered, "ef Ah could on'y strack uh light!"

The rattling ceased for a moment as he stood paralyzed. He waited. It seemed that the snake waited also.

"Oh, fuh de light! Ah thought he'd be too sick"—Sykes was muttering to himself when the whirr began again, closer, right underfoot this time. Long before this, Sykes' ability to think had been flattened down to primitive instinct and he leaped—onto the bed.

Outside Delia heard a cry that might have come from a maddened chimpanzee, a stricken gorilla. All the terror, all the horror, all the rage that man possibly could express, without a recognizable human sound.

A tremendous stir inside there, another series of animal screams, the intermittent whirr of the reptile. The shade torn violently down from the window, letting in the red dawn, a huge brown hand seizing the window stick, great dull blows upon the wooden floor punctuating the gibberish of sound long after the rattle of the snake had abruptly subsided. All this Delia could see and hear from her place beneath the window, and it made her ill. She crept over to the four-o'clocks[7] and stretched herself on the cool earth to recover.

She lay there. "Delia, Delia!" She could hear Sykes calling in a most despairing tone as one who expected no answer. The sun crept on up, and he called. Delia could not move—her legs were gone flabby. She never moved, he called, and the sun kept rising.

"Mah Gawd!" She heard him moan, "Mah Gawd fum Heben!" She heard him stumbling about and got up from her flower-bed. The sun was growing warm. As she approached the door she heard him call out hopefully, "Delia, is dat you Ah heah?"

She saw him on his hands and knees as soon as she reached the door. He crept an inch or two toward her—all that he was able, and she saw his horribly swollen neck and his one open eye shining with hope. A surge of pity too strong to support bore her away from that eye that must, could not, fail to see the tubs. He would see the lamp. Orlando with its doctors was too far. She could scarcely reach the Chinaberry tree, where she waited in the growing heat while inside she knew the cold river was creeping up and up to extinguish that eye which must know by now that she knew.

[1926]

■ TOPICS FOR DISCUSSION AND WRITING

1. Summarize the relationship of Delia and Sykes before the time of the story.
2. How do the men on Joe Clark's porch further your understanding of Delia and Sykes and of the relationship between the two?
3. To what extent is Delia responsible for Sykes's death? To what extent is Sykes responsible? Do you think that Delia's action (or inaction) at the end of the story is immoral? Why, or why not?
4. To what extent does the relationship between blacks and whites play a role in the lives of the characters in "Sweat" and in the outcome of the story?
5. Are the blacks in "Sweat" portrayed stereotypically, as some of Hurston's critics charged? (See the biographical note, page 531.) How, on the evidence available in this story, might Hurston's fiction be defended from that charge?

■ WILLIAM FAULKNER

William Faulkner (1897–1962), was brought up in Oxford, Mississippi. His great-grandfather had been a Civil War hero, and his father was treasurer of the University of Mississippi in Oxford; the family was no longer rich, but it was still respected. In 1918 he enrolled in the Royal Canadian Air Force, though he never saw overseas service. After the war he returned to Mississippi and went to the university for two years.

[7]**four-o'clocks** tropical American plants, especially *Mirabilis japala*, a garden plant whose yellow, red, or white tubular flowers open in the late afternoon

He then moved to New Orleans, where he became friendly with Sherwood Anderson, who was already an established writer. In New Orleans Faulkner worked for the *Times-Picayune;* still later, even after he had established himself as a major novelist with *The Sound and the Fury* (1929), he had to do some work in Hollywood in order to make ends meet. In 1950 he was awarded the Nobel Prize in Literature.

Almost all of Faulkner's writing is concerned with the people of Yoknapatawpha, an imaginary county in Mississippi. "I discovered," he said, "that my own little postage stamp of native soil was worth writing about and that I would never live long enough to exhaust it." Though he lived for brief periods in Canada, New Orleans, New York, Hollywood, and Virginia (where he died), he spent most of his life in his native Mississippi.

A Rose for Emily

I

When Miss Emily Grierson died, our whole town went to her funeral: the men through a sort of respectful affection for a fallen monument, the women mostly out of curiosity to see the inside of her house, which no one save an old manservant—a combined gardener and cook—had seen in at least ten years.

It was a big, squarish frame house that had once been white, decorated with cupolas and spires and scrolled balconies in the heavily lightsome style of the seventies, set on what had once been our most select street. But garages and cotton gins had encroached the obliterated even the august names of that neighborhood; only Miss Emily's house was left, lifting its stubborn and coquettish decay above the cotton wagons and the gasoline pumps—an eyesore among eyesores. And now Miss Emily had gone to join the representatives of those august names where they lay in the cedar-bemused cemetery among the ranked and anonymous graves of Union and Confederate soldiers who fell at the battle of Jefferson.

Alive, Miss Emily had been a tradition, a duty, and a care; a sort of hereditary obligation upon the town, dating from that day in 1894 when Colonel Sartoris, the mayor—he who fathered the edict that no Negro woman should appear on the streets without an apron—remitted her taxes, the dispensation dating from the death of her father on into perpetuity. Not that Miss Emily would have accepted charity. Colonel Sartoris invented an involved tale to the effect that Miss Emily's father had loaned money to the town, which the town, as a matter of business, preferred this way of repaying. Only a man of Colonel Sartoris' generation and thought could have invented it, and only a woman could have believed it.

When the next generation, with its more modern ideas, became mayors and aldermen, this arrangement created some little dissatisfaction. On the first of the year they mailed her a tax notice. February came, and there was no reply. They wrote her a formal letter, asking her to call at the sheriff's office at her convenience. A week later the mayor wrote her himself, offering to call or to send his car for her, and received in reply a note on paper of an archaic shape, in a thin, flowing calligraphy in faded ink, to the effect that she no longer went out at all. The tax notice was also enclosed, without comment.

They called a special meeting of the Board of Aldermen. A deputation 5 waited upon her, knocked at the door through which no visitor had passed since she ceased giving china-painting lessons eight or ten years earlier. They were admitted by the old Negro into a dim hall from which a staircase mounted into still more shadow. It smelled of dust and disuse—a close, dank smell. The Negro led them into the parlor. It was furnished in heavy, leather-covered furniture. When the Negro opened the blinds of one window they could see that the leather was cracked; and when they sat down, a faint dust rose sluggishly about their thighs, spinning with slow motes in the single sunray. On a tarnished gilt easel before the fireplace stood a crayon portrait of Miss Emily's father.

They rose when she entered—a small, fat woman in black, with a thin gold chain descending to her waist and vanishing into her belt, leaning on an ebony cane with a tarnished gold head. Her skeleton was small and spare; perhaps that was why what would have been merely plumpness in another was obesity in her. She looked bloated, like a body long submerged in motionless water, and of that pallid hue. Her eyes, lost in the fatty ridges of her face, looked like two small pieces of coal pressed into a lump of dough as they moved from one face to another while the visitors stated their errand.

She did not ask them to sit. She just stood in the door and listened quietly until the spokesman came to a stumbling halt. Then they could hear the invisible watch ticking at the end of the gold chain.

Her voice was dry and cold. "I have no taxes in Jefferson. Colonel Sartoris explained it to me. Perhaps one of you can gain access to the city records and satisfy yourselves."

"But we have. We are the city authorities, Miss Emily. Didn't you get a notice from the sheriff, signed by him?"

"I received a paper, yes," Miss Emily said. "Perhaps he considers him- 10 self the sheriff. . . . I have no taxes in Jefferson."

"But there is nothing on the books to show that, you see. We must go by the—".

"See Colonel Sartoris. I have no taxes in Jefferson."

"But, Miss Emily—"

"See Colonel Sartoris." (Colonel Sartoris had been dead almost ten years.) "I have no taxes in Jefferson. Tobe!" The Negro appeared. "Show these gentlemen out."

II

So she vanquished them, horse and foot, just as she had vanquished their 15 fathers thirty years before about the smell. That was two years after her father's death and a short time after her sweetheart—the one we believed would marry her—had deserted her. After her father's death she went out very little; after her sweetheart went away, people hardly saw her at all. A few of the ladies had the temerity to call, but were not received, and the only sign of life about the place was the Negro man—a young man then—going in and out with a market basket.

"Just as if a man—any man—could keep a kitchen properly," the ladies said; so they were not surprised when the smell developed. It was another link between the gross, teeming world and the high and mighty Griersons.

A neighbor, a woman, complained to the mayor, Judge Stevens, eighty years old.

"But what will you have me do about it, madam?" he said.

"Why, send her word to stop it," the woman said. "Isn't there a law?"

"I'm sure that won't be necessary," Judge Stevens said. "It's probably 20 just a snake or a rat that nigger of hers killed in the yard. I'll speak to him about it."

The next day he received two more complaints, one from a man who came in diffident deprecation. "We really must do something about it, Judge. I'd be the last one in the world to bother Miss Emily, but we've got to do something." That night the Board of Aldermen met—three gray-beards and one younger man, a member of the rising generation.

"It's simple enough," he said. "Send her word to have her place cleaned up. Give her a certain time to do it in, and if she don't . . . "

"Dammit, sir," Judge Stevens said, "will you accuse a lady to her face of smelling bad?"

So the next night, after midnight, four men crossed Miss Emily's lawn and slunk about the house like burglars, sniffing along the base of the brick-work and at the cellar openings while one of them performed a regular sowing motion with his hand out of a sack slung from his shoulder. They broke open the cellar door and sprinkled lime there, and in all the out-buildings. As they recrossed the lawn, a window that had been dark was lighted and Miss Emily sat in it, the light behind her, and her upright torso motionless as that of an idol. They crept quietly across the lawn and into the shadow of the locusts that lined the street. After a week or two the smell went away.

That was when people had begun to feel really sorry for her. People in 25 our town remembering how old lady Wyatt, her great-aunt, had gone completely crazy at last, believed that the Griersons held themselves a little too high for what they really were. None of the young men were quite good enough for Miss Emily and such. We had long thought of them as a tableau; Miss Emily a slender figure in white in the background, her father a spraddled silhouette in the foreground, his back to her and clutching a horsewhip, the two of them framed by the back-flung front door. So when she got to be thirty and was still single, we were not pleased exactly, but vindicated; even with insanity in the family she wouldn't have turned down all of her chances if they had really materialized.

When her father died, it got about that the house was all that was left to her; and in a way, people were glad. At last they could pity Miss Emily. Being left alone, and a pauper, she had become humanized. Now she too would know the old thrill and the old despair of a penny more or less.

The day after his death all the ladies prepared to call at the house and offer condolence and aid, as is our custom. Miss Emily met them at the door, dressed as usual and with no trace of grief on her face. She told them that her father was not dead. She did that for three days, with the ministers calling on her, and the doctors, trying to persuade her to let them dispose of the body. Just as they were about to resort to law and force, she broke down, and they buried her father quickly.

We did not say she was crazy then. We believed she had to do that. We remembered all the young men her father had driven away, and we knew that with nothing left, she would have to cling to that which had robbed her, as people will.

III

She was sick for a long time. When we saw her again, her hair was cut short, making her look like a girl, with a vague resemblance to those angels in colored church windows—sort of tragic and serene.

The town had just let the contracts for paving the sidewalks, and in the summer after her father's death they began to work. The construction company came with niggers and mules and machinery, and a foreman named Homer Barron, a Yankee—a big, dark, ready man, with a big voice and eyes lighter than his face. The little boys would follow in groups to hear him cuss the niggers, and the niggers singing in time to the rise and fall of picks. Pretty soon he knew everybody in town. Whenever you heard a lot of laughing anywhere about the square, Homer Barron would be in the center of the group. Presently we began to see him and Miss Emily on Sunday afternoons driving in the yellow-wheeled buggy and the matched team of bays from the livery stable.

At first we were glad that Miss Emily would have an interest, because the ladies all said, "Of course a Grierson would not think seriously of a Northerner, a day laborer." But there were still others, older people, who said that even grief could not cause a real lady to forget *noblesse oblige*—without calling it *noblesse oblige*. They just said, "Poor Emily. Her kinsfolk should come to her." She had some kin in Alabama; but years ago her father had fallen out with them over the estate of old lady Wyatt, the crazy woman, and there was no communication between the two families. They had not even been represented at the funeral.

And as soon as the old people said, "Poor Emily," the whispering began. "Do you suppose it's really so?" they said to one another. "Of course it is. . . ." This behind their hands; rustling of craned silk and satin behind jalousies closed upon the sun of Sunday afternoon as the thin, swift clop-clop-clop of the matched team passed: "Poor Emily."

She carried her head high enough—even when we believed that she was fallen. It was as if she demanded more than ever the recognition of her dignity as the last Grierson; as if it had wanted that touch of earthiness to reaffirm her imperviousness. Like when she bought the rat poison, the arsenic. That was over a year after they had begun to say "Poor Emily," and while the two female cousins were visiting her.

"I want some poison," she said to the druggist. She was over thirty then, still a slight woman, though thinner than usual, with cold, haughty black eyes in a face the flesh of which was strained across the temples and about the eyesockets as you imagine a lighthousekeeper's face ought to look. "I want some poison," she said.

"Yes, Miss Emily. What kind? For rats and such? I'd recom—"   35

"I want the best you have. I don't care what kind."

The druggist named several. "They'll kill anything up to an elephant. But what you want is—"

"Arsenic," Miss Emily said. "Is that a good one?"

"Is . . . arsenic? Yes ma'am. But what you want—"

"I want arsenic."   40

The druggist looked down at her. She looked back at him, erect, her face like a strained flag. "Why, of course," the druggist said. "If that's what you want. But the law requires you to tell what you are going to use it for."

Miss Emily just stared at him, her head tilted back in order to look him eye for eye, until he looked away and went and got the arsenic and wrapped it up. The Negro delivery boy brought her the package; the druggist didn't come back. When she opened the package at home there was written on the box, under the skull and bones: "For rats."

IV

So the next day we all said, "She will kill herself"; and we said it would be the best thing. When she had first begun to be seen with Homer Barron, we had said, "She will marry him." Then we said, "She will persuade him yet," because Homer himself had remarked—he liked men, and it was known that he drank with the younger men in the Elks' Club—that he was not a marrying man. Later we said, "Poor Emily," behind the jalousies as they passed on Sunday afternoon in the glittering buggy, Miss Emily with her head high and Homer Barron with his hat cocked and a cigar in his teeth, reins and whip in a yellow glove.

Then some of the ladies began to say that it was a disgrace to the town and a bad example to the young people. The men did not want to interfere, but at last the ladies forced the Baptist minister—Miss Emily's people were Episcopal—to call upon her. He would never divulge what happened during that interview, but he refused to go back again. The next Sunday they again drove about the streets, and the following day the minister's wife wrote to Miss Emily's realtions in Alabama.

So she had blood-kin under her roof again and we sat back to watch de-   45
velopments. At first nothing happened. Then we were sure that they were to be married. We learned that Miss Emily had been to the jeweler's and ordered a man's toilet set in silver, with the letter H.B. on each piece. Two days later we learned that she had bought a complete outfit of men's clothing, including a nightshirt, and we said, "They are married." We were really glad. We were glad because the two female cousins were even more Grierson than Miss Emily had ever been.

So we were surprised when Homer Barron—the streets had been finished some time since—was gone. We were a little disappointed that there was not a public blowing-off but we believed that he had gone on to prepare for Miss Emily's coming, or to give a chance to get rid of the cousins. (By that time it was a cabal, and we were all Miss Emily's allies to help circumvent the cousins.) Sure enough, after another week they departed. And, as we had expected all along, within three days Homer Barron was back in town. A neighbor saw the Negro man admit him at the kitchen door at dusk one evening.

And that was the last we saw of Homer Barron. And of Miss Emily for some time. The Negro man went in and out with the market basket, but the front door remained closed. Now and then we would see her at a window for a moment, as the men did that night when they sprinkled the lime, but for almost six months she did not appear on the streets. Then we knew that this was to be expected too; as if that quality of her father which had thwarted her woman's life so many times had been too virulent and too furious to die.

When we next saw Miss Emily, she had grown fat and her hair was turning gray. During the next few years it grew grayer and grayer until it attained an even pepper-and-salt iron-gray, when it ceased turning. Up to the day of her death at seventy-four it was still that vigorous iron-gray, like the hair of an active man.

From that time on her front door remained closed, save for a period of six or seven years, when she was about forty, during which she gave lessons in china-painting. She fitted up a studio in one of the downstairs rooms, where the daughters and granddaughters of Colonel Sartoris' contemporaries were sent to her with the same regularity and in the same spirit that they were sent on Sundays with a twenty-five cent piece for the collection plate. Meanwhile her taxes had been remitted.

Then the newer generation became the backbone and the spirit of the town, and the painting pupils grew up and fell away and did not send their children to her with boxes of color and tedious brushes and pictures cut from the ladies' magazines. The front door closed upon the last one and remained closed for good. When the town got free postal delivery Miss Emily alone refused to let them fasten the metal numbers above her door and attach a mailbox to it. She would not listen to them.

Daily, monthly, yearly we watched the Negro grow grayer and more stooped, going in and out with the market basket. Each December we sent her a tax notice, which would be returned by the post office a week later, unclaimed. Now and then we could see her in one of the downstairs windows—she had evidently shut up the top floor of the house—like the carven torso of an idol in a niche, looking or not looking at us, we could never tell which. Thus she passed from generation to generation—dear, inescapable, impervious, tranquil, and perverse.

And so she died. Fell ill in the house filled with dust and shadows, with only a doddering Negro man to wait on her. We did not even know she was sick; we had long since given up trying to get any information from the Negro. He talked to no one, probably not even to her, for his voice had grown harsh and rusty, as if from disuse.

She died in one of the downstairs rooms, in a heavy walnut bed with a curtain, her gray head propped on a pillow yellow and moldy with age and lack of sunlight.

V

The Negro met the first of the ladies at the front door and let them in, with their hushed, sibilant voices and their quick, curious glances, and then he disappeared. He walked right through the house and out the back and was not seen again.

The two female cousins came at once. They held the funeral on the se- 55 cond day, with the town coming to look at Miss Emily beneath a mass of bought flowers, with the crayon face of her father musing profoundly above the bier and the ladies sibilant and macabre; and the very old men—some in their brushed Confederate uniforms—on the porch and the lawn, talking of Miss Emily as if she had been a contemporary of theirs, believing that they had danced with her and courted her perhaps, confusing time with its mathematical progression, as the old do, to whom all the past is not a diminishing road, but, instead, a huge meadow which no winter ever quite touches, divided from them now by the narrow bottleneck of the most recent decade of years.

Already we knew that there was one room in that region above stairs which no one had seen in forty years, and which would have to be forced. They waited until Miss Emily was decently in the ground before they opened it.

The violence of breaking down the door seemed to fill this room with pervading dust. A thin, acrid pall as of the tomb seemed to lie everywhere upon this room decked and furnished as for a bridal: upon the valance curtains of faded rose color, upon the rose-shaded lights, upon the dressing table, upon the delicate array of crystal and the man's toilet things backed with tarnished silver, silver so tarnished that the monogram was obscured. Among them lay a collar and tie, as if they had just been removed, which, lifted, left upon the surface a pale crescent in the dust. Upon a chair hung the suit, carefully folded; beneath it the two mute shoes and the discarded socks.

The man himself lay in the bed.

For a long while we just stood there, looking down at the profound and fleshless grin. The body had apparently once lain in the attitude of an embrace, but now the long sleep that outlasts love, that conquers even the grimace of love, had cuckolded him. What was left of him, rotted beneath what was left of the nightshirt, had become inextricable from the bed in which he lay; and upon him and upon the pillow beside him lay that even coating of the patient and biding dust.

Then we noticed that in the second pillow was the indentation of a head. 60 One of us lifted something from it, and leaning forward, that faint and invisible dust dry and acrid in the nostrils, we saw a long strand of iron-gray hair.

[1930]

■ TOPICS FOR DISCUSSION AND WRITING

1. Why does the narrator begin with what is almost the end of the story— the death of Miss Emily—rather than save this information for later? What devices does Faulkner use to hold the reader's interest throughout?

2. In a paragraph, offer a conjecture about Miss Emily's attitudes toward Homer Barron after he was last seen alive.

3. In a paragraph or two, characterize Miss Emily, calling attention not only to her eccentricities or even craziness, but also to what you conjecture to be her moral values.

4. In paragraph 44 we are told that the Baptist minister "would never divulge what happened" during the interview with Miss Emily. Why do you suppose that Faulkner does not narrate or describe the interview? Let's assume that in his first draft of the story he *did* give a paragraph of narration or a short dramatic scene. Write such an episode.

5. Suppose that Homer Barron's remains had been discovered before Miss Emily died, and that she was arrested and charged with murder. You are the prosecutor and you are running for a statewide political office. In 500 words, set forth your argument that—despite the fact that she is a public monument—she should be convicted. Or: you are the defense attorney, also running for office. In 500 words, set forth your defense.

6. Assume that Miss Emily kept a journal—perhaps even from her days as a young girl. Write some entries for the journal, giving her thoughts about some of the episodes reported in Faulkner's story.

■ FAY WELDON
_____

Fay Weldon was born in a village in England in 1931. During her early childhood her parents moved to New Zealand (her father was a physician), but they divorced when she was six, and Weldon lived with her mother. When Weldon was fourteen her mother returned to England. Because the mother, Fay, and another daughter lived with the mother's mother, and because Fay attended convent schools, she came to feel that "the world was composed of women." She has also said that her immersion in a female milieu made her forever independent of the need of male approbation.

In 1952 she earned a master's degree from St. Andrews University in Scotland. In 1955, unwed, she bore a son, whom she supported with little assistance from anyone. She began writing fiction in the 1950s, but having no great success in getting it published, she drifted into writing propaganda for the Foreign Office, then into answering problem letters written to the London *Daily Mirror,* and then into writing plays and advertising copy. In 1960 she married and bore three more children. (Marriage, she has said, gave focus to a life that she had "messed up hopelessly" until she met her husband.)

Weldon has now written dozens of plays, radio and television scripts, two books of short stories, and several novels.

In the Great War

Enid's mother Patty didn't stand a chance. That was in the Great War, in the fifties, when women were at war with women. Victory meant a soft bed and an easy life: defeat meant loneliness and the humiliation of the spinster. These days, of course, women have declared themselves allies, and united in a new war, a cold war, against the common enemy, man. But then, in the Great War, things were very different. And Patty didn't stand a chance against Helene. She was, for one thing, badly equipped for battle. Her legs were thick and practical, her breasts floppy, and her features, though pleasant enough, lacked erotic impact. Her blue eyes were watery and her hair frizzy and cut brusquely for easy washing and combing. 'I can't stand all this dolling up,' she'd say. 'What's the point?'

Patty cooked with margarine because it was cheaper than butter and her white sauces were always lumpy. She wouldn't keep pot plants, or souvenirs, or even a cat. What was the point?
She didn't like sex and, though she never refused her husband Arthur, she washed so carefully before and after, she made him feel he must have been really rather dirty.

Patty, in other words, was what she was, and saw no point in pretending to be anything else. Or in cooking with mushrooms or holidaying abroad or buying a new pair of shoes for Enid, her only child, when she had a perfectly good pair already, or going with her husband to the pub. And, indeed, there very often was no point in these things, except surely life must be more than something just to be practically and sensibly *got through?*

Enid thought so. Enid thought she'd do better than her mother in the Great War. Enid buffed her pre-pubertal nails and arranged wild flowers in jam jars and put them on the kitchen table. Perhaps she could see what was coming!

For all Patty's good qualities—cleanliness, honesty, thrift, reliability, kindness, sobriety, and so on—did her no good whatsoever when Helene came along. Or so Enid observed. Patty was asleep on duty, and there all of a sudden was Helene, the enemy at the gate, with her slim legs and her bedroom eyes, enticing Arthur away. 'But what does she *see* in Arthur?' asked Patty, dumbfounded. What you don't! the ten-year-old Enid thought, but did not say.

In fact, the Second World Male War, from 1939 to 1945, which men had waged among themselves in the name of Democracy, Freedom, Racial Supremacy and so forth, to the great detriment of women and children everywhere, had sharpened the savagery of the Female War. There just weren't enough men to go around. In ordinary times Helene would have gone into battle for some unmarried professional man—accountant or executive—but having lost country, home, family and friends in the ruins of Berlin now laid claim to Arthur, Patty's husband, a railway engineer in the north of England, who painted portraits as a hobby. The battle she fought for him was short and sharp. She shaved her shapely legs and flashed her liquid eyes.
'She's no better than a whore,' said Patty. 'Shaving her legs!' If God put hairs on your legs, thought Patty, then a woman's duty, and her husband's, too, is to put up with them.
Helene thought otherwise. And in her eyes Arthur saw the promise of secret bliss, the complicity of abandon, and all the charm of sin: the pink of her rosy nipples suffused the new world she offered him. And so, without much

difficulty Helen persuaded Arthur to leave Patty and Enid, give up his job, paint pictures for a living and think the world well lost for love.

By some wonderful fluke—wonderful, that is, for Arthur and Helene, if infuriating for Patty—Arthur's paintings were an outstanding commercial success. They became the worst bestselling paintings of the sixties, and Arthur, safely divorced from Patty, lived happily ever after with Helene, painting the occasional painting of wide-eyed deer, and sipping champagne by the side of swimming pools. 'Nasty acidy stuff, champagne,' said Patty.

Enid—Patty and Arthur's daughter—never really forgave her mother for losing the war. As if poor Patty didn't have enough to put up with already, without being blamed by her daughter for something she could hardly help! But that's the way these things go—life is the opposite of fair. It stuns you one moment and trips your feet from under you the next, and then jumps up and down on you, pound, pound, pound for good measure.

You should have seen Enid, when she was twelve, twisting the knife in her mother's wounds, poking about among the lumps of the cauliflower cheese, saying: 'Do we *have* to eat this? No wonder Dad left home!' 'Eat it up, it's good for you,' her mother would reply. 'If you want something fancy go and live with your stepmother.'

And, indeed, Enid had been asked, but Enid never went. Enid would twist a knife but not deliver a mortal wound, not to her mother. Instead she took up the armoury her mother never wore, breathed on it, burnished it, sharpened its cutting edges, prepared for war herself. Long after the war was over, Enid was still fighting. She was like some mad Aussie soldier hiding out in the Malayan jungle, still looking for a foe that had years since thrown away its grenades and taken to TV assembly instead.

At sixteen Enid scanned the fashion pages and read hints on make-up and how to be an interesting person; she went weekly to the theatre and art galleries and classical music concerts and exercised every day, and not until she was eighteen did she feel properly prepared to step into the battlefield. She was intelligent, and thought it sensible enough to go to university, although she chose English literature as the subject least likely to put men off.

'Nothing puts a man off like a clever woman,' said Helene when Enid visited. Now warriors in the Great War thought nothing of swapping secrets. Intelligence services of warring countries, hand in glove, glove in hand! It's always been so. Just as there's always been trade with enemy nations, unofficially if not officially. Helene lisped out quite a few secrets to Enid: her accent tinged with all the poise and decadence of a vanished Europe. 'My foreign wife!' Arthur would say, proudly in his honest, northern, jovial, middleaged voice. Arthur was the J. B. Priestley[1] of the art world—good in spite of himself.

Oh, Patty had lost a lovely prize, Enid knew it! Her beloved father! What a victory Patty's could have been—and yet she chose defeat. She'd chosen a bra

---

[1] **J. B. Priestley** John Boynton Priestley (b. 1894), popular English novelist, playwright, and critic

to flatten an already flat chest. 'What's the point?' she asked, when Enid said she was going off to university. Couldn't she even see that?

Little Enid, so bright and knowledgeable and determined! So young, so ruthless—a warrior! And fortune favours the brave, the strong, the ruthless. That was the point. Enid's professor, Walter Walther, looked at Enid in a lingering way, and Enid looked straight back. Take me! Well, not quite take me. Love me now, take me eventually.

Walter Walther was forty-eight. Enid was nineteen. Enid was studying Chaucer. Enid said in an essay that Chaucer's Parfait Gentle Knight was no hero but a crude mercenary, and Chaucer, in his adulation, was being ironic; Walter Walther hadn't thought of that before, and at forty-eight it is delightful to meet someone who says something you haven't thought of before. And she was so young, and dewy, almost downy, so that if she was out in the rain the drops lay like silver balls upon her skin; and she was surprisingly knowledgeable for one so young, and knew all about music and painting, which Walter didn't, much, and she had an interesting, rich father, if a rather dowdy, vague, distant little mother. And Enid was warm.

Oh, Enid was warm! Enid was warm against his body on stolen nights. Walter's wife Rosanne, four years older than he, was over fifty. Rain fell off her like water off a duck's back—her skin being oily, not downy. Enid had met Roseanne once or twice baby-sitting; or rather adolescent-sitting, for Walter and Roseanne's two children, Barbara and Bernadette.

Roseanne didn't stand a chance against Enid. Enid still fought the old, old war, and Roseanne had put away her weapons long ago.

'He's so unhappy with his wife,' said Enid to Margot. 'She's such a cold unfeeling bitch. She's only interested in her career, not in him at all, or the children.' Margot was Enid's friend. Margot had owl-eyes and a limpid handshake and not a hope of seducing, let alone winning, a married professor. But Margot understood Enid, and was a good friend to her, and had most of the qualities Enid's mother Patty had, and one more important one besides—self-doubt.

'Men never leave their wives for their mistresses,' warned Margot. It was a myth much put about, no doubt by wives, in the days of the Great War, to frighten the enemy. Enid knew better: she could tell a savage war mask from the frightened face of a foe in retreat. Enid knew Roseanne was frightened by the way she would follow Enid into the kitchen if Walter Walther was there alone, getting ice for drinks or scraping mud from the children's shoes.

Enid was pleased. A frightened foe seldom wins. The attacker is usually victorious, even if the advantage of surprise is gone, especially if the victim is old: Roseanne was old. She'd had the children late. It wasn't as if Walter Walther had really wanted children. He knew what kind of mother she'd make—cold.

Enid was warm. She knew how to silhouette her head against the sunlight so that her hair made a halo round her head, and then turn her face slowly so that the pure line of youth, the one that runs from ear to chin, showed to advantage. Roseanne had trouble with her back. Trouble with her back! Roseanne was a hag with one foot in the grave and with the iron bonds of matrimony would drag Walter Walther down there with her, if Walter didn't somehow break the bonds.

And Enid knew how to behave in bed, too: always keeping something in reserve, never taking the initiative, always the pupil, never the teacher. Enid had seen the *Art of Love* in Roseanne's bookshelves, and guessed her to be sexually experimental and innovatory. And she was later proved right, when Walter managed to voice one of his few actual complaints about his wife: there was, he felt, something indecent about Roseanne's sexual prowess: something disagreeably insatiable in her desires; it made Walter, from time to humiliating time, impotent.

Otherwise, it wasn't so much lack of love for Roseanne that Walter suffered from, as surfeit of love for Enid.

Enid exulted. And Rosanne was using worn-out old weapons: that particular stage in the war had ended long ago. The battle these days went to the innocent, not to the experienced. Modern man, Enid knew by instinct, especially those with a tendency to impotence, requires docility in bed and admiration and exulation—not excitement and exercise.

'He'll never leave the children,' said Margot. 'Men don't.' But Enid had been left. Enid knew very well that men did. And Barbara and Bernadette were not the most lovable of children—how could they be? With such a mother as Rosanne—a working mother who never even remembered her children's birthdays, never baked a cake, never ironed or darned, never cleaned the oven? Rosanne was a translator with the International Cocoa Board—a genius at languages, but not at motherhood. She was cold, stringy and sour—all the things soft, warm, rounded Enid was not. Walter said so, in bed, and increasingly out of it.

'What are you playing at?' asked Helene, crossly. Her own attitude to the world was moderating. She was an old retired warrior, sitting in a castle she'd won by force of arms, shaking her head at the shockingness of war.

Patty now lived alone in a little council flat in Birmingham. As Enid had left home Arthur no longer paid Patty maintenance. Why should he?

'You want Walter because Walter's Rosanne's,' observed Patty to Enid one day in a rare rush of insight to the head. Patty's doctor had started giving her oestrogen for her hot flushes, and side-effects were beginning to show. There was a geranium in a pot on Patty's windowsill, when Enid went to break the news to her mother that Walter was finally leaving Rosanne. A geranium! Patty, who never could see the point in pot plants!

All the same, something, if only oestrogen, was now putting a sparkle in Patty's eye, and she turned up at Walter and Enid's wedding in a kind of velvet safari jacket which made her look almost sexy, and when Arthur crossed the room to speak to his ex-wife, she did not turn away, but actually saw the point of shaking his hand, and even laying her cheek against his, in affection and forgiveness.

Enid, in her white velvet trouser suit, saw: and a pang of almost physical pain roared through her, and for a second, just a second, looking at Walter, she saw not her great love but an elderly, paunchy, lecherous stranger. Even though he'd slimmed down quite remarkably during the divorce. It wasn't surprising! Rosanne had behaved like a bitch, and it had told on them both. Nevertheless, people remarked at the wedding that they'd never seen Walter looking so well—or Enid so elegant. He'd somehow scaled down to forty, and she up to thirty. Hardly a difference at all!
Barbara and Bernadette were bridesmaids. Rosanne had been against the idea, out of envy and malice mixed. She hadn't even been prepared to make their dresses, which Enid thought particularly spiteful. 'I'd never have made a bridesmaid's dress for you,' said Patty. 'Not to wear at your father's wedding.' 'That's altogether different,' said Enid, hurt and confused by the way Patty was seeing the war almost as if she, Patty, were Rosanne's ally; more Helene's enemy than Enid's mother.

And then Helene upset her. 'I hope you're not thinking of having children,' she said, during the reception. 'Of course I am,' said Enid. 'Some men can't stand it,' said Helene. 'Your father, for one. Why do you think I never had any?' 'Well, I'm sure he could stand me,' said Enid, with a self-confidence she did not feel. For perhaps he just plain couldn't? Perhaps some of the blame for his departure was Enid's, not Patty's. Perhaps if she'd been nicer her father would never have left? And perhaps, indeed, he wouldn't!

Well, if we can't be nice, we can at least try to be perfect. Enid set out on her journey through life with perfection in mind. Doing better! Oh, how neat the corners of the beds she tucked, how fresh the butter, how crisp the tablecloth! Her curtains were always fully lined, her armpits smooth and washed, never merely sprayed. Enid never let her weapons get rusty. She would do better, thank you, than Patty, or Helene, or Rosanne.

Walter Walther clearly adored his Enid and let the world know it. His colleagues half envied, half pitied him. Walter would ring Enid from the Department twice a day and talk baby-talk at her. Until recently he'd talked to his daughter Barbara in just such a manner. His colleagues came to the conclusion, over many a coffee table, that now the daughter had reached puberty the father, in marrying a girl of roughly the same age, was acting out incest fantasies too terrible to acknowledge. No one mentioned the word love: for this was the new language of the post-war age. If there was to be no hate, how could there be love?

In the meantime, for Walter and Enid, there was perpetual trouble with Rosanne. She insisted at first on staying in the matrimonial home, and it took a lawsuit and some fairly sharp accountants to drive her out: presently she lived with the girls in a little council flat. Oddly enough, it was rather like Patty's. Practical, but somehow depressing. 'You see,' said Enid. 'No gift for living! Poor Walter! What a terrible life she gave him.' In the Great War men gave women money, and women gave men life.

Barbara and Bernadette came to stay at weekends. They had their old rooms. Enid prettified them, and lined the curtains. She was a better mother to Barbara and Bernadette than Rosanne had ever been. Walter said so. Enid remembered their birthdays, and saw to their verrucas and had their hair styled. They looked at her with sullen gratitude, like slaves saved from slaughter.

Rosanne lost her job. Rosanne said—of course, it was because the responsibility of being a one-parent family and earning a living was too much for her, but Enid and Walter knew the loss of her job was just a simple matter of redundancy combined with lack of charm. Bernadette's asthma got worse. 'Of course the poor child's ill,' said Enid. 'With such a mother!' Enid didn't believe in truces. She ignored white flags and went in for the kill.

Enid had a pond built in the garden and entertained Walter's friends on Campari[2] and readings of Shakespeare's sonnets. They were literary people, after all, or claimed to be. 'Couldn't we do without the sonnets?' said Walter.

But Enid insisted on the sonnets, and the friends drifted away. 'It's Rosanne's doing,' said Enid. 'She's turned them against us.' And she twined her white, soft, serpent's arms round his grizzly, stranger body and he believed her. His students, he noticed, seemed less respectful of him than they had been: not as if he had grown younger but they had grown older. Air came through the lecture-room windows, on a hot summer's day, like a sigh. Well, at least he was married, playing honestly and fair, unlike his colleagues, who were for the most part hit-and-run seducers. As for Rosanne, he knew she knew how to look after herself. She always had. A man, in the Great War, usually preferred a woman who couldn't.

'Let's have a baby of our own soon,' said Enid. A baby! He hadn't thought of that. She was his baby. Or was he hers?

'We're so happy,' said Enid. 'You and I. It doesn't matter what the world thinks or says. We were just both a little out of step, that's all, time-wise. God meant us for each other. Don't you feel that?'

He queried her use of the word God, but otherwise agreed with what she said. Her words came as definite instruction from some powerful, knowledgeable source. They flowed, unsullied by doubt. He, being older, had to grope

_____

[2] **Campari** a drink of wine blended with herbs

for meanings. He was too wise, and this could only diffuse his certainty, since wisdom is the acknowledgment of ignorance.

'Of course you should have a baby, Enid,' said Patty. 'Why not?' But she wasn't really thinking. She was having an affair with a mini-cab driver, and had forgotten about Enid. 'Your behaviour is obscene and disgusting,' Enid shouted at her mother. '*He's young.*'
'What's the point in your making all this fuss?' asked Patty. 'I deserve a little happiness in my life, and I'm sure you brought me precious little!'

Enid got pregnant, straight away. Walter went out and got drunk when he heard, with old friends of himself and Rosanne. Enid was so upset by this double disloyalty she went and stayed with her friend Margot for at least three days.

Margot was married and pregnant, too, and by one of Walter Walther's students, who had spots and bad breath. They lived on their grants, and beans and cider. Nevertheless, her husband went with her to the antenatal clinic and they pored over baby books together. Walter Walther took the view, common in the Great War, that the begetting of children was something to do with the one-upmanship of woman against woman, and very little to do with the man.

'Look, Enid,' said Walter, a new Walter, briskly and unkindly, 'you just get on with it by yourself.' Arthur had left Patty to get on with it by herself, too. Her very name, Enid, had been a last-minute choice by Patty with the registrar hovering over her hospital bed, because Arthur just left it to her.

'You can't have everything,' was what Helene said, when Enid murmured a complaint or two. 'You can't have status, money, adoration and what Margot has as well.'
'Why not?' demanded Enid. 'I want *everything!*'

Enid saw herself on a mountain top, a million women bowing down before her, acknowledging her victory. Her foot would be heavy on the necks of those she humbled. That was how it ought to be. She pulled herself together. She knew that, in the Great War, being pregnant could make you or break you. Great prizes were to be won—the best mother, the prettiest child, the whitest white—but much was risked. The enemy could swoop down, slender-waisted and laughing and lively, and deliver any number of mortal wounds. So Enid wore her prettiest clothes, and sighed a little but never grunted when the baby lay on some pelvic nerve or other, and never let Walter suffer a moment because of what he had done to her. (In those pre-pill days men made women pregnant: women didn't just get pregnant.)
His boiled egg and toast soldiers and freshly milled coffee and the single flower in the silver vase were always there on the breakfast table at half past eight sharp and they'd eat together, companionably. Rosanne had slopped Sugar Puffs into bowls for the family breakfast, and they'd eaten among the uncleared children's homework and students' essays. Slut!
Walter was protective. 'We have to take extra special care of you,' he'd say,

helping her across roads. But he seemed a little embarrassed. Something grated: she didn't know what. They ate in rather more often than before.

Then Rosanne, who ought by rights to have been lying punch-drunk in some obscure corner of the battlefield, rose up and delivered a nasty body-blow. Barbara and Bernadette were to come to live with Enid and Walter. Rosanne couldn't cope, in such crowded surroundings. She had a new job, and couldn't always be rushing home for Bernadette's asthma. Could she?

'A new boyfriend, more like,' said Walter, bitterly. Enid restrained from pointing out that Rosanne was an old, old woman with a bad back and hardly in the field for admirers.

Now six perfectly cooked boiled eggs on the table each morning—Bernadette and Barbara demanded two each—is twelve times as difficult to achieve as two. By the time the last one's in, the first one's cooked, but which one is it?

Walter looked at his bowl of Sugar Puffs one morning and said, 'Just like old times,' and the girls looked knowingly and giggled. They looked at Enid and her swelling tum with contempt and pity. They borrowed her clothes and her make-up. They refused to be taken to art galleries, or theatres; they refused even to play Monopoly, let alone Happy Families. They referred to their father as the Old Goat.

Sometimes she hated them. But Walter would not let her. 'Look,' said Walter, 'you did come along and disrupt their lives. You owe them something, at least.' As if it was all nothing to do with him. Which in a way it wasn't. It was between Rosanne and Enid.

Enid locked herself out of the house one day and, though she knew the girls were inside, when she knocked they wouldn't let her in. It was raining. Afterwards they just said they hadn't heard. And she'd fallen and hurt her knee trying to climb in the window, and might have lost the baby. Bernadette threw a bad asthma attack and got all the attention.

Walter spent more and more time in the department. She and he hardly made love at all any more. It didn't seem right.

Enid went into labour at eight o'clock one evening. She rang Walter Walther at the English Department where he said he was, but he wasn't. She rang Margot and wept, and Margot said, 'I don't think I've ever known you cry, Enid,' and Margot's spotty husband said, 'You'll probably find him round at Rosanne's. I wouldn't tell you, if it wasn't an emergency.'

'Yes,' said Barbara and Bernadette. 'He goes round to see Mum quite a lot. We didn't like to tell you because we didn't want to upset you.

'Really,' they said, 'the whole thing was a plot to get rid of us. The thing is, neither of them can stand us.' (Barbara and Bernadette went to one of the large new comprehensive schools, where there were pupil-counsellors, who could explain everything and anything, and were never lost for words.)

Enid screamed and wept all through her labour, not just from pain. They'd never known a noisier mother, they said: and she'd been so quiet and elegant and self-controlled throughout her pregnancy.

Enid gave birth to a little girl. Now in the Great War, the birth of a girl was, understandably, and unlike now, cause for commiseration rather than rejoicing. Nevertheless, Enid rejoiced. And in so doing, abandoned a battle which was really none of her making; she laid down her arms: she kissed her mother and Helene when they came to visit her, clasped her baby and admitted weakness and distress to Barbara and Bernadette, who actually then seemed quite to like her.

Walter Walther did not come home. He stayed with Rosanne. Enid, Barbara and Bernadette lived in the same house, shared suspender belts, shampoo and boyfriends, and looked after baby Belinda. Walter and Rosanne visited, sheepishly, from time to time, and sent money. Enid went back to college and took a degree in psychology, and was later to earn a good living as a research scientist.

Later still she was to become something of a propagandist in the new cold war against men; she wore jeans and a donkey jacket and walked round linked arm-in-arm with women. But that was, perhaps, hardly surprising, so treacherous had the old male allies turned out to be. All the same, yesterday's enemy, tomorrow's friend! Who is to say what will happen next?

[1985]

■ TOPICS FOR DISCUSSION AND WRITING

1. What is the narrator's tone in the first paragraph? By the end of the story, do you share the narrator's attitude (so far as it can be discerned) toward the characters? Exactly what is your attitude toward each major character?

2. The final paragraph informs us that Enid's late friendship with women was "hardly surprising." Did you expect it? Why or why not?

3. Most short stories cover only a brief period of time and contain only a few episodes. What is the effect of packing so much plot into this story?

4. Reviewing Weldon's collection of stories in which "In the Great War" appears, Jan Freeman in the *Boston Globe* commented on "her talent for dialogue, her aphoristic wit, her dexterity at tying up a fable with a neat moral. . . . [Her stories] are bright, shiny boxes that sometimes tick ominously but pop open to reveal a rueful jack-in-the-box." Does "In the Great War" fit this description? (Think about Freeman's words carefully, especially his references to "aphoristic wit," "fable with a neat moral," "tick ominously," and "rueful jack-in-the-box.")

■ RAYMOND CARVER

Raymond Carver (1938–1988) was born in Clatskanie, a logging town in Oregon. In 1963 he graduated from Humboldt State College in northern California and then did further study at the University of Iowa.

His early years were not easy—he married while still in college, divorced a little later, and sometimes suffered from alcoholism. In his last years he found domestic happiness, but he died of cancer at the age of fifty.

As a young man he wrote poetry while working at odd jobs (janitor, delivery man, etc.); later he turned to fiction, though he continued to write poetry. Most of his fiction is of a sort called "minimalist," narrating in a spare, understated style stories about bewildered and sometimes exhausted men and women. His later work, by his own admission, was "larger." (Two of the later stories appear elsewhere in this book.)

Popular Mechanics

Early that day the weather turned and the snow was melting into dirty water. Streaks of it ran down from the little shoulder-high window that faced the backyard. Cars slushed by on the street outside, where it was getting dark. But it was getting dark on the inside too.

He was in the bedroom pushing clothes into a suitcase when she came to the door.

I'm glad you're leaving! I'm glad you're leaving! she said. Do you hear?

He kept on putting his things into the suitcase.

Son of a bitch! I'm so glad you're leaving! She began to cry. You can't even look me in the face, can you?

Then she noticed the baby's picture on the bed and picked it up.

He looked at her and she wiped her eyes and stared at him before turning and going back to the living room.

Bring that back, he said.

Just get your things and get out, she said.

He did not answer. He fastened the suitcase, put on his coat, looked around the bedroom before turning off the light. Then he went out to the living room.

She stood in the doorway of the little kitchen, holding the baby.

I want the baby, he said.

Are you crazy?

No, but I want the baby. I'll get someone to come by for his things.

You're not touching this baby, she said.

The baby had begun to cry and she uncovered the blanket from around his head.

Oh, oh, she said, looking at the baby.

He moved toward her.

For God's sake! she said. She took a step back into the kitchen.

I want the baby.

Get out of here!

She turned and tried to hold the baby over in a corner behind the stove.

But he came up. He reached across the stove and tightened his hands on the baby.

Let go of him, he said.

Get away, get away! she cried.

The baby was red-faced and screaming. In the scuffle they knocked down a flowerpot that hung behind the stove.

He crowded her into the wall then, trying to break her grip. He held on to the baby and pushed with all his weight.

Let go of him, he said.

Don't, she said. You're hurting the baby, she said.

I'm not hurting the baby, he said.

The kitchen window gave no light. In the near-dark he worked on her fisted fingers with one hand and with the other hand he gripped the screaming baby up under an arm near the shoulder.

She felt her fingers being forced open. She felt the baby going from her. No! she screamed just as her hands came loose.

She would have it, this baby. She grabbed for the baby's other arm. She caught the baby around the wrist and leaned back.

But he would not let go. He felt the baby slipping out of his hands and he pulled back very hard.

In this manner, the issue was decided.

[1981]

■ TOPICS FOR DISCUSSION AND WRITING

1. Some readers object to "minimalist" writings (briefly defined in the biographical note on p. 558) on the grounds that the stories (1) lack ideas, (2) do not describe the characters in depth, and (3) are written in a drab style. Does Carver's story seem to you to suffer from these alleged weaknesses? Explain.

2. Here is the first paragraph of the story:

    Early that day the weather turned and the snow was melting into dirty water. Streaks of it ran down from the little shoulder-high window that faced the back yard. Cars slushed by on the street outside, where it was getting dark. But it was getting dark on the inside too.

    When Carver first published the story, the paragraph was slightly different. Here is the earlier version:

    During the day the sun had come out and the snow melted into dirty water. Streaks of water ran down from the little, shoulder-high window that faced the back yard. Cars slushed by on the street outside. It was getting dark, outside and inside.

    How would you account for the changes?

3. The last line—"In this manner, the issue was decided"—in the original version ran thus:

    In this manner they decided the issue.

    Do you consider the small change an improvement? Why, or why not?

4. What do you think happens at the end of the story?
5. The original title was "Mine." Again, what do you think of the change, and why?
6. In an essay of roughly 1000 words compare "Popular Mechanics" with John Cheever's "The Enormous Radio" (p. 273). Some points you might want to consider: the economic and social class of the characters in each story; descriptions of setting; the use of dialogue; the theme of violence.

POETRY

■ WILLIAM SHAKESPEARE

Shakespeare (1564–1616) was born into a middle-class family in Stratford-upon-Avon. Although we have a fair number of records about his life—documents concerning marriage, the birth of children, the purchase of property, and so forth—it is not known exactly why and when he turned to the theater. What we do know, however, is important: He was an actor and a shareholder in a playhouse, and he *did* write the plays that are attributed to him. The dates of some of the plays can be set precisely, but the dates of some others can be only roughly set. *The Taming of the Shrew* probably was written sometime between 1592 and 1594, *Hamlet* between 1600 and 1601. Most of Shakespeare's 154 sonnets were probably written in the late 1590s, but they were not published until 1609.

Sonnet 29

When, in disgrace with Fortune and men's eyes,
I all alone beweep my outcast state,
And trouble deaf heaven with my bootless° cries.
And look upon myself and curse my fate,   4
Wishing me like to one more rich in hope,
Featured like him, like him° with friends possessed,
Desiring this man's art and that man's scope,
With what I most enjoy contented least;   8
Yet in these thoughts myself almost despising,
Haply° I think on thee, and then my state,
Like to the lark at break of day arising
From sullen earth, sings hymns at heaven's gate;   12
    For thy sweet love rememb'red such wealth brings,
    That then I scorn to change my state with kings.
                                      [c. 1600]

3 **bootless** useless 6 **like him, like him** like a second man, like a third man
10 **Haply** perchance

■ TOPICS FOR DISCUSSION AND WRITING

1. Paraphrase the first eight lines. Then, in a sentence, sumamrize the speaker's state of mind to this point in the poem.

2. Summarize the speaker's state of mind in lines 9–12. What does "sullen earth" (line 12) suggest to you?

3. Notice that every line in the poem except line 11 ends with a comma or semicolon, indicating a pause. How does the lack of punctuation at the end of line 11 affect your reading of this line and your understanding of the speaker's emotion?

4. In the last two lines of a sonnet Shakespeare often summarizes the preceding lines. In this sonnet, how does the *structure* (the organization) of the summary differ from that of the statement in the first twelve lines? Why? (Try reading the last lines as if they were reversed. Thus:

   For then I scorn to change my state with kings,
   Since thy sweet love rememb'red such wealth brings.

   Which version do you like better? Why?

5. The "thee" of this poem is almost certainly a man, not a woman. Is the "love" of the poem erotic love, or can it be taken as something like brotherly love or even as loving-kindness?

6. Write a paragraph (or a sonnet) describing how thinking of someone you love—or hate—changes your mood.

Sonnet 116

Let me not to the marriage of true minds
Admit impediments; love is not love
Which alters when it alteration finds,
Or bends with the remover to remove.   4
O, no, it is an ever-fixed mark°
That looks on tempests and is never shaken;
It is the star° to every wand'ring bark,
Whose worth's unknown, although his height be taken.   8
Love's not Time's fool,° though rosy lips and cheeks
Within his bending sickle's compass° come;
Love alters not with his° brief hours and weeks
But bears° it out even to the edge of doom.°   12
   If this be error and upon° me proved,
   I never writ, nor no man ever loved.

                                                        [c. 1600]

5 **ever-fixed mark** seamark, guide to mariners   7 **the star** the North Star   9 **fool** plaything   10 **compass** range, circle   11 **his** Time's   12 **bears** survives   12 **doom** Judgment Day   13 **upon** against

■ TOPICS FOR DISCUSSION AND WRITING

1. Paraphrase (that is, put into your own words) "Let me not to the marriage of true minds / Admit impediments." Is there more than one appropriate meaning of "Admit"?
2. Notice that the poem celebrates "the marriage of true minds," not bodies. In a sentence or two, using only your own words, summarize Shakespeare's idea of the nature of such love, both what it is and what is is not.
3. Paraphrase lines 13–14. What is the speaker's tone here? Would you say that the tone is different from the tone in the rest of the poem?
4. Write a paragraph or a poem defining either love or hate. Or see if you can find such a definition in a popular song. Bring the lyrics to class.

■ JOHN DONNE
_____

John Donne (1572–1631) was born into a Roman Catholic family in England, but in the 1590s he abandoned that faith. In 1615 he became an Anglican priest and soon was known as a great preacher. A hundred and sixty of his sermons survive, including one with the famous line, "No man is an island, entire of itself; every man is a piece of the continent, a part of the main; if a clod be washed away by the sea, Europe is the less . . . ; and therefore never send to know for whom the bell tolls; it tolls for thee." From 1621 until his death he was dean of St. Paul's Cathedral in London. His love poems (often bawdy and cynical) are said to be his early work, and his "Holy Sonnets" (among the greatest religious poems written in English) his later work.

A Valediction: Forbidding Mourning

As virtuous men pass mildly away;
    And whisper to their souls, to go,
Whilst some of their sad friends do say,
    "The breath goes now," and some say, "No":   4

So let us melt, and make no noise.
    No tear-floods, nor sigh-tempests move.
'Twere profanation of our joys
    To tell the laity our love.   8

Moving of the earth° brings harms and fears,
    Men reckon what it did and meant;

_____
9 **Moving of the earth** an earthquake

But trepidation of the spheres,
    Though greater far, is innocent.°   12

Dull sublunary° lovers' love
(Whose soul is sense) cannot admit
Absence, because it doth remove
    Those things which elemented it.   16

But we, by a love so much refined
    That our selves know not what it is,
Inter-assurèd of the mind,
    Care less, eyes, lips, and hands to miss.   20

Our two souls therefore, which are one,
    Though I must go, endure not yet
A breach, but an expansion,
    Like gold to airy thinness beat.   24

If they be two, they are two so
    As stiff twin compasses° are two:
Thy soul, the fixed foot, makes no show
    To move, but doth, if the other do.   28

And though it in the center sit,
    Yet when the other far doth roam,
It leans, and hearkens after it,
    And grows erect, as that comes home.   32

Such wilt thou be to me, who must
    Like the other foot, obliquely run:
Thy firmness makes my circle just,
    And makes me end where I begun.   36

[1611]

■ TOPICS FOR DISCUSSION AND WRITING

1. The first stanza describes the death of "virtuous men." To what is their death compared in the second stanza?
2. Who is the speaker of this poem? To whom does he speak and what is the occasion? Explain the title.
3. What is the meaning of "laity" in line 8? What does it imply about the speaker and his beloved?
4. In the fourth stanza the speaker contrasts the love of "dull sublunary

---

11–12 **But trepidation . . . innocent** But the movement of the heavenly spheres (in Ptolemaic astronomy), though far greater, is harmless   13 **sublunary** under the moon, i.e., earthly   26 **compasses** i.e., a carpenter's compass lovers" (i.e., ordinary mortals) with the love he and his beloved share. What is the difference?

5. In the figure of the carpenter's or draftsperson's compass (lines 25–36) the speaker offers reasons—some stated clearly, some not so clearly— why he will end where he began. In 250 words explain these reasons.

6. In line 35 Donne speaks of his voyage as a "circle." Explain in a paragraph why the circle is traditionally a symbol of perfection.

7. Write a farewell note—or poem—to someone you love (or hate).

■ ANDREW MARVELL
_____

Born in 1621 near Hull in England, Marvell attended Trinity College, Cambridge, and graduated in 1638. During the Civil War he was tutor to the daughter of Sir Thomas Fairfax in Yorkshire at Nun Appleton House, where most of his best-known poems were written. In 1657 he was appointed assistant to John Milton, the Latin Secretary for the Commonwealth. After the Restoration of the monarchy in 1659 until his death, Marvell represented Hull as a member of parliament. Most of his poems were not published until after his death in 1678.

To His Coy Mistress

Had we but world enough, and time,
This coyness, lady, were no crime.
We would sit down, and think which way
To walk, and pass our long love's day.
Thou by the Indian Ganges' side   5
Should'st rubies find: I by the tide
Of Humber° would complain.° I would
Love you ten years before the Flood,
And you should, if you please, refuse   10
Till the conversion of the Jews.
My vegetable° love should grow
Vaster than empires, and more slow.
An hundred years should go to praise
Thine eyes, and on thy forehead gaze:
Two hundred to adore each breast: 15
But thirty thousand to the rest.
An age at least to every part,
And the last age should show your heart.
For, lady, you deserve this state,
Nor would I love at lower rate,   20
    But at my back I always hear
Time's winged chariot hurrying near;

7 **Humber** river in England; **complain** write love poems   11 **vegetable** slowly growing

And yonder all before us lie
Deserts of vast eternity.
Thy beauty shall no more be found,   25
Nor in thy marble vault shall sound
My echoing song; then worms shall try
That long preserved virginity,
And your quaint honor turn to dust,
And into ashes all my lust.   30
The grave's a fine and private place,
But none, I think, do there embrace.
   Now therefore, while the youthful hue
Sits on thy skin like morning dew,
And while thy willing soul transpires   35
At every pore with instant fires,
Now let us sport us while we may;
And now, like am'rous birds of prey,
Rather at once our time devour,
Than languish in his slow-chapt° power,   40
Let us roll all our strength, and all
Our sweetness, up into one ball;
And tear our pleasures with rough strife
Thorough° the iron gates of life.
Thus, though we cannot make our sun   45
Stand still, yet we will make him run.
[1641]

■ TOPICS FOR DISCUSSION AND WRITING

1. What does "coy" mean in the title, and "coyness" in line 2?
2. Do you think that the speaker's claims in lines 1–20 are so inflated that
   we detect behind them a playfully ironic tone? Explain. Why does the
   speaker say in line 8 that he would love "ten years before the Flood,"
   rather than merely "since the Flood"?
3. What do you make of lines 21–24? Why is time behind the speaker, and
   eternity in front of him? Is this "eternity" the same as the period discussed in lines 1–20? Discuss the change in the speaker's tone after line
   20.

■ EDGAR ALLAN POE

   Edgar Allan Poe (1809–1849) was the son of traveling actors. His
father abandoned the family almost immediately, and his mother died
when Poe was two. The child was adopted—though never legally—by a
prosperous merchant and his wife in Richmond. The tensions were great,
aggravated by Poe's drinking and heavy gambling, and in 1827 Poe left
Richmond for Boston. He wrote, served briefly in the army, attended
West Point but left within a year, and became an editor for the remaining

40 **slow-chapt** slowly devouring 44 **Thorough** through

eighteen years of his life. It was during these years, too, that he wrote the poems, essays, and fiction—especially detective stories and horror stories—that have made him famous.

*To Helen**

Helen, thy beauty is to me
    Like those Nicean° barks of yore,
That gently, o'er a perfumed sea,
    The weary, way-worn wanderer bore
    To his own native shore.   5

On desperate seas long wont to roam,
    Thy hyacinth hair,° thy classic face,
Thy Naiad° airs have brought me home
    To the glory that was Greece
And the grandeur that was Rome.   10

Lo! in yon brilliant window-niche
    How statue-like I see thee stand!
    The agate lamp within thy hand,
Ah! Psyche,° from the regions which
    Are Holy Land!°   15
                   [1831–1843]

■   TOPICS FOR DISCUSSION AND WRITING

1.   In the first stanza, to what is Helen's beauty compared? To whom does the speaker apparently compare himself? What does "wayworn" in line 4 suggest to you? To what in the speaker's experience might the "native shore" in line 5 correspond?
2.   What do you take "desperate seas" to mean in line 6, and who has been traveling them? To what are they contrasted in line 8? How does "home" seem to be defined in this stanza (stanza 2)?
3.   What further light is shed on the speaker's home or destination in stanza 3?
4.   Do you think that "To Helen" can be a love poem and also a poem about spiritual beauty or about the love of art? Explain.

*Helen Helen of Troy, considered the most beautiful woman of ancient times
2 Nicean perhaps referring to Nicea, an ancient city associated with the god Dionysus, or perhaps meaning "victorious," from Nike, Greek goddess of Victory   7 hyacinth hair naturally curling hair, like that of Hyacinthus, beautiful Greek youth beloved by Apollo   8 Naiad a nymph associated with lakes and streams   14 Psyche Greek for "soul"   15 Holy Land ancient Rome or Athens, i.e., a sacred realm of art

■ ROBERT BROWNING

Born in a suburb of London into a middle-class family, Browning
(1812–1889) was educated primarily at home, where he read widely. For
a while he wrote for the stage, and in 1846 he married Elizabeth
Barrett—herself a poet—and lived with her in Italy until her death in
1861. He then returned to England and settled in London with their son.
Regarded as one of the most distinguished poets of the Victorian period,
he is buried in Westminster Abbey.

Porphyria's Lover

The rain set early in tonight,
    The sullen wind was soon awake,
It tore the elm-tops down for spite,
    And did its worst to vex the lake:
I listened with heart fit to break.   5
When glided in Porphyria; straight
    She shut the cold out and the storm,
And kneeled and made the cheerless grate
    Blaze up, and all the cottage warm;
Which done, she rose, and from her form   10
Withdrew the dripping cloak and shawl,
    And laid her soiled gloves by, untied
Her hat and let the damp hair fall,
    And, last, she sat down by my side
And called me. When no voice replied,   15
She put my arm about her waist,
    And made her smooth white shoulder bare
And all her yellow hair displaced,
    And stooping, made my cheek lie there,
And spread, o'er all, her yellow hair,   20
Murmuring how she loved me—she
    Too weak, for all her heart's endeavor,
To set its struggling passion free
    From pride, and vainer ties dissever,
And give herself to me forever.   25
But passion sometimes would prevail,
    Nor could tonight's gay feast restrain
A sudden thought of one so pale
    For love of her, and all in vain:
So, she was come through wind and rain.   30
Be sure I looked up at her eyes
    Happy and proud; at last I knew
Porphyria worshiped me; surprise
    Made my heart swell, and still it grew
While I debated what to do.   35

That moment she was mine, mine, fair,
    Perfectly pure and good: I found
A thing to do, and all her hair
    In one long yellow string I wound
Three times her little throat around,   40
And strangled her. No pain felt she;
    I am quite sure she felt no pain.
As a shut bud that holds a bee,
    I warily opened her lids: again
Laughed the blue eyes without a stain.   45
And I untightened next the tress
    About her neck; her cheek once more
Blushed bright beneath my burning kiss:
    I propped her head up as before,
Only, this time my shoulder bore   50
Her head, which droops upon it still:
    The smiling rosy little head,
So glad it has its utmost will,
    That all it scorned at once is fled,
And I, its love, am gained instead!   55
Porphyria's love: she guessed not how
 Her darling one wish would be heard.
And thus we sit together now,
    And all night long we have not stirred,
And yet God has not said a word!

[1834]

■ TOPICS FOR DISCUSSION AND WRITING

1.   Exactly why did the speaker murder Porphyria?
2.   You are a lawyer assigned to defend the speaker against the charge of
    murder. In 500 to 750 words, write your defense.

My Last Duchess

FERRARA*

That's my last Duchess painted on the wall,
Looking as if she were alive. I call
That piece a wonder, now; Frà Pandolf's° hands
Worked busily a day, and there she stands.
Will't please you sit and look at her? I said   5
"Frà Pandolf" by design, for never read
Strangers like you that pictured countenance,

   *Ferrara** town in Italy
3 **Frà Pandolf** a fictitious painter

The depth and passion of its earnest glance,
But to myself they turned (since none puts by
The curtain I have drawn for you, but I)   10
And seemed as they would ask me, if they durst,
How such a glance came there; so, not the first
Are you to turn and ask thus. Sir, 'twas not
Her husband's presence only, called that spot
Of joy into the Duchess' cheek; perhaps   15
Frà Pandolf chanced to say "Her mantle laps
Over my lady's wrist too much," or, "Paint
Must never hope to reproduce the faint
Half-flush that dies along her throat." Such stuff
Was courtesy, she thought, and cause enough   20
For calling up that spot of joy. She had
A heart—how shall I say?—too soon made glad,
Too easily impressed; she liked whate'er
She looked on, and her looks went everywhere.
Sir, 'twas all one! My favor at her breast,   25
The dropping of the daylight in the west,
The bough of cherries some officious fool
Broke in the orchard for her, the white mule
She rode with round the terrace—all and each
Would draw from her alike the approving speech,   30
Or blush, at least. She thanked men—good! but thanked
Somehow—I know not how—as if she ranked
My gift of a nine-hundred-years-old name
With anybody's gift. Who'd stoop to blame
This sort of trifling? Even had you skill   35
In speech—(which I have not)—to make your will
Quite clear to such an one, and say, "Just this
Or that in you disgusts me; here you miss,
Or there exceed the mark"—and if she let
Herself be lessoned so, nor plainly set   40
Her wits to yours, forsooth, and made excuse,
—E'en then would be some stooping; and I choose
Never to stoop. Oh, Sir, she smiled, no doubt,
Whene'er I passed her; but who passed without
Much the same smile? This grew; I gave commands;   45
Then all smiles stopped together. There she stands
As if alive. Will't please you rise? We'll meet
The company below, then. I repeat,
The Count your master's known munificence
Is ample warrant that no just pretense   50
Of mine for dowry will be disallowed;
Though his fair daughter's self, as I avowed
At starting, is my object. Nay, we'll go
Together down, Sir. Notice Neptune, though,   55

Taming a sea-horse, thought a rarity,
Which Claus of Innsbruck° cast in bronze for me!

[1842]

■ TOPICS FOR DISCUSSION AND WRITING

1. Who is speaking to whom? On what occasion?
2. What words or lines especially convey the speaker's arrogance? What is
    our attitude toward the speaker? Loathing? Fascination? Respect?
    Explain.
3. The time and place are Renaissance Italy; how do they affect our atti-
    tude toward the duke? What would be the effect if the poem were set in
    the twentieth century?
4. Years after writing this poem, Browning explained that the duke's
    "commands" (line 45) were "that she should be put to death, or he
    might have had her shut up in a convent." Should the poem have been
    more explicit? Does Browning's later uncertainty indicate that the poem
    is badly thought out? Suppose we did not have Browning's comment on
    line 45; could the line then mean only that he commanded her to stop
    smiling and that she obeyed? Explain.
5. Elizabeth Barrett (not yet Mrs. Browning) wrote to Robert Browning
    that it was not "by the dramatic medium that poets teach most impres-
    sively. . . . It is too difficult for the common reader to analyze, and to
    discern between the vivid and the earnest." She went on, urging him to
    teach "in the directest and most impressive way, the mask thrown off."
    What teaching, if any, is in this poem? If there is any teaching here,
    would it be more impressive if Browning had not used the mask of a
    Renaissance duke? Explain.
6. You are the envoy, writing to the Count, your master, a 500-word
    report of your interview with the duke. What do you write?
7. You are the envoy, writing to the count, advising—as diplomatically as
    possible—for or against this marriage. Notice that this exercise, unlike
    #6, which calls for a *report*, calls for an *argument*.

■ EDNA ST. VINCENT MILLAY

Edna St. Vincent Millay (1892–1950) was born in Rockland, Maine.
Even as a child she wrote poetry, and by the time she graduated from
Vassar College (1917) she had achieved some note as a poet. Millay settled for a while in Greenwich Village, a center of Bohemian activity in
New York City, where she wrote, performed in plays, and engaged in
feminist causes. In 1923, the year she married, she became the first
woman to win the Pulitzer Prize for Poetry. Numerous other awards followed. Though she is best known as a lyric poet—especially as a writer
of sonnets—she also wrote memorable political poetry and nature poetry
as well as short stories, plays, and a libretto for an opera.

57 **Claus of Innsbruck** a fictitious sculptor

The Spring and the Fall

In the spring of the year, in the spring of the year,
I walked the road beside my dear.
The trees were black where the bark was wet.
I see them yet, in the spring of the year.
He broke me a bough of the blossoming peach   5
That was out of the way and hard to reach.

In the fall of the year, in the fall of the year,
I walked the road beside my dear.
The rooks went up with a raucous trill.
I hear them still, in the fall of the year.   10
He laughed at all I dared to praise,
And broke my heart, in little ways.

Year be springing or year be falling,
The bark will drip and the birds be calling.
There's much that's fine to see and hear   15
In the spring of a year, in the fall of a year.
'Tis not love's going hurts my days,
But that it went in little ways.

[1923]

■ TOPICS FOR DISCUSSION AND WRITING

1. The first stanza describes the generally happy beginning of a love story.
   Where do you find the first hint of an unhappy ending?
2. Describe the rhyme scheme of the first stanza, including internal rhymes.
   Do the second and third stanzas repeat the pattern, or are there some
   variations? What repetition of sounds other than rhyme do you note?
3. Paraphrase the last two lines. How do you react to them; that is, do you
   find the conclusion surprising, satisfying (or unsatisfying), recognizable
   from your own experience, anticlimactic, or what?
4. In two or three paragraphs explain how the imagery of the poem contributes to its meaning.

Love Is Not All: It Is Not Meat nor Drink

Love is not all: it is not meat nor drink
Nor slumber nor a roof against the rain;
Nor yet a floating spar to men that sink
And rise and sink and rise and sink again;   4
Love can not fill the thickened lung with breath,
Nor clean the blood, nor set the fractured bone;
Yet many a man is making friends with death
Even as I speak, for lack of love alone.   8

It well may be that in a difficult hour,
Pinned down by pain and moaning for release,
Or nagged by want past resolution's power,
I might be driven to sell your love for peace,   12
Or trade the memory of this night for food.
It well may be. I do not think I would.

[1931]

■ TOPICS FOR DISCUSSION AND WRITING

1. "Love Is Not All" is a sonnet. Using your own words, briefly summarize
    the argument of the octet (the first 8 lines). Next, paraphrase the sestet,
    line by line. On the whole, does the sestet repeat the idea of the octet,
    or does it add a new idea? Whom did you imagine to be speaking the oc-
    tet? What does the sestet add to your knowledge of the speaker and the
    occasion? (And how did you paraphrase line 11?)
2. The first and last lines of the poem consist of words of one syllable, and
    both lines have a distinct pause in the middle. Do you imagine the lines
    to be spoken in the same tone of voice? If not, can you describe the
    difference and account for it?
3. Lines 7 and 8 appear to mean that the absence of love can be a cause of
    death. To what degree do you believe that to be true?
4. Would you call "Love Is Not All" a love poem? Why or why not? Describe
    the kind of person who might include the poem in a love letter or valen-
    tine, or who would be happy to receive it. (One of our friends recited it
    at her wedding. What do you think of that idea?)

■ ROBERT FROST

Robert Frost (1874–1963) was born in California. After his father's death
in 1885 Frost's mother brought the family to New England, where she taught
in high schools in Massachusetts and New Hampshire. Frost studied for part
of one term at Dartmouth College in New Hampshire, then did odd jobs (including teaching), and from 1897 to 1899 was enrolled as a special student at
Harvard. He later farmed in New Hampshire, published a few poems in local
newspapers, left the farm and taught again, and in 1912 left for England,
where he hoped to achieve more popular success as a writer. By 1915 he
had won a considerable reputation, and he returned to the United States,
settling on a farm in New Hampshire and cultivating the image of the
country-wise farmer-poet. In fact he was well read in the classics, in the
Bible, and in English and American literature.

Among Frost's many comments about literature, here are three:
"Writing is unboring to the extent that it is dramatic"; "Every poem
is . . . a figure of the will braving alien entanglements"; and, finally, a poem
"begins in delight and ends in wisdom. . . . It runs a course of lucky events,
and ends in a clarification of life—not necessarily a great clarification, such
as sects and cults are founded on, but in a momentary stay against
confusion."

The Silken Tent

She is as in a field a silken tent
At midday when a sunny summer breeze
Has dried the dew and all its ropes relent,
So that in guys it gently sways at ease,   4
And its supporting central cedar pole,
That is its pinnacle to heavenward
And signifies the sureness of the soul,
Seems to owe naught to any single cord,   8
But strictly held by none, is loosely bound
By countless silken ties of love and thought
To everything on earth the compass round,
And only by one's going slightly taut   12
In the capriciousness of summer air
Is of the slightest bondage made aware.

                                    [1943]

■ TOPICS FOR DISCUSSION AND WRITING

1. The second line places the scene at "midday" in "summer." In addition
    to giving us the concreteness of a setting, do these words help to charac-
    terize the woman whom the speaker describes? If so, how?
2. The tent is supported by "guys" (not men, but the cords or "ties" of line
    10) and by its "central cedar pole." What does Frost tell us about these
    ties? What does he tell us about the pole?
3. What do you make of lines 12–14?
4. In a sentence, a paragraph, or a poem, construct a simile that explains a
    relationship.

■ ADRIENNE RICH

Adrienne Rich, born in 1929 in Baltimore, was educated at Radcliffe
College. Her first book of poems, *A Change of World*, published in 1951
when she was still an undergraduate, was selected by W. H. Auden for
the Yale Series of Younger Poets. In 1953 she married an economist and
had three sons, but as she indicates in several books, she felt confined by
the full-time domestic role that she was expected to play, and the marriage did not last. Much of her poetry is concerned with issues of gender
and power. When her ninth book, *Diving into the Wreck* (1973), won the
National Book Award, Rich accepted the award not as an individual but on
behalf of women everywhere.

Diving into the Wreck

First having read the book of myths,
and loaded the camera,
and checked the edge of the knife-blade,

I put on
the body-armor of black rubber   5
the absurd flippers
the grave and awkward mask.
I am having to do this
not like Cousteau° with his
assiduous team   10
aboard the sun-flooded schooner
but here alone.

There is a ladder.
The ladder is always there
hanging innocently   15
close to the side of the schooner.
We know what it is for,
we who have used it.
Otherwise
it's a piece of maritime floss   20
some sundry equipment.

I go down.
Rung after rung and still
the oxygen immerses me
the blue light   25
the clear atoms

of our human air.
I go down.
My flippers cripple me,
I crawl like an insect down the ladder   30
and there is no one
to tell me when the ocean
will begin.

First the air is blue and then
it is bluer and then green and then   35
black I am blacking out and yet
my mask is powerful
it pumps my blood with power
the sea is another story
the sea is not a question of power   40
I have to learn alone
to turn my body without force
in the deep element.

And now: it is easy to forget
what I came for   45

9 **Cousteau** Jacques Cousteau (b. 1910) French underwater explorer

among so many who have always
lived here
swaying their crenellated fans
between the reefs
and besides   50
you breathe differently down here.

I came to explore the wreck.
The words are purposes.
The words are maps.
I came to see the damage that was done   55
and the treasures that prevail.
I stroke the beam of my lamp
slowly along the flank
of something more permanent
than fish or weed   60

the thing I came for:
the wreck and not the story of the wreck
the thing itself and not the myth
the drowned face always staring
toward the sun   65
the evidence of damage

worn by salt and sway into this threadbare beauty
the ribs of the disaster
curving their assertion
among the tentative haunters.   70

This is the place.
And I am here, the mermaid whose dark hair
streams black, the merman in his armored body
We circle silently
about the wreck   75
we dive into the hold.
I am she: I am he

whose drowned face sleeps with open eyes
whose breasts still bear the stress
whose silver, copper, vermeil cargo lies   80
obscurely inside barrels
half-wedged and left to rot
we are the half-destroyed instruments
that once held to a course
the water-eaten log   85
the fouled compass

We are, I am, you are
by cowardice or courage
the one who find our way

back to this scene   90
carrying a knife, a camera
a book of myths
in which
our names do not appear.

[1973]

■ TOPICS FOR DISCUSSION AND WRITING

1. Do you think the "wreck" can be defined fairly precisely? In any case, what do you think the wreck is?

2. In lines 62–63 the speaker says that she came to explore "the wreck and not the story of the wreck / the thing itself and not the myth." Lines 1 and 92 speak of a "book of myths." What sort of "myths" do you think the poet is talking about?

3. In line 72 the speaker is a mermaid; in line 73, a merman; in lines 74 and 76, "we"; and in line 77, "I am she: I am he." What do you make of this?

DRAMA

■ WILLIAM SHAKESPEARE

       Shakespeare (1564–1616) was born into a middle-class family in Stratford-upon-Avon. Although we have a fair number of records about his life—documents concerning marriage, the birth of children, the purchase of property, and so forth—it is not known exactly why and when he turned to the theater. What we do know, however, is important: He was an actor and a shareholder in a playhouse, and he *did* write the plays that are attributed to him. The dates of some of the plays can be set precisely, but the dates of some others can be only roughly set. *The Taming of the Shrew* probably was written sometime between 1592 and 1594, *Hamlet* between 1600 and 1601. Most of Shakespeare's 154 sonnets were probably written in the late 1590s, but they were not published until 1609.

The Taming of the Shrew

[Dramatis Personae

Induction (and ending of Act I, Scene i)
     CHRISTOPHER SLY, *a tinker*
     HOSTESS *of an alehouse*
     A LORD

HUNTSMEN *and* SERVANTS *of the Lord*
PLAYERS *in a traveling company*
BARTHOLOMEW, *a page*

Acts I–V
BAPTISTA MINOLA, *of Padua, father of Kate and Bianca*
KATE, *the shrew*
BIANCA
PETRUCHIO, *of Verona, suitor of Kate*
LUCENTIO (*Cambio*) ⎫
GREMIO, *a pantaloon* ⎬ *suitors of Bianca*
HORTENSIO (*Litio*) ⎭
VINCENTIO, *of Pisa, father of Lucentio*
A PEDANT (*impersonating Vincentio*)
TRANIO (*later impersonating* ⎫
    Lucentio) ⎬ *servants of Lucentio*
BIONDELLO ⎭
GRUMIO ⎫
CURTIS ⎬ *servants of Petruchio*
NATHANIEL, NICHOLAS
JOSEPH, PHILIP, PETER ⎭
A TAILOR
A HABERDASHER
A WIDOW
SERVANTS *of Baptista and Lucentio*

Scene: Warwick (Induction);
Padua; the country near Verona]

Scene I. [*Outside rural alehouse.*]

Enter HOSTESS *and* BEGGAR, CHRISTOPHERO SLY.

SLY. I'll pheeze°[1] you, in faith.
HOSTESS. A pair of stocks,° you rogue!
SLY. Y'are a baggage, the Slys are no rogues. Look in the
    chronicles: we came in with Richard° Conqueror. There-
    fore, *paucas pallabris;*° let the world slide.° Sessa!°   5
HOSTESS. You will not pay for the glasses you have burst?
SLY. No, not a denier.° Go, by St. Jeronimy,° go to thy cold
    bed and warm thee.

---

[1] The degree sign (°) indicates a footnote, which is keyed to the text by line
number. Text references are printed in **boldface**; the annotation follows in roman type.
Ind.i.1 **pheeze** do for (cf. *faze*) 2 **stocks** (threatened punishment) 4 **Richard** (he
means William) 5 *paucas pallabris* few words (Spanish *pocas palabras*) 5 **slide** go
by (proverb; cf. Ind.ii.143) 5 **Sessa** scram (?) shut up (?) 7 **denier** very small coin
(cf. "a copper") 7 **Jeronimy** (Sly's oath inaccurately reflects a line in Kyd's *Spanish
Tragedy*)

HOSTESS. I know my remedy: I must go fetch the thirdbor-
  ough.°   [*Exit.*]   10
SLY. Third or fourth or fifth borough, I'll answer him, by law.
  I'll not budge an inch, boy;° let him come and kindly.°
                                              Falls asleep.
            Wind° horns. Enter a LORD *from hunting,*
                        with his train.
LORD. Huntsman, I charge thee, tender° well my hounds.
  Broach° Merriman—the poor cur is embossed°—
  And couple Clowder with the deep-mouthed brach.°   15
  Saw'st thou not, boy, how Silver made it good
  At the hedge-corner in the coldest fault?°
  I would not lose the dog for twenty pound.
FIRST HUNTSMAN. Why, Bellman is as good as he, my lord;
  He cried upon it at the merest loss°   20
  And twice today picked out the dullest scent.
  Trust me, I take him for the better dog.
LORD. Thou art a fool. If Echo were as fleet,
  I would esteem him worth a dozen such.
  But sup them well and look unto them all.   25
  Tomorrow I intend to hunt again.
FIRST HUNTSMAN. I will, my lord.
LORD. What's here? One dead or drunk? See, doth he
  breathe?
SECOND HUNTSMAN. He breathes, my lord. Were he not
  warmed with ale,
  This were a bed but cold to sleep so soundly.   30
LORD. O monstrous beast, how like a swine he lies!
  Grim death, how foul and loathsome is thine image!
  Sirs, I will practice on° this drunken man.
  What think you, if he were conveyed to bed,
  Wrapped in sweet clothes, rings put upon his fingers,   35
  A most delicious banquet by his bed,
  And brave° attendants near him when he wakes—
  Would not the beggar then forget himself?
FIRST HUNTSMAN. Believe me, lord, I think he cannot choose.
SECOND HUNTSMAN. It would seem strange unto him when he waked. 40
LORD. Even as a flatt'ring dream or worthless fancy.
  Then take him up and manage well the jest.
  Carry him gently to my fairest chamber
  And hang it round with all my wanton° pictures;
  Balm° his foul head in warm distillèd waters   45

9–10 **thirdborough** constable 12 **boy** wretch 12 **kindly** by all means
12.s.d. **Wind** blow 13 **tender** look after 14 **Broach** bleed, i.e., medicate (some
editors emend to *Breathe*) 14 **embossed** foaming at the mouth 15 **brach** hunting
bitch 17 **fault** lost ("cold") scent 20 **cried...loss** gave cry despite complete loss (of
scent) 33 **practice on** play a trick on 37 **brave** well dressed 44 **wanton**
roguish 45 **Balm** bathe

And burn sweet wood to make the lodging sweet.
Procure me music ready when he wakes
To make a dulcet° and a heavenly sound;
And if he chance to speak, be ready straight°
And with a low submissive reverence   50
Say, "What is it your honor will command?"
Let one attend him with a silver basin
Full of rose water and bestrewed with flowers;
Another bear the ewer, the third a diaper,°
And say, "Will't please your lordship cool your hands?"   55
Some one be ready with a costly suit
And ask him what apparel he will wear,
Another tell him of his hounds and horse
And that his lady mourns at his disease.
Persuade him that he hath been lunatic,   60
And when he says he is,° say that he dreams,
For he is nothing but a mighty lord.
This do, and do it kindly,° gentle sirs.
It will be pastime passing excellent
If it be husbanded with modesty.°   65

FIRST HUNTSMAN. My lord, I warrant you we will play our part
 As° he shall think by our true diligence
 He is no less than what we say he is.

LORD. Take him up gently and to bed with him,
 And each one to his office° when he wakes.   70
      [SLY *is carried out*.] *Sound trumpets.*
 Sirrah,° go see what trumpet 'tis that sounds.
        [*Exit* SERVINGMAN.]
 Belike° some noble gentleman that means,
 Traveling some journey, to repose him here.
      Enter SERVINGMAN.
 How now? Who is it?

SERVINGMAN.   An't° please your honor, players
 That offer service to your lordship.   75
      Enter PLAYERS.

LORD. Bid them come near.
     Now, fellows, you are welcome.

PLAYERS. We thank your honor.

LORD. Do you intend to stay with me tonight?

A PLAYER. So please your lordship to accept our duty.°

LORD. With all my heart. This fellow I remember   80
 Since once he played a farmer's eldest son;
 'Twas where you wooed the gentlewoman so well.

---

48 **dulcet** sweet 49 **straight** without delay 54 **diaper** towel 61 **is** i.e., is "lunatic"
now 63 **kindly** naturally 65 **husbanded with modesty** carried out with modera-
tion 67 **As** so that 70 **office** assignment 71 **Sirrah** (term of address used to
inferiors) 72 **Belike** likely 74 **An't** if it 79 **duty** respectful greeting

I have forgot your name, but sure that part
Was aptly fitted° and naturally performed.
SECOND PLAYER. I think 'twas Soto° that your honor means.   85
LORD. 'Tis very true; thou didst it excellent.
    Well, you are come to me in happy° time,
    The rather for° I have some sport in hand
    Wherein your cunning° can assist me much.
    There is a lord will hear you play tonight.   90
    But I am doubtful of your modesties,°
    Lest over-eyeing° of his odd behavior—
    For yet his honor never heard a play—
    You break into some merry passion°
    And so offend him, for I tell you, sirs,   95
    If you should smile he grows impatient.
A PLAYER. Fear not, my lord, we can contain ourselves
    Were he the veriest antic° in the world.
LORD. Go, sirrah, take them to the buttery°
    And give them friendly welcome every one.   100
    Let them want° nothing that my house affords.
                              Exit one with the PLAYERS.
    Sirrah, go you to Barthol'mew my page
    And see him dressed in all suits° like a lady.
    That done, conduct him to the drunkard's chamber
    And call him "madam"; do him obeisance.   105
    Tell him from me—as he will° win my love—
    He bear himself with honorable action
    Such as he hath observed in noble ladies
    Unto their lords, by them accomplishèd.°
    Such duty to the drunkard let him do   110
    With soft low tongue and lowly courtesy,
    And say, "What is't your honor will command
    Wherein your lady and your humble wife
    May show her duty and make known her love?"
    And then, with kind embracements, tempting kisses,   115
    And with declining head into his bosom,
    Bid him shed tears, as being overjoyed
    To see her noble lord restored to health
    Who for this seven years hath esteemèd him
    No better than a poor and loathsome beggar.   120
    And if the boy have not a woman's gift
    To rain a shower of commanded tears,

---

84 **aptly fitted** well suited (to you) 85 **Soto** (in John Fletcher's *Women Pleased*, 1620;
reference possibly inserted here later) 87 **in happy** at the right 88 **The rather for**
especially because 89 **cunning** talent 91 **modesties** self-restraint 92 **over-eyeing**
seeing 94 **merry passion** fit of merriment 98 **antic** odd person 99 **buttery** liquor
pantry, bar 101 **want** lack 103 **suits** respects (with pun) 106 **as he will** if he
wishes to 109 **by them accomplishèd** i.e., as carried out by the ladies

An onion will do well for such a shift,°
Which in a napkin° being close conveyed°
Shall in despite° enforce a watery eye.   125
See this dispatched with all the haste thou canst;
Anon° I'll give thee more instructions.

                                            Exit a SERVINGMAN.

I know the boy will well usurp° the grace,
Voice, gait, and action of a gentlewoman.
I long to hear him call the drunkard husband,   130
And how my men will stay themselves from laughter
When they do homage to this simple peasant.
I'll in to counsel them; haply° my presence
May well abate the over-merry spleen°
Which otherwise would grow into extremes.   [*Exeunt.*]   135

[Scene II. *Bedroom in the* LORD's *house.*]

Enter aloft° the Drunkard [SLY] *with* ATTENDANTS—
*some with apparel, basin and ewer, and
other appurtenances—and* LORD.

SLY. For God's sake, a pot of small° ale!
FIRST SERVINGMAN. Will't please your lordship drink a cup of sack?°
SECOND SERVINGMAN. Will't please your honor taste of these conserves?°
THIRD SERVINGMAN. What raiment will your honor wear today?
SLY. I am Christophero Sly; call not me "honor" nor "lord-   5
    ship." I ne'er drank sack in my life, and if you give me
    any conserves, give me conserves of beef.° Ne'er ask
    me what raiment I'll wear, for I have no more doub-
    lets° than backs, no more stockings than legs nor no
    more shoes than feet—nay, sometime more feet   10
    than shoes or such shoes as my toes look through the
    overleather.
LORD. Heaven cease this idle humor° in your honor!
    O that a mighty man of such descent,
    Of such possessions and so high esteem,   15
    Should be infusèd with so foul a spirit!
SLY. What, would you make me mad? Am not I Christopher
    Sly, old Sly's son of Burton-heath,° by birth a peddler,
    by education a cardmaker,° by transmutation a bear-
    herd,° and now by present profession a tinker? Ask   20

123 **shift** purpose   124 **napkin** handkerchief   124 **close conveyed** secretly carried
125 **Shall in despite** can't fail to   127 **Anon** then   128 **usurp** take on   133 **haply**
perhaps   134 **spleen** spirit   Ind.ii.s.d. **aloft** (on balcony above stage at back)
1 **small** thin, diluted (inexpensive)   2 **sack** imported sherry (costly)   3 **conserves**
i.e., of fruit   7 **conserves of beef** salt beef   8-9 **doublets** close-fitting jackets   13
idle humor unreasonable fantasy   18 **Burton-heath** (probably Barton-on-the Heath,
south of Stratford)   19 **cardmaker** maker of cards, or combs, for arranging wool fibers
before spinning   19-20 **bearherd** leader of a tame bear

Marian Hacket, the fat ale-wife of Wincot,° if she
she know me not. If she say I am not fourteen pence on
the score° for sheer ale,° score me up for the lying'st
knave in Christendom. What, I am not bestraught!°
Here's—   25
THIRD SERVINGMAN. O, this it is that makes your lady mourn.
SECOND SERVINGMAN. O, this is it that makes your servants droop.
LORD. Hence comes it that your kindred shuns your house
    As beaten hence by your strange lunacy.
    O noble lord, bethink thee of thy birth,   30
    Call home thy ancient thoughts° from banishment
    And banish hence these abject lowly dreams.
    Look how thy servants do attend on thee,
    Each in his office ready at thy beck.
    Wilt thou have music? Hark, Apollo° plays,   *Music.*   35
    And twenty cagèd nightingales do sing.
    Or wilt thou sleep? We'll have thee to a couch
    Softer and sweeter than the lustful bed
    On purpose trimmed up for Semiramis.°
    Say thou wilt walk, we will bestrow° the ground.   40
    Or wilt thou ride? Thy horses shall be trapped,°
    Their harness studded all with gold and pearl.
    Dost thou love hawking? Thou hast hawks will soar
    Above the morning lark. Or wilt thou hunt?
    Thy hounds shall make the welkin° answer them.   45
    And fetch shrill echoes from the hollow earth.
FIRST SERVINGMAN. Say thou wilt course,° thy greyhounds are as swift
    As breathèd° stags, ay, fleeter than the roe.°
SECOND SERVINGMAN. Dost thou love pictures? We will fetch thee
        straight
    Adonis° painted by a running brook   50
    And Cytherea all in sedges° hid,
    Which seem to move and wanton° with her breath
    Even as the waving sedges play with wind.
LORD. We'll show thee Io° as she was a maid
    And how she was beguilèd and surprised,   55
    As lively° painted as the deed was done.

21 **Wincot** village near Stratford (some Hackets lived there)   23 **score** charge account
23 **sheer ale** ale alone (?) undiluted ale (?)   24 **bestraught** distraught, crazy
31 **ancient thoughts** original sanity   35 **Apollo** here, god of music   39 **Semiramis**
mythical Assyrian queen, noted for beauty and sexuality (cf. *Titus Andronicus*, II.i.22,
II.iii.118)   40 **bestrow** cover   41 **trapped** decorated   45 **welkin** sky   47 **course** hunt
hares   48 **breathèd** having good wind   48 **roe** small deer   50 **Adonis** young hunter
loved by Venus (Cytherea) and killed by wild boar   51 **sedges** grasslike plant growing in
marshy places   52 **wanton** sway sinuously   54 **Io** mortal loved by Zeus and changed
into a heifer   56 **lively** lifelike

THIRD SERVINGMAN. Or Daphne° roaming through a thorny wood,
    Scratching her legs that one shall swear she bleeds,
    And at that sight shall sad Apollo weep,
    So workmanly the blood and tears are drawn.   60
LORD. Thou art a lord and nothing but a lord.
    Thou hast a lady far more beautiful
    Than any woman in this waning° age.
FIRST SERVINGMAN. And till the tears that she hath shed for thee
    Like envious floods o'errun her lovely face,   65
    She was the fairest creature in the world,
    And yet° she is inferior to none.
SLY. Am I a lord, and have I such a lady?
    Or do I dream? Or have I dreamed till now?
    I do not sleep: I see, I hear, I speak,   70
    I smell sweet savors and I feel soft things.
    Upon my life, I am a lord indeed
    And not a tinker nor Christopher Sly.
    Well, bring our lady hither to our sight,
    And once again a pot o' th' smallest° ale.   75
SECOND SERVINGMAN. Will't please your mightiness to wash your hands?
    O, how we joy to see your wit° restored!
    O, that once more you knew but what you are!
    These fifteen years you have been in a dream,
    Or when you waked so waked as if you slept.   80
SLY. These fifteen years! By my fay,° a goodly nap.
    But did I never speak of° all that time?
FIRST SERVINGMAN. O yes, my lord, but very idle words,
    For though you lay here in this goodly chamber,
    Yet would you say ye were beaten out of door   85
    And rail upon the hostess of the house°
    And say you would present her at the leet°
    Because she brought stone jugs and no sealed° quarts.
    Sometimes you would call out for Cicely Hacket.
SLY. Ay, the woman's maid of the house.   90
THIRD SERVINGMAN. Why, sir, you know no house nor no such maid
    Nor no such men as you have reckoned up,
    As Stephen Sly° and old John Naps of Greece,°
    And Peter Turph and Henry Pimpernell,
    And twenty more such names and men as these   95
    Which never were nor no man ever saw.
SLY. Now, Lord be thankèd for my good amends!°

---

57 **Daphne** nymph loved by Apollo and changed into laurel to evade him 63 **waning**
decadent 67 **yet** now, still 75 **smallest** weakest 77 **wit** mind 81 **fay** faith 82 **of** in
86 **house** inn 87 **present her at the leet** accuse her at the court under lord of a
manor 88 **sealed** marked by a seal guaranteeing quantity 93 **Stephen Sly** Stratford
man (Naps, etc., may also be names of real persons) 93 **Greece** the Green (?) Greet,
hamlet not far from Stratford (?) 97 **amends** recovery

ALL. Amen.
                Enter [*the* PAGE, *as a*] *Lady, with* ATTENDANTS.
SLY. I thank thee; thou shalt not lose by it.
PAGE. How fares my noble lord?   100
SLY. Marry,° I fare well, for here is cheer enough.
    Where is my wife?
PAGE. Here, noble lord. What is thy will with her?
SLY. Are you my wife and will not call me husband?
    My men should call me "lord"; I am your goodman.°   105
PAGE. My husband and my lord, my lord and husband,
    I am your wife in all obedience.
SLY. I know it well. What must I call her?
LORD. Madam.
SLY. Al'ce madam or Joan madam?   110
LORD. Madam and nothing else. So lords call ladies.
SLY. Madam wife, they say that I have dreamed
    And slept above some fifteen year or more.
PAGE. Ay, and the time seems thirty unto me,
    Being all this time abandoned° from your bed.   115
SLY. 'Tis much. Servants, leave me and her alone.
    Madam, undress you and come now to bed.
PAGE. Thrice noble lord, let me entreat of you
    To pardon me yet for a night or two
    Or, if not so, until the sun be set.   120
    For your physicians have expressly charged,
    In peril to incur° your former malady,
    That I should yet absent me from your bed.
    I hope this reason stands for my excuse.
SLY. Ay, it stands so° that I may hardly tarry so long,   125
    but I would be loath to fall into my dreams again.
    I will therefore tarry in despite of the flesh and the
    blood.
                Enter a MESSENGER.
MESSENGER. Your Honor's players, hearing your amendment,
    Are come to play a pleasant comedy.   130
    For so your doctors hold it very meet,
    Seeing too much sadness hath congealed your blood,
    And melancholy is the nurse of frenzy.°
    Therefore they thought it good you hear a play
    And frame your mind to mirth and merriment,   135
    Which bars a thousand harms and lengthens life.
SLY. Marry, I will let them play it. Is not a comontie° a
    Christmas gambold° or a tumbling trick?

---

101 **Marry** in truth (originally, [by St.] Mary) 105 **goodman** husband
115 **abandoned** excluded 122 **In peril to incur** because of the danger of a return
of 125 **stands so** will do (with phallic pun, playing on "reason," which was pronounced
much like "raising") 133 **frenzy** mental illness 137 **comontie** comedy (as pronounced
by Sly 138 **gambold** gambol (game, dance, frolic)

PAGE. No, my good lord, it is more pleasing stuff.
SLY. What, household stuff?°   140
PAGE. It is a kind of history.
SLY. Well, we'll see't. Come, madam wife, sit by my side
    And let the world slip.° We shall ne'er be younger.

[ACT I

Scene I. *Padua. A street.*]

Flourish.° Enter LUCENTIO *and his man°* TRANIO.

LUCENTIO. Tranio, since for the great desire I had
    To see fair Padua,° nursery of arts,
    I am arrived for fruitful Lombardy,
    The pleasant garden of great Italy,
    And by my father's love and leave am armed   5
    With his good will and thy good company,
    My trusty servant well approved° in all,
    Here let us breathe and haply institute
    A course of learning and ingenious° studies.
    Pisa, renownèd for grave citizens,   10
    Gave me my being and my father first,°
    A merchant of great traffic° through the world,
    Vincentio, come of the Bentivolii.
    Vincentio's son, brought up in Florence,
    It shall become to serve° all hopes conceived,   15
    To deck his fortune with his virtuous deeds;
    And therefore, Tranio, for the time I study,
    Virtue and that part of philosophy
    Will I apply° that treats of happiness
    By virtue specially to be achieved.   20
    Tell me thy mind, for I have Pisa left
    And am to Padua come, as he that leaves
    A shallow plash° to plunge him in the deep
    And with satiety seeks to quench his thirst.
TRANIO. *Mi perdonato,*° gentle master mine,   25
    I am in all affected° as yourself,
    Glad that you thus continue your resolve
    To suck the sweets of sweet philosophy.
    Only, good master, while we do admire
    This virtue and this moral discipline,   30

---

140 **stuff** (with sexual innuendo; see Eric Partridge, *Shakespeare's Bawdy*) 143 **slip** go by
I.i.s.d. **Flourish** fanfare of trumpets s.d. **man** servant 2 **Padua** (noted for its university) 7 **approved** proved, found reliable 9 **ingenious** mind-training 11 **first** i.e., before that 12 **traffic** business 15 **serve** work for 19 **apply** apply myself to 23 **plash**
pool 25 *Mi perdonato* pardon me 26 **affected** inclined

Let's be no stoics nor no stocks,° I pray,
Or so devote° to Aristotle's checks°
As° Ovid° be an outcast quite abjured.
Balk logic° with acquaintance that you have
And practice rhetoric in your common talk.   35
Music and poesy use to quicken° you.
The mathematics and the metaphysics,
Fall to them as you find your stomach° serves you.
No profit grows where is no pleasure ta'en.
In brief, sir, study what you most affect.°   40
LUCENTIO. Gramercies,° Tranio, well dost thou advise.
  If, Biondello, thou wert come ashore,
  We could at once put us in readiness
  And take a lodging fit to entertain
  Such friends as time in Padua shall beget.   45
  But stay awhile, what company is this?
TRANIO. Master, some show to welcome us to town.
            Enter BAPTISTA *with his two daughters,* KATE *and*
            BIANCA; GREMIO, *a pantaloon;*° [*and*] HORTENSIO,
                suitor to BIANCA. LUCENTIO [*and*]
                    TRANIO *stand by.*°
BAPTISTA. Gentlemen, importune me no farther,
  For how I firmly am resolved you know,
  That is, not to bestow my youngest daughter   50
  Before I have a husband for the elder.
  If either of you both love Katherina,
  Because I know you well and love you well,
  Leave shall you have to court her at your pleasure.
GREMIO. To cart° her rather. She's too rough for me.   55
  There, there, Hortensio, will you any wife?
KATE. I pray you, sir, is it your will
  To make a stale° of me amongst these mates?°
HORTENSIO. Mates, maid? How mean you that? No mates for you
  Unless you were of gentler, milder mold.   60
KATE. I' faith, sir, you shall never need to fear:
  Iwis° it° is not halfway to her° heart.
  But if it were, doubt not her care should be
  To comb your noddle with a three-legged stool
  And paint° your face and use you like a fool.   65

---

31 **stocks** sticks (with pun on Stoics) 32 **devote** devoted 32 **checks** restraints
33 **As** so that 33 **Ovid** Roman love poet (cf. III.i.28–29, IV.ii.8) 34 **Balk logic** engage in arguments 36 **quicken** make alive 38 **stomach** taste, preference 40 **affect**
like 41 **Gramercies** many thanks 47s.d. **pantaloon** laughable old man (a stock
character with baggy pants, in Italian Renaissance comedy) 47s.d. **by** nearby 55 **cart**
drive around in an open cart (a punishment for prostitutes) 58 **stale** (1) laughingstock
(2) prostitute 58 **mates** low fellows (with pun on *stalemate* and leading to pun on
mate=husband) 62 **Iwis** certainly 62 **it** i.e., getting a mate 62 **her** Kate's 65 **paint**
i.e., red with blood

HORTENSIO. From all such devils, good Lord deliver us!

GREMIO. And me too, good Lord!

TRANIO. [*Aside*] Husht, master, here's some good pastime toward.°
　　That wench is stark mad or wonderful froward.°

LUCENTIO. [*Aside*] But in the other's silence do I see　　　　　　70
　　Maid's mild behavior and sobriety.
　　Peace, Tranio.

TRANIO. [*Aside*] Well said, master. Mum, and gaze your fill.

BAPTISTA. Gentlemen, that I may soon make good
　　What I have said: Bianca, get you in,　　　　　　　　　　75
　　And let it not displease thee, good Bianca,
　　For I will love thee ne'er the less, my girl.

KATE. A pretty peat!° It is best
　　Put finger in the eye,° and° she knew why.

BIANCA. Sister, content you in my discontent.　　　　　　　80
　　Sir, to your pleasure humbly I subscribe.
　　My books and instruments shall be my company,
　　On them to look and practice by myself.

LUCENTIO. [*Aside*] Hark, Tranio, thou mayst hear Minerva° speak.

HORTENSIO. Signior Baptista, will you be so strange?°　　　　85
　　Sorry am I that our good will effects
　　Bianca's grief.

GREMIO.　　　　　　Why will you mew° her up,
　　Signior Baptista, for this fiend of hell
　　And make her bear the penance of her tongue?

BAPTISTA. Gentlemen, content ye. I am resolved.　　　　　　90
　　Go in, Bianca.　　　　　　　　　　　[*Exit* BIANCA.]
　　And for° I know she taketh most delight
　　In music, instruments, and poetry,
　　Schoolmasters will I keep within my house,
　　Fit to instruct her youth. If you, Hortensio,　　　　　　95
　　Or Signior Gremio, you, know any such,
　　Prefer° them hither; for to cunning° men
　　I will be very kind, and liberal
　　To mine own children in good bringing up.
　　And so, farewell. Katherina, you may stay,　　　　　　100
　　For I have more to commune with° Bianca.　　　　　*Exit.*

KATE. Why, and I trust I may go too, may I not?
　　What, shall I be appointed hours, as though, belike,°
　　I knew not what to take and what to leave? Ha!　　　*Exit.*

GREMIO. You may go to the devil's dam;° your gifts are so　　105
　　good, here's none will hold you. Their love is not so

---

68 **toward** coming up　69 **froward** willful　78 **peat** pet (cf. "teacher's pet")　79 **Put finger in the eye** cry　79 **and** if　84 **Minerva** goddess of wisdom　85 **strange** rigid　87 **mew** cage (falconry term)　92 **for** because　97 **Prefer** recommend　97 **cunning** talented　101 **commune with** communicate to　103 **belike** it seems likely　105 **dam** mother (used of animals)

great,° Hortensio, but we may blow our nails together°
and fast it fairly out. Our cake's dough on both sides.°
Farewell. Yet for the love I bear my sweet Bianca,
if I can by any means light on a fit man to teach   110
her that wherein she delights, I will wish° him to her
father.

HORTENSIO. So will I, Signior Gremio. But a word, I pray.
Though the nature of our quarrel yet never brooked
parle,° know now, upon advice,° it toucheth° us both—   115
that we may yet again have access to our fair mistress and be happy rivals in Bianca's love—to labor
and effect one thing specially.

GREMIO. What's that, I pray?

HORTENSIO. Marry, sir, to get a husband for her sister.   120

GREMIO. A husband! A devil.

HORTENSIO. I say, a husband.

GREMIO. I say, a devil. Think'st thou, Hortensio, though
her father be very rich, any man is so very° a fool to°
be married to hell?   125

HORTENSIO. Tush, Gremio, though it pass your patience
and mine to endure her loud alarums,° why, man,
there be good fellows in the world, and° a man could
light on them, would take her with all faults, and
money enough.   130

GREMIO. I cannot tell, but I had as lief° take her dowry
with this condition, to be whipped at the high cross°
every morning.

HORTENSIO. Faith, as you say, there's small choice in rotten
apples. But come, since this bar in law° makes us   135
friends, it shall be so far forth° friendly maintained,
till by helping Baptista's eldest daughter to a husband,
we set his youngest free for a husband, and then
have to't° afresh. Sweet Bianca! Happy man be his
dole!° He that runs fastest gets the ring. How say you,   140
Signior Gremio?

GREMIO. I am agreed, and would I had given him the
best horse in Padua to begin his wooing, that° would

thoroughly woo her, wed her, and bed her and rid the
house of her. Come on.   145
               Exeunt ambo.° Manet° TRANIO *and* LUCENTIO.
TRANIO. I pray, sir, tell me, is it possible
    That love should of a sudden take such hold?
LUCENTIO. O Tranio, till I found it to be true
    I never thought it possible or likely.
    But see, while idly I stood looking on,   150
    I found the effect of love-in-idleness°
    And now in plainness do confess to thee,
    That art to me as secret° and as dear
    As Anna° to the Queen of Carthage was,
    Tranio, I burn, I pine, I perish, Tranio,   155
    If I achieve not this young modest girl.
    Counsel me, Tranio, for I know thou canst.
    Assist me, Tranio, for I know thou wilt.
TRANIO. Master, it is no time to chide you now.
    Affection is not rated° from the heart.   160
    If love have touched you, naught remains but so,°
    "Redime te captum, quam queas minimo."°
LUCENTIO. Gramercies,° lad, go forward. This contents.
    The rest will comfort, for thy counsel's sound.
TRANIO. Master, you looked so longly° on the maid,   165
    Perhaps you marked not what's the pith of all.°
LUCENTIO. O yes, I saw sweet beauty in her face,
    Such as the daughter of Agenor° had,
    That made great Jove to humble him to her hand
    When with his knees he kissed the Cretan strond.°   170
TRANIO. Saw you no more? Marked you not how her sister
    Began to scold and raise up such a storm
    That mortal ears might hardly endure the din?
LUCENTIO. Tranio, I saw her coral lips to move
    And with her breath she did perfume the air.   175
    Sacred and sweet was all I saw in her.
TRANIO. Nay, then, 'tis time to stir him from his trance.
    I pray, awake, sir. If you love the maid,

145s.d. **ambo** both   145s.d. **Manet** remain (though the Latin plural is properly *manent*,
the singular with a plural subject is common in Elizabethan texts)   151 **love-in-
idleness** popular name for pansy (believed to have mysterious power in love; cf.
Midsummer Night's Dream, II.i.165ff.)   153 **to me as secret as** much in my confidence   154 **Anna** sister and confidante of Queen Dido   160 **rated** scolded   161 **so** to
act thus   162 **Redime . . . minimo** ransom yourself, a captive, at the smallest possible
price (from Terence's play *The Eunuch*, as quoted inaccurately in Lilly's *Latin Grammar*)   163 **Gramercies** many thanks   165 **longly** (1) longingly (2) interminably
166 **pith of all** heart of the matter   168 **daughter of Agenor** Europa, loved by
Jupiter, who, in the form of a bull, carried her to Crete   170 **strond** strand, shore

Bend thoughts and wits to achieve her. Thus it stands:
Her elder sister is so curst and shrewd°   180
That till the father rid his hands of her,
Master, your love must live a maid at home;
And therefore has he closely mewed° her up,
Because° she will not be annoyed with suitors.
LUCENTIO. Ah, Tranio, what a cruel father's he!   185
But art thou not advised° he took some care
To get her cunning° schoolmasters to instruct her?
TRANIO. Ay, marry, am I, sir—and now 'tis plotted!°
LUCENTIO. I have it, Tranio!
TRANIO.   Master, for° my hand,
Both our inventions° meet and jump in one.°   190
LUCENTIO. Tell me thine first.
TRANIO.   You will be schoolmaster
And undertake the teaching of the maid.
That's your device.
LUCENTIO.   It is. May it be done?
TRANIO. Not possible, for who shall bear° your part
And be in Padua here Vincentio's son?   195
Keep house and ply his book, welcome his friends,
Visit his countrymen and banquet them?
LUCENTIO. *Basta,*° content thee, for I have it full.°
We have not yet been seen in any house,
Nor can we be distinguished by our faces   200
For man or master. Then it follows thus:
Thou shalt be master, Tranio, in my stead,
Keep house and port° and servants as I should.
I will some other be—some Florentine,
Some Neapolitan, or meaner° man of Pisa.   205
'Tis hatched and shall be so. Tranio, at once
Uncase° thee, take my colored° hat and cloak.
When Biondello comes he waits on thee,
But I will charm° him first to keep his tongue.
TRANIO. So had you need.   210
In brief, sir, sith° it your pleasure is
And I am tied° to be obedient—
For so your father charged me at our parting;
"Be serviceable to my son," quoth he,
Although I think 'twas in another sense—   215

---

180 **curst and shrewd** sharp-tempered and shrewish 183 **mewed** caged
184 **Because** so that 186 **advised** informed 187 **cunning** knowing 188 **'tis plotted**
I've a scheme 189 **for** I bet 190 **inventions** schemes 190 **jump in one** are identical
194 **bear** act 198 *Basta* enough (Italian) 198 **full** fully (worked out) 203 **port**
style 205 **meaner** of lower rank 207 **Uncase** undress 207 **colored** (masters
dressed colorfully; servants wore dark blue) 209 **charm** exercise power over (he tells
him a fanciful tale, lines 225–34) 211 **sith** since 212 **tied** obligated

I am content to be Lucentio
Because so well I love Lucentio.
LUCENTIO. Tranio, be so, because Lucentio loves,
And let me be a slave, t'achieve that maid
Whose sudden sight hath thralled° my wounded eye.   220
                  Enter BIONDELLO
Here comes the rogue. Sirrah, where have you been?
BIONDELLO. Where have I been? Nay, how now, where are you?
Master, has my fellow Tranio stol'n your clothes,
Or you stol'n his, or both? Pray, what's the news?
LUCENTIO. Sirrah, come hither. 'Tis no time to jest,   225
And therefore frame your manners to the time.°
Your fellow Tranio, here, to save my life,
Puts my apparel and my count'nance° on,
And I for my escape have put on his,
For in a quarrel since I came ashore   230
I killed a man and fear I was descried.°
Wait you on him, I charge you, as becomes,
While I make way from hence to save my life.
You understand me?
BIONDELLO.   I, sir? Ne'er a whit.
LUCENTIO. And not a jot of Tranio in your mouth.   235
Tranio is changed into Lucentio.
BIONDELLO. The better for him. Would I were so too.
TRANIO. So could I, faith, boy, to have the next wish after,
That Lucentio indeed had Baptista's youngest daughter.
But, sirrah, not for my sake but your master's, I advise   240
You use your manners discreetly in all kind of companies.
When I am alone, why, then I am Tranio,
But in all places else your master, Lucentio.
LUCENTIO. Tranio, let's go.
One thing more rests,° that thyself execute°—   245
To make one among these wooers. If thou ask me why,
Sufficeth my reasons are both good and weighty.   *Exeunt.*
               The Presenters° above speaks.
FIRST SERVINGMAN. My lord, you nod; you do not mind° the play.
SLY. Yes, by Saint Anne, do I. A good matter, surely.
Comes there any more of it?   250
PAGE. My lord, 'tis but begun.
SLY. 'Tis a very excellent piece of work, madam lady.
Would 'twere done!   *They sit and mark.*°

---

220 **thralled** enslaved 226 **frame your manners to the time** adjust your conduct to
the situation 228 **count'nance** demeanor 231 **descried** seen, recognized 245 **rests**
remains 245 **execute** are to perform 247s.d. **Presenters** commentators, actors
thought of collectively, hence the singular verb 248 **mind** pay attention to 253s.d.
mark observe

[Scene II. *Padua. The street in front of*
HORTENSIO's *house.*]

Enter PETRUCHIO° *and his man* GRUMIO.

PETRUCHIO. Verona, for a while I take my leave
    To see my friends in Padua, but of all
    My best belovèd and approvèd friend,
    Hortensio, and I trow° this is his house.
    Here, sirrah Grumio, knock, I say.   5
GRUMIO. Knock, sir? Whom should I knock? Is there any
    man has rebused° your worship?
PETRUCHIO. Villain, I say, knock me here° soundly.
GRUMIO. Knock you here, sir? Why, sir, what am I, sir, that
    I should knock you here, sir?   10
PETRUCHIO. Villain, I say, knock me at this gate°
    And rap me well or I'll knock your knave's pate.°
GRUMIO. My master is grown quarrelsome. I should knock you first,
    And then I know after who comes by the worst.
PETRUCHIO. Will it not be?   15
    Faith, sirrah, and° you'll not knock, I'll ring° it;
    I'll try how you can *sol, fa,*° and sing it.
                                        He wrings him by the ears.
GRUMIO. Help, masters, help! My master is mad.
PETRUCHIO. Now, knock when I bid you, sirrah villain.
                    Enter HORTENSIO.
HORTENSIO. How now, what's the matter? My old friend   20
    Grumio, and my good friend Petruchio! How do you
    all at Verona?
PETRUCHIO. Signior Hortensio, come you to part the fray?
    Con tutto il cuore ben trovato,° may I say.
HORTENSIO. *Alla nostra casa ben venuto, molto honorato*   25
    signior mio Petruchio.°
    Rise, Grumio, rise. We will compound° this quarrel.
GRUMIO. Nay, 'tis no matter, sir, what he 'leges° in Latin.°
    If this be not a lawful cause for me to leave his ser-
    vice—look you, sir, he bid me knock him and rap him   30
    soundly, sir. Well, was it fit for a servant to use his
    master so, being perhaps, for aught I see, two-and-
    thirty, a peep out?°

I.ii.s.d. **Petruchio** (correct form *Petrucio*, with *c* pronounced *tch*)   4 **trow** think
7 **rebused** (Grumio means *abused*)   8 **knock me here** knock here for me (Grumio
plays game of misunderstanding, taking "me here" as "my ear")   11 **gate** door
12 **pate** head   16 **and** if   16 **ring** (pun on *wring*)   17 **sol, fa** go up and down the
scales (possibly with puns on meanings now lost)   24 **Con . . . trovato** with all [my]
heart well found (i.e., welcome)   25–26 **Alla . . . Petruchio** welcome to our house, my
much honored Signior Petruchio   27 **compound** settle   28 **'leges** alleges   28 **Latin**
(as if he were English, Grumio does not recognize Italian)   33 **two-and-thirty, a peep
out** (1) an implication that Petruchio is aged (2) a term from cards, slang for "drunk"
(*peep* is an old form of *pip*, a marking on a card)

Whom would to God I had well knocked at first,
Then had not Grumio come by the worst.   35
PETRUCHIO. A senseless villain! Good Hortensio,
    I bade the rascal knock upon your gate
    And could not get him for my heart° to do it.
GRUMIO. Knock at the gate? O heavens! Spake you not
    these words plain, "Sirrah, knock me here, rap me   40
    here, knock me well, and knock me soundly"? And
    come you now with "knocking at the gate"?
PETRUCHIO. Sirrah, be gone or talk not, I advise you.
HORTENSIO. Petruchio, patience, I am Grumio's pledge
    Why, this's a heavy chance° 'twixt him and you,   45
    Your ancient, trusty, pleasant servant Grumio.
    And tell me now, sweet friend, what happy gale
    Blows you to Padua here from old Verona?
PETRUCHIO. Such wind as scatters young men through the world
    To seek their fortunes farther than at home,   50
    Where small experience grows. But in a few,°
    Signior Hortensio, thus it stands with me:
    Antonio my father is deceased,
    And I have thrust myself into this maze,°
    Happily° to wive and thrive as best I may.   55
    Crowns in my purse I have and goods at home
    And so am come abroad to see the world.
HORTENSIO. Petruchio, shall I then come roundly° to thee
    And wish thee to a shrewd ill-favored° wife?
    Thou'ldst thank me but a little for my counsel—   60
    And yet I'll promise thee she shall be rich,
    And very rich—but thou'rt too much my friend,
    And I'll not wish thee to her.
PETRUCHIO. Signior Hortensio, 'twixt such friends as we
    Few words suffice; and therefore if thou know   65
    One rich enough to be Petruchio's wife—
    As wealth is burthen° of my wooing dance—
    Be she as foul° as was Florentius'° love,
    As old as Sibyl,° and as curst and shrewd
    As Socrates' Xanthippe° or a worse,   70
    She moves me not, or not removes, at least,
    Affection's edge in me, were she as rough
    As are the swelling Adriatic seas.

---

38 **heart** life 45 **heavy chance** sad happening 51 **few** i.e., words 54 **maze** traveling; uncertain course 55 **Happily** haply, perchance 58 **come roundly** talk frankly 59 **shrewd ill-favored** shrewish, poorly qualified 67 **burthen** burden (musical ac-
companiment) 68 **foul** homely 68 **Florentius** knight in Gower's *Confessio Amantis*
(cf. Chaucer's Wife of Bath's Tale; knight marries hag who turns into beautiful girl)
69 **Sibyl** prophetess in Greek and Roman myth 70 **Xanthippe** Socrates' wife, legen-
darily shrewish

I come to wive it wealthily in Padua;
If wealthily, then happily in Padua.   75

GRUMIO. Nay, look you, sir, he tells you flatly what his
  mind is. Why, give him gold enough and marry him
  to a puppet or an aglet-baby° or an old trot° with
  ne'er a tooth in her head, though she have as many
  diseases as two-and-fifty horses. Why, nothing come   80
  amiss so money comes withal.°

HORTENSIO. Petruchio, since we are stepped thus far in,
  I will continue that° I broached in jest.
  I can, Petruchio, help thee to a wife
  With wealth enough and young and beauteous,   85
  Brought up as best becomes a gentlewoman.
  Her only fault—and that is faults enough—
  Is that she is intolerable curst°
  And shrewd and froward,° so beyond all measure
  That were my state° far worser than it is,   90
  I would not wed her for a mine of gold.

PETRUCHIO. Hortensio, peace. Thou know'st not gold's effect.
  Tell me her father's name, and 'tis enough,
  For I will board° her though she chide as loud
  As thunder when the clouds in autumn crack.°   95

HORTENSIO. Her father is Baptista Minola,
  An affable and courteous gentleman.
  Her name is Katherina Minola,
  Renowned in Padua for her scolding tongue.

PETRUCHIO. I know her father though I know not her,   100
  And he knew my deceasèd father well.
  I will not sleep, Hortensio, till I see her,
  And therefore let me be thus bold with you,
  To give you over° at this first encounter
  Unless you will accompany me thither.   105

GRUMIO. I pray you, sir, let him go while the humor° lasts.
  A° my word, and° she knew him as well as I do, she
  would think scolding would do little good° upon him.
  She may perhaps call him half a score knaves or
  so—why, that's nothing. And he begin once, he'll   110
  rail in his rope-tricks.° I'll tell you what, sir, and she
  stand° him but a little, he will throw a figure in her

---

78 **aglet-baby** small female figure forming metal tip of cord or lace (French *aiguillette*,
point) 78 **trot** hag 81 **withal** with it 83 **that** what 88 **intolerable curst** intolerably sharp-tempered 89 **froward** willful 90 **state** estate, revenue 94 **board** naval
term, with double sense: (1) accost (2) go on board 95 **crack** make explosive
roars 104 **give you over** leave you 106 **humor** mood 107 **A** on 107 **and** if (also at
lines 110 and 112) 108 **do little good** have little effect 111 **rope-tricks** (1) Grumio's
version of *rhetoric*, going with *figure* just below (2) rascally conduct, deserving hanging
(3) possible sexual innuendo, as in following lines 112 **stand** withstand

face and so disfigure her with it that she shall have
no more eyes to see withal than a cat. You know him
not, sir.   115
HORTENSIO. Tarry, Petruchio, I must go with thee,
  For in Baptista's keep° my treasure is.
  He hath the jewel of my life in hold,°
  His youngest daughter, beautiful Bianca,
  And her withholds from me and other more,   120
  Suitors to her and rivals in my love,
  Supposing it a thing impossible,
  For° those defects I have before rehearsed,
  That ever Katherina will be wooed.
  Therefore this order° hath Baptista ta'en,   125
  That none shall have access unto Bianca
  Till Katherine the curst have got a husband.
GRUMIO. Katherine the curst!
  A title for a maid of all titles the worst.
HORTENSIO. Now shall my friend Petruchio do me grace°   130
  And offer° me, disguised in sober robes,
  To old Baptista as a schoolmaster
  Well seen° in music, to instruct Bianca,
  That so I may, by this device, at least
  Have leave and leisure to make love to her   135
  And unsuspected court her by herself.
                  Enter GREMIO, *and* LUCENTIO *disguised*
                     [*as a schoolmaster,* CAMBIO].
GRUMIO. Here's no knavery! See, to beguile the old folks,
  how the young folks lay their heads together! Master,
  master, look about you. Who goes there, ha?   140
HORTENSIO. Peace, Grumio. It is the rival of my love.
  Petruchio, stand by awhile.
                                                          [*They eavesdrop.*]
GRUMIO. A proper stripling,° and an amorous!
GREMIO. O, very well, I have perused the note.°
  Hark you, sir, I'll have them very fairly bound—   145
  All books of love, see that at any hand,°
  And see you read no other lectures° to her.
  You understand me. Over and beside
  Signior Baptista's liberality,
  I'll mend it with a largess.° Take your paper° too   150
  And let me have them° very well perfumed,

---

117 **keep** heavily fortified inner tower of castle 118 **hold** stronghold 123 **For** because
of 125 **order** step 130 **grace** a favor 131 **offer** present, introduce 133 **seen**
trained 143 **proper stripling** handsome youth (sarcastic comment on Gremio)
144 **note** memorandum (reading list for Bianca) 146 **at any hand** in any case
147 **read no other lectures** assign no other readings 150 **mend it with a largess**
add a gift of money to it 150 **paper** note (line 144) 151 **them** i.e., the books

For she is sweeter than perfume itself
To whom they go to. What will you read to her?
LUCENTIO. Whate'er I read to her, I'll plead for you
    As for my patron, stand you so assured,   155
    As firmly as° yourself were still in place°—
    Yea, and perhaps with more successful words
    Than you unless you were a scholar, sir.
GREMIO. O this learning, what a thing it is!
GRUMIO [*Aside*]. O this woodcock,° what an ass it is!   160
PETRUCHIO. Peace, sirrah!
HORTENSIO. Grumio, mum! [*Coming forward*] God save
    you, Signior Gremio.
GREMIO. And you are well met, Signior Hortensio.
    Trow° you whither I am going? To Baptista Minola.
    I promised to inquire carefully   165
    About a schoolmaster for the fair Bianca,
    And, by good fortune, I have lighted well
    On this young man—for° learning and behavior
    Fit for her turn,° well read in poetry
    And other books, good ones I warrant ye.   170
HORTENSIO. 'Tis well. And I have met a gentleman
    Hath promised me to help me to° another,
    A fine musician to instruct our mistress.
    So shall I no whit be behind in duty
    To fair Bianca, so beloved of me.   175
GREMIO. Beloved of me, and that my deeds shall prove.
GRUMIO. [*Aside*] And that his bags° shall prove.
HORTENSIO. Gremio, 'tis now no time to vent° our love.
    Listen to me, and if you speak me fair,
    I'll tell you news indifferent° good for either.   180
    Here is a gentleman whom by chance I met,
    Upon agreement from us to his liking,°
    Will undertake° to woo curst Katherine,
    Yea, and to marry her if her dowry please.
GREMIO. So said, so done, is well.   185
    Hortensio, have you told him all her faults?
PETRUCHIO. I know she is an irksome, brawling scold;
    If that be all, masters, I hear no harm.
GREMIO. No, say'st me so, friend? What countryman?
PETRUCHIO. Born in Verona, old Antonio's son.   190
    My father dead, my fortune lives for me,
    And I do hope good days and long to see.

---

156 **as** as if you   156 **in place** present   160 **woodcock** bird easily trapped, so considered silly   164 **Trow** know   168 **for** in   169 **turn** situation (with unconscious bawdy pun on the sense of "copulation")   172 **help me to** (1) find (2) become (Hortensio's jest)   177 **bags** i.e., of money   178 **vent** express   180 **indifferent** equally
182 **Upon...liking** if we agree to his terms (paying costs)   183 **undertake** promise

GREMIO. O, sir, such a life with such a wife were strange.
　　But if you have a stomach,° to't a° God's name;
　　You shall have me assisting you in all.　　　　　　　　195
　　But will you woo this wildcat?
PETRUCHIO.　　　　　　　　　　　　Will I live?
GRUMIO. [*Aside*] Will he woo her? Ay, or I'll hang her.
PETRUCHIO. Why came I hither but to that intent?
　　Think you a little din can daunt mine ears?
　　Have I not in my time heard lions roar?　　　　　　　200
　　Have I not heard the sea, puffed up with winds,
　　Rage like an angry boar chafèd with sweat?
　　Have I not heard great ordnance° in the field
　　And heaven's artillery thunder in the skies?
　　Have I not in a pitchèd battle heard　　　　　　　　205
　　Loud 'larums,° neighing steeds, trumpets' clang?
　　And do you tell me of a woman's tongue,
　　That gives not half so great a blow to hear
　　As will a chestnut in a farmer's fire?
　　Tush, tush, fear° boys with bugs.°
GRUMIO. [*Aside*]　　　　　　　For he fears none.　　　210
GREMIO. Hortensio, hark.
　　This gentleman is happily arrived,
　　My mind presumes, for his own good and ours.
HORTENSIO. I promised we would be contributors
　　And bear his charge of° wooing, whatsoe'er.　　　　　215
GREMIO. And so we will, provided that he win her.
GRUMIO. [*Aside*] I would I were as sure of a good dinner.

　　　　　　Enter TRANIO *brave*° [*as Lucentio*] *and* BIONDELLO.

TRANIO. Gentlemen, God save you. If I may be bold,
　　Tell me, I beseech you, which is the readiest way
　　To the house of Signior Baptista Minola?　　　　　220
BIONDELLO. He that has the two fair daughters? Is't he you mean?
TRANIO. Even he, Biondello.
GREMIO. Hark you, sir. You mean not her to—
TRANIO. Perhaps, him and her, sir. What have you to do?°
PETRUCHIO. Not her that chides, sir, at any hand,° I pray.　225
TRANIO. I love no chiders, sir. Biondello, let's away.
LUCENTIO. [*Aside*] Well begun, Tranio.
HORTENSIO.　　　　　　　　　Sir, a word ere you go.
　　Are you a suitor to the maid you talk of, yea or no?
TRANIO. And if I be, sir, is it any offense?
GREMIO. No, if without more words you will get you hence.　230
TRANIO. Why, sir, I pray, are not the streets as free
　　For me as for you?

---

194 **stomach** inclination　194 **a** in　203 **ordnance** cannon　206 **'larums** calls to arms, sudden attacks　210 **fear** frighten　210 **bugs** bugbears　215 **his charge of** the cost of his　217s.d. **brave** elegantly attired　224 **to do** i.e., to do with this　225 **at any hand** in any case

GREMIO.   But so is not she.
TRANIO. For what reason, I beseech you?
GREMIO. For this reason, if you'll know,
  That she's the choice° love of Signior Gremio.   235
HORTENSIO. That she's the chosen of Signior Hortensio.
TRANIO. Softly, my masters! If you be gentlemen,
  Do me this right: hear me with patience.
  Baptista is a noble gentleman
  To whom my father is not all unknown,   240
  And were his daughter fairer than she is,
  She may more suitors have, and me for one.
  Fair Leda's daughter° had a thousand wooers;
  Then well one more may fair Bianca have.
  And so she shall. Lucentio shall make one,   245
  Though Paris° came° in hope to speed° alone.
GREMIO. What, this gentleman will out-talk us all.
LUCENTIO. Sir, give him head. I know he'll prove a jade.°
PETRUCHIO. Hortensio, to what end are all these words?
HORTENSIO. Sir, let me be so bold as ask you,   250
  Did you yet ever see Baptista's daughter?
TRANIO. No, sir, but hear I do that he hath two,
  The one as famous for a scolding tongue
  As is the other for beauteous modesty.
PETRUCHIO. Sir, sir, the first's for me; let her go by.   255
GREMIO. Yea, leave that labor to great Hercules,
  And let it be more than Alcides'° twelve.
PETRUCHIO. Sir, understand you this of me in sooth:°
  The youngest daughter, whom you hearken° for,
  Her father keeps from all access of suitors   260
  And will not promise her to any man
  Until the elder sister first be wed.
  The younger then is free, and not before.
TRANIO. If it be so, sir, that you are the man
  Must stead° us all, and me amongst the rest,   265
  And if you break the ice and do this feat,
  Achieve° the elder, set the younger free
  For our access, whose hap° shall be to have her
  Will not so graceless be to be ingrate.°
HORTENSIO. Sir, you say well, and well you do conceive,°   270
  And since you do profess to be a suitor,

---

235 **choice** chosen   243 **Leda's daughter** Helen of Troy   246 **Paris** lover who took
Helen to Troy (legendary cause of Trojan War)   246 **came** should come   246 **speed**
succeed   248 **prove a jade** soon tire (cf. "jaded")   257 **Alcides** Hercules (after
Alcaeus, a family ancestor)   258 **sooth** truth   259 **hearken** long   265 **stead** aid
267 **Achieve** succeed with   268 **whose hap** the man whose luck   269 **to be ingrate**
as to be ungrateful   270 **conceive** put the case

You must, as we do, gratify° this gentleman
To whom we all rest° generally beholding.°
TRANIO. Sir, I shall not be slack, in sign whereof,
Please ye we may contrive° this afternoon   275
And quaff carouses° to our mistress' health
And do as adversaries° do in law,
Strive mightily but eat and drink as friends.
GRUMIO, BIONDELLO. O excellent motion! Fellows, let's be gone.
HORTENSIO. The motion's good indeed, and be it so.   280
Petruchio, I shall be your *ben venuto.*°   *Exeunt.*

[ACT II

Scene I. *In* BAPTISTA*'s house.*]

Enter KATE *and* BIANCA [*with her hands tied*].

BIANCA. Good sister, wrong me not nor wrong yourself
To make a bondmaid and a slave of me.
That I disdain. But for these other gawds,°
Unbind my hands, I'll pull them off myself,
Yea, all my raiment, to my petticoat,   5
Or what you will command me will I do,
So well I know my duty to my elders.
KATE. Of all thy suitors, here I charge thee, tell
Whom thou lov'st best. See thou dissemble not.
BIANCA. Believe me, sister, of all the men alive   10
I never yet beheld that special face
Which I could fancy more than any other.
KATE. Minion,° thou liest. Is't not Hortensio?
BIANCA. If you affect° him, sister, here I swear
I'll plead for you myself but you shall have him.   15
KATE. O then, belike,° you fancy riches more:
You will have Gremio to keep you fair.°
BIANCA. Is it for him you do envy° me so?
Nay, then you jest, and now I well perceive
You have but jested with me all this while.   20
I prithee, sister Kate, untie my hands.
KATE. If that be jest then all the rest was so.   *Strikes her.*
                    Enter BAPTISTA.
BAPTISTA. Why, how now, dame, whence grows this insolence?
Bianca, stand aside. Poor girl, she weeps.
Go ply thy needle; meddle not with her.   25

---

272 **gratify** compensate   273 **rest** remain   273 **beholding** indebted   275 **contrive**
pass   276 **quaff carouses** empty our cups   277 **adversaries** attorneys
281 **ben venuto** welcome (i.e., host)   II.i.3 **gawds** adornments   13 **Minion**
impudent creature   14 **affect** like   16 **belike** probably   17 **fair** in fine clothes
18 **envy** hate

For same, thou hilding° of a devilish spirit,
Why dost thou wrong her that did ne'er wrong thee?
When did she cross thee with a bitter word?
KATE. Her silence flouts me and I'll be revenged.

                                Flies after BIANCA.

BAPTISTA. What, in my sight? Bianca, get thee in.   *Exit* [BIANCA].   30
KATE. What, will you not suffer° me? Nay, now I see
    She is your treasure, she must have a husband;
    I must dance barefoot on her wedding day,°
    And, for your love to her, lead apes in hell.°
    Talk not to me; I will go sit and weep   35
    Till I can find occasion of revenge.   [*Exit.*]
BAPTISTA. Was ever gentleman thus grieved as I?
    But who comes here?

Enter GREMIO, LUCENTIO *in the habit of a mean° man*
            [*Cambio*], PETRUCHIO, *with* [HORTENSIO *as a music*
            teacher, Lito, and] TRANIO [*as Lucentio*], *with his*
            boy [BIONDELLO] *bearing a lute and books.*

GREMIO. Good morrow, neighbor Baptista.
BAPTISTA. Good morrow, neighbor Gremio. God save you,   40
    gentlemen.
PETRUCHIO. And you, good sir. Pray, have you not a daughter
    Called Katherina, fair and virtuous?
BAPTISTA. I have a daughter, sir, called Katherina.
GREMIO. [*Aside*] You are too blunt; go to it orderly.°   45
PETRUCHIO. [*Aside*] You wrong me, Signior Gremio, give me leave.
    [*To* BAPTISTA] I am a gentleman of Verona, sir,
    That, hearing of her beauty and her wit,
    Her affability and bashful modesty,
    Her wondrous qualities and mild behavior,   50
    Am bold to show myself a forward° guest
    Within your house, to make mine eye the witness
    Of that report which I so oft have heard.
    And, for an entrance to° my entertainment,°
    I do present you with a man of mine,   [*presenting* HORTENSIO]   55
    Cunning in music and the mathematics,
    To instruct her fully in those sciences,
    Whereof I know she is not ignorant.
    Accept of him, or else you do me wrong.
    His name is Litio, born in Mantua.   60
BAPTISTA. Y'are welcome, sir, and he for your good sake.
    But for my daughter Katherine, this I know,
    She is not for your turn,° the more my grief.

---

26 **hilding** base wretch   31 **suffer** permit (i.e., to deal with you)   33 **dance . . . day**
(expected of older maiden sisters)   34 **lead apes in hell** (proverbial occupation of old
maids; cf. *Much Ado About Nothing,* II.i.41)   38s.d. **mean** lower class   45 **orderly**
gradually   51 **forward** eager   54 **entrance to** price of admission for   54 **entertainment** reception   63 **turn** purpose (again, with bawdy pun)

PETRUCHIO. I see you do not mean to part with her,
    Or else you like not of my company.   65
BAPTISTA. Mistake me not; I speak but as I find.
    Whence are you, sir? What may I call your name?
PETRUCHIO. Petruchio is my name, Antonio's son,
    A man well known throughout all Italy.
BAPTISTA. I know him well. You are welcome for his sake.   70
GREMIO. Saving° your tale, Petruchio, I pray,
    Let us, that are poor petitioners, speak too.
    Backare,° you are marvelous° forward.
PETRUCHIO. O pardon me, Signior Gremio, I would fain° be doing.°
GREMIO. I doubt it not, sir, but you will curse your wooing.   75
    Neighbor, this is a gift very grateful° I am sure of it.
    To express the like kindness myself, that° have been
    more kindly beholding to you than any, freely give unto
    you this young scholar [*presenting* LUCENTIO] that
    hath been long studying at Rheims—as cunning in   80
    Greek, Latin, and other languages, as the other in
    music and mathematics. His name is Cambio.° Pray
    accept his service.
BAPTISTA. A thousand thanks, Signior Gremio. Welcome,
    good Cambio. [*To* TRANIO] But, gentle sir, methinks you   85
    walk like° a stranger. May I be so bold to know the
    cause of your coming?
TRANIO. Pardon me, sir, the boldness is mine own,
    That,° being a stranger in this city here,
    Do make myself a suitor to your daughter,   90
    Unto Bianca, fair and virtuous.
    Nor is your firm resolve unknown to me
    In the preferment of° the eldest sister.
    This liberty is all that I request,
    That, upon knowledge of my parentage,   95
    I may have welcome 'mongst the rest that woo
    And free access and favor° as the rest.
    And, toward the education of your daughters
    I here bestow a simple instrument,°
    And this small packet of Greek and Latin books.   100
    If you accept them, then their worth is great.
BAPTISTA. [*Looking at books*] Lucentio is your name.
    Of whence, I pray?
TRANIO. Of Pisa, sir, son to Vincentio.

---

71 **Saving** with all respect for   73 *Backare* back (proverbial quasi-Latin)   73 **marvelous** very   74 **would fain** am eager to   74 **doing** (with a sexual jest)   76 **grateful**
worthy of gratitude   77 **myself, that** I myself, who   82 **Cambio** (Italian for
"exchange")   86 **walk like** have the bearing of   89 **That** who   93 **preferment of**
giving priority to   97 **favor** countenance, acceptance   99 **instrument** i.e., the lute

BAPTISTA. A mighty man of Pisa; by report
    I know him° well. You are very welcome, sir.   105
    [*To* HORTENSIO] Take you the lute, [*to* LUCENTIO] and you the
      set of books;
    You shall go see your pupils presently.°
    Holla, within!
                Enter a SERVANT.
          Sirrah, lead these gentlemen
    To my daughters and tell them both
    These are their tutors; bid them use them well.   110
                  [*Exit* SERVANT, *with* LUCENTIO,
               HORTENSIO, *and* BIONDELLO *following.*]
    We will go walk a little in the orchard°
    And then to dinner. You are passing° welcome,
    And so I pray you all to think yourselves.
PETRUCHIO. Signior Baptista, my business asketh haste,
    And every day I cannot come to woo.   115
    You knew my father well, and in him me,
    Left solely heir to all his lands and goods,
    Which I have bettered rather than decreased.
    Then tell me, if I get your daughter's love
    What dowry shall I have with her to wife?   120
BAPTISTA. After my death the one half of my lands,
    And in possession° twenty thousand crowns.
PETRUCHIO. And, for that dowry, I'll assure her of
    Her widowhood,° be it that she survive me,
    In all my lands and leases whatsoever.   125
    Let specialties° be therefore drawn between us
    That covenants may be kept on either hand.
BAPTISTA. Ay, when the special thing is well obtained,
    That is, her love, for that is all in all.
PETRUCHIO. Why, that is nothing, for I tell you, father,   130
    I am as peremptory° as she proud-minded.
    And where two raging fires meet together
    They do consume the thing that feeds their fury.
    Though little fire grows great with little wind,
    Yet extreme gusts will blow out fire and all.   135
    So I to her, and so she yields to me,
    For I am rough and woo not like a babe.
BAPTISTA. Well mayst thou woo, and happy be thy speed!°
    But be thou armed for some unhappy words.

---

105 **him** his name   107 **presently** at once   111 **orchard** garden   112 **passing**
very   122 **possession** i.e., at the time of marriage   124 **widowhood** estate settled on
a widow (Johnson)   126 **specialties** special contracts   131 **peremptory** resolved
138 **speed** progress

PETRUCHIO. Ay, to the proof,° as mountains are for winds   140
    That shakes not, though they blow perpetually.
                Enter HORTENSIO *with his head broke.*
BAPTISTA. How now, my friend, why dost thou look so pale?
HORTENSIO. For fear, I promise you, if I look pale.
BAPTISTA. What, will my daughter prove a good musician?
HORTENSIO. I think she'll sooner prove a soldier.   145
    Iron may hold with her,° but never lutes.
BAPTISTA. Why, then thou canst not break° her to the lute?
HORTENSIO. Why, no, for she hath broke the lute to me.
    I did but tell her she mistook her frets°
    And bowed° her hand to teach her fingering,   150
    When, with a most impatient devilish spirit,
    "Frets, call you these?" quoth she; "I'll fume with them."
    And with that word she stroke° me on the head,
    And through the instrument my pate made way.
    And there I stood amazèd for a while   155
    As on a pillory,° looking through the lute,
    While she did call me rascal, fiddler,
    And twangling Jack,° with twenty such vile terms
    As° had she studied° to misuse me so.
PETRUCHIO. Now, by the world, it is a lusty° wench!   160
    I love her ten times more than e'er I did.
    O how I long to have some chat with her!
BAPTISTA. [*To* HORTENSIO] Well, go with me, and be not so discomfited.
    Proceed in practice° with my younger daughter;
    She's apt° to learn and thankful for good turns.   165
    Signior Petruchio, will you go with us
    Or shall I send my daughter Kate to you?
                Exit [BAPTISTA, *with* GREMIO, TRANIO, *and*
                    HORTENSIO]. *Manet* PETRUCHIO.°
PETRUCHIO. I pray you do. I'll attend° but here
    And woo her with some spirit when she comes.
    Say that she rail,° why then I'll tell her plain   170
    She sings as sweetly as a nightingale.
    Say that she frown, I'll say she looks as clear
    As morning roses newly washed with dew.
    Say she be mute and will not speak a word,
    Then I'll commend her volubility   175
    And say she uttereth piercing eloquence.

140 **to the proof** in tested steel armor   146 **hold with her** stand her treatment
147 **break** train   149 **frets** ridges where strings are pressed   150 **bowed** bent
153 **stroke** struck   156 **pillory** i.e., with a wooden collar (old structure for public
punishment)   158 **Jack** (term of contempt)   159 **As** as if   159 **studied** prepared
160 **lusty** spirited   164 **practice** instruction   165 **apt** disposed   167s.d. (is in the F
position, which need not be changed; Petruchio speaks to the departing Baptista)
168 **attend** wait for   170 **rail** scold, scoff

If she do bid me pack,° I'll give her thanks
As though she bid me stay by her a week.
If she deny° to wed, I'll crave the day
When I shall ask the banns° and when be marrièd.   180
But here she comes, and now, Petruchio, speak.
                    Enter KATE.
Good morrow, Kate, for that's your name, I hear.
KATE. Well have you heard,° but something hard of hearing.
    They call me Katherine that do talk of me.
PETRUCHIO. You lie, in faith, for you are called plain Kate,   185
    And bonny° Kate, and sometimes Kate the curst.
    But, Kate, the prettiest Kate in Christendom,
    Kate of Kate Hall,° my super-dainty Kate,
    For dainties° are all Kates,° and therefore, Kate,
    Take this of me, Kate of my consolation.   190
    Hearing thy mildness praised in every town,
    Thy virtues spoke of, and thy beauty sounded°—
    Yet not so deeply as to thee belongs—
    Myself am moved to woo thee for my wife.
KATE. Moved! In good time,° let him that moved you hither   195
    Remove you hence. I knew you at the first
    You were a movable.°
PETRUCHIO.   Why, what's a movable?
KATE. A joint stool.°
PETRUCHIO.   Thou hast hit it; come sit on me.
KATE. Asses are made to bear° and so are you.
PETRUCHIO. Women are made to bear° and so are you.   200
KATE. No such jade° as you, if me you mean.
PETRUCHIO. Alas, good Kate, I will not burden thee,
    For, knowing thee to be but young and light—
KATE. Too light for such a swain° as you to catch
    And yet as heavy as my weight should be.   205
PETRUCHIO. Should be!° Should—buzz!
KATE.   Well ta'en, and like a buzzard.°
PETRUCHIO. O slow-winged turtle,° shall a buzzard take° thee?
KATE. Ay, for a turtle, as he takes a buzzard.°

177 **pack** go away   179 **deny** refuse   180 **banns** public announcement in church of intent to marry   183 **heard** (pun: pronounced like *hard*)   186 **bonny** big, fine (perhaps with pun on *bony*, the F spelling)   188 **Kate Hall** (possible topical reference; several places have been proposed)   189 **dainties** delicacies   189 **Kates** i.e., *cates*, delicacies   192 **sounded** (1) measured (effect of *deeply*) (2) spoken of (pun)   195 **In good time** indeed   197 **movable** article of furniture (with pun)   198 **joint stool** stool made by a joiner (standard term of disparagement)   199 **bear** carry   200 **bear** i.e., bear children (with second sexual meaning in Petruchio's "I will not burden thee")   201 **jade** worn-out horse (Kate has now called him both "ass" and "sorry horse")   204 **swain** country boy   206 **be** (pun on *bee;* hence *buzz,* scandal, i.e., about "light" woman)   206 **buzzard** hawk unteachable in falconry (hence idiot)   207 **turtle** turtledove, noted for affectionateness   207 **take** capture (with pun, "mistake for," in next line)   208 **buzzard** buzzing insect (hence "wasp")

PETRUCHIO. Come, come, you wasp, i' faith you are too angry.

KATE. If I be waspish, best beware my sting.   210

PETRUCHIO. My remedy is then to pluck it out.

KATE. Ay, if the fool could find it where it lies.

PETRUCHIO. Who knows not where a wasp does wear his sting?
     In his tail.

KATE.   In his tongue.

PETRUCHIO.   Whose tongue?

KATE. Yours, if you talk of tales,° and so farewell.   215

PETRUCHIO. What, with my tongue in your tail? Nay, come again.
     Good Kate, I am a gentleman—

KATE.   That I'll try.   *She strikes him.*

PETRUCHIO. I swear I'll cuff you if you strike again.

KATE. So may you lose your arms:°
     If you strike me you are no gentleman,   220
     And if no gentleman, why then no arms.

PETRUCHIO. A herald,° Kate? O, put me in thy books.°

KATE. What is your crest?° A coxcomb?°

PETRUCHIO. A combless° cock, so° Kate will be my hen.

KATE. No cock of mine; you crow too like a craven.°   225

PETRUCHIO. Nay, come, Kate, come, you must not look so sour.

KATE. It is my fashion when I see a crab.°

PETRUCHIO. Why, here's no crab, and therefore look
     not sour.

KATE. There is, there is.

PETRUCHIO. Then show it me.

KATE.   Had I a glass° I would.   230

PETRUCHIO. What, you mean my face?

KATE.   Well aimed of° such a young one.

PETRUCHIO. Now, by Saint George, I am too young for you.

KATE. Yet you are withered.

PETRUCHIO.   'Tis with cares.

KATE.   I care not.

PETRUCHIO. Nay, hear you, Kate, in sooth° you scape° not so.

KATE. I chafe° you if I tarry. Let me go.   235

PETRUCHIO. No, not a whit. I find you passing gentle.
     'Twas told me you were rough and coy° and sullen,
     And now I find report a very liar,
     For thou art pleasant, gamesome, passing courteous,
     But slow in speech, yet sweet as springtime flowers.   240
     Thou canst not frown, thou canst not look askance,
     Nor bite the lip as angry wenches will,

215 **of tales** idle tales (leading to bawdy pun on *tail*=pudend)   219 **arms** (pun on "coat of arms")   222 **herald** one skilled in heraldry   222 **books** registers of heraldry (with pun on "in your good books")   223 **crest** heraldic device   223 **coxcomb** identifying feature of court Fool's cap; the cap itself   224 **combless** i.e., unwarlike   224 **so** if   225 **craven** defeated cock   227 **crab** crab apple   230 **glass** mirror   231 **well aimed of** a good shot (in the dark)   234 **sooth** truth   234 **scape** escape   235 **chafe** (1) annoy (2) warm up   237 **coy** offish

Nor hast thou pleasure to be cross in talk,
But thou with mildness entertain'st thy wooers,
With gentle conference,° soft and affable.   245
Why does the world report that Kate doth limp?
O sland'rous world! Kate like the hazel-twig
Is straight and slender, and as brown in hue
As hazelnuts and sweeter than the kernels.
O, let me see thee walk. Thou dost not halt.°   250
KATE. Go, fool, and whom thou keep'st° command.
PETRUCHIO. Did ever Dian° so become a grove
    As Kate this chamber with her princely gait?
    O, be thou Dian and let her be Kate,
    And then let Kate be chaste and Dian sportful!°   255
KATE. Where did you study all this goodly speech?
PETRUCHIO. It is extempore, from my mother-wit.°
KATE. A witty mother! Witless else° her son.
PETRUCHIO. Am I not wise?
KATE.   Yes,° keep you warm.
PETRUCHIO. Marry, so I mean, sweet Katherine, in thy bed.   260
    And therefore, setting all this chat aside,
    Thus in plain terms: your father hath consented
    That you shall be my wife, your dowry 'greed on,
    And will you, nill° you, I will marry you.
    Now, Kate, I am a husband for your turn,°   265
    For, by this light, whereby I see thy beauty—
    Thy beauty that doth make me like thee well—
    Thou must be married to no man but me.
                    Enter BAPTISTA, GREMIO, TRANIO.
    For I am he am born to tame you, Kate,
    And bring you from a wild Kate° to a Kate   270
    Conformable° as other household Kates.
    Here comes your father. Never make denial;
    I must and will have Katherine to my wife.
BAPTISTA. Now, Signior Petruchio, how speed° you with my daughter?
PETRUCHIO. How but well, sir? How but well?   275
    It were impossible I should speed amiss.
BAPTISTA. Why, how now, daughter Katherine, in your dumps?°
KATE. Call you me daughter? Now, I promise° you
    You have showed a tender fatherly regard
    To wish me wed to one half lunatic,   280

---

245 **conference** conversation 250 **halt** limp 251 **whom thou keep'st** i.e., your
servants 252 **Dian** Diana, goddess of hunting and virginity 255 **sportful** (i.e., in the
game of love) 257 **mother-wit** natural intelligence 258 **else** otherwise would be
259 **Yes** yes, just enough to (refers to a proverbial saying) 264 **nill** won't
265 **turn** advantage (with bawdy second meaning) 270 **wild Kate** (pun on "wildcat")
271 **Conformable** submissive 274 **speed** get on 277 **dumps** low spirits
278 **promise** tell

A madcap ruffian and a swearing Jack
That thinks with oaths to face° the matter out.
PETRUCHIO. Father, 'tis thus: yourself and all the world
   That talked of her have talked amiss of her.
   If she be curst it is for policy,°   285
   For she's not froward but modest as the dove.
   She is not hot° but temperate as the morn;
   For patience she will prove a second Grissel°
   And Roman Lucrece° for her chastity.
   And to conclude, we have 'greed so well together   290
   That upon Sunday is the wedding day.
KATE. I'll see thee hanged on Sunday first.
GREMIO. Hark, Petruchio, she says she'll see thee hanged first.
TRANIO. Is this your speeding?° Nay, then good night our part!
PETRUCHIO. Be patient, gentlemen, I choose her for myself.   295
   If she and I be pleased, what's that to you?
   'Tis bargained 'twixt us twain, being alone,
   That she shall still be curst in company.
   I tell you, 'tis incredible to believe
   How much she loves me. O, the kindest Kate,   300
   She hung about my neck, and kiss on kiss
   She vied° so fast, protesting oath on oath,
   That in a twink° she won me to her love.
   O, you are novices. 'Tis a world° to see
   How tame, when men and women are alone,   305
   A meacock° wretch can make the curstest shrew.
   Give me thy hand, Kate. I will unto Venice
   To buy apparel 'gainst° the wedding day.
   Provide the feast, father, and bid the guests;
   I will be sure my Katherine shall be fine.°   310
BAPTISTA. I know not what to say, but give me your hands.
   God send you joy, Petruchio! 'Tis a match.
GREMIO, TRANIO. Amen, say we. We will be witnesses.
PETRUCHIO. Father, and wife, and gentlemen, adieu.
   I will to Venice; Sunday comes apace.   315
   We will have rings and things and fine array,
   And, kiss me, Kate, "We will be married a Sunday."°
                        Exit PETRUCHIO *and* KATE.
GREMIO. Was ever match clapped° up so suddenly?
BAPTISTA. Faith, gentlemen, now I play a merchant's part
   And venture madly on a desperate mart.°   320

---

282 **face** brazen 285 **policy** tactics 287 **hot** intemperate 288 **Grissel** Griselda
(patient wife in Chaucer's Clerk's Tale) 289 **Lucrece** (killed herself after Tarquin raped
her) 294 **speeding** success 302 **vied** made higher bids (card-playing terms), i.e.,
kissed more frequently 303 **twink** twinkling 304 **world** wonder 306 **meacock**
timid 308 **'gainst** in preparation for 310 **fine** well dressed 317 **"We . . . Sunday"**
(line from a ballad) 318 **clapped** fixed 320 **mart** "deal"

TRANIO. 'Twas a commodity° lay fretting° by you;
   'Twill bring you gain or perish on the seas.
BAPTISTA. The gain I seek is quiet in the match.
GREMIO. No doubt but he hath got a quiet catch.
   But now, Baptista, to your younger daughter;   325
   Now is the day we long have lookèd for.
   I am your neighbor and was suitor first.
TRANIO. And I am one that love Bianca more
   Than words can witness or your thoughts can guess.
GREMIO. Youngling, thou canst not love so dear as I.   330
TRANIO. Graybeard, thy love doth freeze.
GREMIO.   But thine doth fry.
   Skipper,° stand back, 'tis age that nourisheth.
TRANIO. But youth in ladies' eyes that flourisheth.
BAPTISTA. Content you, gentlemen; I will compound° this strife.
   'Tis deeds must win the prize, and he of both°   335
   That can assure my daughter greatest dower°
   Shall have my Bianca's love.
   Say, Signior Gremio, what can you assure her?
GREMIO. First, as you know, my house within the city
   Is richly furnishèd with plate and gold,   340
   Basins and ewers to lave° her dainty hands;
   My hangings all of Tyrian° tapestry;
   In ivory coffers I have stuffed my crowns,
   In cypress chests my arras counterpoints,°
   Costly apparel, tents,° and canopies,   345
   Fine linen, Turkey cushions bossed° with pearl,
   Valance° of Venice gold in needlework,
   Pewter and brass, and all things that belongs
   To house or housekeeping. Then, at my farm
   I have a hundred milch-kine to the pail,°   350
   Six score fat oxen standing in my stalls
   And all things answerable to this portion.°
   Myself am struck° in years, I must confess,
   And if I die tomorrow, this is hers,
   If whilst I live she will be only mine.   355
TRANIO. That "only" came well in. Sir, list to me.
   I am my father's heir and only son.
   If I may have your daughter to my wife,
   I'll leave her houses three or four as good,

---

321 **commodity** (here a coarse term for women; see Partridge, *Shakespeare's Bawdy*)
321 **fretting** decaying in storage (with pun)   332 **Skipper** skipping (irresponsible)
fellow   334 **compound** settle   335 **he of both** the one of you two   336 **dower** man's
gift to bride   341 **lave** wash   342 **Tyrian** purple   344 **arras counterpoints** counter-
panes woven in Arras   345 **tents** bed tester (hanging cover)   346 **bossed** embroidered   347 **Valance** bed fringes and drapes   350 **milch-kine to the pail** cows
producing milk for human use   352 **answerable to this portion** corresponding to this
settlement (?)   353 **struck** advanced

Within rich Pisa walls, as any one   360
Old Signior Gremio has in Padua,
Besides two thousand ducats° by the year
Of° fruitful land, all which shall be her jointure.°
What, have I pinched° you, Signior Gremio?

GREMIO. [*Aside*] Two thousand ducats by the year of land!   365
My land amounts not to so much in all.
[*To others*] That she shall have besides an argosy°
That now is lying in Marcellus' road.°
What, have I choked you with an argosy?

TRANIO. Gremio, 'tis known my father hath no less   370
Than three great argosies, besides two galliasses°
And twelve tight° galleys. These I will assure her
And twice as much, whate'er thou off'rest next.

GREMIO. Nay, I have off'red all. I have no more,
And she can have no more than all I have.   375
If you like me, she shall have me and mine.

TRANIO. Why, then the maid is mine from all the world
By your firm promise. Gremio is outvied.°

BAPTISTA. I must confess your offer is the best,
And let your father make her the assurance,°   380
She is your own; else you must pardon me.
If you should die before him, where's her dower?

TRANIO. That's but a cavil.° He is old, I young.

GREMIO. And may not young men die as well as old?

BAPTISTA. Well gentlemen,   385
I am thus resolved. On Sunday next, you know,
My daughter Katherine is to be married.
Now on the Sunday following shall Bianca
Be bride to you if you make this assurance;
If not, to Signior Gremio.   390
And so I take my leave and thank you both.   *Exit.*

GREMIO. Adieu, good neighbor. Now I fear thee not.
Sirrah° young gamester,° your father were° a fool
To give thee all and in his waning age
Set foot under thy table.° Tut, a toy!°   395
An old Italian fox is not so kind, my boy.   *Exit.*

TRANIO. A vengeance on your crafty withered hide!
Yet I have faced it with a card of ten.°
'Tis in my head to do my master good.
I see no reason but supposed Lucentio   400

---

362 **ducats** Venetian gold coins 363 **Of** from 363 **jointure** settlement 364 **pinched**
put the screws on 367 **argosy** largest type of merchant ship 368 **Marcellus' road**
Marseilles' harbor 371 **galliasses large** galleys 372 **tight** watertight 378 **outvied**
outbid 380 **assurance** guarantee 383 **cavil** small point 393 **Sirrah** (used contemptuously) 393 **gamester** gambler 393 **were** would be 395 **Set foot under thy
table** be dependent on you 395 **a toy** a joke 398 **faced it with a card of ten**
bluffed with a ten-spot

Must get° a father, called "supposed Vincentio,"
And that's a wonder. Fathers commonly
Do get their children, but in this case of wooing
A child shall get a sire if I fail not of my cunning.   *Exit.*

ACT III

[Scene I. *Padua. In Baptista's house.*]

Enter LUCENTIO [*as Cambio*], HORTENSIO [*as Litio*],
and BIANCA.

LUCENTIO. Fiddler, forbear. You grow too forward, sir.
Have you so soon forgot the entertainment°
Her sister Katherine welcomed you withal?

HORTENSIO. But, wrangling pedant, this is
The patroness of heavenly harmony.   5
Then give me leave to have prerogative,°
And when in music we have spent an hour,
Your lecture° shall have leisure for as much.

LUCENTIO. Preposterous° ass, that never read so far
To know the cause why music was ordained!   10
Was it not to refresh the mind of man
After his studies or his usual pain?°
Then give me leave to read° philosophy,
And while I pause, serve in your harmony.

HORTENSIO. Sirrah, I will not bear these braves° of thine.   15

BIANCA. Why, gentlemen, you do me double wrong
To strive for that which resteth in my choice.
I am no breeching° scholar° in the schools.
I'll not be tied to hours nor 'pointed times,
But learn my lessons as I please myself.   20
And, to cut off all strife, here sit we down.
[*To* HORTENSIO] Take you your instrument, play you the whiles;°
His lecture will be done ere you have tuned.

HORTENSIO. You'll leave his lecture when I am in tune?

LUCENTIO. That will be never. Tune your instrument.   25

BIANCA. Where left we last?

LUCENTIO. Here, madam:
Hic ibat Simois, hic est Sigeia tellus,
Hic steterat Priami regia celsa senis.°

---

401 **get** beget   III.i.2 **entertainment** i.e., "pillorying" him with the lute
6 **prerogative** priority   8 **lecture** instruction   9 **Preposterous** putting later things
(*post-*) first (*pre-*)   12 **pain** labor   13 **read** give a lesson in   15 **braves** defiances
18 **breeching** (1) in breeches (young) (2) whippable   18 **scholar** schoolboy   22 **the
whiles** meanwhile   28–29 *Hic. . .senis* here flowed the Simois, here is the Sigeian
(Trojan) land, here had stood old Priam's high palace (Ovid)

BIANCA. Conster° them.   30
LUCENTIO. *Hic ibat*, as I told you before, *Simois,* I am
    Lucentio, *hic est,* son unto Vincentio of Pisa, *Sigeia*
    tellus, disguised thus to get your love, *Hic steterat,*
    and that Lucentio that comes a wooing, *Priami,* is
    my man Tranio, *regia,* bearing my port,° *celsa senis,*   35
    that we might beguile the old pantaloon.°
HORTENSIO. [*Breaks in*] Madam, my instrument's in tune.
BIANCA. Let's hear. O fie, the treble jars.°
LUCENTIO. Spit in the hole, man, and tune again.
BIANCA. Now let me see if I can conster it. *Hic ibat*   40
    Simois, I know you not, *hic est Sigeia tellus,* I trust
    you not, *Hic steterat Priami,* take heed he hear us
    not, *regia,* presume not, *celsa senis,* despair not.
HORTENSIO. [*Breaks in again*] Madam, 'tis now in tune.
LUCENTIO.   All but the bass.
LUCENTIO. The bass is right; 'tis the base knave that jars.   45
    [*Aside*] How fiery and forward our pedant is!
    Now, for my life, the knave doth court my love.
    Pedascule,° I'll watch you better yet.
BIANCA. In time I may believe, yet I mistrust.
LUCENTIO. Mistrust it not, for sure Aeacides   50
    Was Ajax,° called so from his grandfather.
BIANCA. I must believe my master; else, I promise you,
    I should be arguing still upon that doubt.
    But let it rest. Now, Litio, to you.
    Good master, take it not unkindly, pray,   55
    That I have been thus pleasant° with you both.
HORTENSIO. [*To* LUCENTIO] You may go walk and give me leave° a while.
    My lessons make no music in three parts.°
LUCENTIO. Are you so formal, sir? [*Aside*] Well, I must wait
    And watch withal,° for but° I be deceived,   60
    Our fine musician groweth amorous.
HORTENSIO. Madam, before you touch the instrument,
    To learn the order of my fingering,
    I must begin with rudiments of art
    To teach you gamut° in a briefer sort,   65
    More pleasant, pithy, and effectual,
    Than hath been taught by any of my trade;
    And there it is in writing, fairly drawn.
BIANCA. Why, I am past my gamut long ago.

---

30 **Conster** construe   35 **bearing my port** taking on my style   36 **pantaloon** Gremio
(see I.i.47.s.d. note)   38 **treble jars** highest tone is off   48 *Pedascule* little pedant
(disparaging quasi-Latin)   50–51 **Aeacides / Was Ajax** Ajax, Greek warrior at Troy,
was grandson of Aeacus (Lucentio comments on next passage in Ovid)   56 **pleasant**
merry   57 **give me leave** leave me alone   58 **in three parts** for three voices
60 **withal** besides   60 **but** unless   65 **gamut** the scale

HORTENSIO. Yet read the gamut of Hortensio.   70
BIANCA. [*Reads*]
    Gamut I am, the ground° of all accord.°
       A re, to plead Hortensio's passion:
    B mi, Bianca, take him for thy lord,
       C fa ut, that loves with all affection;
    D sol re, one clef, two notes have I: 75
       E la mi show pity or I die.

    Call you this gamut? Tut, I like it not.
    Old fashions please me best; I am not so nice°
    To change true rules for odd inventions.
                    Enter a MESSENGER.
MESSENGER. Mistress, your father prays you leave your books   80
    And help to dress your sister's chamber up.
    You know tomorrow is the wedding day.
BIANCA. Farewell, sweet masters both, I must be gone.
             [*Exeunt* BIANCA *and* MESSENGER.]
LUCENTIO. Faith, mistress, then I have no cause to stay.   [*Exit.*]
LUCENTIO. But I have cause to pry into this pedant.   85
    Methinks he looks as though he were in love.
    Yet if thy thoughts, Bianca, be so humble
    To cast thy wand'ring eyes on every stale,°
    Seize thee that list.° If once I find thee ranging,°
    Hortensio will be quit with thee by changing.°   *Exit.*   90

        [Scene II. *Padua. The street in front of*
                 BAPTISTA*'s house.*]

      Enter BAPTISTA, GREMIO, TRANIO [*as Lucentio*], KATE,
            BIANCA, [LUCENTIO *as Cambio*]
            and others, ATTENDANTS.
BAPTISTA. [*To* TRANIO] Signior Lucentio, this is the 'pointed day
    That Katherine and Petruchio should be marrièd,
    And yet we hear not of our son-in-law.
    What will be said? What mockery will it be
    To want° the bridegroom when the priest attends   5
    To speak the ceremonial rites of marriage!
    What says Lucentio to this shame of ours?
KATE. No shame but mine. I must, forsooth, be forced
    To give my hand opposed against my heart
    Unto a mad-brain rudesby,° full of spleen°   10
    Who wooed in haste and means to wed at leisure.
    I told you, I, he was a frantic fool,

---

71 **ground** beginning, first note   71 **accord** harmony   78 **nice** whimsical
88 **stale** lure (as in hunting)   89 **Seize thee that list** let him who likes capture
you   89 **ranging** going astray   90 **changing** i.e., sweethearts
III.ii.5 **want** be without   10 **rudesby** uncouth fellow   10 **spleen** caprice

Hiding his bitter jests in blunt behavior.
And to be noted for° a merry man,
He'll woo a thousand, 'point the day of marriage,   15
Make friends, invite,° and proclaim the banns,
Yet never means to wed where he hath wooed.
Now must the world point at poor Katherine
And so, "Lo, there is mad Petruchio's wife,
If it would please him come and marry her."   20

TRANIO. Patience, good Katherine, and Baptista too.
Upon my life, Petruchio means but well,
Whatever fortune stays° him from his word.
Though he be blunt, I know him passing° wise;
Though he be merry, yet withal he's honest.   25

KATE. Would Katherine had never seen him though!
Exit weeping [*followed by* BIANCA *and others*].

BAPTISTA. Go, girl, I cannot blame thee now to weep.
For such an injury would vex a very saint,
Much more a shrew of thy impatient humor.°
Enter BIONDELLO.

BIONDELLO. Master, master, news! And such old° news   30
as you never heard of!

BAPTISTA. Is it new and old too? How may that be?

BIONDELLO. Why, is it not news to hear of Petruchio's
coming?

BAPTISTA. Is he come?   35

BIONDELLO. Why, no, sir.

BAPTISTA. What then?

BIONDELLO. He is coming.

BAPTISTA. When will he be here?

BIONDELLO. When he stands where I am and sees you   40
there.

TRANIO. But, say, what to thine old news?

BIONDELLO. Why, Petruchio is coming in a new hat and
an old jerkin;° a pair of old breeches thrice turned;°
a pair of boots that have been candle-cases,° one   45
buckled, another laced; an old rusty sword ta'en
out of the town armory, with a broken hilt and
chapeless;° with two broken points;° his horse hipped°
(with an old mothy saddle and stirrups of no kindred),°
besides, possessed with the glanders° and like tomose   50
in the chine;° troubled with the lampass,° in-

14 **noted for** reputed   16 **Make friends, invite** (some editors emend to "Make feast,
invite friends")   23 **stays** keeps   24 **passing** very   29 **humor** temper   30 **old** strange
44 **jerkin** short outer coat   44 **turned** i.e., inside out (to conceal wear and tear)
45 **candle-cases** worn-out boots used to keep candle ends in   48 **chapeless** lacking
the metal mounting at end of scabbard   48 **points** laces to fasten hose to garment
above   48 **hipped** with dislocated hip   49 **of no kindred** not matching   50 **glanders**
bacterial disease affecting mouth and nose   51 **mose in the chine** (1) glanders
(2) nasal discharge   51 **lampass** swollen mouth

fected with the fashions,° full of windgalls,° sped
with spavins,° rayed° with the yellows,° past cure
of the fives,° stark spoiled with the staggers,° begnawn with the bots,° swayed° in the back, and   55
shoulder-shotten;° near-legged before,° and with a
half-cheeked° bit and a head-stall° of sheep's leather,°
which, being restrained° to keep him from stumbling, hath been often burst and now repaired with
knots; one girth° six times pieced,° and a woman's   60
crupper° of velure,° which hath two letters for her
name fairly set down in studs,° and here and there
pieced with packthread.°

BAPTISTA. Who comes with him?

BIONDELLO. O sir, his lackey, for all the world caparisoned°   65
like the horse: with a linen stock° on one leg and a
kersey boot-hose° on the other, gart'red with a red and
blue list;° an old hat, and the humor of forty fancies°
pricked° in't for a feather—a monster, a very monster
in apparel, and not like a Christian footboy° or a gentle-   70
man's lackey.

TRANIO. 'Tis some odd humor° pricks° him to this fashion,
Yet oftentimes he goes but mean-appareled.

BAPTISTA. I am glad he's come, howsoe'er he comes.

BIONDELLO. Why, sir, he comes not.   75

BAPTISTA. Didst thou not say he comes?

BIONDELLO. Who? That Petruchio came?

BAPTISTA. Ay, that Petruchio came.

BIONDELLO. No, sir, I say his horse comes, with him
on his back.   80

BAPTISTA. Why, that's all one.°

---

52 **fashions** tumors (related to glanders)   52 **windgalls** swellings on lower leg
53 **spavins** swellings on upper hind leg   53 **rayed** soiled   53 **yellows** jaundice
54 **fives** vives: swelling of submaxillary glands   54 **staggers** nervous disorder causing
loss of balance   54–55 **begnawn with the bots** gnawed by parasitic worms (larvae
of the botfly)   55 **swayed** sagging   56 **shoulder-shotten** with dislocated shoulder
56 **near-legged before** with forefeet knocking together   57 **half-cheeked** wrongly
adjusted to bridle and affording less control   57 **head-stall** part of bridle which
surrounds head   57 **sheep's leather** (weaker than pigskin)   58 **restrained** pulled back
60 **girth** saddle strap under belly   60 **pieced** patched   61 **crupper** leather loop under
horse's tail to help steady saddle   61 **velure** velvet   63 **studs** large-headed nails of
brass or silver   63 **pieced with packthread** tied together with coarse thread
65 **caparisoned** outfitted   66 **stock** stocking   67 **kersey boot-hose** coarse
stocking worn with riding boot   68 **list** strip of discarded border-cloth
68 **humor of forty fancies** fanciful decoration (in place of feather)   69 **pricked**
pinned   70 **footboy** page in livery   72 **humor** mood, fancy   72 **pricks** incites
81 **all one** the same thing

BIONDELLO. [*Sings*]

Nay, by Saint Jamy,
I hold° you a penny,
A horse and a man
Is more than one   85
And yet not many.

Enter PETRUCHIO *and* GRUMIO.

PETRUCHIO. Come, where be these gallants?° Who's at home?
BAPTISTA. You are welcome, sir.
PETRUCHIO.   And yet I come not well.
BAPTISTA. And yet you halt° not.
TRANIO.   Not so well appareled
   As I wish you were.   90
PETRUCHIO. Were it better,° I should rush in thus.
   But where is Kate? Where is my lovely bride?
   How does my father? Gentles,° methinks you frown.
   And wherefore gaze this goodly company
   As if they saw some wondrous monument,°   95
   Some comet or unusual prodigy?°
BAPTISTA. Why, sir, you know this is your wedding day.
   First were we sad, fearing you would not come,
   Now sadder that you come so unprovided.°
   Fie, doff this habit,° shame to your estate,°   100
   An eyesore to our solemn festival.
TRANIO. And tell us what occasion of import°
   Hath all so long detained you from your wife
   And sent you hither so unlike yourself.
PETRUCHIO. Tedious it were to tell and harsh to hear.   105
   Sufficeth, I am come to keep my word
   Though in some part enforcèd to digress,°
   Which, at more leisure, I will so excuse
   As you shall well be satisfied with all.
   But where is Kate? I stay too long from her.   110
   The morning wears, 'tis time we were at church.
TRANIO. See not your bride in these unreverent robes.
   Go to my chamber; put on clothes of mine.
PETRUCHIO. Not I, believe me; thus I'll visit her.
BAPTISTA. But thus, I trust, you will not marry her.   115
PETRUCHIO. Good sooth,° even thus; therefore ha' done with words.
   To me she's married, not unto my clothes.
   Could I repair what she will wear° in me

---

83 **hold** bet   87 **gallants** men of fashion   89 **halt** limp (pun on *come* meaning
"walk")   91 **Were it better** even if I were better   93 **Gentles** sirs   95 **monument**
warning sign   96 **prodigy** marvel   99 **unprovided** ill-outfitted   100 **habit** costume
100 **estate** status   102 **of import** important   107 **enforcèd to digress** forced to depart
(perhaps from his plan to "buy apparel 'gainst the wedding day," II.i.308)   116 **Good
sooth** yes indeed   118 **wear** wear out

As I can change these poor accoutrements,
'Twere well for Kate and better for myself.   120
But what a fool am I to chat with you
When I should bid good morrow to my bride
And seal the title° with a lovely° kiss.   *Exit [with* GRUMIO].
TRANIO. He hath some meaning in his mad attire.
We will persuade him, be it possible,   125
To put on better ere he go to church.
BAPTISTA. I'll after him and see the event° of this.
                    Exit [with GREMIO *and* ATTENDANTS].
TRANIO. But to her love concerneth us to add
Her father's liking, which to bring to pass,
As I before imparted to your worship,   130
I am to get a man—whate'er he be
It skills° not much, we'll fit him to our turn°—
And he shall be Vincentio of Pisa,
And make assurance° here in Padua
Of greater sums than I have promisèd.   135
So shall you quietly enjoy your hope
And marry sweet Bianca with consent.
LUCENTIO. Were it not that my fellow schoolmaster
Doth watch Bianca's steps so narrowly,
'Twere good, methinks to steal our marriage,°   5
Which once performed, let all the world say no,
I'll keep mine own despite of all the world.
TRANIO. That by degrees we mean to look into
And watch our vantage° in this business.
We'll overreach° the graybeard, Gremio,   10
The narrow-prying father, Minola,
The quaint° musician, amorous Litio—
All for my master's sake, Lucentio.
                    Enter GREMIO.
Signior Gremio, came you from the church?
GREMIO. As willingly as e'er I came from school.   15
TRANIO. And is the bride and bridegroom coming home?
GREMIO. A bridegroom say you? 'Tis a groom° indeed,
A grumbling groom, and that the girl shall find.
TRANIO. Curster than she? Why, 'tis impossible.
GREMIO. Why, he's a devil, a devil, a very fiend.   20
TRANIO. Why, she's a devil, a devil, the devil's dam.°
GREMIO. Tut, she's a lamb, a dove, a fool to° him.
I'll tell you, Sir Lucentio, when the priest
Should ask, if Katherine should be his wife,

123 **title** i.e., as of ownership 123 **lovely** loving 127 **event** upshot, outcome
132 **skills** matters 132 **turn** purpose 134 **assurance** guarantee 140 **steal our
marriage** elope 144 **vantage** advantage 145 **overreach** get the better of
147 **quaint** artful 152 **groom** menial (i.e., coarse fellow) 156 **dam** mother
157 **fool to** harmless person compared with

"Ay, by goggs woones!"° quoth he and swore so loud   25
That, all amazed, the priest let fall the book,
And as he stooped again to take it up,
This mad-brained bridegroom took° him such a cuff
That down fell priest and book and book and priest.
"Now, take them up," quoth he, "if any list."°   30

TRANIO. What said the wench when he rose again?

GREMIO. Trembled and shook, for why° he stamped and swore
As if the vicar meant to cozen° him.
But after many ceremonies done
He calls for wine. "A health!" quoth he as if   35
He had been aboard, carousing° to his mates
After a storm; quaffed off the muscadel°
And threw the sops° all in the sexton's face,
Having no other reason
But that his beard grew thin and hungerly,°   40
And seemed to ask him sops as he was drinking.
This done, he took the bride about the neck
And kissed her lips with such a clamorous smack
That at the parting all the church did echo,
And I, seeing this, came thence for very shame.   45
And after me, I know, the rout° is coming.
Such a mad marriage never was before.
Hark, hark, I hear the minstrels play.   *Music plays.*

    Enter PETRUCHIO, KATE, BIANCA, HORTENSIO [*as Litio*],
        BAPTISTA [*with* GRUMIO *and others*].

PETRUCHIO. Gentlemen and friends, I thank you for your pains.
I know you think to dine with me today   50
And have prepared great store of wedding cheer,°
But so it is, my haste doth call me hence
And therefore here I mean to take my leave.

BAPTISTA. Is't possible you will away tonight?

PETRUCHIO. I must away today, before night come.   55
Make it no wonder;° if you knew my business,
You would entreat me rather go than stay.
And, honest company, I thank you all
That have beheld me give away myself
To this most patient, sweet, and virtuous wife.   60
Dine with my father, drink a health to me,
For I must hence, and farewell to you all.

TRANIO. Let us entreat you stay till after dinner.

PETRUCHIO. It may not be.

GREMIO.   Let me entreat you.

---

160 **goggs woones** by God's wounds (a common oath) 163 **took** gave 165 **list**
pleases to 167 **for why** because 168 **cozen** cheat 171 **carousing** calling "Bottoms
up" 172 **muscadel** sweet wine, conventionally drunk after marriage service 173 **sops**
pieces of cake soaked in wine; dregs 175 **hungerly** as if poorly nourished 181 **rout**
crowd 186 **cheer** food and drink 191 **Make it no wonder** don't be surprised

PETRUCHIO. It cannot be.

KATE.   Let me entreat you.   200

PETRUCHIO. I am content.

KATE.   Are you content to stay?

PETRUCHIO. I am content you shall entreat me stay,
    But yet not stay, entreat me how you can.

KATE. Now if you love me, stay.

PETRUCHIO.   Grumio, my horse!°

GRUMIO. Ay, sir, they be ready; the oats have eaten   205
    the horses.°

KATE. Nay then,
    Do what thou canst, I will not go today,
    No, nor tomorrow, not till I please myself.
    The door is open, sir, there lies your way.   210
    You may be jogging whiles your boots are green;°
    For me, I'll not be gone till I please myself.
    'Tis like you'll prove a jolly° surly groom,
    That take it on you° at the first so roundly.°

PETRUCHIO. O Kate, content thee; prithee,° be not angry.   215

KATE. I will be angry. What hast thou to do?°
    Father, be quiet; he shall stay my leisure.°

GREMIO. Ay, marry, sir, now it begins to work.

KATE. Gentlemen, forward to the bridal dinner.
    I see a woman may be made a fool   220
    If she had not a spirit to resist.

PETRUCHIO. They shall go forward, Kate, at thy command.
    Obey the bride, you that attend on her.
    Go to the feast, revel and domineer,°
    Carouse full measure to her maidenhead,   225
    Be mad and merry, or go hang yourselves.
    But for my bonny Kate, she must with me.
    Nay, look not big,° nor stamp, nor stare,° nor fret;
    I will be master of what is mine own.
    She is my goods, my chattels; she is my house,   230
    My household stuff, my field, my barn,
    My horse, my ox, my ass, my anything,°
    And here she stands. Touch her whoever dare,
    I'll bring mine action° on the proudest he
    That stops my way in Padua. Grumio,   235
    Draw forth thy weapon, we are beset with thieves.
    Rescue thy mistress, if thou be a man.

---

204 **horse** horses   205–206 **oats have eaten the horses** (1) a slip of the tongue or
(2) an ironic jest   211 **You . . . green** (proverbial way of suggesting departure to a guest,
green = new, cleaned)   213 **jolly** domineering   214 **take it on you** do as you
please   214 **roundly** roughly   215 **prithee** I pray thee   216 **What hast thou to do**
what do you have to do with it   217 **stay my leisure** await my willingness
224 **domineer** cut up in a lordly fashion   228 **big** challenging   228 **stare** swagger
232 **My horse . . . anything** (echoing Tenth Commandment)   234 **action** lawsuit

> Fear not, sweet wench; they shall not touch thee, Kate.
> I'll buckler° thee against a million.
>   *Exeunt* PETRUCHIO, KATE [*and* GRUMIO].

BAPTISTA. Nay, let them go, a couple of quiet ones.   240
GREMIO. Went they not quickly, I should die with laughing.
TRANIO. Of all mad matches never was the like.
LUCENTIO. Mistress, what's your opinion of your sister?
BIANCA. That being mad herself, she's madly mated.
GREMIO. I warrant him, Petruchio is Kated.   245
BAPTISTA. Neighbors and friends, though bride and bridegroom wants°
> For to supply the places at the table,
> You know there wants no junkets° at the feast.
> [*To Tranio*] Lucentio, you shall supply the bridegroom's place,
> And let Bianca take her sister's room.   250
TRANIO. Shall sweet Bianca practice how to bride it?
BAPTISTA. She shall, Lucentio. Come, gentlemen, let's go.   *Exeunt.*

[ACT IV

Scene I. PETRUCHIO'*s country house.*]

Enter GRUMIO.

GRUMIO. Fie, fie, on all tired jades,° on all mad masters,
> and all foul ways!° Was ever man so beaten? Was ever
> man so rayed?° Was ever man so weary? I am sent
> before to make a fire, and they are coming after to
> warm them. Now were not I a little pot and soon   5
> hot,° my very lips might freeze to my teeth, my tongue
> to the roof of my mouth, my heart in my belly, ere
> I should come by a fire to thaw me. But I with blow-
> ing the fire shall warm myself, for considering the
> weather, a taller° man than I will take cold. Holla,   10
> ho, Curtis!

Enter CURTIS [*a Servant*].

CURTIS. Who is that calls so coldly?
GRUMIO. A piece of ice. If thou doubt it, thou mayst
> slide from my shoulder to my heel with no greater a
> run° but my head and my neck. A fire, good   15
> Curtis.
CURTIS. Is my master and his wife coming, Grumio?
GRUMIO. O ay, Curtis, ay, and therefore fire, fire; cast on no
> water.°

---

239 **buckler** shield   246 **wants** are lacking   248 **junkets** sweetmeats, confections
IV.i.1 **jades** worthless horses   2 **foul ways** bad roads   3 **rayed** befouled   5-6 **little
pot and soon hot** (proverbial for small person of short temper)   10 **taller** sturdier
(with allusion to "little pot")   15 **run** running start   18-19 **cast on no water** (alters
"Cast on more water" in a well-known round)

CURTIS. Is she so hot a shrew as she's reported?   20

GRUMIO. She was, good Curtis, before this frost, but thou
    know'st winter tames man, woman, and beast; for
    it hath tamed my old master, and my new mistress,
    and myself, fellow Curtis.

CURTIS. Away, you three-inch° fool! I am no beast.   25

GRUMIO. Am I but three inches? Why, thy horn° is a foot,
    and so long am I at the least. But wilt thou make
    a fire, or shall I complain on thee to our mistress,
    whose hand—she being now at hand—thou shalt soon
    feel, to thy cold comfort, for being slow in thy hot   30
    office?°

CURTIS. I prithee, good Grumio, tell me, how goes the
    world?

GRUMIO. A cold world, Curtis, in every office but thine,
    and therefore, fire. Do thy duty and have thy duty,°   35
    for my master and mistress are almost frozen to
    death.

CURTIS. There's fire ready, and therefore, good Grumio,
    the news.

GRUMIO. Why, "Jack boy, ho boy!"° and as much news as   40
    wilt thou.

CURTIS. Come, you are so full of cony-catching.°

GRUMIO. Why therefore fire, for I have caught extreme
    cold. Where's the cook? Is supper ready, the house
    trimmed, rushes strewed,° cobwebs swept, the serv-   45
    ingmen in their new fustian,° the white stockings, and
    every officer° his wedding garment on? Be the jacks°
    fair within, the jills° fair without, the carpets° laid
    and everything in order?

CURTIS. All ready, and therefore, I pray thee, news.   50

GRUMIO. First, know my horse is tired, my master and mis-
    tress fall'n out.

CURTIS. How?

GRUMIO. Out of their saddles into the dirt—and thereby
    hangs a tale.   55

CURTIS. Let's ha't, good Grumio.

GRUMIO. Lend thine ear.

CURTIS. Here.

GRUMIO. There.   [*Strikes him.*]

CURTIS. This 'tis to feel a tale, not to hear a tale.   60

---

25 **three-inch** (1) another allusion to Grumio's small stature (2) a phallic jest, the first
of several   26 **horn** (symbol of cuckold)   30–31 **hot office** job of making a fire
35 **thy duty** what is due thee   40 **"Jack boy, ho boy!"** (from another round or
catch)   42 **cony-catching** rabbit-catching (i.e., tricking simpletons; with pun on *catch*,
the song)   45 **strewed** i.e., on floor (for special occasion)   46 **fustian** coarse cloth
(cotton and flax)   47 **officer** servant   47 **jacks** (1) menservants (2) half-pint leather
drinking cups   48 **jills** (1) maids (2) gill-size metal drinking cups   48 **carpets** table
covers

GRUMIO. And therefore 'tis called a sensible° tale, and this
    cuff was but to knock at your ear and beseech list'ning.
    Now I begin. *Imprimis,*° we came down a foul° hill,
    my master riding behind my mistress—
CURTIS. Both of° one horse?   65
GRUMIO. What's that to thee?
CURTIS. Why, a horse.
GRUMIO. Tell thou the tale. But hadst thou not crossed°
    me thou shouldst have heard how her horse fell
    and she under her horse. Thou shouldst have   70
    heard in how miry a place, how she was bemoiled,°
    how he left her with the horse upon her, how
    he beat me because her horse stumbled, how
    she waded through the dirt to pluck him off me;
    how he swore, how she prayed that never prayed   75
    before; how I cried, how the horses ran away, how
    her bridle was burst, how I lost my crupper, with
    many things of worthy memory which now shall die
    in oblivion, and thou return unexperienced° to thy
    grave.   80
CURTIS. By this reck'ning° he is more shrew than she.
GRUMIO. Ay, and that thou and the proudest of you all
    shall find when he comes home. But what° talk I
    of this? Call forth Nathaniel, Joseph, Nicholas, Philip,
    Walter, Sugarsop, and the rest. Let their heads be   85
    slickly° combed, their blue° coats brushed, and their
    garters of an indifferent° knit. Let them curtsy with
    their left legs and not presume to touch a hair of
    my master's horsetail till they kiss their hands. Are they
    all ready?   90
CURTIS. They are.
GRUMIO. Call them forth.
CURTIS. Do you hear, ho? You must meet my master to
    countenance° my mistress.
GRUMIO. Why, she hath a face of her own.   95
CURTIS. Who knows not that?
GRUMIO. Thou, it seems, that calls for company to coun-
    tenance her.
CURTIS. I call them forth to credit° her.
GRUMIO. Why, she comes to borrow nothing of them.   100
                Enter four or five SERVINGMEN.
NATHANIEL. Welcome home, Grumio!
PHILIP. How now, Grumio?
JOSEPH. What, Grumio!

---

61 **sensible** (1) rational (2) "feel"-able 63 **Imprimis** first 63 **foul** muddy 65 **of**
on 68 **crossed** interrupted 71 **bemoiled** muddied 79 **unexperienced** uninformed 81 **reck'ning** account 83 **what** why 86 **slickly** smoothly 86 **blue** (usual
color of servants' clothing) 87 **indifferent** matching (?) appropriate (?) 94 **countenance** show respect to (with puns following) 99 **credit** honor

NICHOLAS. Fellow Grumio!

NATHANIEL. How now, old lad!   105

GRUMIO. Welcome, you; how now, you; what, you; fellow,
    you; and thus much for greeting. Now, my spruce com-
    panions, is all ready and all things neat?

NATHANIEL. All things is ready. How near is our mas-
    ter?   110

GRUMIO. E'en at hand, alighted by this,° and therefore
    be not—Cock's° passion, silence! I hear my mas-
    ter.

Enter PETRUCHIO *and* KATE.

PETRUCHIO. Where be these knaves? What, no man at door
    To hold my stirrup nor to take my horse?   115
    Where is Nathaniel, Gregory, Philip?

ALL SERVINGMEN. Here, here, sir, here, sir.

PETRUCHIO. Here, sir, here, sir, here, sir, here, sir!
    You loggerheaded° and unpolished grooms!
    What, no attendance? No regard? No duty?   120
    Where is the foolish knave I sent before?

GRUMIO. Here, sir, as foolish as I was before.

PETRUCHIO. You peasant swain!° You whoreson° malt-horse drudge!°
    Did I not bid thee meet me in the park°
    And bring along these rascal knaves with thee?   125

GRUMIO. Nathaniel's coat, sir, was not fully made
    And Gabrel's pumps were all unpinked° i' th' heel.
    There was no link° to color Peter's hat,
    And Walter's dagger was not come from sheathing.°
    There were none fine but Adam, Rafe, and Gregory;   130
    The rest were ragged, old, and beggarly.
    Yet, as they are, here are they come to meet you.

PETRUCHIO. Go, rascals, go, and fetch my supper in.

Exeunt SERVANTS.

    [*Sings*] "Where is the life that late I led?"°
    Where are those°—Sit down, Kate, and welcome.   135
    Soud,° soud, soud, soud!

Enter SERVANTS *with supper.*

    Why, when,° I say?—Nay, good sweet Kate, be merry.—
    Off with my boots, you rogues, you villains! When?
    [*Sings*] "It was the friar of orders gray,

111 **this** now   112 **Cock's** God's (i.e., Christ's)   119 **loggerheaded** blockheaded
123 **swain** bumpkin   123 **whoreson** bastardly   123 **malt-horse drudge** slow horse on
brewery treadmill   124 **park** country-house grounds   127 **unpinked** lacking embellish-
ment made by pinking (making small holes in leather)   128 **link** torch, providing blacking   129 **sheathing** repairing scabbard   134 **"Where...led?"** (from an old ballad)
135 **those** servants   136 **Soud** (exclamation variously explained; some editors emend to
Food)   137 **when** (exclamation of annoyance, as in next line)

As he forth walkèd on his way"° —   140
Out, you rogue, you pluck my foot awry!
Take that, and mend° the plucking of the other.   [*Strikes him.*]
Be merry, Kate. Some water here! What ho!
                    Enter one with water.
 Where's my spaniel Troilus? Sirrah, get you hence
And bid my cousin Ferdinand come hither—   [*Exit* SERVANT.]   145
One, Kate, that you must kiss and be acquainted with.
Where are my slippers? Shall I have some water?
Come, Kate, and wash, and welcome heartily.
You whoreson villain, will you let it fall?   [*Strikes him.*]
KATE. Patience, I pray you. 'Twas a fault unwilling.   150
PETRUCHIO. A whoreson, beetle-headed,° flap-eared knave!
Come, Kate, sit down; I know you have a stomach.°
Will you give thanks,° sweet Kate, or else shall I?
What's this? Mutton?
FIRST SERVINGMAN.   Ay.
PETRUCHIO.   Who brought it?
PETER.   I.
PETRUCHIO. 'Tis burnt, and so is all the meat.   155
What dogs are these! Where is the rascal cook?
How durst you, villains, bring it from the dresser,°
And serve it thus to me that love it not?
There, take it to you, trenchers,° cups, and all,
                    [*Throws food and dishes at them.*]
You heedless joltheads° and unmannered slaves!   160
What, do you grumble? I'll be with° you straight.°
KATE. I pray you, husband, be not so disquiet.
The meat was well if you were so contented.°
PETRUCHIO. I tell thee, Kate, 'twas burnt and dried away,
And I expressly am forbid to touch it,   165
For it engenders choler,° planteth anger,
And better 'twere that both of us did fast—
Since of ourselves, ourselves are choleric°—
Than feed it° with such overroasted flesh.
Be patient. Tomorrow't shall be mended,°   170
And for this night we'll fast for company.°
Come, I will bring thee to thy bridal chamber.   *Exeunt.*

139–40 **"It was...his way"** (from another old song) 142 **mend** improve
151 **beetle-headed** mallet-headed 152 **stomach** (1) hunger (2) irascibility 153 **give
thanks** say grace 157 **dresser** sideboard 159 **trenchers** wooden platters 160 **jolt-
heads** boneheads (*jolt* is related to *jaw* or *jowl*) 161 **with** even with 161 **straight**
directly 163 **so contented** willing to see it as it was 166 **choler** bile, the "humor"
(fluid) supposed to produce anger 168 **choleric** bilious, i.e., hot-tempered
169 **it** i.e., their choler 170 **'t shall be mended** things will be better 171 **for company** together

Enter SERVANTS *severally*.

NATHANIEL. Peter, didst ever see the like?

PETER. He kills her in her own humor.°

           Enter CURTIS, *a Servant*.

GRUMIO. Where is he?   175

CURTIS. In her chamber, making a sermon of continency
   to her.
   And rails and swears and rates,° that she, poor soul,
   Knows not which way to stand, to look, to speak,
   And sits as one new-risen from a dream.   180
   Away, away, for he is coming hither.   [*Exeunt.*]

           Enter PETRUCHIO.

PETRUCHIO. Thus have I politicly° begun my reign,
   And 'tis my hope to end successfully.
   My falcon° now is sharp° and passing empty,
   And till she stoop° she must not be full gorged,°   185
   For then she never looks upon her lure.°
   Another way I have to man° my haggard,°
   To make her come and know her keeper's call,
   That is, to watch° her as we watch these kites°
   That bate and beat° and will not be obedient.   190
   She eat° no meat today, nor none shall eat.
   Last night she slept not, nor tonight she shall not.
   As with the meat, some undeservèd fault
   I'll find about the making of the bed,
   And here I'll fling the pillow, there the bolster,°   195
   This way the coverlet, another way the sheets.
   Ay, and amid this hurly° I intend°
   That all is done in reverent care of her,
   And in conclusion she shall watch° all night.
   And if she chance to nod I'll rail and brawl   200
   And with the clamor keep her still awake.
   This is a way to kill a wife with kindness,°
   And thus I'll curb her mad and headstrong humor.
   He that knows better how to tame a shrew,°
   Now let him speak— 'tis charity to show.   *Exit.*   205

---

174 **kills her in her own humor** conquers her by using her own disposition
178 **rates** scolds   182 **politicly** with a calculated plan   184 **falcon** hawk trained for
hunting (falconry figures continue for several lines)   184 **sharp** pinched with hunger
185 **stoop** (1) obey (2) swoop to the lure   185 **full gorged** fully fed   186 **lure** device
used in training a hawk to return from flight   187 **man** (1) tame (2) be a man to
187 **haggard** hawk captured after reaching maturity   189 **watch** keep from sleep
189 **kites** type of small hawk   190 **bate and beat** flap and flutter (i.e., in jittery
resistance to training)   191 **eat** ate (pronounced *et*, as still in Britain)   195 **bolster**
cushion extending width of bed as under-support for pillows   197 **hurly** disturbance
197 **intend** profess   199 **watch** stay awake   202 **kill a wife with kindness** (ironic
allusion to proverb on ruining a wife by pampering)   204 **shrew** (rhymes with "show")

[Scene II. *Padua. The street in front of*
BAPTISTA*'s house.*]

Enter TRANIO [*as Lucentio*] *and* HORTENSIO [*as Litio*].

TRANIO. Is't possible, friend Litio, that Mistress Bianca
    Doth fancy° any other but Lucentio?
    I tell you, sir, she bears me fair in hand.°
HORTENSIO. Sir, to satisfy you in what I have said,
    Stand by and mark the manner of his teaching.   5
                           [*They eavesdrop.*]

Enter BIANCA [*and* LUCENTIO *as Cambio*].

LUCENTIO. Now mistress, profit you in what you read?
BIANCA. What, master, read you? First resolve° me that.
LUCENTIO. I read that° I profess,° the Art to love.°
BIANCA. And may you prove, sir, master of your art.
LUCENTIO. While you, sweet dear, prove mistress of my heart.   10
                              [*They court.*]
HORTENSIO. Quick proceeders,° marry!° Now, tell me, I pray,
    You that durst swear that your mistress Bianca
    Loved none in the world so well as Lucentio.
TRANIO. O despiteful° love! Unconstant womankind!
    I tell thee, Litio, this is wonderful.°   15
HORTENSIO. Mistake no more. I am not Litio,
    Nor a musician, as I seem to be,
    But one that scorn to live in this disguise,
    For such a one as leaves a gentleman
    And makes a god of such a cullion.°   20
    Know, sir, that I am called Hortensio.
TRANIO. Signior Hortensio, I have often heard
    Of your entire affection to Bianca,
    And since mine eyes are witness of her lightness,°
    I will with you, if you be so contented,   25
    Forswear° Bianca and her love forever.
HORTENSIO. See, how they kiss and court! Signior Lucentio,
    Here is my hand and here I firmly vow
    Never to woo her more, but do forswear her,
    As one unworthy all the former favors°   30
    That I have fondly° flattered her withal.
TRANIO. And here I take the like unfeignèd oath,
    Never to marry with her though she would entreat.
    Fie on her! See how beastly° she doth court him.
HORTENSIO. Would all the world but he had quite forsworn.°   35
    For me, that I may surely keep mine oath,

IV.ii.2 **fancy** like 3 **bears me fair in hand** leads me on 7 **resolve** answer 8 **that**
what 8 **profess** avow, practice 8 **Art to Love** (i.e., Ovid's *Ars Amandi*)
11 **proceeders** (pun on idiom "proceed Master of Arts"; cf. line 9) 11 **marry** by Mary
(mild exclamation) 14 **despiteful** spiteful 15 **wonderful** causing wonder 20 **cullion**
low fellow (literally, testicle) 24 **lightness** (cf. "light woman") 26 **Forswear** "swear
off" 30 **favors** marks of esteem 31 **fondly** foolishly 34 **beastly** unashamedly
35 **Would...forsworn** i.e., would she had only one lover

I will be married to a wealthy widow
Ere three days pass, which° hath as long loved me
As I have loved this proud disdainful haggard.°
And so farewell, Signior Lucentio.   40
Kindness in women, not their beauteous looks,
Shall win my love, and so I take my leave
In resolution as I swore before.   [*Exit.*]

TRANIO. Mistress Bianca, bless you with such grace
As 'longeth to a lover's blessèd case.   45
Nay, I have ta'en you napping,° gentle love,
And have forsworn you with Hortensio.

BIANCA. Tranio, you jest. But have you both forsworn me?

TRANIO. Mistress, we have.

LUCENTIO.   Then we are rid of Litio.

TRANIO. I' faith, he'll have a lusty° widow now,   50
That shall be wooed and wedded in a day.

BIANCA. God give him joy!

TRANIO. Ay, and he'll tame her.

BIANCA.   He says so, Tranio.

TRANIO. Faith, he is gone unto the taming school.

BIANCA. The taming school! What, is there such a place?   55

TRANIO. Ay, mistress, and Petruchio is the master,
That teacheth tricks eleven and twenty long°
To tame a shrew and charm her chattering tongue.

                        Enter BIONDELLO.

BIONDELLO. O master, master, I have watched so long
That I am dog-weary, but at last I spied   60
An ancient angel° coming down the hill
Will serve the turn.°

TRANIO.   What° is he, Biondello?

BIONDELLO. Master, a mercatante° or a pedant,°
I know not what, but formal in apparel,
In gait and countenance° surely like a father.   65

LUCENTIO. And what of him, Tranio?

TRANIO. If he be credulous and trust my tale,
I'll make him glad to seem Vincentio,
And give assurance to Baptista Minola
As if he were the right Vincentio.   70
Take in your love and then let me alone.

                        [*Exeunt* LUCENTIO *and* BIANCA.]

---

38 **which** who   39 **haggard** (cf. IV.i.187)   46 **ta'en you napping** seen you "kiss and
court" (line 27)   50 **lusty** lively   57 **tricks eleven and twenty long** (1) many tricks
(2) possibly an allusion to card game "thirty-one" (cf.I.ii.33)   61 **ancient angel** man of
good old stamp (*angel* = coin; cf. "gentleman of the old school")   62 **Will serve the
turn** who will do for our purposes   62 **What** what kind of man   63 **mercatante**
merchant   63 **pedant** schoolmaster   65 **gait and countenance** bearing and style

Enter a PEDANT.

PEDANT. God save you, sir.

TRANIO.   And you, sir. You are welcome.
Travel you far on, or are you at the farthest?

PEDANT. Sir, at the farthest for a week or two,
But then up farther and as far as Rome,   75
And so to Tripoli if God lend me life.

TRANIO. What countryman,° I pray?

PEDANT.   Of Mantua.

TRANIO. Of Mantua, sir? Marry, God forbid!
And come to Padua, careless of your life?

PEDANT. My life, sir? How, I pray? For that goes hard.°   80

TRANIO. 'Tis death for anyone in Mantua
To come to Padua. Know you not the cause?
Your ships are stayed° at Venice and the Duke,
For private quarrel 'twixt your duke and him,
Hath published and proclaimed it openly.   85
'Tis marvel, but that you are but newly come,
You might have heard it else proclaimed about.

PEDANT. Alas, sir, it is worse for me than so,°
For I have bills for money by exchange
From Florence and must here deliver them.   90

TRANIO. Well, sir, to do you courtesy,
This will I do and this I will advise° you.
First tell me, have you ever been at Pisa?

PEDANT. Ay, sir, in Pisa have I often been—
Pisa, renownèd for grave citizens.   95

TRANIO. Among them, know you one Vincentio?

PEDANT. I know him not but I have heard of him—
A merchant of incomparable wealth.

TRANIO. He is my father, sir, and, sooth to say,
In count'nance somewhat doth resemble you.   100

BIONDELLO. [*Aside*] As much as an apple doth an oyster,
and all one.°

TRANIO. To save your life in this extremity,
This favor will I do you for his sake,
And think it not the worst of all your fortunes   105
That you are like to Sir Vincentio.
His name and credit° shall you undertake,°
And in my house you shall be friendly lodged.
Look that you take upon you° as you should.
You understand me, sir? So shall you stay   110
Till you have done your business in the city.
If this be court'sy, sir, accept of it.

77 **What countryman** a man of what country 80 **goes hard** (cf. "is rough")
83 **stayed** held 88 **than so** than it appears so far 92 **advise** explain to 102 **all one**
no difference 107 **credit** standing 107 **undertake** adopt 109 **take upon you** assume
your role

PEDANT. O sir, I do, and will repute° you ever
    The patron of my life and liberty.
TRANIO. Then go with me to make the matter good.   115
    This, by the way,° I let you understand:
    My father is here looked for every day
    To pass assurance° of a dower in marriage
    'Twixt me and one Baptista's daughter here.
    In all these circumstances I'll instruct you.   120
    Go with me to clothe you as becomes you.   *Exeunt.*

[Scene III. *In* PETRUCHIO's *house.*]

Enter KATE *and* GRUMIO.

GRUMIO. No, no, forsooth, I dare not for my life.
KATE. The more my wrong,° the more his spite appears.
    What, did he marry me to famish me?
    Beggars that come unto my father's door,
    Upon entreaty have a present° alms;   5
    If not, elsewhere they meet with charity.
    But I, who never knew how to entreat
    Nor never needed that I should entreat,
    Am starved for meat,° giddy for lack of sleep,
    With oaths kept waking and with brawling fed.   10
    And that which spites me more than all these wants,
    He does it under name of perfect love,
    As who should say,° if I should sleep or eat
    'Twere deadly sickness or else present death.
    I prithee go and get me some repast,   15
    I care not what, so° it be wholesome food.
GRUMIO. What say you to a neat's° foot?
KATE. 'Tis passing good; I prithee let me have it.
GRUMIO. I fear it is too choleric° a meat.
    How say you to a fat tripe finely broiled?   20
KATE. I like it well. Good Grumio, fetch it me.
GRUMIO. I cannot tell, I fear 'tis choleric.
    What say you to a piece of beef and mustard?
KATE. A dish that I do love to feed upon.
GRUMIO. Ay, but the mustard is too hot a little.   25
KATE. Why then, the beef, and let the mustard rest.
GRUMIO. Nay then, I will not. You shall have the mustard
    Or else you get no beef of Grumio.
KATE. Then both or one, or anything thou wilt.
GRUMIO. Why then, the mustard without the beef.   30

113 **repute** esteem 116 **by the way** as we walk along 118 **pass assurance** give a
guarantee IV.iii.2 **The more my wrong** the greater the wrong done me 5 **present**
prompt 9 **meat** food 13 **As who should say** as if to say 16 **so** as long as
17 **neat's** ox's or calf's 19 **choleric** temper-producing

KATE. Go, get thee gone, thou false deluding slave,   *Beats him.*
    That feed'st me with the very name° of meat.
    Sorrow on thee and all the pack of you
    That triumph thus upon my misery.
    Go, get thee gone, I say.   35
         Enter PETRUCHIO *and* HORTENSIO *with meat.*
PETRUCHIO. How fares my Kate? What, sweeting, all amort?°
HORTENSIO. Mistress, what cheer?°
KATE.   Faith, as cold° as can be.
PETRUCHIO. Pluck up thy spirits; look cheerfully upon me.
    Here, love, thou seest how diligent I am
    To dress thy meat° myself and bring it thee.   40
    I am sure, sweet Kate, this kindness merits thanks.
    What, not a word? Nay then, thou lov'st it not,
    And all my pains is sorted to no proof.°
    Here, take away this dish.
KATE.   I pray you, let it stand.
PETRUCHIO. The poorest service is repaid with thanks,   45
    And so shall mine before you touch the meat.
KATE. I thank you, sir.
HORTENSIO. Signior Petruchio, fie, you are to blame.
    Come, Mistress Kate, I'll bear you company.
PETRUCHIO. [*Aside*] Eat it up all, Hortensio, if thou lovest me;   50
    Much good do it unto thy gentle heart.
    Kate, eat apace. And now, my honey love,
    Will we return unto thy father's house
    And revel it as bravely° as the best,
    With silken coats and caps and golden rings,   55
    With ruffs° and cuffs and fardingales° and things,
    With scarfs and fans and double change of brav'ry,°
    With amber bracelets, beads, and all this knav'ry.°
    What, hast thou dined? The tailor stays thy leisure°
    To deck thy body with his ruffling° treasure.   60
             Enter TAILOR.
    Come, tailor, let us see these ornaments.
            Enter HABERDASHER.
    Lay forth the gown. What news with you, sir?
HABERDASHER. Here is the cap your Worship did bespeak.°
PETRUCHIO. Why, this was molded on a porringer°—
    A velvet dish. Fie, fie, 'tis lewd° and filthy.   65

32 **very name** name only 36 **all amort** depressed, lifeless (cf. "mortified")
37 **what cheer** how are things 37 **cold** (cf. "not so hot"; "cold comfort," IV.i.30)
40 **To dress thy meat** in fixing your food 43 **sorted to no proof** have come to
nothing 54 **bravely** handsomely dressed 56 **ruffs** stiffly starched, wheel-shaped
collars 56 **fardingales** farthingales, hooped skirts of petticoats 57 **brav'ry** handsome
clothes 58 **knav'ry** girlish things 59 **stays thy leisure** awaits your permission
60 **ruffling** gaily ruffled 63 **bespeak** order 64 **porringer** soup bowl 65 **lewd** vile

Why, 'tis a cockle° or a walnut shell,
A knack,° a toy, a trick,° a baby's cap.
Away with it! Come, let me have a bigger.
KATE. I'll have no bigger. This doth fit the time,°
    And gentlewomen wear such caps as these.   70
PETRUCHIO. When you are gentle you shall have one too,
    And not till then.
HORTENSIO. [*Aside*] That will not be in haste.
KATE. Why, sir, I trust I may have leave to speak,
    And speak I will. I am no child, no babe.
    Your betters have endured me say my mind,   75
    And if you cannot, best you stop your ears.
    My tongue will tell the anger of my heart,
    Or else my heart, concealing it, will break,
    And rather than it shall I will be free
    Even to the uttermost, as I please, in words.   80
PETRUCHIO. Why, thou sayst true. It is a paltry cap,
    A custard-coffin,° a bauble, a silken pie.°
    I love thee well in that thou lik'st it not.
KATE. Love me or love me not, I like the cap,
    And it I will have or I will have none.   [*Exit* HABERDASHER.]   85
PETRUCHIO. Thy gown? Why, ay. Come, tailor, let us see't.
    O mercy, God! What masquing° stuff is here?
    What's this? A sleeve? 'Tis like a demi-cannon.°
    What, up and down,° carved like an apple tart?
    Here's snip and nip and cut and slish and slash,   90
    Like to a censer° in a barber's shop.
    Why, what, a° devil's name, tailor, call'st thou this?
HORTENSIO. [*Aside*] I see she's like to have neither cap nor gown.
TAILOR. You bid me make it orderly and well,
    According to the fashion and the time.   95
PETRUCHIO. Marry, and did, but if you be rememb'red,
    I did not bid you mar it to the time.°
    Go, hop me over every kennel° home,
    For you shall hop without my custom, sir.
    I'll none of it. Hence, make your best of it.   100
KATE. I never saw a better-fashioned gown,
    More quaint,° more pleasing, nor more commendable.
    Belike° you mean to make a puppet of me.
PETRUCHIO. Why, true, he means to make a puppet of thee.
TAILOR. She says your worship means to make a puppet of her.   105
PETRUCHIO. O monstrous arrogance!
    Thou liest, thou thread, thou thimble,

---

66 **cockle** shell of a mollusk   67 **knack** knick-knack   67 **trick** plaything   69 **doth fit the time** is in fashion   82 **custard-coffin** custard crust   82 **pie** meat pie   87 **masquing** for masquerades or actors' costumes   88 **demi-cannon** big cannon   89 **up and down** entirely   91 **censer** incense burner with perforated top   92 **a** in the   97 **to the time** for all time (cf. line 95, in which "the time" is "the contemporary style")   98 **kennel** gutter (canal)   102 **quaint** skillfully made   103 **Belike** no doubt

Thou yard, three-quarters, half-yard, quarter, nail!°
Thou flea, thou nit,° thou winter cricket thou!
Braved° in mine own house with° a skein of thread!　　　110
Away, thou rag, thou quantity,° thou remnant,
Or I shall so bemete° thee with thy yard
As thou shalt think on prating° whilst thou liv'st.
I tell thee, I, that thou hast marred her gown.

TAILOR. Your worship is deceived. The gown is made　　　115
　　Just as my master had direction.°
　　Grumio gave order how it should be done.

GRUMIO. I gave him no order; I gave him the stuff.

TAILOR. But how did you desire it should be made?

GRUMIO. Marry, sir, with needle and thread.　　　120

TAILOR. But did you not request to have it cut?

GRUMIO. Thou hast faced° many things.

TAILOR. I have.

GRUMIO. Face° not me. Thou hast braved° many men;
　　brave° not me. I will neither be faced nor braved. I　　　125
　　say unto thee, I bid thy master cut out the gown,
　　but I did not bid him cut it to pieces. *Ergo,*° thou
　　liest.

TAILOR. Why, here is the note° of the fashion to testify.

PETRUCHIO. Read it.　　　130

GRUMIO. The note lies in's throat° if he° say I said so.

TAILOR. *"Imprimis,*° a loose-bodied gown."°

GRUMIO. Master, if ever I said loose-bodied gown, sew me
　　in the skirts of it and beat me to death with a bottom°
　　of brown thread. I said, a gown.　　　135

PETRUCHIO. Proceed.

TAILOR. "With a small compassed° cape."

GRUMIO. I confess the cape.

TAILOR. "With a trunk° sleeve."

GRUMIO. I confess two sleeves.　　　140

TAILOR. "The sleeves curiously° cut."

PETRUCHIO. Ay, there's the villainy.

GRUMIO. Error i' th' bill,° sir, error i' the' bill. I commanded
　　the sleeves should be cut out and sewed up again,
　　and that I'll prove upon° thee, though thy little finger be　　　145
　　armed in a thimble.

---

108 **nail** 1/16 of a yard　109 **nit** louse's egg　110 **Braved** defied　110 **with** by
111 **quantity** fragment　112 **bemete** (1) measure (2) beat　113 **think on prating**
remember your silly talk　116 **had direction** received orders　122 **faced** trimmed
124 **Face** challenge　124 **braved** equipped with finery　125 **brave** defy　127 **Ergo**
therefore　129 **note** written notation　131 **in's throat** from the heart, with premedita-
tion　131 **he** it　132 **Imprimis** first　132 **loose-bodied gown** (worn by prostitutes,
with *loose* in pun)　134 **bottom** spool　137 **compassed** with circular edge　139 **trunk**
full (cf. line 88)　141 **curiously** painstakingly　143 **bill** i.e., the "note"　145 **prove**
upon test by dueling with

TAILOR. This is true that I say. And° I had thee in place
    where,° thou shouldst know it.
GRUMIO. I am for° thee straight.° Take thou the bill,° give
    me thy mete-yard,° and spare not me.   150
HORTENSIO. God-a-mercy, Grumio, then he shall have no
    odds.
PETRUCHIO. Well, sir, in brief, the gown is not for me.
GRUMIO. You are i' th' right, sir; 'tis for my mistress.
PETRUCHIO. Go, take it up unto° thy master's use.°   155
  GRUMIO. Villain, not for thy life! Take up my mistress' gown
    for thy master's use!
PETRUCHIO. Why sir, what's your conceit° in that?
  GRUMIO. O sir, the conceit is deeper than you think for.
    Take up my mistress' gown to his master's use! O,   160
    fie, fie, fie!
PETRUCHIO. [*Aside*] Hortensio, say thou wilt see the tailor paid.
    [*To* TAILOR] Go take it hence; be gone and say no more.
HORTENSIO. Tailor, I'll pay thee for thy gown tomorrow;
    Take no unkindness of his hasty words.   165
    Away, I say, commend me to thy master.   *Exit* TAILOR.
PETRUCHIO. Well, come, my Kate, we will unto your father's,
    Even in these honest mean habiliments.°
    Our purses shall be proud, our garments poor,
    For 'tis the mind that makes the body rich,   170
    And as the sun breaks through the darkest clouds
    So honor peereth° in the meanest habit.°
    What, is the jay more precious than the lark
    Because his feathers are more beautiful?
    Or is the adder better than the eel   175
    Because his painted skin contents the eye?
    O no, good Kate, neither art thou the worse
    For this poor furniture° and mean array.
    If thou account'st it shame, lay° it on me,
    And therefore frolic. We will hence forthwith   180
    To feast and sport us at thy father's house.
    [*To* GRUMIO] Go call my men, and let us straight to him;
    And bring our horses unto Long-lane end.
    There will we mount, and thither walk on foot.
    Let's see, I think 'tis now some seven o'clock,   185
    And well we may come there by dinnertime.°
KATE. I dare assure you, sir, 'tis almost two,
    And 'twill be suppertime ere you come there.

---

147 **And** if 147–148 **place where** the right place 149 **for** ready for 149 **straight** right
now 149 **bill** (1) written order (2) long-handled weapon 150 **mete-yard** yardstick
155 **up unto** away for 155 **use** i.e., in whatever way he can; Grumio uses these words
for a sex joke 158 **conceit** idea 168 **habiliments** clothes 172 **peereth** is recognized
172 **habit** clothes 178 **furniture** outfit 179 **lay** blame 186 **dinnertime** midday

PETRUCHIO. It shall be seven ere I go to horse.
    Look what° I speak or do or think to do,   190
    You are still crossing° it. Sirs, let't alone:
    I will not go today, and ere I do,
    It shall be what o'clock I say it is.
HORTENSIO. [*Aside*] Why, so this gallant will command
    the sun.   [*Exeunt.*]

[Scene IV. *Padua. The street in front
of* BAPTISTA'*s house.*]

Enter TRANIO [*as Lucentio*] *and the* PEDANT
dressed like Vincentio.

TRANIO. Sir, this is the house. Please it you that I call?
PEDANT. Ay, what else? And but° I be deceived,
    Signior Baptista may remember me
    Near twenty years ago in Genoa,
    Where we were lodgers at the Pegasus.°   5
TRANIO. 'Tis well, and hold your own° in any case
    With such austerity as 'longeth to a father.
PEDANT. I warrant° you. But sir, here comes your boy;
    'Twere good he were schooled.°
Enter BIONDELLO.
TRANIO. Fear you not him. Sirrah Biondello,   10
    Now do your duty throughly,° I advise you.
    Imagine 'twere the right Vincentio.
BIONDELLO. Tut, fear not me.
TRANIO. But hast thou done thy errand to Baptista?
BIONDELLO. I told him that your father was at Venice   15
    And that you looked for him this day in Padua.
TRANIO. Th' art a tall° fellow. Hold thee that° to drink.
    Here comes Baptista. Set your countenance, sir.
Enter BAPTISTA *and* LUCENTIO [*as Cambio*].
PEDANT *booted and bareheaded.*°
    Signior Baptista, you are happily met.
    [*To the* PEDANT] Sir, this is the gentleman I told you of.   20
    I pray you, stand good father to me now,
    Give me Bianca for my patrimony.
PEDANT. Soft,° son.
    Sir, by your leave. Having come to Padua
    To gather in some debts, my son Lucentio   25

---

190 **Look what** whatever 191 **crossing** obstructing, going counter to IV.iv.2 **but**
unless 3–5 **Signior Baptista . . . Pegasus** (the Pedant is practicing as Vincentio)
5 **Pegasus** common English inn name (after mythical winged horse symbolizing poetic
inspiration) 6 **hold your own** act your role 8 **warrant** guarantee 9 **schooled**
informed (about his role) 11 **throughly** thoroughly 17 **tall** excellent 17 **Hold thee
that** i.e., take this tip 18 s.d. **booted and bareheaded** i.e., arriving from a journey
and courteously greeting Baptista 23 **Soft** take it easy

Made me acquainted with a weighty cause°
Of love between your daughter and himself.
And—for the good report I hear of you,
And for the love he beareth to your daughter,
And she to him—to stay° him not too long,   30
I am content, in a good father's care,
To have him matched. And if you please to like°
No worse than I, upon some agreement
Me shall you find ready and willing
With one consent to have her so bestowed,   35
For curious° I cannot be with you,
Signior Baptista, of whom I hear so well.

BAPTISTA. Sir, pardon me in what I have to say.
     Your plainness and your shortness° please me well.
     Right true it is, your son Lucentio here   40
     Doth love my daughter and she loveth him—
     Or both dissemble deeply their affections—
     And therefore, if you say no more than this,
     That like a father you will deal with him
     And pass° my daughter a sufficient dower,   45
     The match is made, and all is done.
     Your son shall have my daughter with consent.

TRANIO. I thank you, sir. Where, then, do you know° best
     We be affied° and such assurance ta'en
     As shall with either part's° agreement stand?   50

BAPTISTA. Not in my house, Lucentio, for you know
     Pitchers have ears, and I have many servants.
     Besides, old Gremio is heark'ning still,°
     And happily° we might be interrupted.

TRANIO. Then at my lodging and it like° you.   55
     There doth my father lie,° and there this night
     We'll pass° the business privately and well.
     Send for your daughter by your servant here;
     My boy shall fetch the scrivener° presently.
     The worst is this, that at so slender warning°   60
     You are like to have a thin and slender pittance.°

BAPTISTA. It likes° me well. Cambio, hie you home
     And bid Bianca make her ready straight,
     And, if you will, tell what hath happenèd:
     Lucentio's father is arrived in Padua,   65
     And how she's like to be Lucentio's wife.   [*Exit* LUCENTIO.]

BIONDELLO. I pray the gods she may with all my heart!   *Exit.*

---

26 **weighty cause** important matter   30 **stay** delay   32 **like** i.e., the match
36 **curious** overinsistent on fine points   39 **shortness** conciseness   45 **pass** legally
settle upon   48 **know** think   49 **affied** formally engaged   50 **part's** party's
53 **heark'ning still** listening constantly   54 **happily** perchance   55 **and it like**
if it please   56 **lie** stay   57 **pass** settle   59 **scrivener** notary   60 **slender warning**
short notice   61 **pittance** meal   62 **likes** pleases

TRANIO. Dally not with the gods, but get thee gone.
　　Signior Baptista, shall I lead the way?
　　Welcome, one mess° is like to be your cheer.°   70
　　Come, sir, we will better it in Pisa.
BAPTISTA. I follow you.   *Exeunt.*
　　　　　Enter LUCENTIO [*as Cambio*] *and* BIONDELLO.
BIONDELLO. Cambio!
LUCENTIO. What sayst thou, Biondello?
BIONDELLO. You saw my master° wink and laugh upon you?   75
LUCENTIO. Biondello, what of that?
BIONDELLO. Faith, nothing, but has° left me here behind
　　to expound the meaning or moral of his signs and
　　tokens.   80
LUCENTIO. I pray thee, moralize° them.
BIONDELLO. Then thus. Baptista is safe, talking with the de-
　　ceiving father of a deceitful son.
LUCENTIO. And what of him?
BIONDELLO. His daughter is to be brought by you to the   85
　　supper.
LUCENTIO. And then?
BIONDELLO. The old priest at Saint Luke's church is at your
　　command at all hours.
LUCENTIO. And what of all this?   90
BIONDELLO. I cannot tell, except they are busied about a
　　counterfeit assurance.° Take you assurance° of her,
　　"cum previlegio ad impremendum solem."° To th'
　　church! Take the priest, clerk, and some sufficient
　　honest witnesses.   95
　　If this be not that you look for, I have no more to say,
　　But bid Bianca farewell forever and a day.
LUCENTIO. Hear'st thou, Biondello?
BIONDELLO. I cannot tarry. I knew a wench married in an
　　afternoon as she went to the garden for parsley to stuff   100
　　a rabbit. And so may you, sir. And so adieu, sir. My
　　master hath appointed me to go to Saint Luke's, to bid
　　the priest be ready to come against you come° with
　　your appendix.°   *Exit.*
LUCENTIO. I may, and will, if she be so contented.   105
　　She will be pleased; then wherefore should I doubt?
　　Hap what hap may, I'll roundly° go about° her.
　　It shall go hard if Cambio go without her.   *Exit.*

---

70 **mess** dish   70 **cheer** entertainment   75 **my master** i.e., Tranio; cf. line 59
78 **has** he has   81 **moralize** "expound"   92 **assurance** betrothal document
92 **Take you assurance** make sure   93 **cum . . . solem** (Biondello's version of *cum
privilegio ad imprimendum solum*, "with right of sole printing," a licensing phrase, with
sexual pun in *imprimendum*, literally "pressing upon")   104 **against you come** in
preparing for your coming   104 **appendix** (1) servant (2) wife (another metaphor from
printing)   107 **roundly** directly   107 **about** after

[Scene V. *The road to Padua*.]

Enter PETRUCHIO, KATE, HORTENSIO
[*with* SERVANTS.]

PETRUCHIO. Come on, a° God's name, once more toward our father's.
    Good Lord, how bright and goodly shines the moon.
KATE. The moon? The sun. It is not moonlight now.
PETRUCHIO. I say it is the moon that shines so bright.
KATE. I know it is the sun that shines so bright.   110
PETRUCHIO. Now, by my mother's son, and that's myself,
    It shall be moon or star or what I list,°
    Or ere° I journey to your father's house.
    [*To* SERVANTS] Go on and fetch our horses back again.
    Evermore crossed and crossed, nothing but crossed!°   115
HORTENSIO. [*To* KATE] Say as he says or we shall never go.
KATE. Forward, I pray, since we have come so far,
    And be it moon or sun or what you please.
    And if you please to call it a rush-candle,°
    Henceforth I vow it shall be so for me.   120
PETRUCHIO. I say it is the moon.
KATE.   I know it is the moon.
PETRUCHIO. Nay, then you lie. It is the blessèd sun.
KATE. Then God be blessed, it is the blessèd sun.
    But sun it is not when you say it is not,
    And the moon changes even as your mind.   125
    What you will have it named, even that it is,
    And so it shall be so for Katherine.
HORTENSIO. [*Aside*] Petruchio, go thy ways. The field is won.
PETRUCHIO. Well, forward, forward! Thus the bowl° should run
    And not unluckily against the bias.°   130
    But soft,° company° is coming here.

Enter VINCENTIO.

[*To* VINCENTIO] Good morrow, gentle mistress; where away?
    Tell me, sweet Kate, and tell me truly too,
    Hast thou beheld a fresher° gentlewoman?
    Such war of white and red within her cheeks!   135
    What stars do spangle heaven with such beauty
    As those two eyes become that heavenly face?
    Fair lovely maid, once more good day to thee.
    Sweet Kate, embrace her for her beauty's sake.
HORTENSIO. [*Aside*] 'A° will make the man mad, to   140
    make a woman of him.
KATE. Young budding virgin, fair and fresh and sweet,
    Whither away, or where is thy abode?

IV.v.1 **a** in 7 **list** please 8 **Or ere** before 10 **crossed** opposed, challenged 14 **rush-candle** rush dipped in grease and used as candle 24 **bowl** bowling ball 25 **against the bias** not in the planned curving route, made possible by a lead insertion (bias) weighting one side of the ball 26 **soft** hush 26 **company** someone 29 **fresher** more radiant 35 **'A** he

Happy the parents of so fair a child!
Happier the man whom favorable stars   145
Allots thee for his lovely bedfellow!
PETRUCHIO. Why, how now, Kate, I hope thou are not mad.
This is a man, old, wrinkled, faded, withered,
And not a maiden, as thou sayst he is.
KATE. Pardon, old father, my mistaking eyes   150
That have been so bedazzled with the sun
That everything I look on seemeth green.°
Now I perceive thou art a reverend father;
Pardon, I pray thee, for my mad mistaking.
PETRUCHIO. Do, good old grandsire, and withal make known   155
Which way thou travelest. If along with us,
We shall be joyful of thy company.
VINCENTIO. Fair sir, and you my merry mistress,
That with your strange encounter° much amazed me,
My name is called Vincentio, my dwelling Pisa,   160
And bound I am to Padua, there to visit
A son of mine which long I have not seen.
PETRUCHIO. What is his name?
VINCENTIO.   Lucentio, gentle sir.
PETRUCHIO. Happily met, the happier for thy son.
And now by law as well as reverend age,   165
I may entitle thee my loving father.
The sister to my wife, this gentlewoman,
Thy son by this° hath married. Wonder not
Nor be not grieved. She is of good esteem,
Her dowry wealthy, and of worthy birth;   170
Beside, so qualified° as may beseem°
The spouse of any noble gentleman.
Let me embrace with old Vincentio
And wander we to see thy honest son,
Who will of thy arrival be full joyous.   175
VINCENTIO. But is this true, or is it else your pleasure,
Like pleasant° travelers, to break a jest
Upon the company you overtake?
HORTENSIO. I do assure thee, father, so it is.
PETRUCHIO. Come, go along, and see the truth hereof,   180
For our first merriment hath made thee jealous.°
                          Exeunt [all but HORTENSIO].
HORTENSIO. Well, Petruchio, this has put me in heart.
Have to° my widow, and if she be froward,°
Then hast thou taught Hortensio to be untoward.°   *Exit.*

47 **green** young   54 **encounter** mode of address   63 **this** now   66 **so qualified**
having qualities   66 **beseem** befit   72 **pleasant** addicted to pleasantries
76 **jealous** suspicious   78 **Have to** on to   78 **froward** fractious   79 **untoward** difficult

[ACT V

Scene I. *Padua. The street in front of*
LUCENTIO*'s house.*]

Enter BIONDELLO, LUCENTIO [*as Cambio*], *and*
BIANCA; GREMIO *is out before.*°

BIONDELLO. Softly and swiftly, sir, for the priest is
ready.
LUCENTIO. I fly, Biondello. But they may chance to need
thee at home; therefore leave us.

Exit [*with* BIANCA].

BIONDELLO. Nay, faith, I'll see the church a your back,° and   5
then come back to my master's as soon as I can.

[*Exit.*]

GREMIO. I marvel Cambio comes not all this while.

Enter PETRUCHIO, KATE, VINCENTIO [*and*] GRUMIO,
with ATTENDANTS.

PETRUCHIO. Sir, here's the door, this is Lucentio's house.
My father's bears° more toward the marketplace;
Thither must I, and here I leave you, sir.   10
VINCENTIO. You shall not choose but drink before you go.
I think I shall command your welcome here,
And by all likelihood some cheer is toward.°   *Knock.*
GREMIO. They're busy within. You were best knock louder.

PEDANT [*as Vincentio*] *looks out of*
the window [*above*].

PEDANT. What's° he that knocks as he would beat down the   15
gate?
VINCENTIO. Is Signior Lucentio within, sir?
PEDANT. He's within, sir, but not to be spoken withal.°
VINCENTIO. What if a man bring him a hundred pound or
two, to make merry withal?   20
PEDANT. Keep your hundred pounds to yourself; he shall
need none so long as I live.
PETRUCHIO. Nay, I told you your son was well beloved in
Padua. Do you hear, sir? To leave frivolous circum-
stances,° I pray you tell Signior Lucentio that his   25
father is come from Pisa and here at the door to speak
with him.
PEDANT. Thou liest. His father is come from Padua° and
here looking out at the window.
VINCENTIO. Art thou his father?   30

V.i.s.d. **out before** precedes, and does not see, the others   5 **a your back** on your
back (see you enter the church? or, married?)   9 **bears** lies   13 **toward** at hand
15 **What's** who is   18 **withal** with   24–25 **frivolous circumstances** trivial
matters   28 **Padua** (perhaps Shakespeare's slip of the pen for *Pisa*, home of the real
Vincentio, or *Mantua*, where the Pedant comes from; cf. IV.ii.77)

PEDANT. Ay sir, so his mother says, if I may believe her.

PETRUCHIO. [*To* VINCENTIO] Why how now, gentleman? Why
this is flat° knavery, to take upon you another man's
name.

PEDANT. Lay hands on the villain. I believe 'a° means to   35
cozen° somebody in this city under my countenance.°

Enter BIONDELLO.

BIONDELLO. I have seen them in the church together; God
send 'em good shipping.° But who is here? Mine old
master, Vincentio! Now we are undone° and brought to
nothing.°   40

VINCENTIO. Come hither, crack-hemp.°

BIONDELLO. I hope I may choose,° sir.

VINCENTIO. Come hither, you rogue. What, have you forgot
me?

BIONDELLO. Forgot you? No, sir. I could not forget you, for   45
I never saw you before in all my life.

VINCENTIO. What, you notorious° villain, didst thou never
see thy master's father, Vincentio?

BIONDELLO. What, my old worshipful old master? Yes,
marry, sir, see where he looks out of the window.

VINCENTIO. Is't so, indeed?   *He beats* BIONDELLO.   50

BIONDELLO. Help, help, help! Here's a madman will murder
me.   [*Exit.*]

PEDANT. Help, son! Help, Signior Baptista!

[*Exit from above.*]

PETRUCHIO. Prithee, Kate, let's stand aside and see the end
of this controversy.   55

[*They stand aside.*]

Enter PEDANT [*below*] *with* SERVANTS, BAPTISTA,
[*and*] TRANIO [*as Lucentio*].

TRANIO. Sir, what are you that offer° to beat my servant?

VINCENTIO. What am I, sir? Nay, what are you, sir? O immortal gods! O fine° villain! A silken doublet, a velvet
hose, a scarlet cloak, and a copatain° hat! O, I am un-   60
done, I am undone! While I play the good husband°
at home, my son and my servant spend all at the university.

TRANIO. How now, what's the matter?

BAPTISTA. What, is the man lunatic?   65

TRANIO. Sir, you seem a sober ancient gentleman by your
habit,° but your words show you a madman. Why sir,

---

33 **flat** unvarnished 36 **'a** he 36 **cozen** defraud 36 **countenance** identity
38 **shipping** journey 39 **undone** defeated 40 **brought to nothing** (cf. "annihilated")
41 **crack-hemp** rope-stretcher (i.e., subject for hanging) 42 **choose** have some choice
(in the matter) 47 **notorious** extraordinary 57 **offer** attempt 59 **fine** well dressed
60 **copatain** high conical 61 **husband** manager 67 **habit** manner

what 'cerns° it you if I wear pearl and gold? I thank
my good father, I am able to maintain it.

VINCENTIO. Thy father! O villain, he is a sailmaker in   70
Bergamo.

BAPTISTA. You mistake, sir, you mistake, sir. Pray, what do
you think is his name?

VINCENTIO. His name! As if I knew not his name! I have
brought him up ever since he was three years old,   75
and his name is Tranio.

PEDANT. Away, away, mad ass! His name is Lucentio, and
he is mine only son and heir to the lands of me, Signior
Vincentio.

VINCENTIO. Lucentio! O he hath murd'red his master. Lay   80
hold on him, I charge you in the Duke's name. O my
son, my son! Tell me, thou villain, where is my son
Lucentio?

TRANIO. Call forth an officer.
                    [*Enter an* OFFICER.]
Carry this mad knave to the jail. Father Baptista, I   85
charge you see that he be forthcoming.°

VINCENTIO. Carry me to the jail!

GREMIO. Stay, officer. He shall not go to prison.

BAPTISTA. Talk not, Signior Gremio. I say he shall go to
prison.   90

GREMIO. Take heed, Signior Baptista, lest you be cony-
catched° in this business. I dare swear this is the
right Vincentio.

PEDANT. Swear, if thou dar'st.

GREMIO. Nay, I dare not swear it.   95

TRANIO. Then thou wert best° say that I am not Lucentio.

GREMIO. Yes, I know thee to be Signior Lucentio.

BAPTISTA. Away with the dotard,° to the jail with him!

VINCENTIO. Thus strangers may be haled° and abused. O
monstrous villain!   100
                Enter BIONDELLO, LUCENTIO, *and* BIANCA.

BIONDELLO. O we are spoiled°—and yonder he is. Deny him,
forswear him, or else we are all undone.
            Exit BIONDELLO, TRANIO, *and* PEDANT *as fast as may be.*

LUCENTIO. Pardon, sweet father.   *Kneel.*

VINCENTIO.   Lives my sweet son?

BIANCA. Pardon, dear father.

BAPTISTA.   How hast thou offended?
Where is Lucentio?

68 **'cerns** concerns   86 **forthcoming** available (for trial)   92 **cony-catched** fooled
96 **thou wert best** maybe you'll dare   98 **dotard** old fool   99 **haled** pulled about
101 **spoiled** ruined

LUCENTIO.   Here's Lucentio,   105
    Right son to the right Vincentio,
    That have by marriage made thy daughter mine
    While counterfeit supposes° bleared thine eyne.°
GREMIO. Here's packing,° with a witness,° to deceive us
    all!   110
VINCENTIO. Where is that damnèd villain Tranio
    That faced and braved° me in this matter so?
BAPTISTA. Why, tell me, is not this my Cambio?
BIANCA. Cambio is changed into Lucentio.
LUCENTIO. Love wrought these miracles. Bianca's love   115
    Made me exchange my state with Tranio
    While he did bear my countenance° in the town,
    And happily I have arrived at the last
    Unto the wishèd haven of my bliss.
    What Tranio did, myself enforced him to.   120
    Then pardon him, sweet father, for my sake.
VINCENTIO. I'll slit the villain's nose that would have sent
    me to the jail.
BAPTISTA. [*To* LUCENTIO] But do you hear, sir? Have
    you married my daughter without asking my good   125
    will?
VINCENTIO. Fear not, Baptista; we will content you, go to.°
    But I will in, to be revenged for this villainy.
                                Exit.
BAPTISTA. And I, to sound the depth° of this knavery.
                                  Exit.
LUCENTIO. Look not pale, Bianca. Thy father will not   130
    frown.   *Exeunt* [LUCENTIO *and* BIANCA].
GREMIO. My cake is dough,° but I'll in among the rest
    Out of hope of all but my share of the feast.   [*Exit.*]
KATE. Husband, let's follow, to see the end of this ado.
PETRUCHIO. First kiss me, Kate, and we will.   135
KATE. What, in the midst of the street?
PETRUCHIO. What, art thou ashamed of me?
KATE. No sir, God forbid, but ashamed to kiss.
PETRUCHIO. Why, then let's home again. [*To* GRUMIO] Come sirrah, let's away.
KATE. Nay, I will give thee a kiss. Now pray thee, love, stay.   140
PETRUCHIO. Is not this well? Come, my sweet Kate.
    Better once° than never, for never too late.°   *Exeunt.*

---

108 **supposes** pretendings (evidently an allusion to Gascoigne's play *Supposes,* one of
Shakespeare's sources) 108 **eyne** eyes 109 **packing** plotting 109 **with a witness**
outright, unabashed 112 **faced and braved** impudently challenged and defied
117 **bear my countenance** take on my identity 127 **go to** (mild remonstrance; cf. "go
on," "come, come," "don't worry") 129 **sound the depth** get to the bottom of
132 **cake is dough** project hasn't worked out (proverbial; cf. I.i.108–09) 141 **once**
at some time 141 **Better...late** better late than never

[Scene II. *Padua. In* LUCENTIO*'s house.*]

Enter BAPTISTA, VINCENTIO, GREMIO, *the* PEDANT,
LUCENTIO, *and* BIANCA, [PETRUCHIO, KATE, HORTENSIO,]
TRANIO, BIONDELLO, GRUMIO, *and* WIDOW; *the*
SERVINGMEN *with* TRANIO *bringing in a banquet.*°

LUCENTIO. At last, though long,° our jarring notes agree,
    And time it is, when raging war is done,
    To smile at 'scapes and perils overblown.°
    My fair Bianca, bid my father welcome
    While I with self-same kindness welcome thine.   5
    Brother Petruchio, sister Katherina,
    And thou, Hortensio, with thy loving widow,
    Feast with the best and welcome to my house.
    My banquet is to close our stomachs° up
    After our great good cheer.° Pray you, sit down,   10
    For now we sit to chat as well as eat.
PETRUCHIO. Nothing but sit and sit, and eat and eat.
BAPTISTA. Padua affords this kindness, son Petruchio.
PETRUCHIO. Padua affords nothing but what is kind.
HORTENSIO. For both our sakes I would that word were true.   15
PETRUCHIO. Now, for my life, Hortensio fears° his widow.
WIDOW. Then never trust me if I be afeard.°
PETRUCHIO. You are very sensible and yet you miss my sense:
    I mean Hortensio is afeard of you.
WIDOW. He that is giddy thinks the world turns round.   20
PETRUCHIO. Roundly° replied.
KATE.   Mistress, how mean you that?
WIDOW. Thus I conceive by° him.
PETRUCHIO. Conceives by° me! How likes Hortensio that?
HORTENSIO. My widow says, thus she conceives her tale.°
PETRUCHIO. Very well mended. Kiss him for that, good widow.   25
KATE. "He that is giddy thinks the world turns round."
    I pray you, tell me what you meant by that.
WIDOW. Your husband, being troubled with a shrew,
    Measures° my husband's sorrow by his° woe,
    And now you know my meaning.   30
KATE. A very mean° meaning.
WIDOW.   Right, I mean you.
KATE. And I am mean° indeed, respecting you.
PETRUCHIO. To her, Kate!

V.ii.s.d. **banquet** dessert   1 **At last, though long** at long last   3 **over-blown** that
have blown over   9 **stomachs** (with pun on "irascibility"; cf. IV.i.52)   10 **cheer**
(reception at Baptista's)   16 **fears** is afraid of (the Widow puns on the meaning
"frightens")   17 **afeard** (1) frightened (2) suspected   21 **Roundly** outspokenly
22 **conceive by** understand   23 **Conceives by** is made pregnant by   24 **conceives
her tale** understands her statement (with another pun)   29 **Measures** estimates
29 **his** his own   31 **mean** paltry   32 **am mean** (1) am moderate (2) have a low
opinion

HORTENSIO. To her, widow!

PETRUCHIO. A hundred marks, my Kate does put her down.°   35

HORTENSIO. That's my office.°

PETRUCHIO. Spoke like an officer. Ha'° to thee, lad.

> *Drinks to* HORTENSIO.

BAPTISTA. How likes Gremio these quick-witted folks?

GREMIO. Believe me, sir, they butt° together well.

BIANCA. Head and butt!° An hasty-witted body   40
  Would say your head and butt were head and horn.°

VINCENTIO. Ay, mistress bride, hath that awakened you?

BIANCA. Ay, but not frighted me; therefore I'll sleep again.

PETRUCHIO. Nay, that you shall not. Since you have begun,
  Have at you° for a bitter° jest or two.   45

BIANCA. Am I your bird?° I mean to shift my bush,
  And then pursue me as you draw your bow.
  You are welcome all.

> *Exit* BIANCA [*with* KATE *and* WIDOW].

PETRUCHIO. She hath prevented me.° Here, Signior Tranio,
  This bird you aimed at, though you hit her not;   50
  Therefore a health to all that shot and missed.

TRANIO. O sir, Lucentio slipped° me, like his greyhound.
  Which runs himself and catches for his master.

PETRUCHIO. A good swift° simile but something currish.

TRANIO. 'Tis well, sir, that you hunted for yourself;   55
  'Tis thought your deer° does hold you at a bay.°

BAPTISTA. O, O, Petruchio, Tranio hits you now.

LUCENTIO. I thank thee for that gird,° good Tranio.

HORTENSIO. Confess, confess, hath he not hit you here?

PETRUCHIO. 'A has a little galled° me, I confess,   60
  And as the jest did glance away from me,
  'Tis ten to one it maimed you two outright.

BAPTISTA. Now, in good sadness,° son Petruchio,
  I think thou hast the veriest° shrew of all.

PETRUCHIO. Well, I say no. And therefore, for assurance,°   65
  Let's each one send unto his wife,
  And he whose wife is most obedient
  To come at first when he doth send for her
  Shall win the wager which we will propose.

HORTENSIO. Content. What's the wager?

---

35 **put her down** defeat her (with sexual pun by Hortensio)   36 **office** job   37 **Ha'**
here's, hail   39 **butt** (perhaps also "but," i.e., argue or differ)   40 **butt** (with pun on
"bottom")   41 **horn** (1) butting instrument (2) symbol of cuckoldry (3) phallus
45 **Have at you** let's have   45 **bitter** biting (but good-natured)   46 **bird** prey
49 **prevented me** beaten me to it   52 **slipped** unleashed   54 **swift** quick-witted
56 **deer** (1) doe (2) dear   56 **at a bay** at bay (i.e., backed up at a safe distance)
58 **gird** gibe   60 **galled** chafed   63 **sadness** seriousness   64 **veriest** most genuine
65 **assurance** proof

LUCENTIO. Twenty crowns. 70
PETRUCHIO. Twenty crowns!
    I'll venture so much of° my hawk or hound,
    But twenty times so much upon my wife.
LUCENTIO. A hundred then.
HORTENSIO. Content.°
PETRUCHIO. A match,° tis done.
HORTENSIO. Who shall begin?
LUCENTIO. That will I. 75
    Go Biondello, bid your mistress come to me.
BIONDELLO. I go. *Exit.*
BAPTISTA. Son, I'll be your half,° Bianca comes.
LUCENTIO. I'll have no halves; I'll bear it all myself.
Enter BIONDELLO.
    How now,° what news?
BIONDELLO. Sir, my mistress sends you word 80
    That she is busy and she cannot come.
PETRUCHIO. How?° She's busy and she cannot come?
    Is that an answer?
GREMIO. Ay, and a kind one too.
    Pray God, sir, your wife send you not a worse.
PETRUCHIO. I hope, better. 85
HORTENSIO. Sirrah Biondello, go and entreat my wife
    To come to me forthwith.° *Exit* BIONDELLO.
PETRUCHIO. O ho, entreat her!
    Nay, then she must needs come.
HORTENSIO. I am afraid, sir,
    Do what you can, yours will not be entreated.
Enter BIONDELLO.
    Now where's my wife? 90
BIONDELLO. She says you have some goodly jest in hand.
    She will not come. She bids you come to her.
PETRUCHIO. Worse and worse. She will not come. O vile,
    Intolerable, not to be endured!
    Sirrah Grumio, go to your mistress; say 95
    I command her come to me. *Exit* [GRUMIO].
HORTENSIO. I know her answer.
PETRUCHIO. What?
HORTENSIO. She will not.
PETRUCHIO. The fouler fortune mine, and there an end.
Enter KATE.
BAPTISTA. Now, by my holidame,° here comes Katherina.
KATE. What is your will, sir, that you send for me? 100
PETRUCHIO. Where is your sister and Hortensio's wife?

---

72 **of** on 74 **Content** agreed 74 **A match** (it's) a bet 78 **be your half** assume half
your bet 80 **How now** (mild exclamation; cf. "well") 82 **How** what 87 **forthwith**
right away 99 **hollidame** holy dame (some editors emend to *halidom,* sacred place or
relic)

KATE. They sit conferring° by the parlor fire.
PETRUCHIO. Go fetch them hither. If they deny° to come,
   Swinge° me them soundly° forth unto their husbands.
   Away, I say, and bring them hither straight.   [*Exit* KATE.]   105
LUCENTIO. Here is a wonder, if you talk of a wonder.
HORTENSIO. And so it is. I wonder what it bodes.
PETRUCHIO. Marry, peace it bodes, and love, and quiet life,
   An awful° rule and right supremacy;
   And, to be short, what not° that's sweet and happy.   110
BAPTISTA. Now fair befall° thee, good Petruchio.
   The wager thou hast won, and I will add
   Unto their losses twenty thousand crowns,
   Another dowry to another daughter,
   For she is changed as she had never been.   115
PETRUCHIO. Nay, I will win my wager better yet
   And show more sign of her obedience,
   Her new-built virtue and obedience.
         Enter KATE, BIANCA *and* WIDOW.
   See where she comes and brings your froward° wives
   As prisoners to her womanly persuasion.   120
   Katherine, that cap of yours becomes you not.
   Off with that bauble, throw it under foot.   [*She throws it.*]
WIDOW. Lord, let me never have a cause to sigh
   Till I be brought to such a silly pass.°
BIANCA. Fie, what a foolish—duty call you this?   125
LUCENTIO. I would your duty were as foolish too.
   The wisdom of your duty, fair Bianca,
   Hath cost me five hundred° crowns since suppertime.
BIANCA. The more fool you for laying° on my duty.
PETRUCHIO. Katherine, I charge thee, tell these head-strong women   130
   What duty they do owe their lords and husbands.
WIDOW. Come, come, you're mocking. We will have no telling.
PETRUCHIO. Come on, I say, and first begin with her.
WIDOW. She shall not.
PETRUCHIO. I say she shall—and first begin with her.   135
KATE. Fie, fie, unknit that threatening unkind° brow
   And dart not scornful glances from those eyes
   To wound thy lord, thy king, thy governor.
   It blots thy beauty as frosts do bite the meads,
   Confounds thy fame° as whirlwinds shake° fair buds,   140
   And in no sense is meet or amiable.

---

102 **conferring** conversing 103 **deny** refuse 104 **Swinge** thrash 104 **soundly**
thoroughly (cf. "sound beating") 109 **awful** inspiring respect 110 **what not** i.e.,
everything 111 **fair befall** good luck to 119 **froward** uncooperative 124 **pass**
situation 128 **five hundred** (1) Lucentio makes it look worse than it is, or (2) he made
several bets, or (3) the text errs (some editors emend to "a hundred," assuming that
the manuscript's "a" was misread as the Roman numeral v) 129 **laying** betting
136 **unkind** hostile 140 **Confounds thy fame** spoils people's opinion of you
140 **shake** shake off

A woman moved° is like a fountain troubled,
Muddy, ill-seeming, thick, bereft of beauty,
And while it is so, none so dry or thirsty
Will deign to sip or touch one drop of it.   145
Thy husband is thy lord, thy life, thy keeper,
Thy head, thy sovereign—one that cares for thee,
And for thy maintenance commits his body
To painful labor both by sea and land,
To watch° the night in storms, the day in cold,   150
Whilst thou li'st warm at home, secure and safe;
And craves no other tribute at thy hands
But love, fair looks, and true obedience:
Too little payment for so great a debt.
Such duty as the subject owes the prince,   155
Even such a woman oweth to her husband,
And when she is froward, peevish, sullen, sour,
And not obedient to his honest° will,
What is she but a foul contending rebel
And graceless traitor to her loving lord?   160
I am ashamed that women are so simple°
To offer war where they should kneel for peace,
Or seek for rule, supremacy, and sway,
When they are bound to serve, love, and obey.
Why are our bodies soft and weak and smooth,   165
Unapt to° toil and trouble in the world,
But that our soft conditions° and our hearts
Should well agree with our external parts?
Come, come, you froward and unable worms,°
My mind hath been as big° as one of yours,   170
My heart as great, my reason haply more,
To bandy word for word and frown for frown.
But now I see our lances are but straws,
Our strength as weak, our weakness past compare,
That seeming to be most which we indeed least are.   175
Then vail your stomachs,° for it is no boot,°
And place your hands below your husband's foot,
In token of which duty, if he please,
My hand is ready, may it° do him ease.
PETRUCHIO. Why, there's a wench! Come on and kiss me, Kate.   180
LUCENTIO. Well, go thy ways, old lad, for thou shalt ha't.
VINCENTIO. 'Tis a good hearing° when children are toward.°

---

142 **moved** i.e., by ill temper   150 **watch** stay awake, be alert during   158 **honest**
honorable   161 **simple** silly   166 **Unapt to** unfitted for   167 **conditions** qualities
169 **unable worms** weak, lowly creatures   170 **big** inflated (cf. "think big")
176 **vail your stomachs** fell your pride   176 **no boot** useless, profitless   179 **may it**
(1) I hope it may (2) if it may   182 **hearing** thing to hear; report   182 **toward** tractable

LUCENTIO. But a harsh hearing when women are froward.

PETRUCHIO. Come, Kate, we'll to bed.

We three are married, but you two are sped.°   185

'Twas I won the wager, [*to* LUCENTIO] though you hit the white,°

And, being a winner, God give you good night.

                            Exit PETRUCHIO [*with* KATE].

HORTENSIO. Now, go thy ways; thou hast tamed a curst shrow.

LUCENTIO. 'Tis a wonder, by your leave, she will be tamèd so.

                                        [*Exeunt.*]

FINIS

[1593–94]

■ TOPICS FOR DISCUSSION AND WRITING

1. In a paragraph characterize Lucentio. In a second paragraph explain why you do or do not find him comic.

2. In a paragraph characterize Bianca. In your characterization, be sure to take account of III.i.16–20.

3. In an essay of 250 words, characterize Gremio (*not* Grumio), paying special attention to his romantic pretensions. In your discussion, compare Gremio to his rival, Lucentio.

4. One critic (a male) has said that Petruchio "is every woman's dream of a kind of ideal lover—coming to take her by storm, to club her to his cave, and then to become gentle." First, what do you think he means by this, and, second, do you think he is correct?

5. *The Taming of the Shrew* is a play, not a case history. Do you suppose that watching the play you would be offended by Petruchio's treatment of Kate? Why, or why not?

6. One critic has said that the play is a criticism of the Elizabethan view that marriage is a commercial arrangement, and a celebration of another Elizabethan view, that marriage is a true union of hearts and minds. Evaluate this opinion.

7. An anonymous play called *The Taming of a Shrew* (customarily called *A Shrew*, in contrast to Shakespeare's *The Shrew*), ends with a return to the characters of the induction. We print this ending here. Read it, and then write an essay of 500 words in which you explain why, if you were staging Shakespeare's play, you would or would not add this ending.

Then enter two bearing of SLY *in his own apparel again, and leaves him where they found him, and then gets out. Then enter the* TAPSTER.

TAPSTER. Now that the darksome night is overpast,

And dawning day appears in crystal sky,

Now must I haste abroad. But soft, who's this?

What, Sly? O wondrous, hath he lain here all night?

I'll wake him; I think he's starved by this   5

185 **sped** done for   186 **white** (1) bull's eye (2) *Bianca* means white

But that his belly was so stuffed with ale.
What now, Sly, awake for shame!

SLY. Sim, gi's some more wine. What's all the players gone?
   Am not I a lord?

TAPSTER. A lord with a murrain.° Come, art thou drunken   10
   still?

SLY. Who's this? Tapster? O Lord, sirrah, I have had the
   bravest° dream tonight° that ever thou heardest in all
   thy life.

TAPSTER. Ay, marry,° but you had best get you home, for   15
   your wife will corse you for dreaming here tonight.

SLY. Will she? I know now how to tame a shrew: I dreamt
   upon it all this night till now, and thou hast waked me
   out of the best dream that I ever had in my life. But
   I'll to my wife presently and tame her too an if she anger   20
   me.

TAPSTER. Nay tarry, Sly, for I'll go home with thee. And
   hear the rest that thou hast dreamt tonight.   [*Exit all.*]

---

10 **murrain** plague 13 **bravest** most splendid; **tonight** last night 15 **Ay, marry** a
mild oath, from "By Mary"

CHAPTER 11

American Dreams

and Nightmares

ESSAYS

■ THOMAS JEFFERSON

Thomas Jefferson (1743–1826) was a congressman, the governor of Virginia, the first Secretary of State, and the president of the United States, but he said he wished to be remembered for only three things: drafting the Declaration of Independence, writing the Virginia Statute for Religious Freedom, and founding the University of Virginia. All three were efforts to promote freedom.

Jefferson was born in Virginia and educated at William and Mary College in Williamsburg, Virginia. After graduating he studied law, was admitted to the bar, and in 1769 was elected to the Virginia House of Burgesses, his first political office. In 1776 he went to Philadelphia as a delegate to the second Continental Congress, where he was elected to a committee of five to write the Declaration of Independence. Jefferson drafted the document, which was then subjected to some changes by the other members of the committee and by the Congress. Although he was unhappy with the changes (especially with the deletion of a passage against slavery), his claim to have written the Declaration is just.

The Declaration of Independence

In CONGRESS, July 4, 1776.

THE UNANIMOUS DECLARATION

OF THE THIRTEEN UNITED STATES OF AMERICA.

When in the Course of human events, it becomes necessary for one peo-ple to dissolve the political bands which have connected them with another, and to assume among the powers of the earth, the separate and equal station to which the Laws of Nature and Nature's God entitle them, a decent respect to the opinions of mankind requires that they should declare the causes which impel them to the separation.

We hold these truths to be self-evident, that all men are created equal, that they are endowed by their Creator with certain unalienable Rights, that among these are Life, Liberty and the pursuit of Happiness.

That to secure these rights, Governments are instituted among Men, deriving their just powers from the consent of the governed.

That whenever any Form of Government becomes destructive of these ends, it is the Right of the people to alter or to abolish it, and to institute new Government, laying its foundation on such principles and organizing its powers in such form, as to them shall seem most likely to effect their Safety and Happiness. Prudence, indeed, will dictate that Governments long established should not be changed for light and transient causes; and accordingly all experience hath shewn, that mankind are more disposed to suffer, while evils are sufferable, than to right themselves by abolishing the forms to which they are
accustomed. But when a long train of abuses and usurpations, pursuing invariably the same Object evinces a design to reduce them under absolute Depotism, it is their right, it is their duty, to throw off such Government, and to provide new Guards for their future security.

Such has been the patient sufferance of these Colonies; and such is now 5 the necessity which constrains them to alter their former Systems of Government. The history of the present King of Great Britain is a history of repeated injuries and usurpations, all having in direct object the establishment of an absolute Tyranny over these States. To prove this, let Facts be submitted to a candid world.

He has refused his Assent to Laws, the most wholesome and necessary for the public good.

He has forbidden his Governors to pass Laws of immediate and pressing importance, unless suspended in their operation till his Assent should be obtained; and when so suspended, he has utterly neglected to attend to them.

He has refused to pass other Laws for the accommodation of large districts of people, unless those people would relinquish the right of Representation in the Legislature, a right inestimable to them and formidable to tyrants only.

He has called together legislative bodies at places unusual, uncomfortable, and distant from the depository of their public Records, for the sole purpose of fatiguing them into compliance with his measures.

He has dissolved Representative Houses repeatedly, for opposing with 10 manly firmness his invasions on the rights of people.

He has refused for a long time, after such dissolutions, to cause others to be elected; whereby the Legislative powers, incapable of Annihilation, have returned to the people at large for their exercise; the State remaining in the mean time exposed to all the dangers of invasion from without, and convulsions within.

He has endeavoured to prevent the population of these States; for that purpose obstructing the Laws for Naturalization of Foreigners; refusing to pass others to encourage their migrations hither, and raising the conditions of new Appropriations of Lands.

He has obstructed the Administration of Justice, by refusing his Assent to Laws for establishing Judiciary powers.

He has made Judges dependent on his Will alone, for the tenure of their offices, and the amount and payment of their salaries.

He has erected a multitude of New Offices, and sent hither swarms of 15 Officers to harass our people, and eat out their substance.

He has kept among us, in times of peace, Standing Armies without the Consent of our legislatures.

He has affected to render the Military independent of and superior to the Civil power.

He has combined with others to subject us to a jurisdiction foreign to our constitution, and unacknowledged by our laws; giving his Assent to their Acts of pretended Legislation:

For Quartering large bodies of armed troops among us:

For protecting them, by a mock Trial, from punishment for any Murders 20 which they should commit on the Inhabitants of these States:

For cutting off our Trade with all parts of the world:

For imposing Taxes on us without our Consent:

For depriving us in many cases, of the benefits of Trial by Jury:

For transporting us beyond Seas to be tried for pretended offenses:

For abolishing the free System of English Laws in a neighbouring 25 Province, establishing therein an Arbitrary government, and enlarging its Boundaries so as to render it at once an example and fit instrument for introducing the same absolute rule into these Colonies:

For taking away our Charters, abolishing our most valuable Laws, and altering fundamentally the Forms of our Governments:

For suspending our own Legislatures, and declaring themselves invested with power to legislate for us in all cases whatsoever.

He has abdicated Government here, by declaring us out of his Protection and waging War against us:

He has plundered our seas, ravaged our Coasts, burnt our towns, and destroyed the lives of our people.

He is at this time transporting large Armies of foreign Mercenaries to 30 compleat the works of death, desolation and tyranny, already begun with circumstances of Cruelty & perfidy scarcely paralleled in the most barbarous ages, and totally unworthy the Head of a civilized nation.

He has constrained our fellow Citizens taken Captive on the high Seas to bear Arms against their Country, to become the executioners of their friends and Brethren, or to fall themselves by their Hands.

He has excited domestic insurrections amongst us, and has endeavoured to bring on the inhabitants of our frontiers, the merciless Indian Savages, whose known rule of warfare, is an undistinguished destruction of all ages, sexes and conditions. In every stage of these Oppressions We have Petitioned for Redress in the most humble terms: Our repeated Petitions have been answered only by repeated injury. A Prince, whose character is thus marked by every act which may define a Tyrant, is unfit to be the ruler of a free people. Nor have We been wanting in attentions to our British brethren. We have warned them from time to time of attempts by their legislature to extend an unwarrantable jurisdiction over us. We have reminded them of the circumstances of our emigration and settlement here. We have appealed to their native justice and magnanimity, and we have conjured them by the ties of our common kindred to disavow these usurpations, which, would inevitably interrupt our connections and correspondence. They too have been deaf to the voice of justice and of consanguinity. We must, therefore, acquiesce in the necessity, which denounces our Separation, and hold them, as we hold the rest of mankind, Enemies in War, in Peace Friends.

WE, THEREFORE, the Representatives of the UNITED STATES OF AMERICA, in General Congress Assembled, appealing to the Supreme Judge of the world for the rectitude of our intentions, do, in the Name and by Authority of the good People of these Colonies, solemnly publish and declare, That these United Colonies are, and of Right ought to be FREE AND INDEPENDENT STATES; that they are Absolved from all Allegiance to the British Crown, and that all political connection between them and the State of Great Britain, is and ought to be totally dissolved; and that as Free and Independent States, they have full Power to levy War, conclude Peace, contract Alliances, establish Commerce, and to do all other Acts and Things which Independent States may of right do.

And for the support of this Declaration, with a firm reliance on the protection of divine Providence, we mutually pledge to each other our Lives, our Fortunes and our sacred Honor.

[1776]

■ TOPICS FOR DISCUSSION AND WRITING

1. In a paragraph, define "happiness," and then in a second paragraph explain why, in your opinion, Jefferson spoke of a right to "the pursuit of happiness" rather than of a right to "happiness."

2. In a paragraph, argue that the assertion that "all men are created equal" is clearly nonsense, or, on the other hand, that it makes sense.

3. Write a persuasive Declaration of Independence for some imagined group. Some possible examples include adolescents who declare that their parents have no right to govern them; young adolescents who declare that they should not be compelled to attend school; parents who declare that the state has no right to regulate the education of their children; college students who declare that they should not be required to take certain courses.

4. You are one of King George's trusted ministers. Draft a reply to the colonists for the king to sign.

■ CHIEF SEATTLE

Seattle (1786–1866), for whom the city in Washington is named, was a chief of the Suquamish and Duwamish tribes on the coast of the Pacific Northwest region of what is now the United States. There is some uncertainty about exactly when he delivered this speech—perhaps late in 1853, when the white governor of the Washington Territory first visited the territory, or perhaps early in 1855, when Seattle signed the Port Elliott Treaty, which confined the tribes to a reservation.

Seattle spoke little or no English. The speech was given through an interpreter and was transcribed by Henry Smith, who published it in 1887, with a concluding note saying, "The above is but a fragment of his speech." Because Smith's notes are not extant, it is now impossible to know exactly what Seattle said, but one point can be made: The text we print here is based entirely on Smith's version, the only text with any claim to authenticity. Since 1931 Smith's version has occasionally been reprinted with embellishments, the most popular of which is the addition of three sentences at the end: "Dead—did I say? There is no death. Only a change of worlds." Fine words, but they belong to an editor of 1931, not to Seattle.

My People

Yonder sky has wept tears of compassion on our fathers for centuries untold, and which, to us, looks eternal, may change. To-day it is fair, to-morrow it may be overcast with clouds. My words are like the stars that never set. What Seattle says the great chief, Washington, (the Indians in early times thought that Washington was still alive. They knew the name to be that of a president, and when they heard of the president at Washington they mistook the name of the city for the name of the reigning chief. They thought, also, that King George was still England's monarch, because the Hudson Bay traders called themselves "King George men." This innocent deception the company was shrewd enough not to explain away for the Indians had more respect for them than they would have had, had they known England was ruled by a woman. Some of us have learned better.) can rely upon, with as much certainty as our pale-face brothers can rely upon the return of the seasons. The son of the white chief says his father sends us greetings of friendship and good-will. This is kind, for we know he has little need of our friendship in return, because his people are many. They are like the grass that covers the vast prairies, while my people are few, and resemble the scattering trees of a wind-swept plain.

The great, and I presume also good, white chief sends us word that he wants to buy our lands but is willing to allow us to reserve enough to live on comfortably. This indeed appears generous, for the red man no longer has rights that he need respect, and the offer may be wise, also, for we are no longer in need of a great country. There was a time when our people covered the whole land as the waves of a wind-ruffled sea cover its shell-paved floor. But that time has long since passed away with the greatness of tribes almost forgotten. I will not mourn over our untimely decay, nor reproach my pale-face brothers with hastening it, for we, too, may have been somewhat to blame.

When our young men grow angry at some real or imaginary wrong and disfigure their faces with black paint, their hearts, also, are disfigured and turn black, and then their cruelty is relentless and knows no bounds, and our old men are not able to restrain them.

But let us hope that hostilities between the red man and his pale face brothers may never return. We would have everything to lose and nothing to gain.

True it is that revenge, with our young braves, is considered gain, even at the cost of their own lives, but old men who stay at home in times of war, and old women who have sons to lose, know better.

Our great father Washington, for I presume he is now our father as well as yours, since George has moved his boundaries to the north; our great and good father, I say, sends us word by his son, who, no doubt, is a great chief among his people, that if we do as he desires, he will protect us. His brave armies will be to us a bristling wall of strength, and his great ships of war will fill our harbors so that our ancient enemies far to the northward, the Simsiams and Hydas, will no longer frighten our women and old men. Then he will be our father and we will be his children. But can this ever be? Your God loves your people and hates mine; he folds his strong arms lovingly around the white man and leads him as a father leads his infant son, but he has forsaken his red children; he makes your people wax strong every day, and soon they will fill the land; while our people are ebbing away like a fast-receding tide, that will never flow again. The white man's God cannot love his red children or he would protect them. They seem to be orphans and can look nowhere for help. How then can we become brothers? How can your father become our father and bring us prosperity and awaken in us dreams of returning greatness?

Your God seems to be partial. He came to the white man. We never saw Him; never even heard His voice; He gave the white man laws but He had no word for His red children whose teeming millions filled this vast continent as the stars fill the firmament. No, we are two distinct races and must ever remain so. There is little in common between us. The ashes of our ancestors are sacred and their final resting place is hallowed ground, while you wander away from the tombs of your fathers seemingly without regret.

Your religion was written on tables of stone by the iron finger of an angry God, lest you might forget it. The red man could never remember nor comprehend it.

Our religion is the traditions of our ancestors, the dreams of our old men, given them by the great Spirit, and the visions of our sachems, and is written in the hearts of our people.

Your dead cease to love you and the homes of their nativity as soon as they pass the portals of the tomb. They wander off beyond the stars, are soon forgotten and never return. Our dead never forget the beautiful world that gave them being. They still love its winding rivers, its great mountains and its sequestered vales, and they ever yearn in tenderest affection over the lonely hearted living and often return to visit and comfort them.

Day and night cannot dwell together. The red man has ever fled the approach of the white man, as the changing mists on the mountain side flee before the blazing morning sun.

However, your proposition seems a just one, and I think my folks will accept it and will retire to the reservation you offer them, and we will dwell apart and in peace, for the words of the great white chief seem to be the voice of nature speaking to my people out of the thick darkness that is fast gathering around them like a dense fog floating inward from a midnight sea.

It matters but little where we pass the remainder of our days. They are not many. The Indian's night promises to be dark. No bright star hovers about the horizon. Sad-voiced winds moan in the distance. Some grim Nemesis of our race is on the red man's trail, and wherever he goes he will still hear the sure approaching footsteps of the fell destroyer and prepare to meet his doom, as does the wounded doe that hears the approaching footsteps of the hunter. A few more moons, a few more winters and not one of all the mighty hosts that once filled this broad land or that now roam in fragmentary bands through these vast solitudes will remain to weep over the tombs of a people once as powerful and as hopeful as your own.

But why should we repine? Why should I murmur at the fate of my people? Tribes are made up of individuals and are no better than they. Men come and go like the waves of the sea. A tear, a tamanamus, a dirge, and they are gone from our longing eyes forever. Even the white man, whose God walked and talked with him, as friend to friend, is not exempt from the common destiny. We *may* be brothers after all. We shall see.

We will ponder your proposition, and when we have decided we will tell you. But should we accept it, I here and now make this the first condition: That we will not be denied the privilege, without molestation, of visiting at will the graves of our ancestors and friends. Every part of this country is sacred to my people. Every hillside, every valley, every plain and grove has been hallowed by some fond memory or some sad experience of my tribe. Even the rocks that seem to lie dumb as they swelter in the sun along the silent seashore in solemn grandeur thrill with memories of past events connected with the fate of my people, and the very dust under your feet responds more lovingly to our footsteps than to yours, because it is the ashes of our ancestors, and our bare feet are conscious of the sympathetic touch, for the soil is rich with the life of our kindred.

The sable braves, and fond mothers, and glad-hearted maidens, and the little children who lived and rejoiced here, and whose very names are now forgotten, still love these solitudes, and their deep fastnesses at eventide grow shadowy with the presence of dusky spirits. And when the last red man shall have perished from the earth and his memory among white men shall have become a myth, these shores shall swarm with the invisible dead of my tribe, and when your children's children shall think themselves alone in the field, the shop, upon the highway or in the silence of the woods they will not be alone. In all the earth there is no place dedicated to solitude. At night when the streets of your cities and villages shall be silent, and you think them deserted, they will throng with the returning hosts that once filled and still love this beautiful land. The white man will never be alone. Let him be just and deal kindly with my people, for the dead are not altogether powerless.

[c. 1835]

■ TOPICS FOR DISCUSSION AND WRITING

1. In a paragraph explain why Chief Seattle believes white people have a different God from that of Native Americans.
2. Chief Seattle says that he thinks the offer of the whites is "fair" and that he thinks his people will accept the offer and retire to the reservation.

Judging from his speech, do you think his main reason for approving the proposal is that it is fair?

3. In 250 words explain why Chief Seattle believes that whites and Native Americans can never be reconciled, and evaluate his view.

4. Chief Seattle's speech is rich in metaphors and other figures of speech. (On these terms, see pages 212–213.) List three of his figures. From what areas are most of his figures drawn?

■ ELIZABETH CADY STANTON
_____

Elizabeth Cady Stanton (1815–1902), born into a prosperous conservative family in Johnstone, New York, became one of the most radical advocates of women's rights in the nineteenth century. In 1840 she married Henry Brewster Stanton, an ardent abolitionist lecturer. In the same year, at the World Anti-Slavery Convention in England—which refused to seat the women delegates—she met Lucretia Mott, and the two women resolved to organize a convention to discuss women's rights. Not until 1848, however, did the convention materialize. Of the 300 or so people who attended the Seneca Falls convention, 68 women and 32 men signed the Declaration of Sentiments, but the press on the whole was unfavorable. Not until 1920, with the passage of the Nineteenth Amendment, did women gain the right to vote. (For further details about her life and times, see Stanton's *Eighty Years & More: Reminiscences 1815–1897.*)

Declaration of Sentiments and Resolutions

When, in the course of human events, it becomes necessary for one portion of the family of man to assume among the people of the earth a position different from that which they have hitherto occupied, but one to which the laws of nature and of nature's God entitle them, a decent respect to the opinions of mankind requires that they should declare the causes that impel them to such a course.

We hold these truths to be self-evident: that all men and women are created equal; that they are endowed by their Creator with certain inalienable rights; that among these are life, liberty, and the pursuit of happiness; that to secure these rights governments are instituted, deriving their just powers from the consent of the governed. Whenever any form of government becomes destructive of these ends, it is the right of those who suffer from it to refuse allegiance to it, and to insist upon the institution of a new government, laying its foundation on such principles, and organizing its powers in such form, as to them shall seem most likely to effect their safety and happiness. Prudence, indeed, will dictate that governments long established should not be changed for light and transient causes; and accordingly all experience hath shown that mankind are more disposed to suffer, while evils are sufferable, than to right themselves by abolishing the forms to which they were accustomed. But when a long train of abuses and usurpations, pursuing invariably the same object, evinces a design to reduce them under absolute despotism, it is their duty to throw off such government, and to provide new guards for their future security. Such has been the patient sufferance of the women under this government, and such is now the necessity which constrains them to demand the equal station to which they are entitled.

The history of mankind is a history of repeated injuries and usurpations on the part of man toward woman, having in direct object the establishment of an absolute tyranny over her. To prove this, let facts be submitted to a candid world.

He has never permitted her to exercise her inalienable right to the elective franchise. 4

He has compelled her to submit to laws, in the formation of which she had no voice.

He has withheld from her rights which are given to the most ignorant and degraded men—both natives and foreigners.

Having deprived her of this first right of a citizen, the elective franchise, thereby leaving her without representation in the halls of legislation, he has oppressed her on all sides.

He has made her, if married, in the eye of the law, civilly dead. 8

He has taken from her all right in property, even to the wages she earns.

He has made her, morally, an irresponsible being, as she can commit many crimes with impunity, provided they be done in the presence of her husband. In the covenant of marriage, she is compelled to promise obedience to her husband, he becoming to all intents and purposes, her master—the law giving him power to deprive her of her liberty, and to administer chastisement.

He has so framed the laws of divorce, as to what shall be the proper causes, and in case of separation, to whom the guardianship of the children shall be given, as to be wholly regardless of the happiness of women—the law, in all cases, going upon a false supposition of the supremacy of man, and giving all power into his hands.

After depriving her of all rights as a married woman, if single, and the 12 owner of property, he has taxed her to support a government which recognizes her only when her property can be made profitable to it.

He has monopolized nearly all the profitable employments, and from those she is permitted to follow, she receives but a scanty remuneration. He closes against her all the avenues to wealth and distinction which he considers most honorable to himself. As a teacher of theology, medicine, or law, she is not known.

He has denied her the facilities for obtaining a thorough education, all colleges being closed against her.

He allows her in Church, as well as State, but a subordinate position, claiming Apostolic authority for her exclusion from the ministry, and, with some exceptions, from any public participation in the affairs of the Church.

He has created a false public sentiment by giving to the world a different 16 code of morals for men and women, by which moral delinquencies which exclude women from society, are not only tolerated, but deemed of little account in man.

He has usurped the prerogative of Jehovah himself, claiming it as his right to assign for her a sphere of action, when that belongs to her conscience and to her God.

He has endeavored, in every way that he could, to destroy her confidence in her own powers, to lessen her self-respect, and to make her willing to lead a dependent and abject life.

Now, in view of this entire disfranchisement of one-half the people of this country, their social and religious degradation—in view of the unjust laws above mentioned, and because women do feel themselves aggrieved, oppressed, and fraudulently deprived of their most sacred rights, we insist that they have immediate admission to all the rights and privileges which belong to them as citizens of the United States.

In entering upon the great work before us, we anticipate no small amount 20 of misconception, misrepresentation, and ridicule; but we shalll use every instrumentality within our power to effect our object. We shall employ agents, circulate tracts, petition the State and National legislatures, and endeavor to enlist the pulpit and the press in our behalf. We hope this Convention will be followed by a series of Conventions embracing every part of the country.

[The following resolutions were discussed by Lucretia Mott, Thomas and Mary Ann McClintock, Amy Post, Catharine A. F. Stebbins, and others, and were adopted:]

Whereas, The great precept of nature is conceded to be, that "man shall pursue his own true and substantial happiness." Blackstone in his Commentaries remarks, that this law of Nature being coeval with mankind, and dictated by God himself, is of course superior in obligation to any other. It is binding over all the globe, in all countries, and at all times; no human laws are of any validity if contrary to this, and such of them as are valid, derive all their force, and all their validity, and all their authority, mediately and immediately, from this original; threfore,

Resolved, That such laws as conflict, in any way, with the true and substantial happiness of woman, are contrary to the great precept of nature and of no validity, for this is "superior in obligation to any other."

Resolved, That all laws which prevent woman from occupying such a station in society as her conscience shall dictate, or which place her in a position inferior to that of man, are contrary to the great precept of nature, and therefore of no force or authority.

Resolved, That woman is man's equal—was intended to be so by the Cre- 24 ator, and the highest good of the race demands that she should be recognized as such.

Resolved, That the women of this country ought to be enlightened in regard to the laws under which they live, that they may no longer publish their degradation by declaring themselves satisfied with their present position, nor their ignorance, by asserting that they have all the rights they want.

Resolved, That inasmuch as man, while claiming for himself intellectual superiority, does accord to woman moral superiority, it is preeminently his duty to encourage her to speak and teach, as she has an opportunity, in all religious assemblies.

Resolved, That the same amount of virtue, delicacy, and refinement of behavior that is required of woman in the social state, should also be required of man, and the same transgressions should be visited with equal severity on both man and woman.

Resolved, That the objection of indelicacy and impropriety, which is so 28 often brought against woman when she addresses a public audience, comes with a very ill-grace from those who encourage, by their attendance, her appearance on the stage, in the concert, or in feats of the circus.

Resolved, That woman has too long rested satisfied in the circumscribed limits which corrupt customs and a perverted application of the Scriptures have marked out for her, and that it is time she should move in the enlarged sphere which her great Creator has assigned her.

Resolved, That it is the duty of the women of this country to secure to themselves their sacred right to the elective franchise.

Resolved, That the equality of human rights results necessarily from the fact of the identity of the race in capabilities and responsibilities.

Resolved, therefore, That, being invested by the Creator with the same 32 capabilities, and the same consciousness of responsibility for their exercise, it is demonstrably the right and duty of woman, equally with man, to promote every righteous cause by every righteous means; and especially in regard to the great subjects of morals and religion, it is self-evidently her right to participate with her brother in teaching them, both in private and in public, by writing and by speaking, by any instrumentalities proper to be used, and in any assemblies proper to be held; and this being a self-evident truth growing out of the divinely implanted principles of human nature, any custom or authorities adverse to it, whether modern or wearing the hoary sanction of antiquity, is to be regarded as a self-evident falsehood, and at war with mankind.

[At the last session Lucretia Mott offered and spoke to the following resolution:]

Resolved, That the speedy success of our cause depends upon the zealous and untiring efforts of both men and women, for the overthrow of the monopoly of the pulpit, and for the securing to woman an equal participation with men in the various trades, professions, and commerce.

[1848]

■ TOPICS FOR DISCUSSION AND WRITING

1. Stanton echoes the Declaration of Independence because she wishes to associate her ideas and the movement she supports with a document and a movement that her readers esteem. And of course she must have believed that if readers esteem the Declaration of Independence, they must grant the justice of her goals. Does her strategy work, or does it backfire by making her essay seem strained?

2. The Declaration claims that women have "the same capabilities" as men (para. 32). Yet in 1848 Stanton and the others at Seneca Falls knew, or should have known, that history recorded no example of an outstanding woman philosopher to compare with Plato or Kant, a great composer to compare with Beethoven or Chopin, a scientist to compare with Galileo or Newton, or a creative mathematician to compare with Euclid or Des-

cartes. Do these facts contradict the Declaration's claim? If not, why not? How else but by different intellectual capabilities do you think such facts are to be explained?

3. Stanton's Declaration is almost 150 years old. Have all of the issues she raised been satisfactorily resolved? If not, which ones remain?

4. In our society, children have very few rights. For instance, a child cannot decide to drop out of elementary school or high school, and a child cannot decide to leave his or her parents in order to reside with some other family that he or she finds more compatible. Whatever your view of children's rights, compose the best Declaration of the Rights of Children that you can.

■ MARTIN LUTHER KING, JR.

Martin Luther King (1929–1968), the son and grandson of ministers, after graduating from Morehouse College and Crozier Theological Seminary, earned a Ph.D. at Boston University. King first achieved national attention while serving as pastor of a Baptist church in Montgomery, Alabama, when he advocated civil disobedience as a means of protesting segregated seating on public transportation. In 1957 he organized the Southern Christian Leadership Conference, and in the following year he moved its headquarters to Atlanta, where he served as pastor of the Ebenezer Baptist Church. In 1964 he was awarded the Nobel Peace Prize. Four years later he was assassinated in Memphis, while supporting striking garbage workers.

"I Have a Dream" was delivered in 1963 from the steps of Lincoln Memorial, in Washington, D.C., on the hundredth anniversary of the Emancipation Proclamation.

I Have a Dream

Five score years ago, a great American, in whose symbolic shadow we stand, signed the Emancipation Proclamation. This momentous decree came as a great beacon light of hope to millions of Negro slaves who had been seared in the flames of withering injustice. It came as a joyous daybreak to end the long night of captivity.

But one hundred years later, we must face the tragic fact that the Negro is still not free. One hundred years later, the life of the Negro is still sadly crippled by the manacles of segregation and the chains of discrimination. One hundred years later, the Negro lives on a lonely island of poverty in the midst of a vast ocean of material prosperity. One hundred years later, the Negro is still languishing in the corners of American society and finds himself an exile in his own land. So we have come here today to dramatize an appalling condition.

In a sense we have come to our nation's Capitol to cash a check. When the architects of our republic wrote the magnificent words of the Constitution and the Declaration of Independence, they were signing a promissory note to which every American was to fall heir. This note was a promise that all men would be guaranteed the unalienable rights of life, liberty, and the pursuit of happiness.

It is obvious today that America has defaulted on this promissory note insofar as her citizens of color are concerned. Instead of honoring this sacred obligation, America has given the Negro people a bad check; a check which has come back marked "insufficient funds." But we refuse to believe that the bank of justice is bankrupt. We refuse to believe that there are insufficient funds in the great vaults of opportunity of this nation. So we have come to cash this check—a check that will give us upon demand the riches of freedom and the security of justice. We have also come to this hallowed spot to remind America of the fierce urgency of *now*. This is no time to engage in the luxury of cooling off or to take the tranquilizing drug of gradualism. *Now* is the time to make real the promises of Democracy. *Now* is the time to rise from the dark and desolate valley of segregation to the sunlit path of racial justice. *Now* is the time to open the doors of opportunity to all of God's children. *Now* is the time to lift our nation from the quicksands of racial injustice to the solid rock of brotherhood.

It would be fatal for the nation to overlook the urgency of the moment 5 and to underestimate the determination of the Negro. This sweltering summer of the Negro's legitimate discontent will not pass until there is an invigorating autumn of freedom and equality. 1963 is not an end, but a beginning. Those who hope that the Negro needed to blow off steam and will now be content will have a rude awakening if the nation returns to business as usual. There will be neither rest nor tranquility in America until the Negro is granted his citizenship rights. The whirlwinds of revolt will continue to shake the foundations of our nation until the bright day of justice emerges.

But there is something I must say to my people who stand on the warm threshold which leads into the palace of justice. In the process of gaining our rightful place we must not be guilty of wrongful deeds. Let us not seek to satisfy our thirst for freedom by drinking from the cup of bitterness and hatred. We must forever conduct our struggle on the high plane of dignity and discipline. We must not allow our creative protest to degenerate into physical violence. Again and again we must rise to the majestic heights of meeting physical force with soul force. The marvelous new militancy which has engulfed the Negro community must not lead us to a distrust of all white people, for many of our white brothers, as evidenced by their presence here today, have come to realize that their destiny is tied up with our destiny and their freedom is inextricably bound to our freedom. We cannot walk alone.

And as we walk, we must make the pledge that we shall march ahead. We cannot turn back. There are those who are asking the devotees of civil rights, "When will you be satisfied?" We can never be satisfied as long as the Negro is the victim of the unspeakable horrors of police brutality. We can never be satisfied as long as our bodies, heavy with the fatigue of travel, cannot gain lodging in the motels of the highways and the hotels of the cities. We cannot be satisfied as long as the Negro's basic mobility is from a smaller ghetto to a larger one. We can never be satisfied as long as a Negro in Mississippi cannot vote and a Negro in New York believes he has nothing for which to vote. No, no, we are not satisfied, and we will not be satisfied until justice rolls down like waters and righteousness like a mighty stream.

I am not unmindful that some of you have come here out of great trials and tribulations. Some of you have come fresh from narrow jail cells. Some of you have come from areas where your quest for freedom left you battered by the storms of persecution and staggered by the winds of policy brutality. You have been the veterans of creative suffering. Continue to work with the faith that unearned suffering is redemptive.

Go back to Mississippi, go back to Alabama, go back to South Carolina, go back to Georgia, go back to Louisiana, go back to the slums and ghettoes of our northern cities, knowing that somehow this situation can and will be changed. Let us not wallow in the valley of despair.

I say to you today, my friends, that in spite of the difficulties and frustra- 10 tions of the moment I still have a dream. It is a dream deeply rooted in the American dream.

I have a dream that one day this nation will rise up and live out the true meaning of its creed: "We hold these truths to be self-evident; that all men are created equal."

I have a dream that one day on the red hills of Georgia the sons of former slaves and the sons of former slaveowners will be able to sit down together at the table of brotherhood.

I have a dream that the state of Mississippi, a desert state sweltering with the heat of injustice and oppression, will be transformed into an oasis of freedom and justice.

I have a dream that my four little children will one day live in a nation where they will not be judged by the color of their skin but by the content of their character.

I have a dream today.   15

I have a dream that the state of Alabama, whose governor's lips are presently dripping with the words of interposition and nullification, will be transformed into a situation where little black boys and black girls will be able to join hands with little white boys and white girls and walk together as sisters and brothers.

I have a dream today.

I have a dream that one day every valley shall be exalted, every hill and mountain shall be made low, the rough places will be made plain, and the crooked places will be made straight, and the glory of the Lord shall be revealed, and all flesh shall see it together.

This is our hope. This is the faith with which I return to the South. With this faith we will be able to hew out of the mountain of despair a stone of hope. With this faith we will be able to transform the jangling discords of our nation into a beautiful symphony of brotherhood. With this faith we will be able to work together, to pray together, to struggle together, to go to jail together, to stand up for freedom together, knowing that we will be free one day.

This will be the day when all of God's children will be able to sing with 20 new meaning.

My country, tis of thee
Sweet land of liberty,
    Of thee I sing:
Land where my fathers died,
Land of the pilgrims' pride,
From every mountainside
    Let freedom ring.

And if America is to be a great nation this must become true. So let freedom ring from the prodigious hilltops of New Hampshire. Let freedom ring from the mighty mountains of New York. Let freedom ring from the heightening Alleghenies of Pennsylvania!

Let freedom ring from the snowcapped Rockies of Colorado!

Let freedom ring from the curvaceous peaks of California!

But not only that; let freedom ring from Stone Mountain of Georgia!

Let freedom ring from Lookout Mountain of Tennessee!

Let freedom ring from every hill and molehill of Mississippi. From every mountainside, let freedom ring.

When we let freedom ring, when we let it ring from every village and ev-   25
ery hamlet, from every state and every city, we will be able to speed up that day when all of God's children, black men and white men, Jews and Gentiles, Protestants and Catholics, will be able to join hands and sing in the words of the old Negro spiritual, "Free at last! free at last! thank God almighty, we are free at last!"

[1963]

■ TOPICS FOR DISCUSSION AND WRITING

1. "I Have a Dream" was originally a speech, not an essay. What words in the speech indicate King's relationship to his audience?

2. Clearly this is not ordinary talk, of the sort that can be heard on a bus. How does it differ? What devices do you find that might also be found in a poem?

3. In a paragraph, examine the analogy (in the second and third paragraphs) of the check King and his audience have come to cash. Is it effective, and if so, why?

4. Consider the organization of the talk. In a sentence, summarize the gist of the first four paragraphs. Next, summarize the gist of the next four paragraphs (through the paragraph beginning "Go back to Mississippi"). Finally, summarize the remainder of the speech. Then consider what purpose the first part serves.

5. Exactly what is King asking for on behalf of blacks?

6. The speech is directed to whites as well as blacks. What is King saying to whites?

7. King delivered this speech on 28 August 1963 in Washington, D.C. Do you believe that his dream has been fulfilled? Or is near fulfillment? Explain.

8. Do you believe that members of the clergy should be politically active?
    Why, or why not?

■ STUDS TERKEL
  _____

    Studs Terkel (his real name is Louis Terkel) was born in New York
City in 1912. After earning a Ph.D. and a law degree from the University
of Chicago he worked as a civil servant and an actor before becoming a
radio and television broadcaster. Much of his broadcasting work consisted
of interviewing people for "Studs' Place," and he later published numerous books of interviews.

Arnold Schwarzenegger's Dream*

Call me Arnold.

I was born in a little Austrian town, outside Graz. It was a 300-year-old
house.

When I was ten years old, I had the dream of being the best in the world
in something. When I was fifteen, I had a dream that I wanted to be the best
body builder in the world and the most muscular man. It was not only a dream
I dreamed at night. It was also a daydream. It was so much in my mind that
I felt it had to become a reality. It took me five years of hard work. Five years
later, I turned this dream into reality and became Mr. Universe, the best-built
man in the world.

"Winning" is a very important word. There is one that achieves what he
wanted to achieve and there are hundreds of thousands that failed. It singles
you out: the winner.

I came out second three times, but that is not what I call losing. The bot-   5
tom line for me was: Arnold has to be the winner. I have to win more often
the Mr. Universe title than anybody else. I won it five times consecutively.
I hold the record as Mr. Olympia, the top professional body-building championship. I won it six times. That's why I retired. There was nobody even close
to me. Everybody gave up competing against me. That's what I call a winner.

When I was a small boy, my dream was not to be big physically, but big
in a way that everybody listens to me when I talk, that I'm a very important
person, that people recognize me and see me as something special. I had a
big need for being singled out.

Also my dream was to end up in America. When I was ten years old, I
dreamed of being an American. At the time I didn't know much about America, just that it was a wonderful country. I felt it was where I belonged. I didn't
like being in a little country like Austria. I did everything possible to get out.
I did so in 1968, when I was twenty-one years old.

If I would believe in life after death, I would say my before-life I was living
in America. That's why I feel so good here. It is the country where you can

_____

*Terkel's *American Dreams* presents transcriptions of interviews that Terkel recorded.

turn your dream into reality. Other countries don't have those things. When I came over here to America, I felt I was in heaven. In America, we don't have an obstacle. Nobody's holding you back.

Number One in America pretty much takes care of the rest of the world. You kind of run through the rest of the world like nothing. I'm trying to make people in America aware that they should appreciate what they have here. You have the best tax advantages here and the best prices here and the best products here.

One of the things I always had was a business mind. When I was in high 10 school, a majority of my classes were business classes. Economics and accounting and mathematics. When I came over here to this country, I really didn't speak English almost at all. I learned English and then started taking business courses, because that's what America is best known for: business. Turning one dollar into a million dollars in a short period of time. Also when you make money, how do you keep it?

That's one of the most important things when you have money in your hand, how can you keep it? Or make more out of it? Real estate is one of the best ways of doing that. I own apartment buildings, office buildings, and raw land. That's my love, real estate.

I have emotions. But what you do, you keep them cold or you store them away for a time. You must control your emotions, you must have command over yourself. Three, four months before a competition, I could not be interfered by other people's problems. This is sometimes called selfish. It's the only way you can be if you want to achieve something. Any emotional things inside me, I try to keep cold so it doesn't interfere with my training.

Many times things really touched me. I felt them and I felt sensitive about them. But I had to talk myself out of it. I had to suppress those feelings in order to go on. Sport is one of those activities where you really have to concentrate. You must pay attention a hundred percent to the particular thing you're doing. There must be nothing else on your mind. Emotions must not interfere. Otherwise, you're thinking about your girlfriend. You're in love, your positive energies get channeled into another direction rather than going into your weight room or making money.

You have to choose at a very early date what you want: a normal life or to achieve things you want to achieve. I never wanted to win a popularity contest in doing things the way people want me to do it. I went the road I thought was best for me. A few people thought I was cold, selfish. Later they found out that's not the case. After I achieve my goal, I can be Mr. Nice Guy. You know what I mean?

California is to me a dreamland. It is the absolute combination of every- 15 thing I was always looking for. It has all the money in the world there, show business there, wonderful weather there, beautiful country, ocean is there. Snow skiing in the winter, you can go in the desert the same day. You have beautiful-looking people there. They all have a tan.

I believe very strongly in the philosophy of staying hungry. If you have a dream and it becomes a reality, don't stay satisfied with it too long. Make up a new dream and hunt after that one and turn it into reality. When you have that dream achieved, make up a new dream.

I am a strong believer in Western philosophy, the philosophy of success, of progress, of getting rich. The Eastern philosophy is passive, which I believe in maybe three percent of the times, and the ninety-seven percent is Western, conquering and going on. It's a beautiful philosophy, and America should keep it up.

[1980]

■ TOPICS FOR DISCUSSION AND WRITING

1. After saying that America "is the country where you can turn your dream into reality. Other countries don't have those things," Schwarzenegger goes on to say, "In America . . . nobody's holding you back." What do you suppose he means by "those things," and by saying that here "nobody's holding you back"?

2. If you have some firsthand knowledge of another country, in an essay of 250–500 words indicate in what ways that country might differ from America in the matter of allowing individuals to fulfill their dreams. By the way, is it your guess that Schwarzenegger's particular dream ("to be the best body builder in the world") is more easily fulfilled in the United States than elsewhere—say in Canada, or Cuba, or Russia, or Austria? Why?

3. In a paragraph set forth what you think Schwarzenegger's view of America is.

4. In one paragraph, sketch Schwarzenegger as objectively as possible, as you perceive him in this interview. In a second paragraph, again drawing only on this interview, evaluate him, calling attention to what you think are his strengths and weaknesses.

5. If you have read Arthur Miller's *Death of a Salesman*, write an essay of 500 words comparing Arnold Schwarzenegger and Willy Loman.

■ JEANNE WAKATSUKI HOUSTON
and JAMES D. HOUSTON

Jeanne Wakatsuki, the daughter of immigrants from Japan, was born in Inglewood, California. When she was seven the Japanese attack on Pearl Harbor aroused such fear and resentment that Japanese and Japanese-Americans on the Pacific coast of the United States were relocated, and her family was forced to spend three-and-a-half years at Manzanar, a camp in Owens Valley, California. Later she graduated from San Jose State University, married James D. Houston, and took up writing as a career.

James D. Houston was born in San Francisco. The author of five novels and six books of nonfiction, he teaches writing at the University of California, Santa Cruz.

"The Girl of My Dreams" is a chapter in *Farewell to Manzanar*. Written as a first-person memoir, the book is based on Jeanne Wakatsuki Houston's experience and memories of the years during World War II. It was written in collaboration with her husband.

The Girl of My Dreams

That bow was from the world I wanted out of, while the strutting, sequined partnership I had with Radine was exactly how I wanted my life to go.[1] My path through the next few years can be traced by its relationship to hers. It was a classic situation.

In many ways we had started even. Poor whites from west Texas, her family was so badly off sometimes she'd come to school with no lunch and no money and we would split whatever I had brought along. At the same time we were both getting all this attention together with the drum and bugle corps. After three years at our junior high school, in a ghetto neighborhood that included many Asians, Blacks, Mexicans, and other white migrants from the south, we had ended up close to being social equals.

We stayed best friends until we moved to Long Beach Polytechnic. There everything changed. Our paths diverged. She was asked to join high school sororities. The question of whether or not I should be asked was never even raised. The boys I had crushes on would not ask me out. They would flirt with me in the hallways or meet me after school, but they would ask Radine to the dances, or someone like Radine, someone they could safely be *seen* with. Meanwhile she graduated from baton twirler to song girl, a much more prestigious position in those days. It was unthinkable for a Nisei[2] to be a song girl. Even choosing me as majorette created problems.

The band teacher knew I had more experience than anyone else competing that year. He told me so. But he was afraid to use me. He had to go speak to the board about it, and to some of the parents, to see if it was allowable for an Oriental to represent the high school in such a visible way. It had never happened before. I was told that this inquiry was being made, and my reaction was the same as when I tried to join the Girl Scouts. I was apologetic for imposing such a burden on those who had to decide. When they finally assented, I was grateful. After all, I *was* the first Oriental majorette they'd ever had. Even if my once enviable role now seemed vaguely second-rate, still I determined to try twice as hard to prove they'd made the right choice.

This sort of treatment did not discourage me. I was used to it. I expected 5 it, a condition of life. What demoralized me was watching Radine's success. We had shared everything, including all the values I'd learned from the world I wanted into, not only standards of achievement but ideas about how a girl should look and dress and talk and act, and ideas of male beauty—which was why so many of the boys I liked were Caucasian. Because I so feared never being asked, I often simply made myself unavailable for certain kinds of dates. If one of them had asked me, of course, I would have been mortified. That

---

[1] **That bow. . .to go** The preceding chapter ends by reporting how, at a PTA meeting, Jeanne was humiliated when her father, on being introduced to the group, "gave . . . . a slow, deep Japanese bow from the waist. . . . Twelve years old at the time, I wanted to scream. I wanted to slide out of sight under the table and dissolve." The chapter also describes Jeanne's friendship with Radine, a Caucasian girl, to whom Jeanne taught baton-twirling.

[2] **Nisei** second generation, i.e., the child of a Japanese immigrant

would mean coming to Cabrillo Homes[3] to pick me up, and the very thought of one of his daughters dating a Caucasian would have started Papa raving. He would have chased the fellow across the grass. This was my dilemma. Easy enough as it was to adopt white American values, I still had a Japanese father to frighten my boyfriends and a Japanese face to thwart my social goals.

I never wanted to change my face or to be someone other than myself. What I wanted was the kind of acceptance that seemed to come so easily to Radine. To this day I have a recurring dream, which fills me each time with a terrible sense of loss and desolation. I see a young, beautifully blond and blue-eyed high school girl moving through a room full of others her own age, much admired by everyone, men and women both, myself included, as I watch through a window. I feel no malice toward this girl. I don't even envy her. Watching, I am simply emptied, and in the dream I want to cry out, because she is something I can never be, some possibility in my life that can never be fulfilled.

It is a schoolgirl's dream, one I tell my waking self I've long since out-grown. Yet it persists. Once or twice a year she will be there, the boyfriend-surrounded queen who passed me by. Surely her example spurred me on to pursue what now seems ludicrous, but at the time was the height of my post-Manzanar ambitions.

It didn't happen in Long Beach. There I felt defeated. I watched Radine's rise, and I knew I could never compete with that. Gradually I lost interest in school and began hanging around on the streets. I would probably have dropped out for good, but it was just about this time that Papa decided to go back into farming and finally moved us out of Cabrillo Homes.

A few months earlier he had almost killed himself on a combination of whiskey and some red wine made by an Italian drinking buddy of his. He had been tippling steadily for two days, when he started vomiting blood from his mouth and nose. It sobered him up permanently. He never touched alcohol again. After that he pulled himself together, and when the chance came along to lease and sharecrop a hundred acres from a big strawberry grower up north in Santa Clara Valley, he took it. That's where he stayed until he died, raising premium berries, outside of San Jose.

I was a senior when we moved. In those days, 1951, San Jose was a large 10 town, but not yet a city. Coming from a big high school in southern California gave me some kind of shine, I suppose. It was a chance to start over, and I made the most of it. By the spring of that year, when it came time to elect the annual carnival queen from the graduating seniors, my homeroom chose me. I was among fifteen girls nominated to walk out for inspection by the as-sembled student body on voting day.

I knew I couldn't beat the other contestants at their own game, that is, look like a bobbysoxer. Yet neither could I look too Japanese-y. I decided to go exotic, with a flower-print sarong, black hair loose and a hibiscus flower behind my ear. When I walked barefooted out onto the varnished gymnasium floor, between the filled bleachers, the howls and whistles from the boys were

[3] **Cabrillo Homes** a housing project in west Long Beach, built by the government for defense plant workers

double what had greeted any of the other girls. It sounded like some winning basket had just been made in the game against our oldest rivals.

It was pretty clear what the outcome would be, but ballots still had to be cast and counted. The next afternoon I was standing outside my Spanish class when Leonard Rodriguez, who sat next to me, came hurrying down the hall with a revolutionary's fire in his eye. He helped out each day in the administration office. He had just overheard some teachers and a couple of secretaries counting up the votes.

"They're trying to stuff the ballot box," he whispered loudly. "They're fudging on the tally. They're afraid to have a Japanese girl be queen. They've never had one before. They're afraid of what some of the parents will say."

He was pleased he had caught them, and more pleased to be telling this to me, as if some long-held suspicion of conspiracy had finally been confirmed. I shared it with him. Whether this was true or not, I was prepared to believe that teachers would stuff the batllot box to keep me from being queen. For that reason I couldn't afford to get my hopes up.

I said, "So what?"   15

He leaned toward me eagerly, with final proof. "They want Lois Carson to be queen. I heard them say so."

If applause were any measure, Lois Carson wasn't even in the running. She was too slim and elegant for beauty contests. But her father had contributed a lot to the school. He was on the board of trustees. She was blond, blue-eyed. At that point her name might as well have been Radine. I was ready to capitulate without a groan.

"If she doesn't make carnival queen this year," Leonard went on smugly, "she'll never be queen of anything anywhere else for the rest of her life."

"Let her have it then, if she wants it so much."

"No! We can't do that! *You* can't do that!"   20

I could do that very easily. I wasn't going to be caught caring about this, or needing it, the way I had needed the majorette position. I already sensed, though I couldn't have said why, that I would lose either way, no matter how it turned out. My face was indifferent.

"How can I stop them from fudging," I said, "if that's what they want to do?"

He hesitated. He looked around. He set his brown face. My champion. "You can't," he said. "But I can."

He turned and hurried away toward the office. The next morning he told me he had gone in there and "raised holy hell," threatened to break this news to the student body and make the whole thing more trouble than it would ever be worth. An hour later the announcement came over the intercom that I had been chosen. I didn't believe it. I couldn't let myself believe it. But, for the classmates who had nominated me, I had to look overjoyed. I glanced across at Leonard and he winked, shouting and whooping now with all the others.

At home that evening, when I brought this news, no one whooped. Papa   25
was furious. I had not told them I was running for queen. There was no use mentioning it until I had something to mention. He asked me what I had worn at the tryouts. I told him.

"No wonder those *hakajin*[4] boys vote for you!" he shouted. "It is just like those majorette clothes you wear in the street. Showing off your body. Is that the kind of queen you want to be?"

I didn't say anything. When Papa lectured, you listened. If anyone spoke up it would be Mama, trying to mediate.

"Ko," she said now, "these things are important to Jeannie. She is . . ."

"Important? I'll tell you what is important. Modesty is important. A graceful body is important. You don't show your legs all the time. You don't walk around like this."

He did an imitation of a girl's walk, with shoulders straight, an assertive   30
stride, and lips pulled back in a baboon's grin. I started to laugh.

"Don't laugh! This is not funny. You become this kind of woman and what Japanese boy is going to marry you? Tell me that. You put on tight clothes and walk around like Jean Harlow[5] and the *hakajin* boys make you the queen. And pretty soon you end up marrying a *hakajin* boy . . ."

He broke off. He could think of no worse end result. He began to stomp back and forth across the floor, while Mama looked at me cautiously, with a glance that said, "Be patient, wait him out. After he has spoken his piece, you and I can talk sensibly."

He saw this and turned on her. "Hey! How come your daughter is seventeen years old and if you put a sack over her face you couldn't tell she was Japanese from anybody else on the street?"

"Ko," Mama said quietly. "Jeannie's in high school now. Next year she's going to go to college. She's learning other things . . ."

"Listen to me. It's not too late for her to learn Japanese ways of move-   35
ment. The Buddhist church in San Jose gives odori[6] class twice a week. Jeannie, I want you to phone the teacher and tell her you are going to start taking lessons. Mama has kimonos you can wear. She can show you things too. She used to know all the dances. We have pictures somewhere. Mama, what happened to all those pictures?"

I had seen them, photos of Mama when she lived in Spokane, twelve years old and her round face blanched with rice powder. I remembered the afternoon I spent with the incomprehensible old geisha at Manzanar.

"Papa," I complained.

"Don't make faces. You want to be the carnival queen? I tell you what. I'll make a deal with you. You can be the queen if you start odori lessons at the Buddhist church as soon as school is out."

He stood there, hands on hips, glaring at me, and not at all satisfied with this ultimatum. It was far too late for odori classes to have any effect on me and Papa knew this. But he owed it to himself to make one more show of resistance. When I signed up, a few weeks later, I lasted about ten lessons. The teacher herself sent me away. I smiled too much and couldn't break the habit. Like a majorette before the ever-shifting sidewalk crowd, I smiled during performances, and in Japanese dancing that is equivalent to a concert violinist walking onstage in a bathing suit.

[4] *hakajin* Caucasian
[5] **Jean Harlow** a popular Hollywood movie star
[6] **odori** Japanese dancer

Papa didn't mention my queenship again. He just glared at me from time 40
to time, with great distaste, as if I had betrayed him. Yet in that glare I sometimes detected a flicker of approval, as if this streak of independence, this
refusal to be shaped by him reflected his own obstinance. At least, these
glances seemed to say, she has inherited *that*.

Mama, of course, was very proud. She took charge and helped me pick
out the dress I would wear for the coronation. We drove to San Jose and spent
an afternoon in the shops downtown. She could take time for such things now
that Papa was working again. This was one of the few days she and I ever
spent together, just the two of us, and it confirmed something I'd felt since
early childhood. In her quiet way, she had always supported me, alongside of
or underneath Papa's demands and expectations. Now she wanted for me the
same thing I thought I wanted. Acceptance, in her eyes, was simply another
means for survival.

Her support and Papa's resistance had one point in common: too much
exposure was unbecoming. All the other girls—my four attendants—were going strapless. Mama wouldn't allow this. By the time we finished shopping,
I had begun to agree with her. When she picked out a frilly ball gown that
covered almost everything and buried my legs under layers of ruffles, I
thought it was absolutely right. I had used a low-cut sarong to win the contest. But once chosen I would be a white-gowned figure out of *Gone With the
Wind*; I would be respectable.

On coronation night the gym was lit like a church, with bleachers in half-
dark and a throne at one end, flooded brightly from the ceiling. The throne
was made of plywood, its back shaped in a fleur-de-lis all covered with purple
taffeta that shone like oily water under moonlight. Bed sheets were spread
to simulate a wide, white carpet the length of the gym, from the throne to
the door of the girls' locker room where, with my attendants, we waited for
the PA system to give us our musical cue.

Lois Carson, the trustee's daughter, was one of them. She wore a very
expensive strapless gown and a huge orchid corsage. Her pool-browned
shoulders glowed in harsh bulb light above the lockers.

"Oh Jeannie," she had said, as we took off our coats. "What a marvelous 45
idea!"

I looked at her inquisitively.

"The high *neck*," she explained, studying my dress. "You look so . . . *sedate*. Just perfect for a queen."

As the other girls arrived, she made sure they all agreed with this.
"Don't you *wish* you'd thought of it," she would say. And then to me, during
a silence she felt obliged to fill, "I just *love* Chinese food." The others exclaimed that they too loved Chinese food, and talked about recipes and
restaurants until the music faded in:

> *Girl of my dreams, I love you,*
> *Honest I do,*
> *You are so sweet.*

It swelled during the opening bars to cover all other sounds in the gym.
I stepped out into blue light that covered the first sheet, walking very slowly,

like you do at weddings, carrying against the white bodice of my gown a bouquet of pink carnations.

A burst of applause resounded beneath the music, politely enthusiastic, 50 followed by a steady murmur. The gym was packed, and the lights were intense. Suddenly it was too hot out there. I imagined that they were all murmuring about my dress. They saw the girls behind me staring at it. The throne seemed blocks away, and now the dress was stifling me. I had never before worn such an outfit. It was not at all what I should have on. I wanted my sarong. But then thought, NO. That would have been worse. Papa had been right about the sarong. Maybe he was right about everything. What was I doing out there anyway, trying to be a carnival queen? The teachers who'd counted the votes certainly didn't think it was such a good idea. Neither did the trustees. The students wanted me though. Their votes proved that. I kept walking my processional walk, thinking of all the kids who had voted for me, not wanting to let them down, although in a way I already had. It wasn't the girl in this old-fashioned dress they had voted for. But if not her, who *had* they voted for? Somebody I wanted to be. And wasn't. Who was I then? According to the big wall speakers now saxophoning through the gym, I was the girl of somebody's dream:

> *Since you've been gone, dear,*
> *Life don't seem the same.*
> *Please come back again . . .*

I looked ahead at the throne. It was even further away, a purple carriage receding as I approached. I glanced back. My four attendants seemed tiny. Had they stopped back there? Afterward there would be a little reception in one of the classrooms, punch and cookies under fluorescent tubes. Later, at Lois Carson's house, there'd be a more intimate, less public gathering, which I'd overheard a mention of but wouldn't be invited to. Champagne in the foothills. Oyster dip. I wanted to laugh. I wanted to cry. I wanted to be ten years old again, so I could believe in princesses and queens. It was too late. Too late to be an odori dancer for Papa, too late to be this kind of heroine. I wanted the carnival to end so I could go somewhere private, climb out of my stuffy dress, and cool off. But all eyes were on me. It was too late now not to follow this make-believe carpet to its plywood finale, and I did not yet know of any truer destination.

[1973]

■ TOPICS FOR DISCUSSION AND WRITING

1. In the second paragraph Jeanne Wakatsuki Houston reports that she and Radine were friends throughout junior high school, but then their "paths diverged." If you have had a similar experience with a childhood friend of a different race, religion, or culture, try to account for the separation, perhaps in an essay of about 750 words.
2. Do you think that Houston's comments about her father are objectionable? Explain your position.
3. What do you make of Lois Carson's praise of Jeanne and her assertion

that she "loves" Chinese food (paragraphs 47–48)? (In your response, consider also the final paragraph of the essay.)

4. Drawing on your own experience in high school, do you think that the sort of racism described in this essay—for instance the hesitation to appoint an Asian-American majorette or carnival queen—is completely a thing of the past? What evidence can you cite to support your view?

FICTION

■ SHERWOOD ANDERSON

Sherwood Anderson (1876–1941) was born in Camden, Ohio. At 14 he dropped out of school—his attendance had already been irregular, partly because, like the narrator in "The Egg," his family drifted from small town to small town. He worked at odd jobs, such as newsboy, house painter, and stable groom, and in 1898 served briefly in the Spanish-American War. He then turned to advertising and business, and by 1904 he was a fairly prosperous manager of paint factories in Ohio. In 1912, however, in the midst of dictating a business letter he walked out of the office and disappeared for several days. He went to Chicago, where he fell in with such writers as Carl Sandburg and Theodore Dreiser, and he soon began writing poems, stories, and novels. At the age of 43, after publishing two unsuccessful novels, he achieved fame with *Winesburg, Ohio* (1919), a collection of related stories about life in a small town. "The Egg" comes from a later collection of stories, *The Triumph of the Egg* (1921).

The Egg

My father was, I am sure, intended by nature to be a cheerful, kindly man. Until he was thirty-four years old he worked as a farmhand for a man named Thomas Butterworth whose place lay near the town of Bidwell, Ohio. He had then a horse of his own, and on Saturday evenings drove into town to spend a few hours in social intercourse with other farmhands. In town he drank several glasses of beer and stood about in Ben Head's saloon—crowded on Saturday evenings with visiting farmhands. Songs were sung and glasses thumped on the bar. At ten o'clock father drove home along a lonely country road, made his horse comfortable for the night, and himself went to bed, quite happy in his position in life. He had at that time no notion of trying to rise in the world.

It was in the spring of his thirty-fifth year that father married my mother, then a country school-teacher, and in the following spring I came wriggling and crying into the world. Something happened to the two people. They became ambitious. The American passion for getting up in the world took possession of them.

It may have been that mother was responsible. Being a school-teacher she had no doubt read books and magazines. She had, I presume, read of how Garfield, Lincoln, and other Americans rose from poverty to fame and greatness, and as I lay beside her—in the days of her lying-in—she may have dreamed that I would some day rule men and cities. At any rate she induced father to give up his place as a farmhand, sell his horse, and embark on an independent enterprise of his own. She was a tall silent woman with a long nose and troubled gray eyes. For herself she wanted nothing. For father and myself she was incurably ambitious.

The first venture into which the two people went turned out badly. They rented ten acres of poor stony land on Grigg's Road, eight miles from Bidwell and launched into chicken-raising. I grew into boyhood on the place and got my first impressions of life there. From the beginning they were impressions of disaster, and if, in my turn, I am a gloomy man inclined to see the darker side of life, I attribute it to the fact that what should have been for me the happy joyous days of childhood were spent on a chicken farm.

One unversed in such matters can have no notion of the many and tragic 5 things that can happen to a chicken. It is born out of an egg, lives for a few weeks as a tiny fluffy thing such as you will see pictured on Easter cards, then becomes hideously naked, eats quantities of corn and meal bought by the sweat of your father's brow, gets diseases called pip, cholera, and other names, stands looking with stupid eyes at the sun, becomes sick and dies. A few hens and now and then a rooster, intended to serve God's mysterious ends, struggle through to maturity. The hens lay eggs out of which come other chickens and the dreadful cycle is thus made complete. It is all unbelievably complex. Most philosophers must have been raised on chicken farms. One hopes for so much from a chicken and is so dreadfully disillusioned. Small chickens, just setting out on the journey of life, look so bright and alert and they are in fact so dreadfully stupid. They are so much like people they mix one up in one's judgments of life. If disease does not kill them, they wait until your expectations are thoroughly aroused and then walk under the wheels of a wagon—to go squashed and dead back to their maker. Vermin infest their youth, and fortunes must be spent for curative powders. In later life I have seen how a literature has been built up on the subject of fortunes to be made out of the raising of chickens. It is intended to be read by the gods who have just eaten of the tree of the knowledge of good and evil. It is a hopeful literature and declares that much may be done by simple ambitious people who own a few hens. Do not be led astray by it. It was not written for you. Go hunt for gold on the frozen hills of Alaska, put your faith in the honesty of a politician, believe if you will that the world is daily growing better and that good will triumph over evil, but do not read and believe the literature that is written concerning the hen. It was not written for you.

I, however, digress. My tale does not primarily concern itself with the hen. If correctly told it will center on the egg. For ten years my father and mother struggled to make our chicken farm pay and then they gave up their struggle and began another. They moved into the town of Bidwell, Ohio, and embarked in the restaurant business. After ten years of worry with incubators that did not hatch, and with tiny—and in their own way lovely—balls of fluff that passed on into seminaked pullethood and from that into dead henhood, we threw all aside and, packing our belongings on a wagon, drove down Grigg's Road toward Bidwell, a tiny caravan of hope looking for a new place from which to start on our upward journey through life.

We must have been a sad-looking lot, not, I fancy, unlike refugees fleeing from a battlefield. Mother and I walked in the road. The wagon that contained our goods had been borrowed for the day from Mr. Albert Griggs, a neighbor. Out of its side stuck the legs of cheap chairs, and at the back of the pile of beds, tables, and boxes filled with kitchen utensils was a crate of live chickens, and on top of that the baby carriage in which I had been wheeled about in my infancy. Why we stuck to the baby carriage I don't know. It was unlikely other children would be born and the wheels were broken. People who have few possessions cling tightly to those they have. That is one of the facts that make life so discouraging.

Father rode on top of the wagon. He was then a bald-headed man of forty-five, a little fat, and from long association with mother and the chickens he had become habitually silent and discouraged. All during our ten years on the chicken farm he had worked as a laborer on neighboring farms and most of the money he had earned had been spent for remedies to cure chicken diseases, on Wilmer's White Wonder Cholera Cure or Professor Bidlow's Egg Producer or some other preparations that mother found advertised in the poultry papers. There were two little patches of hair on father's head just above his ears. I remember that as a child I used to sit looking at him when he had gone to sleep in a chair before the stove on Sunday afternoons in the winter. I had at that time already begun to read books and have notions of my own, and the bald path that led over the top of his head was, I fancied, something like a broad road, such a road as Caesar might have made on which to lead his legions out of Rome and into the wonders of an unknown world. The tufts of hair that grew above father's ears were, I thought, like forests. I fell into a half-sleeping, half-waking state and dreamed I was a tiny thing going along the road into a far beautiful place where there were no chicken farms and where life was a happy eggless affair.

One might write a book concerning our flight from the chicken farm into town. Mother and I walked the entire eight miles—she to be sure that nothing fell from the wagon and I to see the wonders of the world. On the seat of the wagon beside father was his greatest treasure. I will tell you of that.

On a chicken farm, where hundreds and even thousands of chickens 10 come out of eggs, surprising things sometimes happen. Grotesques are born out of eggs as out of people. The accident does not often occur—perhaps once in a thousand births. A chicken is, you see, born that has four legs, two pairs of wings, two heads, or what not. The things do not live. They go quickly back to the hand of their maker that has for a moment trembled. The fact that the poor little things could not live was one of the tragedies of life to father. He had some sort of notion that if he could but bring into henhood or roosterhood a five-legged hen or a two-headed rooster his fortune would be made. He dreamed of taking the wonder about the county fairs and of growing rich by exhibiting it to other farmhands.

At any rate, he saved all the little monstrous things that had been born on our chicken farm. They were preserved in alcohol and put each in its own glass bottle. These he had carefully put into a box, and on our journey into town it was carried on the wagon seat beside him. He drove the horses with one hand and with the other clung to the box. When we got to our destination, the box was taken down at once and the bottles removed. All during our days as keepers of a restaurant in the town of Bidwell, Ohio, the grotesques in their little glass bottles sat on a shelf back of the counter. Mother sometimes protested, but father was a rock on the subject of his treasure. The grotesques were, he declared, valuable. People, he said, liked to look at strange and wonderful things.

Did I say that we embarked in the restaurant business in the town of Bidwell, Ohio? I exaggerated a little. The town itself lay at the foot of a low hill and on the shore of a small river. The railroad did not run through the town and the station was a mile away to the north at a place called Pickleville. There had been a cider mill and pickle factory at the station, but before the time of our coming they had both gone out of business. In the morning and in the evening busses came down to the station along a road called Turner's Pike from the hotel on the main street of Bidwell. Our going to the out-of-the-way place to embark in the restaurant business was mother's idea. She talked of it for a year and then one day went off and rented an empty store building opposite the railroad station. It was her idea that the restaurant would be profitable. Traveling men, she said, would be always waiting around to take trains out of town and town people would come to the station to await incoming trains. They would come to the restaurant to buy pieces of pie and drink coffee. Now that I am older I know that she had another motive in going. She was ambitious for me. She wanted me to rise in the world, to get into a town school and become a man of the towns.

At Pickleville father and mother worked hard, as they always had done. At first there was the necessity of putting our place into shape to be a restaurant. That took a month. Father built a shelf on which he put tins of vegetables. He painted a sign on which he put his name in large red letters. Below his name was the sharp command—"EAT HERE"—that was so seldom obeyed. A showcase was bought and filled with cigars and tobacco. Mother scrubbed the floors and the walls of the room. I went to school in the town and was glad to be away from the farm, from the presence of the discouraged, sad-looking chickens. Still I was not very joyous. In the evening I walked home from school along Turner's Pike and remembered the children I had seen playing in the town school yard. A troop of little girls had gone hopping about and singing. I tried that. Down along the frozen road I went hopping solemnly on one leg. "Hippity Hop To The Barber Shop," I sang shrilly. Then I stopped and looked doubtfully about. I was afraid of being seen in my gay mood. It must have seemed to me that I was doing a thing that should not be done by one who, like myself, had been raised on a chicken farm where death was a daily visitor.

Mother decided that our restaurant should remain open at night. At ten in the evening a passenger train went north past our door followed by a local freight. The freight crew had switching to do in Pickleville, and when the work was done they came to our restaurant for hot coffee and food. Sometimes one of them ordered a fried egg. In the morning at four they returned north-bound and again visited us. A little trade began to grow up. Mother slept at night and during the day tended the restaurant and fed our boarders while father slept. He slept in the same bed mother had occupied during the night and I went off to the town of Bidwell and to school. During the long nights, while mother and I slept, father cooked meats that were to go into sandwiches for the lunch baskets of our boarders. Then an idea in regard to getting up in the world came into his head. The American spirit took hold of him. He also became ambitious.

In the long nights when there was little to do, father had time to think. 15 That was his undoing. He decided that he had in the past been an unsuccessful man because he had not been cheerful enough and that in the future he would adopt a cheerful outlook on life. In the early morning he came upstairs and got into bed with mother. She woke and the two talked. From my bed in the corner I listened.

It was father's idea that both he and mother should try to entertain the people who came to eat at our restaurant. I cannot now remember his words, but he gave the impression of one about to become in some obscure way a kind of public entertainer. When people, particularly young people from the town of Bidwell, came into our place, as on very rare occasions they did, bright entertaining conversation was to be made. From father's words I gathered that something of the jolly innkeeper effect was to be sought. Mother must have been doubtful from the first, but she said nothing discouraging. It was father's notion that a passion for the company of himself and mother would spring up in the breasts of the younger people of the town of Bidwell. In the evening bright happy groups would come singing down Turner's Pike. They would troop shouting with joy and laughter into our place. There would be song and festivity. I do not mean to give the impression that father spoke so elaborately of the matter. He was, as I have said, an uncommunicative man. "They want some place to go. I tell you they want some place to go," he said over and over. That was as far as he got. My own imagination has filled in the blanks.

For two or three weeks this notion of father's invaded our house. We did not talk much, but in our daily lives tried earnestly to make smiles take the place of glum looks. Mother smiled at the boarders and I, catching the infection, smiled at our cat. Father became a little feverish in his anxiety to please. There was, no doubt, lurking somewhere in him, a touch of the spirit of the showman. He did not waste much of his ammunition on the railroad men he served at night, but seemed to be waiting for a young man or woman from Bidwell to come in to show what he could do. On the counter in the restaurant there was a wire basket kept always filled with eggs, and it must have been before his eyes when the idea of being entertaining was born in his brain. There was something pre-natal about the way eggs kept themselves connected with the development of his idea. At any rate, an egg ruined his new impulse in life. Late one night I was awakened by a roar of anger coming from father's throat. Both mother and I sat upright in our beds. With trembling hands she lighted a lamp that stood on a table by her head. Downstairs the front door of our restaurant went shut with a bang and in a few minutes father tramped up the stairs. He held an egg in his hand and his hand trembled as though he were having a chill. There was a half-insane light in his eyes. As he stood glaring at us I was sure he intended throwing the egg at either mother or me. Then he laid it gently on the table beside the lamp and dropped on his knees beside mother's bed. He began to cry like a boy, and I, carried away by his grief, cried with him. The two of us filled the little upstairs room with our wailing voices. It is ridiculous, but of the picture we made I can remember only the fact that mother's hand continually stroked the bald path that ran across the top of his head. I have forgotten what mother said to him and how she induced him to tell her of what had happened downstairs. His explanation also has gone out of my mind. I remember only my own grief and fright and the shiny path over father's head glowing in the lamplight as he knelt by the bed.

As to what happened downstairs. For some unexplainable reason I know the story as well as though I had been a witness to my father's discomfiture. One in time gets to know many unexplainable things. On that evening young Joe Kane, son of a merchant of Bidwell, came to Pickleville to meet his father, who was expected on the ten-o'clock evening train from the South. The train was three hours late and Joe came into our place to loaf about and to wait for its arrival. The local freight train came in and the freight crew were fed. Joe was left alone in the restaurant with father.

From the moment he came into our place the Bidwell young man must have been puzzled by my father's actions. It was his notion that father was angry at him for hanging around. He noticed that the restaurant-keeper was apparently disturbed by his presence and he thought of going out. However, it began to rain and he did not fancy the long walk to town and back. He bought a five-cent cigar and ordered a cup of coffee. He had a newspaper in his pocket and took it out and began to read. "I'm waiting for the evening train. It's late," he said apologetically.

For a long time father, whom Joe Kane had never seen before, remained 20 silently gazing at his visitor. He was no doubt suffering from an attack of stage fright. As so often happens in life he had thought so much and so often of the situation that now confronted him that he was somewhat nervous in its presence.

For one thing, he did not know what to do with his hands. He thrust one of them nervously over the counter and shook hands with Joe Kane. "How-de-do," he said. Joe Kane put his newspaper down and stared at him. Father's eyes lighted on the basket of eggs that sat on the counter and he began to talk. "Well," he began hesitatingly, "well, you have heard of Christopher Columbus, eh?" He seemed to be angry. "That Christopher Columbus was a cheat," he declared emphatically. "He talked of making an egg stand on its end. He talked, he did, and then he went and broke the end of the egg."

My father seemed to his visitor to be beside himself at the duplicity of Christopher Columbus. He muttered and swore. He declared it was wrong to teach children that Christopher Columbus was a great man when, after all, he cheated at the critical moment. He had declared he would make an egg stand on end and then, when his bluff had been called, he had done a trick. Still grumbling at Columbus, father took an egg from the basket on the counter and began to walk up and down. He rolled the egg between the palms of his hands. He smiled genially. He began to mumble words regarding the effect to be produced on an egg by the electricity that comes out of the human body. He declared that, without breaking its shell and by virtue of rolling it back and forth in his hands, he could stand the egg on its end. He explained that the warmth of his hands and the gentle rolling movement he gave the egg created a new center of gravity, and Joe Kane was mildly interested. "I have handled thousands of eggs," father said. "No one knows more about eggs than I do."

He stood the egg on the counter and it fell on its side. He tried the trick again and again, each time rolling the egg between the palms of his hands and saying the words regarding the wonders of electricity and the laws of gravity. When after a half-hour's effort he did succeed in making the egg stand for a moment, he looked up to find that his visitor was no longer watching. By the time he had succeeded in calling Joe Kane's attention to the success of his effort, the egg had again rolled over and lay on its side.

Afire with the showman's passion and at the same time a good deal disconcerted by the failure of his first effort, father now took the bottles containing the poultry monstrosities down from their place on the shelf and began to show them to his visitor. "How would you like to have seven legs and two heads like this fellow?" he asked, exhibiting the most remarkable of his treasures. A cheerful smile played over his face. He reached over the counter and tried to slap Joe Kane on the shoulder as he had seen men do in Ben Head's saloon when he was a young farmhand and drove to town on Saturday evenings. His visitor was made a little ill by the sight of the body of the terribly deformed bird floating in the alcohol in the bottle and got up to go. Coming from behind the counter, father took hold of the young man's arm and led him back to his seat. He grew a little angry and for a moment had to turn his face away and force himself to smile. Then he put the bottles back on the shelf. In an outburst of generosity he fairly compelled Joe Kane to have a fresh cup of coffee and another cigar at his expense. Then he took a pan and filling it with vinegar, taken from a jug that sat beneath the counter, he declared himself about to do a new trick. "I will heat this egg in this pan of vinegar," he said. "Then I will put it through the neck of a bottle without breaking the shell. When the egg is inside the bottle it will resume its normal shape and the shell will become hard again. Then I will give the bottle with the egg in it to you. You can take it about with you wherever you go. People will want to know how you got the egg in the bottle. Don't tell them. Keep them guessing. That is the way to have fun with this trick."

Father grinned and winked at his visitor. Joe Kane decided that the man 25 who confronted him was mildly insane but harmless. He drank the cup of coffee that had been given him and began to read his paper again. When the egg had been heated in vinegar, father carried it on a spoon to the counter and going into a back room got an empty bottle. He was angry because his visitor did not watch him as he began to do this trick, but nevertheless went cheerfully to work. For a long time he struggled, trying to get the egg to go through the neck of the bottle. He put the pan of vinegar back on the stove, intending to reheat the egg, then picked it up and burned his fingers. After a second bath in the hot vinegar, the shell of the egg had been softened a little, but not enough for his purpose. He worked and worked and a spirit of desperate determination took possession of him. When he thought that at last the trick was about to be consummated, the delayed train came in at the station and Joe Kane started to go nonchalantly out at the door. Father made a last desperate effort to conquer the egg and make it do the thing that would establish his reputation as one who knew how to entertain guests who came into his restaurant. He worried the egg. He attempted to be somewhat rough with it. He swore and the sweat stood out on his forehead. The egg broke under his hand. When the contents spurted over his clothes, Joe Kane, who had stopped at the door, turned and laughed.

A roar of anger rose from my father's throat. He danced and shouted a string of inarticulate words. Grabbing another egg from the basket on the counter, he threw it, just missing the head of the young man as he dodged through the door and escaped.

Father came upstairs to mother and me with an egg in his hand. I do not know what he intended to do. I imagine he had some idea of destroying it, of destroying all eggs, and that he intended to let mother and me see him begin. When, however, he got into the presence of mother, something happened to him. He laid the egg gently on the table and dropped on his knees by the bed as I have already explained. He later decided to close the restaurant for the night and to come upstairs and get into bed. When he did so, he blew out the light and after much muttered conversation both he and mother went to sleep. I suppose I went to sleep also, but my sleep was troubled. I awoke at dawn and for a long time looked at the egg that lay on the table. I wondered why eggs had to be and why from the egg came the hen who again laid the egg. The question got into my blood. It has stayed there, I imagine, because I am the son of my father. At any rate, the problem remains unsolved in my mind. And that, I conclude, is but another evidence of the complete and final triumph of the egg—at least as far as my family is concerned.

[1920]

■ TOPICS FOR DISCUSSION AND WRITING

1. In a paragraph or two characterize the father, including in your discussion a comment on whether or not he is hypocritical. Then discuss, in an additional paragraph or two, whether his failure is based on his own inadequacies.

2. What do you make out of the narrator's statement that the story "if correctly told . . . will center on the egg"?

3. In a sentence state the theme of the story. Then in the remainder of the paragraph, offer support for your view of the theme.

4. Characterize the narrator.

5. In 250–500 words, recount a story of someone you know. The story should reveal the person's character, and convey to the reader a sense of the character's view of life. Your own view—for example, admiration,

amusement, or sorrow—should be implicit, but do not state this view
explicitly.

■ RALPH ELLISON
_____

Ralph Ellison was born in Oklahoma City in 1914. His father died
when Ellison was three, and his mother supported herself and her child
byworking as a domestic. A trumpeter since boyhood, after graduating
from high school Ellison went to study music at Tuskegee Institute, a
black college in Alabama, founded by Booker T. Washington. In 1936 he
dropped out of Tuskegee and went to Harlem to study music composition
and the visual arts. There he met Langston Hughes and Richard Wright,
who encouraged him to turn to fiction. He published stories and essays
and in 1942 became the managing editor of *Negro Quarterly;* but in the
following year he entered the Merchant Marine, where he served during
the Second World War. He then returned to writing, and later to teaching
in universities.

Ellison's novel, *The Invisible Man* (1952), was a book cited by *Book-
Week* as "the most significant work of fiction written by an American" in
the years between 1945 and 1965. In addition to publishing stories and
one novel, Ellison has published critical essays, some of which are collected in *Shadow and Act* (1964).

King of the Bingo Game

The woman in front of him was eating roasted peanuts that smelled so
good that he could barely contain his hunger. He could not even sleep and
wished they'd hurry and begin the bingo game. There, on his right, two fellows were drinking wine out of a bottle wrapped in a paper bag, and he could
hear soft gurgling in the dark. His stomach gave a low, gnawing growl. "If this
was down South," he thought, "all I'd have to do is lean over and say, 'Lady,
gimme a few of those peanuts, please ma'am,' and she'd pass me the bag and
never think nothing of it." Or he could ask the fellows for a drink in the same
way. Folks down South stuck together that way; they didn't even have to
know you. But up here it was different. Ask somebody for something, and
they'd think you were crazy. Well, I ain't crazy. I'm just broke, 'cause I got
no birth certificate to get a job, and Laura 'bout to die 'cause we got no money
for a doctor. But I ain't crazy. And yet a pinpoint of doubt was focused in his
mind as he glanced toward the screen and saw the hero stealthily entering
a dark room and sending the beam of a flashlight along a wall of bookcases.
This is where he finds the trapdoor, he remembered. The man would pass
abruptly through the wall and find the girl tied to a bed, her legs and arms
spread wide, and her clothing torn to rags. He laughed softly to himself. He
had seen the picture three times, and this was one of the best scenes.

On his right the fellow whispered wide-eyed to his companion, "Man,
look a-yonder!"

"Damn!"

"Wouldn't I like to have her tied up like that . . ."

"Hey! That fool's letting her loose!"   5

"Aw, man, he loves her."

"Love or no love!"

The man moved impatiently beside him, and he tried to involve himself in the scene. But Laura was on his mind. Tiring quickly of watching the picture he looked back to where the white beam filtered from the projection room above the balcony. It started small and grew large, specks of dust dancing in its whiteness as it reached the screen. It was strange how the beam always landed right on the screen and didn't mess up and fall somewhere else. But they had it all fixed. Everything was fixed. Now suppose when they showed that girl with her dress torn the girl started taking off the rest of her clothes, and when the guy came in he didn't untie her but kept her there and went to taking off his own clothes? *That* would be something to see. If a picture got out of hand like that those guys up there would go nuts. Yeah, and there'd be so many folks in here you couldn't find a seat for nine months! A strange sensation played over his skin. He shuddered. Yesterday he'd seen a bedbug on a woman's neck as they walked out into the bright street. But exploring his thigh through a hole in his pocket he found only goose pimples and old scars.

The bottle gurgled again. He closed his eyes. Now a dreamy music was accompanying the film and train whistles were sounding in the distance, and he was a boy again walking along a railroad trestle down South, and seeing the train coming, and running back as fast as he could go, and hearing the whistle blowing, and getting off the trestle to solid ground just in time, with the earth trembling beneath his feet, and feeling relieved as he ran down the cinder-strewn embankment onto the highway, and looking back and seeing with terror that the train had left the track and was following him right down the middle of the street, and all the white people laughing as he ran screaming . . .

"Wake up there buddy! What the hell do you mean hollering like that?   10
Can't you see we trying to enjoy this here picture?"

He stared at the man with gratitude.

"I'm sorry, old man," he said. "I musta been dreaming."

"Well, here, have a drink. And don't be making no noise like that, damn!"

His hands trembled as he tilted his head. It was not wine, but whiskey. Cold rye whiskey. He took a deep swoller, decided it was better not to take another, and handed the bottle back to its owner.

"Thanks, old man," he said.   15

Now he felt the cold whiskey breaking a warm path straight through the middle of him, growing hotter and sharper as it moved. He had not eaten all day, and it made him light-headed. The smell of the peanuts stabbed him like a knife, and he got up and found a seat in the middle aisle. But no sooner did he sit than he saw a row of intense-faced young girls, and got up again, thinking, "You chicks musta been Lindy-hopping[1] somewhere." He found a seat

[1] **Lindy-hopping** dancing

several rows ahead as the lights came on, and he saw the screen disappear
behind a heavy red and gold curtain; then the curtain rising, and the man with
the microphone and a uniformed attendant coming on the stage.

He felt for his bingo cards, smiling. The guy at the door wouldn't like it
if he knew about his having *five* cards. Well, not everyone played the bingo
game; and even with five cards he didn't have much of a chance. For Laura,
though, he had to have faith. He studied the cards, each with its different
numerals, punching the free center hole in each and spreading them neatly
across his lap; and when the lights faded he sat slouched in his seat so that
he could look from his cards to the bingo wheel with but a quick shifting of
his eyes.

Ahead, at the end of the darkness, the man with the microphone was
pressing a button attached to a long cord and spinning the bingo wheel and
calling out the number each time the wheel came to rest. And each time the
voice rang out his finger raced over the cards for the number. With five cards
he had to move fast. He became nervous; there were too many cards, and
the man went too fast with his grating voice. Perhaps he should just select
one and throw the others away. But he was afraid. He became warm. Wonder
how much Laura's doctor would cost? Damn that, watch the cards! And with
despair he heard the man call three in a row which he missed on all five cards.
This way he'd never win . . .

When he saw the row of holes punched across the third card, he sat paralyzed and heard the man call three more numbers before he stumbled forward, screaming.

"Bingo! Bingo!"

"Let that fool up there," someone called.

"Get up there, man!"

He stumbled down the aisle and up the steps to the stage into a light so
sharp and bright that for a moment it blinded him, and he felt that he had
moved into the spell of some strange, mysterious power. Yet it was as familiar
as the sun, and he knew it was the perfectly familiar bingo.

The man with the microphone was saying something to the audience as
he held out his card. A cold light flashed from the man's finger as the card
left his hand. His knees trembled. The man stepped closer, checking the card
against the numbers chalked on the board. Suppose he had made a mistake?
The pomade on the man's hair made him feel faint, and he backed away. But
the man was checking the card over the microphone now, and he had to stay.
He stood tense, listening.

"Under the O, forty-four," the man chanted. "Under the I, seven. Under 25
the G, three. Under the B, ninety-six. Under the N, thirteen!"

His breath came easier as the man smiled at the audience.

"Yessir, ladies and gentlemen, he's one of the chosen people!"

The audience rippled with laughter and applause.

"Step right up to the front of the stage."

He moved slowly forward, wishing that the light was not so bright. 30

"To win to-night's jackpot of $36.90 the wheel must stop between the
double zero, understand?"

He nodded, knowing the ritual from the many days and nights he had watched the winners march across the stage to press the button that controlled the spinning wheel and receive the prizes. And now he followed the instructions as though he'd crossed the slippery stage a million prize-winning times.

The man was making some kind of a joke, and he nodded vacantly. So tense had he become that he felt a sudden desire to cry and shook it away. He felt vaguely that his whole life was determined by the bingo wheel; not only that which would happen now that he was at last before it, but all that had gone before, since his birth, and his mother's birth and the birth of his father. It had always been there, even though he had not been aware of it, handing out the unlucky cards and numbers of his days. The feeling persisted, and he started quickly away. I better get down from here before I make a fool of myself, he thought.

"Here, boy," the man called. "You haven't started yet."

Someone laughed as he went hesitantly back.   35

"Are you all reet?"

He grinned at the man's jive talk, but no words would come, and he knew it was not a convincing grin. For suddenly he knew that he stood on the slippery brink of some terrible embarrassment.

"Where are you from, boy?" the man asked.

"Down South."

"He's from down South, ladies and gentlemen," the man said. "Where   40 from? Speak right into the mike."

"Rocky Mont," he said. "Rock' Mont, North Car'lina."

"So you decided to come down off that mountain to the U. S.," the man laughed. He felt that the man was making a fool of him, but then suddenly something cold was placed in his hand, and the lights were no longer behind him.

Standing before the wheel he felt alone, but that was somehow right, and he remembered his plan. He would give the wheel a short quick twirl. Just a touch of the button. He had watched it many times, and always it came close to double zero when it was short and quick. He steeled himself; the fear had left, and he felt a profound sense of promise, as though he were about to be repaid for all the things he'd suffered all his life. Trembling, he pressed the button. There was a whirl of lights, and in a second he realized with finality that though he wanted to, he could not stop. It was as though he held a high-powered line in his naked hand. His nerves tightened. As the wheel increased its speed it seemed to draw him more and more into its power, as though it held his fate; and with it came a deep need to submit, to whirl, to lose himself in its swirl of color. He could not stop it now. So let it be.

The button rested snugly in his palm where the man had placed it. And now he became aware of the man beside him, advising him through the microphone, while behind the shadowy audience hummed with noisy voices. He shifted his feet. There was still that feeling of helplessness within him, making part of him desire to turn back, even now that the jackpot was right in his hand. He squeezed the button until his fist ached. Then, like the sudden shriek of a subway whistle, a doubt tore through his head. Suppose he did not spin the wheel long enough? What could he do, and how could he tell? And then he knew, even as he wondered, that as long as he pressed the but-

ton, he could control the jackpot. He and only he could determine whether
or not it was to be his. Not even the man with the microphone could do anything about it now. He felt drunk. Then, as though he had come down from
a high hill into a valley of people, he heard the audience yelling.

"Come down from there, you jerk!"   45

"Let somebody else have a chance . . ."

"Ole Jack thinks he done found the end of the rainbow . . ."

The last voice was not unfriendly, and he turned and smiled dreamily into
the yelling mouths. Then he turned his back squarely on them.

"Don't take too long, boy," a voice said.

He nodded. They were yelling behind him. Those folks did not under-   50
stand what had happened to him. They had been playing the bingo game day
in and night out for years, trying to win rent money or hamburger change.
But not one of those wise guys had discovered this wonderful thing. He
watched the wheel whirling past the numbers and experienced a burst of exal-
tation: This is God! This is the really truly God! He said it aloud, "This is
God!"

He said it with such absolute conviction that he feared he would fall faint-
ing into the footlights. But the crowd yelled so loud that they could not hear.
Those fools, he thought. I'm here trying to tell them the most wonderful
secret in the world, and they're yelling like they gone crazy. A hand fell upon
his shoulder.

"You'll have to make a choice now, boy. You've taken too long."

He brushed the hand violently away.

"Leave me alone, man. I know what I'm doing!"

The man looked surprised and held on to the microphone for support.   55
And because he did not wish to hurt the man's feelings he smiled, realizing
with a sudden pang that there was no way of explaining to the man just why
he had to stand there pressing the button forever.

"Come here," he called tiredly.

The man approached, rolling the heavy microphone across the stage.

"Anybody can play this bingo game, right?" he said.

"Sure, but . . ."

He smiled, feeling inclined to be patient with this slick looking white man 60
with his blue shirt and his sharp gabardine suit.

"That's what I thought," he said. "Anybody can win the jackpot as long
as they get the lucky number, right?"

"That's the rule, but after all . . ."

"That's what I thought," he said. "And the big prize goes to the man who
knows how to win it?"

The man nodded speechlessly.

"Well then, go on over there and watch me win like I want to. I ain't going 65
to hurt nobody," he said, "and I'll show you how to win. I mean to show the
whole world how it's got to be done."

And because he understood, he smiled again to let the man know that he
held nothing against him for being white and impatient. Then he refused
to see the man any longer and stood pressing the button, the voices of the
crowd reaching him like sounds in distant streets. Let them yell. All the
Negroes down there were just ashamed because he was black like them. He

smiled inwardly, knowing how it was. Most of the time he was ashamed of what Negroes did himself. Well, let them be ashamed for something this time. Like him. He was like a long thin black wire that was being stretched and wound upon the bingo wheel; wound until he wanted to scream; wound, but this time himself controlling the winding and the sadness and the shame, and because he did, Laura would be all right. Suddenly the lights flickered. He staggered backwards. Had something gone wrong? All this noise. Didn't they know that although he controlled the wheel, it also controlled him, and unless he pressed the button forever and forever and ever it would stop, leaving him high and dry, dry and high on this hard high slippery hill and Laura dead? There was only one chance; he had to do whatever the wheel demanded. And gripping the button in despair, he discovered with surprise that it imparted a nervous energy. His spine tingled. He felt a certain power.

Now he faced the ringing crowd with defiance, its screams penetrating his eardrums like trumpets shrieking from a juke-box. The vague faces glowing in the bingo lights gave him a sense of himself that he had never known before. He was running the show, by God! They had to react to him, for he was their luck. This is *me*, he thought. Let the bastards yell. Then someone was laughing inside him, and he realized that somehow he had forgotten his own name. It was a sad, lost feeling to lose your name, and a crazy thing to do. That name had been given him by the white man who had owned his grandfather a long lost time ago down South. But maybe those wise guys knew his name.

"Who am I?" he screamed.

"Hurry up and bingo, you jerk!"

They didn't know either, he thought sadly. They didn't even know their 70 own names, they were all poor nameless bastards. Well, he didn't need that old name; he was reborn. For as long as he pressed the button he was The-man-who-pressed-the-button-who-held-the-prize-who-was-the-King-of-Bingo. That was the way it was, and he'd have to press the button even if nobody understood, even though Laura did not understand.

"Live!" he shouted.

The audience quieted like the dying of a huge fan.

"Live, Laura, baby. I got holt of it now, sugar. Live!"

He screamed it, tears streaming down his face. "I got nobody but YOU!"

The screams tore from his very guts. He felt as though the rush of blood 75 to his head would burst out in baseball seams of small red droplets, like a head beaten by police clubs. Bending over he saw a trickle of blood splashing the toe of his shoe. With his free hand he searched his head. It was his nose. God, suppose something has gone wrong? He felt that the whole audience had somehow entered him and was stamping its feet in his stomach and he was unable to throw them out. They wanted the prize, that was it. They wanted the secret for themselves. But they'd never get it; he would keep the bingo wheel whirling forever, and Laura would be safe in the wheel. But would she? It had to be, because if she were not safe the wheel would cease to turn; it could not go on. He had to get away, *vomit* all, and his mind formed an image of himself running with Laura in his arms down the tracks of the subway just ahead of an A train, running desperately *vomit* with people screaming for him to come out but knowing no way of leaving the tracks because to stop would bring the train crushing down upon him and to attempt to leave across the other tracks would mean to run into a hot third rail as high as his waist which threw blue sparks that blinded his eyes until he could hardly see.

He heard singing and the audience was clapping its hands.

Shoot the liquor to him, Jim, boy!
Clap-clap-clap
Well a-calla the cop
He's blowing his top!
Shoot the liquor to him, Jim, boy!

Bitter anger grew within him at the singing. They think I'm crazy. Well let 'em laugh. I'll do what I got to do.

He was standing in an attitude of intense listening when he saw that they were watching something on the stage behind him. He felt weak. But when he turned he saw no one. If only his thumb did not ache so. Now they were applauding. And for a moment he thought that the wheel had stopped. But that was impossible, his thumb still pressed the button. Then he saw them. Two men in uniform beckoned from the end of the stage. They were coming toward him, walking in step, slowly, like a tap-dance team returning for a third encore. But their shoulders shot forward, and he backed away, looking wildly about. There was nothing to fight them with. He had only the long black cord which led to a plug somewhere back stage, and he couldn't use that because it operated the bingo wheel. He backed slowly, fixing the men with his eyes as his lips stretched over his teeth in a tight, fixed grin; moved toward the end of the stage and realizing that he couldn't go much further, for suddenly the cord became taut and he couldn't afford to break the cord. But he had to do something. The audience was howling. Suddenly he stopped dead, seeing the men halt, their legs lifted as in an interrupted step of a slow-motion dance. There was nothing to do but run in the other direction and he dashed forward, slipping and sliding. The men fell back, surprised. He struck out violently going past.

"Grab him!"

He ran, but all too quickly the cord tightened, resistingly, and he turned 80 and ran back again. This time he slipped them, and discovered by running in a circle before the wheel he could keep the cord from tightening. But this way he had to flail his arms to keep the men away. Why couldn't they leave a man alone? He ran, circling.

"Ring down the curtain," someone yelled. But they couldn't do that. If they did the wheel flashing from the projection room would be cut off. But they had him before he could tell them so, trying to pry open his fist, and he was wrestling and trying to bring his knees into the fight and holding on to the button, for it was his life. And now he was down, seeing a foot coming down, crushing his wrist cruelly, down, as he saw the wheel whirling serenely above.

"I can't give it up," he screamed. Then quietly, in a confidential tone, "Boys, I really can't give it up."

It landed hard against his head. And in the blank moment they had it away from him, completely now. He fought them trying to pull him up from the stage as he watched the wheel spin slowly to a stop. Without surprise he saw it rest at double zero.

"You see," he pointed bitterly.

"Sure, boy, sure, it's O. K.," one of the men said smiling.   85

And seeing the man bow his head to someone he could not see, he felt very, very happy; he would receive what all the winners received.

But as he warmed in the justice of the man's tight smile he did not see the man's slow wink, nor see the bow-legged man behind him step clear of the swiftly descending curtain and set himself for a blow. He only felt the dull pain exploding in his skull, and he knew even as it slipped out of him that his luck had run out on the stage.

[1944]

■ TOPICS FOR DISCUSSION AND WRITING

1. What foreshadowing do you find in the first paragraph?
2. Describe the setting of the story. How does it contribute to, or help us to understand, the main character's state of mind?
3. Would you call the wheel symbolic? If so, what does it symbolize?
4. In your opinion, why is the protagonist afraid to stop the wheel?
5. In paragraph 66 we are told that "somehow he had forgotten his own name," and, as readers, we are never told what his name is. What does his forgetting his name reveal about his psychological state? What else does his namelessness—even for himself—suggest about his place in society?
6. Explain the irony of the title. What other instances of irony do you find in the story?

■ SHIRLEY JACKSON

Shirley Jackson (1919–1965) was born in San Francisco but went to college in New York, first at the University of Rochester and then at Syracuse University. Although one of her stories was published in *The Best American Short Stories 1944*, she did not receive national attention until 1948, when *The New Yorker* published "The Lottery." The magazine later reported that none of its earlier publications had produced so strong a response.

In 1962 she experienced a breakdown and was unable to write, but she recovered and worked on a new novel. Before completing the book, however, she died of cardiac arrest at the age of 48. The book was published posthumously under the title *Come Along With Me*.

Two of her books, *Life Among the Savages* (1953) and *Raising Demons* (1957), are engaging self-portraits of a harried mother in a house full of children. But what seems amusing also has its dark underside. After her breakdown Jackson said, "I think all my books laid end to end would be one long documentary of anxiety."

Her husband, Stanley Edgar Hyman (her college classmate and later a professor of English), said of Jackson, "If she uses the resources of supernatural terror, it was to provide metaphors for the all-too-real terrors of the natural."

The Lottery

The morning of June 27th was clear and sunny, with the fresh warmth of a full-summer day; the flowers were blossoming profusely and the grass was richly green. The people of the village began to gather in the square, between the post office and the bank, around ten o'clock; in some towns there were so many people that the lottery took two days and had to be started on June 26th, but in this village, where there were only about three hundred people, the whole lottery took less than two hours, so it could begin at ten o'clock in the morning and still be through in time to allow the villagers to get home for noon dinner.

The children assembled first, of course. School was recently over for the summer, and the feeling of liberty sat uneasily on most of them; they tended to gather together quietly for a while before they broke into boisterous play, and their talk was still of the classroom and the teacher, of books and reprimands. Bobby Martin had already stuffed his pockets full of stones, and the other boys soon followed his example, selecting the smoothest and roundest stones; Bobby and Harry Jones and Dickie Delacroix—the villagers pronounced this name "Dellacroy"—eventually made a great pile of stones in one corner of the square and guarded it against the raids of the other boys. The girls stood aside, talking among themselves, looking over their shoulders at the boys, and the very small children rolled in the dust or clung to the hands of their older brothers or sisters.

Soon the men began to gather, surveying their own children, speaking of planting and rain, tractors and taxes. They stood together, away from the pile of stones in the corner, and their jokes were quiet and they smiled rather than laughed. The women, wearing faded house dresses and sweaters, came shortly after their menfolk. They greeted one another and exchanged bits of gossip as they went to join their husbands. Soon the women, standing by their husbands, began to call to their children, and the children came reluctantly, having to be called four or five times. Bobby Martin ducked under his mother's grasping hand and ran, laughing, back to the pile of stones. His father spoke up sharply, and Bobby came quickly and took his place between his father and his oldest brother.

The lottery was conducted—as were the square dances, the teenage club, the Halloween program—by Mr. Summers, who had time and energy to devote to civic activities. He was a round-faced, jovial man and he ran the coal business, and people were sorry for him, because he had no children and his wife was a scold. When he arrived in the square, carrying the black wooden box, there was a murmur of conversation among the villagers and he waved and called, "Little late today, folks." The postmaster, Mr. Graves, followed him, carrying a three-legged stool, and the stool was put in the center of the square and Mr. Summers set the black box down on it. The villagers kept their distance, leaving a space between themselves and the stool, and when Mr. Summers said, "Some of you fellows want to give me a hand?" there was a hesitation before two men, Mr. Martin and his oldest son, Baxter, came forward to hold the box steady on the stool while Mr. Summers stirred up the papers inside it.

The original paraphernalia for the lottery had been lost long ago, and the 5 black box now resting on the stool had been put into use even before Old Man Warner, the oldest man in town, was born. Mr. Summers spoke frequently to the villagers about making a new box, but no one liked to upset even as much tradition as was represented by the black box. There was a story that the present box had been made with some pieces of the box that had preceded it, the one that had been constructed when the first people settled down to make a village here. Every year, after the lottery, Mr. Summers began talking again about a new box, but every year the subject was allowed to fade off without anything's being done. The black box grew shabbier each year; by now it was no longer completely black but splintered badly along one side to show the original wood color, and in some places faded or stained.

Mr. Martin and his oldest son, Baxter, held the black box securely on the stool until Mr. Summers had stirred the papers thoroughly with his hand. Because so much of the ritual had been forgotten or discarded, Mr. Summers had been successful in having slips of paper substituted for the chips of wood that had been used for generations. Chips of wood, Mr. Summers had argued, had been all very well when the village was tiny, but now that the population was more than three hundred and likely to keep on growing, it was necessary to use something that would fit more easily into the black box. The night before the lottery, Mr. Summers and Mr. Graves made up the slips of paper and put them in the box, and it was then taken to the safe of Mr. Summers's coal company and locked up until Mr. Summers was ready to take it to the square next morning. The rest of the year, the box was put away, sometimes one place, sometimes another; it had spent one year in Mr. Graves's barn and another year underfoot in the post office, and sometimes it was set on a shelf in the Martin grocery and left there.

There was a great deal of fussing to be done before Mr. Summers declared the lottery open. There were lists to make up— of heads of families, heads of households in each family, members of each household in each family. There was the proper swearing-in of Mr. Summers by the postmaster, as the official of the lottery; at one time, some people remembered, there had been a recital of some sort, performed by the official of the lottery, a perfunctory, tuneless chant that had been rattled off duly each year; some people believed that the official of the lottery used to stand just so when he said or sang it, others believed that he was supposed to walk among the people, but years and years ago this part of the ritual had been allowed to lapse. There had been, also, a ritual salute, which the official of the lottery had had to use in addressing each person who came up to draw from the box, but this also had changed with time, until now it was felt necessary only for the official to speak to each person approaching. Mr. Summers was very good at all this; in his clean white shirt and blue jeans, with one hand resting carelessly on the black box, he seemed very proper and important as he talked interminably to Mr. Graves and the Martins.

Just as Mr. Summers finally left off talking and turned to the assembled villagers, Mrs. Hutchinson came hurriedly along the path to the square, her sweater thrown over her shoulders, and slid into place in the back of the crowd. "Clean forgot what day it was," she said to Mrs. Delacroix, who stood next to her, and they both laughed softly. "Thought my old man was out back stacking wood," Mrs. Hutchinson went on, "and then I looked out the window and the kids were gone, and then I remembered it was the twenty-seventh and came a-running." She dried her hands on her apron, and Mrs. Delacroix said, "You're in time, though. They're still talking away up there."

Mrs. Hutchinson craned her neck to see through the crowd and found her husband and children standing near the front. She tapped Mrs. Delacroix on the arm as a farewell and began to make her way through the crowd. The people separated goodhumoredly to let her through; two or three people said, in voices just loud enough to be heard across the crowd, "Here comes your Missus, Hutchinson," and "Bill, she made it after all." Mrs. Hutchinson reached her husband, and Mr. Summers, who had been waiting, said cheerfully, "Thought we were going to have to get on without you, Tessie." Mrs. Hutchinson said, grinning, "Wouldn't have me leave m'dishes in the sink, now would you, Joe?," and soft laughter ran through the crowd as the people stirred back into position after Mrs. Hutchinson's arrival.

"Well, now," Mr. Summers said. soberly, "guess we better get started, 10 get this over with, so's we can go back to work. Anybody ain't here?"

"Dunbar," several people said. "Dunbar, Dunbar."

Mr. Summers consulted his list. "Clyde Dunbar," he said. "That's right. He's broke his leg, hasn't he? Who's drawing for him?"

"Me, I guess," a woman said, and Mr. Summers turned to look at her. "Wife draws for her husband," Mr. Summers said. "Don't you have a grown boy to do it for you, Janey?" Although Mr. Summers and everyone else in the village knew the answer perfectly well, it was the business of the official of the lottery to ask such questions formally. Mr. Summers waited with an expression of polite interest while Mrs. Dunbar answered.

"Horace's not but sixteen yet," Mrs. Dunbar said regretfully. "Guess I gotta fill in for the old man this year."

"Right," Mr. Summers said. He made a note on the list he was holding. 15 Then he asked, "Watson boy drawing this year?"

A tall boy in the crowd raised his hand. "Here," he said. "I'm drawing for m'mother and me." He blinked his eyes nervously and ducked his head as several voices in the crowd said things like "Good fellow, Jack," and "Glad to see your mother's got a man to do it."

"Well," Mr. Summers said, "guess that's everyone. Old Man Warner make it?"

"Here," a voice said, and Mr. Summers nodded.

A sudden hush fell on the crowd as Mr. Summers cleared his throat and looked at the list. "All ready?" he called. "Now, I'll read the names—heads of families first—and the men come up and take a paper out of the box. Keep the paper folded in your hand without looking at it until everyone has had a turn. Everything clear?"

The people had done it so many times that they only half listened to the 20
directions, most of them were quiet, wetting their lips, not looking around.
Then Mr. Summers raised one hand high and said, "Adams." A man disen-
gaged himself from the crowd and came forward. "Hi, Steve," Mr. Summers
said, and Mr. Adams said, "Hi, Joe." They grinned at one another humorless-
ly and nervously. Then Mr. Adams reached into the black box and took out
a folded paper. He held it firmly by one corner as he turned and went hastily
back to his place in the crowd, where he stood a little apart from his family,
not looking down at his hand.

"Allen," Mr. Summers said. "Anderson. . . . Bentham."

"Seems like there's no time at all between lotteries any more," Mrs.
Delacroix said to Mrs. Graves in the back row. "Seems like we got through
with the last one only last week."

"Time sure goes fast," Mrs. Graves said.

"Clark. . . . Delacroix."

"There goes my old man," Mrs. Delacroix said. She held her breath 25
while her husband went forward.

"Dunbar," Mr. Summers said, and Mrs. Dunbar went steadily to the box
while one of the women said, "Go on, Janey," and another said, "There she
goes."

"We're next," Mrs. Graves said. She watched while Mr. Graves came
around from the side of the box, greeted Mr. Summers gravely, and selected
a slip of paper from the box. By now, all through the crowd there were men
holding the small folded papers in their large hands, turning them over and
over nervously. Mrs. Dunbar and her two sons stood together, Mrs. Dunbar
holding the slip of paper.

"Harburt. . . . Hutchinson."

"Get up there, Bill," Mrs. Hutchinson said, and the people near her
laughed.

"Jones."   30

"They do say," Mr. Adams said to Old Man Warner, who stood next to
him, "that over in the north village they're talking of giving up the lottery."

Old Man Warner snorted, "Pack of crazy fools," he said. "Listening to
the young folks, nothing's good enough for *them*. Next thing you know, they'll
be wanting to go back to living in caves, nobody work any more, live *that* way
for a while. Used to be a saying about 'Lottery in June, corn be heavy soon.'
First thing you know, we'd all be eating stewed chickweed and acorns. There's
always been a lottery," he added petulantly. "Bad enough to see young Joe
Summers up there joking with everybody."

"Some places have already quit lotteries," Mrs. Adams said.

"Nothing but trouble in *that*," Old Man Warner said stoutly. "Pack of
young fools."

"Martin." And Bobby Martin watched his father go forward. "Over- 35
dyke. . . . Percy."

"I wish they'd hurry," Mrs. Dunbar said to her older son. "I wish they'd
hurry."

"They're almost through," her son said.

"You get ready to run tell Dad," Mrs. Dunbar said.

Mr. Summers called his own name and then stepped forward precisely and selected a slip from the box. Then he called, "Warner."

"Seventy-seventh year I been in the lottery," Old Man Warner said as he 40 went through the crowd. "Seventy-seventh time."

"Watson." The tall boy came awkwardly through the crowd. Someone said, "Don't be nervous, Jack," and Mr. Summers said, "Take your time, son."

"Zanini."

After that, there was a long pause, a breathless pause, until Mr. Summers, holding his slip of paper in the air, said, "All right, fellows." For a minute, no one moved, and then all the slips of paper were opened. Suddenly, all women began to speak at once, saying, "Who is it?," "Who's got it?," "Is it the Dunbars?," "Is it the Watsons?" Then the voices began to say, "It's Hutchinson. It's Bill." "Bill Hutchinson's got it."

"Go tell your father," Mrs. Dunbar said to her older son.

People began to look around to see the Hutchinsons. Bill Hutchinson was 45 standing quiet, staring down at the paper in his hand. Suddenly, Tessie Hutchinson shouted to Mr. Summers, "You didn't give him time enough to take any paper he wanted. I saw you. It wasn't fair!"

"Be a good sport, Tessie," Mrs. Delacroix called, and Mrs. Graves said, "All of us took the same chance."

"Shut up, Tessie," Bill Hutchinson said.

"Well, everyone," Mr. Summers said, "that was done pretty fast, and now we've got to be hurrying a little more to get it done in time." He consulted his next list. "Bill," he said, "you draw for the Hutchinson family. You got any other households in the Hutchinsons?"

"There's Don and Eva," Mrs. Hutchinson yelled. "Make *them* take their chance!"

"Daughters draw with their husbands' families, Tessie," Mr. Summers 50 said gently. "You know that as well as anyone else."

"It wasn't fair," Tessie said.

"I guess not, Joe," Bill Hutchinson said regretfully. "My daughter draws with her husband's family, that's only fair. And I've got no other family except the kids."

"Then, as far as drawing for families is concerned, it's you," Mr. Summers said in explanation, "and as far as drawing for households is concerned, that's you, too. Right?"

"Right," Bill Hutchinson said.

"How many kids, Bill?" Mr. Summers asked formally. 55

"Three," Bill Hutchinson said. "There's Bill, Jr., and Nancy, and little Dave. And Tessie and me."

"All right, then," Mr. Summers said. "Harry, you got their tickets back?"

Mr. Graves nodded and held up the slips of paper. "Put them in the box, then," Mr. Summers directed. "Take Bill's and put it in."

"I think we ought to start over," Mrs. Hutchinson said, as quietly as she could. "I tell you it wasn't *fair*. You didn't give him time enough to choose. *Everybody* saw that."

Mr. Graves had selected the five slips and put them in the box, and he 60
dropped all the papers but those onto the ground, where the breeze caught
them and lifted them off.

"Listen, everybody," Mrs. Hutchinson was saying to the people around
her.

"Ready, Bill?" Mr. Summers asked, and Bill Hutchinson, with one quick
glance around at his wife and children, nodded.

"Remember," Mr. Summers said, "take the slips and keep them folded
until each person has taken one. Harry, you help little Dave." Mr. Graves took
the hand of the little boy, who came willingly with him up to the box. "Take
a paper out of the box, Davy," Mr. Summers said. Davy put his hand into the
box and laughed. "Take just *one* paper," Mr. Summers said. "Harry, you hold
it for him." Mr. Graves took the child's hand and removed the folded paper
from the tight fist and held it while little Dave stood next to him and looked
up at him wonderingly.

"Nancy next," Mr. Summers said. Nancy was twelve, and her school
friends breathed heavily as she went forward, switching her skirt, and took
a slip daintily from the box. "Bill, Jr.," Mr. Summers said, and Billy, his face
red and his feet over-large, nearly knocked the box over as he got a paper
out. "Tessie," Mr. Summers said. She hesitated for a minute, looking around
defiantly, and then set her lips and went up to the box. She snatched a paper
out and held it behind her.

"Bill," Mr. Summers said, and Bill Hutchinson reached into the box and 65
felt around, bringing his hand out at last with the slip of paper in it.

The crowd was quiet. A girl whispered, "I hope it's not Nancy," and the
sound of the whisper reached the edges of the crowd.

"It's not the way it used to be," Old Man Warner said clearly. "People
ain't the way they used to be."

"All right," Mr. Summers said. "Open the papers. Harry, you open little
Dave's."

Mr. Graves opened the slip of paper and there was a general sigh through
the crowd as he held it up and everyone could see that it was blank. Nancy
and Bill, Jr., opened theirs at the same time, and both beamed and laughed,
turning around to the crowd and holding their slips of paper above their heads.

"Tessie," Mr. Summers said. There was a pause, and then Mr. Summers 70
looked at Bill Hutchinson, and Bill unfolded his paper and showed it. It was
blank.

"It's Tessie," Mr. Summers said, and his voice was hushed. "Show us
her paper, Bill."

Bill Hutchinson went over to his wife and forced the slip of paper out of
her hand. It had a black spot on it, the black spot Mr. Summers had made
the night before with the heavy pencil in the coal-company office. Bill Hutchinson held it up, and there was a stir in the crowd.

"All right, folks," Mr. Summers said, "let's finish quickly."

Although the villagers had forgotten the ritual and lost the original black
box, they still remembered to use stones. The pile of stones the boys had
made earlier was ready; there were stones on the ground with the blowing
scraps of paper that had come out of the box. Mrs. Delacroix selected a stone

so large she had to pick it up with both hands and turned to Mrs. Dunbar. "Come on," she said. "Hurry up."

Mrs. Dunbar had small stones in both hands, and she said, gasping for 75 breath, "I can't run at all. You'll have to go ahead and I'll catch up with you."

The children had stones already, and someone gave little Davy Hutchinson a few pebbles.

Tessie Hutchinson was in the center of a cleared space by now, and she held her hands out desperately as the villagers moved in on her. "It isn't fair," she said. A stone hit her on the side of the head.

Old Man Warner was saying, "Come on, come on, everyone." Steve Adams was in the front of the crowd of villagers, with Mrs. Graves beside him.

"It isn't fair, it isn't right," Mrs. Hutchinson screamed, and then they were upon her.

[1948]

■ TOPICS FOR DISCUSSION AND WRITING

1. What is the community's attitude toward tradition?
2. Doubtless a good writer could tell this story effectively from the point of view of a participant, but Jackson chose a nonparticipant point of view. What does she gain?
3. Let's say you were writing this story, and you had decided to write it from Tessie's point of view. What would you first paragraph, or your first 250 words, be?
4. Suppose someone claimed that the story is an attack on religious orthodoxy. What might be your response? (Whether you agree or disagree, set forth your reasons.)

■ TONI CADE BAMBARA

Toni Cade Bambara was born in 1939 in New York City and grew up in black districts of the city. After studying at the University of Florence and at City College in New York, where she received a master's degree, she worked for a while as a case investigator for the New York State Welfare Department. Later she directed a recreation program for hospital patients. Now that her literary reputation is established, she spends most of her time writing, though she has also served as writer in residence at Spelman College in Atlanta.

The Lesson

Back in the days when everyone was old and stupid or young and foolish and me and Sugar were the only ones just right, this lady moved on our block with nappy hair and proper speech and no makeup. And quite naturally we laughed at her, laughed the way we did at the junk man who went about his business like he was some big-time president and his sorry-ass horse his secretary. And we kinda hated her too, hated the way we did the winos who cluttered up our parks and pissed on our handball walls and stank up our hallways and stairs so you couldn't halfway play hide-and-seek without a goddamn gas mask. Miss Moore was her name. The only woman on the block with no first name. And she was black as hell, cept for her feet, which were fish-white and spooky. And she was always planning these boring-ass things for us to do, us being my cousin, mostly, who lived on the block cause we all moved North the same time and to the same apartment then spread out gradual to breathe. And our parents would yank our heads into some kinda shape and crisp up our clothes so we'd be presentable for travel with Miss Moore, who always looked like she was going to church, though she never did. Which is just one of the things the grownups talked about when they talked behind her back like a dog. But when she came calling with some sachet she'd sewed up or some gingerbread she'd made or some book, why then they'd all be too embarrassed to turn her down and we'd get handed over all spruced up. She'd been to college and said it was only right that she should take responsibility for the young ones' education, and she not even related by marriage or blood. So they'd go for it. Specially Aunt Gretchen. She was the main gofer in the family. You got some ole dumb shit foolishness you want somebody to go for, you send for Aunt Gretchen. She been screwed into the go-along for so long, it's a blood-deep natural thing with her. Which is how she got saddled with me and Sugar and Junior in the first place while our mothers were in a la-de-da apartment up the block having a good ole time.

So this one day Miss Moore rounds us all up at the mailbox and it's pure-dee hot and she's knockin herself out about arithmetic. And school suppose to let up in summer I heard, but she don't never let up. And the starch in my pinafore scratching the shit outta me and I'm really hating this nappy-head bitch and her goddamn college degree. I'd much rather go to the pool or to the show where it's cool. So me and Sugar leaning on the mailbox being surly, which is a Miss Moore word. And Flyboy checking out what everybody brought for lunch. And Fat Butt already wasting his peanut-butter-and-jelly sandwich like the pig he is. And Junebug punchin on Q.T.'s arm for potato chips. And Rosie Giraffe shifting from one hip to the other waiting for somebody to step on her foot or ask her if she from Georgia so she can kick ass, preferably Mercedes'. And Miss Moore asking us do we know what money is, like we a bunch of retards. I mean real money, she say, like it's only poker chips or monopoly papers we lay on the grocer. So right away I'm tired of this and say so. And would much rather snatch Sugar and go to the Sunset and terrorize the West Indian kids and take their hair ribbons and their money too. And Miss Moore files that remark away for next week's lesson on brotherhood, I can tell. And finally I say we oughta get to the subway cause it's cooler and besides we might meet some cute boys. Sugar done swiped her mama's lipstick, so we ready.

So we heading down the street and she's boring us silly about what things cost and what our parents make and how much goes for rent and how money ain't divided up right in this country. And then she gets to the part about we all poor and live in the slums, which I don't feature. And I'm ready to speak on that, but she steps out in the street and hails two cabs just like that. Then she hustles half the crew in with her and hands me a five-dollar bill and tells me to calculate 10 percent tip for the driver. And we're off. Me and Sugar and

Junebug and Flyboy hangin out the window and hollering to everybody, putting lipstick on each other cause Flyboy a faggot anyway, and making farts with our sweaty armpits. But I'm mostly trying to figure how to spend this money. But they all fascinated with the meter ticking and Junebug starts laying bets to how much it'll read when Flyboy can't hold his breath no more. Then Sugar lays bets as to how much it'll be when we get there. So I'm stuck. Don't nobody want to go for my plan, which is to jump out at the next light and run off to the first bar-b-que we can find. Then the driver tells us to get the hell out cause we there already. And the meter reads eighty-five cents. And I'm stalling to figure out the tip and Sugar say give him a dime. And I decide he don't need it as bad as I do, so later for him. But then he tries to take off with Junebug foot still in the door so we talk about his mama something ferocious. Then we check out that we on Fifth Avenue and everybody dressed up in stockings. One lady in a fur coat, hot as it is. White folks crazy.

"This is the place," Miss Moore say, presenting it to us in the voice she uses at the museum. "Let's look in the windows before we go in."

"Can we steal?" Sugar asks very serious like she's getting the ground 5 rules squared away before she plays. "I beg your pardon," say Miss Moore, and we fall out. So she leads us around the windows of the toy store and me and Sugar screamin, "This is mine, that's mine, I gotta have that, that was made for me, I was born for that," till Big Butt drowns us out.

"Hey, I'm goin to buy that there."

"That there? You don't even know what it is, stupid."

"I do so," he say punchin on Rosie Giraffe. "It's a microscope."

"Whatcha gonna do with a microscope, fool?"

"Look at things."   10

"Like what, Ronald?" ask Miss Moore. And Big Butt ain't got the first notion. So here go Miss Moore gabbing about the thousands of bacteria in a drop of water and the somethinorother in a speck of blood and the million and one living things in the air around us is invisible to the naked eye. And what she say that for? Junebug go to town on that "naked" and we rolling. Then Miss Moore ask what it cost. So we all jam into the window smudgin it up and the price tag say $300. So then she ask how long'd take for Big Butt and Junebug to save up their allowances. "Too long," I say. "Yeh," adds Sugar, "outgrown it by that time." And Miss Moore say no, you never outgrow learning instruments. "Why, even medical students and interns and," blah, blah, blah. And we ready to choke Big Butt for bringing it up in the first damn place.

"This here costs four hundred eighty dollars," say Rosie Giraffe. So we pile up all over her to see what she pointin out. My eyes tell me it's a chunk of glass cracked with something heavy, and different-color inks dripped into the splits, then the whole thing put into a oven or something. But for $480 it don't make sense.

"That's a paperweight made of semi-precious stones fused together under tremendous pressure," she explains slowly, and her hands doing the mining and all the factory work.

"So what's a paperweight?" asks Rosie Giraffe.

"To weigh paper with, dumbbell," say Flyboy, the wise man from the 15 East.

"Not exactly," say Miss Moore, which is what she say when you warm or way off too. "It's to weigh paper down so it won't scatter and make your desk untidy." So right away me and Sugar curtsy to each other and then to Mercedes who is more the tidy type.

"We don't keep paper on top of the desk in my class," say Junebug, figuring Miss Moore crazy or lyin one.

"At home, then," she say. "Don't you have a calendar and a pencil case and a blotter and a letter-opener on your desk at home where you do your homework?" And she know damn well what our homes look like cause she nosys around in them every chance she gets.

"I don't even have a desk," say Junebug. "Do we?"

"No. And I don't get no homework neither," says Big Butt.   20

"And I don't even have a home," say Flyboy like he do at school to keep the white folks off his back and sorry for him. Send this poor kid to camp posters, is his specialty.

"I do," says Mercedes. "I have a box of stationery on my desk and a picture of my cat. My godmother bought the stationery and the desk. There's a big rose on each sheet and the envelopes smell like roses."

"Who wants to know about your smelly-ass stationery," say Rosie Giraffe fore I can get my two cents in.

"It's important to have a work area all your own so that . . ."

"Will you look at this sailboat, please," say Flyboy, cuttin her off and   25 pointin to the thing like it was his. So once again we tumble all over each other to gaze at this magnificent thing in the toy store which is just big enough to maybe sail two kittens across the pond if you strap them to the posts tight. We all start reciting the price tag like we in assembly. "Hand-crafted sailboat of fiberglass at one thousand one hundred ninety-five dollars."

"Unbelievable," I hear myself say and am really stunned. I read it again for myself just in case the group recitation put me in a trance. Same thing. For some reason this pisses me off. We look at Miss Moore and she lookin at us, waiting for I dunno what.

"Who'd pay all that when you can buy a sailboat set for a quarter at Pop's, a tube of glue for a dime, and a ball of string for eight cents? It must have a motor and a whole lot else besides," I say. "My sailboat cost me about fifty cents."

"But will it take water?" say Mercedes with her smart ass.

"Took mine to Alley Pond Park once," say Flyboy. "String broke. Lost it. Pity."

"Sailed mine in Central Park and it keeled over and sank. Had to ask my   30 father for another dollar."

"And you got the strap," laugh Big Butt. "The jerk didn't even have a string on it. My old man wailed on his behind."

Little Q.T. was staring hard at the sailboat and you could see he wanted it bad. But he too little and somebody'd just take it from him. So what the hell. "This boat for kids, Miss Moore?"

"Parents silly to buy something like that just to get all broke up," say Rosie Giraffe.

"That much money it should last forever," I figure.

"My father'd buy it for me if I wanted it." 35

"Your father, my ass," say Rosie Giraffe getting a chance to finally push Mercedes.

"Must be rich people shop here," say Q.T.

"You are a very bright boy," say Flyboy. "What was your first clue?" And he rap him on the head with the back of his knuckles, since Q.T. the only one he could get away with. Though Q.T. liable to come up behind you years later and get his licks in when you half expect it.

"What I want to know is," I says to Miss Moore though I never talk to her, I wouldn't give the bitch that satisfaction, "is how much a real boat costs? I figure a thousand'd get you a yacht any day."

"Why don't you check that out," she says, "and report back to the 40 group?" Which really pains my ass. If you gonna mess up a perfectly good swim day least you could do is have some answers. "Let's go in," she say like she got something up her sleeve. Only she don't lead the way. So me and Sugar turn the corner to where the entrance is, but when we get there I kinda hang back. Not that I'm scared, what's there to be afraid of, just a toy store. But I feel funny, shame. But what I got to be shamed about? Got as much right to go in as anybody. But somehow I can't seem to get hold of the door, so I step away for Sugar to lead. But she hangs back too. And I look at her and she looks at me and this is ridiculous. I mean, damn, I have never ever been shy about doing nothing or going nowhere. But then Mercedes steps up and then Rosie Giraffe and Big Butt crowd in behind and shove, and next thing we all stuffed into the doorway with only Mercedes squeezing past us, smoothing out her jumper and walking right down the aisle. Then the rest of us tumble in like a glued-together jigsaw done all wrong. And people lookin at us. And it's like the time me and Sugar crashed into the Catholic church on a dare. But once we got in there and everything so hushed and holy and the candles and the bowin and the handkerchiefs on all the drooping heads, I just couldn't go through with the plan. Which was for me to run up to the altar and do a tap dance while Sugar played the nose flute and messed around in the holy water. And Sugar kept givin me the elbow. Then later teased me so bad I tied her up in the shower and turned it on and locked her in. And she'd be there till this day if Aunt Gretchen hadn't finally figured I was lyin about the boarder takin a shower.

Same thing in the store. We all walkin on tiptoe and hardly touchin the games and puzzles and things. And I watched Miss Moore who is steady watchin us like she waitin for a sign. Like Mama Drewery watches the sky and sniffs the air and takes note of just how much slant is in the bird formation. Then me and Sugar bump smack into each other, so busy gazing at the toys, 'specially the sailboat. But we don't laugh and go into our fat-lady bump-stomach routine. We just stare at that price tag. Then Sugar run a finger over the whole boat. And I'm jealous and want to hit her. Maybe not her, but I sure want to punch somebody in the mouth.

"Whatcha bring us here for, Miss Moore?"

"You sound angry, Sylvia. Are you mad about something?" Givin me one of them grins like she tellin a grown-up joke that never turns out to be funny. And she's lookin very closely at me like maybe she plannin to do my portrait from memory. I'm mad, but I won't give her that satisfaction. So I slouch around the store bein very bored and say, "Let's go."

Me and Sugar at the back of the train watchin the tracks whizzin by large then small then gettin gobbled up in the dark. I'm thinkin about this tricky toy I saw in the store. A clown that somersaults on a bar then does chin-ups just cause you yank lightly at his leg. Cost $35. I could see me askin my mother for a $35 birthday clown. "You wanna who that costs what?" she'd say, cocking her head to the side to get a better view of the hole in my head. Thirty-five dollars could buy new bunk beds for Junior and Gretchen's boy. Thirty-five dollars and the whole household could go visit Granddaddy Nelson in the country. Thirty-five dollars would pay for the rent and the piano bill too. Who are these people that spend that much for performing clowns and $1000 for toy sailboats? What kinda work they do and how they live and how come we ain't in on it? Where we are is who we are, Miss Moore always pointin out. But it don't necessarily have to be that way, she always adds then waits for somebody to say that poor people have to wake up and demand their share of the pie and don't none of us know what kind of pie she talkin about in the first damn place. But she ain't so smart cause I still got her four dollars from the taxi and she sure ain't gettin it. Messin up my day with this shit. Sugar nudges me in my pocket and winks.

Miss Moore lines us up in front of the mailbox where we started from, 45 seem like years ago, and I got a headache for thinkin so hard. And we lean all over each other so we can hold up under the draggy-ass lecture she always finishes us off with at the end before we thank her for borin us to tears. But she just looks at us like she readin tea leaves. Finally she say, "Well, what do you think of F. A. O. Schwarz?"

Rosie Giraffe mumbles, "White folks crazy."

"I'd like to go there again when I get my birthday money," says Mercedes, and we shove her out the pack so she has to lean on the mailbox by herself.

"I'd like a shower. Tiring day," say Flyboy.

Then Sugar surprises me by sayin, "You know, Miss Moore, I don't think all of us here put together eat in a year what that sailboat costs." And Miss Moore lights up like somebody goosed her. "And?" she say, urging Sugar on. Only I'm standin on her foot so she don't continue.

"Imagine for a minute what kind of society it is in which some people 50 can spend on a toy what it would cost to feed a family of six or seven. What do you think?"

"I think," say Sugar pushing me off her feet like she never done before, cause I whip her ass in a minute, "that this is not much of a democracy if you ask me. Equal chance to pursue happiness means an equal crack at the dough, don't it?" Miss Moore is besides herself and I am disgusted with Sugar's treachery. So I stand on her foot one more time to see if she'll shove me. She shuts up, and Miss Moore looks at me, sorrowfully I'm thinkin. And somethin weird is goin on, I can feel it in my chest.

"Anybody else learn anything today?" lookin dead at me. I walk away and Sugar has to run to catch up and don't even seem to notice when I shrug her arm off my shoulder.

"Well, we got four dollars anyway," she says.

"Uh hunh."

"We could go to Hascombs and get half a chocolate layer and then go to 55 the Sunset and still have plenty money for potato chips and ice cream sodas."

"Uh hunh."

"Race you to Hascombs," she say.

We start down the block and she gets ahead which is O.K. by me cause I'm going to the West End and then over to the Drive to think this day through. She can run if she want to and even run faster. But ain't nobody gonna beat me at nuthin.

[1972]

■ TOPICS FOR DISCUSSION AND WRITING

1. What is the point of Miss Moore's lesson? Why does Sylvia resist it?
2. Describe the relationship between Sugar and Sylvia. What is Sugar's function in the story?
3. What does the last line of the story suggest?
4. In a paragraph or two, characterize the narrator. Do not summarize the story—assume that your reader is familiar with it—but support your characterization by some references to episodes in the story and perhaps by a few brief quotations.

■ AMY TAN

Amy Tan was born in 1952 in Oakland, California, two-and-a-half years after her parents had emigrated from China. She entered Linfield College in Oregon but then followed a boyfriend to California State University at San Jose, where she shifted her major from premedical studies to English. Because her mother had wanted her to become a physician as well as a pianist, Tan's change in her studies caused a break between mother and daughter; for some six months they did not speak to each other. After earning a master's degree in linguistics from San Jose, Tan worked as a language consultant and then, under the name of May Brown, as a freelance business writer. In 1985, having decided to try her hand at fiction, she joined the Squaw Valley Community of Writers, a fiction workshop. In 1987 she visited China with her mother; on her return to the United States she learned that her agent had sold her first novel, *The Joy Luck Club*, a collection of 16 interwoven stories about four Chinese mothers and their four American daughters.

Two Kinds

My mother believed you could be anything you wanted to be in America. You could open a restaurant. You could work for the government and get good retirement. You could buy a house with almost no money down. You could become rich. You could become instantly famous.

"Of course, you can be prodigy, too," my mother told me when I was nine. "You can be best anything. What does Auntie Lindo know? Her daughter, she is only best tricky."

America was where all my mother's hopes lay. She had come to San Francisco in 1949 after losing everything in China: her mother and father, her family home, her first husband, and two daughters, twin baby girls. But she never looked back with regret. Things could get better in so many ways.

We didn't immediately pick the right kind of prodigy. At first my mother thought I could be a Chinese Shirley Temple. We'd watch Shirley's old movies on TV as though they were training films. My mother would poke my arm and say, "*Ni kan*. You watch." And I would see Shirley tapping her feet, or singing a sailor song, or pursing her lips into a very round O while saying "Oh, my goodness."

"*Ni kan*," my mother said, as Shirley's eyes flooded with tears. "You already know how. Don't need talent for crying!"

Soon after my mother got this idea about Shirley Temple, she took me to the beauty training school in the Mission District and put me in the hands of a student who could barely hold the scissors without shaking. Instead of getting big fat curls, I emerged with an uneven mass of crinkly black fuzz. My mother dragged me off to the bathroom and tried to wet down my hair.

"You look like Negro Chinese," she lamented, as if I had done this on purpose.

The instructor of the beauty training school had to lop off these soggy clumps to make my hair even again. "Peter Pan is very popular these days," the instructor assured my mother. I now had hair the length of a boy's, with curly bangs that hung at a slant two inches above my eyebrows. I liked the haircut, and it made me actually look forward to my future fame.

In fact, in the beginning I was just as excited as my mother, maybe even more so. I pictured this prodigy part of me as many different images, and I tried each one on for size. I was a dainty ballerina girl standing by the curtain, waiting to hear the music that would send me floating on my tiptoes. I was like the Christ child lifted out of the straw manger, crying with holy indignity. I was Cinderella stepping from her pumpkin carriage with sparkly cartoon music filling the air.

In all of my imaginings I was filled with a sense that I would soon become perfect. My mother and father would adore me. I would be beyond reproach. I would never feel the need to sulk, or to clamor for anything.

But sometimes the prodigy in me became impatient. "If you don't hurry up and get me out of here, I'm disappearing for good," it warned. "And then you'll always be nothing."

Every night after dinner my mother and I would sit at the Formica-topped kitchen table. She would present new tests, taking her examples from stories of amazing children that she read in *Ripley's Believe It or Not* or *Good Housekeeping, Reader's Digest,* or any of a dozen other magazines she kept in a pile in our bathroom. My mother got these magazines from people whose houses she cleaned. And since she cleaned many houses each week, we had a great assortment. She would look through them all, searching for stories about remarkable children.

The first night she brought out a story about a three-year-old boy who knew the capitals of all the states and even of most of the European countries.

A teacher was quoted as saying that the little boy could also pronounce the names of the foreign cities correctly. "What's the capital of Finland?" my mother asked me, looking at the story.

All I knew was the capital of California, because Sacramento was the name of the street we lived on in Chinatown. "Nairobi!" I guessed, saying the most foreign word I could think of. She checked to see if that might be one way to pronounce *Helsinki* before showing me the answer.

The tests got harder—multiplying numbers in my head, finding the queen of hearts in a deck of cards, trying to stand on my head without using my hands, predicting the daily temperatures in Los Angeles, New York, and London. One night I had to look at a page from the Bible for three minutes and then report everything I could remember. "Now Jehoshaphat had riches and honor in abundance and . . . that's all I remember, Ma," I said.

And after seeing, once again, my mother's disappointed face, something inside me began to die. I hated the tests, the raised hopes and failed expectations. Before going to bed that night I looked in the mirror above the bathroom sink, and when I saw only my face staring back—and understood that it would always be this ordinary face—I began to cry. Such a sad, ugly girl! I made high-pitched noises like a crazed animal, trying to scratch out the face in the mirror.

And then I saw what seemed to be the prodigy side of me—a face I had never seen before. I looked at my reflection, blinking so that I could see more clearly. The girl staring back at me was angry, powerful. She and I were the same. I had new thoughts, willful thoughts—or, rather, thoughts filled with lots of won'ts. I won't let her change me, I promised myself. I won't be what I'm not.

So now when my mother presented her tests, I performed listlessly, my head propped on one arm. I pretended to be bored. And I was. I got so bored that I started counting the bellows of the foghorns out on the bay while my mother drilled me in other areas. The sound was comforting and reminded me of the cow jumping over the moon. And the next day I played a game with myself, seeing if my mother would give up on me before eight bellows. After a while I usually counted only one bellow, maybe two at most. At last she was beginning to give up hope.

Two or three months went by without any mention of my being a prodigy. And then one day my mother was watching the *Ed Sullivan Show* on TV. The TV was old and the sound kept shorting out. Every time my mother got halfway up from the sofa to adjust the set, the sound would come back on and Sullivan would be talking. As soon as she sat down, Sullivan would go silent again. She got up—the TV broke into loud piano music. She sat down—silence. Up and down, back and forth, quiet and loud. It was like a stiff, embraceless dance between her and the TV set. Finally, she stood by the set with her hand on the sound dial.

She seemed entranced by the music, a frenzied little piano piece with a mesmerizing quality, which alternated between quick, playful passages and teasing, lilting ones.

"*Ni kan,*" my mother said, calling me over with hurried hand gestures. "Look here."

I could see why my mother was fascinated by the music. It was being pounded out by a little Chinese girl, about nine years old, with a Peter Pan haircut. The girl had the sauciness of a Shirley Temple. She was proudly modest, like a proper Chinese child. And she also did a fancy sweep of a curtsy, so that the fluffy skirt of her white dress cascaded to the floor like the petals of a large carnation.

In spite of these warning signs, I wasn't worried. Our family had no piano and we couldn't afford to buy one, let alone reams of sheet music and piano lessons. So I could be generous in my comments when my mother badmouthed the little girl on TV.

"Play note right, but doesn't sound good!" my mother complained. "No singing sound."

"What are you picking on her for?" I said carelessly. "She's pretty good. Maybe she's not the best, but she's trying hard." I knew almost immediately that I would be sorry I had said that.

"Just like you," she said. "Not the best. Because you not trying." She gave a little huff as she let go of the sound dial and sat down on the sofa.

The little Chinese girl sat down also, to play an encore of "Anitra's Tanz," by Grieg.[1] I remember the song, because later on I had to learn how to play it.

Three days after watching the *Ed Sullivan Show* my mother told me what my schedule would be for piano lessons and piano practice. She had talked to Mr. Chong, who lived on the first floor of our apartment building. Mr. Chong was a retired piano teacher, and my mother had traded housecleaning services for weekly lessons and a piano for me to practice on every day, two hours a day, from four until six.

When my mother told me this, I felt as though I had been sent to hell. I whined, and then kicked my foot a little when I couldn't stand it anymore.

"Why don't you like me the way I am?" I cried. "I'm *not* a genius! I can't play the piano. And even if I could, I wouldn't go on TV if you paid me a million dollars!"

My mother slapped me. "Who ask you to be genius?" she shouted. "Only ask you be your best. For you sake. You think I want you to be genius? Hnnh! What for! Who ask you!"

"So ungrateful," I heard her mutter in Chinese. "If she had as much talent as she has temper, she'd be famous now."

Mr. Chong, whom I secretly nicknamed Old Chong, was very strange, always tapping his fingers to the silent music of an invisible orchestra. He looked ancient in my eyes. He had lost most of the hair on the top of his head, and he wore thick glasses and had eyes that always looked tired. But he must have been younger than I thought, since he lived with his mother and was not yet married.

I met Old Lady Chong once, and that was enough. She had a peculiar smell, like a baby that had done something in its pants, and her fingers felt

<hr />

[1] **"Anitra's Tanz," by Grieg** a section from the incidental music that Edvard Grieg (1843–1907) wrote for *Peer Gynt,* a play by Henrik Ibsen

like a dead person's, like an old peach I once found in the back of the refrigerator; its skin just slid off the flesh when I picked it up.

I soon found out why Old Chong had retired from teaching piano. He was deaf. "Like Beethoven!" he shouted to me. "We're both listening only in our head!" And he would start to conduct his frantic silent sonatas.

Our lessons went like this. He would open the book and point to different things, explaining their purpose: "Key! Treble! Bass! No sharps or flats! So this is C major! Listen now and play after me!"

And then he would play the C scale a few times, a simple cord, and then, as if inspired by an old unreachable itch, he would gradually add more notes and running trills and a pounding bass until the music was really something quite grand.

I would play after him, the simple scale, the simple chord, and then just play some nonsense that sounded like a cat running up and down on top of garbage cans. Old Chong would smile and applaud and say, "Very good! But now you must learn to keep time!"

So that's how I discovered that Old Chong's eyes were too slow to keep up with the wrong notes I was playing. He went through the motions in half time. To help me keep rhythm, he stood behind me and pushed down on my right shoulder for every beat. He balanced pennies on top of my wrists so that I would keep them still as I slowly played scales and arpeggios. He had me curve my hand around an apple and keep that shape when playing chords. He marched stiffly to show me how to make each finger dance up and down, staccato, like an obedient little soldier.

He taught me all these things, and that was how I also learned I could be lazy and get away with mistakes, lots of mistakes. If I hit the wrong notes because I hadn't practiced enough, I never corrected myself. I just kept playing in rhythm. And Old Chong kept conducting his own private reverie.

So maybe I never really gave myself a fair chance. I did pick up the basics pretty quickly, and I might have become a good pianist at that young age. But I was so determined not to try, not to be anybody different, and I learned to play only the most ear-splitting preludes, the most discordant hymns.

Over the next year I practiced like this, dutifully in my own way. And then one day I heard my mother and her friend Lindo Jong both talking in a loud, bragging tone of voice so that others could hear. It was after church, and I was leaning against a brick wall, wearing a dress with stiff white petticoats. Auntie Lindo's daughter, Waverly, who was my age, was standing farther down the wall, about five feet away. We had grown up together and shared all the closeness of two sisters, squabbling over crayons and dolls. In other words, for the most part, we hated each other. I thought she was snotty. Waverly Jong had gained a certain amount of fame as "Chinatown's Littlest Chinese Chess Champion."

"She bring home too many trophy," Auntie Lindo lamented that Sunday. "All day she play chess. All day I have no time do nothing but dust off her winnings." She threw a scolding look at Waverly, who pretended not to see her.

"You lucky you don't have this problem," Auntie Lindo said with a sigh to my mother.

And my mother squared her shoulders and bragged: "Our problem worser than yours. If we ask Jing-mei wash dish, she hear nothing but music. It's like you can't stop this natural talent."

And right then I was determined to put a stop to her foolish pride.

A few weeks later Old Chong and my mother conspired to have me play in a talent show that was to be held in the church hall. But then my parents had saved up enough to buy me a secondhand piano, a black Wurlitzer spinet with a scarred bench. It was the showpiece of our living room.

For the talent show I was to play a piece called "Pleading Child," from Schumann's *Scenes From Childhood*.[2] It was a simple, moody piece that sounded more difficult than it was. I was supposed to memorize the whole thing. But I dawdled over it, playing a few bars and then cheating, looking up to see what notes followed. I never really listened to what I was playing. I daydreamed about being somewhere else, about being someone else.

The part I liked to practice best was the fancy curtsy: right foot out, touch the rose on the carpet with a pointed foot, sweep to the side, bend left leg, look up, and smile.

My parents invited all the couples from their social club to witness my debut. Auntie Lindo and Uncle Tin were there. Waverly and her two older brothers had also come. The first two rows were filled with children either younger or older than I was. The littlest ones got to go first. They recited simple nursery rhymes, squawked out tunes on miniature violins, and twirled hula hoops in pink ballet tutus, and when they bowed or curtsied, the audience would sigh in unison, "*Awww*," and then clap enthusiastically.

When my turn came, I was very confident. I remember my childish excitement. It was as if I knew, without a doubt, that the prodigy side of me really did exist. I had no fear whatsoever, no nervousness. I remember thinking, This is it! This is it! I looked out over the audience, at my mother's blank face, my father's yawn, Auntie Lindo's stiff-lipped smile, Waverly's sulky expression. I had on a white dress, layered with sheets of lace, and a pink bow in my Peter Pan haircut. As I sat down, I envisioned people jumping to their feet and Ed Sullivan rushing up to introduce me to everyone on TV.

And I started to play. Everything was so beautiful. I was so caught up in how lovely I looked that I wasn't worried about how I would sound. So I was surprised when I hit the first wrong note. And then I hit another, and another. A chill started at the top of my head and began to trickle down. Yet I couldn't stop playing, as though my hands were bewitched. I kept thinking my fingers would adjust themselves back, like a train switching to the right track. I played this strange jumble through to the end, the sour notes staying with me all the way.

When I stood up, I discovered my legs were shaking. Maybe I had just been nervous, and the audience, like Old Chong, had seen me go through the right motions and had not heard anything wrong at all. I swept my right foot out, went down on my knee, looked up, and smiled. The room was quiet, except for Old Chong, who was beaming and shouting, "Bravo! Bravo! Well

---

[2] **Scenes from Childhood** piano work by Robert Schumann (1810–1856) with twelve titled sections and an epilogue

done!" But then I saw my mother's face, her stricken face. The audience clapped weakly, and as I walked back to my chair, with my whole face quivering as I tried not to cry, I heard a little boy whisper loudly to his mother, "That was awful," and the mother whispered, "Well, she certainly tried."

And now I realized how many people were in the audience—the whole world, it seemed. I was aware of eyes burning into my back. I felt the shame of my mother and father as they sat stiffly through the rest of the show.

We could have escaped during intermission. Pride and some strange sense of honor must have anchored my parents to their chairs. And so we watched it all: The eighteen-year-old boy with a fake moustache who did a magic show and juggled flaming hoops while riding a unicycle. The breasted girl with white makeup who sang an aria from *Madame Butterly* and got an honorable mention. And the eleven-year-old boy who won first prize playing a tricky violin song that sounded like a busy bee.

After the show the Hsus, the Jongs, and the St. Clairs, from the Joy Luck Club, came up to my mother and father.

"Lots of talented kids," Auntie Lindo said vaguely, smiling broadly.

"That was somethin' else," my father said, and I wondered if he was referring to me in a humorous way, or whether he even remembered what I had done.

Waverly looked at me and shrugged her shoulders. "You aren't a genius like me," she said matter-of-factly. And if I hadn't felt so bad, I would have pulled her braids and punched her stomach.

But my mother's expression was what devastated me: a quiet, blank look that said she had lost everything. I felt the same way, and everybody seemed now to be coming up, like gawkers at the scene of an accident, to see what parts were actually missing.

When we got on the bus to go home, my father was humming the busy-bee tune and my mother was silent. I kept thinking she wanted to wait until we got home before shouting at me. But when my father unlocked the door to our apartment, my mother walked in and went straight to the back, into the bedroom. No accusations. No blame. And in a way, I felt disappointed. I had been waiting for her to start shouting, so that I could shout back and cry and blame her for all my misery.

I had assumed that my talent-show fiasco meant that I would never have to play the piano again. But two days later, after school, my mother came out of the kitchen and saw me watching TV.

"Four clock," she reminded me, as if it were any other day. I was stunned, as though she were asking me to go through the talent-show torture again. I planted myself more squarely in front of the TV.

"Turn off TV," she called from the kitchen five minutes later.

I didn't budge. And then I decided. I didn't have to do what my mother said anymore. I wasn't her slave. This wasn't China. I had listened to her before, and look what happened. She was the stupid one.

She came out of the kitchen and stood in the arched entryway of the living room. "Four clock," she said once again, louder.

"I'm not going to play anymore," I said nonchalantly. "Why should I? I'm not a genius."

She stood in front of the TV. I saw that her chest was heaving up and down in an angry way.

"No!" I said, and I now felt stronger, as if my true self had finally emerged. So this was what had been inside me all along.

"No! I won't!" I screamed.

She snapped off the TV, yanked me by the arm and pulled me off the floor. She was frighteningly strong, half pulling, half carrying me toward the piano as I kicked the throw rugs under my feet. She lifted me up and onto the hard bench. I was sobbing by now, looking at her bitterly. Her chest was heaving even more and her mouth was open, smiling crazily as if she were pleased that I was crying.

"You want me to be someone that I'm not!" I sobbed. "I'll never be the kind of daughter you want me to be!"

"Only two kinds of daughters," she shouted in Chinese. "Those who are obedient and those who follow their own mind! Only one kind of daughter can live in this house. Obedient daughter!"

"Then I wish I weren't your daughter. I wish you weren't my mother," I shouted. As I said these things I got scared. It felt like worms and toads and slimy things crawling out of my chest, but it also felt good, that this awful side of me had surfaced, at last.

"Too late change this," my mother said shrilly.

And I could sense her anger rising to its breaking point. I wanted to see it spill over. And that's when I remembered the babies she had lost in China, the ones we never talked about. "Then I wish I'd never been born!" I shouted. "I wish I were dead! Like them."

It was as if I had said magic words. Alakazam!—her face went blank, her mouth closed, her arms went slack, and she backed out of the room, stunned, as if she were blowing away like a small brown leaf, thin, brittle, lifeless.

It was not the only disappointment my mother felt in me. In the years that followed, I failed her many times, each time asserting my will, my right to fall short of expectations. I didn't get straight *A*s. I didn't become class president. I didn't get into Stanford. I dropped out of college.

Unlike my mother, I did not believe I could be anything I wanted to be. I could only be me.

And for all those years we never talked about the disaster at the recital or my terrible declarations afterward at the piano bench. Neither of us talked about it again, as if it were a betrayal that was now unspeakable. So I never found a way to ask her why she had hoped for something so large that failure was inevitable.

And even worse, I never asked her about what frightened me the most: Why had she given up hope? For after our struggle at the piano, she never mentioned my playing again. The lessons stopped. The lid to the piano was closed, shutting out the dust, my misery, and her dreams.

So she surprised me. A few years ago she offered to give me the piano, for my thirtieth birthday. I had not played in all those years. I saw the offer as a sign of forgiveness, a tremendous burden removed.

"Are you sure?" I asked shyly. "I mean, won't you and Dad miss it?"

"No, this your piano," she said firmly. "Always your piano. You only one can play."

"Well, I probably can't play anymore," I said. "It's been years."

"You pick up fast," my mother said, as if she knew this was certain. "You have natural talent. You could be genius if you want to."

"No, I couldn't."

"You just not trying," my mother said. And she was neither angry nor sad. She said it as if announcing a fact that could never be disproved. "Take it," she said.

But I didn't at first. It was enough that she had offered it to me. And after that, every time I saw it in my parents' living room, standing in front of the bay window, it made me feel proud, as if it were a shiny trophy that I had won back.

Last week I sent a tuner over to my parents' apartment and had the piano reconditioned, for purely sentimental reasons. My mother had died a few months before, and I had been getting things in order for my father, a little bit at a time. I put the jewelry in special silk pouches. The sweaters she had knitted in yellow, pink, bright orange—all the colors I hated—I put in moth-proof boxes. I found some old Chinese silk dresses, the kind with little slits up the sides. I rubbed the old silk against my skin, and then wrapped them in tissue and decided to take them home with me.

After I had the piano tuned, I opened the lid and touched the keys. It sounded even richer than I remembered. Really, it was a very good piano. Inside the bench were the same exercise notes with handwritten scales, the same secondhand music books with their covers held together with yellow tape.

I opened up the Schumann book to the dark little piece I had played at the recital. It was on the left-hand page, "Pleading Child." It looked more difficult than I remembered. I played a few bars, surprised at how easily the notes came back to me.

And for the first time, or so it seemed, I noticed the piece on the right-hand side. It was called "Perfectly Contented." I tried to play this one as well. It had a lighter melody but with the same flowing rhythm and turned out to be quite easy. "Pleading Child" was shorter but slower; "Perfectly Contented" was longer but faster. And after I had played them both a few times, I realized they were two halves of the same song.

[1989]

■ TOPICS FOR DISCUSSION AND WRITING

1. Try to recall your responses when you had finished reading the first three paragraphs. At that point, how did the mother strike you? Now that you have read the entire story, is your view of her different? If so, in what way(s)?

2. When the narrator looks in the mirror, she discovers "the prodigy side," a face she "had never seen before." What do you think she is discovering?

3. If you enjoyed the story, point out two or three passages that you found particularly engaging, and briefly explain why they appeal to you.

4. Do you think this story is interesting only because it may give a glimpse of life in a Chinese-American family? Or do you find it interesting for additional reasons? Explain.

POETRY

■ EDWIN ARLINGTON ROBINSON

Edwin Arlington Robinson (1869–1935) grew up in Gardiner, Maine, spent two years at Harvard, and then returned to Maine, where he published his first book of poetry in 1896. Though he received encouragement from neighbors, his finances were precarious, even after President Theodore Roosevelt, having been made aware of the book, secured for him an appointment as customs inspector in New York from 1905 to 1909. Additional books won fame for Robinson, and in 1922 he was awarded the first of the three Pulitzer Prizes for poetry that he would win.

Richard Cory

Whenever Richard Cory went down town,
We people on the pavement looked at him:
He was a gentleman from sole to crown,
Clean favored, and imperially slim.   4

And he was always quietly arrayed,
And he was always human when he talked;
But still he fluttered pulses when he said,
"Good-morning," and he glittered when he walked.   8

And he was rich—yes, richer than a king—
And admirably schooled in every grace:
In fine,[1] we thought that he was everything
To make us wish that we were in his place.   12

So on we worked, and waited for the light,
And went without the meat, and cursed the bread;

[1] **In fine** In short

And Richard Cory, one calm summer night,
Went home and put a bullet through his head.   16
                        [1896]

■ TOPICS FOR DISCUSSION AND WRITING

1. Consult the entry on "irony" in the glossary. Then read the pages
    referred to in the entry. Finally, write an essay of 500 words on irony in
    "Richard Cory."
2. What do you think were Richard Cory's thoughts shortly before he "put a
    bullet through his head"? In 500 words, set forth his thoughts and actions
    (what he sees and does). If you wish, you can write in the first person,
    from Cory's point of view. Further, if you wish, your essay can be in the
    form of a suicide note.

■ ROBERT HAYDEN

    Robert Hayden (1913–1980) was born in Detroit, Michigan. His par-
ents divorced when he was a child, and he was brought up by a neighboring family, whose name he adopted. In 1942, at the age of 29, he graduated from Detroit City College (now Wayne State University), and he
received a master's degree from the University of Michigan. He taught at
Fisk University from 1946 to 1969 and after that, for the remainder of
his life, at the University of Michigan. In 1979 he was appointed Consultant in Poetry to the Library of Congress, the first African-American to
hold the post.

*Frederick Douglass**

When it is finally ours, this freedom, this liberty, this beautiful
and terrible thing, needful to man as air,
usable as earth; when it belongs at last to all,
when it is truly instinct, brain matter, diastole, systole,
reflex action; when it is finally won; when it is more   5
than the gaudy mumbo jumbo of politicians:
this man, this Douglass, this former slave, this Negro
beaten to his knees, exiled, visioning a world
where none is lonely, none hunted, alien,
this man, superb in love and logic, this man   10
shall be remembered. Oh, not with statues' rhetoric,
not with legends and poems and wreaths of bronze alone,
but with the lives grown out of his life, the lives
fleshing his dream of the beautiful, needful thing.
                        [1947]

   *Frederick Douglass Born a slave, Douglass (1817–1895) escaped and became
an important spokesman for the abolitionist movement and later for civil rights for
African-Americans.

■ TOPICS FOR DISCUSSION AND WRITING

1. When, according to Hayden, will Douglass "be remembered"? And *how* will he be remembered?

2. "Frederick Douglass" consists of two sentences (or one sentence and a fragment). In what line do you find the subject of the first sentence? What is the main verb (the predicate) and where do you find it? How would you describe the effect of the long delaying of the subject? And of the predicate?

3. Does Hayden assume or seem to predict that there *will* come a time when freedom "is finally ours" (line 1), and "belongs at last to all" (line 3)?

4. Hayden wrote "Frederick Douglass" in 1947. In your opinion are we closer now to Hayden's vision or farther away? (You may find that we are closer in some ways and farther in others.) In your answer—perhaps an essay of 500 words—try to be as specific as possible.

5. "Frederick Douglass" consists of fourteen lines. Is it a sonnet? (For a discussion of the sonnet form, see pages 229–230.)

■ ALLEN GINSBERG

    Allen Ginsberg, born in Newark, New Jersey, in 1926, graduated from Columbia University in 1948. After eight months in Columbia Psychiatric Institute—Ginsberg had pleaded insanity to avoid prosecution when the police discovered that a friend stored stolen goods in Ginsberg's apartment—he worked at odd jobs and finally left the nine-to-five world for a freer life in San Francisco. In the 1950s he established a reputation as an uninhibited declamatory poet whose chief theme was a celebration of those who were alienated from a repressive America. Ginsberg has received many awards and, though he now lives on a farm in New Jersey, often reads at college campuses throughout the country.

A Supermarket in California

    What thoughts I have of you tonight, Walt Whitman, for I walked down the sidestreets under the trees with a headache self-conscious looking at the full moon.

    In my hungry fatigue, and shopping for images, I went into the neon fruit supermarket, dreaming of your enumerations!

    What peaches and what penumbras! Whole families shopping at night! Aisles full of husbands! Wives in the avocados, babies in the tomatoes!—and you, García Lorca,[1] what were you doing down by the watermelons?

    I saw you, Walt Whitman, childless, lonely old grubber,

---

[1] **García Lorca** Federico García Lorca (1899–1936), Spanish poet (and, like Whitman and Ginsberg, a homosexual)

poking among the meats in the refrigerator and eyeing the grocery
boys.

I heard you asking questions of each: Who killed the pork
chops? What price bananas? Are you my Angel?   5

I wandered in and out of the brilliant stacks of cans following
you, and followed in my imagination by the store detective.

We strode down the open corridors together in our solitary
fancy tasting artichokes, possessing every frozen delicacy, and never
passing the cashier.

Where are we going, Walt Whitman? The doors close in an
hour. Which way does your beard point tonight?

(I touch your book and dream of our odyssey in the supermarket and feel absurd.)

Will we walk all night through solitary streets? The trees
add shade to shade, lights out in the houses, we'll both be
lonely.   10

Will we stroll dreaming of the lost America of love past blue
automobiles in driveways, home to our silent cottage?

Ah, dear father, graybeard, lonely old courage-teacher, what
America did you have when Charon quit poling his ferry and you
got out on a smoking bank and stood watching the boat disappear
on the black water of Lethe?[2]

[1956]

■ TOPICS FOR DISCUSSION AND WRITING

1. Would you say that the setting in the poem is symbolic? If so, symbolic of
    what?
2. In line 11 Ginsberg speaks of "the lost America of love." Does the poem
    indicate what sort of "love" Ginsberg has in mind? Do you think that
    "love" (in whatever sense you wish to take the word) was more abundant
    in Whitman's America (the second half of the nineteenth century) than in
    the America of today?

■ PAT MORA

Pat Mora did her undergraduate work at Texas Western College, and
then earned a master's degree at the University of Texas at El Paso,
where she then served as Assistant to the Vice President for Academic
Affairs, Director of the University Museum, and then (1981–1989) as Assistant to the President. She has published essays on Hispanic culture as
well as a children's book, *Tomás and the Library Lady*, but she is best

---

[2] **Charon . . . Lethe** In Greek mythology, Charon ferries across a river, the Styx,
into Hades; a drink from Lethe, another river, causes the dead to forget the world of
the living.

known for her books of poems. Mora has received several awards, including one from the Southwest Council of Latin American Studies.

Immigrants

wrap their babies in the American flag,
feed them mashed hot dogs and apple pie,
name them Bill and Daisy,
buy them blonde dolls that blink blue
eyes or a football and tiny cleats   5
before the baby can even walk,
speak to them in thick English,
    hallo, babee, hallo.
whisper in Spanish or Polish
when the babies sleep, whisper   10
in a dark parent bed, that dark
parent fear, "Will they like
our boy, our girl, our fine american
boy, our fine american girl?"

[1986]

■ TOPICS FOR DISCUSSION AND WRITING

1. To say that someone—for example, a politician—"wraps himself in the American flag" is to suggest disapproval or even anger or contempt. What behavior does the phrase usually describe? What does Mora mean when she says that immigrants "wrap their babies in the American flag"?
2. What do you suppose is Mora's attitude toward the immigrants? Do you think the poet fully approves of their hopes? On what do you base your answer?
3. Does Mora's description of the behavior of immigrants ring true of the immigrant group you are part of or know best? What is your attitude toward their efforts to assimilate? Explain in an essay of 750–1000 words.

■ SHARON OLDS

Sharon Olds was born in San Francisco in 1942 and was educated at Stanford University and Columbia University. She has published several volumes of poetry and has received major awards.

I Go Back to May 1937

I see them standing at the formal gates of their colleges,
I see my father strolling out
under the ochre sandstone arch, the
red tiles glinting like bent
plates of blood behind his head, I   5

see my mother with a few light books at her hip
standing at the pillar made of tiny bricks with the
wrought-iron gate still open behind her, its
sword-tips black in the May air,
they are about to graduate, they are about to get married,   10
they are kids, they are dumb, all they know is they are
innocent, they would never hurt anybody.
I want to go up to them and say Stop,
don't do it—she's the wrong woman,
he's the wrong man, you are going to do things   15
you cannot imagine you would ever do,
you are going to do bad things to children,
you are going to suffer in ways you never heard of,
you are going to want to die. I want to go
up to them there in the late May sunlight and say it,   20
her hungry pretty blank face turning to me,
his pitiful beautiful untouched body,
his arrogant handsome blind face turning to me,
his pitiful beautiful untouched body,
but I don't do it. I want to live. I   25
take them up like the male and female
paper dolls and bang them together
at the hips like chips of flint as if to
strike sparks from them, I say
Do what you are going to do, and I will tell about it.   30

[1987]

■ TOPICS FOR DISCUSSION AND WRITING

1. Having read the poem, how do you understand its title? How does Olds
    seem to define "I"? What does she mean by "Go Back to"? And why
    "May 1937"?

2. In the first line Olds says, "I see them." *How* does she see them? Actu-
    ally? In imagination? In photographs? Or can't we know?

3. Consider the comparisons, such as the simile in lines 4–5 ("red tiles
    glinting like bent / plates of blood") and the metaphor in lines 8–9 (the
    uprights of the wrought-iron fence are "sword-tips"). What do they tell us
    about the speaker's view of things?

4. Observe where the sentences of the poem begin and end. Can you ex-
    plain these sentence boundaries? What shifts of meaning or mood accom-
    pany the end of one sentence and the beginning of the next?

5. How are the mother and father characterized when young? Are these
    characterizations consistent or inconsistent with the violent emotions of
    lines 13–19?

6. How do you read the last line? Do you feel that the speaker is, for
    example, angry, or vengeful, or sympathetic, or resigned? How do you
    interpret "and I will tell about it."? To whom will she "tell about it," and
    how?

DRAMA

■ EDWARD ALBEE

Edward Albee (b. 1928) in infancy was adopted by the multimillion-aires who owned the chain of Albee theaters. Though surrounded by material comfort, he was an unhappy child who disliked his adoptive parents. The only member of his family with whom he seems to have had an affectionate relationship was his grandmother. His work at school and in college was poor, but he wrote a good deal even as an adolescent; when in 1960 he achieved sudden fame with *Zoo Story* (written in 1958), he had already written plays for more than a decade. Among his other plays are *The Death of Bessie Smith* (1960), *The Sandbox* (1960), *The American Dream* (1961), *Who's Afraid of Virginia Woolf* (1962), *A Delicate Balance* (1966), and *The Man Who Had Three Arms* (1983).

The Sandbox

The Players
THE YOUNG MAN *25, a good looking, well-built boy in a bathing suit*
MOMMY, *55, a well-dressed, imposing woman*
DADDY, *60, a small man; gray, thin*
GRANDMA, *86, a tiny, wizened woman with bright eyes*
THE MUSICIAN, *no particular age, but young would be nice*

Note: When, in the course of the play, MOMMY *and* DADDY *call each other by these names, there should be no suggestion of regionalism. These names are of empty affection and point up the pre-senility and vacuity of their characters.*

The Scene: A bare stage, with only the following: Near the footlights, far stage-right, two simple chairs set side by side, facing the audience; near the footlights, far stage-left, a chair facing stage-right with a music stand before it; farther back, and stage-center, slightly elevated and raked, a large child's sandbox with a toy pail and shovel; the background is the sky, which alters from brightest day to deepest night.
At the beginning, it is brightest day, the YOUNG MAN *is alone on stage, to the rear of the sandbox, and to one side. He is doing calisthenics; he does calisthenics until quite at the very end of the play. These calisthenics, employing the arms only, should suggest the beating and fluttering of wings. The* YOUNG MAN *is, after all, the Angel of Death.*

MOMMY *and* DADDY *enter from the stage-left,* MOMMY *first.*
MOMMY [*motioning to* DADDY]. Well, here we are; this is the beach.
DADDY [*whining*]. I'm cold.
MOMMY [*dismissing him with a little laugh*]. Don't be silly; it's as warm as toast. Look at that nice young man over there: *he* doesn't think it's cold. [*Waves to the* YOUNG MAN.] Hello.

YOUNG MAN [*with an endearing smile*]. Hi!

MOMMY [*looking about*]. This will do perfectly . . . don't you think so, Daddy? There's sand there . . . and the water beyond. What do you think, Daddy?

DADDY [*vaguely*]. Whatever you say, Mommy.

MOMMY [*with the same little laugh*]. Well, of course . . . whatever I say. Then, it's settled, is it?

DADDY [*shrugs*]. She's *your* mother, not mine.

MOMMY. *I* know she's my mother. What do you take me for? [*A pause.*] All right, now; let's get on with it. [*She shouts into the wings, stage-left.*] You! Out there! You can come in now.

The MUSICIAN *enters, seats himself in the chair, stage-left, places music on the music stand, is ready to play.* MOMMY *nods approvingly.*

MOMMY. Very nice; very nice. Are you ready, Daddy? Let's go get Grandma.

DADDY. Whatever you say, Mommy.

MOMMY [*Leading the way out, stage-left*]. Of course, whatever I say. [*To the* MUSICIAN.] You can begin now.

The MUSICIAN *begins playing;* MOMMY *and* DADDY *exit; the* MUSICIAN, *all the while playing nods to the* YOUNG MAN.

YOUNG MAN [*with the same endearing smile*]. Hi!

After a moment, MOMMY *and* DADDY *re-enter, carrying* GRANDMA. *She is borne in by their hands under her armpits; she is quite rigid; her legs are drawn up; her feet do not touch the ground; the expression on her ancient face is that of puzzlement and fear.*

DADDY. Where do we put her?

MOMMY [*the same little laugh*]. Wherever I say, of course. Let me see . . . well . . . all right, over there . . . in the sandbox. [*Pause.*] Well, what are you waiting for Daddy? . . . The sandbox!

Together they carry GRANDMA *over to the sandbox and more or less dump her in.*

GRANDMA [*righting herself to a sitting position; her voice a cross between a baby's laugh and cry*]. Ahhhhhh! Graaaaa!

DADDY [*dusting himself*]. What do we do now?

MOMMY [*to the* MUSICIAN]. You can stop now. [*The* MUSICIAN *stops.*] [*Back to* DADDY.] What do you mean, what do we do now? We go over there and sit down, of course. [*To the* YOUNG MAN.] Hello there.

YOUNG MAN [*again smiling*]. Hi!

MOMMY *and* DADDY *move to the chairs, stage-right, and sit down. A pause.*

GRANDMA [*same as before*]. Ahhhhhh! Ahhaaaaaa! Graaaaaa!

DADDY. Do you think . . . do you think she's . . . comfortable?

MOMMY [*impatiently*]. How would I know?

DADDY [*pause*]. What do we do now?

MOMMY [*as if remembering*]. We . . . wait. We . . . sit here . . . and we wait . . . that's what we do.

DADDY [*after a pause*]. Shall we talk to each other?

MOMMY [*with that little laugh; picking something off her dress*]. Well, *you* can talk, if you want to . . . if you can think of anything to *say* . . . if you can think of anything *new.*

DADDY [*thinks*]. No . . . I suppose not.

MOMMY [*with a triumphant laugh*]. Of course not!

GRANDMA [*banging the toy shovel against the pail*]. Haaaaaa! Ah-haaaaaa!

MOMMY [*out over the audience*]. Be quiet, Grandma . . . just be quiet, and wait.

GRANDMA *throws a shovelful of sand at* MOMMY.

MOMMY [*still out over the audience*]. She's throwing sand at me! You stop that, Grandma; you stop throwing sand at Mommy! [*To* DADDY.] She's throwing sand at me.

DADDY *looks around at* GRANDMA, *who screams at him.*

GRANDMA. GRAAAAAA!

MOMMY. Don't look at her. Just . . . sit here . . . be very still . . . and wait. [*To the* MUSICIAN.] You . . . uh . . . you go ahead and do whatever it is you do.

The MUSICIAN *plays.*

MOMMY *and* DADDY *are fixed, staring out beyond the audience.* GRANDMA *looks at them, looks at the* MUSICIAN, *looks at the sandbox, throws down the shovel.*

GRANDMA. Ah-haaaaaa! Graaaaaa! [*Looks for reaction; gets none. Now . . . directly to the audience.*] Honestly! What a way to treat an old woman! Drag her out of the house . . . stick her in a car . . . bring her out here from the city . . . dump her in a pile of sand . . . and leave her here to set. I'm eighty-six years old! I was married when I was seventeen. To a farmer. He died when I was thirty. [*To the* MUSICIAN.] Will you stop that, please?

The MUSICIAN *stops playing.*

I'm a feeble old woman . . . how do you expect anybody to hear me over that peep! peep! peep! [*To herself.*] There's no respect around here. [*To the* YOUNG MAN.] There's no respect around here!

YOUNG MAN [*same smile*]. Hi!

GRANDMA [*after a pause, a mild double-take, continues, to the audience*]. My husband died when I was thirty [*indicates* MOMMY], and I had to raise that big cow over there all by my lonesome. You can imagine what *that* was like. Lordy! [*To the* YOUNG MAN.] Where'd they get *you?*

YOUNG MAN. Oh . . . I've been around for a while.

GRANDMA. I'll bet you have! Heh, heh, heh. Will you look at you!

YOUNG MAN [*flexing his muscles*]. Isn't that something? [*Continues his calisthenics.*]

GRANDMA. Boy, oh boy; I'll say. Pretty good.

YOUNG MAN [*sweetly*]. I'll say.

GRANDMA. Where ya from?

YOUNG MAN. Southern California.

GRANDMA [*nodding*]. Figgers, figgers. What's your name, honey?

YOUNG MAN. I don't know. . . .

GRANDMA [*to the audience*]. Bright, too!

YOUNG MAN. I mean . . . I mean, they haven't given me one yet . . . the studio . . .

GRANDMA [*giving him the once-over*]. You don't say . . . you don't say. Well . . . uh, I've got to talk some more . . . don't you go 'way.

YOUNG MAN. Oh, no.

GRANDMA [*turning her attention back to the audience*]. Fine; fine. [*Then, once more, back to the* YOUNG MAN.] You're . . . you're an actor, hunh?

YOUNG MAN [*beaming*]. Yes. I am.

GRANDMA [*to the audience again; shrugs*]. I'm smart that way. *Anyhow, I* had to raise . . . *that* over there all by my lonesome; and what's next to her there . . . that's what she married. Rich? I tell you . . . money, money, money. They took me off the *farm* . . . which was real decent of them . . . and they moved me into the big town house with *them* . . . fixed a nice place for me under the stove . . . gave me an army blanket . . . and my own dish . . . my very own dish! So, what have I got to complain about? Nothing, of course. I'm not complaining. [*She looks up at the sky, shouts to someone offstage.*] Shouldn't it be getting dark now, dear?

The lights dim; night comes on. The MUSICIAN *begins to play; it becomes deepest night. There are spots on all the players, including the* YOUNG MAN, *who is, of course, continuing his calisthenics.*

DADDY [*stirring*]. It's nighttime.

MOMMY. Shhhh. Be still . . . wait.

DADDY [*whining*]. It's so hot.

MOMMY. Shhhhhh. Be still . . . wait.

GRANDMA [*to herself*]. That's better. Night. [*To the* MUSICIAN.] Honey, do you play all through this part?

The MUSICIAN *nods.*

Well, keep it nice and soft; that's a good boy.

The MUSICIAN *nods again; plays softly.*

That's nice.

There is an off-stage rumble.

DADDY [*starting*]. What was that?

MOMMY [*beginning to weep*]. It was nothing.

DADDY. It was . . . it was . . . thunder . . . or a wave breaking . . . or something.

MOMMY [*whispering, through her tears*]. It was an off-stage rumble . . . and you know what *that* means. . . .

DADDY. I forget. . . .

MOMMY [*barely able to talk*]. It means the time has come for poor Grandma . . . and I can't bear it!

DADDY [*vacantly*]. I . . . I suppose you've got to be brave.

GRANDMA [*mocking*]. That's right, kid; be brave. You'll bear up; you'll get over it.

[*Another off-stage rumble . . . louder.*]

MOMMY. Ohhhhhhhhhh . . . poor Grandma. . . poor Grandma. . . .

GRANDMA [*to* MOMMY]. I'm fine! I'm all right! It hasn't happened yet!

A violent off-stage rumble. All the lights go out, save the spot on the YOUNG MAN; *the* MUSICIAN *stops playing.*

MOMMY. Ohhhhhhhhhh . . . . Ohhhhhhhhhh. . . .

Silence.

GRANDMA. Don't put the lights up yet . . . I'm not ready; I'm not quite ready. [*Silence.*] All right, dear . . . I'm about done.

The lights come up again, to brightest day; the MUSICIAN *begins to play.* GRANDMA *is discovered, still in the sandbox, lying on her side, propped up on an elbow, half covered, busily shoveling sand over herself.*

GRANDMA. [*muttering*]. I don't know how I'm supposed to do anything with this goddam toy shovel. . . .

DADDY. Mommy! It's daylight!

MOMMY [*brightly*]. So it is! Well! Our long night is over. We must put away our tears, take off our mourning . . . and face the future. It's our duty.

GRANDMA [*still shoveling; mimicking*] . . . take off our mourning . . . face the future. . . . Lordy!

MOMMY *and* DADDY *rise, stretch.* MOMMY *waves to the* YOUNG MAN.

YOUNG MAN [*with that smile*]. Hi!

GRANDMA *plays dead.* (!) MOMMY *and* DADDY *go over to look at her; she is a little more than half buried in the sand; the toy shovel is in her hands, which are crossed on her breast.*

MOMMY [*before the sandbox; shaking her head*]. Lovely! It's . . . it's hard to be sad . . . she looks . . . so happy. [*With pride and conviction.*] It pays to do things well. [*To the* MUSICIAN.] All right, you can stop now, if you want to. I mean, stay around for a swim, or something; it's all right with us. [*She sighs heavily.*] Well, Daddy . . . off we go.

DADDY. Brave Mommy!

MOMMY. Brave Daddy!

They exit, stage-left.

GRANDMA [*after they leave; lying quite still*]. It pays to do things well. . . . Boy, oh boy! [*She tries to sit up*] . . . well, kids . . . [*but she finds she can't*] . . . I . . . I can't get up, I . . . I can't move . . . .

The YOUNG MAN *stops his calisthenics, nods to the* MUSICIAN, *walks over to* GRANDMA, *kneels down by the sandbox.*

GRANDMA. I . . . can't move. . . .

YOUNG MAN. Shhhhh . . . be very still. . . .

GRANDMA. I . . . I can't move. . . .

YOUNG MAN. Uh . . . ma'am; I . . . I have a line here.

GRANDMA. Oh, I'm sorry, sweetie; you go right ahead.

YOUNG MAN. I am . . . uh . . .

GRANDMA. Take your time, dear.

YOUNG MAN [*prepares; delivers the line like a real amateur*]. I am the Angel of Death. I am . . . uh . . . I am come for you.

GRANDMA. What . . . wha . . . [*Then, with resignation.*] . . . ohhhh . . . ohhhh, I see.

The YOUNG MAN *bends over, kisses* GRANDMA *gently on the forehead.*

GRANDMA [*her eyes closed, her hands folded on her breast again, the shovel between her hands, a sweet smile on her face*]. Well . . . that was very nice, dear . . .

YOUNG MAN [*still kneeling*]. Shhhhhh . . . be still. . . .

GRANDMA. What I mean was . . . you did that very well, dear. . . .

YOUNG MAN [*blushing*] . . . oh . . .

GRANDMA. No; I mean it. You've got that . . . you've got a quality.

YOUNG MAN [*with his endearing smile*]. Oh . . . thank you; thank you very much . . . ma'am.

GRANDMA [*slowly; softly—as the* YOUNG MAN *puts his hands on top of* GRANDMA'*s*]. You're . . . you're welcome . . . dear.

Tableau. The MUSICIAN *continues to play as the curtain slowly comes down.*

Curtain

[1960]

■ TOPICS FOR DISCUSSION AND WRITING

1. In a sentence characterize Mommy, and in another sentence characterize Daddy.
2. Of the four characters in the play, which is the most sympathetic? Set forth your answer, with supporting evidence, in two paragraphs, devoting the first to the three less sympathetic characters, the second to the most sympathetic character.
3. In a longer play, *The American Dream,* Albee uses the same four characters that he uses in *The Sandbox.* Of *The American Dream,* he wrote:

   The play is . . . a condemnation of complacency, cruelty, emasculation and vacuity; it is a stand against the fiction that everything in this slipping land of ours is peachy-keen.

   To what extent does this statement help you to understand (and to enjoy) *The Sandbox?*
4. In *The New York Times Magazine,* 25 February 1962, Albee protested against the view that his plays, and others of the so-called Theater of the Absurd, are depressing. He includes a quotation from Martin Esslin's book, *The Theatre of the Absurd:*

   Ultimately . . . the Theatre of the Absurd does not reflect despair or a return to dark irrational forces but expresses modern man's endeavor to come to terms with the world in which he lives. It attempts to make him face up to the human condition as it really is, to free him from illusions that are bound to cause constant maladjustment and disappointment. . . . For the dignity of man lies in his ability to face reality in all its senselessness; to accept it freely, without fear, without illusions—and to laugh at it.

   In what ways is this statement helpful? In what ways is it not helpful? Explain.

■ TENNESSEE WILLIAMS

Tennessee Williams (1914–1983) was born Thomas Lanier Williams in Columbus, Mississippi. During his childhood his family moved to St. Louis, where his father had accepted a job as manager of a shoe company. Williams has written that neither he nor his sister Rose could adjust to the change from the South to the Midwest, but the children had already been deeply troubled. Nevertheless, at the age of 16 he achieved some distinction as a writer when his prize-winning essay in a nationwide contest was published. After high school he attended the University of Missouri but flunked ROTC and was therefore withdrawn from school by his father. He worked in a shoe factory for a while, then attended Washington University, where he wrote several plays. He finally graduated from the University of Iowa with a major in playwrighting. After graduation he continued to write, supporting himself with odd jobs such as waiting on tables and running elevators. His first commercial success was *The Glass Menagerie* (produced in Chicago in 1944, and in New York in 1945); among his other plays are *A Streetcar Named Desire* (1947), *Cat on a Hot Tin Roof* (1955), and *Suddenly Last Summer* (1958).

The Glass Menagerie

Nobody, not even the rain, has such small hands.
　　　　　　　　　　　　—E. E. Cummings

List of Characters

AMANDA WINGFIELD, the mother. A little woman of great but confused vitality clinging frantically to another time and place. Her characterization must be carefully created, not copied from type. She is not paranoiac, but her life is paranoia. There is much to admire in Amanda, and as much to love and pity as there is to laugh at. Certainly she has endurance and a kind of heroism, and though her foolishness makes her unwittingly cruel at times, there is tenderness in her slight person.

LAURA WINGFIELD, her daughter. Amanda, having failed to establish contact with reality, continues to live vitally in her illusions, but Laura's situation is even graver. A childhood illness has left her crippled, one leg slightly shorter than the other, and held in a brace. This defect need not be more than suggested on the stage. Stemming from this, Laura's separation increases till she is like a piece of her own glass collection, too exquisitely fragile to move from the shelf.

TOM WINGFIELD, her son. And the narrator of the play. A poet with a job in a warehouse. His nature is not remorseless, but to escape from a trap he has to act without pity.

JIM O'CONNOR, the gentleman caller. A nice, ordinary, young man.

Scene. An alley in St. Louis.
Part I. Preparation for a Gentleman Caller.
Part II. The Gentleman Calls.

Time. Now and the Past.

SCENE I

　　The Wingfield apartment is in the rear of the building, one of those vast hive-like conglomerations of cellular living-units that flower as warty growths in overcrowded urban centers of lower middle-class population and are symptomatic of the impulse of this largest and fundamentally enslaved section of American society to avoid fluidity and differentiation and to exist and function as one interfused mass of automatism.

This is a scene from the opening production of *The Glass Menagerie* at The Playhouse in New York on March 31, 1945, starring Lorette Taylor, Julie Hayden, Eddie Dowling, and Anthony Ross. Reproduced by courtesy of the New York Public Library, The Billy Rose Theater Collection.

The apartment faces an alley and is entered by a fire-escape, a structure whose name is a touch of accidental poetic truth, for all of these huge buildings are always burning with the slow and implacable fires of human desperation. The fire-escape is included in the set—that is, the landing of it and steps descending from it.

The scene is memory and is therefore nonrealistic. Memory takes a lot of poetic license. It omits some details; others are exaggerated, according to the emotional value of the articles it touches, for memory is seated predominantly in the heart. The interior is therefore rather dim and poetic.

At the rise of the curtain, the audience is faced with the dark, grim rear wall of the Wingfield tenement. This building, which runs parallel to the footlights, is flanked on both sides by dark, narrow alleys which run into murky canyons of tangled clotheslines, garbage cans and the sinister latticework of neighboring fire-escapes. It is up and down these side alleys that exterior entrances and exits are made, during the play. At the end of Tom's opening commentary, the dark tenement wall slowly reveals (by means of a transparency) the interior of the ground floor Wingfield apartment.

Downstage is the living room, which also serves as a sleeping room for Laura, the sofa unfolding to make her bed. Upstage, center, and divided by a wide arch or second proscenium with transparent faded portieres (or second curtain), is the dining room. In an old-fashioned what-not in the living room are seen scores of transparent glass animals. A blown-up photograph of the father hangs on the wall of the living room, facing the audience, to the left of the archway. It is the face of a very handsome young man in a doughboy's First World War cap. He is gallantly smiling, ineluctably smiling, as if to say, "I will be smiling forever."

The audience hears and sees the opening scene in the dining room through both the transparent fourth wall of the building and the transparent gauze portieres of the dining-room arch. It is during this revealing scene that the fourth wall slowly ascends, out of sight.

This transparent exterior wall is not brought down again until the very end of the play, during Tom's final speech.

The narrator is an undisguised convention of the play. He takes whatever license with dramatic convention as is convenient to his purposes.

Tom enters dressed as a merchant sailor from alley, stage left, and strolls across the front of the stage to the fire-escape. There he stops and lights a cigarette. He addresses the audience.

TOM. Yes, I have tricks in my pocket, I have things up my sleeve. But I am the opposite of a stage magician. He gives you illusion that has the appearance of truth. I give you truth in the pleasant disguise of illusion. To begin with, I turn back time. I reverse it to that quaint period, the thirties, when the huge middle class of America was matriculating in a school for the blind. Their eyes had failed them, or they had failed their eyes, and so they were having their fingers pressed forcibly down on the fiery Braille alphabet of a dissolving economy. In Spain there was revolution. Here there was only shouting and confusion. In Spain there was Guernica. Here there were disturbances of labor, sometimes pretty violent, in otherwise peaceful cities such as Chicago, Cleveland, Saint Louis. . . . This is the social background of the play.

[*Music.*]

The play is memory. Being a memory play, it is dimly lighted, it is sentimental, it is not realistic. In memory everything seems to happen to music. That explains the fiddle in the wings. I am the narrator of the play, and also a character in it. The other characters are my mother, Amanda, my sister, Laura, and a gentleman caller who appears in the final scenes. He is the most realistic character in the play, being an emissary from a world of reality that we were somehow set apart from. But since I have a poet's weakness for symbols, I am using this character also as a symbol; he is the long delayed but always expected something that we live for. There is a fifth character in the play who doesn't appear except in this larger-than-life photograph over the mantel. This is our father who left us a long time ago. He was a telephone man who fell in love with long distances; he gave up his job with the telephone company and skipped the light fantastic out of town. . . . The last we heard of him was a picture post-card from Mazatlan, on the Pacific coast of Mexico, containing a message of two words—"Hello—Goodbye!" and no address. I think the rest of the play will explain itself. . . .

Amanda's voice becomes audible through the portieres.

[*Legend on Screen: "Où Sont les Neiges?"*]

He divides the portieres and enters the upstage area.

Amanda and Laura are seated at a drop-leaf table. Eating is indicated by gestures without food or utensils. Amanda faces the audience. Tom and Laura are seated in profile.

The interior has lit up softly and through the scrim we see Amanda and Laura seated at the table in the upstage area.

AMANDA [*calling*]. Tom?

TOM. Yes, Mother.

AMANDA. We can't say grace until you come to the table!

TOM. Coming, Mother. [*He bows slightly and withdraws, reappearing a few moments later in his place at the table.*]

AMANDA [*to her son*]. Honey, don't *push* with your *fingers*. If you have to push with something, the thing to push with is a crust of bread. And chew—chew! Animals have sections in their stomachs which enable them to digest food without mastication, but human beings are supposed to chew their food before they swallow it down. Eat food leisurely, son, and really enjoy it. A well-cooked meal has lots of delicate flavors that have to be held in the mouth for appreciation. So chew your food and give your salivary glands a chance to function!

Tom deliberately lays his imaginary fork down and pushes his chair back from the table.

TOM. I haven't enjoyed one bite of this dinner because of your constant directions on how to eat it. It's you that makes me rush through meals with your hawk-like attention to every bite I take. Sickening—spoils my appetite—all this discussion of animals' secretion—salivary glands—mastication!

AMANDA [*lightly*]. Temperament like a Metropolitan star! [*He rises and crosses downstage.*] You're not excused from the table.

TOM. I am getting a cigarette.

AMANDA. You smoke too much.

Laura rises.

LAURA. I'll bring in the blanc mange.

He remains standing with his cigarette by the portieres during the following.

AMANDA [*rising*]. No, sister, no, sister—you be the lady this time and I'll be the darky.

LAURA. I'm already up.

AMANDA. Resume your seat, little sister—I want you to stay fresh and pretty—for gentlemen callers!

LAURA. I'm not expecting any gentlemen callers.

AMANDA [*crossing out to kitchenette. Airily*]. Sometimes they come when they are least expected! Why, I remember one Sunday afternoon in Blue Mountain—[*Enters kitchenette.*]

TOM. I know what's coming!

LAURA. Yes. But let her tell it.

TOM. Again?

LAURA. She loves to tell it.

Amanda returns with bowl of dessert.

AMANDA. One Sunday afternoon in Blue Mountain—your mother received—*seventeen!*—gentlemen callers! Why, sometimes there weren't chairs enough to accommodate them all. We had to send the nigger over to bring in folding chairs from the parish house.

Tom [*remaining at portieres*]. How did you entertain those gentlemen callers?

AMANDA. I understood the art of conversation!

TOM. I bet you could talk.

AMANDA. Girls in those days *knew* how to talk, I can tell you.

TOM. Yes?

[*Image: Amanda as a Girl on a Porch Greeting Callers.*]

AMANDA. They knew how to entertain their gentlemen callers. It wasn't enough for a girl to be possessed of a pretty face and a graceful figure—although I wasn't slighted in either respect. She also needed to have a nimble wit and a tongue to meet all occasions.

TOM. What did you talk about?

AMANDA. Things of importance going on in the world! Never anything coarse or common or vulgar. [*She addresses Tom as though he were seated in the vacant chair at the table though he remains by portieres. He plays this scene as though he held the book.*] My callers were gentlemen—all! Among my callers were some of the most prominent young planters of the Mississippi Delta—planters and sons of planters!

Tom motions for music and a spot of light on Amanda.

Her eyes lift, her face glows, her voice becomes rich and elegiac.

[*Screen Legend: "Où Sont les Neiges?"*]

There was young Champ Laughlin who later became vice-president of the Delta Planters Bank. Hadley Stevenson who was drowned in Moon Lake and left his widow one hundred and fifty thousand in Government bonds. There were the Cutrere brothers, Wesley and Bates. Bates was one of my bright particular beaux! He got in a quarrel with that wild Wainright boy. They shot it out on the floor of Moon Lake Casino. Bates was shot through the stomach. Died in the ambulance on his way to Memphis. His widow was also well-provided for, came into eight or ten thousand acres, that's all. She married him on the rebound—never loved her—carried my picture on him the night he died! And there was that boy that every girl in Delta had set her cap for! That beautiful, brilliant young Fitzhugh boy from Green County!

TOM. What did he leave his widow?

AMANDA. He never married! Gracious, you talk as though all of my old admirers had turned up their toes to the daisies!

TOM. Isn't this the first you mentioned that still survives?

AMANDA. That Fitzhugh boy went North and made a fortune—came to be known as the Wolf of Wall Street! He had the Midas touch, whatever he touched turned to gold! And I could have been Mrs. Duncan J. Fitzhugh, mind you! But—I picked your *father!*

LAURA [*rising*]. Mother, let me clear the table.

AMANDA. No dear, you go in front and study your typewriter chart. Or practice your shorthand a little. Stay fresh and pretty!—It's almost time for our gentlemen callers to start arriving. [*She flounces girlishly toward the kitchenette.*] How many do you suppose we're going to entertain this afternoon?

Tom throws down the paper and jumps up with a groan.

LAURA [*alone in the dining room*]. I don't believe we're going to receive any, Mother.

AMANDA [*reappearing, airily*]. What? No one—not one? You must be joking! [*Laura nervously echoes her laugh. She slips in a fugitive manner through the half-open portieres and draws them gently behind her. A shaft of very clear light is thrown on her face against the faded tapestry of the curtains.*] [*Music: "The Glass Menagerie" Under Faintly.*] [*Lightly.*] Not one gentleman caller? It can't be true! There must be a flood, there must have been a tornado!

LAURA. It isn't a flood, it's not a tornado, Mother. I'm just not popular like you were in Blue Mountain. . . . [*Tom utters another groan. Laura glances at him with a faint, apologetic smile. Her voice catching a little.*] Mother's afraid I'm going to be an old maid.

[*The Scene Dims Out with "Glass Menagerie" Music.*]

SCENE II

"Laura, Haven't You Ever Liked Some Boy?"

On the dark stage the screen is lighted with the image of blue roses. Gradually Laura's figure becomes apparent and the screen goes out. The music subsides.

Laura is seated in the delicate ivory chair at the small clawfoot table.

She wears a dress of soft violet material for a kimono—her hair tied back from her forehead with a ribbon.

She is washing and polishing her collection of glass.

Amanda appears on the fire-escape steps. At the sound of her ascent, Laura catches her breath, thrusts the bowl of ornaments away and seats herself stiffly before the diagram of the typewriter keyboard as though it held her spellbound. Something has happened to Amanda. It is written in her face as she climbs to the landing: a look that is grim and hopeless and a little absurd.

She has on one of those cheap or imitation velvety-looking cloth coats with imitation fur collar. Her hat is five or six years old, one of those dreadful cloche hats that were worn in the late twenties, and she is clasping an enormous black patent-leather pocketbook with nickel clasp and initials. This is her full-dress outfit, the one she usually wears to the D.A.R.

Before entering she looks through the door.

She purses her lips, opens her eyes wide, rolls them upward and shakes her head.

Then she slowly lets herself in the door. Seeing her mother's expression Laura touches her lips with a nervous gesture.

LAURA. Hello, Mother, I was—[*She makes a nervous gesture toward the chart on the wall. Amanda leans against the shut door and stares at Laura with a martyred look.*]

AMANDA. Deception? Deception? [*She slowly removes her hat and gloves, continuing the swift suffering stare. She lets the hat and gloves fall on the floor—a bit of acting.*]

LAURA [*shakily*]. How was the D.A.R. meeting? [*Amanda slowly opens her purse and removes a dainty white handkerchief which she shakes out delicately and delicately touches to her lips and nostrils.*] Didn't you go to the D.A.R. meeting, Mother?

AMANDA [*faintly, almost inaudibly*].—No.—No. [*Then more forcibly.*] I did not have the strength—to go to the D.A.R. In fact, I did not have the courage! I wanted to find a hole in the ground and hide myself in it forever! [*She crosses slowly to the wall and removes the diagram of the typewriter keyboard. She holds it in front of her for a second, staring at it sweetly and sorrowfully—then bites her lips and tears it in two pieces.*]

LAURA [*faintly*]. Why did you do that, Mother? [*Amanda repeats the same procedure with the chart of the Gregg Alphabet.*] Why are you—

AMANDA. Why? Why? How old are you, Laura?

LAURA. Mother, you know my age.

AMANDA. I thought that you were an adult; it seems that I was mistaken. [*She crosses slowly to the sofa and sinks down and stares at Laura.*]

LAURA. Please don't stare at me, Mother.

Amanda closes her eyes and lowers her head. Count ten.

AMANDA. What are we going to do, what is going to become of us, what is the future?

Count ten.

LAURA. Has something happened, Mother? [*Amanda draws a long breath and takes out the handkerchief again. Dabbing process.*] Mother, has—something happened?

AMANDA. I'll be all right in a minute. I'm just bewildered—[*count five*]—
by life. . . .

LAURA. Mother, I wish that you would tell me what's happened.

AMANDA. As you know, I was supposed to be inducted into my office at
the D.A.R. this afternoon. [*Image: A Swarm of Typewriters.*] But I stopped
off at Rubicam's Business College to speak to your teachers about your having
a cold and ask them what progress they thought you were making down
there.

LAURA. Oh. . . .

AMANDA. I went to the typing instructor and introduced myself as your
mother. She didn't know who you were. Wingfield, she said. We don't have
any such student enrolled at the school! I assured her she did, that you had
been going to classes since early in January. "I wonder," she said, "if you
could be talking about that terribly shy little girl who dropped out of school
after only a few days' attendance?" "No," I said, "Laura, my daughter, has
been going to school every day for the past six weeks!" "Excuse me," she
said. She took the attendance book out and there was your name, unmistaka-
bly printed, and all the dates you were absent until they decided that you had
dropped out of school. I still said, "No, there must have been some mistake!
There must have been some mix-up in the records!" And she said, "No—I
remember her perfectly now. Her hand shook so that she couldn't hit the
right keys! The first time we gave a speed-test, she broke down completely—
was sick at the stomach and almost had to be carried into the wash-room!
After that morning she never showed up any more. We phoned the house
but never got any answer"—while I was working at Famous and Barr, I
suppose, demonstrating those—Oh! I felt so weak I could barely keep on
my feet. I had to sit down while they got me a glass of water! Fifty dollars'
tuition, all of our plans—my hopes and ambitions for you—just gone up the
spout, just gone up the spout like that. [*Laura draws a long breath and gets
awkwardly to her feet. She crosses to the victrola and winds it up.*] What are
you doing?

LAURA. Oh! [*She releases the handle and returns to her seat.*]

AMANDA. Laura, where have you been going when you've gone out
pretending that you were going to business college?

LAURA. I've just been going out walking.

AMANDA. That's not true.

LAURA. It is. I just went walking.

AMANDA. Walking? Walking? In winter? Deliberately courting pneumonia
in that light coat? Where did you walk to, Laura?

LAURA. It was the lesser of two evils, Mother. [*Image: Winter Scene in
Park.*] I couldn't go back up. I—threw up—on the floor!

AMANDA. From half past seven till after five every day you mean to tell
me you walked around in the park, because you wanted to make me think that
you were still going to Rubicam's Business College?

LAURA. It wasn't as bad as it sounds. I went inside places to get warmed
up.

AMANDA. Inside where?

LAURA. I went in the art museum and the bird-houses at the Zoo. I visited the penguins every day! Sometimes I did without lunch and went to the movies. Lately I've been spending most of my afternoons in the Jewel-box, that big glass house where they raise the tropical flowers.

AMANDA. You did all this to deceive me, just for the decepton? [*Laura looks down.*] Why?

LAURA. Mother, when you're disappointed, you get that awful suffering look on your face, like the picture of Jesus' mother in the museum!

AMANDA. Hush!

LAURA. I couldn't face it.

Pause. A whisper of strings.

[*Legend: "The Crust of Humility."*]

AMANDA [*hopelessly fingering the huge pocketbook*]. So what are we going to do the rest of our lives? Stay home and watch the parades go by? Amuse ourselves with the glass menagerie, darling? Eternally play those worn-out phonograph records your father left as a painful reminder of him? We won't have a business career—we've given that up because it gave us nervous indigestion! [*Laughs wearily.*] What is there left but dependency all our lives? I know so well what becomes of unmarried women who aren't prepared to occupy a position. I've seen such pitiful cases in the South—barely tolerated spinsters living upon the grudging patronage of sister's husband or brother's wife!—stuck away in some little mousetrap of a room—encouraged by one in-law to visit another—little birdlike women without any nest—eating the crust of humility all their life! Is that the future that we've mapped out for ourselves? I swear it's the only alternative I can think of! It isn't a very pleasant alternative, is it? Of course—some girls *do marry.* [*Laura twists her hands nervously.*] Haven't you ever liked some boy?

LAURA. Yes. I liked one once. [*Rises.*] I came across his picture a while ago.

AMANDA [*with some interest*]. He gave you his picture?

LAURA. No, it's in the year-book.

AMANDA [*disappointed*]. Oh—a high-school boy.

[*Screen Image: Jim as a High-School Hero Bearing a Silver Cup.*]

LAURA. Yes. His name was Jim. [*Laura lifts the heavy annual from the clawfoot table.*] Here he is in *The Pirates of Penzance.*

AMANDA [*absently*]. The what?

LAURA. The operetta the senior class put on. He had a wonderful voice and we sat across the aisle from each other Mondays, Wednesdays and Fridays in the Aud. Here he is with the silver cup for debating! See his grin?

AMANDA [*absently*]. He must have had a jolly disposition.

LAURA. He used to call me—Blue Roses.

[*Image: Blue Roses.*]

AMANDA. Why did he call you such a name as that?

LAURA. When I had that attack of pleurosis—he asked me what was the matter when I came back. I said pleurosis—he thought that I said Blue Roses! So that's what he always called me after that. Whenever he saw me, he'd holler, "Hello, Blue Roses!" I didn't care for the girl that he went out with. Emily Meisenbach. Emily was the best-dressed girl at Soldan. She never struck me, though, as being sincere. . . . It says in the Personal

Section—they're engaged. That's—six years ago! They must be married by now.

AMANDA. Girls that aren't cut out for business careers usually wind up married to some nice man. [*Gets up with a spark of revival.*] Sister, that's what you'll do!

Laura utters a startled, doubtful laugh. She reaches quickly for a piece of glass.

LAURA. But, Mother—

AMANDA. Yes? [*Crossing to photograph.*]

LAURA [*in a tone of frightened apology*]. I'm—crippled!

[*Image: Screen.*]

AMANDA. Nonsense! Laura, I've told you never, never to use that word. Why, you're not crippled, you just have a little defect—hardly noticeable, even! When people have some slight disadvantage like that, they cultivate other things to make up for it—develop charm—and vivacity—and—*charm!* That's all you have to do! [*She turns again to the photograph.*] One thing your father had *plenty of*—was *charm!*

Tom motions to the fiddle in the wings.

[*The Scene Fades out with Music.*]

Scene III

[*Legend on the Screen: "After the Fiasco—"*]
Tom speaks from the fire-escape landing.

TOM. After the fiasco at Rubicam's Business College, the idea of getting a gentleman caller for Laura began to play a more important part in Mother's calculations. It became an obsession. Like some archetype of the universal unconscious, the image of the gentleman caller haunted our small apartment. . . . [*Image: Young Man at Door with Flowers.*] An evening at home rarely passed without some allusion to this image, this specter, this hope. . . . Even when he wasn't mentioned, his presence hung in Mother's preoccupied look and in my sister's frightened, apologetic manner—hung like a sentence passed upon the Wingfields! Mother was a woman of action as well as words. She began to take logical steps in the planned direction. Late that winter and in the early spring—realizing that extra money would be needed to properly feather the nest and plume the bird—she conducted a vigorous campaign on the telephone, roping in subscribers to one of those magazines for matrons called *The Home-maker's Companion,* the type of journal features the serialized sublimations of ladies of letters who think in terms of delicate cuplike breasts, slim, tapering waists, rich, creamy thighs, eyes like wood-smoke in autumn, fingers that soothe and caress like strains of music, bodies as powerful as Etruscan sculpture.

[*Screen Image: Glamor Magazine Cover.*]

Amanda enters with phone on long extension cord. She is spotted in the dim stage.

AMANDA. Ida Scott? This is Amanda Wingfield! We *missed* you at the D.A.R. last Monday! I said to myself: She's probably suffering with that sinus condition! How is that sinus condition? Horrors! Heaven have mercy!—You're a Christian martyr, yes, that's what you are, a Christian martyr! Well, I just now happened to notice that your subscription to the *Companion's* about to expire! Yes, it expires with the next issue, honey!—just when that wonderful new serial by Bessie Mae Hopper is getting off to such an exciting start. Oh, honey, it's something that you can't miss! You remember how *Gone With the Wind* took everybody by storm? You simply couldn't go out if you hadn't read it. All everybody *talked* was Scarlett O'Hara. Well, this is a book that critics already compare to *Gone With the Wind*. It's the *Gone With the Wind* of the post-World War generation!—What?—Burning?—Oh, honey, don't let them burn, go take a look in the oven and I'll hold the wire! Heavens—I think she's hung up!

[*Dim Out.*]

[*Legend on Screen: "You Think I'm in Love with Continental Shoemakers?"*]

Before the stage is lighted, the violent voices of Tom and Amanda are heard. They are quarreling behind the portieres. In front of them stands Laura with clenched hands and panicky expression.

A clear pool of light on her figure throughout this scene.

TOM. What in Christ's name am I—

AMANDA [*shrilly*]. Don't you use that—

TOM. Supposed to do!

AMANDA. Expression! Not in my—

TOM. Ohhh!

AMANDA. Presence! Have you gone out of your senses?

TOM. I have, that's true, *driven* out!

AMANDA. What is the matter with you, you—big—big—IDIOT!

TOM. Look—I've got *no thing*, no single thing—

AMANDA. Lower your voice!

TOM. In my life here that I can call my OWN! Everything is—

AMANDA. Stop that shouting!

TOM. Yesterday you confiscated my books! You had the nerve to—

AMANDA. I took that horrible novel back to the library—yes! That hideous book by that insane Mr. Lawrence. [*Tom laughs wildly.*] I cannot control the output of diseased minds or people who cater to them—[*Tom laughs still more wildly.*] BUT I WON'T ALLOW SUCH FILTH BROUGHT INTO MY HOUSE! No, no, no, no, no!

TOM. House, house! Who pays rent on it, who makes a slave of himself to—

AMANDA [*fairly screeching*]. Don't you DARE to—

TOM. No, no, *I* musn't say things! *I've* got to just—

AMANDA. Let me tell you—

TOM. I don't want to hear any more! [*He tears the portieres open. The up-stage area is lit with a turgid smoky red glow.*]

Amanda's hair is in metal curlers and she wears a very old bathrobe, much too large for her slight figure, a relic of the faithless Mr. Wingfield.

An upright typewriter and a wild disarray of manuscripts are on the drop-leaf table. The quarrel was probably precipitated by Amanda's interruption of his creative labor. A chair lying overthrown on the floor.

Their gesticulating shadows are cast on the ceiling by the fiery glow.

AMANDA. You *will* hear more, you—

TOM. No, I won't hear more, I'm going out!

AMANDA. You come right back in—

TOM. Out, out, out! Because I'm—

AMANDA. Come back here, Tom Wingfield! I'm not through talking to you!

TOM. Oh, go—

LAURA [*desperately*]. Tom!

AMANDA. You're going to listen, and no more insolence from you! I'm at the end of my patience! [*He comes back toward her.*]

TOM. What do you think I'm at? Aren't I supposed to have any patience to reach the end of, Mother? I know, I know. It seems unimportant to you, what I'm *doing*—what I *want* to do—having a little *difference* between them! You don't think that—

AMANDA. I think you've been doing things that you're ashamed of. That's why you act like this. I don't believe that you go every night to the movies. Nobody goes to the movies night after night. Nobody in their right minds goes to the movies as often as you pretend to. People don't go to the movies at nearly midnight, and movies don't let out at two A.M. Come in stumbling. Muttering to yourself like a maniac! You get three hours' sleep and then go to work. Oh, I can picture the way you're doing down there. Moping, doping, because you're in no condition.

TOM [*wildly*]. No, I'm in no condition!

AMANDA. What right have you got to jeopardize your job? Jeopardize the security of us all? How do you think we'd manage if you were—

TOM. Listen! You think I'm crazy *about* the *warehouse*? [*He bends fiercely toward her slight figure.*] You think I'm in love with the Continental Shoemakers? You think I want to spend fifty-five *years* down there in that—*celotex interior!* with—*fluorescent—tubes!* Look! I'd rather somebody picked up a crowbar and battered out my brains—than go back mornings! *I go!* Every time you come in yelling that God damn *"Rise and Shine!" "Rise and Shine!"* I say to myself "How *lucky dead* people are!" But I get up. I *go!* For sixty-five dollars a month I give up all that I dream of doing and being *ever!* And you say self—*self's* all I ever think of. Why, listen, if self is what I thought of, Mother, I'd be where he is— GONE! [*Pointing to father's picture.*] As far as the system of transportation reaches! [*He starts past her. She grabs his arm.*] Don't grab at me, Mother!

AMANDA. Where are you going?

TOM. I'm going to the *movies!*

AMANDA. I don't believe that lie!

TOM [*crouching toward her, overtowering her tiny figure. She backs away, gasping*]. I'm going to opium dens! Yes, opium dens, dens of vice and criminals' hang-outs, Mother. I've joined the Hogan gang, I'm a hired assassin, I carry a tommy-gun in a violin case! I run a string of cat-houses in the Valley! They call me Killer, Killer Wingfield, I'm leading a double-life, a simple, honest warehouse worker by day, by night a dynamic *czar* of the *underworld*, *Mother.* I go to gambling casinos, I spin away fortunes on the roulette table! I wear a patch over one eye and a false mustache, sometimes I put on green whiskers. On those occasions they call me—*El Diablo!* Oh, I could tell you things to make you sleepless! My enemies plan to dynamite this place.

They're going to blow us all sky-high some night! I'll be glad, very happy, and
so will you! You'll go up, up on a broomstick, over Blue Mountain with seventeen gentlemen callers! You ugly—babbling old—*witch.* . . . (*He goes through
a series of violent, clumsy movements, seizing his overcoat, lunging to the door,
pulling it fiercely open. The women watch him, aghast. His arm catches in the
sleeve of the coat as he struggles to pull it on. For a moment he is pinioned by
the bulky garment. With an outraged groan he tears the coat off again, splitting
the shoulders of it, and hurls it across the room. It strikes against the shelf of
Laura's glass collection, there is a tinkle of shattering glass. Laura cries out
as if wounded.*]

[*Music Legend: "The Glass Menagerie."*]

LAURA [*shrilly*]. My glass!—menagerie. . . . [*She covers her face and
turns away.*]

*But Amanda is still stunned and stupefied by the "ugly witch" so that she
barely notices this occurrence. Now she recovers her speech.*

AMANDA [*in an awful voice*]. I won't speak to you—until you apologize!
[*She crosses through portieres and draws them together behind her. Tom is left
with Laura. Laura clings weakly to the mantel with her face averted. Tom stares
at her stupidly for a moment. Then he crosses to shelf. Drops awkwardly to his
knees to collect the fallen glass, glancing at Laura as if he would speak but
couldn't.*)

"The Glass Menagerie" steals in as
[*The Scene Dims Out.*]

SCENE IV

The interior is dark. Faint light in the alley.

*A deep-voiced bell in a church is tolling the hour of five as the scene
commences.*

*Tom appears at the top of the alley. After each solemn boom of the bell in
the tower, he shakes a little noise-maker or rattle as if to express the tiny
spasm of man in contrast to the sustained power and dignity of the Almighty.
This and the unsteadiness of his advance make it evident that he has been
drinking.*

*As he climbs the few steps to the fire-escape landing light steals up in-
side. Laura appears in night-dress, observing Tom's empty bed in the front
room.*

*Tom fishes in his pockets for the door-key, removing a motley assort-
ment of articles in the search, including a perfect shower of movie-ticket stubs
and an empty bottle. At last he finds the key, but just as he is about to in-
sert it, it slips from his fingers. He strikes a match and crouches below the
door.*

TOM [*bitterly*]. One crack—and it falls through!

Laura opens the door.

LAURA. Tom! Tom, what are you doing?

TOM. Looking for a door-key.

LAURA. Where have you been all this time?

TOM. I have been to the movies.

LAURA. All this time at the movies?

TOM. There was a very long program. There was a Garbo picture and a Mickey Mouse and a travelogue and a newsreel and a preview of coming attractions. And there was an organ solo and a collection for the milk-fund—simultaneously—which ended up in a terrible fight between a fat lady and an usher!

LAURA [*innocently*]. Did you have to stay through everything?

TOM. Of course! And, oh, I forgot! There was a big stage show! The headliner on this stage show was Malvolio the Magician. He performed wonderful tricks, many of them, such as pouring water back and forth between pitchers. First it turned to wine and then it turned to beer and then it turned to whiskey. I know it was whiskey it finally turned into because he needed somebody to come up out of the audience to help him, and I came up—both shows! It was Kentucky Straight Bourbon. A very generous fellow, he gave souvenirs. [*He pulls from his back pocket a shimmering rainbow-colored scarf.*] He gave me this. This is his magic scarf. You can have it, Laura. You wave it over a canary cage and you get a bowl of gold-fish. You wave it over the gold-fish bowl and they fly away canaries. . . . But the wonderfullest trick of all was the coffin trick. We nailed him into a coffin and he got out of the coffin without removing one nail. [*He has come inside.*] There is a trick that would come in handy for me—get me out of this 2 by 4 situation! [*Flops onto bed and starts removing shoes.*]

LAURA. Tom—Shhh!

TOM. What you shushing me for?

LAURA. You'll wake up Mother.

TOM. Goody, goody! Pay 'er back for all those "Rise an' Shines." [*Lies down, groaning.*] You know it don't take much intelligence to get yourself into a nailed-up coffin, Laura. But who in hell ever got himself out of one without removing one nail?

As if in answer, the father's grinning photograph lights up.

[*Scene Dims Out.*]

Immediately following: The church bell is heard striking six. At the sixth stroke the alarm clock goes off in Amanda's room, and after a few moments we hear her calling: "Rise and Shine! Rise and Shine! Laura, go tell your brother to rise and shine!"

TOM [*sitting up slowly*]. I'll rise—but I won't shine.

The light increases.

AMANDA. Laura, tell your brother his coffee is ready.

Laura slips into front room.

LAURA. Tom! it's nearly seven. Don't make Mother nervous. [*He stares at her stupidly. Beseechingly.*] Tom, speak to Mother this morning. Make up with her, apologize, speak to her!

TOM. She won't to me. It's her that started not speaking.

LAURA. If you just say you're sorry she'll start speaking.

TOM. Her not speaking—is that such a tragedy?

LAURA. Please—please!

AMANDA [*calling from kitchenette*]. Laura, are you going to do what I asked you to do, or do I have to get dressed and go out myself?

LAURA. Going, going—soon as I get on my coat! [*She pulls on a shapeless* felt hat with nervous, jerky movement, pleadingly glancing at Tom. Rushes awkwardly for coat. The coat is one of Amanda's, inaccurately made-over, the sleeves too short for Laura.] Butter and what else?

AMANDA [*entering upstage*]. Just butter. Tell them to charge it.

LAURA. Mother, they make such faces when I do that.

AMANDA. Sticks and stones may break my bones, but the expression on Mr. Garfinkel's face won't harm us! Tell your brother his coffee is getting cold.

LAURA [*at door*]. Do what I asked you, will you, will you, Tom?

He looks sullenly away.

AMANDA. Laura, go now or just don't go at all!

LAURA [*rushing out*]. Going—going! [*A second later she cries out. Tom springs up and crosses to the door. Amanda rushes anxiously in. Tom opens the door.*]

TOM. Laura?

LAURA. I'm all right. I slipped, but I'm all right.

AMANDA [*peering anxiously after her*]. If anyone breaks a leg on those fire-escape steps, the landlord ought to be sued for every cent he possesses! [*She shuts door. Remembers she isn't speaking and returns to other room.*]

As Tom enters listlessly for his coffee, she turns her back to him and stands rigidly facing the window on the gloomy gray vault of the areaway. Its light on her face with its aged but childish features is cruelly sharp, satirical as a Daumier print.

[*Music Under: "Ave Maria."*]

Tom glances sheepishly but sullenly at her averted figure and slumps at the table. The coffee is scalding hot; he sips it and gasps and spits it back in the cup. At his gasp, Amanda catches her breath and half turns. Then catches herself and turns back to window.

Tom blows on his coffee, glancing sidewise at his mother. She clears her throat. Tom clears his. He starts to rise. Sinks back down again, scratches his head, clears his throat again. Amanda coughs. Tom raises his cup in both hands to blow on it, his eyes staring over the rim of it at his mother for several moments. Then he slowly sets the cup down and awkwardly and hesitantly rises from the chair.

TOM [*hoarsely*]. Mother. I—I apologize. Mother. [*Amanda draws a quick, shuddering breath. Her face works grotesquely. She breaks into childlike tears.*] I'm sorry for what I said, for everything that I said, I didn't mean it.

AMANDA [*sobbingly*]. My devotion has made me a witch and so I make myself hateful to my children!

TOM. No you *don't*.

AMANDA. I worry so much, don't sleep, it makes me nervous!

TOM [*gently*]. I understand that.

AMANDA. I've had to put up a solitary battle all these years. But you're my right-hand bower! Don't fall down, don't fail!

TOM [*gently*]. I try Mother.

AMANDA [*with great enthusiasm*]. Try and you will SUCCEED! [*The notion makes her breathless.*] Why, you—you're just *full* of natural endowments! Both of my children—they're *unusual* children! Don't you think I know it? I'm so—*proud!* Happy and—feel I've—so much to be thankful for but—Promise me one thing, son!

TOM. What, Mother?

AMANDA. Promise, son, you'll—never be a drunkard!

TOM [*turns to her grinning*]. I will never be a drunkard, Mother.

AMANDA. That's what frightened me so, that you'd be drinking! Eat a bowl of Purina!

TOM. Just coffee, Mother.

AMANDA. Shredded wheat biscuit?

TOM. No. No, Mother, just coffee.

AMANDA. You can't put in a day's work on an empty stomach. You've got ten minutes—don't gulp! Drinking too-hot liquids makes cancer of the stomach. . . . Put cream in.

TOM. No, thank you.

AMANDA. To cool it.

TOM. No! No, thank you, I want it black.

AMANDA. I know, but it's not good for you. We have to do all that we can to build ourselves up. In these trying times we live in, all that we have to cling to is—each other. . . . That's why it's so important to—Tom, I—I sent out your sister so I could discuss something with you. If you hadn't spoken I would have spoken to you. [*Sits down.*]

TOM [*gently*]. What is it, Mother, that you want to discuss?

AMANDA. Laura!

Tom puts his cup down slowly.

[*Legend on Screen: "Laura."*]

[*Music: "The Glass Menagerie."*]

TOM. —Oh.—Laura . . .

AMANDA [*touching his sleeve*]. You know how Laura is. So quiet but—still water runs deep! She notices things and I think she—broods about them. [*Tom looks up.*] A few days ago I came in and she was crying.

TOM. What about?

AMANDA. You.

TOM. Me?

AMANDA. She has an idea that you're not happy here.

TOM. What gave her that idea?

AMANDA. What gives her any idea? However, you do act strangely. I—I'm not criticizing, understand *that!* I know your ambitions do not lie in the warehouse, that like everybody in the whole wide world—you've had to—make sacrifices, but—Tom—Tom—life's not easy, it calls for—Spartan endurance! There's so many things in my heart that I cannot describe to you! I've never told you but I—*loved* your father. . . .

TOM [*gently*]. I know that, Mother.

AMANDA. And you—when I see you taking after his ways! Staying out late—and—well, you *had* been drinking the night you were in that—terrifying condition! Laura says that you hate the apartment and that you go out nights to get away from it! Is that true, Tom?

TOM. No. You say there's so much in your heart that you can't describe to me. That's true of me, too. There's so much in my heart that I can't describe to *you!* So let's respect each other's—

AMANDA. But, why—*why*, Tom—are you always so *restless?* Where do you go to, nights?

TOM. I—go to the movies.

AMANDA. Why do you go to the movies so much, Tom?

TOM. I go to the movies because—I like adventure. Adventure is something I don't have much of at work, so I go to the movies.

AMANDA. But, Tom, you go to the movies *entirely too much!*

TOM. I like a lot of adventure.

Amanda looks baffled, then hurt. As the familiar inquisition resumes he becomes hard and impatient again. Amanda slips back into her querulous attitude toward him.

[*Image on Screen: Sailing Vessel with Jolly Roger.*]

AMANDA. Most young men find adventure in their careers.

TOM. Then most young men are not employed in a warehouse.

AMANDA. The world is full of young men employed in warehouses and offices and factories.

TOM. Do all of them find adventure in their careers?

AMANDA. They do or they do without it! Not everybody has a craze for adventure.

TOM. Man is by instinct a lover, a hunter, a fighter, and none of those instincts are given much play at the warehouse!

AMANDA. Man is by instinct! Don't quote instinct to me! Instinct is something that people have got away from! It belongs to animals! Christian adults don't want it!

TOM. What do Christian adults want, then, Mother?

AMANDA. Superior things! Things of the mind and the spirit! Only animals have to satisfy insticts! Surely your aims are somewhat higher than theirs! Than monkeys—pigs—

TOM. I reckon they're not.

AMANDA. You're joking. However, that isn't what I wanted to discuss.

TOM [*rising*]. I haven't much time.

AMANDA [*pushing his shoulders*]. Sit down.

TOM. You want me to punch in red at the warehouse, Mother?

AMANDA. You have five minutes. I want to talk about Laura.

[*Legend: "Plans and Provisions."*]

TOM. All right! What about Laura?

AMANDA. We have to be making plans and provisions for her. She's older than you, two years, and nothing has happened. She just drifts along doing nothing. It frightens me terribly how she just drifts along.

TOM. I guess she's the type that people call home girls.

AMANDA. There's no such type, and if there is, it's a pity! That is unless the home is hers, with a husband!

TOM. What?

AMANDA. Oh, I can see the handwriting on the wall as plain as I see the nose in the front of my face! It's terrifying! More and more you remind me of your father! He was out all hours without explanation—Then *left! Goodbye!* And me with the bag to hold. I saw that letter you got from the Merchant Marine. I know what you're dreaming of. I'm not standing here blindfolded. Very well, then. Then *do* it! But not till there's somebody to take your place.

TOM. What do you mean?

AMANDA. I mean that as soon as Laura has got somebody to take care

of her, married, a home of her own, independent—why, then you'll be free
to go wherever you please, on land, on sea, whichever way the wind blows!
But until that time you've got to look out for your sister. I don't say me because I'm old and don't matter! I say for your sister because she's young and
dependent. I put her in business college—a dismal failure! Frightened her so
it made her sick to her stomach. I took her over to the Young People's League
at the church. Another fiasco. She spoke to nobody, nobody spoke to her.
Now all she does is fool with those pieces of glass and play those worn-out
records. What kind of a life is that for a girl to lead!

TOM. What can I do about it?

AMANDA. Overcome selfishness! Self, self, self is all that you ever think
of! [*Tom springs up and crosses to get his coat. It is ugly and bulky. He pulls
on a cap with earmuffs.*] Where is your muffler? Put your wool muffler on!
[*He snatches it angrily from the closet and tosses it around his neck and pulls
both ends tight.*] Tom! I haven't said what I had in mind to ask you.

TOM. I'm too late to—

AMANDA [*catching his arms—very importunately. Then shyly*]. Down at
the warehouse, aren't there some—nice young men?

TOM. No!

AMANDA. There *must* be—*some*.

TOM. Mother—

Gesture.

AMANDA. Find out one that's clean-living—doesn't drink and—ask him
out for sister!

TOM. What?

AMANDA. For *sister!* To *meet!* Get *acquainted!*

TOM [*stamping to door*]. Oh, my *go-osh!*

AMANDA. Will you? [*He opens door. Imploringly.*] Will you? [*He starts
down.*] Will you? *Will* you dear?

TOM. [*calling back*]. YES!

*Amanda closes the door hesitantly and with a troubled but faintly hopeful
expression.*

[*Screen Image: Glamor Magazine Cover.*]

Spot Amanda at phone.

AMANDA. Ella Cartwright? This is Amanda Wingfield! How are you
honey? How is that kidney condition? [*Count five.*] Horrors! [*Count five.*]
You're a Christian martyr, yes, honey, that's what you are, a Christian martyr!
Well, I just happened to notice in my little red book that your subscription to
the *Companion* has just run out! I knew that you wouldn't want to miss out
on the wonderful serial starting in this new issue. It's by Bessie Mae Hopper,
the first thing she's written since *Honeymoon for Three*. Wasn't that a strange
and interesting story? Well, this one is even lovelier, I believe. It has a
sophisticated society background. It's all about the horsey set on Long Island!

[*Fade Out.*]

SCENE V

[*Legend on Screen: "Annunciation."*] *Fade with music.*

*It is early dusk of a spring evening. Supper has just been finished at the
Wingfield apartment. Amanda and Laura in light colored dresses are removing*

dishes from the table, in the upstage area, which is shadowy, their movements formalized almost as a dance or ritual, their moving forms as pale and silent as moths.

Tom, in white shirt and trousers, rises from the table and crosses toward the fire-escape.

AMANDA [*as he passes her*]. Son, will you do me a favor?

TOM. What?

AMANDA. Comb your hair! You look so pretty when your hair is combed! [*Tom slouches on sofa with evening paper. Enormous caption "Franco Triumphs."*] There is only one respect in which I would like you to emulate your father.

TOM. What respect is that?

AMANDA. The care he always took of his appearance. He never allowed himself to look untidy. [*He throws down the paper and crosses to fire-escape.*] Where are you going?

TOM. I'm going out to smoke.

AMANDA. You smoke too much. A pack a day at fifteen cents a pack. How much would that amount to in a month? Thirty times fifteen is how much, Tom? Figure it out and you will be astounded at what you could save. Enough to give you a night-school course in accounting at Washington U! Just think what a wonderful thing that would be for you, son!

Tom is unmoved by the thought.

TOM. I'd rather smoke. [*He steps out on landing, letting the screen door slam.*]

AMANDA [*sharply*]. I know! That's the tragedy of it. . . . [*Alone, she turns to look at her husband's picture.*]

[*Dance Music: "All the World Is Waiting for the Sunrise!"*]

TOM [*to the audience*]. Across the alley from us was the Paradise Dance Hall. On evenings in spring the windows and doors were open and the music came outdoors. Sometimes the lights were turned out except for a large glass sphere that hung from the ceiling. It would turn slowly about and filter the dusk with delicate rainbow colors. Then the orchestra played a waltz or a tango, something that had a slow and sensuous rhythm. Couples would come outside, to the relative privacy of the alley. You could see them kissing behind ashpits and telephone poles. This was the compensation for lives that passed like mine, without any change or adventure. Adventure and change were imminent in this year. They were waiting around the corner for all these kids. Suspended in the mist over Berchtesgaden, caught in the folds of Chamberlain's umbrella—In Spain there was Guernica! But here there was only hot swing music and liquor, dance halls, bars, and movies, and sex that hung in the gloom like a chandelier and flooded the world with brief, deceptive rainbows. . . . All the world was waiting for bombardments!

Amanda turns from the picture and comes outside.

AMANDA [*sighing*]. A fire-escape landing's a poor excuse for a porch. [*She spreads a newspaper on a step and sits down, gracefully and demurely as if she were settling into a swing on a Mississippi veranda.*] What are you looking at?

TOM. The moon.

AMANDA. Is there a moon this evening?

TOM. It's rising over Garfinkel's Delicatessen.

AMANDA. So it is! A little silver slipper of a moon. Have you made a wish on it yet?

TOM. Um-hum.

AMANDA. What did you wish for?

TOM. That's a secret.

AMANDA. A secret, huh? Well, I won't tell mine either. I will be just as mysterious as you.

TOM. I bet I can guess what yours is.

AMANDA. Is my head so transparent?

TOM. You're not a sphinx.

AMANDA. No, I don't have secrets. I'll tell you what I wished for on the moon. Success and happiness for my precious children! I wish for that whenever there's a moon, and when there isn't a moon, I wish for it, too.

TOM. I thought perhaps you wished for a gentleman caller.

AMANDA. Why do you say that?

TOM. Don't you remember asking me to fetch one?

AMANDA. I remember suggesting that it would be nice for your sister if you brought some nice young man from the warehouse. I think I've made that suggestion more than once.

TOM. Yes, you have made it repeatedly.

AMANDA. Well?

TOM. We are going to have one.

AMANDA. *What?*

TOM. A gentleman caller!

[*The Annunciation Is Celebrated with Music.*]

Amanda rises.

[*Image on Screen: Caller with Bouquet.*]

AMANDA. You mean you have asked some nice young man to come over?

TOM. Yep. I've asked him to dinner.

AMANDA. You really did?

TOM. I did!

AMANDA. You did, and did he—*accept?*

TOM. He did!

AMANDA. Well, well—well, well! That's—lovely!

TOM. I thought that you would be pleased.

AMANDA. It's definite, then?

TOM. Very definite.

AMANDA. Soon?

TOM. Very soon.

AMANDA. For heaven's sake, stop putting on and tell me some things, will you?

TOM. What things do you want me to tell you?

AMANDA. Naturally I would like to know when he's *coming!*

TOM. He's coming tomorrow.

AMANDA. *Tomorrow?*

TOM. Yep. Tomorrow.

AMANDA. But, Tom!

TOM. Yes, Mother?

AMANDA. Tomorrow gives me no time!

TOM. Time for what?

AMANDA. Preparations! Why didn't you phone me at once, as soon as you asked him, the minute that he accepted? Then, don't you see, I could have been getting ready!

TOM. You don't have to make any fuss.

AMANDA. Oh, Tom, Tom, Tom, of course I have to make a fuss! I want things nice, not sloppy! Not thrown together. I'll certainly have to do some fast thinking, won't I?

TOM. I don't see why you have to think at all.

AMANDA. You just don't know. We can't have a gentleman caller in a pigsty! All my wedding silver has to be polished, the monogrammed table linen ought to be laundered! The windows have to be washed and fresh curtains put up. And how about clothes? We have to *wear* something, don't we?

TOM. Mother, this boy is no one to make a fuss over!

AMANDA. Do you realize he's the first young man we've introduced to your sister? It's terrible, dreadful, disgraceful that poor little sister has never received a single gentleman caller! Tom, come inside! [*She opens the screen door.*]

TOM. What for?

AMANDA. I want to ask you some things.

TOM. If you're going to make such a fuss, I'll call it off, I'll tell him not to come.

AMANDA. You certainly won't do anything of the kind. Nothing offends people worse than broken engagements. It simply means I'll have to work like a Turk! We won't be brilliant, but we'll pass inspection. Come on inside. [*Tom follows, groaning.*] Sit down.

TOM. Any particular place you would like me to sit?

AMANDA. Thank heavens I've got that new sofa! I'm also making payments on a floor lamp I'll have sent out! And put the chintz covers on, they'll brighten things up! Of course I'd hoped to have these walls repapered. . . . What is the young man's name?

TOM. His name is O'Connor.

AMANDA. That, of course, means fish—tomorrow is Friday! I'll have that salmon loaf—with Durkee's dressing! What does he do? He works at the warehouse?

TOM. Of course! How else would I—

AMANDA. Tom, he—doesn't drink?

TOM. Why do you ask me that?

AMANDA. Your father *did!*

TOM. Don't get started on that!

AMANDA. He *does* drink, then?

TOM. Not that I know of!

AMANDA. Make sure, be certain! The last thing I want for my daughter's a boy who drinks!

TOM. Aren't you being a little premature? Mr. O'Connor has not yet appeared on the scene!

AMANDA. But will tomorrow. To meet your sister, and what do I know about his character? Nothing! Old maids are better off than wives of drunkards!

TOM. Oh, my God!

AMANDA. Be still!

TOM [*leaning forward to whisper*]. Lots of fellows meet girls whom they don't marry!

AMANDA. Oh, talk sensibly, Tom—and don't be sarcastic! [*She has gotten a hairbrush.*]

TOM. What are you doing?

AMANDA. I'm brushing that cow-lick down! What is this young man's position at the warehouse?

TOM [*submitting grimly to the brush and the interrogation*]. This young man's position is that of a shipping clerk, Mother.

AMANDA. Sounds to me like a fairly responsible job, the sort of a job *you* would be in if you just had more *get-up*. What is his salary? Have you got any idea?

TOM. I would judge it to be approximately eighty-five dollars a month.

AMANDA. Well—not princely, but—

TOM. Twenty more than I make.

AMANDA. Yes, how well I know! But for a family man, eighty-five dollars a month is not much more than you can just get by on. . . .

TOM. Yes, but Mr. O'Connor is not a family man.

AMANDA. He might be, mightn't he? Some time in the future?

TOM. I see. Plans and provisions.

AMANDA. You are the only man that I know of who ignores the fact that the future becomes the present, the present the past, and the past turns into everlasting regret if you don't plan for it!

TOM. I will think that over and see what I can make of it.

AMANDA. Don't be supercilious with your mother! Tell me some more about this—what do you call him?

TOM. James D. O'Connor. The D. is for Delaney.

AMANDA. Irish on *both* sides! *Gracious!* And doesn't drink?

TOM. Shall I call him up and ask him right this minute?

AMANDA. The only way to find out about those things is to make discreet inquiries at the proper moment. When I was a girl in Blue Mountain and it was suspected that a young man drank, the girl whose attentions he had been receiving, if any girl *was*, would sometimes speak to the minister of his church, or rather her father would if her father was living, and sort of feel him out on the young man's character. That is the way such things are discreetly handled to keep a younng woman from making a tragic mistake!

TOM. Then how did you happen to make a tragic mistake?

AMANDA. That innocent look of your father's had everyone fooled! He *smiled*—the world was *enchanted!* No girl can do worse than put herself at the mercy of a handsome appearance! I hope that Mr. O'Connor is not too good-looking.

TOM. No, he's not too good-looking. He's covered with freckles and hasn't too much of a nose.

AMANDA. He's not right-down homely, though?

TOM. Not right-down homely. Just medium homely, I'd say.

AMANDA. Character's what to look for in a man.

TOM. That's what I've always said, Mother.

AMANDA. You've never said anything of the kind and I suspect you would never give it a thought.

TOM. Don't be suspicious of me.

AMANDA. At least I hope he's the type that's up and coming.

TOM. I think he really goes in for self-improvement.

AMANDA. What reason have you to think so?

TOM. He goes to night school.

AMANDA [*beaming*]. Splendid! What does he do, I mean study?

TOM. Radio engineering and public speaking!

AMANDA. Then he has visions of being advanced in the world! Any young man who studies public speaking is aiming to have an executive job some day! And radio engineering? A thing for the future! Both of these facts are very illuminating. Those are the sort of things that a mother should know concerning any young man who comes to call on her daughter. Seriously or—not.

TOM. One little warning. He doesn't know about Laura. I didn't let on that we had dark ulterior motives. I just said, why don't you come have dinner with us? He said okay and that was the whole conversation.

AMANDA. I bet it was! You're eloquent as an oyster. However, he'll know about Laura when he gets here. When he sees how lovely and sweet and pretty she is, he'll thank his lucky stars he was asked to dinner.

TOM. Mother, you mustn't expect too much of Laura.

AMANDA. What do you mean?

TOM. Laura seems all those things to you and me because she's ours and we love her. We don't even notice she's crippled any more.

AMANDA. Don't say crippled! You know that I never allow that word to be used!

TOM. But face facts, Mother. She is and—that's not all—

AMANDA. What do you mean "not all"?

TOM. Laura is very different from other girls.

AMANDA. I think the difference is all to her advantage.

TOM. Not quite all—in the eyes of others—strangers—she's terribly shy and lives in a world of her own and those things make her seem a little peculiar to people outside the house.

AMANDA. Don't say peculiar.

TOM. Face the facts. She is.

[*The Dance-Hall Music Changes to a Tango that Has a Minor and Somewhat Ominous Tone.*]

AMANDA. In what way is she peculiar—may I ask?

TOM [*gently*]. She lives in a world of her own—a world of—little glass ornaments, Mother. . . . [*Gets up. Amanda remains holding brush, looking at him, troubled.*] She plays old phonograph records and—that's about all—[*He glances at himself in the mirror and crosses to door.*]

AMANDA [*sharply*]. Where are you going?

TOM. I'm going to the movies. [*Out screen door.*]

AMANDA. Not to the movies, every night to the movies! [*Follows quickly* to screen door.] I don't believe you always go to the movies! [*He is gone. Amanda looks worriedly after him for a moment. Then vitality and optimism return and she turns from the door. Crossing to portieres.*] Laura! Laura! [*Laura answers from kitchenette.*]

LAURA. Yes, Mother.

AMANDA. Let those dishes go and come in front! [*Laura appears with dish towel. Gaily.*] Laura, come here and make a wish on the moon!

LAURA [*entering*]. Moon—moon?

AMANDA. A little silver slipper of a moon. Look over your left shoulder, Laura, and make a wish! [*Laura looks faintly puzzled as if called out of sleep. Amanda seizes her shoulders and turns her at angle by the door.*] Now! Now, darling, *wish!*

LAURA. What shall I wish for, Mother?

AMANDA [*her voice trembling and her eyes suddenly filling with tears*]. Happiness! Good Fortune!

The violin rises and the stage dims out.

SCENE VI

[*Image: High School Hero.*]

TOM. And so the following evening I brought Jim home to dinner. I had known Jim slightly in high school. In high school Jim was a hero. He had tremendous Irish good nature and vitality with the scrubbed and polished look of white chinaware. He seemed to move in a continual spotlight. He was a star in basketball, captain of the debating club, president of the senior class and the glee club and he sang the male lead in the annual light operas. He was always running or bounding, never just walking. He seemed always at the point of defeating the law of gravity. He was shooting with such velocity through his adolescence that you would logically expect him to arrive at nothing short of the White House by the time he was thirty. But Jim apparently ran into more interference after his graduation from Soldan. His speed had definitely slowed. Six years after he left high school he was holding a job that wasn't much better than mine.

[*Image: Clerk.*]

He was the only one at the warehouse with whom I was on friendly terms. I was valuable to him as someone who could remember his former glory, who had seen him win basketball games and the silver cup in debating. He knew of my secret practice of retiring to a cabinet of the washroom to work on poems when business was slack in the warehouse. He called me Shakespeare. And while the other boys in the warehouse regarded me with suspicious hostility, Jim took a humorous attitude toward me. Gradually his attitude affected the others, their hostility wore off and they also began to smile at me as people smile at an oddly fashioned dog who trots across their path at some distance.

I knew that Jim and Laura had known each other at Soldan, and I had heard Laura speak admiringly of his voice. I didn't know if Jim remembered her or not. In high school Laura had been as unobtrusive as Jim had been astonishing. If he did remember Laura, it was not as my sister, for when I asked him to dinner, he grinned and said, "You know, Shakespeare, I never thought of you as having folks!"

He was about to discover that I did. . . .

[*Light up Stage.*]

[*Legend on Screen: "The Accent of a Coming Foot."*]

Friday evening. It is about five o'clock of a late spring evening which comes "scattering poems in the sky."

A delicate lemony light is in the Wingfield apartment.

Amanda has worked like a Turk in preparation for the gentleman caller. The results are astonishing. The new floor lamp with its rose-silk shade is in place, a colored paper lantern conceals the broken light fixture in the ceiling, new billowing white curtains are at the windows, chintz covers are on chairs and sofa, a pair of new sofa pillows make their initial appearance.

Open boxes and tissue paper are scattered on the floor.

Laura stands in the middle with lifted arms while Amanda crouches before her, adjusting the hem of the new dress, devout and ritualistic. The dress is colored and designed by memory. The arrangement of Laura's hair is changed; it is softer and more becoming. A fragile, unearthly prettiness has come out in Laura: she is like a piece of translucent glass touched by light, given a momentary radiance, not actual, not lasting.

AMANDA [*impatiently*]. Why are you trembling?

LAURA. Mother, you've made me so nervous!

AMANDA. How have I made you nervous?

LAURA. By all this fuss! You make it seem so important!

AMANDA. I don't understand you, Laura. You couldn't be satisfied with just sitting home, and yet whenever I try to arrange something for you, you seem to resist it. [*She gets up.*] Now take a look at yourself. No, wait! Wait just a moment—I have an idea!

LAURA. What is it now?

Amanda produces two powder puffs which she wraps in handkerchiefs and stuffs in Laura's bosom.

LAURA. Mother, what are you doing?

AMANDA. They call them "Gay Deceivers"!

LAURA. I won't wear them!

AMANDA. You will!

LAURA. Why should I?

AMANDA. Because, to be painfully honest, your chest is flat.

LAURA. You make it seem like we were setting a trap.

AMANDA. All pretty girls are a trap, a pretty trap, and men expect them to be. [*Legend: "A Pretty Trap."*] Now look at yourself, young lady. This is the prettiest you will ever be! I've got to fix myself now! You're going to be surprised by your mother's appearance! [*She crosses through portieres, humming gaily.*]

Laura moves slowly to the long mirror and stares solemnly at herself.

A wind blows the white curtains inward in a slow, graceful motion and with a faint, sorrowful sighing.

AMANDA [*off stage*]. It isn't dark enough yet. [*She turns slowly before the mirror with a troubled look.*]

[*Legend on Screen: "This Is My Sister: Celebrate Her with Strings!"
Music.*]

AMANDA [*laughing, off*]. I'm going to show you something. I'm going to
make a spectacular appearance!

LAURA. What is it, Mother?

AMANDA. Possess your soul in patience—you will see! Something I've
resurrected from that old trunk! Styles haven't changed so terribly much after
all. . . . [*She parts the portieres.*] Now just look at your mother! [*She wears
a girlish frock of yellowed voile with a blue silk sash. She carries a bunch of
jonquils—the legend of her youth is nearly revived. Feverishly.*] This is the
dress in which I led the cotillion. Won the cakewalk twice at Sunset Hill, wore
one spring to the Governor's ball in Jackson! See how I sashayed around the
ballroom, Laura? [*She raises her skirt and does a mincing step around the
room.*] I wore it on Sundays for my gentlemen callers! I had it on the day I
met your father—I had malaria fever all that spring. The change of climate
from East Tennessee to the Delta—weakened resistance—I had a little temperature all the time—not enough to be serious—just enough to make me
restless and giddy! Invitations poured in—parties all over the Delta!—"Stay in
bed," said Mother, "you have fever!"—but I just wouldn't.—I took quinine but
kept on going, going!—Evenings, dances!—Afternoons, long, long rides!
Picnics—lovely!—So lovely, that country in May.—All lacy with dogwood, literally flooded with jonquils!—That was the spring I had the craze for jonquils.
Jonquils became an absolute obsession. Mother said, "Honey, there's no
more room for jonquils." And still I kept bringing in more jonquils. Whenever,
wherever I saw them, I'd say, "Stop! Stop! I see jonquils!" I made the young
men help me gather the jonquils! It was a joke, Amanda and her jonquils! Finally there were no more vases to hold them, every available space was filled
with jonquils. No vases to hold them? All right, I'll hold them myself! And then
I—[*She stops in front of the picture.*] [*Music.*] met your father! Malaria fever
and jonquils and then—this—boy. . . . [*She switches on the rose-colored
lamp.*] I hope they get here before it starts to rain. [*She crosses upstage and
places the jonquils in bowl on table.*] I gave your brother a little extra change
so he and Mr. O'Connor could take the service car home.

LAURA [*with altered look*]. What did you say his name was?

AMANDA. O'Connor.

LAURA. What is his first name?

AMANDA. I don't remember. Oh, yes, I do. It was—Jim!

Laura sways slightly and catches hold of a chair.

[*Legend on Screen: "Not Jim!"*]

LAURA [*faintly*]. Not—Jim!

AMANDA. Yes, that was it, it was Jim! I've never known a Jim that wasn't
nice!

[*Music: Ominous.*]

LAURA. Are you sure his name is Jim O'Connor?

AMANDA. Yes. Why?

LAURA. Is he the one that Tom used to know in high school?

AMANDA. He didn't say so. I think he just got to know him at the
warehouse.

LAURA. There was a Jim O'Connor we both knew in high school—[*Then, with effort.*] If that is the one that Tom is bringing to dinner—you'll have to excuse me, I won't come to the table.

AMANDA. What sort of nonsense is this?

LAURA. You asked me once if I'd ever liked a boy. Don't you remember I showed you this boy's picture?

AMANDA. You mean the boy you showed me in the year book?

LAURA. Yes, that boy.

AMANDA. Laura, Laura, were you in love with that boy?

LAURA. I don't know, Mother. All I know is I couldn't sit at the table if it was him!

AMANDA. It won't be him! It isn't the least bit likely. But whether it is or not, you will come to the table. You will not be excused.

LAURA. I'll have to be, Mother.

AMANDA. I don't intend to humor your silliness, Laura. I've had too much from you and your brother, both! So just sit down and compose yourself till they come. Tom has forgotten his key so you'll have to let them in, when they arrive.

LAURA [*panicky*]. Oh, Mother—*you* answer the door!

AMANDA [*lightly*]. I'll be in the kitchen—busy!

LAURA. Oh, Mother, please answer the door, don't make me do it!

AMANDA [*crossing into kitchenette*]. I've got to fix the dressing for the salmon. Fuss, fuss—silliness!—over a gentleman caller!

Door swings shut. Laura is left alone.

[*Legend: "Terror!"*]

She utters a low moan and turns off the lamp—sits stiffly on the edge of the sofa, knotting her fingers together.

[*Legend on Screen: "The Opening of a Door!"*]

Tom and Jim appear on the fire-escape steps and climb to landing. Hearing their approach, Laura rises with a panicky gesture. She retreats to the portieres.

The doorbell. Laura catches her breath and touches her throat. Low drums.

AMANDA [*calling*]. Laura, sweetheart! The door!

Laura stares at it without moving.

JIM. I think we just beat the rain.

TOM. Uh-huh. [*He rings again, nervously. Jim whistles and fishes for a cigarette.*]

AMANDA [*very, very gaily*]. Laura, that is your brother and Mr. O'Connor! Will you let them in, darling?

Laura crosses toward kitchenette door.

LAURA [*breathlessly*]. Mother—you go to the door!

Amanda steps out of kitchenette and stares furiously at Laura. She points imperiously at the door.

LAURA. Please, please!

AMANDA [*in a fierce whisper*]. What is the matter with you, you silly thing?

LAURA [*desperately*]. Please, you answer it, *please!*

AMANDA. I told you I wasn't going to humor you, Laura. Why have you chosen this moment to lose your mind?

LAURA. Please, please, please, you go!

AMANDA. You'll have to go to the door because I can't!

LAURA [*despairingly*]. I can't either!

AMANDA. Why?

LAURA. I'm *sick!*

AMANDA. I'm sick, too—of your nonsense! Why can't you and your brother be normal people? Fantastic whims and behavior! [*Tom gives a long ring.*] Preposterous goings on! Can you give me one reason—[*Calls out lyrically.*] COMING! JUST ONE SECOND!—why should you be afraid to open a door? Now you answer it, Laura!

LAURA. Oh, oh, oh . . . [*She returns through the portieres. Darts to the victrola and winds it frantically and turns it on.*]

AMANDA. Laura Wingfield, you march right to that door!

LAURA. Yes—yes, Mother!

A faraway, scratchy rendition of "Dardanella" softens the air and gives her strength to move through it. She slips to the door and draws it cautiously open. Tom enters with caller, Jim O'Connor.

TOM. Laura, this is Jim. Jim, this is my sister, Laura.

JIM [*stepping inside*]. I didn't know that Shakespeare had a sister!

LAURA [*retreating stiff and trembling from the door*]. How—how do you do?

JIM [*heartily extending his hand*]. Okay!

Laura touches it hesitantly with hers.

JIM. Your hand's *cold*, Laura!

LAURA. Yes, well—I've been playing the victrola. . . .

JIM. Must have been playing classical music on it! You ought to play a little hot swing music to warm you up!

LAURA. Excuse me—I haven't finished playing the victrola. . . .

She turns awkwardly and hurries into the front room. She pauses a second by the victrola. Then catches her breath and darts through the portieres like a frightened deer.

JIM [*grinning*]. What was the matter?

TOM. Oh—with Laura? Laura is—terribly shy.

JIM. Shy, huh? It's unusual to meet a shy girl nowadays. I don't believe you ever mentioned you had a sister.

TOM. Well, now you know. I have one. Here is the *Post Dispatch*. You want a piece of it?

JIM. Uh-huh.

TOM. What piece? The comics?

JIM. Sports! [*Glances at it.*] Ole Dizzy Dean is on his bad behavior.

TOM [*disinterest*]. Yeah? [*Lights cigarette and crosses back to fire-escape door.*]

JIM. Where are *you* going?

TOM. I'm going out on the terrace.

JIM [*goes after him*]. You know, Shakespeare—I'm going to sell you a bill of goods!

TOM. What goods?

JIM. A course I'm taking.

TOM. Huh?

JIM. In public speaking! You and me, we're not the warehouse type.

TOM. Thanks—that's good news. But what has public speaking got to do with it?

JIM. It fits you for—executive positions!

TOM. Awww.

JIM. I tell you it's done a helluva lot for me.

[*Image: Executive at Desk.*]

TOM. In what respect?

JIM. In every! Ask yourself what is the difference between you an' me and men in the office down front? Brains?—No!—Ability?—No! Then what? Just one little thing—

TOM. What is that one little thing?

JIM. Primarily it amounts to—social poise! Being able to square up to people and hold your own on any social level!

AMANDA [*off stage*]. Tom?

TOM. Yes, Mother?

AMANDA. Is that you and Mr. O'Connor?

TOM. Yes, Mother.

AMANDA. Well, you just make yourselves comfortable in there.

TOM. Yes, Mother.

AMANDA. Ask Mr. O'Connor if he would like to wash his hands.

JIM. Aw—no—no—thank you—I took care of that at the warehouse. Tom—

TOM. Yes?

JIM. Mr. Mendoza was speaking to me about you.

TOM. Favorably?

JIM. What do you think?

TOM. Well—

JIM. You're going to be out of a job if you don't wake up.

TOM. I am waking up—

JIM. You show no signs.

TOM. The signs are interior.

[*Image on Screen: The Sailing Vessel with Jolly Roger Again.*]

TOM. I'm planning to change. [*He leans over the rail speaking with quiet exhilaration. The incandescent marquees and signs of the first-run movie houses light his face from across the alley. He looks like a voyager.*] I'm right at the point of committing myself to a future that doesn't include the warehouse and Mr. Mendoza or even a night-school course in public speaking.

JIM. What are you gassing about?

TOM. I'm tired of the movies.

JIM. Movies!

TOM. Yes, movies! Look at them—[*a wave toward the marvels of Grand Avenue.*] All of those glamorous people—having adventures—hogging it all, gobbling the whole thing up! You know what happens? People go to the *movies* instead of *moving*! Hollywood characters are supposed to have all the adventures for everybody in America, while everybody in America sits in a dark room and watches them have them! Yes, until there's a war. That's when adventure becomes available to the masses! *Everyone's* dish, not only Gable's!

Then the people in the dark room come out of the dark room to have some adventures themselves—Goody, goody—It's our turn now, to go to the South Sea Island—to make a safari—to be exotic, far-off—But I'm not patient. I don't want to wait till then. I'm tired of the *movies* and I am *about* to *move!*

JIM [*incredulously*]. Move?

TOM. Yes.

JIM. When?

TOM. Soon!

JIM. Where? Where?

[*Theme Three: Music Seems to Answer the Question, while Tom Thinks it Over. He Searches among his Pockets.*]

TOM. I'm starting to boil inside. I know I seem dreamy, but inside—well, I'm boiling! Whenever I pick up a shoe, I shudder a little thinking how short life is and what I am doing!—Whatever that means. I know it doesn't mean shoes—except as something to wear on a traveler's feet [*Finds paper.*] Look—

JIM. What?

TOM. I'm a member.

JIM [*reading*]. The Union of Merchant Seamen.

TOM. I paid my dues this month, instead of the light bill.

JIM. You will regret it when they turn the lights off.

TOM. I won't be here.

JIM. How about your mother?

TOM. I'm like my father. The bastard son of a bastard! See how he grins? And he's been absent going on sixteen years!

JIM. You're just talking, you drip. How does your mother feel about it?

TOM. Shhh—Here comes Mother! Mother is not acquainted with my plans!

AMANDA [*enters portieres*]. Where are you all?

TOM. On the terrace, Mother.

They start inside. She advances to them. Tom is distinctly shocked at her appearance. Even Jim blinks a little. He is making his first contact with girlish Southern vivacity and in spite of the nightschool course in public speaking is somewhat thrown off the beam by the unexpected outlay of social charm.

Certain responses are attempted by Jim but are swept aside by Amanda's gay laughter and chatter. Tom is embarrassed but after the first shock Jim reacts very warmly. Grins and chuckles, is altogether won over.

[*Image: Amanda as a Girl.*]

AMANDA [*coyly smiling, shaking her girlish ringlets*]. Well, well, well, so this is Mr. O'Connor. Introductions entirely unnecessary. I've heard so much about you from my boy. I finally said to him, Tom—good gracious!—why don't you bring this paragon to supper? I'd like to meet this nice young man at the warehouse!—Instead of just hearing him sing your praises so much! I don't know why my son is so standoffish—that's not Southern behavior! Let's sit down and—I think we could stand a little more air in here! Tom, leave the door open. I felt a nice fresh breeze a moment ago. Where has it gone? Mmm, so warm already! And not quite summer, even. We're going to burn up when summer really gets started. However, we're having—we're having a very light supper. I think light things are better fo' this time of year. The same as light clothes are. Light clothes an' light food are what warm weather calls fo'. You know our blood gets so thick during th' winter—it takes a while fo' us to *adjust* ou'selves!—when the season changes . . . It's come so quick this year. I wasn't prepared. All of a sudden—heavens! Already summer!—I ran to the trunk an' pulled out this light dress—Terribly old! Historical almost! But feels so good—so good an' co-ol, y'know. . . .

TOM. Mother—

AMANDA. Yes, honey?

TOM. How about—supper?

AMANDA. Honey, you go ask Sister if supper is ready! You know that Sister is in full charge of supper! Tell her you hungry boys are waiting for it. [*To Jim.*] Have you met Laura?

JIM. She—

AMANDA. Let you in? Oh, good, you've met already! It's rare for a girl as sweet an' pretty as Laura to be domestic! But Laura is, thank heavens, not only pretty but also very domestic. I'm not at all. I never was a bit. I never could make a thing but angel-food cake. Well, in the South we had so many servants. Gone, gone, gone. All vestiges of gracious living! Gone completely! I wasn't prepared for what the future brought me. All of my gentlemen callers were sons of planters and so of course I assumed that I would be married to one and raise my family on a large piece of land with plenty of servants. But man proposes—and woman accepts the proposal!—To vary that old, old saying a little bit—I married no planter! I married a man who worked for the telephone company!—that gallantly smiling gentleman over there! [*Points to the picture.*] A telephone man who—fell in love with long distance!—Now he travels and I don't even know where!—But what am I going on for about my—tribulations! Tell me yours—I hope you don't have any! Tom?

TOM [*returning*]. Yes, Mother?

AMANDA. Is supper nearly ready?

TOM. It looks to me like supper is on the table.

AMANDA. Let me look—[*She rises prettily and looks through portieres.*] Oh, lovely—But where is Sister?

TOM. Laura is not feeling well and she says that she thinks she'd better not come to the table.

AMANDA. What?—Nonsense!—Laura? Oh, Laura!

LAURA [*off stage, faintly*]. Yes, Mother.

AMANDA. You really must come to the table. We won't be seated until you come to the table! Come in, Mr. O'Connor. You sit over there and I'll—Laura? Laura Wingfield! You're keeping us waiting, honey! We can't say grace until you come to the table!

The back door is pushed weakly open and Laura comes in. She is obviously quite faint, her lips trembling, her eyes wide and staring. She moves unsteadily toward the table.

[*Legend: "Terror!"*]

Outside a summer storm is coming abruptly. The white curtains billow inward at the windows and there is a sorowful murmur and deep blue dusk.

Laura suddenly stumbles—She catches a chair with a faint moan.

TOM. Laura!

AMANDA. Laura! [*There is a clap of thunder.*] [*Legend: "Ah!"*] [*Despairingly.*] Why, Laura, you *are* sick, darling! Tom, help your sister into the living room, dear! Sit in the living room, Laura—rest on the sofa. Well! [*To the gentleman caller.*] Standing over the hot stove made her ill!—I told her that it was just too warm this evening, but—[*Tom comes back in. Laura is on the sofa.*] Is Laura all right now?

TOM. Yes.

AMANDA. What *is* that? Rain? A nice cool rain has come up! [*She gives the gentleman caller a frightened look.*] I think we may—have grace—now . . . [*Tom looks at her stupidly.*] Tom, honey—you say grace!

TOM. Oh . . . "For these and all thy mercies—" [*They bow their heads, Amanda stealing a nervous glance at Jim. In the living room Laura, stretched on the sofa, clenches her hand to her lips, to hold back a shuddering sob.*] God's Holy Name be praised—

[*The Scene Dims Out.*]

SCENE VII

A Souvenir

Half an hour later. Dinner is just being finished in the upstage area which is concealed by the drawn portieres.

As the curtain rises Laura is still huddled upon the sofa, her feet drawn under her, her head resting on a pale blue pillow, her eyes wide and mysteriously watchful. The new floor lamp with its shade of rose-colored silk gives a soft, becoming light to her face, bringing out the fragile, unearthly prettiness which usually escapes attention. There is a steady murmur of rain, but it is slackening and stops soon after the scene begins; the air outside becomes pale and luminous as the moon breaks out.

A moment after the curtain rises, the lights in both rooms flicker and go out.

JIM. Hey, there, Mr. Light Bulb!

Amanda laughs nervously.

[*Legend: "Suspension of a Public Service."*]

AMANDA. Where was Moses when the lights went out? Ha-ha. Do you know the answer to that one, Mr. O'Connor?

JIM. No, Ma'am, what's the answer?

AMANDA. In the dark! [*Jim laughs appreciatively.*] Everybody sit still. I'll light the candles. Isn't it lucky we have them on the table? Where's a match? Which of you gentlemen can provide a match?

JIM. Here.

AMANDA. Thank you, sir.

JIM. Not at all, Ma'am!

AMANDA. I guess the fuse has burnt out. Mr. O'Connor, can you tell a burnt-out fuse? I know I can't and Tom is a total loss when it comes to mechanics. [*Sound: Getting Up: Voices Recede a Little to Kitchenette.*] Oh, be careful you don't bump into something. We don't want our gentleman caller to break his neck. Now wouldn't that be a fine howdy-do?

JIM. Ha-ha! Where is the fuse-box?

AMANDA. Right here next to the stove. Can you see anything?

JIM. Just a minute.

AMANDA. Isn't electricity a mysterious thing? Wasn't it Benjamin Franklin who tied a key to a kite? We live in such a mysterious universe, don't we? Some people say that science clears up all the mysteries for us. In my opinion it only creates more! Have you found it yet?

JIM. No, Ma'am. All these fuses look okay to me.

AMANDA. Tom!

TOM. Yes, Mother?

AMANDA. That light bill I gave you several days ago. The one I told you we got the notices about?

TOM. Oh.—Yeah.

[*Legend: "Ha!"*]

AMANDA. You didn't neglect to pay it by any chance?

TOM. Why, I—

AMANDA. Didn't! I might have known it!

JIM. Shakespeare probably wrote a poem on that light bill, Mrs. Wingfield.

AMANDA. I might have known better than to trust him with it! There's such a high price for negligence in this world!

JIM. Maybe the poem will win a ten-dollar prize.

AMANDA. We'll just have to spend the remainder of the evening in the nineteenth century, before Mr. Edison made the Mazda lamp!

JIM. Candlelight is my favorite kind of light.

AMANDA. That shows you're romantic! But that's no excuse for Tom. Well, we got through dinner. Very considerate of them to let us get through dinner before they plunged us into everlasting darkness, wasn't it, Mr. O'Connor?

JIM. Ha-ha!

AMANDA. Tom, as a penalty for your carelessness you can help me with the dishes.

JIM. Let me give you a hand.

AMANDA. Indeed you will not!

JIM. I ought to be good for something.

AMANDA. Good for something? [*Her tone is rhapsodic.*] *You?* Why, Mr. O'Connor, nobody, *nobody's* given me this much entertainment in years—as you have!

JIM. Aw, now, Mrs. Wingfield!

AMANDA. I'm not exaggerating, not one bit! But Sister is all by her lonesome. You go keep her company in the parlor! I'll give you this lovely old candelabrum that used to be on the altar at the church of the Heavenly Rest. It was melted a little out of shape when the church burnt down. Lightning struck it one spring. Gypsy Jones was holding a revival at the time and he intimated that the church was destroyed because the Episcopalians gave card parties.

JIM. Ha-ha.

AMANDA. And how about coaxing Sister to drink a little wine? I think it would be good for her! Can you carry both at once?

JIM. Sure. I'm Superman!

AMANDA. Now, Thomas, get into this apron!

The door of kitchenette swings closed on Amanda's gay laughter; the flickering light approaches the portieres.

Laura sits up nervously as he enters. Her speech at first is low and breathless from the almost intolerable strain of being alone with a stranger.

[*Legend: "I Don't Suppose You Remember Me at All!"*]

In her first speeches in this scene, before Jim's warmth overcomes her paralyzing shyness, Laura's voice is thin and breathless as though she has run up a steep flight of stairs.

Jim's attitude is gently humorous. In playing this scene it should be stressed that while the incident is apparently unimportant, it is to Laura the climax of her secret life.

JIM. Hello, there, Laura.

LAURA [*faintly*]. Hello. [*She clears her throat.*]

JIM. How are you feeling now? Better?

LAURA. Yes. Yes, thank you.

JIM. This is for you. A little dandelion wine. [*He extends it toward her with extravagant gallantry.*]

LAURA. Thank you.

JIM. Drink it—but don't get drunk! [*He laughs heartily. Laura takes the glass uncertainly; laughs shyly.*] Where shall I set the candles?

LAURA. Oh—oh, anywhere . . .

JIM. How about here on the floor? Any objections?

LAURA. No.

JIM. I'll spread a newspaper under to catch the drippings. I like to sit on the floor. Mind if I do?

LAURA. Oh, no.

JIM. Give me a pillow?

LAURA. What?

JIM. A pillow!

LAURA. Oh . . . [*Hands him one quickly.*]

JIM. How about you? Don't you like to sit on the floor?

LAURA. Oh—yes.

JIM. Why don't you, then?

LAURA. I—will.

JIM. Take a pillow! [*Laura does. Sits on the other side of the candelabrum. Jim crosses his legs and smiles engagingly at her.*] I can't hardly see you sitting way over there.

LAURA. I can—see you.

JIM. I know, but that's not fair, I'm in the limelight. [*Laura moves her pillow closer.*] Good! Now I can see you! Comfortable?

LAURA. Yes.

JIM. So am I. Comfortable as a cow. Will you have some gum?

LAURA. No, thank you.

JIM. I think that I will indulge, with your permission. [*Musingly unwraps it and holds it up.*] Think of the fortune made by the guy that invented the first piece of chewing gum. Amazing, huh? The Wrigley Building is one of the sights of Chicago.—I saw it summer before last when I went up to the Century of Progress. Did you take in the Century of Progress?

LAURA. No, I didn't.

JIM. Well, it was quite a wonderful exposition. What impressed me most was the Hall of Science. Gives you an idea of what the future will be in America, even more wonderful than the present time is! [*Pause. Smiling at her.*] Your brother tells me you're shy. Is that right, Laura?

LAURA. I—don't know.

JIM. I judge you to be an old-fashioned type of girl. Well, I think that's a pretty good type to be. Hope you don't think I'm being too personal—do you?

LAURA [*hastily, out of embarrassment*]. I believe I *will* take a piece of gum, if you—don't mind. [*Clearing her throat.*] Mr. O'Connor, have you—kept up with your singing?

JIM. Singing? Me?

LAURA. Yes. I remember what a beautiful voice you had.

JIM. When did you hear me sing?

[*Voice Offstage in the Pause*]

Voice [*offstage*].

    O blow, ye winds, heigh-ho.

    A-roving I will go!

    I'm off to my love

    With a boxing glove—

    Ten thousand miles away!

JIM. You say you've heard me sing?

LAURA. Oh, yes! Yes, very often . . . I—don't suppose you remember me—at all?

JIM [*smiling doubtfully*]. You know I have an idea I've seen you before. I had that idea soon as you opened the door. It seemed almost like I was about to remember your name. But the name that I started to call you—wasn't a name! And so I stopped myself before I said it.

LAURA. Wasn't it—Blue Roses?

JIM [*springs up, grinning*]. Blue Roses! My gosh, yes—Blue Roses! That's what I had on my tongue when you opened the door! Isn't it funny what tricks your memory plays? I didn't connect you with the high school somehow or other. But that's where it was; it was high school. I didn't even know you were Shakespeare's sister! Gosh, I'm sorry.

LAURA. I didn't expect you to. You—barely knew me!

JIM. But we did have a speaking acquaintance, huh?

LAURA. Yes, we—spoke to each other.

JIM. When did you recognize me?

LAURA. Oh, right away!

JIM. Soon as I came in the door?

LAURA. When I heard your name I thought it was probably you. I knew that Tom used to know you a little in high school. So when you came in the door—Well, then I was—sure.

JIM. Why didn't you *say* something, then?

LAURA [*breathlessly*]. I didn't know what to say, I was—too surprised!

JIM. For goodness' sakes! You know, this sure is funny!

LAURA. Yes! Yes, isn't it, though. . . .

JIM. Didn't we have a class in something together?

LAURA. Yes, we did.

JIM. What class was that?

JIM. It was—singing—Chorus!

JIM. Aw!

LAURA. I sat across the aisle from you in the Aud.

JIM. Aw.

LAURA. Mondays, Wednesdays and Fridays.

JIM. Now I remember—you always came in late.

LAURA. Yes, it was so hard for me, getting upstairs. I had a brace on my leg—it clumped so loud!

JIM. I never heard any clumping.

LAURA [*wincing at the recollection*]. To me it sounded like—thunder!

JIM. Well, well, well. I never even noticed.

LAURA. And everybody was seated before I came in. I had to walk in front of all those people. My seat was in the back row. I had to go clumping all the way up the aisle with everyone watching!

JIM. You shouldn't have been self-conscious.

LAURA. I know, but I was. It was always such a relief when the singing started.

JIM. Aw, yes, I've placed you now! I used to call you Blue Roses. How was it that I got started calling you that?

LAURA. I was out of school a little while with pleurosis. When I came back you asked me what was the matter. I said I had pleurosis—you thought I said Blue Roses. That's what you always called me after that!

JIM. I hope you didn't mind.

LAURA. Oh, no—I liked it. You see, I wasn't acquainted with many—people. . . .

JIM. As I remember you sort of stuck by yourself.

LAURA. I—I—never had much luck at—making friends.

JIM. I don't see why you wouldn't.

LAURA. Well, I—started out badly.

JIM. You mean being—

LAURA. Yes, it sort of—stood between me—

JIM. You shouldn't have let it!

LAURA. I know, but it did, and—

JIM. You were shy with people!

LAURA. I tried not to be but never could—

JIM. Overcome it?

LAURA. No, I—I never could!

JIM. I guess being shy is something you have to work out of kind of gradually.

LAURA [*sorrowfully*]. Yes—I guess it—

JIM. Takes time!

LAURA. Yes—

JIM. People are not so dreadful when you know them. That's what you have to remember! And everybody has problems, not just you, but practically everybody has got some problems. You think of yourself as having the only problems, as being the only one who is disappointed. But just look around you and you will see lots of people as disappointed as you are. For instance, I hoped when I was going to high school that I would be further along at this time, six years after, than I am now—You remember that wonderful write-up I had in *The Torch?*

LAURA. Yes! [*She rises and crosses to table.*]

JIM. It said I was bound to succeed in anything I went into! [*Laura returns with the annual.*] Holy Jeez! *The Torch!* [*He accepts it reverently. They smile across it with mutual wonder. Laura crouches beside him and they begin to turn through it. Laura's shyness is dissolving in his warmth.*]

LAURA. Here you are in *Pirates of Penzance!*

JIM [*wistfully*]. I sang the baritone lead in that operetta.

LAURA [*rapidly*]. So—*beautifully!*

JIM [*protesting*]. Aw—

LAURA. Yes, yes—beautifully—beautifully!

JIM. You heard me?

LAURA. All three times!

JIM. No!

LAURA. Yes!

JIM. All three performances?

LAURA [*looking down*]. Yes.

JIM. Why?

LAURA. I—wanted to ask you to—autograph my program.

JIM. Why didn't you ask me to?

LAURA. You were always surrounded by your own friends so much that I never had a chance to.

JIM. You should have just—

LAURA. Well, I—thought you might think I was—

JIM. Thought I might think you was—what?

LAURA. Oh—

JIM [*with reflective relish*]. I was beleaguered by females in those days.

LAURA. You were terribly popular!

JIM. Yeah—

LAURA. You had such a—friendly way—

JIM. I was spoiled in high school.

LAURA. Everybody—liked you!

JIM. Including you?

LAURA. I—yes, I—I did, too—[*She gently closes the book in her lap.*]

JIM. Well, well, well!—Give me that program, Laura. [*She hands it to him. He signs it with a flourish.*] There you are—better late than never!

LAURA. Oh, I—what a—surprise!

JIM. My signature isn't worth very much right now. But some day—maybe—it will increase in value! Being disappointed is one thing and being discouraged is something else. I am disappointed but I'm not discouraged. I'm twenty-three years old. How old are you?

LAURA. I'll be twenty-four in June.

JIM. That's not old age!

LAURA. No, but—

JIM. You finished high school?

LAURA [*with difficulty*]. I didn't go back.

JIM. You mean you dropped out?

LAURA. I made bad grades in my final examinations. [*She rises and replaces the book and the program. Her voice strained.*] How is—Emily Meisenbach getting along?

JIM. Oh, that kraut-head!

LAURA. Why do you call her that?

JIM. That's what she was.

LAURA. You're not still—going with her?

JIM. I never see her.

LAURA. It said in the Personal Section that you were—engaged!

JIM. I know, but I wasn't impressed by that—propaganda!

LAURA. It wasn't—the truth?

JIM. Only in Emily's optimistic opinion!

LAURA. Oh—

[*Legend: "What Have You Done since High School?"*)

Jim lights a cigarette and leans indolently back on his elbows smiling at Laura with a warmth and charm which light her inwardly with altar candles. She remains by the table and turns in her hands a piece of glass to cover her tumult.

JIM [*after several reflective puffs on a cigarette*]. What have you done since high school? [*She seems not to hear him.*] Huh? [*Laura looks up.*] I said what have you done since high school, Laura?

LAURA. Nothing much.

JIM. You must have been doing something these six long years.

LAURA. Yes.

JIM. Well, then, such as what?

LAURA. I took a business course at business college—

JIM. How did that work out?

LAURA. Well, not very—well—I had to drop out, it gave me—indigestion—

Jim laughs gently.

JIM. What are you doing now?

LAURA. I don't do anything—much. Oh, please don't think I sit around doing nothing! My glass collection takes up a good deal of my time. Glass is something you have to take good care of.

JIM. What did you say—about glass?

LAURA. Collection I said—I have one—[*She clears her throat and turns away again, acutely shy.*]

JIM [*abruptly*]. You know what I judge to be the trouble with you? Inferiority complex! Know what that is? That's what they call it when someone low-rates himself! I understand it because I had it, too. Although my case was not so aggravated as yours seems to be. I had it until I took up public speaking, developed my voice, and learned that I had an aptitude for science. Before that time I never thought of myself as being outstanding in any way whatsoever! Now I've never made a regular study of it, but I have a friend who says I can analyze people better than doctors that make a profession of it. I don't claim that to be necessarily true, but I can sure guess a person's psychology, Laura! [*Takes out his gum.*] Excuse me, Laura. I always take it out when the flavor is gone. I'll use this scrap of paper to wrap it in. I know how it is to get it stuck on a shoe. Yep—that's what I judge to be your principal trouble. A lack of confidence in yourself as a person. You don't have the proper amount of faith in yourself. I'm basing that fact on a number of your remarks and also on certain observations I've made. For instance that clumping you thought was so awful in high school. You say that you even dreaded to walk into class. You see what you did? You dropped out of school, you gave up an education because of a clump, which as far as I know was practically nonexistent! A little physical defect is what you have. Hardly noticeable even! Magnified thousands of times by imagination! You know what my strong advice to you is? Think of yourself as *superior* in some way!

LAURA. In what way would I think?

JIM. Why, man alive, Laura! Just look about you a little. What do you see? A world full of common people! All of 'em born and all of 'em going to die! Which of them has one-tenth of your good points! Or mine! Or anyone else's, as far as that goes—Gosh! Everybody excels in some one thing. Some in many! [*Unconsciously glances at himself in the mirror.*] All you've got to do is discover in *what!* Take me, for instance. [*He adjusts his tie at the mirror.*] My interest happens to lie in electrodynamics. I'm taking a course in radio engineering at night school, Laura, on top of a fairly responsible job at the warehouse. I'm taking that course and studying public speaking.

LAURA. Ohhhh.

JIM. Because I believe in the future of televison! [*Turning back to her.*] I wish to be ready to go up right along with it. Therefore I'm planning to get in on the ground floor. In fact, I've already made the right connections and all that remains is for the industry itself to get under way! Full steam—[*His eyes are starry.*] *Knowledge*—Zzzzzp! *Money*—Zzzzzzp!—*Power!* That's the cycle democracy is built on! [*His attitude is convincingly dynamic. Laura stares at him, even her shyness eclipsed in her absolute wonder. He suddenly grins.*] I guess you think I think a lot of myself!

LAURA. No—o-o-o, I—

JIM. Now how about you? Isn't there something you take more interest in than anything else?

LAURA. Well, I do—as I said—have my—glass collection—

A peal of girlish laughter from the kitchen.

JIM. I'm not right sure I know what you're talking about. What kind of glass is it?

LAURA. Little articles of it, they're ornaments mostly! Most of them are little animals made out of glass, the tiniest little animals in the world. Mother calls them a glass menagerie! Here's an example of one, if you'd like to see it! This one is one of the oldest. It's nearly thirteen. [*He stretches out his hand.*] [*Music: "The Glass Menagerie."*] Oh, be careful—if you breathe, it breaks!

JIM. I'd better not take it. I'm pretty clumsy with things.

LAURA. Go on, I trust you with him! [*Places it in his palm.*] There now—you're holding him gently! Hold him over the light, he loves the light! You see how the light shines through him?

JIM. It sure does shine!

LAURA. I shouldn't be partial, but he is my favorite one.

JIM. What kind of a thing is this one supposed to be?

LAURA. Haven't you noticed the single horn on his forehead?

JIM. A unicorn, huh?

LAURA. Mmm-hmmm!

JIM. Unicorns, aren't they extinct in the modern world?

LAURA. I know!

JIM. Poor little fellow, he must feel sort of lonesome.

LAURA [*smiling*]. Well, if he does he doesn't complain about it. He stays on a shelf with some horses that don't have horns and all of them seem to get along nicely together.

JIM. How do you know?

LAURA [*lightly*]. I haven't heard any arguments among them!

JIM [*grinning*]. No arguments, huh? Well, that's a pretty good sign! Where shall I set him?

LAURA. Put him on the table. They all like a change of scenery once in a while!

JIM [*stretching*]. Well, well, well, well—Look how big my shadow is when I stretch!

LAURA. Oh, oh, yes—it stretches across the ceiling!

JIM [*crossing to door*]. I think it's stopped raining. [*Opens fire-escape door.*] Where does the music come from?

LAURA. From the Paradise Dance Hall across the alley.

JIM. How about cutting the rug a little, Miss Wingfield?

LAURA. Oh, I—

JIM. Or is your program filled up? Let me have a look at it. [*Grasps imaginary card.*] Why, every dance is taken! I'll just have to scratch some out. [*Waltz Music: "La Golondrina."*] Ahhh, a waltz! [*He executes some sweeping turns by himself then holds his arms toward Laura.*]

LAURA [*breathlessly*]. I—can't dance!

JIM. There you go, that inferiority stuff!

LAURA. I've never danced in my life!

JIM. Come on, try!

LAURA. Oh, but I'd step on you!

JIM. I'm not made out of glass.

LAURA. How—how—how do we start?

JIM. Just leave it to me. You hold your arms out a little.

LAURA. Like this?

JIM. A little bit higher. Right. Now don't tighten up, that's the main thing about it—relax.

LAURA [*laughing breathlessly*]. It's hard not to.

JIM. Okay.

LAURA. I'm afraid you can't budge me.

JIM. What do you bet I can't? [*He swings her into motion.*]

LAURA. Goodness, yes, you can!

JIM. Let yourself go, now, Laura, just let yourself go.

LAURA. I'm—

JIM. Come on!

LAURA. Trying!

JIM. Not so stiff—Easy does it!

LAURA. I know but I'm—

JIM. Loosen th' backbone! There now, that's a lot better.

LAURA. Am I?

JIM. Lots, lots better! [*He moves her about the room in a clumsy waltz.*]

LAURA. Oh, my!

JIM. Ha-ha!

LAURA. Goodness, yes you can!

JIM. Ha-ha-ha! [*They suddenly bump into the table. Jim stops.*] What did we hit on?

LAURA. Table.

JIM. Did something fall off it? I think—

LAURA. Yes.

JIM. I hope that it wasn't the little glass horse with the horn!

LAURA. Yes.

JIM. Aw, aw, aw. Is it broken?

LAURA. Now it is just like all the other horses.

JIM. It's lost its—

LAURA. Horn! It doesn't matter. Maybe it's a blessing in disguise.

JIM. You'll never forgive me. I bet that that was your favorite piece of glass.

LAURA. I don't have favorites much. It's no tragedy, Freckles. Glass breaks so easily. No matter how careful you are. The traffic jars the shelves and things fall off them.

JIM. Still I'm awfully sorry that I was the cause.

LAURA [*smiling*]. I'll just imagine he had an operation. The horn was removed to make him feel less—freakish! [*They both laugh.*] Now he will feel more at home with the other horses, the ones that don't have horns. . .

JIM. Ha-ha, that's very funny! [*Suddenly serious.*] I'm glad to see that you have a sense of humor. You know—you're—well—very different! Surprisingly different from anyone else I know! [*His voice becomes soft and hesitant with a genuine feeling.*] Do you mind me telling you that? [*Laura is abashed beyond speech.*] You make me feel sort of—I don't know how to put it! I'm usually pretty good at expressing things, but—This is something that I don't know how to say! [*Laura touches her throat and clears it—turns the broken unicorn in her hands.*] [*Even softer.*] Has anyone ever told you that you were pretty? [*Pause: Music.*] [*Laura looks up slowly, with wonder, and shakes her head.*] Well, you are! In a very different way from anyone else. And all the nicer because of the difference, too. [*His voice becomes low and husky. Laura turns away, nearly faint with the novelty of her emotions.*] I wish that you were my sister. I'd teach you to have some confidence in yourself. The different people are not like other people, but being different is nothing to be ashamed of. Because other people are not such wonderful people. They're one hundred times one thousand. You're one times one! They walk all over the earth. You just stay here. They're common as—weeds, but—you—well, you're *Blue Roses*!

[*Image on Screen: Blue Roses.*]

[*Music Changes.*]

LAURA. But blue is wrong for—roses. . .

JIM. It's right for you—You're—pretty!

LAURA. In what respect am I pretty?

JIM. In all respects—believe me! Your eyes—your hair—are pretty! Your hands are pretty! [*He catches hold of her hand.*] You think I'm making this up because I'm invited to dinner and have to be nice. Oh, I could do that! I could put on an act for you, Laura, and say lots of things without being very sincere. But this time I am. I'm talking to you sincerely. I happened to notice you had this inferiority complex that keeps you from feeling comfortable with people. Somebody needs to build your confidence up and make you proud instead of shy and turning away and—blushing—Somebody ought to—ought to—*kiss* you. Laura! [*His hand slips slowly up her arm to her shoulder.*] [*Music Swells Tumultuously.*] [*He suddenly turns her about and kisses her on the lips. When he releases her Laura sinks on the sofa with a bright, dazed look. Jim backs away and fishes in his pocket for a cigarette.*] [*Legend on Screen: "Souvenir."*] Stumble-john! [*He lights the cigarette, avoiding her look. There is a peal of girlish laughter from Amanda in the kitchen. Laura slowly raises and opens her hand. It still contains the little broken glass animal. She looks at it with a tender, bewildered expression.*] Stumble-john! I shouldn't have done that— That was way off the beam. You don't smoke, do you? [*She looks up, smiling, not hearing the question. He sits beside her a little gingerly. She looks at him speechlessly—waiting. He coughs decorously and moves a little farther aside as he considers the situation and senses her feelings, dimly, with perturbation. Gently.*] Would you—care for a—mint? [*She doesn't seem to hear him but her look grows brighter even.*] Peppermint—Life Saver? My pocket's a regular drug store—wherever I go . . . [*He pops a mint in his mouth. Then gulps and decides to make a clean breast of it. He speaks slowly and gingerly.*] Laura, you know, if I had a sister like you, I'd do the same thing as Tom. I'd bring out fellows—introduce her to them. The right type of boys of a type to— appreciate her. Only—well—he made a mistake about me. Maybe I've got no call to be saying this. That may not have been the idea in having me over. But what if it was? There's nothing wrong about that. The only trouble is that in my case—I'm not in a situation to—do the right thing. I can't take down your number and say I'll phone. I can't call up next week and—ask for a date. I thought I had better explain the situation in case you misunderstood it and— hurt your feelings. . . . [*Pause. Slowly, very slowly, Laura's look changes, her eyes returning slowly from his to the ornament in her palm.*]

Amanda utters another gay laugh in the kitchen.

LAURA [*faintly*]. You—won't—call again?

JIM. No, Laura, I can't. [*He rises from the sofa.*] As I was just explaining, I've—got strings on me, Laura, I've—been going steady! I go out all the time with a girl named Betty. She's a home-girl like you, and Catholic, and Irish, and in a great many ways we—get along fine. I met her last summer on a moonlight boat trip up the river to Alton, on the *Majestic.* Well—right away from the start it was—love! [*Legend: Love!*] [*Laura sways slightly forward and grips the arm of the sofa. He fails to notice, now enrapt in his own comfortable being.*] Being in love has made a new man of me! [*Leaning stiffly forward, clutching the arm of the sofa, Laura struggles visibly with her storm. But Jim is oblivious, she is a long way off.*] The power of love is really pretty tremendous! Love is something that—changes the whole world, Laura! [*The storm abates a little and Laura leans back. He notices her again.*] It happened that Betty's aunt took sick, she got a wire and had to go to Centralia. So Tom—when he asked me to dinner—I naturally just accepted the invitation, not knowing that you—that he—that I—[*He stops awkwardly.*] Huh—I'm a stumble-john! [*He flops back on the sofa. The holy candles in the altar of Laura's face have been snuffed out! There is a look of almost infinite desolation. Jim glances at her uneasily.*] I wish that you would—say something. [*She bites her lip which was trembling and then bravely smiles. She opens her hand again on the broken glass ornament. Then she gently takes his hand and raises it level with her own. She carefully places the unicorn in the palm of his hand, then pushes his fingers closed upon it.*] What are you—doing that for? You want me to have him?—Laura? [*She nods.*] What for?

LAURA. A—souvenir . . .

She rises unsteadily and crouches beside the victrola to wind it up.

[*Legend on Screen: "Things Have a Way of Turning Out So Badly."*]

[*Or Image: "Gentleman Caller Waving Good-Bye!—Gaily."*]

At this moment Amanda rushes brightly back in the front room. She bears a pitcher of fruit punch in an old-fashioned cut-glass pitcher and a plate of macaroons. The plate has a gold border and poppies painted on it.

AMANDA. Well, well, well! Isn't the air delightful after the shower? I've made you children a little liquid refreshment. [*Turns gaily to the gentleman caller.*] Jim, do you know that song about lemonade?

"Lemonade, lemonade
Made in the shade and stirred with a spade—
Good enough for any old maid!"

JIM [*uneasily*]. Ha-ha! No—I never heard it.

AMANDA. Why, Laura! You look so serious!

JIM. We were having a serious conversation.

AMANDA. Good! Now you're better acquainted!

JIM [*uncertainly*]. Ha-ha! Yes.

AMANDA. You modern young people are much more serious-minded than my generation. I was so gay as a girl!

JIM. You haven't changed, Mrs. Wingfield.

AMANDA. Tonight I'm rejuvenated! The gaiety of the occasion, Mr. O'Connor! [*She tosses her head with a peal of laughter. Spills lemonade.*] Oooo! I'm baptizing myself!

JIM. Here—let me—

AMANDA [*setting the pitcher down*]. There now. I discovered we had some maraschino cherries. I dumped them in, juice and all!

JIM. You shouldn't have gone to that trouble, Mrs. Wingfield.

AMANDA. Trouble, trouble? Why it was loads of fun! Didn't you hear me cutting up in the kitchen? I bet your ears were burning! I told Tom how outdone with him I was for keeping you to himself so long a time! He should have brought you over much, much sooner! Well, now that you've found your way, I want you to be a very frequent caller! Not just occasional but all the time. Oh, we're going to have a lot of gay times together! I see them coming! Mmm, just breathe that air! So fresh, and the moon's so pretty! I'll skip back out—I know where my place is when young folks are having a—serious conversation!

JIM. Oh, don't go out, Mrs. Wingfield. The fact of the matter is I've got to be going.

AMANDA. Going, now? You're joking! Why, it's only the shank of the evening, Mr. O'Connor!

JIM. Well, you know how it is.

AMANDA. You mean you're a young workingman and have to keep workingmen's hours. We'll let you off early tonight. But only on the condition that next time you stay later. What's the best night for you? Isn't Saturday night the best night for you workingmen?

JIM. I have a couple of time-clocks to punch, Mrs. Wingfield. One at morning, another one at night!

AMANDA. My, but you *are* ambitious! You work at night, too?

JIM. No, Ma'am, not work but—Betty! [*He crosses deliberately to pick up his hat. The band at the Paradise Dance Hall goes into a tender waltz.*]

AMANDA. Betty? Betty? Who's—Betty! [*There is an ominous cracking sound in the sky.*]

JIM. Oh, just a girl. The girl I go steady with! [*He smiles charmingly. The sky falls.*]

[*Legend: "The Sky Falls."*]

AMANDA [*a long-drawn exhalation*]. Ohhh . . . Is it a serious romance, Mr. O'Connor?

JIM. We're going to be married the second Sunday in June.

AMANDA. Ohhhh—how nice! Tom didn't mention that you were engaged to be married.

JIM. The cat's not out of the bag at the warehouse yet. You know how they are. They call you Romeo and stuff like that. [*He stops at the oval mirror to put on his hat. He carefully shapes the brim and the crown to give a discreetly dashing effect.*] It's been a wonderful evening, Mrs. Wingfield. I guess this is what they mean by Southern hospitality.

AMANDA. It really wasn't anything at all.

JIM. I hope it don't seem like I'm rushing off. But I promised Betty I'd pick her up at the Wabash depot, an' by the time I get my jalopy down there her train'll be in. Some women are pretty upset if you keep 'em waiting.

AMANDA. Yes, I know—The tyranny of women! [*Extends her hand.*] Goodbye, Mr. O'Connor. I wish you luck—and happiness—and success! All three of them, and so does Laura!—Don't you, Laura?

LAURA. Yes!

JIM [*taking her hand*]. Goodbye, Laura. I'm certainly going to treasure that souvenir. And don't you forget the good advice I gave you. [*Raises his voice to a cheery shout.*] So long, Shakespeare! Thanks again, ladies—good night!

He grins and ducks jauntily out.

Still bravely grimacing, Amanda closes the door on the gentleman caller.

Then she turns back to the room with a puzzled expression. She and Laura don't dare to face each other. Laura crouches beside the victrola to wind it.

AMANDA [*faintly*]. Things have a way of turning out so badly. I don't believe that I would play the victrola. Well, well—well—Our gentleman caller was engaged to be married! Tom!

TOM [*from back*]. Yes, Mother?

AMANDA. Come in here a minute. I want to tell you something awfully funny.

TOM [*enters with macaroon and a glass of the lemonade*]. Has the gentleman caller gotten away already?

AMANDA. The gentleman caller has made an early departure. What a wonderful joke you played on us!

TOM. How do you mean?

AMANDA. You didn't mention that he was engaged to be married.

TOM. Jim? Engaged?

AMANDA. That's what he just informed us.

TOM. I'll be jiggered! I didn't know about that.

AMANDA. That seems very peculiar.

TOM. What's peculiar about it?

AMANDA. Didn't you call him your best friend down at the warehouse?

TOM. He is, but how did I know?

AMANDA. It seems extremely peculiar that you wouldn't know your best friend was going to be married!

TOM. The warehouse is where I work, not where I know things about people!

AMANDA. You don't know things anywhere! You live in a dream; you manufacture illusions! [*He crosses to door.*] Where are you going?

TOM. I'm going to the movies.

AMANDA. That's right, now that you've had us make such fools of ourselves. The effort, the preparations, all the expense! The new floor lamp, the rug, the clothes for Laura! All for what? To entertain some other girl's fiancé! Go to the movies, go! Don't think about us, a mother deserted, an unmarried sister who's crippled and has no job! Don't let anything interfere with your selfish pleasure! Just go, go, go—to the movies!

TOM. All right, I will! The more you shout about my selfishness to me the quicker I'll go, and I won't go to the movies!

AMANDA. Go, then! Then go to the moon—you selfish dreamer!

Tom smashes his glass on the floor. He plunges out on the fire-escape, slamming the door. Laura screams—cut by door.

Dance-hall music up. Tom goes to the rail and grips it desperately, lifting his face in the chill white moonlight penetrating the narrow abyss of the alley.

[*Legend on Screen: "And So Good-Bye . . ."*]

Tom's closing speech is timed with the interior pantomime. The interior scene is played as though viewed through sound-proof glass. Amanda appears to be making a comforting speech to Laura who is huddled upon the sofa. Now that we cannot hear the mother's speech, her silliness is gone and she has dignity and tragic beauty. Laura's dark hair hides her face until at the end of the speech she lifts it to smile at her mother. Amanda's gestures are slow and grace-

ful, almost dancelike, as she comforts the daughter. At the end of her speech she glances a moment at the father's picture—then withdraws through the portieres. At close of Tom's speech, Laura blows out the candles, ending the play.

TOM. I didn't go to the moon, I went much further—for time is the longest distance between two places—Not long after that I was fired for writing a poem on the lid of a shoe-box. I left Saint Louis. I descended the steps of this fire-escape for a last time and followed, from then on, in my father's footsteps, attempting to find in motion what was lost in space— I traveled around a great deal. The cities swept about me like dead leaves, leaves that were brightly colored but torn away from the branches. I would have stopped, but I was pursued by something. It always came upon me unawares, taking me altogether by surprise. Perhaps it was a familiar bit of music. Perhaps it was only a piece of transparent glass—Perhaps I am walking along a street at night, in some strange city, before I have found companions. I pass the lighted window of a shop where perfume is sold. The window is filled with pieces of colored glass, tiny transparent bottles in delicate colors, like bits of a shattered rainbow. Then all at once my sister touches my shoulder. I turn around and look into her eyes . . . Oh, Laura, Laura, I tried to leave you behind me, but I am more faithful than I intended to be! I reach for a cigarette, I cross the street, I run into the movies or a bar, I buy a drink, I speak to the nearest stranger—anything that can blow your candles out! [*Laura bends over the candles.*]—for nowadays the world is lit by lightning! Blow out your candles, Laura—and so goodbye . . .

She blows the candles out.

[*The Scene Dissolves.*]

[1944]

Production Notes

Being a "memory play," *The Glass Menagerie* can be presented with unusual freedom of convention. Because of its considerably delicate or tenuous material, atmospheric touches and subtleties of direction play a particularly important part. Expressionism and all other unconventional techniques in drama have only one valid aim, and that is a closer approach to truth. When a play employs unconventional techniques, it is not, or certainly shouldn't be, trying to escape its responsibility of dealing with reality, or interpreting experience, but is actually or should be attempting to find a closer approach, a more penetrating and vivid expression of things as they are. The straight realistic play with its genuine frigidaire and authentic ice cubes, its characters that speak exactly as its audience speaks, corresponds to the academic landscape and has the same virtue of a photographic likeness. Everyone should know nowadays the unimportance of the photographic in art: that truth, life, or reality is an organic thing which the poetic imagination can represent or suggest, in essence, only through transformation, through changing into other forms than those which were merely present in appearance.

These remarks are not meant as comments only on this particular play. They have to do with a conception of a new, plastic theater which must take the place of the exhausted theater of realistic conventions if the theater is to resume vitality as a part of our culture.

THE SCREEN DEVICE

There is *only one important difference between the original and acting version of the play* and that is the *omission* in the latter of the device which I tentatively included in my *original* script. This device was the use of a screen on which were projected magic-lantern slides bearing images or titles. I do not regret the omission of this device from the . . . Broadway production. The extraordinary power of Miss Taylor's performance made it suitable to have the utmost simplicity in the physical production. But I think it may be interesting to some readers to see how this device was conceived. So I am putting it into the published manuscript. These images and legends, projected from behind, were cast on a section of wall between the front-room and dining-room areas, which should be indistinguishable from the rest when not in use.

The purpose of this will probably be apparent. It is to give accent to certain values in each scene. Each scene contains a particular point (or several) which is structurally the most important. In an episodic play, such as this, the basic structure or narrative line may be obscured from the audience; the effect may seem fragmentary rather than architectural. This may not be the fault of the play so much as a lack of attention in the audience. The legend or image upon the screen will strengthen the effect of what is merely allusion in the writing and allow the primary point to be made more simply and lightly than if the entire responsibility were on the spoken lines. Aside from this structural value, I think the screen will have a definite emotional appeal, less definable but just as important. An imaginative producer or director may invent many other uses for this device than those indicated in the present script. In fact the possibilities of the device seem much larger to me than the instance of this play can possibly utilize.

THE MUSIC

Another extra-literary accent in this play is provided by the use of music. A single recurring tune, "The Glass Menagerie," is used to give emotional emphasis to suitable passages. This tune is like circus music, not when you are on the grounds or in the immediate vicinity of the parade, but when you are at some distance and very likely thinking of something else. It seems under those circumstances to continue almost interminably and it weaves in and out of your preoccupied consciousness; then it is the lightest, most delicate music in the world and perhaps the saddest. It expresses the surface vivacity of life with the underlying strain of immutable and inexpressible sorrow. When you look at a piece of delicately spun glass you think of two things: how beautiful it is and how easily it can be broken. Both of those ideas should be woven into the recurring tune, which dips in and out of the play as if it were carried on a wind that changes. It serves as a thread of connection and allusion beween the narrator with his separate point in time and space and the subject of his story. Between each episode it returns as reference to the emotion, nostalgia, which is the first condition of the play. It is primarily Laura's music and therefore comes out most clearly when the play focuses upon her and the lovely fragility of glass which is her image.

THE LIGHTING

The lighting in the play is not realistic. In keeping with the atmosphere of memory, the stage is dim. Shafts of light are focused on selected areas or actors, sometimes in contradistinction to what is the apparent center. For instance, in the quarrel scene between Tom and Amanda, in which Laura has no active part, the clearest pool of light is on her figure. This is also true of the supper scene. The light upon Laura should be distinct from the others, having a peculiar pristine clarity such as light used in early religious portraits of female saints or madonnas. A certain correspondence to light in religious paintings, such as El Greco's, where the figures are radiant in atmosphere that is relatively dusky, could be effectively used throughout the play. (It will also permit a more effective use of the screen.) A free, imaginative use of light can be of enormous value in giving a mobile, plastic quality to plays of a more or less static nature.

■ TOPICS FOR DISCUSSION AND WRITING

1. When produced in New York, the magic-lantern slides were omitted. Is the device an extraneous gimmick? Might it even interfere with the play, by oversimplifying and thus in a way belittling the actions?

2. What does the victrola offer to Laura? Why is the typewriter a better symbol (for the purposes of the play) than, say, a piano? After all, Laura could have been taking piano lessons. Explain the symbolism of the unicorn, and the loss of its horn. What is Laura saying to Jim in the gesture of giving him the unicorn?

3. Laura escapes to her glass menagerie. To what do Amanda and Tom escape? How complete is Tom's escape at the end of the play?

4. What is meant at the end when Laura blows out the candles? Is she blowing out illusions? Or life? Or both?

5. Did Williams make a slip in having Amanda say Laura is "crippled" on page 766?

6. There is an implication that had Jim not been going steady he might have rescued Laura, but Jim also seems to represent (for example, in his lines about money and power) the corrupt outside world that no longer values humanity. Is this a slip on Williams's part, or is it an interesting complexity?

7. On page 766 Williams says, in a stage direction, "Now that we cannot hear the mother's speech, her silliness is gone and she has dignity and tragic beauty." Is Williams simply dragging in the word "tragic" because of its prestige, or is it legitimate? "Tragedy" is often distinguished

from "pathos": in the tragic, the suffering is experienced by persons who act and are in some measure responsible for their suffering; in the pathetic, the suffering is experienced by the passive and the innocent. For example, in discussing Aeschylus's *The Suppliants* (in *Greek Tragedy*), H. D. F. Kitto says: "The Suppliants are not only pathetic, as the victims of outrage, but also tragic, as the victims of their own misconceptions." Given this distinction, to what extent are Amanda and Laura tragic? Pathetic?

▪ CHAPTER 12

The Individual

and Society

ESSAYS

▪ SULLIVAN BALLOU

Sullivan Ballou (1827–1861) was born in Smithfield, Rhode Island. He spent his youth in New York and Massachusetts, but in 1846 he returned to Rhode Island to enter Brown University. Two years later he left Brown for National Law School in Ballston, New York. Ballou was admitted to the Rhode Island bar in 1853, practiced law, married Sarah Hart Shumway in 1855, served in the Rhode Island House of Representatives from 1857 until the outbreak of the Civil War. He then enlisted as an officer in the 2nd Rhode Island Volunteers. On 21 July 1861, at the first Battle of Bull Run, Major Ballou was wounded in the leg by a cannonball that killed his horse. He was carried from the battlefield but died of his wounds later in the day. He left a widow and two sons.

The original letter is lost. We give the earliest printed version, with some repunctuation. Later versions, including the one recited in the PBS documentary, *The Civil War*, differ slightly.

My Very Dear Wife

Washington, Camp Clarke, July 14th, 1861

My very dear Sarah:

The indications are very strong that we shall move in a few days— 1 perhaps tomorrow. And lest I should not be able to write to you again, I feel impelled to write a few lines that may fall under your eye when I shall be no more. Our movement may be one of a few days' duration and be full of pleasure. And it may be one of severe conflict and death to me. "Not my will but thine O God be done." If it is necessary that I should fall on the battlefield for my Country I am ready. I have no misgivings about, or lack of confidence in, the cause in which I am engaged, and my courage does not halt or falter. I know how strongly American Civilization now leans on the triumph of the Government, and how great a debt we owe to those who went before us through the blood and suffering of the Revolution. And I am willing—perfectly willing—to lay down all my joys in this life, to help maintain this Government, and to pay that debt.

But my dear wife, when I know that with my own joys I lay down nearly 2 all of yours, and replace them in this life with cares and sorrows, when after having eaten for long years the bitter fruit of orphanage myself, I must offer it as the only sustenance to my dear little children, is it weak or dishonorable that while the banner of my purpose floats calmly and proudly in the breeze, underneath, my unbounded love for you my darling wife and children should struggle in fierce though useless contest with my love of Country?

I cannot describe to you my feelilngs on this calm summer Sabbath night, 3 when two thousand men are sleeping around me, many of them enjoying the last, perhaps, before that of Death. And I am suspicious that Death is creeping behind me with his fatal dart, and communing with God, my Country, and thee. I have sought most closely and diligently and often in my breast for a wrong motive in thus hazarding the happiness of all those I loved, and I could find none. A pure love of my Country and of the principles I have often advocated before the people, another name of honor that I love more than I fear death, has called upon me and I have obeyed.

Sarah, my love for you is deathless. It seems to bind me with mighty ca- 4 bles that nothing but Omnipotence could break; and yet my love of Country comes over me like a strong wind and bears me irresistibly on, with all these chains to the battle-field.

The memories of all the blissful moments I have enjoyed with you come 5 creeping over me, and I feel most deeply grateful to God and to you that I have enjoyed them so long. And how hard it is for me to give them up, and burn to ashes the hopes of future years, when, God willing, we might still have lived and loved together, and seen our boys grow up to honorable manhood around us. I know I have but few and small claims upon Divine Providence, but something whispers to me—perhaps it is the wafted prayer of my little Edgar, that I shall return to my loved ones unharmed. If I do not, my dear Sarah, never forget how much I love you, nor that when my last breath escapes me on the battle-field, it will whisper your name.

Forgive my many faults, and the many pains I have caused you. How 6 thoughtless, how foolish I have oftentimes been! How gladly would I wash out with my tears every little spot upon your happiness and struggle with all the misfortunes of this world to shield you and my children from harm. But I cannot; I must watch you from the spirit-land, and hover near you while you buffet the storms with your precious little freight, and wait with sad patience till we meet to part no more.

But, O Sarah, if the dead can come back to this earth and flit unseen 7 around those they loved, I shall be always with you in the gladdest day and in the darkest night, amidst your happiest scenes and gloomiest hours— __

always, always, and if there be a soft breeze upon your cheek, it shall be my breath; or the cool air cools your throbbing temple, it shall be my spirit passing by. Sarah, do not mourn me dead; think I am gone, and wait for me for we shall meet again. . . .

Sullivan

■ TOPICS FOR DISCUSSION AND WRITING

1. In the fall of 1990, an abridged version of Sullivan Ballou's letter to his wife was read on PBS during Ken Burns's documentary series entitled *The Civil War.* The series received the highest rating of any in PBS history, and Ballou's letter prompted so many telephone calls that the letter was repeated at the conclusion of the series.

   Reading the letter, without the benefit of television images and music, do you find it moving? Can you explain why it evoked such an outpouring of response from TV viewers?

2. If you saw the television series, do you remember what pictures were shown while the letter was being read? If you do not remember, or if you didn't see the series, what visual and musical backgrounds would you suggest for a reading of the letter?

3. The documents used on this series were read by a number of well-known people, including Garrison Keillor, Arthur Miller, and Sam Waterston. (They did not, however, appear on the screen.) If you were casting the role of Sullivan Ballou, whose voice would you use and why?

■ MAY SARTON

May Sarton, born in Belgium in 1912, was brought to the United States in 1916; in 1924 she became a citizen. A teacher of writing and a distinguished writer herself, she has received numerous awards for her fiction, poetry, and essays.

The Rewards of Living a Solitary Life

The other day an acquaintance of mine, a gregarious and charming man, told me he had found himself unexpectedly alone in New York for an hour or two between appointments. He went to the Whitney and spent the "empty" time looking at things in solitary bliss. For him it proved to be a shock nearly as great as falling in love to discover that he could enjoy himself so much alone.

What had he been afraid of, I asked myself? That, suddenly alone, he would discover that he bored himself, or that there was, quite simply, no self there to meet? But having taken the plunge, he is now on the brink of adventure; he is about to be launched into his own inner space, space as immense, unexplored, and sometimes frightening as outer space to the astronaut. His every perception will come to him with a new freshness and, for a time, seem startlingly original. For anyone who can see things for himself with a naked eye becomes, for a moment or two, something of a genius. With another human being present vision becomes double vision, inevitably. We are busy wondering, what does my companion see or think of this, and what do I think of it?. The original impact gets lost, or diffused.

"Music I heard with you was more than music." Exactly. And therefore music *itself* can only be heard alone. Solitude is the salt of personhood. It brings out the authentic flavor of every experience.

"Alone one is never lonely: the spirit adventures, walking/In a quiet garden, in a cool house, abiding single there."

Loneliness is most acutely felt with other people, for with others, even with a lover sometimes, we suffer from our differences of taste, temperament, mood. Human intercourse often demands that we soften the edge of perception, or withdraw at the very instant of personal truth for fear of hurting, or of being inappropriately present, which is to say naked, in a social situation. Alone we can afford to be wholly whatever we are, and to feel whatever we feel absolutely. That is a great luxury!

For me the most interesting thing about a solitary life, and mine has been that for the last twenty years, is that it becomes increasingly rewarding. When I can wake up and watch the sun rise over the ocean, as I do most days, and know that I have an entire day ahead, uninterrupted, in which to write a few pages, take a walk with my dog, lie down in the afternoon for a long think (why does one think better in a horizontal position?), read and listen to music, I am flooded with happiness.

I am lonely only when I am overtired, when I have worked too long without a break, when for the time being I feel empty and need filling up. And I am lonely sometimes when I come back home after a lecture trip, when I have seen a lot of people and talked a lot, and am full to the brim with experience that needs to be sorted out.

Then for a little while the house feels huge and empty, and I wonder where my self is hiding. It has to be recaptured slowly by watering the plants, perhaps, and looking again at each one as though it were a person, by feeding the two cats, by cooking a meal.

It takes a while, as I watch the surf blowing up in fountains at the end of the field, but the moment comes when the world falls away, and the self emerges again from the deep unconscious, bringing back all I have recently experienced to be explored and slowly understood, when I can converse again with my hidden powers, and so grow, and so be renewed, till death do us part.

[1974]

■ TOPICS FOR DISCUSSION AND WRITING

1. What does Sarton mean when she says: "Anyone who can see things for himself with a naked eye becomes, for a moment or two, something of a genius"? Does your own experience confirm her comment? Explain.

2. What phrase in the last paragraph connects the ending with the first paragraph?

3. Drawing on Sarton's essay, explain in 500 words the distinction between being "alone" and being "lonely."

■ JUDY BRADY

Born in San Francisco in 1937, Judy Brady married in 1960 and two years later earned a bachelor's degree in painting at the University of Iowa. Active in the women's movement and in other political causes, she has worked as an author, an editor, and a secretary. The essay reprinted here, written before she and her husband separated, appeared originally in the first issue of *Ms.* in 1972, when the author used her married name, Judy Syfers.

I Want a Wife

I belong to that classification of people known as wives. I am A Wife. And, not altogether incidentally, I am a mother.

Not too long ago a male friend of mine appeared on the scene fresh from a recent divorce. He had one child, who is, of course, with his ex-wife. He is looking for another wife. As I thought about him while I was ironing one evening, it suddenly occurred to me that I, too, would like to have a wife. Why do I want a wife?

I would like to go back to school so that I can become economically independent, support myself, and, if need be, support those dependent upon me. I want a wife who will work and send me to school. And while I am going to school I want a wife to take care of my children. I want a wife to keep track of the children's doctor and dentist appointments. And to keep track of mine, too. I want a wife to make sure my children eat properly and are kept clean. I want a wife who will wash the children's clothes and keep them mended. I want a wife who is a good nurturant attendant to my children, who arranges for their schooling, makes sure that they have an adequate social life with their peers, takes them to the park, the zoo, etc. I want a wife who takes care of the children when they are sick, a wife who arranges to be around when the children need special care, because, of course, I cannot miss classes at school. My wife must arrange to lose time at work and not lose the job. It may mean a small cut in my wife's income from time to time, but I guess I can tolerate that. Needless to say, my wife will arrange and pay for the care of the children while my wife is working.

I want a wife who will take care of *my* physical needs. I want a wife who will keep my house clean. A wife who will pick up after my children, a wife who will pick up after me. I want a wife who will keep my clothes clean, ironed, mended, replaced when need be, and who will see to it that my personal things are kept in their proper place so that I can find what I need the minute I need it. I want a wife who cooks the meals, a wife who is a *good* cook. I want a wife who will plan the menus, do the necessary grocery shopping, prepare the meals, serve them pleasantly, and then do the cleaning up while I do my studying. I want a wife who will care for me when I am sick and sympathize with my pain and loss of time from school. I want a wife to go along when our family takes a vacation so that someone can continue to care for me and my children when I need a rest and change of scene.

I want a wife who will not bother me with rambling complaints about a 5 wife's duties. But I want a wife who will listen to me when I feel the need to explain a rather difficult point I have come across in my course of studies. And I want a wife who will type my papers for me when I have written them.

I want a wife who will take care of the details of my social life. When my wife and I are invited out by my friends, I want a wife who will take care of the babysitting arrangements. When I meet people at school that I like and want to entertain, I want a wife who will have the house clean, will prepare a special meal, serve it to me and my friends, and not interrupt when I talk about things that interest me and my friends. I want a wife who will have arranged that the children are fed and ready for bed before my guests arrive so that the children do not bother us. I want a wife who takes care of the needs of my guests so that they feel comfortable, who makes sure that they have an ashtray, that they are passed the hors d'oeuvres, that they are offered a second helping of the food, that their wine glasses are replenished when necessary, that their coffee is served to them as they like it. And I want a wife who knows that sometimes I need a night out by myself.

I want a wife who is sensitive to my sexual needs, a wife who makes love passionately and eagerly when I feel like it, a wife who makes sure that I am satisfied. And, of course, I want a wife who will not demand sexual attention when I am not in the mood for it. I want a wife who assumes the complete responsibility for birth control, because I do not want more children. I want a wife who will remain sexually faithful to me so that I do not have to clutter up my intellectual life with jealousies. And I want a wife who understands that *my* sexual needs may entail more than strict adherence to monogamy. I must, after all, be able to relate to people as fully as possible.

If, by chance, I find another person more suitable as a wife than the wife I already have, I want the liberty to replace my present wife with another one. Naturally, I will expect a fresh, new life; my wife will take the children and be solely responsible for them so that I am left free.

When I am through with school and have a job, I want my wife to quit working and remain at home so that my wife can more fully and completely take care of a wife's duties.

My God, who *wouldn't* want a wife?   10

[1971]

■ TOPICS FOR DISCUSSION AND WRITING

1. Brady uses the word "wife" in sentences where one ordinarily would use "she" or "her." Why? And why does she begin paragraphs 4, 5, 6 and 7 with the same words, "I want a wife"?

2. Drawing on your experience as observer of the world around you (and perhaps as husband, wife, or ex-spouse), do you think Brady's picture of a wife's role is grossly exaggerated? Or is it (allowing for some serious playfulness) fairly accurate, even though it was written in 1971? If grossly exaggerated, is the essay therefore meaningless? If fairly accurate, what attitudes and practices does it encourage you to support? Explain.

3. Whether or not you agree with Brady's vision of marriage in our society, write an essay (500 words) titled "I Want a Husband," imitating her style

and approach. Write the best possible essay, and then decide which of the two essays makes a fairer comment on current society. Or, if you believe Brady is utterly misleading, write an essay titled "I Want a Wife," seeing the matter in a different light.

4. If you feel that you have been pressed into an unappreciated, unreasonable role—built-in babysitter, listening post, or girl (or boy or man or woman) Friday—write an essay of 500 words that will help the reader to see both your plight and the injustice of the system. (*Hint:* A little humor will help to keep your essay from seeming to be a prolonged whine.)

■ NEIL MILLER

Neil Miller was born in Kingston, New York. After graduating in 1967 from Brown University he traveled in the Middle East and for two years taught high school English to the children of Moroccan and Iraqi immigrants in Israel. When he returned to the United States he worked in bookstores, taught English in a Berlitz language school, and in 1975 became the news editor of the *Gay Community News*, a nonprofit Boston-based paper. Later he became a feature writer for the *Boston Phoenix*, an alternative newspaper, though he continued to be active in gay causes. In an effort to learn more about gay life in America, in 1987 and 1988 he traveled throughout the United States. He presented his findings in a book, *In Search of Gay America*, from which the following excerpt comes.

In Search of Gay America: Ogilvie, Minnesota (Population 374)

I missed the Minnesota State Fair by three weeks. As an easterner living in a large urban area, I am not particularly conscious of state fairs. And I never assumed that the beef and poultry barn or the cattle barn of a state fair would be a particularly good place to observe gay and lesbian life.

I was wrong. At the Minnesota State Fair, held at the end of August at the St. Paul fairgrounds, a brown and white fifteen hundred pound bull belonging to Al Philipi and John Ritter was named the 1987 state champion. Al and John are two gay dairy farmers who live sixty-five miles north of the Twin Cities. At the awards ceremony, they received a wooden plaque in the shape of the state of Minnesota with the state seal embossed in gold. Tears were streaming down Al's face, John told me.

In the Twin Cities of Minneapolis and St. Paul, you can't help but be aware of the state's agricultural roots. The farm is always just a generation away, despite the air of urban sophistication, the experimental theatre and the recording studios and the take-out Szechuan restaurants, the punk rockers and the long-haired graduate students pedalling their ten-speeds down Hennepin Avenue as if it were Harvard Square. The connection to the land is as true for gay people as anyone else. Karen Clark, the openly lesbian state representative from an inner-city district of Minneapolis, told me with pride that she had grown up on a farm in southwestern Minnesota; she advertised her rural background in her campaign literature. On the office wall of Allan Spear, the gay state senator and chairman of the Minnesota Senate Judiciary Committee, were large framed photographs of Floyd Olson and Elmer Benson, the two agrarian reforming governors of the thirties elected on the ticket of the Farmer Labor party. So when the managing editor of *Equal Time,* the gay newspaper in Minneapolis, suggested I interview one of their editors who lived on a farm and whose lover was a full-time dairy farmer, I was eager to do so. Orwell[1] had written that the coal miner was second in importance to the man who plowed the soil. I had found the first after such travail; two genuine dairy farmers were as close as I expected to get to the second.

When I arrived at Al and John's farm, late on a Saturday afternoon, autumn was beginning to wane, though it was only September. The leaves had turned to dull yellows and oranges, the cornfields along the side of the road were a russet brown, the days were crisp and clear, and the nights felt colder. Al and John were in high spirits. They had just returned from an overnight trip to the Guernsey Breeders Association cattle sale in Hutchinson, Minnesota, a few hours' drive away. Their friend Paul Leach, a gay dairy farmer who lived an hour to the north, had come by to do the milking and keep an eye on things. Al and John had bought three new cows in Hutchinson, and their prize-winning bull had been displayed on the cover of the auction catalog. John told me later that Al hadn't slept for the entire week before the auction.

Al didn't tend to sleep much anyway. He had put his cows on an unusual schedule, milking and feeding five times in each two-day period, at nine and a half hour intervals, with the schedule changing every other day. The cycle began with a milking at midnight; other milkings followed at nine thirty the next morning and seven in the evening. The next day he milked at four thirty in the morning, at two in the afternoon, and once again at midnight. (Most farmers had a saner schedule, milking regularly at five in the morning and five in the evening.) Al started on this routine to increase cash flow. "Your operation can either get larger and generate more product," he said, "or you can generate more product per unit." Buying more cows was just too expensive, with prices ranging from $750 to $1,600 a head, so Al opted for getting more milk out of the cows he had. The arrangement seemed to work, with production up eighteen percent since they had started on the new schedule. One result was that Al and John had a coffee pot going twenty-four hours a day, and Al took frequent catnaps.

I had never been on a dairy farm before and didn't realize how demanding the work could be. John and Al had fifty cows, twenty of which were milking. Almost all their livestock was brown and white Guernseys, and the two farmers were extremely partial to the breed. Guernsey cattle, they told me, tended to produce higher solids in their milk, which was good for making cheese. Their farm produced six hundred pounds of milk each day, which John and Al sold to a dairy cooperative that resold it to small cheese plants in Wisconsin. Each milking and feeding lasted about two and a half hours.

The evening I arrived, I fell asleep before the midnight milking (or "melking," as John and Al pronounce it) but was at the barn promptly at nine thirty

[1] **Orwell** George Orwell (1903–1950), English writer

the following morning. There, in a sweatshirt, jeans, and high galoshes, John was lugging a forty-five pound steel milking unit from cow to cow and transferring the milk to a big steel vat at the entrance to the barn; then he washed and cleaned the cows' teats, swept the stalls, and shoveled manure. Paul, the visiting farmer, was in charge of the feeding. Al was shoring up a broken stall and giving the cows a dessert of beet pulp.

Like a proud father, Al introduced me to every cow by name, personality, and production value. First came Lilly, lone Brown Swiss among Guernseys, a cow Al described as "heavy, aggressive, good producing. She will finish with 21,000 to 22,000 pounds of milk this year." Then, Honors: "a people cow." Isabel: "on her first lactation." Teardrop: "Our gay friends love her. She has incredibly beautiful eyes." And so on, through fifty cows, eight crested Polish chickens (whose coloration made them look as if they were wearing hats), sixteen lambs (Al hoped to increase that number to one or two hundred soon; both the wool and lamb market had been up recently), two lavender angora rabbits (whose fur could be spun into yarn), and three horses. Never far away was Nellie, a diminutive white poodle who made a rather humorous farm dog.

Al compared looking after his cows to bringing up fifty children. "They are very dependent on humans and very individual," he said. "With them, there are tremendous difficulties and tremendous disappointments. They can have structural problems, heart attacks. You play doctor and nurse to them. They can lay down and die one day for no apparent reason. In this business, the profit margins are slim, the tension and stress can be awful." The rewards made it all worthwhile, nonetheless: "the renewing experience" of calving, the "tremendous joy" of working with animals.

Al was an unusual combination of urban camp sensibility and country 10 style and values. He wore two earrings in his left ear and a bangle on his wrist; his shirt was open almost to his navel. He gave his cows names like "You Tell 'Em Dorothy" and "Fashion Design" and called one sheep "Dottie of Fergus Falls" (after an ice-cream commercial). He divided the cows that weren't milking into three categories: "debs, minnies, and nymphettes." Inside the farmhouse, gay paperback gothics and mysteries filled the shelves. Three movie-theatre seats provided living room furniture, someone's idea of trendy but not particularly comfortable "gay" decor. On the dining room wall was a photograph of someone standing in the barn dressed in black stockings, lace panties, and black jacket, with a cow looking on incredulously in the background. On closer inspection, the person in the photograph turned out to bear a striking resemblance to Al. Also on that wall was the wooden plaque Al and John's bull won at the State Fair. "1987 Minnesota State Fair Grand Champion," it read.

Al, at thirty-seven, was the dreamer, the impractical one, living out his passion—his love of animals. John, at thirty-two, complemented him—he was solid and forthright, bringing sense, balance, and some hard-headed financial realism to the operation and to their life together. When Al described the cows as "a commodity," John assured me, "He doesn't really mean that. He picked up that phrase from me." Unlike Al, John had a life beyond the farm. He commuted five days a week to the Twin Cities, where he worked as a reporter-editor for *The Farmer*, a monthly magazine that covers midwestern agriculture. He also worked part-time as regional news editor for *Equal Time*, the gay and lesbian paper. While Al called dairy farming "my career," John considered himself a journalist first and a farmer second.

Weekdays, John left for work at seven in the morning, often not returning until as late as eleven in the evening, especially if he was doing a story for *Equal Time*. Sometimes he could be gone for days at a stretch covering South Dakota, his beat. John's absences left the management of the farm almost completely in Al's hands. Al became the one to negotiate with the banks and the dairy cooperative and the salesmen who came to the farm to sell feed and semen, to talk to the veterinarian and the county agent. He spent his days like most other dairy farmers in the Midwest: milking and feeding cows, cleaning barns, hauling manure, mowing lawns, confronting crises, and grabbing a few hours of sleep when he could.

Al and John had been dairy farmers for four years and lovers for eight and a half. They leased a five-acre farm near the town of Ogilvie, where the exurbia of Minneapolis gives way to the bait shops and mobile homes of Kanabec County. One demographer recently annointed the county the next area for growth in Minnesota, but there were few signs of development yet, at least in the area where Al and John lived. Ogilvie, the nearest town and where the two did their shopping, looks as if it is out of a painting by Edward Hopper. The country is flat and cheerless, crossed by Highway 65, the route that hunters and fishermen from the Twin Cities take to their cabins on the lakes farther north. The farms are poor and relatively small; the visitor misses the intimacy of the rolling country of Iowa to the south or the dramatic expanses of the wheat belt of the Dakotas to the west.

There was nothing particularly bucolic about John and Al's Blue Spur Farm. They didn't grow their own feed or even have a vegetable garden. The farmhouse, located virtually on the highway, was plain and slightly rundown. Just behind the house, the cattle barn, with its characteristic grey-shingled silo, was badly in need of paint. Connected to it was a tin-roofed, functional structure for the dry cows and baby heifers and a shed for the lambs. A few acres of pasture behind the barn completed the picture.

I went off with John and Paul, the visiting farmer, in John's pickup to have   15
dinner at the Sportsman's Cafe, the nearest watering hole, about ten minutes down the road at Mora. Sportsman's was a joint with a large counter in the middle and booths along the side wall. It was open twenty-four hours a day to serve fishermen and hunters and state troopers, and John knew all the waitresses, women in their forties and fifties who have spent their lives standing on their feet. "Where's your friend?" one of them asked John as soon as we walked in. "I haven't seen either one of you in weeks."

At Sportsman's, we ate homemade oyster stew and pecan pie, and John drank several cups of coffee to keep awake for the late-night milking. John told me that he and Al had both grown up on dairy farms—Al in northern Minnesota, sixty miles from the Canadian border, where his father raised Guernseys; John to the west of the Twin Cities, where his family still raised Holsteins. John had always intended to get away from farming; the work was too hard. He met Al at the wedding of a mutual friend in Grand Forks, North Dakota. At the time, John was living in the Twin Cities and working on a newspaper;

Al was farming with his father. Soon after, Al moved down to St. Paul to live with John, working in retail clothing stores.

But the attractions of urban life dwindled, and the focus of their lives began to shift back towards the farm. John moved into ag-journalism, writing for *The Farmer*, partly because he was frustrated by the long hours of news writing but also because of Al's continuing interest in the subject. More and more, they began to fantasize about returning to a rural setting, if not to farming itself. Their friends refused to take them seriously, dismissing the idea as "cute" or "a nice little dream." Al and John bought some horses and moved just outside St. Paul. A few cows wouldn't be too much trouble, they decided, and then they moved out even farther. John was somewhat reluctant; he is the cautious one, after all, and also the one who really wanted to get away from farming. But Al pressed, and John gave in.

John stressed that in returning to the farm, he and Al had made a conscious effort to do things differently from most gay farmers in the past. Traditionally, he said, in order to stay in agriculture, gay farmers either married someone of the opposite sex or completely sacrificed any possibility of a relationship. Whatever their strategy for survival, they remained in the closet. Although John and Al weren't going to advertise their homosexuality, they were determined not to hide it either, letting people draw their own conclusions instead. "I have run into people in town who thought we were brothers, even though our names are different," said John. "They are more comfortable thinking that way." Some people were suspicious, he admitted, and others knew they were gay and didn't approve, sometimes telling them so directly. But he thought that to half of them, the possiblity of his and Al's homosexuality "doesn't occur at all."

Al agreed. "Most farmers are more interested in how the livestock in our farming operation performs," he told me later. When a story about them as gay farmers (including photos) appeared on the front page of the daily newspaper in nearby St. Cloud, there was no visible reaction from their neighbors.

Their friend Paul had had a more traditionally closeted experience, 20 however. He was a sweet and unassuming man in his late twenties, with curly brown hair and a neatly clipped beard. Four and a half years ago, while living in the Twin Cities, he became the lover of an older man. The two bought a farm together in a predominantly Finnish area about two and a half hours north of Minneapolis. The older man had died of lung cancer a few months before; Paul still spoke of his lover in the present tense. Paul stayed on at the farm with only three small calves, rebuilding a barn and hoping to establish a viable livestock business. Paul said the main issue for the neighbors had not been the couple's homosexuality but the fact that he and his lover were German Catholics, not Finnish Protestants. "First they thought my lover was my father until they realized we didn't have the same last name," he said. "Then they thought I was just his hired man." Now, his neighbors were beginning to wonder. "They are thinking, 'This is weird. The hired man is still living there,' " Paul observed. Just a week before, in the small town nearby, he had heard someone mutter "There goes a queer," as he was leaving a store. "I presume they were talking about me," he said. "I guess I'm 'out' now."

For their part, Al and John had not been particularly active in the organization of local Guernsey farmers, but this was changing. The award their bull received at the state fair and the fact they were advertising their livestock in the Guernsey breeders' magazine had given them increased visibility among local farmers. Now, "people notice us," said John. "The ad gave people an opportunity to say something to us." In fact, the following week Al and John were holding a potluck picnic at their farm for the Northeast District Guernsey Breeders Association. They expected about twenty dairy farmers to attend.

There had been one disturbing episode, however. Al had been coaching the 4-H county dairy cattle judging team, composed of kids aged fourteen to sixteen. One parent complained to the county agent who supervises the 4-H that Al was gay. The agent apparently failed to back Al up, and Al resigned as coach. He hoped to be invited back the following year, noting that the kids involved in the organization had been supportive. But John, always the more realistic one, was doubtful this would happen.

In the process of living in the country, they had increasingly discovered other farmers like themselves—a gay male couple nearby who raised sheep, a lesbian couple who had dairy goats, and two other men with a hog farm. Three years ago, Al and John took out a classified advertisement in *Equal Time*, announcing they would be at the state fair and inviting other gay people to stop by the cattle barn and say hello. They were startled by the constant stream of visitors. This summer, *Equal Time* published John's "Gay Guide to the State Fair" as its cover article. One result was that Paul came by the cattle barn, introduced himself to them, and all three became fast friends.

The fact that John and Al were open about their sexuality put them in a pivotal spot in helping to develop a close-knit rural gay community in Minnesota. (John and Al, it should be noted, were not the first gay farmers in the state to come out publicly. Dick Hanson, farmer, farm activist, and member of the Democratic National Committee, was openly gay and quite well-known. Hanson died of AIDS in late July 1987.) "Unless you are willing to be 'out,' it is hard to connect with people," John observed. "A lot of these gay farmers thought they were the only ones doing this." Now Al and John's social circle was shifting. Although they remained close with many of their urban gay friends, especially those who were interested in what they were doing, only a special occasion could persuade them to trek into the Twin Cities.

To me, one of the most interesting aspects of John and Al's return to the 25 farm was that it had brought about a reconciliation with their parents. Several years ago, when John first told his parents he was gay, they were traumatized, he said. But out of seven sons of a farm family, John was the only one currently involved in agriculture. For his father, who was still operating the family farm, the return of his gay son to the land was "the least expected thing," said John. His father had been supportive of their operation and both father and son tried to help each other whenever possible, trading advice and material assistance. As John noted, they were both in the same business and faced the "same questions and troubles."

None of Al's two brothers and two sisters were farming either, and his parents had retired. But family ties to the land remained strong. One sister, who lived in Denver, was "absolutely thrilled," he said, when their bull won the state fair championship. Although she lived in a city, she was eager for her children to have some connection with the family's rural roots. "And it just so happens that in our family Uncle Al and Uncle John are the only ones who are farming," her brother pointed out.

The ability of both sets of parents to identify with Al and John's occupation appeared to provide a counterweight to their difficulties in accepting their sons' homosexuality. If they had lived in the Twin Cities and worked at jobs their parents couldn't identify with, the gay issue might loom larger between the generations, Al and John thought. John noted that from the time he went to college until he began farming, he had had little in common with his family. That certainly wasn't true these days. "As far as sexuality goes, they accept it but they are not supportive," he said. "But they are supportive of the rest of my life.

Al and John maintained that living on the farm had strengthened their own relationship as well, and noted that they had been together the longest in their circle of gay couples. John believed that doing what they wanted to do with their lives—in Al's case, farming, in John's, a combination of farming and journalism—gave their relationship a strength it might not have had if they had sacrificed their aspirations and opted for a more conventional urban gay life. The fact they were business partners as well as lovers provided another tie; it would take months to dissolve their financial bonds. "This is not just a personal relationship, but an economic one, too," Al said.

Although they had left the big city behind, they were reluctant to cut their links to the larger gay world. They had been exploring the notion of combining farming with managing a gay-oriented bed and breakfast. (By the end of my travels, I was convinced that running a B and B is the dream of half the gay men in the United States.) The farm they currently leased wouldn't be appropriate, so they were looking at property slightly closer to the Twin Cities. "It is a dream," John admitted. He also conceded that combining milking cows and raising sheep with changing sheets and cooking breakfast for guests might turn out to be more than they could handle. Nonetheless, they were just not the kind of farmers who want to be "isolated and secluded," as John put it. The presence of a large and active gay community in the Twin Cities offered them a connection and a potential for involvement that other gay farmers who lived farther away didn't have.

Few urban gays were following in Al and John's footsteps. The dismal 30 state of the farm economy argued against any major migration back to the farm; large numbers of farmers, both gay and straight, were packing up and leaving the land, as it was. And many gay men and lesbians who grew up on farms and in rural areas didn't necessarily recall their formative years with fondness. "You grow up on the farm and as you realize your sexuality, you feel you just don't fit," Al told me. "You don't fit in at Sunday church dinners or the PTA or picnics. You become frustrated and you search for others like yourself, and they are not real visible in a rural area. So you tend to leave."

But the pull of one's roots is a powerful thing. "As you mature," Al added, "you tend to go back."

[1989]

■ TOPICS FOR DISCUSSION AND WRITING

1. In the first paragraph Miller says he had "never assumed" that a state fair "would be a particularly good place to observe gay and lesbian life." What prior assumptions had he presumably made about farmers and state fairs, or about gays and lesbians? How valid do you think these assumptions are? What evidence, if any, can you offer to support your view?

2. The essay, as far as we can discern, has no thesis sentence. Does it have a thesis idea? If so, try to formulate the thesis idea in a sentence or two.

3. "But the pull of one's roots is a powerful thing," Miller tells us in his last paragraph. To which Al adds, "As you mature, . . . you tend to go back." Do these sentiments ring true for your own life? Are you likely at some future time (or do you now) live a life similar to the one you knew as a child? Do you see yourself in the occupation of either of your parents? Explain in an essay of approximately 750–1000 words.

4. In paragraph 19 we are told that an article about Al and John "as gay farmers" appeared in a daily newspaper. Drawing on Miller's essay, write the article (500 words).

FICTION

■ NATHANIEL HAWTHORNE

Nathaniel Hawthorne (1804–1864) was born in Salem, Massachusetts, the son of a sea captain. Two of his ancestors were judges; one had persecuted Quakers, another had served at the Salem witch trials. After graduating from Bowdoin College in Maine he went back to Salem in order to write in relative seclusion. In 1831 he published "My Kinsman, Major Molineux"; in 1835 he published "Young Goodman Brown" and "The Maypole of Merry Mount"; and in 1837 he published "Dr. Heidegger's Experiment."

From 1839 to 1841 Hawthorne worked in the Boston Customs House and then spent a few months as a member of a communal society, Brook Farm. In 1842 he married. From 1846 to 1849 he was a surveyor at the Salem Customs House; from 1849 to 1850 he wrote *The Scarlet Letter,* the book that made him famous. From 1853 to 1857 he served as American consul in Liverpool, England, a plum awarded him in exchange for writing a campaign biography of a former college classmate, President Franklin Pierce. In 1860, after living in England and Italy, he returned to the United States, settling in Concord, Massachusetts.

In his stories and novels Hawthorne keeps returning to the Puritan past, studying guilt, sin, and isolation.

The Maypole of Merry Mount

There is an admirable foundation for a philosophic romance in the curious history of the early settlement of Mount Wollaston, or Merry Mount. In the slight sketch here attempted, the facts, recorded on the grave pages of our New England annalists, have wrought themselves, almost spontaneously, into a sort of allegory. The masques, mummeries, and festive customs, described in the text, are in accordance with the manners of the age. Authority on these points may be found in Strutt's Book of English Sports and Pastimes.

Bright were the days at Merry Mount, when the Maypole was the banner staff of that gay colony! They who reared it, should their banner be triumphant, were to pour sunshine over New England's rugged hills, and scatter flower seeds throughout the soil. Jollity and gloom were contending for an empire. Midsummer eve had come, bringing deep verdure to the forest, and roses in her lap, of a more vivid hue than the tender buds of Spring. But May, or her mirthful spirit, dwelt all the year round at Merry Mount, sporting with the Summer months, and revelling with Autumn, and basking in the glow of Winter's fireside. Through a world of toil and care she flitted with a dreamlike smile, and came hither to find a home among the lightsome hearts of Merry Mount.

Never had the Maypole been so gayly decked as at sunset on midsummer eve. This venerated emblem was a pine-tree, which had preserved the slender grace of youth, while it equalled the loftiest height of the old wood monarchs. From its top streamed a silken banner, colored like the rainbow. Down nearly to the ground the pole was dressed with birchen boughs, and others of the liveliest green, and some with silvery leaves, fastened by ribbons that fluttered in fantastic knots of twenty different colors, but no sad ones. Garden flowers, and blossoms of the wilderness, laughed gladly forth amid the verdure, so fresh and dewy that they must have grown by magic on that happy pine-tree. Where this green and flowery splendor terminated, the shaft of the Maypole was stained with the seven brilliant hues of the banner at its top. On the lowest green bough hung an abundant wreath of roses, some that had been gathered in the sunniest spots of the forest, and others, of still richer blush, which the colonists had reared from English seed. O, people of the Golden Age, the chief of your husbandry was to raise flowers!

But what was the wild throng that stood hand in hand about the Maypole? It could not be that the fauns and nymphs, when driven from their classic groves and homes of ancient fable, had sought refuge, as all the persecuted did, in the fresh woods of the West. These were Gothic monsters, though perhaps of Grecian ancestry. On the shoulders of a comely youth uprose the head and branching antlers of a stag; a second, human in all other points, had the grim visage of a wolf; a third, still with the trunk and limbs of a mortal man, showed the beard and horns of a venerable he-goat. There was the likeness of a bear erect, brute in all but his hind legs, which were adorned with pink silk stockings. And here again, almost as wondrous, stood a real bear of the dark forest, lending each of his fore paws to the grasp of a human hand, and as ready for the dance as any in that circle. His inferior nature rose half way, to meet his companions as they stooped. Other faces wore the similitude of man or woman, but distorted or extravagant, with red noses pendulous before their mouths, which seemed of awful depth, and stretched from ear to ear in an eternal fit of laughter. Here might be seen the Savage Man, well known in heraldry, hairy as a baboon, and girdled with green leaves. By his side, a noble figure, but still a counterfeit, appeared an Indian hunter, with feathery crest and wampum belt. Many of this strange company wore foolscaps, and had little bells appended to their garments, tinkling with a silvery sound, responsive to the inaudible music of their gleesome spirits. Some youths and maidens were of soberer garb, yet well maintained their places in the irregular throng by the expression of wild revelry upon their features. Such were the colonists of Merry Mount, as they stood in the broad smile of sunset round their venerated Maypole.

Had a wanderer, bewildered in the melancholy forest, heard their mirth, and stolen a half-affrighted glance, he might have fancied them the crew of Comus,[1] some already transformed to brutes, some midway between man and beast, and the others rioting in the flow of tipsy jollity that foreran the change. But a band of Puritans, who watched the scene, invisible themselves, compared the masques to those devils and ruined souls with whom their superstition peopled the black wilderness.

Within the ring of monsters appeared the two airiest forms that had ever 5 trodden on any more solid footing than a purple and golden cloud. One was a youth in glistening apparel, with a scarf of the rainbow pattern crosswise on his breast. His right hand held a gilded staff, the ensign of high dignity among the revellers, and his left grasped the slender fingers of a fair maiden, not less gayly decorated than himself. Bright roses glowed in contrast with the dark and glossy curls of each, and were scattered round their feet, or had sprung up spontaneously there. Behind this lightsome couple, so close to the Maypole that its boughs shaded his jovial face, stood the figure of an English priest, canonically dressed, yet decked with flowers, in heathen fashion, and wearing a chaplet of the native vine leaves. By the riot of his rolling eye, and the pagan decorations of his holy garb, he seemed the wildest monster there, and the very Comus of the crew.

"Votaries of the Maypole," cried the flower-decked priest, "merrily, all day long, have the woods echoed to your mirth. But be this your merriest hour, my hearts! Lo, here stand the Lord and Lady of the May, whom I, a clerk of Oxford, and high priest of Merry Mount, am presently to join in holy matrimony. Up with your nimble spirits, ye morris-dancers, green men, and glee maidens, bears and wolves, and horned gentlemen! Come; a chorus now, rich with the old mirth of Merry England, and the wilder glee of this fresh forest; and then a dance, to show the youthful pair what life is made of, and how airily they should go through it! All ye that love the Maypole, lend your voices to the nuptial song of the Lord and Lady of the May!"

[1] A classical deity of revelry

This wedlock was more serious than most affairs of Merry Mount, where jest and delusion, trick and fantasy, kept up a continual carnival. The Lord and Lady of the May, though their titles must be laid down at sunset, were really and truly to be partners for the dance of life, beginning the measure that same bright eve. The wreath of roses, that hung from the lowest green bough of the Maypole, had been twined for them, and would be thrown over both their heads, in symbol of their flowery union. When the priest had spoken, therefore, a riotous uproar burst from the rout of monstrous figures.

"Begin you the stave, reverend Sir," cried they all; "and never did the woods ring to such a merry peal as we of the Maypole shall send up!"

Immediately a prelude of pipe, cithern, and viol, touched with practised minstrelsy, began to play from a neighboring thicket, in such a mirthful cadence that the boughs of the Maypole quivered to the sound. But the May Lord, he of the gilded staff, chancing to look into his Lady's eyes, was wonder struck at the almost pensive glance that met his own.

"Edith, sweet Lady of the May," whispered he reproachfully, "is yon 10 wreath of roses a garland to hang above our graves, that you look so sad? O, Edith, this is our golden time! Tarnish it not by any pensive shadow of the mind; for it may be that nothing of futurity will be brighter than the mere remembrance of what is now passing."

"That was the very thought that saddened me! How came it in your mind too?" said Edith, in a still lower tone than he, for it was high treason to be sad at Merry Mount. "Therefore do I sigh amid this festive music. And besides, dear Edgar, I struggle as with a dream, and fancy that these shapes of our jovial friends are visionary, and their mirth unreal, and that we are no true Lord and Lady of the May. What is the mystery in my heart?"

Just then, as if a spell had loosened them, down came a little shower of withering rose leaves from the Maypole. Alas, for the young lovers! No sooner had their hearts glowed with real passion than they were sensible of something vague and unsubstantial in their former pleasures, and felt a dreary presentiment of inevitable change. From the moment that they truly loved, they had subjected themselves to earth's doom of care and sorrow, and troubled joy, and had no more a home at Merry Mount. That was Edith's mystery. Now leave we the priest to marry them, and the masquers to sport round the Maypole, till the last sunbeam be withdrawn from its summit, and the shadows of the forest mingle gloomily in the dance. Meanwhile, we may discover who these gay people were.

Two hundred years ago, and more, the old world and its inhabitants became mutually weary of each other. Men voyaged by thousands to the West: some to barter glass beads, and such like jewels, for the furs of the Indian hunter; some to conquer virgin empires; and one stern band to pray. But none of these motives had much weight with the colonists of Merry Mount. Their leaders were men who had sported so long with life, that when Thought and Wisdom came, even these unwelcome guests were led astray by the crowd of vanities which they should have put to flight. Erring Thought and perverted Wisdom were made to put on masques, and play the fool. The men of whom we speak, after losing the heart's fresh gayety, imagined a wild philosophy of pleasure, and came hither to act out their latest day-dream.

They gathered followers from all that giddy tribe whose whole life is like the festal days of soberer men. In their train were minstrels, not unknown in London streets; wandering players, whose theatres had been the halls of noblemen; mummers, rope-dancers, and mountebanks, who would long be missed at wakes, church ales, and fairs; in a word, mirth makers of every sort, such as abounded in that age, but now began to be discountenanced by the rapid growth of Puritanism. Light had their footsteps been on land, and as lightly they came across the sea. Many had been maddened by their previous troubles into a gay despair; others were as madly gay in the flush of youth, like the May Lord and his Lady; but whatever might be the quality of their mirth, old and young were gay at Merry Mount. The young deemed themselves happy. The elder spirits, if they knew that mirth was but the counterfeit of happiness, yet followed the false shadow wilfully, because at least her garments glittered brightest. Sworn triflers of a lifetime, they would not venture among the sober truths of life not even to be truly blest.

All the hereditary pastimes of Old England were transplanted hither. The King of Christmas was duly crowned, and the Lord of Misrule bore potent sway. On the Eve of St. John, they felled whole acres of the forest to make bonfires, and danced by the blaze all night, crowned with garlands, and throwing flowers into the flame. At harvest time, though their crop was of the smallest, they made an image with the sheaves of Indian corn, and wreathed it with autumnal garlands, and bore it home triumphantly. But what chiefly characterized the colonists of Merry Mount was their veneration for the Maypole. It has made their true history a poet's tale. Spring decked the hallowed emblem with young blossoms and fresh green boughs; Summer brought roses of the deepest blush, and the perfected foliage of the forest; Autumn enriched it with that red and yellow gorgeousness which converts each wildwood leaf into a painted flower; and Winter silvered it with sleet, and hung it round with icicles, till it flashed in the cold sunshine, itself a frozen sunbeam. Thus each alternate season did homage to the Maypole, and paid it a tribute of its own richest splendor. Its votaries danced round it, once, at least, in every month; sometimes they called it their religion, or their altar; but always, it was the banner staff of Merry Mount.

Unfortunately, there were men in the new world of a sterner faith than 15 those Maypole worshippers. Not far from Merry Mount was a settlement of Puritans, most dismal wretches, who said their prayers before daylight, and then wrought in the forest or the cornfield till evening made it prayer time again. Their weapons were always at hand to shoot down the straggling savage. When they met in conclave, it was never to keep up the old English mirth, but to hear sermons three hours long, or to proclaim bounties on the heads of wolves and the scalps of Indians. Their festivals were fast days and their chief pastime the singing of psalms. Woe to the youth or maiden who did but dream of a dance! The selectman nodded to the constable; and there sat the light-heeled reprobate in the stocks; or if he danced, it was round the whipping-post, which might be termed the Puritan Maypole.

A party of these grim Puritans, toiling through the difficult woods, each with a horseload of iron armor to burden his footsteps, would sometimes draw near the sunny precincts of Merry Mount. There were the silken colonists, sporting round their Maypole; perhaps teaching a bear to dance, or striving to communicate their mirth to the grave Indian; or masquerading in the skins of deer and wolves, which they had hunted for that especial purpose. Often, the whole colony were playing at blindman's buff, magistrates and all, with their eyes bandaged, except a single scapegoat, whom the blinded sinners pursued by the tinkling of the bells at his garments. Once, it is said, they were seen following a flower-decked corpse, with merriment and festive music, to his grave. But did the dead man laugh? In their quietest times, they sang ballads and told tales, for the edification of their pious visitors; or perplexed them with juggling tricks; or grinned at them through horse collars; and when sport itself grew wearisome, they made game of their own stupidity, and began a yawning match. At the very least of these enormities, the men of iron shook their heads and frowned so darkly that the revellers looked up imagining that a momentary cloud had overcast the sunshine, which was to be perpetual there. On the other hand, the Puritans affirmed that, when a psalm was pealing from their place of worship, the echo which the forest sent them back seemed often like the chorus of a jolly catch, closing with a roar of laughter. Who but the fiend, and his bond slaves, the crew of Merry Mount, had thus disturbed them? In due time, a feud arose, stern and bitter on one side, and as serious on the other as anything could be among such light spirits as had sworn allegiance to the Maypole. The future complexion of New England was involved in this important quarrel. Should the grizzly saints establish their jurisdiction over the gay sinners, then would their spirits darken all the clime, and make it a land of clouded visages, of hard toil, of sermon and psalm forever. But should the banner staff of Merry Mount be fortunate, sunshine would break upon the hills, and flowers would beautify the forest, and late posterity do homage to the Maypole.

After these authentic passages from history, we return to the nuptials of the Lord and Lady of the May. Alas! we have delayed too long, and must darken our tale too suddenly. As we glance again at the Maypole, a solitary sunbeam is fading from the summit, and leaves only a faint, golden tinge blended with the hues of the rainbow banner. Even that dim light is now withdrawn, relinquishing the whole domain of Merry Mount to the evening gloom, which has rushed so instantaneously from the black surrounding woods. But some of these black shadows have rushed forth in human shape.

Yes, with the setting sun, the last day of mirth had passed from Merry Mount. The ring of gay masquers was disordered and broken; the stag lowered his antlers in dismay; the wolf grew weaker than a lamb; the bells of the morris-dancers tinkled with tremulous affright. The Puritans had played a characteristic part in the Maypole mummeries. Their darksome figures were intermixed with the wild shapes of their foes, and made the scene a picture of the moment, when waking thoughts start up amid the scattered fantasies of a dream. The leader of the hostile party stood in the centre of the circle, while the route of monsters cowered around him, like evil spirits in the presence of a dread magician. No fantastic foolery could look him in the face. So stern was the energy of his aspect, that the whole man, visage, frame, and soul, seemed wrought of iron, gifted with life and thought, yet all of one substance with his headpiece and breastplate. It was the Puritan of Puritans; it was Endicott himself!

"Stand off, priest of Baal!" said he, with a grim frown, and laying no reverent hand upon the surplice. "I know thee, Blackstone![2] Thou art the man who couldst not abide the rule even of thine own corrupted church, and hast come hither to preach iniquity, and to give example of it in thy life. But now shall it be seen that the Lord hath sanctified this wilderness for his peculiar people. Woe unto them that would defile it! And first, for this flower-decked abomination, the altar of thy worship!"

And with his keen sword Endicott assaulted the hallowed Maypole. Nor   20
long did it resist his arm. It groaned with a dismal sound; it showered leaves and rosebuds upon the remorseless enthusiast; and finally, with all its green boughs and ribbons and flowers, symbolic of departed pleasures, down fell the banner staff of Merry Mount. As it sank, tradition says, the evening sky grew darker, and the woods threw forth a more sombre shadow.

"There," cried Endicott, looking triumphantly on his work, "there lies the only Maypole in New England! The thought is strong within me that, by its fall, is shadowed forth the fate of light and idle mirth makers, amongst us and our posterity. Amen, saith John Endicott."

"Amen!" echoed his followers.

But the votaries of the Maypole gave one groan for their idol. At the sound, the Puritan leader glanced at the crew of Comus, each a figure of broad mirth, yet, at this moment, strangely expressive of sorrow and dismay.

"Valiant captain," quoth Peter Palfrey, the Ancient of the band, "what order shall be taken with the prisoners?"

"I thought not to repent me of cutting down a Maypole," replied En-   25
dicott, "yet now I could find in my heart to plant it again, and give each of these bestial pagans one other dance round their idol. It would have served rarely for a whipping-post!"

"But there are pine-trees enow," suggested the lieutenant.

"True, good Ancient," said the leader. "Wherefore, bind the heathen crew, and bestow on them a small matter of stripes apiece, as earnest of our future justice. Set some of the rogues in the stocks to rest themselves, so soon as Providence shall bring us to one of our own well-ordered settlements where such accommodations may be found. Further penalties, such as branding and cropping of ears, shall be thought of hereafter."

"How many stripes for the priest?" inquired Ancient Palfrey.

"None as yet," answered Endicott, bending his iron frown upon the culprit. "It must be for the Great and General Court to determine, whether stripes and long imprisonment, and other grievous penalty, may atone for his transgressions. Let him look to himself! For such as violate our civil order, it may be permitted us to show mercy. But woe to the wretch that troubleth our religion."

"And this dancing bear," resumed the officer. "Must he share the stripes   30
of his fellows?"

"Shoot him through the head!" said the energetic Puritan. "I suspect witchcraft in the beast."

---

[2] Did Governor Endicott speak less positively, we should suspect a mistake here. The Rev. Mr. Blackstone, though an eccentric, is not known to have been an immoral man. We rather doubt his identity with the priest of Merry Mount. [Hawthorne's note]

"Here be a couple of shining ones," continued Peter Palfrey, pointing his weapon at the Lord and Lady of the May. "They seem to be of high station among these misdoers. Methinks their dignity will not be fitted with less than a double share of stripes."

Endicott rested on his sword, and closely surveyed the dress and aspect of the hapless pair. There they stood, pale, downcast, and apprehensive. Yet there was an air of mutual support and of pure affection, seeking aid and giving it, that showed them to be man and wife, with the sanction of a priest upon their love. The youth, in the peril of the moment, had dropped his gilded staff, and thrown his arm about the Lady of the May, who leaned against his breast, too lightly to burden him, but with weight enough to express that their destinies were linked together, for good or evil. They looked first at each other, and then into the grim captain's face. There they stood, in the first hour of wedlock, while the idle pleasures, of which their companions were the emblems, had given place to the sternest cares of life, personified by the dark Puritans. But never had their youthful beauty seemed so pure and high as when its glow was chastened by adversity.

"Youth," said Endicott, "ye stand in an evil case thou and thy maiden wife. Make ready presently, for I am minded that ye shall both have a token to remember your wedding day!"

"Stern man," cried the May Lord, "how can I move thee? Were the means at hand, I would resist to the death. Being powerless, I entreat! Do with me as thou wilt, but let Edith go untouched!"

"Not so," replied the immitigable zealot. "We are not wont to show an idle courtesy to that sex, which requireth the stricter discipline. What sayest thou, maid? Shall thy silken bridegroom suffer thy share of the penalty, besides his own?"

"Be it death," said Edith, "and lay it all on me!"

Truly, as Endicott had said, the poor lovers stood in a woful case. Their foes were triumphant, their friends captive and abased, their home desolate, the benighted wilderness around them, and a rigorous destiny, in the shape of the Puritan leader, their only guide. Yet the deepening twilight could not altogether conceal that the iron man was softened; he smiled at the fair spectacle of early love; he almost sighed for the inevitable blight of early hopes.

"The troubles of life have come hastily on this young couple," observed Endicott. "We will see how they comport themselves under their present trials ere we burden them with greater. If, among the spoil, there be any garments of a more decent fashion, let them be put upon this May Lord and his Lady, instead of their glistening vanities. Look to it, some of you."

"And shall not the youth's hair be cut?" asked Peter Palfrey, looking with abhorrence at the lovelock and long glossy curls of the young man.

"Crop it forthwith, and that in the true pumpkin-shell fashion," answered the captain. "Then bring them along with us, but more gently than their fellows. There be qualities in the youth, which may make him valiant to fight, and sober to toil, and pious to pray; and in the maiden, that may fit her to become a mother in our Israel, bringing up babes in better nurture than her own hath been. Nor think ye, young ones, that they are the happiest, even in our lifetime of a moment, who misspend it in dancing round a Maypole!"

And Endicott, the severest Puritan of all who laid the rock foundation of New England, lifted the wreath of roses from the ruin of the Maypole, and threw it, with his own gauntleted hand, over the heads of the Lord and Lady of the May. It was a deed of prophecy. As the moral gloom of the world overpowers all systematic gayety, even so was their home of wild mirth made desolate amid the sad forest. They returned to it no more. But as their flowery garland was wreathed of the brightest roses that had grown there, so, in the tie that united them, were intertwined all the purest and best of their early joys. They went heavenward, supporting each other along the difficult path which it was their lot to tread, and never wasted one regretful thought of the vanities of Merry Mount.

[1835]

■ TOPICS FOR DISCUSSION AND WRITING

1. In his brief headnote, Hawthorne says that the facts as "recorded on the grave pages of our New England annalists, have wrought themselves, almost spontaneously, into a sort of allegory." In a paragraph or two explain the allegory.
2. What words or phrases in the first two paragraphs suggest that there is something illusionary or insubstantial or transient in the life of Merry Mount?
3. In a paragraph, characterize Endicott.

■ HERMAN MELVILLE

Herman Melville (1819–1891) was born into a poor family in New York City. The bankruptcy and death of his father when Melville was 12 forced the boy to leave school. During these early years he worked first as a bank clerk, then as a farm laborer, then as a store clerk and bookkeeper, and then as a schoolmaster. In 1837 he sailed to England as a cabin boy and signed on for other voyages, notably on whalers in the South Pacific, where he spent time in the Marquesas Islands and Tahiti. Out of his maritime adventures he produced commercially successful books, *Typee* (1846), *Omoo* (1847), *Mardi* (1849), and *Redburn* (1849), but *Moby-Dick* (1851) was a commercial failure, and so was a later book, *Pierre* (1852). Melville next turned to writing short fiction, but, again commercially unsuccessful, he stopped trying to live by his pen. In "Bartleby" (1853), Melville's first published short story, many readers see an image of the author withdrawing from the commercial-literary world. He continued, however, to write—poetry as well as prose.

Bartleby, the Scrivener

A STORY OF WALL STREET

I am a rather elderly man. The nature of my avocations, for the last thirty years, has brought me into more than ordinary contact with what would seem an interesting and somewhat singular set of men, of whom, as yet, nothing, that I know of, has ever been written—I mean, the law-copyists, or scriveners. I have known very many of them, professionally and privately, and, if I pleased, could relate divers histories, at which good-natured gentlemen might smile, and sentimental souls might weep. But I waive the biographies of all other scriveners, for a few passages in the life of Bartleby, who was a scrivener, the strangest I ever saw, or heard of. While, of other law-copyists, I might write the complete life, of Bartleby nothing of that sort can be done. I believe that no materials exist, for a full and satisfactory biography of this man. It is an irreparable loss to literature. Bartleby was one of those beings of whom nothing is ascertainable, except from the original sources, and, in his case, those are very small. What my own astonished eyes saw of Bartleby, *that* is all I know of him, except, indeed, one vague report, which will appear in the sequel.

Ere introducing the scrivener, as he first appeared to me, it is fit I make some mention of myself, my *employés*, my business, my chambers, and general surroundings, because some such description is indispensable to an adequate understanding of the chief character about to be presented. Imprimis:[1] I am a man who, from his youth upwards, has been filled with a profound conviction that the easiest way of life is the best. Hence, though I belong to a profession proverbially energetic and nervous, even to turbulence, at times, yet nothing of that sort have I ever suffered to invade my peace. I am one of those unambitious lawyers who never address a jury, or in any way draw down public applause; but, in the cool tranquility of a snug retreat, do a snug business among rich men's bonds, and mortgages, and title-deeds. All who know me, consider me an eminently *safe* man. The late John Jacob Astor,[2] a personage little given to poetic enthusiasm, had no hesitation in pronouncing my first grand point to be prudence; my next, method. I do not speak it in vanity, but simply record the fact, that I was not unemployed in my profession by the late John Jacob Astor; a name which, I admit, I love to repeat; for it hath a rounded and orbicular sound to it, and rings like unto bullion. I will freely add, that I was not insensible to the late John Jacob Astor's good opinion.

Some time prior to the period at which this little history begins, my avocations had been largely increased. The good old office, now extinct in the State of New York, of a Master in Chancery,[3] had been conferred upon me. It was not a very arduous office, but very pleasantly remunerative. I seldom lose my temper; much more seldom indulge in dangerous indignation at wrongs and outrages; but I must be permitted to be rash here and declare, that I consider the sudden and violent abrogation of the office of Master in Chancery, by the new Constitution, as a——premature act; inasmuch as I had counted upon a life-lease of the profits, whereas I only received those of a few short years. But this is by the way.

My chambers were up stairs, at No. — Wall Street. At one end, they looked upon the white wall of the interior of a spacious skylight shaft, penetrating the building from top to bottom.

[1] **Imprimis** Latin for "in the first place," often used in legal documents

[2] **John Jacob Astor** Astor (1763–1848) was a German-born immigrant who made a fortune in New York City real estate and in the fur trade.

[3] **Chancery** courts in which decisions were often negotiated. No matter who won, the Master always collected a fee.

This view might have been considered rather tame than otherwise, deficient in what landscape painters call "life." But, if so, the view from the other end of my chambers offered, at least, a contrast, if nothing more. In that direction, my windows commanded an unobstructed view of a lofty brick wall, black by age and everlasting shade; which wall required no spy-glass to bring out its lurking beauties, but, for the benefit of all near-sighted spectators, was pushed up to within ten feet of my window-panes. Owing to the great height of the surrounding buildings, and my chambers being on the second floor, the interval between this wall and mine not a little resembled a huge square cistern.

At the period just preceding the advent of Bartleby, I had two persons as copyists in my employment, and a promising lad as an office-boy. First, Turkey; second, Nippers; third, Ginger Nut. These may seem names, the like of which are not usually found in the Directory. In truth, they were nick-names, mutually conferred upon each other by my three clerks, and were deemed expressive of their respective persons or characters. Turkey was a short, pursy Englishman, of about my own age—that is, somewhere not far from sixty. In the morning, one might say, his face was of a fine florid hue, but after twelve o'clock, meridian—his dinner hour—it blazed like a grate full of Christmas coals; and continued blazing—but, as it were, with a gradual wane—till six o'clock, P.M., or thereabouts; after which, I saw no more of the proprietor of the face, which gaining its meridian with the sun, seemed to set with it, to rise, culminate, and decline the following day, with the like regularity and undiminished glory. There are many singular coincidences I have known in the course of my life, not the least among which was the fact, that, exactly when Turkey displayed his fullest beams from his red and radiant countenance, just then, too, at that critical moment, began the daily period when I considered his business capacities as seriously disturbed for the remainder of the twenty-four hours. Not that he was absolutely idle, or averse to business then; far from it. The difficulty was, he was apt to be altogether too energetic. There was a strange, inflamed, flurried, flighty recklessness of activity about him. He would be incautious in dipping his pen into his ink-stand. All his blots upon my documents were dropped there after twelve o'clock, meridian. Indeed, not only would he be reckless, and sadly given to making blots in the afternoon, but some days, he went further, and was rather noisy. At such times, too, his face flamed with augmented blazonry, as if cannel coal[4] had been heaped on anthracite. He made an unpleasant racket with his chair; spilled his sand-box; in mending his pens, impatiently split them all to pieces, and threw them on the floor in a sudden passion; stood up, and leaned over his table, boxing his papers about in a most indecorous manner, very sad to behold in an elderly man like him. Nevertheless, as he was in many ways a most valuable person to me, and all the time before twelve o'clock, meridian, was the quickest, steadiest creature, too, accomplishing a great deal of work in a style not easily to be matched—for these reasons, I was willing to overlook his eccentricities, though, indeed, occasionally, I remonstrated with him. I did this very gently, however, because, though the

---

[4] **cannel coal** bituminous coal, which burns more brightly than anthracite coal

civilest, nay, the blandest and most reverential of men in the morning, yet, in the afternoon, he was disposed, upon provocation, to be slightly rash with his tongue—in fact, insolent. Now, valuing his morning services as I did, and resolved not to lose them—yet, at the same time, made uncomfortable by his inflamed ways after twelve o'clock—and being a man of peace, unwilling by my admonitions to call forth unseemly retorts from him, I took upon me, one Saturday noon (he was always worse on Saturdays) to hint to him, very kindly, that, perhaps, now that he was growing old, it might be well to abridge his labors; in short, he need not come to my chambers after twelve o'clock, but, dinner over, had best go home to his lodgings, and rest himself till tea-time. But no; he insisted upon his afternoon devotions. His countenance became intolerably fervid, as he oratorically assured me—gesticulating with a long ruler at the other end of the room—that if his services in the morning were useful, how indispensable, then, in the afternoon?

"With submission, sir," said Turkey, on this occasion, "I consider myself your right-hand man. In the morning I but marshal and deploy my columns; but in the afternoon I put myself at their head, and gallantly charge the foe, thus"—and he made a violent thrust with the ruler.

"But the blots, Turkey," intimated I.

"True; but, with submission, sir, behold these hairs! I am getting old. Surely, sir, a blot or two of a warm afternoon is not to be severely urged against gray hairs. Old age—even if it blot the page—is honorable. With submission, sir, we *both* are getting old."

This appeal to my fellow-feeling was hardly to be resisted. At all events, I saw that go he would not. So, I made up my mind to let him stay, resolving, nevertheless, to see to it that, during the afternoon, he had to do with my less important papers.

Nippers, the second on my list, was a whiskered, sallow, and, upon the whole, rather piratical-looking young man, of about five-and-twenty. I always deemed him the victim of two evil powers—ambition and indigestion. The ambition was evinced by a certain impatience of the duties of a mere copyist, an unwarrantable usurpation of strictly professional affairs such as original drawing up of legal documents. The indigestion seemed betokened in an occasional nervous testiness and grinning irritability, causing the teeth to audibly grind togehter over mistakes committed in copying; unnecessary maledictions, hissed, rather than spoken, in the heat of business; and especially by a continual discontent with the height of the table where he worked. Though of a very ingenious mechanical turn, Nippers could never get this table to suit him. He put chips under it, blocks of various sorts, bits of pasteboard, and at last went so far as to attempt an exquisite adjustment, by final pieces of folded blotting-paper. But no invention would answer. If, for the sake of easing his back, he brought the table-lid at a sharp angle well up towards his chin, and wrote there like a man using the steep roof of a Dutch house for his desk, then he declared that it stopped the circulation in his arms. If now he lowered the table to his waistbands, and stooped over it in writing, then there was a sore aching in his back. In short, the truth of the matter was, Nippers knew not what he wanted. Or, if he wanted anything, it was to be rid of a scrivener's table altogether. Among the manifestations of his diseased ambition was a fondness he had for receiving visits from certain ambiguous-looking fellows in seedy coats, whom he called his clients. Indeed, I was aware that not only was he, at times, considerable of a ward-politician, but he occasionally did a little business at the justices' courts, and was not unknown on the steps of the Tombs.[5] I have good reason to believe, however, that one individual who called upon him at my chambers, and who, with a grand air, he insisted was his client, was no other than a dun, and the alleged title-deed, a bill. But, with all his failings, and the annoyances he caused me, Nippers, like his compatriot Turkey, was a very useful man to me; wrote a neat, swift hand; and, when he chose, was not deficient in a gentlemanly sort of deportment. Added to this, he always dressed in a gentlemanly sort of way; and so, incidentally, reflected credit upon my chambers. Whereas, with respect to Turkey, I had much ado to keep him from being a reproach to me. His clothes were apt to look oily, and smell of eating-houses. He wore his pantaloons very loose and baggy in summer. His coats were execrable, his hat not to be handled. But while the hat was a thing of indifference to me, inasmuch as his natural civility and deference, as a dependent Englishman, always led him to doff it the moment he entered the room, yet his coat was another matter. Concerning his coats, I reasoned with him; but with no effect. The truth was, I suppose, that a man with so small an income could not afford to sport such a lustrous face and a lustrous coat at one and the same time. As Nippers once observed, Turkey's money went chiefly for red ink. One winter day, I presented Turkey with a highly respectable-looking coat of my own—a padded gray coat, of a most comfortable warmth, and which buttoned straight up from the knee to the neck. I thought Turkey would appreciate the favor, and abate his rashness and obstreperousness of afternoons. But no; I verily believe that buttoning himself up in so downy and blanket-like a coat had a pernicious effect upon him—upon the same principle that too much oats are bad for horses. In fact, precisely as a rash, restive horse is said to feel his oats, so Turkey felt his coat. It made him insolent. He was a man whom prosperity harmed.

Though, concerning the self-indulgent habits of Turkey, I had my own private surmises, yet, touching Nippers, I was well persuaded that, whatever might be his faults in other respects, he was, at least, a temperate young man. But, indeed, nature herself seemed to have been his vintner, and, at his birth, charged him so thoroughly with an irritable, brandy-like disposition, that all subsequent potations were needless. When I consider how, amid the stillness of my chambers, Nippers would sometimes impatiently rise from his seat, and stooping over his table, spread his arms wide apart, seize the whole desk, and move it, and jerk it, with a grim, grinding motion on the floor, as if the table were a perverse voluntary agent, intent on thwarting and vexing him, I plainly perceive that, for Nippers, brandy-and-water were altogether superfluous.

It was fortunate for me that, owing to its peculiar cause—indigestion— the irritability and consequent nervousness of Nippers were mainly observable in the morning, while in the afternoon he was comparatively mild. So that, Turkey's paroxysms only coming on about twelve o'clock, I never had to do with their eccentricities at one time. Their fits relieved each other, like

[5] **the Tombs** nickname for the city prison

guards. When Nippers' was on, Turkey's was off; and *vice versa*. This was a good natural arrangement, under the circumstances.

Ginger Nut, the third on my list, was a lad, some twelve years old. His father was a carman, ambitious of seeing his son on the bench instead of a cart, before he died. So he sent him to my office, as student at law, errandboy, cleaner, and sweeper, at the rate of one dollar a week. He had a little desk to himself, but he did not use it much. Upon inspection, the drawer exhibited a great array of the shells of various sorts of nuts. Indeed, to this quick-witted youth, the whole noble science of the law was contained in a nutshell. Not the least among the employments of Ginger Nut, as well as one which he discharged with the most alacrity, was his duty as cake and apple purveyor for Turkey and Nippers. Copying lawpapers being proverbially a dry, husky sort of business, my two scriveners were fain to moisten their mouths very often with Spitzenbergs,[6] to be had at the numerous stalls nigh the Custom House and Post Office. Also, they sent Ginger Nut very frequently for that peculiar cake—small, flat, round, and very spicy—after which he had been named by them. Of a cold morning, when business was but dull, Turkey would gobble up scores of these cakes, as if they were mere wafers—indeed, they sell them at the rate of six or eight for a penny—the scrape of his pen blending with the crunching of the crisp particles in his mouth. Of all the fiery afternoon blunders and flurried rashness of Turkey, was his once moistening a ginger-cake between his lips, and clapping it on to a mortgage, for a seal. I came within an ace of dismissing him then. But he mollified me by making an oriental bow, and saying—

"With submission, sir, it was generous of me to find you in stationery on my own account."

Now my original business—that of a conveyancer and title hunter, and drawer-up of recondite documents of all sorts—was considerably increased by receiving the Master's office. There was now great work for scriveners. Not only must I push the clerks already with me, but I must have additional help.

In answer to my advertisement, a motionless young man one morning stood upon my office threshold, the door being open, for it was summer. I can see that figure now—pallidly neat, pitiably respectable, incurably forlorn! It was Bartleby.

After a few words touching his qualifications, I engaged him, glad to have among my corps of copyists a man of so singularly sedate an aspect, which I thought might operate beneficially upon the flighty temper of Turkey, and the fiery one of Nippers.

I should have stated before that ground-glass folding-doors divided my premises into two parts, one of which was occupied by my scriveners, the other by myself. According to my humor, I threw open these doors, or closed them. I resolved to assign Bartleby a corner by the folding-doors, but on my side of them, so as to have this quiet man within easy call, in case any trifling thing was to be done. I placed his desk close up to a small side-window in that part of the room, a window which originally had afforded a lateral view of certain grimy brickyards and bricks, but which, owing to subsequent erections, commanded as present no view at all, though it gave some light. Within

[6] **Spitzenbergs** a kind of apple

three feet of the panes was a wall, and the light came down from far above, between two lofty buildings, as from a very small opening in a dome. Still further to a satisfactory arrangement, I procured a high green folding screen, which might entirely isolate Bartleby from my sight, though not remove him from my voice. And thus, in a manner, privacy and society were conjoined.

At first, Bartleby did an extraordinary quantity of writing. As if long famishing for something to copy, he seemed to gorge himself on my documents. There was no pause for digestion. He ran a day and night line, copying by sunlight and by candle-light. I should have been quite delighted with his application, had he been cheerfully industrious. But he wrote on silently, palely, mechanically.

It is, of course, an indispensable part of a scrivener's business to verify the accuracy of his copy, word by word. Where there are two or more scriveners in an office, they assist each other in this examination, one reading from the copy, the other holding the original. It is a very dull, wearisome, and lethargic affair. I can readily imagine that, to some sanguine temperaments, it would be altogether intolerable. For example, I cannot credit that the mettlesome poet, Byron, would have contentedly sat down with Bartleby to examine a law document of, say five hundred pages, closely written in a crimpy hand.

Now and then, in the haste of business, it had been my habit to assist in comparing some brief document myself, calling Turkey or Nippers for this purpose. One object I had, in placing Bartleby so handy to me behind the screen, was, to avail myself of his services on such trivial occasions. It was on the third day, I think, of his being with me, and before any necessity had arisen for having his own writing examined, that, being much hurried to complete a small affair I had in hand, I abruptly called to Bartleby. In my haste and natural expectancy of instant compliance, I sat with my head bent over the original on my desk, and my right hand sideways, and somewhat nervously extended with the copy, so that, immediately upon emerging from his retreat, Bartleby might snatch it and proceed to business without the least delay.

In this very attitude did I sit when I called to him, rapidly stating what it was I wanted him to do—namely, to examine a small paper with me. Imagine my surprise, nay, my consternation, when, without moving from his privacy, Bartleby, in a singularly mild, firm voice, replied, "I would prefer not to."

I sat awhile in perfect silence, rallying my stunned faculties. Immediately it occurred to me that my ears had deceived me, or Bartleby had entirely misunderstood my meaning. I repeated my request in the clearest tone I could assume; but in quite as clear a one came the previous reply, "I would prefer not to."

"Prefer not to," echoed I, rising in high excitement, and crossing the room with a stride. "What do you mean? Are you moonstruck? I want you to help me compare this sheet here—take it," and I thrust it towards him.

"I would prefer not to," said he.

I looked at him steadfastly. His face was leanly composed; his gray eye dimly calm. Not a wrinkle of agitation rippled him. Had there been the least uneasiness, anger, impatience, or impertinence in his manner; in other words, had there been anything ordinarily human about him, doubtless I should have violently dismissed him from the premises. But as it was, I should have as soon thought of turning my pale plaster-of-paris bust of Cicero[7] out of doors. I stood gazing at him awhile, as he went on with his own writing, and then reseated myself at my desk. This is very strange, thought I. What had one best do? But my business hurried me. I concluded to forget the matter for the present, reserving it for my future leisure. So, calling Nippers from the other room, the paper was speedily examined.

A few days after this, Bartleby concluded four lengthy documents, being quadruplicates of a week's testimony taken before me in my High Court of Chancery. It became necessary to examine them. It was an important suit, and great accuracy was imperative. Having all things arranged, I called Turkey, Nippers, and Ginger Nut, from the next room, meaning to place the four copies in the hands of my four clerks, while I should read from the original. Accordingly, Turkey, Nippers, and Ginger Nut had taken their seats in a row, ech with his document in his hand, when I called to Bartleby to join this interesting group.

"Bartleby! quick, I am waiting."

I heard a slow scrape of his chair legs on the uncarpeted floor, and soon he appeared standing at the entrance of his hermitage.

"What is wanted?" said he, mildly.

"The copies, the copies," said I, hurriedly. "We are going to examine them. There" —and I held toward him the fourth quadruplicate.

"I would prefer not to," he said, and gently disappeared behind the screen.

For a few moments I was turned into a pillar of salt, standing at the head of my seated column of clerks. Recovering myself, I advanced towards the screen, and demanded the reason for such extraordinary conduct.

"*Why* do you refuse?"

"I would prefer not to."

With any other man I should have flown outright into a dreadful passion, scorned all further words, and thrust him ignominiously from my presence. But there was something about Bartleby that not only strangely disarmed me, but, in a wonderful manner, touched and disconcerted me. I began to reason with him.

"These are your own copies we are about to examine. It is labor saving to you, because one examination will answer for your four papers. It is common usage. Every copyist is bound to help examine his copy. Is it not so? Will you not speak? Answer!"

"I prefer not to," he replied in a flute-like tone. It seemed to me that, while I had been addressing him, he carefully revolved every statement that I made; fully comprehended the meaning; could not gainsay the irresistible conclusion; but, at the same time, some paramount consideration prevailed with him to reply as he did.

"You are decided, then, not to comply with my request—a request made according to common usage and common sense?"

[7] **Cicero** Roman orator (106–43 B.C.), famous as a defense lawyer

He briefly gave me to understand, that on that point my judgment was sound. Yes: his decision was irreversible.

It is not seldom the case that, when a man is browbeaten in some unprecedented and violently unreasonable way, he begins to stagger in his own plainest faith. He begins, as it were, vaguely to surmise that, wonderful as it may be, all the justice and all the reason is on the other side. Accordingly, if any disinterested persons are present, he turns to them for some reinforcement for his own faltering mind.

"Turkey," said I, "what do you think of this? Am I not right?"

"With submission, sir" said Turkey, in his blandest tone, "I think that you are."

"Nippers," said I, "what do *you* think of it?"

"I think I should kick him out of the office."

(The reader of nice perceptions will have perceived that, it being morning, Turkey's answer is couched in polite and tranquil terms, but Nippers replies in ill-tempered ones. Or, to repeat a previous sentence, Nippers' ugly mood was on duty, and Turkey's off.)

"Ginger Nut," said I, willing to enlist the smallest suffrage in my behalf, "what do *you* think of it?"

"I think, sir, he's a little *luny*," replied Ginger Nut, with a grin.

"You hear what they say," said I, turning towards the screen, "come forth and do your duty."

But he vouchsafed no reply. I pondered a moment in sore perplexity. But once more business hurried me. I determined again to postpone the consideration of this dilemma to my future leisure. With a little trouble we made out to examine the papers without Bartleby, though at every page or two Turkey deferentially dropped his opinion, that this proceeding was quite out of the common; while Nippers, twitching in his chair with a dyspeptic nervousness, ground out, between his set teeth, occasional hissing maledictions against the stubborn oaf behind the screen. And for his (Nippers') part, this was the first and the last time he would do another man's business without pay.

Meanwhile Bartleby sat in his hermitage, oblivious to everything but his own peculiar business there.

Some days passed, the scrivener being employed upon another lengthy work. His late remarkable conduct led me to regard his ways narrowly. I observed that he never went to dinner; indeed, that he never went anywhere. As yet I had never, of my personal knowledge, known him to be outside of my office. He was a perpetual sentry in the corner. At about eleven o'clock though, in the morning, I noticed that Ginger Nut would advance towards the opening in Bartleby's screen, as if silently beckoned thither by a gesture invisible to me where I sat. The boy would then leave the office, jingling a few pence, and reappear with a handful of ginger-nuts, which he delivered in the hermitage, receiving two of the cakes for his trouble.

He lives, then, on ginger-nuts, thought I; never eats a dinner, properly speaking; he must be a vegetarian, then, but no; he never eats even vegetables, he eats nothing but ginger-nuts. My mind then ran on in reveries concerning the probable effects upon the human constitution of living entirely on ginger-nuts. Ginger-nuts are so called, because they contain ginger as one of their peculiar constituents, and the final flavoring one. Now, what was ginger? A hot, spicy thing. Was Bartleby hot and spicy? Not at all. Ginger, then, had no effect upon Bartleby. Probably he preferred it should have none.

Nothing so aggravates an earnest person as a passive resistance. If the individual so resisted be of a not inhumane temper, and the resisting one perfectly harmless in his passivity, then, in the better moods of the former, he will endeavor charitably to construe to his imagination what proves impossible to be solved by his judgment. Even so, for the most part, I regarded Bartleby and his ways. Poor fellow! thought I, he means no mischief; it is plain he intends no insolence; his aspect sufficiently evinces that his eccentricities are involuntary. He is useful to me. I can get along with him. If I turn him away, the chances are he will fall in with some less indulgent employer, and then he will be rudely treated, and perhaps driven forth miserably to starve. Yes. Here I can cheaply purchase a delicious self-approval. To befriend Bartleby; to humor him in his strange wilfulness, will cost me little or nothing, while I lay up in my soul what will eventually prove a sweet morsel for my conscience. But this mood was not invariable with me. The passiveness of Bartleby sometimes irritated me. I felt strangely goaded on to encounter him in new opposition—to elicit some angry spark from him answerable to my own. But, indeed, I might as well have essayed to strike fire with my knuckles against a bit of Windsor soap. But one afternoon the evil impulse in me mastered me, and the following little scene ensued:

"Bartleby," said I, "when those papers are all copied, I will compare them with you."

"I would prefer not to."

"How? Surely you do not mean to persist in that mulish vagary?"

No answer.

I threw open the folding-doors nearby, and turning upon Turkey and Nippers, exclaimed:

"Bartleby a second time says, he won't examine his papers. What do you think of it, Turkey?"

It was afternoon, be it remembered. Turkey sat glowing like a brass boiler; his bald head steaming; his hands reeling among his blotted papers.

"Think of it?" roared Turkey. "I think I'll just step behind his screen, and black his eyes for him!"

So saying, Turkey rose to his feet and threw his arms into a pugilistic position. He was hurrying away to make good his promise, when I detained him, alarmed at the effect of incautiously rousing Turkey's combativeness after dinner.

"Sit down, Turkey," said I, "and hear what Nippers has to say. What do you think of it, Nippers? Would I not be justified in immediately dismissing Bartleby?"

"Excuse me, that is for you to decide, sir. I think his conduct quite unusual, and, indeed, unjust, as regards Turkey and myself. But it may only be a passing whim."

"Ah," exclaimed I, "you have strangely changed your mind, then—you speak very gently of him now."

"All beer," cried Turkey; "gentleness is effects of beer—Nippers and I dined together to-day. You see how gentle *I* am, sir. Shall I go and black his eyes?"

"You refer to Bartleby, I suppose. No, not to-day, Turkey," I replied; "pray, put up your fists."

I closed the doors, and again advanced towards Bartleby. I felt additional incentives tempting me to my fate. I burned to be rebelled against again. I remembered that Bartleby never left the office.

"Bartleby," said I, "Ginger Nut is away; just step around to the Post Office, won't you?" (it was but a three minutes' walk) "and see if there is anything for me."

"I would prefer not to."

"You *will* not?"

"I *prefer* not."

I staggered to my desk, and sat there in a deep study. My blind inveteracy returned. Was there any other thing in which I could procure myself to be ignominiously repulsed by this lean, penniless wight?—my hired clerk? What added thing is there, perfectly reasonable, that he will be sure to refuse to do?

"Bartleby!"

No answer.

"Bartleby," in a louder tone.

No answer.

"Bartleby," I roared.

Like a very ghost, agreeably to the laws of magical invocation, at the third summons, he appeared at the entrance of his hermitage.

"Go to the next room, and tell Nippers to come to me."

"I prefer not to," he respectfully and slowly said, and mildly disappeared.

"Very good, Bartleby," said I, in a quiet sort of serenely-severe self-possessed tone, intimating the unalterable purpose of some terrible retribution very close at hand. At the moment I half intended something of the kind. But upon the whole, as it was drawing towards my dinner-hour, I thought it best to put on my hat and walk home for the day, suffering much from perplexity and distress of mind.

Shall I acknowledge it? The conclusion of this whole business was, that it soon became a fixed fact of my chambers, that a pale young scrivener, by the name of Bartleby, had a desk there; that he copied for me at the usual rate of four cents a folio (one hundred words); but he was permanently exempt from examining the work done by him, that duty being transferred to Turkey and Nippers, out of compliment, doubtless, to their superior acuteness; moreover, said Bartleby was never, on any account, to be dispatched on the most trivial errand of any sort; and that even if entreated to take upon him such a matter, it was generally understood that he would "prefer not to"—in other words, that he would refuse point-blank.

As days passed on, I became considerably reconciled to Bartleby. His steadiness, his freedom from all dissipation, his incessant industry (except when he chose to throw himself into a standing revery behind his screen), his great stillness, his unalterableness of demeanor under all circumstances, made him a valuable acquisition. One prime thing was this—*he was always there*—first in the morning, continually through the day, and the last at night.

I had a singular confidence in his honesty. I felt my most precious papers perfectly safe in his hands. Sometimes, to be sure, I could not, for the very soul of me, avoid falling into sudden spasmodic passions with him. For it was exceeding difficult to bear in mind all the time those strange peculiarities, privileges, and unheard-of exemptions, forming the tacit stipulations on Bartleby's part under which he remained in my office. Now and then, in the eagerness of dispatching pressing business, I would inadvertently summon Bartleby, in a short, rapid tone, to put his finger, say, on the incipient tie of a bit of red tape with which I was about compressing some papers. Of course, from behind the screen the usual answer, "I prefer not to," was sure to come; and then, how could a human creature, with the common infirmities of our nature, refrain from bitterly exclaiming upon such perverseness—such unreasonableness? However, every added repulse of this sort which I received only tended to lessen the probability of my repeating the inadvertence.

Here it must be said, that, according to the custom of most legal gentlemen occupying chambers in densely populated law buildings, there were several keys to my door. One was kept by a woman residing in the attic, which person weekly scrubbed and daily swept and dusted my apartments. Another was kept by Turkey for convenience sake. The third I sometimes carried in my own pocket. The fourth I knew not who had.

Now, one Sunday morning I happened to go to Trinity Church, to hear a celebrated preacher, and finding myself rather early on the ground I thought I would walk round to my chambers for a while. Luckily I had my key with me; but upon applying it to the lock, I found it resisted by something inserted from the inside. Quite surprised, I called out; when to my consternation a key was turned from within; and thrusting his lean visage at me, and holding the door ajar, the apparition of Bartleby appeared, in his shirt-sleeves, and otherwise in a strangely tattered *deshabille*,[8] saying quietly that he was sorry, but he was deeply engaged just then, and—preferred not admitting me at present. In a brief word or two, he moreover added, that perhaps I had better walk round the block two or three times, and by that time he would probably have concluded his affairs.

Now, the utterly unsurmised appearance of Bartleby, tenanting my law-chambers of a Sunday morning, with his cadaverously gentlemanly *nonchalance*, yet withal firm and self-possessed, had such a strange effect upon me, that incontinently I slunk away from my own door, and did as desired. But not without sundry twinges of impotent rebellion against the mild effrontery of this unaccountable scrivener. Indeed, it was his wonderful mildness chiefly, which not only disarmed me, but unmanned me, as it were. For I consider that one, for the time, is a sort of unmanned when he tranquilly permits his hired clerk to dictate to him, and order him away from his own premises. Furthermore, I was full of uneasiness as to what Bartleby could possibly be doing in my office in his shirt-sleeves, and in an otherwise dismantled condition of a Sunday morning. Was anything amiss going on? Nay, that was out of the question. It was not to be thought of for a moment that Bartleby was an immoral person. But what could he be doing there?—copying? Nay again, whatever might be his eccentricities, Bartleby was an eminently decorous

[8]**deshabille** disorderly dress

person. He would be the last man to sit down to his desk in any state approaching to nudity. Besides, it was Sunday; and there was something about Bartleby that forbade the supposition that he would by any secular occupation violate the properties of the day.

Nevertheless, my mind was not pacified; and full of a restless curiosity, at last I returned to the door. Without hindrance I inserted my key, opened it, and entered. Bartleby was not to be seen. I looked round anxiously, peeped behind his screen; but it was very plain that he was gone. Upon more closely examining the place, I surmised that for an indefinite period Bartleby must have ate, dressed, and slept in my office, and that too without plate, mirror, or bed. The cushioned seat of a rickety old sofa in one corner bore the faint impress of a lean, reclining form. Rolled away under his desk, I found a blanket; under the empty grate, a blacking box and brush; on a chair, a tin basin, with soap and a ragged towel; in a newspaper a few crumbs of ginger-nuts and a morsel of cheese. Yes, thought I, it is evident enough that Bartleby has been making his home here, keeping bachelor's hall all by himself. Immediately then the thought came sweeping across me, what miserable friendliness and loneliness are here revealed! His poverty is great; but his solitude, how horrible! Think of it. Of a Sunday, Wall Street is deserted as Petra;[9] and every night of every day it is an emptiness. This building, too, which of weekdays hums with industry and life, at nightfall echoes with sheer vacancy, and all through Sunday is forlorn. And here Bartleby makes his home; sole spectator of a solitude which he has seen all populous—a sort of innocent and transformed Marius[10] brooding among the ruins of Carthage!

For the first time in my life a feeling of overpowering stinging melancholy seized me. Before, I had never experienced aught but a not unpleasing sadness. The bond of a common humanity now drew me irresistibly to gloom. A fraternal melancholy! For both I and Bartleby were sons of Adam. I remembered the bright silks and sparkling faces I had seen that day, in gala trim, swan-like sailing down the Mississippi of Broadway; and I contrasted them with the pallid copyist, and thought to myself, Ah, happiness courts the light, so we deem the world is gay; but misery hides aloof, so we deem that misery there is none. These sad fancyings—chimeras, doubtless, of a sick and silly brain—led on to other and more special thoughts, concerning the eccentricities of Bartleby. Presentiments of strange discoveries hovered round me. The scrivener's pale form appeared to me laid out, among uncaring strangers, in its shivering winding-sheet.

Suddenly I was attracted by Bartleby's closed desk, the key in open sight left in the lock.

I mean no mischief, seek the gratification of no heartless curiosity, thought I; besides, the desk is mine, and its contents, too, so I will make bold to look within. Everything was methodically arranged, the papers smoothly placed. The pigeon-holes were deep, and removing the files of documents,

[9]**Petra** ancient city in what is now Jordan. It was once an important trading city, but later was deserted for a thousand years.

[10]**Marius** Gaius Marius (157?–1586 B.C.), a Roman general who after considerable military and political success was banished. He fled to Carthage, in North Africa.

I groped into their recesses. Presently I felt something there, and dragged it out. It was an old bandanna handkerchief, heavy and knotted. I opened it, and saw it was a saving's bank.

I now recalled all the quiet mysteries which I had noted in the man. I remembered that he never spoke but to answer; that, though at intervals he had considerable time to himself, yet I had never seen him reading—no, not even a newspaper; that for long periods he would stand looking out, at his pale window behind the screen, upon the dead brick wall; I was quite sure he never visited any refectory or eating-house; while his pale face clearly indicated that he never drank beer like Turkey; or tea and coffee even, like other men; that he never went anywhere in particular that I could learn; never went out for a walk, unless, indeed, that was the case at present; that he had declined telling who he was, or whence he came, or whether he had any relatives in the world; that though so thin and pale, he never complained of ill-health. And more than all, I remembered a certain unconscious air of pallid—how shall I call it?—of pallid haughtiness, say, or rather an austere reserve about him, which has positively awed me into my tame compliance with his eccentricities, when I had feared to ask him to do the slightest incidental thing for me, even though I might know, from his long-continued motionless, that behind his screen he must be standing in one of those dead-wall reveries of his.

Revolving all these things, and coupling them with the recently discovered fact, that he made my office his constant abiding place and home, and not forgetful of his morbid moodiness; revolving all these things, a prudential feeling began to steal over me. My first emotions had been those of pure melancholy and sincerest pity; but just in proportion as the forlornness of Bartleby grew and grew to my imagination, did that same melancholy merge into fear, and pity into repulsion. So true it is, and so terrible, too, that up to a certain point the thought or sight of misery enlists our best affections; but, in certain special cases, beyond that point it does not. They err who would assert that invariably this is owing to the inherent selfishness of the human heart. It rather proceeds from a certain hopelessness of remedying excessive and organic ill. To a sensitive being, pity is not seldom pain. And when at last it is perceived that such pity cannot lead to effectual succor, common sense bids the soul be rid of it. What I saw that morning persuaded me that the scrivener was the victim of innate and incurable disorder. I might give alms to his body; but his body did not pain him; it was his soul that suffered, and his soul I could not reach.

I did not accomplish the purpose of going to Trinity Church that morning. Somehow, the things I had seen disqualified me for the time from church-going. I walked homeword, thinking what I would do with Bartleby. Finally, I resolved upon this—I would put certain calm questions to him the next morning, touching his history, etc., and if he declined to answer them openly and unreservedly (and I supposed he would prefer not), then to give him a twenty dollar bill over and above whatever I might owe him, and tell him his services were no longer required; but that if in any other way I could assist him, I would be happy to do so, especially if he desired to return to his native place, wherever that might be, I would willingly help to defray the expenses.

Moreover, if, after reaching home, he found himself at any time in want of aid, a letter from him would be sure of a reply.

The next morning came.

"Bartleby," said I, gently calling to him behind his screen.

No reply.

"Bartleby," said I, in a still gentler tone, "come here; I am not going to ask you to do anything you would prefer not to do—I simply wish to speak to you."

Upon this he noiselessly slid into view.

"Will you tell me, Bartleby, where you were born?"

"I would prefer not to."

"Will you tell me *anything* about yourself?"

"I would prefer not to."

"But what reasonable objection can you have to speak to me? I feel friendly towards you."

He did not look at me while I spoke, but kept his glance fixed upon my bust of Cicero, which, as I then sat, was directly behind me, some six inches above my head.

"What is your answer Bartleby?" said I, after waiting a considerable time for a reply, during which his countenance remained immovable, only there was the faintest conceivable tremor of the white attenuated mouth.

"At present I prefer to give no answer," he said, and retired into his hermitage.

It was rather weak in me I confess, but his manner, on this occasion, nettled me. Not only did there seem to lurk in it a certain calm disdain, but his perverseness seemed ungrateful, considering the undeniable good usage and indulgence he had received from me.

Again I sat ruminating what I should do. Mortified as I was at his behavior, and resolved as I had been to dismiss him when I entered my office, nevertheless I strangely felt something superstitious knocking at my heart, and forbidding me to carry out my purpose, and denouncing me for a villain if I dared to breathe one bitter word against this forlornest of mankind. At last, familiarly drawing my chair behind his screen, I sat down and said: "Bartleby, never mind, then, about revealing your history; but let me entreat you, as a friend, to comply as far as may be with the usages of this office. Say now, you will help to examine papers tomorrow or next day: in short, say now, that in a day or two you will begin to be a little reasonable:—say so, Bartleby."

"At present I would prefer not to be a little reasonable," was his mildly cadaverous reply.

Just then the folding-doors opened, and Nippers approached. He seemed suffering from an unusually bad night's rest, induced by severer indigestion than common. He overheard those final words of Bartleby.

"*Prefer not*, eh?" gritted Nippers—"I'd *prefer* him, if I were you, sir," addressing me—"I'd *prefer* him; I'd give him preferences, the stubborn mule! What is it, sir, pray, that he *prefers* not to do now?"

Bartleby moved not a limb.

"Mr. Nippers," said I, "I'd prefer that you would withdraw for the present."

Somehow, of late, I had got into the way of involuntarily using this word "prefer" upon all sorts of not exactly suitable occasions. And I trembled to think that my contact with the scrivener had already and seriously affected me in a mental way. And what further and deeper aberration might it not yet produce? This apprehension had not been without efficacy in determining me to summary measures.

As Nippers, looking very sour and sulky, was departing, Turkey blandly and deferentially approached.

"With submission, sir," said he, "yesterday I was thinking about Bartleby here, and I think that if he would but prefer to take a quart of good ale every day, it would do much towards mending him, and enabling him to assist in examining his papers."

"So you have got the word, too," said I, slightly excited.

"With submission, what word, sir?" asked Turkey, respectfully crowding himself into the contracted space behind the screen, and by so doing, making me jostle the scrivener. "What word, sir?"

"I would prefer to be left alone here," said Bartleby, as if offended at being mobbed in his privacy.

"*That's* the word, Turkey," said I—"*that's* it."

"Oh, *prefer?* oh yes—queer word. I never use it myself. But, sir, as I was saying, if he would but prefer—"

"Turkey," interrupted I, "you will please withdraw."

"Oh certainly, sir, if you prefer that I should."

As he opened the folding-door to retire, Nippers at his desk caught a glimpse of me, and asked whether I would prefer to have a certain paper copied on blue paper or white. He did not in the least roguishly accent the word "prefer." It was plain that it involuntarily rolled from his tongue. I thought to myself, surely I must get rid of a demented man, who already has in some degree turned the tongues, if not the heads of myself and clerks. But I thought it prudent not to break the dismission at once.

The next day I noticed that Bartleby did nothing but stand at his window in his dead-wall revery. Upon asking him why he did not write, he said that he had decided upon doing no more writing.

"Why, how now? what next?" exclaimed I, "do no more writing?"

"No more."

"And what is the reason?"

"Do you not see the reason for yourself?" he indifferently replied.

I looked steadfastly at him, and perceived that his eyes looked dull and glazed. Instantly it occurred to me, that his unexampled diligence in copying by his dim window for the first few weeks of his stay with me might have temporarily impaired his vision.

I was touched. I had something in condolence with him. I hinted that of course he did wisely in abstaining from writing for a while; and urged him to embrace that opportunity of taking wholesome exercise in the open air. This, however, he did not do. A few days after this, my other clerks being absent, and being in a great hurry to dispatch certain letters by the mail, I thought that, having nothing else earthly to do, Bartleby would surely be less inflexible than usual, and carry these letters to the Post Office. But he blankly declined. So much to my inconvenience, I went myself.

Still added days went by. Whether Bartleby's eyes improved or not, I could not say. To all appearance, I thought they did. But when I asked him if they did, he vouchsafed no answer. At all events, he would do no copying. At last, in replying to my urgings, he informed me that he had permanently given up copying.

"What!" exclaimed I; "suppose your eyes should get entirely well— better than ever before—would you not copy then?"

"I have given up copying," he answered, and slid aside.

He remained as ever, a fixture in my chamber. Nay—if that were possible—he became still more of a fixture than before. What was to be done? He would do nothing in the office; why should he stay there? In plain fact, he had now become a millstone to me, not only useless as a necklace, but afflictive to bear. Yet I was sorry for him. I speak less than truth when I say that, on his own account, he occasioned me uneasiness. If he would but have named a single relative or friend, I would instantly have written, and urged their taking the poor fellow away to some convenient retreat. But he seemed alone, absolutely alone in the universe. A bit of wreck in the mid-Atlantic. At length, necessities connected with my business tyrannized over all other considerations. Decently as I could, I told Bartleby that in six days' time he must unconditionally leave the office. I warned him to take measures, in the interval, for procuring some other abode. I offered to assist him in this endeavor, if he himself would but take the first step towards a removal. "And when you finally quit me, Bartleby," added I, "I shall see that you go not away entirely unprovided. Six days from this hour, remember."

At the expiration of that period, I peeped behind the screen, and lo! Bartleby was there.

I buttoned up my coat, balanced myself; advanced slowly towards him, touched his shoulder, and said, "The time has come; you must quit this place; I am sorry for you; here is money; but you must go."

"I would prefer not," he replied, with his back still towards me.

"You *must*."

He remained silent.

Now I had an unbounded confidence in this man's common honesty. He had frequently restored to me sixpences and shillings carelessly dropped upon the floor, for I am apt to be very reckless in such shirt-button affairs. The proceeding, then, which followed will not be deemed extraordinary.

"Bartleby," said I, "I owe you twelve dollars on account; here are thirty-two; the odd twenty are yours—Will you take it?" and I handed the bills towards him.

But he made no motion.

"I will leave them here, then," putting them under a weight on the table. Then taking my hat and cane and going to the door, I tranquilly turned and added—"After you have removed your things from these offices, Bartleby, you will of course lock the door—since every one is now gone for the day but you—and if you please, slip your key underneath the mat, so that I may have it in the morning. I shall not see you again; so good-bye to you. If, hereafter, in your new place of abode, I can be of any service to you, do not fail to advise me by letter. Good-bye, Bartleby, and fare you well."

But he answered not a word; like the last column of some ruined temple, he remained standing mute and solitary in the middle of the otherwise deserted room.

As I walked home in a pensive mood, my vanity got the better of my pity. I could not but highly plume myself on my masterly management in getting rid of Bartleby. Masterly I call it, and such it much appear to any dispassionate thinker. The beauty of my procedure seemed to consist in its perfect quietness. There was no vulgar bullying, no bravado of any sort, no choleric hectoring, and striding to and fro across the apartment, jerking out vehement commands for Bartleby to bundle himself off with his beggarly traps. Nothing of the kind. Without loudly bidding Bartleby depart—as an inferior genius might have done—I *assumed* the ground that depart he must; and upon that assumption built all I had to say. The more I thought over my procedure, the more I was charmed with it. Nevertheless, next morning, upon awakening, I had my doubts—I had somehow slept off the fumes of vanity. One of the coolest and wisest hours a man has, is just after he awakes in the morning. My procedure seemed as sagacious as ever—but only in theory. How it would prove in practice—there was the rub. It was truly a beautiful thought to have assumed Bartleby's departure; but, after all, that assumption was simply my own, and none of Bartleby's. The great point was, not whether I had assumed that he would quit me, but whether he would prefer to do so. He was more a man of preferences than assumptions.

After breakfast, I walked down town, arguing the probabilities *pro* and *con*. One moment I thought it would prove a miserable failure, and Bartleby would be found all alive at my office as usual; the next moment it seemed certain that I should find his chair empty. And so I kept veering about. At the corner of Broadway and Canal Street, I saw quite an excited group of people standing in earnest conversation.

"I'll take odds he doesn't," said a voice as I passed.

"Doesn't go?—done!" said I, "put up your money."

I was instinctively putting my hands in my pocket to produce my own, when I remembered that this was an election day. The words I had overheard bore no reference to Bartleby, but to the success or non-success of some candidate for the mayoralty. In my intent frame of mind, I had, as it were, imagined that all Broadway shared in my excitement, and were debating the same question with me. I passed on, very thankful that the uproar of the street screened my momentary absent-mindedness.

As I had intended, I was earlier than usual at my office door. I stood listening for a moment. All was still. He must be gone. I tried the knob. The door was locked. Yes, my procedure had worked to a charm; he indeed must be vanished. Yet a certain melancholy mixed with this: I was almost sorry for my brilliant success. I was fumbling under the door mat for the key, which Bartleby was to have left there for me, when accidentally my knee knocked against a panel, producing a summoning sound, and in response a voice came to me from within— "Not yet; I am occupied."

It was Bartleby.

I was thunderstruck. For an instant I stood like the man who, pipe in mouth, was killed one cloudless afternoon long ago in Virginia, by summer lightning; at his own warm open window he was killed, and remained leaning out there upon the dreamy afternoon, till some one touched him, when he fell.

"Not gone!" I murmured at last. But again obeying that wondrous ascendancy which the inscrutable scrivener had over me, and from which ascendancy, for all my chafing, I could not completely escape, I slowly went down stairs and out into the street, and while walking round the block, considered what I should next do in this unheard-of perplexity. Turn the man out by an actual thrusting I could not; to drive him away by calling him hard names would not do; calling in the police was an unpleasant idea; and yet, permit him to enjoy his cadaverous triumph over me—this, too, I could not think of. What was to be done? or, if nothing could be done, was there anything further that I could *assume* in the matter? Yes, as before I had prospectively assumed that Bartleby would depart, so now I might retrospectively assume that departed he was. In the legitimate carrying out of this assumption, I might enter my office in a great hurry, and pretending not to see Bartleby at all, walk straight against him as if he were air. Such a proceeding would in a singular degree have the appearance of a home-thrust. It was hardly possible that Bartleby could withstand such an application of the doctrine of assumption. But upon second thoughts the success of the plan seemed rather dubious. I resolved to argue the matter over with him again.

"Bartleby," said I, entering the office, with a quietly severe expression, "I am seriously displeased. I am pained, Bartleby. I had thought better of you. I had imagined you of such a gentlemanly organization, that in any delicate dilemma a slight hint would suffice—in short, an assumpton. But it appears I am deceived. Why," I added, unaffectedly starting, "you have not even touched that money yet," pointing to it, just where I had left it the evening previous.

He answered nothing.

"Will you, or will you not, quit me?" I now demanded in a sudden passion, advancing close to him.

"I would prefer *not* to quit you," he replied, gently emphasizing the *not*.

"What earthly right have you to stay here? Do you pay any rent? Do you pay my taxes? or is this property yours?"

He answered nothing.

"Are you ready to go on and write now? Are your eyes recovered? Could you copy a small paper for me this morning? or help examine a few lines? or step round to the Post Office? In a word, will you do anything at all, to give me a coloring to your refusal to depart the premises?"

He silently retired into his hermitage.

I was now in such a state of nervous resentment that I thought it but prudent to check myself at present from further demonstrations. Bartleby and I were alone. I remembered the tragedy of the unfortunate Adams and the still more unfortunate Colt[11] in the solitary office of the latter; and how poor Colt, being dreadfully incensed by Adams, and imprudently permitting himself to get wildly excited, was at unawares hurried into his fatal act—an act which

[11] **Colt** John C. Colt murdered Samuel Adams in 1842. He was convicted and sentenced to death, but committed suicide a few minutes before his scheduled execution.

certainly no man could possibly deplore more than the actor himself. Often it had occurred to me in my ponderings upon the subject that had that altercation taken place in the public street, or at a private residence, it would not have terminated as it did. It was the circumstance of being alone in a solitary office, up stairs, of a building entirely unhallowed by humanizing domestic associations—an uncarpeted office, doubtless, of a dusty, haggard sort of appearance—this it must have been, which greatly helped to enhance the irritable desperation of the hapless Colt.

But when this old Adam of Resentment rose in me and tempted me concering Bartleby, I grappled him and threw him. How? Why, simply by recalling the divine injunction: "A new commandment give I unto you, that ye love one another." Yes, this it was that saved me. Aside from higher considerations, charity often operates as a vastly wise and prudent principle—a great safeguard to its possessor. Men have committed murder for jealousy's sake, and anger's sake, and hatred's sake, and selfishness' sake, and spiritual pride's sake; but no man, that ever I heard of, ever committed a diabolical murder for sweet charity's sake. Mere self-interest, then, if no better motive can be enlisted, should, especially with high-tempered men, prompt all beings to charity and philanthropy. At any rate, upon the occasion in question, I strove to drown my exasperated feelings toward the scrivener by benevolently construing his conduct. Poor fellow, poor fellow! thought I, he don't mean anything; and besides, he has seen hard times, and ought to be indulged.

I endeavored, also, immediately to occupy myself, and at the same time to comfort my despondency. I tried to fancy, that in the course of the morning, at such time as might prove agreeable to him, Bartleby, of his own free accord, would emerge from his hermitage and take up some decided line of march in the direction of the door. But no. Half-past twelve o'clock came; Turkey began to glow in the face, overturn his inkstand, and become generally obstreperous; Nippers abated down into quietude and courtesy; Ginger Nut munched his noon apple; and Bartleby remained standing at his window in one of his profoundest dead-wall reveries. Will it be credited? Ought I to acknowledge it? That afternoon I left the office without saying one further word to him.

Some days now passed, during which, at leisure intervals I looked a little into "Edwards on the Will," and "Priestly[12] on Necessity." Under the circumstances, those books induced a salutary feeling. Gradually I slid into the persuasion that these troubles of mine, touching the scrivener, had been all predestined from eternity, and Bartleby was billeted upon me for some mysterious purpose of an all-wise Providence, which it was not for a mere mortal like me to fathom. Yes, Bartleby, stay there behind your screen, thought I; I shall persecute you no more; you are harmless and noiseless as any of these old chairs; in short, I never feel so private as when I know you are here. At last I see it, I feel it; I penetrate to the predestined purpose of my life. I am content. Others may have loftier parts to enact; but my mission in this world,

---

[12]**Edwards...Priestley** Jonathan Edwards, an American theologian, in *Freedom of the Will* (1754) set forth the Calvinist doctrine of predestination. Joseph Priestly, (1733–1804), an English scientist, rejected Calvinism but argued for determinism on a scientific basis of cause and effect.

Bartleby, is to furnish you with office-room for such period as you may see fit to remain.

I believe that this wise and blessed frame of mind would have continued with me, had it not been for the unsolicited and uncharitable remarks obtruded upon me by my professional friends who visited the rooms. But thus it often is, that the constant friction of illiberal minds wears out at last the best resolves of the more generous. Though to be sure, when I reflected upon it, it was not strange that people entering my office should be struck by the peculiar aspect of the unaccountable Bartleby, and so be tempted to throw out some sinister observations concerning him. Sometimes an attorney, having business with me, and calling at my office, and finding no one but the scrivener there, would undertake to obtain some sort of precise information from him touching my whereabouts; but without heeding his idle talk, Bartleby would remain standing immovable in the middle of the room. So after contemplating him in that position for a time, the attorney would depart, no wiser than he came.

Also, when a reference was going on, and the room full of lawyers and witnesses, and business driving fast, some deeply-occupied legal gentleman present, seeing Bartleby wholly unemployed, would request him to run round to his (the legal gentleman's office) and fetch some papers for him. Thereupon, Bartleby would tranquilly decline, and yet remain idle as before. Then the lawyer would give a great stare, and turn to me. And what could I say? At last I was made aware that all through the circle of my professional acquaintance, a whisper of wonder was running round, having reference to the strange creature I kept at my office. This worried me very much. And as the idea came upon me of his possibly turning out a long-lived man, and keeping occupying my chambers, and denying my authority; and perplexing my visitors; and scandalizing my professional reputation; and casting a general gloom over the premises; keeping soul and body together to the last upon his savings (for doubtless he spent but half a dime a day), and in the end perhaps outlive me, and claim possession of my office by right of his perpetual occupancy: as all these dark anticipations crowded upon me more and more, and my friends continually intruded their relentless remarks upon the apparition in my room; a great change was wrought in me. I resolved to gather all my faculties together, and forever rid me of this intolerable incubus.

Ere revolving any complicated project, however, adapted to this end, I first simply suggested to Bartleby the propriety of his permanent departure. In a calm and serious tone, I commended the idea to his careful and mature consideration. But, having taken three days to meditate upon it, he apprised me, that his original determination remained the same; in short, that he still preferred to abide with me.

What shall I do? I now said to myself, buttoning up my coat to the last button. What shall I do? what ought I to do? what does conscience say I *should* do with this man, or, rather, ghost. Rid myself of him, I must; go, he shall. But how? You will not thrust him, the poor, pale, passive mortal—you will not thrust such a helpless creature out of your door? you will not dishonor yourself by such cruelty? No, I will not, I cannot do that. Rather would I let him live and die here, and then mason up his remains in the wall. What, then, will you do? For all your coaxing, he will not budge. Bribes he leaves under your own paper-weight on your table; in short, it is quite plain that he prefers to cling to you.

Then something severe, something unusual must be done. What! surely you will not have him collared by a constable, and commit his innocent pallor to the common jail? And upon what ground could you procure such a thing to be done?—a vagrant, is he? What! he a vagrant, a wanderer, who refuses to budge? It is because he will *not* be a vagrant, then, that you seek to count him *as* a vagrant. That is too absurd. No visible means of support: there I have him. Wrong again: for indubitably he *does* support himself, and that is the only unanswerable proof that any man can show of his possessing the means so to do. No more, then. Since he will not quit me, I must quit him. I will change my offices; I will move elsewhere, and give him fair notice, that if I find him on my new premises I will then proceed against him as a common trespasser.

Acting accordingly, next day I thus addressed him: "I find these chambers too far from the City Hall; the air is unwholesome. In a word, I propose to remove my offices next week, and shall no longer require your services. I tell you this now, in order that you may seek another place."

He made no reply, and nothing more was said.

On the appointed day I engaged carts and men, proceeded to my chambers, and, having but little furniture, everything was removed in a few hours. Throughout, the scrivener remained standing behind the screen, which I directed to be removed the last thing. It was withdrawn; and being folded up like a huge folio, left him the motionless occupant of a naked room. I stood in the entry watching him a moment, while something from within me upbraided me.

I re-entered, with my hand in my pocket—and—and my heart in my mouth.

"Good-bye, Bartleby; I am going—good-bye, and God some way bless you; and take that," slipping something in his hand. But it dropped upon the floor, and then—strange to say—I tore myself from him whom I had so longed to be rid of.

Established in my new quarters, for a day or two I kept the door locked, and started at every footfall in the passages. When I returned to my rooms, after any little absence, I would pause at the threshold for an instant, and attentively listen, ere applying my key. But these fears were needless. Bartleby never came nigh me.

I thought all was going well, when a perturbed-looking stranger visited me, inquiring whether I was the person who had recently occupied rooms at No. — Wall Street.

Full of forebodings, I replied that I was.

"Then, sir," said the stranger, who proved a lawyer, "you are responsible for the man you left there. He refuses to do any copying; he refuses to do anything; he says he prefers not to; and he refuses to quit the premises."

"I am very sorry, sir," said I, with assumed tranquillity, but an inward tremor, "but, really, the man you allude to is nothing to me—he is no relation or apprentice of mine, that you should hold me responsible for him."

"In mercy's name, who is he?"

"I certainly cannot inform you. I know nothing about him. Formerly I employed him as a copyist; but he has done nothing for me now for some past time."

"I shall settle him, then—good morning, sir."

Several days passed, and I heard nothing more; and, though I often felt a charitable prompting to call at the place and see poor Bartleby, yet a certain squeamishness, of I know not what, withheld me.

All is over with him, by this time, thought I, at last, when, through another week, no further intelligence reached me. But, coming to my room the day after, I found several persons waiting at my door in a high state of nervous excitement.

"That's the man—here he comes," cried the foremost one, whom I recognized as the lawyer who had previously called upon me alone.

"You must take him away, sir, at once," cried a portly person among them, advancing upon me, and whom I knew to be the landlord of No. — Wall Street. "These gentlemen, my tenants, cannot stand it any longer; Mr. B—
," pointing to the lawyer, "has turned him out of his room, and he now persists in haunting the building generally, sitting upon the banisters of the stairs by day, and sleeping in the entry by night. Everybody is concerned; clients are leaving the offices; some fears are entertained of a mob; something you must do, and that without delay."

Aghast at this torrent, I fell back before it, and would fain have locked myself in my new quarters. In vain I persisted that Bartleby was nothing to me—no more than to any one else. In vain—I was the last person known to have anything to do with him, and they held me to the terrible account. Fearful then, of being exposed in the papers (as one person present obscurely threatened), I considered the matter, and, at length, said, that if the lawyer would give me a confidential interview with the scrivener, in his (the lawyer's) own room, I would, that afternoon, strive my best to rid them of the nuisance they complained of.

Going up stairs to my old haunt, there was Bartleby silently sitting upon the banister at the landing.

"What are you doing here, Bartleby?" said I.

"Sitting upon the banister," he mildly replied.

I motioned him into the lawyer's room, who then left us.

"Bartleby," said I, "are you aware that you are the cause of great tribulation to me, by persisting in occupying the entry after being dismissed from the office?"

No answer.

"Now one of two things must take place. Either you must do something, or something must be done to you. Now what sort of business would you like to engage in? Would you like to re-engage in copying for someone?"

"No; I would prefer not to make any change."

"Would you like a clerkship in a dry-goods store?"

"There is too much confinement about that. No, I would not like a clerkship; but I am not particular."

"Too much confinement," I cried, "why, you keep yourself confined all the time!"

"I would prefer not to take a clerkship," he rejoined, as if to settle that little item at once.

"How would a bar-tender's business suit you? There is no trying of the eye-sight in that."

"I would not like that at all; though, as I said before, I am not particular."

His unwonted wordiness inspirited me. I returned to the charge.

"Well, then, would you like to travel through the country collecting bills for the merchants? That would improve your health."

"No, I would prefer to be doing something else."

"How, then, would going as a companion to Europe, to entertain some young gentleman with your conversation—how would that suit you?"

"Not at all. It does not strike me that there is anything definite about that. I like to be stationary. But I am not particular."

"Stationary you shall be, then," I cried, now losing all patience, and, for the first time in all my exasperating connection with him, fairly flying into a passion. "If you do not go away from these premises before night, I shall feel bound—indeed, I *am* bound—to—to—to quit the premises myself!" I rather absurdly concluded, knowing not with what possible threat to try to frighten his immobility into compliance. Despairing of all further efforts, I was precipitately leaving him, when a final thought occurred to me—one which had not been wholly unindulged before.

"Bartleby," said I, in the kindest tone I could assume under such exciting cirumstances, "will you go home with me now—not to my office, but my dwellling—and remain there till we can conclude upon some convenient arrangement for you at our leisure? Come, let us start now, right away."

"No: at present I would prefer not to make any change at all."

I answered nothing; but, effectually dodging every one by the suddenness and rapidity of my flight, rushed from the building, ran up Wall Street towards Broadway, and, jumping into the first omnibus, was soon removed from pursuit. As soon as tranquillity returned, I distinctly perceived that I had now done all that I possibly could, both in respect to the demands of the landlord and his tenants, and with regard to my own desire and sense of duty, to benefit Bartleby, and shield him from rude persecution. I now strove to be entirely care-free and quiescent; and my conscience justified me in the attempt; though, indeed, it was not so successful as I could have wished. So fearful was I of being again hunted out by the incensed landlord and his exasperated tenants, that, surrendering my business to Nippers, for a few days, I drove about the upper part of the town and through the suburbs, in my rockaway;[13] crossed over to Jersey City and Hoboken, and paid fugitive visits to Manhattanville and Astoria. In fact, I almost lived in my rockaway for the time.

When again I entered my office, lo, a note from the landlord lay upon the desk. I opened it with trembling hands. It informed me that the writer had sent to the police, and had Bartleby removed to the Tombs as a vagrant. Moreover, since I knew more about him than any one else, he wished me to appear at that place, and make a suitable statement of the facts. These tidings had a conflicting effect upon me. At first I was indignant; but, at last, almost approved. The landlord's energetic, summary disposition, had led him to

[13] **rockaway** a light, open carriage

adopt a procedure which I do not think I would have decided upon myself; and yet, as a last resort, under such peculiar circumstances, it seemed the only plan.

As I afterwards learned, the poor scrivener, when told he must be conducted to the Tombs, offered not the slightest obstacle, but, in his pale, unmoving way, silently acquiesced.

Some of the compassionate and curious by-standers joined the party; and headed by one of the constables arm-in-arm with Bartleby, the silent procession filed its way through all the noise, and heat, and joy of the roaring thoroughfares at noon.

The same day I received the notice, I went to the Tombs, or, to speak more properly, the Halls of Justice. Seeking the right officer, I stated the purpose of my call, and was informed that the individual I described was, indeed, within. I then assured the functionary that Bartleby was a perfectly honest man, and greatly to be compassionated, however unaccountably eccentric. I narrated all I knew, and closed by suggesting the idea of letting him remain in as indulgent confinement as possible, till something less harsh might be done—though, indeed, I hardly knew what. At all events, if nothing else could be decided upon, the alms-house must receive him. I then begged to have an interview.

Being under no disgraceful charge, and quite serene and harmless in all his ways, they had permitted him freely to wander about the prison, and, especially, in the inclosed grass-plated yards thereof. And so I found him there, standing all alone in the quietest of the yards, his face towards a high wall, while all around, from the narrow slits of the jail windows, I thought I saw peering out upon him the eyes of murderers and thieves.

"Bartleby!"

"I know you," he said, without looking round—"and I want nothing to say to you."

"It was not I that brought you here, Bartleby," said I, keenly pained at his implied suspicion. "And to you, this should be not so vile a place. Nothing reproachful attaches to you by being here. And see, it is not so sad a place as one might think. Look, there is the sky, and here is the grass."

"I know where I am," he replied, but would say nothing more, and so I left him.

As I entered the corridor again, a broad meat-like man, in an apron, accosted me, and, jerking his thumb over his shoulder, said—"Is that your friend?"

"Yes."

"Does he want to starve? If he does, let him live on the prison fare, that's all."

"Who are you?" asked I, not knowing what to make of such an unofficially speaking person in such a place.

"I am the grub-man. Such gentlemen as have friends here, hire me to provide them with something good to eat."

"Is this so?" said I, turning to the turnkey.

He said it was.

"Well, then," said I, slipping some silver into the grub-man's hands (for so they called him), "I want you to give particular attention to my friend there; let him have the best dinner you can get. And you must be as polite to him as possible."

"Introduce me, will you?" said the grub-man, looking at me with an expression which seemed to say he was all impatience for an opportunity to give a specimen of his breeding.

Thinking it would prove of benefit to the scrivener, I acquiesced; and, asking the grub-man his name, went up with him to Bartleby.

"Bartleby, this is a friend; you will find him very useful to you."

"Your sarvant, sir, your sarvant," said the grub-man, making a low salutation behind his apron. "Hope you find it pleasant here, sir; nice grounds—cool apartments—hope you'll stay with us some time—try to make it agreeable. What will you have for dinner to-day?"

"I prefer not to dine to-day," said Bartleby, turning away. "It would disagree with me; I am unused to dinners." So saying, he slowly moved to the other side of the inclosure, and took up a position fronting the deadwall.

"How's this?" said the grub-man, addressing me with a stare of astonishment. "He's odd, ain't he?"

"I think he is a little deranged," said I, sadly.

"Deranged? deranged is it? Well, now, upon my word, I thought that friend of yourn was a gentleman forger; they are always pale and genteel-like, them forgers. I can't help pity 'em—can't help it, sir. Did you know Monroe Edwards?"[14] he added, touchingly, and paused. Then, laying his hand piteously on my shoulder, sighed, "he died of consumption at Sing-Sing. So you weren't acquainted with Monroe?"

"No, I was never socially acquainted with any forgers. But I cannot stop longer. Look to my friend yonder. You will not lose by it. I will see you again."

Some few days after this, I again obtained admission to the Tombs, and went through the corridors in quest of Bartleby; but without finding him.

"I saw him coming from his cell not long ago," said a turnkey, "may be he's gone to loiter in the yards."

So I went in that direction.

"Are you looking for the silent man?" said another turnkey, passing me. "Yonder he lies—sleeping in the yard there. 'Tis not twenty minutes since I saw him lie down."

The yard was entirely quiet. It was not accessible to the common prisoners. The surrounding walls, of amazing thickness, kept off all sounds behind them. The Egyptian character of the masonry weighed upon me with its gloom. But a soft imprisoned turf grew under foot. The heart of the eternal pyramids, it seemed, wherein, by some strange magic, through the clefts, grass-seed, dropped by birds, had sprung.

Strangely huddled at the base of the wall, his knees drawn up, and lying on his side, his head touching the cold stones, I saw the wasted Bartleby. But nothing stirred. I paused; then went close to him; stooped over, and saw that his dim eyes were open; otherwise he seemed profoundly sleeping. Some-

[14]**Monroe Edwards** a swindler and forger, convicted in 1842. He died in Sing-Sing, a prison at Ossining, New York.

thing prompted me to touch him. I felt his hand, when a tingling shiver ran up my arm and down my spine to my feet.

The round face of the grub-man peered upon me now. "His dinner is ready. Won't he dine to-day, either? Or does he live without dining?"

"Lives without dining," said I, and closed the eyes.

"Eh!—He's asleep, ain't he?"

"With kings and counselors," [15] murmured I.

There would seem little need for proceeding further in this history. Imagination will readily supply the meagre recital of poor Bartleby's interment. But, ere parting with the reader, let me say, that if this little narrative has sufficiently interested him, to awaken curiosity as to who Bartleby was, and what manner of life he led prior to the present narrator's making his acquaintance, I can only reply, that in such curiosity I fully share, but am wholly unable to gratify it. Yet here I hardly know whether I should divulge one little item of rumor, which came to my ear a few months after the scrivener's decease. Upon what basis it rested, I could never ascertain; and hence, how true it is I cannot now tell. But, inasmuch as this vague report has not been without a certain suggestive interest to me, however sad, it may prove the same with some others; and so I will briefly mention it. The report was this: that Bartleby had been a subordinate clerk in the Dead Letter Office at Washington, from which he had been suddenly removed by a change in the administration. When I think over this rumor, hardly can I express the emotions which seize me. Dead letters! does it not sound like dead men? Conceive a man by nature and misfortune prone to a pallid hopelessness, can any business seem more fitted to heighten it than that of continually handling these dead letters, and assorting them for the flames? For by the cart-load they are annually burned. Sometimes from out the folded paper the pale clerk takes a ring—the finger it was meant for, perhaps, moulders in the grave; a bank-note sent in swiftest charity—he whom it would relieve, nor eats nor hungers any more; pardon for those who died despairing; hope for those who died unhoping; good tidings for those who died stifled by unrelieved calamities. On errands of life, these letters speed to death.

Ah, Bartleby! Ah, humanity!

[1853]

■ TOPICS FOR DISCUSSION

1. Suppose the narrator were Turkey, Nippers, or Ginger Nut, or even Bartleby. What might the opening paragraph sound like?

2. Why do you suppose Melville bothered to include Turkey, Nippers, and Ginger Nut? To make contrasts with Bartleby? With the lawyer-narrator? Or what?

3. Characterize the narrator. Do you think that his association with Bartleby changes him? If so, how?

4. We learn that Bartleby had worked in the Dead Letter Office. What effect did this information have on you when you encountered it in the story?

[15] **With kings and counselors** a quotation from Job 3:14. Job, afflicted with disasters, wishes he had never been born: "Then had I been at rest with kings and counselors of the earth. . . ."

Do you think that Melville should have given the reader the information earlier? Why or why not?

■ TILLIE OLSEN

Tillie Olsen was born in 1913 in Omaha of a family that had fled persecution in czarist Russia. She left school after completing the eleventh grade and at 19 began a novel called *Yonnonido,* which was not published until 1947. Her first publications, in the *Partisan Review* in 1934, were some poems and a story (the story was the opening chapter of her novel); in the next 20 years, however, when she was wife, mother of four children, office worker, and political activist, she published nothing. In *Silences* (1978), a collection of essays, she comments on the difficulty of working "fulltime on temporary jobs . . . , wandering from office to office, always hoping to manage two, three writing months ahead."

Her first published book was *Tell Me a Riddle* (1961), a collection of six stories, including "I Stand Here Ironing." (This story, written in 1953–1954, first appeared in a journal in 1956, under the title "Help Her to Believe.") Her stories are marked by their concentration on what the author obviously feels are immensely important emotions and experiences; she is scarcely concerned with seeming to be objective or with the creation of mere verisimilitude.

I Stand Here Ironing

I stand here ironing, and what you asked me moves tormented back and forth with the iron.

"I wish you would manage the time to come in and talk with me about your daughter. I'm sure you can help me understand her. She's a youngster who needs help and whom I'm deeply interested in helping."

"Who needs help." . . . Even if I came, what good would it do? You think because I am her mother I have a key, or that in some way you could use me as a key? She has lived for nineteen years. There is all that life that has happened outside of me, beyond me.

And when is there time to remember, to sift, to weigh, to estimate, to total? I will start and there will be an interruption and I will have to gather it all together again. Or I will become engulfed with all I did or did not do, with what should have been and what cannot be helped.

She was a beautiful baby. The first and only one of our five that was beau-   5
tiful at birth. You do not guess how new and uneasy her tenancy in her now-loveliness. You did not know her all those years she was thought homely, or see her poring over her baby pictures, making me tell her over and over how beautiful she had been—and would be, I would tell her—and was now, to the seeing eye. But the seeing eyes were few or non-existent. Including mine.

I nursed her. They feel that's important nowadays. I nursed all the children, but with her, with all the fierce rigidity of first motherhood, I did like the books then said. Though her cries battered me to trembling and my breasts ached with swollenness, I waited till the clock decreed.

Why do I put that first? I do not even know if it matters, or if it explains anything.

She was a beautiful baby. She blew shining bubbles of sound. She loved motion, loved light, loved color and music and textures. She would lie on the floor in her blue overalls patting the surface so hard in ectasy her hands and feet would blur. She was a miracle to me, but when she was eight months old I had to leave her daytimes with the woman downstairs to whom she was no miracle at all, for I worked or looked for work and for Emily's father, who "could no longer endure" (he wrote in his good-bye note) "sharing want with us."

I was nineteen. It was the pre-relief, pre-WPA world of the depression. I would start running as soon as I got off the streetcar, running up the stairs, the place smelling sour, and awake or asleep to startle awake, when she saw me she would break into a clogged weeping that could not be comforted, a weeping I can hear yet.

After a while I found a job hashing at night so I could be with her days, 10 and it was better. But it came to where I had to bring her to his family and leave her.

It took a long time to raise the money for her fare back. Then she got chicken pox and I had to wait longer. When she finally came, I hardly knew her, walking quick and nervous like her father, looking like her father, thin, and dressed in a shoddy red that yellowed her skin and glared at the pock-marks. All the baby loveliness gone.

She was two. Old enough for nursery school they said, and I did not know then what I know now—the fatigue of the long day, and the lacerations of group life in the kinds of nurseries that are only parking places for children.

Except that it would have made no difference if I had known. It was the only place there was. It was the only way we could be together, the only way I could hold a job.

And even without knowing, I knew. I knew the teacher that was evil because all these years it has curdled into my memory, the little boy hunched in the corner, her rasp, "why aren't you outside, because Alvin hits you? that's no reason, go out, scaredy." I knew Emily hated it even if she did not clutch and implore "don't go Mommy" like the other children, mornings.

She always had a reason why we should say home. Momma, you look 15 sick. Momma, I feel sick. Momma, the teachers aren't there today, they're sick. Momma, we can't go, there was a fire there last night. Momma, it's a holiday today, no school, they told me.

But never a direct protest, never rebellion. I think of our others in their three-four-year-oldness—the explosions, the tempers, the denunciations, the demands—and I feel suddenly ill. I put the iron down. What in me demanded that goodness in her? And what was the cost, the cost to her of such goodness?

The old man living in the back once said in his gentle way: "You should smile at Emily more when you look at her." What *was* in my face when I looked at her? I loved her. There were all the acts of love.

It was only with the others I remembered what he said, and it was the face of joy, and not of care or tightness or worry I turned to them—too late for Emily. She does not smile easily, let alone almost always as her brothers and sisters do. Her face is closed and sombre, but when she wants, how fluid. You must have seen it in her pantomimes, you spoke of her rare gift for comedy on the stage that rouses a laughter out of the audience so dear they applaud and do not want to let her go.

Where does it come from, that comedy? There was none of it in her when she came back to me that second time, after I had had to send her away again. She had a new daddy now to learn to love, and I think perhaps it was a better time.

Except when we left her alone nights, telling ourselves she was old enough.   20

"Can't you go some other time, Mommy, like tomorrow?" she would ask. "Will it be just a little while you'll be gone? Do you promise?"

The time we came back, the front door open, the clock on the floor in the hall. She rigid awake. "It wasn't just a little while. I didn't cry. Three times I called you, just three times, and then I ran downstairs to open the door so you could come faster. The clock talked loud. I threw it away, it scared me what it talked."

She said the clock talked loud again that night I went to the hospital to have Susan. She was delirious with the fever that comes before red measles, but she was fully conscious all the week I was gone and the week after we were home when she could not come near the new baby or me.

She did not get well. She stayed skeleton thin, not wanting to eat, and night after night she had nightmares. She would call for me, and I would rouse from exhaustion to sleepily call back: "You're all right, darling, go to sleep, it's just a dream," and if she still called, in a sterner voice, "now go to sleep, Emily, there's nothing to hurt you." Twice, only twice, when I had to get up for Susan anyhow, I went in to sit with her.

Now when it is too late (as if she would let me hold and comfort her like   25 I do the others) I get up and go to her at once at her moan or restless stirring. "Are you awake, Emily? Can I get you something?" And the answer is always the same: "No, I'm all right, go back to sleep, Mother."

They persuaded me at the clinic to send her away to a convalescent home in the country where "she can have the kind of food and care you can't manage for her, and you'll be free to concentrate on the new baby." They still send children to that place. I see pictures on the society page of sleek young women planning affairs to raise money for it, or dancing at the affairs, or decorating Easter eggs or filling Christmas stockings for the children.

They never have a picture of the children so I do not know if the girls still wear those gigantic red bows and the ravaged looks on the every other Sunday when parents can come to visit "unless otherwise notified" —as we were notified the first six weeks.

Oh it is a handsome place, green lawns and tall trees and fluted flower beds. High up on the balconies of each cottage the children stand, the girls in their red bows and white dresses, the boys in white suits and giant red ties. The parents stand below shrieking up to be heard and the children shriek down to be heard, and between them the invisible wall: "Not to Be Contaminated by Parental Germs or Physical Affection."

There was a tiny girl who always stood hand in hand with Emily. Her parents never came. One visit she was gone. "They moved her to Rose Cottage," Emily shouted in explanation. "They don't like you to love anybody here."

She wrote once a week, the labored writing of a seven-year-old. "I am 30 fine. How is the baby. If I write my leter nicly I will have a star. Love." There never was a star. We wrote every other day, letters she could never hold or keep but only hear read—once. "We simply do not have room for children to keep any personal possessions," they patiently explained when we pieced one Sunday's shrieking together to plead how much it would mean to Emily, who loved so to keep things, to be allowed to keep her letters and cards.

Each visit she looked frailer. "She isn't eating," they told us.

(They had runny eggs for breakfast or mush with lumps, Emily said later, I'd hold it in my mouth and not swallow. Nothing ever tasted good, just when they had chicken.)

It took us eight months to get her released home, and only the fact that she gained back so little of her seven lost pounds convinced the social worker.

I used to try to hold and love her after she came back, but her body would stay stiff, and after a while she'd push away. She ate little. Food sickened her, and I think much of life too. Oh she had physical lightness and brightness, twinkling by on skates, bouncing like a ball up and down up and down over the jump rope, skimming over the hill: but these were momentary.

She fretted about her appearance, thin and dark and foreign-looking at 35 a time when every little girl was supposed to look or thought she should look a chubby blonde replica of Shirley Temple. The doorbell sometimes rang for her, but no one seemed to come and play in the house or be a best friend. Maybe because we moved so much.

There was a boy she loved painfully through two school semesters. Months later she told me how she had taken pennies from my purse to buy him candy. "Licorice was his favorite and I brought him some every day, but he still liked Jennifer better'n me. Why, Mommy?" The kind of question for which there is no answer.

School was a worry to her. She was not glib or quick in a world where glibness and quickness were easily confused with ability to learn. To her overworked and exasperated teachers she was an overconscientious "slow learner" who kept trying to catch up and was absent entirely too often.

I let her be absent, though sometimes the illness was imaginary. How different from my now-strictness about attendance with the others. I wasn't working. We had a new baby, I was home anyhow. Sometimes, after Susan grew old enough, I would keep her home school, too, to have them all together.

Mostly Emily had asthma, and her breathing, harsh and labored, would fill the house with a curiously tranquil sound. I would bring the two old dresser mirrors and her boxes of collections to her bed. She would select beads and single earrings, bottle tops and shells, dried flowers and pebbles, old postcards and scraps, all sorts of oddments; then she and Susan would play Kingdom, setting up landscapes and furniture, peopling them with action.

Those were the only times of peaceful companionship between her and 40

Susan. I have edged away from it, that poisonous feeling between them, that terrible balancing of hurts and needs I had to do between the two, and did so badly, those earlier years.

Oh there are conflicts between the others too, each one human, needing, demanding, hurting, taking—but only between Emily and Susan, no, Emily toward Susan that corroding resentment. It seems so obvious on the surface, yet it is not obvious. Susan, the second child, Susan, golden- and curly-haired and chubby, quick and articulate and assured, everything in appearance and manner Emily was not; Susan, not able to resist Emily's precious things, losing or sometimes clumsily breaking them; Susan telling jokes and riddles to company for applause while Emily sat silent (to say to me later: that was *my* riddle, Mother, I told it to Susan); Susan, who for all the five years' difference in age was just a year behind Emily in developing physically.

I am glad for that slow physical development that widened the difference between her and her contemporaries, though she suffered over it. She was too vulnerable for that terrible world of youthful competition, of preening and parading, of constant measuring of yourself against every other, of envy, "If I had that copper hair," "If I had that skin . . . ." She tormented herself enough about not looking like the others, there was enough of the unsureness, the having to be conscious of words before you speak, the constant caring—what are they thinking of me? without having it all magnified by the merciless physical drives.

Ronnie is calling. He is wet and I change him. It is rare there is such a cry now. That time of motherhood is almost behind me when the ear is not one's own but must always be racked and listening for the child cry, the child call. We sit for a while and I hold him, looking out over the city spread in charcoal with its soft aisles of light. "*Shoogily*," he breathes and curls closer. I carry him back to bed, asleep. *Shoogily*. A funny word, a family word, inherited from Emily, invented by her to say: *comfort*.

In this and other ways she leaves her seal, I say aloud. And startle at my saying it. What do I mean? What did I start to gather together, to try to make coherent? I was at the terrible, growing years. War years. I do not remember them well. I was working, there were four smaller ones now, there was not time for her. She had to help be a mother, and a housekeeper, and shopper. She had to set her seal. Mornings of crisis and near hysteria trying to get lunches packed, hair combed, coats and shoes found, everyone to school or Child Care on time, the baby ready for transportation. And always the paper scribbled on by a smaller one, the book looked at by Susan then mislaid, the homework not done. Running out to that huge school where she was one, she was lost, she was a drop; suffering over the unpreparedness, stammering and unsure in her classes.

There was so little time left at night after the kids were bedded down. She would struggle over books, always eating (it was in those years she developed her enormous appetite that is legendary in our family) and I would be ironing, or preparing food for the next day, or writing V-mail to Bill, or tending the baby. Sometimes, to make me laugh, or out of her despair, she would imitate happenings or types at school.

I think I said once: "Why don't you do something like this in the school amateur show?" One morning she phoned me at work, hardly understandable through the weeping: "Mother, I did it. I won, I won; they gave me first prize; they clapped and clapped and wouldn't let me go."

Now suddenly she was Somebody, and as imprisoned in her difference as she had been in anonymity.

She began to be asked to perform at other high schools, even in colleges, then at city and statewide affairs. The first one we went to, I only recognized her that first moment when thin, shy, she almost drowned heself into the curtains. Then: Was this Emily? The control, the command, the convulsing and deadly clowning, the spell, then the roaring, stamping audience, unwilling to let this rare and precious laughter out of their lives.

Afterwards: You ought to do something about her with a gift like that—but without money or knowing how, what does one do? We have left it all to her, and the gift has as often eddied inside, clogged and clotted, as been used and growing.

She is coming. She runs up the stairs two at a time with her light graceful 50 step, and I know she is happy tonight. Whatever it was that occasioned your call did not happen today.

"Aren't you ever going to finish the ironing, Mother? Whistler painted his mother in a rocker. I'd have to paint mine standing over an ironing board." This is one of her communicative nights and she tells me everything and nothing as she fixes herself a plate of food out of the icebox.

She is so lovely. Why did you want me to come in at all? Why were you concerned? She will find her way.

She starts up the stairs to bed. "Don't get me up with the rest in the morning." "But I thought you were having midterms." "Oh, those," she comes back in, kisses me, and says quite lightly, "in a couple of years when we'll all be atom-dead they won't matter a bit."

She has said it before. She *believes* it. But because I have been dredging the past, and all that compounds a human being is so heavy and meaningful in me, I cannot endure it tonight.

I will never total it all. I will never come in to say: She was a child seldom 55 smiled at. Her father left me before she was a year old. I had to work her first six years when there was work, or I sent her home and to his relatives. There were years she had care she hated. She was dark and thin and foreign-looking in a world where the prestige went to blondeness and curly hair and dimples, she was slow where glibness was prized. She was a child of anxious, not proud, love. We were poor and could not afford for her the soil of easy growth. I was a young mother, I was a distracted mother. There were other children pushing up, demanding. Her younger sister seemed all that she was not. There were years she did not want me to touch her. She kept too much in herself, her life was such she had to keep too much in herself. My wisdom came too late. She has much to her and probably little will come of it. She is a child of her age, of depression, of war, of fear.

Let her be. So all that is in her will not bloom—but in how many does it? There is still enough left to live by. Only help her to know—help make it so there is cause for her to know—that she is more than this dress on the ironing board, helpless before the iron.

[1954]

■ TOPICS FOR DISCUSSION AND WRITING

1. Who is the "you" whom the mother speaks of? Do you think the mother will visit the "you"? Why, or why not?
2. What do you make of Emily's telling her mother not to awaken her for the midterm examination on the next morning?
3. In what way(s) did your response toward the mother change as you progressed through the story?
4. What, if anything, has the mother learned about life?

■ ALICE MUNRO
_____

   Alice Munroe was born in 1931 in Wingham, Ontario, Canada, a relatively rural community and the sort of place in which she sets much of her fiction. She began publishing stories when she was an undergraduate at the University of Western Ontario. She left Western after two years, worked in a library and in a bookstore, then married, moved to Victoria, British Columbia, and founded a bookstore there. She continued to write while raising three children. She divorced and remarried; much of her fiction concerns marriage or divorce, which is to say it concerns shifting relationships in a baffling world.

Boys and Girls

   My father was a fox farmer. That is, he raised silver foxes, in pens; and in the fall and early winter, when their fur was prime, he killed them and skinned them and sold their pelts to the Hudson's Bay Company or the Montreal Fur Traders. These companies supplied us with heroic calendars to hang, one on each side of the kitchen door. Against a background of cold blue sky and black pine forests and treacherous northern rivers, plumed adventurers planted the flags of England or of France; magnificent savages bent their backs to the portage.

   For several weeks before Christmas, my father worked after supper in the cellar of our house. The cellar was whitewashed, and lit by a hundred-watt bulb over the worktable. My brother Laird and I sat on the top step and watched. My father removed the pelt inside-out from the body of the fox, which looked surprisingly small, mean and rat-like, deprived of its arrogant weight of fur. The naked, slippery bodies were collected in a sack and buried at the dump. One time the hired man, Henry Bailey, had taken a swipe at me with this sack, saying, "Christmas present!" My mother thought that was not funny. In fact she disliked the whole pelting operation—that was what the killing, skinning, and preparation of the furs was called—and wished it did not have to take place in the house. There was the smell. After the pelt had been stretched inside-out on a long board my father scraped away delicately, removing the little clotted webs of blood vessels, the bubbles of fat; the smell of blood and animal fat, with the strong primitive odor of the fox itself, penetrated all parts of the house. I found it reassuringly seasonal, like the smell of oranges and pine needles.

   Henry Bailey suffered from bronchial troubles. He would cough and cough until his narrow face turned scarlet, and his light blue, derisive eyes filled up with tears; then he took the lid off the stove, and, standing well back, shot out a great clot of phlegm—hsss—straight into the heart of the flames. We admired him for this performance and for his ability to make his stomach growl at will, and for his laughter, which was full of high whistlings and gurglings and involved the whole faulty machinery of his chest. It was sometimes hard to tell what he was laughing at, and always possible that it might be us.

After we had been sent to bed we could still smell fox and still hear Henry's laugh, but these things, reminders of the warm, safe, brightly lit downstairs world, seemed lost and diminished, floating on the stale cold air upstairs. We were afraid at night in the winter. We were not afraid of *outside* though this was the time of year when snowdrifts curled around our house like sleeping whales and the wind harassed us all night, coming up from the buried fields, the frozen swamp, with its old bugbear chorus of threats and misery. We were afraid of *inside*, the room where we slept. At this time the upstairs of our house was not finished. A brick chimney went up one wall. In the middle of the floor was a square hole, with a wooden railing around it; that was where the stairs came up. On the other side of the stairwell were the things that nobody had any use for any more—a soldiery roll of linoleum, standing on end, a wicker baby carriage, a fern basket, china jugs and basins with cracks in them, a picture of the Battle of Balaclava, very sad to look at. I had told Laird, as soon as he was old enough to understand such things, that bats and skeletons lived over there; whenever a man escaped from the country jail, twenty miles away, I imagined that he had somehow let himself in the window and was hiding behind the linoleum. But we had rules to keep us safe. When the light was on, we were safe as long as we did not step off the square of worn carpet which defined our bedroom-space; when the light was off no place was safe but the beds themselves. I had to turn out the light kneeling on the end of my bed, and stretching as far as I could to reach the cord.

In the dark we lay on our beds, our narrow life rafts, and fixed our eyes 5 on the faint light coming up the stairwell, and sang songs. Laird sang "Jingle Bells," which he would sing any time, whether it was Christmas or not, and I sang "Danny Boy." I loved the sound of my own voice, frail and supplicating, rising in the dark. We could make out the tall frosted shapes of the windows now, gloomy and white. When I came to the part, *When I am dead, as dead I well may be*—a fit of shivering caused not by the cold sheets but by pleasurable emotion almost silenced me. *You'll kneel and say, an Ave there above me*— What was an Ave? Every day I forgot to find out.

Laird went straight from singing to sleep. I could hear his long, satisfied, bubbly breaths. Now for the time that remained to me, the most perfectly private and perhaps the best time of the whole day, I arranged myself tightly under the covers and went on with one of the stories I was telling myself from night to night. These stories were about myself, when I had grown a little older; they took place in a world that was recognizably mine, yet one that presented opportunities for courage, boldness and self-sacrifice, as mine never did. I rescued people from a bombed building (it discouraged me that the real war had gone on so far away from Jubilee). I shot two rabid wolves who were menacing the schoolyard (the teachers cowered terrified at my back). I rode a fine horse spiritedly down the main street of Jubilee, acknowledging the townspeople's gratitude for some yet-to-be-worked-out piece of heroism (nobody ever rode a horse there, except King Billy in the Orangemen's Day[1] parade). There was always riding and shooting in these stories, though I had only been on a horse twice—bareback because we did not own a saddle—and the second time I had slid right around and dropped under the horse's feet; it had stepped placidly over me. I really was learning to shoot, but I could not hit anything yet, not even tin cans on fence posts.

Alive, the foxes inhabited a world my father made for them. It was surrounded by a high guard fence, like a medieval town, with a gate that was padlocked at night. Along the streets of this town were ranged large, sturdy pens. Each of them had a real door that a man could go through, a wooden ramp along the wire, for the foxes to run up and down on, and a kennel—something like a clothes chest with airholes—where they slept and stayed in winter and had their young. There were feeding and watering dishes attached to the wire in such a way that they could be emptied and cleaned from the outside. The dishes were made of old tin cans, and the ramps and kennels of odds and ends of old lumber. Everything was tidy and ingenious; my father was tirelessly inventive and his favorite book in the world was Robinson Crusoe. He had fitted a tin drum on a wheelbarrow, for bringing water to the pens. This was my job in summer, when the foxes had to have water twice a day. Between nine and ten o'clock in the morning, and again after supper, I filled the drum at the pump and trundled it down through the barnyard to the pens, where I parked it, and filled my watering can and went along the streets. Laird came too, with his little cream and green gardening can, filled too full and knocking against his legs and slopping water on his canvas shoes. I had the real watering can, my father's, though I could only carry it three-quarters full.

The foxes all had names, which were printed on a tin plate and hung beside their doors. They were not named when they were born, but when they survived the first year's pelting and were added to the breeding stock. Those my father had named were called names like Prince, Bob, Wally and Betty. Those I had named were called Star or Turk, or Maureen or Diana. Laird named one Maud after a hired girl we had when he was little, one Harold after a boy at school, and one Mexico, he did not say why.

Naming them did not make pets out of them, or anything like it. Nobody but my father ever went into the pens, and he had twice had blood-poisoning from bites. When I was bringing them their water they prowled up and down on the paths they had made inside their pens, barking seldom—they saved that for night-time, when they might get up a chorus of community frenzy—but always watching me, their eyes burning, clear gold, in their pointed, malevolent faces. They were beautiful for their delicate legs and heavy, aristocratic tails and the bright fur sprinkled on dark down their backs—which gave them their name—but especially for their faces, drawn exquisitely sharp in pure hostility, and their golden eyes.

[1] The Orange Society is named for William of Orange, who, as King William III of England, defeated James II of England at the Battle of the Boyne on 12 July 1609. It sponsors an annual procession on 12 July.

Besides carrying water I helped my father when he cut the long grass, 10 and the lamb's quarter and flowering money-musk, that grew between the pens. He cut with the scythe and I raked into piles. Then he took a pitchfork and threw fresh-cut grass all over the top of the pens to keep the foxes cooler and shade their coats, which were browned by too much sun. My father did not talk to me unless it was about the job we were doing. In this he was quite different from my mother, who, if she was feeling cheerful, would tell me all sorts of things—the name of a dog she had when she was a little girl, the names of boys she had gone out with later on when she was grown up, and what certain dresses of hers had looked like—she could not imagine now what had become of them. Whatever thoughts and stories my father had were private, and I was shy of him and would never ask him questions. Nevertheless I worked willingly under his eyes, and with a feeling of pride. One time a feed salesman came down into the pens to talk to him and my father said, "Like to have you meet my new hired man." I turned away and raked furiously, red in the face with pleasure.

"Could of fooled me," said the salesman. "I thought it was only a girl."

After the grass was cut, it seemed suddenly much later in the year. I walked on stubble in the earlier evening, aware of the reddening skies, the entering silences, of fall. When I wheeled the tank out of the gate and put the padlock on, it was almost dark. One night at this time I saw my mother and father standing on the little rise of ground we called the gangway, in front of the barn. My father had just come from the meathouse; he had his stiff bloody apron on, and a pail of cut-up meat in his hand.

It was an odd thing to see my mother down at the barn. She did not often come out of the house unless it was to do something—hang out the wash or dig potatoes in the garden. She looked out of place, with her bare lumpy legs, not touched by the sun, her apron still on and damp across the stomach from the supper dishes. Her hair was tied up in a kerchief, wisps of it falling out. She would tie her hair up like this in the morning, saying she did not have time to do it properly, and it would stay tied up all day. It was true, too; she really did not have time. These days our back porch was piled with baskets of peaches and grapes and pears, bought in town, and onions and tomatoes and cucumbers grown at home, all waiting to be made into jelly and jam and preserves, pickles and chili sauce. In the kitchen there was a fire in the stove all day, jars clinked in boiling water, sometimes a cheesecloth bag was strung on a pole between two chairs straining blue-black grape pulp for jelly. I was given jobs to do and I would sit at the table peeling peaches that had been soaked in the hot water, or cutting up onions, my eyes smarting and streaming. As soon as I was done I ran out of the house, trying to get out of earshot before my mother thought of what she wanted me to do next. I hated the hot dark kitchen in summer, the green blinds and the flypapers, the same old oilcloth table and wavy mirror and bumpy linoleum. My mother was too tired and preoccupied to talk to me, she had no heart to tell about the Normal School Graduation Dance; sweat trickled over her face and she was always counting under her breath, pointing at jars, dumping cups of sugar. It seemed to me that work in the house was endless, dreary and peculiarly depressing; work done out of doors, and in my father's service, was ritualistically important.

I wheeled the tank up to the barn, where it was kept, and I heard my mother saying, "Wait till Laird gets a little bigger, then you'll have a real help."

What my father said I did not hear. I was pleased by the way he stood 15 listening, politely as he would to a salesman or a stranger, but with an air of wanting to get on with his real work. I felt my mother had no business down here and I wanted him to feel the same way. What did she mean about Laird? He was no help to anybody. Where was he now? Swinging himself sick on the swing, going around in circles, or trying to catch caterpillars. He never once stayed with me till I was finished.

"And then I can use her more in the house," I heard my mother say. She had a dead-quiet, regretful way of talking about me that always made me uneasy. "I just get my back turned and she runs off. It's not like I had a girl in the family at all."

I went and sat on a feed bag in the corner of the barn, not wanting to appear when this conversation was going on. My mother, I felt, was not to be trusted. She was kinder than my father and more easily fooled, but you could not depend on her, and the real reasons for the things she said and did were not to be known. She loved me, and she sat up late at night making a dress of the difficult style I wanted, for me to wear when school started, but she was also my enemy. She was always plotting. She was plotting now to get me to stay in the house more, although she knew I hated it (*because* she knew I hated it) and keep me from working for my father. It seemed to me she would do this simply out of perversity, and to try her power. It did not occur to me that she could be lonely, or jealous. No grown-up could be; they were too fortunate. I sat and kicked my heels monotonously against a feed bag, raising dust, and did not come out till she was gone.

At any rate, I did not expect my father to pay any attention to what she said. Who could imagine Laird doing my work—Laird remembering the padlock and cleaning out the watering dishes with a leaf on the end of a stick, or even wheeling the tank without it tumbling over? It showed how little my mother knew about the way things really were.

I have forgotten to say what the foxes were fed. My father's bloody apron reminded me. They were fed horsemeat. At this time most farmers still kept horses, and when a horse got too old to work, or broke a leg or got down and would not get up, as they sometimes did, the owner would call my father, and he and Henry went out to the farm in the truck. Usually they shot and butchered the horse there, paying the farmer from five to twelve dollars. If they had already too much meat on hand, they would bring the horse back alive, and keep it for a few days or weeks in our stable, until the meat was needed. After the war the farmers were buying tractors and gradually getting rid of horses altogether, so it sometimes happened that we got a good healthy horse, that there was just no use for any more. If this happened in the winter we might keep the horse in our stable till spring, for we had plenty of hay and if there was a lot of snow—and the plow did not always get our road cleared— it was convenient to be able to go to town with a horse and cutter.[2]

The winter I was eleven years old we had two horses in the stable. We 20 did not know what names they had had before, so we called them Mack and

[2] A small sleigh

Flora. Mack was an old black workhorse, sooty and indifferent. Flora was a sorrel mare, a driver. We took them both out in the cutter. Mack was slow and easy to handle. Flora was given to fits of violent alarm, veering at cars and even at other horses, but we loved her speed and high-stepping, her general air of gallantry and abandon. On Saturdays we went down to the stable and as soon as we opened the door on its cosy, animal-smelling darkness Flora threw up her head, rolled her eyes, whinnied despairingly and pulled herself through a crisis of nerves on the spot. It was not safe to go into her stall; she would kick.

This winter also I began to hear a great deal more on the theme my mother had sounded when she had been talking in front of the barn. I no longer felt safe. It seemed that in the minds of the people around me there was a steady undercurrent of thought, not to be deflected, on this one subject. The word *girl* had formerly seemed to me innocent and unburdened, like the word *child*; now it appeared that it was no such thing. A girl was not, as I had supposed, simply what I was; it was what I had to become. It was a definition, always touched with emphasis, with reproach and disappointment. Also it was a joke on me. Once Laird and I were fighting, and for the first time ever I had to use all my strength against him; even so, he caught and pinned my arm for a moment, really hurting me. Henry saw this, and laughed, saying, "Oh, that there Laird's gonna show you, one of these days!" Laird was getting a lot bigger. But I was getting bigger too.

My grandmother came to stay with us for a few weeks and I heard other things. "Girls don't slam doors like that." "Girls keep their knees together when they sit down." And worse still, when I asked some questions, "That's none of girls' business." I continued to slam the doors and sit as awkwardly as possible, thinking by such measures I kept myself free.

When spring came, the horses were let out in the barnyard. Mack stood against the barn wall trying to scratch his neck and haunches, but Flora trotted up and down and reared at the fences, clattering her hooves against the rails. Snow drifts dwindled quickly, revealing the hard gray and brown earth, the familiar rise and fall of the ground, plain and bare after the fantastic landscape of winter. There was a great feeling of opening-out, of release. We just wore rubbers now, over our shoes; our feet felt ridiculously light. One Saturday we went to the stable and found all the doors open, letting in the unaccustomed sunlight and fresh air. Henry was there, just idling around looking at his collection of calendars which were tacked up behind the stalls in a part of the stable my mother had probably never seen.

"Come to say goodbye to your old friend Mack?" Henry said. "Here, you give him a taste of oats." He poured some oats in Laird's cupped hands and Laird went to feed Mack. Mack's teeth were in bad shape. He ate very slowly, patiently shifting the oats around in his mouth, trying to find a stump of a molar to grind it on. "Poor old Mac," said Henry mournfully. "When a horse's teeth's gone, he's gone. That's about the way."

"Are you going to shoot him today?" I said. Mack and Flora had been in the stable so long I had almost forgotten they were going to be shot.

Henry didn't answer me. Instead he started to sing in a high, trembly, mocking-sorrowful voice. *Oh, there's no more work, for poor Uncle Ned, he's gone where the good darkies go.* Mack's thick, blackish tongue worked diligently at Laird's hand. I went out before the song was ended and sat down on the gangway.

I had never seen them shoot a horse, but I knew where it was done. Last summer Laird and I had come upon a horse's entrails before they were buried. We had thought it was a big black snake, coiled up in the sun. That was around in the field that ran up beside the barn. I thought that if we went inside the barn, and found a wide crack or a knothole to look through, we would be able to see them do it. It was not something I wanted to see; just the same, if a thing really happened, it was better to see, and know.

My father came down from the house, carrying the gun.

"What are you doing here?" he said.

"Nothing."   30

"Go on up and play around the house."

He sent Laird out of the stable. I said to Laird, "Do you want to see them shoot Mack?" and without waiting for an answer led him around to the front door of the barn, opened it carefully, and went in. "Be quiet or they'll hear us," I said. We could hear Henry and my father talking in the stable; then the heavy, shuffling steps of Mack being backed out of his stall.

In the loft it was cold and dark. Thin crisscrossed beams of sunlight fell through the cracks. The hay was low. It was a rolling country, hills and hollows, slipping under our feet. About four feet up was a beam going around the walls. We piled hay up in one corner and I boosted Laird up and hoisted myself. The beam was not very wide; we crept along it with our hands flat on the barn walls. There were plenty of knotholes, and I found one that gave me the view I wanted—a corner of the barnyard, the gate, part of the field. Laird did not have a knothole and began to complain.

I showed him a widened crack between two boards. "Be quiet and wait. If they hear you you'll get us in trouble."

My father came in sight carrying the gun. Henry was leading Mack by   35
the halter. He dropped it and took out his cigarette papers and tobacco; he rolled cigarettes for my father and himself. While this was going on Mack nosed around in the old, dead grass along the fence. Then my father opened the gate and they took Mack through. Henry led Mack way from the path to a patch of ground and they talked together, not loud enough for us to hear. Mack again began searching for a mouthful of fresh grass, which was not to be found. My father walked away in a straight line, and stopped short a distance which seemed to suit him. Henry was walking away from Mack too, but sideways, still negligently holding on to the halter. My father raised the gun and Mack looked up as if he had noticed something and my father shot him.

Mack did not collapse at once but swayed, lurched sideways and fell, first on his side; then he rolled over on his back and, amazingly, kicked his legs for a few seconds in the air. At this Henry laughed, as if Mack had done a trick for him. Laird, who had drawn a long, groaning breath of surprise when the shot was fired, said out loud, "He's not dead." And it seemed to me it might be true. But his legs stopped, he rolled on his side again, his muscles quivered and sank. The two men walked over and looked at him in a businesslike way; they bent down and examined his forehead where the bullet had gone in, and now I saw his blood on the brown grass.

"Now they just skin him and cut him up," I said. "Let's go." My legs were a little shaky and I jumped gratefully down into the hay. "Now you've seen how they shoot a horse," I said in a congratulatory way, as if I had seen it many times before. "Let's see if any barn cat's had kittens in the hay." Laird jumped. He seemed young and obedient again. Suddenly I remembered how, when he was little, I had brought him into the barn and told him to climb the ladder to the top beam. That was in the spring, too, when the hay was low. I had done it out of a need for excitement, a desire for something to happen so that I could tell about it. He was wearing a little bulky brown and white checked coat, made down from one of mine. He went all the way up just as I told him, and sat down on the top beam with the hay far below him on one side, and the barn floor and some old machinery on the other. Then I ran screaming to my father, "Laird's up on the top beam!" My father came, my mother came, my father went up the ladder talking very quietly and brought Laird down under his arm, at which my mother leaned against the ladder and began to cry. They said to me, "Why weren't you watching him?" but nobody ever knew the truth. Laird did not know enough to tell. But whenever I saw the brown and white checked coat hanging in the closet, or at the bottom of the rag bag, which was where it ended up, I felt a weight in my stomach, the sadness of unexorcised guilt.

I looked at Laird, who did not even remember this, and I did not like the look on this thin, winter-pale face. His expression was not frightened or up-set, but remote, concentrating. "Listen," I said, in an unusually bright and friendly voice, "you aren't going to tell, are you?"

"No," he said absently.

"Promise." 40

"Promise," he said. I grabbed the hand behind his back to make sure he was not crossing his fingers. Even so, he might have a nightmare; it might come out that way. I decided I had better work hard to get all thoughts of what he had seen out of his mind—which, it seemed to me, could not hold very many things at a time. I got some money I had saved and that afternoon we went into Jubilee and saw a show, with Judy Canova,[3] at which we both laughed a great deal. After that I thought it would be all right.

Two weeks later I knew they were going to shoot Flora. I knew from the night before, when I heard my mother ask if the hay was holding out all right, and my father said, "Well, after tomorrow there'll just be the cow, and we should be able to put her out to grass in another week." So I knew it was Flora's turn in the morning.

This time I didn't think of watching it. That was something to see just one time. I had not thought about it very often since, but sometimes when I was busy working at school, or standing in front of the mirror combing my hair and wondering if I would be pretty when I grew up, the whole scene would flash into my mind: I would see the easy, practiced way my father raised the gun, and hear Henry laughing when Mack kicked his legs in the air. I did not have any great feeling of horror and opposition, such as a city child might have had; I was too used to seeing the death of animals as a necessity by

[3] American comedian, popular in films in the 1940s

which we lived. Yet I felt a little ashamed, and there was a new wariness, a sense of holding-off, in my attitude to my father and his work.

It was a fine day, and we were going around the yard picking up tree branches that had been torn off in winter storms. This was something we had been told to do, and also we wanted to use them to make a teepee. We heard Flora whinny, and then my father's voice and Henry's shouting, and we ran down to the barnyard to see what was going on.

The stable door was open. Henry had just brought Flora out, and she 45 had broken away from him. She was running free in the barnyard, from one end to the other. We climbed up on the fence. It was exciting to see her running, whinnying, going up on her hind legs, prancing and threatening like a horse in a Western movie, an unbroken ranch horse, though she was just an old driver, an old sorrel mare. My father and Henry ran after her and tried to grab the dangling halter. They tried to work her into a corner, and they had almost succeeded when she made a run between them, wild-eyed, and disappeared around the corner of the barn. We heard the rail clatter down as she got over the fence, and Henry yelled. "She's into the field now!"

That meant she was in the long L-shaped field that ran up by the house. If she got around the center, heading toward the lane, the gate was open; the truck had been driven into the field this morning. My father shouted to me, because I was on the other side of the fence, nearest the lane, "Go shut the gate!"

I could run very fast. I ran across the garden, past the tree where our swing was hung, and jumped across a ditch into the lane. There was the open gate. She had not got out, I could not see her up the road; she must have run to the other end of the field. The gate was heavy. I lifted it out of the gravel and carried it across the roadway. I had it halfway across when she came in sight, galloping straight toward me. There was just time to get the chain on. Laird came scrambling through the ditch to help me.

Instead of shutting the gate, I opened it as wide as I could. I did not make any decision to do this, it was just what I did. Flora never slowed down; she galloped straight past me, and Laird jumped up and down, yelling "Shut it, shut it!" even after it was too late. My father and Henry appeared in the field a moment too late to see what I had done. They only saw Flora heading for the township road. They would think I had not got there in time.

They did not waste any time asking about it. They went back to the barn and got the gun and the knives they used, and put these in the truck; then they turned the truck around and came bouncing up the field toward us. Laird called to them, "Let me go too, let me go too!" and Henry stopped the truck and they took him in. I shut the gate after they were all gone.

I supposed Laird would tell. I wondered what would happen to me. I had 50 never disobeyed my father before, and I could not understand why I had done it. Flora would not really get away. They would catch up with her in the truck. Or if they did not catch her this morning somebody would see her and telephone us this afternoon or tomorrow. There was no wild country here for her to run to, only farms. What was more, my father had paid for her, we needed the meat to feed the foxes, we needed the foxes to make our living. All I had done was make more work for my father who worked hard enough already.

And when my father found out about it he was not going to trust me any more; he would know that I was not entirely on his side. I was on Flora's side, and that made me no use to anybody, not even to her. Just the same, I did not regret it; when she came running at me and I held the gate open, that was the only thing I could do.

I went back to the house, and my mother said. "What's all the commotion?" I told her that Flora had kicked down the fence and got away. "Your poor father," she said, "now he'll have to go chasing over the countryside. Well, there isn't any use planning dinner before one." She put up the ironing board. I wanted to tell her, but thought better of it and went upstairs and sat on my bed.

Lately I had been trying to make my part of the room fancy, spreading the bed with old lace curtains, and fixing myself a dressing table with some leftovers of cretonne for a skirt. I planned to put up some kind of barricade between my bed and Laird's, to keep my section separate from his. In the sunlight, the lace curtains were just dusty rags. We did not sing at night any more. One night when I was singing Laird said, "You sound silly," and I went right on but the next night I did not start. There was not so much need to anyway, we were no longer afraid. We knew it was just old furniture over there, old jumble and confusion. We did not keep to the rules. I still stayed awake after Laird was asleep and told myself stories, but even in these stories something different was happening, mysterious alterations took place. A story might start off in the old way, with a spectacular danger, a fire or wild animals, and for a while I might rescue people; then things would change around, and instead, somebody would be rescuing me. It might be a boy from our class at school, or even Mr. Campbell, our teacher, who tickled girls under the arms. And at this point the story concerned itself at great length with what I looked like—how long my hair was, and what kind of dress I had on; by the time I had these details worked out the real excitement of the story was lost.

It was later than one o'clock when the truck came back. The tarpaulin was over the back, which meant there was meat in it. My mother had to heat dinner up all over again. Henry and my father had changed from their bloody overalls into ordinary working overalls in the barn, and they washed their arms and necks and faces at the sink, and splashed water on their hair and combed it. Laird lifted his arm to show off a streak of blood. "We shot old Flora," he said, "and cut her up in fifty pieces."

"Well I don't want to hear about it," my mother said. "And don't come to my table like that."

My father made him go and wash the blood off.   55

We sat down and my father said grace and Henry pasted his chewing gum on the end of his fork, the way he always did; when he took it off he would have us admire the pattern. We began to pass the bowls of steaming, overcooked vegetables. Laird looked across the table at me and said proudly, distinctly, "Anyway it was her fault Flora got away."

"What?" my father said.

"She could of shut the gate and she didn't. She just open' it up and Flora run out."

"Is that right?" my father said.

Everybody at the table was looking at me. I nodded, swallowing food with 60
great difficulty. To my shame, tears flooded my eyes.

My father made a curt sound of disgust. "What did you do that for?"

I did not answer. I put down my fork and waited to be sent from the table,
still not looking up.

But this did not happen. For some time nobody said anything, then Laird
said matter-of-factly, "She's crying."

"Never mind," my father said. He spoke with resignation, even good
humor, the words which absolved and dismissed me for good. "She's only a
girl," he said.

I didn't protest that, even in my heart. Maybe it was true.   65

1968]

■ TOPICS FOR DISCUSSION AND WRITING

1. Explain, in a paragraph, what the narrator means when she says (para-
    graph 21), "The word *girl* had formerly seemed to me innocent and un-
    burdened, like the world *child*; now it appeared that it was no such thing.
    A girl was not, as I had supposed, simply what I was; it was what I had
    to become."

2. The narrator says that she "could not understand" why she disobeyed
    her father and allowed the horse to escape. Can you explain her action to
    her? If so, do so.

3. In a paragraph, characterize the mother.

POETRY

■ RICHARD LOVELACE

Richard Lovelace (1618–1657) was born into a prominent English
family. Rich, handsome, witty, and favored by King Charles and Queen
Henrietta Maria, he supported the Royalists against the Parliamentarians
during the Civil War (1642–1652). In 1642 the Parliamentarians imprisoned him, and it was during his stay in prison that he wrote "To Althea,
from Prison," a poem that includes his most famous lines: "Stone walls
do not a prison make, / Nor iron bars a cage." He was released and exiled, fought in France against the Spanish, returned to England and in
1648 was again imprisoned. Soon after his release from prison he died,
penniless.

"To Lucasta, Going to the Wars," written during his second imprisonment, alludes to his support of the royalist cause.

To Lucasta, Going to the Wars

Tell me not, sweet, I am unkind
That from the nunnery
Of thy chaste breast and quiet mind,
To war and arms I fly.   4

True, a new mistress now I chase,
The first foe in the field;
And with a stronger faith embrace
A sword, a horse, a shield.   8

Yet this inconstancy is such
As you too shall adore;
I could not love thee, dear, so much,
Loved I not honor more.   12

[1649]

■ TOPICS FOR DISCUSSION AND WRITING

1. The speaker of this poem explains to his beloved, Lucasta, why he is
    willing to leave her. What words or lines particularly suggest her
    presence?
2. In the second stanza, who (or what) is the "new mistress" the speaker
    chases?
3. How does the speaker justify leaving his beloved? In your answer, take
    special account of the last two lines.
4. Judging from the tone of this poem, do you assume that his beloved will
    understand and agree? Explain.

■ ROBERT FROST

Robert Frost (1874–1963) was born in California. After his father's
death in 1885 Frost's mother brought the family to New England, where
she taught in high schools in Massachusetts and New Hampshire. Frost
studied for part of one term at Dartmouth College in New Hampshire,
then did odd jobs (including teaching), and from 1897 to 1899 was enrolled as a special student at Harvard. He then farmed in New Hampshire, published a few poems in local newspapers, left the farm and
taught again, and in 1912 left for England, where he hoped to achieve
more popular success as a writer. By 1915 he had won a considerable
reputation, and he returned to the United States, settling on a farm in
New Hampshire and cultivating the image of the country-wise farmer-
poet. In fact he was well read in the classics, the Bible, and in English
and American literature.

Among Frost's many comments about literature, here are three:
"Writing is unboring to the extent that it is dramatic"; "Every poem
is . . . a figure of the will braving alien entanglements"; and, finally, a
poem "begins in delight and ends in wisdom. . . . It runs a course of

lucky events, and ends in a clarification of life—not necessarily a great clarification, such as sects and cults are founded on, but in a momentary stay against confusion."

Stopping by Woods on a Snowy Evening

Whose woods these are I think I know.
His house is in the village though;
He will not see me stopping here
To watch his woods fill up with snow.   4

My little horse must think it queer
To stop without a farmhouse near
Between the woods and frozen lake
The darkest evening of the year.   8

He gives his harness bells a shake
To ask if there is some mistake.
The only other sound's the sweep
Of easy wind and downy flake.   12

The woods are lovely, dark and deep.
But I have promises to keep,
And miles to go before I sleep,
And miles to go before I sleep.   16

[1923]

■ TOPICS FOR DISCUSSION AND WRITING

1. Line 5 originally read: "The steaming horses think it queer." Line 7 read: "Between a forest and a lake." Evaluate the changes.
2. The rhyming words in the first stanza can be indicated by *aaba;* the second stanza picks up the *b* rhyme: *bbcb.* Indicate the rhymes for the third stanza. For the fourth. Why is it appropriate that the rhyme scheme differs in the fourth stanza?
3. Hearing that the poem had been interpreted as a "death poem," Frost said. "I never intended that, but I did have the feeling it was loaded with ulteriority." What do you understand "ulteriority" to mean in regards to this poem? For example, what significance do you attach to the time of day and year?
4. How does the horse's attitude contrast with the man's?

Mending Wall

Something there is that doesn't love a wall,
That sends the frozen-ground-swell under it,
And spills the upper boulder, in the sun;

And makes gaps even two can pass abreast.
The work of hunters is another thing: 5
I have come after them and made repair
Where they have left not one stone on a stone,
But they would have the rabbit out of hiding,
To please the yelping dogs. The gaps I mean,
No one has seen them made or heard them made,   10
But at spring mending-time we find them there.
I let my neighbor know beyond the hill;
And on a day we meet to walk the line
And set the wall between us once again.
We keep the wall between us as we go.   15
To each the boulders that have fallen to each.
And some are loaves and some so nearly balls
We have to use a spell to make them balance:
"Stay where you are until our backs are turned!"
We wear our fingers rough with handling them.   20
Oh, just another kind of outdoor game,
One on a side. It comes to little more:
There where it is we do not need the wall:
He is all pine and I am apple orchard.
My apple trees will never get across   25
And eat the cones under his pines, I tell him.
He only says, "Good fences make good neighbors."
Spring is the mischief in me, and I wonder
If I could put a notion in his head:
"*Why* do they make good neighbors? Isn't it   30
Where there are cows? But here there are no cows.
Before I built a wall I'd ask to know
What I was walling in or walling out,
And to whom I was like to give offense.
Something there is that doesn't love a wall,   35
That wants it down." I could say "Elves" to him,
But it's not elves exactly, and I'd rather
He said it for himself. I see him there
Bringing a stone grasped firmly by the top
In each hand, like an old-stone savage armed.   40
He moves in darkness as it seems to me,
Not of woods only and the shade of trees.
He will not go behind his father's saying,
And he likes having thought of it so well
He says again, "Good fences make good neighbors."   45

                              [1914]

■   TOPICS FOR DISCUSSION AND WRITING

1.   The poem includes a scene, or action, in which the speaker and a neigh-
     bor are engaged. Briefly summarize the scene. What indicates that the
     scene has been enacted before and will be again?

2. Compare and contrast the speaker and the neighbor.
3. Notice that the speaker, not the neighbor, initiates the business of repairing the wall (line 12). Why do you think he does this?
4. Both the speaker and the neighbor repeat themselves; they each make one point twice in identical language. What do they say? And why does Frost allow the neighbor to have the last word?
5. "Something there is that doesn't love a wall" adds up to "Something doesn't love a wall." Or does it? Within the context of the poem, what is this difference between the two statements?
6. Write an essay of 500 words, telling of an experience in which you came to conclude that "good fences make good neighbors." Or tell of an experience that led you to conclude that fences (they can be figurative fences, of course) are "like to give offense" (see lines 32–34).

The Road Not Taken

Two roads diverged in a yellow wood,
And sorry I could not travel both
And be one traveler, long I stood
And looked down one as far as I could
To where it bent in the undergrowth;   5

Then took the other, as just as fair,
And having perhaps the better claim,
Because it was grassy and wanted wear
Though as for that the passing there
Had worn them really about the same,   10

And both that morning equally lay
In leaves no step had trodden black.
Oh, I kept the first for another day!
Yet knowing how way leads on to way,
I doubted if I should ever come back.   15

I shall be telling this with a sigh
Somewhere ages and ages hence:
Two roads diverged in a wood, and I—
I took the one less traveled by,
And that has made all the difference.   20

[1916]

■ TOPICS FOR DISCUSSION AND WRITING

1. Would it make any difference if instead of "yellow" in the first line the poet had written "bright green" (or "dark green")?
2. What reason does the speaker give for choosing the road he takes? Why was it a difficult choice?

3. Frost called the poem "The Road Not Taken." Why didn't he call it "The Road Taken"? Which do you think is the better title, and why?

4. What do you think that the speaker says that he will later be telling this story "with a sigh"? Set forth your response in a paragraph.

5. Consider a choice that you made, perhaps almost unthinkingly, and offer your reflections on how your life might have been different if you had chosen otherwise. Are you now regretful, pleased, puzzled, indifferent, or what? (For instance, what seemed to be a big choice may in retrospect have been a decision of no consequence.)

■ T. S. ELIOT

Thomas Stearns Eliot (1888–1965) was born into a New England family that had moved to St. Louis. He attended a preparatory school in Massachusetts, then graduated from Harvard and did further study in literature and philosophy in France, Germany, and England. In 1914 he began working for Lloyd's Bank in London, and three years later he published his first book of poems (it included "Prufrock"). In 1925 he joined a publishing firm, and in 1927 he became a British citizen and a member of the Church of England. Much of his later poetry, unlike "The Love Song of J. Alfred Prufrock," is highly religious. In 1948 Eliot received the Nobel Prize for Literature.

The Love Song of J. Alfred Prufrock

S'io credesse che mia risposta fosse
A persona che mai tornasse al mondo,
Questa fiamma staria senza piu scosse.
Ma perciocche giammai di questo fondo
Non torno vivo alcun, s' i' odo il vero,
*Senza tema d'infama ti rispondo.**

Let us go then, you and I,
When the evening is spread out against the sky
Like a patient etherized upon a table;
Let us go, through certain half-deserted streets,
The muttering retreats   5
Of restless nights in one-night cheap hotels
And sawdust restaurants with oyster-shells:
Streets that follow like a tedious argument

*In Dante's *Inferno* XXVII:61–66, a damned soul who had sought absolution before committing a crime addresses Dante, thinking that his words will never reach the earth: "If I believed that my answer were to a person who could ever return to the world, this flame would no longer quiver. But because no one ever returned from this depth, if what I hear is true, without fear of infamy, I answer you."

Of insidious intent
To lead you to an overwhelming question...   10
Oh, do not ask, "What is it?"
Let us go and make our visit.

In the room the women come and go
Talking of Michelangelo.

The yellow fog that rubs its back upon the window-panes,   15
The yellow smoke that rubs its muzzle on the window-panes
Licked its tongue into the corners of the evening,
Lingered upon the pools that stand in drains,
Let fall upon its back the soot that falls from chimneys,
Slipped by the terrace, made a sudden leap,   20
And seeing that it was a soft October night,
Curled once about the house, and fell asleep.

And indeed there will be time
For the yellow smoke that slides along the street,
Rubbing its back upon the window-panes;   25
There will be time, there will be time
To prepare a face to meet the faces that you meet;
There will be time to murder and create,
And time for all the works and days° of hands
That lift and drop a question on your plate;   30
Time for you and time for me,
And time yet for a hundred indecisions,
And for a hundred visions and revisions,
Before the taking of a toast and tea.

In the room the women come and go   35
Talking of Michelangelo.

And indeed there will be time
To wonder, "Do I dare?" and, "Do I dare?"
Time to turn back and descend the stair,
With a bald spot in the middle of my hair—   40
[They will say: "How his hair is growing thin!"]
My morning coat, my collar mounting firmly to the chin,
My necktie rich and modest, but asserted by a simple pin—
[They will say: "But how his arms and legs are thin!"]
Do I dare   45
Disturb the universe?

29 **works and days** "Works and Days" is the title of a poem on farm life by Hesiod
(eighth century B.C.).

In a minute there is time
For decisions and revisions which a minute will reverse.

For I have known them all already, known them all:—
Have known the evenings, mornings, afternoons,   50
I have measured out my life with coffee spoons;
I know the voices dying with a dying fall°
Beneath the music from a farther room.
        So how should I presume?

And I have known the eyes already, known them all—   55
The eyes that fix you in a formulated phrase,
And when I am formulated, sprawling on a pin,
When I am pinned and wriggling on the wall,
Then how should I begin
To spit out all the butt-ends of my days and ways?   60
        And how should I presume?

And I have known the arms already, known them all—
Arms that are braceleted and white and bare
[But in the lamplight, downed with light brown hair!]

Is it perfume from a dress   65
That makes me so digress?
Arms that lie along a table, or wrap about a shawl.
        And should I then presume?
        And how should I begin?
                    . . . . .
Shall I say, I have gone at dusk through narrow streets   70
And watched the smoke that rises from the pipes
Of lonely men in shirt-sleeves, leaning out of windows?. . .

I should have been a pair of ragged claws
Scuttling across the floors of silent seas.
                    . . . . .
And the afternoon, the evening, sleeps so peacefully!   75
Smoothed by long fingers,
Asleep . . . tired . . . or it malingers,
Stretched on the floor, here beside you and me.
Should I, after tea and cakes and ices,
Have the strength to force the moment to its crisis?   80
But though I have wept and fasted, wept and prayed,
Though I have seen my head [grown slightly bald]
        brought in upon a platter,°
I am no prophet—and here's no great matter;

52 **dying fall** This line echoes Shakespeare's *Twelfth Night* I.i.4   81–83 These lines
allude to John the Baptist (see Matthew 14:1–11).

I have seen the moment of my greatness flicker,
And I have seen the eternal Footman hold my coat, and snicker,   85
And in short, I was afraid.

And would it have been worth it, after all,
After the cups, the marmalade, the tea,
Among the porcelain, among some talk of you and me,
Would it have been worth while,   90
To have bitten off the matter with a smile,
To have squeezed the universe into a ball°
To roll it toward some overwhelming question,
To say: "I am Lazarus,° come from the dead,
Come back to tell you all, I shall tell you all"—   95
If one, settling a pillow by her head,
        Should say: "That is not what I meant at all.
        That is not it, at all."

And would it have been worth it, after all,
Would it have been worth while,   100
After the sunsets and the dooryards and the sprinkled streets,
After the novels, after the teacups, after the skirts
        that trail along the floor—
And this, and so much more?—
It is impossible to say just what I mean!
But as if a magic lantern threw the nerves in patterns
        on a screen: 105
Would it have been worth while
If one, settling a pillow or throwing off a shawl,
And turning toward the window, should say:
        "That is not it at all,
        That is not what I meant, at all."   110
                              . . . . .
No! I am not Prince Hamlet, nor was meant to be;
Am an attendant lord, one that will do
To swell a progress, start a scene or two,
Advise the prince; no doubt, an easy tool,
Deferential, glad to be of use,   115
Politic, cautious, and meticulous;
Full of high sentence, but a bit obtuse;°
At times, indeed, almost ridiculous—
Almost, at times, the Fool.

I grow old . . . I grow old . . .   120

92 This line echoes lines 41–42 of Marvell's "To His Coy Mistress" (see page 564).
94 **Lazarus** See Luke 16 and John 11   112–117 These lines allude to Polonius and
perhaps other figures in Hamlet (pages 407–512).   **full of high sentence** See
Chaucer's description of the Clerk of Oxford in the *Canterbury Tales*.

I shall wear the bottoms of my trousers rolled.

Shall I part my hair behind? Do I dare to eat a peach?
I shall wear white flannel trousers, and walk upon the beach.
I have heard the mermaids singing, each to each.
I do not think that they will sing to me.   125

I have seen them riding seaward on the waves
Combing the white hair of the waves blown back
When the wind blows the water white and black.

We have lingered in the chambers of the sea
By sea-girls wreathed with seaweed red and brown   130
Till human voices wake us, and we drown.

                                        [1910–1911]

■ TOPICS FOR DISCUSSION AND WRITING

1. How does the speaker's name help to characterize him? What
    suggestions—of class, race, personality—do you find in it? Does the title
    of this poem strike you as ironic? If so, how or why?
2. What qualities of big-city life are suggested in the poem? How are these
    qualities linked to the speaker's mood? What other details of the
    setting—the weather, the time of day—express or reflect his mood? What
    images do you find especially striking?
3. The speaker's thoughts are represented in a stream-of-consciousness
    monologue, that is, in what appears to be an unedited flow of thought.
    Nevertheless, they reveal a story. What is the story?
4. In a paragraph, characterize Prufrock as he might be characterized by one
    of the women in the poem, and then, in a paragraph or two, offer your
    own characterization of him.
5. Consider the possibility that the "you" whom Prufrock is addressing is
    not a listener but is one aspect of Prufrock, and the "I" is another.
    Given this possibility, in a paragraph characterize the "you," and in
    another paragraph characterize the "I."
6. Prufrock has gone to a therapist, psychiatrist, or member of the clergy
    for help. Write a 500-word transcript of their session.

■ W. H. AUDEN

    Wystan Hugh Auden (1907–1973) was born in York, England, and
educated at Oxford. In the 1930s his witty Left-wing poetry earned him
wide acclaim as the leading poet of his generation. He went to Spain
during the Spanish Civil War, intending to serve as an ambulance driver
for the Republicans in their struggle against Fascism, but he was so dis-
tressed by the violence of the Republicans that he almost immediately
returned to England. In 1939 he came to America, and in 1946 he
became a citizen of the United States, though he spent his last years in

England. Much of his poetry is characterized by a combination of colloquial diction and technical dexterity.

Musée des Beaux Arts[1]

About suffering they were never wrong,
The Old Masters: how well they understood
Its human position; how it takes place
While someone else is eating or opening a window or just walking dully along;
How, when the aged are reverently, passionately waiting   5
For the miraculous birth, there always must be
Children who did not specially want it to happen, skating
On a pond at the edge of the wood:
They never forgot
That even the dreadful martyrdom must run its course   10
Anyhow in a corner, some untidy spot
Where the dogs go on with their doggy life and the torturer's horse
Scratches its innocent behind on a tree.

In Brueghel's *Icarus*,[2] for instance: how everything turns away
Quite leisurely from the disaster; the plowman may   15
Have heard the splash, the forsaken cry,
But for him it was not an important failure; the sun shone
As it had to on the white legs disappearing into the green
Water; and the expensive delicate ship that must have seen
Something amazing, a boy falling out of the sky,   20
Had somewhere to get to and sailed calmly on.

[1938]

- ## TOPICS FOR DISCUSSION AND WRITING

1. In your own words sum up what, according to the speaker (in lines 1–13),
   the Old Masters understood about human suffering. (The Old Masters
   were the great European painters who worked from about 1500 to about
   1750.)
2. In line 15, to what "disaster" does the speaker refer? (If you're not sure,
   look up "Icarus" in any college dictionary or in a handbook of classical
   mythology.)
3. Note the instances of rhyme in the poem. In the first stanza, for example: *wrong/along, understood/wood, waiting/skating, forgot/spot,* and so on.
   If you were surprised to find rhymes in this poem, can you explain why
   you were surprised?

[1] Museum of Fine Arts (French)
[2] Painting by the Flemish painter Pieter Brueghel (c. 1522–1569) that now hangs in
the Brussels Museum of Fine Arts

4. Suppose the first lines read:

   The Old Masters were never wrong about suffering.
   They understood its human position well.

   What (beside the particular rhymes you've noted) would change or be lost?

5. Find, if you can, a reproduction of Pieter Brueghel's painting *Icarus*. (Most libraries will have at least one book with reproductions of Brueghel's paintings, for instance, Timothy Foote's *The World of Brueghel*.) In your opinion, has Auden chosen a good example of what he sees as the Old Masters' understanding of suffering? Again, in your opinion, does Auden's poem help you to understand Brueghel's *Icarus?* How would you explain your answer to either question to someone who had read the poem but was baffled by it?

6. Reread the poem (preferably over the course of several days) a number of times, jotting down your chief reponses after reach reading. Then, in connection with a final reading, study your notes, and write an essay of 500 words setting forth the history of your final response to the poem. For example, you may want to report that certain difficulties soon were clarified and that your enjoyment increased. Or, conversely, you may want to report that the poem became less interesting (for reasons you will set forth) the more you studied it. Probably your history will be somewhat more complicated than these simple examples. Try to find a chief pattern in your experience and shape it into a thesis.

7. Consider a picture, either in a local museum or reproduced in a book, and write a 500-word reflection on it. If the picture is not well known, include a reproduction (a postcard from the museum or a photocopy of a page of the book) with your essay.

The Unknown Citizen

(To JS/07/M/378
This Marble Monument
Is Erected by the State)

He was found by the Bureau of Statistics to be
One against whom there was no official complaint,
And all the reports on his conduct agree
That, in the modern sense of an old-fashioned word, he was a saint,
For in everything he did he served the Greater Community.   5
Except for the War till the day he retired
He worked in a factory and never got fired,
But satisfied his employers, Fudge Motors Inc.
Yet he wasn't a scab or odd in his views,
For his Union reports that he paid his dues.   10
(Our report on his Union shows it was sound)
And our Social Psychology workers found

That he was popular with his mates and liked a drink.
The press are convinced that he bought a paper every day
And that his reactions to advertisements were normal in every way.   15
Policies taken out in his name prove that he was fully insured,
And his Health-card shows he was once in hospital but left it cured.
Both Producers Research and High-Grade Living declare
He was fully sensible to the advantages of the Installment Plan
And had everything necessary to the Modern Man,   20
A phonograph, radio, a car and a frigidaire.
Our researches into Public Opinion are content
That he held the proper opinions for the time of year;
When there was peace, he was for peace; when there was war, he went.
He was married and added five children to the population,   25
Which our Eugenist says was the right number for a parent of his generation,
And our teachers report that he never interfered with their education.
Was he free? Was he happy? The question is absurd:
Had anything been wrong, we should certainly have heard.

[1940]

■ TOPICS FOR DISCUSSION AND WRITING

1. Who is the speaker, and on what occasion is he supposed to be speaking?
2. What do the words "The Unknown Citizen" suggest to you?
3. How does Auden suggest that he doesn't share the attitudes of the speaker and is, in fact, satirizing them? What else does he satirize?
4. If Auden were writing the poem today, what might he substitute for "Installment Plan" in line 19 and the items listed in line 21?
5. Explicate the last two lines.
6. Write a tribute to The Unknown Student or The Unknown Professor or Politician or Professional Athlete or some other object of your well-deserved scorn.

■ MITSUYE YAMADA

Mitsuye Yamada, the daughter of Japanese immigrants to the United States, was born in Japan in 1923, during her mother's return visit to her native land. Yamada was raised in Seattle, but in 1942 she and her family were incarcerated and then relocated in a camp in Idaho, when Executive Order 9066 gave military authorities the right to remove any and all persons from "military areas." In 1954 she became an American citizen. A professor of English at Cypress Junior College in San Luis Obispo, California, she is the author of poems and stories.

To the Lady

The one in San Francisco who asked:
Why did the Japanese Americans let

the government put them in
those camps without protest?

Come to think of it I   5
    should've run off to Canada
    should've hijacked a plane to Algeria
    should've pulled myself up from my
    bra straps
    and kicked'm in the groin   10
    should've bombed a bank
    should've tried self-immolation
    should've holed myself up in a
    woodframe house
    and let you watch me   15
    burn up on the six o'clock news
    should've run howling down the street
    naked and assaulted you at breakfast
    by AP wirephoto
    should've screamed bloody murder   20
    like Kitty Genovese[1]

    Then
YOU would've
    come to my aid in shining armor
    laid yourself across the railroad track   25
    marched on Washington
    tatooed a Star of David on your arm
    written six million enraged
    letters to Congress

    But we didn't draw the line   30
    anywhere
    law and order Executive Order 9066[2]
    social order moral order internal order

    YOU let'm
    I let'm   35
    All are punished.
                [1976]

   [1]**Kitty Genovese** In 1964 Kitty Genovese of Kew Gardens, New York, was
stabbed to death when she left her car and walked toward her home. Thirty-eight persons heard her screams, but no one came to her assistance.
   [2]**Executive Order 9066** an authorization, signed in 1941 by President Franklin
D. Roosevelt, allowing military authorities to relocate Japanese and Japanese-Americans
who resided on the Pacific Coast of the United States

■ TOPICS FOR DISCUSSION AND WRITING

1. Has the lady's question (lines 2–4) ever crossed your mind? If so, what answers did you think of?
2. What, in effect, is the speaker really saying in lines 5–21? And in lines 24–29?
3. Explain the last line.

■ MARGE PIERCY

Marge Piercy, born in Detroit in 1936, was the first member of her family to attend college. After earning a bachelor's degree from the University of Michigan in 1957 and a master's degree from Northwestern University in 1958, she moved to Chicago. There she worked at odd jobs while writing novels (unpublished) and engaging in action on behalf of women and blacks and against the war in Vietnam. In 1970—the year she moved to Wellfleet, Massachusetts, where she still lives—she published her first book, a novel. Since then she has published other novels, short stories, poems, and essays.

Barbie Doll

This girlchild was born as usual
and presented dolls that did pee-pee
and miniature GE stoves and irons
and wee lipsticks the color of cherry candy.
Then in the magic of puberty, a classmate said: 5
You have a great big nose and fat legs.

She was healthy, tested intelligent,
possessed strong arms and back,
abundant sexual drive and manual dexterity.
She went to and fro apologizing.   10
Everyone saw a fat nose on thick legs.

She was advised to play coy,
exhorted to come on hearty,
exercise, diet, smile and wheedle.
Her good nature wore out   15
like a fan belt.
So she cut off her nose and her legs
and offered them up.
In the casket displayed on satin she lay
with the undertaker's cosmetics painted on,   20
a turned-up putty nose,
dressed in a pink and white nightie.
Doesn't she look pretty? everyone said.

Consummation at last.
To every woman a happy ending.   [1969]   25

■ TOPICS FOR DISCUSSION AND WRITING

1. Do you have any particular attitude(s) toward Barbie Dolls? Do you find them attractive? Repellent? Whatever your response, set it forth in a paragraph.
2. In a paragraph explain why the poem is called "Barbie Doll."
3. What voice do you hear in lines 1–4? Line 6 is, we are told, the voice of "a classmate." How do these voices differ? What voice do you hear in the first three lines of the second stanza?
4. Explain in your own words what Piercy is saying about women in this poem. Does her view seem to you fair, slightly exaggerated, or greatly exaggerated?

What's That Smell in the Kitchen?

All over America women are burning dinners.
It's lambchops in Peoria; it's haddock
in Providence; it's steak in Chicago;
tofu delight in Big Sur; red
rice and beans in Dallas.   5
All over America women are burning
food they're supposed to bring with calico
smile on platters glittering like wax.
Anger sputters in her brainpan, confined
but spewing out missiles of hot fat.   10
Carbonized despair presses like a clinker
from a barbecue against the back of her eyes.
If she wants to grill anything, it's
her husband spitted over a slow fire.
If she wants to serve him anything   15
it's a dead rat with a bomb in its belly
ticking like the heart of an insomniac.
Her life is cooked and digested,
nothing but leftovers in Tupperware.
Look, she says, once I was roast duck   20
on your platter with parsley but now I am Spam.
Burning dinner is not incompetence but war.
                                            [1980]

■ TOPICS FOR DISCUSSION AND WRITING

1. Suppose a friend told you that she didn't understand lines 20–21. How would you paraphrase the lines?
2. Who speaks the title?

3. If a poem begins, "All over America women are . . . ," what words might
    a reader reasonably expect next?

4. Do you take the poem to be chiefly comic? Superficially but essentially
    comic but a work with a serious purpose? Or what?

5. If you have ever used apparent "incompetence" as "war" (line 22), nar-
    rate the episode so that the reader understands not only *what* happened
    but also *why* it happened.

A Work of Artifice

The bonsai tree
in the attractive pot
could have grown eighty feet tall
on the side of a mountain
till split by lightning.   5
But a gardener
carefully pruned it.
It is nine inches high.
Every day as he
whittles back the branches   10
the gardener croons,
It is your nature
to be small and cozy,
domestic and weak;
how lucky, little tree,   15
to have a pot to grow in.
With living creatures
one must begin very early
to dwarf their growth:
the bound feet,   20
the crippled brain,
the hair in curlers,
the hands you
love to touch.

                    [1973]

■ TOPICS FOR DISCUSSION AND WRITING

1. Piercy uses a bonsai tree as a metaphor—but a metaphor for what? (If
    you have never seen a bonsai tree, try to visit a florist or a nursery to
    take a close look at one. You can find a picture of a bonsai in *The Ameri-
    can Heritage Dictionary.*)

2. The gardener "croons" (line 11) a song to the bonsai tree. If the tree
    could respond, what might it say?

3. Explain lines 17–24 to someone who doesn't get the point. In your
    response, explain how these lines are connected with "hair in curlers."
    Explain, too, what "the hands you / love to touch" has to do with the

rest of the poem. What tone of voice do you hear in "the hands
you / love to touch"?

4.   How does the form of the poem suggest its subject?

■ CAROLYN FORCHÉ

Carolyn Forché was born in Detroit in 1950. After earning a
bachelor's degree from Michigan State University and a master's degree
from Bowling Green State University, she traveled widely in the Southwest, living among Pueblo Indians. Between 1978 and 1986 she made
several visits to El Salvador, documenting human rights violations for Am-
nesty International. Her first book of poems, *Gathering the Tribes*, won
the Yale Younger Poets award in 1975. Her second book of poems, *The
Country Between Us* (1981), includes "The Colonel," which has been
called a prose-poem. (The term "prose-poem" is sometimes applied to a
short work that looks like prose but that is highly rhythmical or rich in
images, or both.)

The Colonel

What you have heard is true. I was in his house. His wife carried a tray of
coffee and sugar. His daughter filed her nails, his son went out for the night.
There were daily papers, pet dogs, a pistol on the cushion beside him. The
moon swung bare on its black cord over the house. On the television was a
cop show. It was in English. Broken bottles were embedded in the walls
around the house to scoop the kneecaps from a man's legs or cut his hands
to lace. On the windows there were gratings like those in liquor stores. We
had dinner, rack of lamb, good wine, a gold bell was on the table for calling
the maid. The maid brought green mangoes, salt, a type of bread. I was asked
how I enjoyed the country. There was a brief commercial in Spanish. His wife
took everything away. There was some talk then of how difficult it had become
to govern. The parrot said hello on the terrace. The colonel told it to shutup,
and pushed himself from the table. My friend said to me with his eyes: say
nothing. The colonel returned with a sack used to bring groceries home. He
spilled many human ears on the table. They were like dried peach halves.
There is no other way to say this. He took one of them in his hands, shook
it in our faces, dropped it into a water glass. It came alive there. I am tired
of fooling around he said. As for the rights of anyone, tell your people they
can go fuck themselves. He swept the ears to the floor with his arm and held
the last of his wine in the air. Something for your poetry, no? he said. Some
of the ears on the floor caught this scrap of his voice. Some of the ears on
the floor were pressed to the ground.

May 1978

[1982]

- ## TOPICS FOR DISCUSSION AND WRITING

1. How would you characterize the colonel in a few sentences?
2. We are told that the colonel spoke of "how difficult it had become to govern." What do you suppose the colonel assumes is the purpose of government? What do you assume its purpose is?
3. How much do we know about the narrator? Can we guess the narrator's purpose in visiting the colonel? How would you characterize the narrator's tone? Do you believe the narrator?
4. What do you make of the last two lines?

DRAMA

- ## HENRIK IBSEN

Henrik Ibsen (1828–1906) was born in Skien, Norway, of wealthy parents who soon after his birth lost their money. Ibsen worked as a pharmacist's apprentice, but at the age of 22 he had written his first play, a promising melodrama entitled *Cataline*. He engaged in theater work first in Norway and then in Denmark and Germany. By 1865 his plays had won him a state pension that enabled him to settle in Rome. After writing romantic, historic, and poetic plays, he turned to realistic drama with *The League of Youth* (1869). Among the major realistic "problem plays" are *A Doll's House* (1879), *Ghosts* (1881), and *An Enemy of the People* (1882). In *The Wild Duck* (1884) he moved toward a more symbolic tragic comedy, and his last plays, written in the nineties, are highly symbolic. *Hedda Gabler* (1890) looks backward to the plays of the eighties rather than forward to the plays of the nineties.

A Doll's House

Translated by Otto Reinert

List of Characters

TORVALD HELMER, *a lawyer*
NORA, *his wife*
DR. RANK
MRS. LINDE
KROGSTAD
THE HELMERS' THREE SMALL CHILDREN

Claire Bloom starred as Nora in the 1971 production of *A Doll's House*. Photograph by Martha Swope. Used by permission.

ANNE-MARIE, *the children's nurse*
A HOUSEMAID
A PORTER

Scene: The Helmers' living room

ACT I

A pleasant, tastefully but not expensively furnished, living room. A door
on the rear wall, right, leads to the front hall, another door, left, to HELMER'S
study. Between the two doors a piano. A third door in the middle of the left wall;
further front a window. Near the window a round table with easy chairs and
a small couch. Towards the rear of the right wall a fourth door; further front
a tile stove with a rocking chair and a couple of arm chairs in front of it. Between the stove and the side door a small table. Copperplate etchings on the
walls. A whatnot with porcelain figurines and other small objects. A small
bookcase with deluxe editions. A rug on the floor; fire in the stove. Winter day.

The doorbell rings, then the sound of the front door opening. NORA,
dressed for outdoors, enters, humming cheerfully. She carries several packages,
which she puts down on the table, right. She leaves the door to the front hall
open; there a PORTER is seen holding a Christmas tree and a basket. He gives
them to THE MAID, who has let them in.

NORA. Be sure to hide the Christmas tree, Helen. The children mustn't
see it before tonight when we've trimmed it. [*Opens her purse; to the* PORT-
ER.] How much?

PORTER. Fifty øre.

NORA. Here's a crown. No, keep the change. [*The* PORTER *thanks her,
leaves.* NORA *closes the door. She keeps laughing quietly to herself as she takes
off her coat, etc. She takes a bag of macaroons from her pocket and eats a couple. She walks cautiously over to the door to the study and listens.*] Yes, he's
home. [*Resumes her humming, walks over to the to table, right.*]

HELMER [*in his study*]. Is that my little lark twittering out there?

NORA [*opening some of the packages*]. That's right.

HELMER. My squirrel bustling about?

NORA. Yes.

HELMER. When did squirrel come home?

NORA. Just now. [*Puts the bag of macaroons back in her pocket, wipes her
mouth.*] Come out here, Torvald. I want to show you what I've bought.

HELMER. I'm busy! [*After a little while he opens the door and looks in, pen
in hand.*] Bought, eh? All that? So little wastrel has been throwing money
around again?

NORA. Oh but Torvald, this Christmas we can be a little extravagant,
can't we? It's the first Christmas we don't have to scrimp.

HELMER. I don't know about that. We certainly don't have money to
waste.

NORA. Yes, Torvald, we do. A little, anyway. Just a tiny little bit? Now
that you're going to get that big salary and make lots and lots of money.

HELMER. Starting at New Year's, yes. But payday isn't till the end of the quarter.

NORA. That doesn't matter. We can always borrow.

HELMER. Nora! [*Goes over to her and playfully pulls her ear.*] There you go being irresponsible again. Suppose I borrowed a thousand crowns today and you spent it all for Christmas and on New Year's Eve a tile hit me in the head and laid me out cold.

NORA [*putting her hand over his mouth*]. I won't have you say such horrid things.

HELMER. But suppose it happened. Then what?

NORA. If it did, I wouldn't care whether we owed money or not.

HELMER. But what about the people I had borrowed from?

NORA. Who cares about them! They are strangers.

HELMER. Nora, Nora, you are a woman. No, really! You know how I feel about that. No debts! A home in debt isn't a free home, and if it isn't free it isn't beautiful. We've managed nicely so far, you and I, and that's the way we'll go on. It won't be for much longer.

NORA [*walks over toward the stove*]. All right, Torvald. Whatever you say.

HELMER [*follows her*]. Come, come, my little songbird mustn't droop her wings. What's this? Can't have a pouty squirrel in the house, you know. [*Takes out his wallet.*] Nora, what do you think I have here?

NORA [*turns around quickly*]. Money!

HELMER. Here. [*Gives her some bills*]. Don't you think I know Christmas is expensive?

NORA [*counting*]. Ten—twenty—thirty—forty. Thank you, thank you, Torvald. This helps a lot.

HELMER. I certainly hope so.

NORA. It does, it does. But I want to show you what I got. It was cheap, too. Look. New clothes for Ivar. And a sword. And a horse and trumpet for Bob. And a doll and a little bed for Emmy. It isn't any good, but it wouldn't last anyway. And here's some dress material and scarves for the maids. I feel bad about old Anne-Marie, though. She really should be getting much more.

HELMER. And what's in here?

NORA [*cries*]. Not till tonight!

HELMER. I see. But now what does my little prodigal have in mind for herself?

NORA. Oh, nothing. I really don't care.

HELMER. Of course you do. Tell me what you'd like. Within reason.

NORA. Oh, I don't know. Really, I don't. The only thing—

HELMER. Well?

NORA [*fiddling with his buttons, without looking at him*]. If you really want to give me something, you might—you could—

HELMER. All right, let's have it.

NORA [*quickly*]. Some money, Torvald. Just as much as you think you can spare. Then I'll buy myself something one of these days.

HELMER. No, really Nora—

NORA. Oh yes, please, Torvald. Please? I'll wrap the money in pretty gold paper and hang it on the tree. Won't that be nice?

HELMER. What's the name for little birds that are always spending money?

NORA. Wastrels, I know. But please let's do it my way, Torvald. Then I'll have time to decide what I need most. Now that's sensible, isn't it?

HELMER [*smiling*]. Oh, very sensible. That is, if you really bought yourself something you could use. But it all disappears in the household expenses or you buy things you don't need. And then you come back to me for more.

NORA. Oh, but Torvald—

HELMER. That's the truth, dear little Nora, and you know it. [*Puts his arm around her.*] My wastrel is a little sweetheart, but she does go through an awful lot of money awfully fast. You've no idea how expensive it is for a man to keep a wastrel.

NORA. That's not fair, Torvald. I really save all I can.

HELMER [*laughs*]. Oh, I believe that. All you can. Meaning, exactly nothing!

NORA [*hums, smiles mysteriously*]. You don't know all the things we songbirds and squirrels need money for, Torvald.

HELMER. You know, you're funny. Just like your father. You're always looking for ways to get money, but as soon as you do it runs through your fingers and you can never say what you spent it for. Well, I guess I'll just have to take you the way you are. It's in your blood. Yes, that sort of thing is hereditary, Nora.

NORA. In that case, I wish I had inherited many of Daddy's qualities.

HELMER. And I don't want you any different from just what you are—my own sweet little songbird. Hey!—I think I just noticed something. Aren't you looking—what's the word?—a little—sly—?

NORA. I am?

HELMER. You definitely are. Look at me.

NORA [*looks at him*]. Well?

HELMER [*wagging a finger*]. Little sweet-tooth hasn't by any chance been on a rampage today, has she?

NORA. Of course not. Whatever makes you think that?

HELMER. A little detour by the pastryshop maybe?

NORA. No, I assure you, Torvald—

HELMER. Nibbled a little jam?

NORA. Certainly not!

HELMER. Munched a macaroon or two?

NORA. No, really, Torvald, I honestly—

HELMER. All right. Of course I was only joking.

NORA [*walks toward the table, right*]. You know I wouldn't do anything to displease you.

HELMER. I know. And I have your promise. [*Over to her.*] All right, keep your little Christmas secrets to yourself, Nora darling. They'll all come out tonight, I suppose, when we light the tree.

NORA. Did you remember to invite Rank?

HELMER. No, but there's no need to. He knows he'll have dinner with us. Anyway, I'll see him later this morning. I'll ask him then. I did order some good wine. Oh Nora, you've no idea how much I'm looking forward to tonight!

NORA. Me too. And the children, Torvald! They'll have such a good time!

HELMER. You know, it *is* nice to have a good, safe job and a comfortable income. Feels good just thinking about it. Don't you agree?

NORA. Oh, it's wonderful!

HELMER. Remember last Christmas? For three whole weeks you shut yourself up every evening till long after midnight, making ornaments for the Christmas tree and I don't know what else. Some big surprise for all of us, anyway. I'll be damned if I've ever been so bored in my whole life!

NORA. I wasn't bored at all.

HELMER [*smiling*]. But you've got to admit you didn't have much to show for it in the end.

NORA. Oh, don't tease me again about that! Could I help it that the cat got in and tore up everything?

HELMER. Of course you couldn't, my poor little Nora. You just wanted to please the rest of us, and that's the important thing. But I am glad the hard times are behind us. Aren't you?

NORA. Oh yes. I think it's just wonderful.

HELMER. This year I won't be bored and lonely. And you won't have to strain your dear eyes and your delicate little hands—

NORA [*claps her hands*]. No I won't, will I, Torvald? Oh, how wonderful, how lovely, to hear you say that! [*Puts her arm under his.*] Let me tell you how I think we should arrange things, Torvald. Soon as Christmas is over— [*The doorbell rings.*] Someone's at the door. [*Straightens things up a bit.*] A caller, I suppose. Bother!

HELMER. Remember, I'm not home for visitors.

THE MAID [*in the door to the front hall*]. Ma'am, there's a lady here—

NORA. All right. Ask her to come in.

THE MAID [*to* HELMER]. And the Doctor just arrived.

HELMER. Is he in the study?

THE MAID. Yes, sir.

HELMER *exits into his study.* THE MAID *shows* MRS. LINDE *in and closes the door behind her as she leaves.* MRS. LINDE *is in travel dress.*

MRS. LINDE [*timid and a little hesitant*]. Good morning, Nora.

NORA [*uncertainly*]. Good morning.

MRS. LINDE. I don't believe you know who I am.

NORA. No—I'm not sure—Though I know I should—Of course! Kristine! It's you!

MRS. LINDE. Yes, it's me.

NORA. And I didn't even recognize you! I had no idea! [*In a lower voice.*] You've changed, Kristine.

MRS. LINDE. I'm sure I have. It's been nine or ten long years.

NORA. Has it really been that long? Yes, you're right. I've been so happy these last eight years. And now you're here. Such a long trip in the middle of winter. How brave!

MRS. LINDE. I got in on the steamer this morning.

NORA. To have some fun over the holidays, of course. That's lovely. For we *are* going to have fun. But take off your coat! You aren't cold, are you? [*Helps her.*] There, now! Let's sit down here by the fire and just relax and talk.

No, you sit there. I want the rocking chair. [*Takes her hands.*] And now you've got your old face back. It was just for a minute, right at first—Though you are a little more pale, Kristine. And maybe a little thinner.

MRS. LINDE. And much, much older, Nora.

NORA. Maybe a little older. Just a teeny-weeny bit, not much. [*Interrupts herself, serious.*] Oh, but how thoughtless of me, chatting away like this! Sweet, good Kristine, can you forgive me?

MRS. LINDE. Forgive you what, Nora?

NORA [*in a low voice*]. You poor dear, you lost your husband, didn't you?

MRS. LINDE. Three years ago, yes.

NORA. I know. I saw it in the paper. Oh please believe me, Kristine. I really meant to write you, but I never got around to it. Something was always coming up.

MRS. LINDE. Of course, Nora. I understand.

NORA. No, that wasn't very nice of me. You poor thing, all you must have been through. And he didn't leave you much, either, did he?

MRS. LINDE. No.

NORA. And no children?

MRS. LINDE. No.

NORA. Nothing at all, in other words?

MRS. LINDE. Not so much as a sense of loss—a grief to live on—

NORA [*incredulous*]. But Kristine, how can that *be?*

MRS. LINDE [*with a sad smile, strokes* NORA*'s hair*]. That's the way it sometimes is, Nora.

NORA. All alone. How awful for you. I have three darling children. You can't see them right now, though; they're out with their nurse. But now you must tell me everything—

MRS. LINDE. No, no; I'd rather listen to you.

NORA. No, you begin. Today I won't be selfish. Today I'll think only of you. Except there's one thing I've just got to tell you first. Something marvelous that's happened to us just these last few days. You haven't heard, have you?

MRS. LINDE. No; tell me.

NORA. Just think. My husband's been made manager of the Mutual Bank.

MRS. LINDE. Your husband—! Oh, I'm so glad!

NORA. Yes, isn't that great? You see, private law practice is so uncertain, especially when you won't have anything to do with cases that aren't—you know—quite nice. And of course Torvald won't do that, and I quite agree with him. Oh, you've no idea how delighted we are! He takes over at New Year's, and he'll be getting a big salary and all sorts of extras. From now on we'll be able to live in quite a different way—exactly as we like. Oh, Kristine! I feel so carefree and happy! It's lovely to have lots and lots of money and not have to worry about a thing! Don't you agree?

MRS. LINDE. It would be nice to have enough, at any rate.

NORA. No, I don't mean just enough. I mean lots and lots!

MRS. LINDE [*smiles*]. Nora, Nora, when are you going to be sensible? In school you spent a great deal of money.

NORA [*quietly laughing*]. Yes, and Torvald says I still do. [*Raises her finger at* MRS. LINDE.] But "Nora, Nora" isn't so crazy as you all think. Believe me, we've had nothing to be extravagant with. We've both had to work.

MRS. LINDE. You too?

NORA. Yes. Oh, it's been little things mostly—sewing, crocheting, embroidery—that sort of thing. [*Casually.*] And other things too. You know, of course, that Torvald left government service when we got married? There was no chance of promotion in his department, and of course he had to make more money than he had been making. So for the first few years he worked altogether too hard. He had to take jobs on the side and work night and day. It turned out to be too much for him. He became seriously ill. The doctors told him he needed to go south.

MRS. LINDE. That's right; you spent a year in Italy, didn't you?

NORA. Yes, we did. But you won't believe how hard it was to get away. Ivar had just been born. But of course we had to go. Oh, it was a wonderful trip. And it saved Torvald's life. But it took a lot of money, Kristine.

MRS. LINDE. I'm sure it did.

NORA. Twelve hundred specie dollars. Four thousand eight hundred crowns. That's a lot of money.

MRS. LINDE. Yes. So it's lucky you have it when something like that happens.

NORA. Well, actually we got the money from Daddy.

MRS. LINDE. I see. That was about the time your father died, I believe.

NORA. Yes, just about then. And I couldn't even go and take care of him. I was expecting little Ivar any day. And I had poor Torvald to look after, desperately sick and all. My dear, good Daddy! I never saw him again, Kristine. That's the saddest thing that's happened to me since I got married.

MRS. LINDE. I know you were very fond of him. But then you went to Italy?

NORA. Yes, for now we had the money, and the doctors urged us to go. So we left about a month later.

MRS. LINDE. And when you came back your husband was well again?

NORA. Healthy as a horse!

MRS. LINDE. But—the doctor?

NORA. What do you mean?

MRS. LINDE. I thought the maid said it was the doctor, that gentleman who came the same time I did.

NORA. Oh, that's Dr. Rank. He doesn't come as a doctor. He's our closest friend. He looks in at least once every day. No, Torvald hasn't been sick once since then. And the children are strong and healthy, too, and so am I. [*Jumps up and claps her hands.*] Oh God, Kristine! Isn't it wonderful to be alive and happy—Isn't it just lovely!—But now I'm being mean again, talking only about myself and my things. [*Sits down on a footstool close to* MRS. LINDE *and puts her arm on her lap.*] Please, don't be angry with me! Tell me, is it really true that you didn't care for your husband? Then why did you marry him?

MRS. LINDE. Mother was still alive then, but she was bedridden and helpless. And I had my two younger brothers to look after. I didn't think I had the right to turn him down.

NORA. No, I suppose not. So he had money then?

MRS. LINDE. He was quite well off, I think. But it was an uncertain business, Nora. When he died, the whole thing collapsed and there was nothing left.

NORA. And then—?

MRS. LINDE. Well, I had to manage as best I could. With a little store and a little school and anything else I could think of. The last three years have been one long work day for me, Nora, without any rest. But now it's over. My poor mother doesn't need me any more. She passed away. And the boys are on their own too. They've both got jobs and support themselves.

NORA. What a relief for you—

MRS. LINDE. No, not relief. Just a great emptiness. Nobody to live for any more. [*Gets up, restlessly.*] That's why I couldn't stand it any longer in that little hole. Here in town it has to be easier to find something to keep me busy and occupy my thoughts. With a little luck I should be able to find a permanent job, something in an office—

NORA. Oh but Kristine, that's exhausting work, and you look worn out already. It would be much better for you to go to a resort.

MRS. LINDE [*walks over to the window*]. I don't have a Daddy who can give me the money, Nora.

NORA [*getting up*]. Oh, don't be angry with me.

MRS. LINDE [*over to her*]. Dear Nora, don't *you* be angry with *me*. That's the worst thing about my kind of situation: you become so bitter. You've nobody to work for, and yet you have to look out for yourself, somehow. You've got to keep on living, and so you become selfish. Do you know—when you told me about your husband's new position I was delighted not so much for your sake as for my own.

NORA. Why was that? Oh, I see. You think maybe Torvald can give you a job?

MRS. LINDE. That's what I had in mind.

NORA. And he will too, Kristine. Just leave it to me. I'll be ever so subtle about it. I'll think of something nice to tell him, something he'll like. Oh I so much want to help you.

MRS. LINDE. That's very good of you, Nora—making an effort like that for me. Especially since you've known so little trouble and hardship in your own life.

NORA. I—?—have known so little—?

MRS. LINDE [*smiling*]. Oh well, a little sewing or whatever it was. You're still a child, Nora.

NORA [*with a toss of her head, walks away*]. You shouldn't sound so superior.

MRS. LINDE. I shouldn't?

NORA. You're just like all the others. None of you think I'm good for anything really serious.

MRS. LINDE. Well, now—

NORA. That I've never been through anything difficult.

MRS. LINDE. But Nora! You just told me all your troubles!

NORA. That's nothing. [*Lowers her voice.*] I haven't told you about *it*.

MRS. LINDE. It? What's that? What do you mean?

NORA. You patronize me, Kristine, and that's not fair. You're proud that you worked so long and so hard for your mother.

MRS. LINDE. I don't think I patronize anyone. But it *is* true that I'm both proud and happy that I could make mother's last years comparatively easy.

NORA. And you're proud of all you did for your brothers.

MRS. LINDE. I think I have the right to be.

NORA. And so do I. But now I want to tell you something, Kristine. I have something to be proud and happy about too.

MRS. LINDE. I don't doubt that for a moment. But what exactly do you mean?

NORA. Not so loud! Torvald mustn't hear—not for anything in the world. Nobody must know about this, Kristine. Nobody but you.

MRS. LINDE. But what is it?

NORA. Come here. [*Pulls her down on the couch beside her.*] You see, I *do* have something to be proud and happy about. I've saved Torvald's life.

MRS. LINDE. Saved—? How do you mean—"saved"?

NORA. I told you about our trip to Italy. Torvald would have died if he hadn't gone.

MRS. LINDE. I understand that. And so your father gave you the money you needed.

NORA [*smiles*]. Yes, that's what Torvald and all the others think. But—

MRS. LINDE. But what?

NORA. Daddy didn't give us a penny. *I* raised that money.

MRS. LINDE. *You* did? That whole big amount?

NORA. Twelve hundred specie dollars. Four thousand eight hundred crowns. *Now* what do you say?

MRS. LINDE. But Nora, how could you? Did you win in the state lottery?

NORA [*contemptuously*]. State lottery! [*Snorts.*] What is so great about that?

MRS. LINDE. Where did it come from then?

NORA [*humming and smiling, enjoying her secret*]. Hmmm. Tra-la-la-la-la!

MRS. LINDE. You certainly couldn't have borrowed it.

NORA. Oh? And why not?

MRS. LINDE. A wife can't borrow money without her husband's consent.

NORA [*with a toss of her head*]. Oh, I don't know—take a wife with a little bit of a head for business—a wife who knows how to manage things—

MRS. LINDE. But Nora, I don't understand at all—

NORA. You don't have to. I didn't say I borrowed the money, did I? I could have gotten it some other way. [*Leans back.*] An admirer may have given it to me. When you're as tolerably goodlooking as I am—

MRS. LINDE. Oh, you're crazy.

NORA. I think you're dying from curiosity, Kristine.

MRS. LINDE. I'm beginning to think you've done something very foolish, Nora.

NORA [*sits up*]. Is it foolish to save your husband's life?

MRS. LINDE. I say it's foolish to act behind his back.

NORA. But don't you see: he couldn't be told! You're missing the whole point, Kristine. We couldn't even let him know how seriously ill he was. The doctors came to *me* and told me his life was in danger, that nothing could save him but a stay in the south. Don't you think I tried to work on him? I told him how lovely it would be if I could go abroad like other young wives. I cried and begged. I said he'd better remember what condition I was in, that he had to be nice to me and do what I wanted. I even hinted he could borrow the money. But that almost made him angry with me. He told me I was being irresponsible and that it was his duty as my husband not to give in to my moods and whims—I think that's what he called it. All right, I said to myself, you've got to be saved somehow, and so I found a way—

MRS. LINDE. And your husband never learned from your father that the money didn't come from him?

NORA. Never. Daddy died that same week. I thought of telling him all about it and ask him not to say anything. But since he was sick—It turned out I didn't have to—

MRS. LINDE. And you've never told your husband?

NORA. Of course not! Good heavens, how could I? He, with his strict principles! Besides, you know how men are. Torvald would find it embarrassing and humiliating to learn that he owed me anything. It would upset our whole relationship. Our happy, beautiful home would no longer be what it is.

MRS. LINDE. Aren't you ever going to tell him?

NORA [*reflectively, half smiling*]. Yes—one day, maybe. Many, many years from now, when I'm no longer young and pretty. Don't laugh! I mean when Torvald no longer feels about me the way he does now, when he no longer thinks it's fun when I dance for him and put on costumes and recite for him. Then it will be good to have something in reserve—[*Interrupts herself*] Oh, I'm just being silly! That day will never come.—Well, now, Kristine, what do you think of my great secret? Don't you think I'm good for something too?— By the way, you wouldn't believe all the worry I've had because of it. It's been very hard to meet my obligations on schedule. You see, in business there's something called quarterly interest and something called installments on the principal, and those are terribly hard to come up with. I've had to save a little here and a little there, whenever I could. I couldn't use much of the housekeeping money, for Torvald has to eat well. And I couldn't use what I got for clothes for the children. They have to look nice, and I didn't think it would be right to spend less than I got—the sweet little things!

MRS. LINDE. Poor Nora! So you had to take it from your own allowance?

NORA. Yes, of course. After all, it was my affair. Every time Torvald gave me money for a new dress and things like that, I never used more than half of it. I always bought the cheapest, simplest things for myself. Thank God, everything looks good on me, so Torvald never noticed. But it was hard many times, Kristine, for it's fun to have pretty clothes. Don't you think?

MRS. LINDE. Certainly.

NORA. Anyway, I had other ways of making money too. Last winter I was lucky enough to get some copying work. So I locked the door and sat up writing every night till quite late. God! I often got so tired—! But it was great fun, too, working and making money. It was almost like being a man.

MRS. LINDE. But how much have you been able to pay off this way?

NORA. I couldn't tell you exactly. You see, it's very difficult to keep track of business like that. All I know is I have been paying off as much as I've been able to scrape together. Many times I just didn't know what to do. [*Smiles.*] Then I used to imagine a rich old gentleman had fallen in love with me—

MRS. LINDE. What! What old gentleman?

NORA. Phooey! And now he was dead and they were reading his will, and there it said in big letters, "All my money is to be paid in cash immediately to the charming Mrs. Nora Helmer."

MRS. LINDE. But dearest Nora—who was this old gentleman?

NORA. For heaven's sake, Kristine, don't you see! There was no old gentleman. He was just somebody I made up when I couldn't think of any way to raise the money. But never mind him. The old bore can be anyone he likes to for all I care. I have no use for him or his last will, for now I don't have a single worry in the world. [*Jumps up.*] Dear God, what a lovely thought that is! To be able to play and have fun with the children, to have everything nice and pretty in the house, just the way Torvald likes it! Not a care! And soon spring will be here, and the air will be blue and high. Maybe we can travel again. Maybe I'll see the ocean again! Oh, yes, yes!—it's wonderful to be alive and happy!

The doorbell rings.

MRS. LINDE [*getting up*]. There's the doorbell. Maybe I better be going.

NORA. No, please stay. I'm sure it's just someone for Torvald—

THE MAID [*in the hall door*]. Excuse me, ma'am. There's a gentleman here who'd like to see Mr. Helmer.

NORA. You mean the bank manager.

THE MAID. Sorry, ma'am; the bank manager. But I didn't know—since the Doctor is with him—

NORA. Who is the gentleman?

KROGSTAD [*appearing in the door*]. It's just me, Mrs. Helmer.

MRS. LINDE *starts, looks, turns away toward the window.*

NORA [*takes a step toward him, tense, in a low voice*]. You? What do you want? What do you want with my husband?

KROGSTAD. Bank business—in a way. I have a small job in the Mutual, and I understand your husband is going to be our new manager—

NORA. So it's just—

KROGSTAD. Just routine business, ma'am. Nothing else.

NORA. All right. In that case, why don't you go through the door to the office.

Dismisses him casually as she closes the door. Walks over to the stove and tends the fire.

MRS. LINDE. Nora—who was that man?

NORA. His name's Krogstad. He's a lawyer.

MRS. LINDE. So it *was* him.

NORA. Do you know him?

MRS. LINDE. I used to—many years ago. For a while he clerked in our part of the country.

NORA. Right. He did.

MRS. LINDE. He has changed a great deal.

NORA. I believe he had a very unhappy marriage.

MRS. LINDE. And now he's a widower, isn't he?

NORA. With many children. There now; it's burning nicely again. [*Closes the stove and moves the rocking chair a little to the side.*]

MRS. LINDE. They say he's into all sorts of business.

NORA. Really? Maybe so. I wouldn't know. But let's not think about business. It's such a bore.

DR. RANK [*appears in the door to* HELMER's *study*]. No, I don't want to be in the way. I'd rather talk to your wife a bit. [*Closes the door and notices* MRS. LINDE.] Oh, I beg your pardon. I believe I'm in the way here too.

NORA. No, not at all. [*Introduces them.*] Dr. Rank. Mrs. Linde.

RANK. Aha. A name often heard in this house. I believe I passed you on the stairs coming up.

MRS. LINDE. Yes. I'm afraid I climb stairs very slowly. They aren't good for me.

RANK. I see. A slight case of inner decay, perhaps?

MRS. LINDE. Overwork, rather.

RANK. Oh, is that all? And now you've come to town to relax at all the parties?

MRS. LINDE. I have come to look for a job.

RANK. A proven cure for overwork, I take it?

MRS. LINDE. One has to live, Doctor.

RANK. Yes, that seems to be the common opinion.

NORA. Come on, Dr. Rank—you want to live just as much as the rest of us.

RANK. Of course I do. Miserable as I am, I prefer to go on being tortured as long as possible. All my patients feel the same way. And that's true of the moral invalids too. Helmer is talking with a specimen right this minute.

MRS. LINDE [*in a low voice*]. Ah!

NORA. What do you mean?

RANK. Oh, this lawyer, Krogstad. You don't know him. The roots of his character are decayed. But even he began by saying something about having *to live*—as if it were a matter of the highest importance.

NORA. Oh? What did he want with Torvald?

RANK. I don't really know. All I heard was something about the bank.

NORA. I didn't know that Krog—that this Krogstad had anything to do with the Mutual Bank.

RANK. Yes, he seems to have some kind of job there. [*To Mrs. Linde.*] I don't know if you are familiar in your part of the country with the kind of person who is always running around trying to sniff out cases of moral decrepitude and as soon as he finds one puts the individual under observation in some excellent position or other. All the healthy ones are left out in the cold.

MRS. LINDE. I should think it's the sick who need looking after the most.

RANK [*shrugs his shoulders*]. There we are. That's the attitude that turns society into a hospital.

NORA, *absorbed in her own thoughts, suddenly starts giggling and clapping her hands.*

RANK. What's so funny about that? Do you even know what society is?

NORA. What do I care about your stupid society! I laughed at something entirely different—something terribly amusing. Tell me, Dr. Rank—all the employees in the Mutual Bank, from now on they'll all be dependent on Torvald, right?

RANK. Is that what you find so enormously amusing?

NORA [*smiles and hums*]. That's my business, that's my business! [*Walks around.*] Yes, I do think it's fun that we—that Torvald is going to have so much influence on so many people's lives. [*Brings out the bag of macaroons.*] Have a macaroon, Dr. Rank.

RANK. Well, well—macaroons. I thought they were banned around here.

NORA. Yes, but these were some that Kristine gave me.

MRS. LINDE. What! I?

NORA. That's all right. Don't look so scared. You couldn't know that Torvald won't let me have them. He's afraid they'll ruin my teeth. But who cares! Just once in a while—! Right, Dr. Rank? Have one! [*Puts a macaroon into his mouth.*] You too, Kristine. And one for me. A very small one. Or at most two. [*Walks around again.*] Yes, I really feel very, very happy. Now there's just one thing I'm dying to do.

RANK. Oh? And what's that?

NORA. Something I'm dying to say so Torvald could hear.

RANK. And why can't you?

NORA. I don't dare to, for it's not nice.

MRS. LINDE. Not nice?

RANK. In that case, I guess you'd better not. But surely to the two of us—? What is it you'd like to say for Helmer to hear?

NORA. I want to say, "Goddammit!"

RANK. Are you out of your mind!

MRS. LINDE. For heaven's sake, Nora!

RANK. Say it. Here he comes.

NORA [*hiding the macaroons*]. Shhh!

HELMER *enters from his study, carrying his hat and overcoat.*

NORA [*going to him*]. Well, dear, did you get rid of him?

HELMER. Yes, he just left.

NORA. Torvald, I want you to meet Kristine. She's just come to town.

HELMER. Kristine—? I'm sorry; I don't think—

NORA. Mrs. Linde, Torvald dear. Mrs. Kristine Linde.

HELMER. Ah, yes. A childhood friend of my wife's, I suppose.

MRS. LINDE. Yes, we've known each other for a long time.

NORA. Just think; she has come all this way just to see you.

HELMER. I'm not sure I understand—

MRS. LINDE. Well, not really—

NORA. You see, Kristine is an absolutely fantastic secretary, and she would so much like to work for a competent executive and learn more than she knows already—

HELMER. Very sensible, I'm sure, Mrs. Linde.

NORA. So when she heard about your appointment—they got a wire about it—she came here as fast as she could. How about it, Torvald? Couldn't you do something for Kristine? For my sake. Please?

HELMER. Quite possibly. I take it you're a widow, Mrs. Linde?

MRS. LINDE. Yes.

HELMER. And you've had office experience?

MRS. LINDE. Some—yes.

HELMER. In that case I think it's quite likely that I'll be able to find you a position.

NORA [claps her hands]. I knew it! I knew it!

HELMER. You've arrived at a most opportune time, Mrs. Linde.

MRS. LINDE. Oh, how can I ever thank you—

HELMER. Not at all, not at all. [Puts his coat on.] But today you'll have to excuse me—

RANK. Wait a minute; I'll come with you. [Gets his fur coat from the front hall, warms it by the stove.]

NORA. Don't be long, Torvald.

HELMER. An hour or so; no more.

NORA. Are you leaving, too, Kristine?

MRS. LINDE [putting on her things]. Yes, I'd better go and find a place to stay.

HELMER. Good. Then we'll be going the same way.

NORA [helping her]. I'm sorry this place is so small, but I don't think we very well could—

MRS. LINDE. Of course! Don't be silly, Nora. Goodbye, and thank you for everything.

NORA. Goodbye. We'll see you soon. You'll be back this evening, of course. And you too, Dr. Rank; right? If you feel well enough? Of course you will. Just wrap yourself up.

General small talk as all exit into the hall. Children's voices are heard on the stairs.

NORA. There they are! There they are! [She runs and opens the door. The nurse ANNE-MARIE enters with the children.]

NORA. Come in! Come in! [Bends over and kisses them.] Oh, you sweet, sweet darlings! Look at them, Kristine! Aren't they beautiful!

RANK. No standing around in the draft!

HELMER. Come along, Mrs. Linde. This place isn't fit for anyone but mothers right now.

DR. RANK, HELMER, and MRS. LINDE go down the stairs. The NURSE enters the living room with the children. Nora follows, closing the door behind her.

NORA. My, how nice you all look! Such red cheeks! Like apples and roses. [The children all talk at the same time.] You've had so much fun? I bet you have. Oh, isn't that nice! You pulled both Emmy and Bob on your sleigh? Both at the same time? That's very good, Ivar. Oh, let me hold her for a minute, Anne-Marie. My sweet little doll baby! [Takes the smallest of the children from the NURSE and dances with her.] Yes, yes, of course; Mama'll dance with you too, Bob. What? You threw snowballs? Oh, I wish I'd been there! No, no; I want to take their clothes off, Anne-Marie. Please let me; I think it's so much fun. You go on in. You look frozen. There's hot coffee on the stove.

The NURSE exits into the room to the left. NORA takes the children's wraps off and throws them all around. They all keep telling her things at the same time.

NORA. Oh, really? A big dog ran after you? But it didn't bite you. Of course not. Dogs don't bite sweet little doll babies. Don't peek at the packages, Ivar! What's in them? Wouldn't you like to know! No, no; that's something terrible! Play? You want to play? What do you want to play? Okay, let's play hide-and-seek. Bob hides first. You want *me* to? All right. I'll go first.

Laughing and shouting, NORA *and the children play in the living room and in the adjacent room, right. Finally,* NORA *hides herself under the table; the children rush in, look for her, can't find her. They hear her low giggle, run to the table, lift the rug that covers it, see her. General hilarity. She crawls out, pretends to scare them. New delight. In the meantime there has been a knock on the door between the living room and the front hall, but nobody has noticed. Now the door is opened halfway;* KROGSTAD *appears. He waits a little. The playing goes on.*

KROGSTAD. Pardon me, Mrs. Helmer—

NORA [*with a muted cry turns around, jumps up*]. Ah! What do you want?

KROGSTAD. I'm sorry. The front door was open. Somebody must have forgotten to close it—

NORA [*standing up*]. My husband isn't here, Mr. Krogstad.

KROGSTAD. I know.

NORA. So what do you want?

NORA. I'd like a word with you.

NORA. With—? [*To the children in a low voice.*] Go in to Anne-Marie. What? No, the strange man won't do anything bad to Mama. When he's gone we'll play some more.

She takes the children into the room to the left and closes the door.

NORA [*tense, troubled*]. You want to speak with me?

KROGSTAD. Yes I do.

NORA. Today—? It isn't the first of the month yet.

KROGSTAD. No, it's Christmas Eve. It's up to you what kind of holiday you'll have.

NORA. What do you want? I can't possibly—

KROGSTAD. Let's not talk about that just yet. There's something else. You do have a few minutes, don't you?

NORA. Yes. Yes, of course. That is—

KROGSTAD. Good. I was sitting in Olsen's restaurant when I saw your husband go by.

NORA. Yes—?

KROGSTAD. —with a lady.

NORA. What of it?

KROGSTAD. May I be so free as to ask: wasn't that lady Mrs. Linde?

NORA. Yes.

KROGSTAD. Just arrived in town?

NORA. Yes, today.

KROGSTAD. She's a good friend of yours, I understand?

NORA. Yes, she is. But I fail to see—

KROGSTAD. I used to know her myself.

NORA. I know that.

KROGSTAD. So you know about that. I thought as much. In that case, let me ask you a simple question. Is Mrs. Linde going to be employed in the bank?

NORA. What makes you think you have the right to cross-examine me like this, Mr. Krogstad—you, one of my husband's employees? But since you ask, I'll tell you. Yes, Mrs. Linde is going to be working in the bank. And it was I who recommended her, Mr. Krogstad. Now you know.

KROGSTAD. So I was right.

NORA [*walks up and down*]. After all, one does have a little influence, you know. Just because you're a woman, it doesn't mean that—Really, Mr. Krogstad, people in a subordinate position should be careful not to offend someone who—oh well—

KROGSTAD. —has influence?

NORA. Exactly.

KROGSTAD [*changing his tone*]. Mrs. Helmer, I must ask you to be good enough to use your influence on my behalf.

NORA. What do you mean?

KROGSTAD. I want you to make sure that I am going to keep my subordinate position in the bank.

NORA. I don't understand. Who is going to take your position away from you?

KROGSTAD. There's no point in playing ignorant with me, Mrs. Helmer. I can very well appreciate that your friend would find it unpleasant to run into me. So now I know who I can thank for my dismissal.

NORA. But I assure you—

KROGSTAD. Never mind. Just want to say you still have time. I advise you to use your influence to prevent it.

NORA. But Mr. Krogstad, I don't have any influence—none at all.

KROGSTAD. No? I thought you just said—

NORA. Of course I didn't mean it that way. I! Whatever makes you think that I have any influence of that kind on my husband?

KROGSTAD. I went to law school with your husband. I have no reason to think that the bank manager is less susceptible than other husbands.

NORA. If you're going to insult my husband, I'll ask you to leave.

KROGSTAD. You're brave, Mrs. Helmer.

NORA. I'm not afraid of you any more. After New Year's I'll be out of this thing with you.

KROGSTAD [*more controlled*]. Listen, Mrs. Helmer. If necessary, I'll fight as for my life to keep my little job in the bank.

NORA. So it seems.

KROGSTAD. It isn't just the money; that's really the smallest part of it. There is something else—Well, I guess I might as well tell you. It's like this. I'm sure you know, like everybody else, that some years ago I committed—an impropriety.

NORA. I believe I've heard it mentioned.

KROGSTAD. The case never came to court, but from that moment all doors were closed to me. So I took up the kind of business you know about. I had to do something, and I think I can say about myself that I have not been among the worst. But now I want to get out of all that. My sons are growing up. For their sake I must get back as much of my good name as I can. This job in the bank was like the first rung on the ladder. And now your husband wants to kick me down and leave me back in the mud again.

NORA. But I swear to you, Mr. Krogstad; it's not at all in my power to help you.

KROGSTAD. That's because you don't want to. But I have the means to force you.

NORA. You don't mean you're going to tell my husband I owe you money?

KROGSTAD. And if I did?

NORA. That would be a mean thing to do. [*Almost crying.*] That secret, which is my joy and my pride—for him to learn about it in such a coarse and ugly manner—to learn it from you—! It would be terribly unpleasant for me.

KROGSTAD. Just unpleasant?

NORA [*heatedly*]. But go ahead! Do it! It will be worse for you than for me. When my husband realizes what a bad person you are, you'll be sure to lose your job.

KROGSTAD. I asked you if it was just domestic unpleasantness you were afraid of?

NORA. When my husband finds out, of course he'll pay off the loan, and then we won't have anything more to do with you.

KROGSTAD [*stepping closer*]. Listen, Mrs. Helmer—either you have a very bad memory, or you don't know much about business. I think I had better straighten you out on a few things.

NORA. What do you mean?

KROGSTAD. When your husband was ill, you came to me to borrow twelve hundred dollars.

NORA. I knew nobody else.

KROGSTAD. I promised to get you the money—

NORA. And you did.

KROGSTAD. I promised to get you the money on certain conditions. At the time you were so anxious about your husband's health and so set on getting him away that I doubt very much that you paid much attention to the details of our transaction. That's why I remind you of them now. Anyway, I promised to get you the money if you would sign an I.O.U., which I drafted.

NORA. And which I signed.

KROGSTAD. Good. But below your signature I added a few lines, making your father security for the loan. Your father was supposed to put his signature to those lines.

NORA. Supposed to—? He did.

KROGSTAD. I had left the date blank. That is, your father was to date his own signature. You recall that, don't you, Mrs. Helmer?

NORA. I guess so—

KROGSTAD. I gave the note to you. You were to mail it to your father. Am I correct?

NORA. Yes.

KROGSTAD. And of course you did so right away, for no more than five or six days later you brought the paper back to me, signed by your father. Then I paid you the money.

NORA. Well? And haven't I been keeping up with the payments?

KROGSTAD. Fairly well, yes. But to get back to what we were talking about—those were difficult days for you, weren't they, Mrs. Helmer?

NORA. Yes, they were.

KROGSTAD. Your father was quite ill, I believe.

NORA. He was dying.

KROGSTAD. And died shortly afterwards?

NORA. That's right.

KROGSTAD. Tell me, Mrs. Helmer; do you happen to remember the date of your father's death? I mean the exact day of the month?

NORA. Daddy died on September 29.

KROGSTAD. Quite correct. I have ascertained that fact. That's why there is something peculiar about this [*takes out a piece of paper*], which I can't account for.

NORA. Peculiar? How? I don't understand—

KROGSTAD. It seems very peculiar, Mrs. Helmer, that your father signed this promissory note three days after his death.

NORA. How so? I don't see what—

KROGSTAD. Your father died on September 29. Now look. He has dated his signature October 2. Isn't that odd?

NORA *remains silent.*

KROGSTAD. Can you explain it?

NORA *is still silent.*

KROGSTAD. I also find it striking that the date and the month and the year are not in your father's handwriting but in a hand I think I recognize. Well, that might be explained. Your father may have forgotten to date his signature and somebody else may have done it here, guessing at the date before he had learned of your father's death. That's all right. It's only the signature itself that matters. And that is genuine, isn't it, Mrs. Helmer? Your father did put his name to this note?

NORA [*after a brief silence tosses her head back and looks defiantly at him*]. No, he didn't. *I* wrote Daddy's name.

KROGSTAD. Mrs. Helmer—do you realize what a dangerous admission you just made?

NORA. Why? You'll get your money soon.

KROGSTAD. Let me ask you something. Why didn't you mail this note to your father?

NORA. Because it was impossible. Daddy was sick—you know that. If I had asked him to sign it, I would have had to tell him what the money was for. But I couldn't tell him, as sick as he was, that my husband's life was in danger. That was impossible. Surely you can see that.

KROGSTAD. Then it would have been better for you if you had given up your trip abroad.

NORA. No, that was impossible! That trip was to save my husband's life. I couldn't give it up.

KROGSTAD. But didn't you realize that what you did amounted to fraud against me?

NORA. I couldn't let that make any difference. I didn't care about you at all. I hated the way you made all those difficulties for me, even though you knew the danger my husband was in. I thought you were cold and unfeeling.

KROGSTAD. Mrs. Helmer, obviously you have no clear idea of what you have done. Let me tell you that what I did that time was no more and no worse. And it ruined my name and reputation.

NORA. You! Are you trying to tell me that you did something brave once in order save your wife's life?

KROGSTAD. The law doesn't ask about motives.

NORA. Then it's a bad law.

KROGSTAD. Bad or not—if I produce this note in court you'll be judged according to the law.

NORA. I refuse to believe you. A daughter shouldn't have the right to spare her dying old father worry and anxiety? A wife shouldn't have the right to save her husband's life? I don't know the laws very well, but I'm sure that somewhere they make allowance for cases like that. And you, a lawyer, don't know that? I think you must be a bad lawyer, Mr. Krogstad.

KROGSTAD. That may be. But business—the kind of business you and I have with one another—don't you think I know something about that? Very well. Do what you like. But let me tell you this: if I'm going to be kicked out again, you'll keep me company. [*He bows and exits through the front hall.*]

NORA [*pauses thoughtfully; then, with a defiant toss of her head*]. Oh, nonsense! Trying to scare me like that! I'm not all that silly. [*Starts picking up the children's clothes; soon stops.*] But—? No! That's impossible! I did it for love!

THE CHILDREN [*in the door to the left*]. Mama, the strange man just left. We saw him.

NORA. Yes, yes; I know. But don't tell anybody about the strange man. Do you hear? Not even Daddy.

THE CHILDREN. We won't. But now you'll play with us again, won't you, Mama?

NORA. No, not right now.

THE CHILDREN. But Mama—you promised.

NORA. I know, but I can't just now. Go to your own room. I've so much to do. Be nice now, my little darlings. Do as I say. [*She nudges them gently into the other room and closes the door. She sits down on the couch, picks up a piece of embroidery, makes a few stitches, then stops.*] No! [*Throws the embroidery down, goes to the hall door and calls out.*] Helene! Bring the Christmas tree in here, please! [*Goes to the table, left, opens the drawer, halts.*] No—that's impossible!

THE MAID [*with the Christmas tree*]. Where do you want it, ma'am?

NORA. There. The middle of the floor.

THE MAID. You want anything else?

NORA. No, thanks. I have everything I need. [THE MAID *goes out.* NORA *starts trimming the tree.*] I want candles—and flowers—That awful man! Oh, nonsense! There's nothing wrong. This will be a lovely tree. I'll do everything you want me to, Torvald. I'll sing for you—dance for you—

HELMER, *a bundle of papers under his arm, enters from outside.*

NORA. Ah—you're back already?

HELMER. Yes. Has anybody been here?

NORA. Here? No.

HELMER. That's funny. I saw Krogstad leaving just now.

NORA. Oh? Oh yes, that's right. Krogstad was here for just a moment.

HELMER. I can tell from your face that he came to ask you to put in a word for him.

NORA. Yes.

HELMER. And it was supposed to be your own idea, wasn't it? You were not to tell me he'd been here. He asked you that too, didn't he?

NORA. Yes, Torvald, but—

HELMER. Nora, Nora, how could you! Talk to a man like that and make him promises! And lying to me about it afterwards—!

NORA. Lying—?

HELMER. Didn't you say nobody had been here? [*Shakes his finger at her.*] My little songbird must never do that again. Songbirds are supposed to have clean beaks to chirp with—no false notes. [*Puts his arm around her waist.*] Isn't that so? Of course it is. [*Lets her go.*] And that's enough about that. [*Sits down in front of the fireplace.*] Ah, it's nice and warm in here. [*Begins to leaf through his papers.*]

NORA [*busy with the tree; after a brief pause*]. Torvald.

HELMER. Yes.

NORA. I'm looking forward so much to the Stenborgs' costume party day after tomorrow.

HELMER. And I can't wait to find out what you're going to surprise me with.

NORA. Oh, that silly idea!

HELMER. Oh?

NORA. I can't think of anything. It all seems so foolish and pointless.

HELMER. Ah, my little Nora admits that?

NORA [*behind his chair, her arms on the back of the chair*]. Are you very busy, Torvald?

HELMER. Well—

NORA. What are all those papers?

HELMER. Bank business.

NORA. Already?

HELMER. I've asked the board to give me the authority to make certain changes in organization and personnel. That's what I'll be doing over the holidays. I want it all settled before New Year's.

NORA. So that's why this poor Krogstad—

HELMER. Hm.

NORA [*leisurely playing with the hair on his neck*]. If you weren't so busy, Torvald, I'd ask you for a great big favor.

HELMER. Let's hear it, anyway.

NORA. I don't know anyone with better taste than you, and I want so much to look nice at the party. Couldn't you sort of take charge of me, Torvald, and decide what I'll wear—Help me with my costume?

HELMER. Aha! Little Lady Obstinate is looking for someone to rescue her?

NORA. Yes, Torvald. I won't get anywhere without your help.

HELMER. All right. I'll think about it. We'll come up with something.

NORA. Oh, you *are* nice! [*Goes back to the Christmas tree. A pause.*] Those red flowers look so pretty.—Tell me, was it really all that bad what this Krogstad fellow did?

HELMER. He forged signatures. Do you have any idea what that means?

NORA. Couldn't it have been because he felt he had to?

HELMER. Yes, or like so many others he may simply have been thoughtless. I'm not so heartless as to condemn a man absolutely because of a single imprudent act.

NORA. Of course not, Torvald!

HELMER. People like him can redeem themselves morally by openly confessing their crime and taking their punishment.

NORA. Punishment?

HELMER. But that was not the way Krogstad chose. He got out of it with tricks and evasions. That's what has corrupted him.

NORA. So you think that if—?

HELMER. Can't you imagine how a guilty person like that has to lie and fake and dissemble wherever he goes—putting on a mask before everybody he's close to, even his own wife and children. It's this thing with the children that's the worst part of it, Nora.

NORA. Why is that?

HELMER. Because when a man lives inside such a circle of stinking lies he brings infection into his own home and contaminates his whole family. With every breath of air his children inhale the germs of something ugly.

NORA [*moving closer behind him*]. Are you so sure of that?

HELMER. Of course I am. I have seen enough examples of that in my work. Nearly all young criminals have had mothers who lied.

NORA. Why mothers—particularly?

HELMER. Most often mothers. But of course fathers tend to have the same influence. Every lawyer knows that. And yet, for years this Krogstad has been poisoning his own children in an atmosphere of lies and deceit. That's why I call him a lost soul morally. [*Reaches out for her hands.*] And that's why my sweet little Nora must promise me never to take his side again. Let's shake on that.—What? What's this? Give me your hand. There! Now that's settled. I assure you, I would find it impossible to work in the same room with that man. I feel literally sick when I'm around people like that.

NORA [*withdraws her hand and goes to the other side of the Christmas tree*]. It's so hot in here. And I have so much to do.

HELMER [*gets up and collects his papers*]. Yes, and I really should try to get some of this reading done before dinner. I must think about your costume too. And maybe just possibly I'll have something to wrap in gilt paper and hang on the Christmas tree. [*Puts his hand on her head.*] Oh my adorable little songbird! [*Enters his study and closes the door.*]

NORA [*after a pause, in a low voice*]. It's all a lot of nonsense. It's not that way at all. It's impossible. It has to be impossible.

THE NURSE [*in the door, left*]. The little ones are asking ever so nicely if they can't come in and be with their mamma.

NORA. No, no, no! Don't let them in here! You stay with them, Anne-Marie.

THE NURSE. If you say so, ma'am. [*Closes the door.*]

NORA [*pale with terror*]. Corrupt my little children—! Poison my home—? [*Brief pause; she lifts her head.*] That's not true. Never. Never in a million years.

ACT II

The same room. The Christmas tree is in the corner by the piano, stripped shabby-looking, with burnt-down candles. Nora's outside clothes are on the couch. NORA *is alone. She walks around restlessly. She stops by the couch and picks up her coat.*

NORA [*drops the coat again*]. There's somebody now! [*Goes to the door, listens.*] No. Nobody. Of course not—not on Christmas. And not tomorrow either[1] —But perhaps—[*Opens the door and looks.*] No, nothing in the mailbox. All empty. [*Comes forward.*] How silly I am! Of course he isn't serious. Nothing like that could happen. After all, I have three small children.

THE NURSE *enters from the room, left, carrying a big carton.*

THE NURSE. Well, at last I found it—the box with your costume.

NORA. Thanks. Just put it on the table.

NURSE [*does so*]. But it's all a big mess, I'm afraid.

NORA. Oh, I wish I could tear the whole thing to little pieces!

NURSE. Heavens! It's not as bad as all that. It can be fixed all right. All it takes is a little patience.

NORA. I'll go over and get Mrs. Linde to help me.

NURSE. Going out again? In this awful weather? You'll catch a cold.

NORA. That might not be such a bad thing. How are the children?

NURSE. The poor little dears are playing with their presents, but—

NORA. Do they keep asking for me?

NURSE. Well, you know, they're used to being with their mamma.

NORA. I know. But Anne-Marie, from now on I can't be with them as much as before.

NURSE. Oh well. Little children get used to everything.

NORA. You think so? Do you think they'll forget their mamma if I were gone altogether?

NURSE. Goodness me—gone altogether?

NORA. Listen, Anne-Marie—something I've wondered about. How could you bring yourself to leave your child with strangers?

NURSE. But I had to, if I were to nurse you.

NORA. Yes, but how could you *want* to?

NURSE. When I could get such a nice place? When something like that happens to a poor young girl, she'd better be grateful for whatever she gets. For *he* didn't do a thing for me—the louse!

NORA. But your daughter has forgotten all about you, hasn't she?

NURSE. Oh no! Not at all! She wrote to me both when she was confirmed and when she got married.

---

[1] **And not tomorrow either** In Norway both December 25 and 26 are legal holidays.

NORA [*putting her arms around her neck*]. You dear old thing—you were a good mother to me when I was little.

NURSE. Poor little Nora had no one else, you know.

NORA. And if my little ones didn't, I know you'd—oh, I'm being silly! [*Opens the carton.*] Go in to them, please. I really should—Tomorrow you'll see how pretty I'll be.

NURSE. I know. There won't be anybody at that party half as pretty as you, ma'am. [*Goes out, left.*]

NORA [*begins to take clothes out of the carton; in a moment she throws it all down*]. If only I dared to go out. If only I knew nobody would come. That nothing would happen while I was gone.—How silly! Nobody'll come. Just don't think about it. Brush the muff. Beautiful gloves. Beautiful gloves. Forget it. Forget it. One, two, three, four, five, six—[*Cries out.*] There they are! [*Moves toward the door, stops irresolutely.*]

MRS. LINDE *enters from the hall. She has already taken off her coat.*

NORA. Oh, it's you, Kristine. There's no one else out there, is there? I'm so glad you're here.

MRS. LINDE. They told me you'd asked for me.

NORA. I just happened to walk by. I need your help with something—badly. Let's sit here on the couch. Look. Torvald and I are going to a costume party tomorrow night—at Consul Stenborg's upstairs—and Torvald wants me to go as a Neapolitan fisher girl and dance the tarantella. I learned it when we were on Capri.

MRS. LINDE. Well, well! So you'll be putting on a whole show?

NORA. Yes. Torvald thinks I should. Look, here's the costume. Torvald had it made for me while we were there. But it's all so torn and everything. I just don't know—

MRS. LINDE. Oh, that can be fixed. It's not that much. The trimmings have come loose in a few places. Do you have needle and thread? Ah, here we are. All set.

NORA. I really appreciate it, Kristine.

MRS. LINDE [*sewing*]. So you'll be in disguise tomorrow night, eh? You know—I may come by for just a moment, just to look at you.—Oh dear. I haven't even thanked you for the nice evening last night.

NORA [*gets up, moves around*]. Oh, I don't know. I don't think last night was as nice as it usually is.—You should have come to town a little earlier, Kristine.—Yes, Torvald knows how to make it nice and pretty around here.

MRS. LINDE. You too, I should think. After all, you're your father's daughter. By the way, is Dr. Rank always as depressed as he was last night?

NORA. No, last night was unusual. He's a very sick man, you know—very sick. Poor Rank, his spine is rotting away. Tuberculosis, I think. You see, his father was a nasty old man with mistresses and all that sort of thing. Rank has been sickly ever since he was a little boy.

MRS. LINDE [*dropping her sewing to her lap*]. But dearest Nora, where have you learned about things like that?

NORA [*still walking about*]. Oh, you know—with three children you sometimes get to talk with—other wives. Some of them know quite a bit about medicine. So you pick up a few things.

MRS. LINDE [*resumes her sewing; after a brief pause*]. Does Dr. Rank come here every day?

NORA. Every single day. He's Torvald's oldest and best friend, after all. And my friend too, for that matter. He's part of the family, almost.

MRS. LINDE. But tell me, is he quite sincere? I mean, isn't he the kind of man who likes to say nice things to people?

NORA. No, not at all. Rather the opposite, in fact. What makes you say that?

MRS. LINDE. When you introduced us yesterday, he told me he'd often heard my name mentioned in this house. But later on it was quite obvious that your husband really had no idea who I was. So how could Dr. Rank—?

NORA. You're right, Kristine, but I can explain that. You see, Torvald loves me so very much that he wants me all to himself. That's what he says. When we were first married he got almost jealous when I as much as mentioned anybody from back home that I was fond of. So of course I soon stopped doing that. But with Dr. Rank I often talk about home. You see, he likes to listen to me.

MRS. LINDE. Look here, Nora. In many ways you're still a child. After all, I'm quite a bit older than you and have had more experience. I want to give you a piece of advice. I think you should get out of this thing with Dr. Rank.

NORA. Get out of what thing?

MRS. LINDE. Several things in fact, if you want my opinion. Yesterday you said something about a rich admirer who was going to give you money—

NORA. One who doesn't exist, unfortunately. What of it?

MRS. LINDE. Does Dr. Rank have money?

NORA. Yes, he does.

MRS. LINDE. And no dependents?

NORA. No. But—?

MRS. LINDE. And he comes here every day?

NORA. Yes, I told you that already.

MRS. LINDE. But how can that sensitive man be so tactless?

NORA. I haven't the slightest idea what you're talking about.

MRS. LINDE. Don't play games with me, Nora. Don't you think I know who you borrowed the twelve hundred dollars from?

NORA. Are you out of your mind! The very idea—! A friend of both of us who sees us every day—! What a dreadfully—uncomfortable position that would be!

MRS. LINDE. So it really isn't Dr. Rank?

NORA. Most certainly not! I would never have dreamed of asking him—not for a moment. Anyway, he didn't have any money then. He inherited it afterwards.

MRS. LINDE. Well, I still think it may have been lucky for you, Nora dear.

NORA. The idea! It would never have occurred to me to ask Dr. Rank—Though I'm sure that if I *did* ask him—

MRS. LINDE. But of course you wouldn't.

NORA. Of course not. I can't imagine that that would ever be necessary. But I am quite sure that if I told Dr. Rank—

MRS. LINDE. Behind your husband's back?

NORA. I must get out of—this other thing. That's also behind his back. I must get out of it.

MRS. LINDE. That's what I told you yesterday. But—

NORA [*walking up and down*]. A man manages these things so much better than a woman—

MRS. LINDE. One's husband, yes.

NORA. Silly, Silly! [*Stops.*] When you've paid off all you owe, you get your I.O.U. back; right?

MRS. LINDE. Yes, of course.

NORA. And you can tear it into a hundred thousand little pieces and burn it—that dirty, filthy, paper!

MRS. LINDE [*looks hard at her, puts down her sewing, rises slowly*]. Nora—you're hiding something from me.

NORA. Can you tell?

MRS. LINDE. Something's happened to you, Nora, since yesterday morning. What is it?

NORA [*going to her*]. Kristine! [*Listens.*] Shhh. Torvald just came back. Listen. Why don't you go in to the children for a while. Torvald can't stand having sewing around. Get Anne-Marie to help you.

MRS. LINDE [*gathers some of the sewing things together*]. All right, but I'm not leaving here till you and I have talked.

She goes out left, just as HELMER *enters from the front hall.*

NORA [*towards him*]. I have been waiting and waiting for you, Torvald.

HELMER. Was that the dressmaker?

NORA. No, it was Kristine. She's helping me with my costume. Oh Torvald, just wait till you see how nice I'll look!

HELMER. I told you. Pretty good idea I had, wasn't it?

NORA. Lovely! And wasn't it nice of me to go along with it?

HELMER [*his hand under her chin*]. Nice? To do what your husband tells you? All right, you little rascal; I know you didn't mean it that way. But don't let me interrupt you. I suppose you want to try it on.

NORA. And you'll be working?

HELMER. Yes. [*Shows her a pile of papers.*] Look. I've been down to the bank. [*Is about to enter his study.*]

HELMER. Torvald.

HELMER [*halts*]. Yes?

NORA. What if your little squirrel asked you ever so nicely—

HELMER. For what?

NORA. Would you do it?

HELMER. Depends on what it is.

NORA. Squirrel would run around and do all sorts of fun tricks if you'd be nice and agreeable.

HELMER. All right. What is it?

NORA. Lark would chirp and twitter in all the rooms, up and down—

HELMER. So what? Lark does that anyway.

NORA. I'll be your elfmaid and dance for you in the moonlight, Torvald.

HELMER. Nora, don't tell me it's the same thing you mentioned this morning?

NORA [*closer to him*]. Yes, Torvald. I beg you!

HELMER. You really have the nerve to bring that up again?

NORA. Yes. You've just got to do as I say. You *must* let Krogstad keep his job.

HELMER. My dear Nora. It's his job I intend to give to Mrs. Linde.

NORA. I know. And that's ever so nice of you. But can't you just fire somebody else?

HELMER. This is incredible! You just don't give up, do you? Because you make some foolish promise, *I* am supposed to—!

NORA. That's not the reason, Torvald. It's for your own sake. That man writes for the worst newspapers. You've said so yourself. There's no telling what he may do to you. I'm scared to death of him.

HELMER. Ah, I understand. You're afraid because of what happened before.

NORA. What do you mean?

HELMER. You're thinking of your father, of course.

NORA. Yes. Yes, you're right. Remember the awful things they wrote about Daddy in the newspapers. I really think they might have forced him to resign if the ministry hadn't sent you to look into the charges and if you hadn't been so helpful and understanding.

HELMER. My dear little Nora, there is a world of difference between your father and me. Your father's official conduct was not above reproach. Mine is, and I intend for it to remain that way as long as I hold my position.

NORA. Oh, but you don't know what vicious people like that may think of. Oh, Torvald! Now all of us could be so happy together here in our own home, peaceful and carefree. Such a good life, Torvald, for you and me and the children! That's why I implore you—

HELMER. And it's exactly because you plead for him that you make it impossible for me to keep him. It's already common knowledge in the bank that I intend to let Krogstad go. If it gets out that the new manager has changed his mind because of his wife—

NORA. Yes? What then?

HELMER. No, of course, that wouldn't matter at all as long as little Mrs. Pighead here got her way! Do you want me to make myself look ridiculous before my whole staff—make people think I can be swayed by just anybody— by outsiders? Believe me, I would soon enough find out what the consequences would be! Besides, there's another thing that makes it absolutely impossible for Krogstad to stay on in the bank now that I'm in charge.

NORA. What's that?

HELMER. I suppose in a pinch I could overlook his moral shortcomings—

NORA. Yes, you could; couldn't you, Torvald?

HELMER. And I understand he's quite a good worker, too. But we've known each other for a long time. It's one of those imprudent relationships you get into when you're young that embarrass you for the rest of your life. I guess I might as well be frank with you: he and I are on a first name basis. And that tactless fellow never hides the fact even when other people are around. Rather, he seems to think it entitles him to be familiar with me. Every chance he gets he comes out with his damn "Torvald, Torvald." I'm telling you, I find it most awkward. He would make my position in the bank intolerable.

NORA. You don't really mean any of this, Torvald.

HELMER. Oh? I don't? And why not?

NORA. No, for it's all so petty.

HELMER. What! Petty? You think I'm being petty!

NORA. No, I *don't* think you are petty, Torvald dear. That's exactly why I—

HELMER. Never mind. You think my reasons are petty, so it follows that I must be petty too. Petty! Indeed! By God, I'll put an end to this right now! [*Opens the door to the front hall and calls out.*] Helene!

NORA. What are you doing?

HELMER [*searching among his papers*]. Making a decision. [THE MAID *enters.*] Here. Take this letter. Go out with it right away. Find somebody to deliver it. But quick. The address is on the envelope. Wait. Here's money.

THE MAID. Very good, sir. [*She takes the letter and goes out.*]

HELMER [*collecting his papers*]. There now, little Mrs. Obstinate!

NORA [*breathless*]. Torvald—what was that letter?

HELMER. Krogstad's dismissal.

NORA. Call it back, Torvald! There's still time! Oh Torvald, please—call it back! For my sake, for your own sake, for the sake of the children! Listen to me, Torvald! Do it! You don't know what you're doing to all of us!

HELMER. Too late.

NORA. Yes. Too late.

HELMER. Dear Nora, I forgive you this fear you're in, although it really is an insult to me. Yes, it is! It's an insult to think that I am scared of a shabby scrivener's revenge. But I forgive you, for it's such a beautiful proof how much you love me. [*Takes her in his arms.*] And that's the way it should be, my sweet darling. Whatever happens, you'll see that when things get really rough I have both strength and courage. You'll find out that I am man enough to shoulder the whole burden.

NORA [*terrified*]. What do you mean by that?

HELMER. All of it, I tell you—

NORA [*composed*]. You'll never have to do that.

HELMER. Good. Then we'll share the burden, Nora—like husband and wife, the way it ought to be. [*Caresses her.*] Now are you satisfied? There, there, there. Not that look in your eyes—like a frightened dove. It's all your own foolish imagination.—Why don't you practice the tarantella—and your tambourine, too. I'll be in the inner office and close both doors, so I won't hear you. You can make as much noise as you like. [*Turning in the doorway.*] And when Rank comes, tell him where to find me. [*He nods to her, enters his study carrying his papers, and closes the door.*]

NORA [*transfixed by terror, whispers*]. He would do it. He'll do it. He'll do it in spite of the whole world.—No, this mustn't happen. Anything rather than that! There must be a way—! [*The doorbell rings.*] Dr. Rank! Anything rather than that! Anything—anything at all!

She passes her hand over her face, pulls herself together, and opens the door to the hall. DR. RANK *is out there, hanging up his coat. Darkness begins to fall during the following scene.*

NORA. Hello there, Dr. Rank. I recognized your ringing. Don't go in to Torvald yet. I think he's busy.

RANK. And you?

NORA [*as he enters and she closes the door behind him*]. You know I always have time for you.

RANK. Thanks. I'll make use of that as long as I can.

NORA. What do you mean by that—As long as you can?

RANK. Does that frighten you?

NORA. Well, it's a funny expression. As if something was going to happen.

RANK. Something is going to happen that I've long been expecting. But I admit I hadn't thought it would come quite so soon.

NORA [*seizes his arm*]. What is it you've found out? Dr. Rank—tell me!

RANK [*sits down by the stove*]. I'm going downhill fast. There's nothing to do about that.

NORA [*with audible relief*]. So it's *you*—

RANK. Who else? No point in lying to myself. I'm in worse shape than any of my other patients, Mrs. Helmer. These last few days I've been conducting an audit on my inner condition. Bankrupt. Chances are that within a month I'll be rotting up in the cemetery.

NORA. Shame on you! Talking that horrid way!

RANK. The thing itself is horrid—damn horrid. The worst of it, though, is all that other horror that comes first. There is only one more test I need to make. After that I'll have a pretty good idea when I'll start coming apart. There is something I want to say to you. Helmer's refined nature can't stand anything hideous. I don't want him in my sick room.

NORA. Oh, but Dr. Rank—

RANK. I don't want him there. Under no circumstance. I'll close my door to him. As soon as I have full certainty that the worst is about to begin I'll give you my card with a black cross on it. Then you'll know the last horror of destruction has started.

NORA. Today you're really quite impossible. And I had hoped you'd be in a particularly good mood.

RANK. With death on my hands? Paying for someone else's sins? Is there justice in that? And yet there isn't a single family that isn't ruled by that same law of ruthless retribution, in one way or another.

NORA [*puts her hands over her ears*]. Poppycock! Be fun! Be fun!

RANK. Well, yes. You may just as well laugh at the whole thing. My poor, innocent spine is suffering for my father's frolics as a young lieutenant.

NORA [*over by the table, left*]. Right. He was addicted to asparagus and goose liver paté, wasn't he?

RANK. And truffles.

NORA. Of course. Truffles. And oysters too, I think.

RANK. And oysters. Obviously.

NORA. And all the port and champagne that go with it. It's really too bad that goodies like that ruin your backbone.

RANK. Particularly an unfortunate backbone that never enjoyed any of it.

NORA. Ah yes, that's the saddest part of it all.

RANK [*looks searchingly at her*]. Hm—

NORA [*after a brief pause*]. Why did you smile just then?

RANK. No, it was you that laughed.

NORA. No, it was you that smiled, Dr. Rank!

RANK [*gets up*]. You're more of a mischief-maker than I thought.

NORA. I feel in the mood for mischief today.

RANK. So it seems.

NORA [*with both her hands on his shoulders*]. Dear, dear Dr. Rank, don't you go and die and leave Torvald and me.

RANK. Oh, you won't miss me for very long. Those who go away are soon forgotten.

NORA [*with an anxious look*]. Do you believe that?

RANK. You'll make new friends, and then—

NORA. Who'll make new friends?

RANK. Both you and Helmer, once I'm gone. You yourself seem to have made a good start already. What was this Mrs. Linde doing here last night?

NORA. Aha—Don't tell me you're jealous of poor Kristine?

RANK. Yes, I am. She'll be my successor in this house. As soon as I have made my excuses, that woman is likely to—

NORA. Shh—not so loud. She's in there.

RANK. Today too? There you are!

NORA. She's mending my costume. My God, you really *are* unreasonable. [*Sits down on the couch.*] Now be nice, Dr. Rank. Tomorrow you'll see how beautifully I'll dance, and then you are to pretend I'm dancing just for you—and for Torvald too, of course. [*Takes several items out of the carton.*] Sit down, Dr. Rank; I want to show you something.

RANK [*sitting down*]. What?

NORA. Look.

RANK. Silk stockings.

NORA. Flesh-colored. Aren't they lovely? Now it's getting dark in here, but tomorrow—No, no. You only get to see the foot. Oh well, you might as well see all of it.

RANK. Hmm.

NORA. Why do you look so critical? Don't you think they'll fit?

RANK. That's something I can't possibly have a reasoned opinion about.

NORA [*looks at him for a moment*]. Shame on you. [*Slaps his ear lightly with the stocking.*] That's what you get. [*Puts the things back in the carton.*]

RANK. And what other treasures are you going to show me?

NORA. Nothing at all, because you're naughty. [*She hums a little and rummages in the carton.*]

RANK [*after a brief silence*]. When I sit here like this, talking confidently with you, I can't imagine—I can't possibly imagine what would have become of me if I hadn't had you and Helmer.

NORA [*smiles*]. Well, yes—I do believe you like being with us.

RANK [*in a lower voice, lost in thought*]. And then to have to go away from it all—

NORA. Nonsense. You are not going anywhere.

RANK [*as before*].—and not to leave behind as much as a poor little token of gratitude, hardly a brief memory of someone missed, nothing but a vacant place that anyone can fill.

NORA. And what if I were to ask you—? No—

RANK. Ask me what?

NORA. For a great proof of your friendship—

RANK. Yes, yes—?

NORA. No, I mean—for an enormous favor—

RANK. Would you really for once make me as happy as all that?

NORA. But you don't even know what it is.

RANK. Well, then; tell me.

NORA. Oh, but I can't, Dr. Rank. It's altogether too much to ask—It's advice and help and a favor—

RANK. So much the better. I can't even begin to guess what it is you have in mind. So for heaven's sake tell me! Don't you trust me?

NORA. Yes, I trust you more than anyone else I know. You are my best and most faithful friend. I know that. So I will tell you. All right, Dr. Rank. There is something you can help me prevent. You know how much Torvald loves me—beyond all words. Never for a moment would he hesitate to give his life for me.

RANK [leaning over to her]. Nora—do you really think he's the only one—?

NORA [with a slight start]. Who—?

RANK. —would gladly give his life for you.

NORA [heavily]. I see.

RANK. I have sworn an oath to myself to tell you before I go. I'll never find a better occasion.—All right, Nora; now you know. And now you also know that you can confide in me more than in anyone else.

NORA [gets up; in a calm, steady voice]. Let me get by.

RANK [makes room for her but remains seated]. Nora—

NORA [in the door to the front hall]. Helene, bring the lamp in here, please. [Walks over to the stove.] Oh, dear Dr. Rank. That really wasn't very nice of you.

RANK [gets up]. That I have loved you as much as anybody—was that not nice?

NORA. No, not that. But that you told me. There was no need for that.

RANK. What do you mean? Have you known—?

THE MAID enters with the lamp, puts it on the table, and goes out.

RANK. Nora—Mrs. Helmer—I'm asking you: did you know?

NORA. Oh, how can I tell what I knew and didn't know! I really can't say—But that you could be so awkward, Dr. Rank! Just when everything was so comfortable.

RANK. Well, anyway, now you know that I'm at your service with my life and soul. And now you must speak.

NORA [looks at him]. After what just happened?

RANK. I beg of you—let me know what it is.

NORA. There is nothing I can tell you now.

RANK. Yes, yes. You mustn't punish me this way. Please let me do for you whatever anyone can do.

NORA. Now there is nothing you can do. Besides, I don't think I really need any help, anyway. It's probably just my imagination. Of course that's all it is. I'm sure of it! [Sits down in the rocking chair, looks at him, smiles.] Well,

well, well, Dr. Rank! What a fine gentleman you turned out to be! Aren't you ashamed of yourself, now that we have light?

RANK. No, not really. But perhaps I ought to leave—and not come back?

NORA. Don't be silly; of course not! You'll come here exactly as you have been doing. You know perfectly well that Torvald can't do without you.

RANK. Yes, but what about you?

NORA. Oh, I always think it's perfectly delightful when you come.

RANK. That's the very thing that misled me. You are a riddle to me. It has often seemed to me that you'd just as soon be with me as with Helmer.

NORA. Well, you see, there are people you love, and there are other people you'd almost rather be with.

RANK. Yes, there is something in that.

NORA. When I lived at home with Daddy, of course I loved him most. But I always thought it was so much fun to sneak off down to the maids' room, for they never gave me good advice and they always talked about such fun things.

RANK. Aha! So it's *their* place I have taken.

NORA [*jumps up and goes over to him*]. Oh dear, kind Dr. Rank, you know very well I didn't mean it that way. Can't you see that with Torvald it is the way it used to be with Daddy?

THE MAID *enters from the front hall.*

THE MAID. Ma'am! [*Whispers to her and gives her a caller's card.*]

NORA [*glances at the card*]. Ah! [*Puts it in her pocket.*]

RANK. Anything wrong?

NORA. No, no; not at all. It's nothing—just my new costume—

RANK. But your costume is lying right there!

NORA. Oh yes, that one. But this is another one. I ordered it. Torvald mustn't know—

RANK. Aha. So that's the great secret.

NORA. That's it. Why don't you go in to him, please. He's in the inner office. And keep him there for a while—

RANK. Don't worry. He won't get away. [*Enters* HELMER's *study.*]

NORA [*to* THE MAID]. You say he's waiting in the kitchen?

THE MAID. Yes. He came up the back stairs.

NORA. But didn't you tell him there was somebody with me?

THE MAID. Yes, but he wouldn't listen.

NORA. He won't leave?

THE MAID No, not till he's had a word with you, ma'am.

NORA. All right. But try not to make any noise. And, Helene—don't tell anyone he's here. It's supposed to be a surprise for my husband.

THE MAID. I understand, ma'am—[*She leaves.*]

NORA. The terrible is happening. It's happening, after all. No, no, no. It can't happen. It won't happen. [*She bolts the study door.*]

THE MAID *opens the front hall door for* KROGSTAD *and closes the door behind him. He wears a fur coat for traveling, boots, and a fur hat.*

NORA [*toward him*]. Keep your voice down. My husband's home.

KROGSTAD. That's all right.

NORA. What do you want?

KROGSTAD. To find out something.

NORA. Be quick, then. What is it?

KROGSTAD. I expect you know I've been fired.

KROGSTAD. I couldn't prevent it, Mr. Krogstad. I fought for you as long and as hard as I could, but it didn't do any good.

KROGSTAD. Your husband doesn't love you any more than that? He knows what I can do to you, and yet he runs the risk—

NORA. Surely you didn't think I'd tell him?

KROGSTAD. No, I really didn't. It wouldn't be like Torvald Helmer to show that kind of guts—

NORA. Mr. Krogstad, I insist that you show respect for my husband.

KROGSTAD. By all means. All due respect. But since you're so anxious to keep this a secret, may I assume that you are a little better informed than yesterday about exactly what you have done?

NORA. Better than *you* could ever teach me.

KROGSTAD. Of course. Such a bad lawyer as I am—

NORA. What do you want of me?

KROGSTAD. I just wanted to find out how you are, Mrs. Helmer. I've been thinking about you all day. You see, even a bill collector, a pen pusher, a— anyway, someone like me—even he has a little of what they call a heart.

NORA. Then show it. Think of my little children.

KROGSTAD. Have you and your husband thought of mine? Never mind. All I want to tell you is that you don't need to take this business too seriously. I have no intention of bringing charges right away.

NORA. Oh no, you wouldn't; would you? I knew you wouldn't.

KROGSTAD. The whole thing can be settled quite amiably. Nobody else needs to know anything. It will be between the three of us.

NORA. My husband must never find out about this.

KROGSTAD. How are you going to prevent that? Maybe you can pay me the balance on the loan?

NORA. No, not right now.

KROGSTAD. Or do you have a way of raising the money one of these next few days?

NORA. None I tend to make use of.

KROGSTAD. It wouldn't do you any good, anyway. Even if you had the cash in your hand right this minute, I wouldn't give you your note back. It wouldn't make any difference *how* much money you offered me.

NORA. Then you'll have to tell me what you plan to use the note *for*.

KROGSTAD. Just keep it; that's all. Have it on hand, so to speak. I won't say a word to anybody else. So if you've been thinking about doing something desperate—

NORA. I have.

KROGSTAD. —like leaving house and home—

NORA. I have!

KROGSTAD. —or even something worse—

NORA. How did you know?

KROGSTAD. —then: don't.

NORA. How did you know I was thinking of *that*?

KROGSTAD. Most of us do, right at first. I did, too, but when it came down to it I didn't have the courage—

NORA [*tonelessly*]. Nor do I.

KROGSTAD [*relieved*]. See what I mean? I thought so. You don't either.

NORA. I don't. I don't.

KROGSTAD. Besides, it would be very silly of you. Once that first domestic blow-up is behind you—. Here in my pocket is a letter for your husband.

NORA. Telling him everything?

KROGSTAD. As delicately as possible.

NORA [*quickly*]. He mustn't get that letter. Tear it up. I'll get you the money somehow.

KROGSTAD. Excuse me, Mrs. Helmer. I thought I just told you—

NORA. I'm not talking about the money I owe you. Just let me know how much money you want from my husband, and I'll get it for you.

KROGSTAD. I want no money from your husband.

NORA. Then, what *do* you want?

KROGSTAD. I'll tell you, Mrs. Helmer. I want to rehabilitate myself; I want to get up in the world; and your husband is going to help me. For a year and a half I haven't done anything disreputable. All that time I have been struggling with the most miserable circumstances. I was content to work my way up step by step. Now I've been kicked out, and I'm no longer satisfied just getting my old job back. I want more than that; I want to get to the top. I'm being quite serious. I want the bank to take me back but in a higher position. I want your husband to create a new job for me—

NORA. He'll never do that!

KROGSTAD. He will. I know him. He won't dare not to. And once I'm back inside and he and I are working together, you'll see! Within a year I'll be the manager's right hand. It will be Nils Krogstad and not Torvald Helmer who'll be running the Mutual Bank!

NORA. You'll never see that happen!

KROGSTAD. Are you thinking of—?

NORA. Now I *do* have the courage.

KROGSTAD. You can't scare me. A fine, spoiled lady like you—

NORA. You'll see, you'll see!

KROGSTAD. Under the ice, perhaps? Down into that cold, black water? Then spring comes, and you float up again—hideous, can't be identified, hair all gone—

NORA. You don't frighten me.

KROGSTAD. Nor you me. One doesn't do that sort of thing, Mrs. Helmer. Besides, what good would it do? He'd still be in my power.

NORA. Afterwards? When I'm no longer—?

KROGSTAD. Aren't you forgetting that your reputation would be in my hands?

NORA *stares at him, speechless.*

KROGSTAD. All right; now I've told you what to expect. So don't do anything foolish. When Helmer gets my letter I expect to hear from him. And don't you forget that it's your husband himself who forces me to use such means again. That I'll never forgive him. Goodbye, Mrs. Helmer. [*Goes out through the hall.*]

NORA [*at the door, opens it a little, listens*]. He's going. And no letter. Of course not! That would be impossible! [*Opens the door more.*] What's he doing? He's still there. Doesn't go down. Having second thoughs—? Will he—?

The sound of a letter dropping into the mailbox. Then KROGSTAD*'s steps are heard going down the stairs, gradually dying away.*

NORA [*with a muted cry runs forward to the table by the couch; brief pause*]. In the mailbox. [*Tiptoes back to the door to the front hall.*] There it is. Torvald, Torvald—now we're lost!

MRS. LINDE [*enters from the left, carrying* NORA*'s Capri costume*]. There now. I think it's all fixed. Why don't we try it on you—

NORA [*in a low, hoarse voice*]. Kristine, come here.

MRS. LINDE. What's wrong with you? You look quite beside yourself.

NORA. Come over here. Do you see that letter? There, look—through the glass in the mailbox.

MRS. LINDE. Yes, yes; I see it.

NORA. That letter is from Krogstad.

MRS. LINDE. Nora—it was Krogstad who lent you the money!

NORA. Yes, and now Torvald will find out about it.

MRS. LINDE. Oh believe me, Nora. That's the best thing for both of you.

NORA. There's more to it than you know. I forged a signature—

MRS. LINDE. Oh my God—!

NORA. I just want to tell you this, Kristine, that you must be my witness.

MRS. LINDE. Witness? How? Witness to what?

NORA. If I lose my mind—and that could very well happen—

MRS. LINDE. Nora!

NORA. —or if something were to happen to me—something that made it impossible for me to be here—

MRS. LINDE. Nora, Nora! You're not yourself!

NORA. —and if someone were to take all the blame, assume the whole responsibility—Do you understand—?

MRS. LINDE. Yes, yes; but how can you think—!

NORA. —then you are to witness that that's not so, Kristine. I am not beside myself. I am perfectly rational, and what I'm telling you is that nobody else has known about this. I've done it all by myself, the whole thing. Just remember that.

MRS. LINDE. I will. But I don't understand any of it.

NORA. Oh, how could you! For it's the wonderful that's about to happen.

MRS. LINDE. The wonderful?

MRS. LINDE. Yes, the wonderful. But it's so terrible, Kristine. It mustn't happen for anything in the whole world!

MRS. LINDE. I'm going over to talk to Krogstad right now.

NORA. No, don't. Don't go to him. He'll do something bad to you.

MRS. LINDE. There was a time when he would have done anything for me.

NORA. He!

MRS. LINDE. Where does he live?

NORA. Oh, I don't know—Yes, wait a minute—[*Reaches into her pocket.*] here's his card—But the letter, the letter—

HELMER [*in his study, knocks on the door*]. Nora!

NORA [*cries out in fear*]. Oh, what is it? What do you want?

HELMER. That's all right. Nothing to be scared about. We're not coming in. For one thing, you've bolted the door, you know. Are you modeling your costume?

NORA. Yes, yes; I am. I'm going to be so pretty, Torvald.

MRS. LINDE [*having looked at the card*]. He lives just around the corner.

NORA. Yes, but it's no use. Nothing can save us now. The letter is in the mailbox.

MRS. LINDE. And your husband has the key?

NORA. Yes. He always keeps it with him.

MRS. LINDE. Krogstad must ask for his letter back, unread. He's got to think up some pretext or other—

NORA. But this is just the time of day when Torvald—

MRS. LINDE. Delay him. Go in to him. I'll be back as soon as I can. [*She hurries out through the hall door.*]

NORA [*walks over to* HELMER's *door, opens it, and peeks in*]. Torvald!

HELMER [*still offstage*]. Well, well! So now one's allowed in one's own living room again. Come on, Rank. Now we'll see— [*In the doorway.*] But what's this?

NORA. What, Torvald dear?

HELMER. Rank prepared me for a splendid metamorphosis.

RANK [*in the doorway*]. That's how I understood it. Evidently I was mistaken.

NORA. Nobody gets to admire me in my costume before tomorrow.

HELMER. But, dearest Nora—you look all done in. Have you been practicing too hard?

NORA. No, I haven't practiced at all.

HELMER. But you'll have to, you know.

NORA. I know it, Torvald. I simply must. But I can't do a thing unless you help me. I have forgotten everything.

HELMER. Oh it will all come back. We'll work on it.

NORA. Oh yes, please, Torvald. You just have to help me. Promise? I am so nervous. That big party—. You mustn't do anything else tonight. Not a bit of business. Don't even touch a pen. Will you promise, Torvald?

HELMER. I promise. Tonight I'll be entirely at your service—you helpless little thing.—Just a moment, though. First I want to—[*Goes to the door to the front hall.*]

NORA. What are you doing out there?

HELMER. Just looking to see if there's any mail.

NORA. No, no! Don't, Torvald!

HELMER. Why not?

NORA. Torvald, I beg you. There is no mail.

HELMER. Let me just look, anyway. [*Is about to go out.*]

NORA *by the piano, plays the first bars of the tarantella dance.*

HELMER [*halts at the door*]. Aha!

NORA. I won't be able to dance tomorrow if I don't get to practice with you.

HELMER [*goes to her*]. Are you really all that scared, Nora dear?

NORA. Yes, so terribly scared. Let's try it right now. There's still time before we eat. Oh please, sit down and play for me, Torvald. Teach me, coach me, the way you always do.

HELMER. Of course I will, my darling, if that's what you want. [*Sits down at the piano.*]

NORA *takes the tambourine out of the carton, as well as a long, many-colored shawl. She quickly drapes the shawl around herself, then leaps into the middle of the floor.*

NORA. Play for me! I want to dance!

HELMER *plays and* NORA *dances.* DR. RANK *stands by the piano behind* HELMER *and watches.*

HELMER [*playing*]. Slow down, slow down!

NORA. Can't!

HELMER. Not so violent, Nora!

NORA. It has to be this way.

HELMER [*stops playing*]. No, no. This won't do at all.

NORA [*laughing, swinging her tambourine*]. What did I tell you?

RANK. Why don't you let me play?

HELMER [*getting up*]. Good idea. Then I can direct her better.

RANK *sits down at the piano and starts playing.* NORA *dances more and more wildly.* HELMER *stands over by the stove, repeatedly correcting her. She doesn't seem to hear. Her hair comes loose and falls down over her shoulders. She doesn't notice but keeps on dancing.* MRS. LINDE *enters.*

MRS. LINDE [*stops by the door, dumbfounded*]. Ah—!

NORA [*dancing*]. We're having such fun, Kristine!

HELMER. My dearest Nora, you're dancing as if it were a matter of life and death!

NORA. It is! It is!

HELMER. Rank, stop. This is sheer madness. Stop it, I say!

RANK *stops playing;* NORA *suddenly stops dancing.*

HELMER [*goes over to her*]. If I hadn't seen it I wouldn't have believed it. You've forgotten every single thing I ever taught you.

NORA [*tosses away the tambourine*]. See? I told you.

HELMER. Well! You certainly need coaching.

NORA. Didn't I tell you I did? Now you've seen for yourself. I'll need your help till the very minute we're leaving for the party. Will you promise, Torvald?

HELMER. You can count on it.

NORA. You're not to think of anything except me—not tonight and not tomorrow. You're not to read any letters—not to look in the mailbox—

HELMER. Ah, I see. You're still afraid of that man.

NORA. Yes—yes, that too.

HELMER. Nora, I can tell from looking at you. There's a letter from him out there.

NORA. I don't know. I think so. But you're not to read it now. I don't want anything ugly to come between us before it's all over.

RANK [*to* HELMER *in a low voice*]. Better not argue with her.

HELMER [*throws his arm around her*]. The child shall have her way. But tomorrow night, when you've done your dance—

NORA. Then you'll be free.

THE MAID [*in the door, right*]. Dinner can be served any time, ma'am.

NORA. We want champagne, Helene.

THE MAID. Very good, ma'am. [*Goes out.*]

HELMER. Aha! Having a party, eh?

NORA. Champagne from now till sunrise! [*Calls out.*] And some maca-roons, Helene. Lots!—just this once.

HELMER [*taking her hands*]. There, there—I don't like this wild—frenzy—Be my own sweet little lark again, the way you always are.

NORA. Oh, I will. But you go on in. You too, Dr. Rank. Kristine, please help me put up my hair.

RANK [*in a low voice to* HELMER *as they go out*]. You don't think she is—you know—expecting—?

HELMER. Oh no. Nothing like that. It's just this childish fear I was telling you about. [*They go out, right.*]

NORA. Well?

MRS. LINDE. Left town.

NORA. I saw it in your face.

MRS. LINDE. He'll be back tomorrow night. I left him a note.

NORA. You shouldn't have. I don't want you to try to stop anyting. You see, it's a kind of ecstasy, too, this waiting for the wonderful.

MRS. LINDE. But what is it you're waiting *for*?

NORA. You wouldn't understand. Why don't you go in to the others. I'll be there in a minute.

MRS. LINDE *enters the dining room, right.*

NORA [*stands still for a little while, as if collecting herself; she looks at her watch*]. Five o'clock. Seven hours till midnight. Twenty-four more hours till next midnight. Then the tarantella is over. Twenty-four plus seven—thirty-one more hours to live.

HELMER [*in the door, right*]. What's happening to my little lark?

NORA [*to him, with open arms*]. Here's your lark!

ACT III

The same room. The table by the couch and the chairs around it have been moved to the middle of the floor. A lighted lamp is on the table. The door to the front hall is open. Dance music is heard from upstairs.

MRS. LINDE *is seated by the table, idly leafing through the pages of a book. She tries to read but seems unable to concentrate. Once or twice she turns her head in the direction of the door, anxiously listening.*

MRS. LINDE [*looks at her watch*]. Not yet. It's almost too late. If only he hasn't—[*Listens again.*] Ah! There he is. [*She goes to the hall and opens the front door carefully. Quiet footsteps on the stairs. She whispers.*] Come in. There's nobody here.

KROGSTAD [*in the door*]. I found your note when I got home. What's this all about?

MRS. LINDE. I've got to talk to you.

KROGSTAD. Oh? And it has to be here?

MRS. LINDE. It couldn't be at my place. My room doesn't have a separate entrance. Come in. We're all alone. The maid is asleep and the Helmers are at a party upstairs.

KROGSTAD [*entering*]. Really? The Helmers are dancing tonight, are they?

MRS. LINDE. And why not?

KROGSTAD. You're right. Why not, indeed.

MRS. LINDE. All right, Krogstad. Let's talk, you and I.

KROGSTAD. I didn't know we had anything to talk about.

MRS. LINDE. We have much to talk about.

KROGSTAD. I didn't think so.

MRS. LINDE. No, because you've never really understood me.

KROGSTAD. What was there to understand? What happened was perfectly commonplace. A heartless woman jilts a man when she gets a more attractive offer.

MRS. LINDE. Do you think I'm all that heartless? And do you think it was easy for me to break with you?

KROGSTAD. No?

MRS. LINDE. You really thought it was?

KROGSTAD. If it wasn't, why did you write the way you did that time?

MRS. LINDE. What else could I do? If I had to make a break, I also had the duty to destroy whatever feelings you had for me.

KROGSTAD [*clenching his hands*]. So that's the way it was. And you did— *that*—just for money!

KROGSTAD. Don't forget I had a helpless mother and two small brothers. We couldn't wait for you, Krogstad. You know yourself how uncertain your prospects were then.

KROGSTAD. All right. But you still didn't have the right to throw me over for somebody else.

MRS. LINDE. I don't know. I have asked myself that question many times. Did I have that right?

KROGSTAD [*in a lower voice*]. When I lost you I lost my footing. Look at me now. A shipwrecked man on a raft.

MRS. LINDE. Rescue may be near.

KROGSTAD. It *was* near. Then you came between.

MRS. LINDE. I didn't know that, Krogstad. Only today did I find out it's your job I'm taking over in the bank.

KROGSTAD. I believe you when you say so. But now that you *do* know, aren't you going to step aside?

MRS. LINDE. No, for it wouldn't do you any good.

KROGSTAD. Whether it would or not—*I* would do it.

MRS. LINDE. I have learned common sense. Life and hard necessity have taught me that.

KROGSTAD. And life has taught me not to believe in pretty speeches.

MRS. LINDE. Then life has taught you a very sensible thing. But you do believe in actions, don't you?

KROGSTAD. How do you mean?

MRS. LINDE. You referred to yourself just now as a shipwrecked man.

KROGSTAD. It seems to me I had every reason to do so.

MRS. LINDE. And I am a shipwrecked woman. No one to grieve for, no one to care for.

KROGSTAD. You made your choice.

MRS. LINDE. I had no other choice that time.

KROGSTAD. Let's say you didn't. What then?

MRS. LINDE. Krogstad, how would it be if we two shipwrecked people got together?

KROGSTAD. What's this!

MRS. LINDE. Two on one wreck are better off than each on his own.

KROGSTAD. Kristine!

MRS. LINDE. Why do you think I came to town?

KROGSTAD. Surely not because of me?

MRS. LINDE. If I'm going to live at all I must work. All my life, for as long as I can remember, I have worked. That's been my one and only pleasure. But now that I'm all alone in the world I feel nothing but this terrible emptiness and desolation. There is no joy in working just for yourself. Krogstad— give me someone and something to work for.

KROGSTAD. I don't believe this. Only hysterical females go in for that kind of high-minded self-sacrifice.

MRS. LINDE. Did you ever know me to be hysterical?

KROGSTAD. You really could do this? Listen—do you know about my past? All of it?

MRS. LINDE. Yes, I do.

KROGSTAD. Do you also know what people think of me around here?

MRS. LINDE. A little while ago you sounded as if you thought that together with me you might have become a different person.

KROGSTAD. I'm sure of it.

MRS. LINDE. Couldn't that still be?

KROGSTAD. Kristine—do you know what you are doing? Yes, I see you do. And you think you have the courage?

KROGSTAD. I need someone to be a mother to, and your children need a mother. You and I need one another. Nils, I believe in you—in the real you. Together with you I dare to do anything.

KROGSTAD [*seizes her hands*]. Thanks, thanks, Kristine—now I know I'll raise myself in the eyes of others. —Ah, but I forget—!

MRS. LINDE [*listening*]. Shh!—There's the tarantella. You must go; hurry!

KROGSTAD. Why? What is it?

MRS. LINDE. Do you hear what they're playing up there? When the dance is over they'll be down.

KROGSTAD. All right. I'm leaving. The whole thing is pointless, anyway. Of course you don't know what I'm doing to the Helmers.

MRS. LINDE. Yes, Krogstad; I do know.

KROGSTAD. Still, you're brave enough—?

MRS. LINDE. I very well understand to what extremes despair can drive a man like you.

KROGSTAD. If only it could be undone!

MRS. LINDE. It could, for your letter is still out there in the mailbox.

KROGSTAD. Are you sure?

MRS. LINDE. Quite sure. But—

KROGSTAD [*looks searchingly at her*]. Maybe I'm beginning to understand. You want to save your friend at any cost. Be honest with me. That's it, isn't it?

MRS. LINDE. Krogstad, you may sell yourself once for somebody else's sake, but you don't do it twice.

KROGSTAD. I'll demand my letter back.

MRS. LINDE. No, no.

KROGSTAD. Yes, of course. I'll wait here till Helmer comes down. Then I'll ask him for my letter. I'll tell him it's just about my dismissal—that he shouldn't read it.

MRS. LINDE. No, Krogstad. You are not to ask for that letter back.

KROGSTAD. But tell me—wasn't that the real reason you wanted to meet me here?

MRS. LINDE. At first it was, because I was so frightened. But that was yesterday. Since then I have seen the most incredible things going on in this house. Helmer must learn the whole truth. This miserable secret must come out in the open; those two must come to a full understanding. They simply can't continue with all this concealment and evasion.

KROGSTAD. All right; if you want to take that chance. But there is one thing I *can* do, and I'll do that right now.

MRS. LINDE [*listening*]. But hurry! Go! The dance is over. We aren't safe another minute.

KROGSTAD. I'll be waiting for you downstairs.

MRS. LINDE. Yes, do. You must see me home.

KROGSTAD. I've never been so happy in my whole life. [*He leaves through the front door. The door between the living room and the front hall remains open.*]

MRS. LINDE [*straightens up the room a little and gets her things ready*]. What a change! Oh yes!—what a change! People to work for—to live for—a home to bring happiness to. I can't wait to get to work—! If only they'd come soon—[*Listens.*] Ah, there they are. Get my coat on—[*puts on her coat and hat.*]

HELMER's *and* NORA's *voices are heard outside. A key is turned in the lock, and* HELMER *almost forces* NORA *into the hall. She is dressed in her Italian costume, with a big black shawl over her shoulders. He is in evening dress under an open black domino.*

NORA [*in the door, still resisting*]. No, no, no! I don't want to! I want to go back upstairs. I don't want to leave so early.

HELMER. But dearest Nora—

NORA. Oh please, Torvald—please! I'm asking you as nicely as I can— just another hour!

HELMER. Not another minute, sweet. You know we agreed. There now. Get inside. You'll catch a cold out here. [*She still resists, but he guides her gently into the room.*]

MRS. LINDE. Good evening.

NORA. Kristine!

HELMER. Ah, Mrs. Linde. Still here?

MRS. LINDE. I know. I really should apologize, but I so much wanted to see Nora in her costume.

NORA. You've been waiting up for me?

MRS. LINDE. Yes, unfortunately I didn't get here in time. You were already upstairs, but I just didn't feel like leaving till I had seen you.

HELMER [*removing* NORA*'s shawl*]. Yes, do take a good look at her, Mrs. Linde. I think I may say she's worth looking at. Isn't she lovely?

MRS. LINDE. She certainly is—

HELMER. Isn't she a miracle of loveliness, though? That was the general opinion at the party, too. But dreadfully obstinate—that she is, the sweet little thing. What can we do about that? Will you believe it—I practically had to use force to get her away.

NORA. Oh Torvald, you're going to be sorry you didn't give me even half an hour more.

HELMER. See what I mean, Mrs. Linde? She dances the tarantella—she is a tremendous success—quite deservedly so, though perhaps her performance was a little too natural—I mean, more than could be reconciled with the rules of art. But all right! The point is: she's a success, a tremendous success. So should I let her stay after that? Spoil the effect? Of course not. So I take my lovely little Capri girl—I might say, my capricious little Capri girl—under my arm—a quick turn around the room—a graceful bow in all directions, and—as they say in the novels—the beautiful apparition is gone. A finale should always be done for effect, Mrs. Linde, but there doesn't seem to be any way of getting that into Nora's head. Poooh—! It's hot in here. [*Throws his cloak down on a chair and opens the door to his room.*] Why, it's dark in here! Of course. Excuse me—[*Goes inside and lights a couple of candles.*]

NORA [*in a hurried, breathless whisper*]. Well?

MRS. LINDE [*in a low voice*]. I have talked to him.

NORA. And—?

MRS. LINDE. Nora—you've got to tell your husband everything.

NORA [*no expression in her voice*]. I knew it.

MRS. LINDE. You have nothing to fear from Krogstad. But you must speak.

NORA. I'll say nothing.

MRS. LINDE. Then the letter will.

NORA. Thank you, Kristine. Now I know what I have to do. Shh!

HELMER [*returning*]. Well, Mrs. Linde, have you looked your fill?

MRS. LINDE. Yes. And now I'll say goodnight.

HELMER. So soon? Is that your knitting?

MRS. LINDE [*takes it*]. Yes, thank you. I almost forgot.

HELMER. So you knit, do you?

MRS. LINDE. Oh yes.

HELMER. You know—you ought to take up embroidery instead.

MRS. LINDE. Oh? Why?

HELMER. Because it's so much more beautiful. Look. You hold the embroidery so—in your left hand. Then with your right you move the needle—like this—in an easy, elongated arc—you see?

MRS. LINDE. Maybe you're right—

HELMER. Knitting, on the other hand, can never be anything but ugly. Look here: arms pressed close to the sides—the needles going up and down—there's something Chinese about it somehow—. That really was an excellent champagne they served us tonight.

MRS. LINDE. Well, goodnight, Nora. And don't be obstinate any more.

HELMER. Well said, Mrs. Linde!

MRS. LINDE. Goodnight, sir.

HELMER [*sees her to the front door*]. Goodnight, goodnight. I hope you'll get home all right? I'd be very glad to—but of course you don't have far to walk, do you? Goodnight, goodnight. [*She leaves. He closes the door behind her and returns to the living room.*] There! At last we got rid of her. She really is an incredible bore, that woman.

NORA. Aren't you very tired, Torvald?

HELMER. No, not in the least.

NORA. Not sleepy either?

HELMER. Not at all. Quite the opposite. I feel enormously—animated. How about you? Yes, you do look tired and sleepy.

NORA. Yes, I am very tired. Soon I'll be asleep.

HELMER. What did I tell you? I was right, wasn't I? Good thing I didn't let you stay any longer.

NORA. Everything you do is right.

HELMER [*kissing her forehead*]. Now my little lark is talking like a human being. But did you notice what splendid spirits Rank was in tonight?

NORA. Was he? I didn't notice. I didn't get to talk with him.

HELMER. Nor did I—hardly. But I haven't seen him in such a good mood for a long time. [*Looks at her, comes closer to her.*] Ah! It does feel good to be back in our own home again, to be quite alone with you—my young, lovely, ravishing woman!

NORA. Don't look at me like that, Torvald!

HELMER. Am I not to look at my most precious possession? All that loveliness that is mine, nobody's but mine, all of it mine.

NORA [*walks to the other side of the table*]. I won't have you talk to me like that tonight.

HELMER [*follows her*]. The tarantella is still in your blood. I can tell. That only makes you all the more alluring. Listen! The guests are beginning to leave. [*Softly.*] Nora—soon the whole house will be quiet.

NORA. Yes, I hope so.

HELMER. Yes, don't you, my darling? Do you know—when I'm at a party with you, like tonight—do you know why I hardly ever talk to you, why I keep away from you, only look at you once in a while—a few stolen glances—do you know why I do that? It's because I pretend that you are my secret love, my young, secret bride-to-be, and nobody has the slightest suspicion that there is anything between us.

NORA. Yes, I know. All your thoughts are with me.

HELMER. Then when we're leaving and I lay your shawl around your delicate young shoulders—around that wonderful curve of your neck—then I imagine you're my young bride, that we're coming away from the wedding, that I am taking you to my home for the first time—that I am alone with you for the first time—quite alone with you, you young, trembling beauty! I have desired you all evening—there hasn't been a longing in me that hasn't been for you. When you were dancing the tarantella, chasing, inviting—my blood was on fire; I couldn't stand it any longer—that's why I brought you down so early—

NORA. Leave me now, Torvald. Please! I don't want all this.

HELMER. What do you mean? You're only playing your little teasing bird game with me; aren't you, Nora? Don't want to? I'm your husband, aren't I?

There is a knock on the front door.

NORA [*with a start*]. Did you hear that—?

HELMER [*on his way to the hall*]. Who is it?

RANK [*outside*]. It's me. May I come in for a moment?

HELMER [*in a low voice, annoyed*]. Oh, what does he want now? [*Aloud.*] Just a minute. [*Opens the door.*] Well! How good of you not to pass by our door.

RANK. I thought I heard your voice, so I felt like saying hello. [*Looks around.*] Ah yes—this dear, familiar room. What a cozy, comfortable place you have here, you two.

HELMER. Looked to me as if you were quite comfortable upstairs too.

RANK. I certainly was. Why not? Why not enjoy all you can in this world? As much as you can for as long as you can, anyway. Excellent wine.

HELMER. The champagne, particularly.

RANK. You noticed that too? Incredible how much I managed to put away.

NORA. Torvald drank a lot of champagne tonight, too.

RANK. Did he?

NORA. Yes, he did, and then he's always so much fun afterwards.

RANK. Well, why not have some fun in the evening after a well spent day?

HELMER. Well spent? I'm afraid I can't claim that.

RANK [*slapping him lightly on the shoulder*]. But you see, I can!

NORA. Dr. Rank, I believe you must have been conducting a scientific test today.

RANK. Exactly.

HELMER. What do you know—little Nora talking about scientific tests!

NORA. May I congratulate you on the result?

RANK. You may indeed.

NORA. It was a good one?

RANK. The best possible for both doctor and patient—certainty.

NORA [*a quick query*]. Certainty?

RANK. Absolute certainty. So why shouldn't I have myself an enjoyable evening afterwards?

NORA. I quite agree with you, Dr. Rank. You should.

HELMER. And so do I. If only you don't pay for it tomorrow.

RANK. Oh well—you get nothing for nothing in this world.

NORA. Dr. Rank—you are fond of costume parties, aren't you?

RANK. Yes, particularly when there is a reasonable number of amusing disguises.

NORA. Listen—what are the two of us going to be next time?

HELMER. You frivolous little thing! Already thinking about the next party!

RANK. You and I? That's easy. You'll be Fortune's Child.

HELMER. Yes, but what is a fitting costume for that?

RANK. Let your wife appear just the way she always is.

HELMER. Beautiful. Very good indeed. But how about yourself? Don't you know what you'll go as?

RANK. Yes, my friend. I know precisely what I'll be.

HELMER. Yes?

RANK. At the next masquerade I'll be invisible.

HELMER. That's a funny idea.

RANK. There's a certain big, black hat—you've heard about the hat that makes you invisible, haven't you? You put that on, and nobody can see you.

HELMER [*suppressing a smile*]. I guess that's right.

RANK. But I'm forgetting what I came for. Helmer, give me a cigar—one of your dark Havanas.

HELMER. With the greatest pleasure. [*Offers him his case.*]

RANK [*takes one and cuts off the tip*]. Thanks.

NORA [*striking a match*]. Let me give you a light.

RANK. Thanks. [*She holds the match; he lights his cigar.*] And now goodbye!

HELMER. Goodbye, goodbye, my friend.

NORA. Sleep well, Dr. Rank.

RANK. I thank you.

NORA. Wish me the same.

RANK. You? Well, if you really want me to—. Sleep well. And thanks for the light. [*He nods to both of them and goes out.*]

HELMER [*in a low voice*]. He had had quite a bit to drink.

NORA [*absently*]. Maybe so.

HELMER *takes out his keys and goes out into the hall.*

NORA. Torvald—what are you doing out there?

HELMER. Got to empty the mailbox. It is quite full. There wouldn't be room for the newspapers in the morning—

NORA. Are you going to work tonight?

HELMER. You know very well I won't.—Say! What's this? Somebody's been at the lock.

NORA. The lock—?

HELMER. Yes. Why, I wonder. I hate to think that any of the maids—. Here's a broken hairpin. It's one of yours, Nora.

NORA [*quickly*]. Then it must be one of the children.

HELMER. You better make damn sure they stop that. Hm, hm.— There! I got it open, finally. [*Gathers up the mail, calls out to the kitchen.*] Helene?— Oh Helene—turn out the light here in the hall, will you? [*He comes back into the living room and closes the door.*] Look how it's been piling up. [*Shows her the bundle of letters. Starts leafing through it.*] What's this?

NORA [*by the window*]. The letter! Oh no, no, Torvald!

HELMER. Two calling cards—from Rank.

NORA. From Dr. Rank?

HELMER [*looking at them*]. "Doctor medicinae Rank." They were on top. He must have put them there when he left just now.

NORA. Anything written on them?

HELMER. A black cross above the name. Look. What a macabre idea. Like announcing his own death.

NORA. That's what it is.

HELMER. Hm? You know about this? Has he said anything to you?

NORA. That card means he has said goodbye to us. He'll lock himself up to die.

HELMER. My poor friend. I knew of course he wouldn't be with me very long. But so soon—. And hiding himself away like a wounded animal—

NORA. When it has to be, it's better it happens without words. Don't you think so, Torvald?

HELMER [*walking up and down*]. He'd grown so close to us. I find it hard to think of him as gone. With his suffering and loneliness he was like a clouded background for our happy sunshine. Well, it may be better this way. For him, at any rate. [*Stops.*] And perhaps for us, too, Nora. For now we have nobody but each other. [*Embraces her.*] Oh you—my beloved wife! I feel I just can't hold you close enough. Do you know, Nora—many times I have wished some great danger threatened you, so I could risk my life and blood and everything—everything, for your sake.

NORA [*frees herself and says in a strong and firm voice*]. I think you should go and read your letters now, Torvald.

HELMER. No, no—not tonight. I want to be with you, my darling.

NORA. With the thought of your dying friend—?

HELMER. You are right. This has shaken both of us. Something not beautiful has come between us. Thoughts of death and dissolution. We must try to get over it—out of it. Till then—we'll each go to our own room.

NORA [*her arms around his neck*]. Torvald—goodnight! Goodnight!

HELMER [*kisses her forehead*]. Goodnight, my little songbird. Sleep well, Nora. Now I'll read my letters. [*He goes into his room, carrying the mail. Closes the door.*]

NORA [*her eyes desperate, her hands groping, finds* HELMER*'s domino and throws it around her; she whispers, quickly, brokenly, hoarsely*]. Never see him again. Never. Never. Never. [*Puts her shawl over her head.*] And never see the children again either. Never; never.—The black, icy water—fathomless— this—! If only it was all over.—Now he has it. Now he's reading it. No, no; not yet. Torvald—goodbye—you—the children—

She is about to hurry through the hall, when HELMER *flings open the door to his room and stands there with an open letter in his hand.*

HELMER. Nora!

NORA [*cries out*]. Ah—!

HELMER. What is it? You know what's in this letter?

NORA. Yes, I do! Let me go! Let me out!

HELMER [*holds her back*]. Where do you think you're going?

NORA [*trying to tear herself loose from him*]. I won't let you save me, Torvald!

HELMER [*tumbles back*]. True! Is it true what he writes? Oh my God! No, no—this can't possibly be true.

NORA. It is true. I have loved you more than anything else in the whole world.

HELMER. Oh, don't give me any silly excuses.

NORA [*taking a step towards him*]. Torvald—

HELMER. You wretch! What have you done!

NORA. Let me go. You are not to sacrifice yourself for me. You are not to take the blame.

HELMER. No more playacting. [*Locks the door to the front hall.*] You'll stay here and answer me. Do you understand what you have done? Answer me! Do you understand?

NORA [*gazes steadily at him with an increasingly frozen expression*]. Yes. Now I'm beginning to understand.

HELMER [*walking up and down*]. What a dreadful awakening. All these years—all these eight years—she, my pride and my joy—a hypocrite, a liar—oh worse! worse!—a criminal! Oh, the bottomless ugliness in all this! Damn! Damn! Damn!

NORA, *silent, keeps gazing at him.*

HELMER [*stops in front of her*]. I ought to have guessed that something like this would happen. I should have expected it. All your father's loose principles—Silence! You have inherited every one of your father's loose principles. No religion, no morals, no sense of duty—. Now I am being punished for my leniency with him. I did it for your sake, and this is how you pay me back.

NORA. Yes. This is how.

HELMER. You have ruined all my happiness. My whole future—that's what you have destroyed. Oh, it's terrible to think about. I am at the mercy of an unscrupulous man. He can do with me whatever he likes, demand anything of me, command me and dispose of me just as he pleases—I dare not say a word! To go down so miserably, to be destroyed—all because of an irresponsible woman!

NORA. When I am gone from the world, you'll be free.

HELMER. No noble gestures, please. Your father was always full of such phrases too. What good would it do me if you were gone from the world, as you put it? Not the slightest good at all. He could still make the whole thing public, and if he did I wouldn't be surprised if people thought I'd put you up to it. They might even think it was my idea—that it was I who urged you to do it! And for all this I have you to thank—you, whom I've borne on my hands through all the years of our marriage. *Now* do you understand what you've done to me?

NORA [*with cold calm*]. Yes.

HELMER. I just can't get it into my head that this is happening; it's all so incredible But we have to come to terms with it somehow. Take your shawl off. Take it off, I say! I have to satisfy him one way or another. The whole affair must be kept quiet at whatever cost.—And as far as you and I are concerned, nothing must seem to have changed. I'm talking about appearances, of course. You'll go on living here; that goes without saying. But I won't let you bring up the children; I dare not trust you with them.—Oh! Having to say this to one I have loved so much, and whom I still—! But all that is past. It's not a question of happiness any more but of hanging on to what can be salvaged—pieces, appearances—[*The doorbell rings.*]

HELMER [*jumps*]. What's that? So late. Is the worst—? Has he—! Hide, Nora! Say you're sick.

NORA *doesn't move.* HELMER *opens the door to the hall.*

THE MAID [*half dressed, out in the hall*]. A letter for your wife, sir.

HELMER. Give it to me. [*takes the letter and closes the door.*] Yes, it's from him. But I won't let you have it. I'll read it myself.

NORA. Yes—you read it.

HELMER [*by the lamp*]. I hardly dare. Perhaps we're lost, both you and I. No; I've got to know. [*Tears the letter open, glances through it, looks at enclosure; a cry of joy.*] Nora!

Nora looks at him with a question in her eyes.

HELMER. Nora!—No I must read it again.—Yes, yes; it is so! I'm saved! Nora, I'm saved!

NORA. And I?

HELMER. You too, of course; we're both saved, both you and I. Look! He's returning your note. He writes that he's sorry, he regrets, a happy turn in his life—oh, it doesn't matter what he writes. We're saved, Nora! Nobody can do anything to you now. Oh Nora, Nora—. No, I want to get rid of this disgusting thing first. Let me see—[*Looks at the signature.*] No, I don't want to see it. I don't want it to be more than a bad dream, the whole thing. [*Tears up the note and both letters, throws the pieces in the stove, and watches them burn.*] There! Now it's gone.—He wrote that ever since Christmas Eve—. Good God, Nora, these must have been three terrible days for you.

NORA. I have fought a hard fight these last three days.

HELMER. And been in agony and seen no other way out than—. No, we won't think of all that ugliness. We'll just rejoice and tell ourselves it's over, it's all over! Oh, listen to me, Nora. You don't seem to understand. It's over. What *is* it? Why do you look like that—that frozen expression on your face? Oh my poor little Nora, don't you think I know what it is? You can't make yourself believe that I have forgiven you. But I have, Nora; I swear to you, I have forgiven you for everything. Of course I know that what you did was for love of me.

NORA. That is true.

HELMER. You have loved me the way a wife ought to love her husband. You just didn't have the wisdom to judge the means. But do you think I love you any less because you don't know how to act on your own? Of course not. Just lean on me. I'll advise you; I'll guide you. I wouldn't be a man if I didn't find you twice as attractive because of your womanly helplessness. You mustn't pay any attention to the hard words I said to you right at first. It was just that first shock when I thought everything was collapsing all around me. I have forgiven you, Nora. I swear to you—I really have forgiven you.

NORA. I thank you for your forgiveness. [*She goes out through the door, right.*]

HELMER. No, stay—[*Looks into the room she entered.*] What are you doing in there?

NORA [*within*]. Getting out of my costume.

HELMER [*by the open door*]. Good, good. Try to calm down and compose yourself, my poor little frightened songbird. Rest safely; I have broad wings to cover you with. [*Walks around near the door.*] What a nice and cozy home we have, Nora. Here's shelter for you. Here I'll keep you safe like a hunted dove I have rescued from the hawk's talons. Believe me: I'll know how to quiet your beating heart. It will happen by and by, Nora; you'll see. Why, tomorrow you'll look at all this in quite a different light. And soon everything will be just the way it was before. I won't need to keep reassuring you that I have forgiven you; you'll feel it yourself. Did you really think I could have abandoned you, or even reproached you? Oh, you don't know a real man's heart, Nora. There is something unspeakably sweet and satisfactory for a man to know deep in himself he has forgiven his wife—forgiven her in all the fullness of his honest heart. You see, that way she becomes his very own all over again—in a double sense, you might say. He has, so to speak, given her a second birth; it is as if she had become his wife and his child, both. From now on that's what you'll be to me, you lost and helpless creature. Don't worry about a thing, Nora. Only be frank with me, and I'll be your will and your conscience.—What's this? You're not in bed? You've changed your dress—!

NORA [*in an everyday dress*]. Yes, Torvald. I have changed my dress.

HELMER. But why—now—this late?

NORA. I'm not going to sleep tonight.

HELMER. But my dear Nora—

NORA [*looks at her watch*]. It isn't all that late. Sit down here with me, Torvald. You and I have much to talk about. [*Sits down at the table.*]

HELMER. Nora—what is this all about? That rigid face—

NORA. Sit down. This will take a while. I have much to say to you.

HELMER [*sits down, facing her across the table*]. You worry me, Nora. I don't understand you.

NORA. No, that's just it. You don't understand me. And I have never understood you—not till tonight. No, don't interrupt me. Just listen to what I have to say.—This is a settling of accounts, Torvald.

HELMER. What do you mean by that?

NORA [*after a brief silence*]. Doesn't one thing strike you, now that we are sitting together like this?

HELMER. What would that be?

NORA. We have been married for eight years. Doesn't it occur to you that this is the first time that you and I, husband and wife, are having a serious talk?

HELMER. Well—serious—. What do you mean by that?

NORA. For eight whole years—longer, in fact—ever since we first met, we have never talked seriously to each other about a single serious thing.

HELMER. You mean I should forever have been telling you about worries you couldn't have helped me with anyway?

NORA. I am not talking about worries. I'm saying we have never tried seriously to get to the bottom of anything together.

HELMER. But dearest Nora, I hardly think that would have been someting *you*—

NORA. That's the whole point. You have never understood me. Great wrong has been done to me, Torvald. First by Daddy and then by you.

HELMER. What! By us two? We who have loved you more deeply than anyone else?

NORA [*shakes her head*]. You never loved me—neither Daddy nor you. You only thought it was fun to be in love with me.

HELMER. But, Nora—what an expression to use!

NORA. That's the way it has been, Torvald. When I was home with Daddy, he told me all his opinions, and so they became my opinions too. If I disagreed with him I kept it to myself, for he wouldn't have liked that. He called me his little doll baby, and he played with me the way I played with my dolls. Then I came to your house—

HELMER. What a way to talk about our marriage!

NORA [*imperturbably*]. I mean that I passed from Daddy's hands into yours. You arranged everything according to your taste, and so I came to share it—or I pretended to; I'm not sure which. I think it was a little of both, now one and now the other. When I look back on it now, it seems to me I've been living here like a pauper—just a hand-to-mouth kind of existence. I have earned my keep by doing tricks for you, Torvald. But that's the way you wanted it. You have great sins against me to answer for, Daddy and you. It's your fault that nothing has become of me.

HELMER. Nora, you're being both unreasonable and ungrateful. Haven't you been happy here?

NORA. No, never. I thought I was, but I wasn't.

HELMER. Not—not happy!

NORA. No; just having fun. And you have always been very good to me. But our home has never been more than a playroom. I have been your doll wife here, just the way I used to be Daddy's doll child. And the children have been my dolls. I thought it was fun when you played with me, just as they thought it was fun when I played with them. That's been our marriage, Torvald.

HELMER. There is something in what you are saying—exaggerated and hysterical though it is. But from now on things will be different. Playtime is over; it's time for growing up.

NORA. Whose growing up—mine or the children's?

HELMER. Both yours and the children's, Nora darling.

NORA. Oh Torvald, you're not the man to bring me up to be the right kind of wife for you.

HELMER. How can you say that?

NORA. And I—? What qualifications do I have for bringing up the children?

HELMER. Nora!

NORA. You said so yourself a minute ago—that you didn't dare to trust me with them.

HELMER. In the first flush of anger, yes. Surely, you're not going to count that.

NORA. But you were quite right. I am *not* qualified. Something else has to come first. Somehow I have to grow up myself. And you are not the man to help me do that. That's a job I have to do by myself. And that's why I'm leaving you.

HELMER [*jumps up*]. What did you say!

NORA. I have to be myself if I am to find out about myself and about all the other things too. So I can't stay here with you any longer.

HELMER. Nora, Nora!

NORA. I'm leaving now. I'm sure Kristine will put me up for tonight.

HELMER. You're out of your mind! I won't let you! I forbid you!

NORA. You can't forbid me anything any more; it won't do any good. I'm taking my own things with me. I won't accept anything from you, either now or later.

HELMER. But this is madness!

NORA. Tomorrow I'm going home—I mean back to my old hometown. It will be easier for me to find some kind of job there.

HELMER. Oh, you blind, inexperienced creature—!

NORA. I must see to it that I get experience, Torvald.

HELMER. Leaving your home, your husband, your children! Not a thought of what people will say!

NORA. I can't worry about that. All I know is that I have to leave.

HELMER. Oh, this is shocking! Betraying your most sacred duties like this!

NORA. And what do you consider my most sacred duties?

HELMER. Do I need tell you that? They are your duties to your husband and your children.

NORA. I have other duties equally sacred.

HELMER. You do not. What duties would they be?

NORA. My duties to myself.

HELMER. You are a wife and a mother before you are anything else.

NORA. I don't believe that any more. I believe I am first of all a human being, just as much as you—or at any rate that I must try to become one. Oh, I know very well that most people agree with you, Torvald, and that it says something like that in all the books. But what people say and what the books say is no longer enough for me. I have to think about these things myself and see if I can't find the answers.

HELMER. You mean to tell me you don't know what your proper place in your own home is? Don't you have a reliable guide in such matters? Don't you have religion?

NORA. Oh but Torvald—I don't really know what religion is.

HELMER. What are you saying!

NORA. All I know is what the Reverend Hansen told me when he prepared me for confirmation. He said that religion was *this* and it was *that*. When I get by myself, away from here, I'll have to look into that, too. I have to decide if what the Reverend Hansen said was right, or anyway if it is right for *me*.

HELMER. Oh, this is unheard of in a young woman! If religion can't guide you, let me appeal to your conscience. For surely you have moral feelings? Or—answer me—maybe you don't?

NORA. Well, you see, Torvald, I don't really know what to say. I just don't know. I am confused about these things. All I know is that my ideas are quite different from yours. I have just found out that the laws are different from what I thought they were, but in no way can I get it into my head that those laws are right. A woman shouldn't have the right to spare her dying old father or save her husband's life! I just can't believe that.

HELMER. You speak like a child. You don't understand the society you live in.

NORA. No, I don't. But I want to find out about it. I have to make up my mind who is right, society or I.

HELMER. You are sick, Nora; you have a fever. I really don't think you are in your right mind.

NORA. I have never felt so clearheaded and sure of myself as I do tonight.

HELMER. And clearheaded and sure of yourself you're leaving your husband and children?

NORA. Yes.

HELMER. Then there is only one possible explanation.

NORA. What?

HELMER. You don't love me any more.

NORA. No, that's just it.

HELMER. Nora! Can you say that?

NORA. I am sorry, Torvald, for you have always been so good to me. But I can't help it. I don't love you any more.

HELMER [*with forced composure*]. And this too is a clear and sure conviction?

NORA. Completely clear and sure. That's why I don't want to stay here any more.

HELMER. And are you ready to explain to me how I came to forfeit your love?

NORA. Certainly I am. It was tonight, when the wonderful didn't happen. That was when I realized you were not the man I thought you were.

HELMER. You have to explain. I don't understand.

NORA. I have waited patiently for eight years, for I wasn't such a fool that I thought the wonderful is something that happens any old day. Then this— thing—came crashing in on me, and then there wasn't a doubt in my mind that now—now comes the wonderful. When Krogstad's letter was in that mailbox, never for a moment did it ever occur to me that you would submit to his conditions. I was so absolutely certain that you would say to him: make the whole thing public—tell everybody. And when that had happened—

HELMER. Yes, then what? When I had surrendered my own wife to shame and disgrace—!

NORA. When that had happened, I was absolutely certain that you would stand up and take the blame and say, "I'm the guilty one."

HELMER. Nora!

NORA. You mean I never would have accepted such a sacrifice from you? Of course not. But what would my protests have counted against yours? *That* was the wonderful I was waiting for in hope and terror. And to prevent that I was going to kill myself.

HELMER. I'd gladly work nights and days for you, Nora—endure sorrow and want for your sake. But nobody sacrifices his *honor* for his love.

NORA. A hundred thousand women have done so.

HELMER. Oh, you think and talk like a silly child.

NORA. All right. But you don't think and talk like the man I can live with. When you had gotten over your fright—not because of what threatened *me* but because of the risk to *you*—and the whole danger was past, then you acted as if nothing at all had happened. Once again I was your little songbird, your doll, just as before, only now you had to handle her even more carefully, because she was so frail and weak. [*Rises.*] Torvald—that moment I realized that I had been living here for eight years with a stranger and had borne him three children—Oh, I can't stand thinking about it! I feel like tearing myself to pieces!

HELMER [*heavily*]. I see it, I see it. An abyss has opened up between us.—Oh but Nora—surely it can be filled?

NORA. The way I am now I am no wife for you.

HELMER. I have it in me to change.

NORA. Perhaps—if your doll is taken from you.

HELMER. To part—to part from you! No, no, Nora! I can't grasp that thought!

NORA [*goes out, right*]. All the more reason why it has to be. [*She returns with her outdoor clothes and a small bag, which she sets down on the chair by the table.*]

HELMER. Nora, Nora! Not now! Wait till tomorrow.

NORA [*putting on her coat*]. I can't spend the night in a stranger's rooms.

HELMER. But couldn't we live here together like brother and sister—?

NORA [*tying on her hat*]. You know very well that wouldn't last long—. [*Wraps her shawl around her.*] Goodbye, Torvald. I don't want to see the children. I know I leave them in better hands than mine. The way I am now I can't be anything to them.

HELMER. But some day, Nora—some day?

NORA. How can I tell? I have no idea what's going to become of me.

HELMER. But you're still my wife, both as you are now and as you will be.

NORA. Listen, Torvald—when a wife leaves her husband's house, the way I am doing now, I have heard he has no more legal responsibilities for her. At any rate, I now release you from all responsibility. You are not to feel yourself obliged to me for anything, and I have no obligations to you. There has to be full freedom on both sides. Here is your ring back. Now give me mine.

HELMER. Even this?

NORA. Even this.

HELMER. Here it is.

NORA. There. So now it's over. I'm putting the keys here. The maids know everything about the house—better than I. Tomorrow, after I'm gone, Kristine will come over and pack my things from home. I want them sent after me.

HELMER. Over! It's all over! Nora, will you never think of me?

NORA. I'm sure I'll often think of you and the children and this house.

HELMER. May I write to you, Nora?

NORA. No—never. I won't have that.

HELMER. But send you things—? You must let me.

NORA. Nothing, nothing.

HELMER. —help you, when you need help—

NORA. I told you, no; I won't have it. I'll accept nothing from strangers.

HELMER. Nora—can I never again be more to you than a stranger?

NORA [*picks up her bag*]. Oh Torvald—then the most wonderful of all would have to happen—

HELMER. Tell me what that would be—!

NORA. For that to happen, both you and I would have to change so that—Oh Torvald; I no longer believe in the wonderful.

HELMER. But I *will* believe. Tell me! Change, so that—?

NORA. So that our living together would become a true marriage. Goodbye. [*She goes out through the hall.*]

HELMER [*sinks down on a chair near the door and covers his face with his hands*]. Nora! Nora! [*Looks around him and gets up.*] All empty. She's gone. [*With sudden hope.*] The most wonderful—?!

From downstairs comes the sound of a heavy door slamming shut.

[1879]

■ TOPICS FOR DISCUSSION AND WRITING

1. Near the beginning of the play, how does Mrs. Linde's presence help to define Nora's character? How does Nora's response to Krogstad's entrance tell us something about Nora?

2. What does Dr. Rank contribute to the play? If he were eliminated, what would be lost?

3. Ibsen very reluctantly acceded to a request for an alternate ending for a German production. In the new ending Helmer forces Nora to look at their sleeping children and reminds her that "tomorrow, when they wake up and call for their mother, they will be—motherless." Nora "struggles with herself" and concludes by saying, "Oh, this is a sin against myself, but I cannot leave them." In view of the fact that the last act several times seems to be moving toward a "happy ending" (e.g., Krogstad promises to recall his letter), what is wrong with this alternate ending?

4. Can it be argued that although at the end Nora goes out to achieve self-realization, her abandonment of her children—especially to Torvald's loathsome conventional morality—is a crime? (By the way, exactly why does Nora leave the children? She seems to imply, in some passages, that because she forged a signature she is unfit to bring them up. But do you agree with her?)

5. Michael Meyer, in his splendid biography *Henrik Ibsen*, says that the play is not so much about women's rights as about "the need of every individual to find out the kind of person he or she really is, and to strive to become that person." What evidence can you offer to support this interpretation?

6. In *The Quintessence of Ibsenism* Bernard Shaw says that Ibsen, reacting against a common theatrical preference for strange situations, "saw that . . . the more familiar the situation, the more interesting the play. Shakespear had put ourselves on the stage but not our situations. Our uncles seldom murder our fathers and . . . marry our mothers. . . .

Ibsen gives us not only ourselves, but ourselves in our own situations. The things that happen to his stage figures are things that happen to us. One consequence is that his plays are much more important to us than Shakespear's. Another is that they are capable both of hurting us cruelly and of filling us with excited hopes of escape from idealistic tyrannies, and with visions of intenser life in the future." How much of this do you believe?

7. In about 250 words (perhaps two paragraphs), sketch Nora's character. In your discussion, indicate to what degree she may be a victim and to what degree she may be at fault.

CHAPTER 13

Men, Women,
God, and Gods

ESSAYS

■ WILLIAM JAMES

William James (1842–1910), brother of Alice James and of the novelist Henry James, was born into a wealthy family in New York City. He at first studied to be a painter, then turned to chemistry and biology and took a degree in medicine. Though given to depression and hallucinations, it seems that he saved himself by an act of will or of faith: "My first act of free will," he said, "shall be to believe in free will." James accepted a position as instructor in physiology at Harvard, but, considering his uncertain health, he decided that he did not have the strength to do laboratory work, and he turned to philosophy and psychology. "I never had any philosophic instruction, the first lecture on psychology I ever heard being the first I ever gave." He published his first book, *Principles of Psychology* (1890), when he was forty-eight.

James developed his ideas partly under the influence of Darwin's writing, but he gave Darwinism a decidely special twist. Impressed by Darwin's findings that "variations" assisted some creatures to survive in a changing environment, James saw the human mind as a potent force, not as a consciousness that merely receives external impressions. "Mental interests, hypotheses, postulates, so far as they are the basis for human action—action which to a great extent transforms the world—help to *make* the truth which they declare."

In 1897 James published a book of essays titled *The Will to Believe*. Part of one essay is reprinted here.

Religious Faith[1]

Religion has meant many things in human history; but when from now onward I use the word I mean to use it in the supernaturalist sense, as declaring that the so-called order of nature, which constitutes this world's experience, is only one portion of the total universe, and that there stretches beyond this visible world an unseen world of which we now know nothing positive, but in its relation to which the true significance of our present mundane life consists. A man's religious faith (whatever more special items of doctrine it may involve) means for me essentially his faith in the existence of an unseen order of some kind in which the riddles of the natural order may be found explained. In the more developed religions the natural world has always been regarded as the mere scaffolding or vestibule of a truer, more eternal world, and affirmed to be a sphere of education, trial, or redemption. In these religions, one must in some fashion die to the natural life before one can enter into life eternal. The notion that this physical world of wind and water, when the sun rises and the moon sets, is absolutely and ultimately the divinely aimed-at and established thing, is one which we find only in very early religions. . . . It is this natural religion (primitive still, in spite of the fact that poets and men of science whose good-will exceeds their perspicacity keep publishing it in new editions tuned to our contemporary ears) that, as I said a while ago, has suffered definitive bankruptcy in the opinion of a circle of persons, among whom I must count myself, and who are growing more numerous every day. For such persons the physical order of nature, taken simply as science knows it, cannot be held to reveal any one harmonious spiritual intent. It is mere *weather*, as Chauncey Wright called it, doing and undoing without end.

Now, I wish to make you feel, if I can in the short remainder of this hour, that we have a right to believe the physical order to be only a partial order; that we have a right to supplement it by an unseen spiritual order which we assume on trust, if only thereby life may seem to us better worth living again. But as such a trust will seem to some of you sadly mystical and execrably unscientific, I must first say a word or two to weaken the veto which you may consider that science opposes to our act.

There is included in human nature an ingrained naturalism and materialism of mind which can only admit facts that are actually tangible. Of this sort of mind the entity called "science" is the idol. Fondness of the word "scientist" is one of the notes by which you may know its votaries; and its short way of killing any opinion that it disbelieves in is to call it "unscientific." It must be granted that there is no slight excuse for this. Science has made such glorious leaps in the last three hundred years, and extended our knowledge of nature so enormously both in general and in detail; men of science, moreover, have as a class displayed such admirable virtues—that it is no wonder if the worshippers of science lose their head. In this very University, accordingly, I have heard more than one teacher say that all the fundamental conceptions of truth have already been found by science, and that the future has only the

[1] Editors' title. From *The Will to Believe*

details of the picture to fill in. But the slightest reflection on the real conditions will suffice to show how barbaric such notions are. They show such a
lack of scientific imagination, that it is hard to see how one who is actively
advancing any part of science can make a mistake so crude. Think how many
absolutely new scientific conceptions have arisen in our own generation, how
many new problems have been formulated that were never thought of before,
and then cast an eye upon the brevity of science's career. It began with
Galileo, not three hundred years ago. Four thinkers since Galileo, each informing his successor of what discoveries his own lifetime had seen achieved,
might have passed the torch of science into our hands as we sit here in this
room. Indeed, for the matter of that, an audience much smaller than the
present one, an audience of some five or six score people, if each person in
it could speak for his own generation, would carry us away to the black
unknown of the human species, to days without a document or monument to
tell their tale. Is it credible that such a mushroom knowledge, such a growth
overnight as this, *can* represent more than the minutest glimpse of what the
universe will really prove to be when adequately understood? No! our science
is a drop, our ignorance a sea. Whatever else be certain, this at least is
certain—that the world of our present natural knowledge *is* enveloped in a
larger world of *some* sort of whose residual properties we at present can
frame no positive idea.

Agnostic positivism,[2] of course, admits this principle theoretically in the
most cordial terms, but insists that we must not turn it to any practical use.
We have no right, this doctrine tells us, to dream dreams, or suppose anything
about the unseen part of the universe, merely because to do so may be for
what we are pleased to call our highest interests. We must always wait for
sensible evidence for our beliefs; and where such evidence is inaccessible we
must frame no hypotheses whatever. Of course this is a safe enough position
in asbtracto. If a thinker had no stake in the unknown, no vital needs, to live
or languish according to what the unseen world contained, a philosophic neutrality and refusal to believe either one way or the other would be his wisest
cue. But, unfortunately, neutrality is not only inwardly difficult, it is also outwardly unrealizable, where our relations to an alternative are practical and vital. This is because, as the psychologists tell us, belief and doubt are living
attitudes, and involve conduct on our part. Our only way, for example, of
doubting, or refusing to believe, that a certain thing *is*, is continuing to act
as if it were *not*. If, for instance, I refuse to believe that the room is getting
cold, I leave the windows open and light no fire just as if it still were warm.
If I doubt that you are worthy of my confidence, I keep you uninformed of all
my secrets just as if you were *un*worthy of the same. If I doubt the need of
insuring my house, I leave it uninsured as much as if I believed there were
no need. And so if I must not believe that the world is divine, I can only express that refusal be declining ever to act distinctively as if it were so, which
can only mean acting on certain critical occasions as if it were *not* so, or in
an irreligious way. There are, you see, inevitable occasions in life when inaction is a kind of action, and must count as action, and when not to be for is

---

[2] A belief that human knowledge must be based on sense perceptions

to be practically against; and in all such cases strict and consistent neutrality is an unattainable thing.

And, after all, is not this duty of neutrality where only our inner interests 5 would lead us to believe, the most ridiculous of commands? Is it not sheer dogmatic folly to say that our inner interests can have no real connection with the forces that the hidden world may contain? In other cases divinations based on inner interests have proved prophetic enough. Take science itself! Without an imperious inner demand on our part for ideal logical and mathematical harmonies, we should never have attained to proving that such harmonies lie hidden between all the chinks and interstices of the crude natural world. Hardly a law has been established in science, hardly a fact ascertained, which was not first sought after, often with sweat and blood, to gratify an inner need. Whence such needs come from we do not know: we find them in us, and biological psychology so far only classes them with Darwin's "accidental variations." But the inner need of believing that this world of nature is a sign of something more spiritual and eternal than itself is just as strong and authoritative in those who feel it, as the inner need of uniform laws of causation ever can be in a professionally scienctific head. The toil of many generations has proved the latter need prophetic. Why *may* not the former one be prophetic, too? And if needs of ours outrun the visible universe, why *may* not that be a sign than an invisible universe is there? What, in short, has authority to debar us from trusting our religious demands? Science as such assuredly has no authority, for she can only say what is, not what is not; and the agnostic "thou shalt not believe without coercive sensible evidence" is simply an expression (free to any one to make) of private personal appetite for evidence of a certain peculiar kind.

Now, when I speak of trusting our religious demands, just what do I mean by "trusting"? Is the word to carry with it license to define in detail an invisible world, and to anathematize and excommunicate those whose trust is different? Certainly not! Our faculties of belief were not primarily given us to make orthodoxies and heresies withal; they were given us to live by. And to trust our religious demands means first of all to live in the light of them, and to act as if the invisible world which they suggest were real. It is a fact of human nature, that men can live and die by the help of a sort of faith that goes without a single dogma or definition. The bare assurance that this natural order is not ultimate but a mere sign or vision, the external staging of a many-storied universe, in which spiritual forces have the last word and are eternal—this bare assurance is to such men enough to make life seem worth living in spite of every contrary presumption suggested by its circumstances on the natural plane. Destroy this inner assurance, however, vague as it is, and all the light and radiance of existence is extinguished for these persons at a stroke. Often enough the wild-eyed look at life—the suicidal mood—will then set in.

And now the application comes directly home to you and me. Probably to almost every one of us here the most adverse life would seem well worth living, if we only could be *certain* that our bravery and patience with it were terminating and eventuating and bearing fruit somewhere in an unseen spiritual world. But granting we are not certain, does it then follow that a bare trust in such a world is a fool's paradise and lubberland, or rather that it is a living attitude in which we are free to indulge? Well, we are free to trust at our own risks anything that is not impossible, and that can bring analogies to bear in its behalf. That the world of physics is probably not absolute, all the converging multitude of arguments that make in favor of idealism tend to prove; and that our whole physical life may lie soaking in a spiritual atmosphere, a dimension of being that we at present have no organ for apprehending, is vividly suggested to us by the analogy of the life of our domestic animals. Our dogs, for example, are in our human life but not of it. They witness hourly the outward body of events whose inner meaning cannot, by any possible operation, be revealed to their intelligence—events in which they themselves often play the cardinal part. My terrier bites a teasing boy, for example, and the father demands damages. The dog may be present at every step of the negotiations, and see the money paid, without an inkling of what it all means, without a suspicion that it has anything to do with *him;* and he never *can* know in his natural dog's life. Or take another case which used greatly to impress me in my medical-student days. Consider a poor dog whom they are vivisecting in a laboratory. He lies strapped on a board and shrieking at his executioners, and to his own dark consciousness is literally in a sort of hell. He cannot see a single redeeming ray in the whole business; and yet all these diabolical-seeming events are often controlled by human intentions with which, if his poor benighted mind could only be made to catch a glimpse of them, all that is heroic in him would religiously acquiesce. Healing truth, relief to future sufferings of beast and man, are to be bought by them. It may be genuinely a process of redemption. Lying on his back on the board there he may be performing a function incalculably higher than any that prosperous canine life admits of; and yet, of the whole performance, this function is the one portion that must remain absolutely beyond his ken.

Now turn from this to the life of man. In the dog's life we see the world invisible to him because we live in both worlds. In human life, although we only see our world, and his within it, yet encompassing both these worlds a still wider world may be there, as unseen by us as our world is by him; and to believe in that world *may* be the most essential function that our lives in this world have to perform. But *"may* be! *may* be!" one now hears the positivist contemptuously exclaim; "what use can a scientific life have for maybes?" Well, I reply, the "scientific" life itself has much to do with maybes, and human life at large has everything to do with them. So far as man stands for anything, and is productive or originative at all, his entire vital function may be said to have to deal with maybes. Not a victory is gained, not a deed of faithfulness or courage is done, except upon a maybe; not a service, not a sally of generosity, not a scientific exploration or experiment or textbook, that may not be a mistake. It is only by risking our persons from one hour to another that we live at all. And often enough our faith beforehand in an uncertified result *is the only thing that makes the result come true.* Suppose, for instance, you are climbing a mountain, and have worked yourself into a position from which the only escape is by a terrible leap. Have faith that you can successfully make it, and your feet are nerved to its accomplishment. But mistrust yourself, and think of all the sweet things you have heard the scientists say of *maybes*, and you will hesitate so long that, at least, all unstrung and trembling, and launching yourself in a moment of despair, you roll in the abyss. In such a case (and it belongs to an enormous class), the part of wisdom as well as of courage is to *believe what is in the line of your needs*, for only by such belief is the need fulfilled. Refuse to believe, and you shall indeed be right, for you shall irretrievably perish. But believe, and again you shall be right, for you shall save yourself. You make one or the other of two possible universes true by your trust or mistrust—both universes having been only *maybes*, in this particular, before you contributed your act.

Now, it appears to me that the question whether life is worth living is subject to conditions logically much like these. It does, indeed, depend on you *the liver*. If you surrender to the nightmare view and crown the evil edifice by your own suicide, you have indeed made a picture totally black. Pessimism, completed by your act, is true beyond a doubt, so far as your world goes. Your mistrust of life has removed whatever worth your own enduring existence might have given to it; and now, throughout the whole sphere of possible influence of that existence, the mistrust has proved itself to have had divining power. But suppose, on the other hand, that instead of giving way to the nightmare view you cling to it that this world is not the *ultimatum*. Suppose you find yourself a very well-spring, as Wordsworth says, of—

> Zeal, and the virtue to exist by faith
> As soldiers live by courage; as, by strength
> Of heart, the sailor fights with roaring seas.

Suppose, however thickly evils crowd upon you, that your unconquerable subjectivity proves to be their match, and that you find a more wonderful joy than any passive pleasure can bring in trusting ever in the larger whole. Have you not now made life worth living on these terms? What sort of a thing would life really be, with your qualities ready for a tussle with it, if it only brought fair weather and gave these higher faculties of yours no scope? Please remember that optimism and pessimism are definitions of the world, and that our own reactions on the world, small as they are in bulk, are integral parts of the whole thing, and necessarily help to determine the definition. They may even be the decisive elements in determining the definition. A large mass can have its unstable equilibrium overturned by the addition of a feather's weight; a long phrase may have its sense reversed by the addition of the three letters *n-o-t*. This life *is* worth living, we can say, *since it is what we make it, from the moral point of view;* and we are determined to make it from that point of view, so far as we have anything to do with it, a success.

Now, in this description of faiths that verify themselves I have assumed 10 that our faith in an invisible order is what inspires those efforts and that patience which make this visible order good for moral men. Our faith in the seen world's goodness (goodness now meaning fitness for successful moral and religious life) has verified itself by leaning on our faith in the unseen world. But will our faith in the unseen world similarly verify itself? Who knows?

Once more it is a case of *maybe;* and once more *maybes* are the essence of the situation. I confess that I do not see why the very existence of an invisible world may not in part depend on the personal response which any one of us may make to the religious appeal. God himself, in short, may draw vital strength and increase of very being from our fidelity. For my own part, I do not know what the sweat and blood and tragedy of this life mean, if they mean anything short of this. If this life be not a real fight, in which something is eternally gained for the universe by success, it is no better than a game of private theatricals from which one may withdraw at will. But it *feels* like a real fight— as if there were something really wild in the universe which we, with all our idealities and faithfulnesses, are needed to redeem; and first of all to redeem our own hearts from atheisms and fears. For such a half-wild, half-saved universe our nature is adapted. The deepest thing in our nature is the *Binnenleben* (as a German doctor lately has called it), this dumb region of the heart in which we dwell alone with our willingness and unwillingness, our faiths and fears. As through the cracks and crannies of caverns those waters exude from the earth's bosom which then form the fountain-heads of springs, so in these crepuscular depths of personality the sources of all our outer deeds and decisions take their rise. Here is our deepest organ of communication with the nature of things; and compared with these concrete movements of our soul all abstract statements and scientific arguments—the veto, for example, which the strict positivist pronounces upon our faith—sound to us like the mere chatterings of the teeth. For here possibilities, not finished facts, are the realities with which we have actively to deal; and to quote my friend William Salter, of the Philadelphia Ethical Society, "as the essence of courage is to stake one's life on a possibility, so the essence of faith is to believe that the possibility exists."

These, then, are my last words to you: Be not afraid of life. Believe that life *is* worth living, and your belief will help create the fact. The "scientific proof" that you are right may not be clear before the day of judgment (or some stage of being which that expression may serve to symbolize) is reached. But the faithful fighter of this hour, or the beings that then and there will represent them, may then turn to the faint-hearted, who here decline to go on, with words like those with which Henry IV[3] greeted the tardy Crillon after a great victory had been gained: "Hang yourself, brave Crillon! We fought at Arques, and you were not there."

[1897]

■ TOPICS FOR DISCUSSION AND WRITING

1. James says (paragraph 6) that, believing only in "the bare assurance that this natural order is not ultimate but a mere sign or vision . . . of a many-storied universe, in which spiritual forces have the last word," people can live and die by the help of a sort of faith that goes without a single dogma or definition. But what principles *would* guide such a believer? For instance, would such a believer necessarily have only one spouse? Or be charitable? Explain.

2. In 250 to 500 words, define what a "Christian" is and then discuss whether James can reasonably be called a Christian.

[3] At the Battle of Arques, 1589, Henry IV of France put down a rebellion.

■ JILL TWEEDIE

Jill Tweedie was born in 1936 of an English family in the Middle East. She grew up in England and then lived ten years in Canada before returning to England. The author of a novel and of books of essays (some of the essays have been collected under the title *It's Only Me*), she now lives in London and writes articles for the *Guardian*.

God the Mother Rules—OK?

Recently I read a snippet about women in the United States who were altering prayers and hymns by substituting Her for Him, Mother for Father and Goddess for God. Oh ho ho, did you ever, sniggered the writer. Put them in straitjackets and take them off to the funny farm.

One of the continuing small surprises for the enquiring atheist is the widespread ignorance of believers about their belief. A viewpoint peculiarly limited—parochial is, I suppose, the *mot juste*.[1] It is wildly unfair to say that if you picked the first avowed Christian off any pew and set him the religious equivalent of the 11-plus,[2] he would fail?

The one I picked was quite hot on the Church version of Jesus's life: who he was born to, where he was born, how he died and where he died, though in between was a bit of a blank, apart from a vague image of white robes, long hair, sheep and children. He knew about Judas and he listed three miracles, including the resurrection but he didn't know the number of apostles and only remembered five of their names. As to any historical realities of the time, nothing. The Sadducees, the Philistines, the Pharisees and the Samaritans were simply emotive words, the Old Testament an almost complete blank other than the bit about Moses in the cradle and parting the Red Sea. Nor had he any idea at all about the beliefs of the Jews (except that they killed Jesus, of course), the Buddhists, Islam, Taoism, Shintoism, Hinduism or any other ism. Religions that preceded Christianity? The Greeks had a lot of different gods and the Indians (Red) had the totem pole.

Indeed, without wishing to be unduly critical, my experience even of those who have taken up religion fulltime, priests and vicars, monks and nuns, is that though they may have a detailed knowledge of the mystical side of things, the mysteries, the ritual, the dogma, they are almost as ignorant as my random sample of historical realities. Which is, of course, not entirely accidental. Historical realities and, worse, historical perspectives, have a frightening way of shedding light and reason on corners that, to the believer, are best left dark.

That reporter from the States automatically assumed that his readers would join him in his titters at the absurdity of women who, not content with equal rights, are now pretending God could be female. He has, like most of us, the comforting idea that history started yesterday and will stay that way

---

[1] *Mot juste* exact word (French)
[2] 11-plus school examination

for ever. Because God and God's son are male today, so they always were and always will be, amen.

Brother, you couldn't be wronger. Slowly but surely a vast and ancient international jig-saw is being pieced together: antique temples here, swollen statues there, papyri drawings, carvings and writings from all over. And already the puzzle, half-finished though it is, is as exciting and significant as would be the revelation of a mother to a child who supposed itself an orphan from birth. Because it appears increasingly certain that a male God is an *arriviste,* a mere *nouveau riche*[3] upon the contemporary scene. Before Him, for literally thousands of years, disappearing back into the trackless wastes of pre-history, the people of the world shared one central figure of worship. A She, a Her, a Mother. The Goddess.

Merlin Stone, sculptor and art historian, has spent over 10 years on the trail of the Goddess and the results of her detective work in museums and ancient sites in the Near and Middle East have been published in *The Paradise Papers.* It makes a beautiful whole of many scattered clues until now undiscovered, ignored, misinterpreted, or—shamefully often—unacknowledged; an anthology of archaeological material that fairly bellows Ms Stone's central thesis. The impulse to worship came from the mystery of birth and the performer of that mystery, apparently entirely on her own, was woman.

So the explanation of a Goddess, the original Mother of humanity, came about as naturally and, when you think about it, as obviously as all the other apparent miracles of life and the Goddess was made manifest in the millions of statues, large and small, of big-bellied women. Statues we all know about and we have all been encouraged to dismiss as unimportant, mere fertility symbols, evidence only of cults, of strange rites practised in corners by heretics instead of what they surely are—endless variations of the same central belief held by many peoples over anything up to 25,000 years.

The face behind the clouds is a woman's face, women are her chosen priestesses and handmaidens and unto women shall go all kinship lines and rights of inheritance. Call her Ishtar in Babylon, Ashtoreth in Israel, Astarte in Phoenicia, Athar in Syria or Ate in Cicilia, call her what you will in the Mediterranean, the Near or the Middle East, even in old Ireland—by any other name she is the Goddess, the Queen of Heaven.

Ms Stone opines that the core of all theological thought is the quest for   10
the ultimate source of life and ancestry worship occurs (and occurred) among tribal people the world over. Add that fact to the observations of anthropologists like Margaret Mead and James Frazer—that in the most ancient human societies coitus was not linked with reproduction—and you have woman the life-giver, the sex that gives birth.

What, then, more logical than to posit a First Ancestress in the sky? Robertson Smith, writing of the precedence of the female deity among the Arab and Hebrew peoples, says: "It was the mother's, not the father's, blood which formed the original bond of kinship among the Semites as among other early people and in this stage of society, if the tribal deity was thought of as the parent of the stock, a goddess, not a god, would necessarily have been the object of worship."

[3] *arriviste . . . nouveau riche* upstart . . . one who has lately become rich (French)

How did women fare when the Goddess reigned in their lands? Merlin Stone brings together the researches of many archaeologists and anthropologist to find out and the answer is as predictable as it is revealing of the purpose of religion. If you have a God in heaven, men rule on earth. If you have a Goddess, women take charge. Diodorus of Sicily, observant traveller BC, reported that the ladies of Ethiopia carried arms, practised communal marriage and raised their children communally. Of the warrier women in Libya he says: "All authority was vested in the woman, who discharged every kind of public duty. The men looked after domestic affairs and did as they were told by their wives.

"They were not allowed to undertake war service or to exercise any functions of government or to fill any public office, such as might have given them more spirit to set themselves up against the women. The children were handed over immediately after birth to the men." Are you listening, Colonel Gaddafi?

Professor Cyrus Gordon, writing of life in ancient Egypt, says: "In family life women had a peculiarly important position for inheritance passed through the mother . . . this system may well hark back to prehistoric times when only the obvious relationship between mother and child was recognized." The message is as clear and as apposite today as ever. Though you gain power through error (the misunderstanding about the father's part in reproduction), once the system is working for you (matrilineal descent) you can hang on for a very long time in the face of the most damning facts. Patriarchal gods know all about this, too.

Mind you, in spite of probable male suppression under a goddess, there 15 is a plethora of evidence that the goddess made it well worth their while and that under her sexually permissive reign there were more tempting compensations for being a mere man than ever there were for a mere woman in a god's world. Subjugation, says the God, is your punishment. Subjugation, said the Goddess, can be fun. Because one thing is certain. It took eons of bloody struggle to put the Goddess down. They came out of the northern countries, those eventual victors, migrating in waves over perhaps a thousand, even three thousand years, to the lands of the Goddess, armed with their God and the realization that power for men could only come when a man knew his own son. And how could a man know his own son? By caging women, by making her male property, by scaring her into believing that all hell would break loose if *she* did, that only by cleaving to one man from virginity to death could she hope to save her soul by a male God's intervention.

So battle commenced, fought as much against the desires of many men as against the sexual freedom of women. All over the territories of the Goddess are the myths that mark the traces of that battle. For years I have wondered at the stories of men fighting dragons—what did a dragon represent, what was its factual origin? Merlin Stone drops in another piece of the puzzle. The snake (serpent, dragon) was the widespread Goddess symbol and the living companion of her priestesses. So what was St. George doing, fighting his dragon? He was the new religion fighting the old, the male squaring off with the female, an historical reality told in snake/man struggles in hundreds of nations and tribes from India to Turkey, from Babylon to Assyria, from Ireland to Israel and Jehovah's battle with the serpent Leviathan.

"But it was upon the last assaults by the Hebrews and eventually by the Christians of the first centuries after Christ that the religion ws finally suppressed and nearly forgotten," says Merlin Stone. The struggle rages still in the pages of the Bible, pages that as a girl amazed and fascinated me, with their constant emphasis on whores; whores of Babylon, whores of Sodom and Gomorrah, whores like Lilith and Jezebel, painted whores to be spurned by the sons and daughters of Israel. I had thought it then a sort of kink, a kind of mental aberration common to Jews and Christians. Not at all. The truth is far more tangible. The whore was the Garden, the old religion. The sin—adherence to the old religion. The real sin—ignorance of paternity, female promiscuity.

And that whole battle, so bitterly fought over so many years, produced as its apogee the fable of the Garden of Eden. There is the serpent, creature of the Goddess, of the old religion. There is Eve, the woman, handmaiden to the Goddess and traitress at the heart of the new religion, potentially promiscuous and, therefore, potentially the underminer of male power, of patrilineal descent. She must be warned, threatened, terrified in order to save Adam from the temptations of the Goddess. If she will not accept a male God and reject the Goddess, if she will not accept one man and one man only, all her life, she will be thrown out of Paradise and bear her children in agony.

It is all there in *The Paradise Papers* and, for me at least, Merlin Stone crystallizes what has all along been obvious, however submerged. Even today, in the dour Protestant religions, the last lingering trace of the Goddess (Mary, carefully a virgin) is hardly allowed to surface. The Catholics, always more opportunist, gave Mary her place in the sun but exacted from the ordinary women a terrible price for this concession.

Yesterday, I thought the leaders of all contemporary religions a blind and   20
prejudiced lot for their refusal to allow women any more power within their churches than the arrangement of flowers upon the altars. Now I know they are simply afraid, afraid that the Goddess may return from her long exile and take over again, and that is curiously comforting, an explanation from weakness rather than strength.

This, then, was the original battle of the sexes. A Goddess reigned for thousands of years, a God for two thousand. Shall we soon, perhaps, learn to do without either?

[1976]

■ TOPICS FOR DISCUSSION AND WRITING

1. In paragraph 3 Tweedie ridicules a Christian who didn't know the number of the apostles and could name only five. If you are a Christian, could you pass Tweedie's test? If you are a Christian and couldn't pass, would you agree that you are deficient in essential knowledge of the faith—or, on the other hand, would you argue that her test is invalid? (If you are a member of some faith other than Christianity, apply a comparable test to yourself.)

2. Drawing on the writing of Merlin Stone, in paragraph 7 Tweedie asserts that "The impulse to worship came from the mystery of birth, and the performer of that mystery, apparently entirely on her own, was woman."

Given the rest of Tweedie's essay, in an essay of 500 words explain why you are willing or not willing to accept this assertion.

FICTION

■ LUKE

Luke, the author of the third of the four Gospels, was a second-generation Christian, a fellow-worker with Paul. He probably was a Roman, though some early accounts refer to him as a Syrian; in any case, he wrote in Greek, probably composing the Gospel about A.D. 80–85. Jesus' Parable of the Prodigal Son (a parable is an extremely brief story from which a moral may be drawn) occurs only in this Gospel, in Chapter 15, verses 11–32.

The Parable of The Prodigal Son

And he said, "A certain man had two sons: and the younger of them said to his father, 'Father, give me a portion of goods that falleth to me.' And he divided unto them his living. And not many days after, the younger son gathered all together, and took his journey into a far country, and there wasted his substance with riotous living.

"And when he had spent all, there arose a mighty famine in that land, and he began to be in want. And he went and joined himself to a citizen of that country, and he sent him into his fields to feed swine. And he would fain have filled his belly with the husks that the swine did eat: and no man gave unto him. And when he came to himself, he said, 'How many hired servants of my father's have bread enough and to spare, and I perish with hunger? I will arise and go to my father, and will say unto him, "Father, I have sinned against heaven, and before thee, and am no more worthy to be called thy son: make me as one of thy hired servants."'

"And he arose, and came to his father. But when he was yet a great way off, his father saw him, and had compassion, and ran, and fell on his neck, and kissed him. And the son said unto him, 'Father, I have sinned against heaven, and in thy sight, and am no more worthy to be called thy son.' But the father said to his servants, 'Bring forth the best robe, and put it on him, and put a ring on his hand, and shoes on his feet. And bring hither the fatted calf, and kill it, and let us eat, and be merry. For this my son was dead, and is alive again; he was lost, and is found.' And they began to be merry.

"Now his elder son was in the field, and as he came and drew nigh to the house, he heard music and dancing. And he called one of the servants, and asked what these things meant. And he said unto him 'Thy brother is come, and thy father hath killed the fatted calf, because he hath received him safe and sound.' And he was angry, and would not go in: therefore came his father out, and entreated him. And he answering said to his father 'Lo, these many years do I serve thee, neither transgressed I at any time thy commandment, and yet thou never gavest me a kid, that I might make merry with friends: but as soon as this thy son was come, which hath devoured thy living with harlots, thou hast killed for him the fatted calf.' And he said unto him, 'Son, thou art ever with me, and all that I have is thine. It was meet that we should make merry, and be glad: for this thy brother was dead, and is alive again: and was lost, and is found.' "

■ TOPICS FOR DISCUSSION AND WRITING

1.   What is the function of the older brother? Characterize him, and compare him with the younger brother.
2.   Is the father foolish and sentimental? Do we approve or disapprove of his behavior at the end? Explain.

■ NATHANIEL HAWTHORNE

Nathaniel Hawthorne (1804–1864) was born in Salem, Massachusetts, the son of a sea captain. Two of his ancestors were judges; one had persecuted Quakers, and another had served at the Salem witch trials. After graduating from Bowdoin College in Maine he went back to Salem in order to write in relative seclusion. In 1831 he published "My Kinsman, Major Molineux"; in 1835 he published "Young Goodman Brown" and "The Maypole of Merry Mount"; and in 1837 he published "Dr. Heidegger's Experiment."

From 1839 to 1841 Hawthorne worked in the Boston Customs House and then spent a few months as a member of a communal society, Brook Farm. In 1842 he married. From 1846 to 1849 he was a surveyor at the Salem Customs House; from 1849 to 1850 he wrote *The Scarlet Letter,* the book that made him famous. From 1853 to 1857 he served as American consul in Liverpool, England, a plum awarded him in exchange for writing a campaign biography of a former college classmate, President Franklin Pierce. In 1860, after living in England and Italy, he returned to the United States, settling in Concord, Massachusetts.

In his stories and novels Hawthorne keeps returning to the Puritan past, studying guilt, sin, and isolation.

Young Goodman Brown

Young Goodman Brown came forth at sunset into the street at Salem village; but put his head back, after crossing the threshold, to exchange a parting kiss with his young wife. And Faith, as the wife was aptly named, thrust her own pretty head into the street, letting the wind play with the pink ribbons of her cap while she called to Goodman Brown.

"Dearest heart," whispered she, softly and rather sadly, when her lips were close to his ear, "prithee put off your journey until sunrise and sleep in your own bed to-night. A lone woman is troubled with such dreams and such thoughts that she's afeared of herself sometimes. Pray tarry with me this night, dear husband, of all nights in the year."

"My love and my Faith," replied young Goodman Brown, "of all nights in the year, this one night must I tarry away from thee. My journey, as thou callest it, forth and back again, must needs be done 'twixt now and sunrise. What, my sweet, pretty wife, dost thou doubt me already, and we but three months married?"

"Then God bless you!" said Faith, with the pink ribbons; "and may you find all well when you come back."

"Amen!" cried Goodman Brown. "Say thy prayers, dear Faith, and go to   5
bed at dusk, and no harm will come to thee."

So they parted; and the young man pursued his way until, being about to turn the corner by the meeting-house, he looked back and saw the head of Faith still peeping after him with a melancholy air, in spite of her pink ribbons.

"Poor little Faith!" thought he, for his heart smote him. "What a wretch am I to leave her on such an errand! She talks of dreams, too. Methought as she spoke there was trouble in her face, as if a dream had warned her what work is to be done to-night. But no, no; 'twould kill her to think it. Well, she's a blessed angel on earth; and after this one night I'll cling to her skirts and follow her to heaven."

With this excellent resolve for the future, Goodman Brown felt himself justified in making more haste on his present evil purpose. He had taken a dreary road, darkened by all the gloomiest trees of the forest, which barely stood aside to let the narrow path creep through, and closed immediately behind. It was all as lonely as could be; and there is this peculiarity in such a solitude, that the traveler knows not who may be concealed by the innumerable trunks and the thick boughs overhead; so that with lonely footsteps he may yet be passing through an unseen multitude.

"There may be a devilish Indian behind every tree," said Goodman Brown to himself; and he glanced fearfully behind him as he added, "What if the devil himself should be at my very elbow!"

His head being turned back, he passed a crook of the road, and, looking   10
forward again, beheld the figure of a man, in grave and decent attire, seated at the foot of an old tree. He arose at Goodman Brown's approach and walked onward side by side with him.

"You are late, Goodman Brown," said he. "The clock of the Old South was striking as I came through Boston, and that is full fifteen minutes agone."

"Faith kept me back a while," replied the young man, with a tremor in his voice, caused by the sudden appearance of his companion, though not wholly unexpected.

It was now deep dusk in the forest, and deepest in that part of it where these two were journeying. As nearly as could be discerned, the second traveller was about fifty years old, apparently in the same rank of life as Goodman Brown, and bearing a considerable resemblance to him, though perhaps more in expression than features. Still they might have been taken for father and son. And yet, though the elder person was as simply clad as the younger, and as simple in manner too, he had an indescribable air of one who knew the world, and who would not have felt abashed at the governor's dinner table or in King William's court, were it possible that his affairs should call him thither. But the only thing about him that could be fixed upon as remarkable was his staff, which bore the likeness of a great black snake, so curiously wrought that it might almost be seen to twist and wriggle itself like a living serpent. This, of course, must have been an ocular deception, assisted by the uncertain light.

"Come, Goodman Brown," cried his fellow-traveller, "this is a dull pace for the beginning of a journey. Take my staff, if you are so soon weary."

"Friend," said the other, exchanging his slow pace for a full stop, "Having 15 kept covenant by meeting thee here, it is my purpose now to return whence I came. I have scruples touching the matter thou wot'st of."

"Sayest thou so?" replied he of the serpent, smiling apart. "Let us walk on, nevertheless, reasoning as we go; and if I convince thee not thou shalt turn back. We are but a little way in the forest yet."

"Too far! too far!" exclaimed the goodman, unconsciously resuming his walk. "My father never went into the woods on such an errand, nor his father before him. We have been a race of honest men and good Christians since the days of the martyrs; and shall I be the first of the name of Brown that ever took this path and kept—"

"Such company, thou wouldst say," observed the elder person, interpreting his pause. "Well said, Goodman Brown! I have been as well acquainted with your family as with ever a one among the Puritans; and that's no trifle to say. I helped your grandfather, the constable, when he lashed the Quaker woman so smartly through the streets of Salem; and it was I that brought your father a pitch-pine knot, kindled at my own hearth, to set fire to an Indian village, in King Philip's war. They were my good friends, both; and many a pleasant walk have we had along this path, and returned merrily after midnight. I would fain be friends with you for their sake."

"If it be as thou sayest," replied Goodman Brown, "I marvel they never spoke of these matters; or, verily, I marvel not, seeing that the least rumor of the sort would have driven them from New England. We are a people of prayer, and good works to boot, and abide no such wickedness."

"Wickedness or not," said the traveller with the twisted staff, "I have a 20 very general acquaintance here in New England. The deacons of many a church have drunk the communion wine with me; the selectmen of divers towns make me their chairman; and a majority of the Great and General Court are firm supporters of my interest. The governor and I, too—But these are state secrets."

"Can this be so?" cried Goodman Brown, with a stare of amazement at his undisturbed companion. "Howbeit, I have nothing to do with the governor and council; they have their own ways, and are no rule for a simple husbandman like me. But, were I to go on with thee, how should I meet the eye of that good old man, our minister, at Salem village? Oh, his voice would make me tremble both Sabbath day and lecture day."

Thus far the elder traveller had listened with due gravity; but now burst into a fit of irrepressible mirth, shaking himself so violently that his snakelike staff actually seemed to wriggle in sympathy.

"Ha! ha! ha!" shouted he again and again; then composing himself, "Well, go on, Goodman Brown, go on; but, prithee, don't kill me with laughing."

"Well, then, to end the matter at once," said Goodman Brown, considerably nettled, "there is my wife, Faith. It would break her dear little heart; and I'd rather break my own."

"Nay, if that be the case," answered the other, "e'en go thy ways, Good- 25 man Brown. I would not for twenty old women like the one hobbling before us that Faith should come to any harm."

As he spoke he pointed his staff at a female figure on the path, in whom Goodman Brown recognized a very pious and exemplary dame, who had taught him his catechism in youth, and was still his moral and spiritual adviser, jointly with the minister and Deacon Gookin.

"A marvel, truly, that Goody Cloyse should be so far in the wilderness at nightfall," said he. "But with your leave, friend, I shall take a cut through the woods until we have left this Christian woman behind. Being a stranger to you, she might ask whom I was consorting with and whither I was going."

"Be it so," said his fellow-traveller. "Betake you the woods, and let me keep the path."

Accordingly the young man turned aside, but took care to watch his companion, who advanced softly along the road until he had come within a staff's length of the old dame. She, meanwhile, was making the best of her way, with singular speed for so aged a woman, and mumbling some indistinct words—a prayer, doubtless—as she went. The traveller put forth his staff and touched her withered neck with what seemed the serpent's tail.

"The devil!" screamed the pious old lady. 30

"Then Good Cloyse knows her old friend?" observed the traveller, confronting her and leaning on his writhing stick.

"Ah, forsooth, and is it your worship indeed?" cried the good dame. "Yea, truly is it, and in the very image of my old gossip, Goodman Brown, the grandfather of the silly fellow that now is. But—would your worhsip believe it?—my broomstick hath strangely disappeared, stolen, as I suspect, by that unhanged witch, Goody Cory, and that, too, when I was all anointed with the juice of smallage, and cinquefoil, and wolf's bane—"

"Mingled with fine wheat and the fat of a new-born babe," said the shape of old Goodman Brown.

"Ah, your worship knows the recipe," cried the old lady, cackling aloud. "So, as I was saying, being all ready for the meeting, and no horse to ride on, I made up my mind to foot it; for they tell me there is a nice young man to be taken into communion to-night. But now your good worship will lend me your arm, and we shall be there in a twinkling."

"That can hardly be," answered her friend. "I may not spare you my arm, 35 Goody Cloyse; but here is my staff, if you will."

So saying, he threw it down at her feet, where, perhaps, it assumed life, being one of the rods which its owner had formerly lent to the Egyptian magi. Of this fact, however, Goodman Brown could not take cognizance. He had cast up his eyes in astonishment, and, looking down again, beheld neither Goody Cloyse nor the serpentine staff, but his fellow-traveller alone, who waited for him as calmly as if nothing had happened.

"That old woman taught me my catechism," said the young man; and there was a world of meaning in this simple comment.

They continued to walk onward, while the elder traveller exhorted his companion to make good speed and persevere in the path, discoursing so aptly that his arguments seemed rather to spring up in the bosom of his auditor than to be suggested by himself. As they went, he plucked a branch of maple to serve for a walking stick, and began to strip it of the twigs and the little boughs, which were wet with evening dew. The moment his fingers touched them they became strangely withered and dried up as with a week's sunshine. Thus the pair proceeded, at a good free pace, until suddenly, in a gloomy hollow of the road, Goodman Brown sat himself down on the stump of a tree and refused to go any farther.

"Friend," said he, stubbornly, "my mind is made up. Not another step will I budge on this errand. What if a wretched old woman do choose to go to the devil when I thought she was going to heaven: is that any reason why I should quit my dear Faith and go after her?"

"You will think better of this by and by," said his acquaintance, composed- 40 ly. "Sit here and rest yourself a while; and when you feel like moving again, there is my staff to help you along."

Without more words, he threw his companion the maple stick, and was as speedily out of sight as if he had vanished into the deepening gloom. The young man sat a few moments by the roadside, applauding himself greatly, and thinking with how clear a conscience he should meet the minister in his morning walk, nor shrink from the eye of good old Deacon Gookin. And what calm sleep would be his that very night, which was to have been spent so wickedly, but so purely and sweetly now, in the arms of Faith! Amidst these pleasant and praiseworthy meditations, Goodman Brown heard the tramp of horses along the road, and deemed it advisable to conceal himself within the verge of the forest, conscious of the guilty purpose that had brought him thither, though now so happily turned from it.

On came the hoof tramps and the voices of the riders, two grave old voices, conversing soberly as they drew near. These mingled sounds appeared to pass along the road, within a few yards of the young man's hiding-place; but, owing doubtless to the depth of the gloom at that particular spot, neither the travellers nor their steeds were visible. Though their figures brushed the small boughs by the wayside, it could not be seen that they intercepted, even for a moment, the faint gleam from the strip of bright sky athwart which they must have passed. Goodman Brown alternately crouched and stood on tiptoe, pulling aside the branches and thrusting forth his head as far as he durst without discerning so much as a shadow. It vexed him the more, because he could have sworn, were such a thing possible, that he recognized the voices of the minister and Deacon Gookin, jogging along quietly, as they were wont to do, when bound to some ordination or ecclesiastical council. While yet within hearing, one of the riders stopped to pluck a switch.

"Of the two, reverend sir," said the voice like the deacon's, "I had rather miss an ordination dinner than to-night's meeting. They tell me that some of our community are to be here from Falmouth and beyond, and others from Connecticut and Rhode Island, besides several of the Indian powwows, who, after their fashion, know almost as much deviltry as the best of us. Moreover, there is a goodly young woman to be taken into communion."

"Mighty well, Deacon Gookin!" replied the solemn old tones of the minister. "Spur up, or we shall be late. Nothing can be done, you know, until I get on the ground."

The hoofs clattered again; and the voices, talking so strangely in the 45 empty air, passed on through the forest, where no church had ever been gathered or solitary Christian prayed. Whither, then, could these holy men be journeying so deep into the heathen wilderness? Young Goodman Brown caught hold of a tree for support, being ready to sink down on the ground, faint and overburdened with the heavy sickness of his heart. He looked up to the sky, doubting whether there really was a heaven above him. Yet there was the blue arch, and the stars brightening in it.

"With heaven above and Faith below, I will yet stand firm against the devil!" cried Goodman Brown.

While he still gazed upward into the deep arch of the firmament and had lifted his hands to pray, a cloud, though no wind was stirring, hurried across the zenith and hid the brightening stars. The blue sky was still visible, except directly overhead, where this black mass of cloud was sweeping swiftly north-ward. Aloft in the air, as if from the depths of the cloud, came a confused and doubtful sound of voices. Once the listener fancied that he could distinguish the accents of townspeople of his own, men and women, both pious and un-godly, many of whom he had met at the communion table, and had seen others rioting at the tavern. The next moment, so indistinct were the sounds, he doubted whether he had heard aught but the murmur of the old forest, whispering without a wind. Then came a stronger swell of those familiar tones, heard daily in the sunshine at Salem village, but never until now from a cloud of night. There was one voice, of a young woman, uttering lamenta-tions, yet with an uncertain sorrow, and entreating for some favor, which, perhaps, it would grieve her to obtain; and all the unseen multitude, both saints and sinners, seemed to encourage her onward.

"Faith!" shouted Goodman Brown, in a voice of agony and desperation; and the echoes of the forest mocked him, crying, "Faith! Faith!" as if bewil-derd wretches were seeking her all through the wilderness.

The cry of grief, rage, and terror was yet piercing the night, when the unhappy husband held his breath for a response. There was a scream, drowned immediately in a louder murmur of voices, fading into far-off laugh-ter, as the dark cloud swept away, leaving the clear and silent sky above Good-man Brown. But something fluttered lightly down through the air and caught on the branch of a tree. The young man seized it, and beheld a pink ribbon.

"My Faith is gone!" cried he, after one stupefied moment. "There is no 50 good on earth; and sin is but a name. Come, devil; for to thee is this world given."

And, maddened with despair, so that he laughed loud and long, did Good-man Brown grasp his staff and set forth again, at such a rate that he seemed to fly along the forest path rather than to walk or run. The road grew wilder and drearier and more faintly traced, and vanished at length, leaving him in the heart of the dark wilderness, still rushing onward with the instinct that guides mortal man to evil. The whole forest was peopled with frightful sounds—the creaking of the trees, the howling of wild beasts, and the yell of Indians; while sometimes the wind tolled like a distant church bell, and sometimes gave a broad roar around the traveller, as if all Nature were laughing him to scorn. But he was himself the chief horror of the scene, and shrank not from its other horrors.

"Ha! ha! ha!" roared Goodman Brown when the wind laughed at him. "Let us hear which will laugh loudest. Think not to frighten me with your deviltry. Come witch, come wizard, come Indian powwow, come devil himself, and here comes Goodman Brown. You may as well fear him as he fear you."

In truth, all through the haunted forest there could be nothing more frightful than the figure of Goodman Brown. On he flew among the black pines, brandishing his staff with frenzied gestures, now giving vent to an inspiration of horrid blasphemy, and now shouting forth such laughter as set all the echoes of the forest laughing like demons around him. The fiend in his own shape is less hideous than when he rages in the breast of man. Thus sped the demoniac on his course, until, quivering among the trees, he saw a red light before him, as when the felled trunks and branches of a clearing have been set on fire, and throw up their lurid blaze against the sky, at the hour of midnight. He paused, in a lull of the tempest that had driven him onward, and heard the swell of what seemed a hymn, rolling solemnly from a distance with the weight of many voices. He knew the tune; it was a familiar one in the choir of the village meeting-house. The verse died heavily away, and was lengthened by a chorus, not of human voices, but of all the sounds of the benighted wilderness pealing in awful harmony together. Goodman Brown cried out, and his cry was lost to his own ear by its unison with the cry of the desert.

In the interval of silence he stole forward until the light glared full upon his eyes. At one extremity of an open space, hemmed in by the dark wall of the forest, arose a rock, bearing some rude, natural resemblance either to an altar or a pulpit, and surrounded by four blazing pines, their tops aflame, their stems untouched, like candles at an evening meeting. The mass of foliage that had overgrown the summit of the rock was all on fire, blazing high into the night and fitfully illuminating the whole field. Each pendent twig and leafy festoon was in a blaze. As the red light arose and fell, a numerous congregation alternately shone forth, then disappeared in shadow, and again grew, as it were, out of the darkness, peopling the heart of the solitary woods at once.

"A grave and dark-clad company," quoth Goodman Brown.   55

In truth they were such. Among them, quivering to and fro between gloom and splendor, appeared faces that would be seen next day at the council board of the province, and others which, Sabbath after Sabbath, looked devoutly heavenward, and benignantly over the crowded pews, from the holiest pulpits in the land. Some affirm that the lady of the governor was there. At least three were high dames well known to her, and wives of honored husbands, and widows, a great multitude, and ancient maidens, all of excellent repute, and fair young girls, who trembled lest their mothers should espy them. Either the sudden gleams of light flashing over the obscure field bedazzled Goodman Brown, or he recognized a score of the church members of Salem village famous for their especial sanctity. Good old Deacon Gookin had arrived, and waited at the skirts of that venerable saint, his revered pastor. But, irreverently consorting with these grave, reputable, and pious people, these elders of the church, these chaste dames and dewy virgins, there were men of dissolute lives and women of spotted fame, wretches given over to all mean and filthy vice, and suspected even of horrid crimes. It was strange to see that the good shrank not from the wicked, nor were the sinners abashed by the saints. Scattered also among their pale-faced enemies were the Indian priests, or powwows, who had often scared their native forest with more hideous incantations than any known to English witchcraft.

"But where is Faith?" thought Goodman Brown; and, as hope came into his heart, he trembled.

Another verse of the hymn arose, a slow and mournful strain, such as the pious love, but joined to words which expresed all that our nature can conceive of sin, and darkly hinted at far more. Unfathomable to mere mortals is the lore of fiends. Verse after verse was sung; and still the chorus of the desert swelled between like the deepest tone of a mighty organ; and with the final peal of that dreadful anthem there came a sound, as if the roaring wind, the rushing streams, the howling beasts, and every other voice of the unconcerted wilderness were mingling and according with the voice of guilty man in homage to the prince of all. The four blazing pines threw up a loftier flame, and obscurely discovered shapes and visages of horror on the smoke wreaths above the impious assembly. At the same moment the fire on the rock shot redly forth and formed a glowing arch above its base, where now appeared a figure. With reverence be it spoken, the figure bore no slight similitude, both in garb and manner, to some grave divine of the New England churches.

"Bring forth the converts!" cried a voice that echoed through the field and rolled into the forest.

At the word, Goodman Brown stepped forth from the shadow of the 60 trees and approached the congregation, with whom he felt a loathful brotherhood by the sympathy of all that has wicked in his heart. He could have wellnigh sworn that the shape of his own dead father beckoned him to advance, looking downard from a smoke wreath, while a woman, with dim features of despair, threw out her hand to warn him back. Was it his mother? But he had no power to retreat one step, nor to resist, even in thought, when the minister and good old Deacon Gookin seized his arms and led him to the blazing rock. Thither came also the slender form of a veiled female, led between Goody Cloyse, that pious teacher of the catechism, and Martha Carrier, who had received the devil's promise to be queen of hell. A rampant hag was she. And there stood the proselytes beneath the canopy of fire.

"Welcome, my children," said the dark figure, "to the communion of your race. Ye have found thus young your nature and your destiny. My children, look behind you!"

They turned; and flashing forth, as it were, in a sheet of flame, the fiend worshippers were seen; the smile of welcome gleamed darkly on every visage.

"There," resumed the sable form, "are all whom ye have reverenced from youth. Ye deemed them holier than yourselves, and shrank from your own sin, contrasting it with their lives of righteousness and prayerful aspirations heavenward. Yet here are they all in my worshipping assembly. This night it shall be granted you to know their secret deeds: how hoary-bearded elders of the church have whispered wanton words to the young maids of their households; how many a woman, eager for widows' weeds, has given her husband a drink at bedtime and let him sleep his last sleep in her bosom; how beardless youths have made haste to inherit their fathers' wealth; and how fair damsels—blush not, sweet ones—have dug little graves in the garden, and bidden me, the sole guest, to an infant's funeral. By the sympathy of your human hearts for sin ye shall scent out all the places—whether in church, bed-chamber, street, field, or forest—where crime has been committed, and shall exult to behold the whole earth one stain of guilt, one mighty blood spot. Far more than this. It shall be yours to penetrate, in every bosom, the deep mystery of sin, the fountain of all wicked arts, and which inexhaustibly supplies more evil impulses than human power—than my power at its utmost—can make manifest in deeds. And now, my children, look upon each other."

They did so; and, by the blaze of the hell-kindled torches, the wretched man beheld his Faith, and the wife her husband, trembling before that unhallowed altar.

"Lo, there ye stand, my children," said the figure, in a deep and solemn   65
tone, almost sad with its despairing awfulness, as if his once angelic nature could yet mourn for our miserable race. "Depending upon one another's hearts, ye had still hoped that virtue were not all a dream. Now are ye undeceived. Evil is the nature of mankind. Evil must be your only happiness. Welcome again, my children, to the communion of your race."

"Welcome," repeated the fiend worshippers, in one cry of despair and triumph.

And there they stood, the only pair, as it seemed, who were yet hesitating on the verge of wickedness in this dark world. A basin was hollowed, naturally, in the rock. Did it contain water, reddened by the lurid light? or was it blood? or, perchance, a liquid flame? Herein did the shape of evil dip his hand and prepare to lay the mark of baptism upon their foreheads, that they might be partakers of the mystery of sin, more conscious of the secret guilt of others, both in deed and thought, than they could now be of their own. The husband cast one look at his pale wife, and Faith at him. What polluted wretches would the next glance show them to each other, shuddering alike at what they disclosed and what they saw!

"Faith! Faith!" cried the husband, "look up to heaven, and resist the wicked one."

Whether Faith obeyed he knew not. Hardly had he spoken when he found himself amid calm night and solitude, listening to a roar of the wind which died heavily away through the forest. He staggered against the rock, and felt it chill and damp; while a hanging twig, that had been all on fire, besprinkled his cheek with the coldest dew.

The next morning young Goodman Brown came slowly into the street of 70 Salem village, staring around him like a bewildered man. The good old minister was taking a walk along the graveyard to get the appetite for breakfast and meditate his sermon, and bestowed a blessing, as he passed, on Goodman Brown. He shrank from the venerable saint as if to avoid an anathema. Old Deacon Gookin was at domestic worship, and the holy words of his prayer were heard through the open window. "What God doth the wizard pray to?" quoth Goodman Brown. Goody Cloyse, that excellent old Christian, stood in the early sunshine at her own lattice, catechizing a little girl who had brought her a pint of morning's milk. Goodman Brown snatched away the child as from the grasp of the fiend himself. Turning the corner by the meeting-house, he spied the head of Faith, with the pink ribbons, gazing anxiously forth, and bursting into such joy at sight of him that she skipped along the street and almost kissed her husband before the whole village. But Goodman Brown looked sternly and sadly into her face, and passed on without a greeting.

Had Goodman Brown fallen asleep in the forest and only dreamed a wild dream of a witch-meeting?

Be it so if you will; but alas! it was a dream of evil omen for young Goodman Brown. A stern, a sad, a darkly meditative, a distrustful, if not a desperate man did he become from the night of that fearful dream. On the Sabbath day, when the congregation were singing a holy psalm, he could not listen because an anthem of sin rushed loudly upon his ear and drowned all the blessed strain. When the minister spoke from the pulpit and power and fervid eloquence, and, with his hand on the open Bible, of the sacred truths of our religion, and of saint-like lives and triumphant deaths, and of future bliss or misery unutterable, then did Goodman Brown turn pale, dreading lest the roof should thunder down upon the gray blasphemer and his hearers. Often, awaking suddenly at midnight, he shrank from the bosom of Faith; and at mourning or eventide, when the family knelt down at prayer, he scowled and muttered to himself, and gazed sternly at his wife, and turned away. And when he had lived long, and was borne to his grave a hoary corpse, followed by Faith, an aged woman, and children and grandchildren, a goodly procession, besides neighbors not a few, they carved no hopeful verse upon his tombstone, for his dying hour was gloom.

[1835]

■ TOPICS FOR DISCUSSION AND WRITING

1. What do you think Hawthorne gains (or loses) by the last sentence?
2. Evaluate the view that when Young Goodman Brown enters the dark forest he is really entering his own evil mind. Why, by the way, does he go into the forest at night? (Hawthorne gives no explicit reason, but you may want to offer a conjecture.)
3. In a sentence or two summarize the plot, and then in another sentence or two state the theme of the story. (On theme, see pages 119–120.)

4.   If you have undergone a religious experience, write an essay discussing your condition before, during, and after the experience.

■ KATHERINE ANNE PORTER

Katherine Anne Porter (1890–1980) had the curious habit of inventing details in her life, but it is true that she was born in a log cabin in Indian Creek, Texas, that she was originally named Callie Russell Porter, that her mother died when the child was 2 years old, and that Callie was brought up by her maternal grandmother in Kyle, Texas. She was sent to convent schools, where, in her words, she received a "strangely useless and ornamental education." When she was 16 she left school, married (and soon divorced), and worked as a reporter, first in Texas and later in Denver and Chicago. She moved around a good deal, both within the United States and abroad; she lived for a while in Mexico, Belgium, Switzerland, France, and Germany.

Even as a child she was interested in writing, but she did not publish her first story until she was 33. She wrote essays and one novel (*Ship of Fools*), but she is best known for her stories. Porter's *Collected Stories* won the Pulitzer Prize and the National Book Award in 1965.

The Jilting of Granny Weatherall

She flicked her wrist neatly out of Doctor Harry's pudgy careful fingers and pulled the sheet up to her chin. The brat ought to be in knee breeches. Doctoring around the country with spectacles on his nose! "Get along now, take your schoolbooks and go. There's nothing wrong with me."

Doctor Harry spread a warm paw like a cushion on her forehead where the forked green vein danced and made her eyelids twitch. "Now, now, be a good girl, and we'll have you up in no time."

"That's no way to speak to a woman nearly eighty years old just because she's down. I'd have you respect your elders, young man."

"Well, Missy, excuse me." Doctor Harry patted her cheek. "But I've got to warn you, haven't I? You're a marvel, but you must be careful or you're going to be good and sorry."

"Don't tell me what I'm going to be. I'm on my feet now, morally speak-   5 ing. It's Cornelia. I had to go to bed to get rid of her."

Her bones felt loose, and floated around in her skin, and Doctor Harry floated like a balloon around the foot of the bed. He floated and pulled down his waistcoat and swung his glasses on a cord. "Well, stay where you are, it certainly can't hurt you."

"Get along and doctor your sick," said Granny Weatherall. "Leave a well woman alone. I'll call for you when I want you. . . . Where were you forty years ago when I pulled through milk-leg and double pneumonia? You weren't even born. Don't let Cornelia lead you on," she shouted, because Doctor Harry appeared to float up to the ceiling and out. "I pay my own bills, and I don't throw my money away on nonsense!"

She meant to wave good-bye, but it was too much trouble. Her eyes closed of themselves, it was like a dark curtain drawn around the bed. The pillow rose and floated under her, pleasant as a hammock in a light wind. She listened to the leaves rustling outside the window. No, somebody was swishing newspapers: no, Cornelia and Doctor Harry were whispering together. She leaped broad awake, thinking they whispered in her ear.

"She was never like this, *never* like this!" "Well, what can we expect?" "Yes, eighty years old. . . ."

Well, and what if she was? She still had ears. It was like Cornelia to 10 whisper around doors. She always kept things secret in such a public way. She was always being tactful and kind. Cornelia was dutiful; that was the trouble with her. Dutiful and good: "So good and dutiful," said Granny, "and I'd like to spank her." She saw herself spanking Cornelia and making a fine job of it.

"What'd you say, Mother?"

Granny felt her face tying up in hard knots.

"Can't a body think, I'd like to know?"

"I thought you might want something."

"I do. I want a lot of things. First off, go away and don't whisper." 15

She lay and drowsed, hoping in her sleep that the children would keep out and let her rest a minute. It had been a long day. Not that she was tired. It was always pleasant to snatch a minute now and then. There was always so much to be done, let me see: tomorrow.

Tomorrow was far away and there was nothing to trouble about. Things were finished somehow when the time came; thank God there was always a little margin over for peace; then a person could spread out the plan of life and tuck in the edges orderly. It was good to have everything clean and folded away, with the hair brushes and tonic bottles sitting straight on the white embroidered linen: the day started without fuss and the pantry shelves laid out with rows of jelly glasses and brown jugs and white stone-china jars and blue whirligigs and words painted on them: coffee, tea, sugar, ginger, cinnamon, allspice: and the bronze clock with the lion on top nicely dusted off. The dust that lion could collect in twenty-four hours! The box in the attic with all those letters tied up, she'd have to go through that tomorrow. All those letters— George's letters and John's letters and her letters to them both—lying around for the children to find afterwards made her uneasy. Yes, that would be tomorrow's business. No use to let them know how silly she had been once.

While she was rummaging around she found death in her mind and it felt clammy and unfamiliar. She had spent so much time preparing for death there was no need for bringing it up again. Let it take care of itself now. When she was sixty she had felt very old, finished, and went around making farewell trips to see her children and grandchildren, with a secret in her mind: This is the very last of your mother, children! Then she made her will and came down with a long fever. That was all just a notion like a lot of other things, but it was lucky too, for she had once for all got over the idea of dying for a long time. Now she couldn't be worried. She hoped she had better sense now. Her father had lived to be one hundred and two years old and had drunk a noggin of strong hot toddy at his last birthday. He told the reporters it was his daily habit, and he owed his long life to that. He had made quite a scandal and was very pleased about it. She believed she'd just plague Cornelia a little.

"Cornelia! Cornelia!" No footsteps, but a sudden hand on her cheek. "Bless you, where have you been?"

"Here, Mother."   20

"Well, Cornelia, I want a noggin of hot toddy."

"Are you cold, darling?"

"I'm chilly, Cornelia. Lying in bed stops the circulation. I must have told you that a thousand times."

Well, she could just hear Cornelia telling her husband that Mother was getting a little childish and they'd have to humor her. The thing that most annoyed her was that Cornelia thought she was deaf, dumb, and blind. Little hasty glances and tiny gestures tossed around her and over her head saying, "Don't cross her, let her have her way, she's eighty years old," and she sitting there as if she lived in a thin glass cage. Sometimes Granny almost made up her mind to pack up and move back to her own house where nobody could remind her every minute that she was old. Wait, wait, Cornelia, till your own children whisper behind your back!

In her day she had kept a better house and had got more work done. She   25 wasn't too old yet for Lydia to be driving eighty miles for advice when one of the children jumped the track, and Jimmy still dropped in and talked things over: "Now, Mammy, you've a good business head, I want to know what you think of this? . . ." Old. Cornelia couldn't change the furniture around without asking. Little things, little things! They had been so sweet when they were little. Granny wished the old days were back again with the children young and everything to be done over. It had been a hard pull, but not too much for her. When she thought of all the food she had cooked, and all the clothes she had cut and sewed, and all the gardens she had made—well, the children showed it. There they were, made out of her, and they couldn't get away from that. Sometimes she wanted to see John again and point to them and say, Well, I didn't do so badly, did I? But that would have to wait. That was for tomorrow. She used to think of him as a man, but now all the children were older than their father, and he would be a child beside her if she saw him now. It seemed strange and there was something wrong in the idea. Why, he couldn't possibly recognize her. She had fenced in a hundred acres once, digging the post holes herself and clamping the wires with just a negro boy to help. That changed a woman. John would be looking for a young woman with the peaked Spanish comb in her hair and the painted fan. Digging post holes changed a woman. Riding country roads in the winter when women had their babies was another thing: sitting up nights with sick horses and sick negroes and sick children and hardly ever losing one. John, I hardly ever lost one of them! John would see that in a minute, that would be something he could understand, she wouldn't have to explain anything!

It made her feel like rolling up her sleeves and putting the whole place to rights again. No matter if Cornelia was determined to be everywhere at once, there were a great many things left undone on this place. She would start tomorrow and do them. It was good to be strong enough for everything, even if all you made melted and changed and slipped under your hands, so that by the time you finished you almost forgot what you were working for. What was it I set out to do? she asked herself intently, but she could not remember. A fog rose over the valley, she saw it marching across the creek swallowing the trees and moving up the hill like an army of ghosts. Soon it would be at the near edge of the orchard, and then it was time to go in and light the lamps. Come in, children, don't stay out in the night air.

Lighting the lamps had been beautiful. The children huddled up to her and breathed like little calves waiting at the bars in the twilight. Their eyes followed the match and watched the flame rise and settle in a blue curve, then they moved away from her. The lamp was lit, they didn't have to be scared and hang on to mother any more. Never, never, never more. God, for all my life I thank Thee. Without Thee, my God, I could never have done it. Hail, Mary, full of grace.

I want you to pick all the fruit this year and see that nothing is wasted. There's always someone who can use it. Don't let good things rot for want of using. You waste life when you waste good food. Don't let things get lost. It's bitter to lose things. Now, don't let me get to thinking, not when I am tired and taking a little nap before supper. . . .

The pillow rose about her shoulders and pressed against her heart and the memory was being squeezed out of it: oh, push down that pillow, somebody: it would smother her if she tried to hold it. Such a fresh breeze blowing and such a green day with no threats in it. But he had not come, just the same. What does a woman do when she has put on the white veil and set out the white cake for a man and he doesn't come? She tried to remember. No, I swear he never harmed me but in that. He never harmed me but in that . . . and what if he did? There was the day, the day, but a whirl of dark smoke rose and covered it, crept up and over into the bright field where everything was planted so carefully in orderly rows. That was hell, she knew hell when she saw it. For sixty years she had prayed against remembering him and against losing her soul in the deep pit of hell, and now the two things were mingled in one and the thought of him was a smoky cloud from hell that moved and crept in her head when she had just got rid of Doctor Harry and was trying to rest a minute. Wounded vanity, Ellen, said a sharp voice in the top of her mind. Don't let your wounded vanity get the upper hand of you. Plenty of girls get jilted. You were jilted, weren't you? Then stand up to it. Her eyelids wavered and let in streamers of blue-gray light like tissue paper over her eyes. She must get up and pull the shades down or she'd never sleep. She was in bed again and the shades were not down. How could that happen? Better turn over, hide from the light, sleeping in the light gave you nightmares. "Mother, how do you feel now?" and a stinging wetness on her forehead. But I don't like having my face washed in cold water!

Hapsy? George? Lydia? Jimmy? No, Cornelia, and her features were swollen and full of little puddles. "They're coming, darling, they'll all be here soon." Go wash your face, child, you look funny.

Instead of obeying, Cornelia knelt down and put her head on the pillow. She seemed to be talking but there was no sound. "Well, are you tongue-tied? Whose birthday is it? Are you going to give a party?"

Cornelia's mouth moved urgently in strange shapes. "Don't do that, you bother me, daughter."

"Oh, no, Mother. Oh, no. . . ."

Nonsense. It was strange about children. They disputed your every word. "No what, Cornelia?"

"Here's Doctor Harry."   35

"I won't see that boy again. He just left five minutes ago."

"That was this morning, Mother. It's night now. Here's the nurse."

"This is Doctor Harry, Mrs. Weatherall. I never saw you look so young and happy!"

"Ah, I'll never be young again—but I'd be happy if they'd let me lie in peace and get rested."

She thought she spoke up loudly, but no one answered. A warm weight   40
on her forehead, a warm bracelet on her wrist, and a breeze went on whispering, trying to tell her something. A shuffle of leaves in the everlasting hand of God. He blew on them and they danced and rattled. "Mother, don't mind, we're going to give you a little hypodermic." "Look here, daughter, how do ants get in this bed? I saw sugar ants yesterday." Did you send for Hapsy too?

It was Hapsy she really wanted. She had to go a long way back through a great many rooms to find Hapsy standing with a baby on her arm. She seemed to herself to be Hapsy also, and the baby on Hapsy's arm was Hapsy and himself and herself, all at once, and there was no surprise in the meeting. Then Hapsy melted from within and turned flimsy as gray gauze and the baby was a gauzy shadow, and Hapsy came up close and said, "I thought you'd never come," and looked at her very searchingly and said, "You haven't changed a bit!" They leaned forward to kiss, when Cornelia began whispering from a long way off, "Oh, is there anything you want to tell me? Is there anything I can do for you?"

Yes, she had changed her mind after sixty years and she would like to see George. I want you to find George. Find him and be sure to tell him I forgot him. I want him to know I had my husband just the same and my children and my house like any other woman. A good house too and a good husband that I loved and fine children out of him. Better than I hoped for even. Tell him I was given back everything he took away and more. Oh, no, oh, God, no, there was something else besides the house and the man and the children. Oh, surely they were not all? What was it? Something not given back. . . . Her breath crowded down under her ribs and grew into a monstrous frightening shape with cutting edges; it bored up into her head, and the agony was unbelievable: Yes, John, get the doctor now, no more talk, my time has come.

When this one was born it should be the last. The last. It should have been born first, for it was the one she had truly wanted. Everything came in good time. Nothing left out, left over. She was strong, in three days she would be as well as ever. Better. A woman needed milk in her to have her full health.

"Mother, do you hear me?"

"I've been telling you—"   45

"Mother, Father Connolly's here."

"I went to Holy Communion only last week. Tell him I'm not so sinful as all that."

"Father just wants to speak to you."

He could speak as much as he pleased. It was like him to drop in and inquire about her soul as if it were a teething baby, and then stay on for a cup of tea and a round of cards and gossip. He always had a funny story of some sort, usually about an Irishman who made his little mistakes and confessed them, and the point lay in some absurd thing he would blurt out in the confessional showing his struggles between native piety and original sin. Granny felt easy about her soul. Cornelia, where are your manners? Give Father Connolly a chair. She had her secret comfortable understanding with a few favorite saints who cleared a straight road to God for her. All as surely signed and sealed as the papers for the new Forty Acres. Forever . . . heirs and assigns forever. Since the day the wedding cake was not cut, but thrown out and wasted. The whole bottom dropped out of the world, and there she was blind and sweating and nothing under her feet and the walls falling away. His hand had caught her under the breast, she had not fallen, there was the freshly polished floor with the green rug on it, just as before. He had cursed like a sailor's parrot and said, "I'll kill him for you." Don't lay a hand on him, for my sake leave something to God. "Now, Ellen, you must believe what I tell you. . . ."

So there was nothing, nothing to worry about any more, except some- 50
times in the night one of the children screamed in a nightmare, and they both hustled out shaking and hunting for the matches and calling, "There, wait a minute, here we are!" John, get the doctor now, Hapsy's time has come. But there was Hapsy standing by the bed in a white cap. "Cornelia, tell Hapsy to take off her cap. I can't see her plain."

Her eyes opened very wide and the room stood out like a picture she had seen somewhere. Dark colors with the shadows rising toward the ceiling in long angles. The tall black dresser gleamed with nothing on it but John's picture, enlarged from a little one, with John's eyes very black when they should have been blue. You never saw him, so how do you know how he looked? But the man insisted the copy was perfect, it was very rich and handsome. For a picture, yes, but it's not my husband. The table by the bed had a linen cover and a candle and a crucifix. The light was blue from Cornelia's silk lampshades. No sort of light at all, just frippery. You had to live forty years with kerosene lamps to appreciate honest electricity. She felt very strong and she saw Doctor Harry with a rosy nimbus around him.

"You look like a saint, Doctor Harry, and I vow that's as near as you'll ever come to it."

"She's saying something."

"I heard you, Cornelia. What's all this carrying on?"

"Father Connolly's saying—" 55

Cornelia's voice staggered and bumped like a cart in a bad road. It rounded corners and turned back again and arrived nowhere. Granny stepped up in the cart very lightly and reached for the reins, but a man sat beside her and she knew him by his hands, driving the cart. She did not look in his face, for she knew without seeing, but looked instead down the road where the trees leaned over and bowed to each other and a thousand birds were singing a Mass. She felt like singing too, but she put her hand in the bosom of her dress and pulled out a rosary, and Father Connolly murmured Latin in a very solemn voice and tickled her feet. My God, will you stop that nonsense? I'm a married woman. What if he did run away and leave me to face the priest by myself? I found another a whole world better. I wouldn't have exchanged my husband for anybody except St. Michael himself, and you may tell him that for me with a thank you in the bargain.

Light flashed on her closed eyelids, and a deep roaring shook her. Cornelia, is that lightning? I hear thunder. There's going to be a storm. Close all the windows. Call the children in. . . . "Mother, here we are, all of us." "Is that you, Hapsy?" "Oh, no, I'm Lydia. We drove as fast as we could." Their faces drifted above her, drifted away. The rosary fell out of her hands and Lydia put it back. Jimmy tried to help, their hands fumbled together, and Granny closed two fingers around Jimmy's thumb. Beads wouldn't do, it must be something alive. She was so amazed her thoughts ran round and round. So, my dear Lord, this is my death and I wasn't even thinking about it. My children have come to see me die. But I can't, it's not time. Oh, I always hated surprises. I wanted to give Cornelia the amethyst set—Cornelia, you're to have the amethyst set, but Hapsy's to wear it when she wants, and, Doctor Harry, do shut up. Nobody sent for you. Oh, my dear Lord, do wait a minute. I meant to do something about the Forty Acres, Jimmy doesn't need it and Lydia will later on, with that worthless husband of hers. I meant to finish the altar cloth and send six bottles of wine to Sister Borgia for her dyspepsia. I want to send six bottles of wine to Sister Borgia, Father Connolly, now don't let me forget.

Cornelia's voice made short turns and tilted over and crashed. "Oh, Mother, oh, Mother, oh, Mother. . . ."

"I'm not going, Cornelia. I'm taken by surprise. I can't go."

You'll see Hapsy again. What about her? "I thought you'd never come." 60 Granny made a long journey outward, looking for Hapsy. What if I don't find her? What then? Her heart sank down and down, there was no bottom to death, she couldn't come to the end of it. The blue light from Cornelia's lampshade drew into a tiny point in the center of her brain, it flickered and winked like an eye, quietly it fluttered and dwindled. Granny lay curled down within herself, amazed and watchful, starting at the point of light that was herself; her body was now only a deeper mass of shadow in an endless darkness and this darkness would curl around the light and swallow it up, God, give a sign!

For the second time there was no sign. Again no bridegroom and the priest in the house. She could not remember any other sorrow because this grief wiped them all away. Oh, no, there's nothing more cruel than this—I'll never forgive it. She stretched herself with a deep breath and blew out the light.

[1929]

■ TOPICS FOR DISCUSSION AND WRITING

1. In a paragraph, characterize Granny Weatherall. In another paragraph, evaluate her claim that the anguish of the jilting has been compensated for by her subsequent life.

2. The final paragraph alludes to Christ's parable of the bridegroom (Mat-

thew 25: 1–13). With this allusion in mind, write a paragraph explaining the title of the story.

■ ERNEST HEMINGWAY

Ernest Hemingway (1899–1961) was born in Oak Park, Illinois. After graduating from high school in 1917 he worked on the Kansas City *Star,* but left to serve as a volunteer ambulance driver in Italy, where he was wounded in action. He returned home, married, and then served as European correspondent for the Toronto *Star,* but he soon gave up journalism for fiction. In 1922 he settled in Paris, where he moved in a circle of American expatriates that included Ezra Pound, Gertrude Stein, and F. Scott Fitzgerald. He served as a journalist during the Spanish Civil War and during the Second World War, but he was also something of a private soldier.

After the Second World War his reputation sank, though he was still active as a writer (for instance, he wrote *The Old Man and the Sea* in 1952). In 1954 he was awarded the Nobel Prize in Literature, but in 1961, depressed by a sense of failing power, he took his own life.

A Clean, Well-Lighted Place[1]

It was late and every one had left the café except an old man who sat in the shadow the leaves of the tree made against the electric light. In the day time the street was dusty, but at night the dew settled the dust and the old man liked to sit late because he was deaf and now at night it was quiet and he felt the difference. The two waiters inside the café knew that the old man was a little drunk, and while he was a good client they knew that if he became too drunk he would leave without paying, so they kept watch on him.

"Last week he tried to commit suicide," one waiter said.

"Why?"

"He was in despair."

"What about?" 5

"Nothing."

"How do you know it was nothing?"

"He has plenty of money."

They sat together at a table that was close against the wall near the door of the café and looked at the terrace where the tables were all empty except where the old man sat in the shadow of the leaves of the tree that moved slightly in the wind. A girl and a soldier went by in the street. The street light shone on the brass number on his collar. The girl wore no head covering and hurried beside him.

"The guard will pick him up," one waiter said. 10

[1] The story uses a few Spanish words: *bodega* = wineshop; *nada* = nothing; *nada y pues nada* nothing and then nothing; *otro loco mas* = another madman; *copita* = little cup

"What does it matter if he gets what he's after?"

"He had better get off the street now. The guard will get him. They went by five minutes ago."

The old man sitting in the shadow rapped on his saucer with his glass. The younger waiter went over to him.

"What do you want?"

The old man looked at him. "Another brandy," he said.   15

"You'll be drunk," the waiter said. The old man looked at him. The waiter went away.

"He'll stay all night," he said to his colleague. "I'm sleepy now. I never get into bed before three o'clock. He should have killed himself last week."

The waiter took the brandy bottle and another saucer from the counter inside the café and marched out to the old man's table. He put down the saucer and poured the glass full of brandy.

"You should have killed yourself last week," he said to the deaf man. The old man motioned with his finger. "A little more," he said. The waiter poured on into the glass so that the brandy slopped over and ran down the stem into the top saucer of the pile. "Thank you," the old man said. The waiter took the bottle back inside the café. He sat down at the table with his colleague again.

"He's drunk now," he said.   20

"He's drunk every night."

"What did he want to kill himself for?"

"How should I know."

"How did he do it?"

"He hung himself with a rope."   25

"Who cut him down?"

"His niece."

"Why did they do it?"

"Fear for his soul."

"How much money has he got?"   30

"He's got plenty."

"He must be eighty years old."

"Anyway I should say he was eighty."

"I wish he would go home. I never get to bed before three o'clock. What kind of hour is that to go to bed?"

"He stays up because he likes it."   35

"He's lonely. I'm not lonely. I have a wife waiting in bed for me."

"He had a wife once too."

"A wife would be no good to him now."

"You can't tell. He might be better with a wife."

"His niece looks after him. You said she cut him down."   40

"I know."

"I wouldn't want to be that old. An old man is a nasty thing."

"Not always. This old man is clean. He drinks without spilling. Even now, drunk. Look at him."

"I don't want to look at him. I wish he would go home. He has no regard for those who must work."

The old man looked from his glass across the square, then over at the waiters.

"Another brandy," he said, pointing to his glass. The waiter who was in a hurry came over.

"Finished," he said, speaking with that omission of syntax stupid people employ when talking to drunken people or foreigners. "No more tonight. Close now."

"Another," said the old man.

"No. Finished." The waiter wiped the edge of the table with a towel and shook his head.

"The old man stood up, slowly counted the saucers, took a leather coin purse from his pocket and paid for the drinks, leaving half a peseta tip.

The waiter watched him go down the street, a very old man walking unsteadily but with dignity.

"Why didn't you let him stay and drink?" the unhurried waiter asked. They were putting up the shutters. "It is not half-past two."

"I want to go home to bed."

"What is an hour?"

"More to me than to him."

"An hour is the same."

"You talk like an old man yourself. He can buy a bottle and drink at home."

"It's not the same."

"No, it is not," agreed the waiter with a wife. He did not wish to be unjust. He was only in a hurry.

"And you? You have no fear of going home before your usual hour?"

"Are you trying to insult me?"

"No, hombre, only to make a joke."

"No," the waiter who was in a hurry said, rising from pulling down the metal shutters. "I have confidence. I am all confidence."

"You have youth, confidence, and a job," the old waiter said. "You have everything."

"And what do you lack?"

"Everything but work."

"You have everything I have."

"No. I have never had confidence and I am not young."

"Come on. Stop talking nonsense and lock up."

"I am of those who like to stay late at the café," the older waiter said. "With all those who do not want to go to bed. With all those who need a light for the night."

"I want to go home and into bed."

"We are of two different kinds," the older waiter said. He was now dressed to go home. "It is not only a question of youth and confidence although those things are very beautiful. Each night I am reluctant to close up because there may be some one who needs the café."

"Hombre, there are bodegas open all night long."

"You do not understand. This is a clean and pleasant café. It is well lighted. The light is very good and also, now, there are shadows of the leaves."

"Good night," said the younger waiter.   75

"Good night," the other said. Turning off the electric light he continued the conversation with himself. It is the light of course but it is necessary that the place be clean and pleasant. You do not want music. Certainly you do not want music. Nor can you stand before a bar with dignity although that is all that is provided for these hours. What did he fear? It was not fear or dread. It was a nothing that he knew too well. It was all a nothing and a man was nothing too. It was only that and light was all it needed and a certain cleanness and order. Some lived in it and never felt it but he knew it all was nadas y pues nada y pues nada. Our nada who art in nada, nada be thy name thy kingdom nada thy will be nada in nada as it is in nada. Give us this nada our daily nada and nada us our nada as we nada our nadas and nada us not into nada but deliver us from nada; pues nada. Hail nothing full of nothing, nothing is with thee. He smiled and stood before a bar with a shining steam pressure coffee machine.

"What's yours?" asked the barman.

"Nada."

"Otro loco mas," said the barman and turned away.

"A little cup," said the waiter.   80

The barman poured it for him.

"The light is very bright and pleasant but the bar is unpolished," the waiter said.

The barman looked at him but did not answer. It was too late at night for conversation.

"You want another copita?" the barman asked.

"No, thank you," said the waiter and went out. He disliked bars and   85 bodegas. A clean, well-lighted café was a very different thing. Now, without thinking further, he would go home to his room. He would lie in the bed and finally, with daylight, he would go to sleep. After all, he said to himself, it is probably only insomnia. Many must have it.

[1933]

■ TOPICS FOR DISCUSSION AND WRITING

1. In an essay of 500 words compare and contrast the two waiters. What does the young waiter believe in? Does the older waiter believe in anything? In your answer devote some space to each waiter's view of the café.

2. What is the point of the parody of the Lord's Prayer? In this context, note, too, the setting in which it is spoken: a bar in a *bodega* equipped with a steam-pressure coffee machine.

3. In 250 words explain why, if the older waiter is a nihilist (Latin *nihl*, like Spanish *nada* = nothing), he is concerned that there be a clean, well-lighted place.

4. Reread the story, draw some conclusions about Hemingway's style, and then write a paragraph or a short dialogue in his style. Or write a parody of Hemingway's style. (The writing of a parody usually employs the style of the victim, but in circumstances that make the language amusing. For example, you might have two infants, or two duchesses, talking like Hemingway's waiters.)

■ FLANNERY O'CONNOR

Flannery O'Connor (1925–1964)—her first name was Mary but she did not use it—was born in Savannah, Georgia, but spent most of her life in Milledgeville, Georgia, where her family moved when she was 12. She was educated at parochial schools and at the local college and then went to School for Writers at the University of Iowa, where she earned an M.F.A. in 1946. For a few months she lived at a writers' colony in Saratoga Springs, New York and then spent a few weeks in New York City, but she lived most of her life in Milledgeville, where she tended her peacocks and wrote stories, novels, essays (posthumously published as *Mystery and Manners* [1970]), and letters (posthumously published under the title of *The Habit of Being* [1979]).

In 1951, when she was 25, Flannery O'Connor discovered that she was a victim of lupus erythematosus, an incurable degenerative blood disease that had crippled and then killed her father ten years before. She died at the age of 39. O'Connor faced her illness with Stoic courage and Christian fortitude and tough humor. Here is a glimpse, from one of her letters, of how she dealt with those who pitied her:

> An old lady got on the elevator behind me and as soon as I turned around she fixed me with a moist gleaming eye and said in a loud voice, "Bless you, darling!" I felt exactly like the Misfit [in "A Good Man Is Hard To Find"] and I gave her a weakly lethal look, whereupon greatly encouraged she grabbed my arm and whispered (very loud) in my ear, "Remember what they said to John at the gate, darling!" It was not my floor but I got off and I suppose the old lady was astounded at how quick I could get away on crutches. I have a one-legged friend and I asked her what they said to John at the gate. She said she reckoned they said, "The lame shall enter first." This may be because the lame will be able to knock everybody else aside with their crutches.

A Good Man Is Hard to Find

The grandmother didn't want to go to Florida. She wanted to visit some of her connections in east Tennessee and she was seizing at every chance to change Bailey's mind. Bailey was the son she lived with, her only boy. He was sitting on the edge of his chair at the table, bent over the orange sports section of the *Journal*. "Now look here, Bailey," she said, "see here, read this," and she stood with one hand on her thin hip and the other rattling the newspaper at his bald head. "Here this fellow that calls himself The Misfit is aloose from the Federal Pen and headed toward Florida and you read here what it says he did to these people. Just you read it. I wouldn't take my children in any direction with a criminal like that aloose in it. I couldn't answer to my conscience if I did."

Bailey didn't look up from his reading so she wheeled around then and faced the children's mother, a young woman in slacks, whose face was as broad and innocent as a cabbage and was tied round with a green headkerchief that had two points on the top like rabbit's ears. She was sitting on the sofa, feeding the baby his apricots out of a jar. "The children have been to Florida before," the old lady said. "You all ought to take them somewhere else for a change so they would see different parts of the world and be broad. They never have been to east Tennessee."

The children's mother didn't seem to hear her but the eight-year-old boy, John Wesley, a stocky child with glasses, said, "If you don't want to go to Florida, why dontcha stay at home?" He and the little girl, June Star, were reading the funny papers on the floor.

"She wouldn't stay at home to be queen for a day," June Star said without raising her yellow head.

"Yes and what would you do if this fellow, The Misfit, caught you?" the   5 grandmother asked.

"I'd smack his face," John Wesley said.

"She wouldn't stay at home for a million bucks," June Star said. "Afraid she'd miss something. She has to go everywhere we go."

"All right, Miss," the grandmother said. "Just remember that the next time you want me to curl you hair."

June Star said her hair was naturally curly.

The next morning the grandmother was the first one in the car, ready   10 to go. She had her big black valise that looked like the head of a hippopotamus in one corner, and underneath it she was hiding a basket with Pitty Sing, the cat, in it. She didn't intend for the cat to be left alone in the house for three days because he would miss her too much and she was afraid he might brush against one of the gas burners and accidentally asphyxiate himself. Her son, Bailey, didn't like to arrive at a motel with a cat.

She sat in the middle of the back seat with John Wesley and June Star on either side of her. Bailey and the children's mother and the baby sat in the front and they left Atlanta at eight forty-five with the mileage on the car at 55890. The grandmother wrote this down because she thought it would be interesting to say how many miles they had been when they got back. It took them twenty minutes to reach the outskirts of the city.

The old lady settled herself comfortably, removing her white cotton gloves and putting them up with her purse on the shelf in front of the back window. The children's mother still had on slacks and still had her head tied up in a green kerchief, but the grandmother had on a navy blue straw sailor hat with a bunch of white violets on the brim and a navy blue dress with a small white dot in the print. Her collar and cuffs were white organdy trimmed with lace and at her neckline she had pinned a purple spray of cloth violets containing a sachet. In case of an accident, anyone seeing her dead on the highway would know at once that she was a lady.

She said she thought it was going to be a good day for driving, neither too hot nor too cold, and she cautioned Bailey that the speed limit was fifty-five miles an hour and that the patrolmen hid themselves behind billboards and small clumps of trees and sped out after you before you had a chance to slow down. She pointed out interesting details of the scenery: Stone Mountain; the blue granite that in some places came up to both sides of the highway; the brilliant red clay banks slightly streaked with purple; and the various crops that made rows of green lace-work on the ground. The trees were full of silver-white sunlight and the meanest of them sparkled. The children were reading comic magazines and their mother had gone back to sleep.

"Let's go through Georgia fast so we won't have to look at it much," John Wesley said.

"If I were a little boy," said the grandmother, "I wouldn't talk about my 15 native state that way. Tennessee has the mountains and Georgia has the hills."

"Tennessee is just a hillbilly dumping ground," John Wesley said, "and Georgia is a lousy state too."

"You said it," June Star said.

"In my time," said the grandmother, folding her thin veined fingers, "children were more respectful of their native states and their parents and everything else. People did right then. Oh look at the cute little pickaninny!" she said and pointed to a Negro child standing in the door of a shack. "Wouldn't that make a picture, now?" she asked and they all turned and looked at the little Negro out of the back window. He waved.

"He didn't have any britches on," June Star said.

"He probably didn't have any," the grandmother explained. "Little niggers in the country don't have things like we do. If I could paint, I'd paint that picture," she said.

The children exchanged comic books.

The grandmother offered to hold the baby and the children's mother passed him over the front seat to her. She set him on her knee and bounced him and told him about the things they were passing. She rolled her eyes and screwed up her mouth and stuck her leathery thin face into his smooth bland one. Occasionally he gave her a faraway smile. They passed a large cotton field with five or six graves fenced in the middle of it, like a small island. "Look at the graveyard!" the grandmother said, pointing it out. "That was the old family burying ground. That belonged to the plantation."

"Where's the plantation?" John Wesley asked.

"Gone with the Wind," said the grandmother. "Ha. Ha."

When the children finished all the comic books they had brought, they 25 opened the lunch and ate it. The grandmother ate a peanut butter sandwich and an olive and would not let the children throw the box and the paper napkins out the window. When there was nothing else to do they played a game by choosing a cloud and making the other two guess what shape it suggested. John Wesley took one the shape of a cow and June Star guessed a cow and John Wesley said, no, an automobile, and June Star said he didn't play fair, and they began to slap each other over the grandmother.

The grandmother said she would tell them a story if they would keep quiet. When she told a story, she rolled her eyes and waved her head and was very dramatic. She said once when she was a maiden lady she had been courted by a Mr. Edgar Atkins Teagarden from Jasper, Georgia. She said he was a very good-looking man and a gentleman and that he brought her a watermelon every Saturday afternoon with his initials cut in it. E. A. T. Well, one Saturday, she said, Mr. Teagarden brought the watermelon and there was nobody at home and he left it on the front porch and returned in his buggy to Jasper, but she never got the watermelon, she said, because a nigger boy ate it when he saw the initials, E. A. T.! This story tickled John Wesley's funny bone and he giggled and giggled but June Star didn't think it was any good. She said she wouldn't marry a man that just brought her a watermelon on Saturday. The grandmother said she would have done well to marry Mr. Teagarden because he was a gentleman and had bought Coca-Cola stock when it first came out and that he had died only a few years ago, a very wealthy man.

They stopped at The Tower for barbecued sandwiches. The Tower was a part stucco and part wood filling station and dance hall set in a clearing outside of Timothy. A fat man named Red Sammy Butts ran it and there were signs stuck here and there on the building and for miles up and down the highway saying, TRY RED SAMMY'S FAMOUS BARBECUE. NONE LIKE FAMOUS RED SAMMY'S! RED SAM! THE FAT BOY WITH THE HAPPY LAUGH. A VETERAN! RED SAMMY'S YOUR MAN!

Red Sammy was lying on the bare ground outside The Tower with his head under a truck while a gray monkey about a foot high, chained to a small chinaberry tree, chattered nearby. The monkey sprang back into the tree and got on the highest limb as soon as he saw the children jump out of the car and run toward him.

Inside, The Tower was a long dark room with a counter at one end and tables at the other and dancing space in the middle. They all sat down at a broad table next to the nickelodeon and Red Sam's wife, a tall burnt-brown woman with hair and eyes lighter than her skin, came and took their order. The children's mother put a dime in the machine and played "The Tennessee Waltz," and the grandmother said that tune always made her want to dance. She asked Bailey if he would like to dance but he only glared at her. He didn't have a naturally sunny disposition like she did and trips made him nervous. The grandmother's brown eyes were very bright. She swayed her head from side to side and pretended she was dancing in her chair. June Star said play something she could tap to so the children's mother put in another dime and played a fast number and June Star stepped out onto the dance floor and did her tap routine.

"Ain't she cute?" Red Sam's wife said, leaning over the counter. "Would 30 you like to come be my little girl?"

"No I certainly wouldn't," June Star said. "I wouldn't live in a broken-down place like this for a million bucks!" and she ran back to the table.

"Ain't she cute?" the woman repeated, stretching her mouth politely.

"Aren't you ashamed?" hissed the grandmother.

Red Sam came in and told his wife to quit lounging on the counter and hurry up with these people's order. His khaki trousers reached just to his hip bones and his stomach hung over them like a sack of meal swaying under his shirt. He came over and sat down at a table nearby and let out a combination sigh and yodel. "You can't win," he said. "You can't win," and he wiped his sweating red face off with a gray handkerchief. "These days you don't know who to trust," he said. "Ain't that the truth?"

"People are certainly not nice like they used to be," said the grand- 35 mother.

"Two fellers come in here last week," Red Sammy said, "driving a Chrysler. It was a old beat-up car but it was a good one and these boys looked all right to me. Said they worked at the mill and you know I let them fellers charge the gas they bought? Now why did I do that?"

"Because you're a good man!" the grandmother said at once.

"Yes'm, I suppose so," Red Sam said as if he were struck with the answer.

His wife brought the orders, carrying the five plates all at once without a tray, two in each hand and one balanced on her arm. "It isn't a soul in this green world of God's that you can trust," she said. "And I don't count anybody out of that, not nobody," she repeated, looking at Red Sammy.

"Did you read about that criminal, The Misfit, that's escaped?" asked the 40 grandmother.

"I wouldn't be a bit surprised if he didn't attact this place right here," said the woman. "If he hears about it being here, I wouldn't be none surprised to see him. If he hears it's two cent in the cash register, I wouldn't be a tall surprised if he. . ."

"That'll do," Red Sam said. "Go bring these people their Co'Colas," and the woman went off to get the rest of the order.

"A good man is hard to find," Red Sammy said. "Everything is getting terrible. I remember the day you could go off and leave your screen door un-latched. Not no more."

He and the grandmother discussed better times. The old lady said that in her opinion Europe was entirely to blame for the way things were now. She said the way Europe acted you would think we were made of money and Red Sam said it was no use talking about it, she was exactly right. The children ran outside into the white sunlight and looked at the monkey in the lacy chinaberry tree. He was busy catching fleas on himself and biting each one carefully between his teeth as if it were a delicacy.

They drove off again into the hot afternoon. The grandmother took cat 45 naps and woke up every few minutes with her own snoring. Outside of Toombsboro she woke up and recalled an old plantation that she had visited in this neighborhood once when she was a young lady. She said the house had six white columns across the front and that there was an avenue of oaks leading up to it and two little wooden trellis arbors on either side in front where you sat down with your suitor after a stroll in the garden. She recalled exactly which road to turn off to get to it. She knew that Bailey would not be willing to lose any time looking at an old house, but the more she talked about it, the more she wanted to see it once again and find out if the little twin arbors were still standing. "There was a secret panel in this house," she said craftily, not telling the truth but wishing that she were, "and the story went that all the family silver was hidden in it when Sherman came through but it was never found. . ."

"Hey!" John Wesley said. "Let's go see it! We'll find it! We'll poke all the woodwork and find it! Who lives there? Where do you turn off at? Hey, Pop, can't we turn off there?"

"We never have seen a house with a secret panel!" June Star shrieked. "Let's go to the house with the secret panel! Hey, Pop, can't we go see the house with the secret panel!"

"It's not far from here, I know," the grandmother said. "It wouldn't take over twenty minutes."

Bailey was looking straight ahead. His jaw was as rigid as a horseshoe. "No," he said.

The children began to yell and scream that they wanted to see the house 50 with the secret panel. John Wesley kicked the back of the front seat and June Star hung over her mother's shoulder and whined desperately into her ear that they never had any fun even on their vacation, and that they could never do what THEY wanted to do. The baby began to scream and John Wesley kicked the back of the seat so hard that his father could feel the blows in his kidney.

"All right!" he shouted, and drew the car to a stop at the side of the road. "Will you all shut up? Will you all just shut up for one second? If you don't shut up, we won't go anywhere."

"It would be very educational for them," the grandmother murmured.

"All right," Bailey said, "but get this: this is the only time we're going to stop for anything like this. This is the one and only time."

"The dirt road that you have to turn down is about a mile back," the grandmother directed. "I marked it when we passed."

"A dirt road," Bailey groaned.   55

After they had turned around and were headed toward the dirt road, the grandmother recalled other points about the house, the beautiful glass over the front doorway and the candle-lamp in the hall. John Wesley said that the secret panel was probably in the fireplace.

"You can't go inside this house," Bailey said. "You don't know who lives there."

"While you all talk to the people in front, I'll run around behind and get in a window," John Wesley suggested.

"We'll all stay in the car," his mother said.

They turned onto the dirt road and the car raced roughly along in a swirl 60 of pink dust. The grandmother recalled the times when there were no paved roads and thirty miles was a day's journey. The dirt road was hilly and there were sudden washes in it and sharp curves on dangerous embankments. All at once they would be on a hill, looking down over the blue tops of trees for miles around, then the next minute they would be in a red depression with the dust-coated trees looking down on them.

"This place had better turn up in a minute," Bailey said, "or I'm going to turn around."

The road looked as if no one had traveled on it in months.

"It's not much farther," the grandmother said and just as she said it, a horrible thought came to her. The thought was so embarrassing that she turned red in the face and her eyes dilated and her feet jumped up, upsetting her valise in the corner. The instant the valise moved, the newspaper top she had over the basket under it rose with a snarl and Pitty Sing, the cat, sprang onto Bailey's shoulder.

The children were thrown to the floor and their mother, clutching the baby, was thrown out of the door onto the ground, the old lady was thrown into the front seat. The car turned over once and landed rightside up in a gulch on the side of the road. Bailey remained in the driver's seat with the cat—gray-striped with a broad white face and an orange nose—clinging to his neck like a caterpillar.

As soon as the children saw they could move their arms and legs, they 65 scrambled out of the car, shouting, "We've had an ACCIDENT!" The grandmother was curled up under the dashboard, hoping she was injured so that Bailey's wrath would not come down on her all at once. The horrible thought she had had before the accident was that the house she remembered so vividly was not in Georgia but in Tennessee.

Bailey removed the cat from his neck with both hands and flung it out the window against the side of a pine tree. Then he got out of the car and started looking for the children's mother. She was sitting against the side of a red gutted ditch, holding the screaming baby, but she only had a cut down her face and a broken shoulder. "We've had an ACCIDENT!" the children screamed in a frenzy of delight.

"But nobody's killed," June Star said with disappointment as the grandmother limped out of the car, her hat still pinned to her head but the broken front brim standing up at a jaunty angle and the violet spray hanging off the side. They all sat down in the ditch, except the children, to recover from the shock. They were all shaking.

"Maybe a car will come along," said the children's mother hoarsely.

"I believe I have injured an organ," said the grandmother, pressing her side, but no one answered her. Bailey's teeth were clattering. He had on a yellow sport shirt with bright blue parrots designed in it and his face was as yellow as the shirt. The grandmother decided that she would not mention that the house was in Tennessee.

The road was about ten feet above and they could see only the tops of 70 the trees on the other side of it. Behind the ditch they were setting in there were more woods, tall and dark and deep. In a few minutes they saw a car come some distance away on top of a hill, coming slowly as if the occupants were watching them. The grandmother stood up and waved both arms dramatically to attract their attention. The car continued to come on slowly, disappeared around a bend and then appeared again, moving even slower, on top of the hill they had gone over. It was a big black battered hearselike automobile. There were three men in it.

It came to a stop just over them and for some minutes, the driver looked down with a steady expressionless gaze to where they were sitting, and didn't speak. Then he turned his head and muttered someting to the other two and they got out. One was a fat boy in black trousers and a red sweat shirt with a silver stallion embossed on the front of it. He moved around on the right side of them and stood staring, his mouth partly open in a kind of loose grin. The other had on khaki pants and a blue striped coat and a gray hat pulled down very low, hiding most of his face. He came around slowly on the left side. Neither spoke.

The driver got out of the car and stood by the side of it, looking down at them. He was an older man than the other two. His hair was just beginning to gray and he wore silver-rimmed spectacles that gave him a scholarly look. He had a long creased face and didn't have on any shirt or undershirt. He had on blue jeans that were too tight for him and was holding a black hat and a gun. The two boys also had guns.

"We've had an ACCIDENT!" the children screamed.

The grandmother had the peculiar feeling that the bespectacled man was someone she knew. His face was so familiar to her as if she had known him all her life, but she could not recall who he was. He moved away from the car and began to come down the embankment, placing his feet carefully so that he wouldn't slip. He had on tan and white shoes and no socks, and his ankles were red and thin. "Good afternoon," he said. "I see you all had you a little spill."

"We turned over twice!" said the grandmother.   75

"Oncet," he corrected. "We seen it happen. Try their car and see will it run, Hiram," he said quietly to the boy with the gray hat.

"What you got that gun for?" John Wesley asked. "Whatcha gonna do with that gun?"

"Lady," the man said to the children's mother, "would you mind calling them children to set down by you? Children make me nervous. I want all you all to sit down right together there where you're at."

"What are you telling us what to do for?" June Star asked.

Behind them the line of woods gaped like a dark open mouth. "Come   80 here," said their mother.

"Look here now," Bailey began suddenly, "we're in a predicament! We're in . . ."

"The grandmother shrieked. She scrambled to her feet and stood staring. "You're The Misfit!" she said. "I recognized you at once."

"Yes'm," the man said, smiling slightly as if he were pleased in spite of himself to be known, "but it would have been better for all of you, lady, if you hadn't of recognized me."

Bailey turned his head sharply and said something to his mother that shocked even the children. The old lady began to cry and The Misfit reddened.

"Lady," he said, "don't you get upset. Sometimes a man says things he   85 don't mean. I don't reckon he meant to talk to you thataway."

"You wouldn't shoot a lady, would you?" the grandmother said and removed a clean handkerchief from her cuff and began to slap at her eyes with it.

The Misfit pointed the toe of his shoe into the ground and made a little hole and then covered it up again. "I would hate to have to," he said.

"Listen," the grandmother almost screamed, "I know you're a good man. You don't look a bit like you have common blood. I know you must come from nice people!"

"Yes ma'm," he said, "finest people in the world." When he smiled he showed a row of strong white teeth. "God never made a finer woman than my mother and my daddy's heart was pure gold," he said. The boy with the red sweat shirt had come around behind them and was standing with his gun at his hip. The Misfit squatted down on the ground. "Watch them children, Bobby Lee," he said. "You know they make me nervous." He looked at the six of them huddled together in front of him and he seemed to be embarrassed as if he couldn't think of anything to say. "Ain't a cloud in the sky," he remarked, looking up at it. "Don't see no sun but don't see no cloud neither."

"Yes, it's a beautiful day," said the grandmother. "Listen," she said, "you 90 shouldn't call yourself The Misfit because I know you're a good man at heart. I can just look at you and tell."

"Hush!" Bailey yelled. "Hush! Everybody shut up and let me handle this!" He was squatting in the position of a runner about to sprint forward but he didn't move.

"I pre-chate that, lady," The Misfit said and drew a little circle in the ground with the butt of his gun.

"I'll take a half a hour to fix this here car," Hiram called, looking over the raised hood of it.

"Well, first you and Bobby Lee get him and that little boy to step over yonder with you," The Misfit said, pointing to Bailey and John Wesley. "The boys want to ask you something," he said to Bailey. "Would you mind stepping back in them woods there with them?"

"Listen," Bailey began, "we're in a terrible predicament. Nobody real- 95 izes what this is," and his voice cracked. His eyes were as blue and intense as the parrots on his shirt and he remained perfectly still.

The grandmother reached up to adjust her hat brim as if she were going to the woods with him but it came off in her hand. She stood staring at it and after a second she let it fall on the ground. Hiram pulled Bailey up by the arm as if he were assisting an old man. John Wesley caught hold of his father's hand and Bobby Lee followed. They went off toward the woods and just as they reached the dark edge, Bailey turned and supporting himself against a gray naked pine trunk, he shouted, "I'll be back in a minute, Mamma, wait on me!"

"Come back this instant!" his mother shrilled but they all disappeared into the woods.

"Bailey Boy!" the grandmother called in a tragic voice but she found she was looking at The Misfit squatting on the ground in front of her. "I just know you're a good man," she said desperately. "You're not a bit common!"

"Nome, I ain't a good man," The Misfit said after a second as if he had considered her statement carefully, "but I ain't the worst in the world neither. My daddy said I was a different breed of dog from my brothers and sisters. 'You know,' Daddy said, 'it's some that can live their whole life out without asking about it and it's others has to know why it is, and this boy is one of the latters. He's going to be into everything!' " He put on his black hat and looked up suddenly and then away deep into the woods as if he were embarrassed again. "I'm sorry I don't have on a shirt before you ladies," he said, hunching his shoulders slightly. "We buried our clothes that we had on when we escaped and we're just making do until we can get better. We borrowed these from some nice folks we met," he explained.

"That's perfectly all right," the grandmother said. "Maybe Bailey has an 100 extra shirt in his suitcase."

"I'll look and see terrectly," The Misfit said.

"Where are they taking him?" the children's mother screamed.

"Daddy was a card himself," The Misfit said. "You couldn't put anything over on him. He never got in trouble with the Authorities though. Just had the knack of handling them."

"You could be honest too if you'd only try," said the grandmother. "Think how wonderful it would be to settle down and live a comfortable life and not have to think about somebody chasing you all the time."

The Misfit kept scratching in the ground with the butt of his gun as if 105
he were thinking about it. "Yes'm, somebody is always after you," he murmured.

The grandmother noticed how thin his shoulder blades were just behind his hat because she was standing up looking down on him. "Do you ever pray?" she asked.

He shook his head. All she saw was the black hat wiggle between shoulder blades. "Nome," he said.

There was a pistol shot from the woods, followed closely by another. Then silence. The old lady's head jerked around. She could hear the wind move through the tree tops like a long satisfied insuck of breath. "Bailey Boy!" she called.

"I was a gospel singer for a while," The Misfit said. "I been most everything. Been in the arm service, both land and sea, at home and abroad, been twict married, been an undertaker, been with the railroads, plowed Mother Earth, been in a tornado, see a man burnt alive oncet," and he looked up at the children's mother and the little girl who were sitting close together, their faces white and their eyes glassy; "I even seen a woman flogged," he said.

"Pray, pray," the grandmother began, "pray, pray . . ."   110

"I never was a bad boy that I remember of," The Misfit said in an almost dreamy voice, "but somewhere along the line I done something wrong and got sent to the penitentiary. I was buried alive," and he looked up and held her attention to him by a steady stare.

"That's when you should have started to pray," she said. "What did you do to get sent to the penitentiary that first time?"

"Turn to the right, it was a wall," The Misfit said, looking up again at the cloudless sky. "Turn to the left, it was a wall. Look up it was a ceiling, look down it was a floor. I forgot what I done, lady. I set there and set there, trying to remember what it was I done and I ain't recalled it to this day. Oncet in a while, I would think it was coming to me, but it never come."

"Maybe they put you in by mistake," the old lady said vaguely.

"Nome," he said. "It wasn't no mistake. They had the papers on me."   115

"You must have stolen something," she said.

The Misfit sneered slightly. "Nobody had nothing I wanted," he said. "It was a head-doctor in the penitentiary said what I had done was kill my daddy but I know that for a lie. My daddy died in nineteen ought nineteen of an epidemic flu and I never had a thing to do with it. He was buried in the Mount Hopewell Baptist churchyard and you can go there and see for yourself."

"If you would pray," the old lady said, "Jesus would help you."

"That's right," The Misfit said.

"Well then, why don't you pray?" she asked trembling with delight suddenly.   120

"I don't want no hep," he said. "I'm doing all right by myself."

Bobby Lee and Hiram came ambling back from the woods. Bobby Lee was dragging a yellow shirt with bright blue parrots in it.

"Throw me that shirt, Bobby Lee," The Misfit said. The shirt came flying at him and landed on his shoulder and he put it on. The grandmother couldn't name what the shirt reminded her of. "No, lady," The Misfit said while he was buttoning it up. "I found out the crime don't matter. You can do one thing or you can do another, kill a man or take a tire off his car, because sooner or later you're going to forget what it was you done and just be punished for it."

The children's mother had begun to make heaving noises as if she couldn't get her breath. "Lady," he asked, "would you and that little girl like to step off yonder with Bobby Lee and Hiram and join your husband?"

"Yes, thank you," the mother said faintly. Her left arm dangled helplessly 125 and she was holding the baby, who had gone to sleep, in the other. "Hep that lady up, Hiram," The Misfit said as she struggled to climb out of the ditch, "and Bobby Lee, you hold onto that little girl's hand."

"I don't want to hold hands with him," June Star said. "He reminds me of a pig."

The fat boy blushed and laughed and caught her by the arm and pulled her off into the woods after Hiram and her mother.

Alone with The Misfit, the grandmother found that she had lost her voice. There was not a cloud in the sky nor any sun. There was nothing around her but woods. She wanted to tell him that he must pray. She opened and closed her mouth several times before anything came out. Finally she found herself saying, "Jesus, Jesus," meaning Jesus will help you, but the way she was saying it, it sounded as if she might be cursing.

"Yes'm," The Misfit said as if he agreed. "Jesus thrown everything off balance. It was the same case with Him as with me except He hadn't committed any crime and they could prove I had committed one because they had the papers on me. Of course," he said, "they never shown me my papers. That's why I sign myself now. I said long ago, you get you a signature and sign everything you do and keep a copy of it. Then you'll know what you done and you can hold up the crime to the punishment and see do they match and in the end you'll have something to prove you ain't been treated right. I call myself The Misfit," he said, "because I can't make what all I done wrong fit with all I gone through in punishment."

There was a piercing scream from the woods, followed closely by a pistol 130 report. "Does it seem right to you, lady, that one is punished a heap and another ain't punished at all?"

"Jesus!" the old lady cried. "You've got good blood! I know you wouldn't shoot a lady! I know you come from nice people! Pray! Jesus, you ought not to shoot a lady. I'll give you all the money I've got!"

"Lady," The Misfit said, looking beyond her into the woods, "there never was a body that give the undertaker a tip."

There were two more pistol reports and the grandmother raised her head like a parched old turkey hen crying for water and called, "Bailey Boy, Bailey Boy!" as if her heart would break.

"Jesus was the only One that ever raised the dead," The Misfit continued, "and He shouldn't have done it. He thown everything off balance. If he did what He said, then it's nothing for you to do but thow away everything and follow Him, and if He didn't, then it's nothing for you to do but enjoy the few minutes you got left the best way you can—by killing somebody or burning down his house or doing some other meanness to him. No pleasure but meanness," he said and his voice had become almost a snarl.

"Maybe He didn't raise the dead," the old lady mumbled, now knowing   135
what she was saying and feeling so dizzy that she sank down in the ditch with her legs twisted under her.

"I wasn't there so I can't say He didn't," The Misfit said. "I wisht I had of been there," he said, hitting the ground with his fist. "It ain't right I wasn't there because if I had of been there I would of known. Listen lady," he said in a high voice, "if I had of been there I would of known and I wouldn't be like I am now." His voice seemed about to crack and the grandmother's head cleared for an instant. She saw the man's face twisted close to her own as if he were going to cry and she murmured, "Why you're one of my babies. You're one of my own children!" She reached out and touched him on the shoulder. The Misfit sprang back as if a snake had bitten him and shot her three times through the chest. Then he put his gun down on the ground and took off his glasses and began to clean them.

Hiram and Bobby Lee returned from the woods and stood over the ditch, looking down at the grandmother who half sat and half lay in a puddle of blood with her legs crossed under her like a child's and her face smiling up at the cloudless sky.

Without his glasses, The Misfit's eyes were red-rimmed and pale and defenseless-looking. "Take her off and thow her where you thown the others," he said, picking up the cat that was rubbing itself against his leg.

"She was a talker, wasn't she?" Bobby Lee said, sliding down the ditch with a yodel.

"She would of been a good woman," The Misfit said, "if it had been   140
somebody there to shoot her every minute of her life."

"Some fun!" Bobby Lee said.

"Shut up, Bobby Lee," The Misfit said. "It's no real pleasure in life."

[1953]

■ TOPICS FOR DISCUSSION AND WRITING

1. What are the associations of the names June Star, John Wesley, and Bobby Lee?

2. What are the values of the members of the family?

3. Flannery O'Connor, a Roman Catholic, wrote, "I see from the standpoint of Christian orthodoxy. This means that for me the meaning of life is centered in our Redemption by Christ and what I see in the world I see is its relation to that." In the light of this statement and drawing on "A Good Man Is Hard to Find," explain what O'Connor saw in the world.

4. Let's assume that a reader, unlike O'Connor, does *not* "see from the standpoint of Christian orthodoxy." In an essay of 500 words, explain what interest "A Good Man Is Hard to Find" can have for such a reader.

5. The Misfit says, "I can't make what all I done wrong fit what all I gone through in punishment." What would O'Connor's explanation (i.e., the orthodox Christian explanation) be? In 250 to 500 words, explain what the Misfit means by saying that Jesus has "thown everything off balance."

Revelation

The doctor's waiting room, which was very small, was almost full when the Turpins entered and Mrs. Turpin, who was very large, made it look even smaller by her presence. She stood looming at the head of the magazine table set in the center of it, a living demonstration that the room was inadequate and ridiculous. Her little bright black eyes took in all the patients as she sized up the seating situation. There was one vacant chair and a place on the sofa occupied by a blond child in a dirty blue romper who should have been told to move over and make room for the lady. He was five or six, but Mrs. Turpin saw at once that no one was going to tell him to move over. He was slumped down in the seat, his arms idle at his sides and his eyes idle in his head; his nose ran unchecked.

Mrs. Turpin put a firm hand on Claud's shoulder and said in a voice that included everyone that wanted to listen, "Claud, you sit in that chair there," and gave him a push down into the vacant one. Claud was florid and bald and sturdy, somewhat shorter than Mrs. Turpin, but he sat down as if he were accustomed to doing what she told him to.

Mrs. Turpin remained standing. The only man in the room besides Claud was a lean stringy old fellow with a rusty hand spread out on each knee, whose eyes were closed as if he were asleep or dead or pretending to be so as not to get up and offer her his seat. Her gaze settled agreeably on a well-dressed gray-haired lady whose eyes met hers and whose expression said: If that child belonged to me, he would have some manners and move over—there's plenty of room there for you and him too.

Claud looked up with a sigh and made as if to rise.

"Sit down," Mrs. Turpin said, "You know you're not supposed to stand 5 on that leg. He has an ulcer on his leg," she explained.

Claud lifted his foot onto the magazine table and rolled his leg up to reveal a purple swelling on a plump marble-white calf.

"My!" the pleasant lady said. "How did you do that?"

"A cow kicked him," Mrs. Turpin said.

"Goodness!" said the lady.

Claud rolled his trouser leg down.   10

"Maybe the little boy would move over," the lady suggested, but the child did not stir.

"Somebody will be leaving in a minute," Mrs. Turpin said. She could not understand why a doctor—with as much money as they made charging five dollars a day just to stick his head in the hospital door and look at you—couldn't afford a decent-sized waiting room. This one was hardly bigger than a garage. The table was cluttered with limp-looking magazines and at one end of it there was a big green ash tray full of cigaret butts and cotton wads with little blood spots on them. If she had had anything to do with the running of the place, that would have been emptied every so often. There were no chairs against the wall at the head of the room. It had a rectangular-shaped panel in it that permitted a view of the office where the nurse came and went and the secretary listened to the radio. A plastic fern in a gold pot sat in the opening and trailed its fronds down almost to the floor. The radio was softly playing gospel music.

Just then the inner door opened and a nurse with the highest stack of yellow hair Mr. Turpin had ever seen put her face in the crack and called for the next patient. The woman sitting beside Claud grasped the two arms of her chair and hoisted herself up; she pulled her dress free from her legs and lumbered through the door where the nurse had disappeared.

Mrs. Turpin eased into the vacant chair, which held her tight as a corset. "I wish I could reduce," she said, and rolled her eyes and gave a comic sigh.

"Oh, *you* aren't fat," the stylish lady said.   15

"Ooooo I am too," Mrs. Turpin said. "Claud he eats all he wants to and never weighs over one hundred and seventy-five pounds, but me I just look at something good to eat and gain some weight," and her stomach and shoulders shook with laughter. "You can eat all you want to, can't you, Claud?" she asked turning to him.

Claud only grinned.

"Well, as long as you have a good disposition," the stylish lady said, "I don't think it makes a bit of difference what size you are. You just can't beat a good disposition."

Next to her was a fat girl of eighteen or nineteen, scowling into a thick blue book which Mrs. Turpin saw was entitled *Human Development*. The girl raised her head and directed her scowl at Mrs. Turpin as if she did not like her looks. She appeared annoyed that anyone should speak while she tried to read. The poor girl's face was blue with acne and Mrs. Turpin thought how pitiful it was to have a face like that at any age. She gave the girl a friendly smile but the girl only scowled the harder. Mrs. Turpin herself was fat but she always had good skin, and, though she was forty-seven years old, there was not a wrinkle in her face except around her eyes from laughing too much.

Next to the ugly girl was the child, still in exactly the same position, and 20 next to him was a thin leathery old woman in a cotton print dress. She and Claud had three sacks of chicken feed in their pump house that was in the same print. She had seen from the first that the child belonged with the old woman. She could tell by the way they sat—kind of vacant and white-trashy, as if they would sit there until Doomsday if nobody called and told them to get up. And at right angles but next to the well-dressed pleasant lady was a lank-faced woman who was certainly the child's mother. She had on a yellow sweat shirt and wine-colored slacks, both gritty-looking, and the rims of her lips were stained with snuff. Her dirty yellow hair was tied behind with a little piece of red paper ribbon. Worse than niggers any day, Mrs. Turpin thought.

The gospel hymn playing was, "When I looked up and He looked down," and Mrs. Turpin, who knew it, supplied the last line mentally, "And wona these days I know I'll we-eara crown."

Without appearing to, Mrs. Turpin always noticed people's feet. The well-dressed lady had on red and grey suede shoes to match her dress. Mrs.

Turpin had on her good black patent leather pumps. The ugly girl had on Girl Scout shoes and heavy socks. The old woman had on tennis shoes and the white-trashy mother had on what appeared to be bedroom slippers, black straw with gold braid threaded through them—exactly what you would have expected her to have on.

Sometimes at night when she couldn't go to sleep, Mrs. Turpin would occupy herself with the question of who she would have chosen to be if she couldn't have been herself. If Jesus had said to her before he made her, "There's only two places available for you. You can either be a nigger or white-trash," what would she have said? "Please, Jesus, please," she would have said, "just let me wait until there's another place available," and he would have said, "No, you have to go right now and I have only those two places so make up your mind." She would have wiggled and squirmed and begged and pleaded but it would have been no use and finally she would have said, "All right, make me a nigger then—but that don't mean a trashy one." And he would have made her a neat clean respectable Negro woman, herself but black.

Next to the child's mother was a red-headed youngish woman, reading one of the magazines and working a piece of chewing gum, hell for leather, as Claud would say. Mrs. Turpin could not see the woman's feet. She was not white-trash, just common. Sometimes Mrs. Turpin occupied herself at night naming the classes of people. On the bottom of the heap were most colored people, not the kind she would have been if she had been one, but most of them; then next to them—not above, just away from—were the white-trash; then above them were the homeowners, and above them the home-and-land owners, to which she and Claud belonged. Above she and Claud were people with a lot of money and much bigger houses and much more land. But here the complexity of it would begin to bear in on her, for some of the poeple with a lot of money were common and ought to be below she and Claud and some of the poeple who had good blood had lost their money and had to rent and then there were colored people who owned their homes and land as well. There was a colored dentist in town who had two red Lincolns and a swimming pool and farm with registered white-faced cattle on it. Usually by the time she had fallen asleep all the classes of people were moiling and roiling around in her head, and she would dream they were all crammed in together in a box car, being ridden off to be put in a gas oven.

"That's a beautiful clock," she said and nodded to her right. It was a big 25 wall clock, the face encased in a brass sunburst.

"Yes, it's very pretty," the stylish lady said agreeably. "And right on the dot too," she added, glancing at her watch.

The ugly girl beside her cast an eye upward at the clock, smirked, then looked directly at Mrs. Turpin and smirked again. Then she returned her eyes to her book. She was obviously the lady's daughter because, although they didn't look anything alike as to disposition, they both had the same shape of face and the same blue eyes. On the lady they sparkled pleasantly but in the girl's seared face they appeared alternately to smolder and to blaze.

What if Jesus had said, "All right, you can be white-trash or a nigger or ugly"!

Mrs. Turpin felt an awful pity for the girl, though she thought it was one thing to be ugly and another to act ugly.

The woman with the snuff-stained lips turned around in her chair and looked up at the clock. Then she turned back and appeared to look a little to the side of Mrs. Turpin. There was a cast in one of her eyes. "You want to know wher you can get one of themther clocks?" she asked in a loud voice.

"No, I already have a nice clock," Mrs. Turpin said. Once somebody like her got a leg in the conversation, she would be all over it.

"You can get you one with green stamps," the woman said. "That's most likely wher he got hisn. Save you up enough, you can get you most anythang. I got me some joo'ry."

Ought to have got you a wash rag and some soap, Mrs. Turpin thought.

"I get contour sheets with mine," the pleasant lady said.

The daughter slammed her book shut. She looked straight in front of her, directly through Mrs. Turpin and on through the yellow curtain and the plate glass window which made the wall behind her. The girl's eyes seemed lit all of a sudden with a peculiar light, an unnatural light like night road signs give. Mrs. Turpin turned her head to see if there was anything going on outside that she should see, but she could not see anything. Figures passing cast only a pale shadow through the curtain. There was no reason the girl should single her out for her ugly looks.

"Miss Finley," the nurse said, cracking the door. The gum-chewing woman got up and passed in front of her and Claud and went into the office. She had on red high-heeled shoes.

Directly across the table, the ugly girl's eyes were fixed on Mrs. Turpin as if she had some very special reason for disliking her.

"This is wonderful weather, isn't it?" the girl's mother said.

"It's good weather for cotton if you can get the niggers to pick it," Mrs. Turpin said, "but niggers don't want to pick cotton any more. You can't get the white folks to pick it and now you can't get the niggers—because they got to be right up there with the white folks."

"They gonna *try* anyways," the white-trash woman said, leaning forward.

"Do you have one of those cotton-picking machines?" the pleasant lady asked.

"No," Mrs. Turpin said, "they leave half the cotton in the field. We don't have much cotton anyway. If you want to make it farming now, you have to have a little of everything. We got a couple of acres of cotton and a few hogs and chickens and just enough white-face that Claud can look after them himself."

"One thang I don't want," the white-trash woman said, wiping her mouth with the back of her hand. "Hogs. Nasty stinking things, a-gruntin and a-rootin all over the place."

Mrs. Turpin gave her the merest edge of attention. "Our hogs are not dirty and they don't stink," she said. "They're cleaner than some children I've seen. Their feet never touch the ground. We have a pig-parlor—that's where you raise them on concrete," she explained to the pleasant lady, "and Claud scoots them down with the hose every afternoon and washes off the floor."

Cleaner by far than that child right there, she thought. Poor nasty little thing. He had not moved except to put the thumb of his dirty hand into his mouth.

The woman turned her face away from Mrs. Turpin. "I know I wouldn't 45 scoot down no hog with no hose," she said to the wall.

You wouldn't have no hog to scoot down, Mrs. Turpin said to herself.

"A-gruntin and a-rootin and a-groanin," the woman muttered.

"We got a little of everything," Mrs. Turpin said to the pleasant lady. "It's no use in having more than you can handle yourself with help like it is. We found enough niggers to pick our cotton this year but Claud he has to go after them and take them home again in the evening. They can't walk that half a mile. No they can't. I tell you," she said and laughed merrily, "I sure am tired of buttering up niggers, but you got to love em if you want em to work for you. When they come in the morning, I run out and I say, 'Hi yawl this morning?' and when Claud drives them off to the field I just wave to beat the band and they just wave back." And she waved her hand rapidly to illustrate.

"Like you read out of the same book," the lady said, showing she understood perfectly.

"Child, yes," Mrs. Turpin said. "And when they come in from the field, 50 I run out with a bucket of icewater. That's the way it's going to be from now on," she said. "You may as well face it."

"One thang I know," the white-trash woman said. "Two thangs I ain't going to do: love no niggers or scoot down no hog with no hose." And she let out a bark of contempt.

The look that Mrs. Turpin and the pleasant lady exchanged indicated they both understood that you had to *have* certain things before you could *know* certain things. But every time Mrs. Turpin exchanged a look with the lady, she was aware that the ugly girl's peculiar eyes were still on her, and she had trouble bringing her attention back to the conversation.

"When you got something," she said, "you got to look after it." And when you ain't got a thing but breath and britches, she added to herself, you can afford to come to town every morning and just sit on the Court House coping and spit.

A grotesque revolving shadow passed across the curtain behind her and was thrown palely on the opposite wall. Then a bicycle clattered down against the outside of the building. The door opened and a colored boy glided in with a tray from the drug store. It had two large red and white paper cups on it with tops on them. He was a tall, very black boy in discolored white pants and a green nylon shirt. He was chewing gum slowly, as if to music. He set the tray down in the office opening next to the fern and stuck his head through to look for the secretary. She was not in there. He rested his arms on the ledge and waited, his narrow bottom stuck out, swaying slowly to the left and right. He raised a hand over his head and scratched the base of his skull.

"You see that button there, boy?" Mrs. Turpin said. "You can punch that 55 and she'll come. She's probably in the back somewhere."

"Is that right?" the boy said agreeably, as if he had never seen the button before. He leaned to the right and put his finger on it. "She sometime out," he said and twisted around to face his audience, his elbows behind him on the counter. The nurse appeared and he twisted back again. She handed him a dollar and he rooted in his pocket and made the change and counted it out to her. She gave him fifteen cents for a tip and he went out with the empty tray. The heavy door swung to slowly and closed at length with the sound of suction. For a moment no one spoke.

"They ought to send all them niggers back to Africa," the white-trash woman said. "That's wher they come from in the first place."

"Oh, I couldn't do without my good colored friends," the pleasant lady said.

"There's a heap of things worse than a nigger," Mrs. Turpin agreed. "It's all kinds of them just like it's all kinds of us."

"Yes, and it takes all kinds to make the world go round," the lady said in her musical voice.

As she said it, the raw-complexioned girl snapped her teeth together. Her lower lip turned downwards and inside out, revealing the pale pink inside of her mouth. After a second it rolled back up. It was the ugliest face Mrs. Turpin had ever seen anyone make and for a moment she was certain that the girl had made it at her. She was looking at her as if she had known and disliked her all her life—all of Mrs. Turpin's life, it seemed too, not just all the girl's life. Why, girl, I don't even know you, Mrs. Turpin said silently.

She forced her attention back to the discussion. "It wouldn't be practical to send them back to Africa," she said. "They wouldn't want to go. They got it too good here."

"Wouldn't be what they wanted—if I had anythang to do with it," the woman said.

"It wouldn't be a way in the world you could get all the niggers back over there," Mrs. Turpin said. "They'd be hiding out and lying down and turning sick on you and wailing and hollering and raring and pitching. It wouldn't be a way in the world to get them over there."

"They got over here," the trashy woman said. "Get back like they got 65 over."

"It wasn't so many of them then," Mrs. Turpin explained.

The woman looked at Mrs. Turpin as if here was an idiot indeed but Mrs. Turpin was not bothered by the look, considering where it came from.

"Nooo," she said, "they're going to stay here where they can go to New York and marry white folks and improve their color. That's what they all want to do, every one of them, improve their color."

"You know what comes of that, don't you?" Claud asked.

"No, Claud, what?" Mrs. Turpin said.   70

Claud's eyes twinkled. "White-faced niggers," he said with never a smile.

Everybody in the office laughed except the white-trash and the ugly girl. The girl gripped the book in her lap with white fingers. The trashy woman looked around her from face to face as if she thought they were all idiots. The old woman in the feed sack dress continued to gaze expressionless across the floor at the high-top shoes of the man opposite her, the one who had been pretending to be asleep when the Turpins came in. He was laughing heartily, his hands still spread out on his knees. The child had fallen to the side and was lying now almost face down in the old woman's lap.

While they recovered from their laughter, the nasal chorus on the radio kept the room from silence.

> *You go to blank blank*
> *And I'll go to mine*
> *But we'll all blank along*
> *To-geth-ther*
> *And all along the blank*
> *We'll hep each other out*
> *Smile-ling in any kind of*
> *Weath-ther!*

Mrs. Turpin didn't catch every word but she caught enough to agree with the spirit of the song and it turned her thoughts sober. To help anybody out that needed it was her philosophy of life. She never spared herself when she found somebody in need, whether they were white or black, trash or decent. And of all she had to be thankful for, she was most thankful that this was so. If Jesus had said, "You can be high society and have all the money you want and be thin and svelte-like, but you can't be a good woman with it," she would have had to say, "Well don't make me that then. Make me a good woman and it don't matter what else, how fat or how ugly or how poor!" Her heart rose. He had not made her a nigger or white-trash or ugly! He had made her herself and given her a little of everything. Jesus, thank you! she said. Thank you thank you thank you! Whenever she counted her blessings she felt as buoyant as if she weighed one hundred and twenty-five pounds instead of one hundred and eighty.

"What's wrong with your little boy?" the pleasant lady asked the white-   75
trashy woman.

"He has an ulcer," the woman said proudly. "He ain't give me a minute's peace since he was born. Him and her are just alike," she said, nodding at the old woman, who was running her leather fingers through the child's pale hair. "Look like I can't get nothing down them two but Co'Cola and candy."

That's all you try to get down em, Mrs. Turpin said to herself. Too lazy to light the fire. There was nothing you could tell her about people like them that she didn't know already. And it was not just that they didn't have anything. Because if you gave them everything, in two weeks it would all be broken or filthy or they would have chopped it up for lightwood. She knew all this from her own experience. Help them you must, but help them you couldn't.

All at once the ugly girl turned her lips inside out again. Her eyes were fixed like two drills on Mrs. Turpin. This time there was no mistaking that there was something urgent behind them.

Girl, Mrs. Turpin exclaimed silently, I haven't done a thing to you! The girl might be confusing her with somebody else. There was no need to sit by and let herself be intimidated. "You must be in college," she said boldly, looking directly at the girl. "I see you reading a book there."

The girl continued to stare and pointedly did not answer.   80

Her mother blushed at this rudeness. "The lady asked you a question, Mary Grace," she said under her breath.

"I have ears," Mary Grace said.

The poor mother blushed again. "Mary Grace goes to Wellesley College," she explained. She twisted one of the buttons on her dress. "In Massachusetts," she added with a grimace. "And in the summer she just keeps right on studying. Just reads all the time, a real book worm. She's done real well at Wellesley; she's taking English and Math and History and Psychology and Social Studies," she rattled on, "and I think it's too much. I think she ought to get out and have fun."

The girl looked as if she would like to hurl them all through the plate glass window.

"Way up north," Mrs. Turpin murmured and thought, well, it hasn't done 85 much for her manners.

"I'd almost rather to have him sick," the white-trash woman said, wrenching the attention back to herself. "He's so mean when he ain't. Look like some children just take natural to meanness. It's some gets bad when they get sick but he was the opposite. Took sick and turned good. He don't give me no trouble now. It's me waitin to see the doctor," she said.

If I was going to send anybody back to Africa, Mrs. Turpin thought, it would be your kind, woman. "Yes, indeed," she said aloud, but looking up at the ceiling, "it's a heap of things worse than a nigger." And dirtier than a hog, she added to herself.

"I think people with bad dispositions are more to be pitied than anyone on earth," the pleasant lady said in a voice that was decidely thin.

"I thank the Lord he has blessed me with a good one," Mrs. Turpin said. "The day has never dawned that I couldn't find something to laugh at."

"Not since she married me anyways," Claud said with a comical straight 90 face.

Everybody laughed except the girl and the white-trash.

Mrs. Turpin's stomach shook. "He's such a caution," she said, "that I can't help but laugh at him."

The girl made a loud ugly noise through her teeth.

Her mother's mouth grew thin and tight. "I think the worst thing in the world," she said, "is an ungrateful person. To have everything and not appreciate it. I know a girl," she said, "who has parents who would give her anything, a little brother who loves her dearly, who is getting a good education, who wears the best clothes, but who can never say a kind word to anyone, who never smiles, who just criticizes and complains all day long."

"Is she too old to paddle?" Claud asked.   95

The girl's face was almost purple.

"Yes," the lady said, "I'm afraid there's nothing to do but leave her to her folly. Some day she'll wake up and it'll be too late."

"It never hurt anyone to smile," Mrs. Turpin said. "It just makes you feel better all over."

"Of course," the lady said sadly, "but there are just some people you can't tell anything to. They can't take criticism."

"If it's one thing I am," Mrs. Turpin said with feeling, "it's grateful. When 100 I think who all I could have been besides myself and what all I got, a little of everything, and a good disposition besides, I just feel like shouting, 'Thank you, Jesus for making everything the way it is!' It could have been different!" For one thing, somebody else could have got Claud. At the thought of this, she was flooded with gratitude and a terrible pang of joy ran through her. "Oh thank you, Jesus, Jesus, thank you!" she cried aloud.

The book struck her directly over the left eye. It struck almost at the same instant that she realized the girl was about to hurl it. Before she could utter a sound, the raw face came crashing across the table toward her, howling. The girl's fingers sank like clamps into the soft flesh of her neck. She heard the mother cry out and Claud shout, "Whoa!" There was an instant when she was certain that she was about to be in an earthquake.

All at once her vision narrowed and she saw everything as if it were happening in a small room far away, or as if she were looking at it through the wrong end of a telescope. Claud's face crumpled and fell out of sight. The nurse ran in, then out, then in again. Then the gangling figure of the doctor rushed out of the inner door. Magazines flew this way and that as the table turned over. The girl fell with a thud and Mrs. Turpin's vision suddenly reversed itself and she saw everything large instead of small. The eyes of the white-trashy woman were staring hugely at the floor. There the girl, held down on one side by the nurse and on the other by her mother, was wrenching and turning in their grasp. The doctor was kneeling astride her, trying to hold her arm down. He managed after a second to sink a long needle into it.

Mrs. Turpin felt entirely hollow except for her heart which swung from side to side as if it were agitated in a great empty drum of flesh.

"Somebody that's not busy call for the ambulance," the doctor said in the off-hand voice young doctors adopt for terrible occasions.

Mrs. Turpin could not have moved a finger. The old man who had been 105 sitting next to her skipped nimbly into the office and made the call, for the secretary still seemed to be gone.

"Claud!" Mrs. Turpin called.

He was not in his chair. She knew she must jump up and find him but she felt like some one trying to catch a train in a dream, when everything moves in slow motion and the faster you try to run the slower you go.

"Here I am," a suffocated voice, very unlike Claud's, said.

He was doubled up in the corner on the floor, pale as paper, holding his leg. She wanted to get up and go to him but she could not move. Instead, her gaze was drawn slowly downward to the churning face on the floor, which she could see over the doctor's shoulder.

The girl's eyes stopped rolling and focused on her. They seemed a much 110 lighter blue than before, as if a door that had been tightly closed behind them was now open to admit light and air.

Mrs. Turpin's head cleared and her power of motion returned. She leaned forward until she was looking directly into the fierce brilliant eyes. There was no doubt in her mind that the girl did know her, knew her in some intense and personal way, beyond time and place and condition. "What you got to say to me?" she asked hoarsely and held her breath, waiting, as for a revelation.

The girl raised her head. Her gaze locked with Mrs. Turpin's. "Go back to hell where you came from, you old wart hog," she whispered. Her voice was low but clear. Her eyes burned for a moment as if she saw with pleasure that her message had struck its target.

Mrs. Turpin sank back in her chair.

After a moment the girl's eyes closed and she turned her head wearily to the side.

The doctor rose and handed the nurse the empty syringe. He leaned 115 over and put both hands for a moment on the mother's shoulders, which were shaking. She was sitting on the floor, her lips pressed together, holding Mary Grace's hand in her lap. The girl's fingers were gripped like a baby's around her thumb. "Go on to the hospital," he said. "I'll call and make the arrangements."

"Now let's see that neck," he said in a jovial voice to Mrs. Turpin. He became to inspect her neck with his first two fingers. Two little moon-shaped lines like pink fish bones were indented over her windpipe. There was the beginning of an angry red swelling above her eye. His fingers passed over this also.

"Lea' me be," she said thickly and shook him off. "See about Claud. She kicked him."

"I'll see about him in a minute," he said and felt her pulse. He was a thin grey-haired man, given to pleasantries. "Go home and have yourself a vacation the rest of the day," he said and patted her on the shoulder.

Quit your pattin me, Mrs. Turpin growled to herself.

"And put an ice pack over that eye," he said. Then he went and squatted 120 down beside Claud and looked at his leg. After a moment he pulled him up and Claud limped after him into the office.

Until the ambulance came, the only sounds in the room were the tremulous moans of the girl's mother, who continued to sit on the floor. The white-trash woman did not take her eyes off the girl. Mrs. Turpin looked straight ahead at nothing. Presently the ambulance drew up, a long dark shadow, behind the curtain. The attendants came in and set the stretcher down beside the girl and lifted her expertly onto it and carried her out. The nurse helped the mother gather up her things. The shadow of the ambulance moved silently away and the nurse came back in the office.

"That ther girl is going to be a lunatic, ain't she?" the white-trash woman asked the nurse, but the nurse kept on to the back and never answered her.

"Yes, she's going to be a lunatic," the white-trash woman said to the rest of them.

"Po' critter," the old woman murmured. The child's face was still in her lap. His eyes looked idly out over her knees. He had not moved during the disturbance except to draw one leg up under him.

"I thank Gawd," the white-trash woman said fervently, "I ain't a lunatic." 125

Claud came limping out and the Turpins went home.

As their pick-up truck turned into their own dirt road and made the crest of the hill, Mrs. Turpin gripped the window ledge and looked out suspiciously. The land sloped gracefully down through a field dotted with lavender weeds and at the start of the rise their small yellow frame house, with its little flower beds spread out around it like a fancy apron, sat primly in its accustomed place between two giant hickory trees. She would not have been startled to see a burnt wound between two blackened chimneys.

Neither of them felt like eating so they put on their house clothes and lowered the shade in the bedroom and lay down, Claud with his leg on a pillow and herself with a damp washcloth over her eye. The instant she was flat on her back the image of a razor-backed hog with warts on its face and horns coming out behind its ears snorted into her head. She moaned, a low quiet moan.

"I am not," she said tearfully, "a wart hog. From hell." But the denial had no force. The girl's eyes and her words, even the tone of her voice, low but clear, directed only to her, brooked no repudiation. She had been singled out for the message, though there was trash in the room to whom it might justly have been applied. The full force of this fact struck her only now. There was a woman there who was neglecting her own child but she had been over-looked. The message had been given to Ruby Turpin, a respectable, hard-working, church-going woman. The tears dried. Her eyes began to burn in-stead with wrath.

She rose on her elbow and the washcloth fell into her hand. Claud was   130 lying on his back, snoring. She wanted to tell him what the girl had said. At the same time, she did not wish to put the image of herself as a wart hog from hell into his mind.

"Hey, Claud," she muttered and pushed his shoulder.

Claud opened one pale baby blue eye.

She looked into it warily. He did not think about anything. He just went his way.

"Wha, whasit?" he said and closed the eye again.

"Nothing," she said. "Does your leg pain you?"   135

"Hurts like hell," Claud said.

"It'll quit terreckley," she said and lay back down. In a moment Claud was snoring again. For the rest of the afternoon they lay there. Claud slept. She scowled at the ceiling. Occasionally she raised her fist and made a small stab-bing motion over her chest as if she was defending her innocence to invisible guests who were like the comforters of Job,[1] reasonable-seeming but wrong.

About five-thirty Claud stirred. "Got to go after those niggers," he sighed, not moving.

She was looking straight up as if there were unintelligible handwriting on the ceiling. The protuberance over her eye had turned a greenish-blue. "Listen here," she said.

"What?"   140

"Kiss me."

Claud leaned over and kissed her loudly on the mouth. He pinched her side and their hands interlocked. Her expression of ferocious concentration did not change. Claud got up, groaning and growling, and limped off. She con-tinued to study the ceiling.

She did not get up until she heard the pick-up truck coming back with the Negroes. Then she rose and thrust her feet in her brown oxfords, which

---

[1] **Job** In the Book of Job, in the Hebrew Bible, Job is afflicted terribly. Friends seek to comfort him, but they insist that he must have sinned and offended God. Job rejects their view, insisting on his sinlessness, but at the end, when God addressed him in a whirlwind, Job is humbled and he says, "I abhor myself, and repent in dust and ashes."

she did not bother to lace, and stumped out onto the back porch and got her
red plastic bucket. She emptied a tray of ice cubes into it and filled it half full
of water and went out into the back yard. Every afternoon after Claud brought
the hands in, one of the boys helped him put out hay and the rest waited in
the back of the truck until he was ready to take them home. The truck was
parked in the shade under one of the hickory trees.

"Hi yawl this evening?" Mrs. Turpin asked grimly, appearing with the
bucket and the dipper. There were three women and a boy in the truck.

"Us doing nicely," the oldest woman said. "Hi you doin?" and her gaze   145
stuck immediately on the dark lump on Mrs. Turpin's forehead. "You done fell
down, ain't you?" she asked in a solicitous voice. The old woman was dark
and almost toothless. She had on an old felt hat of Claud's set back on her
head. The other two women were younger and lighter and they both had new
bright green sun hats. One of them had hers on her head; the other had taken
hers off and the boy was grinning beneath it.

Mrs. Turpin set the bucket down on the floor of the truck. "Yawl hep
youselves," she said. She looked around to make sure Claud had gone. "No.
I didn't fall down," she said, folding her arms. "It was something worse than
that."

"Ain't nothing bad happen to you!" the old woman said. She said it as if
they all knew that Mrs. Turpin was protected in some special way by Divine
Providence. "You just had you a little fall."

"We were in town at the doctor's office for where the cow kicked Mr.
Turpin," Mrs. Turpin said in a flat tone that indicated they could leave off their
foolishness. "And there was this girl there. A big fat girl with her face all
broke out. I could look at that girl and tell she was peculiar but I couldn't tell
how. And me and her mama were just talking and going along and all of a sudden WHAM! She throws this big book she was reading at me and . . ."

"Naw!" the old woman cried out.

"And then she jumps over the table and commences to choke me."   150

"Naw!" they all exclaimed, "naw!"

"Hi come she do that?" the old woman asked. "What ail her?"

Mrs. Turpin only glared in front of her.

"Somethin ail her," the old woman said.

"They carried her off in an ambulance," Mrs. Turpin continued, "but be- 155
fore she went she was rolling on the floor and they were trying to hold her
down to give her a shot and she said something to me." She paused. "You
know what she said to me?"

"What she say?" they asked.

"She said," Mrs. Turpin began, and stopped, her face very dark and
heavy. The sun was getting whiter and whiter, blanching the sky overhead so
that the leaves of the hickory tree were black in the face of it. She could not
bring forth the words. "Something real ugly," she muttered.

"She sho shouldn't say nothing ugly to you," the old woman said. "You
so sweet. You the sweetest lady I know."

"She pretty too," the one with the hat on said.

"And stout," the other one said. "I never knowed no sweeter white lady." 160

"That's the truth befo' Jesus," the old woman said. "Amen! You des as
sweet and pretty as you can be."

Mrs. Turpin knew just exactly how much Negro flattery was worth and it added to her rage. "She said," she began again and finished this time with a fierce rush of breath, "that I was an old wart hog from hell."

There was an astounded silence.

"Where she at?" the youngest woman cried in a piercing voice.

"Lemme see her. I'll kill her!   165

"I'll kill her with you!" the other one cried.

"She b'long in the sylum," the old woman said emphatically. "You the sweetest white lady I know."

"She pretty too," the other two said. "Stout as she can be and sweet. Jesus satisfied with her!"

"Deed he is," the old woman declared.

Idiots! Mrs. Turpin growled to herself. You could never say anything in- 170
telligent to a nigger. You could talk at them but not with them. "Yawl ain't drunk your water," she said shortly. "Leave the bucket in the truck when you're finished with it. I got more to do than just stand around and pass the time of day," and she moved off and into the house.

She stood for a moment in the middle of the kitchen. The dark protuber-ance over her eye looked like a miniature tornado cloud which might any mo-ment sweep across the horizon of her brow. Her lower lip protruded danger-ously. She squared her massive shoulders. Then she marched into the front of the house and out the side door and started down the road to the pig parlor. She had the look of a woman going single-handed, weaponless, into battle.

The sun was a deep yellow now like a harvest moon and was riding west-ward very fast over the far tree line as if it meant to reach the hogs before she did. The road was rutted and she kicked several good-sized stones out of her path as she strode along. The pig parlor was on a little knoll at the end of a lane that ran off from the side of the barn. It was a square of concrete as large as a small room, with a board fence about four feet high around it. The concrete floor sloped slightly so that the hog wash could drain off into a trench where it was carried to the field for fertilizer. Claud was standing on the outside, on the edge of the concrete, hanging onto the top board, hosing down the floor inside. The hose was connected to the faucet of a water trough nearby.

Mrs. Turpin climbed up beside him and glowered down at the hogs in-side. There were seven long-snouted bristly shoats in it—tan with liver-colored spots—and an old sow a few weeks off from farrowing. She was lying on her side grunting. The shoats were running about shaking themselves like idiot children, their little slit pig eyes searching the floor for anything left. She had read that pigs were the most intelligent animal. She doubted it. They were supposed to be smarter than dogs. There had even been a pig as-tronaut. He had performed his assignment perfectly but died of a heart attack afterwards because they left him in his electric suit, sitting upright throughout his examination when naturally a hog should be on all fours.

A-gruntin and a-rootin and a-groanin.

"Gimme that hose," she said, yanking it away from Claud. "Go on and 175
carry them niggers home and then get off that leg."

"You look like you might have swallowed a mad dog," Claud observed, but he got down and limped off. He paid no attention to her humors.

Until he was out of earshot, Mrs. Turpin stood on the side of the pen, holding the hose and pointing the stream of water at the hind quarter of any shoat that looked as if it might try to lie down. When he had had time to get over the hill, she turned her head slightly and her wrathful eyes scanned the path. He was nowhere in sight. She turned back again and seemed to gather herself up. Her shoulders rose and she drew in her breath.

"What do you send me a message like that for?" she said in a low fierce voice, barely above a whisper but with the force of a shout in its concentrated fury. "How am I a hog and me both? How am I saved and from hell too?" Her free fist was knotted and with the other she gripped the hose, blindly pointing the stream of water in and out of the eye of the old sow whose outraged squeal she did not hear.

The pig parlor commanded a view of the back pasture where their twenty beef cows were gathered around the hay-bales Claud and the boy had put out. The freshly cut pasture sloped down to the highway. Across it was their cotton field and beyond that a dark green dusty wood which they owned as well. The sun was behind the wood, very red, looking over the paling of trees like a farmer inspecting his own hogs.

"Why me?" she rumbled. "It's no trash around here, black or white, that 180 I haven't given to. And break my back to the bone every day working. And do for the church."

She appeared to be the right size woman to command the arena before her. "How am I a hog?" she demanded. "Exactly how am I like them?" and she jabbed the stream of water at the shoats. "There was plenty of trash there. It didn't have to be me."

"If you like trash better, go get yourself some trash then," she railed. "You could have made me trash. Or a nigger. If trash is what you wanted why didn't you make me trash?" She shook her fist with the hose in it and a watery snake appeared momentarily in the air. "I could quit working and take it easy and be filthy," she growled. "Lounge about the sidewalks all day drinking root beer. Dip snuff and spit in every puddle and have it all over my face. I could be nasty."

"Or you could have made me a nigger. It's too late for me to be a nigger," she said with deep sarcasm, "but I could act like one. Lay down in the middle of the road and stop traffic. Roll on the ground."

In the deepening light everything was taking on a mysterious hue. The pasture was growing a peculiar glassy green and the streak of highway had turned lavender. She braced herself for a final assault and this time her voice rolled out over the pasture. "Go on," she yelled, "call me a hog! Call me a hog again. From hell. Call me a wart hog from hell. Put that bottom rail on top. There'll still be a top and bottom!"

A garbled echo returned to her. 185

A final surge of fury shook her and she roared, "Who do you think you are?"

The color of everything, field and crimson sky, burned for a moment with a transparent intensity. The question carried over the pasture and across the highway and the cotton field and returned to her clearly like an answer from beyond the wood.

She opened her mouth but no sound came out of it.

A tiny truck, Claud's, appeared on the highway, heading rapidly out of sight. Its gears scraped thinly. It looked like a child's toy. At any moment a bigger truck might smash into it and scatter Claud's and the niggers' brains all over the road.

Mrs. Turpin stood there, her gaze fixed on the highway, all her muscles rigid, until in five or six minutes the truck reappeared, returning. She waited until it had had time to turn into their own road. Then like a monumental statue coming to life, she bent her head slowly and gazed, as if through the very heart of the mystery, down into the pig parlor at the hogs. They had settled all in one corner around the old sow who was grunting softly. A red glow suffused them. They appeared to pant with a secret life.

Until the sun slipped finally between the tree line, Mrs. Turpin remained there with her gaze bent to them as if she were absorbing some abysmal life-giving knowledge. At last she lifted her head. There was only a purple streak in the sky, cutting through a field of crimson and leading, like an extension of the highway, into the descending dusk. She raised her hands from the side of the pen in a gesture hieratic and profound. A visionary light settled in her eyes. She saw the streak as a vast swinging bridge extending upward from the earth through a field of living fire. Upon it a vast horde of souls were rumbling toward heaven. There were whole companies of white-trash, clean for the first time in their lives, and bands of black niggers in white robes, and battalions of freaks and lunatics shouting and clapping and leaping like frogs. And bringing up the end of the procession was a tribe of people whom she recognized at once as those who, like herself and Claud, had always had a little of everything and the God-given wit to use it right. She leaned forward to observe them closer. They were marching behind the others with great dignity, accountable as they had always been for good order and common sense and respectable behavior. They alone were on key. Yet she could see by their shocked and altered faces that even their virtues were being burned away. She lowered her hands and gripped the rail of the hog pen, her eyes small but fixed unblinkingly on what lay ahead. In a moment the vision faded but she remained where she was, immobile.

At length she got down and turned off the faucet and made her slow way on the darkening path to the house. In the woods around the invisible cricket choruses had struck up, but what she heard were the voices of the souls climbing upward into the starry field and shouting hallelujah.

[1964]

■ TOPICS FOR DISCUSSION AND WRITING

1. When Mrs. Turpin goes toward the pig parlor, she has "the look of a woman going single-handed, weaponless, into battle" (paragraph 171).
   Once there, she dismisses Claud, uses the hose as a weapon against the pigs, and talks to herself "in a low fierce voice." What is she battling, besides the pigs?

2. In 500 words, characterize Mrs. Turpin before her revelation.

3. If you have read Flannery O'Connor's "A Good Man Is Hard to Find," compare and contrast the grandmother and Mrs. Turpin, paying special

attention to their attitudes toward other people and their concepts of religion.

■ LESLIE MARMON SILKO

Leslie Marmon Silko—part Laguna Pueblo Indian, part Mexican, part Anglo—was born in 1948 in Albuquerque, New Mexico, and grew up on the Laguna Pueblo Reservation. After attending the Bureau of Indian Affairs school, she went to the University of New Mexico and graduated *cum laude* in 1969. She has taught at Navajo Community College and at the University of Arizona. In 1981 the MacArthur Foundation, recognizing Silko as an "exceptionally talented individual," granted her five years of financial support.

The Man to Send Rain Clouds

One

They found him under a big cottonwood tree. His Levi jacket and pants were faded light-blue so that he had been easy to find. The big cottonwood tree stood apart from a small grove of winterbare cottonwoods which grew in the wide, sandy arroyo. He had been dead for a day or more, and the sheep had wandered and scattered up and down the arroyo. Leon and his brother-in-law, Ken, gathered the sheep and left them in the pen at the sheep camp before they returned to the cottonwood tree. Leon waited under the tree while Ken drove the truck through the deep sand to the edge of the arroyo. He squinted up at the sun and unzipped his jacket—it sure was hot for this time of year. But high and northwest the blue mountains were still deep in snow. Ken came sliding down the low, crumbling bank about fifty yards down, and he was bringing the red blanket.

Before they wrapped the old man, Leon took a piece of string out of his pocket and tied a small gray feather in the old man's long white hair. Ken gave him the paint. Across the brown wrinkled forehead he drew a streak of white and along the high cheekbones he drew a strip of blue paint. He paused and watched Ken throw pinches of corn meal and pollen into the wind that fluttered the small gray feather. Then Leon painted with yellow under the old man's broad nose, and finally, when he had painted green across the chin, he smiled.

"Send us rain clouds, Grandfather." They laid the bundle in the back of the pickup and covered it with a heavy tarp before they started back to the pueblo.

They turned off the highway onto the sandy pueblo road. Not long after they passed the store and post office they saw Father Paul's car coming toward them. When he recognized their faces he slowed his car and waved for them to stop. The young priest rolled down the car window.

"Did you find old Teofilo?" he asked loudly.   5

Leon stopped the truck. "Good morning, Father. We were just out to the sheep camp. Everything is O.K. now."

"Thank God for that. Teofilo is a very old man. You really shouldn't allow him to stay at the sheep camp alone."

"No, he won't do that any more now."

"Well, I'm glad you understand. I hope I'll be seeing you at Mass this week—we missed you last Sunday. See if you can get old Teofilo to come with you." The priest smiled and waved at them as they drove away.

Two

Louise and Teresa were waiting. The table was set for lunch, and the   10
coffee was boiling on the black iron stove. Leon looked at Louise and then at Teresa.

"We found him under a cottonwood tree in the big arroyo near sheep camp. I guess he sat down to rest in the shade and never got up again." Leon walked toward the old man's bed. The red plaid shawl had been shaken and spread carefully over the bed, and a new brown flannel shirt and pair of stiff new Levis were arranged neatly beside the pillow. Louise held the screen door open while Leon and Ken carried in the red blanket. He looked small and shriveled, and after they dressed him in the new shirt and pants he seemed more shrunken.

It was noontime now because the church bells rang the Angelus. They ate the beans with hot bread, and nobody said anything until after Teresa poured the coffee.

Ken stood up and put on his jacket. "I'll see about the gravediggers. Only the top layer of soil is frozen. I think it can be ready before dark."

Leon nodded his head and finished his coffee. After Ken had been gone for a while, the neighbors and clanspeople came quietly to embrace Teofilo's family and to leave food on the table because the grave-diggers would come to eat when they were finished.

Three

The sky in the west was full of pale-yellow light. Louise stood outside   15
with her hands in the pockets of Leon's green army jacket that was too big for her. The funeral was over, and the old men had taken their candles and medicine bags and were gone. She waited until the body was laid into the pickup before she said anything to Leon. She touched his arm, and he noticed that her hands were still dusty from the corn meal that she had sprinkled around the old man. When she spoke, Leon could not hear her.

"What did you say? I didn't hear you."

"I said that I had been thinking about something."

"About what?"

"About the priest sprinkling holy water for Grandpa. So he won't be thirsty."

Leon stared at the new moccasins that Teofilo had made for the   20 ceremonial dances in the summer. They were nearly hidden by the red blanket. It was getting colder, and the wind pushed gray dust down the narrow pueblo road. The sun was approaching the long mesa where it disappeared during the winter. Louise stood there shivering and watching his face. Then he zipped up his jacket and opened the truck door. "I'll see if he's there."

Four

Ken stopped the pickup at the church, and Leon got out; and then Ken drove down the hill to the graveyard where people were waiting. Leon knocked at the old carved door with its symbols of the Lamb. While he waited he looked up at the twin bells from the king of Spain with the last sunlight pouring around them in their tower.

The priest opened the door and smiled when he saw who it was. "Come in! What brings you here this evening?"

The priest walked toward the kitchen, and Leon stood with his cap in his hand, playing with the earflaps and examining the living room—the brown sofa, the green armchair, and the brass lamp that hung down from the ceiling by links of chain. The priest dragged a chair out of the kitchen and offered it to Leon.

"No thank you, Father. I only came to ask you if you would bring your holy water to the graveyard."

The priest turned away from Leon and looked out the window at the patio 25 full of shadows and the dining-room windows of the nuns' cloister across the patio. The curtains were heavy, and the light from within faintly penetrated; it was impossible to see the nuns inside eating supper. "Why didn't you tell me he was dead? I could have brought the Last Rites anyway."

Leon smiled. "It wasn't necessary, Father."

The priest stared down at his scuffed brown loafers and the worn hem of his cassock. "For a Christian burial it was necessary."

His voice was distant, and Leon thought that his blue eyes looked tired.

"It's O.K., Father, we just want him to have plenty of water."

The priest sank down in the green chair and picked up a glossy mission- 30 ary magazine. He turned the colored pages full of lepers and pagans without looking at them.

"You know I can't do that, Leon. There should have been the Last Rites and a funeral Mass at the very least."

Leon put on his green cap and pulled the flaps down over his ears. "It's getting late, Father. I've got to go."

When Leon opend the door Father Paul stood up and said, "Wait." He left the room and came back wearing a long brown overcoat. He followed Leon out the door and across the dim churchyard to the adobe steps in front of the church. They both stooped to fit through the low adobe entrance. And when they started down the hill to the graveyard only half of the sun was visible above the mesa.

The priest approached the grave slowly, wondering how they had managed to dig into the frozen ground; and then he remembered that this was

New Mexico, and saw the pile of cold loose sand beside the hole. The people stood close to each other with little clouds of steam puffing from their faces. The priest looked at them and saw a pile of jackets, gloves, and scarves in the yellow, dry tumbleweeds that grew in the graveyard. He looked at the red blanket, not sure that Teofilo was so small, wondering if it wasn't some perverse Indian trick—something they did in March to ensure a good harvest—wondering if maybe old Teofilo was actually at sheep camp corraling the sheep for the night. But there he was, facing into a cold dry wind and squinting at the last sunlight, ready to bury a red wool blanket while the faces of the parishioners were in shadow with the last warmth of the sun on their backs.

His fingers were stiff, and it took them a long time to twist the lid off 35 the holy water. Drops of water fell on the red blanket and soaked into dark icy spots. He sprinkled the grave and the water disappeared almost before it touched the dim, cold sand; it reminded him of something—he tried to remember what it was, because he thought if he could remember he might understand this. He sprinkled more water; he shook the container until it was empty, and the water fell through the light from sundown like August rain that fell while the sun was still shining, almost evaporating before it touched the wilted squash flowers.

The wind pulled at the priest's brown Franciscan robe and swirled away the corn meal and pollen that had been sprinkled on the blanket. They lowered the bundle into the ground, and they didn't bother to untie the stiff pieces of new rope that were tied around the ends of the blanket. The sun was gone, and over on the highway the eastbound lane was full of headlights. The priest walked away slowly. Leon watched him climb the hill, and when he had disappeared within the tall, thick walls, Leon turned to look up at the high blue mountains in the deep snow that reflected a faint red light from the west. He felt good because it was finished, and he was happy about the sprinkling of the holy water; now the old man could send them big thunderclouds for sure.

[1969]

■ TOPICS FOR DISCUSSION AND WRITING

1. How would you describe the response of Leon, Ken, Louise, and Teresa to Teofilo's death? To what degree does it resemble or differ from responses to death that you are familiar with?
2. How do the funeral rites resemble or differ from those of your community?
3. How well does Leon understand the priest? How well does the priest understand Leon?
4. At the end of the story we are told that Leon "felt good." Do you assume that the priest also felt good? Why, or why not?
5. From what point of view is the story told? Mark the passages where the narrator enters a character's mind, and then explain what, in your opinion, Silko gains (or loses?) by doing so.

POETRY

■ JOHN DONNE

John Donne (1572–1631) was born into a Roman Catholic family in England, but in the 1590s he abandoned that faith. In 1615 he became an Anglican priest and soon was known as a great preacher. One hundred and sixty of his sermons survive, including one with the famous line, "No man is an island, entire of itself; every man is a piece of the continent, a part of the main; if a clod be washed away by the sea, Europe is the less . . .; and therefore never send to know for whom the bell tolls; it tolls for thee." From 1621 until his death he was dean of St Paul's Cathedral in London. His love poems (often bawdy and cynical) are said to be his early work, and his "Holy Sonnets" (among the greatest religious poems written in English) his later work.

Holy Sonnet IV

At the round earth's imagined corners, blow
Your trumpets, angels, and arise, arise
From death, you numberless infinities
Of souls, and to your scattered bodies go,   4
All whom the flood did, and fire shall o'erthrow,
All whom war, dearth, age, agues, tyrannies,
Despair, law, chance, hath slain, and you whose eyes,
Shall behold God, and never taste death's woe.   8
But let them sleep, Lord, and me mourn a space,
For, if above all these, my sins abound,
'Tis late to ask abundance of thy grace,
When we are there; here on this lowly ground,   12
Teach me how to repent; for that's as good
As if thou hadst sealed[1] my pardon, with thy blood.

                                        [1633]

■ TOPICS FOR DISCUSSION AND WRITING

1. What is the speaker envisioning in the first four lines? Put into your own words the meaning of line 5.
2. What is the effect of piling up nouns in lines 6–7?
3. In which line is there the most marked change of tone? Why does the change occur?

---

[1] Confirmed, with a seal

Holy Sonnet XIV

Batter my heart, three-personed God; for you
As yet but knock, breathe, shine, and seek to mend;
That I may rise and stand, o'erthrow me, and bend
Your force, to break, blow, burn, and make me new.   4
I, like an usurped town, to another due,
Labor to admit you, but oh, to no end.
Reason, your viceroy in me, me should defend,
But is captived, and proves weak or untrue.   8
Yet dearly I love you, and would be loved fain,
But am betrothed unto your enemy:
Divorce me, untie, or break that knot again,
Take me to you, imprison me, for I   12
Except you enthrall me, never shall be free,
Nor ever chaste, except you ravish me.

[1633]

■ TOPICS FOR DISCUSSION AND WRITING

1. Explain the paradoxes (apparent contradictions) in lines 1, 3, 13, and 14.
   Explain the double meanings of "enthrall" (line 13) and "ravish" (line 14).
2. In lines 1–4, what is God implicitly compared to (considering especially
   lines 2 and 4)? How does this comparison lead into the comparison that
   dominates lines 5–8? What words in lines 9–12 are especially related to
   the earlier lines?
3. What is gained by piling up verbs in lines 2–4?
4. Are sexual references necessarily irreverent in a religious poem? (Donne,
   incidentally, was an Anglican priest.)

■ EMILY DICKINSON

    Emily Dickinson (1830–1886) was born into a proper New England
family in Amherst, Massachusetts. Although she spent her seventeenth
year a few miles away, at Mount Holyoke Seminary (now Mount Holyoke
College), in her twenties and thirties she left Amherst only five or six
times, and in her last twenty years she may never have left her house.
Her brother was probably right when he said that having seen something
of the rest of the world—she had visited Washington with her father
when he was a member of congress— "she could not resist the feeling
that it was painfully hollow. It was to her so thin and unsatisfying in the
face of the Great Realities of Life."

    Dickinson lived with her parents (a somewhat reclusive mother and
an austere, remote father) and a younger sister; a married brother lived
in the house next door. She did, however, form some passionate attachments, to women as well as men. but there is no evidence that they
found physical expression.

By the age of 12 Dickinson was writing witty letters, but she apparently did not write more than an occasional poem before her late twenties. At her death—she died in the house where she was born—she left 1,775 poems, only seven of which had been published (anonymously) during her lifetime.

Those—dying, then

Those—dying, then
Knew where they went
They went to God's Right Hand—
The Hand is amputated now
And God cannot be found—

The abdication of Belief
Makes the Behavior small—
Better an ignis fatuus
Than no illume at all—

[1882]

■ TOPICS FOR DISCUSSION AND WRITING

1. In a sentence or two, state the point of the poem.
2. Is the image in line 4 in poor taste? Explain.
3. What is an *ignis fatuus?* In what ways does it connect visually with traditional images of hell and heaven?
4. If you have read William James's "Religious Faith" (page 909), in an essay of 500 words consider the degree to which these two writers agree.

There's a certain Slant of light

There's a certain Slant of light,
Winter Afternoons—
That oppresses, like the Heft[1]
Of Cathedral Tunes—   4

Heavenly Hurt, it gives us—
We can find no scar,
But internal difference,
Where the Meanings, are—   8

None may teach it—Any—
'Tis the Seal Despair—
An imperial affliction
Sent us of the Air—   12

When it comes, the Landscape listens—
Shadows—hold their breath—

[1] Heaviness, weight

When it goes, 'tis like the Distance
On the look of Death— 16

[c. 1861]

■ TOPICS FOR DISCUSSION AND WRITING

1. In the first stanza, what kind or kinds of music does "Cathedral Tunes" suggest? In what ways might they (and the light to which they are compared) be oppressive?

2. In the second stanza, the effect on us of the light is further described. Try to paraphrase Dickinson's lines, or interpret them. Compare your paraphrase or interpretation with that of a classmate or someone else who has read the poem. Are your interpretations similar? If not, can you account for some of the differences?

3. In the third stanza, how would you interpret "None may teach it"? Is the idea "No one can instruct (or tame) the light to be different"? Or "No one can teach us what we learn from the light"? Or do you have a different reading of this line?

4. "Death" is the last word of the poem. Rereading the poem, how early (and in what words or images) is "death" suggested or foreshadowed?

5. Try to describe the rhyme scheme. Then, a more difficult business, try to describe the effect of the rhyme scheme. Does it work with or against the theme, or meaning, of the poem?

6. What is the relationship in the poem between the light as one might experience it in New England on a winter afternoon and the experience of despair? To put it crudely, does the light itself cause despair, or does Dickinson see the light as an image or metaphor for human despair? And how is despair related to death?

7. Overall, how would you describe the tone of the poem? Anguished? Serene? Resigned?

This World is not Conclusion

This World is not Conclusion.
A Species stands beyond—
Invisible, as Music—
But positive, as Sound— 4
It beckons, and it baffles—
Philosophy—dont know—
And through a Riddle, at the last—
Sagacity, must go— 8
To guess it, puzzles scholars—
To gain it, Men have borne
Contempt of Generations
And Crucifixion, shown— 12
Faith slips—and laughs, and rallies—
Blushes, if any see—
Plucks at a twig of Evidence—
And asks a Vane, the way— 16
Much Gesture, from the Pulpit—

Strong Hallelujahs roll—
Narcotics cannot still the Tooth
That nibbles at the soul—   20
[c. 1862]

■ TOPICS FOR DISCUSSION AND WRITING

1. Given the context of the first two lines, what do you think "Conclusion" means in the first line?

2. Although white spaces here are not used to divide the poem into stanzas, the poem seems to be constructed in units of four lines each. Summarize each four-line unit in a sentence or two.

3. Compare your summaries with those of a classmate. If you substantially disagree, reread the poem to see if, on reflection, one or the other of you seems in closer touch with the poem. Or does the poem (or some part of it) allow for two very different interpretations?

4. In the first four lines the speaker seems (to use a word from line 4) quite "positive." Do some or all of the following stanzas seem less positive? If so, which—and what makes you say so?

5. Would you agree with a reader who said that "Much Gesture, from the Pulpit" (line 17) suggests—by its vigorous action—*a lack* of deep conviction?

■ CHRISTINA ROSSETTI
_____

Christina Rossetti (1830–1894) was the daughter of an exiled Italian patriot who lived in London and the sister of the poet and painter Dante Gabriel Rossetti. After her father became an invalid, she led an extremely ascetic life, devoting most of her life to doing charitable work. Her first and best-known volume of poetry, *Goblin Market and Other Poems*, was published in 1862.

Amor Mundi[1]

"Oh where are you going with your love-locks flowing,
    On the west wind blowing along this valley track?"
"The downhill path is easy, come with me an it please ye,
    We shall escape the uphill by never turning back."   4

So they two went together in glowing August weather,
    The honey-breathing heather lay to their left and right;
And dear she was to doat on, her swift feet seemed to float on
    The air like soft twin pigeons too sportive to alight.   8

"Oh what is that in heaven where grey cloud-flakes are seven,
    Where blackest clouds hang riven just as the rainy skirt?"

_____

[1] **amor mundi:** Latin for "love of the world." "World" here has the sense, common in the New Testament, of an arena of sin, or of human alienation from God.

"Oh that's a meteor sent us, a message dumb, portentous,
    An undeciphered solemn signal of help or hurt." 12

"Oh what is that glides quickly where velvet flowers grow thickly,
    Their scent comes rich and sickly?" "A scaled and hooded worm."
"Oh what's that in the hollow, so pale I quake to follow?"
    "Oh that's a thin dead body which waits the eternal term." 16

"Turn again, O my sweetest, —turn again, false and fleetest:
    This beaten way thou beatest, I fear, is hell's own track."
"Nay, too steep for hill mounting; nay, too late for cost counting:
    This downhill path is easy, but there's no turning back." 20

              [1865]

■ TOPICS FOR DISCUSSION AND WRITING

1   Taking into account "she" in line 7, try to assign all of the quoted passages, giving some to this "she" and the others to (presumably) a "he." Is it clear whether the seducer is male or female?

2.   The speaker of the last line of the poem says, "There's no turning back." Do you assume that the reader is to believe this assertion? Why, or why not? Christina Rossetti was a devout Anglo Catholic, but could one use this poem as evidence that she sometimes had moments of doubt about the possibility of free will and of salvation?

3.   The poem uses anapests, feminine rhymes, and internal rhymes (on these terms, see the Glossary at the rear of this book). What is their cumulative effect here?

Uphill

Does the road wind uphill all the way?
    Yes, to the very end.
Will the day's journey take the whole long day?
    From morn to night, my friend. 4

But is there for the night a resting-place?
    A roof for when the slow dark hours begin.
May not the darkness hide it from my face?
    You cannot miss that inn. 8

Shall I meet other wayfarers at night?
    Those who have gone before.
Then must I knock, or call when just in sight?
    They will not keep you standing at that door. 12

Shall I find comfort, travel-sore and weak?
    Of labor you shall find the sum.
Will there be beds for me and all who seek?
    Yea, beds for all who come. 16

            [1858]

■ TOPICS FOR DISCUSSION AND WRITING

1. Suppose that someone told you this poem is about a person preparing to
    go on a hike. The person is supposedly making inquiries about the road
    and the possible hotel arrangements. What would you reply?
2. Who is the questioner? A woman? A man? All human beings collectively?
    "Uphill," unlike Rossetti's "Amor Mundi" (see the previous poem), does
    not use quotation marks to distinguish between two speakers. Can one
    say that in "Uphill" the questioner and the answerer are the same
    person?
3. Are the answers unambiguously comforting? Or can it, for instance, be
    argued that the "roof" is (perhaps among other things) the lid of a
    coffin—hence the questioner will certainly not be kept "standing at that
    door"? If the poem can be read along these lines, is it chilling rather than
    comforting?

■ GERARD MANLEY HOPKINS

Gerard Manly Hopkins (1844–1889) was born near London and was
educated at Oxford, where he studied Classics. A convert from Anglicanism to Roman Catholicism, he was ordained a Jesuit priest in 1877. After
serving as a parish priest and teacher, he was appointed Professor of
Greek at the Catholic University in Dublin.

Hopkins published only a few poems during his lifetime, partly because he believed that the pursuit of literary fame was incompatible with
his vocation as a priest, and partly because he was aware that his highly
individual style might puzzle readers.

God's Grandeur

The world is charged with the grandeur of God.
    It will flame out, like shining from shook foil;
    It gathers to a greatness, like the ooze of oil
Crushed. Why do men then now not reck his rod?   4
Generations have trod, have trod, have trod;
    And all is seared with trade; bleared, smeared with toil;
    And wears man's smudge and shares man's smell: the soil
Is bare now, nor can foot feel, being shod.   8

And for all this, nature is never spent;
    There lives the dearest freshness deep down things;
And though the last lights off the black West went
    Oh, morning, at the brown brink eastward, springs—   12
Because the Holy Ghost over the bent
    World broods with warm breast and with ah! bright wings.
                      [1877]

■ TOPICS FOR DISCUSSION AND WRITING

1. Hopkins, a Roman Catholic priest, lived in England during the last decades of the nineteenth century—that is, in an industrialized society.
Where in the poem do you find him commenting on his setting? Circle
the words in the poem that can refer both to England's physical appearance and to the sinful condition of human beings.

2. What is the speaker's tone in the first three and a half lines (through
"Crushed")? In the rest of line 4? In lines 5–8? Is the second part of the
sonnet (the next six lines) more unified in *tone* or less? In an essay of
500 words describe the shifting tones of the speaker's voice. Probably after writing a first draft you will be able to form a thesis that describes an
overall pattern. As you revise your drafts, make sure that: (1) the thesis
is clear to the reader, and that (2) it is adequately supported by brief
quotations.

■ KRISTINE BATEY*

Lot's Wife

While Lot, the conscience of a nation,
struggles with the Lord,
she struggles with the housework.
The City of Sin is where
she raises the children.   5
Ba'al or Adonai—
Whoever is God—
the bread must still be made
and the doorsill swept.
The Lord may kill the children tomorrow,   10
but today they must be bathed and fed.
Well and good to condemn your neighbor's religion;
but weren't they there
when the baby was born,
and when the well collapsed?   15
While her husband communes with God
she tucks the children into bed.
In the morning, when he tells her of the judgment,
she puts down the lamp she is cleaning
and calmly begins to pack.   20
In between bundling up the children
and deciding what will go,
she runs for a moment
to say goodbye to the herd,
gently patting each soft head   25

*We have been unable to find any biographical information about Ms. Batey.

with tears in her eyes for the animals that will not understand.
She smiles blindly to the woman
who held her hand at childbed.
It is easy for eyes that have always turned to heaven
not to look back;   30
those that have been—by necessity—drawn to earth
cannot forget that life is lived from day to day.
Good, to a God, and good in human terms
are two different things.
On the breast of the hill, she chooses to be human,   35
and turns, in farewell—
and never regrets
the sacrifice.

[1978]

■ TOPICS FOR DISCUSSION AND WRITING

1. The story of the pious Lot, his wife, and the destruction of the wicked
    city of Sodom is told in the Old Testament, in Genesis 19:1-28. Briefly,
    Lot sheltered two angels who, in the form of men, visited him in Sodom.
    The townspeople sought to rape the angels, and the city was marked for
    destruction, but the angels warned Lot's family and urged them to flee
    and not to look back. Lot's wife, however, looked back and was turned
    into a pillar of salt. What was the message of the biblical tale? What does
    Batey see in the original tale? Do you find her interpretation compelling?
    Why?

2. In line 35, why "breast" instead of, say "crest" or "foot"?

3. Exactly what is "the sacrifice" Lot's wife makes in the last line?

DRAMA

A Note on Greek Tragedy

Little or nothing is known for certain of the origin of Greek tragedy. The
most common hypothesis holds that it developed from improvised speeches
during choral dances honoring Dionysos, a Greek nature god associated with
spring, fertility, and wine. Thespis (who perhaps never existed) is said to
have introduced an actor into these choral performances in the sixth century
B.C. Aeschylus (525–456 B.C.), Greece's first great writer of tragedies, added
the second actor, and Sophocles (496?–406 B.C.) added the third actor and

Greek theater of Epidaurus on the Peloponnesus east of Nauplia. (Photograph: Frederick Ayer, Photo Researchers, Inc.)

fixed the size of the chorus at fifteen. (Because the chorus leader often functioned as an additional actor, and because the actors sometimes doubled in their parts, a Greek tragedy could have more characters than might at first be thought.)

All of the extant great Greek tragedy is of the fifth century B.C. It was performed at religious festivals in the winter and early spring, in large outdoor amphitheaters built on hillsides. Some of these theaters were enormous; the one at Epidaurus held about fifteen thousand people. The audience sat in tiers, looking down on the *orchestra* (a dancing place), with the acting area behind it and the *skene* (the scene building) yet farther back. The scene building served as dressing room, background (suggesting a palace or temple), and place for occasional entrances and exits. Furthermore, this building helped to provide good acoustics, for speech travels well if there is a solid barrier behind the speaker and a hard, smooth surface in front of him, and if the audience sits in tiers. The wall of the scene building provided the barrier; the orchestra provided the surface in front of the actors; and the seats on the hillside fulfilled the third requirement. Moreover, the acoustics were somewhat improved by slightly elevating the actors above the orchestra, but it is not known exactly when this platform was first constructed in front of the scene building.

A tragedy commonly begins with a *prologos* (prologue), during which the exposition is given. Next comes the *parados*, the chorsus's ode of entrance, sung while the chorus marches into the theater, through the side aisles and onto the orchestra. The *epeisodion* (episode) is the ensuing scene; it is followed by a *stasimon* (choral song, ode). Usually there are four or five *epeisodia*, alternating with *stasima*. Each of these choral odes has a *strophe* (lines presumably sung while the chorus dances in one direction) and an *antistrophe* (lines presumably sung while the chorus retraces its steps). Sometimes a third part, an *epode*, concludes an ode. (In addition to odes that are *stasima*, there can be odes within episodes; the fourth episode of *Antigonê* (here called Scene IV) contains an ode complete with *epode*.) After the last part of the last ode comes the *exodos*, the epilogue or final scene.

The actors (all male) wore masks, and seem to have chanted much of the play. Perhaps the total result of combining speech with music and dancing was a sort of music-drama roughly akin to opera with some spoken dialogue, like Mozart's *Magic Flute*.

■ SOPHOCLES

One of the three great writers of tragedies in ancient Greece, Sophocles (496?–406 B.C.) was born in Colonus, near Athens, into a well-to-do family. Well educated, he first won public acclaim as a tragic poet at the age of 27, in 468 B.C., when he defeated Aeschylus in a competition for writing a tragic play. He is said to have written some 120 plays, but only seven tragedies are extant; among them are *Oedipus Rex, Antigone,* and *Oedipus at Colonus.* He died, much honored, in his ninetieth year, in Athens, where he had lived his entire life.

Oedipus Rex

An English Version by Dudley Fitts and Robert Fitzgerald

List of Characters
OEDIPUS
A PRIEST
CREON
TEIRESIAS
IOCASTÊ
MESSENGER
SHEPHERD OF LAÏOS
SECOND MESSENGER
CHORUS OF THEBAN ELDERS

Scene: Before the palace of OEDIPUS, *King of Thebes. A central door and two lateral doors open onto a platform which runs the length of the facade. On the platform, right and left, are altars; and three steps lead down into the "orchestra," or chorus-ground. At the beginning of the action these steps are crowded by* SUPPLIANTS *who have brought branches and chaplets of olive leaves and who lie in various attitudes of despair.* OEDIPUS *enters.*

PROLOGUE

OEDIPUS. My children, generations of the living
    In the line of Kadmos,° nursed at his ancient hearth;
    Why have you strewn yourselves before these altars
    In supplication, with your boughs and garlands?
    The breath of incense rises from the city   5
    With a sound of prayer and lamentation.
                       Children,
    I would not have you speak through messengers,
    And therefore I have come myself to hear you—
    I, Oedipus, who bear the famous name.
    [*To a* PRIEST.] You, there, since you are eldest
        in the company,   10
    Speak for them all, tell me what preys upon you,
    Whether you come in dread, or crave some blessing:
    Tell me, and never doubt that I will help you
    In every way I can; I should be heartless
    Were I not moved to find you suppliant here.   15
PRIEST. Great Oedipus, O powerful King of Thebes!
    You see how all the ages of our people
    Cling to your altar steps: here are boys
    Who can barely stand alone, and here are priests
    By weight of age, as I am a priest of God,   20

2 **Kadmos** mythical founder of Thebes

And young men chosen from those yet unmarried;
As for the others, all that multitude,
They wait with olive chaplets in the squares,
At the two shrines of Pallas,° and where Apollo°
Speaks in the glowing embers.
        Your own eyes   25
Must tell you: Thebes is in her extremity
And cannot lift her head from the surge of death.
A rust consumes the buds and fruits of the earth;
The herds are sick; children die unborn,
And labor is vain. The god of plague and pyre   30
Raids like detestable lightning through the city,
And all the house of Kadmos is laid waste,
All emptied, and all darkened: Death alone
Battens upon the misery of Thebes.
You are not one of the immortal gods, we know; 35
Yet we have come to you to make our prayer
As to the man of all men best in adversity
And wisest in the ways of God. You saved us
From the Sphinx,° that flinty singer, and the tribute
We paid to her so long; yet you were never   40
Better informed than we, nor could we teach you:
It was some god breathed in you to set us free.

Therefore, O mighty King, we turn to you:
Find us our safety, find us a remedy,
Whether by counsel of the gods or the men.   45
A king of wisdom tested in the past
Can act in a time of troubles, and act well.
Noblest of men, restore
Life to your city! Think how all men call you
Liberator for your triumph long ago;   50
Ah, when your years of kingship are remembered,
Let them not say *We rose, but later fell*—
Keep the State from going down in the storm!
Once, years ago, with happy augury,
You brought us fortune; be the same again!   55
No man questions your power to rule the land:
But rule over men, not over a dead city!
Ships are only hulls, citadels are nothing,
When no life moves in the empty passageways.
OEDIPUS. Poor children! You may be sure I know 60
All that you longed for in your coming here.

---

24 **Pallas** Athena, goddess of wisdom, protectress of Athens 24 **Apollo** god of light
and healing 39 **Sphinx** a monster (body of a lion, wings of a bird, face of a woman)
who asked the riddle, "What goes on four legs in the morning, two at noon, and three
in the evening?" and who killed those who could not answer. When Oedipus responded
correctly that man crawls on all fours in infancy, walks upright in maturity, and uses a
staff in old age, the Sphinx destroyed herself.

I know that you are deathly sick; and yet,
Sick as you are, not one is as sick as I.
Each of you suffers in himself alone
His anguish, not another's; but my spirit   65
Groans for the city, for myself, for you.

I was not sleeping, you are not waking me.
No, I have been in tears for a long while
And in my restless thought walked many ways.
In all my search, I found one helpful course,   70
And that I have taken: I have sent Creon,
Son of Menoikeus, brother of the Queen,
To Delphi, Apollo's place of revelation,
To learn there, if he can,
What act or pledge of mine may save the city.   75
I have counted the days, and now, this very day,
I am troubled, for he has overstayed his time.
What is he doing? He has been gone too long.
Yet whenever he comes back, I should do ill
To scant whatever hint the god may give.   80

PRIEST. It is a timely promise. At this instant
They tell me Creon is here.

OEDIPUS.   O Lord Apollo!
May his news be fair as his face is radiant!

PRIEST. It could not be otherwise: he is crowned with bay,
The chaplet is thick with berries.

OEDIPUS.   We shall soon know;   85
He is near enough to hear us now.

Enter CREON.

                                          O Prince:
Brother: son of Menoikeus:
What answer do you bring us from the god?

CREON. It is favorable. I can tell you, great afflictions
Will turn out well, if they are taken well.   90

OEDIPUS. What was the oracle? These vague words
Leave me still hanging between hope and fear.

CREON. Is it your pleasure to hear me with all these
Gathered around us? I am prepared to speak,
But should we not go in?

OEDIPUS.   Let them all hear it.   95
It is for them I suffer, more than myself.

CREON. Then I will tell you what I heard at Delphi.

In plain words
The god commands us to expel from the land of Thebes
An old defilement that it seems we shelter.   100
It is a deathly thing, beyond expiation.
We must not let it feed upon us longer.

OEDIPUS. What defilement? How shall we rid ourselves of it?

CREON. By exile or death, blood for blood. It was
    Murder that brought the plague-wind on the city.   105
OEDIPUS. Murder of whom? Surely the god has named him?
CREON. My lord: long ago Laïos was our king,
    Before you came to govern us.
OEDIPUS.   I know;
    I learned of him from others; I never saw him.
CREON. He was murdered; and Apollo commands us now   110
    To take revenge upon whoever killed him.
OEDIPUS. Upon whom? Where are they? Where shall we find a clue
    To solve that crime, after so many years?
CREON. Here in this land, he said.
                    If we make enquiry,
    We may touch things that otherwise escape us.   115
OEDIPUS. Tell me: Was Laïos murdered in his house,
    Or in the fields, or in some foreign country?
CREON. He said he planned to make a pilgrimage.
    He did not come home again.
OEDIPUS.   And was there no one,
    No witness, no companion, to tell what happened?   120
CREON. They were all killed but one, and he got away
    So frightened that he could remember one thing only.
OEDIPUS. What was that one thing? One may be the key
    To everything, if we resolve to use it.
CREON. He said that a band of highwaymen attacked them,   125
    Outnumbered them, and overwhelmed the King.
OEDIPUS. Strange, that a highwayman should be so daring—
    Unless some faction here bribed him to do it.
CREON. We thought of that. But after Laïos' death
    New troubles arose and we had no avenger.   130
OEDIPUS. What troubles could prevent your hunting
    down the killers?
CREON. The riddling Sphinx's song
    Made us deaf to all mysteries but her own
OEDIPUS. Then once more I must bring what is dark to light.
    It is most fitting that Apollo shows,   135
    As you do, this compunction for the dead.
    You shall see how I stand by you, as I should,
    To avenge the city and the city's god,
    And not as though it were for some distant friend,
    But for my own sake, to be rid of evil.   140
    Whoever killed King Laïos might—who knows?—
    Decide at any moment to kill me as well.
    By avenging the murdered king I protect myself.
    Come, then, my children: leave the altar steps,
    Lift up your olive boughs!
                    One of you go   145

And summon the people of Kadmos to gather here.
I will do all that I can; you may tell them that.   [*Exit a* PAGE.]
So, with the help of God,
We shall be saved—or else indeed we are lost.
PRIEST. Let us rise, children. It was for this we came,   150
And now the King has promised it himself.
Phoibos° has sent us an oracle; may he descend
Himself to save us and drive out the plague.

Exeunt OEDIPUS *and* CREON *into the palace by the central door. The* PRIEST *and
the* SUPPLIANTS *disperse right and left. After a short pause the* CHORUS *enters the
orchestra.*

PÁRODOS

CHORUS. What is God singing in his profound   *Strophe 1*
    Delphi of gold and shadow?
    What oracle for Thebes, the sunwhipped city?
    Fear unjoints me, the roots of my heart tremble.
    Now I remember, O Healer, your power, and wonder;   5
    Will you send doom like a sudden cloud, or weave it
    Like nightfall of the past?
    Speak, speak to us, issue of holy sound:
    Dearest to our expectancy: be tender!

    Let me pray to Athenê, the immortal daughter of Zeus, *Antistrophe 1* 10
    And to Artemis her sister
    Who keeps her famous throne in the market ring,
    And to Apollo, bowman at the far butts of heaven—

    O gods, descend! Like three streams leap against
    The fires of our grief, the fires of darkness;   15
    Be swift to bring us rest!

    As in the old time from the brilliant house
    Of air you stepped to save us, come again!

    Now our afflictions have no end,   *Strophe 2*
    Now all our stricken host lies down   20
    And no man fights off death with his mind;

    The noble plowland bears no grain,
    And groaning mothers cannot bear—
    See, how our lives like birds take wing,
    Like sparks that fly when a fire soars,   25
    To the shore of the god of evening.

    The plague burns on, it is pitiless   *Antistrophe 2*
    Though pallid children laden with death

152 *Phoibos* Phoebus Apollo, the sun god

Lie unwept in the stony ways,
And old gray women by every path
Flock to the strand about the altars

There to strike their breasts and cry
Worship of Phoibos in wailing prayers:
Be kind, God's golden child!

There are no swords in this attack by fire,   *Strophe 3* 35
No shields, but we are ringed with cries.
Send the besieger plunging from our homes
Into the vast sea-room of the Atlantic
Or into the waves that foam eastward of Thrace—
For the day ravages what the night spares—   40

Destroy our enemy, lord of the thunder!
Let him be riven by lightning from heaven!

Phoibos Apollo, stretch the sun's bowstring,   *Antistrophe 3*
That golden cord, until it sing for us,
Flashing arrows in heaven!
                              Artemis, Huntress,   45
Race with flaring lights upon our mountains!
O scarlet god, O golden-banded brow,
O Theban Bacchos° in a storm of Maenads,°

[*Enter* OEDIPUS, *center.*]

Whirl upon Death, that all the Undying hate!
Come with blinding cressets, come in joy!   50

SCENE I

OEDIPUS. Is this your prayer? It may be answered. Come,
Listen to me, act as the crisis demands,
And you shall have relief from all these evils.

Until now I was a stranger to this tale,
As I had been a stranger to the crime.   5
Could I track down the murderer without a clue?
But now, friends,
As one who became a citizen after the murder,
I make this proclamation to all Thebans:
If any man knows by whose hand Laîos, son of Labdakos,   10
Met his death, I direct that man to tell me everything,
No matter what he fears for having so long withheld it.
Let it stand as promised that no further trouble
Will come to him, but he may leave the land in safety.

Moreover: If anyone knows the murderer to be foreign,   15
Let him not keep silent: he shall have his reward from me.

48 **Bacchos** Dionysos, god of wine, thus scarlet-faced 48 **maenads** Dionysos's female
attendants

However, if he does conceal it; if any man
Fearing for his friend or for himself disobeys this edict,
Hear what I propose to do:

I solemnly forbid the people of this country,   20
Where power and throne are mine, ever to receive that man
Or speak to him, no matter who he is, or let him
Join in sacrifice, lustration, or in prayer.
I decree that he be driven from every house,

Being, as he is, corruption itself to us: the Delphic   25
Voice of Zeus has pronounced this revelation.
Thus I associate myself with the oracle
And take the side of the murdered king.

As for the criminal, I pray to God—
Whether it be a lurking thief, or one of a number—   30
I pray that that man's life be consumed in evil and wretchedness.
And as for me, this curse applies no less
If it should turn out that the culprit is my guest here,
Sharing my hearth.
                    You have heard the penalty.
I lay it on you now to attend to this   35
For my sake, for Apollo's, for the sick
Sterile city that heaven has abandoned.
Suppose the oracle had given you no command:
Should this defilement go uncleansed for ever?
You should have found the murderer: your king,   40
A noble king, had been destroyed!
                    Now I,
Having the power that he held before me,
Having his bed, begetting children there
Upon his wife, as he would have, had he lived—
Their son would have been my children's brother,   45
If Laîos had had luck in fatherhood!
(But surely ill luck rushed upon his reign)—
I say I take the son's part, just as though
I were his son, to press the fight for him
And see it won! I'll find the hand that brought   50
Death to Labdakos' and Polydoros' child,
Heir of Kadmos' and Agenor's line.
And as for those who fail me,
May the gods deny them the fruit of the earth,
Fruit of the womb, and may they rot utterly!   55
Let them be wretched as we are wretched, and worse!

For you, for loyal Thebans, and for all
Who find my actions right, I pray the favor
Of justice, and of all the immortal gods.
CHORAGOS. Since I am under oath, my lord, I swear   60
        I did not do the murder, I cannot name

The murderer. Might not the oracle
That has ordained the search tell where to find him?
OEDIPUS. An honest question. But no man in the world
    Can make the gods do more than the gods will.   65
CHORAGOS. There is one last expedient—
OEDIPUS.   Tell me what it is.
    Though it seem slight, you must not hold it back.
CHORAGOS. A lord clairvoyant to the lord Apollo,
    As we all know, is the skilled Teiresias.
    One might learn much about this from him, Oedipus.   70
OEDIPUS. I am not wasting time:
    Creon spoke of this, and I have sent for him—
    Twice, in fact; it is strange that he is not here.
CHORAGOS. The other matter—that old report—seems useless.
OEDIPUS. Tell me. I am interested in all reports.   75
CHORAGOS. The King was said to have been killed by highwaymen.
OEDIPUS. I know. But we have no witnesses to that.
CHORAGOS. If the killer can feel a particle of dread,
    Your curse will bring him out of hiding!
OEDIPUS.   No.
    The man who dared that act will fear no curse.   80

Enter the blind seer TEIRESIAS *led by a* PAGE.

CHORAGOS. But there is one man who may detect the criminal.
    This is Teiresias, this is the holy prophet
    In whom, alone of all men, truth was born.
OEDIPUS. Teiresias: seer: student of mysteries,
    Of all that's taught and all that no man tells,   85
    Secrets of Heaven and secrets of the earth:
    Blind though you are, you know the city lies
    Sick with plague; and from this plague, my lord,
    We find that you alone can guard or save us.

    Possibly you did not hear the messengers?   90
    Apollo, when we sent to him,
    Sent us back word that this great pestilence
    Would lift, but only if we established clearly
    The identity of those who murdered Laïos.
    They must be killed or exiled.
                        Can you use   95
    Birdflight or any art of divination
    To purify yourself, and Thebes, and me
    From this contagion? We are in your hands.
    There is no fairer duty
    Than that of helping others in distress.   100
TEIRESIAS. How dreadful knowledge of the truth can be
    When there's no help in truth! I knew this well,
    But did not act on it: else I should not have come.

OEDIPUS. What is troubling you? Why are your eyes so cold?

TEIRESIAS. Let me go home. Bear your own fate, and I'll   105
    Bear mine. It is better so: trust what I say.

OEDIPUS. What you say is ungracious and unhelpful
    To your native country. Do not refuse to speak.

TEIRESIAS. When it comes to speech, your own is neither temperate
    Nor opportune. I wish to be more prudent.   110

OEDIPUS. In God's name, we all beg you—

TEIRESIAS.   You are all ignorant.
    No; I will never tell you what I know.
    Now it is my misery; then, it would be yours.

OEDIPUS. What! You do know something, and will not tell us?
    You would betray us all and wreck the State?   115

TEIRESIAS. I do not intend to torture myself, or you.
    Why persist in asking? You will not persuade me.

OEDIPUS. What a wicked man you are! You'd try a stone's
    Patience! Out with it! Have you no feeling at all?

TEIRESIAS. You call me unfeeling. If you could only see   120
    The nature of your feelings. . .

OEDIPUS.   Why,
    Who would not feel as I do? Who could endure
    Your arrogance toward the city?

TEIRESIAS.   What does it matter!
    Whether I speak or not, it is bound to come.

OEDIPUS. Then, if "it" is bound to come, you are bound to tell me.   125

TEIRESIAS. No, I will not go on. Rage as you please

OEDIPUS. Rage? Why not!
                And I'll tell you what I think:
    You planned it, you had it done, you all but
    Killed him with your own hands: if you had eyes,
    I'd say the crime was yours, and yours alone.   130

TEIRESIAS. So? I charge you, then,
    Abide by the proclamation you have made.
    From this day forth
    Never speak again to these men or to me;
    You yourself are the pollution of this country.   135

OEDIPUS. You dare say that! Can you possibly think you have
    Some way of going free, after such insolence?

TEIRESIAS. I have gone free. It is the truth sustains me.

OEDIPUS. Who taught you shamelessness? It was not your craft.

TEIRESIAS. You did. You made me speak. I did not want to.   140

OEDIPUS. Speak what? Let me hear it again more clearly.

TEIRESIAS. Was it not clear before? Are you tempting me?

OEDIPUS. I did not understand it. Say it again.

TEIRESIAS. I say that you are the murderer whom you seek.

OEDIPUS. Now twice you have spat out infamy. You'll pay for it!   145

TEIRESIAS. Would you care for more? Do you wish to be really angry?

OEDIPUS. Say what you will. Whatever you say is worthless.

TEIRESIAS. I say you live in hideous shame with those
      Most dear to you. You cannot see the evil.
OEDIPUS. It seems you can go on mouthing like this for ever.   150
TEIRESIAS. I can, if there is power in truth.
OEDIPUS.   There is:
      But not for you, not for you,
      You sightless, witless, senseless, mad old man!
TEIRESIAS. You are the madman. There is no one here
      Who will not curse you soon, as you curse me.   155
OEDIPUS. You child of endless night! You cannot hurt me
      Or any other man who sees the sun.
TEIRESIAS. True: it is not from me your fate will come.
      That lies within Apollo's competence,
      As it is his concern.
OEDIPUS.   Tell me: 160
      Are you speaking for Creon, or for yourself?
TEIRESIAS. Creon is no threat. You weave your own doom.
OEDIPUS. Wealth, power, craft of statesmanship!
      Kingly position, everywhere admired!
      What savage envy is stored up against these,   165
      If Creon, whom I trusted, Creon my friend,
      For this great office which the city once
      Put in my hands unsought—if for this power
      Creon desires in secret to destroy me!

      He has brought this decrepit fortune-teller, this   170
      Collector of dirty pennies, this prophet fraud—
      Why, he is no more clairvoyant than I am!
                              Tell us:
      Has your mystic mummery ever approached the truth?
      When that hellcat the Sphinx was performing here,
      What help were you to these people?   175
      Her magic was not for the first man who came along:
      It demanded a real exorcist. Your birds—
      What good were they? or the gods, for the matter of that?
      But I came by,
      Oedipus, the simple man, who knows nothing—   180
      I thought it out for myself, no birds helped me!
      And this is the man you think you can destroy,
      That you may be close to Creon when he's king!
      Well, you and your friend Creon, it seems to me,
      Will suffer most. If you were not an old man,   185
      You would have paid already for your plot.
CHORAGOS. We cannot see that his words or yours
      Have spoken except in anger, Oedipus,
      And of anger we have no need. How can God's will
      Be accomplished best? That is what most concerns us.   190
TEIRESIAS. You are a king. But where argument's concerned
      I am your man, as much a king as you.

I am not your servant, but Apollo's.
I have no need of Creon to speak for me.

Listen to me. You mock my blindness, do you?   195
But I say that you, with both your eyes, are blind:
You cannot see the wretchedness of your life,
Not in whose house you live, no, nor with whom.
Who are your father and mother? Can you tell me?
You do not even know the blind wrongs   200
That you have done them, on earth and in the world below.
But the double lash of your parents' curse will whip you
Out of this land some day, with only night
Upon your precious eyes.
Your cries then—where will they not be heard?   205
What fastness of Kithairon° will not echo them?
And that bridal-descant of yours—you'll know it then,
The song they sang when you came here to Thebes
And found your misguided berthing.
All this, and more, that you cannot guess at now,   210
Will bring you to yourself among your children.
Be angry, then. Curse Creon. Curse my words.
I tell you, no man that walks upon the earth
Shall be rooted out more horribly than you.
OEDIPUS. Am I to bear this from him?—Damnation   215
     Take you! Out of this place! Out of my sight!
TEIRESIAS. I would not have come at all if you had not asked me.
OEDIPUS. Could I have told that you'd talk nonsense, that
     You'd come here to make a fool of yourself, and of me?
TEIRESIAS. A fool? Your parents thought me sane enough.   220
OEDIPUS. My parents again!—Wait: who were my parents?
TEIRESIAS. This day will give you a father, and break your heart.
OEDIPUS. Your infantile riddles! Your damned abracadabra!
TEIRESIAS. You were a great man once at solving riddles.
OEDIPUS. Mock me with that if you like; you will find it true.   225
TEIRESIAS. It was true enough. It brought about your ruin.
OEDIPUS. But if it saved this town.
TEIRESIAS. [to the PAGE]. Boy, give me your hand.
OEDIPUS. Yes, boy; lead him away.
                         —While you are here
     We can do nothing. Go; leave us in peace.
TEIRESIAS. I will go when I have said what I have to say.   230
     How can you hurt me? And I tell you again:
     The man you have been looking for all this time,
     The damned man, the murderer of Laïos,
     That man is in Thebes. To your mind he is foreignborn,
     But it will soon be shown that he is a Theban,   235

206 **fastness of Kithairon** stronghold in a mountain near Thebes

A revelation that will fail to please
A blind man,
Who has his eyes now; a penniless man, who is rich now;
And he will go tapping the strange earth with his staff;
To the children with whom he lives now he will be
Brother and father—the very same; to her   240
Who bore him, son and husband—the very same
Who came to his father's bed, wet with his father's blood.

Enough. Go think that over.
If later you find error in what I have said,
You may say that I have no skill in prophecy.   245

[*Exit* TEIRESIAS, *led by his* PAGE. OEDIPUS *goes into the palace.*]

ODE I

CHORUS. The Delphic stone of prophecies   *Strophe 1*
    Remembers ancient regicide
    And a still bloody hand.
    That killer's hour of flight has come.
    He must be stronger than riderless   5
    Coursers of untiring wind,
    For the son of Zeus° armed with his father's thunder
    Leaps in lightning after him;
    And the Furies° follow him, the sad Furies.

Holy Parnossos' peak of snow   *Antistrophe 1* 10
    Flashes and blinds that secret man,
    That all shall hunt him down:
    Though he may roam the forest shade
    Like a bull gone wild from pasture
    To rage through glooms of stone.   15
    Doom comes down on him; flight will not avail him;
    For the world's heart calls him desolate,
    And the immortal Furies follow, for ever follow.

But now a wilder thing is heard   *Strophe 2*
From the old man skilled at hearing Fate in the wingbeat of a bird. 20
Bewildered as a blown bird, my soul hovers and cannot find
Foothold in this debate, or any reason or rest of mind.
But no man ever brought—none can bring
Proof of strife between Thebes' royal house,
Labdakos' line,° and the son of Polybos;°   25
And never until now has any man brought word
Of Laïos dark death staining Oedipus the King.

Divine Zeus and Apollo hold   *Antistrophe 2*
Perfect intelligence alone of all tales ever told;

7 **son of Zeus** Apollo 9 **Furies** avenging deities 25 **Labdakos' line** family of Laïos
25 **son of Polybos** Oedipus (so the Chorus believes)

And well though this diviner works, he works in his own night;　30
No man can judge that rough unknown or trust in second sight,
For wisdom changes hands among the wise.
Shall I believe my great lord criminal.
At a raging word that a blind old man let fall?
I saw him, when the carrion woman faced him of old,　35
Prove his heroic mind! These evil words are lies.

SCENE II

CREON. Men of Thebes:
　I am told that heavy accusations
　Have been brought against me by King Oedipus.
　I am not the kind of man to bear this tamely.

　If in these present difficulties　5
　He holds me accountable for any harm to him
　Through anything I have said or done—why, then,
　I do not value life in this dishonor.
　It is not as though this rumor touched upon
　Some private indiscretion. The matter is grave.　10
　The fact is that I am being called disloyal
　To the State, to my fellow citizens, to my friends.
CHORAGOS. He may have spoken in anger, not from his mind.
CREON. But did you hear him say I was the one
　Who seduced the old prophet into lying?　15
CHORAGOS. The thing was said; I do not know how seriously.
CREON. But you were watching him! Were his eyes steady?
　Did he look like a man in his right mind?
CHORAGOS.　　　　　　　　　　I do not know.
　I cannot judge the behavior of great men.
　But here is the King himself.

　[*Enter* OEDIPUS.]
OEDIPUS.　　　　　　　　So you dared come back.　20

　Why? How brazen of you to come to my house,
　You murderer!
　　　　Do you think I do not know
　That you plotted to kill me, plotted to steal my throne?
　Tell me, in God's name: am I coward, a fool,
　That you should dream you could accomplish this?　25
　A fool who could not see your slippery game?
　A coward, not to fight back when I saw it?
　You are the fool, Creon, are you not? hoping
　Without support or friends to get a throne?
　Thrones may be won or bought: you could do neither.　30
CREON. Now listen to me. You have talked; let me talk, too.
　You cannot judge unless you know the facts.

OEDIPUS. You speak well: there is one fact; but I find it hard
    To learn from the deadliest enemy I have.
CREON. That above all I must dispute with you.   35
OEDIPUS. That above all I will not hear you deny.
CREON. If you think there is anything good in being stubborn
    Against all reason, then I say you are wrong.
OEDIPUS. If you think a man can sin against his own kind
    And not be punished for it, I say you are mad.   40
CREON. I agree. But tell me: what have I done to you?
OEDIPUS. You advised me to send for that wizard, did you not?
CREON. I did. I should do it again.
OEDIPUS.   Very well. Now tell me:
    How long has it been since Laïos—
CREON.   What of Laïos?
OEDIPUS. Since he vanished in that onset by the road?   45
CREON. It was long ago, a long time.
OEDIPUS.   And this prophet,
    Was he practicing here then?
CREON.   He was; and with honor, as now.
OEDIPUS. Did he speak of me at that time?
CREON.   He never did;
    At least, not when I was present.
OEDIPUS.   But . . . the enquiry?
    I suppose you held one?
CREON.   We did, but we learned nothing.   50
OEDIPUS. Why did the prophet not speak against me then?
CREON. I do not know; and I am the kind of man
    Who holds his tongue when he has no facts to go on.
OEDIPUS. There's one fact that you know, and you could tell it.
CREON. What fact is that? If I know it, you shall have it.   55
OEDIPUS. If he were not involved with you, he could not say
    That it was I who murdered Laïos.
CREON. If he says that, you are the one that knows it!—
    But now it is my turn to question you.
OEDIPUS. Put your questions. I am no murderer.   60
CREON. First, then: You married my sister?
OEDIPUS.   I married your sister.
CREON. And you rule the kingdom equally with her?
OEDIPUS. Everything that she wants she has from me.
CREON. And I am the third, equal to both of you?
OEDIPUS. That is why I call you a bad friend.   65
CREON. No. Reason it out, as I have done.
    Think of this first. Would any sane man prefer
    Power, with all a king's anxieties,
    To that same power and the grace of sleep?
    Certainly not I.   70
    I have never longed for the king's power—only his rights.
    Would any wise man differ from me in this?

As matters stand, I have my way in everything
With your consent, and no responsibilities.
If I were king, I should be a slave to policy. 　　　　75
How could I desire a scepter more
Than what is now mine—untroubled influence?
No, I have not gone mad; I need no honors,
Except those with the perquisites I have now.
I am welcome everywhere; every man salutes me, 　　　80
And those who want your favor seek my ear,
Since I know how to manage what they ask.
Should I exchange this ease for that anxiety?
Besides, no sober mind is treasonable.
I hate anarchy 　　　　　　　　　　　　　　　85
And never would deal with any man who likes it.

Test what I have said. Go to the priestess
At Delphi, ask if I quoted her correctly.
And as for this other thing: if I am found
Guilty of treason with Teiresias, 　　　　　　　90
Then sentence me to death! You have my word
It is a sentence I should cast my vote for—
But not without evidence!
　　　　　　　　　　　You do wrong
When you take good men for bad, bad men for good.
A true friend thrown aside—why, life itself 　　　95
Is not more precious!
　　　　　　　　　　In time you will know this well:
For time, and time alone, will show the just man,
Though scoundrels are discovered in a day.
CHORAGOS. This is well said, and a prudent man would ponder it.
　　Judgments too quickly formed are dangerous. 　　100
OEDIPUS. But is he not quick in his duplicity?
　　And shall I not be quick to parry him?
　　Would you have me stand still, hold my peace, and let
　　This man win everything, through my inaction?
CREON. And you want—what is it, then? To banish me? 　　105
OEDIPUS. No, not exile. It is your death I want,
　　So that all the world may see what treason means.
CREON. You will persist, then? You will not believe me?
OEDIPUS. How can I believe you?
CREON. 　　　　　　　　　　Then you are a fool.
OEDIPUS. To save myself?
CREON. 　　　　　　　　　In justice, think of me. 　　110
OEDIPUS. You are evil incarnate.
CREON. 　　　　　　　　　　But suppose that you are wrong?
OEDIPUS. Still I must rule.
CREON. 　　　　　　　　But not if you rule badly.
OEDIPUS. O city, city!
CREON. 　　　　　　It is my city, too!

CHORAGOS. Now, my lords, be still. I see the Queen,
 Iocastê, coming from her palace chambers;   115
 And it is time she came, for the sake of you both.
 This dreadful quarrel can be resolved through her.

Enter IOCASTÊ.

IOCASTÊ. Poor foolish men, what wicked din is this?
 With Thebes sick to death, is it not shameful
 That you should rake some private quarrel up?   120
[*To* OEDIPUS.] Come into the house.
          —And you, Creon, go now:
 Let us have no more of this tumult over nothing.
CREON. Nothing? No, sister: what your husband plans for me
 Is one of two great evils: exile or death.
OEDIPUS. He is right.
 Why, woman, I have caught him squarely   125
 Plotting against my life.
CREON.   No! Let me die
 Accurst if ever I have wished you harm!
IOCASTÊ. Ah, believe it, Oedipus!
 In the name of the gods, respect this oath of his
 For my sake, for the sake of these people here!   130

CHORAGOS. Open your mind to her, my lord. Be ruled   *Strophe 1*
 by her, I beg you!
OEDIPUS. What would you have me do?
CHORAGOS. Respect Creon's word. He has never spoken like a fool,
 And now he has sworn an oath.
OEDIPUS. You know what you ask?
CHORAGOS.   I do.
OEDIPUS.   Speak on, then.
CHORAGOS. A friend so sworn should not be baited so,   135
 In blind malice, and without final proof.
OEDIPUS. You are aware, I hope, that what you say
 Means death for me, or exile at the least.

CHORAGOS. No, I swear by Helios,° first in Heaven!   *Strophe 2*
 May I die friendless and accurst,   140
 The worst of deaths, if ever I meant that!
  It is the withering fields
   That hurt my sick heart:
  Must we bear all these ills,
   And now your bad blood as well?   145
OEDIPUS. Then let him go. And let me die, if I must,
 Or be driven by him in shame from the land of Thebes.
 It is your unhappiness, and not his talk,
 That touches me.

139 **Helios** sun god

As for him—
Wherever he is, I will hate him as long as I live.   150
CREON. Ugly in yielding, as you were ugly in rage!
  Natures like yours chiefly torment themelves.
OEDIPUS. Can you not go? Can you not leave me?
CREON.   I can.
  You do not know me; but the city knows me,
  And in its eyes I am just, if not in yours. [*Exit* CREON.]   155

CHORAGOS. Lady Iocastê, did you not ask the King   *Antistrophe 1*
  to go to his chambers?
IOCASTÊ. First tell me what has happened.
CHORAGOS. There was suspicion without evidence; yet it rankled
  As even false charges will.
IOCASTÊ.   On both sides?
CHORAGOS.   On both.
IOCASTÊ.   But what was said?
CHORAGOS. Oh let it rest, let it be done with!   160
  Have we not suffered enough?
OEDIPUS. You see to what your decency has brought you:
  You have made difficulties where my heart saw none.

IOCASTÊ. Oedipus, it is not once only I have told you—   *Antistrophe 2*
  You must know I should count myself unwise   165
  To the point of madness, should I now forsake you—
      You, under whose hand,
          In the storm of another time,
      Our dear land sailed out free,
          But now stand fast at the helm!   170
IOCASTÊ. In God's name, Oedipus, inform your wife as well:
  Why are you so set in this hard anger?
OEDIPUS. I will tell you, for none of these men deserves
  My confidence as you do. It is Creon's work,
  His treachery, his plotting against me.   175
IOCASTÊ. Go on, if you can make this clear to me.
OEDIPUS. He charges me with the murder of Laïos.
IOCASTÊ. Has he some knowledge? Or does he speak from hearsay?
OEDIPUS. He would not commit himself to such a charge,
  But he has brought in that damnable soothsayer   180
  To tell his story.
IOCASTÊ.   Set your mind at rest.
  If it is a question of soothsayers, I tell you
  That you will find no man whose craft gives knowledge
  Of the unknowable.
                  Here is my proof.

An oracle was reported to Laïos once   185
  (I will not say from Phoibos himself, but from
  His appointed ministers, at any rate)

That his doom would be death at the hands of his own son—
His son, born of his flesh and of mine!

Now, you remember the story: Laïos was killed   190
By marauding strangers where three highways meet;
But his child had not been three days in this world
Before the King had pierced the baby's ankles
And left him to die on a lonely mountainside.

Thus, Apollo never caused that child   195
To kill his father, and it was not Laïos fate
To die at the hands of his son, as he had feared.
This is what prophets and prophecies are worth!
Have no dread of them.
                    It is God himself
Who can show us what he wills, in his own way.   200

OEDIPUS. How strange a shadowy memory crossed my mind,
    Just now while you were speaking; it chilled my heart.

IOCASTÊ. What do you mean? What memory do you speak of?

OEDIPUS. If I understand you, Laïos was killed
    At a place where three roads meet.

IOCASTÊ.   So it was said;   205
    We have no later story.

OEDIPUS.   Where did it happen?

IOCASTÊ. Phokis, it is called: at a place where the Theban Way
    Divides into the roads towards Delphi and Daulia.

OEDIPUS. When?

IOCASTÊ.   We had the news not long before you came
    And proved the right to your succession here.   210

OEDIPUS. Ah, what net has God been weaving for me?

IOCASTÊ. Oedipus! Why does this trouble you?

OEDIPUS.   Do not ask me yet.
    First, tell me how Laïos looked, and tell me
    How old he was.

IOCASTE.   He was tall, his hair just touched
    With white; his form was not unlike your own.   215

OEDIPUS. I think that I myself may be accurst
    By my own ignorant edict.

IOCASTÊ.   You speak strangely.
    It makes me tremble to look at you, my King.

OEDIPUS. I am not sure that the blind man cannot see.
    But I should know better if you were to tell me—   220

IOCASTÊ. Anything—though I dread to hear you ask it.

OEDIPUS. Was the King lightly escorted, or did he ride
    With a large company, as a ruler should?

IOCASTÊ. There were five men with him in all: one was a herald;
    And a single chariot, which he was driving.   225

OEDIPUS. Alas, that makes it plain enough!
                         But who—

Who told you how it happened?

IOCASTÊ.   A household servant,
The only one to escape.

OEDIPUS.   And is he still
A servant of ours?

IOCASTÊ.   No; for when he came back at last
And found you enthroned in the place of the dead king,   230
He came to me, touched my hand with his, and begged
That I would send him away to the frontier district
Where only the shepherds go—
As far away from the city as I could send him.
I granted his prayer; for although the man was a slave,   235
He had earned more than this favor at my hands.

OEDIPUS. Can he be called back quickly?

IOCASTÊ.   Easily.
But why?

OEDIPUS.   I have taken too much upon myself
Without enquiry; therefore I wish to consult him.

IOCASTÊ. Then he shall come.
                 But am I not one also   240
To whom you might confide these fears of yours!

OEDIPUS. That is your right; it will not be denied you,
Now least of all; for I have reached a pitch
Of wild foreboding. Is there anyone
To whom I should sooner speak?   245
Polybos of Corinth is my father.
My mother is a Dorian: Meropê.
I grew up chief among the men of Corinth
Until a strange thing happened—
Not worth my passion, it may be, but strange.   250

At a feast, a drunken man maundering in his cups
Cries out that I am not my father's son!

I contained myself that night, though I felt anger
And a sinking heart. The next day I visited
My father and mother, and questioned them. They stormed,   255
Calling it all the slanderous rant of a fool;
And this relieved me. Yet the suspicion
Remained always aching in my mind;
I knew there was talk; I could not rest;
And finally, saying nothing to my parents,   260
I went to the shrine at Delphi.
The god dismissed my question without reply;
He spoke of other things.
                 Some were clear,
Full of wretchedness, dreadful, unbearable:
As, that I should lie with my own mother, breed   265
Children from whom all men would turn their eyes;

And that I should be my father's murderer.

I heard all this, and fled. And from that day
Corinth to me was only in the stars
Descending in that quarter of the sky,   270
As I wandered farther and farther on my way
To a land where I should never see the evil
Sung by the oracle. And I came to this country
Where, so you say, King Laïos was killed.
I will tell you all that happened there, my lady.   275

There were three highways
Coming together at a place I passed;
And there a herald came towards me, and a chariot
Drawn by horses, with a man such as you describe
Seated in it. The groom leading the horses   280
Forced me off the road at his lord's command;
But as this charioteer lurched over toward me
I struck him in my rage. The old man saw me
And brought his double goad down upon my head
As I came abreast.

                         He was paid back, and more!   285
Swinging my club in this right hand I knocked him
Out of his car, and he rolled on the ground.

                                                I killed him.

I killed them all.
Now if that stranger and Laïos were—kin,
Where is a man more miserable than I?   290
More hated by the gods? Citizen and alien alike
Must never shelter me or speak to me—
I must be shunned by all.

                         And I myself
Pronounced this malediction upon myself!

Think of it: I have touched you with these hands,   295
These hands that killed your husband. What defilement!

Am I all evil, then? It must be so,
Since I must flee from Thebes, yet never again
See my own countrymen, my own country,
For fear of joining my mother in marriage   300
And killing Polybos, my father.

                         Ah,
If I was created so, born to this fate,
Who could deny the savagery of God?

O holy majesty of heavenly powers!
May I never see that day! Never!   305
Rather let me vanish from the race of men
Than know the abomination destined me!

CHORAGOS. We too, my lord, have felt dismay at this.
    But there is hope: you have yet to hear the shepherd.
OEDIPUS. Indeed, I fear no other hope is left me.   310
IOCASTÊ. What do you hope from him when he comes?
OEDIPUS.   This much:
    If his account of the murder tallies with yours,
    Then I am cleared.
IOCASTÊ.   What was it that I said
    Of such importance?
OEDIPUS.   Why, "marauders," you said,
    Killed the King, according to this man's story.   315
    If he maintains that still, if there were several,
    Clearly the guilt is not mine: I was alone.
    But if he says one man, singlehanded, did it,
    Then the evidence all points to me.
IOCASTÊ. You may be sure that he said there were several;   320
    And can he call back that story now? He cannot.
    The whole city heard it as plainly as I.
    But suppose he alters some detail of it:
    He cannot ever show that Laïos' death
    Fulfilled the oracle: for Apollo said   325
    My child was doomed to kill him; and my child—
    Poor baby!—it was my child that died first.

    No. From now on, where oracles are concerned,
    I would not waste a second thought on any.
OEDIPUS. You may be right.
                But come: let someone go   330
    For the shepherd at once. This matter must be settled.
IOCASTÊ. I will send for him.
    I would not wish to cross you in anything,
    And surely not in this.—Let us go in.   *Exeunt into the palace.*

ODE II

CHORUS. Let me be reverent in the ways of right,   *Strophe 1*
    Lowly the paths I journey on;
    Let all my words and actions keep
    The laws of the pure universe
    From highest Heaven handed down.   5
    For Heaven is their bright nurse,
    Those generations of the realms of light;
    Ah, never of mortal kind were they begot,
    Nor are they slaves of memory, lost in sleep:
    Their Father is greater than Time, and ages not.   10

    The tyrant is a child of Pride   *Antistrophe 1*
    Who drinks from his great sickening cup

Recklessness and vanity,
Until from his high crest headlong
He plummets to the dust of hope.   15
That strong man is not strong.
But let no fair ambition be denied;
May God protect the wrestler for the State
In government, in comely policy,
Who will fear God, and on His ordinance wait.   20

Haughtiness and the high hand of disdain   *Strophe 2*
Tempt and outrage God's holy law;
And any mortal who dares hold
No immortal Power in awe
Will be caught up in a net of pain: 25
The price for which his levity is sold.
Let each man take due earnings, then,
And keep his hands from holy things,
And from blasphemy stand apart—
Else the crackling blast of heaven   30
Blows on his head, and on his desperate heart;
Though fools will honor impious men,
In their cities no tragic poet sings.

Shall we lose faith in Delphi's obscurities,   *Antistrophe 2*
We who have heard the world's core   35
Discredited, and the sacred wood
Of Zeus at Elis praised no more?
The deeds and the strange prophecies
Must make a pattern yet to be understood.
Zeus, if indeed you are lord of all,   40
Throned in light over night and day,
Mirror this in your endless mind:
Our masters call the oracle
Words on the wind, and the Delphic vision blind!
Their hearts no longer know Apollo,   45
And reverence for the gods has died away.

SCENE III

Enter IOCASTÊ

IOCASTÊ. Princes of Thebes, it has occurred to me
    To visit the altars of the gods, bearing
    These branches as a suppliant, and this incense.
    Our King is not himself: his noble soul
    Is overwrought with fantasies of dread,   5
    Else he would consider
    The new prophecies in the light of the old.
    He will listen to any voice that speaks disaster,
    And my advice goes for nothing.

She approaches the altar, right.

To you, then, Apollo,

Lycean lord, since you are nearest, I turn in prayer.   10
Receive these offerings, and grant us deliverance
From defilement. Our hearts are heavy with fear
When we see our leader distracted, as helpless sailors
Are terrified by the confusion of their helmsman.

Enter MESSENGER.

MESSENGER. Friends, no doubt you can direct me: 15
    Where shall I find the house of Oedipus,
    Or, better still, where is the King himself?
CHORAGOS. It is this very place, stranger; he is inside.
    This is his wife and mother of his children.
MESSENGER. I wish her happiness in a happy house,   20
    Blest in all the fulfillment of her marriage.
IOCASTÊ. I wish as much for you: your courtesy
    Deserves a like good fortune. But now, tell me:
    Why have you come? What have you to say to us?
MESSENGER. Good news, my lady, for your house and your husband.   25
IOCASTÊ. What news? Who sent you here?
MESSENGER.   I am from Corinth.
    The news I bring ought to mean joy for you,
    Though it may be you will find some grief in it.
IOCASTÊ. What is it? How can it touch us in both ways?
MESSENGER. The people of Corinth, they say,   30
    Intend to call Oedipus to be their king.
IOCASTÊ. But old Polybos—is he not reigning still?
MESSENGER. No. Death holds him in his sepulchre.
IOCASTÊ. What are you saying? Polybos is dead?
MESSENGER. If I am not tellling the truth, may I die myself.   35
IOCASTÊ [*To a* MAIDSERVANT]. Go in, go quickly; tell this to your master.

    O riddlers of God's will, where are you now!
    This was the man whom Oedipus, long ago,
    Feared so, fled so, in dread of destroying him—
    But it was another fate by which he died.   40

Enter OEDIPUS, *center.*

OEDIPUS. Dearest Iocastê, why have you sent for me?
IOCASTÊ. Listen to what this man says, and then tell me
    What has become of the solemn prophecies.
OEDIPUS. Who is this man? What is his news for me?
IOCASTÊ. He has come from Corinth to announce your father's death!   45
OEDIPUS. Is it true, stranger? Tell me in your own words.
MESSENGER. I cannot say it more clearly: the King is dead.
OEDIPUS. Was it by treason? Or by an attack of illness?
MESSENGER. A little thing brings old men to their rest.
OEDIPUS. It was sickness, then?

MESSENGER.   Yes, and his many years.   50
OEDIPUS. Ah!
    Why should a man respect the Pythian hearth,° or
    Give heed to the birds that jangle above his head?
    They prophesied that I should kill Polybos,
    Kill my own father; but he is dead and buried,   55
    And I am here—I never touched him, never,
    Unless he died in grief for my departure,
    And thus, in a sense, through me. No Polybos
    Has packed the oracles off with him underground.
    They are empty words.
IOCASTÊ.   Had I not told you so?   60
OEDIPUS. You had; it was my faint heart that betrayed me.
IOCASTÊ. From now on never think of those things again.
OEDIPUS. And yet—must I not fear my mother's bed?
IOCASTÊ. Why should anyone in this world be afraid,
    Since Fate rules us and nothing can be foreseen?   65
    A man should live only for the present day.
    Have no more fear of sleeping with your mother
    How many men, in dreams, have lain with their mothers!
    No reasonable man is troubled by such things.
OEDIPUS. That is true; only—   70
    If only my mother were not still alive!
    But she is alive. I cannot help my dread.
IOCASTÊ. Yet this news of your father's death is wonderful.
OEDIPUS. Wonderful. But I fear the living woman.
MESSENGER. Tell me, who is this woman that you fear?   75
OEDIPUS. It is Meropê, man; the wife of King Polybos.
MESSENGER. Meropê? Why should you be afraid of her?
OEDIPUS. An oracle of the gods, a dreadful saying.
MESSENGER. Can you tell me about it or are you sworn to silence?
OEDIPUS. I can tell you, and I will.   80
    Apollo said through his prophet that I was the man
    Who should marry his own mother, shed his father's blood
    With his own hands. And so, for all these years
    I have kept clear of Corinth, and no harm has come—
    Though it would have been sweet to see my parents again.   85
MESSENGER. And is this the fear that drove you out of Corinth?
OEDIPUS. Would you have me kill my father?
MESSENGER.   As for that
    You must be reassured by the news I gave you.
OEDIPUS. If you could reassure me, I would reward you.
MESSENGER. I had that in mind, I will confess: I thought   90
    I could count on you when you returned to Corinth.
OEDIPUS. No: I will never go near my parents again.
MESSENGER. Ah, son, you still do not know what you are doing—

---

52 **Pythian hearth** Delphi (also called Pytho became a great snake had lived there), where Apollo spoke through a priestess

OEDIPUS. What do you mean? In the name of God tell me!

MESSENGER. —If these are your reasons for not going home, 95

OEDIPUS. I tell you, I fear the oracle may come true.

MESSENGER. And guilt may come upon you through your parents?

OEDIPUS. That is the dread that is always in my heart.

MESSENGER. Can you not see that all your fears are groundless?

OEDIPUS. How can you say that? They are my parents, surely?　　100

MESSENGER. Polybos was not your father.

OEDIPUS. 　　　　　　　　　　　　　Not my father?

MESSENGER. No more your father than the man speaking to you.

OEDIPUS. But you are nothing to me!

MESSENGER. 　　　　　　　　　Neither was he.

OEDIPUS. Then why did he call me son?

MESSENGER. 　　　　　　　　　　　I will tell you:

　　Long ago he had you from my hands, as a gift.　　　　105

OEDIPUS. Then how could he love me so, if I was not his?

MESSENGER. He had no children, and his heart turned to you.

OEDIPUS. What of you? Did you buy me? Did you find me by chance?

MESSENGER. I came upon you in the crooked pass of Kithairon.

OEDIPUS. And what were you doing there?

MESSENGER. 　　　　　　　　　　Tending my flocks.　　　　110

OEDIPUS. A wandering shepherd?

MESSENGER. 　　　　　　　　But your savior, son, that day.

OEDIPUS. From what did you save me?

MESSENGER. 　　　　　　　　　Your ankles should tell you that.

OEDIPUS. Ah, stranger, why do you speak of that childhood pain?

MESSENGER. I cut the bonds that tied your ankles together.

OEDIPUS. I have had the mark as long as I can remember.　　115

MESSENGER. That was why you were given the name you bear.°

OEDIPUS. God! Was it my father or my mother who did it?

　　Tell me!

MESSENGER. I do not know. The man who gave you to me

　　Can tell you better than I.　　　　　　　　120

OEDIPUS. It was not you that found me, but another?

MESSENGER. It was another shepherd gave you to me.

OEDIPUS. Who was he? Can you tell me who he was?

MESSENGER. I think he was said to be one of Laïos' people.

OEDIPUS. You mean the Laïos who was king here years ago?　　125

MESSENGER. Yes; King Laïos; and the man was one of his herdsmen.

OEDIPUS. Is he still alive? Can I see him?

MESSENGER. 　　　　　　　　　　These men here

　　Know best about such things.

OEDIPUS. 　　　　　　　　　　Does anyone here

　　Know this shepherd that he is talking about?

　　Have you seen him in the fields, or in the town?　　130

　　If you have, tell me. It is time things were made plain.

116 **name you bear** "Oedipus" means "swollen-foot."

CHORAGOS. I think the man he means is that same shepherd
          You have already asked to see. Iocastê perhaps
          Could tell you something.
OEDIPUS.   Do you know anything
          About him, Lady? Is he the man we have summoned?   135
          Is that the man this shepherd means?
IOCASTÊ.   Why think of him?
          Forget this herdsman. Forget it all.
          This talk is a waste of time.
OEDIPUS.   How can you say that,
          When the clues to my true birth are in my hands?
IOCASTÊ. For God's love, let us have no more questioning!   140
          Is your life nothing to you?
          My own is pain enough for me to bear.
OEDIPUS. You need not worry. Suppose my mother a slave,
          And born of slaves: no baseness can touch you.
IOCASTÊ. Listen to me, I beg you: do not do this thing!   145
OEDIPUS. I will not listen; the truth must be made known.
IOCASTÊ. Everything that I say is for your own good!
OEDIPUS.   My own good
          Snaps my patience, then: I want none of it.
IOCASTÊ. You are fatally wrong! May you never learn who your are!
OEDIPUS. Go, one of you, and bring the shepherd here.   150
          Let us leave this woman to brag of her royal name.
IOCASTÊ. Ah, miserable!
          That is the only word I have for you now.
          That is the only word I can ever have.   *Exit into the palace.*

CHORAGOS. Why has she left us, Oedipus? Why has she gone   155
          In such a passion of sorrow? I fear this silence:
          Something dreadful may come of it.
OEDIPUS.   Let it come!
          However base my birth, I must know about it.
          The Queen, like a woman, is perhaps ashamed
          To think of my low origin. But I   160
          Am a child of luck; I cannot be dishonored.
          Luck is my mother; the passing months, my brothers,
          Have seen me rich and poor. If this is so,
          How could I wish that I were someone else?
          How could I not be glad to know my birth?   165

ODE III

CHORUS. If ever the coming time were known   *Strophe*
          To my heart's pondering,
          Kithairon, now by Heaven I see the torches
          At the festival of the next full moon,
          And see the dance, and hear the choir sing   5

A grace to your gentle shade:
Mountain where Oedipus was found,
O mountain guard of a noble race!
May the god who heals us lend his aid,
And let that glory come to pass   10
For our king's cradling-ground.

Of the nymphs that flower beyond the years.   *Antistrophe*
Who bore you, royal child,
To Pan of the hills or the timberline Apollo,
Cold in delight where the upland clears.   15
Or Hermês for whom Kyllenê's° heights are piled?
Or flushed as evening cloud,
Great Dionysos, roamer of mountains,
He—was it he who found you there,
And caught you up in his own proud   20
Arms from the sweet god-ravisher
Who laughed by the Muses' fountains?

SCENE IV

OEDIPUS. Sirs: though I do not know the man,
    I think I see him coming, this shepherd we want:
    He is old, like our friend here, and the men
    Bringing him seem to be servants of my house.
    But you can tell, if you have ever seen him.   5

Enter SHEPHERD *escorted by servants.*

CHORAGOS. I know him, he was Laïos' man. You can trust him.
OEDIPUS. Tell me first, you from Corinth: is this the shepherd
    We were discussing?
MESSENGER.   This is the very man.
OEDIPUS [*To* SHEPHERD]. Come here. No, look at me. You must answer
    Everything I ask.—You belonged to Laïos?   10
SHEPHERD. Yes: born his slave, brought up in his house.
OEDIPUS. Tell me: what kind of work did you do for him?
SHEPHERD. I was a shepherd of his, most of my life.
OEDIPUS. Where mainly did you go for pasturage?
SHEPHERD. Sometimes Kithairon, sometimes the hills near-by.   15
OEDIPUS. Do you remember ever seeing this man out there?
SHEPHERD. What would he be doing there? This man?
OEDIPUS. This man standing here. Have you ever seen him before?
SHEPHERD. No. At least, not to my recollection.
MESSENGER. And that is not strange, my lord. But I'll refresh   20
    His memory: he must remember when we two

16 **Hermes . . . Kyllenê's** Hermês, messenger of the gods, was said to have been
born on Mt. Kyllenê.

Spent three whole seasons together, March to September,
On Kithairon or thereabouts. He had two flocks;
I had one. Each autumn I'd drive mine home
And he would go back with his to Laïos' sheepfold.—   25
Is this not true, just as I have described it?
SHEPHERD. True, yes; but it was all so long ago.
MESSENGER. Well, then: do you remember, back in those days
    That you gave me a baby boy to bring up as my own?
SHEPHERD. What if I did? What are you trying to say?   30
MESSENGER. King Oedipus was once that little child.
SHEPHERD. Damn you, hold your tongue!
OEDIPUS.   No more of that!
    It is your tongue needs watching, not this man's.
SHEPHERD. My King, my Master, what is it I have done wrong?
OEDIPUS. You have not answered his question about the boy.   35
SHEPHERD. He does not know . . . He is only making trouble . . .
OEDIPUS. Come, speak plainly, or it will go hard with you.
SHEPHERD. In God's name, do not torture an old man!
OEDIPUS. Come here, one of you; bind his arms behind him.
SHEPHERD. Unhappy king! What more do you wish to learn?   40
OEDIPUS. Did you give this man the child he speaks of?
SHEPHERD.   I did.
    And I would to God I had died that very day.
OEDIPUS. You will die now unless you speak the truth.
SHEPHERD. Yet if I speak the truth, I am worse than dead.
OEDIPUS. Very well; since you insist upon delaying—   45
SHEPHERD. No! I have told you already that I gave him the boy.
OEDIPUS. Where did you get him? From your house?
    From somewhere else?
SHEPHERD. Not from mine, no. A man gave him to me.
OEDIPUS. Is that man here? Do you know whose slave he was?
SHEPHERD. For God's love, my King, do not ask me any more!   50
OEDIPUS. You are a dead man if I have to ask you again.
SHEPHERD. Then . . . Then the child was from the palace of Laïos.
OEDIPUS. A slave child? or a child of his own line?
SHEPHERD. Ah, I am on the brink of dreadful speech!
OEDIPUS. And I of dreadful hearing. Yet I must hear.   55
SHEPHERD. If you must be told, then . . .
                     They said it was Laïos' child,
    But it is your wife who can tell you about that.
OEDIPUS. My wife!—Did she give it to you?
SHEPHERD.   My lord, she did.
OEDIPUS. Do you know why?
SHEPHERD.   I was told to get rid of it.
OEDIPUS. An unspeakable mother!
SHEPHERD.   There had been prophecies . . .   60
OEDIPUS. Tell me.
SHEPHERD.   It was said that the boy would kill his own father.

OEDIPUS. Then why did you give him over to this old man?
SHEPHERD. I pitied the baby, my King,
    And I thought that this man would take him far away
    To his own country.
                      He saved him—but for what a fate!   65
    For if you are what this man says you are,
    No man living is more wretched than Oedipus.
OEDIPUS. Ah God!
            It was true!
                 All the prophecies!
                         —Now,
    O Light, may I look on you for the last time!   70
    I, Oedipus,
    Oedipus, damned in his birth, in his marriage damned,
    Damned in the blood he shed with his own hand!

He rushes into the palace.

ODE IV

CHORUS. Alas for the seed of men.   *Strophe 1*

    What measure shall I give these generations
    That breathe on the void and are void
    And exist and do not exist?

    Who bears more weight of joy   5
    Than mass of sunlight shifting in images,
    Or who shall make his thought stay on
    That down time drifts away?

    Your splendor is all fallen.

    O naked brow of wrath and tears,   10
    O change of Oedipus!
    I who saw your days call no man blest—
    Your great days like ghósts góne.

    That mind was a strong bow.   *Antistrophe 1*
    Deep, how deep you drew it then, hard archer,   15
    At a dim fearful range,
    And brought dear glory down!

    You overcame the stranger—
    The virgin with her hooking lion claws—
    And though death sang, stood like a tower   20
    To make pale Thebes take heart.

    Fortress against our sorrow!

    Divine king, giver of laws,
    Majestic Oedipus!

No prince in Thebes had ever such renown,   25
No prince won such grace of power.

And now of all men ever known   *Strophe 2*
Most pitiful is this man's story:
His fortunes are most changed, his state
Fallen to a low slave's   30
Ground under bitter fate.

O Oedipus, most royal one!
The great door that expelled you to the light
Gave it night—ah, gave night to your glory:
As to the father, to the fathering son.   35

All understood too late.

How could that queen whom Laïos won,
The garden that he harrowed at his height,
Be silent when that act was done?

But all eyes fail before time's eye,   *Antistrophe 2* 40
All actions come to justice there.
Though never willed, though far down the deep past,
Your bed, your dread sirings,
Are brought to book at last.
Child by Laïos doomed to die,   45
Then doomed to lose that fortunate little death,
Would God you never took breath in this air
That with my wailing lips I take to cry:

For I weep the world's outcast.

I was blind, and now I can tell why: 50
Asleep, for you had given ease of breath
To Thebes, while the false years went by.

EXODOS

Enter, from the palace, SECOND MESSENGER.

SECOND MESSENGER. Elders of Thebes, most honored in this land,
    What horrors are yours to see and hear, what weight
    Of sorrow to be endured, if, true to your birth,
    You venerate the line of Labdakos!
    I think neither Istros nor Phasis, those great rivers,   5
    Could purify this place of the corruption
    It shelters now, or soon must bring to light—
    Evil not done unconsciously, but willed.

    The greatest griefs are those we cause ourselves.
CHORAGOS. Surely, friend, we have grief enough already;   10
    What new sorrow do you mean?

SECOND MESSENGER.   The Queen is dead.
CHORAGOS. Iocastê? Dead? But at whose hand?
SECOND MESSENGER.   Her own.
　　The full horror of what happened you cannot know,
　　For you did not see it; but I, who did, will tell you
　　As clearly as I can how she met her death.   15

　　When she had left us,
　　In passionate silence, passing through the court,
　　She ran to her apartment in the house,
　　Her hair clutched by the fingers of both hands.
　　She closed the doors behind her; then, by that bed   20
　　Where long ago the fatal son was conceived—
　　That son who should bring about his father's death—
　　We heard her call upon Laïos, dead so many years,
　　And heard her wail for the double fruit of her marriage,
　　A husband by her husband, children by her child.   25

　　Exactly how she died I do not know:
　　For Oedipus burst in moaning and would not let us
　　Keep vigil to the end: it was by him
　　As he stormed about the room that our eyes were caught.
　　From one to another of us he went, begging a sword,   30
　　Cursing the wife who was not his wife, the mother
　　Whose womb had carried his own children and himself.
　　I do not know: it was none of us aided him,
　　But surely one of the gods was in control!
　　For with a dreadful cry   35
　　He hurled his weight, as though wrenched out of himself,
　　At the twin doors: the bolts gave, and he rushed in.
　　And there we saw her hanging, her body swaying
　　From the cruel cord she had noosed about her neck.
　　A great sob broke from him heartbreaking to hear,   40
　　As he loosed the rope and lowered her to the ground.

　　I would blot out from my mind what happened next!
　　For the King ripped from her gown the golden brooches
　　That were her ornament, and raised them, and plunged them down
　　Straight into his own eyeballs, crying, "No more,   45
　　No more shall you look on the misery about me,
　　The horrors of my own doing! Too long you have known
　　The faces of those whom I should never have seen,
　　Too long been blind to those for whom I was searching!
　　From this hour, go in darkness!" And as he spoke,   50
　　He struck at his eyes—not once, but many times;
　　And the blood spattered his beard,
　　Bursting from his ruined sockets like red hail.

　　So from the unhappiness of two this evil has sprung,
　　A curse on the man and woman alike. The old   55

Happiness of the house of Labdakos
Was happiness enough: where is it today?
It is all wailing and ruin, disgrace, death—all
The misery of mankind that has a name—
And it is wholly and for ever theirs.   60

CHORAGOS. Is he in agony still? Is there no rest for him?
SECOND MESSENGER. He is calling for someone to lead him to
          the gates
So that all the children of Kadmos may look upon
His father's murderer, his mother's—no,
I cannot say it!
                    And then he will leave Thebes,   65
Self-exiled, in order that the curse
Which he himself pronounced may depart from the house.
He is weak, and there is none to lead him,
So terrible is his suffering.
                    But you will see:
Look, the doors are opening; in a moment   70
You will see a thing that would crush a heart of stone.

The central door is opened; OEDIPUS, *blinded, is led in.*

CHORAGOS. Dreadful indeed for men to see.
     Never have my own eyes
     Looked on a sight so full of fear.

     Oedipus!   75
     What madness came upon you, what daemon°
     Leaped on your life with heavier
     Punishment than a mortal man can bear?
     No: I cannot even
     Look at you, poor ruined one.   80
     And I would speak, question, ponder,
     If I were able. No.
     You make me shudder.
OEDIPUS. God. God.
     Is there a sorrow greater?   85
     Where shall I find harbor in this world?
     My voice is hurled far on a dark wind.
     What has God done to me?
CHORAGOS. Too terrible to think of, or to see.

OEDIPUS. O cloud of night,   *Strophe 1* 90
     Never to be turned away: night coming on,
     I cannot tell how: night like a shroud!
     My fair winds brought me here.
                    Oh God. Again
     The pain of the spikes where I had sight,
     The flooding pain   95
     Of memory, never to be gouged out.

76 **daemon** a spirit, not necessarily evil

CHORAGOS. This is not strange.
      You suffer it all twice over, remorse in pain,
      Pain in remorse.

OEDIPUS. Ah dear friend   *Antistrophe 1* 100
      Are you faithful even yet, you alone?
      Are you still standing near me, will you stay here,
      Patient, to care for the blind?
                              The blind man!
      Yet even blind I know who it is attends me,
      By the voice's tone—   105
      Though my new darkness hide the comforter.
CHORAGOS. Oh fearful act!
      What god was it drove you to rake black
      Night across your eyes?

OEDIPUS. Apollo. Apollo. Dear   *Strophe 2* 110
      Children, the god was Apollo.
      He brought my sick, sick fate upon me.
      But the blinding hand was my own!
      How could I bear to see
      When all my sight was horror everywhere?   115
CHORAGOS. Everywhere; that is true.
OEDIPUS. And now what is left?
      Images? Love? A greeting even,
      Sweet to the senses? Is there anything?
      Ah, no, friends: lead me away.   120
      Lead me away from Thebes.
                              Lead the great wreck
      And hell of Oedipus, whom the gods hate.
CHORAGOS. Your fate is clear, you are not blind to that.
      Would God you had never found it out!

OEDIPUS. Death take the man who unbound   *Antistrophe 2* 125
      My feet on that hillside
      And delivered me from death to life! What life?
      If only I had died,
      This weight of monstrous doom
      Could not have dragged me and my darlings down.   130
CHORAGOS. I would have wished the same.
OEDIPUS. Oh never to have come here
      With my father's blood upon me! Never
      To have been the man they call his mother's husband!
      Oh accurst! O child of evil,   135
      To have entered that wretched bed—
                              the selfsame one!
      More primal than sin itself, this fell to me.
CHORAGOS. I do not know how I can answer you.
      You were better dead than alive and blind.
OEDIPUS. Do not counsel me any more. This punishment   140
      That I have laid upon myself is just.

If I had eyes,
I do not know how I could bear the sight
Of my father, when I came to the house of Death,
Or my mother: for I have sinned against them both   145
So vilely that I could not make my peace
By strangling my own life.
                      Or do you think my children,
Born as they were born, would be sweet to my eyes?
Ah never, never! Nor this town with its high walls,
Nor the holy images of the gods.
                   For I,   150
Thrice miserable—Oedipus, noblest of all the line
Of Kadmos, have condemned myself to enjoy
These things no more, by my own malediction
Expelling that man whom the gods declared
To be a defilement in the house of Laïos.   155
After exposing the rankness of my own guilt,
How could I look men frankly in the eyes?
No, I swear it,
If I could have stifled my hearing at its source,
I would have done it and made all this body   160
A tight cell of misery, blank to light and sound:
So I should have been safe in a dark agony
Beyond all recollection.
                Ah Kithairon!
Why did you shelter me? When I was cast upon you,
Why did I not die? Then I should never   165
Have shown the world my execrable birth.

Ah Polybos! Corinth, city that I believed
The ancient seat of my ancestors: how fair
I seemed, your child! And all the while this evil
Was cancerous within me!
                For I am sick   170
In my daily life, sick in my origin.

O three roads, dark ravine, woodland and way
Where three roads met: you, drinking my father's blood,
My own blood, spilled by my own hand: can you remember
The unspeakable things I did there, and the things   175
I went on from there to do?
                  O marriage, marriage!
The act that engendered me, and again the act
Performed by the son in the same bed—
                      Ah, the net
Of incest, mingling fathers, brothers, sons,
With brides, wives, mothers: the last evil   180
That can be known by men: no tongue can say
How evil!
        No. For the love of God, conceal me

Somewhere far from Thebes; or kill me; or hurl me
Into the sea, away from men's eyes for ever.
Come, lead me. You need not fear to touch me.　　　185
Of all men, I alone can bear this guilt.

Enter CREON.

CHORAGOS. We are not the ones to decide; but Creon here
　　　May fitly judge of what you ask. He only
　　　Is left to protect the city in your place.
OEDIPUS. Alas, how can I speak to him? What right have I　　　190
　　　To beg his courtesy whom I have deeply wronged?
CREON. I have not come to mock you, Oedipus,
　　　Or to reproach you, either.
[*To* ATTENDANTS.]　　　　　　　—You, standing there:
　　　If you have lost all respect for man's dignity,
　　　At least respect the flame of Lord Helios:　　　195
　　　Do not allow this pollution to show itself
　　　Openly here, an affront to the earth
　　　And Heaven's rain and the light of day. No, take him
　　　Into the house as quickly as you can.
　　　For it is proper　　　200
　　　That only the close kindred see his grief.
OEDIPUS. I pray you in God's name, since your courtesy
　　　Ignores my dark expectation, visiting
　　　With mercy this man of all men most execrable:
　　　Give me what I ask—for your good, not for mine.　　　205
CREON. And what is it that you would have me do?
OEDIPUS. Drive me out of this country as quickly as may be
　　　To a place where no human voice can ever greet me.
CREON. I should have done that before now—only,
　　　God's will had not been wholly revealed to me.　　　210
OEDIPUS. But his command is plain: the parricide
　　　Must be destroyed. I am that evil man.
CREON. That is the sense of it, yes; but as things are,
　　　We had best discover clearly what is to be done.
OEDIPUS. You would learn more about a man like me?　　　215
CREON. You are ready now to listen to the god.
OEDIPUS. I will listen. But it is to you.
　　　That I must turn for help. I beg you, hear me.

　　　The woman in there—
　　　Give her whatever funeral you think proper:　　　220
　　　She is your sister.
　　　　　　　—But let me go, Creon!
　　　Let me purge my father's Thebes of the pollution
　　　Of my living here, and go out to the wild hills,
　　　To Kithairon, that has won such fame with me,
　　　The tomb my mother and father appointed for me,　　　225
　　　And let me die there, as they willed I should.

And yet I know
Death will not ever come to me through sickness
Or in any natural way: I have been preserved
For some unthinkable fate. But let that be.   230
As for my sons, you need not care for them.
They are men, they will find some way to live.
But my poor daughters, who have shared my table,
Who never before have been parted from their father—
Take care of them, Creon; do this for me.   235
And will you let me touch them with my hands
A last time, and let us weep together?
Be kind, my lord,
Great prince, be kind!
                     Could I but touch them,
They would be mine again, as when I had my eyes.   240

Enter ANTIGONÊ *and* ISMENÊ, *attended.*

Ah, God!
Is it my dearest children I hear weeping?
Has Creon pitied me and sent my daughters?
CREON. Yes, Oedipus: I knew that they were dear to you
In the old days, and know you must love them still.   245
OEDIPUS. May God bless you for this—and be a friendlier
Guardian to you than he has been to me!

Children, where are you?
Come quickly to my hands: they are your brother's—
Hands that have brought your father's once clear eyes   250
To this way of seeing—
                     Ah dearest ones,
I had neither sight nor knowledge then, your father
By the woman who was the source of his life!
And I weep for you—having no strength to see you—,
I weep for you when I think of the bitterness   255
That men will visit upon you all your lives.
What homes, what festivals can you attend
Without being forced to depart again in tears?
And when you come to marriageable age,
Where is the man, my daughters, who would dare   260
Risk the bane that lies on all my children?
Is there any evil wanting? Your father killed
His father; sowed the womb of her who bore him;
Engendered you at the fount of his own existence!
That is what they will say of you.
                              Then, whom   265
Can you ever marry? There are no bridegrooms for you,
And your lives must wither away in sterile dreaming.

O Creon, son of Menoikeus!
You are the only father my daughters have,
Since we, their parents, are both of us gone for ever.　　　270
They are your own blood: you will not let them
Fall into beggary and loneliness;
You will keep them from the miseries that are mine!
Take pity on them; see, they are only children,
Friendless except for you. Promise me this,　　　275
Great Prince, and give me your hand in token of it.

CREON *clasps his right hand.*

Children:
I could say much, if you could understand me,
But as it is, I have only this prayer for you:
Live where you can, be as happy as you can—　　　280
Happier, please God, than God has made your father!
CREON. Enough. You have wept enough. Now go within.
OEDIPUS. I must; but it is hard.
CREON.　　　　　　　　Time eases all things.
OEDIPUS. But you must promise—
CREON.　　　　　　　　Say what you desire.
OEDIPUS. Send me from Thebes!
CREON.　　　　　　　　God grant that I may!　　　285
OEDIPUS. But since God hates me . . .
CREON.　　　　　　　　No, he will grant your wish.
OEDIPUS. You promise?
CREON.　　　　　I cannot speak beyond my knowledge.
OEDIPUS. Then lead me in.
CREON.　　　　　　Come now, and leave your children.
OEDIPUS. No! Do not take them from me!
CREON.　　　　　　　　　　Think no longer
That you are in command here, but rather think　　　290
How, when you were, you served your own destruction.

Exeunt into the house all but the CHORUS; *the* CHORAGOS *chants directly to the audience.*

CHORAGOS. Men of Thebes: look upon Oedipus.
This is the king who solved the famous riddle
And towered up, most powerful of men.
No mortal eyes but looked on him with envy,　　　295

Yet in the end ruin swept over him.
Let every man in mankind's frailty
Consider his last day; and let none
Presume on his good fortune until he find
Life, at his death, a memory without pain.　　　300

[c. 430 B.C.]

■ TOPICS FOR DISCUSSION AND WRITING

1. On the basis of the Prologue, characterize Oedipus. What additional traits are revealed in Scene I and Ode I?

2. How fair is it to say that Oedipus is morally guilty? Does he argue that he is morally innocent because he did not intend to do immoral deeds? Can it be said that he is guilty of *hybris* but that *hybris* has nothing to do with his fall?

3. Oedipus says that he blinds himself in order not to look upon people he should not. What further reasons can be given? Why does he not (like his mother) commit suicide?

4. How fair is it to say that the play shows the contemptibleness of man's efforts to act intelligently?

5. How fair is it to say that in *Oedipus* the gods are evil?

6. Are the choral odes lyrical interludes that serve to separate the scenes, or do they advance the dramatic action?

7. Matthew Arnold said that Sophocles saw life steadily and saw it whole. But in this play is Sophocles facing the facts of life, or, on the contrary, is he avoiding life as it usually is and presenting a series of unnatural and outrageous coincidences?

8. Can you describe your emotions at the end of the play? Do they include pity for Oedipus? Pity for all human beings, including yourself? Fear that you might be punished for some unintended transgression? Awe, engendered by a perception of the interrelatedness of things? Relief that the story is only a story? Exhilaration?

Antigonê

An English Version by Dudley Fitts and Robert Fitzgerald

List of Characters

ANTIGONÊ
ISMENÊ
EURYDICÊ
CREON
HAIMON
TEIRESIAS
A SENTRY
A MESSENGER
CHORUS

Scene: Before the palace of CREON, *king of Thebes. A central double door, and two lateral doors. A platform extends the length of the façade, and from this platform three steps lead down into the "orchestra," or chorus-ground.*

Time: Dawn of the day after the repulse of the Argive army from the assault on Thebes.

PROLOGUE

ANTIGONÊ *and* ISMENÊ *enter from the central door of the palace.*

ANTIGONÊ. Ismenê, dear sister,
　　You would think that we had already suffered enough
　　For the curse on Oedipus.°
　　I cannot imagine any grief
　　That you and I have not gone through. And now— 　　　　　　5
　　Have they told you of the new decree of our King Creon?
ISMENÊ. I have heard nothing: I know
　　That two sisters lost two brothers, a double death
　　In a single hour; and I know that the Argive army
　　Fled in the night; but beyond this, nothing. 　　　　　　10
ANTIGONÊ. I thought so. And this is why I wanted you
　　To come out here with me. There is something we must do.
ISMENÊ. Why do you speak so strangely?
ANTIGONÊ. Listen, Ismenê:
　　Creon buried our brother Eteoclês 　　　　　　15
　　With military honors, gave him a soldier's funeral,
　　And it was right that he should; but Polyneicês,
　　Who fought as bravely and died as miserably,—
　　They say that Creon has sworn
　　No one shall bury him, no one mourn for him, 　　　　　　20
　　But his body must lie in the fields, a sweet treasure
　　For carrion birds to find as they search for food.
　　That is what they say, and our good Creon is coming here
　　To announce it publicly; and the penalty—
　　Stoning to death in the public square!
　　　　　　　　　　　　　　　There it is, 　　　　　　25
　　And now you can prove what you are:
　　A true sister, or a traitor to your family.
ISMENÊ. Antigonê, you are mad! What could I possibly do?
ANTIGONÊ. You must decide whether you will help me or not.
ISMENÊ. I do not understand you. Help you in what? 　　　　　　30
ANTIGONÊ. Ismenê, I am going to bury him. Will you come?
ISMENÊ. Bury him! You have just said the new law forbids it.
ANTIGONÊ. He is my brother. And he is your brother, too.
ISMENÊ. But think of the danger! Think what Creon will do!
ANTIGONÊ. Creon is not strong enough to stand in my way. 　　　　　　35
ISMENÊ. Ah sister!
　　Oedipus died, everyone hating him

---

3 **Oedipus,** once King of Thebes, was the father of Antigonê and Ismenê, and of their
brothers Polyneicês and Eteoclês. Oedipus unwittingly killed his father, Laïos, and married his own mother Iocastê. When he learned what he had done, he blinded himself
and left Thebes. Eteoclês and Polyneicês quarreled; Polyneicês was driven out but
returned to assault Thebes. In the battle each brother killed the other; Creon became
king and ordered that Polyneicês be left to rot unburied on the battlefield as a traitor.

For what his own search brought to light, his eyes
Ripped out by his own hand; and Iocastê died,
His mother and wife at once: she twisted the cords   40
That strangled her life; and our two brothers died,
Each killed by the other's sword. And we are left:
But oh, Antigonê,
Think how much more terrible than these
Our own death would be if we should go against Creon   45
And do what he has forbidden! We are only women,
We cannot fight with men, Antigonê!
The law is strong, we must give in to the law
In this thing, and in worse. I beg the Dead
To forgive me, but I am helpless: I must yield   50
To those in authority. And I think it is dangerous business
To be always meddling.

ANTIGONÊ.   If that is what you think,
I should not want you, even if you asked to come.
You have made your choice, you can be what you want to be.
But I will bury him; and if I must die,   55
I say that this crime is holy: I shall lie down
With him in death, and I shall be as dear
To him as he to me.
                    It is the dead,
Not the living, who make the longest demands:
We die for ever . . . .
                    You may do as you like.   60
Since apparently the laws of the gods mean nothing to you.

ISMENÊ. They mean a great deal to me; but I have no strength
To break laws that were made for the public good.

ANTIGONÊ. That must be your excuse, I suppose. But as for me,
I will bury the brother I love.

ISMENÊ.   Antigonê,   65
I am so afraid for you!

ANTIGONÊ.   You need not be:
You have yourself to consider, after all.

ISMENÊ. But no one must hear of this, you must tell no one!
I will keep it a secret, I promise!

ANTIGONÊ.   O tell it! Tell everyone!
Think how they'll hate you when it all comes out   70
If they learn that you knew about it all the time!

ISMENÊ. So fiery! You should be cold with fear.

ANTIGONÊ. Perhaps. But I am doing only what I must.

ISMENÊ. But can you do it? I say that you cannot.

ANTIGONÊ. Very well: when my strength gives out,
I shall do no more.   75

ISMENÊ. Impossible things should not be tried at all.

ANTIGONÊ. Go away, Ismenê:
I shall be hating you soon, and the dead will too,

For your words are hateful. Leave me my foolish plan:
I am not afraid of the danger; if it means death,   80
It will not be the worst of deaths—death without honor.
ISMENÊ. Go then, if you feel that you must.
You are unwise,
But a loyal friend indeed to those who love you.

Exit into the palace. ANTIGONÊ *goes off, left. Enter the* CHORUS.

PÁRODOS

CHORUS. Now the long blade of the sun, lying   *Strophe 1*
    Level east to west, touches with glory
    Thebes of the Seven Gates. Open, unlidded
    Eye of golden day! O marching light
    Across the eddy and rush of Dircê's stream,°   5
    Striking the white shields of the enemy
    Thrown headlong backward from the blaze of morning!
CHORAGOS.° Polyneicês their commander
    Roused them with windy phrases,
    He the wild eagle screaming   10
    Insults above our land,
    His wings their shields of snow,
    His crest their marshalled helms.

CHORUS. Against our seven gates in a yawning ring   *Antistrophe 1*
    The famished spears came onward in the night: 15
    But before his jaws were sated with our blood,
    Or pinefire took the garland of our towers,
    He was thrown back; and as he turned, great Thebes—
    No tender victim for his noisy power—
    Rose like a dragon behind him, shouting war.   20
CHORAGOS. For God hates utterly
    The bray of bragging tongues;
    And when he beheld their smiling,
    Their swagger of golden helms,
    The frown of his thunder blasted   25
    Their first man from our walls.

CHORUS. We heard his shout of triumph high in the air   *Strophe 2*
    Turn to a scream; far out in a flaming arc
    He fell with his windy torch, and the earth struck him.
    And others storming in fury no less than his   30
    Found shock of death in the dusty joy of battle.
CHORAGOS. Seven captains at seven gates
    Yielded their clanging arms to the god
    That bends the battle-line and breaks it.

5 **Dircê's stream** a stream west of Thebes   8 **Choragos** leader of the Chorus

These two only, brothers in blood,   35
Face to face in matchless rage.
Mirroring each the other's death,
Clashed in long combat.

CHORUS. But now in the beautiful morning of victory   *Antistrophe 2*
Let Thebes of the many chariots sing for joy!   40
With hearts for dancing we'll take leave of war:
Our temples shall be sweet with hymns of praise,
And the long nights shall echo with our chorus.

SCENE I

CHORAGOS. But now at last our new King is coming:
Creon of Thebes, Menoikeus' son.
In this auspicious dawn of his rein
What are the new complexities
That shifting Fate has woven for him?   5
What is his counsel? Why has he summoned
The old men to hear him?

Enter CREON *from the palace, center. He addresses the* CHORUS
from the top step.

CREON. Gentlemen: I have the honor to inform you that our
Ship of State, which recent storms have threatened to
destroy, has come safely to harbor at last, guided by   10
the merciful wisdom of Heaven. I have summoned you
here this morning because I know that I can depend
upon you: your devotion to King Laïos was absolute;
you never hesitated in your duty to our late ruler
Oedipus; and when Oedipus died, your loyalty was   15
transferred to his children. Unfortunately, as you
know, his two sons, the princes Eteoclês and Polyneicês, have killed each other in battle; and I, as the
next in blood, have succeeded to the full power of the
throne.   20

I am aware, of course, that no Ruler can expect
complete loyalty from his subjects until he has been
tested in office. Nevertheless, I say to you at the very
outset that I have nothing but contempt for the kind
of Governor who is afraid, for whatever reason, to fol-   25
low the course that he knows is best for the State; and
as for the man who sets private friendship above the
public welfare,—I have no use for him, either. I call
God to witness that if I saw my country headed for
ruin, I should not be afraid to speak out plainly; and   30
I need hardly remind you that I would never have any
dealings with an enemy of the people. No one values
friendship more highly than I: but we must remember

that friends made at the risk of wrecking our Ship are
not real friends at all.   35

      These are my principles, at any rate, and that is
why I have made the following decision concerning the
sons of Oedipus: Eteoclês, who died as a man should
die, fighting for his country, is to be buried with full
military honors, with all the ceremony that is usual   40
when the greatest heroes die; but his brother Polyneicês, who broke his exile to come back with fire and
sword against his native city and the shrines of his
fathers' gods, whose one idea was to spill the blood of
his blood and sell his own people into slavery—   45
Polyneicês, I say, is to have no burial: no man is to touch
him or say the least prayer for him; he shall lie on
the plain, unburied; and the birds and the scavenging
dogs can do with him whatever they like.

      This is my command, and you can see the wis-   50
dom behind it. As long as I am King, no traitor is going
to be honored with the loyal man. But whoever shows
by word and deed that he is on the side of the State,—
he shall have my respect while he is living and my reverence when he is dead.   55

CHORAGOS. If that is your will, Creon son of Menoikeus,
   You have the right to enforce it: we are yours.
CREON. That is my will. Take care that you do your part.
CHORAGOS. We are old men: let the younger ones carry it out.
CREON. I do not mean that: the sentries have been appointed.   60
CHORAGOS. Then what is it that you would have us do?
CREON. You will give no support to whoever breaks this law.
CHORAGOS. Only a crazy man is in love with death!
CREON. And death it is; yet money talks, and the wisest
Have sometimes been known to count a few coins too many.   65

Enter SENTRY *from left.*

SENTRY. I'll not say that I'm out of breath from running,
   King, because every time I stopped to think about what
   I have to tell you, I felt like going back. And all the time
   a voice kept saying, "You fool, don't you know you're
   walking straight into trouble?"; and then another voice: 70
   "Yes, but if you let somebody else get the news to
   Creon first, it will be even worse than that for you!"
   But good sense won out, at least I hope it was good
   sense, and here I am with a story that makes no sense
   at all; but I'll tell it anyhow, because, as they say, what's   75
   going to happen's going to happen and—
CREON. Come to the point. What have you to say?
SENTRY. I did not do it. I did not see who did it. You must
   not punish me for what someone else has done.

CREON. A comprehensive defense! More effective, perhaps.　　　　80
　　　If I knew its purpose. Come: what is it?
SENTRY. A dreadful thing . . . I don't know how to put it—
CREON. Out with it!
SENTRY.　　　　　　　Well, then;
　　　The dead man—
　　　　　　　　　Polyneicês—

Pause. The SENTRY *is overcome, fumbles for words.* CREON *waits impassively.*

　　　　　　　　　　　out there—
　　　　　　　　　　　　　someone,—
New dust on the slimy flesh!　　　　85

Pause. No sign from CREON.

Someone has given it burial that way, and
Gone . . . .

Long pause. CREON *finally speaks with deadly control.*

CREON. And the man who dared do this?
SENTRY.　　　　　　　　　　I swear I
　　　Do not know! You must believe me!
　　　　　　　　　　　　　Listen:
　　　The ground was dry, not a sign of digging, no,　　　　90
　　　Not a wheeltrack in the dust, no trace of anyone.
　　　It was when they relieved us this morning: and one of them,
　　　The corporal, pointed to it.
　　　　　　　　　　There it was,
　　　The strangest—
　　　　　　　Look:
　　　The body, just mounded over with light dust: you see?　　　　95
　　　Not buried really, but as if they'd covered it
　　　Just enough for the ghost's peace. And no sign
　　　Of dogs or any wild animal that had been there.

　　　And then what a scene there was! Every man of us
　　　Accusing the other: we all proved the other man did it,　　　　100
　　　We all had proof that we could not have done it.
　　　We were ready to take hot iron in our hands,
　　　Walk through fire, swear by all the gods,
　　　It was not I!
　　　I do not know who it was, but it was not I!　　　　105

CREON'S *rage has been mounting steadily,* but the SENTRY *is too intent upon his story to notice it.*

　　　And then, when this came to nothing, someone said
　　　A thing that silenced us and made us stare
　　　Down at the ground: you had to be told the news,
　　　And one of us had to do it! We threw the dice,

And the bad luck fell to me. So here I am,   110
No happier to be here than you are to have me:
Nobody likes the man who brings bad news.

CHORAGOS. I have been wondering, King: can it be that the gods
    have done this?

CREON [*furiously*]. Stop!   115
    Must you doddering wrecks
Go out of your heads entirely? "The gods"!
Intolerable!
The gods favor this corpse? Why? How had he served them?
Tried to loot their temples, burn their images,   120
Yes, and the whole State, and its laws with it!
Is it your senile opinion that the gods love to honor bad men?
A pious thought!—
                    No, from the very beginning
There have been those who have whispered together,
Stiff-necked anarchists, putting their heads together,   125
Scheming against me in alleys. These are the men,
And they have bribed my own guard to do this thing.
[*Sententiously.*] Money!
There's nothing in the world so demoralizing as money.
Down go your cities,   130
Homes gone, men gone, honest hearts corrupted.
Crookedness of all kinds, and all for money!
[*To* SENTRY.]   But you—!
I swear by God and by the throne of God,
The man who has done this thing shall pay for it!
Find that man, bring him here to me, or your death   135
Will be the least of your problems: I'll string you up
Alive, and there will be certain ways to make you
Discover your employer before you die;
And the process may teach you a lesson you seem to have missed:
The dearest profit is sometimes all too dear: 140
That depends on the source. Do you understand me?
A fortune won is often misfortune.

SENTRY. King, may I speak?

CREON.   Your very voice distresses me.

SENTRY. Are you sure that it is my voice, and not your conscience?

CREON. By God, he wants to analyze me now!   145

SENTRY. It is not what I say, but what has been done, that hurts you.

CREON. You talk too much.

SENTRY.   Maybe; but I've done nothing.

CREON. Sold your soul for some silver: that's all you've done.

SENTRY. How dreadful it is when the right judge judges wrong!

CREON. Your figures of speech   150
    May entertain you now; but unless you bring me the man,
You will get little profit from them in the end.

Exit CREON *into the palace.*

SENTRY. "Bring me the man"—!
　　I'd like nothing better than bringing him the man!
　　But bring him or not, you have seen the last of me here.　　155
　　At any rate, I am safe! [*Exit* SENTRY.]

ODE I

CHORUS. Numberless are the world's wonders, but not　　　*Strophe 1*
　　More wonderful than man; the stormgray sea
　　Yields to his prows, the huge crests bear him high;
　　Earth, holy and inexhaustible, is graven
　　With shining furrows where his plows have gone　　5
　　Year after year, the timeless labor of stallions.

　　The lightboned birds and beasts that cling to　　　*Antistrophe 1*
　　　　cover,
　　The lithe fish lighting their reaches of dim water,
　　All are taken, tamed in the net of his mind;
　　The lion on the hill, the wild horse windy-maned,　　10
　　Resign to him; and his blunt yoke has broken
　　The sultry shoulders of the mountain bull.

　　Words also, and thought as rapid as air,　　　*Strophe 2*
　　He fashions to his good use; statecraft is his,
　　And his the skill that deflects the arrows of snow,　　15
　　The spears of winter rain: from every wind
　　He has made himself secure—from all but one:
　　In the late wind of death he cannot stand.

　　O clear intelligence, force beyond all measure!　　　*Antistrophe 2*
　　O fate of man, working both good and evil!　　20
　　When the laws are kept, how proudly his city stands!
　　When the laws are broken, what of his city then?
　　Never may the anárchic man find rest at my hearth,
　　Never be it said that my thoughts are his thoughts.

SCENE II

Reenter SENTRY *leading* ANTIGONÊ

CHORAGOS. What does this mean? Surely this captive woman
　　Is the Princess, Antigonê. Why should she be taken?
SENTRY. Here is the one who did it! We caught her
　　In the very act of burying him.—Where is Creon?
CHORAGOS. Just coming from the house.

Enter CREON, *center.*

CREON.　　　　　　　　　　What has happened?　　5
　　Why have you come back so soon?

SENTRY [*expansively*].   O King,
    A man should never be too sure of anything:
    I would have sworn
    That you'd not see me here again: your anger
    Frightened me so, and the things you threatened
            me with;   10
    But how could I tell then
    That I'd be able to solve the case so soon?
    No dice-throwing this time: I was only too glad to come!
    Here is this woman. She is the guilty one:
    We found her trying to bury him.   15
    Take her, then; question her; judge her as you will.
    I am through with the whole thing now, and glad of it.
CREON. But this is Antigonê! Why have you brought her here?
SENTRY. She was burying him, I tell you!
CREON [*severely*].   Is this the truth?
SENTRY. I saw her with my own eyes. Can I say more?   20
CREON. The details: come, tell me quickly!
SENTRY.   It was like this:
    After those terrible threats of yours, King,
    We went back and brushed the dust away from the body.
    The flesh was soft by now, and stinking,
    So we sat on a hill to windward and kept guard.   25
    No napping this time! We kept each other awake.
    But nothing happened until the white round sun
    Whirled in the center of the round sky over us:
    Then, suddenly,
    A storm of dust roared up from the earth, and the sky   30
    Went out, the plain vanished with all its trees
    In the stinging dark. We closed our eyes and endured it.
    The whirlwind lasted a long time, but it passed;
    And then we looked, and there was Antigonê!
    I have seen   35
    A mother bird come back to a stripped nest, heard
    Her crying bitterly a broken note or two
    For the young ones stolen. Just so, when this girl
    Found the bare corpse, and all her love's work wasted,
    She wept, and cried on heaven to damn the hands   40
    That had done this thing.
                            And then she brought more dust
    And sprinkled wine three times for her brother's ghost.

    We ran and took her at once. She was not afraid,
    Not even when we charged her with what she had done.
    She denied nothing.
                        And this was a comfort to me,   45
    And some uneasiness: for it is a good thing
    To escape from death, but it is no great pleasure

To bring death to a friend.
                              Yet I always say
There is nothing so comfortable as your own safe skin!
CREON [*slowly, dangerously*]. And you, Antigonê,   50
    You with your head hanging,—do you confess this thing?
ANTIGONÊ. I do. I deny nothing.
CREON [*to* SENTRY].   You may go. [*Exit* SENTRY.]
    [*To* ANTIGONÊ.] Tell me, tell me briefly:
    Had you heard my proclamation touching this matter?
ANTIGONÊ. It was public. Could I help hearing it?   55
CREON. And yet you dared defy the law.
ANTIGONÊ.   I dared.
    It was not God's proclamation. That final Justice
    That rules the world below makes no such laws.

    Your edict, King, was strong,
    But all your strength is weakness itself against   60
    The immortal unrecorded laws of God.
    They are not merely now: they were, and shall be,
    Operative for ever, beyond man utterly.
    I knew I must die, even without your decree:
    I am only mortal. And if I must die   65
    Now, before it is my time to die,
    Surely this is no hardship: can anyone
    Living, as I live, with evil all about me,
    Think Death less than a friend? This death of mine
    Is of no importance; but if I had left my brother   70
    Lying in death unburied, I should have suffered.
    Now I do not.
                    You smile at me. Ah Creon,
    Think me a fool, if you like; but it may well be
    That a fool convicts me of folly.
CHORAGOS. Like father, like daughter: both headstrong,
        deaf to reason!   75
    She has never learned to yield:
CREON.   She has much to learn.
    The inflexible heart breaks first, the toughest iron
    Cracks first, and the wildest horses bend their necks
    At the pull of the smallest curb.
                              Pride? In a slave?
    This girl is guilty of a double insolence,   80
    Breaking the given laws and boasting of it.
    Who is the man here,
    She or I, if this crime goes unpunished?
    Sister's child, or more than sister's child,
    Or closer yet in blood—she and her sister   85
    Win bitter death for this!
    [*To* SERVANTS.] Go, some of you,
    Arrest Ismenê. I accuse her equally.

Bring her: you will find her sniffling in the house there.

Here mind's a traitor: crimes kept in the dark
Cry for light, and the guardian brain shudders;   90
But how much worse than this
Is brazen boasting of barefaced anarchy!
ANTIGONÊ. Creon, what more do you want than my death?
CREON.   Nothing.
That gives me everything.
ANTIGONÊ.   Then I beg you: kill me.
This talking is a great weariness: your words   95
Are distasteful to me, and I am sure that mine
Seem so to you. And yet they should not seem so:
I should have praise and honor for what I have done.
All these men here would praise me
Were their lips not frozen shut with fear of you.   100
[*Bitterly.*] Ah the good fortune of kings,
Licensed to say and do whatever they please!
CREON. You are alone here in that opinion.
ANTIGONÊ. No, they are with me. But they keep their tongues in leash.
CREON. Maybe. But you are guilty, and they are not.   105
ANTIGONÊ. There is no guilt in reverence for the dead.
CREON. But Eteoclês—was he not your brother too?
ANTIGONÊ. My brother too.
CREON.   And you insult his memory?
ANTIGONÊ [*softly*]. The dead man would not say that I insult it.
CREON. He would: for you honor a traitor as much as him.   110
ANTIGONÊ. His own brother, traitor or not, and equal in blood.
CREON. He made war on his country. Eteoclês defended it.
ANTIGONÊ. Nevertheless, there are honors due all the dead.
CREON. But not the same for the wicked as for the just.
ANTIGONÊ. Ah Creon, Creon,   115
Which of us can say what the gods hold wicked?
CREON. An enemy is an enemy, even dead.
ANTIGONÊ. It is my nature to join in love, not hate.
CREON [*finally losing patience*]. Go join them then; if you must
        have your love,
Find it in hell!   120
CHORAGOS. But see, Ismenê comes:

Enter ISMENÊ, *guarded.*

Those tears are sisterly, the cloud
That shadows her eyes rains down gentle sorrow.
CREON. You too, Ismenê,
Snake in my ordered house, sucking my blood   125
Stealthily—and all the time I never knew
That these two sisters were aiming at my throne!
                                                        Ismenê,
Do you confess your share in this crime, or deny it?

Answer me.

ISMENÊ. Yes, if she will let me say so. I am guilty.   130

ANTIGONÊ [*coldly*]. No. Ismenê. You have no right to say so.
    You would not help me, and I will not have you help me.

ISMENÊ. But now I know what you meant; and I am here
    To join you, to take my share of punishment.

ANTIGONÊ. The dead man and the gods who rule the dead   135
    Know whose act this was. Words are not friends.

ISMENÊ. Do you refuse me, Antigonê? I want to die with you:
    I too have a duty that I must discharge to the dead.

ANTIGONÊ. You shall not lessen my death by sharing it.

ISMENÊ. What do I care for life when you are dead?   140

ANTIGONÊ. Ask Creon. You're always hanging on his opinions.

ISMENÊ. You are laughing at me. Why, Antigonê?

ANTIGONÊ. It's a joyless laughter, Ismenê.

ISMENÊ.   But can I do nothing?

ANTIGONÊ. Yes. Save yourself. I shall not envy you.
    There are those who will praise you; I shall have honor, too.   145

ISMENÊ. But we are equally guilty!

ANTIGONÊ.   No more, Ismenê.
    You are alive, but I belong to Death.

CREON [*to the* CHORUS]. Gentlemen, I beg you to observe these girls:
    One has just now lost her mind; the other,
    It seems, has never had a mind at all.   150

ISMENÊ. Grief teaches the steadiest minds to waver, King.

CREON. Yours certainly did, when you assumed guilt with the guilty!

ISMENÊ. But how could I go on living without her?

CREON.   You are.
    She is already dead.

ISMENÊ.   But your own son's bride!

CREON. There are places enough for him to push his plow.   155
    I want no wicked women for my sons!

ISMENÊ. O dearest Haimon, how your father wrongs you!

CREON. I've had enough of your childish talk of marriage!

CHORAGOS. Do you really intend to steal this girl from your son?

CREON. No; Death will do that for me.

CHORAGOS.   Then she must die?   160

CREON [*ironically*]. You dazzle me.
                  —But enough of this talk!
    [*To* GUARDS.] You, there, take them away and guard them well:
    For they are but women, and even brave men run
    When they see Death coming.

    Exeunt ISMENÊ, ANTIGONÊ, *and* GUARDS.

ODE II

CHORUS. Fortunate is the man who has never tasted   *Strophe 1*
    God's vengeance!

Where once the anger of heaven has struck, that house is shaken
For ever: damnation rises behind each child
Like a wave cresting out of the black northeast,
When the long darkness under sea roars up   5
And bursts drumming death upon the windwhipped sand.

I have seen this gathering sorrow from time long past   *Antistrophe 1*
Loom upon Oedipus' children: generation from generation
Takes the compulsive rage of the enemy god.
So lately this last flower of Oedipus' line   10
Drank the sunlight! but now a passionate word
And a handful of dust have closed up all its beauty.

What mortal arrogance   *Strophe 2*
Transcends the wrath of Zeus?
Sleep cannot lull him nor the effortless long months   15
Of the timeless gods: but he is young for ever,
And his house is the shining day of high Olympos.
All that is and shall be,
And all the past, is his.
No pride on earth is free of the curse of heaven.   20

The straying dreams of men   *Antistrophe 2*
May bring them ghosts of joy:
But as they drowse, the waking embers burn them;
Or they walk with fixed eyes, as blind men walk.
But the ancient wisdom speaks for our own time: 25
    Fate works most for woe
    With Folly's fairest show.
Man's little pleasure is the spring of sorrow.

SCENE III

CHORAGOS. But here is Haimon, King, the last of all your sons
    Is it grief for Antigonê that brings him here,
    And bitterness at being robbed of his bride?

Enter HAIMON.

CREON. We shall soon see, and no need of diviners.
                           —Son,
    You have heard my final judgment on that girl: 5
    Have you come here hating me, or have you come
    With deference and with love, whatever I do?
HAIMON. I am your son, father. You are my guide.
    You make things clear for me, and I obey you.
    No marriage means more to me than your continuing wisdom.   10
CREON. Good. That is the way to behave: subordinate
    Everything else, my son, to your father's will.
    This is what a man prays for, that he may get
    Sons attentive and dutiful in his house,

Each one hating his father's enemies,　　　　　　　　　　　15
Honoring his father's friends. But if his sons
Fail him, if they turn out unprofitably,
What has he fathered but trouble for himself
And amusement for the malicious?
　　　　　　　　　　　　　　　So you are right
Not to lose your head over this woman.　　　　　　　　　　20
Your pleasure with her would soon grow cold, Haimon,
And then you'd have a hellcat in bed and elsewhere.
Let her find her husband in Hell!
Of all the people in this city, only she
Has had contempt for my law and broken it.　　　　　　　　25

Do you want me to show myself weak before the people?
Or to break my sworn word? No, and I will not.
The woman dies.
I suppose she'll plead "family ties." Well, let her.
If I permit my own family to rebel,　　　　　　　　　　30
How shall I earn the world's obedience?
Show me the man who keeps his house in hand,
He's fit for public authority.
　　　　　　　　　　　　I'll have no dealings
With lawbreakers, critics of the government:
Whoever is chosen to govern should be obeyed—　　　　　35
Must be obeyed, in all things, great and small,
Just and unjust! O Haimon,
The man who knows how to obey, and that man only,
Knows how to give commands when the time comes.
You can depend on him, no matter how fast　　　　　　　40
The spears come: he's a good soldier, he'll stick it out.

Anarchy, anarchy! Show me a greater evil!
This is why cities tumble and the great houses rain down,
This is what scatters armies!
No, no: good lives are made so by discipline.　　　　　　45
We keep the laws then, and the lawmakers,
And no woman shall seduce us. If we must lose,
Let's lose to a man, at least! Is a woman stronger than we?
CHORAGOS. Unless time has rusted my wits,
What you say, King, is said with point and dignity.　　　50
HAIMON [*boyishly earnest*]. Father:
Reason is God's crowning gift to man, and you are right
To warn me against losing mine. I cannot say—
I hope that I shall never want to say!—that you
Have reasoned badly. Yet there are other men　　　　　55
Who can reason, too; and their opinions might be helpful.
You are not in a position to know everything
That people say or do, or what they feel:
Your temper terrifies—everyone

Will tell you only what you like to hear.   60
But I, at any rate, can listen; and I have heard them
Muttering and whispering in the dark about this girl.
They say no woman has ever, so unreasonably,
Died so shameful a death for a generous act:
"She covered her brother's body. Is this indecent?   65
She kept him from dogs and vultures. Is this a crime?
Death?—She should have all the honor that we can give her!"

This is the way they talk out there in the city.

You must believe me:
Nothing is closer to me than your happiness.   70
What could be closer? Must not any son
Value his father's fortune as his father does his?
I beg you, do not be unchangeable:
Do not believe that you alone can be right.
The man who thinks that,   75
The man who maintains that only he has the power
To reason correctly, the gift to speak, the soul—
A man like that, when you know him, turns out empty.

It is not reason never to yield to reason!

In flood time you can see how some trees bend,   80
And because they bend, even their twigs are safe,
While stubborn trees are torn up, roots and all.
And the same thing happens in sailing:
Make your sheet fast, never slacken,—and over you go,
Head over heels and under: and there's your voyage.   85
Forget you are angry! Let yourself be moved!
I know I am young; but please let me say this:
The ideal condition
Would be, I admit, that men should be right by instinct;
But since we are all too likely to go astray,   90
The reasonable thing is to learn from those who can teach.
CHORAGOS. You will do well to listen to him, King,
If what he says is sensible. And you, Haimon,
Must listen to your father.—Both speak well.
CREON. You consider it right for a man of my years and experience   95
To go to school to a boy?
HAIMON.   It is not right
If I am wrong. But if I am young, and right,
What does my age matter?
CREON. You think it right to stand up for an anarchist?
HAIMON. Not at all. I pay no respect to criminals.   100
CREON. Then she is not a criminal?
HAIMON. The City would deny it, to a man.
CREON. And the City proposes to teach me how to rule?
HAIMON. Ah. Who is it that's talking like a boy now?

CREON. My voice is the one voice giving orders in this City!   105
HAIMON. It is no City if it takes orders from one voice.
CREON. The State is the King!
HAIMON.   Yes, if the State is a desert.

> *Pause.*

CREON. This boy, it seems, has sold out to a woman.
HAIMON. If you are a woman: my concern is only for you.
CREON. So? Your "concern"! In a public brawl with your father!   110
HAIMON. How about you, in a public brawl with justice?
CREON. With justice, when all that I do is within my rights?
HAIMON. You have no right to trample on God's right.
CREON [*completely out of control*]. Fool, adolescent fool! Taken
     in by a woman!
HAIMON. You'll never see me taken in by anything vile.   115
CREON. Every word you say is for her!
HAIMON [*quietly, darkly*].   And for you.
     And for me. And for the gods under the earth.
CREON. You'll never marry her while she lives.
HAIMON. Then she must die.—But her death will cause another.
CREON. Another?   120
     Have you lost your senses? Is this an open threat?
HAIMON. There is no threat in speaking to emptiness.
CREON. I swear you'll regret this superior tone of yours!
     You are the empty one!
HAIMON.   If you were not my father,
     I'd say you were perverse.   125
CREON. You girlstruck fool, don't play at words with me!
HAIMON. I am sorry. You prefer silence.
CREON.   Now, by God—
     I swear, by all the gods in heaven above us,
     You'll watch it, I swear you shall!
     [*To the* SERVANTS.]   Bring her out!
     Bring the woman out! Let her die before his eyes!   130
     Here, this instant, with her bridegroom beside her!
HAIMON. Not here, no; she will not die here, King.
     And you will never see my face again.
     Go on raving as long as you've a friend to endure you.
                              [*Exit* HAIMON.]
CHORAGOS. Gone, gone.   135
     Creon, a young man in a rage is dangerous!
CREON. Let him do, or dream to do, more than a man can.
     He shall not save these girls from death.
CHORAGOS.   These girls?
     You have sentenced them both?
CREON.   No, you are right.
     I will not kill the one whose hands are clean.   140
CHORAGOS. But Antigonê?

CREON [*somberly*]. I will carry her far away
    Out there in the wilderness, and lock her
    Living in a vault of stone. She shall have food,
    As the custom is, to absolve the State of her death.
    And there let her pray to the gods of hell: 145
    They are her only gods:
    Perhaps they will show her an escape from death,
    Or she may learn,
                though late,
    That piety shown the dead is pity in vain. [*Exit* CREON.]

ODE III

CHORUS. Love, unconquerable   *Strophe*
    Waster of rich men, keeper
    Of warm lights and all-nigh vigil
    In the soft face of a girl:
    Sea-wanderer, forest-visitor!   5
    Even the pure Immortals cannot escape you,
    And the mortal man, in his one day's dusk,
    Trembles before your glory.

    Surely you swerve upon ruin   *Antistrophe*
    The just man's consenting heart,
    As here you have made bright anger
    Strike between father and son—
    And none has conquered by Love!
    A girl's glánce wórking the will of heaven:
    Pleasure to her alone who mocks us,   15
    Merciless Aphroditê.°

SCENE IV

CHORAGOS. [*as* ANTIGONE *enters guarded*]. But I can no longer
        stand in awe of this,
    Nor, seeing what I see, keep back my tears.
    Here is Antigonê, passing to that chamber
    Where all find sleep at last.

ANTIGONÊ. Look upon me, friends, and pity me   *Strophe 1* 5
    Turning back at the night's edge to say
    Good-by to the sun that shines for me no longer;
    Now sleepy Death
    Summons me down to Acheron,° that cold shore:
    There is no bridesong there, nor any music.   10

16 **Aphroditê** goddess of love
Scene IV: 9 **Acheron** a river of the underworld, which was ruled by Hades

CHORUS. Yet not unpraised, not without a kind of honor,
　　You walk at last into the underworld;
　　Untouched by sickness, broken by no sword.
　　What woman has ever found your way to death?

ANTIGONÊ. How often I have heard the story of Niobê,°　　　*Antistrophe 1* 15
　　Tantalos' wretched daughter, how the stone
　　Clung fast about her, ivy-close: and they say
　　The rain falls endlessly
　　And sifting soft snow; her tears are never done.
　　I feel the loneliness of her death in mine.　　　　　　　20
CHORUS. But she was born of heaven, and you
　　Are woman, woman-born. If her death is yours,
　　A mortal woman's, is this not for you
　　Glory in our world and in the world beyond?

ANTIGONÊ. You laugh at me. Ah, friends, friends,　　　　*Strophe 2* 25
　　Can you not wait until I am dead? O Thebes,
　　O men many-charioted, in love with Fortune,
　　Dear springs of Dircê, sacred Theban grove,
　　Be witnesses for me, denied all pity,
　　Unjustly judged! and think a word of love　　　　　　30
　　For her whose path turns
　　Under dark earth, where there are no more tears.
CHORUS. You have passed beyond human daring and come at last
　　Into a place of stone where Justice sits.
　　I cannot tell　　　　　　　　　　　　　　　　　　35
　　What shape of your father's guilt appears in this.
ANTIGONÊ. You have touched it at last:　　　　　　　*Antistrophe 2*
　　That bridal bed
　　Unspeakable, horror of son and mother mingling:
　　Their crime, infection of all our family!
　　O Oedipus, father and brother!　　　　　　　　　40
　　Your marriage strikes from the grave to murder mine.
　　I have been a stranger here in my own land:
　　All my life
　　The blasphemy of my birth has followed me.
CHORUS. Reverence is a virtue, but strength　　　　　　45
　　Lives in established law: that must prevail.
　　You have made your choice,
　　Your death is the doing of your conscious hand.
ANTIGONÊ. Then let me go, since all your words are bitter,　　*Epode*
　　And the very light of the sun is cold to me.　　　　　50
　　Lead me to my vigil, where I must have
　　Neither love nor lamentation; no song, but silence.

15 **Niobê** (Niobê boasted of her numerous children, provoking Leto, the mother of Apollo, to destroy them. Niobê wept profusely, and finally was turned to stone on Mount Sipylus, whose streams are her tears).

CREON *interrupts impatiently.*

CREON. If dirges and planned lamentations could put off death,
    Men would be singing for ever.
    [*To the* SERVANTS.]   Take her, go!
    You know your orders: take her to the vault   55
    And leave her alone there. And if she lives or dies,
    That's her affair, not ours: our hands are clean.

ANTIGONÊ. O tomb, vaulted bride-bed in eternal rock,
    Soon I shall be with my own again
    Where Persephonê° welcomes the thin ghosts underground: 60
    And I shall see my father again, and you, mother,
    And dearest Polyneicês—
                    dearest indeed
    To me, since it was my hand
    That washed him clean and poured the ritual wine:
    And my reward is death before my time!   65

    And yet, as men's hearts know, I have done no wrong,
    I have not sinned before God. Or if I have,
    I shall know the truth in death. But if the guilt
    Lies upon Creon who judged me, then, I pray,
    May his punishment equal my own.
CHORAGOS.   O passionate heart,   70
    Unyielding, tormented still by the same winds!
CREON. Her guards shall have good cause to regret their delaying.
ANTIGONÊ. Ah! That voice is like the voice of death!
CREON. I can give you no reason to think you are mistaken.
ANTIGONÊ. Thebes, and you my fathers' gods,   75
    And rulers of Thebes, you see me now, the last
    Unhappy daughter of a line of kings,
    Your kings, led away to death. You will remember
    What things I suffer, and at what men's hands,
    Because I would not transgress the laws of heaven.   80
    [*To the* GUARDS, *simply.*] Come: let us wait no longer.
                    [*Exit* ANTIGONÊ, *left, guarded.*]

ODE IV

CHORUS. All Danaê's beauty was locked away   *Strophe 1*
    In a brazen cell where the sunlight could not come:
    A small room still as any grave, enclosed her.
    Yet she was a princess too,
    And Zeus in a rain of gold poured love upon her.   5
    O child, child,

60 **Persephonê** queen of the underworld

No power in wealth or war
Or tough sea-blackened ships
Can prevail against untiring Destiny!

And Dryas' son° also, that furious king,   *Antistrophe 1* 10
Bore the god's prisoning anger for his pride:
Sealed up by Dionysos in deaf stone,
His madness died among echoes.
So at the last he learned what dreadful power
His tongue had mocked: 15
For he had profaned the revels,
And fired the wrath of the nine
Implacable Sisters° that love the sound of the flute.

And old men tell a half-remembered tale   *Strophe 2*
Of horror where a dark ledge splits the sea   20
And a double surf beats on the gráy shóres:
How a king's new woman°, sick
With hatred for the queen he had imprisoned,
Ripped out his two sons' eyes with her bloody hands
While grinning Arês° watched the shuttle plunge   25
Four times: four blind wounds crying for revenge,

Crying, tears and blood mingled.—Piteously born,   *Antistrophe 2*
Those sons whose mother was of heavenly birth!
Her father was the god of the North Wind
And she was cradled by gales,   30
She raced with young colts on the glittering hills
And walked untrammeled in the open light:
But in her marriage deathless Fate found means
To build a tomb like yours for all her joy.

SCENE V

Enter blind TEIRESIAS, *led by a boy. The opening speeches of* TEIRESIAS
should be in singsong contrast to the realistic lines of CREON.

TEIRESIAS. This is the way the blind man comes, Princes, Princes,
Lock-step, two heads lit by the eyes of one.
CREON. What new thing have you to tell us, old Teiresias?
TEIRESIAS. I have much to tell you: listen to the prophet, Creon.
CREON. I am not aware that I have ever failed to listen.   5
TEIRESIAS. Then you have done wisely, King, and ruled well.
CREON. I admit my debt to you. But what have you to say?
TEIRESIAS. This, Creon: you stand once more on the edge of fate.

10 **Dryas' son** Lycurgus, King of Thrace   18 **Sisters** the Muses   22 **king's new**
woman Eidothea, second wife of King Phineus, blinded her stepsons. Their mother,
Cleopatra, had been imprisoned in a cave. Phineus was the son of a king, and
Cleopatra, his first wife, was the daughter of Boreas, the North wind, but this illustrious
ancestry could not protect his sons from violence and darkness.   25 **Arês** god of war

CREON. What do you mean? Your words are a kind of dread.
TEIRESIAS. Listen, Creon: 10
    I was sitting in my chair of augury, at the place
    Where the birds gather about me. They were all a-chatter,
    As is their habit, when suddenly I heard
    A strange note in their jangling, a scream, a
    Whirring fury; I knew that they were fighting,   15
    Tearing each other, dying
    In a whirlwind of wings clashing. And I was afraid.
    I began the rites of burnt-offering at the altar,
    But Hephaistos° failed me: instead of bright flame,
    There was only the sputtering slime of the fat thigh-flesh   20
    Melting: the entrails dissolved in gray smoke,
    The bare bone burst from the welter. And no blaze!

    This was a sign from heaven. My boy described it,
    Seeing for me as I see for others.

    I tell you, Creon, you yourself have brought   25
    This new calamity upon us. Our hearths and altars
    Are stained with the corruption of dogs and carrion birds
    That glut themselves on the corpse of Oedipus' son.
    The gods are deaf when we pray to them, their fire
    Recoils from our offering, their birds of omen   30
    Have no cry of comfort, for they are gorged
    With the thick blood of the dead.
                  O my son,
    These are no trifles! Think: all men make mistakes,
    But a good man yields when he knows his course is wrong,
    And repairs the evil. The only crime is pride.   35

    Give in to the dead man, then: do not fight with a corpse—
    What glory is it to kill a man who is dead?
    Think, I beg you:
    It is for your own good that I speak as I do.
    You should be able to yield for your own good.   40
CREON. It seems that prophets have made me their especial province.
    All my life long
    I have been a kind of butt for the dull arrows
    Of doddering fortune-tellers!
                  No, Teiresias:
    If your birds—if the great eagles of God himself   45
    Should carry him stinking bit by bit to heaven,
    I would not yield. I am not afraid of pollution:
    No man can defile the gods.
                 Do what you will,
    Go into business, make money, speculate
    In India gold or that synthetic gold from Sardis,   50

19 **Hephaistos** god of fire

Get rich otherwise than by my consent to bury him.
Teiresias, it is a sorry thing when a wise man
Sells his wisdom, lets out his words for hire!

TEIRESIAS. Ah Creon! Is there no man left in the world—

CREON. To do what?—Come, let's have the aphorism!   55

TEIRESIAS. No man who knows that wisdom outweighs any wealth?

CREON. As surely as bribes are baser than any baseness.

TEIRESIAS. You are sick, Creon! You are deathly sick!

CREON. As you say: it is not my place to challenge a prophet.

TEIRESIAS. Yet you have said my prophecy is for sale.   60

CREON. The generation of prophets has always loved gold.

TEIRESIAS. The generation of kings has always loved brass.

CREON. You forget yourself! You are speaking to your King.

TEIRESIAS. I know it. You are a king because of me.

CREON. You have a certain skill; but you have sold out.   65

TEIRESIAS. King, you will drive me to words that—

CREON.   Say them, say them!
Only remember: I will not pay you for them.

TEIRESIAS. No, you will find them too costly.

CREON.   No doubt. Speak:
Whatever you say, you will not change my will.

TEIRESIAS. Then take this, and take it to heart!   70
The time is not far off when you shall pay back
Corpse for corpse, flesh of your own flesh.
You have thrust the child of this world into living night,
You have kept from the gods below the child that is theirs:
The one in a grave before her death, the other,   75
Dead, denied the grave. This is your crime:
And the Furies and the dark gods of Hell
Are swift with terrible punishment for you.

Do you want to buy me now, Creon?

                         Not many days,
And your house will be full of men and women weeping,   80
And curses will be hurled at you from far
Cities grieving for sons unburied, left to rot
Before the walls of Thebes.

These are my arrows, Creon: they are all for you.

[*To* BOY.] But come, child: lead me home.   85
Let him waste his fine anger upon younger men.
Maybe he will learn at last
To control a wiser tongue in a better head. [*Exit* TEIRESIAS.]

CHORAGOS. The old man has gone, King, but his words
Remain to plague us. I am old, too,   90
But I cannot remember that he was ever false.

CREON. That is true. . . . . . It troubles me.
Oh it is hard to give in! but it is worse
To risk everything for stubborn pride.

CHORAGOS. Creon: take my advice.
CREON.   What shall I do?   95
CHORAGOS. Go quickly: free Antigonê from her vault
    And build a tomb for the body of Polyneicês.
CREON. You would have me do this!
CHORAGOS.   Creon, yes!
    And it must be done at once: God moves
    Switftly to cancel the folly of stubborn men.   100
CREON. It is hard to deny the heart! But I
    Will do it: I will not fight with destiny.
CHORAGOS. You must go yourself, you cannot leave it to others.
CREON. I will go.
            —Bring axes, servants:
    Come with me to the tomb. I buried her, I   105
    Will set her free.
                        Oh quickly!
    My mind misgives—
    The laws of the gods are might, and a man must serve them
    To the last day of his life!   [*Exit* CREON.]

PAEAN°

CHORAGOS. God of many names   *Strophe 1*
CHORUS.   O Iacchos
                                son
    of Kadmeian Sémelê
                    O born of the Thunder!
    Guardian of the West
                    Regent
    of Eleusis' plain
                    O Prince of maenad Thebes
    and the Dragon Field by rippling Ismenós:°   5
CHORAGOS. God of many names   *Antistrophe 1*
CHORUS.   the flame of torches
    flares on our hills
                    the nymphs of Iacchos
    dance at the spring of Castalia:°
    from the vine-close mountain
                            come ah come in ivy:
    Evohé evohé! sings through the streets of Thebes   10

CHORAGOS. God of many names   *Strophe 2*

Paean a hymn (here dedicated to Iacchos, also called Dionysos. His father was Zeus, his mother was Sémelé, daughter of Kadmos. Iacchos's worshipers were the Maenads, whose cry was *"Evohé evohé"*) 5 **Ismenós** a river east of Thebes (from a dragon's teeth, sown near the river, there sprang men who became the ancestors of the Theban nobility) 8 **Castalia** a spring on Mount Parnasos

CHORUS.   Iacchos of Thebes
      heavenly Child
                    of Sémelê bride of the Thunderer!
      The shadow of plague is upon us:
                              come
      with clement feet
                    oh come from Parnasos
      down the long slopes
                              across the lamenting water   15
CHORAGOS. Iô Fire! Chorister of the throbbing stars!   *Antistrophe 2*
      O purest among the voices of the night!
      Thou son of God, blaze for us!
CHORUS. Come with choric rapture of circling Maenads
      Who cry *Iô Iacche!*
                    God of many names!   20

EXODOS

Enter MESSENGER *from left.*

MESSENGER. Men of the line of Kadmos,° you who live
      Near Amphion's citadel,°
                    I cannot say
      Of any condition of human life "This is fixed,
      This is clearly good, or bad." Fate raises up,
      And Fate casts down the happy and unhappy alike: 5
      No man can foretell his Fate.
                    Take the case of Creon:
      Creon was happy once, as I count happiness:
      Victorious in battle, sole governor of the land,
      Fortunate father of children nobly born.
      And now it has all gone from him! Who can say   10
      That a man is still alive when his life's joy fails?
      He is a walking dead man. Grant him rich,
      Let him live like a king in his great house:
      If his pleasure is gone, I would not give
      So much as the shadow of smoke for all he owns.   15
CHORAGOS. Your words hint at sorrow: what is your news for us?
MESSENGER. They are dead. The living are guilty of their death.
CHORAGOS. Who is guilty? Who is dead? Speak!
MESSENGER.   Haimon.
      Haimon is dead; and the hand that killed him
      Is his own hand.
CHORAGOS. His father's? or his own?   20

1 **Kadmos,** who sowed the dragon's teeth, was founder of Thebes. 2 **Amphion's citadel** Amphion played so sweetly on his lyre that he charmed stones to form a wall around Thebes.

MESSENGER. His own, driven mad by the murder his father had done.
CHORAGOS. Teiresias, Teiresias, how clearly you saw it all!
MESSENGER. This is my news: you must draw what conclusions
       you can from it.
CHORAGOS. But look: Eurydicê, our Queen:
    Has she overheard us?   25
    Enter EURYDICÊ *from the palace, center.*
EURYDICÊ. I have heard something, friends:
    As I was unlocking the gate of Pallas'° shrine,
    For I needed her help today, I heard a voice
    Telling of some new sorrow. And I fainted
    There at the temple with all my maidens about me.   30
    But speak again: whatever it is, I can bear it:
    Grief and I are no strangers.
MESSENGER.   Dearest Lady,
    I will tell you plainly all that I have seen.
    I shall not try to comfort you: what is the use,
    Since comfort could lie only in what is not true?   35
    The truth is always best.
               I went with Creon
    To the outer plain where Polyneicês was lying,
    No friend to pity him, his body shredded by dogs.
    We made our prayers in the place to Hecatê
    And Pluto,° that they would be merciful. And we bathed   40
    The corpse with holy water, and we brought
    Fresh-broken branches to burn what was left of it,
    And upon the urn we heaped up a towering barrow
    Of the earth of his own land.
                  When we were done, we ran
    To the vault where Antigonê lay on her couch of stone.   45
    One of the servants had gone ahead,
    And while he was yet far off he heard a voice
    Grieving within the chamber, and he came back
    And told Creon. And as the King went closer,
    The air was full of wailing, the words lost,   50
    And he begged us to make all haste. "Am I a prophet?"
    He said, weeping, "And must I walk this road,
    The saddest of all that I have gone before?
    My son's voice calls me on. Oh quickly, quickly!
    Look through the crevice there, and tell me   55
    If it is Haimon, or some deception of the gods!"

    We obeyed; and in the cavern's farthest corner
    We saw her lying:
    She had made a noose of her fine linen veil
    And hanged herself. Haimon lay beside her,   60

27 **Pallas** Pallas Athene, goddess of wisdom
40 **Hecatê / And Pluto** Hecatê and Pluto (also known as Hades) were deities of the
underworld.

His arms about her waist, lamenting her,
His love lost under ground, crying out
That his father had stolen her away from him.

When Creon saw him the tears rushed to his eyes
And he called to him: "What have you done, child?
Speak to me.   65
What are you thinking that makes your eyes so strange?
O my son, my son, I come to you on my knees!"
But Haimon spat in his face. He said not a word,
Staring—
     And suddenly drew his sword
And lunged. Creon shrank back, the blade missed; and the boy,   70
Desperate against himself, drove it half its length
Into his own side, and fell. And as he died
He gathered Antigonê close in his arms again,
Choking, his blood bright red on her white check.
And now he lies dead with the dead, and she is his   75
At last, his bride in the house of the dead.

          Exit EURYDICÊ *into the palace.*

CHORAGOS. She has left us without a word. What can this mean?
MESSENGER. It troubles me, too; yet she knows what is best,
    Her grief is too great for public lamentation,
    And doubtless she has gone to her chamber to weep   80
    For her dead son, leading her maidens in his dirge.

    Pause.

CHORAGOS. It may be so: but I fear this deep silence.
MESSENGER. I will see what she is doing. I will go in.
        Exit MESSENGER *into the palace.*

Enter CREON *with attendants, bearing* HAIMON's *body.*

CHORAGOS. But here is the king himself: oh look at him,
    Bearing his own damnation in his arms.   85
CREON. Nothing you say can touch me any more.
    My own blind heart has brought me
    From darkness to final darkness, Here you see
    The father murdering, the murdered son—
    And all my civic wisdom!   90

    Haimon my son, so young, so young to die,
    I was the fool, not you; and you died for me.
CHORAGOS. That is the truth; but you were late in learning it.
CREON. This truth is hard to bear. Surely a god
    Has crushed me beneath the hugest weight of heaven,   95
    And driven me headlong a barbaric way
    To trample out the thing I held most dear.

    The pains that men will take to come to pain!

Enter MESSENGER *from the palace.*

MESSENGER. The burden you carry in your hands is heavy,
   But it is not all: you will find more in your house.   100
CREON. What burden worse than this shall I find there?
MESSENGER. The Queen is dead.
CREON. O port of death, deaf world,
   Is there no pity for me? And you, Angel of evil,
   I was dead, and your words are death again.   105
   Is it true, boy? Can it be true?
   Is my wife dead? Has death bred death?
MESSENGER. You can see for yourself.

The doors are opened and the body of EURYDICÊ *is disclosed within.*

CREON. Oh pity!
   All true, all true, and more than I can bear!   110
   O my wife, my son!
MESSENGER. She stood before the altar, and her heart
   Welcomed the knife her own hand guided,
   And a great cry burst from her lips for Megareus° dead,
   And for Haimon dead, her sons; and her last breath   115
   Was a curse for their father, the murderer of her sons.
   And she fell, and the dark flowed in through her closing eyes.
CREON. O God, I am sick with fear.
   Are there no swords here? Has no one a blow for me?
MESSENGER. Her curse is upon you for the deaths of both.   120
CREON. It is right that it should be. I alone am guilty.
   I know it, and I say it. Lead me in,
   Quickly, friends.
   I have neither life nor substance. Lead me in.
CHORAGOS. You are right, if there can be right in so much wrong.   125
   The briefest way is best in a world of sorrow.
CREON. Let it come,
   Let death come quickly, and be kind to me.
   I would not ever see the sun again.
CHORAGOS. All that will come when it will; but we, meanwhile,   130
   Have much to do. Leave the future to itself.
CREON. All my heart was in that prayer!
CHORAGOS. Then do not pray any more: the sky is deaf.
CREON. Lead me away. I have been rash and foolish.
   I have killed my son and my wife.   135
   I look for comfort; my comfort lies here dead.
   Whatever my hands have touched has come to nothing.
   Fate has brought all my pride to a thought of dust.

As CREON *is being led into the house, the* CHORAGOS *advances and
speaks directly to the audience.*

CHORAGOS. There is no happiness where there is no wisdom;
   No wisdom but in submission to the gods.   140

---

114 **Megareus** Megareus, brother of Haimon, had died in the assault on Thebes.

Big words are always punished,
And proud men in old age learn to be wise.

[c.441 B.C.]

■ TOPICS FOR DISCUSSION AND WRITING

1. Would you use masks for some (or all) of the characters? If so, would they be masks that fully cover the face, Greek-style, or some sort of half-masks? (A full mask enlarges the face, and conceivably the mouth-piece can amplify the voice, but only an exceptionally large theater might require such help. Perhaps half-masks are enough if the aim is chiefly to distance the actors from the audience and from daily reality, and to force the actors to develop resources other than facial gestures. One director, arguing in favor of half-masks, has said that an actor who wears even a half-mask learns to act not with his eyes but with his neck.)

2. How would you costume the players? Would you dress them as the Greeks might have? Why? One argument sometimes used by those who hold the modern productions of Greek drama should use classical costumes is that Greek drama *ought* to be remote and ritualistic. Evaluate this view. What sort of modern dress might be effective?

3. If you were directing a college production of *Antigone,* how large a chorus would you use? (Sophocles is said to have used a chorus of 15.) Would you have the chorus recite (or chant) the odes in unison, or would you assign lines to single speakers?

4. If you have read *Oedipus Rex,* compare and contrast the Creon of *Antigone* with the Creon of *Oedipus.*

5. Although Sophocles called his play *Antigone,* many critics say that Creon is the real tragic hero, pointing out that Antigone is absent from the last third of the play. Evaluate this view.

6. In some Greek tragedies, fate plays a great role in bringing about the downfall of the tragic hero. Though there are references to the curse on the House of Oedipus in *Antigone,* do we feel that Antigone goes to her death as a result of the workings of fate? Do we feel that fate is responsible for Creon's fall? Are both Antigone and Creon the creators of their own tragedy?

7. Are the words *hamartia* (page 161) and *hybris* (page 159) relevant to Antigone? To Creon?

8. Why does Creon, contrary to the Chorus's advice (lines 1065–1066), bury the body of Polyneices before he releases Antigone? Does his action show a zeal for piety as short-sighted as his earlier zeal for law? Is his action plausible, in view of the facts that Teiresias has dwelt on the wrong done to Polyneices and that Antigone has ritual food to sustain her? Or are we not to worry about Creon's motive?

9. A *foil* is a character who, by contrast, sets off or helps define another character. To what extent is Ismene a foil to Antigone? Is she entirely without courage?

10. What function does Eurydice serve? How deeply do we feel about her fate?

■ APPENDIX A

Research Papers

What Research is Not, and What Research Is

Jeff, in a Mutt and Jeff cartoon, sells jars of honey. He includes in each jar a dead bee as proof that the product is genuine. Some writers—even some professionals—seem to think that a hiveful of dead quotations or footnotes is proof of research. But research requires much more than the citation of authorities. What it requires, briefly, is informed, *thoughtful* analysis.

Because a research paper requires its writer to collect and interpret evidence—usually including the opinions of earlier investigators—one sometimes hears that a research paper, unlike a critical essay, is not the expression of personal opinion. But such a view is unjust both to criticism and to research. A critical essay is not a mere expression of personal opinions; if it is any good, it offers evidence that supports the opinions and thus persuades the reader of their objective rightness. And a research paper is in the final analysis largely personal, because the author continuously uses his or her own judgment to evaluate the evidence, deciding what is relevant and convincing. A research paper is not the mere presentation of what a dozen scholars have already said about a topic; it is a thoughtful evaluation of the available evidence, and so it is, finally, an expression of what the author thinks the evidence adds up to.

Research can be a tedious and frustrating business; there are hours spent reading books and articles that prove to be irrelevant, there are contradictory pieces of evidence, and there is never enough time.

Still, even though research is time-consuming, those who engage in it feel (at least sometimes) an exhilaration, a sense of triumph at having studied a problem thoroughly and arrived at conclusions that—for the moment, anyway—seem objective and irrefutable. Later, new evidence may turn up and require a new conclusion, but until that time one has built something that will endure wind and weather.

Primary and Secondary Materials

The materials of literary research can be conveniently divided into two sorts, primary and secondary. The *primary materials* or sources are the real subject of study; the *secondary materials* are critical and historical accounts already written about these primary materials. For example, if you want to know whether Shakespeare's attitude toward Julius Caesar was highly traditional or highly original (or a little of each), you read the primary materials (*Julius Caesar*, and other Elizabethan writings about Caesar); and since research requires that you be informed about the present state of thought on your topic, you also read the secondary materials (post-Elizabethan essays, books on Shakespeare, and books on Elizabethan attitudes toward Caesar, or, more generally, on Elizabethan attitudes toward Rome and toward monarchs).

The line between these two kinds of sources is not always clear. For example, if you are concerned with the degree to which Joyce's *A Portrait of the Artist as a Young Man* is autobiographical, primary materials include not only *Portrait* and Joyce's letters, but perhaps also his brother Stanislaus's diary and autobiography. The diary and autobiography might be considered secondary sources (certainly a scholarly biography about Joyce or about his brother would be a secondary source), but because Stanislaus's books are more or less contemporary with your subject and are more or less Joycean, they can reasonably be called primary sources.

From Topic to Thesis

Almost every literary work lends itself to research. We have already mentioned that a study of Shakespeare's attitude toward Julius Caesar would lead to a study of other Elizabethan works and of modern critical works. Similarly, a study of the ghost of Caesar—does it have a real, objective existence or is it merely a figment of Brutus's imagination?—could lead to a study of Shakespeare's other ghosts (for instance, those in *Hamlet* and *Macbeth*), and a study of Elizabethan attitudes toward ghosts. Or, to take an example from our own century, a reader of Edward Albee's *The Sandbox* might want to study the early, critical reception of the play. Did the reviewers like it? More precisely, did the reviewers in academic journals evaluate it differently from those in popular magazines and newspapers? Or, what has Albee himself said about the play in the decades that have passed since he wrote it? Do his comments in essays and interviews indicate that he now sees the play as something different from what he saw when he wrote it? Or, to take yet another example of a work from the middle of our century, a reader might similarly study George Orwell's *1984*, looking at its critical reception, or Orwell's own view of it, or, say, at the sources of Orwell's inspiration. Let's look, for a few minutes, at this last topic.

Assume that you have read George Orwell's *1984* and that, in preparing to do some research on it, browsing through *The Collected Essays, Journalism, and Letters,* you come across a letter (17 February 1944) in which Orwell says that he has been reading Evgenii Zamyatin's *We* and that he himself had been keeping notes for "that kind of book." And in *The Collected Essays, Journalism, and Letters* you also come across a review (4 January 1946) Orwell wrote of *We,* from which it is apparent that *We* resembles *1984.* Or perhaps you learned in a preface to an edition of *1984* that Orwell was influenced by *We,* and you have decided to look into the matter. You want to know exactly how great the influence is. You borrow *We* from the library, read it, and perceive resemblances in plot, character, and theme. But it's not simply a question of listing resemblances between the two books. Your topic is: What do the resemblances add up to? After all, Orwell in the letter said he had already been working in Zamyatin's direction without even knowing Zamyatin's book, so your investigation may find, for example, that the closest resemblances are in relatively trivial details and that there is really nothing important in *1984* that was not already implicit in Orwell's earlier books; or your investigation may find that Zamyatin gave a new depth to Orwell's thought; or it may find that though Orwell borrowed heavily from Zamyatin, he missed the depth of *We.* In the earliest stage of your research, then, you don't know what you will find, so you cannot yet formulate a thesis (or, at best, you can formulate only a tentative thesis). But you know that there is a topic, that it interests you, and that you are ready to begin the necessary legwork.

Locating Material: First Steps

First, prepare a working bibliography, that is, a list of books and articles that must be looked at. The catalog of your library is an excellent place to begin. If your topic is Orwell and Zamyatin, you'll want at least to glance at whatever books by and about these two authors are available. When you have looked over the most promising portions of this material (in secondary sources, chapter headings and indexes will often guide you), you will have found some interesting things. But you want to get a good idea of the state of current scholarship on your topic, and you realize that you must go beyond the card catalog's listings under *Orwell, Zamyatin,* and such obviously related topics as *utopian literature.* Doubtless there are pertinent articles in journals, but you cannot start thumbing through them at random.

The easiest way to locate articles and books on literature written in a modern language—that is, on a topic other than the literature of the ancient world—is to consult the *MLA International Bibliography,* which until 1969 was published as part of *PMLA* (*Publications of the Modern Language Association*) and since 1969 has been published separately. This bibliography, published annually, lists scholarly studies published in a given year; you look, therefore, in the most recent issue under *Orwell* (in the section on *Engligh Literature,* the subsection on *Twentieth Century*) to see if anything is listed that sounds relevant. A look at *Zamyatin* may also turn up material. (Note that in the past few years the number of entries in the *MLA International Bibliography* has so increased that for each year from 1969 the annual bibliography consists of more than one volume. Writings on literature in English are in one

volume, writings on European literature in another; so the volume that gives
you information about Orwell will not be the one that gives you information
about Zamyatin.)

If, by the way, you are indeed working on Orwell, when you consult the
MLA International Bibliography for 1975 you'll find you are lucky; it lists an
article, in an issue of a periodical entitled *Modern Fiction Studies,* that is itself
a bibliography of writings on Orwell. If you consult this article, you'll see that
it is a supplement to an earlier bibliography of writings on Orwell, published
in *Bulletin of Bibliography* in 1974. This last item, of course, could also have
been located by looking at the *MLA International Bibliography* for 1974.

Because your time is severely limited, you probably cannot read everything published on your two authors. At least for the moment, therefore, you
will use only the last ten years of this bibliography. Presumably any important
earlier material will have been incorporated into some of the recent studies
listed, and if when you come to read these recent studies you find references
to an article of, say, 1958 that sounds essential, of course you will read that
article too.

Other Bibliographic Aids

The *MLA International Bibliography* is not the only valuable guide to
scholarship. The *Year's Work in English Studies,* though concerned only with
English authors (hence it will have nothing on Zamyatin, a Russian, unless an
article links Zamyatin with an English author), and though not nearly so comprehensive even on English authors as the *MLA International Bibliography,*
is useful partly because it is selective—presumably listing only the more significant items—and partly because it includes some evaluative comments on
the books and articles it lists.

For topics in American literature, there is a similar annual publication,
American Literary Scholarship (1965–), valuable for its broad coverage of articles and books on major and minor writers and for its evaluative comments.
There are two useful guides to scholarly and critical studies of some canonical
American figures. James Woodress et al., eds., *Eight American Authors: A
Review of Research and Criticism,* rev. ed. (New York: Norton, 1972), covering Poe, Emerson, Hawthorne, Thoreau, Melville, Whitman, Mark Twain,
and Henry James, is of course now dated, but it remains a good guide to early
studies of these authors. Jackson R. Bryer, ed., *Sixteen Modern American
Authors: A Survey of Research and Criticism* (Durham, N.C.: Duke University
Press, 1974), covering such figures as Sherwood Anderson, Willa Cather, Eugene O'Neill, and Ezra Pound (living authors were excluded) is also dated, but
a supplement is in preparation at the time of this writing and may now be
available.

A fair number of recent guides focus on authors who until a decade ago
were relatively neglected. Two examples will have to suffice. *American Wom-
en Writers: Bibliographical Essays* (Westport, Conn.: Greenwood, 1983),
edited by Maurice Duke, Jackson R. Bryer, and M. Thomas Inge, includes
scholarship through 1981 on 24 authors, including Bradstreet, Jewett, Chopin,
Stein, O'Connor, Hurston, and Plath. *Black American Writers: Bibliographi-*

cal Essays (New York: St. Martin's, 1978), edited by M. Thomas Inge, Maurice Duke, and Jackson R. Bryer, covers slave narratives as well as such later writers as Hughes, Ellison, and Baldwin.

None of the bibliographic aids mentioned thus far covers ancient writers; there is no point, then, in looking at these aids if you are writing about the Book of Job, or Greek conceptions of the tragic hero, or Roman conceptions of comedy. For articles on ancient literature as well as on literature in modern languages, consult the annual volumes of *Humanities Index,* issued since 1974; for the period from 1965 to 1974 it was entitled *Social Sciences and Humanities Index,* and before that (1907–1964) it was *International Index.* In *Humanities Index* (to use the current title) you can find listings of articles in periodicals on a wide range of topics. This breadth is bought at the cost of depth, for *Humanities Index,* though it includes the chief scholarly journals, includes neither the less well known scholarly journals nor the most popular magazines, nor does it include books.

For the more popular magazines, consult the *Readers' Guide to Periodical Literature.* If, for example, you want to do a research paper on the reception given to Laurence Olivier's films of Shakespeare, the *Readers' Guide* can quickly lead you to reviews in such magazines as *Time, Newsweek,* and *Atlantic.*

Bibliographies of the sort mentioned are guides, and there are so many of them that there are guides to these guides. Two invaluable guides to reference works (that is, to bibliographies and also to such helpful compilations as handbooks of mythology, place names, and critical terms) are James L. Harner, *Literary Research Guide: A Guide to Reference Sources for the Study of Literature in English and Related Topics* (New York: MLA, 1989); and Michael J. Marcuse, *A References Guide for English Studies* (Berkeley: University of California Press, 1990).

And there are guides to these guides to guides: reference librarians. If you don't know where to turn to find something, turn to the librarian.

Taking Notes

Let's assume now that you have checked some bibliographies and that you have a fair number of references to things you feel you must read to have a substantial knowledge of the evidence and the common interpretations of the evidence. Most researchers find it convenient, when examining bibliographies and the card catalog, to write down each reference on a 3 × 5 index card—one title per card. On the card put the author's full name (last name first), the exact title of the book or of the article, and the name of the journal (with dates and pages). Titles of books and periodicals (publications issued periodically—for example, monthly or four times a year) are underlined; titles of articles and of essays in books are put within quotation marks. It's also a good idea to put the library catalog number on the card, to save time if you need to get the item for a second look.

Next, you have to start reading or scanning the materials whose titles you have collected. Some of these items will prove irrelevant or silly; others will prove valuable in themselves and also in the leads they give you to further references, which you should duly record on 3×5 cards. Notes—aside from these bibliographic notes—are best taken on 4×6 cards. Smaller cards do not provide enough space for summaries of useful materials, but 4×6 cards—rather than larger cards—will serve to remind you that you should not take notes on everything. Be selective in taking notes.

1. In taking notes, write brief *summaries* rather than paraphrases. There is rarely any point to paraphrasing; generally speaking, either quote exactly (and put the passage in quotation marks, with a notation of the source, including the page numbers), or summarize, reducing a page or even an entire article or chapter of a book to a single 4×6 card. Even when you summarize, indicate your source on the card, so you can give appropriate credit in your paper. (On plagiarism, see pages 1056–1057.)

2. Of course, in your summary you will sometimes quote a phrase or a sentence—putting it in quotation marks—but quote sparingly. You are not doing stenography but rather thinking and assimilating knowledge; for the most part, then, you should digest your source rather than engorge it whole. Thinking now while taking notes will also help you avoid plagiarism later. If, on the other hand, you mindlessly copy material at length when taking notes, when you are writing the paper later you may be tempted to copy it yet again, perhaps without giving credit. Similarly, if you photocopy pages from articles or books and then merely underline some passages, you will probably not be thinking; you will just be underlining. But if you make a terse summary on a note card, you will be forced to think and to find your own words for the idea. Most of the direct quotations you copy should be effectively stated passages or especially crucial passages or both. In your finished paper some of these quotations will provide authority and emphasis.

3. If you quote but omit some irrelevant material within the quotation, be sure to indicate the omission by three spaced periods, as explained on page 1071.

4. *Never* copy a passage changing an occasional word under the impression that you are thereby putting it into your own words. Notes of this sort will find their way into your paper, your reader will sense a style other than your own, and suspicions of plagiarism may follow.

5. In the upper corner of each note card, write a brief key—for example, "Orwell's first reading of *We*," or "Characterization," or "Thought control"—so that later you can tell at a glance what is on the card.

As you work, you'll find yourself returning again and again to your primary materials—and you'll probably find to your surprise that a good deal of the secondary material is unconvincing or even wrong, despite the fact that it is printed in a handsome book or a scholarly journal. There are times when, under the weight of evidence, you will have to abandon some of your earlier views, but there are also times when you will feel that your ideas have more validity than those you are reading. One of the things we learn from research is that not everything in print is true; this discovery is one of the pleasures we get from research.

Drafting the Paper

There remains the difficult job of writing up your findings, but if you have taken good notes and have put useful headings on each card, you are well on your way. Read through the cards and sort them into packets of related material. Discard all notes, however interesting, that you now see are irrelevant to your paper. Go through the cards again and again, sorting and resorting, putting together what belongs together. Probably you will find that you have to do a little additional research—somehow you are aren't quite clear about this or that—but after you have done this additional research, you should be able to arrange the packets in a reasonable and consistent sequence. You how now have a kind of first draft or at least a tentative organization for your paper. Two further pieces of advice:

1. Beware of the compulsion to include every note card in your essay; that is, beware of telling the reader, "*A* says . . . ; *B* says . . . ; *C* says . . . . "
2. You must have a point, a thesis.

Remember: As you studied the evidence, you increasingly developed or documented or corrected a thesis. You may, for example, have become convinced that the influence of Zamyatin was limited to a few details of plot and character and that Orwell had already developed the framework and the chief attitudes that are implicit in *1984*. Similarly, now, as you write and revise your paper, you will probably still be modifying your thesis to some extent, discovering what in fact the evidence implies.

The final version of the paper, however, should be a finished piece of work, without the inconsistencies, detours, and occasional dead ends of an early draft. Your readers should feel that they are moving toward a conclusion (by means of your thoughtful evaluation of the evidence) rather than merely reading an anthology or commentary on the topic. And so we should get some such structure as: "There are three common views on . . . The first two are represented by *A* and *B;* the third, and by far the most reasonable, is *C*'s view that . . . *A* argues . . . but . . . The second view, *B*'s, is based on . . . but . . . Although the third view, *C*'s, is not conclusive, still . . . Moreover, *C*'s point can be strengthened when we consider a piece of evidence that he does not make use of. . . . "

Be sure, when you quote, to *write a lead-in,* such as "*X* concisely states the common view," or "*Z*, without offering any proof, asserts that . . ." Let the reader know where you are going, or, to put it a little differently, let the reader know how the quotation fits into your argument.

Quotations and summaries, in short, are accompanied by judicious analysis of your own, so that by the end of the paper your readers not only have read a neatly typed paper (see pages 1068–1069) and have gained an idea of what previous writers have said, but also are persuaded that under your guidance they have seen the evidence, heard the arguments justly summarized, and reached a sound conclusion.

A bibliography or list of works consulted (see pages 1060–1067) is usually appended to a research paper so readers may easily look further into the primary and secondary material if they wish; but if you have done your job well, readers will be content to leave the subject where you left it, grateful that you have set matters straight.

Documentation

WHAT TO DOCUMENT: AVOIDING PLAGIARISM

Honesty requires that you acknowledge your indebtedness for material, not only when you quote directly from a work, but also when you appropriate an idea that is not common knowledge. Not to acknowledge such borrowing is plagiarism. If in doubt as to whether or not to give credit, give credit.

You ought, however, to develop a sense of what is considered **common knowledge.** Definitions in a dictionary can be considered common knowledge, so there is no need to say, "According to Webster, a novel is . . ." (This is weak in three ways: It's unnecessary, it's uninteresting, and it's unclear, since "Webster" appears in the titles of several dictionaries, some good and some bad.) Similarly, the date of first publication of *The Scarlet Letter* can be considered common knowledge. Few can give it when asked, but it can be found out from innumerable sources, and no one need get the credit for providing you with the date. The idea that Hamlet delays is also a matter of common knowledge. But if you are impressed by So-and-so's argument that Claudius has been much maligned, you should give credit to So-and-so.

Suppose that you happen to come across Frederick R. Karl's statement in the revised edition of *A Reader's Guide to the Contemporary English Novel* (New York: Farrar, Straus & Giroux, 1972) that George Orwell was "better as a man than as a novelist." This is an interesting and an effectively worded idea. You cannot use these words without giving credit to Karl. Nor can you retain the idea but alter the words, for example, to "Orwell was a better human being than he was a writer of fiction," presenting the idea as your own, for here you are simply lifting Karl's idea—and putting it less effectively. If you want to use Karl's point, give him credit and—since you can hardly summarize so brief a statement—use his exact words and put them within quotation marks.

But what about a longer passage that strikes you favorably? Let's assume that in reading Alex Zwerdling's *Orwell and the Left* (New Haven: Yale, 1974) you find the following passage from page 105 interesting:

> *1984* might be said to have a predominantly negative goal, since it is much more concerned to fight *against* a possible future society than *for* one. Its tactics are primarily defensive. Winston Smith is much less concerned with the future than with the past—which is of course the reader's present.

You certainly *cannot* say:

> The goal of <u>1984</u> can be said to be chiefly negative,
> because it is devoted more to opposing some future
> society than it is to fighting for a future society.

> Smith is more concerned with the past (our present)
> than he is with the future.

This passage is simply a theft of Zwerdling's property: The writer has stolen Zwerdling's automobile and put a different color paint on it. How, then, can a writer use Zwerdling's idea? (1) Give Zwerdling credit and quote directly, or (2) give Zwerdling credit and summarize his point in perhaps a third of the length, or (3) give Zwerdling credit and summarize the point but include—within quotation marks—some phrase you think is especially quotable. Thus:

1. *Direct quotation.* In a study of Orwell's politics, Alex Zwerdling says, "*1984* might be said to have a predominantly negative goal, since it is much more concerned to fight *against* a possible future society than *for* one" (105).
2. *Summary.* The goal of *1984,* Zwerdling points out, is chiefly opposition to, rather than advocacy of, a certain kind of future society (105).
3. *Summary with selected quotation.* Zwerdling points out that the goal of *1984* is "predominantly negative," opposition to, rather than advocacy of, a certain kind of future society (105).

If for some reason you do not wish to name Zwerdling in your lead-in, you will have to give his name with the parenthetical citation so that a reader can identify the source:

> The goal of <u>1984</u>, one critic points out, is "predomin-
> antly negative" (Zwerdling 105), opposition to, rather
> than advocacy of, a certain kind of future society.

But it is hard to imagine why the writer preferred to say "one critic," rather than to name Zwerdling immediately, since Zwerdling sooner or later must be identified.

HOW TO DOCUMENT: FOOTNOTES AND INTERNAL PARENTHETICAL CITATIONS

Documentation tells your reader exactly what your sources are. Until recently, the standard form was the footnote, which, for example, told the reader that the source of such-and-such a quotation was a book by So-and-so. But in 1984 the Modern Language Association, which had established the footnote form used in hundreds of journals, university presses, and classrooms, substituted a new form. It is this new form—parenthetical citations *within* the text (rather than at the foot of the page or the end of the essay)—that we will discuss at length. Keep in mind, though, that footnotes still have their uses.

Footnotes. If you are using only one source your instructor may advise you to give the source in a footnote. (Check with your instructors to find out their preferred forms of documentation.)

Let's say that your only source is this textbook. Let's say, too, that all of your quotations will be from a single story—Kate Chopin's "The Story of an Hour"—printed in this book on pages 12–14. The simplest way to cite your source is to type the digit 1 (elevated, and *without* a period after it) after your first reference to (or quotation from) the story, and then to put a footnote at the bottom of the page, explaining where the story can be found. After the last line of type on the page, triple-space, indent five spaces from the left-hand margin, raise the typewriter carriage half a line, and type the arabic number 1. Do *not* put a period after it. Then lower the carriage half a line, hit the space bar once, and type a statement (double-spaced) to the effect that all references are to this book. Notice that although the footnote begins by being indented five spaces, if the note runs to more than one line the subsequent lines are given flush left.

> [1]Chopin's story appears in Sylvan Barnet, et al.,
>
> eds, <u>Literature for Composition</u>, 3rd ed. (New York:
>
> HarperCollins, 1992), 12–14

(If a book has more than three authors or editors, as here, give only the name of the first author or editor, and follow it with a comma and et al., the Latin abbreviation for "and others.")

Even if you are writing a comparison of, say, two stories in this book, you can use a note of this sort. It might run thus:

> [1]All page references, given parenthetically within
>
> the essay, refer to stories in Sylvan Barnet et al.,
>
> eds., <u>Literature for Composition</u>, 3rd ed. (New York:
>
> HarperCollins, 1992).

If you use such a note, you do not need to use a footnote after each quotation that follows. You can give the citations right in the body of the paper, by putting the page references in parentheses after the quotations.

Internal Parenthetical Citations

On page 1071 we distinguish between embedded quotations (which are short, are run right into your own sentence, and are enclosed within quotation marks) and quotations that are set off on the page (for example, three or more lines of poetry, five or more lines of typed prose that are not enclosed within quotation marks).

For an embedded quotation, put the page reference in parentheses immediately after the closing quotation mark, *without* any intervening punctuation. Then, after the parenthesis that follows the number, put the necessary punctuation (for instance, a comma or a period).

> Woolf says that there was "something marvelous as
>
> well as pathetic" about the struggling moth (93). She
>
> goes on to explain . . . .

Notice that the period comes *after* the parenthetical citation. Notice, similarly, that in the next example *no* punctuation comes after the first citation—because none is needed—and a comma comes *after* (not before or within) the second citation, because a comma is needed in the sentence.

> This is ironic because almost at the start of the
> story, in the second paragraph, Richards with the best
> of motives "hastened" (12) to bring his sad message; if
> he had at the start been "too late" (14), Mallard
> would have arrived at home first.

For a quotation that is not embedded within the text but is set off (by being indented ten spaces), put the parenthetical citation on the last line of the quotation, two spaces *after* the period that ends the quoted sentence.

> Long sentences are not necessarily hard to follow. For
> instance, a reader has no trouble with this sentence,
> from Juanita Miranda's essay:
>> The Philistine's scorn when he sees David,
>> David's reply (a mixture of scorn and pity,
>> for David announces that he comes "in the
>> name of the Lord"), the observation that
>> David was eager to do battle (he "<u>ran</u> toward
>> the army to meet the Philistine"), the
>> explanation that David cut off Goliath's
>> head with Goliath's own sword--all of these
>> details help us to see the scene, to believe
>> in the characters, and yet of course the
>> whole story is, on the literal level, remote
>> from our experience. (249)
> Why is the sentence easy to follow? Partly because
> it uses parallel constructions ("The Philistine's
> scorn..., David's reply"; "the observation that...,
> the explanation that"; "to see,...to believe"), and
> partly because Miranda does not hesitate to repeat the
> names of David and Goliath. In certain places if she
> had (as we might normally expect) substituted the
> pronoun "he," the passage probably would have become

```
muddled. For instance, we have no trouble with "David
cut off Goliath's head with Goliath's own sword," but
we might have been at least briefly uncertain if
Miranda had written "David cut off Goliath's head with
his own sword."
```

Notice that the indented quotation ends with a period. After the period there are two spaces, and then the citation in parentheses.

Four additional points:

1. "p.," "pg.," and "pp." are *not* used in citing pages.
2. If a story is very short—perhaps running for only a page or two—your instructor may tell you there is no need to keep citing the page reference for each quotation. Simply mention in the footnote that the story appears on, say, pages 200–202.
3. If you are referring to a poem, your instructor may tell you to use parenthetical citations of line numbers rather than of page numbers. But, again, your footnote will tell the reader that the poem can be found in this book, and on what page.
4. If you are referring to a play with numbered lines, your instructor may prefer that in your parenthetical citations you give act, scene, and line, rather than page numbers. Use arabic (not roman) numerals, separating the act from the scene, and the scene from the line, by periods. Here, then, is how a reference to act three, scene two, line 118 would be given:

(3.2.118)

Parenthetical Citations and List of Works Cited

Footnotes have fallen into disfavor. Parenthetical citations are now usually clarified not by means of a footnote but by means of a list, headed Works Cited, given at the end of the essay. In this list you give, alphabetically (last name first), the authors and titles that you have quoted or referred to in the essay.

Briefly, the idea is that the reader of your paper encounters an author's name and a parenthetical citation of pages. By checking the author's name in Works Cited, the reader can find the passage in the book. Suppose the writer is writing about Kate Chopin's "The Story of an Hour." Let's assume that the writer has already mentioned the author and title of the story—that is, has let the reader know what the subject of the essay is—and now uses a quotation from the story, in a sentence such as this. (Notice the parenthetical citation of page numbers immediately after the quotation.)

```
True, Mrs. Mallard at first expresses grief when she
hears the news, but soon (unknown to her friends) she
finds joy in it. So, Richards's "sad message" (12),
though sad in Richards's eyes, is in fact a happy
message.
```

Turning to Works Cited, the reader, knowing the quoted words are by Chopin, looks for Chopin and finds the following:

Chopin, Kate. "The Story of an Hour." Literature

    for Composition, 3rd ed. Eds. Sylvan Barnet

    et al. New York: HarperCollins, 1992. 12–14.

Thus the essayist is informing the reader that the quoted words ("sad message") are to be found on page 12 of this anthology.

If the writer had not mentioned Chopin's name in some sort of lead-in, the name would have to be given within the parentheses so that the reader would know the author of the quoted words:

What are we to make out of a story that ends by telling

us that the leading character has died "of joy that

kills" (Chopin 14)?

(Notice, by the way, that the closing quotation marks come immediately after the last word of the quotation; the citation and the final punctuation—in this case, the essayist's question mark—come *after* the closing quotation marks.)

If you are comparing Chopin's story with Gilman's "The Yellow Wallpaper," in Works Cited you will give a similar entry for Gilman—her name, the title of the story, the book in which it is reprinted, and the page numbers that the story occupies.

If you are referring to several works reprinted within one volume, instead of listing each item fully, it is acceptable in Works Cited to list each item simply by giving the author's name, the title of the work, then a period, two spaces, and the name of the anthologist followed by the page numbers that the selection spans. Thus a reference to Chopin's "The Story of an Hour" would be followed only by: Barnet, 12–14. This form, of course, requires that the anthology itself be cited under the name of the first-listed editor, thus:

Barnet, Sylvan, et al., eds. Literature for

    Composition. 3rd ed. New York: HarperCollins, 1992.

If you are writing a research paper, you will of course use many sources. Within the essay itself you will mention an author's name, and then will quote or summarize from this author, and follow the quotation or summary with a parenthetical citation of the pages. In Works Cited, you will give the full title, place of publication, and other bibliographic material.

Forms of Citation in Works Cited

In looking over the following samples of entries in Works Cited, remember:

1. The list of Works Cited is arranged alphabetically by author (last name first).
2. If a work is anonymous, list it under the first word of the title unless the first word is *A, An,* or *The,* in which case list it under the second word.

3. If a work is by two authors, although the book is listed alphabetically under the first author's last name, the second author's name is given in the normal order, first name first.
4. If you list two or more works by the same author, the author's name is not repeated but is represented by three hyphens followed by a period and two spaces.
5. Each item begins flush left, but if an entry is longer than one line, subsequent lines in the entry are indented five spaces.

For details about almost every imaginable kind of citation, consult Joseph Gibaldi and Walter S. Achtert, *MLA Handbook for Writers of Research Papers*, 2nd ed. (New York: Modern Language Association, 1984).

Here are samples of the citations of the kinds of publications you are most likely to include in your list of Works Cited.

Entries (arranged alphabetically) begin flush with the left margin. If an entry runs more than one line, indent the subsequent line or lines five spaces from the left margin.

A book by one author

Douglas, Ann. The Feminization of American Culture.
     New York: Knopf, 1977.

Notice that the author's last name is given first, but otherwise the name is given as on the title page. Do not substitute initials for names written out on the title page. But you may shorten the publisher's name—for example, from Little, Brown and Company to Little.

Take the title from the title page, not from the cover or the spine. But disregard unusual typography—for instance, the use of only capital letters, or the use of & for *and*. Underline the title and subtitle with one continuous underline, but do not underline the period. The place of publication is indicated by the name of the city. But if the city is not well known, or if several cities have the same name (for instance, Cambridge, Massachusetts, and Cambridge, England) the name of the state is added. If the title page lists several cities, give only the first.

A book by more than one author

Gilbert, Sandra, and Susan Gubar, The Madwoman in the
     Attic: The Woman Writer and the Nineteenth-
     Century Literary Imagination. New Haven: Yale UP,
     1979.

Notice that the book is listed under the last name of the first author (Gilbert) and that the second author's name is then given with first name (Susan) first. *If the book has more than three authors*, give the name of the first author only (last name first) and follow it with et al. (Latin for "and others.")

A book in several volumes

McQuade, Donald, et al., eds. The Harper American
        Literature. 2 vols. New York: HarperCollins, 1987.

Pope, Alexander. The Correspondence of Alexander Pope.
        5 vols. Ed. George Sherburn. Oxford: Clarendon, 1956.

Notice that the total number of volumes is given after the title, regardless of
the number that you have used.

If you have used more than one volume, within your essay you will paren-
thetically indicate a reference to, for instance, page 30 of volume 3 thus:
(3: 30). But if you have used only one volume of a multivolume work—let's
say you used only volume 2 of McQuade's anthology—in your entry in Works
Cited write, after the period following the date, Vol. 2. In your parenthetical
citation within the essay you will therefore cite only the page reference
(without the volume number), since the reader will (on consulting Works Cited) understand that in this example the reference is in volume 2.

If, instead of using the volumes as whole, you used only an independent
work within one volume—say a poem in volume 2—in Works Cited omit the
abbreviation "Vol." Instead give an arabic 2 (indicating volume 2) followed by
a colon, a space, and the page numbers that encompass the selection you
used.

Didion, Joan. "Some Dreamers of the Golden Dream."
        The Harper American Literature. Ed. Donald McQuade
        et al. 2 vols. New York: HarperCollins, 1987.
        2: 2198–2210.

Notice that this entry for Didion specifies not only that the book consists of
two volumes, but also that only one selection ("Some Dreamers," occupying
pages 2198–2210 in volume 2) was used. If you use this sort of citation in
Works Cited, in the body of your essay a documentary reference to this work
will be only to the page; the volume number will *not* be added.

A book with a separate title in a set of volumes

Churchill, Winston. The Age of Revolution. Vol. 3 of
        A History of the English-Speaking Peoples.
        New York: Dodd, 1957.

Jonson, Ben. The Complete Masques. Ed. Stephen Orgel.
        Vol. 4 of The Yale Ben Jonson. New Haven: Yale UP,
        1969.

A revised edition of a book

Ellmann, Richard. James Joyce. Rev. ed. New York:
        Oxford UP, 1982.

Chaucer, Geoffrey. <u>The Works of Geoffrey Chaucer</u>. Ed.
F. N. Robinson. 2nd ed. Boston: Houghton, 1957.

A reprint, for instance, a paperback version of an older clothbound book

Rourke, Constance, <u>American Humor</u>. 1931. Garden City,
New York: Doubleday, 1953.

Notice that the entry cites the original date (1931) but indicates that the writer is using the Doubleday reprint of 1953.

An edited book other than an anthology

Keats, John. <u>The Letters of John Keats</u>. Ed Hyder Edward
Rollins. 2 vols. Cambridge, Mass.: Harvard UP,
1958.

An anthology. You can list an anthology either under the editor's name or under the title.

A work in a volume of works by one author

Sontag, Susan, "The Aesthetics of Silence." In <u>Styles
of Radical Will</u>. New York: Farrar, 1969. 3–34.

This entry indicates that Sontag's essay, called "The Aesthetics of Silence," appears in a book of hers entitled *Styles of Radical Will*. Notice that the page numbers of the short work are cited (not page numbers that you may happen to refer to, but the page numbers of the entire piece).

A work in an anthology, that is, in a collection of works by several authors. Begin with the author and the title of the work you are citing, not with the name of the anthologist or the title of the anthology. The entry ends with the pages occupied by the selection you are citing.

Bowen, Elizabeth. "Hand in Glove." <u>The Oxford Book of
English Ghost Stories</u>. Ed. Michael Cox and R. A.
Gilbert. Oxford: Oxford UP, 1986. 444–52.

Porter, Katherine Anne. "The Jilting of Granny
Weatherall." <u>Literature for Composition</u>. Ed.
Sylvan Barnet, et al. 3rd ed. New York:
HarperCollins. 1992. 930–36.

Normally you will give the title of the work you are citing (probably an essay, short story or poem) in quotation marks. But if you are referring to a book-length work (for instance, a novel or a full-length play), underline it to indicate italics. If the work is translated, after the period that follows the title, write "Trans." and give the name of the translator, followed by a period and the name of the anthology.

If the collection is a multivolume work, and you are using only one volume, in Works Cited you will specify the volume, as in the example (page 1063) of Didion's essay. Because the list of Works Cited specifies the volume, your parenthetical documentary reference within your essay will specify (as mentioned earlier) only the page numbers, not the volume. Thus, although Didion's essay appears on pages 2198–2210 in the second volume of a two-volume work, a parenthetical citation will refer only to the page numbers because the citation in Works Cited specifies the volume.

Remember that the pages specified in the entry in your list of Works Cited are to the *entire selection*, not simply to pages you may happen to refer to within your paper.

If you are referring to a *reprint of a scholarly article*, give details of the original publication, as in the following example:

Mack, Maynard. "The World of Hamlet." Yale Review 41
(1952): 502–23. Rpt. in Hamlet. By William
Shakespeare. Ed. Edward Hubler. New York: New
American Library, 1963. 234–56.

Two or more works in an anthology. If you are referring to more than one work in an anthology (for example, in this book), in order to avoid repeating all the information about the anthology in each entry in Works Cited, under each author's name (in the appropriate alphabetical place) you can give the author and title of the work, then a period, two spaces, and the name of the anthologist followed by the page numbers that the selection spans. Thus, a reference to Shakespeare's *Hamlet* would be followed only by

Barnet 407–512

rather than by a full citation of this book. But this form of course requires that the anthology itself also be listed, under Barnet.

Two or more works by the same author. Notice that the works are given in alphabetical order (*Fables* precedes *Fools*) and that the author's name is not repeated but is represented by three hyphens followed by a period and two spaces. If the author is the translator or editior of a volume, the three hyphens are followed not by a period but by a comma, then a space, then the appropriate abbreviation (trans. or ed.), then (two spaces after the period) the title.

Frye, Northrop. Fables of Identity: Studies in Poetic
Mythology. New York: Harcourt, 1963.
---. Fools of Time: Studies in Shakespearian Tragedy.
Toronto: U of Toronto P, 1967.

A translated book

Gogol, Nikolai. <u>Dead Souls</u>. Trans. Andrew McAndrew.

New York: New American Library. 1961.

If, however, you are discussing the translation itself, as opposed to the book, list the work under the translator's name. Then put a comma, a space, and "trans." After the period following "trans." skip two spaces, then give the title of the book, a period, two spaces, and then "by" and the author's name, first name first. Continue with information about the place of publication, publisher, and date, as in any entry to a book.

An introduction, foreword, or afterword, or other editorial apparatus

Fromm, Erich. Afterword. <u>1984</u>. By George Orwell. New

American Library, 1961.

Usually a book with an introduction or some such comparable material is listed under the name of the author of the book rather than the name of the author of the editorial material (see the citation to Pope on page 1063). But if you are referring to the editor's apparatus rather than to the work itself, use the form just given.

Words such as preface, introduction, afterword, and conclusion are capitalized in the entry but are neither enclosed within quotation marks nor underlined.

A book review. First, an example of a review that does not have a title.

Vendler, Helen. Rev. of <u>Essays on Style</u>. Ed. Roger

Fowler. <u>Essays in Criticism</u> 16 (1966): 457–63.

If the review has a title, give the title after the period following the reviewer's name, before the word "Rev." If the review is unsigned, list it under the first word of the title, or the second word if the first word is *A, An,* or *The.* If an unsigned review has no title, begin the entry with "Rev. of" and alphabetize it under the title of the work being reviewed.

An encyclopedia. The first example is for a signed article, the second for an unsigned article:

Lang, Andrew. "Ballads." <u>Encyclopaedia Britannica</u>.

1910 ed.

"Metaphor." <u>The New Encyclopaedia Britannica</u>:

<u>Micropaedia</u>. 1974 ed.

An article in a scholarly journal. Some journals are paginated consecutively—that is, the pagination of the second issue picks up where the first is-

sue left off. Other journals begin each issue with a new page one. The forms of the citations in Works Cited differ slightly.

First, the citation of *a journal that uses continuous pagination:*

> Burbick, Joan. "Emily Dickinson and the Economics of
>
> Desire." American Literature 58 (1986): 361-78.

This article appeared in volume 58, which was published in 1986. (Notice that the volume number is followed by a space, then by the year, in parentheses, then by a colon, a space, and the page numbers of the entire article.) Although each volume consists of four issues, you do *not* specify the issue number when the journal is paginated continuously.

For *a journal that paginates each issue separately* (if the journal is a quarterly, there will be four page 1's each year), give the issue number directly after the volume number and a period, with no spaces before or after the period.

> Spillers, Hortense J. "Martin Luther King and the
>
> Style of the Black Sermon." The Black Scholar 3.1
>
> (1971), 14-27.

An article in a weekly, biweekly, or monthly publication

> McCabe, Bernard. "Taking Dickens Seriously."
>
> Commonweal 14 May 1965.

Notice that the volume number and the issue number are omitted for popular weeklies or monthlies such as *Time* and *Atlantic*.

An article in a newspaper. Because newspapers usually consist of several sections, a section number may precede the page number. The example indicates that an article begins on page 1 of section 2 and is continued on a later page.

> Wu, Jim. "Authors Praise New Forms." New York Times
>
> 8 March 1987, Sec. 2: 1 +.

Remarks about

Manuscript Form

Basic Manuscript Form

Much of what follows is nothing more than common sense.

1. Use 8½" × 11" paper of good weight. Do *not* use pages torn out of a spiral notebook.
2. If you typewrite, use a reasonably fresh ribbon, double-space, and type on one side of the page only. If you submit a handwritten copy, use lined paper and write on one side of the page only, in black or dark blue ink, on every other line. Most instructors do *not* want papers to be enclosed in any sort of binder. And most instructors want papers to be clipped together in the upper left corner; do not crimp or crease corners and expect them to hold together.
3. Leave an adequate margin—an inch or an inch and a half—at top, bottom, and sides.
4. Number the pages consecutively, using arabic numerals in the upper right-hand corner.
5. Put your name and class or course number in the upper right-hand corner of the first page. It is a good idea to put your name in the upper corner of each page so that if a page gets separated it can easily be restored to the proper essay.
6. Create your own title—one that reflects your topic or thesis. For example, a paper on Shirley Jackson's "The Lottery" should *not* be called "The Lottery" but might be called

    ```
    Suspense in Shirley Jackson's "The Lottery"
    ```

    or

Is "The Lottery" Rigged?

or

Jackson's "The Lottery" and Scapegoat Rituals

These titles do at least a little in the way of rousing a reader's interest.

7.   Center the title of your essay below the top margin of the first page. Begin the first word of the title with a capital letter, and capitalize each subsequent word except articles (*a, an, the*), conjunctions (*and, but, if, when,* etc.), and prepositions (*in, on, with,* etc.), thus:

A Word on Behalf of Mrs. Walter Mitty

Notice that you do *not* enclose your title within quotation marks, nor do you underline it—though if it includes the title of a story, *that* is enclosed within quotation marks, as in the following example:

Illusion and Reality in
Hawthorne's "Young Goodman Brown"

8.   Begin the essay an inch or two below the title.
9.   Your extensive revisions should have been made in your drafts, but minor last-minute revisions may be made—neatly—on the finished copy. Proofreading may catch some typographical errors, and you may notice some small weaknesses. You can make corrections with the following proofreader's symbols.

Corrections in the Manuscript

1.   *Changes* in wording may be made by crossing through words and re-writing them:

The influence of Poe and Hawthorne ~~have~~ greatly
diminished.
(*has* written above *have*)

2.   *Additions* should be made above the line, with a caret below the line at the appropriate place:

The influence of Poe and Hawthorne has ∧ diminished.
(*greatly* written above)

3.   *Transpositions* of letters may be made thus:

The in(fl)uence of Poe and Hawthorne has greatly
diminished.

4.   *Deletions* are indicated by a horizontal line through the word or words to be deleted. Delete a single letter by drawing a vertical or diagonal line through it, and indicate whether the letters on either side are to be closed up by drawing a connecting arc:

The influence of Poe and Hawthorne has greatl̸y, diminished.

5. *Separation* of words accidentally run together is indicated by a vertical line, *closure* by a curved line connecting the letters to be closed up:

The influence̸of Poe and Hawthorne has g reatly diminished.

6. *Paragraphing* may be indicated by the symbol ¶ before the word that is to begin the new paragraph:

The influence of Poe and Hawthorne has greatly diminished. ¶ The influence of Borges has very largely replaced that of earlier writers of fantasy.

Quotations and Quotation Marks

First, a word about the *point* of using quotations. Don't use quotations to pad the length of a paper. Rather, give quotations from the work you are discussing so that your readers will see the material you are discussing and (especially in a research paper) so that your readers will know what some of the chief interpretations are and what your responses to them are.

Note: The next few paragraphs do *not* discuss how to include citations of pages, a topic discussed in the preceding appendix under the heading "How to Document."

The Golden Rule: If you quote, *comment on* the quotation. Let the reader know what you make of it and why you quote it.

Additional principles:

1. **Identify the speaker or writer of the quotation** so that the reader is not left with a sense of uncertainty. Usually, in accordance with the principle of letting readers know where they are going, this identification precedes the quoted material, but occasionally it may follow the quotation, especially if it will provide something of a pleasant surprise. For instance, in a discussion of Flannery O'Connor's stories, you might quote a disparaging comment on one of the stories and then reveal that O'Connor herself was the speaker.

2. **If the quotation is part of your own sentence, be sure to fit the quotation grammatically and logically into your sentence.**

   Incorrect: Holden Caulfield tells us very little about "what my lousy childhood was like."

   Correct: Holden Caulfield tells us very little about what his "lousy childhood was like."

3. **Indicate any omissions or additions.** The quotation must be exact. Any material that you add—even one or two words—must be enclosed within square brackets, thus:

Hawthorne tells us that "owing doubtless to the depth
of the gloom at that particular spot [in the forest],
neither the travellers nor their steeds were visible."

If you wish to omit material from within a quotation, indicate the ellipsis
by three spaced periods. If your sentence ends in an omission, add a
closed-up period and then three spaced periods to indicate the omission.
The following example is based on a quotation from the sentences immediately above this one:

The instructions say that "if you...omit material from
within a quotation, [you must] indicate the
ellipsis.... If your sentence ends in an omission, add
a closed-up period and then three spaced periods...."

Notice that although material preceded "If you," periods are not needed
to indicate the omission because "If you" began a sentence in the original. Customarily, initial and terminal omissions are indicated only when
they are part of the sentence you are quoting. Even such omissions need
not be indicated when the quoted material is obviously incomplete—
when, for instance, it is a word or phrase.

4. **Distinguish between short and long quotations,** and treat each
appropriately. *Short quotations* (usually defined as fewer than five lines
of typed prose) are enclosed within quotation marks and are embedded,
that is they are run into the text (rather than being set off, without quotation marks), as in the following example:

Hawthorne begins the story by telling us that "Young
Goodman Brown came forth at sunset into the street at
Salem village," thus at the outset connecting the
village with daylight. A few paragraphs later, when
Hawthorne tells us that the road Brown takes was
"darkened by all of the gloomiest trees of the forest,"
he begins to associate the forest with darkness—and a
very little later with evil.

To set off a *long quotation* (more than four typed lines of prose), indent the entire quotation ten spaces from the left margin. Usually a long
quotation is introduced by a clause ending with a colon; for instance,
"The following passage will make this point clear:" or "The closest we
come to hearing an editorial voice is a long passage in the middle of the
story:" or some such lead-in. After typing your lead-in, double-space,
and then type the quotation, indented and double-spaced. See page
1059.

5. Commas and periods go inside the quotation marks.

   Chopin tells us in the first sentence that "Mrs.
   Mallard was afflicted with heart trouble," and in the
   last sentence the doctors say that Mrs. Mallard "died
   of heart disease."

   Exception: If the quotation is immediately followed by material in parentheses or in square brackets, close the quotation, then give the parenthetic or bracketed material, and then—after closing the parenthesis or bracket—put the comma or period.

   Chopin tells us in the first sentence that "Mrs.
   Mallard was afflicted with heart trouble" (17), and in
   the last sentence the doctors say that Mrs. Mallard
   "died of heart disease" (18).

6. **Semicolons, colons, and dashes** go outside the closing quotation marks.

7. **Question marks and exclamation points** go inside if they are part of the quotation, outside if they are your own.

   In the following passage from a student's essay, notice that because the second question mark is the student's, it comes after the closing quotation marks.

   The older man says to Goodman Brown, "Sayest thou so?"
   Doesn't a reader become uneasy when the man immediately
   adds, "We are but a little way in the forest yet"?

8. **Quotation marks versus underlining.** Use quotation marks around titles of short stories and other short works—that is, titles of chapters in books, essays, and poems that might not be published by themselves. Underline (to indicate italics) titles of books, periodicals, collections of essays, plays, and long poems such as *The Rime of the Ancient Mariner.*

■ APPENDIX C

Glossary of

Literary Terms

The terms briefly defined here are for the most part more fully defined earlier in the text. Hence many of the entries below are followed by page references to the earlier discussions.

Absurd, Theater of the   plays, especially written in the 1950s and 1960s, that call attention to the incoherence of character and of action, the inability of people to communicate, and the apparent purposelessness of existence

accent   stress given to a syllable (225–226)

act   a major division of a play

action   (1) the happenings in a narrative or drama, usually physical events (*B* marries *C*, *D* kills *E*), but also mental changes (*F* moves from innocence to experience); in short, the answer to the question, "What happens?" (2) less commonly, the theme or underlying idea of a work (162–163)

allegory   a work in which concrete elements (for instance, a pilgrim, a road, a splendid city) stand for abstractions (humanity, life, salvation), usually in an unambiguous, one-to-one relationship. The literal items (the pilgrim, and so on) thus convey a meaning, which is usually moral, religious, or political. To take a nonliterary example: The Statue of Liberty holds a torch (enlightenment, showing the rest of the world the way to freedom), and at her feet are broken chains (tyranny overcome). A caution: Not all of the details in an allegorical work are meant to be interpreted. For example, the hollowness of the Statue of Liberty does not stand for the insubstantiality or emptiness of liberty.

alliteration   repetition of consonant sounds, especially at the beginnings of words (*f*ree, *f*orm, *ph*antom) (228)

allusion   an indirect reference; thus when Lincoln spoke of "a nation dedicated to the proposition that all men are created equal," he was making an allusion to the Declaration of Independence.

ambiguity   multiplicity of meaning, often deliberate, that leaves the reader uncertain about the intended significance

anagnorisis   a recognition or discovery, especially in tragedy—for example, when the hero understands the reason for his or her fall (161)

analysis   an examination, which usually proceeds by separating the object of study into parts (34–43, 54–55)

anapest   a metrical foot consisting of two unaccented syllables followed by an accented one. Example, showing three anapests: "As I came / to the edge / of the wood" (226)

anecdote   a short narrative, usually reporting an amusing event in the life of an important person

antagonist   a character or force that opposes (literally, "wrestles") the main character

apostrophe   address to an absent figure or to a thing as if it were present and could listen. Example: "Oh rose, thou art sick!" (213)

approximate rhyme   only the final consonant-sounds are the same, as in *crown/alone,* or *pail/fall*

archetype   a theme, image, motive, or pattern that occurs so often in literary works it seems to be universal. Examples: a dark forest (for mental confusion), the sun (for illumination)

assonance   repetition of similar vowel sounds in stressed syllables. Example: *light/bride* (228)

atmosphere   the emotional tone (for instance, joy, or horror) in a work, most often established by the setting (114–115)

ballad   a short narrative poem, especially one that is sung or recited, often in a stanza of four lines, with 8, 6, 8, 6 syllables, with the second and fourth lines rhyming. A **popular ballad** is a narrative song that has been transmitted orally by what used to be called "the folk"; a **literary ballad** is a conscious imitation (without music) of such a work, often with complex symbolism. (306–307)

blank verse   unrhymed iambic pentameter, that is, unrhymed lines of ten syllables, with every second syllable stressed (230)

cacophony   an unpleasant combination of sounds

caesura   a strong pause within a line of verse (227)

catastrophe   the concluding action, especially in a tragedy

catharsis   Aristotle's term for the purgation or purification of the pity and terror supposedly experienced while witnessing a tragedy

character   (1) a person in a literary work (Romeo); (2) the personality of such a figure (sentimental lover, or whatever). Characters (in the first sense) are sometimes classified as either "flat" (one-dimensional) or "round" (fully realized, complex).

characterization the presentation of a character, whether by direct description, by showing the character in action, or by the presentation of other characters who help to define each other (166–169)

cliché an expression that through overuse has ceased to be effective. Examples: acid test, sigh of relief, the proud possessor

climax the culmination of a conflict; a turning point, often the point of greatest tension in a plot (163)

comedy a literary work, especially a play, characterized by humor and by a happy ending (161–162)

comparison and contrast to compare is strictly to note similarities, whereas to contrast is to note differences. But *compare* is now often used for both activities.

complication an entanglement in a narrative or dramatic work that causes a conflict

conflict a struggle between a character and some obstacle (for example, another character or fate) or between internal forces, such as divided loyalties (163, 174–175)

connotation the associations (suggestions, overtones) of a word or expression. Thus *seventy* and *three score and ten* both mean "one more than sixty-nine," but because *three score and ten* is a biblical expression, it has an association of holiness; see *denotation*. (70–71, 206–207)

consonance repetition of consonant sounds, especially in stressed syllables. Also called half rhyme or slant rhyme. Example: *arouse/doze* (228)

convention a pattern (for instance, the 14-line poem, or sonnet) or motif (for instance, the bumbling police officer in detective fiction) or other device occurring so often that it is taken for granted. Thus it is a convention that actors in a performance of *Julius Caesar* are understood to be speaking Latin, though in fact they are speaking English. Similarly, the soliloquy (a character alone on the stage speaks his or her thoughts aloud) is a convention, for in real life sane people do not talk aloud to themselves.

couplet a pair of lines of verse, usually rhyming (229)

crisis a high point in the conflict that leads to the turning point (163)

criticism the analysis or evaluation of a literary work

dactyl a metrical foot consisting of a stressed syllable followed by two unstressed syllables. Example: *underwear* (226)

denotation the dictionary meaning of a word. Thus *soap opera* and *daytime serial* have the same denotation, but the connotations (associations, emotional overtones) of *soap opera* are less favorable. (206–207)

dénouement the resolution or the outcome (literally, the "unknotting") of a plot (163)

deus ex machina   literally, "a god out of a machine"; any unexpected and artificial way of resolving the plot—for example, by introducing a rich uncle, thought to be dead, who arrives on the scene and pays the debts that otherwise would overwhelm the young hero

dialogue   exchange of words between characters; speech

diction   the choice of vocabulary and of sentence structure. There is a difference in diction between "One never knows" and "You never can tell." (206–207, 232)

didactic   pertaining to teaching; having a moral purpose

dimeter   a line of poetry containing two feet (226)

discovery   see *anagnorisis* (161)

drama   (1) a play; (2) conflict or tension, as in "The story lacks drama" (153–176)

dramatic irony   see *irony*

dramatic monologue   a poem spoken entirely by one character but addressed to one or more other characters whose presence is strongly felt

effaced narrator   a narrator who reports but who does not editorialize or enter into the minds of any of the characters in the story

elegy   a lyric poem, usually a meditation on a death

elision   omission (usually of a vowel or unstressed syllable), as in *o'er* (for *over*) and in "Th' inevitable hour"

end rhyme   identical sounds at the ends of lines of poetry (228)

end-stopped line   a line of poetry that ends with a pause because the grammatical structure and the sense reach (at least to some degree) completion (227)

English (or Shakespearean) sonnet   a poem of 14 lines (three quatrains and a couplet), rhyming *ababcdcdefefgg* (230)

enjambment   a line of poetry in which the grammatical and logical sense run on, without pause, into the next line or lines (227)

epic   a long narrative, especially in verse, that usually records heroic material in an elevated style

epigram   a brief, witty poem or saying

epigraph   a quotation at the beginning of the work, just after the title, often giving a clue to the theme

epiphany   a "showing forth," as when an action reveals a character with particular clarity

episode   an incident or scene that has unity in itself but is also a part of a larger action

epistle   a letter, in prose or verse

essay   a work, usually in prose and usually fairly short, that purports to be true and that treats its subject tentatively. In most literary essays the reader's interest is as much in the speaker's personality as in any argument that is offered. (69–88)

euphony   literally, "good sound," a pleasant combination of sounds

explication   a line-by-line unfolding of the meaning of a text (220–224)

exposition   a setting-forth of information. In fiction and drama, introductory material introducing characters and the situation; in an essay, the presentation of information, as opposed to the telling of a story or the setting forth of an argument (163–164)

eye rhyme   words that look as though they rhyme, but do not rhyme when pronounced. Example: *come/home* (228)

fable   a short story (often involving speaking animals) with an easily grasped moral

farce   comedy based not on clever language or on subtleties of characters but on broadly humorous situations (for instance, a man mistakenly enters the ladies' locker room)

feminine rhyme   a rhyme of two or more syllables, with the stress falling on a syllable other than the last. Examples: *fatter/batter*; *tenderly/slenderly* (227)

fiction   an imaginative work, usually a prose narrative (novel, short story), that reports incidents that did not in fact occur. The term may include all works that invent a world, such as a lyric poem or a play. (108–123)

figurative language   words intended to be understood in a way that is other than literal. Thus *lemon* used literally refers to a citrus fruit, but *lemon* used figuratively refers to a defective machine, especially a defective automobile. Other examples: "He's a beast," "She's a witch," "A sea of troubles." Literally, such expressions are nonsense, but writers use them to express meanings inexpressible in literal speech. Among the commonest kinds of figures of speech are *apostrophe, metaphor,* and *simile* (see the discussions of these words in this glossary). (211–214)

flashback   an interruption in a narrative that presents an earlier episode

flat character   a one-dimensional character (for instance, the figure who is only and always the jealous husband or the flirtatious wife) as opposed to a round or many-sided character. (111–112)

fly-on-the-wall narrator   a narrator who never editorializes and never enters a character's mind but reports only what is said and done

foil   a character who makes a contrast with another, especially a minor character who helps to set off a major character (112, 166)

foot   a metrical unit, consisting of two or three syllables, with a specified arrangement of the stressed syllable or syllables. Thus the iambic foot consists of an unstressed syllable followed by a stressed syllable. (225–226)

foreshadowing   suggestions of what is to come (113–114, 164)

free verse   poetry in lines of irregular length, usually unrhymed (230)

genre   kind or type, roughly analogous to the biological term *species*. The four chief literary genres are nonfiction, fiction, poetry, and drama, but these can be subdivided into further genres. Thus fiction obviously can be divided into the short story and the novel, and drama obviously can be divided into tragedy and comedy. But these can be still further divided—for instance, tragedy into heroic tragedy and bourgeois tragedy, comedy into romantic comedy and satirical comedy.

gesture   physical movement, especially in a play (164–165, 175)

half rhyme   repetition in accented syllables of the final consonant sound but without identity in the preceding vowel sound; words of similar but not identical sound. Also called near rhyme, slant rhyme, approximate rhyme, and off-rhyme. Examples: *light/bet*; *affirm/perform* (228)

hamartia   a flaw in the tragic hero, or an error made by the tragic hero (161)

heptameter   a metrical line of seven feet (226)

hero, heroine   the main character (not necessarily heroic or even admirable) in a work; cf. *protagonist*

heroic couplet   an end-stopped pair of rhyming lines of iambic pentameter (229)

hexameter   a metrical line of six feet (226)

hubris, hybris   a Greek word, usually translated as "overweening pride," "arrogance," "excessive ambition," and often said to be characteristic of tragic figures (159–160)

hyperbole   figurative language using overstatement, as in "He died a thousand deaths" (215)

iamb, iambic   a poetic foot consisting of an unaccented syllable followed by an accented one. Example: *alone* (226)

image, imagery   imagery is established by language that appeals to the senses, especially sight ("deep blue sea") but also other senses ("tinkling bells," "perfumes of Arabia") (214–215)

innocent eye   a naive narrator in whose narration the reader sees more than the narrator sees

internal rhyme   rhyme within a line (228)

interpretation   the exposition of meaning, chiefly by means of analysis

irony   a contrast of some sort. For instance, in **verbal irony** or **Socratic irony** the contrast is between what is said and what is meant ("You're a great guy," meant bitterly). In **dramatic irony** or **Sophoclean irony** the contrast is between what is intended and what is accomplished (Macbeth usurps the throne, thinking he will then be happy, but the action leads him to misery), or between what the audience knows (a murderer waits in the bedroom) and what a character says (the victim enters the bedroom, innocently saying, "I think I'll have a long sleep")

Italian   (or **Petrarchan**) **sonnet** a poem of 14 lines, consisting of an octave (rhyming *abbaabba*) and a sestet (usually *cdecde* or *cdccdc*) (229–230)

litotes   a form of understatement in which an affirmation is made by means of a negation; thus "He was not underweight," meaning "He was grossly overweight"

lyric poem   a short poem, often songlike, with the emphasis not on narrative but on the speaker's emotion or reverie

masculine rhyme   rhyme of one-syllable words (*lies/cries*) or, if more than one syllable, words ending with accented syllables (*behold/foretold*)

melodrama   a narrative, usually in dramatic form, involving threatening situations but ending happily. The characters are usually stock figures (virtuous heroine, villainous landlord).

metaphor   a kind of figurative language equating one thing with another: "This novel is garbage" (a book is equated with discarded and probably inedible food), "a piercing cry" (a cry is equated with a spear or other sharp instrument) (212)

meter   a pattern of stressed and unstressed syllables (225–227)

metonymy   a kind of figurative language in which a word or phrase stands not for itself but for something closely related to it: *saber-rattling* means "militaristic talk or action" (212–213)

monologue   a relatively long, uninterrupted speech by a character

monometer   a metrical line consisting of only one foot (226)

mood   the atmosphere, usually created by descriptions of the settings and characters

motif   a recurrent theme within a work, or a theme common to many works

motivation   grounds for a character's action (166)

myth   (1) a traditional story reflecting primitive beliefs, especially explaining the mysteries of the natural world (why it rains, or the origin of mountains); (2) a body of belief, not necessarily false, especially as set forth by a writer. Thus one may speak of Yeats or Alice Walker as myth-makers, referring to the visions of reality that they set forth in their works.

narrative, narrator   a narrative is a story (an anecdote, a novel); a narrator is one who tells a story (not the author, but the invented speaker of the story). On kinds of narrators, see *point of view*. (115–119, 121–122)

novel   a long work of prose fiction, especially one that is relatively realistic

novella   a work of prose fiction longer than a short story but shorter than a novel, say about 40 to 80 pages

objective point of view   a narrator reports but does not editorialize or enter into the minds of any of the characters in the story (116)

octave, octet   an eight-line stanza, or the first eight lines of a sonnet, especially of an Italian sonnet (230)

octosyllabic couplet   a pair of rhyming lines, each line with four iambic feet

ode   a lyric exalting someone (for instance, a hero) or something (for instance, a season)

omniscient narrator   a speaker who knows the thoughts of all of the characters in the narrative (116)

onomatopoeia   words (or the use of words) that sound like what they mean. Examples: *buzz, whirr* (228–229)

oxymoron   a compact paradox, as in "a mute cry," "a pleasing pain," "proud humility"

parable   a short narrative that is at least in part allegorical and that illustrates a moral or spiritual lesson

paradox   an apparent contradiction, as in Christ's words: "Whosoever will save his life shall lose it; but whosoever will lose his life for my sake, the same shall save it" (215)

paraphrase   a restatement that sets forth an idea in diction other than that of the original (211, 1054)

parody   a humorous imitation of a literary work, especially of its style

pathos   pity, sadness

pentameter   a line of verse containing five feet (226)

peripeteia   a reversal in the action (161)

persona   literally, a mask; the "I" or speaker of a work, sometimes identified with the author but usually better regarded as the voice or mouthpiece created by the author (69–71, 205–207)

personification   a kind of figurative language in which an inanimate object, animal, or other nonhuman is given human traits. Examples: "the creeping tide" (the tide is imagined as having feet), "the cruel sea" (the sea is imagined as having moral qualities) (213)

plot   the episodes in a narrative or dramatic work—that is, what happens—or the particular arrangement (sequence) of these episodes (111–113, 163–164)

poem   an imaginative work in meter or in free verse, usually employing figurative language

point of view   the perspective from which a story is told—for example, by a major character or a minor character or a fly on the wall; see also *narrative, narrator* (115–119, 121–122)

prosody   the principles of versification (225–230)

protagonist   the chief actor in any literary work. The term is usually preferable to *hero* and *heroine* because it can include characters—for example, villainous or weak ones—who are not aptly called heroes or heroines.

quatrain   a stanza of four lines (229)

realism   presentation of plausible characters (usually middle-class) in plausible (usually everyday) circumstances, as opposed, for example, to heroic characters engaged in improbable adventures. Realism in literature seeks to give the illusion of reality.

recognition   see *anagnorisis* (161)

refrain   a repeated phrase, line, or group of lines in a poem, especially in a ballad

resolution   the dénouement or untying of the complication of the plot

reversal   a change in fortune, often an ironic twist (161)

rhetorical question   a question to which no answer is expected or to which only one answer is plausible. Example: "Do you think I am unaware of your goings-on?"

rhyme   similarity or identity of accented sounds in corresponding positions, as, for example, at the ends of lines: *love/dove*; *tender/slender* (228)

rhythm   in poetry, a pattern of stressed and unstressed sounds; in prose, some sort of recurrence (for example, of a motif) at approximately identical intervals (224–230)

rising action   in a story or play, the events that lead up to the climax (163)

rising meter   a foot (for example, iambic or anapestic) ending with a stressed syllable

romance   narrative fiction, usually characterized by improbable adventures and love

round character   a many-sided character, one who does not always act predictably, as opposed to a "flat" or one-dimensional, unchanging character

run-on line   a line of verse whose syntax and meaning require the reader to go on, without a pause, to the next line; an enjambed line (227)

sarcasm   crudely mocking or contemptuous language; heavy verbal irony

satire   literature that entertainingly attacks folly or vice; amusingly abusive writing

scansion   description of rhythm in poetry; metrical analysis (227)

scene   (1) a unit of a play, in which the setting is unchanged and the time continuous; (2) the setting (locale, and time of the action); (3) in fiction, a dramatic passage, as opposed to a passage of description or of summary

selective omniscience   a point of view in which the author enters the mind of one character and for the most part sees the other characters only from the outside (116–117)

sentimentality   excessive emotion, especially excessive pity, treated as appropriate rather than as disproportionate

sestet   a six-line stanza, or the last six lines of an Italian sonnet (230)

sestina a poem with six stanzas of six lines each and a concluding stanza of three lines. The last word of each line in the first stanza appears as the last word of a line in each of the next five stanzas but in a different order. In the final (three-line) stanza, each line ends with one of these six words, and each line includes in the middle of the line one of the other three words.

setting the time and place of a story, play, or poem (for instance, a Texas town in winter, about 1900) (114–115, 165–166, 176)

short story a fictional narrative, usually in prose, rarely longer than 30 pages and often much briefer

simile a kind of figurative language explicitly making a comparison—for example, by using *as, like,* or a verb such as *seems* (212)

soliloquy a speech in a play, in which a character alone on the stage speaks his or her thoughts aloud

sonnet a lyric poem of 14 lines; see *English sonnet, Italian sonnet* (229–230)

speaker see *persona* (205–207, 231)

spondee a metrical foot consisting of two stressed syllables (226)

stage direction a playwright's indication to the actors or readers—for example, offering information about how an actor is to speak a line

stanza a group of lines forming a unit that is repeated in a poem (229–230)

stereotype a simplified conception, especially an oversimplification—for example, a stock character such as the heartless landlord, the kindly old teacher, the prostitute with a heart of gold. Such a character usually has only one personality trait, and this is boldly exaggerated.

stream of consciousness the presentation of a character's unrestricted flow of thought, often with free associations, and often without punctuation (117)

stress relative emphasis on one syllable as compared with another (225–226)

structure the organization of a work, the relationship between the chief parts, the large-scale pattern—for instance, a rising action or complication followed by a crisis and then a resolution

style the manner of expression, evident not only in the choice of certain words (for instance, colloquial language) but in the choice of certain kinds of sentence structure, characters, settings, and themes (81, 83–87, 117–119)

subplot a sequence of events often paralleling or in some way resembling the main story

summary a synopsis or condensation (74–80)

symbol a person, object, action, or situation that, charged with meaning, suggests another thing (for example, a dark forest may suggest confusion, or perhaps evil), though usually with less specificity and more ambiguity than an allegory. A symbol usually differs from a metaphor in that a symbol is expanded or repeated and works by accumulating associations. (115, 214)

synecdoche   a kind of figurative language in which the whole stands for a part ("the law," for a police officer), or a part ("all hands on deck," for all persons) stands for the whole (212)

tale   a short narrative, usually less realistic and more romantic than a short story; a yarn

tercet   a unit of three lines of verse (229)

tetrameter   a verse line of four feet (226)

theme   what the work is about; an underlying idea of a work; a conception of human experience suggested by the concrete details. Thus the theme of *Macbeth* is often said to be that "Vaulting ambition o'erleaps itself." (119–120, 162–163)

thesis   the point or argument that a writer announces and develops. A thesis differs from a *topic* by making an assertion. "The fall of Oedipus" is a topic, but "Oedipus falls because he is impetuous" is a thesis, as is "Oedipus is impetuous, but his impetuosity has nothing to do with his fall." (18, 41–42)

third-person narrator   the teller of a story who does not participate in the happenings (116–117)

tone   the prevailing attitude (for instance, ironic, genial, objective) as perceived by the reader. Notice that a reader may feel that the tone of the persona of the work is genial while the tone of the author of the same work is ironic. (70–71, 206–207, 231)

topic   a subject, such as "Hamlet's relation to Horatio." A topic becomes a *thesis* when a predicate is added to this subject, thus: "Hamlet's relation to Horatio helps to define Hamlet." (41, 71–72)

tragedy   a serious play showing the protagonist moving from good fortune to bad and ending in death or a deathlike state (159–161)

tragic flaw   a supposed weakness (for example, arrogance) in the tragic protagonist (161)

tragicomedy   a mixture of tragedy and comedy, usually a play with serious happenings that expose the characters to the threat of death but that ends happily

transition   a connection between one passage and the next (52)

trimeter   a verse line with three feet (226)

triplet   a group of three lines of verse, usually rhyming (229)

trochee   a metrical foot consisting of a stressed syllable followed by an unstressed syllable. Example: garden (226)

understatement   a figure of speech in which the speaker says less than what he or she means; an ironic minimizing, as in "You've done fairly well for yourself" said to the winner of a multimillion-dollar lottery (215)

unity   harmony and coherence of parts, absence of irrelevance

verse   (1) a line of poetry; (2) a stanza of a poem

vers libre   free verse, unrhymed poetry (230, 1078)

villanelle   a poem with five stanzas of three lines rhyming *aba*, and a concluding stanza of four lines, rhyming *abaa*. The first and third lines of the first stanza rhyme. The entire first line is repeated as the third line of the second and fourth stanzas; the entire third line is repeated as the third line of the third and fifth stanzas. These two lines form the final two lines of the last (four-line) stanza.

voice   see *persona, style,* and *tone* (205–207)

ques, University of New Mexico Press. Reprinted by permission of José Armas.

W. H. Auden, "Musée des Beaux Arts" and "The Unknown Citizen" from *W. H. Auden: Collected Poems* by W. H. Auden, edit. by E. Mendelson. Copyright © 1976 by Edward Mendelson, William Meredith, and Monroe K. Spears, Executors of the Estate of W. H. Auden. Reprinted by permission of Random House, Inc. and Faber and Faber Ltd.

Toni Cade Bambara, "The Lesson" from *Gorilla, My Love* by Toni Cade Bambara. Copyright © 1971 by Toni Cade Bambara. Reprinted by permission of Random House, Inc.

Kristine Batey, "Lot's Wife" from *Jam Today #6* (1978). Copyright © 1978 by Jam Today.

Elizabeth Bishop, "The Fish" from *The Complete Poems, 1927–1979* by Elizabeth Bishop. Copyright © 1940 by Elizabeth Bishop. Copyright © 1979, 1983 by Alice Helen Methfessel. Reprinted by permission of Farrar, Straus and Giroux, Inc.

Elizabeth Bowen, "The Demon Lover" from *The Collected Stories of Elizabeth Bowen* by Elizabeth Bowen. Copyright 1946 and renewed 1974 by Elizabeth Bowen. Reprinted by permission of Alfred A. Knopf, Inc.

Ray Bradbury, "The Million Year Picnic" from *Planet Stories* by Ray Bradbury. Copyright © 1946, renewed 1974 by Ray Bradbury. Reprinted by permission of Don Congdon Associates, Inc.

Judy Brady, "I Want a Wife" from *Ms.* (Vol. 1, No. 1, December 31, 1971). Reprinted by permission of Judy Brady.

Raymond Carver, "Popular Mechanics" from *What We Talk About When We Talk About Love* by Raymond Carver. Copyright © 1981 by Raymond Carver. Reprinted by permission of Alfred A. Knopf, Inc.

John Cheever, "The Enormous Radio" from *The Stories of John Cheever* by John Cheever. Copyright 1947 by John Cheever. Reprinted by permission of Alfred A. Knopf, Inc.

Kate Chopin, "The Storm" reprinted by permission of Louisiana State University Press from *The Complete Works of Kate Chopin,* edited by Per Seyersted. Copyright © 1969 by Louisiana State University Press.

E. E. Cummings, "anyone lived in a pretty how town" is reprinted from *Complete Poems, 1913–1962,* by E. E. Cummings, by permission of Liveright Publishing Corporation. Copyright © 1923, 1925, 1931, 1935, 1938, 1939, 1940, 1944, 1945, 1946, 1947, 1948, 1961, 1962 by the Trustees for the E. E. Cummings Trust. Copyright © 1961, 1963, 1968 by Marion Morehouse Cummings.

Emily Dickinson, poems numbered 712, 986, 258, 1551, and 1624 reprinted by permission of the publishers and the Trustees of Amherst College from *The Poems of Emily Dickinson,* Thomas H. Johnson, ed., Cambridge, Mass.: The Belknap Press of Harvard University Press, Copyright 1951, © 1955, 1979, 1983 by the President and Fellows of Harvard College.

Joan Didion, "Los Angeles Notebook" from *Slouching Towards Bethlehem* by Joan Didion. Copyright © 1965, 1966, 1967, 1968 by Joan Didion. Reprinted by permission of Farrar, Straus and Giroux, Inc.

T. S. Eliot, "The Love Song of J. Alfred Prufrock" from *Collected Poems 1909–1962* by T. S. Eliot, copyright 1936 by Harcourt Brace Jovanovich, Inc., copyright © 1964, 1963, by T. S. Eliot, reprinted by permission of Harcourt Brace Jovanovich, Inc. and Faber and Faber Ltd.

Ralph Ellison, "The King of the Bingo Game" copyright © 1944 by Ralph Ellison. Reprinted by permission of William Morris Agency, Inc. on behalf of the author.

William Faulkner, "A Rose for Emily" from *Collected Stories of William Faulkner* by William Faulkner. Copyright 1930 and renewed 1958 by William Faulkner. Reprinted by permission of Random House, Inc.

Harvey Fierstein, *On Tidy Endings.* Reprinted with permission of Atheneum Publishers, an imprint of Macmillan Publishing Company, from *Safe Sex* by Harvey Fierstein. Copyright © 1987 by Harvey Fierstein.

Carolyn Forché, "The Colonel" from *The Country Between Us* by Carolyn Forché. Copyright © 1980 by Carolyn Forché. Reprinted by permission of HarperCollins Publishers.

E. M. Forster, "My Wood" from *Abinger Harvest* by E. M. Forster. Copyright 1936 and renewed 1964 by E. M. Forster, reprinted by permission of Harcourt Brace Jovanovich, Inc. and Hodder & Stoughton Limited.

Robert Frost, "Design," "The Need of Being Versed in Country Things," "The Road Not Taken," "The Silken Tent," "Stopping by Woods on a Snowy Evening" and "The Telephone" from *The Poetry of Robert Frost* edited by Edward Connery Lathem. Copyright 1916, 1923, © 1969 by Holt, Rinehart and Winston. Copyright 1936, 1942, 1944, 1951 by Robert Frost.

■ INDEX

of Authors, Titles, and

First Lines of Poems

■ INDEX
of Terms

TO THE STUDENT

Please help us make *Literature for Composition,* Third Edition, an even better book. When we revise our textbooks, we take into account the experiences of both instructors and students with the previous edition. At some time, your instructor will be asked to comment extensively on *Literature for Composition,* Third Edition. Now we would like to hear from you.

Please complete this questionnaire and return it to:

English Literature Acquisitions Editor
HarperCollins Publishers
College Division
10 East 53rd Street
New York, New York 10022–5299

SCHOOL _____

COURSE TITLE _____

OTHER TEXTS REQUIRED _____

INSTRUCTOR'S FULL NAME _____

1. Did you like the book overall? Why or why not?

2. Did you find Part One, "Getting Started," useful preparation for the work you did later in the course? Why or why not?

3. Please rate the selections you were assigned in Part One, "Getting Started."

	Liked best				Liked least	Didn't read
CHAPTER 1 Fiction						
Kate Chopin RIPE FIGS	5	4	3	2	1	___
CHAPTER 2 Fiction						
Kate Chopin THE STORY OF AN HOUR	5	4	3	2	1	___
Kate Chopin THE STORM	5	4	3	2	1	___
CHAPTER 3 Poetry						
Langston Hughes HARLEM	5	4	3	2	1	___
Fiction						
James Thurber THE SECRET LIFE OF WALTER MITTY	5	4	3	2	1	___

	Liked best				Liked least	Didn't read
Alice Walker EVERYDAY USE	5	4	3	2	1	____
José Armas EL TONTO DEL BARRIO	5	4	3	2	1	____

CHAPTER 4
Essays

Brent Staples BLACK MEN AND PUBLIC SPACE	5	4	3	2	1	____
Joan Didion LOS ANGELES NOTEBOOK	5	4	3	2	1	____
Virginia Woolf PROFESSIONS FOR WOMEN	5	4	3	2	1	____
Virginia Woolf THE DEATH OF THE MOTH	5	4	3	2	1	____
E. M. Forster MY WOOD	5	4	3	2	1	____
Langston Hughes SALVATION	5	4	3	2	1	____
Alice Walker THE CIVIL RIGHTS MOVEMENT: WHAT GOOD WAS IT?	5	4	3	2	1	____

CHAPTER 5
Fiction

Grace Paley SAMUEL	5	4	3	2	1	____
Lola Lee Loveall THE TICKET	5	4	3	2	1	____
Edgar Allan Poe THE CASK OF AMONTILLADO	5	4	3	2	1	____
Shiga Naoya HAN'S CRIME	5	4	3	2	1	____
Eudora Welty A WORN PATH	5	4	3	2	1	____
John Updike A & P	5	4	3	2	1	____

CHAPTER 6
Drama

Susan Glaspell TRIFLES	5	4	3	2	1	____
Harvey Fierstein ON TIDY ENDINGS	5	4	3	2	1	____

CHAPTER 7
Poetry

Emily Dickinson WILD NIGHTS—WILD NIGHTS	5	4	3	2	1	____
Robert Frost THE TELEPHONE	5	4	3	2	1	____
William Blake THE SICK ROSE	5	4	3	2	1	____
Robert Herrick UPON JULIA'S CLOTHES	5	4	3	2	1	____
Christina Rossetti IN AN ARTIST'S STUDIO	5	4	3	2	1	____
William Butler Yeats THE BALLOON OF THE MIND	5	4	3	2	1	____
Emily Dickinson A NARROW FELLOW IN THE GRASS	5	4	3	2	1	____
Emily Dickinson APPARENTLY WITH NO SUR-PRISE	5	4	3	2	1	____
Gerard Manley Hopkins PIED BEAUTY	5	4	3	2	1	____
Thomas Hardy TRANSFORMATIONS	5	4	3	2	1	____
Robert Frost THE NEED OF BEING VERSED IN COUNTRY THINGS	5	4	3	2	1	____
Robert Frost DESIGN	5	4	3	2	1	____
Elizabeth Bishop THE FISH	5	4	3	2	1	____
William Stafford TRAVELING THROUGH THE DARK	5	4	3	2	1	____
A. R. Ammons MOUNTAIN TALK	5	4	3	2	1	____
N. Scott Momaday THE EAGLE-FEATHER FAN	5	4	3	2	1	____

4. Please rate the selections you were assigned in Part Two, "A Thematic Anthology."

CHAPTER 8 *Strange Worlds* Essays	Liked best				Liked least	Didn't read
Juanita Miranda IN DEFENSE OF FANTASY	5	4	3	2	1	___
Fiction						
Edgar Allan Poe THE FALL OF THE HOUSE OF USHER	5	4	3	2	1	___
Jean Rhys I USED TO LIVE HERE ONCE	5	4	3	2	1	___
Elizabeth Bowen THE DEMON LOVER	5	4	3	2	1	___
John Cheever THE ENORMOUS RADIO	5	4	3	2	1	___
Ray Bradbury OCTOBER 2026: THE MILLION-YEAR PICNIC	5	4	3	2	1	___
Gabriel García Márquez A VERY OLD MAN WITH ENORMOUS WINGS	5	4	3	2	1	___
Joyce Carol Oates WHERE ARE YOU GOING, WHERE HAVE YOU BEEN?	5	4	3	2	1	___
Poetry						
Anonymous THE WIFE OF USHER'S WELL	5	4	3	2	1	___
Anonymous THE DEMON LOVER	5	4	3	2	1	___
John Keats LA BELLE DAME SANS MERCI	5	4	3	2	1	___
Emily Dickinson BECAUSE I COULD NOT STOP FOR DEATH	5	4	3	2	1	___
John Hall Wheelock EARTH	5	4	3	2	1	___
Craig Raine A MARTIAN SENDS A POSTCARD HOME	5	4	3	2	1	___
Drama						
W. W. Jacobs and Louis N. Parker THE MONKEY'S PAW	5	4	3	2	1	___

CHAPTER 9 *Innocence and Experience* Essays						
Plato THE MYTH OF THE CAVE	5	4	3	2	1	___
Maya Angelou GRADUATION	5	4	3	2	1	___
Fiction						
James Joyce ARABY	5	4	3	2	1	___
Frank O'Connor GUESTS OF THE NATION	5	4	3	2	1	___
Hisaye Yamamoto YONEKO'S EARTHQUAKE	5	4	3	2	1	___
Alice Munro HOW I MET MY HUSBAND	5	4	3	2	1	___
Liliana Heker THE STOLEN PARTY	5	4	3	2	1	___
Jamaica Kincaid GIRL	5	4	3	2	1	___
Jamaica Kincaid COLUMBUS IN CHAINS	5	4	3	2	1	___
Poetry						
William Blake THE LAMB	5	4	3	2	1	___
William Blake THE TYGER	5	4	3	2	1	___
Gerard Manley Hopkins SPRING AND FALL: TO A YOUNG CHILD	5	4	3	2	1	___
A. E. Housman WHEN I WAS ONE-AND-TWENTY	5	4	3	2	1	___
E. E. Cummings ANYONE LIVED IN A PRETTY HOW TOWN	5	4	3	2	1	___

	Liked best				Liked least	Didn't read

Ralph Ellison KING OF THE BINGO GAME   5 4 3 2 1 ____
Shirley Jackson THE LOTTERY   5 4 3 2 1 ____
Toni Cade Bambara THE LESSON   5 4 3 2 1 ____
Amy Tan TWO KINDS   5 4 3 2 1 ____

Poetry

Edwin Arlington Robinson RICHARD CORY   5 4 3 2 1 ____
Robert Hayden FREDERICK DOUGLASS   5 4 3 2 1 ____
Allen Ginsberg A SUPERMARKET IN CALIFORNIA   5 4 3 2 1 ____
Pat Mora IMMIGRANTS   5 4 3 2 1 ____
Sharon Olds I GO BACK TO MAY 1937   5 4 3 2 1 ____

Drama

Edward Albee THE SANDBOX   5 4 3 2 1 ____
Tennessee Williams THE GLASS MENAGERIE   5 4 3 2 1 ____

CHAPTER 12
The Individual and Society

Essays

Sullivan Ballou MY VERY DEAR SARAH   5 4 3 2 1 ____
May Sarton THE REWARDS OF LIVING A SOLITARY LIFE   5 4 3 2 1 ____
Judy Brady I WANT A WIFE   5 4 3 2 1 ____
Neil Miller IN SEARCH OF GAY AMERICA: OGILVIE, MINNESOTA (POPULATION 374)   5 4 3 2 1 ____

Fiction

Nathaniel Hawthorne THE MAYPOLE OF MERRY MOUNT   5 4 3 2 1 ____
Herman Melville BARTLEBY, THE SCRIVENER   5 4 3 2 1 ____
Tillie Olsen I STAND HERE IRONING   5 4 3 2 1 ____
Alice Munro BOYS AND GIRLS   5 4 3 2 1 ____

Poetry

Richard Lovelace TO LUCASTA, GOING TO THE WARS   5 4 3 2 1 ____
Robert Frost STOPPING BY WOODS ON A SNOWY EVENING   5 4 3 2 1 ____
Robert Frost MENDING WALL   5 4 3 2 1 ____
Robert Frost THE ROAD NOT TAKEN   5 4 3 2 1 ____
T. S. Eliot THE LOVE SONG OF J. ALFRED PRUFROCK   5 4 3 2 1 ____
W. H. Auden MUSÉE DES BEAUX ARTS   5 4 3 2 1 ____
W. H. Auden THE UNKNOWN CITIZEN   5 4 3 2 1 ____
Mitsuye Yamada TO THE LADY   5 4 3 2 1 ____
Marge Piercy BARBIE DOLL   5 4 3 2 1 ____
Marge Piercy WHAT'S THAT SMELL IN THE KITCHEN?   5 4 3 2 1 ____
Marge Piercy A WORK OF ARTIFICE   5 4 3 2 1 ____
Carolyn Forché THE COLONEL   5 4 3 2 1 ____

Drama

Henrik Ibsen A DOLL'S HOUSE   5 4 3 2 1 ____

CHAPTER 13
Men, Women, God, and Gods

Essays

William James RELIGIOUS FAITH   5 4 3 2 1 ____

	Liked best				Liked least	Didn't read
Jill Tweedie GOD THE MOTHER RULES—OK?	5	4	3	2	1	____
Fiction						
Luke THE PARABLE OF THE PRODIGAL SON	5	4	3	2	1	____
Nathaniel Hawthorne YOUNG GOODMAN BROWN	5	4	3	2	1	____
Katherine Anne Porter THE JILTING OF GRANNY WEATHERALL	5	4	3	2	1	____
Ernest Hemingway A CLEAN, WELL-LIGHTED PLACE	5	4	3	2	1	____
Flannery O'Connor A GOOD MAN IS HARD TO FIND	5	4	3	2	1	____
Flannery O'Connor REVELATION	5	4	3	2	1	____
Leslie Marmon Silko THE MAN TO SEND RAIN CLOUDS	5	4	3	2	1	____
Poetry						
John Donne HOLY SONNET IV (At the round earth's imagined corners)	5	4	3	2	1	____
John Donne HOLY SONNET XIV (Batter my heart, three-personed God)	5	4	3	2	1	____
Emily Dickinson THOSE—DYING, THEN	5	4	3	2	1	____
Emily Dickinson THERE'S A CERTAIN SLANT OF LIGHT	5	4	3	2	1	____
Emily Dickinson THIS WORLD IS NOT CONCLUSION	5	4	3	2	1	____
Christina Rossetti AMOR MUNDI	5	4	3	2	1	____
Christina Rossetti UPHILL	5	4	3	2	1	____
Gerard Manley Hopkins GOD'S GRANDEUR	5	4	3	2	1	____
Kristine Batey LOT'S WIFE	5	4	3	2	1	____
Drama						
Sophocles OEDIPUS REX	5	4	3	2	1	____
Sophocles ANTIGONE	5	4	3	2	1	____

5. Are there other authors or topics you would like to see added?

6. Were Appendixes A, B, and C assigned? _____ Were they useful in completing your writing assignments?

7. Please add any comments or suggestions on how we might improve this book.

YOUR NAME _____ DATE _____

MAILING ADDRESS _____

_____

May we quote you either in promotion for this book or in future publishing ventures?

YES _____ NO _____

Thank you.